Elizabeth Barrett
Browning

The Works of
Elizabeth Barrett Browning

*with an Introduction by Karen Hill,
and Bibliography*

The Wordsworth Poetry Library

This edition published 1994 by Wordsworth Editions Ltd,
Cumberland House, Crib Street, Ware, Hertfordshire SG12 9ET.

ISBN 1-85326-424-5

Printed and bound in Denmark by Nørhaven.

The paper in this book is produced from pure wood
pulp, without the use of chlorine or any other substance
harmful to the environment. The energy used in its
production consists almost entirely of hydroelectricity
and heat generated from waste materials, thereby
conserving fossil fuels and contributing little to the
greenhouse effect.

INTRODUCTION

As VIRGINIA WOOLF pointed out in 1932, the Brownings are

> far better known in the flesh than they have ever been in the spirit.
> Passionate lovers, in curls and side whiskers, oppressed, defiant,
> eloping – in this guise thousands of people must know and love
> the Brownings who never read a line of their poetry...We all know
> how Miss Barrett lay on her sofa; how she escaped from the dark
> house in Wimpole Street one September morning; how she met
> health and happiness, and Robert Browning in the church around the
> corner (1).

Yet whilst critical studies of Robert Browning's poetry prolif-
erate, the library shelf devoted to Elizabeth Barrett Browning
will yield a good deal more biographical than critical materi-
al. Today Barrett Browning is still the romantic heroine in
the well-documented Victorian legend in the popular if not
literary imagination – and various scholars, rightly damning
her exclusion from the literary canon other than as a
composer of suitably sentimental love poems, are lionising
her as a radical social visionary and feminist. However, both
visions are incorrect. According to Margaret Forster, her
recent biographer, Barrett Browning was no damsel in
distress but a woman shaping her own life; and her social and
political commentary was far from radical. Her work deserves
a place with the major Victorian poets – she was seriously
considered as Poet Laureate to replace Wordsworth – and
yet it is not a wholly comfortable fit: neither feminine in the
traditional sense of the word, nor offering a wholehearted
rejection of Victorian values, her work masters yet ultimate-
ly transcends the male poetic tradition to which she was heir.
She defines and brings to her work an unsentimental yet
decidedly womanly perspective on Victorian society and
values, grounded in the centrality of love in the spiritual,
sexual and social dimensions: she makes it clear that this, in
her view, is the role of man, woman and poet.

In 'Fragment of an "Essay on Woman"' (not printed in
this collection) the youthful poet asks 'why must women to

be loved be weak?'. Before even meeting her husband, Elizabeth Barrett had believed that a 'happy marriage was the happiest condition' but wondered 'where were the happy marriages?' (2). She blamed neither love nor marriage themselves but the roles that women were expected to play in them; Victorian women were expected to be beautiful, charming, domestic, and yet 'weak' to the extent of foolishness. She argues against the artificial feminine virtues inculcated in women, and encourages them to cultivate a more womanly strength. Her ballads, often tales of women betrayed, offer a commentary on the roles women are expected to play for and in love: in 'The Romaunt of the Page' a woman follows her husband to the Crusades disguised as a page, saves his life three times and dies fighting in his defence, despite his contention that a woman is 'unwomaned' by such acts. In the narrator's eyes, however, she has died 'woman-proud', a 'truthful woman'; and in 'Bertha in the Lane' another courageous woman is doomed in love, rejected in favour of her sweet, shy, 'bashful' sister, yet remaining 'death-strong' in her sufferings.

The potential for suffering offered by the feminine role is fully explored: the self-deluding Bianca in 'Bianca among the Nightingales' cannot distinguish between a true and a false lover, between love and lust. Despite the pure sexuality of her union with her lover, portrayed tellingly in images of violent penetration, when he deserts her for the superior physical charms of another Bianca blames her rival and convinces herself that she is still loved. The refrain is varied effectively to suggest the mounting anguish resulting from her delusions about love: 'The nightingales, the nightingales' becomes 'And still they sing, the nightingales' and finally 'Our Lady, hush these nightingales'; in 'Catarina to Camoens' Catarina more wisely questions the truth of a lover's words: when asked to sing of your dead lady, she asks,

> Will you tremble
> Yet dissemble, –
> Or sing hoarse, with tears between,
> 'Sweetest eyes were ever seen'?

Barrett Browning is not, however, trying to undermine the

importance of love in women's (or men's) lives; rather she is asking that we give love the intelligent attention that it deserves. Women should be brave, not foolhardy, in love, even, or perhaps especially, when their lovers are not. One way of doing this is by shifting the parameters of the female role. 'Lady Geraldine's Courtship' offers an alternative female role, that of pursuer of a suitably worthy, i.e. virtuous, man. The heroine, Lady Geraldine, falls in love with a poet who although 'lowly born' is 'Very rich...in virtues', and she declares herself to him rather than wait for him to take the initiative. Barrett Browning is adding a twist to the convention of the unworthy poet-lover wooing the unattainable lady, and she does so again and to greater effect in the *Sonnets from the Portuguese*, where instead of the traditional male poet-lover and his silent mistress we have a female poet-lover wooing her beloved. While it is true that the sonnets contain references to her personal experience (for example the poet-lover sends her beloved a lock of her hair, as she did Robert Browning) the general tone of the poems is that of the conventional sonnet: that of an unworthy poet-lover languishing in sorrow and despair for a superior beloved. What *is* different in this sequence is the nature of the beloved that she desires: he jumps down from his pedestal so that their love can be consummated. The distance required by conventional sonneteers is revealed as indicative of a fear of love that is not overcome within the sequence: her beloved embodies this love, and it is a force which must be reckoned with because it has the power to 'behold my soul's true face'. The sexuality as well as the spirituality of their love is celebrated:

> ... The widest land
> Doom takes to part us, leaves thy heart in mine
> With pulses that beat double. What I do
> And what I dream include thee, as the wine
> Must taste of its own grapes.

(VI II. 8-12)

These lovers lie breast to breast, breath on breath, and taste of each other. The final sonnet acknowledges the gift of love offered by the beloved, who has 'brought me many

flowers...all the summer through/And winter', and returned:
she offers him her thoughts plucked from her heart as flowers
whose 'roots are left in me'. In Barrett Browning's sonnet
sequence, then, the silent mistress becomes active wooer of
an honourable yet passionate man; the sequence is celebra-
tory of the mature, passionate, mutual love, possible when
the woman steps out of her assigned role.

Despite the fact that present-day affairs were not consid-
ered the stuff of poetry by influential critics such as Matthew
Arnold, from the start of her career Barrett Browning had
been aware of her desire to speak of love in the public as well
as the private sphere. Her poems commenting on social or
political affairs attempt to inspire that love, or loving action,
in her audience rather than a desire for specific social or
political reform. 'The City of the Children', for instance,
draws attention to the ill treatment of children in Victorian
society, by a 'cruel nation' of 'gold-heapers'. A bloody
revenge will be exacted, she prophesies, for 'the child's sob
in the silence curses deeper/Than the strong man in his
wrath'; in 'A Curse for a Nation', one of a collection of
overtly political poems, a woman realises that her responsi-
bility is to love, and to 'curse' loudly and publicly those who
do not; but a curse is lifted by love in' The Runaway Slave
at Pilgrim's Point'. A dramatic monologue, the speaker is a
female slave and the poem opens as she raises her hand 'to
curse this land'. At the end of the poem, however, she
retracts her curses:

> White men I leave you all curse-free
> In my broken heart's disdain.

The poem is a powerful study of issues of power, race and
sex, but ultimately the debasement the slave suffers is
transcended by her ability to love. The love she shared with
her (slave) lover was not 'strong enough.../To conquer the
world' and the deliberate destruction of this love acts as a
metaphor for slavery as an act of hatred, of un-love; her heart
may have been broken by that act but it was still superior, in
its ability to love and its disdain for hatred, to the hearts of
the white men who destroyed it.

Aurora Leigh, the poem most often seized upon by feminist critics, is an 'Autobiography of a poetess – not me ... [including] a good deal ... upon the social question, and against the socialists' (3). The poem expresses the loneliness of the eponymous heroine 'Our very heart of passionate womanhood,/ ... could not beat so in the verse without/Being present also in the unkissed lips'. Aurora refuse to marry Romney Leigh, her cousin, and join him in his socialist schemes; she asserts that she has the right to her own vocation and that poetry is as necessary to the improvement of society as reforming movements. Yet *Aurora Leigh* espouses neither feminism nor socialism as the answer to society's ills; instead, it falls back on love. Aurora comes to realise that 'God made women, to save men by love'. and she rues the pride that caused her to miss her true role as a woman, for: 'Art is much, but love is more'. This is a role fit for men too: Romney, too, discovers that individual love is the foundation for a true love of mankind that transcends mere ideology.

Love, then, informs Barrett Browning's work in both the private and public spheres, and it may be, paradoxically, that 'being a happy wife and mother *and* a prolific and successful poet was her most radical revision of all' (4); ironically it is this very success that is a major factor in our most unjust neglect of her work.

Karen Hill
Reading 1994

Notes
1. Virginia Woolf, *The Common Reader, Second Series*, London 1932, p202.
2. Glennis Stephenson, *Elizabeth Barrett Browning and the Poetry of Love*, Ann Arbor, Michigan 1989, pp29-34.
3. Quoted in Elizabeth Barrett Browning, *Aurora Leigh*, ed. Kerry McSweeney, Oxford 1993, p(xix).
4. Dorothy Mermin, *Elizabeth Barrett Browning: The Origins of a New Poetry*, Chicago 1989, p5.

x

FURTHER READING

Margaret Forster, *Elizabeth Barrett Browning*, London 1990.
Gardner B. Taplin, *The Life of Elizabeth Barrett Browning*, London 1957.
Dorothy Mermin, *Elizabeth Barrett Browning: The Origins of a New Poetry*, Chicago 1989.
Glennis Stephenson, *Elizabeth Barrett Browning and the Poetry of Love*, Ann Arbor, Michigan 1989.

DEDICATION

TO MY FATHER

WHEN your eyes fall upon this page of dedication, and you start to see to whom it is inscribed, your first thought will be of the time far off when I was a child and wrote verses, and when I dedicated them to you who were my public and my critic. Of all that such a recollection implies of saddest and sweetest to both of us, it would become neither of us to speak before the world; nor would it be possible for us to speak of it to one another, with voices that did not falter. Enough, that what is in my heart when I write thus, will be fully known to yours.

And my desire is that you, who are a witness how if this art of poetry had been a less earnest object to me, it must have fallen from exhausted hands before this day,—that you, who have shared with me in things bitter and sweet, softening or enhancing them, every day,—that you, who hold with me over all sense of loss and transiency, one hope by one Name,—may accept from me the inscription of these volumes, the exponents of a few years of an existence which has been sustained and comforted by you as well as given. Somewhat more faint-hearted than I used to be, it is my fancy thus to seem to return to a visible personal dependence on you, as if indeed I were a child again; to conjure your beloved image between myself and the public, so as to be sure of one smile,—and to satisfy my heart while I sanctify my ambition, by associating with the great pursuit of my life its tenderest and holiest affection.

Your

E. B. B.

LONDON, 50 WIMPOLE STREET,
1844.

CONTENTS

EARLY POEMS, 1820-33

THE BATTLE OF MARATHON [1]

> Behold
> What care employs me now, my vows I pay
> To the sweet Muses, teachers of my youth!—AKENSIDE.
>
> Ancient of days! August Athena! Where,
> Where are thy men of might, thy grand in soul?
> Gone—glimmering through the dream of things that were.
> First in the race that led to glory's goal,
> They won, and passed away.—BYRON.

PREFACE

THAT poetry is the first, and most celebrated of all the fine arts, has not been denied in any age, or by any philosopher. The culture of the soul, which Sallust so nobly describes, is necessary to those refined pleasures, and elegant enjoyments, in which man displays his superiority to brutes. It is alone the elevation of the soul, not the form of the body, which constitutes the proud distinction; according to the learned historian, 'Alterum nobis cum diis, alterum cum belluis commune est.' The noblest of the productions of man, that which inspires the enthusiasm of virtue, the energy of truth, is poetry: poetry elevates the mind to heaven, kindles within it unwonted fires, and bids it throb with feelings exalting to its nature.

This humble attempt may by some be unfortunately attributed to vanity, to an affectation of talent, or to the still more absurd desire of being thought a *genius*. With the humility and deference due to their judgements, I wish to plead not guilty to their accusations, and, with submission, to offer these pages to the perusal of the few kind and partial friends who may condescend to read them, assured that their criticism will be tempered with mercy.

Happily it is not now, as it was in the days of Pope, who was so early in actual danger of thinking himself 'the greatest genius of the age.' Now, even the female may drive her Pegasus through the realms of Parnassus, without being saluted with the most equivocal of all appellations, a learned lady; without being celebrated by her friends as a Sappho, or traduced by her enemies as a pedant; without being abused in the Review, or criticized in society; how justly then may a child hope to pass unheeded!

In these reading days there need be little vulgar anxiety among poets for the fate of their works: the public taste is no longer so epicurean. As the press pours forth profusion, the literary multitude eagerly receive its lavish offerings, while the sublimity of Homer, and the majesty of Virgil, those grand and solitary specimens of ancient poetic excellence, so renowned through the lapse of ages, are by many read only as schoolbooks, and are justly estimated alone by the comparative

---

[1] Dedication to the original edition of 1820: 'To him to whom "I owe the most," and whose admonitions have guided my youthful muse, even from her earliest infancy, to the Father whose never-failing kindness, whose unwearied affection, I never can repay, I offer these pages as a small testimony of the gratitude of his affectionate child, ELIZABETH B. BARRETT.'

few, whose hearts can be touched by the grandeur of their sentiments, or exalted by their kindred fire ; by them this dereliction must be felt, but they can do no more than mourn over this semblance of decline in literary judgement and poetic taste. Yet, in contemplating the poets of our own times—(for there are real poets, though they be mingled with an inferior multitude of the common herd)—who, unsophisticated by prejudice, can peruse those inspired pages emitted from the soul of Byron, or who can be dazzled by the gems sparkling from the rich mine of the imagination of Moore, or captivated by scenes glowing in the descriptive powers of Scott, without a proud consciousness that our day may boast the exuberance of true poetic genius ? And if criticism be somewhat too general in its suffrage, may it not be attributed to an overwhelming abundance of contemporary authors, which induces it to err in discrimination, and may cause its praises to be frequently ill-merited, and its censures ill-deserved ; as the eye, wandering over a garden where flowers are mingled with weeds, harassed by exertion and dimmed by the brilliancy of colours, frequently mistakes the flower for the weed, and the weed for the flower ?

It is worthy of remark, that when Poetry first burst from the mists of ignorance—when first she shone a bright star illumining the then narrow understanding of the Greeks—from that period when Homer, the sublime poet of antiquity, awoke the first notes of poetic inspiration to the praise of valour, honour, patriotism, and, best of all, to a sense of the high attributes of the Deity, though darkly and mysteriously revealed ; then it was, and not till then, that the seed of every virtue, of every great quality, which had so long lain dormant in the souls of the Greeks, burst into the germ ; as when the sun disperses the mist cowering o'er the face of the heavens, illumes with his resplendent rays the whole creation, and speaks to the verdant beauties of nature, joy, peace, and gladness. Then it was that Greece began to give those immortal examples of exalted feeling, and of patriotic virtue, which have since astonished the world ; then it was

that the unenlightened soul of the savage rose above the degradation which assimilated him to the brute creation, and discovered the first rays of social independence, and of limited freedom ; not the freedom of barbarism, but that of a state enlightened by a wise jurisdiction, and restrained by civil laws. From that period man seems to have first proved his resemblance to his Creator, and his superiority to brutes, and the birth of Poetry was that of all the kindred arts ; in the words of Cicero, 'Quo minus ergo honoris erat poetis eo minora studia fuerunt.'

It is no disparagement to an historical poem to enlarge upon its subject ; but where truth is materially outraged, it ceases to be history. Homer, in his *Iliad* and *Odyssey*, and Virgil, in his *Aeneid*, have greatly beautified their subjects, so grand in themselves, and, with true poetic taste and poetic imagery, have contributed with magnificent profusion to adorn those incidents which otherwise would appear tame, barren, and uninteresting. It is certain, however happily they have succeeded, their poems cannot be called strictly historical, because the truth of history is not altogether their undeviated form. Virgil, especially, has introduced in his *Aeneid* 'an anachronism of nearly three hundred years, Dido having fled from Phoenicia that period after the age of Aeneas.' But in that dependence upon the truth of history which I would enforce as a necessary quality in an historical poem, I do not mean to insinuate that it should be mere prose versified, or a suspension of the functions of the imagination, for then it could no longer be poetry. It is evident that an historical poem should possess the following qualifications :—Imagination, invention, judgement, taste, and truth ; the four first are necessary to poetry, the latter to history. He who writes an historical poem must be directed by the pole-star of history, truth ; his path may be laid beneath the bright sun of invention, amongst the varied walks of imagination, with judgement and taste for his guides, but his goal must be that resplendent and unchangeable luminary, truth.

Imagination must be allowed to be the

characteristic, and invention the very foundation, of poetry. The necessity of the latter in all poetic effusions is established by that magnificent translator of the greatest of poets, Pope, in this beautiful passage : 'It is the invention that in different degrees distinguishes all great geniuses : the utmost extent of human study, learning, and industry, which masters everything besides, can never attain to this. It furnishes art with all her materials, and without it, judgement itself can but steal wisely ; for art is only a prudent steward, who lives on managing the riches of nature.' And in this ingenious note the editor, Mr. Wakefield, elegantly exemplifies it : ' For poetry, in its proper acceptation, is absolutely creation, ποίησις or invention. In the three requisites prescribed by Horace of poetic excellence, "Ingenium cui sit cui mens divinior atque os magna sonaturum." The first, "ingenium," or native fertility of intellect, corresponds to the "invention" of Pope.'

The battle of Marathon is not, perhaps, a subject calculated to exercise the powers of the imagination, or of poetic fancy, the incidents being so limited ; but it is a subject every way formed to call forth the feelings of the heart, to awake the strongest passions of the soul. Who can be indifferent, who can preserve his tranquillity, when he hears of one little city rising undaunted, and daring her innumerable enemies, in defence of her freedom—of a handful of men overthrowing the invaders, who sought to molest their rights and to destroy their liberties ? Who can hear unmoved of such an example of heroic virtue, of patriotic spirit, which seems to be crying from the ruins of Athens for honour and immortality ? The heart, which cannot be fired by such a recital, must be cold as the icy waters of the Pole, and must be devoid at once of manly feeling and of patriotic virtue ; for what is it that can awaken the high feelings which sometimes lie dormant in the soul of man, if it be not liberty ? Liberty, beneath whose fostering sun the arts, genius, every congenial talent of the mind, spring up spontaneously, and unite in forming one bright garland of glory around the brow of independence ; liberty, at whose decline virtue sinks before the despotic sway of licentiousness, effeminacy, and vice. At the fall of liberty, the immortal Republics of Rome and Athens became deaf to the call of glory, fame, and manly virtue. ' On vit manifestement (says Montesquieu) pendant le peu de temps que dura la tyrannie des decemvirs, à quel point l'agrandissement de Rome dependoit de sa liberté ; l'état semb!a avoir perdu l'âme qui la faisoit mouvoir.' And Bigland thus : ' It was not till luxury had corrupted their manners, and their liberties were on the eve of their extinction, that the principal citizens of Athens and of Rome began to construct magnificent houses, and to display their opulence and splendour in private life.'

It may be objected to my little poem, that the mythology of the ancients is too much called upon to support the most considerable incidents ; it may unhappily offend those feelings most predominant in the breast of a Christian, or it may be considered as injudicious in destroying the simplicity so necessary to the epic. Glover's Leonidas is commended by Lyttelton, because he did not allow himself the liberty so largely taken by his predecessors, of ' wandering beyond the bounds, and out of sight, of common sense in the airy regions of poetic mythology ' ; yet, where is the poet more remarkable for simplicity than Homer, and where is the author who makes more frequent use of heathen mythology ? ' The heathens,' says Rollin, ' addressed themselves to their gods, as beings worthy of adoration.'

He who writes an epic poem must transport himself to the scene of action ; he must imagine himself possessed of the same opinions, manners, prejudices, and beliefs ; he must suppose himself to be the hero he delineates, or his picture can no longer be nature, and what is not natural cannot please. It would be considered ridiculous in the historian or poet describing the ancient manners of Greece, to address himself to that Omnipotent Being who first called the world out of chaos, nor would it be considered less so if he were to be silent upon the whole subject ; for in all nations, in all ages, religion must be the spur of every noble action, and the characteristic of every lofty soul.

Perhaps I have chosen the rimes of Pope, and departed from the noble simplicity of the Miltonic verse, injudiciously. The immortal poet of England, in his apology for the verse of *Paradise Lost*, declares 'rimes to be, to all judicious ears, trivial, and of no true musical delight.' In my opinion, humble as it is, the custom of riming would ere now have been abolished amongst poets, had not Pope, the disciple of the immortal Dryden, awakened the lyre to music, and proved that rime could equal blank verse in simplicity and gracefulness, and vie with it in elegance of composition, and in sonorous melody. No one who has read his translation of Homer, can refuse him the immortality which he merits so well, and for which he laboured so long. He it was who planted rime for ever in the regions of Parnassus, and uniting elegance with strength, and sublimity with beauty, raised the English language to the highest excellence of smoothness and purity.

I confess that I have chosen Homer for a model, and perhaps I have attempted to imitate his style too often and too closely; and yet some imitation is authorized by poets immortalized in the annals of Parnassus, whose memory will be revered as long as man has a soul to appreciate their merits. Virgil's magnificent description of the storm in the first book of the *Aeneid* is almost literally translated from Homer, where Ulysses, quitting the Isle of Calypso for 'Phaeacia's. dusty shore,' is overwhelmed by Neptune. That sublime picture, 'Ponto nox incubat atra,' and the beautiful apostrophe, 'O terque quaterque beati,' is a literal translation of the same incident in Homer. There are many other imitations, which it would be unnecessary and tedious here to enumerate. Even Milton, the pride and glory of English taste, has not disdained to replenish his imagination from the abundant fountains of the first and greatest of poets. It would have been both absurd and presumptuous, young and inexperienced as I am, to have attempted to strike out a path for myself, and to have wandered among the varied windings of Parnassus, without a guide to direct my steps, or to warn me from those fatal quicksands of literary blunders, in which, even with the best guide, I find myself so frequently immersed. There is no humility, but rather folly, in taking inferiority for a model, and there is no vanity, but rather wisdom, in following humbly the footsteps of perfection; for who would prefer quenching his thirst at the stagnant pool, when he may drink the pure waters of the fountain-head? Thus, then, however unworthily, I have presumed to select, from all the poets of ancient or modern ages, Homer, the most perfect of the votaries of Apollo, whom every nation has contributed to immortalize, to celebrate, and to admire.

If I have in these pages proved what I desired, that poetry is the parent of liberty, and of all the fine arts, and if I have succeeded in clearing up some of the obscurities of my little poem, I have attained my only object; but if on the contrary I have failed, it must be attributed to my incapacity, and not to my inclination. Either way, it would be useless to proceed further, for nothing can be more true than the declaration of Bigland, 'that a good book seldom requires, and a worthless never deserves, a long preface.'

HOPE END, 1819.

THE BATTLE OF MARATHON

BOOK I

THE war of Greece with Persia's haughty
King,
No vulgar strain, eternal Goddess, sing!
What dreary ghosts to glutted Pluto fled,
What nations suffered, and what heroes
bled:
Sing Asia's powerful Prince, who en-
vious saw
The fame of Athens, and her might in
war;
And scorns her power, at Cytherea's call
Her ruin plans, and meditates her fall;
How Athens, blinded to th' approaching
chains
By Vulcan's artful spouse, unmoved re-
mains;
Deceived by Venus thus, unconquered
Greece
Forgot her glories in the lap of peace;
While Asia's realms and Asia's lord pre-
pare
T' ensnare her freedom by the wiles of
war:
Hippiast' exalt upon th' Athenian throne,
Where once Pisistratus his father shone.
For yet her son Aeneas' wrongs impart
Revenge and grief to Cytherea's heart;
And still from smoking Troy's once sacred
wall
Does Priam's reeking shade for ven-
geance call.
Minerva saw, and Paphia's Queen defied,
A boon she begged, nor Jove the boon
denied;
That Greece should rise triumphant o'er
her foe,
Disarm th' invaders, and their power
o'erthrow.
Her prayer obtained, the blue-eyed God-
dess flies
As the fierce eagle, thro' the radiant
skies.
To Aristides then she stood confessed,
Shows Persia's arts, and fires his warlike
breast:
Then pours celestial ardour o'er his frame,
And points the way to glory and to fame.

Awe struck the Chief, and swells his
troubled soul,
In pride and wonder thoughts pro-
gressive roll.
He inly groaned and smote his labouring
breast,
At once by Pallas and by care opprest.
Inspired he moved, earth echoed where
he trod,
All full of Heaven, all burning with the
God.
Th' Athenians viewed with awe the
mighty man,
To whom the Chief impassioned thus
began:
'Hear, all ye Sons of Greece! Friends,
Fathers, hear!
The Gods command it, and the Gods
revere!
No madness mine, for mark, O favoured
Greeks!
That by my mouth the martial Goddess
speaks!
This know, Athenians, that proud Persia
now
Prepares to twine thy laurels on her brow;
Behold her princely Chiefs their weapons
wield,
By Venus fired, and shake the brazen
shield.
I hear their shouts that echo to the skies,
I see their lances blaze, their banners
rise,
I hear the clash of arms, the battle's roar,
And all the din and thunder of the war!
I know that Greeks shall purchase just
renown,
And fame impartial shall Athena crown.
Then Greeks, prepare your arms! award
the yoke,
Thus Jove commands.'—Sublime the
hero spoke;
The Greeks assent with shouts, and rend
the skies
With martial clamour and tumultuous
cries.
So struggling winds with rage indignant
sweep
The azure waters of the silent deep,

Sudden the seas rebellowing, frightful
    rise,
And dash their foaming surges to the
    skies ;
Burst the firm sand, and boil with dread-
    ful roar,
Lift their black waves, and combat with
    the shore.
So each brave Greek in thought aspires
    to fame,
Stung by his words, and dread of future
    shame ;
Glory's own fires within their bosom
    rise,
And shouts tumultuous thunder to the
    skies.
But Love's celestial Queen resentful saw
The Greeks (by Pallas warned) prepare
    for war ;
Th' indignant Goddess of the Paphian
    bower
Deceives Themistocles with heavenly
    power ;
The hero, rising, spoke : 'O rashly blind,
What sudden fury thus has seized thy
    mind ?
Boy as thou art, such empty dreams be-
    ware !
Shall we for griefs and wars unsought
    prepare ?
The will of mighty Jove, whate'er it be,
Obey, and own th' Omnipotent decree.
If our disgrace and fall the fates employ,
Why did we triumph o'er perfidious
    Troy ?
Why, say, O Chief, in that eventful hour
Did Grecian heroes crush Dardanian
    power ? '
Him eyeing sternly, thus the Greek
    replies,
Renowned for truth, and as Minerva
    wise :
' O Son of Greece, no heedless boy am I,
Despised in battle's toils, nor first to fly,
Nor dreams or frenzy call my words
    astray,
The heaven-sent mandate pious I obey.
If Pallas did not all my words inspire,
May heaven pursue me with unceasing
    ire !
But if (oh, grant my prayer, almighty
    Jove)
I bear a mandate from the Courts above,

Then thro' yon heaven let awful thunder
    roar
Till Greeks believe my mission, and
    adore ! '
He ceased—and thro' the host one
    murmur ran,
With eyes transfixed upon the godlike
    man.
But hark ! o'er earth expands the
    solemn sound ;
It lengthening grows—heaven's azure
    vaults resound,
While peals of thunder beat the echoing
    ground.
Prostrate, convinced, divine Themisto-
    cles
Embraced the hero's hands, and clasped
    his knees :
' Behold me here ' (the awe-struck
    Chieftain cries,
While tears repentant glisten in his eyes),
' Behold me here, thy friendship to en-
    treat,
Themistocles, a suppliant at thy feet.
Before no haughty despot's royal throne
This knee has bent—it bends to thee
    alone,
Thy mission to adore, thy truth to own.
Behold me, Jove, and witness what I
    swear
By all on earth I love, by all in heaven
    I fear :
Some fiend inspired my words of dark
    design,
Some fiend concealed beneath a robe
    divine ;
Then aid me in my prayer, ye Gods
    above,
Bid Aristides give me back his love ! '
He spake and wept ; benign the godlike
    man
Felt tears descend, and paused, then thus
    began :
' Thrice worthy Greek, for this shall we
    contend ?
Ah no ! I feel thy worth, thou more than
    friend.
Pardon sincere, Themistocles, receive ;
The heart declares 'tis easy to forgive.'
He spake divine, his eye with Pallas
    burns,
He spoke and sighed, and sighed and
    wept by turns.

Themistocles beheld the Chief opprest,
Awe-struck he paused, then rushed upon
    his breast,
Whom sage Miltiades with joy addressed :
' Hero of Greece, worthy a hero's name,
Adored by Athens, fav'rite child of fame !
Glory's own spirit does with truth com-
    bine
To form a soul so godlike, so divine !
O Aristides, rise, our Chief ! to save
The fame, the might of Athens from the
    grave.
Nor then refuse thy noble arm to lend
To guard Athena, and her state defend.
First I, obedient, 'customed homage pay
To own a hero's and a leader's sway.'
He said, and would have knelt ; the man
    divine
Perceived his will, and stayed the Sire's
    design.
' Not mine, O Sage, to lead this gallant
    band,'
He generous said, and grasped his agèd
    hand,
' Proud as I am in glory's arms to rise,
Athenian Greeks, to shield your liberties,
Yet 'tis not mine to lead your powerful
    state,
Enough it is to tempt you to be great ;
Be 't for Miltiades, experienced sage,
To curb your ardour and restrain your
    rage,
Your souls to temper—by his skill prepare
To succour Athens, and conduct the
    war.
More fits my early youth to purchase
    fame
By deeds in arms t' immortalize my name.'
Firmly he spake, his words the Greek
    inspire,
And all were hushed to listen and admire.
The Sage thus : ' Most Allied to Gods !
    the fame,
The pride, the glory of the Grecian name,
E'en by thee, Chief, I swear, to whom
    is given
The sacred mandate of yon marble
    heaven—
To lead, not undeserving of thy love,
T' avert the yoke, if so determines Jove.'
Amidst the host imagination rose
And paints the combat, but disdains the
    woes.

And heaven-born fancy, with dishevelled
    hair,
Points to the ensanguined field, and
    victory there.
But soon, too soon, these empty dreams
    are driven
Forth from their breasts.   But soothing
    hope is given :
Hope sprung from Jove, man's sole and
    envied heaven.
Then all his glory Aristides felt,
And begged the Chieftain's blessing as
    he knelt :
Miltiades his pious arms outspread,
Called Jove's high spirit on the hero's
    head ;
Nor called unheard—sublime in upper
    air
The bird of Jove appeared to bless his
    prayer.
Lightning he breathed, not harsh, not
    fiercely bright,
But one pure stream of heaven-collected
    light :
Jove's sacred smile lulls every care to
    rest,
Calms every woe, and gladdens every
    breast.
But what shrill blast thus bursts upon the
    ear ?
What banners rise, what heralds' forms
    appear ?
That haughty mien, and that commanding
    face
Bespeak them Persians, and of noble
    race ;
One on whose hand Darius' signet
    beamed,
Superior to the rest, a leader seemed,
With brow contracted and with flashing
    eye
Thus threatening spoke, in scornful
    majesty :
' Know Greeks that I, a sacred herald,
    bring
The awful mandate of the Persian King,
To force allegiance from the sons of
    Greece ;
Then earth and water give, nor scorn his
    peace.
For if, for homage, back reproof I bear,
To meet his wrath, his vengeful wrath,
    prepare ;

For not in vain ye scorn his dread com-
    mand
When Asia's might comes thundering in
    his hand.'
To whom Miltiades with kindling eye :
'We scorn Darius, and his threats defy ;
And now, proud herald, shall we stoop
    to shame ?
Shall Athens tremble at a tyrant's name ?
Persian, away ! such idle dreams forbear,
And shun our anger and our vengeance
    fear.'
'Oh ! vain thy words,' the herald fierce
    began ;
'Thrice vain thy dotaged words, O
    powerless man,
Sons of a desert, hoping to withstand
All the joint forces of Darius' hand ;
Fools, fools, the King of millions to defy,
For freedom's empty name to ask to die !
Yet stay, till Persia's powers their ban-
    ners rear,
Then shall ye learn our forces to revere,
And ye, O impotent, shall deign to fear !'
To whom great Aristides : rising ire
Boiled in his breast, and set his soul on
    fire :
'O wretch accurst,' the hero cried, 'to
    seek
T' insult experienced age, t' insult a
    Greek !
Inglorious slave ! whom truth and heaven
    deny,
Unfit to live, yet more unfit to die :
But, trained to pass the goblet at the board
And servile kiss the footsteps of thy lord,
Whose wretched life no glorious deeds
    beguile,
Who lives upon the semblance of a smile,
Die ! thy base shade to gloomy regions
    fled,
Join there the shivering phantoms of the
    dead.
Base slave, return to dust !' His victim
    then
In fearful accents cried : 'O best of men,
Most loved of Gods, most merciful, most
    just,
Behold me humbled, grovelling in the
    dust :
Not mine th' offence, the mandate stern
    I bring
From great Darius, Asia's tyrant King.

Oh, strike not, Chief ; not mine the
    guilt, not mine.
Ah, o'er those brows severe let mercy
    shine,
So dear to heaven, of origin divine !
Tributes, lands, gold, shall wealthy
    Persia give,
All, and yet more, but bid me, wretched,
    live ! '
He trembling, thus persuades with fond
    entreat
And nearer pressed, and clasped the
    hero's feet.
Forth from the Grecian's breast all rage
    is driven,
He lifts his arms, his eyes, his soul to
    heaven.
'Hear, Jove omnipotent, all wise, all
    great,
To whom all fate is known, whose will
    is fate ;
Hear, thou all-seeing one, hear, Sire
    divine,
Teach me thy will, and be thy wisdom
    mine !
Behold this suppliant ! life or death de-
    cree ;
Be thine the judgement, for I bend to
    thee.'
And thus the Sire of Gods and men replies,
While pealing thunder shakes the groan-
    ing skies ;
The awful voice thro' spheres unknown
    was driven,
Resounding thro' the dark'ning realms
    of heaven ;
Aloft in air sublime the echo rode,
And earth resounds the glory of the God :
'Son of Athena, let the coward die,
And his pale ghost to Pluto's empire fly ;
Son of Athena, our command obey,
Know thou our might, and then adore
    our sway.'
Th' Almighty spake—the heavens con-
    vulsive start,
From the black clouds the whizzing
    lightnings dart
And dreadful dance along the troubled
    sky,
Struggling with fate in awful mystery.
The hero heard, and Jove his breast in-
    spired,
Nor now by pity touched, but anger fired ;

While his big heart within his bosom
    burns,
Off from his feet the clinging slave he
    spurns.
Vain were his cries, his prayers 'gainst
    fate above,
Jove wills his fall, and who can strive
    with Jove?
To whom the hero : ' Hence to Pluto's
    sway,
To realms of night ne'er lit by Cynthia's
    ray ;
Hence—from yon gulf the earth and
    water bring
And crown with victory your mighty
    King.'
He said ; and where the gulf of death
    appeared,
Where raging waves, with rocks sub-
    limely reared,
He hurled the wretch, at once of hope
    bereaved ;
Struggling he fell, the roaring flood re-
    ceived.
E'en now for life his shrieks, his groans
    implore,
And now death's latent agony is o'er,
He struggling sinks, and sinks to rise no
    more.
The train, amazed, behold their herald
    die,
And Greece in arms—they tremble and
    they fly.
So some fair herd upon the verdant
    mead
See by the lion's jaws their foremost
    bleed ;
Fearful they fly, lest what revolving fate
Had doomed their leader, should them-
    selves await.
Then shouts of glorious war and fame
    resound,
Athena's brazen gates receive the lofty
    sound.
But she whom Paphia's radiant climes
    adore
From her own bower the work of Pallas
    saw :
Tumultuous thoughts within her bosom
    rise,
She calls her car, and at her will it flies.
Th' eternal car with gold celestial burns,
Its polished wheel on brazen axle turns :

This to his spouse by Vulcan's self was
    given,
An offering worthy of the forge of heaven.
The Goddess mounts the seat and seized
    the reins,
The doves celestial cut th' aerial plains ;
Before the sacred birds and car of gold
Self-moved the radiant gates of heaven
    unfold.
She then dismounts, and thus to mighty
    Jove
Begins the Mother and the Queen of
    Love :
' And is it thus, O Sire, that fraud should
    spring
From the pure breast of heaven's eternal
    King ?
Was it for this Saturnius' word was given
That Greece should fall 'mong nations
    curst of heaven ?
Thou swore by hell's black flood, and
    heaven above ;
Is this, oh say, is this the faith of Jove ?
Behold stern Pallas Athens' sons alarms,
Darius' herald crushed, and Greece in
    arms ;
E'en now behold her crested streamers
    fly,
Each Greek resolved to triumph or to die.
Ah me, unhappy ! when shall sorrow
    cease ?
Too well I know the fatal might of Greece ;
Was 't not enough imperial Troy should
    fall,
That Argive hands should raze the god-
    built wall ?
Was 't not enough Anchises' son should
    roam
Far from his native shore and much-loved
    home ?
All this, unconscious of thy fraud, I bore ;
For thou, O Sire, t' allay my vengeance,
    swore
That Athens towering in her might should
    fall
And Rome should triumph on her pros-
    trate wall.
But oh, if haughty Greece should captive
    bring
The great Darius, Persia's mighty King,
What power her pride, what power her
    might shall move ?
Not e'en the Thunderer, not eternal Jove ;

E'en to thy heaven shall rise her tower-
　　ing fame,
And prostrate nations will adore her
　　name.
Rather on me thy instant vengeance take
Than all should fall for Cytherea's sake !
Oh ! hurl me flaming in the burning lake,
Transfix me there unknown to Olympian
　　calm,
Launch thy red bolt, and bare thy crimson
　　arm,
I'd suffer all—more—bid my woes in-
　　crease,
To hear but one sad groan from haughty
　　Greece.'
She thus her grief with fruitless rage
　　expressed,
And pride and anger swelled within her
　　breast.
But he whose thunders awe the troubled
　　sky
Thus mournful spake, and curbed the
　　rising sigh :
' And it is thus celestial pleasures flow ?
E'en here shall sorrow reach and mortal
　　woe ?
Shall strife the heavenly powers for ever
　　move,
And e'en insult the sacred ear of Jove ?
Know, O rebellious, Greece shall rise
　　sublime,
In fame the first, nor, daughter, mine
　　the crime,
In valour foremost, and in virtue great :
Fame's highest glories shall attend her
　　state.
So fate ordains, nor all my boasted power
Can raise those virtues, or those glories
　　lower.
But rest secure, destroying time must
　　come,
And Athens' self must own imperial
　　Rome.'
Then the great Thunderer, and with
　　visage mild,
Shook his ambrosial curls before his child,
And bending awful gave the eternal nod ;
Heaven quaked, and fate adored the
　　parent God.
Joy seized the Goddess of the smiles and
　　loves,
Nor longer care her heavenly bosom
　　moves ;

Hope rose, and o'er her soul its powers
　　displayed,
Nor checked by sorrow, nor by grief
　　dismayed.
She thus : ' O thou, whose awful thunders
　　roll
Thro' heaven's ethereal vaults and shake
　　the Pole,
Eternal Sire, so wonderfully great,
To whom is known the secret page of fate,
Say, shall great Persia, next to Rome
　　most dear
To Venus' breast, shall Persia learn to
　　fear ?
Say, shall her fame and princely glories
　　cease ?
Shall Persia, servile, own the sway of
　　Greece ? '
To whom the Thunderer bent his brow
　　divine,
And thus in accents heavenly and benign :
' Daughter, not mine the secrets to relate,
The mysteries of all-revolving fate.
But ease thy breast ; enough for thee to
　　know,
What powerful fate decrees will Jove
　　bestow ! '
He then her griefs and anxious woes
　　beguiled,
And in his sacred arms embraced his child.
Doubt clouds the Goddess' breast—she
　　calls her car,
And lightly sweeps the liquid fields of air.
When sable night midst silent nature
　　springs,
And o'er Athena shakes her drowsy
　　wings,
The Paphian Goddess from Olympus flies,
And leaves the starry senate of the skies.
To Athens' heaven-blest towers the
　　Queen repairs
To raise more sufferings, and to cause
　　more cares ;
The Pylian Sage she moved, so loved
　　by fame,
In face, in wisdom, and in voice the same.
Twelve Chiefs in sleep absorbed and
　　grateful rest
She first beheld, and them she thus
　　addrest :
' Immortal Chiefs,' the fraudful Goddess
　　cries,
While all the hero kindled in her eyes,

' For you, these agèd arms did I employ,
For you, we razed the sacred walls of
    Troy,
And now for you my shivering shade is
    driven
From Pluto's dreary realms by urgent
    heaven;
Then oh, be wise, nor tempt th' unequal
    fight
In open fields, but wait superior might
Within immortal Athens' sacred wall ;
There strive, there triumph, nor there
    fear to fall !
To own the Thunderer's sway, then
    Greeks prepare.'
Benign she said, and melted into air.

BOOK II

WHEN from the briny deep the orient
    morn
Exalts her purple light and beams
    unshorn,
And when the flaming orb of infant day
Glares o'er the earth and re-illumes the
    sky,
The twelve deceived, with souls on fire,
    arose,
While the false vision fresh in memory
    glows.
The Senate first they sought, whose
    lofty wall
Midst Athens rises, and o'ershadows all ;
The pride of Greece, it lifts its front
    sublime,
Unbent amidst the ravages of time.
High on their towering seats, the heroes
    found
The Chiefs of Athens solemn ranged
    around ;
One of the twelve, the great Clombrotus,
    then,
Renowned for piety, and loved by men :
'Assembled heroes, Chiefs to Pallas dear,
All great in battle and in virtue, hear !
When night with sable wings extended
    rose
And wrapt our weary limbs in sweet
    repose,
I and my friends, Cydoon famed in song,
Thelon the valiant, Herocles the strong,
Cleon and Thermosites, in battle great,
By Pallas loved and blest by partial fate,

To us and other six, while day toils steep
Our eyes in happy dreams and grateful
    sleep,
The Pylian Sage appeared.   But not as
    when
On Troy's last dust he stood, the pride
    of men ;
Driven from the shore of Acheron he
    came
From lower realms to point the path to
    fame.
"O glorious Chiefs," the sacred hero said,
" For you and for your fame all Troy has
    bled ;
Hither for you my shivering shade is
    driven
From Pluto's dreary realms by urgent
    heaven;
Then oh, be wise, nor tempt th' unequal
    fight
In open field, but wait superior might
Within immortal Athens' sacred wall ;
There strive, there triumph, nor there
    fear to fall !
To own the Thunderer's sway, then
    Greeks prepare."
Benign he said, and melted into air.
" Leave us not thus," I cried, " O Pylian
    Sage,
Experienced Nestor, famed for reverend
    age ;
Say first, great hero, shall the trump of
    fame
Our glory publish, or disclose our shame?
Oh, what are Athens' fates ? " In vain
    I said ;
E'en as I spoke the shadowy Chief had
    fled.
Then here we flew to own the vision's
    sway,
And heaven's decrees to adore and to
    obey.'
He thus ; and as before the blackened
    skies
Sound the hoarse breezes, murmuring
    as they rise,
So thro' th' assembled Greeks one mur-
    mur rose,
One long dull echo lengthening as it goes.
Then all was hushed in silence—breath-
    less awe
Opprest each tongue, and trembling they
    adore.

But now uprising from th' astonished
  Chiefs,
Divine Miltiades exposed his griefs;
For well the godlike warrior Sage had
  seen
The frauds deceitful of the Paphian
  Queen,
And feared for Greece—for Greece to
  whom is given
Eternal fame, the purest gift of heaven.
And yet he feared. The pious hero rose,
Majestic in his sufferings, in his woes;
Grief clammed his tongue, but soon his
  spirit woke,
Words burst aloft, and all the Patriot
  spoke.
'O Athens, Athens! all the snares I view;
Thus shalt thou fall, and fall inglorious
  too!
Are all thy boasted dignities no more?
Is all thy might, are all thy glories o'er?
Oh, woe on woe, unutterable grief!
Not Nestor's shade, that cursèd phantom
  chief,
But in that reverend air, that lofty mien,
Behold the frauds of Love's revengeful
  Queen.
Not yet her thoughts does vengeance
  cease t' employ;
Her son Aeneas' wrongs, and burning
  Troy,
Not yet forgotten lie within her breast,
Nor soothed by time, nor by despair
  deprest.
Greeks still extolled by glory and by
  fame—
For yet, O Chiefs! ye bear a Grecian
  name—
If in these walls, these sacred walls, we
  wait
The might of Persia and the will of fate,
Before superior force will Athens fall
And one o'erwhelming ruin bury all.
Then in the open plain your might essay,
Rush on to battle, crush Darius' sway;
The frauds of Venus, warrior Greeks,
  beware,
Disdain the Persian foes, nor stoop to
  fear.'
This said, Clombrotus him indignant
  heard,
Nor felt his wisdom, nor his wrath he
  feared.

With rage the Chief, the godlike Sage,
  beheld,
And passion in his stubborn soul re-
  belled.
'Thrice impious man,' th' infuriate
  Chieftain cries
(Flames black and fearful flashing from
  his eyes),
'Where lies your spirit, Greeks? and
  can ye bow
To this proud upstart of your power so
  low?
What! does his aspect awe ye? is his eye
So full of haughtiness and majesty?
Behold the impious soul, that dares defy
The power of Gods and Sovereign of
  the sky!
And can your hands no sacred weapon
  wield
To crush the tyrant, and your country
  shield?
On, Greeks!—your sons, your homes,
  your country free
From such usurping Chiefs and tyranny!'
He said, and grasped his weapon; at
  his words
Beneath the horizon gleamed ten thou-
  sand swords,
Ten thousand swords e'en in one instant
  raised,
Sublime they danced aloft, and midst
  the Senate blazed;
Nor wisdom checked, nor gratitude re-
  prest,
They rose, and flashed before the Sage's
  breast.
With pride undaunted, greatness un-
  subdued,
'Gainst him in arms the impetuous Greeks
  he viewed,
Unarmed, unawed, before th' infuriate
  bands,
Nor begged for life, nor stretched his
  suppliant hands.
He stood astounded, riveted, opprest
By grief unspeakable, which swelled
  his breast;
Life, feeling, being, sense forgotten lie,
Buried in one wide waste of misery.
Can this be Athens! this her Senate's
  pride?
He asked but gratitude,—was this de-
  nied?

Tho' Europe's homage at his feet were
    hurled
Athens forsakes him—Athens was his
    world.
Unutterable woe! by anguish stung
All his full soul rushed heaving to his
    tongue,
And thoughts of power, of fame, of
    greatness o'er,
He cried 'Athenians!' and he could no
    more.
Awed by that voice of agony, that word,
Hushed were the Greeks, and sheathed
    the obedient sword ;
They stood abashed—to them the ancient
    Chief
Began, and thus relieved his swelling
    grief :
'Athenians ! warrior Greeks ! my words
    revere !
Strike me, but listen—bid me die, but
    hear!
Hear not Clombrotus when he bids you
    wait,
At Athens' walls, Darius and your fate ;
I feel that Pallas' self my soul inspires,
My mind she strengthens, and my bosom
    fires ;
Strike, Greeks ! but hear me ; think not
    to this heart
Yon thirsty swords one breath of fear
    impart !
Such slavish, low-born thoughts, to
    Greeks unknown,
A Persian feels, and cherishes alone !
Hear me, Athenians ! hear me, and
    believe,
See Greece mistaken ! e'en the Gods
    deceive.
But fate yet wavers—yet may wisdom
    move
These threatening woes and thwart the
    Queen of Love.
Obey my counsels, and invoke for aid
The cloud-compelling God and blue-eyed
    maid ;
I fear not for myself the silent tomb ;
Death lies in every shape, and death
    must come.
But ah ! ye mock my truth, traduce my
    fame,
Ye blast my honour, stigmatize my
    name !

Ye call me tyrant when I wish thee free,
Usurper, when I live but, Greece, for
    thee !'
And thus the Chief—and boding silence
    drowned
Each clam'rous tongue, and sullen reigned
    around.
'O Chief !' great Aristides first began,
' Mortal yet perfect, godlike and yet man !
Boast of ungrateful Greece ! my prayer
    attend.
Oh ! be my Chieftain, Guardian, Father,
    Friend !
And ye, O Greeks ! impetuous and
    abhorred,
Again presumptuous, lift the rebel sword,
Again your weapons raise, in hateful
    ire,
To crush the Leader, Hero, Patriot, Sire !
Not such was Greece when Greeks united
    stood
To bathe perfidious Troy in hostile
    blood ;
Not such were Greeks inspired by glory ;
    then
As Gods they conquered, now they're
    less than men !
Degenerate race ! now lost to once-
    loved fame,
Traitors to Greece and to the Grecian
    name !
Who now your honours, who your
    praise will seek ?
Who now shall glory in the name of
    Greek ?
But since such discords your base souls
    divide,
Procure the lots, let Jove and Heaven
    decide.'
To him Clombrotus thus admiring cries :
' Thy thoughts how wondrous, and thy
    words how wise !
So let it be, avert the threatened woes,
And Jove be present and the right dis-
    close ;
But give me, Sire of Gods and powers
    above,
The heavenly vision, and my truth to
    prove !
Give me t' avenge the breach of all thy
    laws,
T' avenge myself, then aid my righteous
    cause !

If this thou wilt, I'll to thine altars lead
Twelve bulls which to thy sacred name
 shall bleed,
Six snow-white heifers of a race divine
Prostrate shall fall, and heap the groaning
 shrine.
Nor this the most—six rams that fearless
 stray
Untouched by man, for thee this arm
 shall slay.'
Thus prayed the Chief, with shouts the
 heavens resound ;
Jove weighs the balance and the lots go
 round !
Declare, O Muse ! for to thy piercing eyes
The book of fate irrevocably lies ;
What lots leapt forth, on that eventful day,
Who won, who lost, all-seeing Goddess,
 say !
First great Clombrotus all his fortune
 tried
And strove with fate, but Jove his prayer
 denied.
Infuriate to the skies his arms are driven,
And raging thus upbraids the King of
 Heaven :
' Is this the virtue of the blest abodes,
And this the justice of the God of Gods ?
Can he who hurls the bolt and shakes
 the sky
The prayer of truth, unblemished truth,
 deny ?
Has he no faith by whom the clouds are
 riven,
Who sits superior on the throne of heaven ?
No wonder earth-born men are prone
 to fall
In sin, or listen to dishonour's call,
When Gods, th' immortal Gods, trans-
 gress the laws
Of truth, and sin against a righteous
 cause.'
Furious he said, by anger's spirit fired,
Then sullen from the Senate walls retired.
'Tis now Miltiades' stern fate to dare,
But first he lifts his pious soul in prayer.
' Daughter of Jove !' the mighty Chief
 began,
' Without thy wisdom, frail and weak
 is man.
A phantom Greece adores ; oh, show
 thy power,
And prove thy love in this eventful hour !

Crown all thy glory, all thy might
 declare ! '
The Chieftain prayed, and Pallas heard
 his prayer.
Swayed by the presence of the power
 divine,
The fated lot, Miltiades, was thine !
That hour the swelling trump of partial
 fame
Diffused eternal glory on thy name !
' Daughter of Jove,' he cries, ' uncon-
 quered maid !
Thy power I own, and I confess thy aid ;
For this twelve ewes upon thy shrine
 shall smoke
Of milk-white fleece, the comeliest of
 their flock,
While hecatombs and generous sacrifice
Shall fume and blacken half th' aston-
 ished skies.'
And thus the Chief—the shouting Greeks
 admire,
While truth's bright spirit sets their
 souls on fire.
Then thus Themistocles : ' Ye Grecian
 host,
Not now the time for triumph or for
 boast.
Now, Greeks ! for graver toils your minds
 prepare,
Not for the strife, but council of the war.
Behold the sacred herald ! sent by
 Greece
To Sparta's vales, now hushed in leagues
 of peace ;
Her Chiefs, to aid the common cause,
 t' implore,
And bid Darius shun the Argive shore ;
Behold him here ! then let the leader
 Greek
Command the bearer of our hopes to
 speak.'
And thus the Sage : ' Where'er the
 herald stands,
Bid him come forth, 'tis Athens' Chief
 commands,
And bid him speak with freedom uncon-
 trolled,
His thoughts deliver and his charge un-
 fold.'
He said and sate—the Greeks impatient
 wait
The will of Sparta and Athena's fate.

Silent they sate—so ere the whirlwinds rise,
Ere billows foam and thunder to the skies,
Nature in death-like calm her breath suspends,
And hushed in silent awe th' approaching storm attends.
Now midst the Senate's walls the herald stands :
' Ye Greeks,' he said, and stretched his sacred hands,
' Assembled heroes, ye Athenian bands,
And thou, beloved of Jove, our Chief, O Sage,
Renowned for wisdom, as renowned for age,
And all ye Chiefs in battle rank divine !
No joyful mission swayed by Pallas mine.
The hardy Spartans with one voice declare
Their will to aid our freedom and our war ;
Instant they armed, by zeal and impulse driven,
But on the plains of the mysterious heaven
Comets and fires were writ—an awful sign,
And dreadful omen of the wrath divine :
While threatened plagues upon their shores appear,
They curb their valour, all subdued by fear ;
The oracles declare the will above,
And of the sister and the wife of Jove,
That not until the moon's bright course was o'er
The Spartan warriors should desert their shore.
Threats following threats succeed the mandate dire,
Plagues to themselves, and to their harvest fire.
The Spartan Chiefs desist, their march delay
To wait th' appointed hour and heaven obey.
Grief smote my heart, my hopes and mission vain ;
Their town I quitted for my native plain,
And when an eminence I gained, in woe
I gazed upon the verdant fields below,

Where Nature's ample reign, extending wide,
Displays her graces with commanding pride ;
Where cool Eurotas winds her limpid floods
Thro' verdant valleys, and thro' shady woods ;
And crowned in majesty o'ertowering all,
In bright effulgence Sparta's lofty wall.
To these I looked farewell, and humbled, bowed
In chastened sorrow to the thundering God.
'Twas thus I mused, when from a verdant grove
That wafts delicious perfume from above,
The monster Pan his form gigantic reared,
And dreadful to my awe-struck sight appeared.
I hailed the God who reigns supreme below,
Known by the horns that started from his brow ;
Up to the hips a goat, but man's his face,
Tho' grim, and stranger to celestial grace.
Within his hand a shepherd's crook he bore,
The gift of Dian on th' Arcadian shore ;
Before th' immortal power I, fearing, bowed,
Congealed with dread, and thus addressed the God :
" Comes Hermes' son, as awful as his sire,
To vent upon the Greeks immortal ire ?
Is't not enough the mandate stern I bring
From Sparta's Chiefs and Sparta's royal King,
That heaven enjoins them to refrain from fight
Till Dian fills again her horns with light ?
Then vain their aid, ere then may Athens fall
And Persia's haughty Chiefs invest her wall."
I said and sighed, the God in accents mild
My sorrow thus and rigid griefs beguiled :
" Not to destroy I come, O chosen Greek,
Not Athens' fall, but Athens' fame I seek.
Then give again to honour and to fame
My power despised and my forgotten name.

At Sparta's doom no longer, Chief, repine,
But learn submission to the will divine ;
Behold e'en now, within this fated hour,
On Marathonian plains, the Persian power !
E'en Hippias' self inspires th' embattled host,
Th' Athenian's terror, as the Persian's boast.
Bid Athens rise and glory's powers attest.
Enough—no more—the fates conceal the rest."
He said, his visage burned with heavenly light ;
He spoke and, speaking, vanished from my sight ;
And awed, I sought where those loved walls invite.
But think not, warrior Greeks, the fault is mine,
If Athens fall—it is by wrath divine.
I vainly, vainly grieve, the evil springs
From him—the God of Gods, the King of Kings !'
The Herald said, and bent his sacred head,
While cherished hope from every bosom fled.
Each dauntless hero, by despair deprest,
Felt the deep sorrow swelling in his breast :
They mourn for Athens, friendless and alone ;
Cries followed cries, and groan succeeded groan.
Th' Athenian matrons, startled at the sound,
Rush from their looms and anxious crowd around.
They ask the cause, the fatal cause is known
By each fond sigh and each renewing groan,
While in their arms some infant love they bear
At once for which they joy, for which they fear.
Hushed on its mother's breast, the cherished child,
Unconscious midst the scene of terror, smiled.

On rush the matrons, they despairing seek
Miltiades, adored by every Greek ;
Him found at length, his counsels they entreat,
Hang on his knees and clasp his sacred feet ;
Their babes before him on the ground they throw
In all the maddening listlessness of woe.
First Delopeia, of the matrons chief,
Thus vents her bursting soul in frantic grief,
While her fond babe she holds aloft in air ;
Thus her roused breast prefers a mother's prayer :
' O Son of Cimon, for the Grecians raise
To heaven thy fame, thy honour, and thy praise.
Thus—thus—shall Athens and her heroes fall,
Shall thus one ruin seize and bury all ?
Say, shall these babes be strangers then to fame,
And be but Greeks in spirit and in name ?
Oh, first, ye Gods ! and hear a mother's prayer,
First let them glorious fall in ranks of war !
If Asia triumph, then shall Hippias reign,
And Athens' free-born sons be slaves again !
O Son of Cimon ! let thy influence call
The souls of Greeks to triumph or to fall !
And guard their own, their children's, country's name,
From foul dishonour and eternal shame !'
Thus thro' her griefs the love of glory broke ;
The mother wept, but 'twas the Patriot spoke :
And as before the Greek she bowed with grace,
The lucid drops bedewed her lovely face.
Their shrieks and frantic cries the matrons cease,
And death-like silence awes the sons of Greece.
Thrice did the mighty Chief of Athens seek
To curb his feelings and essay to speak ;

'Twas vain—the ruthless sorrow wrung
   his breast,
His mind disheartened and his soul op-
   prest.
He thus—while o'er his cheek the
   moisture stole :
' Retire, ye matrons, nor unman my soul !
Tho' little strength this agèd arm re-
   tains,
My swelling soul Athena's foe disdains ;
Hushed be your griefs, to heaven for
   victory cry,
Assured we'll triumph or with freedom
   die.
And ye, O Chiefs, when night disowns
   her sway,
And pensive Dian yields her power to
   day,
To quit these towers for Marathon pre-
   pare,
And brave Darius in the ranks of war.
For yet may Jove protect the Grecian
   name
And crown, in unborn ages, Athens'
   fame.'
He said—and glowing with the warlike
   fire,
And cheered by hope, the godlike Chiefs
   retire.
Now Cynthia rules the earth, the flaming
   God
In ocean sinks, green Neptune's old
   abode ;
Black Erebus on drowsy pinions springs,
And o'er Athena cowers his sable wings.

BOOK III

When from the deep the hour's eternal
   sway
Impels the coursers of the flaming day,
The long-haired Greeks with brazen
   arms prepare
Their freedom to preserve and wage the
   war.
First Aristides from the couch arose,
While his great mind with all Minerva
   glows ;
His mighty limbs his golden arms invest,
The cuirass blazes on his ample breast,
The glittering cuisses both his legs enfold,
And the huge shield's on fire with
   burnished gold ;

His hands two spears uphold of equal
   size,
And fame's bright glories kindle in his
   eyes ;
Upon his helmet plumes of horse-hair
   nod,
And forth he moved, majestic as a God !
Upon his snorting steed the warrior
   sprung,
The courser neighed, the brazen armour
   rung ;
From heaven's ethereal heights the
   martial maid
With conscious pride the hero's might
   surveyed.
Him as she eyed, she shook the gorgon
   shield ;
' Henceforth to me,' she cried, ' let all
   th' immortals yield.
Let monster Mars the Latian regions
   own,
For Attica, Minerva stands alone.'
And now th' unconquered Chief of
   Justice gains
The Senate's walls, and there the steed
   detains,
Whence he dismounts—Miltiades he
   seeks,
Beloved of Jove, the leader of the Greeks :
Nor sought in vain ; there clad in
   armour bright
The Chieftain stood, all eager for the
   fight.
Within his agèd hands two lances shine,
The helmet blazed upon his brows divine :
And as he bends beneath th' unequal
   weight
Youth smiles again, when with gigantic
   might
His nervous limbs immortal arms could
   wield,
Crush foe on foe, and raging, heap the
   field.
Yet tho' such days were past, and ruth-
   less age
Transformed the warrior to the thought-
   ful sage ;
Tho' the remorseless hand of silent time
Impaired each joint and stiffened every
   limb ;
Yet thro' his breast the fire celestial stole,
Throbbed in his veins, and kindled in his
   soul

In thought, the Lord of Asia threats no
  more,
And Hippias bites the dust mid seas of
  gore.
Him as he viewed, the youthful hero's
  breast
Heaved high with joy, and thus the Sage
  addressed :
' Chief, best beloved of Pallas,' he began,
' In fame allied to Gods, O wondrous
  man !
Behold Apollo gilds th' Athenian wall,
Our freedom waits, and fame and glory
  call
To battle ! Asia's King and myriads
  dare,
Swell the loud trump, and swell the din
  of war.'
He said impatient ; then the warrior sage
Began, regardless of the fears of age :
' Not mine, O youth, with caution to
  control
The fire and glory of thy eager soul ;
So was I wont in brazen arms to shine,
Such strength and such impatient fire
  were mine.'
He said, and bade the trumpet's peals
  rebound,
High, and more high, the echoing war-
  notes sound :
Sudden one general shout the din replies,
A thousand lances blazing as they rise,
And Athens' banners wave and float
  along the skies.
So from the marsh the cranes embodied
  fly,
Clap their glad wings and cut the liquid
  sky ;
With thrilling cries they mount their
  joyful way,
Vig'rous they spring, and hail the new-
  born day.
So rose the shouting Greeks, inspired by
  fame
T' assert their freedom and maintain
  their name.
First came Themistocles, in arms re-
  nowned,
Whose steed, impatient, tore the trem-
  bling ground ;
High o'er his helmet snowy plumes arise,
And shade that brow which Persia's
  might defies ;

A purple mantle graceful waves behind,
Nor hides his arms, but floats upon the
  wind ;
His mighty form two crimson belts enfold,
Rich in embroidery and stiff with gold.
Callimachus the Polemarch next came,
The theme of general praise and general
  fame.
Cynaegirus, who e'en the Gods would
  dare,
Heap ranks on ranks, and thunder thro'
  the war ;
His virtues godlike ; man's his strength
  surpassed,
In battle foremost, and in flight the last ;
His ponderous helm's a shaggy lion's hide,
And the huge war-axe clattered at his side;
The mighty Chief a brazen chariot bore,
While fame and glory hail him and adore.
Antenor next his aid to Athens gave,
Like Paris youthful, and like Hector
  brave ;
Cleon, Minerva's priest, experienced
  sage,
Advanced in wisdom, as advanced in age.
Agregoras, Delenus' favourite child ;
The parent's cares the glorious son be-
  guiled ;
But now he leaves his sire to seek his
  doom,
His country's freedom or a noble tomb.
And young Aratus, moved with youthful
  pride,
And heart elated at the hero's side.
Next thou, Cleones, thou triumphant
  moved,
By Athens honoured, by the Greeks be-
  loved :
And Sthenelus the echoing pavements
  trod,
From youth devoted to the martial God.
Honour unspotted crowned the hero's
  name,
Unbounded virtue and unbounded fame.
Such heroes shone the foremost of the
  host,
All Athens' glory and all Athens' boast.
Behind, a sable cloud of warriors rise
With ponderous arms, and shouting rend
  the skies :
These bands with joy Miltiades inspire,
Fame fills his breast and sets his soul on
  fire ;

Aloft he springs into the gold-wrought
car,
While the shrill blast resounds, to war !
to war !
The coursers plunge as conscious of
their load
And, proudly neighing, feel they bear
a God.
The snow-white steeds by Pallas' self
were given,
Which sprung from the immortal breed
of heaven.
The car was wrought of brass and bur-
nished gold,
And divers figures on its bulk were told,
Of heroes who in plunging to the fight
Shrouded Troy's glories in eternal night :
Of fierce Pelides, who relenting gave,
At Priam's prayer, to Hector's corpse a
grave :
Here Spartan Helen flies her native shore
To bid proud Troy majestic stand no
more :
There Hector clasps his consort to his
breast,
Consoles her sufferings, tho' himself op-
prest ;
And there he rushes to the embattled
field
For victory or death, nor e'en in death
to yield :
Here Ilium prostrate feels the Argive ire,
Her heroes perished, and her towers on
fire :
And here old Priam breathes his last-
drawn sigh,
And feels 'tis least of all his griefs to
die :
There his loved sire, divine Aeneas,
bears,
And leaves his own with all a patriot's
tears ;
While in one hand he holds his weeping
boy,
And looks his last on lost unhappy Troy.
The warrior seized the reins, the im-
patient steeds
Foam at the mouth and spring where
glory leads.
The gates the heroes pass, th' Athenian
dames
Bend from their towers, and bid them
save from flames

Their walls, their infant heirs, and fill
the skies
With shouts, entreaties, prayers, and
plaintive cries :
Echo repeats their words, the sounds
impart
New vigour to each Greek's aspiring
heart.
Forward with shouts they press, and
hastening on
Try the bold lance and dream of Mara-
thon.
Meanwhile the Persians on th' embattled
plain
Prepare for combat, and the Greeks dis-
dain.
Twice twenty sable bulls they daily pay,
Unequalled homage, to the God of day ;
Sucn worthy gifts the wealthy warriors
bring,
And such the offerings of the Persian
King ;
While the red wine around his altars
flowed
They beg protection from the flaming
God.
But the bright Patron of the Trojan war
Accepts their offerings, but rejects their
prayer :
The power of love alone dares rigid fate,
To vent on Greece her vengence and
her hate ;
Not love for Persia prompts the venge-
ful dame,
But hate for Athens, and the Grecian
name :
In Phoebus' name the fraudful Queen
receives
The hecatombs, and happy omens gives.
And now the heralds with one voice
repeat
The will of Datis echoing thro' the fleet,
To council, to convene the Persian train,
That Athens' Chiefs should brave their
might in vain.
The Chiefs and Hippias' self his will obey,
And seek the camp—the heralds lead the
way.
There on the couch their leader Datis sate
In ease luxurious, and in kingly state ;
Around his brow pride deep and scornful
played,
A purple robe his slothful limbs arrayed,

Which o'er his form its silken draperies
  fold,
Majestic sweeps the ground, and glows
  with gold ;
While Artaphernes resting at his side
Surveys th' advancing train with con-
  scious pride.
The elder leader, mighty Datis, then :
' Assembled Princes, great and valiant
  men,
And thou thrice glorious Hippias, loved
  by heaven,
To whom, as to thy sire, is Athens
  given ;
Behold the Grecian banners float afar,
Shouting they hail us, and provoke the
  war.
Then, mighty Chiefs and Princes, be it
  yours
To warm and fire the bosoms of our
  powers,
That when the morn has spread her
  saffron light
The Greeks may own and dread Darius'
  might ;
For know, O Chiefs, when once proud
  Athens falls,
When Persian flames shall reach her
  haughty walls,
From her depression wealth to you shall
  spring,
And honour, fame, and glory to your
  King.'
He said ; his words the Princes' breasts
  inspire :
Silent they bend, and with respect retire.
And now the Greeks in able marches
  gain,
By Pallas fired, the Marathonian plain.
Before their eyes th' unbounded ocean
  rolls
And all Darius' fleet—unawed their
  souls :
They fix their banners and the tents they
  raise,
And in the sun their polished javelins
  blaze.
Their leader's self within the brazen car
Their motions orders, and prepares for
  war ;
Their labours o'er, the agèd hero calls
The Chiefs to council midst the canvas
  walls.

And then the Sage : ' How great the
  Persian host !
But let them not their strength or num-
  bers boast ;
Their slothful minds, to love of fame un-
  known,
Sigh not for war, but for the spoil alone
Strangers to honour's pure immortal
  light,
They not as heroes, but as women fight ;
Grovelling as proud, and cowardly as
  vain,
The Greeks they fear, their numbers
  they disdain.
And now, Athenians ! fired by glory, rise
And lift your fame unsullied to the skies,
Your victim Persia, liberty your prize.
And now twice twenty sable bullocks
  bring
To heap the altars of the thundering King,
Bid twelve white heifers of gigantic
  breed
To Jove's great daughter, wise Minerva,
  bleed,
And then in sleep employ the solemn
  night,
Nor till Apollo reigns provoke the fight.'
The hero said ; the warlike council o'er
They raise the lofty altars on the shore.
They pile in heaps the pride of all the
  wood ;
They fall the first, who first in beauty
  stood :
The pine that soars to heaven, the sturdy
  oak,
And cedars crackle at each hero's stroke.
And now two altars stand of equal size,
And lift their forms majestic to the
  skies ;
The heroes then twice twenty bullocks
  bring,
A worthy offering to the thundering King.
The agèd leader seized the sacred knife,
Blow followed blow, out gushed the
  quivering life ;
Thro' their black hides the ruthless steel
  is driven,
The victims groan—Jove thunders from
  his heaven.
And then their bulks upon the pile they
  lay,
The flames rush upward, and the armies
  pray.

Driven by the wind, the roaring fires
    ascend,
And now they hiss in air, and now
    descend ;
With all their sap, the new-cut faggots
    raise
Their flames to heaven, and crackle as
    they blaze.
And then the Sage : 'Oh, thou of powers
    above
The first and mightiest, hear, eternal
    Jove !
Give us, that Athens in her strength may
    rise,
And lift our fame and freedom to the
    skies !'
This said, he ceased—th' assembled
    warriors pour
The sacred incense, and the God adore;
Then partial Jove propitious heard their
    prayer,
Thrice shook the heavens, and thundered
    thro' the air.
With joy the Greeks the favouring sign
    inspires,
And their breasts glow with all the war-
    like fires :
And now twelve heifers white as snow
    they lead
To great Minerva's sacred name to bleed;
They fall—their bulks upon the pile are
    laid,
Sprinkled with oil, and quick in flame
    arrayed.
And now descending midst the darken-
    ing skies
Behold the Goddess of the radiant eyes ;
The ground she touched, beneath the
    mighty load
Earth groaning rocks, and nature hails
    the God.
Within her hand her father's lightnings
    shone,
And shield that blazes near th' eternal
    throne ;
The Greeks with fear her dauntless form
    surveyed,
And trembling bowed before the blue-
    eyed maid.
Then favouring, thus began the power
    divine,
While in her eyes celestial glories
    shine :

'Ye sons of Athens, loved by heaven,'
    she cries,
'Revered by men, be valiant and be wise.
When morn awakes, Darius' numbers
    dare,
Clang your loud arms, and rouse the
    swelling war :
But first to yon proud fleet a herald send
To bid the Persians yield, and fight sus-
    pend ;
For vainly to their God they suppliant
    call,
Jove favours Greece, and Pallas wills
    their fall.'
She said, and thro' the depths of air she
    flies,
Mounts the blue heaven, and scales the
    liquid skies.
The Greeks rejoicing thank the powers
    above,
And Jove's great daughter, and eternal
    Jove ;
And now a herald to the fleet they send
To bid the Persians yield, and war sus-
    pend.
Thro' the divided troops the herald goes,
Thro' Athens' host, and thro' th' un-
    numbered foes ;
Before the holy man the Persian bands
Reverend give way, and ask what
    Greece demands :
He tells not all, but that he, chosen,
    seeks
Datis their Chief, by order of the Greeks.
The mission but in part he sage reveals,
And what his prudence prompts him he
    conceals.
Then to their Chief they lead him, where
    he sate
With pomp surrounded, and in gorgeous
    state ;
Around his kingly couch his arms were
    spread
Flaming in gold, by forge Cyclopean
    made.
And then stern Datis, frowning, thus
    began :
'What hopes deceive thee, miserable
    man ?
What treacherous fate allures thee thus
    to stray
Thro' all our hosts ? What Gods beguile
    the way ?

Think'st thou to 'scape the Persian steel, when Greece
Our herald crushed, and banished hopes of peace ?
But speak, what will the Greeks ? and do they dare
To prove our might, and tempt th' unequal war ?
Or do they deign to own Darius' sway,
And yield to Persia's might th' embattled day ?'
To whom th' Athenian herald made reply :
'The Greeks disdain your terms, and scorn to fly.
Unknown to heroes and to sons of Greece
The shameful slavery of a Persian peace ;
Defiance stern, not servile gifts I bring,
Your bonds detested, and despised your King.
Of equal size, the Greeks two altars raise
To Jove's high glory, and Minerva's praise ;
The God propitious heard, and from the skies
Descends the Goddess of the azure eyes,
And thus began—" Assembled Greeks, give ear,
Attend my wisdom, nor my glory fear ;
When morn awakes, Darius' numbers dare,
Clang your loud arms, and rouse the swelling war :
But first to yon proud fleet a herald send
To bid the Persians yield, and war suspend ;
For vainly to their God they suppliant call,
Jove favours Greece, and Pallas wills their fall."
The Goddess spoke ; th' Athenians own her sway ;
I seek the fleet, and heaven's command obey.
The Greeks disdain your millions in the war,
Nor I, O Chief, your promised vengeance fear.
Strike ! but remember that the God on high
Who rules the heavens, and thunders thro' the sky,
Not unrevenged will see his herald slain,
Nor shall thy threats his anger tempt in vain.'

And thus the Greek : then Datis thus replies,
Flames black and fearful scowling from his eyes :
'Herald, away ! and Asia's vengeance fear ;
Back to your frenzied train my mandate bear,
That Greece and Grecian Gods may threat in vain—
We scorn their anger, and their wrath disdain :
For he who lights the earth and rules the skies
With happy omens to our vows replies ;
When morn uprising breathes her saffron light,
Prepare to dare our millions in the fight.
Thy life I give, Darius' will to say,
And Asia's hate—hence, Chief, no more, away !'
He said, and anger filled the Grecian's breast,
But prudent, he the rising wrath suppressed ;
Indignant, thro' the canvas tents he strode
And silently invoked the thundering God.
Fears for his country in his bosom rose
As on he wandered midst unnumbered foes ;
He strikes his swelling breast and hastens on
O'er the wide plains of barren Marathon.
And now he sees the Grecian banners rise,
And well-armed warriors blaze before his eyes.
Then thus he spoke : 'Ye Grecian bands, give ear,
Ye warrior Chiefs and Attic heroes hear !
Your will to Asia's other Prince I told,
All which you bade me, Chieftains, to unfold ;
But Pallas' vengeance I denounced in vain,
Your threats he scorned, and heard with proud disdain.
The God, he boasts, who lights the earth and skies,
With happy omens to his vows replies ;
Then when the uprising morn extends her light
Prepare, ye Greeks, to dare his powers in fight.'

He said—the Greeks for instant strife declare
Their will, and arm impatient for the war.
Then he, their godlike Chief, as Pallas sage :
'Obey my counsels, and repress your rage,
Ye Greeks,' he cried, ' the sacred night displays
Her shadowy veil, and earth in gloom arrays ;
Her sable shades e'en Persia's Chiefs obey,
And wait the golden mandate of the day :
Such is the will of Jove, and Gods above,
And such the order of the loved of Jove.'
He said—the Greeks their leader's word obey,
They seek their tents, and wait th' approaching day ;
O'er either host celestial Somnus reigns,
And solemn silence lulls th' embattled plains.

BOOK IV

AND now the morn by Jove to mortals given
With rosy fingers opes the gates of heaven.
The Persian Princes and their haughty Lord
Gird on their arms, and seize the flaming sword :
Forth, forth they rush to tempt the battle's roar,
Earth groans, and shouts rebellowing shake the shore.
As when the storm the heavenly azure shrouds
With sable night, and heaps on clouds the clouds,
The Persians rose, and crowd th' embattled plain,
And stretch their warlike millions to the main ;
And now th' Athenians throng the fatal field,
By fame inspired, and swords and bucklers wield ;
In air sublime their floating banners rise,
The lances blaze, the trumpets rend the skies.

And then Miltiades : 'Athenians, hear,
Behold the Persians on the field appear,
Dreadful in arms; remember, Greeks, your fame,
Rush to the war, and vindicate your name ;
Forward ! till low in death the Persians lie,
For freedom triumph or for freedom die.'
He said ; his visage glows with heavenly light ;
He spoke sublime, and rushed into the fight.
And now the fury of the day began—
Lance combats lance, and man 's opposed to man ;
Beneath their footsteps groans the labouring plain,
And shouts re-echoing bellow to the main ;
Mars rages fierce ; by heroes, heroes die ;
Earth rocks, Jove thunders, and the wounded cry.
What mighty Chiefs by Aristides fell,
What heroes perished, heavenly Goddess, tell :
First thou, O Peleus ! felt his conquering hand,
Stretched in the dust and weltering in the sand ;
Thro' thy bright shield the forceful weapon went,
Thyself in arms o'erthrown, thy corselet rent.
Next rash Antennes met an early fate,
And feared, alas ! th' unequal foe too late ;
And Delucus the sage, and Philo fell,
And Crotan sought the dreary gates of hell,
And Mnemon's self with wealth and honour crowned,
Revered for virtue, and for fame renowned ;
He, great in battle, feared the hero's hand,
Groaning he fell, and spurned the reeking sand.
But what bold chief thus rashly dares advance ?
Tho' not in youth, he shakes the dreadful lance ;
Proudly the earth the haughty warrior trod,
He looked a Monarch and he moved a God :

Then on the Greek with rage intrepid
   flew
And with one blow th' unwary Greek
   o'erthrew;
That hour, O Chief, and that eventful
   day,
Had bade thee pass a shivering ghost
   away,
But Pallas, fearful for her fav'rite's life,
Sudden upraised thee to renew the
   strife;
Then Aristides with fresh vigour rose,
Shame fired his breast, his soul with
   anger glows;
With all his force he rushes on the foe,
The warrior bending disappoints the
   blow,
And thus with rage contemptuous:
   'Chieftain, know,
Hippias, the loved of heaven, thine eyes
   behold,
Renowned for strength of arm, in battle
   bold,
But tell thy race, and who the man
   whose might
Dares cope with rebel Athens' King in
   fight.'
Stung to the soul, 'O slave,' the Greek
   returns,
While his big heart within his bosom
   burns,
'Perfidious Prince, to faith and truth
   unknown;
On Athens' ashes raise thy tyrant throne,
When Grecia's chiefs and Grecia's heroes
   fall,
When Persia's fires invest her lofty wall,
When nought but slaves within her
   towers remain;
Then, nor till then, shalt thou, O Hippias,
   reign,
Then, nor till then, will Athens yield her
   fame
To foul dishonour and eternal shame!
Come on! no matter what my race or
   name;
For this, O Prince, this truth unerring
   know,
That in a Greek you meet a noble foe.'
Furious he said, and on the Prince he
   sprung
With all his force, the meeting armour
   rung,

Struggling they raged, and both together
   fell.
That hour the tyrant's ghost had entered
   hell,
But partial fate prolonged the Prince's
   breath,
Renewed the combat, and forbad the
   death.
Meanwhile the hosts the present war
   suspend,
Silent they stand, and heaven's decree
   attend.
First the bright lance majestic Hippias
   threw,
But erringly the missile weapon flew;
Then Aristides hurled the thirsty dart,
Struck the round shield, and nearly
   pierced his heart,
But the bright arms, that shone with
   conscious pride,
Received the blow, and turned the point
   aside.
And thus the Greek: 'Whom your inquir-
   ing eyes
Behold, O Prince,' th' Athenian hero
   cries,
'Is Aristides, called the just, a name
By Athens honoured, nor unknown to
   fame.'
Scared at the sound, and seized by sudden
   fright,
The Prince starts back in mean, inglorious
   flight.
And now Bellona rages o'er the field,
All strive elated, all disdain to yield;
And great Themistocles, in arms re-
   nowned,
Stretched heaps of heroes on the groan-
   ing ground.
First by his hand fell Delos' self, divine,
The last-loved offspring of a noble line;
Straight thro' his neck the reeking dart
   was driven,
Prostrate he sinks, and vainly calls to
   heaven.
Next godlike Phanes, midst the Persians
   just,
Leucon and mighty Caudos bit the
   dust;
And now the Greek, with pride im-
   prudent, dares
Victorious Mandrocles, renowned in
   wars.

The agile Persian swift avoids the blow,
Furious disarms and grasps th' unequal
foe !
Th' intrepid Greek with godlike calm
awaits
His instant fall, and dares th' impending
fates ;
But great Cynaegirus his danger spies
And lashed his steeds—the ponderous
chariot flies,
Then from its brazen bulk he leaps to
ground,
Beneath his clanging arms the plains re-
sound,
And on the Persian rushes fierce, and
raised
The clattering axe on high, which threat-
ening blazed,
And lopped his head ; out spouts the
smoking gore,
And the huge trunk rolled bleeding on
the shore.
And then Cynaegirus : 'Thus, Persian, go
And boast thy victory in the shades
below,
A headless form, and tell who bade thee
bleed,
For know a Greek performed the won-
drous deed :
But thou, Themistocles, O hero ! say
Who bade thee rush, to tempt th' unequal
fray ?
But learn from this thy daring to restrain,
And seek less mighty foes upon the plain.'
With secret wrath the youthful hero
burned,
And thus impetuous to the Chief returned:
' Such thoughts as these, unworthy those
who dare
The battle's rage, and tempt the toils of
war ;
Heedless of death, and by no fears
opprest,
Conquest my aim, I leave to heaven the
rest.'
He said, and glowed with an immortal
light,
Plunged 'midst the foes, and mingled in
the fight.
Zeno, the bravest of the Persian youth,
Renowned for filial piety and truth,
His mother's only joy ; she loved to trace
His father's features in his youthful face :

That sire, in fight o'erwhelmed mid seas
of gore,
Slept unentombed, and cared for fame no
more.
And now as youth in opening manhood
glows,
All his loved father in his visage rose ;
Like him, regardful of his future fame,
Resolved like him to immortalize his
name,
At glory's call he quits his native shore
And feeble parent, to return no more.
Oh ! what prophetic griefs her bosom
wrung
When on his neck in agony she hung !
When on that breast she hid her sorrow-
ing face,
And feared to take, or shun, the last
embrace !
Unhappy youth ! the fates decree thy
doom,
Those flowers, prepared for joy, shall
deck thy tomb ;
Thy mother now no more shall hail thy
name,
So high enrolled upon the lists of fame.
Nor check the widow's tear, the widow's
sigh,
For e'en her son, her Zeno's doom to die ;
Zeno, e'en thou ! for so the Gods decree,
A parents' threshold opes no more for
thee !
On him the hero turned his eye severe,
Nor on his visage saw one mark of fear ;
There manly grace improved each separ-
ate part,
And joined by ties of truth the face and
heart.
The supple javelin then the Grecian tries
With might gigantic, and the youth
defies.
Its point impetuous at his breast he flung,
The brazen shield received, and mocking
rung ;
Then Zeno seized the lance, the Chief
defied,
And scoffing, thus began, in youthful
pride :
' Go, mighty Greek ! to weaker warriors
go,
And fear this arm, and an unequal foe ;
A mother gave the mighty arms I bear,
Nor think with such a gift I cherish fear.'

He hurled the lance, but Pallas' self was there
And turned the point : it passed in empty air.
With hope renewed, again the hero tries
His boasted might ; the thirsty weapon flies ;
In Zeno's breast it sinks, and drank the gore,
And stretched the hero vanquished on the shore ;
Gasping for utterance, and life and breath,
For fame he sighs, nor fears approaching death.
Themistocles perceived, and bending low
Thought of his friends, and tears began to flow
That washed the bleeding bosom of his foe.
Young Zeno then the Grecian hero eyed,
Rejects his offered aid, and all defied,
Breathed one disdainful sigh, and turned his head and died.
Such Persians did the godlike warrior slay,
And bade their groaning spirits pass away.
Epizelus, the valiant and the strong,
Thundered in fight, and carried death along ;
Him not a Greek in strength of arms surpassed,
In battle foremost, but in virtue last.
He, impious man, to combat dared defy
The Gods themselves, and senate of the sky,
E'en earth and heaven, and heaven's eternal sire,
He mocks his thunders and disdains his ire.
But now the retributive hour is come,
And rigid justice seals the boaster's doom :
Theseus he sees within the fight, revealed
To him alone—to all the rest concealed.
To punish guilt, he leaves the shades below
And quits the seat of never-ending woe :
Pale as in death, upon his hands he bore
Th' infernal serpent of the dreadful shore,
To stay his progress should he strive to fly
From Tart'rus far, and gain the upper sky.

This (dreadful sight !) with slippery sinews now
Wreathed round his form, and clasped his ghastly brow ;
With horror struck and seized with sudden awe
The Greek beheld, nor mingled in the war.
Withheld from combat by the force of fear,
He trembling thus : 'Oh say, what God draws near !
But speak thy will, if 'tis a God, oh speak !
Nor vent thy vengence on a single Greek.'
Vainly he suppliant said—o'erpowered with fright,
And instant from his eyeballs fled the sight ;
Confused, distracted, to the skies he throws
His frantic arms, and thus bewails his woes :
'Almighty ! thou by whom the bolts are driven !'
He said, and cast his sightless balls to heaven,
'Restore my sight, unhappy me, restore
My own loved offspring, to behold once more !
So will I honour thy divine abodes,
And learn how dreadful th' avenging Gods !
And if—but oh, forbid !—you mock my prayer
And cruel fate me ever cursed declare,
Give me, to yield to fame alone my life,
And fall immortalized in glorious strife !'
He said—the God who thunders thro' the air
Frowns on his sufferings and rejects his prayer ;
Around his form the dreadful Aegis spread,
And darts fall harmless on his wretched head ;
Condemned by fate in ceaseless pain to groan,
Friendless in grief, in agony alone.
Now Mars and death pervade on every side,
And heroes fall and swell the crimson tide.

Not with less force th' Athenian leader
    shone,
In strife conspicuous, nor to fame un-
    known,
Advanced in wisdom and in honoured
    years ;
He nor for life, but for the battle fears.
Borne swift as winds within the flying car,
Now here, now there, directs the swell-
    ing war,
On every side the foaming coursers
    guides,
Here praises valour, and there rashness
    chides ;
While from his lips persuasive accents
    flow
T' inspire th' Athenians, or unman the
    foe.
The glorious Greeks rush on with daring
    might,
And shout and thunder, and increase the
    fight.
Nor yet inglorious do the Persians shine,
In battle's ranks they strength and valour
    join :
Datis himself impels the ponderous car
Thro' broken ranks, conspicuous in the
    war,
In armour sheathed, and terror round
    him spread,
He whirls his chariot over heaps of dead ;
Where'er he dreadful rushes, warriors
    fly,
Ghosts seek their hell, and chiefs and
    heroes die.
All pale with rage he ranks on ranks
    o'erthrows,
For blood he gasps, and thunders midst
    his foes :
Callimachus, the mighty leader, found
In fight conspicuous, bearing death
    around :
The lance, wheeled instant from the
    Persian's hand,
Transfixed the glorious Grecian in the
    sand ;
Fate ends the hero's life, and stays his
    breath,
And clouds his eyeballs with the shade
    of death :
Erect in air the cruel javelin stood,
Pierced thro' his breast, and drank the
    spouting blood.

Released from life's impending woes and
    care,
The soul immerges in the fields of air :
Then, crowned with laurels, seeks the
    blest abodes
Of awful Pluto and the Stygian floods.
And now with joy great Aristides saw
Again proud Hippias thundering thro'
    the war,
And mocking thus, ' O tyrant, now await
The destined blow, behold thy promised
    fate !
Thrice mighty King, obey my javelin's
    call,
For e'en thy godlike self's decreed to
    fall ! '
He said, and hurled the glittering spear
    on high,
The destined weapon hissed along the
    sky ;
Winged by the hero's all-destroying hand
It pierced the Prince, and stretched him
    on the sand.
Then thro' the air the awful peals were
    driven,
And lightnings blazed along the vast of
    heaven ;
The Persian hosts behold their bulwark
    die,
Fear chills their hearts, and all their
    numbers fly,
And reached the fleet ; the shouting
    Greeks pursue
All Asia's millions, flying in their view.
On, on, they glorious rush, and side by
    side,
Yet red with gore, they plunge into the
    tide ;
For injured freedom's sake th' indignant
    main
With swelling pride receives the crimson
    stain ;
The Persians spread the sail, nor dare
    delay,
And suppliant call upon the King of day,
But vainly to their Gods the cowards
    pray.
Some of the ships th' Athenian warriors
    stay
And fire their bulks ; the flames destroy-
    ing rise,
Rushing they swell, and mount into the
    skies.

Foremost Cynaegirus, with might divine,
While midst the waves his arms majestic shine ;
With blood-stained hand a Persian ship he seized,
The vessel vainly strove to be released ;
With fear the crew the godlike man beheld,
And pride and shame their troubled bosoms swelled.
They lop his limb ; then Pallas fires his frame
With scorn of death, and hope of future fame :
Then with the hand remaining seized the prize,
A glorious spirit kindling in his eyes.
Again the Persians wield the unmanly blow
And wreak their vengeance on a single foe ;

The fainting Greek, by loss of blood opprest,
Still feels the patriot rise within his breast ;
Within his teeth the shattered ship he held,
Nor in his soul one wish for life rebelled.
But strength decaying, fate supprest his breath,
And o'er his brows expand the dews of death ;
The Elysium plains his generous spirit trod,
' He lived a Hero and he died a God.'
By vengeance fired, the Grecians from the deep
With rage and shouting scale the lofty ship,
Then in the briny bosom of the main
They hurl in heaps the living and the slain ;
Thro' the wide shores resound triumphant cries,
Fill all the seas, and thunder thro' the skies.

AN ESSAY ON MIND

Brama assai, poco spera, e nulla chiede.—TASSO.

PREFACE TO THE FIRST EDITION, 1826

IN offering this little volume to the world, it is not my intention to trespass long on its indulgence, ' with prefaces, and passages, and excusations.' As, however, preface-writing strangely reminds one of Bottom's prologuizing device, which so ingeniously showeth the ' disfiguration of moonshine,' and how lion was no lion after all, but plain ' Snug the joiner,' I will treat the subject according to my great prototype ; declaring to those readers who ' cannot abide lions,' that their ' parlous fear ' is here unnecessary, and assuring the public that ' moonshine ' shall be introduced as seldom as is consistent with modern composition.

But something more is necessary ; and since writers commonly make use of their prefaces as opportunities for auricular confession to the absolving reader, I am prepared to acknowledge, with unfeigned humility, that the imputation of presumption is likely to be attached to me, on account of the form and title of this production. And yet, to imagine that a confidence in our powers is undeviatingly shown by our selection of an extensive field for their exertion, is an error ; for the subject supports the writer, as much as it is supported by him. It is not difficult to draw a succession of affecting images from objects intrinsically affecting ; and ideas arising from an elevated subject are naturally elevated. As Tacitus hath it, ' materia aluntur.' Thought catches the light reflected from the object of her contemplation, and, ' expanded by the genius of the spot,' loses much of her material grossness; unless indeed, like Thales, she fall into the water while looking at the stars.

'Ethical poetry,' says that immortal writer we have lost, 'is the highest of all poetry, as the highest of all earthly objects must be moral truth.' I am nevertheless aware how often it has been asserted that poetry is not a proper vehicle for abstract ideas—how far the assertion may be correct, is with me a matter of doubt. We do not deem the imaginative incompatible with the philosophic, for the name of Bacon is on our lips; then why should we expel the argumentative from the limits of the poetic? If indeed we consider Poetry as Plato considered her, when he banished her from his republic; or as Newton, when he termed her 'a kind of ingenious nonsense'; or as Locke, when he pronounced that 'gaming and poetry went usually together'; or as Boileau, when he boasted of being acquainted with two arts equally useful to mankind— 'writing verses, and playing at skittles,'— we shall find no difficulty in assenting to this opinion. But while we behold in poetry the inspiritings to political feeling, the 'monumentum aere perennius' of buried nations, we are loath to believe her unequal to the higher walks of intellect : when we behold the works of the great though erring Lucretius, the sublime Dante, the reasoning Pope—when we hear Quintilian acknowledge the submission due from Philosophers to Poets, and Gibbon declare Homer to be ' the law-giver, the theologian, the historian, and the philosopher of the ancients,' we are *unable* to believe it. Poetry is the enthusiasm of the understanding; and, as Milton finely expresses it, there is ' a high reason in her fancies.'

As, according to the plan of my work, I have dwelt less on the operations of the mind than on their effects, so I have not touched on that point difficult to argue, and impossible to determine—the nature of her substance. The investigation is curious, and the subject a glorious one; but, after all, our closest reasonings thereupon are acquired from analogy, and our most extensive views must be content to take their places among other ingenious speculations. The columns of Hercules are yet unpassed. Metaphysicians have cavilled and confuted; but they have failed in their endeavour to establish any permanent theoretical edifice on that windy site. The effort was vainly made even by our enlightened Locke; and, as in the days of Socratic disputation, it is still given to the learned to ask, though not to answer, ' τί δὲ ἡ ψυχή.' Perhaps, however, the following sensible acknowledgement would better become their human lips, than the most artfully constructed hypothesis—The things we understand are so excellent, that we believe what we do not understand to be likewise excellent[1].

The effects of mental operation, or pro- ductions of the mind, I have divided into two classes—the philosophical, and the poetical; the former of which I have sub- divided into three divisions—History, Physics, and Metaphysics: History, or the doctrine of man, as an active and social being; Physics, or the doctrine of efficient causes; Metaphysics, or the doctrine of abstractions, and final causes. Lord Bacon's comprehensive discernment of the whole, and Locke's acute penetra- tion into parts, have assisted me in my trembling endeavour to trace the outline of these branches of knowledge. To have considered them methodically, and in detail, would have greatly exceeded both the limits of my volume, and, what is more material, the extent of my information : but if I may be allowed to hope that

The lines, though touch'd thus faintly, are drawn right,

I shall have nothing left to wish.

Poetry is treated in as cursory a manner as Philosophy, though not pre- cisely for the same reasons. I have been deterred from a further development of her nature and principles, by observing that no single subject has employed the didactic pen with such frequent success, and by a consequent unwillingness to incur a charge of tediousness, when repeating what is well known, or one of presumption,

1 I here adopt, with some little variation, an expression which fell from Socrates, on the subject of a work by Heraclitus the obscure.

when intruding new-fangled maxims in the place of those deservedly established. The act of white-washing an ancient Gothic edifice would be less indicative of bad taste than the latter attempt. Since the time of Horace, many excellent didactic writers have formed poetic systems from detached passages of that unsystematic work, his *Ars Poetica*. Pope and Boileau, in their Essays on Poetry and Criticism, have with superior method traced his footsteps. And yet, ' haud passibus aequis ' —it is only justice to observe, that though the poem has been excelled, the poet remains unequalled. For the merits of his imitators are, except in arrangement, Horace's merits, while the merits of Horace are his own [1].

I wish that the sublime circuit of intellect, embraced by the plan of my poem, had fallen to the lot of a spirit more powerful than mine. I wish it had fallen to the lot of one familiar with the dwelling-place of Mind, who could search her secret chambers, and call forth those that sleep; or of one who could enter into her temples, and cast out the iniquitous who buy and sell, profaning the sanctuary of God ; or of one who could try the golden links of that chain which hangs from Heaven to earth, and show that it is not placed there for man to covet for lucre's sake, or for him to weigh his puny strength at one end against Omnipotence at the other ; but that it is placed there to join, in mysterious union, the natural and the spiritual, the mortal and the eternal, the creature and the Creator. I wish the subject of my poem had fallen into such hands, that the powers of the execution might have equalled the vastness of the design —and the public will wish so too. But as it is—though I desire this field to be more meritoriously occupied by others—I would mitigate the voice of censure for myself. I would endeavour to show, that while I may have often erred, I have not clung willingly to error ; and that while I may have failed in representing, I have never ceased to love Truth. If there be much to condemn in the following pages, let my narrow capacity, as opposed to the infinite object it would embrace, be generously considered ; if there be any thing to approve, I am ready to acknowledge the assistance which my illustrations have received from the exalting nature of their subject—as the waters of Halys acquire a peculiar taste from the soil over which they flow.

[1] He is indebted to Aristotle, which, however, cannot be said to affect his poetical originality.

AN ESSAY ON MIND

My narrow leaves cannot in, them contayne
The large discourse.—SPENSER.

ANALYSIS OF BOOK I

THE poem commences by remarking the desire, natural to the mind, of investigating its own qualities—qualities the more exalted, as their development has seldom been impeded by external circumstances—The various dispositions of different minds are next considered, and are compared to the varieties of scenic nature ; inequalities in the spiritual not being more wonderful than inequalities in the natural —Byron and Campbell contrasted—The varieties of genius having been thus treated, the art of criticism is briefly alluded to, as generally independent of genius, but always useful to its productions—Jeffrey—The various stages of life in which genius appears, and the different causes by which its influence is discovered—Cowley, Alfieri—Allusion to the story of the emotion of Thucydides on hearing Herodotus recite his History at the Olympic Games—The elements of Mind are thus arranged, Invention, Judgement, Memory, and Association—The creations of mind are next noticed, among which we first behold Philosophy—History, Science, and Metaphysics are included in the studies of Philosophy.

Of History, it is observed, that though on a cursory view her task of recalling the past may appear of little avail, it is in reality one of the highest importance—The living are sent for a lesson to the grave—The present state of Rome alluded to ; and the future state of England anticipated—Condemnation of those who deprive historical facts of their moral inference, and only make use of their basis to render falsehood more secure—Gibbon—Condemnation of those who would colour the political conduct of past ages with their own political feelings—Hume, Mitford—From the writers, we turn to the readers of history—Their extreme scepticism, or credulity—They are recommended to be guided by no faction, but to measure facts by their consistency with reason; to study the personal character and circumstances of an historian before they give entire credit to his representations—The influence of private feeling and prejudice—Miller—Science is introduced—Apostrophe to man—Episode of Archimedes—Parallel between history and science—The pride of the latter considered most excessive—The risk attending knowledge—Buffon, Leibnitz—The advantageous experience to be derived from the errors of others illustrated by an allusion to Southey's Hexameters—Utility the object of Science—An exclusive attention to parts deprecated, since it is impossible even to have a just idea of PARTS without acquiring a knowledge of their relative situation in the whole—The extreme difficulty of enlarging the contemplations of a mind long accustomed to contracted views—The scale of knowledge; every science being linked with the one preceding and succeeding, giving and receiving reciprocal support—Why this system is not calculated, as might be conjectured, either to render scientific men superficial, or to intrude on the operations of genius—That the danger of knowledge originates in PARTIAL knowledge—Apostrophe to Newton.

BOOK I

SINCE Spirit first inspired, pervaded all,
And Mind met Matter at th' Eternal call—
Since dust weighed Genius down, or Genius gave
Th' immortal halo to the mortal's grave—
Th' ambitious soul her essence hath defined,
And Mind hath eulogized the powers of Mind.
Ere Revelation's holy light began
To strengthen Nature, and illumine Man—
When Genius, on Icarian pinions, flew,
And Nature's pencil Nature's portrait drew—
When Reason shuddered at her own wan beam,
And Hope turned pale beneath the sickly gleam,
Even then hath Mind's triumphant influence spoke,
Dust owned the spell, and Plato's spirit woke,
Spread her eternal wings, and rose sublime
Beyond th' expanse of circumstance and time:

Blinded, but free, with faith instinctive soared,
And found her home where prostrate saints adored!

Thou thing of light! that warm'st the breasts of men,
Breath'st from the lips, and tremblest from the pen!
Thou, formed at once t' astonish, fire, beguile—
With Bacon reason, and with Shakespeare smile!
The subtle cause, ethereal essence! say,
Why dust rules dust, and clay surpasses clay;
Why a like mass of atoms should combine
To form a Tully and a Catiline?
Or why, with flesh perchance of equal weight,
One cheers a prize-fight, and one frees a state?
Why do not I the muse of Homer call,
Or why, indeed, did Homer sing at all?
Why wrote not Blackstone upon love's delusion,
Or Moore a libel on the Constitution?
Why must the faithful page refuse to tell
That Dante, Laura sang, and Petrarch, Hell—
That Tom Paine argued in the throne's defence—
That Byron nonsense wrote, and Thurlow sense—
That Southey sighed with all a patriot's cares,
While Locke gave utterance to Hexameters?
Thou thing of light! instruct my pen to find
Th' unequal powers, the various forms of Mind!

O'er Nature's changeful face direct your sight;
View light meet shade, and shade dissolve in light!
Mark, from the plain, the cloud-capped mountain soar;
The sullen ocean spurn the desert shore!
Behold, afar, the playmate of the storm,
Wild Niagara lifts his awful form—
Spits his black foam above the madd'ning floods,
Himself the savage of his native woods—

See him, in air, his smoking torrents
    wheel,
While the rocks totter, and the forests
    reel—
Then, giddy, turn ! lo ! Shakespeare's
    Avon flows,
Charmed, by the green-sward's kiss, to
    soft repose ;
With tranquil brow reflects the smile of
    fame,
And, 'midst her sedges, sighs her Poet's
    name.

Thus, in bright sunshine and alternate
    storms,
Is various mind expressed in various
    forms.
In equal men, why burns not equal fire ?
Why are not valleys hills,—or mountains
    higher ?
Her destined way hath destined Nature
    trod ;
While Matter, Spirit rules, and Spirit,
    God.

Let outward scenes, for inward sense
    designed,
Call back our wand'rings to the world
    of Mind !
Where Reason, o'er her vasty realms,
    may stand,
Convene proud thoughts, and stretch
    her sceptred hand.
Here, classic recollections breathe
    around ;
Here, living Glory consecrates the
    ground ;
And here, Mortality's deep waters span
The shores of Genius and the paths of
    Man !

O'er this imagined land your soul direct—
Mark Byron, the Mont Blanc of intellect,
'Twixt earth and heaven exalt his brow
    sublime,
O'erlook the nations, and shake hands
    with Time !
Stretched at his feet do Nature's beauties
    throng,
The flowers of love, the gentleness of
    song ;
Above, the Avalanche's thunder speaks,
While Terror's spirit walks abroad, and
    shrieks !

To some Utopian strand, some fairy
    shore,
Shall soft-eyed Fancy waft her Campbell
    o'er !
Wont o'er the lyre of Hope his hand to
    fling,
And never waken a discordant string ;
Who ne'er grows awkward by affecting
    grace,
Or ' common sense confounds with com-
    mon-place ' ;
To bright conception adds expression
    chaste,
And human feeling joins to classic taste :
For still, with magic art, he knows, and
    knew,
To touch the heart, and win the judge-
    ment too !

Thus, in uncertain radiance, Genius
    glows,
And fitful gleams on various mind be-
    stows :
While Mind, exulting in th' admitted day,
On various themes reflects its kindling ray.
Unequal forms receive an equal light ;
And Klopstock wrote what Kepler could
    not write.

Yet Fame hath welcomed a less noble
    few,
And Glory hailed whom Genius never
    knew ;
Art laboured Nature's birthright to
    secure,
And forged, with cunning hand, her sig-
    nature.
The scale of life is linked by close degrees ;
Motes float in sunbeams, mites exist in
    cheese ;
Critics seize half the fame which bards
    receive,
And Shakespeare suffers that his friends
    may live ;
While Bentley leaves, on stilts, the
    beaten track,
And peeps at glory from some ancient's
    back.
But though to hold a lantern to the sun
Be not too wise, and were as well un-
    done—
Though, e'en in this inventive age, alas !
A moral darkness can't be cured by gas —

And though we may not reasonably deem
How poets' craniums can be turned by
  steam—
Yet own we, in our juster reasonings,
That lanterns, gas, and steam are useful
  things ;
And oft this truth Reflection ponders
  o'er—
Bards would write worse if critics wrote
  no more.

Let Jeffrey's praise our willing pen en-
  gage,
The lettered critic of a lettered age !
Who justly judges, rightfully discerns,
With wisdom teaches and with candour
  learns.
His name on Scotia's brightest tablet
  lives,
And proudly claims the laurel that it
  gives.

Eternal Genius ! fashioned like the sun,
To make all beautiful thou look'st upon !
Prometheus of our earth ! whose kindling
  smile
May warm the things of clay a little
  while ;
Till by thy touch inspired, thine eyes
  surveyed,
Thou stoop'st to love the glory thou hast
  made,
And weepest, human-like, the mortal's
  fall,
When by and by a breath disperses all.
Eternal Genius ! mystic essence ! say,
How on 'the chosen breast' descends
  thy day !
Breaks it at once in Thought's celestial
  dream,
While Nature trembles at the sudden
  gleam ?
Or steals it gently, like the morning's
  light,
Shedding, unmarked, an influence soft
  and bright,
Till all the landscape gather on the sight ?

As different talents, different breasts in-
  spire,
So different causes wake the latent fire.
The gentle Cowley of our native clime
Lisped his first accents in Aonian rime.

Alfieri's startling muse tuned not her
  strings,
And dumbly looked 'unutterable things';
Till, when six lustrums o'er his head had
  past,
Conception found expression's voice at
  last ;
Broke the bright light, uprose the
  smothered flame,
And Mind and Nature owned their poet's
  fame !
To some the waving woods, the harp of
  spring,
A gently-breathing inspiration bring !
Some hear from Nature's haunts her
  whispered call ;
And Mind hath triumphed by an apple's
  fall.

Wave Fancy's picturing wand ! recall
  the scene
Which Mind hath hallowed—where her
  sons have been—
Where, 'midst Olympia's concourse,
  simply great,
Th' historic sage, the son of Lyxes, sate,
Grasping th' immortal scroll: he breathed
  no sound,
But, calm in strength, an instant looked
  around,
And rose—the tone of expectation rushed
Through th' eager throng—he spake,
  and Greece was hushed !
See, in that breathless crowd, Olorus
  stand,
While one fair boy hangs, list'ning, on
  his hand—
The young Thucydides ! with upward
  brow
Of radiance, and dark eye, that beaming
  now
Full on the speaker, drinks th' inspirèd
  air—
Gazing entranced and turned to marble
  there !
Yet not to marble—for the wild emotion
Is kindling on his cheek, like light on
  ocean,
Coming to vanish ; and his pulses throb
With transport, and the inarticulate sob
Swells to his lip—internal nature leaps
To glorious life, and all th' historian
  weeps !

The mighty master marked the favoured
child—
Did Genius linger there? She did, and
smiled!
Still on itself let Mind its eye direct,
To view the elements of intellect—
How wild Invention (daring artist!)
plies
Her magic pencil, and creating dies;
And Judgement near the living canvas
stands,
To blend the colours for her airy hands;
While Memory waits, with twilight mists
o'ercast,
To mete the length'ning shadows of the
past:
And bold Association, not untaught,
The links of fact unites with links of
thought;
Forming th' electric chains which mystic
bind
Scholastic learning and reflective mind.

Let reasoning Truth's unerring glance
survey
The fair creations of the mental ray;
Her holy lips, with just discernment,
teach
The forms, the attributes, the modes of
each;
And tell, in simple words, the narrow
span
That circles intellect and fetters man;
Where darkling mists o'er Time's last
footstep creep,
And Genius drops her languid wing—to
weep.

See first Philosophy's mild spirit, nigh,
Raise the rapt brow and lift the thought-
ful eye;
Whether the glimmering lamp, that
History gave,
Light her enduring steps to some lone
grave,
The while she dreams on him asleep be-
neath,
And conjures mystic thoughts of life and
death:
Whether, on Science' rushing wings,
she sweep
From concave heaven to earth, and search
the deep;

Showing the pensile globe attraction's
force,
The tides their mistress, and the stars
their course:
Or whether (task with nobler object
fraught)
She turn the powers of thinking back on
thought—
With mind, delineate mind; and dare
define
The point, where human mingles with
divine:
Majestic still, her solemn form shall stand,
To show the beacon on the distant land—
Of thought and nature chronicler sub-
lime!
The world her lesson, and her teacher
Time!

And when, with half a smile and half a
sigh,
She lifts old History's faded tapestry
I' the dwelling of past years, she ay is seen
Point to the shades, where bright'ning
tints had been—
The shapeless forms outworn and mil-
dewed o'er—
And bids us reverence what was loved
before;
Gives the dank wreath and dusty urn to
fame,
And lends its ashes—all she can—a name.
Think'st thou in vain, while pale Time
glides away,
She rakes cold graves and chronicles
their clay?
Think'st thou in vain she counts the bony
things
Once loved as patriots, or obeyed as
kings?
Lifts she in vain the past's mysterious
veil?
Seest thou no moral in her awful tale?
Can man the crumbling pile of nations
scan,
And is their mystic language mute for
man?

Go! let the tomb its silent lesson give,
And let the dead instruct thee how to live!
If Tully's page hath bade thy spirit burn
And lit the raptured cheek—behold his
urn!

If Maro's strains thy soaring fancy guide,
That hail 'th' eternal city' in their pride—
Then turn to mark, in some reflective
    hour,
The immortality of mortal power!
See the crushed column and the ruined
    dome—
'Tis all Eternity has left of Rome!
While travelled crowds, with curious
    gaze, repair
To read the littleness of greatness there!

Alas! alas! so Albion shall decay,
And all my country's glory pass away!
So shall she perish, as the mighty must,
And be Italia's rival—in the dust;
While her ennobled sons, her cities fair,
Be dimly thought of 'midst the things
    that were!
Alas! alas! her fields of pleasant green,
Her woods of beauty, and each well-
    known scene!
Soon o'er her plains shall grisly Ruin
    haste,
And the gay vale become the silent waste!
Ah! soon perchance, our native tongue
    forgot,
The land may hear strange words it
    knoweth not;
And the dear accents which our bosoms
    move
With sounds of friendship, or with tones
    of love,
May pass away; or, conned on mould-
    'ring page,
Gleam 'neath the midnight lamp for
    unborn sage;
To tell our dream-like tale to future years,
And wake th' historian's smile, and
    schoolboy's tears!

Majestic task! to join, though placed afar,
The things that have been with the
    things that are!
Important trust! the awful dead to scan,
And teach mankind to moralize from man!
Stupendous charge! when on the record
    true
Depend the dead, and hang the living too!
And, oh! thrice impious he who dares
    abuse
That solemn charge, and good and ill
    confuse!

Thrice guilty he who, false with 'words
    of sooth,'
Would pay to Prejudice his debt to Truth;
The hallowed page of fleeting Time pro-
    fane,
And prove to Man that man has lived in
    vain;
Pass the cold grave with colder jestings
    by;
And use the truth to illustrate a lie!

Let Gibbon's name be traced in sorrow
    here—
Too great to spurn, too little to revere!
Who followed Reason, yet forgot her
    laws,
And found all causes but the 'great first
    Cause':
The paths of time with guideless footsteps
    trod,
Blind to the light of nature and of God;
Deaf to the voice, amid the past's dread
    hour,
Which sounds His praise and chronicles
    His power!
In vain for *him* was Truth's fair tablet
    spread
When Prejudice, with jaundiced organs,
    read.
In vain for *us* the polished periods flow,
The fancy kindles, and the pages glow,
When one bright hour, and startling
    transport past,
The musing soul must turn—to sigh at
    last.
Still let the page be luminous and just,
Nor private feeling war with public trust;
Still let the pen from narrowing views
    forbear,
And modern faction ancient freedom
    spare.
But, ah! too oft th' historian bends his
    mind
To flatter party—not to serve mankind;
To make the dead in living feuds engage,
And give all time the feelings of his age.
Great Hume hath stooped the Stuarts'
    fame t' increase,
And ultra Mitford soared to libel Greece!

Yet must the candid muse, impartial, learn
To trace the errors which her eyes dis-
    cern;

View every side, investigate each part,
And get the holy scroll of Truth by
    heart ;
No blame misplaced, and yet no fault
    forgot—
Like ink employed to write with—not
    to blot.
Hence, while historians just reproof
    incur,
We find some readers, with their
    authors, err ;
And soon discover, that as few excel
In reading justly, as in writing well.
For prejudice, or ignorance, is such,
That men believe too little or too much ;
Too apt to cavil, or too glad to trust,
With confidence misplaced, or blame
    unjust.

Seek out no faction—no peculiar school—
But lean on Reason as your safest rule ;
Let doubtful facts with patient hand be led,
To take their place on this Procrustean
    bed !
What plainly fits not may be thrown
    aside
Without the censure of pedantic pride :
For nature still to just proportion clings.
And human reason judges natural things.
Moreover, in th' historian's bosom look,
And weigh his feelings ere you trust his
    book ;
His private friendships, private wrongs,
    descry,
Where tend his passions, where his
    interests lie—
And while his proper faults your mind
    engage,
Discern the ruling foibles of his age.
Hence, when on deep research, the
    work you find
A too obtrusive transcript of his mind ;
When you perceive a fact too highly
    wrought,
Which kindly seems to prove a fav'rite
    thought ;
Or some opposing truth traced briefly
    out,
With hand of careless speed—then turn
    to doubt !
For private feeling like the taper glows,
And here a light and there a shadow
    throws.

If some gay picture, vilely daubed, were
    seen
With grass of azure and a sky of green,
Th' impatient laughter we'd suppress in
    vain,
And deem the painter jesting, or insane.
But when the sun of blinding prejudice
Glares in our faces, it deceives our eyes ;
Truth appears falsehood to the dazzled
    sight,
The comment apes the fact, and black
    seems white ;
Commingled hues, their separate colours
    lost,
Dance wildly on, in bright confusion tost ;
And, midst their drunken whirl, the
    giddy eye
Beholds one shapeless blot for earth and
    sky.

Of such delusions let the mind take heed,
And learn to think, or wisely cease to
    read ;
And if a style of laboured grace display
Perverted feelings in a pleasing way—
False tints on real objects brightly laid,
Facts in disguise, and Truth in masquer-
    ade—
If cheating thoughts in beauteous dress
    appear,
With magic sound, to captivate the ear—
Th' enchanting poison of that page
    decline,
Or drink Circean draughts—and turn to
    swine !

We hail with British pride and ready
    praise
Enlightened Miller of our modern days !
Too firm though temp'rate, liberal though
    exact,
To give too much to argument or fact,
To love details and draw no moral thence,
Or seek the comment and forget the sense :
He leaves all vulgar aims, and strives
    alone
To find the ways of Truth, and make them
    known !

Spirit of life ! for ay with heavenly breath
Warm the dull clay and cold abodes of
    death !
Clasp in its urn the consecrated dust,
And bind a laurel round the broken bust ;

While 'mid decaying tombs, thy pensive
    choice,
Thou bid'st the silent utter forth a voice,
To prompt the actors of our busy scene,
And tell what *is*, the tale of what *has been!*

Yet turn, Philosophy! with brow sublime
Shall Science follow on the steps of
    Time!
As o'er Thought's measureless depths we
    bend to hear
The whispered sound which stole on
    Descartes' ear,
Hallowing the sunny visions of his youth
With that eternal mandate, 'Search for
    Truth!'
Yes! search for Truth—the glorious path
    is free;
Mind shows her dwelling, Nature holds
    the key:
Yes! search for Truth—her tongue shall
    bid thee scan
The book of knowledge, for the use of
    Man!

Man! Man! thou poor antithesis of
    power!
Child of all time! yet creature of an hour!
By turns chameleon of a thousand forms,
The lord of empires, and the food of
    worms!
The little conqueror of a petty space,
The more than mighty, or the worse than
    base!
Thou ruined landmark in the desert way,
Betwixt the all of glory and decay!
Fair beams the torch of Science in thine
    hand,
And sheds its brightness o'er the glim-
    mering land;
While in thy native grandeur, bold and
    free,
Thou bid'st the wilds of nature smile for
    thee,
And treadest Ocean's paths full royally!
Earth yields her treasures up; celestial
    air
Receives thy globe of life when, journey-
    ing there,
It bounds from dust, and bends its course
    on high,
And walks in beauty through the wonder-
    ing sky.

And yet, proud clay! thine empire is
    a span,
Nor all thy greatness makes thee more
    than man!
While Knowledge, Science, only serve
    t' impart
The god thou *wouldst* be, and the
    thing thou *art!*

Where stands the Syracusan, while the
    roar
Of men and engines echoes through the
    shore?
Where stands the Syracusan.   Haggard
    Fate,
With ghastly smile, is sitting at the gate;
And Death forgets his silence 'midst the
    crash
Of rushing ruins; and the torches' flash
Waves redly on the straggling forms
    that die;
And masterless steeds beneath that
    gleam dart by,
Scared into madness by the battle-cry;
And sounds are hurtling in the angry air,
Of hate, and pain, and vengeance, and
    despair—
The smothered voice of babes—the long,
    wild shriek
Of mothers, and the curse the dying
    speak!
Where stands the Syracusan? Tranquil
    sage,
He bends sublime o'er Science' splendid
    page,
Walks the high circuit of extended mind,
Surpasses man, and dreams not of man-
    kind;
While on his listless ear the battle-shout
Falls senseless—as if echo breathed about
The hum of many words, the laughing
    glee
Which lingered there when Syracuse
    was free.
Away! away! for louder accents fall—
But not the sounds of joy from marble hall!
Quick steps approach—but not of sylphic
    feet
Whose echo heralded a smile more sweet,
Coming, all sport, th' indulgent sage t'
    upbraid
For lonely hours, to studious musing
    paid.

Be hushed! Destruction bares the flicker-
ing blade!
He asked to live, th' unfinished lines to
fill,
And died—to solve a problem deeper
still.
He died, the glorious! who, with soaring
sight,
Sought some new world to plant his foot
of might;
Thereon in solitary pride to stand,
And lift our planet with a master's hand!
He sank in death—Creation only gave
That thorn-encumbered space which
forms his grave—
An unknown grave, till Tully chanced
to stray,
And named the spot where Archimedes
lay!
Genius! behold the limit of thy power!
Thou fir'st the soul, but, when life's
dream is o'er,
Giv'st not the silent pulse one throb the
more:
And mighty beings come and pass away,
Like other comets, and like other—clay.

Though analysing Truth must still divide
Historic state and scientific pride,
Yet one stale fact our judging thoughts
infer—
Since each is human, each is prone to
err!
Oft in the night of Time doth History
stray,
And lift her lantern and proclaim it day!
And oft when day's eternal glories shine
Doth Science, boasting, cry—'The light
is mine!'
So hard to bear, with unobstructed sight,
Th' excess of darkness or th' extreme of
light.

Yet, to be just, though faults belong to
each,
The themes of one an humbler moral
teach:
And, 'midst th' historian's eloquence
and skill,
The human chronicler is human still.
If on past power his eager thoughts be
cast,
It brings an awful antidote—'tis past!

If deathless fame his ravished organs
scan,
The deathless fame exists for buried
man:
Power and decay at once he turns to view,
And, with the strength, beholds the
weakness too.
Not so doth Science' musing son aspire,
And pierce creation with his eye of fire.
Yon mystic pilgrims of the starry way
No humbling lesson to his soul convey;
No tale of change their changeless course
hath taught,
And works divine excite no earthward
thought.
And still he, reckless, builds the splendid
dream;
And still his pride increases with his
theme;
And still the cause is slighted in th' effect;
And still self-worship follows self-
respect:
Too apt to watch the engines of the
scene,
And lose the hand which moves the vast
machine;
View Matter's form, and not its moving
soul;
Interpret parts, and misconceive the
whole:
While, darkly musing 'twixt the earth
and sky,
His heart grows narrow, as his hopes
grow high;
And quits for ay, with unavailing loss,
The sympathies of earth, but not the
dross;
Till Time sweeps down the fabric of his
trust,
And life and riches turn to death and dust.

And such is Man! 'neath Error's foul
assaults
His noblest moods beget his grossest
faults!
When Knowledge lifts her hues of
varied grace,
The fair exotic of a brighter place,
To keep her stem, from mundane blasts,
enshrined,
He makes a fatal hot-bed of his mind;
Too oft adapted, in their growth, to spoil
The natural beauties of a generous soil.

Ah ! such is Man ! thus strong, and weak
    withal,
His rise oft renders him too prone to fall !
The loftiest hills' fresh tints the soonest
    fade,
And highest buildings cast the deepest
    shade !

So Buffon erred ; amidst his chilling
    dream,
The judgement grew material as the
    theme :
Musing on Matter, till he called away
The modes of Mind to form the modes
    of clay ;
And made, confusing each, with judge-
    ment blind,
Mind stoop to dust, and dust ascend to
    Mind.
So Leibnitz erred, when, in the starry
    hour,
He read no weakness where was written
    ' Power ' ;
Beheld the verdant earth, the circling
    sea,
Nor dreamt so fair a world could cease
    to be !
Yea ! but he heard the Briton's awful
    name,
As, scattering darkness, in his might he
    came.
Girded with Truth, and earnest to confute
What gave to Matter Mind's best attri-
    bute.
Sternly they strove—th' unequal race
    was run !
The owlet met the eagle at the sun !

While such defects their various forms
    unfold,
And rust so foul obscures the brightest
    gold,
Let Science' soaring sons the ballast cast,
But judge their present errors by their
    past ;
As some poor wanderer in the darkness
    goes,
When fitful wind, in hollow murmur,
    blows,
Hailing, with trembling joy, the light-
    ning's ray,
Which threats his safety, but illumes his
    way.

Gross faults buy deep experience. Sages
    tell
That Truth, like Aesop's fox, is in a well ;
And, like the goat his fable prates about,
Fools must stay in, that wise men may
    get out.
What thousand scribblers of our age
    would choose
To throw a toga round the English muse,
Rending her garb of ease, which grace-
    ful grew
From Dryden's loom, beprankt with
    varied hue !
In that dull aim, by Mind unsanctified,
What thousand Wits would have their
    wits belied,
Devoted Southey ! if thou hadst not
    tried !
Use is the aim of Science ; this the end
The wise appreciate, and the good com-
    mend.
For not, like babes, the flaming torch
    we prize,
That sparkling lustre may attract our
    eyes ;
But that, when evening shades impede
    the sight,
It casts on objects round a useful light.

Use is the aim of Science ! give again
A golden sentence to the faithful pen—
Dwell not on parts ! for parts contract
    the mind ;
And knowledge still is useless, when
    confined.
The yearning soul, enclosed in narrow
    bound,
May be ingenious, but is ne'er profound :
Spoiled of its strength, the fettered
    thought grows tame ;
And want of air extinguishes the flame !
And as the sun, beheld in mid-day blaze,
Seems turned to darkness, as we strive
    to gaze ;
So mental vigour, on one object cast,
That object's self becomes obscured at
    last.

'Tis easy, as Experience may aver,
To pass from general to particular,
But most laborious to direct the soul
From studying parts to reason on the
    whole :

Thoughts, trained on narrow subjects, to let fall ;
And learn the unison of each with all.

In Nature's reign a scale of life we find :
A scale of knowledge we behold in mind ;
With each progressive link our steps ascend,
And traverse all before they reach the end ;
Searching, while Reason's powers may farther go,
The things we know not by the things we know.

But hold ! methinks some sons of Thought demand,
' Why strive to form the Trajan's vase in sand ?
Are Reason's paths so few, that Mind may call
Her finite energies to tread them all ?
Lo ! Learning's waves in bounded channel sweep ;
When they flow wider, shall they run as deep ?
Shall that broad surface no dull shallow hide,
Growing dank weeds of superficial pride ?
Then Heaven may leave our giant powers alone,
Nor give each soul a focus of its own !
Genius bestows in vain the chosen page
If all the tome the minds of all engage !'

Nay ! I reply—with free congenial breast
Let each peruse the part which suits him best !
But, lest contracting prejudice mislead,
Regard the context as he turns to read !
Hence, liberal feeling gives th' enlightened soul
The spirit with the letter of the scroll.

With what triumphant joy, what glad surprise,
The dull behold the dullness of the wise !
What insect tribes of brainless impudence
Buzz round the carcass of perverted sense !
What railing idiots hunt, from classic school,
Each flimsy sage and scientific fool,

Crying, ''Tis well ! we see the blest effect
Of watchful night and toiling intellect !'
Yet let them pause, and tremble—vainly glad ;
For too much learning maketh no man mad !
Too *little* dims the sight, and leads us o'er
The twilight path, where fools have been before ;
With not enough of Reason's radiance seen
To track the footsteps where those fools have been.

Divinest Newton ! if my pen may show
A name so mighty in a verse so low—
Still let the sons of Science, joyful, claim
The bright example of that splendid name !
Still let their lips repeat, my page bespeak,
The sage how learnèd ! and the man how meek !
Too wise, to think his human folly less ;
Too great, to doubt his proper littleness ;
Too strong, to deem his weakness passed away ;
Too high in soul, to glory in his clay :
Rich in all nature, but her erring side :
Endowed with all of Science—but its pride.

ANALYSIS OF BOOK II

Metaphysics—Address to Metaphysicians—The most considerable portion of their errors conceived to arise from difficulties attending the use of words—That on one hand, thoughts become obscure without the assistance of language, while on the other, language from its material analogy deteriorates from spiritual meaning—Allusion to a probable mode of communication between spirits after death—That a limited respect, though not a servile submission, is due to verbal distinctions—Clearness of style peculiarly necessary to Metaphysical subjects—The graces of Composition not inconsistent with them—Plato, Bacon, Bolingbroke—The extremes into which Philosophers have fallen with regard to sensation and reflection—Berkeley, Condillac—That subject briefly considered—Abstractions—Longinus, Burke, Price, Payne Knight—Blind submission to authorities deprecated—The Pythagorean saying opposed, and Cicero's unphilosophical assertion alluded to—That, however, it partakes of injustice to love Truth, and yet refuse our homage to the advocates of Truth—How the names of great writers become endeared to us by early recollections—Description of the schoolboy's first intellectual gratifications—That even without reference to the past, some immortal names are entitled to our veneration, since they are connected with Truth—Bacon—Apostrophe to Locke.

Poetry is introduced—More daring than Philosophy, she personifies abstractions, and brings the things unseen before the eye of the Mind—How often reason is indebted to poetic imagery—Irving—The poetry of prose—Plato's ingratitude—Philosophers and Poets contrasted—An attempt to define Poetry—That the passions make use of her language—Nature the poet's study—Shakespeare—Human nature as seen in cities—Scenic nature, and how the mind is affected thereby—That Poetry exists not in the object contemplated but is created by the contemplating mind—The ideal—Observations on the structure of verse, as adapted to the subject treated—Milton, Horace, Pope—The French Drama—Corneille, Racine—Harmony and chasteness of versification—The poem proceeds to argue, that the Muse will refuse her inspiration to a soul unattuned to generous sympathy, unkindled by the deeds of Virtue, or the voice of Freedom—Contemptuous notice of those prompted only by interest to aspire to poetic eminence—What should be the Poet's best guerdon—From the contemplation of motives connected with Freedom, we are led by no unnatural transition to Greece—Her present glorious struggle—Anticipation of her ultimate independence, and the restoration of the Muses to their ancient seats—Allusion to the death of Byron—Reflections on Mortality—The terrors of death as beheld by the light of Nature—The consolations of death as beheld with reference to a future state—Contemplation of the immortality of Mind, and her perfected powers—Conclusion.

BOOK II

But now to higher themes! no more confined
To copy Nature, Mind returns to Mind.
We leave the throng, so nobly and so well
Tracing, in Wisdom's book, things visible,
And turn to things unseen; where, greatly wrought,
Soul questions soul, and thought revolves on thought.
My spirit loves, my voice shall hail ye, now,
Sons of the patient eye and passionless brow!
Students sublime! Earth, man, unmoved, ye view,
Time, circumstance; for what are they to you?

What is the crash of worlds—the fall of kings—
When worlds and monarchs are such brittle things?
What the tost, shattered bark, that blindly dares
A sea of storm? Ye sketch the wave which bears!
The cause, and not th' effect, your thoughts exact;
The principle of action, not the act,—
The soul! the soul! and,'midst so grand a task,
Ye call her rushing passions, and ye ask
Whence are ye? and each mystic thing responds!
I would be all ye are—except those bonds!

Except those bonds! Even here is oft descried
The love to parts, the poverty of pride!
Even here, while Mind in Mind's horizon springs,
Her 'native mud' is weighing on her wings!
Even here, while Truth invites the ardent crowd,
Ixion-like, they rush t' embrace a cloud!
Even here, oh! foul reproach to human wit!
A Hobbes hath reasoned, and Spinoza writ!

Rank pride does much! and yet we justly cry,
Our greatest errors in our weakness lie.
For thoughts unclothed by language are, at best,
Obscure; while grossness injures those exprest
Through words, in whose analysis we find
Th' analogies of Matter, not of Mind:
Hence, when the use of words is graceful brought,
As physical dress to metaphysic thought,
The thought, howe'er sublime its pristine state,
Is by th' expresssion made degenerate;
Its spiritual essence changed, or cramped; and hence
Some hold by words who cannot hold by sense,

And leave the thought behind, and take
th' attire—
Elijah's mantle, but without his fire !
Yet spurn not words ! 'tis needful to
confess
They give ideas a body and a dress !
Behold them traverse Learning's region
round,
The vehicles of thought on wheels of
sound ;
Mind's wingèd strength, wherewith the
height is won,
Unless she trust their frailty to the sun.
Destroy the body !—will the spirit stay ?
Destroy the car !—will Thought pursue
her way ?
Destroy the wings !—let Mind their aid
forgo !
Do no Icarian billows yawn below ?
Ah ! spurn not words with reckless inso-
lence ;
But still admit their influence with the
sense,
And fear to slight their laws ! Perchance
we find
No perfect code transmitted to mankind ;
And yet mankind, till life's dark sands
are run,
Prefers imperfect government to none.
Thus Thought must bend to words !—
Some sphere of bliss
Ere long shall free her from th' alloy of
this :
Some kindred home for Mind—some
holy place
Where spirits look on spirits, ' face to
face,'—
Where souls may see as they themselves
are seen,
And voiceless intercourse may pass
between,
All pure—all free ! as light, which doth
appear
In its own essence incorrupt and clear !
One service, praise ! one age, eternal
youth !
One tongue, intelligence ! one subject,
truth !

Till then, no freedom Learning's search
affords
Of soul from body, or of thought from
words.

For thought may lose, in struggling to
be hence,
The gravitating power of common sense ;
Through all the depths of space with
Phaethon hurled,
T' impair our reason, as he scorched our
world.
Hence this preceptive truth my page
affirms—
Respect the technicality of terms !
Yet not in base submission, lest we find
That, aiding clay, we crouch too low for
Mind ;
Too apt conception's essence to forget,
And place all wisdom in the alphabet.

Still let appropriate phrase the sense
invest ;
That what is well conceived be well
exprest !
Nor e'er the reader's wearied brain en-
gage
In hunting meaning down the mazy page,
With three long periods tortured into one,
The sentence ended, with the sense
begun ;
Nor in details, which schoolboys know
by heart,
Perplex each turning with the terms of art.
To understand, we deem no common
good ;
And 'tis less easy to be *understood*.
But let not clearness be your only praise,
When style may charm a thousand differ-
ent ways ;
In Plato glow, to life and glory wrought,
By high companionship with noblest
thought ;
In Bacon, warm abstraction with a breath,
Catch Poesy's bright beams, and smile
beneath ;
In St. John roll, a generous stream, along,
Correctly free and regularly strong.
Nor scornful deem the effort out of place
With taste to reason, and convince with
grace ;
But ponder wisely, ere you know, too
late,
Contempt of trifles will not prove us
great !
The Cynics, not their tubs, respect en-
gage ;
And dirty tunic never made a sage.

E'en Cato had he owned the Senate's
will,
And washed his toga, had been Cato
still.

Justly we censure, yet are free to own
That indecision is a crime unknown.
For, never faltering, seldom reasoning
long,
And still most positive whene'er most
wrong,
No theoretic sage is apt to fare
Like Mah'met's coffin—hung in middle
air !
No ! fenced by Error's all-sufficient trust.
These stalk 'in nubibus '—those crawl
in dust.
From their proud height, the first demand
to know
If spiritual essence should descend more
low ?
The last, as vainly, from their dunghill cry,
Can body's grossness hope t' aspire more
high ?
And while Reflection's empire these
disclose,
Sensation's sovereign right is told by
those.

Lo ! Berkeley proves an old hypothesis !
' Out on the senses !' (he was out of his !)
' All is idea, and nothing real springs
But God and Reason !'—(not the right
of kings ?)
' Hold !' says Condillac, with profound
surprise—
' Why prate of Reason ? we have ears
and eyes !'

Condillac ! while the dangerous periods
fall
Upon thy page, to stamp sensation *all ;*
While (coldly studious !) thine ingenious
scroll
Endows the mimic statue with a soul
Composed of sense—behold the generous
hound—
His piercing eye, his ear awake to sound,
His scent, most delicate organ ! and
declare
What triumph hath the 'Art of thinking '
there !
What Gall, or Spurzheim, on his front
hath sought
The mystic bumps indicative of Thought?

Or why, if Thought *do* there maintain
her throne,
Will reasoning curs leave logic for a bone ?

Mind is imprisoned in a lonesome tower :
Sensation is its window—hence herb,
flower,
Landscapes all sun, the rush of thousand
springs,
Waft in sweet scents, fair sights, soft
murmurings ;
And in her joy she gazeth—yet ere long
Reason awaketh in her, bold and strong,
And o'er the scene exerting secret laws,
First seeks th' efficient, then the final
cause,
Abstracts from forms their hidden acci-
dents,
And marks in outward substance inward
sense.
Our first perceptions formed, we search,
to find
The operations of the forming mind ;
And turn within by Reason's certain
route,
To view the shadows of the things with-
out,
Discerned, retained, compared, com-
bined, and brought
To mere abstraction by abstracting
Thought.
Hence to discern, retain, compare, con-
nect,
We deem the faculties of Intellect ;
The which, mused on, exert a new con-
trol,
And fresh ideas are opened on the soul.

Sensation is a stream with dashing spray
That shoots in idle speed its arrowy
way ;
When lo ! the mill arrests its waters'
course,
Turning to use their unproductive force :
The cunning wheels by foamy currents
sped,
Reflection triumphs,—and mankind is
fed !

Since Pope hath shown, and Learning
still must show,
' We cannot reason but from what we
know,'

Unfold the scroll of Thought and turn
to find
The undeceiving signature of Mind !
There judge her nature by her nature's
course,
And trace her actions upwards to their
source.
So when the property of Mind we call
An essence or a substance spiritual,
We name her thus by marking how she
clings
Less to the forms than essences of things ;
For body clings to body—objects seen
And substance sensible alone have been
Sensation's study ; while reflective Mind
Essence unseen in objects seen may find,
And, tracing whence her known impres-
sions came,
Give single forms an universal name.

So when particular sounds in concord
rise,
Those sounds as *melody* we generalize ;
When pleasing shapes and colours blend,
the soul
Abstracts th' idea of *beauty* from the whole,
Deducting thus, by Mind's enchanting
spell,
The intellectual from the sensible.
Hence bold Longinus' splendid periods
grew,
' Who was himself the great sublime he
drew ' :
Hence Burke, the poet-reasoner, learned
to trace
His glowing style of energetic grace :
Hence thoughts, perchance, some
favoured bosoms move,
Which Price might own, and classic
Knight approve !

Go ! light a rushlight ere the day is done
And call its glimm'ring brighter than
the sun !
Go ! while the stars in midnight glory
beam,
Prefer their cold reflection in the stream !
But be not that dull slave who only looks
On Reason ' through the spectacles of
books ' !
Rather by Truth determine what is true,
And reasoning works through Reason's
medium view ;

For authors can't monopolize her light :
'Tis yours to read as well as theirs to
write.
To judge is yours !—then why submissive
call
' The master said so ' ?—'tis no rule at
all !
Shall passive sufferance e'en to mind
belong
When right divine in man is human
wrong ?
Shall a high name a low idea enhance
When all may fail, as some succeed—by
chance ?
Shall fixed chimeras unfixed reason
shock ?
And if Locke err, must thousands err
with Locke ?
Men ! claim your charter ! spurn th' unjust
control,
And shake the bondage from the free-
born soul !
Go walk the porticoes ! and teach your
youth
All names are bubbles, but the name of
Truth !
If fools by chance attend to Wisdom's
rules,
'Tis no dishonour to be right with fools ;
If human faults to Plato's page belong,
Not even with Plato willingly go wrong.
But though the judging page declare it
well
To love Truth better than the lips which
tell,
Yet 'twere an error, with injustice classed,
T' adore the former and neglect the last.
Oh ! beats there, Heaven ! a heart of
human frame,
Whose pulses throb not at some kindling
name ?
Some sound which brings high musings
in its track,
Or calls perchance the days of childhood
back
In its dear echo, when, without a sigh,
Swift hoop and bounding ball were first
laid by,
To clasp in joy, from schoolroom tyrant
free,
The classic volume on the little knee,
And con sweet sounds of dearest min-
strelsy,

Or words of sterner lore ; the young
brow, fraught
With a calm brightness which might
mimic thought,
Leant on the boyish hand—as, all the
while,
A half-heaved sigh, or ay th' unconscious
smile,
Would tell how o'er that page the soul
was glowing
In an internal transport, past the know-
ing!
How feelings, erst unfelt, did then ap-
pear,
Give forth a voice, and murmur, ' We
are here !'
As lute-strings which a strong hand
plays upon,
Or Memnon's statue singing 'neath the
sun.
Ah me ! for such are pleasant memories,
And call the tears of fondness to our
eyes
Reposing on this gone-by dream, when
thus
One marbled book was all the world to
us,
The gentlest bliss our innocent thoughts
could find—
The happiest cradle of our infant mind !
And though such hours be past we shall
not less
Think on their joy with grateful tender-
ness,
And bless the page which bade our reason
wake,
And love the prophet for his mission's
sake.
But not alone doth Memory's smoulder-
ing flame
Reflect a radiance on a glorious name ;
For there are names of pride ; and they
who bear
Have walked with Truth, and turned their
footsteps where
We walk not—their beholdings ay have
been
O'er Mind's far countries which we have
not seen.
Our thoughts are not their thoughts!
and oft we dream
That light upon the awful brow doth
gleam,

From that high converse ; as when Moses
trod
Towards the people from the mount of
God
His lips were silent, but his face was
bright,
And prostrate Israel trembled at the sight.

What tongue can syllable our Bacon's
name,
Nor own a heart exulting in his fame ?
Where prejudice' wild blasts were wont
to blow,
And waves of ignorance rolled dark
below,
He raised his sail and left the coast
behind—
Sublime Columbus of the realms of Mind !
Dared folly's mists, opinion's treacherous
sands,
And walked, with godlike step, th' un-
trodden lands !
But ah ! our Muse of Britain, standing
near,
Hath dimmed my tablet with a pensive
tear !
Thrice the proud theme her free-born
voice essays,
And thrice that voice is faltering in his
praise —
Yea ! till her eyes in silent triumph turn
To mark afar her Locke's sepulchral urn !
O urn ! where students rapturous vigils
keep,
Where sages envy, and where patriots
weep!
O name ! that bids my glowing spirit
wake—
To freemen's hearts endeared for Free-
dom's sake !
O soul! too bright in life's corrupting hour
To rise by faction or to crouch to power !
While radiant Genius lifts her heaven-
ward wing,
And human bosoms own the Mind I sing ;
While British writers British thoughts
record,
And England's press is fearless as her
sword ;
While 'mid the seas which gird our
favoured isle
She clasps her chartered rights with
conscious smile—

So long be *thou* her glory and her guide,
Thy page her study and thy name her
    pride!
Oh! ever thus, immortal Locke, belong
First to my heart, as noblest in my song;
And since in thee the Muse enraptured
    find
A moral greatness and creating mind,
Still may thine influence, which with
    honoured light
Beams when I read, illume me as I write!
The page too guiltless, and the soul too
    free,
To call a frown from Truth, or blush
    from thee!
But where Philosophy would fear to soar,
Young Poesy's elastic steps explore!
Her fairy foot, her daring eye pursues
The light of faith—nor trembles as she
    views!
Wont o'er the Psalmist's holy harp to
    hang,
And swell the sacred note which Milton
    sang;
Mingling reflection's chords with fancy's
    lays,
The tones of music with the voice of
    praise!

And while Philosophy, in spirit free,
Reasons, believes, yet cannot plainly *see*,
Poetic Rapture to her dazzled sight
Portrays the shadows of the things of
    light;
Delighting o'er the unseen worlds to roam,
And waft the pictures of perfection home.
Thus Reason oft the aid of fancy seeks,
And strikes Pierian chords—when Irving
    speaks!

Oh! silent be the withering tongue of
    those
Who call each page bereft of measure,
    prose;
Who deem the Muse possessed of such
    faint spells
That, like poor fools, she glories in her
    bells;
Who hear her voice alone in tinkling
    chime,
And find a line's whole magic in its rime;
Forgetting, if the gilded shrine be fair,
What purer spirit may inhabit there!

For such, indignant at her questioned
    might,
Let Genius cease to charm—and Scott
    to write!

Ungrateful Plato! o'er thy cradled rest
The Muse hath hung, and all her love
    exprest;
Thy first imperfect accents fondly taught,
And warmed thy visions with poetic
    thought!
Ungrateful Plato! should her deadliest
    foe
Be found within the breast she tended so?
Spoiled of her laurels, should she weep
    to find
The best beloved become the most un-
    kind?
And was it well or generous, Brutus-like,
To pierce the hand that gave the power
    to strike?

Sages by reason reason's powers direct;
Bards through the heart convince the
    intellect:
Philosophy majestic brings to view
Mind's perfect modes, and fair proportions
    too;
Enchanting Poesy bestows the while,
Upon its sculptured grace, her magic
    smile,
Bids the cold form with living radiance
    glow,
And stamps existence on its marble brow!
For Poesy's whole essence, when defined,
Is elevation of the reasoning mind,
When inward sense from Fancy's page
    is taught,
And moral feeling ministers to Thought.
And hence the natural passions all agree
In seeking Nature's language—poetry.
When Hope, in soft perspective, from afar
Sees lovely scenes more lovely than they
    are,
To deck the landscape tiptoe Fancy brings
Her plastic shapes and bright imaginings;
Or when man's breast by torturing pangs
    is stung,
If fearful silence cease t' enchain his
    tongue,
In metaphor the feelings seek relief,
And all the soul grows eloquent with
    grief.

Poetic fire, like Vesta's, pure and bright,
Should draw from Nature's sun its holy
light.
With Nature should the musing poet
roam,
And steal instruction from her classic
tome ;
When 'neath her guidance, least inclined
to err—
The ablest painter when he copies *her*.

Belovèd Shakespeare! England's dearest
fame !
Dead is the breast that swells not at thy
name !
Whether thine Ariel skim the seas along,
Floating on wings ethereal as his song —
Lear rave amid the tempest—or Macbeth
Question the hags of hell on midnight
heath—
Immortal Shakespeare ! still thy lips
impart
The noblest comment on the human
heart.
And as fair Eve, in Eden newly placed,
Gazed on her form, in limpid waters
traced,
And stretched her gentle arms, with
pleased surprise,
To meet the image of her own bright
eyes—
So Nature on thy magic page surveys
Her sportive graces and untutored ways!
Wondering, the soft reflection doth she
see,
Then laughing owns she loves herself
in thee !

Shun not the haunts of crowded cities,
then ;
Nor e'er, as man, forget to study men !
What though the tumult of the town
intrude
On the deep silence and the lofty mood ;
'Twill make thy human sympathies rejoice
To hear the music of a human voice,
To watch strange brows by various
reason wrought,
To claim the interchange of thought with
thought,
T' associate mind with mind, for Mind's
own weal,
As steel is ever sharpened best by steel.

T' impassioned bards the scenic world is
dear—
But Nature's glorious masterpiece is
here !
All poetry is beauty, but exprest
In inward essence, not in outward vest.
Hence lovely scenes, reflective poets
find,
Awake their lovelier images in Mind :
Nor doth the pictured earth the bard
invite,
The lake of azure or the heaven of light,
But that his swelling breast arouses there
Something less visible, and much more
fair !
There is a music in the landscape round —
A silent voice, that speaks without a
sound—
A witching spirit, that, reposing near,
Breathes to the heart, but comes not to
the ear !
These softly steal, his kindling soul t'
embrace,
And natural beauty gild with moral
grace.
Think not, when summer breezes tell
their tale,
The poet's thoughts are with the summer
gale ;
Think not his Fancy builds her elfin
dream
On painted floweret, or on sighing
stream :
No single objects cause his raptured
starts,
For Mind is narrowed, not inspired, by
parts.
But o'er the scene the poet's spirit broods,
To warm the thoughts that form his
noblest moods,
Peopling his solitude with faëry play,
And beckoning shapes that whisper him
away,
While lilied fields, and hedgerow blos-
soms white,
And hills, and glittering streams, are full
in sight—
The forests wave, the joyous sun be-
guiles,
And all the poetry of Nature smiles !

Such poetry is formed by Mind, and not
By scenic grace of one peculiar spot.

The artist lingers in the moonlit glade,
And light and shade, with him, are—light
    and shade ;
The philosophic chemist wandering there
Dreams of the soil and nature of the air ;
The rustic marks the young herbs' fresh'n-
    ing hue,
And only thinks—his scythe may soon
    pass through !
None 'muse on nature with a Poet's eye,'
None read, but Poets, Nature's poetry !
Its characters are traced in mystic hand,
And all may gaze, but few can understand.

Nor here alone the Poet's dwelling rear,
Though Beauty's voice perchance is
    sweetest here !
Bind not his footsteps to the sylvan scene,
To heathy banks, fair woods, and valleys
    green,
When Mind is all his own ! Her dear
    impress
Shall throw a magic o'er the wilderness
As o'er the blossoming vale, and ay recall
Its shadowy plane and silver waterfall,
Or sleepy crystal pool, reposing by,
To give the earth a picture of the sky !
Such, gazed on by the spirit, are, I ween,
Lovelier than ever prototype was seen ;
For Fancy teacheth Memory's hand to
    trace
Nature's ideal form in Nature's place.
In every theme by lofty Poet sung
The thought should seem to speak, and
    not the tongue.
When godlike Milton lifts th' exalted
    song
The subject bears the burning words
    along—
Resounds the march of Thought, th'
    o'erflowing line,
Full cadence, solemn pause, and strength
    divine !
When Horace chats his neighbour's
    faults away
The sportive measures, like his muse,
    are gay ;
For once Good-humour Satire's byway
    took,
And all his soul is laughing in his book !
On moral Pope's didactic page is found
Sound ruled by sense, and sense made
    clear by sound,

The power to reason and the taste to
    please,
While, as the subject varies in degrees,
He stoops with dignity and soars with
    ease.

Hence let our Poets, with discerning
    glance,
Forbear to imitate the stage of France.
What though Corneille arouse the thrill-
    ing chords,
And walk with Genius o'er th' inspirèd
    boards ;
What though his rival bring, with calmer
    grace,
The classic unities of time and place—
All polish and all eloquence—'twere
    mean
To leave the path of Nature for Racine ;
When Nero's parent, 'midst her woe,
    defines
The wrong that tortures—in two hundred
    lines :
Or when Orestes, maddened by his
    crime,
Forgets life, joy, and everything—but
    rime.

While thus to character and nature true,
Still keep the harmony of verse in view ;
Yet not in changeless concord,—it
    should be,
Though graceful, nervous,—musical,
    though free ;
Not clogged by useless drapery, not beset
By the superfluous word or epithet,
Wherein Conception only dies in state,
As Draco smothered by the garments'
    weight—
But join, Amphion-like (whose magic
    fire
Won the deep music of the Maian lyre,
To call Boeotia's city from the ground),
The just in structure with the sweet in
    sound.

Nor this the whole—the poet's classic
    strain
May flow in smoothest numbers, yet in
    vain ;
And Taste may please, and Fancy sport
    awhile,
And yet Aonia's muse refuse to smile !

For lo! her heavenly lips these words
    reveal—
'The sage may coldly *think*, the bard
    must *feel*!
And if his writings, to his heart untrue,
Would ape the fervent throb it never
    knew;
If generous deeds, and Virtue's noblest
    part,
And Freedom's voice, could never warm
    that heart;
If Interest taxed the produce of the brain,
And fettered Genius followed in her
    train,
Weeping as each unwilling word she
    spoke—
Then hush the lute—its master-string is
    broke!
In vain the skilful hand may linger o'er—
Concord is dead, and music speaks no
    more!'

There are, and have been such—they
    were forgot
If shame could veil their page, if tears
    could blot!
There are, and have been, whose dis-
    honoured lay
Aspired t' enrapture that the world
    might—pay!
Whose life was one long bribe, oft
    counted o'er—
Bribed to think on, and bribed to think
    no more;
Bribed to laugh, weep, nor ask the reason
    why;
Bribed to tell truth, and bribed to gild a
    lie!
O Man! for this, the sensual left behind,
We boast our empire o'er the vast of Mind?
O Mind! reported valueless till sold,
Thought dross till metamorphosed into
    gold
By Midas' touch—breath'st thou im-
    mortal verse
To throw a ducat in an empty purse—
To walk the market at a bellman's cry
For knaves to sell and wondering fools
    to buy?
Can Heaven-born bards, undone by
    lucre's lust,
Crouch thus, like Heaven-born ministers,
    to dust?

Alas! to dust indeed—yet wherefore
    blame?
They keep their profits though they lose
    their fame.

Leave to the dross they seek the grovel-
    ling throng,
And swell with nobler aim th' Aonian
    song!
Enough for thee, uninfluenced and un-
    hired,
If Truth reward the strain herself in-
    spired!
Enough for thee if grateful Man commend,
If Genius love, and Virtue call thee friend!
Enough for thee to wake th' exalted
    mood,
Reprove the erring, and confirm the good;
Excite the tender smile, the generous tear,
Or rouse the thought to loftiest Nature
    dear,
Which rapturous greets amidst the fer-
    vent line
Thy name, O Freedom! glorious Hellas,
    thine!

I love my own dear land—it doth rejoice
The soul to stretch my arms and lift my
    voice,
To tell her of my love! I love her green
And bowery woods, her hills in mossy
    sheen,
Her silver running waters—there's no
    spot
In all her dwelling which my breast loves
    not—
No place not heart-enchanted! Sunnier
    skies
And calmer waves may meet another's
    eyes;
I love the sullen mist, the stormy sea,
The winds of rushing strength which,
    like the land, are free!
Such is my love—yet, turning thus to
    thee,
O Graecia! I must hail with hardly less
Of joy, and pride, and deepening tender-
    ness,
And feelings wild I know not to control,
My other country—country of my soul!
For so, to me, thou art! my lips have sung
Of thee with childhood's lisp, and harp
    unstrung!

In thee, my Fancy's pleasant walks have
been,
Telling her tales, while Memory wept
between !
And now *for* thee I joy, with heart be-
guiled,
As if a dying friend looked up and smiled.

Lo ! o'er Aegaea's waves the shout hath
risen !
Lo ! Hope hath burst the fetters of her
prison !
And Glory sounds the trump along the
shore,
And Freedom walks where Freedom
walked before !
Ipsara glimmers with heroic light.
Redd'ning the waves that lash her flaming
height ;
And Aegypt hurries from that dark blue
sea !
Lo ! o'er the cliffs of famed Thermopylae
And voiceful Marathon the wild winds
sweep,
Bearing this message to the brave who
sleep—
'They come ! they come ! with their
embattled shock,
From Pelion's steep and Paros' foam-
dashed rock !
They come from Tempe's vale and
Helicon's spring,
And proud Eurotas' banks, the river king !
They come from Leuctra, from the waves
that kiss
Athena—from the shores of Salamis ;
From Sparta, Thebes, Euboea's hills of
blue—
To live with Hellas—or to sleep with
you !'

Smile—smile, belovèd land ! and though
no lay
From Doric pipe may charm thy glades
to-day—
Though dear Ionic music murmur not
Adown the vale, its echo all forgot !—
Yet smile, belovèd land ! for soon, around,
Thy silent earth shall utter forth a sound
As whilom ; and, its pleasant groves
among,
The Grecian voice shall breathe the
Grecian song,

While the exilèd muse shall 'habit still
The happy haunts of her Parnassian hill.
Till then, behold the cold, dumb sepul-
chre—
The ruined column—ocean, earth, and
air,
Man and his wrongs !—thou hast Tyrtaeus
there !
And pardon, if across the heaving main
Sound the far melody of minstrel strain
In wild and fitful gust from England's
shore,
For *his* immortal sake, who never more
Shall tread with living foot, and spirit
free,
Her fields, or breathe her passionate
poetry—
The pilgrim bard, who lived and died
for thee,
O land of Memory ! loving thee no less
Than parent—with the filial tenderness
And holy ardour of the Argive son,
Straining each nerve to bear thy chariot
on—
Till when its wheels the place of glory
swept
He laid him down before the shrine—
and slept.

So be it ! at his cold, unconscious bier
We fondly sate, and dropped the natural
tear—
Yet wept not wisely, for he sank to rest
On the dear earth his waking thoughts
loved best,
And gently life's last pulses stole away !
No Moschus sang a requiem o'er his clay,
But Greece was sad ! and breathed above,
below,
The warrior's sigh, the silence, and the
woe !

And is this all ?   Is this the little sum
For which we toil—to which our glories
come ?
Doth History bend her mouldering pages
o'er,
And Science stretch her bulwark from
the shore,
And Sages search the mystic paths of
Thought,
And Poets charm with lays that Genius
taught—

For this? to labour through their little
day,
To weep an hour, then want the tear
they pay—
To ask the urn, their death and life to
teli,
When the dull dust would give that tale
as well!

Man! hast thou seen the gallant vessel
sweep,
Borrowing her moonlight from the
jealous deep,
And gliding with mute foot and silver
wing
Over the waters like a soul-moved thing?
Man, hast thou gazed on this—then
looked again,
And seen no speck on all that desolate
main,
And heard no sound—except the gurgling
cry,
The winds half stifled in their mockery?

Woe unto thee! for thus thy course is
run,
And in the fullness of thy noonday sun
The darkness cometh—yea! thou walk'st
abroad
In glory, Child of Mind, Creation's Lord—
And wisdom's music from thy lips hath
gushed!
Then comes the *Selah !* and the voice is
hushed,
And the light past! we seek where thou
hast been
In beauty—but thy beauty is not seen!
We breathe the air thou breath'dst, we
tread the spot
Thy feet were wont to tread, but find thee
not!
Beyond, sits Darkness with her haggard
face.
Brooding fiend-like above thy burying-
place—

Beneath, let wildest Fancy take her fill!
Shall we seek on? we shudder, and are
still!
Yet woe not unto thee, thou child of
Earth!
Though moonlight sleep on thy deserted
hearth
We will not cry ' alas!' above thy clay!
It was, perchance, thy joyous pride to
stray
On Mind's lone shore, and linger by the
way:
But now thy pilgrim's staff is laid aside,
And on thou journeyest o'er the sullen
tide,
To bless thy wearied sight, and glad
thine heart
With all that Mind's serener skies impart;
Where Wisdom suns the day no shades
destroy,
And Learning ends in Truth, as hope in
joy:
While *we* stand mournful on the desert
beach,
And wait, and wish, thy distant bark to
reach,
And weep to watch it passing from our
sight,
And sound the gun's salute, and sigh our
last ' good night!'

And oh! while thus the spirit glides
away,
Give to the world its memory with its clay!
Some page our country's grateful eyes
may scan;
Some useful truth to bless surviving man;
Some name to honest bosoms justly dear;
Some grave t' exalt the thought and
claim the tear;
So when the pilgrim Sun is travelling o'er
The last blue hill, to gild a distant shore,
He leaves a freshness in the evening scene
That tells Creation where his steps have
been!

SHORTER POEMS

APPENDED TO 'AN ESSAY ON MIND' AND THE FIRST VERSION
OF 'PROMETHEUS BOUND,' 1833

TO MY FATHER ON HIS BIRTH-DAY

Causa fuit Pater his.—HORACE.

AMIDST the days of pleasant mirth,
That throw their halo round our earth;
Amidst the tender thoughts that rise
To call bright tears to happy eyes;
Amidst the silken words that move
To syllable the names we love;
There glides no day of gentle bliss
More soothing to the heart than *this !*
No thoughts of fondness e'er appear
More fond, than those I write of here !
No name can e'er on tablet shine,
My Father! more beloved than *thine !*
'Tis sweet, adown the shady past,
A lingering look of love to cast—
Back th' enchanted world to call,
That beamed around us first of all;
And walk with Memory fondly o'er
The paths where Hope had been before—
Sweet to receive the sylphic sound
That breathes in tenderness around,
Repeating to the listening ear
The names that made our childhood
    dear—
For parted Joy, like Echo, kind,
Will leave her dulcet voice behind,
To tell, amidst the magic air,
How oft she smiled and lingered there.
Oh ! let the deep Aonian shell
Breathe tuneful numbers, clear and well,
While the glad Hours, in fair array,
Lead on this buxom Holiday ;
And Time, as on his way he springs,
Hates the last bard who gave him wings ;
For 'neath thy gentleness of praise,
My Father! rose my early lays !
And when the lyre was scarce awake,
I loved its strings for *thy* loved sake ;
Wooed the kind Muses—but the while
Thought only how to win thy smile—
My proudest fame—my dearest pride—
More dear than all the world beside !
And now, perchance, I seek the tone
For magic that is more its own;
But still my Father's looks remain
The best Maecenas of my strain ;
My gentlest joy, upon his brow
To read the smile, that meets me now—
To hear him, in his kindness. say
The words,—perchance he'll speak to-
    day !

SPENSERIAN STANZAS ON A BOY OF THREE YEARS OLD

CHILD of the sunny lockes and beautifull
    brow !
In thoughtfull tendernesse I gaze on
    thee—
Upon thy daintie cheek Expression's
    glow
Daunceth in tyme to thine heart's
    melodie ;
Ne mortall wight mote lovelier urchin
    see !
Nathlesse it teens this pensive brest of
    mine
To think—belive the innocent revelrie
Shall be eclipsed in those soft blue
    eyne—
Whenso the howre of youth no more for
    thee shall shine.

Ah me! eftsoons thy childhood's
    pleasaunt dais
Shall fly away, and be a whilome thing !
And sweetest mearimake, and birthday
    lais
Be recked not of, except when memo-
    ries bring
Feres to their embers with awaking
    wing,

To make past love rejoyce thy tender
sprite,
Albeit the toyles of daunger thee en-
ring!
Child of the wavy lockes and brow of
light—
Then be thy conscience pure, as *now* thy
face is bright.

VERSES TO MY BROTHER

For we were nursed upon the self-same hill.
Lycidas.

I WILL write down thy name, and
when 'tis writ,
Will turn me from the hum that mortals
keep
In the wide world without, and gaze
on it!
It telleth of the past—calling from sleep
Such dear, yet mournful thoughts, as
make us smile, and weep.

Beloved and best! what thousand
feelings start,
As o'er the paper's course my fingers
move—
My Brother! dearest, kindest as thou
art!
How can these lips my heart's affection
prove?
I could not speak the words, if words
could speak my love.

Together have we passed our infant
hours,
Together sported Childhood's spring
away,
Together culled young Hope's fast
budding flowers,
To wreathe the forehead of each
coming day!
Yes! for the present's sun makes e'en
the future gay.

And when the laughing mood was
nearly o'er,
Together, many a minute did we wile
On Horace' page, or Maro's sweeter
lore;

While one young critic, on the classic
style,
Would sagely try to frown, and make
the other smile.

But now alone thou con'st the ancient
tome—
And sometimes thy dear studies, it
may be,
Are crossed by dearer dreams of me
and home!
Alone I muse on Homer—thoughts
are free—
And if mine often stray, they go in
search of thee!

I may not praise thee *here*—I will not
bless!
Yet all thy goodness doth my memory
bear,
Cherished by more than Friendship's
tenderness—
And, in the silence of my evening
prayer,
Thou shalt not be forgot—thy dear name
shall be there!

STANZAS ON THE DEATH OF
LORD BYRON

λέγε πᾶσιν ἀπώλετο.—BION.

I am not now
That which I have been.—*Childe Harold.*

HE *was*, and *is* not! Graecia's trembl:ng
shore,
Sighing through all her palmy groves,
shall tell
That Harold's pilgrimage at last is
o'er—
Mute the impassioned tongue, and
tuneful shell,
That erst was wont in noblest strains
to swell—
Hushed the proud shouts that rode
Aegaea's wave!
For lo! the great Deliv'rer breathes
farewell!
Gives to the world his mem'ry and a
grave—
Expiring in the land he only lived to save!

Mourn, Hellas, mourn! and o'er thy
    widowed brow,
For ay, the cypress wreath of sorrow
    twine;
And in thy new-formed beauty, deso-
    late, throw
The fresh-culled flowers on *his* sepul-
    chral shrine.
Yes! let that heart whose fervour was
    all thine,
In consecrated urn lamented be!
That generous heart where genius
    thrilled divine,
Hath spent its last most glorious throb
    for thee—
Then sank amid the storm that made thy
    children free!

Britannia's poet! Graecia's hero,
    sleeps!
And Freedom, bending o'er the breath-
    less clay,
Lifts up her voice, and in her anguish
    weeps!
For *us*, a night hath clouded o'er our
    day,
And hushed the lips that breathed our
    fairest lay.
Alas! and must the British lyre resound
A requiem, while the spirit wings away
Of him who on its strings such music
    found,
And taught its startling chords to give so
    sweet a sound!

The theme grows sadder—but my soul
    shall find
A language in these tears! No more—
    no more!
Soon, 'midst the shriekings of the
    tossing wind,
The 'dark blue depths' he sang of,
    shall have bore
Our *all* of Byron to his native shore!
His grave is thick with voices—to the
    ear
Murm'ring an awful tale of greatness
    o'er;
But Memory strives with Death, and
    lingering near,
Shall consecrate the dust of Harold's
    lonely bier!

MEMORY

My Fancy's steps have often strayed
To some fair vale the hills have made;
Where sparkling waters travel o'er,
And hold a mirror to the shore;
Windings with murmurings in and out,
To find the flowers which grow about.
And there, perchance, in childhood bold,
Some little elf, four summers old,
Adown the vales may chance to run,
To hunt his shadow in the sun!
But when the waters meet his eyes,
He starts and stops with glad surprise,
And shouts, with merry voice, to view
The banks of green, the skies of blue,
Th' inverted flocks that bleating go,
Lilies, and trees of apple-blow,
Seeming so beautiful below!
He peeps above—he glances round,
And then looks down, and thinks he's
    found
Reposing in the stream, to woo one,
A world even lovelier than the true one.

Thus, with visions gay and light.
Hath Fancy loved my page to dight;
Yet Thought hath, through a vista, seen
Something less frivolous, I ween:
Then, while my chatting pen runs on,
I'll tell you what she dreamt upon.

Memory's the streamlet of the scene,
Which sweeps the hills of Life between;
And, when our walking hour is past,
Upon its shore we rest at last;
And love to view the waters fair,
And see lost joys depictured there.

My ——, when thy feet are led
To press those banks we all must tread,
May Virtue's smile and Learning's praise
Adorn the waters to thy gaze;
And, o'er their lucid course, be lent
The sunshine of a life well spent!
Then, if a thought should glad thy breast
Of those who loved thee first and best,
My name, perchance, may haunt the
    spot,
Not quite unprized—nor all forgot.

TO ——

Mine is a wayward lay ;
And, if its echoing rimes I try to
    string
  Proveth a truant thing,
Whenso some names I love, send it
    away !

For then, eyes swimming o'er,
And claspèd hands, and smiles in fondness
    meant,
  Are much more eloquent —
So it had fain begone, and speak no more !

Yet shall it come again,
Ah, friend beloved ! if so thy wishes be,
And, with wild melody,
I will, upon thine ear, cadence my
    strain—

Cadence my simple line,
Unfashioned by the cunning hand of Art,
  But coming from my heart,
To tell the message of its love to thine !

As ocean shells, when taken
From Ocean's bed, will faithfully repeat
  Her ancient music sweet—
Ev'n so these words, true to my heart,
    shall waken !

Oh ! while our bark is seen,
Our little bark of kindly, social love,
  Down life's clear stream to move
Toward the summer shores, where all
    is green—

So long thy name shall bring
Echoes of joy unto the grateful gales,
  And thousand tender tales,
To freshen the fond hearts that round
    thee cling !

Hast thou not looked upon
The flowerets of the field in lowly dress ?
  Blame not my simpleness—
Think only of my love !—my song is
    gone.

STANZAS

OCCASIONED BY A PASSAGE IN
MR. EMERSON'S JOURNAL

*Which states that, on the mention of Lord
Byron's name, Captain Demetrius, an
old Roumeliot, burst into tears*

Name not his name, or look afar—
  For when my spirit hears
That name, its strength is turned to
    woe—
  My voice is turned to tears.

Name me the host and battle-storm,
  Mine own good sword shall stem ;
Name me the foeman and the block,
  I have a smile for *them !*

But name *him* not, or cease to mark
  This brow where passions sweep—
Behold, a warrior is a man,
  And as a man may weep !

I could not scorn my Country's foes,
  Did not these tears descend—
I could not love my Country's fame,
  And not my Country's Friend.

Deem not his memory e'er can be
  Upon our spirits dim—
Name us the generous and the free,
  And we must think of *him !*

For his voice resounded through our land
  Like the voice of liberty,
As when the war-trump of the wind
  Upstirs our dark blue sea.

His arm was in the foremost rank,
  Where embattled thousands roll—
His name was in the love of Greece,
  And his spell was on her soul !

But the arm that wielded her good sword,
  The brow that wore the wreath,
The lips that breathed the deathless
    thoughts—
  They went asleep in death.

Ye left his HEART, when ye took away
  The dust in funeral state ;
And we dumbly placed in a little urn
  That home of all things great.

The banner streamed—the war-shout
    rose—
  Our heroes played their part ;
But not a pulse would throb or burn—
  Oh ! could it be *his* heart !

I will not think—'tis worse than vain
  Upon such thoughts to keep ;
Then, Briton, name me not his name—
  I cannot choose but weep !

THE PAST

THERE is a silence upon the Ocean.
Albeit it swells with a feverish motion ;
Like to the battle-camp's fearful calm,
While the banners are spread, and the
    warriors arm.

The winds beat not their drum to the
    waves,
But sullenly moan in the distant caves ;
Talking over, before they rise,
Some of their dark conspiracies.

And so it is in this life of ours,
A calm may be on the present hours,
But the calmest hour of festive glee
May turn the mother of woe to thee.

I will betake me to the Past,
And she shall make my love at last ;
I will find my home in her tarrying-
    place—
I will gaze all day on her deathly face !

Her form, though awful, is fair to view ;
The clasp of her hand, though cold, is
    true ;
Her shadowy brow hath no changeful-
    ness,
And her numbered smiles can grow no
    less !

Her voice is like a pleasant song,
Which we have not heard for very long,
And which a joy on our souls will cast,
Though we know not where we heard
    it last.

She shall walk with me, away, away,
Where'er the mighty have left their
    clay ;
She shall speak to me in places lone,
With a low and holy tone.

Aye ! when I have lit my lamp at night,
She will be present with my sprite ;
And I will say, whate'er it be,
Every word she telleth me !

THE PRAYER

METHOUGHT that I did stand upon a
    tomb—
And all was silent as the dust beneath,
While feverish thoughts upon my soul
    would come,
Losing my words in tears : I thought
    of death ;
And prayed that when my lips gave
    out the breath,
The friends I loved like life might stay
    behind :
So, for a little while, my name might
    eath
Be something dear,—spoken with
    voices kind,
Heard with remembering looks, from
    eyes which tears would blind !

I prayed that I might sink unto my rest
(O foolish, selfish prayer !) before
    them all ;
So I might look my last on those loved
    best—
So never would my voice repining call,
And never would my tears impassioned
    fall
On one familiar face turning to clay !
So would my tune of life be musical,
Albeit abrupt—like airs the Spaniards
    play,
Which in the sweetest part break off,
    and die away.

Methought I looked around ! the scene
    was rife
With little vales, green banks, and
    waters heaving ;
And every living thing did joy in life,

And every thing of beauty did seem
    living—
Oh, then, life's pulse was at my heart
    reviving ;
And then I knew that it was good to bear
Dispensèd woe, that by the spirit's
    grieving
It might be weanèd from a world so
    fair !—
Thus with submissive words mine heart
    did close its prayer.

ON A PICTURE OF RIEGO'S WIDOW

PLACED IN AN EXHIBITION

DAUGHTER of Spain ! a passer by
    May mark the cheek serenely pale—
The dark eyes which dream silently,
    And the calm lip which gives no wail !

Calm ! it bears not a deeper trace
    Of feelings it disdained to show ;
We look upon the Widow's face,
    And only read the Patriot's woe !

No word, no look, no sigh of thine,
    Would make *his* glory seem more dim ;
Thou wouldst not give to vulgar eyne
    The sacred tear which fell for HIM.

Thou wouldst not hold to the world's
    view
Thy ruined joys, thy broken heart—
The jeering world—it only knew
    Of all thine anguish—that thou WERT !

While o'er *his* grave thy steps would go
    With a firm tread,—stilling thy love,—
As if the dust would blush below
    To feel one faltering foot above.

For Spain, *he* dared the noble strife —
    For Spain, he gave his latest breath ;
And he who lived the Patriot's life
    Was dragged to die the traitor's death !

And the shout of thousands swept around,
    As he stood the traitor's block beside ;
But his dying lips gave a free sound—
    Let the foe weep !—THY brow had
      pride !

Yet haply in the midnight air,
    When none might part thy God and
      thee,
The lengthened sob, the passionate
    prayer,
Have spoken thy soul's agony !

But silent else, thou passed away—
    The plaint unbreathed, the anguish
      hid—
More voiceless than the echoing clay
    Which idly knocked thy coffin's lid.

Peace be to thee ! while Britons seek
    This place, if British souls they bear,
'Twill start the crimson in the cheek
    To see Riego's widow THERE !

SONG

WEEP, as if you thought of laughter !
Smile, as tears were coming after !
Marry your pleasures to your woes ;
And think life's green well worth its
    rose !

No sorrow will your heart betide,
Without a comfort by its side ;
The sun may sleep in his sea-bed,
But you have starlight overhead.

Trust not to Joy ! the rose of June,
When opened wide, will wither soon ;
Italian days without twilight
Will turn them suddenly to night.

Joy, most changeful of all things,
Flits away on rainbow wings ;
And when they look the gayest, know,
It is that they are spread to go !

THE DREAM

A FRAGMENT

I HAD a dream !—my spirit was un-
    bound
From the dark iron of its dungeon, clay,
And rode the steeds of Time ;—my
    thoughts had sound,
And spoke without a word,—I went
    away
Among the buried ages, and did lay

The pulses of my heart beneath the touch
Of the rude minstrel Time, that he should play
Thereon a melody which might seem such
As musing spirits love—mournful, but not too much!

I had a dream—and there mine eyes did see
The shadows of past deeds like present things—
The sepulchres of Greece and Hespery,
Aegyptus, and old lands, gave up their kings,
Their prophets, saints, and minstrels, whose lute-strings
Keep a long echo—yea, the dead, white bones
Did stand up by the house whereto Death clings,
And dressed themselves in life, speaking of thrones,
And fame, and power, and beauty, in familiar tones!

I went back further still, for I beheld
What time the earth was one fair Paradise—
And over such bright meads the waters welled,
I wot the rainbow was content to rise
Upon the earth, when absent from the skies!
And there were tall trees that I never knew,
Whereon sate nameless birds in merry guise,
Folding their radiant wings, as the flowers do,
When summer nights send sleep down with the dew.

.   .   .   .   .   .

Anon there came a change—a terrible motion,
That made all living things grow pale and shake!
The dark Heavens bowed themselves unto the ocean,
Like a strong man in strife—Ocean did take

His flight across the mountains; and the lake
Was lashed into a sea where the winds ride—
Earth was no more, for in her merry-make
She had forgot her God—Sin claimed his bride,
And with his vampire breath sucked out her life's fair tide!

Life went back to her nostrils, and she raised
Her spirit from the waters once again—
The lovely sights, on which I erst had gazed,
Were *not*—though she was beautiful as when
The Grecian called her 'Beauty'—sinful men
Walked i' the track of the waters, and felt bold—
Yea, they looked up to Heaven in calm disdain,
As if no eye had seen its vault unfold
Darkness, and fear, and death!—as if a tale were told!

And ages fled away within my dream;
And still Sin made the heart his dwelling-place,
Eclipsing Heaven from men; but it would seem
That two or three dared commune face to face,
And speak of the soul's life, of hope, and grace.
Anon there rose such sounds as angels breathe—
For a God came to die, bringing down peace—
'Pan *was not*'; and the darkness that did wreathe
The earth, passed from the soul—Life came by Death!

.   .   .   .   .   .

RIGA'S LAST SONG

I HAVE looked my last on my native land,
And over these strings I throw my hand,
To say in the death-hour's minstrelsy,
Hellas, my country! farewell to thee!

I have looked my last on my native shore;
I shall tread my country's plains no more;
But my last thought is of her fame;
But my last breath speaketh her name!

And though these lips shall soon be still,
They may now obey the spirit's will;
Though the dust be fettered, the spirit
    is free—
Hellas, my country! farewell to thee!

I go to death—but I leave behind
The stirrings of Freedom's mighty mind;
Her voice shall arise from plain to sky,
Her steps shall tread where my ashes lie!

I looked on the mountains of proud Souli,
And the mountains they seemed to look
    on me;
I spoke my thought on Marathon's plain,
And Marathon seemed to speak again!

And as I journeyed on my way,
I saw an infant group at play;
One shouted aloud in his childish glee,
And showed me the heights of Ther-
    mopylae!

I gazed on peasants hurrying by,—
The dark Greek pride crouched in their
    eye;
So I swear in my death-hour's minstrelsy,
Hellas, my country! thou *shalt* be free!

No more!—I dash my lyre on the
    ground—
I tear its strings from their home of
    sound—
For the music of slaves shall never keep
Where the hand of a freeman was wont
    to sweep!

And I bend my brows above the block,
Silently waiting the swift death shock;
For these lips shall speak what becomes
    the free—
Or—Hellas, my country! farewell to
    thee!

He bowed his head with a Patriot's pride,
And his dead trunk fell the mute lyre
    beside!
The soul of each had passed away—
Soundless the strings—breathless the
    clay!

THE VISION OF FAME

DID ye ever sit on summer noon,
    Half musing and half asleep,
When ye smile in such a dreamy way,
    Ye know not if ye weep—

When the little flowers are thick beneath,
    And the welkin blue above;
When there is not a sound but the cattle's
    low,
    And the voice of the woodland dove?

A while ago, and I dreamèd thus—
    I mused on ancient story,—
For the heart like a minstrel of old doth
    seem,
    It delighteth to sing of glory.

What time I saw before me stand
    A bright and lofty One;
A golden lute was in her hand,
    And her brow drooped thereon.

But the brow that drooped was raisèd
    soon,
    Showing its royal sheen—
It was, I guessed, no human brow,
    Though pleasant to human een.

And this brow of peerless majesty
    With its whiteness did enshroud
Two eyes that, darkly mystical,
    'Gan look up at a cloud.

Like to the hair of Berenice,
    Fetched from its house of light,
Was the hair which wreathed her
    shadowless form—
    And Fame the ladye hight!

But as she wended on to me,
    My heart's deep fear was chidden;
For she called up the sprite of Melody,
    Which in her lute lay hidden.

When ye speak to well-belovèd ones,
    Your voice is tender and low:
The wires methought did love her touch—
    For they did answer so.

And her lips in such a quiet way
    Gave the chant soft and long,—
You might have thought she only
    breathed,
    And that her breath was song:—

' When Death shrouds thy memory,
     Love is no shrine—
The dear eyes that weep for thee
     Soon sleep like thine !
The wail murmured over thee
     Fainteth away;
And the heart which kept love for thee
     Turns into clay !

' But wouldst thou remembered be,
     Make me thy vow ;
This verse that flows gushingly
     Telleth thee how—
Linking thy hand in mine,
     Listen to me,
So not a thought of thine
     Dieth with thee—

' Rifle thy pulsing heart
     Of the gift, love made ;
Bid thine eye's light depart ;
     Let thy cheek fade !
Give me the slumber deep,
     Which night-long seems ;
Give me the joys that creep
     Into thy dreams !

' Give me thy youthful years,
     Merriest that fly—
So the word, spoke in *tears,*
     Liveth for ay !
So thy sepulchral stone,
     Nations may raise—
What time thy soul hath known
     The *worth of praise !* '

She did not sing this chant to me,
     Though I was sitting by ;
But I listened to it with chainèd breath,
     That had no power to sigh.

And ever as the chant went on
     Its measure changed to wail ;
And ever as the lips sang on
     Her face did grow more pale.

Paler and paler—till anon
     A fear came o'er my soul ;
For the flesh curled up from her bones,
     Like to a blasted scroll !

Aye ! silently it dropped away
     Before my wondering sight—
There was only a bleachèd skeleton
     Where erst was ladye bright !

But still the vacant sockets gleamed
     With supernatural fires—
But still the bony hands did ring
     Against the shuddering wires !

Alas, alas ! I wended home,
     With a sorrow and a shame—
Is Fame the rest of our poor hearts ?
     Woe's me ! for THIS IS FAME !

THE TEMPEST

A FRAGMENT

Mors erat ante oculos.—LUCAN, lib. ix.

.   .   .   .

THE forest made my home—the voiceful
     streams
My minstrel throng : the everlasting
     hills, —
Which marry with the firmament, and cry
Unto the brazen thunder, ' Come away,
Come from thy secret place, and try our
     strength,'—
Enwrapped me with their solemn arms.
     Here, light
Grew pale as darkness, scarèd by the
     shade
O'the forest Titans. Here, in piny state,
Reigned Night, the Aethiopian queen,
     and crowned
The charmèd brow of Solitude, her
     spouse.

.   .   .   .

A sign was on creation. You beheld
All things encoloured in a sulph'rous hue,
As day were sick with fear. The hag-
     gard clouds
O'erhung the utter lifelessness of air ;
The top boughs of the forest, all aghast,
Stared in the face of Heaven ; the deep-
     mouthed wind,
That hath a voice to bay the armèd sea,
Fled with a low cry like a beaten hound :
And only that askance the shadows flew
Some open-beakèd birds in wilderment,
Naught stirred abroad. All dumb did
     Nature seem,
In expectation of the coming storm.

It came in power. You soon might hear
     afar
The footsteps of the martial thunder sound

Over the mountain battlements ; the sky
Being deep-stained with hues fantastical,
Red like to blood, and yellow like to fire,
And black like plumes at funerals ; over-
head
You might behold the lightning faintly
gleam
Amid the clouds which thrill and gape
aside,
And straight again shut up their solemn
jaws,
As if to interpose between Heaven's
wrath
And Earth's despair. Interposition brief!
Darkness is gathering out her mighty pall
Above us, and the pent-up rain is loosed,
Down trampling in its fierce delirium.

Was not my spirit gladdened, as with
wine,
To hear the iron rain, and view the mark
Of battle on the banner of the clouds ?
Did I not hearken for the battle-cry,
And rush along the bowing woods to
meet
The riding Tempest—skyey cataracts
Hissing around him with rebellion vain ?
Yea ! and I lifted up my glorying voice
In an ' All hail ' ; when, wildly resonant,
As brazen chariots rushing from the war,
As passioned waters gushing from the
rock,
As thousand crashèd woods, the thunder
cried :
And at his cry the forest tops were shook
As by the woodman's axe ; and far and
near
Staggered the mountains with a muttered
dread.

All hail unto the lightning ! hurriedly
His lurid arms are glaring through the air,
Making the face of Heaven to show like
hell !
Let him go breathe his sulphur stench
about,
And, pale with death's own mission,
lord the storm !
Again the gleam—the glare : I turned
to hail
Death's mission : at my feet there lay the
dead !

The dead—the dead lay there ! I could
not view
(For Night espoused the storm, and made
all dark)
Its features, but the lightning in its course
Shivered above a white and corpse-like
heap,
Stretched in the path, as if to show his
prey,
And have a triumph ere he passed.
Then I
Crouched down upon the ground, and
groped about
Until I touched that thing of flesh, rain-
drenched,
And chill, and soft. Nathless, I did re-
frain
My soul from natural horror ! I did lift
The heavy head, half-bedded in the clay,
Unto my knee ; and passed my fingers o'er
The wet face, touching every lineament,
Until I found the brow ; and chafed its
chill,
To know if life yet lingered in its pulse.
And while I was so busied, there did leap
From out the entrails of the firmament,
The lightning, who his white unblench-
ing breath
Blew in the dead man's face, discovering
it
As by a staring day. I knew that face—
His, who did hate me—his, whom I did
hate !

I shrunk not—spake not—sprang not
from the ground !
But felt my lips shake without cry or
breath,
And mine heart wrestle in my breast to
still
The tossing of its pulses ; and a cold,
Instead of living blood, o'ercreep my
brow.
Albeit such darkness brooded all around,
I had dread knowledge that the open
eyes
Of that dead man were glaring up to mine,
With their unwinking, unexpressive
stare ;
And mine I could not shut nor turn away
The man was my familiar. I had borne
Those eyes to scowl on me their living
hate,

Better than I could bear their deadliness :
I had endured the curses of those lips
Far better than their silence.   Oh, con-
strained
And awful silence!—awful peace of
death !
There is an answer to all questioning,
That one word—*death*.   Our bitterness
can throw
No look upon the face of death, and live.
The burning thoughts that erst my soul
illumed
Were quenched at once ; as tapers in a
pit
Wherein the vapour-witches weirdly
reign
In charge of darkness.   Farewell all the
past !
It was out-blotted from my memory's eyes
When clay's cold silence pleaded for its
sin.

Farewell the elemental war ! farewell
The clashing of the shielded clouds—the
cry
Of scathèd echoes ! I no longer knew
Silence from sound, but wandered far
away
Into the deep Eleusis of mine heart,
To learn its secret things.   When armèd
foes
Meet on one deck with impulse violent,
The vessel quakes thro' all her oaken ribs,
And shivers in the sea ; so with mine
heart :
For there had battled in her solitudes,
Contrary spirits ; sympathy with power,
And stooping unto power ;—the energy
And passiveness,—the thunder and the
death !

Within me was a nameless thought : it
closed
The Janus of my soul on echoing hinge,
And said ' Peace ! ' with a voice like
War's.   I bowed,
And trembled at its voice : it gave a key,
Empowered to open out all mysteries
Of soul and flesh ; of man, who doth begin,
But endeth not ; of life, and *after life*.
.   .   .   .   .   .
Day came at last : her light showed grey
and sad,

As hatched by tempest, and could scarce
prevail
Over the shaggy forest to imprint
Its outline on the sky—expressionless,
Almost sans shadow as sans radiance :
An idiocy of light.   I wakened from
My deep unslumb'ring dream, but uttered
naught.
My living I uncoupled from the dead,
And looked out, 'mid the swart and
sluggish air,
For place to make a grave.   A mighty tree
Above me, his gigantic arms out-
stretched,
Poising the clouds.   A thousand muttered
spells
Of every ancient wind and thund'rous
storm
Had been off-shaken from his scatheless
bark.
He had heard distant years sweet con-
cord yield,
And go to silence ; having firmly kept
Majestical companionship with Time.
Anon his strength waxed proud : his
tusky roots
Forced for themselves a path on every
side,
Riving the earth ; and, in their savage
scorn,
Casting it from them like a thing unclean,
Which might impede his naked clamber-
ing
Unto the heavens.   Now blasted, peeled,
he stood,
By the gone night, whose lightning had
come in
And rent him, even as it rent the man
Beneath his shade : and there the strong
and weak
Communion joined in deathly agony.
There, underneath, I lent my feverish
strength,
To scoop a lodgement for the traveller's
corse.
I gave it to the silence and the pit,
And strewed the heavy earth on all :
and then—
I—I, whose hands had formed that
silent house,—
I could not look thereon, but turned and
wept !   .   .   .   .

O Death—O crownèd Death—pale-
steedèd Death !

Whose name doth make our respiration
brief,

Muffling the spirit's drum ! Thou, whom
men know

Alone by charnel-houses, and the dark

Sweeping of funeral feathers, and the
scath

Of happy days,—love deemed inviolate !

Thou of the shrouded face, which to
have seen

Is to be very awful, like thyself !—

Thou, whom all flesh shall see !—thou,
who dost call,

And there is none to answer !—thou,
whose call

Changeth all beauty into what we fear,

Changeth all glory into what we tread,

Genius to silence, wrath to nothingness,

And love—not love!—thou hast no change
for love !

Thou, who art Life's betrothed, and
bear'st her forth

To scare her with sad sights,—who hast
thy joy

Where'er the peopled towns are dumb
with plague,—

Where'er the battle and the vulture
meet,—

Where'er the deep sea writhes like
Laocoon

Beneath the serpent winds, and vessels
split

On secret rocks, and men go gurgling
down,

Down, down, to lose their shriekings in
the depth !

O universal thou ! who comest ay

Among the minstrels, and their tongue
is tied ;

Among the sophists, and their brain is
still ;

Among the mourners, and their wail is
done ;

Among the dancers, and their tinkling
feet

No more make echoes on the tombing
earth ;

Among the wassail rout, and all the
lamps

Are quenched, and withered the wine-
pouring hands !

Mine heart is armèd not in panoply

Of the old Roman iron, nor assumes

The Stoic valour.   'Tis a human heart,

And so confesses, with a human fear ;—

That only for the hope the cross inspires,

That only for the MAN who died and lives,

'Twould crouch beneath thy sceptre's
royalty,

With faintness of the pulse, and back-
ward cling

To life.   But knowing what I soothly
know,

High-seeming Death, I dare thee ! and
have hope,

In God's good time, of showing to thy face

An unsuccumbing spirit, which sublime

May cast away the low anxieties

That wait upon the flesh—the reptile
moods ;

And enter that eternity to come,

Where live the dead, and only Death
shall die.

A SEA-SIDE MEDITATION

Ut per aquas quae nunc rerum simulacra vide-
mus.—LUCRETIUS.

Go, travel 'mid the hills ! The summer's
hand

Hath shaken pleasant freshness o'er
them all.

Go, travel 'mid the hills ! There, tuneful
streams

Are touching myriad stops, invisible ;

And winds, and leaves, and birds, and
your own thoughts

(Not the least glad) in wordless chorus,
crowd

Around the thymele [1] of Nature.
                                     Go,

And travel onward.   Soon shall leaf and
bird,

Wind, stream, no longer sound.   Thou
shalt behold

Only the pathless sky, and houseless
sward ;

O'er which anon are spied innumerous
sails

Of fisher vessels like the wings o' the hill,

[1] The central point of the choral movements
in the Greek theatre.

And white as gulls above them, and as
    fast,—
But sink they—sink they out of sight.
    And now
The wind is springing upward in your
    face ;
And, with its fresh-toned gushings, you
    may hear
Continuous sound which is not of the
    wind,
Nor of the thunder, nor o' the cataract's
Deep passion, nor o' the earthquake's
    wilder pulse ;
But which rolls on in stern tranquillity,
As memories of evil o'er the soul ;—
Boweth the bare broad Heaven.—What
    view you ? sea—and sea !

The sea—the glorious sea ! from side to
    side
Swinging the grandeur of his foamy
    strength,
And undersweeping the horizon,—on—
On—with his life and voice inscrutable.
Pause : sit you down in silence ! I have
    read
Of that Athenian, who, when ocean
    raged,
Unchained the prisoned music of his lips
By shouting to the billows, sound for
    sound.
I marvel how his mind would let his
    tongue
Affront thereby the ocean's solemnness.
Are we not mute, or speak restrainedly,
When overhead the trampling tempests
    go,
Dashing their lightning from their hoofs ?
    and when
We stand beside the bier ? and when
    we see
The strong bow down to weep—and
    stray among
Places which dust or mind hath sanctified ?
Yea ! for such sights and acts do tear
    apart
The close and subtle clasping of a chain,
Formed not of gold, but of corroded brass,
Whose links are furnished from the
    common mine
Of every day's event, and want, and wish ;
From work-times, diet-times, and sleep-
    ing-times :

And thence constructed, mean and heavy
    links
Within the pandemonic walls of sense
Enchain our deathless part, constrain
    our strength,
And waste the goodly stature of our soul.

Howbeit, we love this bondage ; we do
    cleave
Unto the sordid and unholy thing,
Fearing the sudden wrench required to
    break
Those claspèd links.   Behold ! all sights
    and sounds
In air, and sea, and earth, and under earth,
All flesh, all life, all ends, are mysteries ;
And all that is mysterious dreadful seems,
And all we cannot understand we fear.
Ourselves do scare ourselves : we hide
    our sight
In artificial nature from the true,
And throw sensation's veil associative
On God's creation, man's intelligence ;
Bowing our high imaginings to eat
Dust, like the serpent, once erect as they ;
Binding conspicuous on our reason's brow
Phylacteries of shame ; learning to feel
By rote, and act by rule (man's rule,
    not God's !),
Unto our words grow echoes, and our
    thoughts
A mechanism of spirit.
                        Can this last !
No ! not for ay.   We cannot subject ay
The heaven-born spirit to the earth-born
    flesh.
Tame lions *will* scent blood, and appetite
Carnivorous glare from out their restless
    eyes.
Passions, emotions, sudden changes,
    throw
Our nature back upon us, till we burn.
What warmed Cyrene's fount ? As poets
    sing,
The *change* from light to dark, from dark
    to light.

All that doth force this nature back on us,
All that doth force the mind to view the
    mind,
Engend'reth what is named by men,
    sublime.
Thus when, our wonted valley left, we
    gain

The mountain's horrent brow, and mark
from thence
The sweep of lands extending with the
sky ;
Or view the spanless plain ; or turn our
sight
Upon yon deep's immensity ;—we
breathe
As if our breath were marble : to and fro
Do reel our pulses, and our words are
mute.
We cannot mete by parts, but grapple all ;
We cannot measure with our eye, but
soul ;
And fear is on us. The extent unused,
Our spirit, sends, to spirit's element,
To seize upon abstractions: first on
space,
The which *eternity in place* I deem ;
And then upon eternity ; till thought
Hath formed a mirror from their secret
sense,
Wherein we view ourselves, and back
recoil
At our own awful likeness ; ne'ertheless,
Cling to that likeness with a wonder wild,
And while we tremble, glory—proud in
fear.
So ends the prose of life : and so shall be
Unlocked her poetry's magnific store.
And so, thou pathless and perpetual sea,
So, o'er thy deeps, I brooded and must
brood,
Whether I view thee in thy dreadful
peace,
Like a spent warrior hanging in the sun
His glittering arms, and meditating
death ;
Or whether thy wild visage gath'reth
shades,
What time thou marshall'st forth thy
waves who hold
A covenant of storms, then roar and
wind
Under the racking rocks ; as martyrs lie
Wheel-bound ; and, dying, utter lofty
words !
Whether the strength of day is young
and high,
Or whether, weary of the watch, he sits
Pale on thy wave, and weeps himself to
death ;—
In storm and calm, at morn and eventide,

Still have I stood beside thee, and out-
thrown
My spirit onward on thine element,—
Beyond thine element,—to tremble low
Before those feet which trod thee as
they trod
Earth,—to the holy, happy, peopled
place,
Where there is no more sea. Yea, and
my soul,
Having put on thy vast similitude,
Hath wildly moaned at her proper depth,
Echoed her proper musings, veiled in
shade
Her secrets of decay, and exercised
An elemental strength, in casting up
Rare gems and things of death on fancy's
shore,
Till Nature said 'Enough.'
                    Who longest dreams,
Dreams not for ever; seeing day and
night
And corporal feebleness divide his
dreams,
And on his elevate creations weigh
With hunger, cold, heat, darkness,
weariness :
Else should we be like gods ; else would
the course
Of thought's free wheels, increased in
speed and might
By an eterne volution, oversweep
The heights of wisdom, and invade her
depths :
So, knowing all things, should we have
all power ;
For is not Knowledge power? But
mighty spells
Our operation sear ; the Babel must,
Or ere it touch the sky, fall down to earth :
The web, half formed, must tumble from
our hands,
And, ere they can resume it, lie decayed.
Mind struggles vainly from the flesh.
E'en so,
Hell's angel (saith a scroll apocryphal)
Shall, when the latter days of earth have
shrunk
Before the blast of God, affect his heaven ;
Lift his scarred brow, confirm his rebel
heart,
Shoot his strong wings, and darken pole
and pole,—

Till day be blotted into night ; and shake
The fevered clouds, as if a thousand
　　　storms
Throbbed into life ! Vain hope—vain
　　　strength—vain flight !
God's arm shall meet God's foe, and hurl
　　　him back !

A VISION OF LIFE AND DEATH

MINE ears were deaf to melody,
　　My lips were dumb to sound :
Where didst thou wander, O my soul,
　　When ear and tongue were bound ?

'I wandered by the stream of time,
　　Made dark by human tears :
I threw my voice upon the waves,
　　And *they* did throw me theirs.'

And how did sound the waves, my soul ?
　　And how did sound the waves ?
'Hoarse, hoarse, and wild !—they ever
　　　dashed
　　'Gainst ruined thrones and graves.'

And what sight on the shore, my soul ?
　　And what sight on the shore ?
'Twain beings sate there silently,
　　And sit there evermore.'

Now tell me fast and true, my soul ;
　　Now tell me of those twain.
'One was yclothed in mourning vest,
　　And one, in trappings vain.

'She in the trappings vain was fair,
　　And eke fantastical :
A thousand colours dyed her garb ;
　　A blackness bound them all.

'In part her hair was gaily wreathed,
　　In part was wildly spread :
Her face did change its hue too fast,
　　To say 'twas pale or red.

'And when she looked on earth, I thought
　　She smiled for very glee :
But when she looked to heaven, I knew
　　That tears stood in her ee.

'She held a mirror, there to gaze :
　　It could no cheer bestow ;
For while her beauty cast the shade,
　　Her breath did make it go.

'A harper's harp did lie by her,
　　Without the harper's hest ;
A monarch's crown did lie by her,
　　Wherein an owl had nest :

'A warrior's sword did lie by her,
　　Grown rusty since the fight ;
A poet's lamp did lie by her :—
　　Ah me !—where was its light ?'

And what didst *thou* say, O my soul,
　　Unto that mystic dame ?
'I asked her of her tears, and eke
　　I asked her of her name.

'She said, she built a prince's throne :
　　She said, he ruled the grave ;
And that the levelling worm asked not
　　If he were king or slave.

'She said, she formed a godlike tongue,
　　Which lofty thoughts unsheathed ;
Which rolled its thunder round, and
　　　purged
　　The air the nations breathed.

'She said, that tongue, all eloquent,
　　With silent dust did mate ;
Whereon false friends betrayed long faith,
　　And foes outspat their hate.

'She said, she warmed a student's heart,
　　But heart and brow 'gan fade :
Alas, alas ! those Delphic trees
　　Do cast an upas shade !

'She said, she lighted happy hearths,
　　Whose mirth was all forgot :
She said, she tunèd marriage bells,
　　Which rang when love was *not.*

'She said, her name was Life ; and then
　　Out laughed and wept aloud,—
What time the other being strange
　　Lifted the veiling shroud.

'Yea ! lifted she the veiling shroud,
　　And breathed the icy breath : .
Whereat, with inward shuddering.
　　I knew *her* name was Death.

'Yea ! lifted she her calm, calm brow,
　　Her clear cold smile on me :
Whereat within my deepness, leaped
　　Mine immortality.

'She told me, it did move her smile,
    To witness how I sighed,
Because that what was fragile brake,
    And what was mortal died :

'As if that kings could grasp the earth,
    Who from its dust began ;
As if that suns could shine at night,
    Or glory dwell with man.

'She told me, she had freed *his* soul,
    Who ay did freedom love ;
Who now recked not, were worms below,
    Or ranker worms above !

'She said, the student's heart had beat
    Against its prison dim ;
Until she crushed the bars of flesh,
    And poured truth's light on him.

'She said, that they who left the hearth,
    For ay in sunshine dwell ;
She said, the funeral tolling brought
    More joy than marriage bell !

'And as she spake, she spake less loud ;
    The stream resounded more :
Anon I nothing heard but waves
    That wailed along the shore.'

And what didst thou say, O my soul,
    Upon that mystic strife ?
'I said, that Life was only Death,
    That only Death was Life.'

EARTH

How beautiful is earth ! my starry
        thoughts
Look down on it from their unearthly
        sphere,
And sing symphonious—Beautiful is
        earth !
The lights and shadows of her myriad
        hills ;
The branching greenness of her myriad
        woods ;
Her sky-affecting rocks ; her zoning sea ;
Her rushing, gleaming cataracts ; her
        streams
That race below, the wingèd clouds on
        high ;
Her pleasantness of vale and meadow !—

Hush !
Meseemeth through the leafy trees to ring
A chime of bells to falling waters tuned ;
Whereat comes heathen Zephyrus, out
        of breath
With running up the hills, and shakes
        his hair
From off his gleesome forehead, bold
        and glad
With keeping blythe Dan Phoebus
        company ;—
And throws him on the grass, though
        half afraid ;
First glancing round, lest tempests should
        be nigh ;
And lays close to the ground his ruddy
        lips,
And shapes their beauty into sound, and
        calls
On all the petalled flowers, that sit beneath
In hiding-places from the rain and snow,
To loosen the hard soil, and leave their
        cold
Sad idlesse, and betake them up to him.
They straightway hear his voice—

                            A thought did come,
And press from out my soul the heathen
        dream.
Mine eyes were purgèd.   Straightway
        did I bind
Round me the garment of my strength,
        and heard
Nature's death-shrieking—the hereafter
        cry,
When he o' the lion voice, the rainbow-
        crowned,
Shall stand upon the mountains and the
        sea,
And swear by earth, by Heaven's throne,
        and Him
Who sitteth on the throne, there shall
        be time
No more, no more ! Then, veiled Eternity
Shall straight unveil her awful counten-
        ance
Unto the reeling worlds, and take the
        place
Of seasons, years, and ages. Ay and ay
Shall be the time of day.   The wrinkled
        heaven
Shall yield her silent sun, made blind
        and white

With an exterminating light: the wind,
Unchainèd from the poles, nor having
    charge
Of cloud or ocean, with a sobbing wail
Shall rush among the stars, and swoon
    to death.
Yea, the shrunk earth, appearing livid
    pale
Beneath the red-tongued flame, shall
    shudder by
From out her ancient place, and leave—
    a void.
Yet haply by that void the saints re-
    deemed
May sometimes stray ; when memory of
    sin
Ghost-like shall rise upon their holy souls;
And on their lips shall lie the name of
    earth
In paleness and in silentness ; until
Each looking on his brother, face to face,
And bursting into sudden happy tears
(The only tears undried) shall murmur—
        ' Christ ! '

THE PICTURE GALLERY AT PENSHURST

THEY spoke unto me from the silent
    ground,
They looked unto me from the pictured
    wall :
The echo of my footstep was a sound
Like to the echo of their own footfall,
What time their living feet were in the
    hall.
  I breathed where they had breathed—
    and where they brought
  Their souls to moralize on glory's pall,
  I walked with silence in a cloud of
    thought :
So, what they erst had learned, I mine
    own spirit taught.

  Aye ! with mine eyes of flesh, I did
    behold
  The likeness of their flesh ! They, the
    great dead,
  Stood still upon the canvas, while I told
  The glorious memories to their ashes
    wed.

There, I beheld the Sidneys :—he,
    who bled
Freely for freedom's sake, bore gal-
    lantly
His soul upon his brow ;—he, whose
    lute said
Sweet music to the land, meseemed to
    be
Dreaming, with that pale face, of love
    and Arcadie.

Mine heart had shrinèd these. And
    therefore past
Were these, and such as these, in mine
    heart's pride,
Which deemed death glory's other
    name. At last
I stayed my pilgrim feet, and paused
    beside
A picture [1], which the shadows half
    did hide.
The form was a fair woman's form ;
    the brow
Brightly between the clustering curls
    espied :
The cheek a little pale, yet seeming so
As, if the lips could speak, the paleness
    soon would go.

And rested there the lips, so warm
    and loving,
That, they *could* speak, one might be
    fain to guess :
Only they had been much too bright,
    if moving,
To stay by their own will, all motion-
    less.
One outstretched hand its marble seal
    'gan press
On roses which looked fading ; while
    the eyes,
Uplifted in a calm, proud loveliness,
Seemed busy with their flow'ry
    destinies,
Drawing, for ladye's heart, some moral
    quaint and wise.

She perished like her roses. I did look
On her, as she did look on them—to
    sigh !
Alas, alas ! that the fair-written book
Of her sweet face should be in death
    laid by,

[1] Vandyke's portrait of Waller's Sacharissa.

As any blotted scroll! Its cruelty
Poisoned a heart most gentle-pulsed of all,
And turned it unto song, therein to die:
For grief's stern tension maketh musical,
Unless the strained string break or ere the music fall.

Worship of Waller's heart! no dream of thine
Revealed unto thee, that the lowly one,
Who sate enshadowed near thy beauty's shine,
Should, when the light was out, the life was done,
Record thy name with those by Memory won
From Time's eternal burial. I am wooed
By wholesome thoughts this sad thought hath begun ;
For mind is strengthened when awhile subdued,
As he who touched the earth, and rose with power renewed.

TO A POET'S CHILD

A FAR harp swept the sea above ;
A far voice said thy name in love :
Then silence on the harp was cast ;
The voice was chained—the love went last !

And as I heard the melodie,
Sweet-voicèd Fancy spake of thee :
And as the silence o'er it came,
Mine heart, in silence, sighed thy name.

I thought there was one only place,
Where thou couldst lift thine orphaned face :
A little home for prayer and woe ;—
A stone above—a shroud below ;—

That evermore, that stone beside,
Thy withered joys would form thy pride ;
As palm-trees, on their South Sea bed,
Make islands with the flowers they shed.

Child of the Dead ! my dream of thee
Was sad to tell, and dark to see ;
And vain as many a brighter dream ;
Since thou canst sing by Babel's stream !

For here, amid the worldly crowd,
'Mid common brows, and laughter loud,
And hollow words, and feelings sere,
Child of the Dead ! I meet thee here !

And is thy step so fast and light ?
And is thy smile so gay and bright ?
And *canst* thou smile, with cheek undim,
Upon a world that frowned on *him* ?

The minstrel's harp is on his bier ;
What doth the minstrel's orphan here ?
The loving moulders in the clay ;
The loved,—she keepeth holiday !

'Tis well ! I would not doom thy years
Of golden prime, to only tears.
Fair girl ! 'twere better that thine eyes
Should find a joy in summer skies,

As if their sun were on thy fate.
Be happy ; strive not to be great ;
And go not from thy kind apart,
With lofty soul and stricken heart.

Think not too deeply : shallow thought,
Like open rills, is ever sought
By light and flowers ; while fountains deep
Amid the rocks and shadows sleep.

Feel not too warmly : lest thou be
Too like Cyrene's waters free,
Which burn at night, when all around
In darkness and in chill is found.

Touch not the harp to win the wreath :
Its tone is fame, its echo death !
The wreath may like the laurel grow,
Yet turns to cypress on the brow !

And, as a flame springs clear and bright,
Yet leaveth ashes 'stead of light ;
So genius (fatal gift !) is doomed
To leave the heart it fired, consumed.

For thee, for thee, thou orphaned one,
I make an humble orison !
Love all the world ; and ever dream
That all are true who truly seem.

Forget! for, so, 'twill move thee not,
Or lightly move; to be forgot!
Be streams thy music; hills, thy mirth;
Thy chiefest light, the household hearth.

So, when grief plays her natural part,
And visiteth thy quiet heart;
Shall all the clouds of grief be seen
To show a sky of hope between.

So, when thy beauty senseless lies,
No sculptured urn shall o'er thee rise;
But gentle eyes shall weep at will,
Such tears as hearts like thine distil.

MINSTRELSY

One asked her once the resun why
She hadde delyte in minstrelsie;
She answerèd on this manère.
ROBERT DE BRUNNE.

FOR ever, since my childish looks
Could rest on Nature's pictured books;
For ever, since my childish tongue
Could name the themes our bards have
        sung;
So long, the sweetness of their singing
Hath been to me a rapture bringing!—
Yet ask me not the reason why
I have delight in minstrelsy.

I know that much whereof I sing
Is shapen but for vanishing;
I know that summer's flower and leaf
And shine and shade are very brief,
And that the heart they brighten may,
Before them all, be sheathed in clay!—
I do not know the reason why
I have delight in minstrelsy.

A few there are whose smile and praise
My minstrel hope would kindly raise:
But, of those few—Death may impress
The lips of some with silentness;
While some may friendship's faith resign,
And heed no more a song of mine.—
Ask not, ask not the reason why
I have delight in minstrelsy.

The sweetest song that minstrels sing
Will charm not Joy to tarrying;
The greenest bay that earth can grow
Will shelter not in burning woe;

A thousand voices will not cheer
When *one* is mute that ay is dear!—
Is there, alas! *no* reason why
I have delight in minstrelsy?

I do not know! The turf is green
Beneath the rain's fast-dropping sheen,
Yet asks not why that deeper hue
Doth all its tender leaves renew;—
And I, like-minded, am content,
While music to my soul is sent,
To question not the reason why
I have delight in minstrelsy.

Years pass—my life with them shall pass:
And soon the cricket in the grass,
And summer bird, shall louder sing
Than she who owns a minstrel's string.
Oh, then may some, the dear and few,
Recall her love, whose truth they knew;
When all forget to question why
She had delight in minstrelsy!

TO THE MEMORY OF
SIR UVEDALE PRICE, BART.

FAREWELL!—a word that human lips
        bestow
On all that human hearts delight to know:
On summer skies, and scenes that change
        as fast;
On ocean calms, and faith as fit to last;
On Life, from Love's own arms, that
        breaks away;
On hopes that blind, and glories that
        decay!

And ever thus 'farewell, farewell,' is said,
As round the hills of lengthening time
        we tread;
As at each step the winding ways unfold
Some untried prospect which obscures
        the old;—
Perhaps a prospect brightly coloured o'er,
Yet not with brightness that we loved
        before;
And dull and dark the brightest hue
        appears
To eyes like ours, surcharged and dim
        with tears.
Oft, oft we wish the winding road were
        past,
And yon supernal summit gained at last;

Where all that gradual change removed,
is found
At once, for ever, as you look around ;
Where every scene by tender eyes sur-
veyed,
And lost and wept for, to their gaze is
spread—
No tear to dim the sight, no shade to fall,
But Heaven's own sunshine lighting,
charming all.

Farewell !—a common word—and yet
how drear
And strange it soundeth as I write it here !
How strange that *thou* a place of death
shouldst fill,
Thy brain unlighted, and thine heart
grown chill !
And dark the eye, whose plausive glance
to draw
Incited Nature brake her tyrant's law !
And deaf the ear, to charm whose organ
true
Maeonian music tuned her harp anew !
And mute the lips where Plato's bee
hath roved ;
And motionless the hand that genius
moved !—
Ah, friend ! thou speakest not !—but still
to me
Do Genius, Music, Nature, speak of
thee !—
Still golden fancy, still the sounding line,
And waving wood, recall some word of
thine :
Some word, some look, whose living
light is o'er—
And Memory sees what Hope can see
no more.

Twice, twice, thy voice hath spoken.
Twice there came
To us a change, a joy—to thee, a fame !
Thou spakest once [1], and every pleasant
sight,
Woods waving wild, and fountains gush-
ing bright,
Cool copses, grassy banks, and all the
dyes
Of shade and sunshine gleamed before
our eyes.

Thou spakest twice [2]; and every pleasant
sound
Its ancient silken harmony unwound,
From Doric pipe and Attic lyre that
lay
Enclasped in hands whose cunning is
decay.
And now no more thou speakest ! Death
hath met
And won thee to him ! Oh, remembered
yet !
We cannot *see*, and *hearken*, and forget !

My thoughts are far. I think upon the
time
When Foxley's purple hills and woods
sublime
Were thrilling at thy step ; when thou
didst throw
Thy burning spirit on the vale below,
To bathe its sense in beauty. Lovely
ground !
There, never more shall step of thine re-
sound !
There, Spring again shall come, but find
thee not,
And deck with humid eyes her favourite
spot ;
Strew tender green on paths thy foot
forsakes,
And make that fair, which Memory
saddest makes.
For me, all sorrowful, unused to raise
A minstrel song and dream not of thy
praise,
Upon thy grave my tuneless harp I lay,
Nor try to sing what only tears can
say.
So warm and fast the ready waters
swell—
So weak the faltering voice thou knewest
well !
Thy words of kindness calmed that voice
before ;
Now, thoughts of *them* but make it
tremble more ;
And leave its theme to others, and de-
part
To dwell within the silence where thou
art.

[1] *Essay on the Picturesque.*

[2] *Essay on the Pronunciation of the Ancient
Languages.*

THE AUTUMN

Go, sit upon the lofty hill,
  And turn your eyes around,
Where waving woods and waters wild
  Do hymn an autumn sound.
The summer sun is faint on them—
  The summer flowers depart—
Sit still—as all transformed to stone,
  Except your musing heart.

How there you sate in summer-time,
  May yet be in your mind;
And how you heard the green woods
    sing
  Beneath the freshening wind.
Though the same wind now blows around,
  You would its blast recall;
For every breath that stirs the trees
  Doth cause a leaf to fall.

Oh! like that wind, is all the mirth
  That flesh and dust impart;
We cannot bear its visitings,
  When change is on the heart.
Gay words and jests may make us smile
  When Sorrow is asleep;
But other things must make us smile
  When Sorrow bids us *weep!*

The dearest hands that clasp our hands,—
  Their presence may be o'er;
The dearest voice that meets our ear,
  That tone may come no more!
Youth fades; and then, the joys of
    youth,
  Which once refreshed our mind,
Shall come—as, on those sighing woods,
  The chilling autumn wind.

Hear not the wind — view not the
    woods;
  Look out o'er vale and hill:
In spring, the sky encircled them—
  The sky is round them still.
Come autumn's scathe, come winter's
    cold,
Come change—and human fate!
Whatever prospect HEAVEN doth bound
  Can ne'er be desolate.

THE DEATH-BED OF TERESA DEL RIEGO

Si fia muta ogni altra cosa, al fine
Parlerà il mio morire,
E ti dirà la morte il mio martire.
                        GUARINI.

THE room was darkened; but a wan
    lamp shed
Its light upon a half-uncurtained bed,
Whereon the widowed sate. Blackly
    as death
Her veiling hair hung round her, and no
    breath
Came from her lips to motion it. Between
Its parted clouds, the calm fair face was
    seen
In a snow paleness, and snow silentness,
With eyes unquenchable, whereon did
    press
A little, their white lids, so taught to lie,
By weights of frequent tears wept
    secretly.
Her hands were clasped and raised—the
    lamp did fling
A glory on her brow's meek suffering.

Beautiful form of woman! seeming made
Alone to shine in mirrors, there to braid
The hair and zone the waist—to garland
    flowers—
To walk like sunshine through the orange
    bowers—
To strike her land's guitar—and often see
In other eyes how lovely hers must be—
Grew she acquaint with anguish? Did
    she sever
For ever from the one she loved for ever,
To dwell among the strangers? Aye!
    and she,
Who shone most brightly in that festive
    glee,
Sate down in this despair most patiently.

Some hearts are Niobes! in grief's down-
    sweeping
They turn to very stone from over-
    weeping,
And after, feel no more. Hers did remain
In life, which is the power of feeling
    pain,

Till pain consumed the life so called below.
She heard that he was dead!—she asked
    not how—
For *he* was dead! She wailed not o'er
    his urn,
For *he* was dead—and in *her* hands, should
    burn
His vestal flame of honour radiantly:
Sighing would dim its light—she did not
    sigh.

She only died. They laid her in the
    ground,
Whereon th' unloving tread, and accents
    sound
Which are not of her Spain. She left
    behind,
For those among the strangers who were
    kind
Unto the poor heartbroken, her dark hair.
It once was gauded out with jewels rare;
It swept her dying pillow—it doth lie
Beside me (thank the giver) droopingly,
And very long and bright! Its tale doth go
Half to the dumb grave, half to lifetime
    woe,
Making the heart of man, if manly, ring
Like Dodonaean brass, with echoing.

TO VICTOIRE, ON HER MARRIAGE

VICTOIRE! I knew thee in thy land,
    Where I was strange to all:
I heard thee; and were strange to me
    The words thy lips let fall.

I loved thee—for the Babel curse
    Was meant not for the heart:
I parted from thee, in such way
    As those who love may part.

And now a change hath come to us,
    A sea doth rush between!
I do not know if we can be
    Again as we have been.

I sit down in mine English land,
    Mine English hearth beside;
And thou, to one I never knew,
    Art plighted for a bride.

It will not wrong thy present joy
    With bygone days to wend;
Nor wrongeth it mine English hearth
    To love my Gallic friend.

Bind, bind the wreath! the slender ring
    Thy wedded finger press!
May he who calls thy love his own,
    Call so thine happiness!

Be he Terpander to thine heart,
    And string fresh strings of gold,
Which may outgive new melodies,
    But never mar the old!

And though I clasp no more thy hand
    In my hand, and rejoice—
And though I see thy face no more,
    And hear no more thy voice—

Farewell, farewell!—let thought of me
    Visit thine heart! There is
In mine the very selfish prayer
    That prayeth for thy bliss!

TO A BOY

WHEN my last song was said for thee
Thy golden hair swept, long and free,
Around thee; and a dove-like tone
Was on thy voice—or Nature's own:
And every phrase and word of thine
Went out in lispings infantine!
Thy small steps faltering round our
    hearth—
Thine een out-peering in their mirth—
Blue een! that, like thine heart, seemed
    given
To be, for ever, full of heaven!
Wert thou, in sooth, made up of glee,
When my last song was said for thee?

And now more years are finishèd,—
For thee another song is said.
Thy voice hath lost its cooing tone;
The lisping of thy words is gone:
Thy step treads firm—thine hair not flings
Round thee its length of golden rings—
Departed, like all lovely things!
Yet art thou still made up of glee,
When my *now* song is said for thee.

Wisely and well responded they,
Who cut thy golden hair away,

What time I made the bootless prayer,
That they should pause awhile, and spare.
They said, 'its sheen did less agree
With boyhood than with infancy.'
And thus I know it ay must be :
Before the revel noise is done,
The revel lamps pale one by one.

Aye! Nature loveth not to bring
Crowned victims to life's labouring.
The mirth-effulgent eye appears
Less sparkling—to make room for tears :
After the heart's quick throbs depart,
We lose the gladness of the heart :
And, after we have lost awhile
The rose o' the lip, we lose its smile :
As Beauty could not bear to press
Near the death-pyre of Happiness.

This seemeth but a sombre dream?
It hath more pleasant thoughts than seem.
The older a young tree doth grow
The deeper shade it sheds below ;
But makes the grass more green—the air
More fresh, than had the sun been there.
And thus our human life is found,
Albeit a darkness gather round :
For patient virtues, that their light
May shine to all men, want the night :
And holy Peace, unused to cope,
Sits meekly at the tomb of Hope,
Saying that 'she is risen !'

Then I

Will sorrow not at destiny,—
Though from thine eyes, and from thine
heart,
The glory of their light depart ;
Though on thy voice, and on thy brow,
Should come a fiercer change than now ;
Though thou no more be made of glee,
When my next song is said for thee.

REMONSTRANCE

Oh, say not it is vain to weep
That deafened bier above ;
Where genius has made room for death,
And life is past from love ;
That tears can never his bright looks
And tender words restore :
I know it is most vain to weep—
And therefore weep the more !

Oh, say not I shall cease to weep
When years have withered by ;
That ever I shall speak of joy,
As if he could reply ;
That ever mine unquivering lips
Shall name the name he bore :
I know that I may cease to weep,
And therefore weep the more !

Say, Time, who slew mine happiness,
Will leave to me my woe ;
And woe's own stony strength shall chain
These tears' impassioned flow :
Or say, that these, my ceaseless tears,
May life to death restore ;
For then my soul were wept away,
And I should weep no more !

REPLY

To weep awhile beside the bier,
Whereon his ashes lie,
Is well !—I know that rains must fall
When clouds are in the sky :
I know, *to die—to part*, will cloud
The brightest spirit o'er ;
And yet, wouldst *thou* for ever weep,
When *he* can weep no more?

Fix not thy sight so long and fast
Upon the shroud's despair ;
Look upward unto Zion's hill,
For death was also *there !*
And think, 'The death, the scourge, the
scorn,
My sinless Saviour bore—
The curse—the pang, too deep for
tears—
That *I* should weep no more !'

EPITAPH

Beauty, who softly walkest all thy days
In silken garment to the tunes of praise ;—
Lover, whose dreamings by the green-
banked river,
Where once she wandered, fain would
last for ever ;—
King, whom the nations scan, adoring
scan,
And shout 'a god,' when sin hath marked
thee man ;—

Bard, on whose brow the Hyblan dew
    remains,
Albeit the fever burneth in the veins :—
Hero, whose sword in tyrant's blood is
    hot ;—
Sceptic, who doubting, wouldst be
    doubted not ;—
Man, whosoe'er thou art, whate'er thy
    trust ;—
Respect thyself in me ;—thou treadest
    dust.

THE IMAGE OF GOD

I am God, and there is none like me.
                 Isaiah xlvi. 9.
Christ, who is the image of God.
            2 *Corinthians* iv. 4.

Thou ! art thou like to God ?
(I asked this question of the glorious
    sun)
Thou high unwearied one,
Whose course in heat, and light, and life
    is run ?

Eagles may view thy face—clouds can
    assuage
Thy fiery wrath—the sage
Can mete thy stature—thou shalt fade
    with age.
Thou art not like to God.

Thou ! art thou like to God ?
(I asked this question of the bounteous
    earth)
O thou, who givest birth
To forms of beauty and to sounds of
    mirth ?

In all thy glory works the worm decay—
Thy golden harvests stay
For seed and toil—thy power shall pass
    away.
Thou art not like to God.

Thou ! art thou like to God ?
(I asked this question of my deathless
    soul)
O thou, whose musings roll
Above the thunder, o'er creation's whole ?

Thou art not. Sin, and shame, and agony
Within thy deepness lie :
They utter forth their voice in thee, and
    cry,
'*Thou* art not like to God.'

Then art Thou like to God ;
Thou, who didst bear the sin, and shame,
    and woe—
O Thou, whose sweat did flow—
Whose tears did gush—whose brow was
    dead and low ?

No grief is like Thy grief ; no heart can
    prove
Love like unto Thy love ;
And none, save only Thou,—below,
    above,—
O God, is like to God !

THE APPEAL

Children of our England ! stand
On the shores that girt our land ;
The aegis of whose cloud-white rock
Braveth Time's own battle-shock.
Look above the wide, wide world ;
Where the northern blasts have furled
Their numbèd wings amid the snows,
Mutt'ring in a forced repose—
Or where the maddened sun on high
Shakes his torch athwart the sky,
Till within their prison sere,
Chainèd earthquakes groan for fear !
Look above the wide, wide world,
Where a gauntlet Sin hath hurled
To astonied Life ; and where
Death's gladiatorial smile doth glare,
On making the arena bare.
Shout aloud the words that show
Jesus in the sands and snow ;—
Shout aloud the words that free,
Over the perpetual sea.

Speak ye. As a breath will sweep
Avalanche from Alpine steep,
So the spoken word shall roll
Fear and darkness from the soul.
Are ye men, and love not man ?
Love ye, and permit his ban ?
Can ye, dare ye, rend the chain
Wrought of common joy and pain,
Clasping with its links of gold,
Man to man in one strong hold ?

Lo! if the golden links ye sever,
Ye shall make your heart's flesh quiver;
And wheresoe'er the links are reft,
There shall be a bloodstain left.
To earth's remotest rock repair,
Ye shall find a vulture there:
Though for others sorrowing not,
Your own tears shall still be hot:
Though ye play a lonely part;
Though ye bear an iron heart;—
Woe, like Echetus, still must
Grind your iron into dust.

But, children of our Britain, ye
Rend not man's chain of sympathy;
To those who sit in woe and night,
Denying tears and hiding light.
Ye have stretched your hands abroad
With the Spirit's sheathless sword:
Ye have spoken—and the tone
To earth's extremest verge hath gone:
East and west sublime it rolls,
Echoed by a million souls!
The wheels of rapid circling years,
Erst hot with crime, are quenched in tears.
Rocky hearts wild waters pour,
That were chained in stone before:
Bloody hands, that only bare
Hilted sword, are clasped in prayer:
Savage tongues, that wont to fling
Shouts of war in deathly ring,
Speak the name which angels sing.
Dying lips are lit the while
With a most undying smile,
Which reposing there, instead
Of language, when the lips are dead,
Saith,—'No sound of grief or pain
Shall haunt us when we move again.'

Children of our country! brothers
To the children of all others!
Shout aloud the words that show
Jesus in the sands and snow;—
Shout aloud the words that free,
Over the perpetual sea!

IDOLS

How weak the gods of this world are—
  And weaker yet their worship made
    me!
I have been an idolater
  Of three—and three times they be-
    trayed me!

Mine oldest worshipping was given
  To natural Beauty, ay residing
In bowery earth and starry heaven,
  In ebbing sea, and river gliding.

But natural Beauty shuts her bosom
  To what the natural feelings tell!
Albeit I sighed, the trees would blossom—
  Albeit I smiled, the blossoms fell.

Then left I earthly sights, to wander
  Amid a grove of name divine,
Where bay-reflecting streams meander,
  And Moloch Fame hath reared a shrine.

Not green, but black, is that reflection;
  On rocky beds those waters lie;
That grove hath chillness and dejection—
  How could I sing? I had to sigh.

Last, human Love, thy Lares greeting,
  To rest and warmth I vowed my years.
To rest? how wild my pulse is beating!
  To warmth? ah me! my burning tears.

Aye, *they* may burn—though thou be
    frozen
  By death, and changes wint'ring on!
Fame!—Beauty!—idols madly chosen—
  Were yet of gold; but *thou* art STONE!

Crumble like stone! my voice no longer
  Shall wail their names, who silent be:
There is a voice that soundeth stronger—
  'My daughter, give thine heart to *Me*.'

Lord! take mine heart! O first and
    fairest,
  Whom all creation's ends shall hear;
Who deathless love in death declarest!
  None else is beauteous—famous—
    dear!

HYMN

Lord, I cry unto Thee, make haste unto me.
                              Psalm cxli.
The Lord is nigh unto all them that call upon
  Him.   *Psalm* cxlv.

  SINCE without Thee we do no good,
    And with Thee do no ill,
  Abide with us in weal and woe,—
    In action and in will.

In weal,—that while our lips confess
   The Lord who 'gives,' we may
Remember, with an humble thought,
   The Lord who ' takes away.'

In woe,—that while to drowning tears
   Our hearts their joys resign,
We may remember *who* can turn
   Such water into wine.

By hours of day,—that when our feet
   O'er hill and valley run,
We still may think the light of truth
   More welcome than the sun.

By hours of night,—that when the air
   Its dew and shadow yields,
We still may hear the voice of God
   In silence of the fields.

Oh! then sleep comes on us like death,
   All soundless, deaf, and deep :
Lord! teach us so to watch and pray,
   That death may come like sleep.

Abide with *us*, abide with *us*,
   While flesh and soul agree ;
And when our flesh is only dust,
   Abide our souls with *Thee*.

WEARINESS

MINE eyes are weary of surveying
The fairest things, too soon decaying ;
Mine ears are weary of receiving
The kindest words—ah, past believing !
Weary my hope, of ebb and flow ;
Weary my pulse, of tunes of woe :
My trusting heart is weariest !
I would—I would I were at rest !

For *me*, can earth refuse to fade ?
For *me*, can words be faithful made ?
Will *my* embittered hope be sweet ?
My pulse forgo the human beat ?
No ! Darkness must consume mine eye—
Silence, mine ear—hope cease—pulse
   die—
And o'er mine heart a stone be pressed—
Or vain this,—' Would I were at rest ! '

There is a land of rest deferred :
Nor eye hath seen, nor ear hath heard,
Nor Hope hath trod the precinct o'er ;
For hope beheld is hope no more !
There, human pulse forgets its tone—
There, hearts may know as they are
   known !
Oh, for dove's wings, thou dwelling blest,
To fly to *thee*, and be at rest !

THE SERAPHIM

Some to sing, and some to say,
Some to weep, and some to praye.—SKELTON.

PREFACE TO THE FIRST EDITION, 1838

IT is natural for every writer who has not published frequently to revert, at least in thought, to his last work, in risking the publication of a new one. To me this is most natural, the subject of the principal poem in the present collection having suggested itself to me, though very faintly and imperfectly, when I was engaged upon my translation of the *Prometheus Bound* of Aeschylus.

I thought that, had Aeschylus lived after the incarnation and crucifixion of our Lord Jesus Christ, he might have turned, if not in moral and intellectual yet in poetic faith, from the solitude of Caucasus to the deeper desertness of that crowded Jerusalem where none had any pity; from the 'faded white flower' of the Titanic brow, to the 'withered grass' of a heart trampled on by its own beloved; from the glorying of him who gloried that he could not die, to the sublimer meekness of the Taster of death for every man; from the taunt stung into being by the torment, to His more awful silence, when the agony stood dumb before the love! And I thought how, 'from the height of this great argument,' the scenery of the *Prometheus* would have dwarfed itself even in the eyes of its poet,—how the fissures of his rocks and the innumerous smiles of his ocean would have closed and waned into blankness,—and his demigod stood confessed so human a conception as to fall below the aspiration of his own humanity. He would have turned from such to the rent rocks and darkened sun—rent and darkened by a sympathy thrilling through nature but leaving man's heart untouched—to the multitudes whose victim was their Saviour: to the Victim, whose sustaining thought beneath an unexampled agony was not the Titanic 'I can revenge,' but the celestial 'I can forgive!'

The subjects of my two books lie side by side. The *Prometheus* of Aeschylus is avowedly one of the very noblest of human imaginations; and when we measure it with the eternal counsel we know at once and for ever how wide is the difference between man's ideal and God's divine!

The great tragic soul, though untaught directly of Deity, brooded over His creation with exhaustless faculties, until it gave back to her a thought—vast, melancholy, beneficent, malign—the Titan on the rock, the reflected image of her own fallen immortality; rejoicing in bounty, agonizing in wrong, and triumphant in revenge. This was all. 'Then,' said He, 'Lo I come!' and we knew love, in that He laid down His life for us. 'By this we know love [1]'—love in its intense meaning. 'The splendour in the grass and fragrance in the flower' are the splendour and fragrance of a love beyond them. 'All thoughts, all passions, all delights,' are 'ministers' of a love around us. All citizenship, all brotherhood, all things for which men bless us, saying, 'Surely this is good,'—are manifestations of a love within us. All exaltations of our inward nature, in which we bless ourselves, saying, 'Surely this is great,'—are yearnings to a love above us. And thus, among the fragments of our fallen state, we may guess at love even as Plato guessed at God: but by this, and this only, can we *know* it—that Christ laid down His life for us. Has not love a deeper mystery than wisdom, and a more ineffable lustre than power? I believe it has. I venture to believe those beautiful and often quoted words 'God is love,' to be even less an expression of condescension towards the finite, than an

[1] *Ep. John* i. 5. The modifying expression *of God* which appears in our version is not in the Greek.

assertion of essential dignity in Him who is infinite.

But if my dream be true that Aeschylus might have turned to the subject before us in poetic instinct ; and if in such a case—and here is no dream—its terror and its pathos would have shattered into weakness the strong Greek tongue, and caused the conscious chorus to tremble round the thymele,—how much more may *I* turn from it in the instinct of incompetence ! In a manner I have done so. I have worn no shoes upon this holy ground : I have stood there, but have not walked. I have drawn no copy of the statue of this Great Pan,—but have caught its shadow,—shortened in the dawn of my imperfect knowledge, and distorted and broken by the unevenness of our earthly ground. I have written no work, but a suggestion. Nor has even so little been attempted without as deep a consciousness of weakness as the severest critic and the humblest Christian could desire to impress upon me. I have felt in the midst of my own thoughts upon my own theme, like Homer's 'children in a battle.'

The agents in this poem of imperfect form—a dramatic lyric, rather than a lyrical drama—are those mystic beings who are designated in Scripture the Seraphim. The subject has thus assumed a character of exaggerated difficulty, the full sense of which I have tried to express in my Epilogue. But my desire was, to gather some vision of the supreme spectacle under a less usual aspect—to glance at it, as dilated in seraphic eyes, and darkened and deepened by the near association with blessedness and Heaven. Are we not too apt to measure the depth of the Saviour's humiliation from the common estate of man, instead of from His own peculiar and primaeval one ? To avoid which error I have endeavoured to count some steps of the ladder at Bethel—a very few steps, and as seen between the clouds.

And thus I have endeavoured to mark in my two Seraphic personages, distinctly and predominantly, that shrinking from, and repugnance to, evil, which in my weaker Seraph is expressed by *fear*, and in my stronger one by a more complex

passion ; in order to contrast with such the voluntary debasement of Him who became lower than the angels, and touched in His own sinless being sin and sorrow and death. In my attempted production of such a contrast I have been true to at least my own idea of angelic excellence, as well as to that of His perfection. For one holiness differs from another holiness in glory. To recoil from evil is according to the stature of an angel ; to subdue it is according to the infinitude of a God.

Of the poems which succeed *The Seraphim*, two ballads have been published in *The New Monthly Magazine ;* one, the *Romance of the Ganges*, was written for the illustration of *Finden's Tableaux*, edited by Miss Mitford ; and a few miscellaneous verses have appeared in the *Athenaeum*[1].

Lest in any of these poems a dreaminess be observed upon, while a lawlessness is imputed to their writer, she is anxious to assure whatever reader may think it worth while to listen to her defence, that none of them were written with a lawless purpose. For instance, *The Poet's Vow* was intended to enforce a truth—that the creature cannot be *isolated* from the creature ; and *The Romaunt of Margret*, a corresponding one, that the creature cannot be *sustained* by the creature. And if, indeed, the faintest character of poetry be granted to these compositions, it must be granted to them besides, that they contain a certain verity. For there is no greater fiction than that poetry is fiction. Poetry is essentially truthfulness ; and the very incoherences of poetic dreaming are but the struggle and the strife to reach the True in the Unknown. 'If you please to call it but a dream,' says Cowley, 'I shall not take it ill ; because the father of poets tells us, even dreams, too, are from God[2].'

It was subsequent to my writing the poem called *The Virgin Mary to the Child Jesus* that I read in a selection of religious poetry, made by Mr. James

---

[1] These poems are printed in this edition under the heading ' Poems, 1838-50.'

[2] *Discourse by way of vision, concerning the government of Oliver Cromwell.*

Montgomery, a lyric of the sixteenth century upon the same subject[1], together with an observation of the editor, that no living poet would be daring enough to approach it. As it has here been approached and attempted by the 'weak'st of many,' I would prove by this explanation, that consciously to impugn an opinion of Mr. Montgomery's, and to enter into rivalship with the bold simplicity of an ancient ballad, made no part of the daringness of which I confess myself guilty.

Nothing more is left to me to explain in relation to any particular poem of this collection. I need not defend them for being religious in their general character. The generation of such as held the doctrine of that critic who was *not* Longinus, and believed in the inadmissibility of religion into poetry, may have seen the end of vanity. That 'contemplative piety, or the intercourse between God and the human soul, cannot be poetical,' is true *if* it be true that the human soul having such intercourse is parted from its humanity, or *if* it be true that poetry is not expressive of that humanity's most exalted state. The first supposition is contradicted by man's own experience, and the latter by the testimony of Him who knoweth what is in man. For otherwise David's 'glory' would have awakened with no 'harp and lute'; and Isaiah's poetry of diction would have fallen in ashes from his lips, beneath the fire which cleansed them.

To any less reverent objection I would not willingly reply. 'An irreligious poet,' said Burns, meaning an undevotional one, 'is a monster.' An irreligious poet, he might have said, is no poet at all. The gravitation of poetry is upwards. The poetic wing, if it move, ascends. What did even the heathen Greeks—Homer, Aeschylus, Sophocles, Pindar? Sublimely, because born poets, darkly, because born of Adam and unrenewed in Christ, their spirits wandered like the rushing chariots and winged horses, black and white, of their brother-poet Plato[2], through the

[1] The coincidence consists merely of the choice of subject; the mode of treating it being wholly different.
[2] See his *Phaedrus*.

universe of Deity, seeking if haply they might find Him: and as that universe closed around the seekers, not with the transparency in which it flowed first from His hand, but opaquely, as double-dyed with the transgression of its sons,—they felt though they could not discern the God beyond, and used the gesture though ignorant of the language of worshipping. The blind eagle missed the sun, but soared towards its sphere. Shall the blind eagle soar—and the seeing eagle peck chaff? Surely it should be the gladness and the gratitude of such as are poets among us, that in turning towards the beautiful, they may behold the true face of God.

The disparaging speeches of prefaces are not proverbial for their real humility. I remember smiling over a preface of Pomfret, which intimates that *he* might hope for readers, as even Quarles and Wither found them! He does not add in words,—perhaps he did in thought, '*Fortunati nimium!*'

Without disparaging speeches, and yet with a self-distrust amounting to emotion, I offer to the public, and for the first time in my own name, these poems, which were not written because there is a public, but because they were thought and felt, and perhaps under some of the constraint referred to by Wither himself—for he *has* readers!

> Those that only sip,
> Or but even their fingers dip
> In that sacred fount (poor elves!)
> Of that brood will show themselves:
> Yea, in hope to get them fame,
> *They will speake though to their shame.*

May the omen be averted!

I assume no power of art, except that power of love towards it which has remained with me from my childhood until now. In the power of such a love, and in the event of my life being prolonged, I would fain hope to write hereafter better verses; but I never can feel more intensely than at this moment—nor can it be needful that any should—the sublime uses of poetry, and the solemn responsibilities of the poet.

LONDON, 1838.

THE SERAPHIM

I look for Angels' songs, and hear Him cry.—GILES FLETCHER.

PART THE FIRST

[*It is the time of the Crucifixion ; and the
angels of heaven have departed towards
the earth, except the two seraphim, ADOR
the Strong and ZERAH the Bright One.
The place is the outer side of the shut
heavenly gate.*]

Ador. O SERAPH, pause no more.
Beside this gate of heaven we stand alone.
Zerah. Of heaven !
Ador.   Our brother hosts are
       gone—
Zerah. Are gone before.
Ador. And the golden harps the angels
       bore
To help the songs of their desire,
Still burning from their hands of fire,
Lie without touch or tone
       Upon the glass-sea shore.
Zerah. Silent upon the glass-sea shore !
Ador. There the Shadow from the
       throne
Formless with infinity
Hovers o'er the crystal sea ;
       Awfuller than light derived,
       And red with those primaeval
       heats
       Whereby all life has lived.
Zerah. Our visible God, our heavenly
       seats !
Ador. Beneath us sinks the pomp
       angelical,
       Cherub and seraph, powers and
       virtues, all,—
       The roar of whose descent has died
To a still sound, as thunder into rain.
       Immeasurable space spreads mag-
       nified
With that thick life, along the plane
The worlds slid out on.   What a fall
       And eddy of wings innumerous,
       crossed
       By trailing curls that have not lost
       The glitter of the God-smile shed
On every prostrate angel's head !
       What gleaming up of hands that
       fling

Their homage in retorted rays,
From high instinct of worship-
       ping,
       And habitude of praise.
Zerah. Rapidly they drop below us.
       Pointed palm and wing and hair
       Indistinguishable show us
       Only pulses in the air
       Throbbing with a fiery beat,
       As if a new creation heard
Some divine and plastic word,
And trembling at its new-found
       being,
       Awakened at our feet.
Ador. Zerah, do not wait for seeing.
       His voice, His, that thrills us so
As we our harpstrings, uttered *Go,
Behold the Holy in His woe.*
       And all are gone, save thee and—
Zerah.   Thee !
Ador. I stood the nearest to the throne
       In hierarchical degree,
       What time the Voice said *Go !*
       And whether I was moved alone
       By the storm-pathos of the tone
Which swept through heaven the alien
       name of *woe*,
       Or whether the subtle glory broke
       Through my strong and shielding
       wings,
       Bearing to my finite essence
       Incapacious of their presence,
       Infinite imaginings,
None knoweth save the Throned who
       spoke ;
But I, who at creation stood upright
       And heard the God-breath move
Shaping the words that lightened, ' Be
       there light,'
       Nor trembled but with love,
       Now fell down shudderingly,
My face upon the pavement whence I
       had towered,
As if in mine immortal overpowered
       By God's eternity.
       Zerah. Let me wait !—let me wait !—
       Ador. Nay, gaze not backward through
       the gate.

God fills our heaven with God's own
          solitude
     Till all the pavements glow,
His Godhead being no more subdued
     By itself, to glories low
          Which seraphs can sustain.
     What if thou, in gazing so,
     Shouldst behold but only one
     Attribute, the veil undone—
Even that to which we dare to press
     Nearest, for its gentleness—
          Aye, His love !
     How the deep ecstatic pain
     Thy being's strength would capture !
Without language for the rapture,
     Without music strong to come
          And set the adoration free,
     For ever, ever, wouldst thou be
     Amid the general chorus dumb,
God-stricken to seraphic agony !—
     Or, brother, what if on thine eyes
     In vision bare should rise
The life-fount whence His hand did
          gather
          With solitary force
          Our immortalities !
Straightway how thine own would
          wither,
     Falter like a human breath,
     And shrink into a point like death,
          By gazing on its source !—
     My words have imaged dread.
     Meekly hast thou bent thine head,
     And dropt thy wings in languish-
          ment ;
     Overclouding foot and face,
     As if God's throne were eminent
          Before thee, in the place.
          Yet not—not so,
O loving spirit and meek, dost thou
     fulfil
The supreme Will.
Not for obeisance but obedience,
Give motion to thy wings.   Depart from
     hence.
          The voice said 'Go !'
     Zerah. Beloved, I depart.
His will is as a spirit within my spirit,
A portion of the being I inherit.
His will is mine obedience.   I resemble
A flame all undefilèd though it tremble :
I go and tremble. Love me, O beloved !
     O thou, who stronger art,

And standest ever near the Infinite,
          Pale with the light of Light !
Love me, beloved ! me, more newly made,
          More feeble, more afraid ;
And let me hear with mine thy pinions
          moved,
As close and gentle as the loving are,
That love being near, heaven may not
          seem so far.
     Ador. I am near thee and I love thee.
          Were I loveless, from thee gone,
          Love is round, beneath, above thee,
          God, the omnipresent One.
          Spread the wing, and lift the brow.
          Well-beloved, what fearest thou ?
     Zerah. I fear, I fear—
     Ador.   What fear ?
     Zerah.   The fear of earth.
     Ador. Of earth, the God-created and
          God-praised
In the hour of birth ?
Where every night the moon in light
Doth lead the waters silver-faced ?
Where every day the sun doth lay
A rapture to the heart of all
     The leafy and reeded pastoral,
As if the joyous shout which burst
     From angel lips to see him first,
Had left a silent echo in his ray ?
     Zerah. Of earth—the God created and
          God-curst,
          Where man is, and the thorn :
          Where sun and moon have borne
No light to souls forlorn :
Where Eden's tree of life no more up-
          rears
Its spiral leaves and fruitage, but instead
The yew-tree bows its melancholy head,
And all the undergrasses kills and seres.
     Ador. Of earth the weak,
Made and unmade ?
Where men that faint, do strive for
          crowns that fade ?
Where, having won the profit which
          they seek,
They lie beside the sceptre and the gold
With fleshless hands that cannot wield
          or hold,
And the stars shine in their unwinking
          eyes ?
     Zerah. Of earth the bold,
          Where the blind matter wrings
An awful potence out of impotence,

Bowing the spiritual things
   To the things of sense.
Where the human will replies
With aye and no,
Because the human pulse is quick or slow.
Where Love succumbs to Change,
With only his own memories, for revenge.
And the fearful mystery—
  Ador.   Called Death?
  Zerah. Nay, death is fearful,—but who
    saith
  ' To die,' is comprehensible.
  What's fearfuller, thou knowest well,
  Though the utterance be not for
    thee,
  Lest it blanch thy lips from glory—
  Aye ! the cursèd thing that moved
  A shadow of ill, long time ago,
  Across our heaven's own shining
    floor,
  And when it vanished, some who
    were
  On thrones of holy empire there,
  Did reign — were seen — were —
    never more.
    Come nearer, O beloved !
  Ador. I am near thee.   Didst thou bear
    thee
  Ever to this earth?
  Zerah.   Before.
  When thrilling from His hand along
  Its lustrous path with spheric song
  The earth was deathless, sorrowless.
  Unfearing, then, pure feet might
    press
  The grasses brightening with their
    feet,
  For God's own voice did mix its
    sound
  In a solemn confluence oft
  With the rivers' flowing round,
  And the life-tree's waving soft.
  Beautiful new earth and strange !
  Ador. Hast thou seen it since—the
    change?
  Zerah. Nay, or wherefore should I fear
    To look upon it now?
  I have beheld the ruined things
  Only in depicturings
  Of angels from an earthly mission,—
  Strong one, even upon thy brow,
  When, with task completed, given
  Back to us in that transition,

  I have beheld thee silent stand,
  Abstracted in the seraph band,
    Without a smile in heaven.
  Ador. Then thou wast not one of those
  Whom the loving Father chose
  In visionary pomp to sweep
  O'er Judaea's grassy places,
  O'er the shepherds and the sheep,
  Though thou art so tender?—
    dimming
  All the stars except one star
  With their brighter kinder faces,
  And using heaven's own tune in
    hymning,
While deep response from earth's own
    mountains ran,
  ' Peace upon earth—goodwill to
    man.'
  Zerah. ' Glory to God.'—I said amen
    afar.
And those who from that earthly mission
    are,
  Within mine ears have told
That the seven everlasting Spirits did
    hold
With such a sweet and prodigal constraint
The meaning yet the mystery of the song,
What time they sang it, on their natures
    strong,
That, gazing down on earth's dark
    steadfastness
And speaking the new peace in promises,
The love and pity made their voices faint
Into the low and tender music, keeping
The place in heaven, of what on earth
    is weeping.
  Ador. Peace upon earth.   Come down
    to it.
  Zerah.   Ah me !
I hear thereof uncomprehendingly.
Peace where the tempest, where the
    sighing is,
And worship of the idol, 'stead of His?
  Ador. Yea, peace, where He is.
  Zerah.   He !
Say it again.
  Ador.   Where He is.
  Zerah.   Can it be
That earth retains a tree
Whose leaves, like Eden foliage, can be
    swayed
By the breathing of His voice, nor shrink
    and fade ?

Ador. There is a tree !—it hath no leaf
        nor root ;
Upon it hangs a curse for all its fruit :
    Its shadow on His head is laid.
        For He, the crownèd Son,
        Has left His crown and throne,
        Walks earth in Adam's clay,
        Eve's snake to bruise and slay—
Zerah. Walks earth in clay ?
Ador. And walking in the clay which
        He created,
        He through it shall touch death.
What do I utter ? what conceive ? did
        breath
Of demon howl it ın a blasphemy ?
Or was it mine own voice, informed,
        dilated
By the seven confluent Spirits ?—Speak
        —answer me !
Who said man's victim was his Deity ?
    Zerah. Beloved, beloved, the word
        came forth from thee.
Thine eyes are rolling a tempestuous light
        Above, below, around,
As putting thunder-questions without
        cloud,
        Reverberate without sound,
To universal nature's depth and height.
The tremor of an inexpressive thought
Too self-amazed to shape itself aloud,
O'erruns the awful curving of thy lips ;
    And while thine hands are stretched
        above,
        As newly they had caught
Some lightning from the Throne, or
        showed the Lord
        Some retributive sword,
Thy brows do alternate with wild eclipse
And radiance, with contrasted wrath
        and love,
    As God had called thee to a seraph's
        part,
        With a man's quailing heart.
    Ador. O heart—O heart of man !
        O ta'en from human clay,
    To be no seraph's but Jehovah's own !
        Made holy in the taking,
        And yet unseparate
        From death's perpetual ban,
And human feelings sad and passionate !
Still subject to the treacherous forsakıng
Of other hearts, and its own steadfast
        pain !

O heart of man—of God ! which God
        has ta'en
From out the dust, with its humanity
Mournful and weak yet innocent around
        it,
And bade its many pulses beating lie
Beside that incommunicable stir
Of Deity wherewith He interwound it.
O man ! and is thy nature so defiled,
That all that holy Heart's devout law-
        keeping,
And low pathetic beat in deserts wild,
And gushings pitiful of tender weeping
For traitors who consigned it to such
        woe—
That all could cleanse thee not, without
        the flow
Of blood, the life-blood — *His* — and
        streaming *so* ?
O earth the thundercleft, windshaken,
        where
The louder voice of 'blood and blood'
        doth rise,
Hast thou an altar for this sacrifice ?
        O heaven—O vacant throne !
O crownèd hierarchies, that wear your
        crown
        When His is put away !
Are ye unshamèd that ye cannot dim
Your alien brightness to be liker Him,—
Assume a human passion, and down-lay
Your sweet secureness for congenial
        fears,
And teach your cloudless ever-burning
        eyes
        The mystery of His tears ?
    Zerah. I am strong, I am strong.
    Were I never to see my heaven again,
    I would wheel to earth like the
        tempest rain
    Which sweeps there with an exult-
        ant sound
    To lose its life as it reaches the
        ground.
        I am strong, I am strong.
    Away from mine inward vision swim
    The shining seats of my heavenly
        birth—
    I see but His, I see but Him—
    The Maker's steps on His cruel earth.
    Will the bitter herbs of earth grow
        sweet
    To me, as trodden by His feet ?

Will the vexed, accurst humanity,
As worn by Him, begin to be
A blessed, yea, a sacred thing,
For love, and awe, and ministering?
    I am strong, I am strong.
By our angel ken shall we survey
His loving smile through his woful
    clay?
    I am swift, I am strong—
    The love is bearing me along.
Ador. One love is bearing us along.

PART THE SECOND

[*Mid-air, above Judaea.* ADOR *and* ZERAH
are a little apart from the visible Angelic
Hosts.]

   Ador. BELOVED! dost thou see?—
   Zerah.   Thee,—thee.
Thy burning eyes already are
Grown wild and mournful as a star
Whose occupation is for ay
To look upon the place of clay
    Whereon thou lookest now.
The crown is fainting on thy brow
To the likeness of a cloud,
The forehead's self a little bowed
From its aspect high and holy,
As it would in meekness meet
Some seraphic melancholy.
Thy very wings that lately flung
An outline clear, do flicker here,
And wear to each a shadow hung,
    Dropped across thy feet.
In these strange contrasting glooms
Stagnant with the scent of tombs,
Seraph faces, O my brother,
Show awfully to one another.
   Ador. Dost thou see?
   Zerah.   Even so—I see
Our empyreal company,
    Alone the memory of their brightness
    Left in them, as in thee.
The circle upon circle, tier on tier,
    Piling earth's hemisphere
    With heavenly infiniteness,
    Above us and around,
Straining the whole horizon like a bow!
Their songful lips divorcèd from all sound,
A darkness gliding down their silvery
    glances,—
Bowing their steadfast solemn counten-
    ances

As if they heard God speak, and could
    not glow.
   Ador. Look downward! dost thou see?
   Zerah. And wouldst thou press *that*
    vision on my words?
Doth not Earth speak enough
Of change and of undoing,
Without a seraph's witness? Oceans
    rough
With tempest, pastoral swards
Displaced by fiery deserts, mountains
    ruing
The bolt fallen yesterday,
That shake their piny heads, as who
    would say
'We are too beautiful for our decay'—
Shall seraphs speak of these things?
    Let alone
    Earth, to her earthly moan.
  Voice of all things. Is there no moan
    but hers?
   Ador. Hearest thou the attestation
    Of the rousèd Universe,
    Like a desert lion shaking
    Dews of silence from its mane?
    With an irrepressive passion
      Uprising at once,
    Rising up, and forsaking
    Its solemn state in the circle of suns,
      To attest the pain
    Of Him who stands (O patience
      sweet!)
    In His own hand-prints of creation,
      With human feet?
  Voice of all things. Is there no moan
    but ours?
   Zerah. Forms, Spaces, Motions wide,
    O meek, insensate things,
O congregated matters! who inherit,
    Instead of vital powers,
    Impulsions God-supplied;
    Instead of influent spirit,
    A clear informing beauty;
    Instead of creature-duty,
    Submission calm as rest!
    Lights, without feet or wings,
    In golden courses sliding!
    Glooms, stagnantly subsiding,
Whose lustrous heart away was prest
    Into the argent stars!
    Ye crystal, firmamental bars.
    That hold the skyey waters free
    From tide or tempest's ecstasy!

Airs universal! thunders lorn,
That wait your lightnings in cloud-
    cave
Hewn out by the winds! O brave
And subtle elements! the Holy
Hath charged me by your voice
    with folly [1].
Enough, the mystic arrow leaves its
    wound.
Return ye to your silences inborn,
Or to your inarticulated sound.
   Ador. Zerah.
   Zerah. Wilt *thou* rebuke?
God hath rebuked me, brother.—I am
    weak.
   Ador. Zerah, my brother Zerah!—
    could I speak
Of thee, 'twould be of love to thee.
   Zerah.   Thy look
Is fixed on earth, as mine upon thy face.
Where shall I see His?
              I have thrown
One look upon earth, but one,
Over the blue mountain-lines,
Over the forests of palms and pines,
Over the harvest-lands golden,
Over the valleys that fold in
The gardens and vines—
    He is not there.
All these are unworthy
Those footsteps to bear,
   Before which, bowing down
I would fain quench the stars of my crown
   In the dark of the earthy.
Where shall I see Him?
           No reply?
Hath language left thy lips, to place
   Its vocal in thine eye?
Ador, Ador! are we come
To a double portent, that
Dumb matter grows articulate
   And songful seraphs dumb?
Ador, Ador!
   Ador.   I constrain
The passion of my silence. None
Of those places gazed upon
Are gloomy enow to fit His pain.
Unto Him, whose forming word
Gave to Nature flower and sward,
   She hath given back again,
    For the myrtle, the thorn,

[1] His angels He charged with folly.—*Job*
iv. 18.

For the sylvan calm, the human scorn.
Still, still, reluctant seraph, gaze beneath!
There is a city——
   Zerah.   Temple and tower,
Palace and purple would droop like a
    flower,
   (Or a cloud at our breath)
If He neared in His state
The outermost gate.
   Ador.   Ah me, not so
In the state of a King did the victim go!
And THOU who hangest mute of speech
   'Twixt heaven and earth, with fore-
    head yet
Stainèd by the bloody sweat,
God! man! Thou hast forgone Thy
    throne in each!
   Zerah. Thine eyes behold Him?
   Ador.   Yea, below.
Track the gazing of mine eyes,
Naming God within thine heart
That its weakness may depart
   And the vision rise.
Seest thou yet, beloved?
   Zerah.   I see
Beyond the city, crosses three,
And mortals three that hang thereon,
'Ghast and silent to the sun.
Round them blacken and welter
    and press
Staring multitudes, whose father
Adam was, whose brows are dark
With his Cain's corroded mark,
Who curse with looks. Nay—let
    me rather
Turn unto the wilderness.
   Ador. Turn not. God dwells with men.
   Zerah.   Above
He dwells with angels, and they love.
Can these love? With the living's pride
They stare at those who die,—who hang
In their sight and die. They bear the
    streak
Of the crosses' shadow, black not wide,
To fall on their heads, as it swerves aside
   When the victims' pang
   Makes the dry wood creak.
   Ador. The cross—the cross!
   Zerah.   A woman kneels
The mid cross under,
With white lips asunder,
And motion on each.
They throb, as she feels,

With a spasm, not a speech;
And her lids, close as sleep,
Are less calm, for the eyes
Have made room there to weep
Drop on drop—
Ador.   Weep? Weep blood,
All women, all men!
He sweated it, He,
For your pale womanhood
And base manhood. Agree
That these water-tears, then,
Are vain, mocking like laughter!
Weep blood!—Shall the flood
Of salt curses, whose foam is the dark-
ness, on roll
Forward, on from the strand of the
storm-beaten years,
And back from the rocks of the horrid
hereafter,
And up, in a coil, from the present's
wrath-spring,
Yea, down from the windows of heaven
opening,—
Deep calling to deep as they meet on
His soul,—
And men weep only tears?
Zerah. Little drops in the lapse!
And yet, Ador, perhaps
It is all that they can.
Tears! the lovingest man
Has no better bestowed
Upon man.
Ador.   Nor on God.
Zerah. Do all-givers need gifts?
If the Giver said 'Give,' the first motion
would slay
Our Immortals, the echo would ruin away
The same worlds which He made.
Why, what angel uplifts
Such a music, so clear,
It may seem in God's ear
Worth more than a woman's hoarse
weeping? And thus,
Pity tender as tears, I above thee would
speak,
Thou woman that weepest! weep un-
scorned of us!
I, the tearless and pure, am but loving
and weak.
Ador. Speak low, my brother, low,—
and not of love,
Or human or angelic. Rather stand
Before the throne of that Supreme above,

In whose infinitude the secrecies
Of thine own being lie hid, and lift thine
hand
Exultant, saying, 'Lord God, I am wise!'—
Than utter *here*, 'I love.'
Zerah.   And yet thine eyes
Do utter it. They melt in tender light,
The tears of heaven.
Ador.   Of heaven. Ah me!
Zerah. Ador!
Ador.   Say on.
Zerah.   The crucified are three.
Beloved, they are unlike.
Ador.   Unlike.
Zerah.   For one
Is as a man who has sinned and still
Doth wear the wicked will,
The hard malign life-energy,
Tossed outward, in the parting soul's
disdain,
On brow and lip that cannot change
again.
Ador. And one—
Zerah.   Has also sinned.
And yet (O marvel!) doth the Spirit-wind
Blow white those waters?—Death upon
his face
Is rather shine than shade,
A tender shine by looks belovèd made.
He seemeth dying in a quiet place,
And less by iron wounds in hands and feet
Than heart-broke by new joy too sudden
and sweet.
Ador. And ONE!—
Zerah.   And ONE—
Ador.   Why dost thou pause?
Zerah.   God! God!
Spirit of my spirit! who movest
Through seraph veins in burning deity
To light the quenchless pulses!—
Ador.   But hast trod
The depths of love in Thy peculiar nature,
And not in any Thou hast made and lovest
In narrow seraph hearts!—
Zerah.   Above, Creator!
Within, Upholder!
Ador.   And below, below,
The creature's and the upholden's sacri-
fice!
Zerah. Why do I pause?—
Ador.   There is a silentness
That answers thee enow,—
That, like a brazen sound

Excluding others, doth ensheathe us
    round,—
Hear it ! It is not from the visible skies
    Though they are still,
Unconscious that their own dropped
    dews express
The light of heaven on every earthly hill.
It is not from the hills, though calm and
    bare
    They, since their first creation,
Through midnight cloud or morning's
    glittering air
Or the deep deluge blindness, toward
    the place
Whence thrilled the mystic word's
    creative grace,
    And whence again shall come
    The word that uncreates,
Have lift their brows in voiceless ex-
    pectation.
It is not from the places that entomb
Man's dead—though common Silence
    there dilates
Her soul to grand proportions, worthily
    To fill life's vacant room.
    Not there—not there !
Not yet within those chambers lieth He,
A dead One in His living world ! His south
And west winds blowing over earth and
    sea,
And not a breath on that creating Mouth.
    But now,—a silence keeps
    (Not death's, nor sleep's)
    The lips whose whispered word
Might roll the thunders round rever-
    berated.
    Silent art Thou, O my Lord,
    Bowing down Thy stricken head !
    Fearest Thou, a groan of Thine
Would make the pulse of Thy creation fail
As Thine own pulse?— would rend the veil
Of visible things, and let the flood
Of the unseen Light, the essential God,
Rush in to whelm the undivine ?—
Thy silence, to my thinking, is as dread.
    Zerah. O silence !
    Ador. Doth it say to thee—the NAME,
Slow-learning seraph ?
    Zerah.   I have learnt.
    Ador.   The flame
Perishes in thine eyes.
    Zerah.   He opened His,
And looked. I cannot bear—

    Ador.   Their agony ?
    Zerah. Their love. God's depth is in
    them. From His brows
White, terrible in meekness, didst thou
    see
    The lifted eyes unclose !
He is God, seraph! Look no more on me,
O God—I am not God.
    Ador.   The loving is
Sublimed within them by the sorrowful.
In heaven we could sustain them.
    Zerah.   Heaven is dull,
Mine Ador, to man's earth. The light
    that burns
    In fluent, refluent motion
    Along the crystal ocean ;
The springing of the golden harps be-
    tween
The bowery wings, in fountains of sweet
    sound ;
The winding, wandering music that re-
    turns
Upon itself, exultingly self-bound
In the great spheric round
    Of everlasting praises ;
The God-thoughts in our midst that
    intervene,
Visibly flashing from the súpreme throne
    Full in seraphic faces
Till each astonishes the other, grown
More beautiful with worship and delight!
My heaven ! my home of heaven ! my
    infinite
Heaven-choirs ! what are ye to this dust
    and death,
This cloud, this cold, these tears, this
    failing breath,
Where God's immortal love now issueth
    In this MAN's woe ?
    Ador. His eyes are very deep yet calm.
    Zerah.   No more
On *me*, Jehovah-man—
    Ador.   Calm-deep. They show
A passion which is tranquil. They are
    seeing
No earth, no heaven, no men that slay
    and curse,
    No seraphs that adore ;
Their gaze is on the invisible, the dread,
The things we cannot view or think or
    speak,
Because we are too happy, or too weak,—
The sea of ill, for which the universe,

With all its pilèd space, can find no
  shore,
With all its life, no living foot to tread!
But He, accomplished in Jehovah-being,
  Sustains the gaze adown,
  Conceives the vast despair,
And feels the billowy griefs come up to
  drown,
Nor fears, nor faints, nor fails, till all be
  finished.
  Zerah. Thus, do I find Thee thus?
  My undiminished
And undiminishable God!—my God!
The echoes are still tremulous along
The heavenly mountains, of the latest
  song
Thy manifested glory swept abroad
In rushing past our lips! they echo ay
  'Creator, Thou art strong!—
Creator, Thou art blessèd over all.'
By what new utterance shall I now recall.
Unteaching the heaven-echoes? Dare I
  say,
'Creator, Thou art feebler than Thy
  work!
Creator, Thou art sadder than Thy
  creature!
  A worm, and not a man,
  Yea, no worm, but a curse'?—
I dare not so mine heavenly phrase
  reverse.
Albeit the piercing thorn and thistle-fork
  (Whose seed disordered ran
From Eve's hand trembling when the
  curse did reach her)
Be garnered darklier in Thy soul, the rod
That smites Thee never blossoming, and
  Thou
Grief-bearer for Thy world, with un-
  kinged brow—
I leave to men their song of Ichabod.
I have an angel-tongue—I know but
  praise.
  Ador. Hereaftershall the blood-bought
  captives raise
The passion-song of blood.
  Zerah.   And *we*, extend
Our holy vacant hands towards the
  Throne,
Crying 'We have no music!'
  Ador.   Rather, blend
  Both musics into one.
The sanctities and sanctified above

Shall each to each, with lifted looks
  serene,
  Their shining faces lean,
  And mix the adoring breath
And breathe the full thanksgiving.
  Zerah.   But the love—
The love, mine Ador!
  Ador.   Do we love not?
  Zerah.   Yea,
But not as man shall! not with life for
  death,
New-throbbing through the startled
  being! not
With strange astonished smiles, that ever
  may
Gush passionate like tears and fill their
  place!
Nor yet with speechless memories of what
Earth's winters were, enverduring the
  green
  Of every heavenly palm
  Whose windless, shadeless calm
Moves only at the breath of the Unseen.
Oh, not with this blood on us—and this
  face,—
Still, haply, pale with sorrow that it bore
In our behalf, and tender evermore
With nature all our own, upon us
  ing!—
Nor yet with these forgiving hands up-
  raising
Their unreproachful wounds, alone to
  bless!
Alas, Creator! shall we love Thee less
Than mortals shall?
  Ador.   Amen! so let it be.
We love in our proportion—to the bound
Thine infinite our finite set around,
And that is finitely,—Thou, infinite
And worthy infinite love! And our
  delight
Is watching the dear love poured out to
  Thee
From ever fuller chalice. Blessèd they,
Who love Thee more than we do! blessèd
  we,
Viewing that love which shall exceed
  even this,
And winning in the sight a double bliss,
For all so lost in love's supremacy!
The bliss is better. Only on the sad
  Cold earth there are who say
It seemeth better to be great than glad.

The bliss is better. Love Him more,
O man,
　　Than sinless seraphs can.
Zerah. Yea, love Him more.
Voices of the angelic multitude. Yea, more.
Ador. 　　　　The loving word
Is caught by those from whom we stand
　　apart.
For Silence hath no deepness in her heart
Where love's low name low breathed
　　would not be heard
By angels, clear as thunder.
　Angelic voices. 　　Love him more !
Ador. Sweet voices, swooning o'er
　　The music which ye make !
　　Albeit to love there were not ever
　　given
　　A mournful sound when uttered out
　　of heaven,
　• That angel-sadness ye would fitly
　　take.
　　Of love be silent now ! we gaze
　　adown
　　Upon the incarnate Love who wears
　　no crown.
Zerah. No crown ! the woe instead
　　Is heavy on His head,
　　Pressing inward on His brain
　　With a hot and clinging pain,
　　Till all tears are prest away,
　　And clear and calm His vision may
　　Peruse the black abyss.
　　No rod, no sceptre is
　　Holden in His fingers pale ;
　　They close instead upon the nail,
　　Concealing the sharp dole—
　　Never stirring to put by
　　The fair hair matted with blood,
　　Drooping forward from the rood
　　Helplessly, heavily,
　　On the cheek that waxeth colder,
　　Whiter ever,—and the shoulder
　　Where the government was laid.
　　His glory made the heavens afraid ;
Will He not unearth this cross from
　　its hole ?
His pity makes His piteous state ;
Will He be uncompassionate
Alone to His proper soul ?
Yea, will He not lift up
His lips from the bitter cup,
His brows from the dreary weight,
His hand from the clenching cross,

Crying, ' My Father, give to Me
Again the joy I had with Thee,
Or ere this earth was made for loss ? '—
　　No stir—no sound !
The love and woe being interwound
　　He cleaveth to the woe,
And putteth forth heaven's strength
　　below—
　　　　To bear.
Ador. And that creates His anguish
　　now,
　　Which made His glory there.
Zerah. Shall it indeed be so ?
　　Awake, thou Earth ! behold !
　　Thou, uttered forth of old
　　In all thy life-emotion,
　　In all thy vernal noises,
　　In the rollings of thine ocean,
　　Leaping founts, and rivers run-
　　ning,—
　　In thy woods' prophetic heaving
　　Ere the rains a stroke have given,
　　In thy winds' exultant voices
　　When they feel the hills anear,
　　In the firmamental sunning,
　　And the tempest which rejoices
　　Thy full heart with an awful cheer !
　　Thou, uttered forth of old,
　　And with all thy music rolled
　　In a breath abroad
　　　By the breathing God,—
　　Awake ! He is here ! behold !
　　Even *thou*—
　　　　beseems it good
　　To thy vacant vision dim,
　　That the deadly ruin should,
　　For thy sake, encompass Him ?
　　That the Master-word should lie
　　A mere silence, while His own
　　　Processive harmony,
The faintest echo of His lightest tone,
Is sweeping in a choral triumph by ?
　　Awake ! emit a cry !
　　And say, albeit used
　　From Adam's ancient years
　　To falls of acrid tears,
　　To frequent sighs unloosed,
　　Caught back to press again
　　On bosoms zoned with pain—
　　To corses still and sullen
　　The shine and music dulling
　　With closèd eyes and ears
　　That nothing sweet can enter,

Commoving thee no less
With that forced quietness
Than the earthquake in thy centre—
Thou hast not learnt to bear
This new divine despair !
These tears that sink into thee,
These dying eyes that view thee,
This dropping blood from lifted
    rood,
They darken and undo thee !
Thou canst not, presently, sustain this
    corse !
Cry, cry, thou hast not force !
Cry, thou wouldst fainer keep
Thy hopeless charnels deep,
Thyself a general tomb—
Where the first and the second Death
Sit gazing face to face
And mar each other's breath,
While silent bones through all the place
'Neath sun and moon do faintly glisten,
And seem to lie and listen
For the tramp of the coming Doom.
        Is it not meet
That they who erst the Eden fruit did eat,
    Should champ the ashes ?
That they who wrapt them in the
    thundercloud,
    Should wear it as a shroud,
    Perishing by its flashes ?
That they who vexed the lion, should be
    rent ?
Cry, cry—'I will sustain my punish-
    ment,
The sin being mine ! but take away from
    me
This visioned Dread—this Man—this
    Deity.'
    The Earth. I have groaned—I have
    travailed—I am weary.
I am blind with mine own grief, and
    cannot see,
As clear-eyed angels can, His agony,
And what I see I also can sustain,
Because His power protects me from
    His pain.
I have groaned—I have travailed—I am
    dreary,
Hearkening the thick sobs of my child-
    ren's heart.
    How can I say ' Depart '
To that Atoner making calm and free ?
    Am I a God as He,

To lay down peace and power as will-
    ingly !
    Ador. He looked for some to pity.
        There is none.
All pity is within Him, and not for Him.
His earth is iron under Him, and o'er Him
    His skies are brass.
    His seraphs cry ' Alas '
With hallelujah voice that cannot weep.
And man, for whom the dreadful work is
    done —
Scornful voices from the Earth. If verily
    this *be* the Eternal's son—
    Ador. Thou hearest !—man is grateful !
    Zerah.   Can I hear,
Nor darken into man and cease for ever
    My seraph-smile to wear ?
        Was it for such,
    It pleased Him to overleap
His glory with His love and sever
From the God-light and the throne
And all angels bowing down,
For whom His every look did touch
New notes of joy on the unworn
    string
Of an eternal worshipping ?
    For such, He left His heaven ?
    There, though never bought by
    blood
And tears, we gave Him gratitude !
We loved Him there, though unfor-
    given !
    Ador.   The light is riven
        Above, around,
And down in lurid fragments flung,
That catch the mountain-peak and stream
    With momentary gleam,
Then perish in the water and the ground.
    River and waterfall,
    Forest and wilderness,
Mountain and city, are together wrung
Into one shape, and that is shapelessness ;
    The darkness stands for all.
    Zerah. The pathos hath the day undone :
        The death-look of His eyes
        Hath overcome the sun,
And made it sicken in its narrow skies.
    Ador. Is it to death ? He dieth.
    Zerah.   Through the dark
He still, He only, is discernible—
The naked hands and feet transfixèd stark,
The countenance of patient anguish white,
    Do make themselves a light

More dreadful than the glooms which
    round them dwell,
And therein do they shine.
    Ador.   God ! Father-God !
Perpetual Radiance on the radiant
    throne !
Uplift the lids of inward Deity,
    Flashing abroad
    Thy burning Infinite !
Light up this dark, where there is nought
    to see
Except the unimagined agony
Upon the sinless forehead of the Son.
    Zerah. God, tarry not ! Behold, enow
Hath He wandered as a stranger,
Sorrowed as a victim. Thou
    Appear for Him, O Father !
    Appear for Him, Avenger !
Appear for Him, just One and holy One,
    For He is holy and just !
At once the darkness and dishonour
    rather
To the ragged jaws of hungry chaos rake,
    And hurl aback to ancient dust
    These mortals that make blasphemies
    With their made breath ! this earth and
        skies
    That only grow a little dim,
    Seeing their curse on Him !
    But Him, of all forsaken,
    Of creature and of brother,
    Never wilt thou forsake !
Thy living and Thy loving cannot slacken
Their firm essential hold upon each
    other—
And well Thou dost remember how His
    part
Was still to lie upon Thy breast and be
Partaker of the light that dwelt in Thee
    Ere sun or seraph shone ;
And how while silence trembled round
    the throne,
Thou countedst by the beatings of His
    heart
The moments of Thine own eternity !
    Awaken,
O right Hand with the lightnings !
    Again gather
His glory to thy glory ! What estranger,
What ill supreme in evil, can be thrust
Between the faithful Father and the Son ?
    Appear for Him, O Father !
    Appear for Him, Avenger !

Appear for Him, just One and holy One,
    For He is holy and just.
    Ador. Thy face, upturned toward the
        throne, is dark—
Thou hast no answer, Zerah.
    Zerah.   No reply,
O unforsaking Father ?—
    Ador.   Hark !
Instead of downward voice, a cry
    Is uttered from beneath.
    Zerah. And by a sharper sound than
        death
    Mine immortality is riven.
The heavy darkness which doth tent the
    sky
Floats backward as by a sudden wind—
    But I see no light behind !
    But I feel the farthest stars are all
        Stricken and shaken,
    And I know a shadow sad and broad
        Doth fall—doth fall
On our vacant thrones in heaven.
    Voice from the Cross. MY GOD, MY GOD,
WHY HAST THOU ME FORSAKEN ?
    The Earth. Ah me, ah me, ah me ! the
        dreadful why !
My sin is on Thee, sinless One ! Thou art
God-orphaned, for my burden on Thy
    head.
Dark sin, white innocence, endurance
    dread !
Be still, within your shrouds, my buried
    dead—
Nor work with this quick horror round
    mine heart !
    Zerah. He hath forsaken *Him.* I
        perish—
    Ador.   Hold
Upon His name ! we perish not. Of old
His will—
    Zerah. I seek His will. Seek, seraphim !
My God, my God ! where is it ? Doth
    that curse
Reverberate spare us, seraph or universe ?
    He hath forsaken *Him.*
    Ador. He cannot fail.
    Angel Voices. We faint, we droop—
        Our love doth tremble like fear.
    Voices of Fallen Angels from the earth.
        Do we prevail ?
Or are we lost ?—Hath not the ill we did
    Been heretofore our good ?
Is it not ill that One, all sinless, should

Hang heavy with all curses on a cross?
Nathless, that cry!—With huddled faces
  hid
Within the empty graves which men did
  scoop
To hold more damnèd dead, we shudder
  through
  What shall exalt us or undo,—
  Our triumph, or our loss.
Voice from the Cross. IT IS FINISHED.
Zerah.   Hark, again!
Like a victor speaks the Slain.
  Angel Voices. Finished be the trembling
    vain!
  Ador. Upward. like a well-loved Son,
    Looketh He, the orphaned One.
  Angel Voices. Finished is the mystic
    pain!
  Voices of Fallen Angels. His deathly
    forehead at the word
    Gleameth like a seraph sword.
  Angel Voices. Finished is the demon
    reign!
  Ador. His breath, as living God,
    createth,
    His breath, as dying man, com-
    pleteth.
  Angel Voices. Finished work His hands
    sustain!
  The Earth. In mine ancient sepul-
    chres
    Where my kings and prophets
    freeze,
    Adam dead four thousand years,
    Unwakened by the universe's
    Everlasting moan,
    Ay his ghastly silence, mocking—
    Unwakened by his children's
    knocking
    At his old sepulchral stone,
    'Adam, Adam, all this curse is
    Thine and on us yet!'—
    Unwakened by the ceaseless tears
    Wherewith they made his cere-
    ment wet,
    'Adam, must thy curse re-
    main?'—
    Starts with sudden life, and hears
Through the slow dripping of the
    caverned eaves,—
  Angel Voices. Finished is his bane!
  Voice from the Cross. FATHER! MY
    SPIRIT TO THINE HANDS IS GIVEN!

Ador. Hear the wailing winds that be
  By wings of unclean spirits made!
  They, in that last look, surveyed
The love they lost in losing heaven,
  And passionately flee,—
With a desolate cry that cleaves
The natural storms—though *they* are
  lifting
God's strong cedar-roots like leaves,
And the earthquake and the thunder,
Neither keeping either under,
Roar and hurtle through the glooms!—
And a few pale stars are drifting
Past the Dark, to disappear,
What time, from the splitting tombs,
Gleamingly the Dead arise,
Viewing with their death-calmed eyes
The elemental strategies,
To witness, Victory is the Lord's.
Hear the wail o' the spirits! hear.
Zerah. I hear alone the memory of His
  words.

EPILOGUE

I

My song is done.
My voice that long hath faltered, shall
  be still.
The mystic darkness drops from Calvary's
  hill
Into the common light of this day's sun.

II

I see no more Thy cross, O holy Slain!
I hear no more the horror and the coil
  Of the great world's turmoil,
Feeling thy countenance *too still*,—nor
  yell
Of demons sweeping past it to their prison.
The skies, that turned to darkness with
  Thy pain,
  Make now a summer's day;
And on my changèd ear that sabbath bell
  Records how CHRIST IS RISEN.

III

  And I—ah! what am I
To counterfeit, with faculty earth-
  darkened,
  Seraphic brows of light,

And seraph language never used nor
    hearkened ?
Ah me ! what word that seraphs say,
    could come
From mouth so used to sighs—so soon
    to lie
Sighless, because then breathless, in the
    tomb ?

IV

Bright ministers of God and grace !—of
    grace
Because of God ! — whether ye bow
    adown
In your own heaven, before the living
    face
Of Him who died, and deathless wears
    the crown—
Or whether at this hour ye haply are
Anear, around me, hiding in the night
Of this permitted ignorance your light,
    This feebleness to spare,—
Forgive me, that mine earthly heart
    should dare
Shape images of unincarnate spirits,

And lay upon their burning lips a thought
Cold with the weeping which mine earth
    inherits.
And though ye find in such hoarse music,
    wrought
To copy yours, a cadence all the while
Of sin and sorrow — only pitying
    smile !—
    Ye know to pity, well.

V

I too may haply smile another day
At the far recollection of this lay,
When God may call me in your midst to
    dwell,
To hear your most sweet music's miracle
And see your wondrous faces. May it be !
For His remembered sake, the Slain on
    rood,
Who rolled His earthly garment red in
    blood
(Treading the wine-press) that the weak,
    like me,
Before His heavenly throne should walk
    in white.

QUEEN ANNELIDA AND FALSE ARCITE[1]

I

O THOU fierce God of armies, Mars the red,
Who in thy frosty country callèd Thrace,
Within thy grisly temples full of dread,
Art honoured as the patron of that place,
With the Bellona Pallas, full of grace !
Be present ; guide, sustain this song of mine,
Beginning which, I cry toward thy shrine.

II

For deep the hope is sunken in my mind,
In piteous-hearted English to indite
This story old, which I in Latin find,
Of Queen Annelida and false Arcite :
Since Time, whose rust can all things fret and bite,
In fretting many a tale of equal fame,
Hath from our memory nigh devoured this same.

III

Thy favour, Polyhymnia, also deign,
Who, in thy sisters' green Parnassian glade,
By Helicon, not far from Cirrha's fane,
Singest with voice memorial in the shade,
Under the laurel which can never fade;
Now grant my ship, that some smooth haven win her !
I follow Statius first, and then Corinna.

IV

When Theseus by a long and deathly war
The hardy Scythian race had overcome,
He, laurel-crownèd, in his gold-wrought car,
Returning to his native city home,
The blissful people for his pomp make room,
And throw their shouts up to the stars, and bring
The general heart out for his honouring.

V

Before the Duke, in sign of victory,
The trumpets sound, and in his banner large
Dilates the figure of Mars—and men may see,
In token of glory, many a treasure charge,
Many a bright helm, and many a spear and targe,
Many a fresh knight, and many a blissful rout
On horse and foot, in all the field about.

VI

Hippolyte, his wife, the heroic queen
Of Scythia, conqueress though conquerèd,
With Emily, her youthful sister sheen,
Fair in a car of gold he with him led.
The ground about her car she overspread
With brightness from the beauty in her face,
Which smiled forth largesses of love and grace.

VII

Thus triumphing, and laurel-crownèd thus,
In all the flower of Fortune's high providing,
I leave this noble prince, this Theseus,
Toward the walls of Athens bravely riding,—
And seek to bring in, without more abiding,
Something of that whereof I 'gan to write,
Of fair Annelida and false Arcite.

VIII

Fierce Mars, who in his furious course
of ire,
The ancient wrath of Juno to fulfil,
Had set the nations' mutual hearts on fire
In Thebes and Argos, (so that each
would kill
Either with bloody spears,) grew never
still—
But rushed now here, now there,
among them both,
Till each was slain by each, they were
so wroth.

IX

For when Parthenopaeus and Tydeus
Had perished with Hippomedon,—alsò
Amphiaraus and proud Capaneus,—
And when the wretched Theban brethren
two
Were slain, and King Adrastus home
did go—
So desolate stood Thebes, her halls so
bare,
That no man's love could remedy his
care.

X

And when the old man, Creon, 'gan
espy
How darkly the blood royal was brought
down,
He held the city in his tyranny,
And forced the nobles of that regiòn
To be his friends and dwell within the
town ;
Till half for love of him, and half for fear,
Those princely persons yielded, and
drew near,—

XI

Among the rest the young Armenian
queen,
Annelida, was in that city living.
She was as beauteous as the sun was
sheen,
Her fame to distant lands such glory
giving,
That all men in the world had some
heart-striving
To look on her. No woman, sooth,
can be,
Though earth is rich in fairness, fair as
she.

XII

Young was this queen, but twenty
summers old,
Of middle stature, and such wondrous
beauty,
That Nature, self-delighted, did behold
A rare work in her—while, in steadfast
duty,
Lucretia and Penelope would suit ye
With a worse model—all things under-
stood,
She was, in short, most perfect fair and
good.

XIII

The Theban knight eke, to give all their
due,
Was young, and therewithal a lusty
knight.
But he was double in love, and nothing
true,
Aye, subtler in that craft than any wight,
And with his cunning won this lady
bright ;
So working on her simpleness of nature,
That she him trusted above every crea-
ture.

XIV

What shall I say ? She lovèd Arcite so,
That if at any hour he parted from her,
Her heart seemed ready anon to burst
in two ;
For he with lowliness had overcome her :
She thought she knew the heart which
did foredoom her.
But he was false, and all that softness
feigning,—
I trow men need not *learn* such arts of
paining.

XV

And ne'ertheless full mickle business
Had he, before he might his lady win,—
He swore that he should die of his
distress,
His brain would madden with the fire
within !
Alas, the while ! for it was ruth and sin,
That she, sweet soul, upon his grief
should rue ;
But little reckon false hearts as the true.

XVI

And she to Arcite so subjected her,
That all she did or had seemed his of
    right :
No creature in her house met smile or
    cheer,
Further than would be pleasant to Arcite ;
There was no lack whereby she did
    despite
To his least will—for hers to his was
    bent,
And all things which pleased him made
    her content.

XVII

No kind of letter to her fair hands came,
Touching on love, from any kind of
    wight,
But him she showed it ere she burned
    the same :
So open was she, doing all she might,
That nothing should be hidden from her
    knight,
Lest he for any untruth should upbraid
    her,—
The slave of his unspoken will she made
    her.

XVIII

He played his jealous fancies over her,
And if he heard that any other man
Spoke to her, would beseech her
    straight to swear
To each word—or the speaker had his
    ban ;
And out of her sweet wits she almost ran
For fear ; but all was fraud and flattery,
Since without love he feignèd jealousy.

XIX

All which with so much sweetness
    suffered she,
Whate'er he willed she thought the
    wisest thing ;
And evermore she loved him tenderly,
And did him honour as he were a king.
Her heart was wedded to him with
    a ring,
So eager to be faithful and intent,
That wheresoe'er he wandered, there it
    went.

XX

When she would eat he stole away her
    thought,
Till little thought for food, I ween, was
    kept ;
And when a time for rest the midnight
    brought,
She always mused upon him till she
    slept,—
When he was absent, secretly she wept ;
And thus lived Queen Annelida the fair,
For false Arcite, who worked her this
    despair.

XXI

This false Arcite in his new-fangleness,
Because so gentle were her ways and
    true,
Took the less pleasure in her steadfast-
    ness,
And saw another lady proud and new,
And right anon he clad him in her
    hue ;
I know not whether white, or red, or
    green,
Betraying fair Annelida the Queen.

XXII

And yet it was no thing to wonder on,
Though he were false—It is the way of
    man,
(Since Lamech was, who flourished
    years agone,)
To be in love as false as any can ;
For *he* was the first father who began
To love two ; and I trow, indeed, that he
Invented tents as well as bigamy.

XXIII

And having so betrayed her, false Arcite
Feigned more, that primal wrong to
    justify.
A vicious horse will snort besides his
    bite ;
And so he taunted her with treachery,
Swearing he saw thro' her duplicity,
And how she was not loving, but false-
    hearted—
The perjured traitor swore thus, and
    departed.

XXIV

Alas, alas, what heart could suffer it,
For ruth, the story of her grief to tell?
What thinker hath the cunning and the wit
To image it? what hearer, strength to dwell
A room's length off, while I rehearse the hell
Suffered by Queen Annelida the fair
For false Arcite, who worked her this despair?

XXV

She weepeth, waileth, swooneth piteously;
She falleth on the earth dead as a stone;
Her graceful limbs are cramped convulsively;
She speaketh out wild, as her wits were gone.
No colour, but an ashen paleness—none—
Touched cheek or lips; and no word shook their white,
But 'Mercy, cruel heart! mine own Arcite!'

XXVI

Thus it continued, till she pinèd so,
And grew so weak, her feet no more could bear
Her body, languishing in ceaseless woe.
Whereof Arcite had neither ruth nor care—
His heart had put out new-green shoots elsewhere;
Therefore he deigned not on her grief to think,
And reckoned little, did she float or sink.

XXVII

His fine new lady kept him in such narrow
Strict limit, by the bridle, at the end
O' the whip, he feared her least word as an arrow,—
Her threatening made him, as a bow, to bend,
And at her pleasure did he turn and wend;
Seeing she never granted to this lover
A single grace he could sing 'Ios' over.

XXVIII

She drove him forth—she scarcely deigned to know
That he was servant to her ladyship:
But, lest he should be proud, she kept him low,
Nor paid his service from a smiling lip:
She sent him now to land, and now to ship;
And giving him all danger to his fill,
She thereby had him at her sovereign will.

XXIX

Be taught of this, ye prudent women all,
Warned by Annelida and false Arcite:
Because she chose, himself, 'dear heart' to call
And be so meek, he loved her not aright.
The nature of man's heart is to delight
In something strange—moreover (may Heaven save
The wronged) the thing they cannot, they would have.

XXX

Now turn we to Annelida again,
Who pinèd day by day in languishment.
But when she saw no comfort met her pain,
Weeping once in a woful unconstraint,
She set herself to fashion a complaint,
Which with her own pale hand she 'gan to write,
And sent it to her lover, to Arcite.

THE COMPLAINT OF ANNELIDA TO FALSE ARCITE

I

The sword of sorrow, whetted sharp for me
On false delight, with point of memory
Stabbed so mine heart, bliss-bare and black of hue,
That all to dread is turned my dance's glee,
My face's beauty to despondency—
For nothing it availeth to be true—
And, whosoever is so, she shall rue
Obeying love, and cleaving faithfully
Alway to one, and changing for no new.

II

I ought to know it well as any wight,
For *I* loved one with all my heart and
     might,
More than myself a hundred-thousand
     fold,
And callèd him my heart's dear life, my
     knight,
And was all his, as far as it was right;
His gladness did my blitheness make of
     old,
And in his least disease my death was
     told;
Who, on his side, had plighted lovers'
     plight,
Me, evermore, his lady and love to hold.

III

Now is he false—alas, alas!—although
Unwronged! and acting such a ruthless
     part,
That with a little word he will not deign
To bring the peace back to my mournful
     heart.
Drawn in, and caught up by another's
     art,
Right as he will, he laugheth at my pain;
While *I*—I cannot my weak heart re-
     strain
From loving him—still, ay; yet none I
     know
To whom of all this grief I can complain.

IV

Shall I complain (ah, piteous and harsh
     sound!)
Unto my foe, who gave mine heart a
     wound,
And still desireth that the harm be more?
Now certes, if I sought the whole earth
     round,
No other help, no better leach were
     found!
My destiny hath shaped it so of yore—
I would not other medicine, nor yet lore.
I would be ever where I once was bound;
And what I said, would say for evermore.

V

Alas! and where is gone your gentillesse?
Where gone your pleasant words, your
     humbleness?
Where your devotion full of reverent fear,
Your patient loyalty, your busy address
To me, whom once you callèd nothing less
Than mistress, sovereign lady, i' the
     sphere
O' the world? Ah me! no word, no look
     of cheer,
Will you vouchsafe upon my heaviness!
Alas your love! I bought it all too dear.

VI

Now certes, sweet, howe'er you be
The cause so, and so causelessly,
Of this my mortal agony,
Your reason should amend the failing!
Your friend, your true love, do you flee,
Who never in time nor yet degree
Grieved you: so may the all-knowing
     He
Save my lorn soul from future wailing.

VII

Because I was so plain, Arcite,
In all my doings, your delight,
Seeking in all things, where I might
In honour,—meek and kind and free;
Therefore you do me such despite.
Alas! howe'er through cruelty
My heart with sorrow's sword you
     smite,
You cannot kill its love.—Ah me!

VIII

Ah, my sweet foe, why do you so
          For shame?
Think you that praise, in sooth, will raise
          Your name,
Loving anew, and being untrue
          For ay?
Thus casting down your manhood's crown
          In blame,
And working *me* adversity,
          The same
Who loves you most—(O God, Thou
     know'st!)
          Alway?
Yet turn again—be fair and plain
          Some day;
And then shall this, that seems amiss,
          Be game,
All being forgiven, while yet from heaven
          I stay.

IX

Behold, dear heart, I write this to obtain
Some knowledge, whether I should pray
    or 'plain :
Which way is best to force you to be true?
For either I must have you in my chain,
Or you, sweet, with the death must part
    us twain ;
There is no mean, no other way more
    new :
And, that heaven's mercy on my soul
    may rue
And let you slay me outright with this
    pain,
The whiteness in my cheeks may prove
    to you.

X

For hitherto mine own death have I
    sought ;
Myself I murder with my secret thought,
In sorrow and ruth of your unkindnesses !
I weep, I wail, I fast—all helpeth nought,
I flee all joy (I mean the name of aught),
I flee all company, all mirthfulness—
Why, who can make her boast of more
    distress
Than I ?—To such a plight you have me
    brought,
Guiltless (I need no witness) ne'ertheless.

XI

Shall I go pray and wail my womanhood?
Compared to such a deed, death's self
    were good.
What ! ask for mercy, and guiltless—
    where 's the need ?
And if I wailed my life so,—that you
    would
Care nothing, is less feared than under-
    stood :
And if mine oath of love I dared to plead
In mine excuse,—your scorn would be
    its meed.
Ah, love ! it giveth flowers instead of
    seed—
Full long ago I might have taken heed.

XII

And though I had you back to-morrow
    again,
I might as well hold April from the rain

As hold you to the vows you vowed me
    last.
Maker of all things, and truth's sovereign,
Where is the truth of man, who hath it
    slain,
That she who loveth him should find
    him fast
As in a tempest is a rotten mast?
Is that a *tame* beast which is ever fain
To flee us when restraint and fear are
    past ?

XIII

Now mercy, sweet, if I mis-say ;—
Have I said aught is wrong to-day?
I do not know—my wit 's astray—
I fare as doth the song of one who
    weepeth ;
For now I 'plain, and now I play—
I am so mazed, I die away—
Arcite, you have the key for ay
Of all my world, and all the good it
    keepeth.

XIV

And in this world there is not one
Who walketh with a sadder moan,
And bears more grief than I have done;
And if light slumbers overcome me,
Methinks your image, in the glory
Of skyey azure, stands before me,
Revowing the old love you bore me,
And praying for new mercy from me.

XV

Through the long night, this wondrous
    sight,
                    Bear I,
Which haunteth still, the daylight, till
                    I die :
But nought of this, your heart, I wis,
                    Can reach.
Mine eyes down-pour, they nevermore
                    Are dry.
While to your ruth, and eke your truth,
                    I cry—
But, weladay, too far be they
                    To fetch.
Thus destiny is holding me—
                    Ah, wretch !
And when I fain would break the chain,
                    And try—
Faileth my wit (so weak is it)
                    With speech.

XVI

Therefore I end thus, since my hope is o'er—
I give all up both now and evermore ;
And in the balance ne'er again will lay
My safety, nor be studious in love-lore.
But like the swan who, as I heard of yore,
Singeth life's penance on his deathly day,
So I sing here my life and woes away,—
Aye, how you, cruel Arcite, wounded sore,
With memory's point, your poor Anne-
lida.

XVII

After Annelida, the woful queen,
Had written in her own hand in this wise,
With ghastly face, less pale than white, I ween,
She fell a-swooning ; then she 'gan arise,
And unto Mars voweth a sacrifice
Within the temple, with a sorrowful bearing,
And in such phrase as meets your present hearing.

POEMS, 1838—50

PREFACE TO THE EDITION OF 1844

THE collection here offered to the public consists of Poems which have been written in the interim between the period of the publication of my *Seraphim* and the present; variously coloured, or perhaps shadowed, by the life of which they are the natural expression, and, with the exception of a few contributions to English or American periodicals, are printed now for the first time.

As the first poem of this collection, the *Drama of Exile*, is the longest and most important work (to *me!*) which I ever trusted into the current of publication, I may be pardoned for entreating the reader's attention to the fact, that I decided on publishing it after considerable hesitation and doubt. The subject of the Drama rather fastened on me than was chosen; and the form, approaching the model of the Greek tragedy, shaped itself under my hand, rather by force of pleasure than of design. But when the excitement of composition had subsided I felt afraid of my position. My subject was the new and strange experience of the fallen humanity, as it went forth from Paradise into the wilderness; with a peculiar reference to Eve's allotted grief, which, considering that self-sacrifice belonged to her womanhood, and the consciousness of originating the Fall to her offence, appeared to me imperfectly apprehended hitherto, and more expressible by a woman than a man. There was room, at least, for lyrical emotion in those first steps into the wilderness,—in that first sense of desolation after wrath,—in that first audible gathering of the recriminating 'groan of the whole creation,'—in that first darkening of the hills from the recoiling feet of angels,—and in that first silence of the voice of God. And I took pleasure in driving in, like a pile, stroke upon stroke, the idea of EXILE,—admitting Lucifer as an extreme Adam, to represent the ultimate tendencies of sin and loss,—that it might be strong to bear up the contrary idea of the Heavenly love and purity. But when all was done I felt afraid, as I said before, of my position. I had promised my own prudence to shut close the gates of Eden between Milton and myself, so that none might say I dared to walk in his footsteps. He should be within, I thought, with his Adam and Eve unfallen or falling,—and I, without, with my EXILES,—*I* also an exile! It would not do. The subject, and his glory covering it, swept through the gates, and I stood full in it, against my will, and contrary to my vow, till I shrank back fearing, almost desponding; hesitating to venture even a passing association with our great poet before the face of the public. Whether at last I took courage for the venture by a sudden revival of that love of manuscript which should be classed by moral philosophers among the natural affections, or by the encouraging voice of a dear friend, it is not interesting to the reader to inquire. Neither could the fact affect the question; since I bear, of course, my own responsibilities. For the rest, Milton is too high, and I am too low, to render it necessary for me to disavow any rash emulation of his divine faculty on his own ground; while enough individuality will be granted, I hope, to my poem, to rescue me from that imputation of plagiarism which should be too servile a thing for every sincere thinker. After all, and at the worst, I have only attempted, in respect to Milton, what the Greek dramatists achieved lawfully in respect to Homer. They constructed dramas on Trojan ground; they raised on the buskin and even clasped with the sock, the feet of Homeric heroes; yet they neither imitated their Homer nor emasculated him. The Agamemnon of Aeschylus, who died in the bath, did no harm to, nor suffered any harm from, the Agamemnon of Homer who bearded Achilles. To this analogy—the more favourable to me from the obvious exception in it, that Homer's subject was his own possibly by creation, whereas Milton's was his own by illustration only—I appeal. To this analogy—*not* to this comparison, be it understood—I appeal. For the analogy of the stronger may apply to the weaker; and the reader may have patience with the weakest while she suggests the application.

On a graver point I must take leave to touch, in further reference to my dramatic poem. The divine Saviour is represented in vision towards the close, speaking and transfigured; and it has been hinted to me that the introduction may give offence in quarters where I should be most reluctant to give any. A reproach of the same class, relating to the frequent recurrence of a Great Name in my pages, has already filled me with regret. How shall I answer these things? Frankly, in any case. When the old mysteries represented the Holiest Being in a rude familiar fashion, and the people gazed on, with the faith of children in their earnest eyes, the critics of a succeeding age, who rejoiced in Congreve, cried out 'profane.' Yet Andreini's mystery suggested Milton's epic; and Milton, the most reverent of poets, doubting whether to throw his work into the epic form or the dramatic, left, on the latter basis, a rough ground-plan, in which his intention of introducing the 'Heavenly Love' among the persons of his drama is extant to the present day. But the tendency of the present day is to sunder the daily life from the spiritual creed,—to separate the worshipping from the acting man,—and by no means to 'live by faith.' There is a feeling abroad which appears to me (I say it with deference) nearer to superstition than to religion, that there should be no touching of holy vessels except by consecrated fingers, nor any naming of holy names except in consecrated places. As if life were not a continual sacrament to man, since Christ brake the daily bread of it in His hands! As if the name of God did

not build a church, by the very naming of it! As if the word God were not, everywhere in His creation, and at every moment in His eternity, an appropriate word! As if it could be uttered unfitly, if devoutly! I appeal on these points, which I will not argue, from the conventions of the Christian to his devout heart; and I beseech him generously to believe of me that I have done that in reverence from which, through reverence, he might have abstained; and that where he might have been driven to silence by the principle of adoration, I, by the very same principle, have been hurried into speech.

It should have been observed in another place,—the fact, however, being sufficiently obvious throughout the drama,—that the time is from the evening into the night. If it should be objected that I have lengthened my twilight too much for the East, I might hasten to answer that we know nothing of the length of mornings or evenings before the Flood, and that I cannot, for my own part, believe in an Eden without the longest of purple twilights. The evening, עֶרֶב, of Genesis signifies a 'mingling,' and approaches the meaning of our 'twilight' analytically. Apart from which considerations, my 'exiles' are surrounded, in the scene described, by supernatural appearances; and the shadows that approach them are not only of the night.

The next longest poem to the *Drama of Exile*, in the collection, is the *Vision of Poets*, in which I have endeavoured to indicate the necessary relations of genius to suffering and self-sacrifice. In the eyes of the living generation, the poet is at once a richer and poorer man than he used to be; he wears better broadcloth, but speaks no more oracles: and the evil of this social incrustation over a great idea is eating deeper and more fatally into our literature than either readers or writers may apprehend fully. I have attempted to express in this poem my view of the mission of the poet, of the self-abnegation implied in it, of the great work involved in it, of the duty and glory of what Balzac has beautifully and truly called 'la patience angélique du génie';

and of the obvious truth, above all, that if knowledge is power, suffering should be acceptable as a part of knowledge. It is enough to say of the other poems, that scarcely one of them is unambitious of an object and a significance.

Since my *Seraphim* was received by the public with more kindness than its writer had counted on, I dare not rely on having put away the faults with which that volume abounded and was mildly reproached. Something indeed I may hope to have retrieved, because some progress in mind and in art every active thinker and honest writer must consciously or unconsciously make, with the progress of existence and experience : and, in some sort—since 'we learn in suffering what we teach in song,'—my songs may be fitter to teach. But if it were not presumptuous language on the lips of one to whom life is more than usually uncertain, my favourite wish for this work would be, that it be received by the public as a step in the right track, towards a future indication of more value and acceptability. I would fain do better—and I feel as if I might do better : I aspire to do better. It is no new form of the nympholepsy of poetry, that my ideal should fly before me : and if I cry out too hopefully at

sight of the white vesture receding between the cypresses, let me be blamed gently if justly. In any case, while my poems are full of faults—as I go forward to my critics and confess—they have my heart and life in them : they are not empty shells. If it must be said of me that I have contributed immemorable verses to the many rejected by the age, it cannot at least be said that I have done so in a light and irresponsible spirit. Poetry has been as serious a thing to me as life itself ; and life has been a very serious thing : there has been no playing at skittles for me in either. I never mistook pleasure for the final cause of poetry ; nor leisure, for the hour of the poet. I have done my work, so far, as work—not as mere hand and head work, apart from the personal being, but as the completest expression of that being to which I could attain ; and as work I offer it to the public—feeling its shortcomings more deeply than any of my readers, because measured from the height of my aspiration, but feeling also that the reverence and sincerity with which the work was done should give it some protection with the reverent and sincere.

LONDON, 50 WIMPOLE STREET, 1844.

ADVERTISEMENT TO THE EDITION OF 1850

THIS edition, including my earlier and later writings, I have endeavoured to render as little unworthy as possible of the indulgence of the public. Several poems I would willingly have withdrawn, if it were not almost impossible to extricate what has been once caught and involved in the machinery of the press. The alternative is a request to the generous reader that he may use the weakness of those earlier verses, which no subsequent revision has succeeded in strengthening, less as a reproach to the writer, than as a means of marking some progress in her other attempts. One early failure, a translation of the *Prometheus* of Aeschylus—which, though happily free of the current of publication, may be

remembered against me by a few of my personal friends—I have replaced by an entirely new version, made for them and my conscience, in expiation of a sin of my youth, with the sincerest application of my mature mind. This collection includes, also, various poems hitherto unprinted, which I am glad to have the present opportunity of throwing behind me, so as to leave clear the path before, towards better aims and ends . . . may I hope ? . . . than any which are attained here [1].

FLORENCE, *January* 1850.

[1] Three additional pieces were added in the fourth edition, 1856 (from which the ensuing Poems are printed)—'A Denial,' 'Proof and Disproof,' 'Question and Answer.'

A DRAMA OF EXILE

SCENE.—*The outer side of the gate of Eden shut fast with cloud, from the depth of which revolves a sword of fire self-moved.* ADAM *and* EVE *are seen in the distance flying along the glare.*

LUCIFER, *alone.*

REJOICE in the clefts of Gehenna,
  My exiled, my host!
Earth has exiles as hopeless as when a
  Heaven's empire was lost.
Through the seams of her shaken foundations,
  Smoke up in great joy!
With the smoke of your fierce exultations
  Deform and destroy!
Smoke up with your lurid revenges,
  And darken the face
Of the white heavens and taunt them
  with changes
  From glory and grace.
We, in falling, while destiny strangles,
  Pull down with us all.
Let them look to the rest of their angels!
  Who's safe from a fall?
He saves not. Where's Adam? Can
  pardon
  Requicken that sod?
Unkinged is the King of the Garden,
  The image of God.
Other exiles are cast out of Eden,—
  More curse has been hurled.
Come up, O my locusts, and feed in
  The green of the world.
Come up! we have conquered by evil.
  Good reigns not alone.
I prevail now, and, angel or devil,
  Inherit a throne.

[*In sudden apparition a watch of innumerable angels, rank above rank, slopes up from around the gate to the zenith. The* angel GABRIEL *descends.*

Luc. Hail Gabriel, the keeper of the
  gate!
Now that the fruit is plucked, prince
  Gabriel,
I hold that Eden is impregnable
Under thy keeping.

Gab.   Angel of the sin,
Such as thou standest,—pale in the drear
  light
Which rounds the rebel's work with
  Maker's wrath,—
Thou shalt be an Idea to all souls,
A monumental melancholy gloom
Seen down all ages, whence to mark
  despair
And measure out the distances from good.
Go from us straightway.
  Luc.   Wherefore?
  Gab.   Lucifer,
Thy last step in this place trod sorrow
  up.
Recoil before that sorrow, if not this
  sword.
  Luc. Angels are in the world—wherefore not I?
Exiles are in the world—wherefore not I?
The cursed are in the world—wherefore
  not I?
  Gab. Depart.
  Luc.   And where's the logic of
  'depart'?
Our lady Eve had half been satisfied
To obey her Maker, if I had not learnt
To fix my postulate better. Dost thou
  dream
Of guarding some monopoly in heaven
Instead of earth? Why I can dream with
  thee
To the length of thy wings.
  Gab.   I do not dream.
This is not Heaven, even in a dream, nor
  earth,
As earth was once, first breathed among
  the stars,
Articulate glory from the mouth divine,
To which the myriad spheres thrilled
  audibly
Touched like a lute-string, and the sons
  of God
Said AMEN, singing it. I know that this
Is earth not new created but new cursed—
This, Eden's gate not opened but built up
With a final cloud of sunset. Do I dream?
Alas, not so! this is the Eden lost
By Lucifer the serpent! this the sword

(This sword alive with justice and with
    fire !)
That smote upon the forehead, Lucifer
The angel.   Wherefore, angel, go—de-
    part—
Enough is sinned and suffered.
   Luc.   By no means.
Here 's a brave earth to sin and suffer on.
It holds fast still—it cracks not under
    curse ;
It holds like mine immortal.   Presently
We'll sow it thick enough with graves
    as green
Or greener certes, than its knowledge-
    tree—
We'll have the cypress for the tree of life,
More eminent for shadow :—for the rest
We'll build it dark with towns and
    pyramids,
And temples, if it please you :—we'll
    have feasts
And funerals also, merrymakes and
    wars,
Till blood and wine shall mix and run
    along
Right o'er the edges.   And good Gabriel,
(Ye like that word in Heaven !) *I* too
    have strength—
Strength to behold Him and not worship
    Him,
Strength to fall from Him and not cry
    on Him,
Strength to be in the universe and yet
Neither God nor His servant.   The red
    sign
Burnt on my forehead, which you taunt
    me with,
Is God's sign that it bows not unto God,
The potter's mark upon his work, to show
It rings well to the striker.   I and the
    earth
Can bear more curse.
   Gab.   O miserable earth,
O ruined angel !
   Luc.   Well, and if it be !
I CHOSE this ruin ; I elected it
Of my will, not of service.   What I do,
I do volitient, not obedient,
And overtop thy crown with my despair.
My sorrow crowns me.   Get thee back
    to Heaven,
And leave me to the earth which is mine
    own

In virtue of her ruin, as I hers
In virtue of my revolt ! turn thou from
    both
That bright, impassive, passive angel-
    hood,
And spare to read us backward any more
Of the spent hallelujahs.
   Gab.   Spirit of scorn,
I might say, of unreason ! I might say,
That who despairs, acts ; that who acts,
    connives
With God's relations set in time and
    space ;
That who elects, assumes a something
    good
Which God made possible ; that who
    lives, obeys
The law of a Life-maker . . .
   Luc.   Let it pass.
No more, thou Gabriel ! What if I stand up
And strike my brow against the crystalline
Roofing the creatures,—shall I say, for
    that,
My stature is too high for me to stand,—
Henceforward I must sit ?   Sit *thou.*
   Gab.   I kneel.
   Luc. A heavenly answer.   Get thee
    to thy Heaven,
And leave my earth to me.
   Gab.   Through Heaven and earth
God's will moves freely, and I follow it,
As colour follows light.   He overflows
The firmamental walls with deity,
Therefore with love ; His lightnings go
    abroad,
His pity may do so, His angels must,
Whene'er He gives them charges.
   Luc.   Verily,
I and my demons, who are spirits of scorn,
Might hold this charge of standing with
    a sword
'Twixt man and his inheritance, as well
As the benignest angel of you all.
   Gab. Thou speakest in the shadow of
    thy change.
If thou hadst gazed upon the face of God
This morning for a moment, thou hadst
    known
That only pity fitly can chastise.
Hate but avenges.
   Luc.   As it is, I know
Something of pity.   When I reeled in
    Heaven,

And my sword grew too heavy for my
   grasp,
Stabbing through matter, which it could
   not pierce
So much as the first shell of,—toward
   the throne ;
When I fell back, down,—staring up as
   I fell,—
The lightnings holding open my scathed
   lids,
And that thought of the infinite of God,
Hurled after to precipitate descent ;
When countless angel faces still and
   stern
Pressed out upon me from the level
   heavens
Adown the abysmal spaces, and I fell
Trampled down by your stillness, and
   struck blind
By the sight within your eyes,—'twas
   then I knew
How ye could pity, my kind angelhood !
   Gab. Alas, discrowned one, by the
   truth in me
Which God keeps in me, I would give
   away
All—save that truth and His love keeping
   it,—
To lead thee home again into the light
And hear thy voice chant with the
   morning stars,
When their rays tremble round them
   with much song
Sung in more gladness !
   Luc.   Sing, my Morning Star !
Last beautiful, last heavenly, that I loved !
If I could drench thy golden locks with
   tears,
What were it to this angel ?
   Gab.   What love is.
And now I have named God.
   Luc.   Yet Gabriel,
By the lie in me which I keep myself,
Thou 'rt a false swearer. Were it other-
   wise,
What dost thou here, vouchsafing tender
   thoughts
To that earth-angel or earth-demon—
   which,
Thou and I have not solved the problem
   yet
Enough to argue,—that fallen Adam
   there,—

That red-clay and a breath ! who must,
   forsooth,
Live in a new apocalypse of sense,
With beauty and music waving in his
   trees
And running in his rivers, to make glad
His soul made perfect ?—is it not for hope,
A hope within thee deeper than thy truth,
Of finally conducting him and his
To fill the vacant thrones of me and mine,
Which affront Heaven with their vacuity?
   Gab. Angel, there are no vacant
   thrones in Heaven
To suit thy empty words. Glory and life
Fulfil their own depletions ; and if God
Sighed you far from Him, His next
   breath drew in
A compensative splendour up the vast,
Flushing the starry arteries.
   Luc.   With a change !
So, let the vacant thrones and gardens too
Fill as may please you !—and be pitiful,
As ye translate that word, to the de-
   throned
And exiled, man or angel. The fact
   stands,
That I, the rebel, the cast out and down,
Am here and will not go; while there,
   along
The light to which ye flash the desert out,
Flies your adopted Adam, your red-clay
In two kinds, both being flawed. Why,
   what is this ?
Whose work is this ? Whose hand was
   in the work ?
Against whose hand ? In this last strife,
   methinks,
I am not a fallen angel !
   Gab.   Dost thou know
Aught of those exiles ?
   Luc.   Aye: I know they have fled
Silent all day along the wilderness :
I know they wear, for burden on their
   backs,
The thought of a shut gate of Paradise,
And faces of the marshalled cherubim
Shining against, not for them ; and I know
They dare not look in one another's
   face,—
As if each were a cherub !
   Gab.   Dost thou know
Aught of their future ?
   Luc.   Only as much as this :

That evil will increase and multiply
Without a benediction.
    Gab.   Nothing more ?
    Luc. Why so the angels taunt ! What
    should be more ?
    Gab. God is more.
    Luc.   Proving what ?
    Gab.   That He is God,
And capable of saving. Lucifer,
I charge thee by the solitude He kept
Ere He created,—leave the earth to God !
    Luc. My foot is on the earth, firm as
    my sin.
    Gab. I charge thee by the memory of
    Heaven
Ere any sin was done,—leave earth to
    God !
    Luc. My sin is on the earth, to reign
    thereon.
    Gab. I charge thee by the choral song
    we sang,
When up against the white shore of our
    feet,
The depths of the creation swelled and
    brake,—
And the new worlds, the beaded foam
    and flower
Of all that coil, roared outward into space
On thunder-edges,—leave the earth to
    God !
    Luc. My woe is on the earth, to curse
    thereby.
    Gab. I charge thee by that mournful
    Morning Star
Which trembles . . .
    Luc.   Enough spoken. As the pine
In norland forest drops its weight of
    snows
By a night's growth, so, growing toward
    my ends,
I drop thy counsels. Farewell. Gabriel !
Watch out thy service ; I achieve my will.
And peradventure in the after years,
When thoughtful men shall bend their
    spacious brows
Upon the storm and strife seen every-
    where
To ruffle their smooth manhood and
    break up
With lurid lights of intermittent hope
Their human fear and wrong,—they
    may discern
The heart of a lost angel in the earth.

CHORUS OF EDEN SPIRITS

(Chanting from paradise, while ADAM *and*
EVE *fly across the Sword-glare).*

Hearken, oh hearken ! let your souls
    behind you
    Turn, gently moved !
Our voices feel along the Dread to find you,
    O lost, beloved !
Through the thick-shielded and strong-
    marshalled angels,
    They press and pierce :
Our requiems follow fast on our evan-
    gels,—
    Voice throbs in verse.
We are but orphaned spirits left in Eden
    A time ago.
God gave us golden cups, and we were
    bidden
    To feed you so.
But now our right hand hath no cup
    remaining,
    No work to do,
The mystic hydromel is spilt, and stain-
    ing
    The whole earth through.
Most ineradicable stains, for showing
    (Not interfused !)
That brighter colours were the world's
    foregoing,
    Than shall be used.
Hearken, oh hearken ! ye shall hearken
    surely
    For years and years,
The noise beside you, dripping coldly,
    purely,
    Of spirits' tears.
The yearning to a beautiful denied you,
    Shall strain your powers.
Ideal sweetnesses shall over-glide you,
    Resumed from ours.
In all your music, our pathetic minor
    Your ears shall cross ;
And all good gifts shall mind you of
    diviner,
    With sense of loss.
We shall be near you in your poet-
    languors
    And wild extremes,
What time ye vex the desert with vain
    angers,
    Or mock with dreams.

And when upon you, weary after roaming,
    Death's seal is put,
By the foregone ye shall discern the
    coming,
    Through eyelids shut.

Spirits of the trees.

Hark! the Eden trees are stirring,
Soft and solemn in your hearing!
Oak and linden, palm and fir,
Tamarisk and juniper,
Each still throbbing in vibration
Since that crowning of creation
When the God-breath spake abroad,
Let us make man like to God!
And the pine stood quivering
As the awful word went by,
Like a vibrant music-string
Stretched from mountain-peak to sky.
And the platan did expand
Slow and gradual, branch and head;
And the cedar's strong black shade
Fluttered brokenly and grand.
Grove and wood were swept aslant
In emotion jubilant.

Voice of the same, but softer.

Which divine impulsion cleaves
In dim movements to the leaves
Dropt and lifted, dropt and lifted
In the sunlight greenly sifted,—
In the sunlight and the moonlight
Greenly sifted through the trees.
Ever wave the Eden trees
In the nightlight and the noonlight,
With a ruffling of green branches
Shaded off to resonances,
Never stirred by rain or breeze.
    Fare ye well, farewell!
The sylvan sounds, no longer audible,
    Expire at Eden's door.
Each footstep of your treading
Treads out some murmur which ye
    heard before.
    Farewell! the trees of Eden
    Ye shall hear nevermore.

River-spirits.

Hark! the flow of the four rivers—
    Hark the flow!
How the silence round you shivers,
While our voices through it go,
    Cold and clear.

A softer voice.

Think a little, while ye hear,
    Of the banks
Where the willows and the deer
Crowd in intermingled ranks,
As if all would drink at once
Where the living water runs!—
Of the fishes' golden edges
Flashing in and out the sedges;
Of the swans on silver thrones,
Floating down the winding streams
With impassive eyes turned shoreward
And a chant of undertones,—
And the lotus leaning forward
To help them into dreams.
    Fare ye well, farewell!
The river-sounds, no longer audible,
    Expire at Eden's door.
Each footstep of your treading
Treads out some murmur which ye
    heard before.
    Farewell! the streams of Eden,
    Ye shall hear nevermore.

Bird-spirit.

I am the nearest nightingale
That singeth in Eden after you;
And I am singing loud and true,
And sweet,—I do not fail.
I sit upon a cypress bough,
Close to the gate, and I fling my song
Over the gate and through the mail
Of the warden angels marshalled
    strong,—
    Over the gate and after you!
And the warden angels let it pass,
Because the poor brown bird, alas,
    Sings in the garden, sweet and true.
And I build my song of high pure notes,
    Note over note, height over height,
    Till I strike the arch of the Infinite,
And I bridge abysmal agonies
With strong, clear calms of har-
    monies,—
And something abides, and something
    floats,
In the song which I sing after you.
    Fare ye well, farewell!
The creature-sounds, no longer audible,
    Expire at Eden's door.
Each footstep of your treading
Treads out some cadence which ye
    heard before.

Farewell! the birds of Eden,
Ye shall hear nevermore.

Flower-spirits.

We linger, we linger,
   The last of the throng,
Like the tones of a singer
   Who loves his own song.
We are spirit-aromas
   Of blossom and bloom.
We call your thoughts home as
   Ye breathe our perfume,—
To the amaranth's splendour
   Afire on the slopes;
To the lily-bells tender,
   And grey heliotropes;
To the poppy-plains keeping
   Such dream-breath and blee
That the angels there stepping
   Grew whiter to see:
To the nook, set with moly,
   Ye jested one day in,
Till your smile waxed too holy
   And left your lips praying :
To the rose in the bower-place,
   That dripped o'er you sleeping ;
To the asphodel flower-place,
   Ye walked ankle-deep in !
We pluck at your raiment,
   We stroke down your hair,
We faint in our lament
   And pine into air.
      Fare ye well, farewell !
The Eden scents, no longer sensible,
   Expire at Eden's door.
Each footstep of your treading
Treads out some fragrance which ye
   knew before.
Farewell ! the flowers of Eden,
Ye shall smell nevermore.

[*There is silence.* ADAM *and* EVE *fly on,
and never look back. Only a colossal
shadow, as of the dark* Angel *passing
quickly, is cast upon the Sword-glare.*

SCENE.—*The extremity of the Sword-glare.*

Adam. Pausing a moment on this
   outer edge
Where the supernal sword-glare cuts in
   light
The dark exterior desert,—hast thou
   strength,

Beloved, to look behind us to the gate ?
   Eve. Have I not strength to look up
      to thy face ?
   Adam. We need be strong : yon spec-
      tacle of cloud
Which seals the gate up to the final doom,
Is God's seal manifest. There seem to lie
A hundred thunders in it, dark and dead ;
The unmolten lightnings vein it motion-
   less ;
And, outward from its depth, the self-
   moved sword
Swings slow its awful gnomon of red fire
From side to side, in pendulous horror
   slow,
Across the stagnant, ghastly glare thrown
   flat
On the intermediate ground from that to
   this.
The angelic hosts, the archangelic pomps,
Thrones, dominations, princedoms, rank
   on rank,
Rising sublimely to the feet of God,
On either side and overhead the gate,
Show like a glittering and sustainèd
   smoke
Drawn to an apex. That their faces shine
Betwixt the solemn clasping of their
   wings
Clasped high to a silver point above
   their heads,—
We only guess from hence, and not dis-
   cern.
   Eve. Though we were near enough
      to see them shine,
The shadow on thy face was awfuller,
To me, at least,—to me—than all their
   light.
   Adam. What is this, Eve ? thou
      droppest heavily
In a heap earthward, and thy body heaves
Under the golden floodings of thine hair !
   Eve. O Adam, Adam ! by that name
      of Eve—
Thine Eve, thy life—which suits me
   little now,
Seeing that I now confess myself thy
   death
And thine undoer, as the snake was
   mine,—
I do adjure thee, put me straight away,
Together with my name. Sweet, punish
   me !

O Love, be just! and, ere we pass beyond
The light cast outward by the fiery sword,
Into the dark which earth must be to us,
Bruise my head with thy foot,—as the
        curse said
My seed shall the first tempter's!
        strike with curse,
As God struck in the garden! and as HE,
Being satisfied with justice and with
        wrath,
Did roll His thunder gentler at the
        close,—
Thou, peradventure, mayst at last recoil
To some soft need of mercy. Strike, my
        lord!
I, also, after tempting, writhe on the
        ground,
And I would feed on ashes from thine
        hand,
As suits me, O my tempted!
    Adam.   My beloved,
Mine Eve and life—I have no other name
For thee or for the sun than what ye are,
My utter life and light! If we have fallen,
It is that we have sinned,—we: God is
        just;
And, since His curse doth comprehend
        us both,
It must be that His balance holds the
        weights
Of first and last sin on a level. What!
Shall I who had not virtue to stand straight
Among the hills of Eden, here assume
To mend the justice of the perfect God,
By piling up a curse upon His curse,
Against thee—thee—
    Eve.   For so, perchance, thy God
Might take thee into grace for scorning me;
Thy wrath against the sinner giving proof
Of inward abrogation of the sin.
And so, the blessed angels might come
        down
And walk with thee as erst,—I think
        they would,—
Because I was not near to make them sad
Or soil the rustling of their innocence.
    Adam. They know me. I am deepest
        in the guilt,
If last in the transgression.
    Eve.   THOU!
    Adam.   If God,
Who gave the right and joyaunce of the
        world

Both unto thee and me,—gave thee to me,
The best gift last, the last sin was the
        worst,
Which sinned against more complement
        of gifts
And grace of giving. God! I render back
Strong benediction and perpetual praise
From mortal feeble lips (as incense-
        smoke,
Out of a little censer, may fill heaven),
That Thou, in striking my benumbèd
        hands
And forcing them to drop all other boons
Of beauty and dominion and delight,—
Hast left this well-beloved Eve, this life
Within life, this best gift between their
        palms,
In gracious compensation!
    Eve.   Is it thy voice?
Or some saluting angel's—calling home
My feet into the garden?
    Adam.   O my God!
I, standing here between the glory and
        dark,—
The glory of thy wrath projected forth
From Eden's wall, the dark of our distress
Which settles a step off in that drear
        world—
Lift up to Thee the hands from whence
        hath fallen
Only creation's sceptre,—thanking Thee
That rather Thou hast cast me out with *her*
Than left me lorn of her in paradise,
With angel looks and angel songs around
To show the absence of her eyes and voice,
And make society full desertness
Without her use in comfort!
    Eve.   Where is loss?
Am I in Eden? can another speak
Mine own love's tongue?
    Adam.   Because with *her*, I stand
Upright, as far as can be in this fall,
And look away from heaven which doth
        accuse,
And look away from earth which doth
        convict,
Into her face, and crown my discrowned
        brow
Out of her love, and put the thought of her
Around me, for an Eden full of birds,
And lift her body up—thus—to my heart,
And with my lips upon her lips,—thus,
        thus,—

Do quicken and sublimate my mortal
  breath
Which cannot climb against the grave's
  steep sides
But overtops this grief!
  Eve.   I am renewed.
My eyes grow with the light which is in
  thine;
The silence of my heart is full of sound.
Hold me up—so! Because I comprehend
This human love, I shall not be afraid
Of any human death; and yet because
I know this strength of love, I seem to
  know
Death's strength by that same sign.
  Kiss on my lips,
To shut the door close on my rising soul,—
Lest it pass outwards in astonishment
And leave thee lonely.
  Adam.   Yet thou liest, Eve,
Bent heavily on thyself across mine arm,
Thy face flat to the sky.
  Eve.   Aye! and the tears
Running, as it might seem, my life from
  me,
They run so fast and warm. Let me lie so,
And weep so, as if in a dream or prayer,
Unfastening, clasp by clasp, the hard,
  tight thought
Which clipped my heart and showed me
  evermore
Loathed of thy justice as I loathe the
  snake,
And as the pure ones loathe our sin.
  To-day,
All day, beloved, as we fled across
This desolating radiance cast by swords
Not suns,—my lips prayed soundless to
  myself,
Striking against each other—'O Lord
  God!'
('Twas so I prayed) 'I ask Thee by my sin,
And by thy curse, and by thy blameless
  heavens,
Make dreadful haste to hide me from
  thy face
And from the face of my beloved here
For whom I am no helpmeet, quick away
Into the new dark mystery of death;
I will lie still there, I will make no plaint,
I will not sigh, nor sob, nor speak a word,
Nor struggle to come back beneath the
  sun

Where peradventure I might sin anew
Against Thy mercy and his pleasure.
  Death,
O death, whate'er it be, is good enough
For such as I am.—While for Adam
  here
No voice shall say again, in heaven or
  earth,
It is not good for him to be alone.'
  Adam. And was it good for such
  a prayer to pass,
My unkind Eve, betwixt our mutual lives?
If I am exiled, must I be bereaved?
  Eve. 'Twas an ill prayer: it shall be
  prayed no more;
And God did use it like a foolishness,
Giving no answer. Now my heart has
  grown
Too high and strong for such a foolish
  prayer;
Love makes it strong: and since I was
  the first
In the transgression, with a steady foot
I will be first to tread from this sword-
  glare
Into the outer darkness of the waste,—
And thus I do it.
  Adam.   Thus I follow thee,
As erewhile in the sin.—What sounds!
  what sounds!
I feel a music which comes straight from
  Heaven,
As tender as a watering dew.
  Eve.   I think
That angels—not those guarding Para-
  dise,—
But the love-angels, who came erst to us,
And when we said 'GOD,' fainted un-
  awares
Back from our mortal presence unto God,
(As if He drew them inward in a breath)
His name being heard of them,—I think
  that they
With sliding voices lean from heavenly
  towers,
Invisible but gracious. Hark—how soft!

CHORUS OF INVISIBLE ANGELS.
  Faint and tender.

  Mortal man and woman,
    Go upon your travel!
  Heaven assist the Human
    Smoothly to unravel

All that web of pain
  Wherein ye are holden.
Do ye know our voices
  Chanting down the Golden?
Do ye guess our choice is,
  Being unbeholden,
To be hearkened by you yet again?

This pure door of opal
  God hath shut between us,—
Us, his shining people,
  You, who once have seen us
And are blinded new!
  Yet, across the doorway,
Past the silence reaching,
  Farewells evermore may,
Blessing in the teaching,
  Glide from us to you.

First semichorus.

Think how erst your Eden,
Day on day succeeding,
  With our presence glowed.
We came as if the Heavens were bowed
To a milder music rare.
Ye saw us in our solemn treading,
  Treading down the steps of cloud,
  While our wings, outspreading
  Double calms of whiteness,
  Dropped superfluous brightness
Down from stair to stair.

Second semichorus.

Or oft, abrupt though tender,
  While ye gazed on space,
We flashed our angel-splendour
  In either human face.
With mystic lilies in our hands,
From the atmospheric bands
Breaking with a sudden grace,
  We took you unaware!
While our feet struck glories
  Outward, smooth and fair,
Which we stood on floorwise,
  Platformed in mid air.

First semichorus.

Or oft, when Heaven-descended,
  Stood we in your wondering sight
In a mute apocalypse!
With dumb vibrations on our lips
  From hosannas ended,
  And grand half-vanishings
  Of the empyreal things
  Within our eyes belated,

Till the heavenly Infinité
Falling off from the Created,
Left our inward contemplation
Opened into ministration.

Chorus.

Then upon our axle turning
Of great joy to sympathy,
We sang out the morning
  Broadening up the sky.
  Or we drew
  Our music through
The noontide's hush and heat and shine,
Informed with our intense Divine!
Interrupted vital notes
Palpitating hither, thither,
Burning out into the ether,
Sensible like fiery motes.
  Or, whenever twilight drifted
  Through the cedar masses,
  The globed sun we lifted,
Trailing purple, trailing gold
  Out between the passes
Of the mountains manifold,
  To anthems slowly sung!
While he, aweary, half in swoon
For joy to hear our climbing tune
Transpierce the stars' concentric rings,—
The burden of his glory flung
In broken lights upon our wings.

[*The chant dies away confusedly, and*
  LUCIFER *appears.*

Luc. Now may all fruits be pleasant
  to thy lips,
Beautiful Eve! The times have somewhat
  changed
Since thou and I had talk beneath a tree,
Albeit ye are not gods yet.
  Eve.   Adam! hold
My right hand strongly. It is Lucifer—
And we have love to lose.
  Adam.   I' the name of God,
Go apart from us, O thou Lucifer!
And leave us to the desert thou hast
  made
Out of thy treason. Bring no serpent-
  slime
Athwart this path kept holy to our tears,
Or we may curse thee with their bitter-
  ness.
  Luc. Curse freely! curses thicken.
  Why, this Eve

Who thought me once part worthy of
    her ear
And somewhat wiser than the other
    beasts,—
Drawing together her large globes of eyes,
The light of which is throbbing in and out
Their steadfast continuity of gaze,—
Knots her fair eyebrows in so hard a knot,
And down from her white heights of
    womanhood
Looks on me so amazed,—I scarce should
    fear
To wager such an apple as she plucked,
Against one riper from the tree of life,
That she could curse too—as a woman
    may—
Smooth in the vowels.

Eve.   So—speak wickedly!
I like it best so. Let thy words be
    wounds,—
For, so, I shall not fear thy power to hurt.
Trench on the forms of good by open ill—
For, so, I shall wax strong and grand
    with scorn,
Scorning myself for ever trusting thee
As far as thinking, ere a snake ate dust,
He could speak wisdom.

Luc.   Our new gods, it seems,
Deal more in thunders than in courtesies.
And, sooth, mine own Olympus, which
    anon
I shall build up to loud-voiced imagery
From all the wandering visions of the
    world,
May show worse railing than our lady Eve
Pours o'er the rounding of her argent arm.
But why should this be? Adam pardoned
    Eve.

Adam. Adam loved Eve. Jehovah
    pardon both.

Eve. Adam forgave Eve — because
    loving Eve.

Luc. So, well. Yet Adam was un-
    done of Eve,
As both were by the snake. Therefore
    forgive,
In like wise, fellow-temptress, the poor
    snake—
Who stung there, not so poorly! [*Aside.*

Eve.   Hold thy wrath,
Beloved Adam! let me answer him;
For this time he speaks truth, which
    we should hear,

And asks for mercy, which I most should
    grant,
In like wise, as he tells us—in like wise!
And therefore I thee pardon, Lucifer,
As freely as the streams of Eden flowed
When we were happy by them. So,
    depart;
Leave us to walk the remnant of our time
Out mildly in the desert. Do not seek
To harm us any more or scoff at us,
Or ere the dust be laid upon our face,
To find there the communion of the dust
And issue of the dust.—Go.

Adam.   At once, go.

Luc. Forgive! and go! Ye images
    of clay,
Shrunk somewhat in the mould,—what
    jest is this?
What words are these to use? By what
    a thought
Conceive ye of me? Yesterday—a snake!
To-day—what?

Adam.   A strong spirit.

Eve.   A sad spirit.

Adam. Perhaps a fallen angel.—Who
    shall say!

Luc. Who told thee, Adam?

Adam.   Thou! The prodigy
Of thy vast brows and melancholy eyes
Which comprehend the heights of some
    great fall.
I think that thou hast one day worn a
    crown
Under the eyes of God.

Luc.   And why of God?

Adam. It were no crown else.
    Verily, I think
Thou'rt fallen far. I had not yesterday
Said it so surely, but I know to-day
Grief by grief, sin by sin!

Luc.   A crown, by a crown.

Adam. Aye, mock me! now I know
    more than I knew:
Now I know thou art fallen below hope
Of final re-ascent.

Luc.   Because?

Adam.   Because
A spirit who expected to see God,
Though at the last point of a million
    years,
Could dare no mockery of a ruined man
Such as this Adam.

Luc.   Who is high and bold—

Be it said passing !—of a good red clay
Discovered on some top of Lebanon,
Or haply of Aornus, beyond sweep
Of the black eagle's wing ! A furlong
    lower
Had made a meeker king for Eden. Soh!
Is it not possible, by sin and grief
(To give the things your names) that
    spirits should rise
Instead of falling ?
    Adam.   Most impossible.
The Highest being the Holy and the Glad,
Whoever rises must approach delight
And sanctity in the act.
    Luc.   Ha, my clay-king!
Thou wilt not rule by wisdom very long
The after generations. Earth, methinks,
Will disinherit thy philosophy
For a new doctrine suited to thine heirs,
And class these present dogmas with the
    rest
Of the old-world traditions, Eden fruits
And Saurian fossils.
    Eve.   Speak no more with him,
Beloved ! it is not good to speak with him.
Go from us, Lucifer, and speak no more !
We have no pardon which thou dost not
    scorn,
Nor any bliss, thou seest, for coveting,
Nor innocence for staining. Being bereft,
We would be alone.—Go.
    Luc.   Ah ! ye talk the same,
All of you—spirits and clay—go, and
    depart !
In Heaven they said so ; and at Eden's
    gate,—
And here, reiterant, in the wilderness.
None saith, Stay with me, for thy face
    is fair !
None saith, Stay with me, for thy voice
    is sweet !
And yet I was not fashioned out of clay.
Look on me, woman ! Am I beautiful ?
    Eve. Thou hast a glorious darkness.
    Luc.   Nothing more ?
    Eve. I think, no more.
    Luc.   False Heart—
    thou thinkest more !
Thou canst not choose but think, as
    I praise God,
Unwillingly but fully, that I stand
Most absolute in beauty. As yourselves
Were fashioned very good at best, so *we*

Sprang very beauteous from the creant
    Word
Which thrilled behind us, God Himself
    being moved
When that august work of a perfect shape
His dignities of sovran angel-hood
Swept out into the universe,—divine
With thunderous movements, earnest
    looks of gods,
And silver-solemn clash of cymbal wings !
Whereof was I, in motion and in form,
A part not poorest. And yet,—yet,
    perhaps,
This beauty which I speak of, is not here,
As God's voice is not here, nor even my
    crown—
I do not know. What is this thought
    or thing
Which I call beauty ? is it thought, or
    thing ?
Is it a thought accepted for a thing ?
Or both ? or neither ?—a pretext—a word ?
Its meaning flutters in me like a flame
Under my own breath : my perceptions
    reel
For evermore around it, and fall off,
As if it too were holy.
    Eve.   Which it is.
    Adam. The essence of all beauty,
    I call love.
The attribute, the evidence, and end,
The consummation to the inward sense,
Of beauty apprehended from without,
I still call love. As form, when colour-
    less,
Is nothing to the eye,—that pine-tree
    there,
Without its black and green, being all
    a blank,—
So, without love, is beauty undiscerned
In man or angel. Angel ! rather ask
What love is in thee, what love moves
    to thee,
And what collateral love moves on with
    thee ;
Then shalt thou know if thou art beautiful.
    Luc. Love ! what is love ? I lose it.
    Beauty and love
I darken to the image. Beauty—love !

[*He fades away, while a low music sounds.*

    Adam. Thou art pale, Eve.
    Eve.   The precipice of ill

Down this colossal nature, dizzies me—
And, hark! the starry harmony remote
Seems measuring the heights from
      whence he fell.
   Adam. Think that we have not fallen
      so. By the hope
And aspiration, by the love and faith,
We do exceed the stature of this angel.
   Eve. Happier we are than he is, by
      the death.
   Adam. Or rather, by the life of the
      Lord God!
How dim the angel grows, as if that
      blast
Of music swept him back into the dark.

   [*The music is stronger, gathering itself
      into uncertain articulation.*

   Eve. It throbs in on us like a plaintive
      heart,
Pressing, with slow pulsations, vibrative,
Its gradual sweetness through the yield-
      ing air,
To such expression as the stars may use,
Most starry-sweet and strange! With
      every note
That grows more loud, the angel grows
      more dim,
Receding in proportion to approach,
Until he stand afar,—a shade.
   Adam.   Now, words.

SONG OF THE MORNING STAR TO
      LUCIFER.

*He fades utterly away and vanishes,
      as it proceeds.*

Mine orbèd image sinks
   Back from thee, back from thee,
As thou art fallen, methinks,
   Back from me, back from me.
   O my light-bearer,
   Could another fairer
Lack to thee, lack to thee?
   Ah, ah, Heosphoros!
I loved thee with the fiery love of stars
Who love by burning, and by loving move,
Too near the thronèd Jehovah not to love.
   Ah, ah, Heosphoros!
Their brows flash fast on me from gliding
      cars,
   Pale-passioned for my loss.
   Ah, ah, Heosphoros!

Mine orbèd heats drop cold
   Down from thee, down from thee,
As fell thy grace of old
   Down from me, down from me.
   O my light-bearer,
   Is another fairer
Won to thee, won to thee?
   Ah, ah, Heosphoros,
   Great love preceded loss,
Known to thee, known to thee.
   Ah, ah!
Thou, breathing thy communicable grace
   Of life into my light,
Mine astral faces, from thine angel face,
   Hast inly fed,
And flooded me with radiance overmuch
   From thy pure height.
   Ah, ah!
Thou, with calm, floating pinions both
      ways spread,
   Erect, irradiated,
   Didst sting my wheel of glory
   On, on before thee
Along the Godlight by a quickening touch!
   Ha, ha!
Around, around the firmamental ocean
I swam expanding with delirious fire!
Around, around, around, in blind desire
To be drawn upward to the Infinite—
   Ha, ha!

Until, the motion flinging out the motion
To a keen whirl of passion and avidity,
To a dim whirl of languor and delight,
I wound in girant orbits smooth and
      white
   With that intense rapidity.
   Around, around,
I wound and interwound,
While all the cyclic heavens about me
      spun.
Stars, planets, suns, and moons dilated
      broad,
Then flashed together into a single sun,
   And wound, and wound in one,
And as they wound I wound,—around,
      around,
In a great fire I almost took for God!
   Ha, ha, Heosphoros!

Thine angel glory sinks
   Down from me, down from me—
My beauty falls, methinks,
   Down from thee, down from thee!

O my light-bearer,
O my path-preparer,
Gone from me, gone from me !
Ah, ah, Heosphoros !
I cannot kindle underneath the brow
Of this new angel here, who is not thou.
All things are altered since that time
    ago,—
And if I shine at eve, I shall not know.
    I am strange—I am slow.
        Ah, ah, Heosphoros !
Henceforward, human eyes of lovers be
The only sweetest sight that I shall see,
With tears between the looks raised up
    to me.
        Ah, ah !
When, having wept all night, at break
    of day
Above the folded hills they shall survey
My light, a little trembling, in the grey.
        Ah, ah !
And gazing on me, such shall com-
    prehend,
Through all my piteous pomp at morn
    or even
And melancholy leaning out of heaven,
That love, their own divine, may change
    or end,
    That love may close in loss !
    Ah, ah, Heosphoros !

SCENE.—*Farther on. A wild open coun-
try seen vaguely in the approaching
night.*

Adam. How doth the wide and
    melancholy earth
Gather her hills around us, grey and
    ghast,
And stare with blank significance of loss
Right in our faces ! Is the wind up ?
Eve.   Nay.
Adam. And yet the cedars and the
    junipers
Rock slowly through the mist, without a
    sound,
And shapes which have no certainty of
    shape
Drift duskly in and out between the pines,
And loom along the edges of the hills,
And lie flat, curdling in the open ground—
Shadows without a body, which con-
    tract

And lengthen as we gaze on them.
Eve.   Oh life
Which is not man's nor angel's !   What
    is this?
Adam. No cause for fear.   The circle
    of God's life
Contains all life beside.
Eve.   I think the earth
Is crazed with curse, and wanders from
    the sense
Of those first laws affixed to form and
    space
Or ever she knew sin.
Adam.   We will not fear :
We were brave sinning.
Eve.   Yea, I plucked the fruit
With eyes upturned to heaven and see-
    ing there
Our god-thrones, as the tempter said,—
    not GOD.
My heart, which beat then, sinks.   The
    sun hath sunk
Out of sight with our Eden.
Adam.   Night is near.
Eve. And God's curse, nearest.   Let
    us travel back
And stand within the sword-glare till
    we die,
Believing it is better to meet death
Than suffer desolation.
Adam.   Nay, beloved !
We must not pluck death from the
    Maker's hand,
As erst we plucked the apple : we must
    wait
Until He gives death as He gave us life,
Nor murmur faintly o'er the primal gift
Because we spoilt its sweetness with
    our sin.
Eve. Ah, ah ! dost thou discern what
    I behold?
Adam. I see all.   How the spirits in
    thine eyes
From their dilated orbits bound before
To meet the spectral Dread !
Eve.   I am afraid—
Ah, ah ! the twilight bristles wild with
    shapes
Of intermittent motion, aspect vague
And mystic bearings, which o'ercreep
    the earth,
Keeping slow time with horrors in the
    blood.

How near they reach ... and far! How
    grey they move—
Treading upon the darkness without feet,
And fluttering on the darkness without
    wings!
Some run like dogs, with noses to the
    ground;
Some keep one path, like sheep; some
    rock like trees;
Some glide like a fallen leaf; and some
    flow on
Copious as rivers.
    Adam.   Some spring up like fire—
And some coil ...
    Eve.   Ah, ah! dost thou pause to say
Like what?—coil like the serpent, when
    he fell
From all the emerald splendour of his
    height
And writhed, and could not climb against
    the curse,
Not a ring's length.   I am afraid—
    afraid—
I think it is God's will to make me
    afraid,—
Permitting THESE to haunt us in the place
Of His beloved angels—gone from us
Because we are not pure.   Dear Pity
    of God,
That didst permit the angels to go home
And live no more with us who are not
    pure,
Save *us* too from a loathly company—
Almost as loathly in our eyes, perhaps,
As *we* are in the purest!   Pity us—
Us too! nor shut us in the dark, away
From verity and from stability,
Or what we name such through the
    precedence
Of earth's adjusted uses,—leave us not
To doubt betwixt our senses and our
    souls,
Which are the more distraught and full
    of pain
And weak of apprehension.
    Adam.   Courage, Sweet!
The mystic shapes ebb back from us,
    and drop
With slow concentric movement, each
    on each,—
Expressing wider spaces,—and collapsed
In lines more definite for imagery
And clearer for relation, till the throng

Of shapeless spectra merge into a few
Distinguishable phantasms vague and
    grand
Which sweep out and around us vastily
And hold us in a circle and a calm.
    Eve.   Strange phantasms of pale
        shadow! there are twelve.
Thou who didst name all lives, hast
    names for these?
    Adam.   Methinks this is the zodiac of
        the earth,
Which rounds us with a visionary dread,
Responding with twelve shadowy signs
    of earth,
In fantasque apposition and approach,
To those celestial, constellated twelve
Which palpitate adown the silent nights
Under the pressure of the hand of God
Stretched wide in benediction.   At this
    hour,
Not a star pricketh the flat gloom of
    heaven!
But, girdling close our nether wilderness,
The zodiac-figures of the earth loom
    slow,—
Drawn out, as suiteth with the place
    and time,
In twelve colossal shades instead of stars,
Through which the ecliptic line of
    mystery
Strikes bleakly with an unrelenting
    scope,
Foreshowing life and death.
    Eve.   By dream or sense,
Do we see this?
    Adam.   Our spirits have climbed high
By reason of the passion of our grief,
And, from the top of sense, looked over
    sense,
To the significance and heart of things
Rather than things themselves.
    Eve.   And the dim twelve ...
    Adam.   Are dim exponents of the
        creature-life
As earth contains it.   Gaze on them,
    beloved!
By stricter apprehension of the sight,
Suggestions of the creatures shall assuage
The terror of the shadows,—what is
    known
Subduing the unknown and taming it
From all prodigious dread.   That phan-
    tasm, there,

Presents a lion, albeit twenty times
As large as any lion—with a roar
Set soundless in his vibratory jaws,
And a strange horror stirring in his mane.
And, there, a pendulous shadow seems
  to weigh—
Good against ill, perchance ; and there,
  a crab
Puts coldly out its gradual shadow-claws,
Like a slow blot that spreads,—till all
  the ground,
Crawled over by it, seems to crawl itself.
A bull stands hornèd here with gibbous
  glooms ;
And a ram likewise ! and a scorpion
  writhes
Its tail in ghastly slime and stings the
  dark.
This way a goat leaps with wild blank
  of beard ;
And here, fantastic fishes duskly float,
Using the calm for waters, while their fins
Throb out quick rhythms along the
  shallow air.
While images more human——
    Eve.   How he stands,
That phantasm of a man—who is not *thou!*
Two phantasms of two men !
    Adam.   One that sustains,
And one that strives,—resuming, so, the
  ends
Of manhood's curse of labour[1]. Dost
  thou see
That phantasm of a woman ?—
    Eve.   I have seen,
But look off to those small humanities[2]
Which draw me tenderly across my
  fear,
Lesser and fainter than my womanhood
Or yet thy manhood—with strange
  innocence
Set in the misty lines of head and hand.
They lean together ! I would gaze on
  them

---

[1] Adam recognizes in *Aquarius*, the water-
bearer, and *Sagittarius*, the archer, distinct
types of the man bearing and the man com-
bating,—the passive and active forms of human
labour. I hope that the preceding zodiacal signs
—transferred to the earthly shadow and repre-
sentative purpose—of Aries, Taurus, Cancer,
Leo, Libra, Scorpio, Capricornus, and Pisces,
are sufficiently obvious to the reader.

[2] Her maternal instinct is excited by *Gemini.*

Longer and longer, till my watching
  eyes,
As the stars do in watching anything.
Should light them forward from their
  outline vague
To clear configuration.

[*Two* Spirits, *of organic and inorganic
  nature, arise from the ground.*

                But what Shapes
Rise up between us in the open space,
And thrust me into horror, back from
  hope !
    Adam. Colossal Shapes—twin sovran
  images,
With a disconsolate, blank majesty
Set in their wondrous faces ! with no look,
And yet an aspect—a significance
Of individual life and passionate ends,
Which overcomes us gazing.
                  O bleak sound,
O shadow of sound, O phantasm of thin
  sound !
How it comes, wheeling as the pale
  moth wheels,
Wheeling and wheeling in continuous
  wail
Around the cyclic zodiac, and gains
  ' force,
And gathers, settling coldly like a moth,
On the wan faces of these images
We see before us,—whereby modified,
It draws a straight line of articulate song
From out that spiral faintness of lament,
And, by one voice, expresses many griefs.

First Spirit.

I am the spirit of the harmless earth.
  God spake me softly out among the
    stars,
As softly as a blessing of much worth ;
  And then, His smile did follow un-
    awares,
That all things fashioned so for use and
    duty
Might shine anointed with His chrism
    of beauty—
          Yet I wail !
I drave on with the worlds exultingly,
  Obliquely down the Godlight's gradual
    fall ;
Individual aspect and complexity
  Of giratory orb and interval

Lost in the fluent motion of delight
Toward the high ends of Being beyond
    sight—
       Yet I wail!

Second Spirit.

I am the spirit of the harmless beasts,
    Of flying things, and creeping things,
       and swimming;
Of all the lives, erst set at silent feasts,
    That found the love-kiss on the goblet
       brimming,
And tasted in each drop within the
    measure
The sweetest pleasure of their Lord's
    good pleasure—
       Yet I wail!
What a full hum of life around His lips
    Bore witness to the fullness of creation!
How all the grand words were full-laden
    ships
    Each sailing onward from enunciation
To separate existence,—and each bearing
The creature's power of joying, hoping,
    fearing!
       Yet I wail!

Eve. They wail, beloved! they speak
    of glory and God,
And they wail—wail. That burden of
    the song
Drops from it like its fruit, and heavily falls
Into the lap of silence.
Adam.   Hark, again!

First Spirit.

I was so beautiful, so beautiful,
    My joy stood up within me bold to add
A word to God's,—and, when His work
    was full,
    To 'very good,' responded 'very glad!'
Filtered through roses, did the light
    enclose me,
And bunches of the grape swam blue
    across me—
       Yet I wail!

Second Spirit.

I bounded with my panthers! I rejoiced
    In my young tumbling lions rolled
       together!
My stag, the river at his fetlocks, poised
    Then dipped his antlers through the
       golden weather

In the same ripple which the alligator
Left, in his joyous troubling of the
    water—
       Yet I wail!

First Spirit.

O my deep waters, cataract and flood,
    What wordless triumph did your voices
       render!
O mountain-summits, where the angels
    stood
And shook from head and wing thick
    dews of splendour!
How, with a holy quiet, did your Earthy
Accept that Heavenly, knowing ye were
    worthy!
       Yet I wail!

Second Spirit.

O my wild wood-dogs, with your listen-
    ing eyes!
    My horses—my ground-eagles, for
       swift fleeing!
My birds, with viewless wings of
    harmonies,
    My calm cold fishes of a silver being,
How happy were ye, living and possess-
    ing,
O fair half-souls capacious of full bless-
    ing!
       Yet I wail!

First Spirit.

I wail, I wail! Now hear my charge
    to-day,
    Thou man, thou woman, marked as
       the misdoers
By God's sword at your backs! I lent
    my clay
    To make your bodies, which had grown
       more flowers:
And now, in change for what I lent, ye
    give me
The thorn to vex, the tempest-fire to
    cleave me—
       And I wail!

Second Spirit.

I wail, I wail! Behold ye that I fasten
    My sorrow's fang upon your souls
       dishonoured?
Accursèd transgressors! down the steep
    ye hasten,—
    Your crown's weight on the world, to
       drag it downward

Unto your ruin. Lo! my lions, scenting
The blood of wars, roar hoarse and un-
relenting—
And I wail!

First Spirit.

I wail, I wail! Do you hear that I wail?
I had no part in your transgression—
none.
My roses on the bough did bud not pale,
My rivers did not loiter in the sun ;
I was obedient. Wherefore in my centre
Do I thrill at this curse of death and
winter?—
Do I wail?

Second Spirit.

I wail, I wail! I wail in the assault
Of undeserved perdition, sorely
wounded !
My nightingale sang sweet without a
fault,
My gentle leopards innocently bounded.
We were obedient. What is this con-
vulses
Our blameless life with pangs and fever
pulses?
And I wail!

Eve. I choose God's thunder and His
angels' swords
To die by, Adam, rather than such words.
Let us pass out and flee.
Adam. We cannot flee.
This zodiac of the creatures' cruelty
Curls round us, like a river cold and
drear,
And shuts us in, constraining us to hear.

First Spirit.

I feel your steps, O wandering sinners,
strike
A sense of death to me, and undug
graves !
The heart of earth, once calm, is trem-
bling like
The ragged foam along the ocean-
waves :
The restless earthquakes rock against
each other ;
The elements moan 'round me—'Mother,
mother '—
And I wail!

Second Spirit.

Your melancholy looks do pierce me
through ;
Corruption swathes the paleness of
your beauty.
Why have ye done this thing? What
did we do
That we should fall from bliss as ye
from duty ?
Wild shriek the hawks, in waiting for
their jesses,
Fierce howl the wolves along the wilder-
nesses—
And I wail!

Adam. To thee, the Spirit of the
harmless earth,
To thee, the Spirit of earth's harmless
lives,
Inferior creatures but still innocent,
Be salutation from a guilty mouth
Yet worthy of some audience and respect
From you who are not guilty. If we
have sinned,
God hath rebuked us, who is over us
To give rebuke or death, and if ye wail
Because of any suffering from our sin,
Ye who are under and not over us,
Be satisfied with God, if not with us,
And pass out from our presence in such
peace
As we have left you, to enjoy revenge
Such as the Heavens have made you.
Verily,
There must be strife between us, large
as sin.
Eve. No strife, mine Adam! Let us
not stand high
Upon the wrong we did to reach disdain,
Who rather should be humbler evermore
Since self-made sadder. Adam ! shall
I speak—
I who spake once to such a bitter end—
Shall I speak humbly now, who once
was proud ?
I. schooled by sin to more humility
Than thou hast, O mine Adam, O my
king—
My king, if not the world's ?
Adam. Speak as thou wilt.
Eve. Thus, then—my hand in thine—
.... Sweet, dreadful Spirits !
I pray you humbly in the name of God,

Not to say of these tears, which are im-
    pure—
Grant me such pardoning grace as can
    go forth
From clean volitions toward a spotted
    will,
From the wronged to the wronger, this
    and no more :
I do not ask more. I am 'ware, indeed,
That absolute pardon is impossible
From you to me, by reason of my sin,—
And that I cannot evermore, as once,
With worthy acceptation of pure joy,
Behold the trances of the holy hills
Beneath the leaning stars, or watch the
    vales
Dew-pallid with their morning ecstasy,—
Or hear the winds make pastoral peace
    between
Two grassy uplands,—and the river-wells
Work out their bubbling mysteries under
    ground,—
And all the birds sing, till for joy of song,
They lift their trembling wings as if to
    heave
The too-much weight of music from their
    heart
And float it up the ether. I am 'ware
That these things I can no more apprehend
With a pure organ into a full delight,—
The sense of beauty and of melody
Being no more aided in me by the sense
Of personal adjustment to those heights
Of what I see well-formed or hear well-
    tuned,
But rather coupled darkly and made
    ashamed
By my percipiency of sin and fall
In melancholy of humiliant thoughts.
But, oh! fair, dreadful Spirits—albeit this
Your accusation must confront my soul,
And your pathetic utterance and full gaze
Must evermore subdue me, be content—
Conquer me gently—as if pitying me,
Not to say loving ! let my tears fall thick
As watering dews of Eden, unre-
    proached ;
And when your tongues reprove me,
    make me smooth,
Not ruffled—smooth and still with your
    reproof,
And peradventure better while more sad.
For look to it, sweet Spirits, look well to it,

It will not be amiss in you who kept
The law of your own righteousness, and
    keep
The right of your own griefs to mourn
    themselves,—
To pity me twice fallen, from that, and
    this,
From joy of place, and also right of wail,
'I wail' being not for me—only ' I sin.'
Look to it, O sweet Spirits !—
                              For was I not,
At that last sunset seen in Paradise,
When all the westering clouds flashed
    out in throngs
Of sudden angel-faces, face by face,
All hushed and solemn, as a thought of
    God
Held them suspended,—was I not, that
    hour,
The lady of the world, princess of life,
Mistress of feast and favour? Could I
    touch
A rose with my white hand, but it became
Redder at once ? Could I walk leisurely
Along our swarded garden, but the grass
Tracked me with greenness ? Could I
    stand aside
A moment underneath a cornel-tree,
But all the leaves did tremble as alive
With songs of fifty birds who were made
    glad
Because I stood there ? Could I turn to
    look
With these twain eyes of mine, now
    weeping fast,
Now good for only weeping,—upon man,
Angel, or beast, or bird, but each rejoiced
Because I looked on him ? Alas, alas!
And is not this much woe, to cry 'alas!'
Speaking of joy ? And is not this more
    shame,
To have made the woe myself, from all
    that joy ?
To have stretched my hand, and plucked
    it from the tree,
And chosen it for fruit ? Nay, is not this
Still most despair,—to have halved that
    bitter fruit,
And ruined, so, the sweetest friend I have,
Turning the Greatest to mine enemy ?
    Adam. I will not hear thee speak so.
        Hearken, Spirits !
Our God, who is the enemy of none

But only of their sin, hath set your hope
And my hope, in a promise, on this Head.
Show reverence, then, and never bruise
her more
With unpermitted and extreme re-
proach,—
Lest, passionate in anguish, she fling
down
Beneath your trampling feet, God's gift
to us
Of sovranty by reason and free will,
Sinning against the province of the Soul!
To rule the soulless. Reverence her estate,
And pass out from her presence with no
words.

    Eve. O dearest Heart, have patience
with my heart!
O Spirits, have patience, 'stead of
reverence,
And let me speak, for, not being innocent,
It little doth become me to be proud,
And I am prescient by the very hope
And promise set upon me, that henceforth
Only my gentleness shall make me great,
My humbleness exalt me. Awful Spirits,
Be witness that I stand in your reproof
But one sun's length off from my happi-
ness—
Happy, as I have said, to look around,
Clear to look up!—And now! I need
not speak—
Ye see me what I am ; ye scorn me so,
Because ye see me what I have made
myself
From God's best making! Alas,—peace
foregone,
Love wronged, and virtue forfeit, and
tears wept
Upon all, vainly ! Alas, me ! alas,
Who have undone myself from all that
best,
Fairest and sweetest, to this wretchedest,
Saddest and most defiled—cast out, cast
down—
What word metes absolute loss? let
absolute loss
Suffice you for revenge. For *I*, who lived
Beneath the wings of angels yesterday,
Wander to-day beneath the roofless
world !
I, reigning the earth's empress yesterday,
Put off from me, to-day, your hate with
prayers !

I, yesterday, who answered the Lord
God,
Composed and glad as singing-birds the
sun,
Might shriek now from our dismal
desert, ' God,'
And hear Him make reply, ' What is
thy need,
Thou whom I cursed to-day ? '
    Adam.   Eve !
    Eve.   *I*, at last,
Who yesterday was helpmate and delight
Unto mine Adam, am to-day the grief
And curse-mete for him ! And, so, pity us,
Ye gentle Spirits, and pardon him and me,
And let some tender peace, made of our
pain,
Grow up betwixt us, as a tree might grow,
With boughs on both sides. In the shade
of which,
When presently ye shall behold us
dead,—
For the poor sake of our humility,
Breathe out your pardon on our breath-
less lips,
And drop your twilight dews against our
brows,
And stroking with mild airs our harm-
less hands
Left empty of all fruit, perceive your love
Distilling through your pity over us,
And suffer it, self-reconciled, to pass.

      LUCIFER *rises in the circle.*

    Luc. Who talks here of a complement
of grief ?
Of expiation wrought by loss and fall ?
Of hate subduable to pity ? Eve ?
Take counsel from thy counsellor the
snake,
And boast no more in grief, nor hope
from pain,
My docile Eve ! I teach you to despond,
Who taught you disobedience. Look
around ;—
Earth-spirits and phantasms hear you
talk unmoved,
As if ye were red clay again and talked
What are your words to them ? your
grief to them ?
Your deaths, indeed, to them ? Did the
hand pause
For *their* sake, in the plucking of the fruit,

That they should pause for *you*, in hating you?
Or will your grief or death, as did your sin,
Bring change upon their final doom? Behold,
Your grief is but your sin in the rebound,
And cannot expiate for it.
    Adam.   That is true.
    Luc. Aye, that is true. The clay-king testifies
To the snake's counsel,—hear him!— very true.
    Earth Spirits. I wail, I wail!
    Luc.   And certes, *that* is true.
Ye wail, ye all wail. Peradventure I
Could wail among you. O thou universe,
That holdest sin and woe,—more room for wail!
    Distant starry voice. Ah, ah, Heosphoros! Heosphoros!
    Adam. Mark Lucifer. He changes awfully.
    Eve. It seems as if he looked from grief to God
And could not see Him!—wretched Lucifer!
    Adam. How he stands—yet an angel!
    Earth Spirits.   We all wail!
    Luc. (*after a pause.*) Dost thou remember, Adam, when the curse
Took us in Eden? On a mountain-peak
Half-sheathed in primal woods and glittering
In spasms of awful sunshine at that hour,
A lion couched, part raised upon his paws,
With his calm, massive face turned full on thine,
And his mane listening. When the ended curse
Left silence in the world, right suddenly
He sprang up rampant and stood straight and stiff,
As if the new reality of death
Were dashed against his eyes, and roared so fierce
(Such thick carnivorous passion in his throat
Tearing a passage through the wrath and fear)
And roared so wild, and smote from all the hills
Such fast, keen echoes crumbling down the vales

Precipitately,—that the forest beasts,
One after one, did mutter a response
Of savage and of sorrowful complaint
Which trailed along the gorges. Then, at once,
He fell back, and rolled crashing from the height
Into the dusk of pines.
    Adam.   It might have been.
I heard the curse alone.
    Earth Spirits.   I wail, I wail!
    Luc. That lion is the type of what I am.
And as he fixed thee with his full-faced hate,
And roared, O Adam, comprehending doom,
So, gazing on the face of the Unseen,
I cry out here between the Heavens and Earth
My conscience of this sin, this woe, this wrath,
Which damn me to this depth.
    Earth Spirits.   I wail, I wail!
    Eve. I wail—O God!
    Luc.   I scorn you that ye wail,
Who use your petty griefs for pedestals
To stand on, beckoning pity from without,
And deal in pathos of antithesis
Of what ye *were* forsooth, and what ye are ;—
I scorn you like an angel! Yet, one cry
I, too, would drive up like a column erect,
Marble to marble, from my heart to Heaven,
A monument of anguish to transpierce
And overtop your vapory complaints
Expressed from feeble woes.
    Earth Spirits.   I wail, I wail!
    Luc. For, O ye Heavens, ye are my witnesses,
That *I*, struck out from nature in a blot,
The outcast and the mildew of things good,
The leper of angels, the excepted dust
Under the common rain of daily gifts,—
I the snake, I the tempter, I the cursed,—
To whom the highest and the lowest alike
Say, 'Go from us—we have no need of thee,'—
Was made by God like others. Good and fair,
He did create me!—ask Him, if not fair!
Ask, if I caught not fair and silvery

His blessing for chief angels on my head
Until it grew there, a crown crystallized!
Ask, if He never called me by my name,
Lucifer—kindly said as ' Gabriel '—
Lucifer—soft as 'Michael!' while serene
I, standing in the glory of the lamps,
Answered 'my Father,' innocent of shame
And of the sense of thunder. Ha! ye think,
White angels in your niches,—I repent,
And would tread down my own offences back
To service at the footstool? *that*'s read wrong!
I cry as the beast did, that I may cry—
Expansive, not appealing! Fallen so deep,
Against the sides of this prodigious pit
I cry—cry—dashing out the hands of wail
On each side, to meet anguish everywhere,
And to attest it in the ecstasy
And exaltation of a woe sustained
Because provoked and chosen.
                                    Pass along
Your wilderness, vain mortals! Puny griefs
In transitory shapes, be henceforth dwarfed
To your own conscience, by the dread extremes
Of what I am and have been. If ye have fallen,
It is but a step's fall,—the whole ground beneath
Strewn woolly soft with promise! if ye have sinned,
Your prayers tread high as angels! if ye have grieved,
Ye are too mortal to be pitiable,
The power to die disproves the right to grieve.
Go to! ye call this ruin? I half scorn
The ill I did you! Were ye wronged by me,
Hated and tempted and undone of me,—
Still, what's your hurt to mine of doing hurt,
Of hating, tempting, and so ruining?
This sword's *hilt* is the sharpest, and cuts through
The hand that wields it.
                          Go—I curse you all.

Hate one another—feebly—as ye can ;
I would not certes cut you short in hate :
Far be it from me! hate on as ye can!
I breathe into your faces, spirits of earth,
As wintry blast may breathe on wintry leaves
And lifting up their brownness show beneath
The branches bare. — Beseech you, spirits, give
To Eve, who beggarly entreats your love
For her and Adam when they shall be dead,
An answer rather fitting to the sin
Than to the sorrow—as the Heavens, I trow,
For justice' sake gave theirs.
                          I curse you both,
Adam and Eve! Say grace as after meat,
After my curses. May your tears fall hot
On all the hissing scorns o' the creatures here,—
And yet rejoice. Increase and multiply,
Ye in your generations, in all plagues,
Corruptions, melancholies, poverties,
And hideous forms of life and fears of death,—
The thought of death being alway imminent,
Immovable and dreadful in your life,
And deafly and dumbly insignificant
Of any hope beyond,—as death itself,
Whichever of you lieth dead the first,
Shall seem to the survivor—yet rejoice !
My curse catch at you strongly, body and soul,
And HE find no redemption—nor the wing
Of seraph move your way; and yet rejoice !
Rejoice,—because ye have not, set in you,
This hate which shall pursue you—this fire-hate
Which glares without, because it burns within,—
Which kills from ashes—this potential hate,
Wherein I, angel, in antagonism
To God and his reflex beatitudes,
Moan ever in the central universe
With the great woe of striving against Love—
And gasp for space amid the Infinite,
And toss for rest amid the Desertness,

Self-orphaned by my will, and self-elect
To kingship of resistant agony
Toward the Good round me—hating
    good and love,
And willing to hate good and to hate love,
And willing to will on so evermore,
Scorning the past and damning the To
    come—
Go and rejoice! I curse you.
                [LUCIFER *vanishes.*

Earth Spirits.

And we scorn you! there's no pardon
    Which can lean to you aright.
When your bodies take the guerdon
    Of the death-curse in our sight,
Then the bee that hummeth lowest shall
    transcend you:
Then ye shall not move an eyelid
    Though the stars look down your
        eyes;
And the earth which ye defilèd,
    Shall expose you to the skies,—
'Lo! these kings of ours, who sought
    to comprehend you.'

First Spirit.

And the elements shall boldly
    All your dust to dust constrain.
Unresistedly and coldly
    I will smite you with my rain.
From the slowest of my frosts is no
    receding.

Second Spirit.

And my little worm, appointed
    To assume a royal part,
He shall reign, crowned and anointed,
    O'er the noble human heart.
Give him counsel against losing of that
    Eden!

Adam.

Do ye scorn us? Back your scorn
Towards your faces grey and lorn,
As the wind drives back the rain,
Thus I drive with passion-strife,
I who stand beneath God's sun,
Made like God, and, though undone,
Not unmade for love and life.
Lo! ye utter threats in vain.
By my free will that chose sin,
By mine agony within
Round the passage of the fire,
By the pinings which disclose

That my native soul is higher
    Than what it chose,
We are yet too high, O Spirits, for your
    disdain.

Eve.

Nay, beloved! If these be low,
We confront them from no height.
We have stooped down to their level
By infecting them with evil,
And their scorn that meets our blow
    Scathes aright.
Amen.   Let it be so.

Earth Spirits.

We shall triumph—triumph greatly
    When ye lie beneath the sward.
There, our lily shall grow stately
    Though ye answer not a word,
And her fragrance shall be scornful of
    your silence:
While your throne ascending calmly
We, in heirdom of your soul,
Flash the river, lift the palm-tree,
    The dilated ocean roll
By the thoughts that throbbed within
    you, round the islands.

Alp and torrent shall inherit
    Your significance of will,
And the grandeur of your spirit
    Shall our broad savannahs fill;
In our winds, your exultations shall be
    springing.
Even your parlance which inveigles,
    By our rudeness shall be won.
Hearts poetic in our eagles
    Shall beat up against the sun
And strike downward in articulate clear
    singing.

Your bold speeches, our Behemoth
    With his thunderous jaw shall wield.
Your high fancies, shall our Mammoth
    Breathe sublimely up the shield
Of Saint Michael at God's throne, who
    waits to speed him!
Till the heaven's smooth-groovèd
    thunder
    Spinning back, shall leave them clear,
And the angels smiling wonder
    With dropt looks from sphere to
        sphere,
Shall cry, 'Ho, ye heirs of Adam! ye
    exceed him!'

Adam. Root out thine eyes, Sweet,
    from the dreary ground.
Beloved, we may be overcome by God,
But not by these.
    Eve. By God, perhaps, in these.
    Adam. I think, not so. Had God
        foredoomed despair,
He had not spoken hope. He may destroy
Certes, but not deceive.
    Eve. Behold this rose!
I plucked it in our bower of Paradise
This morning as I went forth, and my
    heart
Has beat against its petals all the day.
I thought it would be always red and full
As when I plucked it—*Is* it?—ye may
    see!
I cast it down to you that ye may see,
All of you!—count the petals lost of it,
And note the colours fainted! ye may see!
And I am as it is, who yesterday
Grew in the same place. Oh ye spirits
    of earth,
I almost, from my miserable heart,
Could here upbraid you for your cruel
    heart,
Which will not let me, down the slope
    of death,
Draw any of your pity after me,
Or lie still in the quiet of your looks,
As my flower, there, in mine.

    [*A bleak wind, quickened with indistinct
    human voices, spins around the earth-
    zodiac, filling the circle with its pre-
    sence; and then wailing off into the
    east, carries the rose away with it.*
    EVE *falls upon her face.* ADAM
    stands erect.

    Adam. So, verily,
The last departs.
    Eve. So Memory follows Hope,
And Life both. Love said to me, 'Do
    not die,'
And I replied, 'O Love, I will not die.
I exiled and I will not orphan Love.'
But now it is no choice of mine to die—
My heart throbs from me.
    Adam. Call it straightway back.
Death's consummation crowns com-
    pleted life,
Or comes too early. Hope being set on
    thee

For others, if for others then for thee,—
For thee and me.

    [*The wind revolves from the east, and
    round again to the east, perfumed by
    the Eden-rose, and full of voices which
    sweep out into articulation as they pass.*

                Let thy soul shake its leaves
To feel the mystic wind—hark!
    Eve. I hear life.

    Infant voices passing in the wind.

Oh we live, oh we live—
And this life that we receive
Is a warm thing and a new,
Which we softly bud into
From the heart and from the brain,—
Something strange that overmuch is
    Of the sound and of the sight,
Flowing round in trickling touches,
    With a sorrow and delight,—
Yet is it all in vain?
                Rock us softly,
Lest it be all in vain.

    Youthful voices passing.

Oh we live, oh we live—
And this life that we achieve
Is a loud thing and a bold,
Which with pulses manifold
Strikes the heart out full and fain—
Active doer, noble liver,
    Strong to struggle, sure to conquer,
Though the vessel's prow will quiver
    At the lifting of the anchor:
Yet do we strive in vain?

    Infant voices passing.

                Rock us softly,
Lest it be all in vain.

    Poet voices passing.

Oh we live, oh we live—
And this life that we conceive
Is a clear thing and a fair,
Which we set in crystal air
That its beauty may be plain!
With a breathing and a flooding
    Of the heaven-life on the whole,
While we hear the forests budding
    To the music of the soul—
Yet is it tuned in vain?

Infant voices passing.

                    Rock us softly,
Lest it be all in vain.

Philosophic voices passing.

Oh we live, oh we live—
And this life that we perceive,
Is a great thing and a grave,
Which for others' use we have,
Duty-laden to remain.
We are helpers, fellow creatures,
  Of the right against the wrong,
We are earnest-hearted teachers
  Of the truth which maketh strong—
Yet do we teach in vain?

Infant voices passing.

                    Rock us softly,
Lest it be all in vain.

Revel voices passing.

Oh we live, oh we live—
And this life that we reprieve,
Is a low thing and a light,
Which is jested out of sight,
And made worthy of disdain!
Strike with bold electric laughter
  The high tops of things divine—
Turn thy head, my brother, after,
  Lest thy tears fall in my wine ;—
For is all laughed in vain?

Infant voices passing.

                    Rock us softly,
Lest it be all in vain.

Eve. I hear a sound of life—of life like
    ours—
Of laughter and of wailing, of grave
    speech,
Of little plaintive voices innocent,
Of life in separate courses flowing out
Like our four rivers to some outward
    main.
I hear life—life!
  Adam.   And, so, thy cheeks
    have snatched
Scarlet to paleness, and thine eyes drink
    fast
Of glory from full cups, and thy moist lips
Seem trembling, both of them, with
    earnest doubts
Whether to utter words or only smile.

Eve. Shall I be mother of the coming
    life?
Hear the steep generations, how they fall
Adown the visionary stairs of Time
Like supernatural thunders—far, yet
    near,—
Sowing their fiery echoes through the
    hills.
Am I a cloud to these—mother to these?
Earth Spirits. And bringer of the curse
    upon all these.
                    [EVE *sinks down again.*

Poet voices passing.

Oh we live, oh we live—
And this life that we conceive,
Is a noble thing and high,
Which we climb up loftily
To view God without a stain ;
Till, recoiling where the shade is,
  We retread our steps again.
And descend the gloomy Hades
  To resume man's mortal pain.
Shall it be climbed in vain?

Infant voices passing.

                    Rock us softly,
Lest it be all in vain.

Love voices passing.

Oh we live, oh we live—
And this life we would retrieve,
Is a faithful thing apart
Which we love in, heart to heart,
Until one heart fitteth twain.
'Wilt thou be one with me?'
'I will be one with thee.'
'Ha, ha!—we love and live!'
Alas! ye love and die.
Shriek—who shall reply?
For is it not loved in vain?

Infant voices passing.

                    Rock us softly,
Though it be all in vain.

Aged voices passing.

Oh we live, oh we live—
And this life we would survive,
Is a gloomy thing and brief,
Which, consummated in grief,
Leaveth ashes for all gain.
Is it not *all* in vain?

Infant voices passing.
　　　　Rock us softly,
Though it be *all* in vain.
　　　　　　[Voices die away.
Earth Spirits. And bringer of the curse
　upon all these.
Eve. The voices of foreshown Hu-
　manity
Die off;—so let me die.
　Adam. 　　　So let us die,
When God's will soundeth the right
　hour of death.
Earth Spirits. And bringer of the
　curse upon all these.
Eve. O spirits! by the gentleness ye use
In winds at night, and floating clouds at
　noon,
In gliding waters under lily-leaves,
In chirp of crickets, and the settling hush
A bird makes in her nest with feet and
　wings,—
Fulfil your natures now!

Earth Spirits.
　　　　Agreed, allowed!
We gather out our natures like a cloud,
And thus fulfil their lightnings! Thus,
　and thus!
　　Hearken, O hearken to us!

First Spirit.
As the storm-wind blows bleakly from
　the norland,
As the snow-wind beats blindly on the
　moorland,
As the simoom drives hot across the
　desert,
As the thunder roars deep in the Un-
　measured,
As the torrent tears the ocean-world to
　atoms,
As the whirlpool grinds it fathoms below
　fathoms,
　　　Thus,—and thus!

Second Spirit.
As the yellow toad, that spits its poison
　chilly,
As the tiger, in the jungle crouching stilly,
As the wild boar, with ragged tusks of
　anger,
As the wolf-dog, with teeth of glittering
　clangour,

As the vultures, that scream against the
　thunder,
As the owlets, that sit and moan asunder,
　　Thus,—and thus!
Eve. Adam! God!
　Adam. 　　Cruel, unrelenting spirits!
By the power in me of the sovran soul
Whose thoughts keep pace yet with the
　angel's march,
I charge you into silence—trample you
Down to obedience.—I am king of you!

Earth Spirits.
Ha, ha! thou art king!
With a sin for a crown,
And a soul undone!
Thou, the antagonized.
Tortured and agonized,
Held in the ring
Of the zodiac!
Now, king, beware!
We are many and strong
Whom thou standest among,—
And we press on the air,
And we stifle thee back,
And we multiply where
Thou wouldst trample us down
From rights of our own
To an utter wrong—
And, from under the feet of thy scorn,
　O forlorn,
We shall spring up like corn,
And our stubble be strong.

Adam. God, there is power in Thee!
　I make appeal
Unto Thy kingship.
　Eve. 　　There is pity in THEE,
O sinned against, great God!—My seed,
　my seed,
There is hope set on THEE—I cry to Thee,
Thou mystic seed that shalt be!—leave
　us not
In agony beyond what we can bear,
Fallen in debasement below thunder-
　mark,
A mark for scorning—taunted and per-
　plext
By all these creatures we ruled yesterday,
Whom Thou, Lord, rulest alway. O my
　Seed,
Through the tempestuous years that rain
　so thick
Betwixt my ghostly vision and Thy face,

Let me have token! for my soul is bruised
Before the serpent's head is.

[*A vision of* CHRIST *appears in the
midst of the zodiac, which pales before
the heavenly light. The Earth Spirits
grow greyer and fainter.*

CHRIST.   I AM HERE!
Adam. This is God!—Curse us not,
    God, any more.
Eve. But gazing so—so—with omnific
    eyes,
Lift my soul upward till it touch Thy feet!
Or lift it only,—not to seem too proud,—
To the low height of some good angel's
    feet,
For such to tread on when he walketh
    straight
And Thy lips praise him.
    CHRIST.   Spirits of the earth,
I meet you with rebuke for the reproach
And cruel and unmitigated blame
Ye cast upon your masters. True, they
    have sinned;
And true their sin is reckoned into loss
For you the sinless. Yet, your innocence,
Which of you praises? since God made
    your acts
Inherent in your lives, and bound your
    hands
With instincts and imperious sanctities
From self-defacement? Which of you
    disdains
These sinners who in falling proved
    their height
Above you by their liberty to fall?
And which of you complains of loss by
    them,
For whose delight and use ye have your
    life
And honour in creation? Ponder it!
This regent and sublime Humanity,
Though fallen, exceeds you! this shall
    film your sun,
Shall hunt your lightning to its lair of
    cloud,
Turn back your rivers, footpath all your
    seas,
Lay flat your forests, master with a look
Your lion at his fasting, and fetch down
Your eagle flying. Nay, without this law
Of mandom, ye would perish,—beast by
    beast

Devouring,—tree by tree, with strang-
    ling roots
And trunks set tuskwise. Ye would
    gaze on God
With imperceptive blankness up the stars,
And mutter, 'Why, God, hast Thou made
    us thus?'
And pining to a sallow idiocy
Stagger up blindly against the ends of
    life,
Then stagnate into rottenness and drop
Heavily—poor, dead matter—piecemeal
    down
The abysmal spaces—like a little stone
Let fall to chaos. Therefore over you
Receive man's sceptre,—therefore be
    content
To minister with voluntary grace
And melancholy pardon, every rite
And function in you, to the human hand.
Be ye to man as angels are to God,
Servants in pleasure, singers of delight,
Suggesters to his soul of higher things
Than any of your highest. So at last,
He shall look round on you with lids too
    straight
To hold the grateful tears, and thank you
    well,
And bless you when he prays his secret
    prayers,
And praise you when he sings his open
    songs
For the clear song-note he has learnt in
    you
Of purifying sweetness, and extend
Across your head his golden fantasies
Which glorify you into soul from sense!
Go, serve him for such price. That not
    in vain
Nor yet ignobly ye shall serve, I place
My word here for an oath, mine oath for
    act
To be hereafter. In the name of which
Perfect redemption and perpetual grace,
I bless you through the hope and through
    the peace
Which are mine,—to the Love, which is
    myself.
Eve. Speak on still, Christ. Albeit Thou
    bless me not
In set words, I am blessed in hearkening
    Thee—
Speak, Christ.

CHRIST.   Speak, Adam. Bless the
    woman, man—
It is thine office.
    Adam.   Mother of the world,
Take heart before this Presence. Lo,
    my voice,
Which, naming erst the creatures, did
    express
(God breathing through my breath) the
    attributes
And instincts of each creature in its name,
Floats to the same afflatus,—floats and
    heaves
Like a water-weed that opens to a wave,
A full-leaved prophecy affecting thee,
Out fairly and wide. Henceforward, rise,
    aspire
To all the calms and magnanimities,
The lofty uses and the noble ends,
The sanctified devotion and full work,
To which thou art elect for evermore,
First woman, wife, and mother.
    Eve.   And first in sin.
    Adam. And also the sole bearer of
    the Seed
Whereby sin dieth! raise the majesties
Of thy disconsolate brows, O well-
    beloved,
And front with level eyelids the To come,
And all the dark o' the world. Rise,
    woman, rise
To thy peculiar and best altitudes
Of doing good and of enduring ill,
Of comforting for ill, and teaching good,
And reconciling all that ill and good
Unto the patience of a constant hope,—
Rise with thy daughters! If sin came
    by thee,
And by sin, death,—the ransom-right-
    eousness,
The heavenly life and compensative rest
Shall come by means of thee. If woe by
    thee
Had issue to the world, thou shalt go forth
An angel of the woe thou didst achieve,
Found acceptable to the world instead
Of others of that name, of whose bright
    steps
Thy deed stripped bare the hills. Be
    satisfied ;
Something thou hast to bear through
    womanhood,
Peculiar suffering answering to the sin,—

Some pang paid down for each new
    human life,
Some weariness in guarding such a life,
Some coldness from the guarded, some
    mistrust
From those thou hast too well served,
    from those beloved
Too loyally some treason ; feebleness
Within thy heart, and cruelty without,
And pressures of an alien tyranny
With its dynastic reasons of larger bones
And stronger sinews. But, go to! thy love
Shall chant itself its own beatitudes
After its own life-working. A child's kiss
Set on thy sighing lips, shall make thee
    glad ;
A poor man served by thee, shall make
    thee rich ;
A sick man helped by thee, shall make
    thee strong ;
Thou shalt be served thyself by every
    sense
Of service which thou renderest. Such
    a crown
I set upon thy head,—Christ witnessing
With looks of prompting love—to keep
    thee clear
Of all reproach against the sin foregone,
From all the generations which succeed.
Thy hand which plucked the apple, I
    clasp close,
Thy lips which spake wrong counsel,
    I kiss close,
I bless thee in the name of Paradise
And by the memory of Edenic joys
Forfeit and lost,—by that last cypress
    tree,
Green at the gate, which thrilled as we
    came out,
And by the blessed nightingale which
    threw
Its melancholy music after us,—
And by the flowers, whose spirits full of
    smells
Did follow softly, plucking us behind
Back to the gradual banks and vernal
    bowers
And fourfold river-courses.—By all these,
I bless thee to the contraries of these,
I bless thee to the desert and the thorns,
To the elemental change and turbulence,
And to the roar of the estrangèd beasts,
And to the solemn dignities of grief,—

To each one of these ends,—and to their
    END
Of Death and the hereafter !
  Eve.   I accept
For me and for my daughters this high
    part
Which lowly shall be counted. Noble
    work
Shall hold me in the place of garden-rest,
And in the place of Eden's lost delight
Worthy endurance of permitted pain ;
While on my longest patience there shall
    wait
Death's speechless angel, smiling in the
    east
Whence cometh the cold wind. I bow
    myself
Humbly henceforward on the ill I did,
That humbleness may keep it in the
    shade.
Shall it be so ? shall I smile, saying so ?
O seed ! O King ! O God, who *shalt* be
    seed,—
What shall I say ? As Eden's fountain
    swelled
Brightly betwixt their banks, so swells
    my soul
Betwixt thy love and power !
            And, sweetest thoughts
Of foregone Eden ! now, for the first time
Since God said 'Adam,' walking through
    the trees,
I dare to pluck you as I plucked erewhile
The lily or pink, the rose or heliotrope.
So pluck I you—so largely—with both
    hands,
And throw you forward on the outer earth
Wherein we are cast out, to sweeten it.
  Adam. As Thou, Christ, to illume it,
    holdest Heaven
Broadly above our heads.

[*The* CHRIST *is gradually transfigured
    during the following phrases of dia-
    logue, into humanity and suffering.*

  Eve.   O Saviour Christ,
Thou standest mute in glory, like the sun.
  Adam. We worship in Thy silence,
    Saviour Christ.
  Eve. Thy brows grow grander with a
    forecast woe,—
Diviner, with the possible of death !

We worship in Thy sorrow, Saviour
    Christ.
  Adam. How do Thy clear, still eyes
    transpierce our souls,
As gazing *through* them toward the
    Father-throne
In a pathetical, full Deity,
Serenely as the stars gaze through the air
Straight on each other.
  Eve.   O pathetic Christ,
Thou standest mute in glory, like the
    moon.
  CHRIST. Eternity stands alway fronting
    God ;
A stern colossal image, with blind eyes
And grand dim lips that murmur ever-
    more
God, God, God ! while the rush of life
    and death,
The roar of act and thought, of evil and
    good,
The avalanches of the ruining worlds
Tolling down space,—the new worlds'
    genesis
Budding in fire,—the gradual humming
    growth
Of the ancient atoms and first forms of
    earth,
The slow procession of the swathing seas
And firmamental waters,—and the noise
Of the broad, fluent strata of pure airs,—
All these flow onward in the intervals
Of that reiterated sound of—GOD !
Which WORD, innumerous angels straight-
    way lift
Wide on celestial altitudes of song
And choral adoration, and then drop
The burden softly, shutting the last notes
In silver wings. Howbeit in the noon
    of time
Eternity shall wax as dumb as Death,
While a new voice beneath the spheres
    shall cry,
'God ! why hast Thou forsaken me, my
    God ?'
And not a voice in Heaven shall answer it.

[*The transfiguration is complete in sadness.*

  Adam. Thy speech is of the Heaven-
    lies, yet, O Christ,
Awfully human are Thy voice and face.
  Eve. My nature overcomes me from
    Thine eyes.

A DRAMA OF EXILE

CHRIST. In the set noon of time, shall
one from Heaven,
An angel fresh from looking upon God,
Descend before a woman, blessing her
With perfect benediction of pure love,
For all the world in all its elements,
For all the creatures of earth, air, and sea,
For all men in the body and in the soul,
Unto all ends of glory and sanctity.

Eve. O pale, pathetic Christ—I wor-
ship Thee!
I thank Thee for that woman!
CHRIST. Then, at last,
I, wrapping round me your humanity,
Which being sustained, shall neither
break nor burn
Beneath the fire of Godhead, will tread
earth,
And ransom you and it, and set strong
peace
Betwixt you and its creatures. With
my pangs
I will confront your sins; and since
those sins
Have sunken to all Nature's heart from
yours,
The tears of my clean soul shall follow
them
And set a holy passion to work clear
Absolute consecration. In my brow
Of kingly whiteness, shall be crowned
anew
Your discrowned human nature. Look
on me!
As I shall be uplifted on a cross
In darkness of eclipse and anguish dread,
So shall I lift up in my piercèd hands,
Not into dark, but light—not unto death,
But life,—beyond the reach of guilt and
grief,
The whole creation. Henceforth in my
name
Take courage, O thou woman,—man,
take hope!
Your grave shall be as smooth as Eden's
sward,
Beneath the steps of your prospective
thoughts,
And, one step past it, a new Eden-gate
Shall open on a hinge of harmony
And let you through to mercy. Ye shall
fall
No more, within that Eden, nor pass out

Any more from it. In which hope, move
on,
First sinners and first mourners. Live
and love,—
Doing both nobly, because lowlily.
Live and work, strongly, because
patiently.
And, for the deed of death, trust it to God
That it be well done, unrepented of,
And not to loss. And thence, with con-
stant prayers
Fasten your souls so high, that constantly
The smile of your heroic cheer may float
Above all floods of earthly agonies,
Purification being the joy of pain.

[*The vision of* CHRIST *vanishes.* ADAM
and EVE *stand in an ecstasy. The
earth-zodiac pales away shade by shade,
as the stars, star by star, shine out in
the sky; and the following chant from
the two* Earth Spirits (*as they sweep
back into the zodiac and disappear
with it*) *accompanies the process of
change.*

Earth Spirits.

By the mighty word thus spoken
Both for living and for dying,
We, our homage-oath once broken,
Fasten back again in sighing,
And the creatures and the elements renew
their covenanting.

Here, forgive us all our scorning;
Here, we promise milder duty:
And the evening and the morning
Shall reorganize in beauty
A sabbath day of sabbath joy, for uni-
versal chanting.

And if, still, this melancholy
May be strong to overcome us,
If this mortal and unholy
We still fail to cast out from us,—
If we turn upon you, unaware, your own
dark influences,—

If ye tremble when surrounded
By our forest pine and palm-trees,
If we cannot cure the wounded
With our gum-trees and our balm-
trees,
And if your souls all mournfully sit down
among your senses,—

Yet, O mortals, do not fear us,
    We are gentle in our languor ;
Much more good ye shall have near us
    Than any pain or anger,
And our God's refracted blessing in our
      blessing shall be given.

By the desert's endless vigil
    We will solemnize your passions,
By the wheel of the black eagle
    We will teach you exaltations,
When he sails against the wind, to the
      white spot up in Heaven.

Ye shall find us tender nurses
    To your weariness of nature,
And our hands shall stroke the curse's
    Dreary furrows from the creature,
Till your bodies shall lie smooth in death,
      and straight and slumberful.

Then, a couch we will provide you
    Where no summer heats shall dazzle,
Strewing on you and beside you
    Thyme and rosemary and basil—
And the yew-tree shall grow overhead
      to keep all safe and cool.

Till the Holy Blood awaited
    Shall be chrism around us running,
Whereby, newly-consecrated
    We shall leap up in God's sunning,
To join the spheric company which
      purer worlds assemble.

While, renewed by new evangels,
    Soul-consummated, made glorious,
Ye shall brighten past the angels,
    Ye shall kneel to Christ victorious,
And the rays around His feet beneath
      your sobbing lips shall tremble.

[*The fantastic vision has all passed ; the
earth-zodiac has broken like a belt,
and is dissolved from the desert. The*
Earth Spirits *vanish, and the stars
shine out above.*

CHORUS OF INVISIBLE ANGELS

while ADAM *and* EVE *advance into the
desert, hand in hand.*

Hear our heavenly promise
    Through your mortal passion !
Love, ye shall have from us,
    In a pure relation.

As a fish or bird
    Swims or flies, if moving,
We unseen are heard
    To live on by loving.
Far above the glances
    Of your eager eyes.
Listen ! we are loving !
Listen, through man's ignorances,
Listen, through God's mysteries.
Listen down the heart of things,—
Ye shall hear our mystic wings
    Murmurous with loving.
Through the opal door
    Listen evermore
How we live by loving.

First semichorus.

When your bodies therefore
    Reach the grave their goal,
Softly will we care for
    Each enfranchised soul.
Softly and unloathly
    Through the door of opal
    Toward the Heavenly people,
Floated on a minor fine
Into the full chant divine,
    We will draw you smoothly,—
While the human in the minor
Makes the harmony diviner.
    Listen to our loving !

Second semichorus.

There, a sough of glory
    Shall breathe on you as you come,
Ruffling round the doorway
    All the light of angeldom.
From the empyrean centre
    Heavenly voices shall repeat,
' Souls redeemed and pardoned, enter,
    For the chrism on you is sweet.'
And every angel in the place
Lowlily shall bow his face,
    Folded fair on softened sounds,
Because upon your hands and feet
    He images his Master's wounds.
    Listen to our loving !

First semichorus.

So, in the universe's
    Consummated undoing,
Our seraphs of white mercies
    Shall hover round the ruin !
Their wings shall stream upon the flame
As if incorporate of the same

In elemental fusion,
And calm their faces shall burn out
With a pale and mastering thought,
And a steadfast looking of desire
From out between the clefts of fire,—
While they cry, in the Holy's name,
  To the final Restitution.
    Listen to our loving!

Second semichorus.

So, when the day of God is
  To the thick graves accompted,
Awaking the dead bodies
  The angel of the trumpet
Shall split and shatter the earth
  To the roots of the grave
Which never before were slackened,
  And quicken the charnel birth
With his blast so clear and brave,
  That the Dead shall start and stand
    erect,
And every face of the burial-place
Shall the awful, single look reflect,
  Wherewith he them awakened.
    Listen to our loving!

First semichorus.

But wild is the horse of Death.
He will leap up wild at the clamour
  Above and beneath.
    And where is his Tamer
  On that last day,
    When he crieth, Ha, ha!
  To the trumpet's blare,
And paweth the earth's Aceldama?
  When he tosseth his head,
  The drear-white steed,
And ghastlily champeth the last moon-
    ray,—
    What angel there
    Can lead him away,
That the living may rule for the Dead?

Second semichorus.

Yet a TAMER shall be found!
One more bright than seraph crowned,
And more strong than cherub bold,
Elder, too, than angel old,
By his grey eternities.
He shall master and surprise
  The steed of Death.
For He is strong, and He is fain.

He shall quell him with a breath,
And shall lead him where He will,
With a whisper in the ear,
    Full of fear—
And a hand upon the mane,
    Grand and still.

First semichorus.

Through the flats of Hades where the
    souls assemble
He will guide the Death-steed calm
    between their ranks,
While, like beaten dogs, they a little
    moan and tremble
To see the darkness curdle from the
    horse's glittering flanks.
Through the flats of Hades where the
    dreary shade is,
Up the steep of Heaven, will the Tamer
    guide the steed,—
Up the spheric circles—circle above
    circle,
We who count the ages, shall count the
    tolling tread—
Every hoof-fall striking a blinder, blanker
    sparkle
From the stony orbs, which shall show
    as they were dead.

Second semichorus.

All the way the Death-steed with tolling
    hoofs shall travel,
Ashen grey the planets shall be motion-
  • less as stones,
Loosely shall the systems eject their
    parts coeval,—
Stagnant in the spaces, shall float the
    pallid moons.
Suns that touch their apogees, reeling
    from their level,
Shall run back on their axles, in wild,
    low, broken tunes.

Chorus.

Up against the arches of the crystal
    ceiling,
From the horse's nostrils shall steam the
    blurting breath.
Up between the angels pale with silent
    feeling,
Will the Tamer, calmly, lead the horse
    of Death.

Semichorus.

Cleaving all that silence, cleaving all
    that glory,
Will the Tamer lead him straightway to
    the Throne;
'Look out, O Jehovah, to this I bring
    before Thee
With a hand nail-piercèd,—I, who am
    Thy Son.'
Then the Eye Divinest, from the Deepest,
    flaming,
On the mystic courser, shall look out in
    fire.
Blind the beast shall stagger where It
    overcame him,
Meek as lamb at pasture—bloodless in
    desire.
Down the beast shall shiver,—slain amid
    the taming,—
And, by Life essential, the phantasm
    Death expire.

Chorus.

Listen, man, through life and death,
Through the dust and through the breath,
    Listen down the heart of things!
    Ye shall hear our mystic wings
    Murmurous with loving.

A Voice from below. Gabriel, thou
    Gabriel!
A Voice from above. What wouldst
    thou with me?
First Voice. I heard thy voice sound
    in the angels' song,
And I would give thee question.
Second Voice.   Question me.
First Voice. Why have I called thrice
    to my Morning Star
And had no answer? All the stars are
    out,
And answer in their places. Only in vain
I cast my voice against the outer rays
Of *my* Star, shut in light behind the
    sun.
No more reply than from a breaking
    string,
Breaking when touched. Or is she *not*
    my Star?
Where *is* my Star—my Star? Have ye
    cast down
Her glory like my glory? has she waxed
Mortal, like Adam? has she learnt to
    hate

Like any angel?
Second Voice. She is sad for thee.
All things grow sadder to thee, one by
    one.

Angel Chorus.

Live, work on, O Earthy!
    By the Actual's tension,
Speed the arrow worthy
    Of a pure ascension.
From the low earth round you,
    Reach the heights above you!
From the stripes that wound you,
    Seek the loves that love you!
God's divinest burneth plain
Through the crystal diaphane
    Of our loves that love you.

First Voice. Gabriel, O Gabriel!
Second Voice. What wouldst *thou*
    with me?
First Voice. Is it true, O thou Gabriel,
    that the crown
Of sorrow which I claimed, another
    claims?
That HE claims THAT too?
Second Voice. Lost one, it is true.
First Voice. That HE will be an exile
    from His Heaven,
To lead those exiles homeward?
Second Voice.   It is true.
First Voice. That HE will be an exile
    by His will,
As I by mine election?
Second Voice.   It is true.
First Voice. That *I* shall stand sole
    exile finally,—
Made desolate for fruition?
Second Voice.   It is true.
First Voice. Gabriel!
Second Voice.   I hearken.
First Voice.   Is it true besides—
Aright true—that mine orient Star will
    give
Her name of 'Bright and Morning-Star'
    to HIM,—
And take the fairness of His virtue
    back,
To cover loss and sadness?
Second Voice.   It is true.
First Voice. UNTRUE, UNTRUE!
    Morning-Star, O MINE.
Who sittest secret in a veil of light
Far up the starry spaces, say—*Untrue.*

Speak but so loud as doth a wasted moon
To Tyrrhene waters.   I am Lucifer.
    [A pause.   Silence in the stars.
All things grow sadder to me, one by one.

Angel Chorus.

Exiled human creatures,
    Let your hope grow larger
Larger grows the vision
    Of the new delight.
From this chain of Nature's
    God is the Discharger,
And the Actual's prison
    Opens to your sight.

Semichorus.

Calm the stars and golden,
    In a light exceeding :
What their rays have measured,
    Let your feet fulfil !
These are stars beholden
    By your eyes in Eden,
Yet, across the desert,
    See them shining still.

Chorus.

Future joy and far light
    Working such relations,
Hear us singing gently
    Exiled is not lost.
God, above the starlight,
    God, above the patience,
Shall at last present ye
    Guerdons worth the cost.
Patiently enduring,
    Painfully surrounded,
Listen how we love you,
    Hope the uttermost.
Waiting for that curing
    Which exalts the wounded,
Hear us sing above you—
    EXILED, BUT NOT LOST !

[The stars shine on brightly, while
ADAM *and* EVE *pursue their way into
the far wilderness.   There is a sound
through the silence, as of the falling
tears of an angel.*

PROMETHEUS BOUND

FROM THE GREEK OF AESCHYLUS

PREFACE TO THE FIRST EDITION, 1833

ALTHOUGH, among the various versions which have appeared of various ancient writers, we may recognize the dead, together with much of the living letter; a literal version, together with a transfusion of poetical spirit ;—why should we, on that account, consider ourselves charmed away from attempting another translation ? A mirror may be held in different lights by different hands ; and, according to the position of those hands, will the light fall. A picture may be imitated in different ways,—by steel engraving, or stone engraving ; and, according to the vocation of the artist, will the copy be.   According to Dr. Bentley, Pope's translation of Homer is not Homer ; it is Spondanus : he might have said, it is not even Spondanus—it is Pope.   Cowper's translation is a different Homer altogether ; not Spondanus, nor Pope, nor the right Homer either.   We do not blame Pope and Cowper for not having faithfully represented Homer : we do not blame Pope and Cowper for being Pope and Cowper.   It is the nature of the human mind to communicate its own character to whatever substance it conveys, whether it convey metaphysical impressions from itself to another mind, or literary compositions from one to another language.   It is therefore desirable that the same composition should be conveyed by different minds, that the character of the medium may not be necessarily associated with the thing conveyed.   All men, since Aesop's time and before it, have worn various-coloured spectacles.   They cannot part with their colour, which is their individuality; but they may correct the effects of that individuality by itself. If Potter show us Aeschylus through green spectacles, and another translator, though in a very inferior manner, show us Aeschylus through yellow ones, it will become clear to the English reader that green and yellow are not inherent properties of the Greek poet: and in this respect, both the English reader and the Greek poet are benefited.

But the present age says, it has no need of translations from classic authors. It is, or it would be, an original age: it will not borrow thoughts with long genealogies, nor walk upon a *pavé*, nor wear a costume, like Queen Anne's authors and the French dramatists. Its poetry shall not be cold and polished and imitative poetry; but shall dream undreamt of dreams, and glow with an unearthly frenzy. If its dreams be noble dreams, may they be dreamt on; if its frenzy be the evidence of inspiration, 'may I,' as Prometheus says, 'be mad.' But let the age take heed: there is one step from dreaming nobly to sleeping inertly; and one, from frenzy to imbecility.

I do not ask, I would not obtain, that our age should be servilely imitative of any former age. Surely it may think its own thoughts and speak its own words, yet not turn away from those who *have* thought and spoken well. The contemplation of excellence produces excellence, if not similar, yet parallel. We do not turn from green hills and waving forests, because we build and inhabit palaces; nor do we turn towards them, that we may model them in painted wax. We make them subjects of contemplation, in order to abstract from them those ideas of beauty, afterwards embodied in our own productions; and, above all, in order to consider their and our Creator under every manifestation of His goodness and His power. All beauties, whether in nature or art, whether in physics or morals, whether in composition or abstract reasoning, are multiplied reflections, visible in different distances and under different positions, of one archetypal beauty. If we owe gratitude to Him

who created and unveiled its form, should we refuse to gaze upon those reflections? Because they rest even upon heathen scrolls, should we turn away from those scrolls? Because thorns and briers are the product of the earth, should we avert our eyes from that earth? The mind of man and the earth of man are cursed alike.

But the age would not be 'classical.' 'Oh, that profaned name!' What does it mean, and what is it made to mean? It does not mean what it is made to mean: it does not mean what is necessarily regular, and polished, and unimpassioned. The ancients, especially the ancient Greeks, felt, and thought, and wrote antecedently to rules: they felt passionately, and thought daringly; and wrote because they felt and thought. Shakespeare is a more classical writer than Racine.

Perhaps, of all the authors of antiquity, no one stands so forward to support this hypothesis as Aeschylus: and of all the works of Aeschylus, no one stands more forward to support it than his work of the *Prometheus Bound*. He is a fearless and impetuous, not a cautious and accomplished poet. His excellences could not be acquired by art, nor could his defects exist separately from genius. It would be nearly equally impossible for the mere imitator to compass either; for if we would stand in the mist, we must stand also on the mountain. His excellences consist chiefly in a vehement imaginativeness, a strong but repressed sensibility, a high tone of morality, a fervency of devotion, and a rolling energetic diction: and as sometimes his fancy rushes in, where his judgement fears to tread, and language, even the most copious and powerful of languages, writhes beneath its impetuosity; an occasional mixing of metaphor, and frequent obscurity of style, are named among his chief defects. He is pompous too, sometimes; but his pomposity has not any modern, any rigid, frigid effect. When he walks, like his actors, on cothurni, we do not say 'how stiff he is!' but 'how majestic!'

Whether the *Prometheus* be, or be not, the finest production of its author, it will not, I think, be contested, that Prometheus himself is the character in the conception and development of which its author has concentrated his powers in the most full and efficient manner. There is more gorgeousness of imagery in the *Seven Chiefs* and more power in the *Eumenides*; and I should tremble to oppose any one scene in *Prometheus* to the Cassandra scene in *Agamemnon*. The learned Mr. Boyd, who, in addition to many valuable and well-known translations, has furnished the public with an able version of that obscure tragedy, considers the scene in question to be 'unapproached and unapproachable by any rival.' But I would rest the claims of the *Prometheus* upon one fulcrum, the conception of character. It is not in the usual manner of Aeschylus to produce upon his canvas any very prominent figure, to which every other is made subordinate, and to which the interest of the spectator is very strongly and almost exclusively attached. Agamemnon's πληγὴν ἔχω we do not feel within our hearts. In the *Seven Chiefs*, there is a clear division of interest; and the reader willingly agrees with Antigone, that Polynices should be as honourably buried as Eteocles. In the *Supplices* we are called upon to exercise universal charity towards fifty heroines. In the *Persae*, we cannot weep with Atossa over the misfortunes of Xerxes; not even over what she most femininely considers to be his greatest misfortune—μάλιστα δ᾽ ἥδε συμφορὰ δάκνει—his wearing a tattered garment. Perhaps we know more of Orestes than of any personage, always excepting Prometheus, introduced by Aeschylus : and yet both in the *Choëphoroe* and *Eumenides* we are interested in his calamities, rather from their being calamities than from their being his. But Prometheus stands eminent and alone; one of the most original, and grand, and attaching characters ever conceived by the mind of man. That conception sank deeply into the soul of Milton, and, as has been observed, rose from thence in the likeness of his Satan. But the Satan of Milton and the Prometheus of Aeschylus stand upon ground as unequal as do the

sublime of sin and the sublime of virtue. Satan suffered from his ambition; Prometheus from his humanity : Satan for himself; Prometheus for mankind : Satan dared perils which he had not weighed; Prometheus devoted himself to sorrows which he had foreknown. 'Better to rule in hell,' said Satan; 'Better to serve this rock,' said Prometheus. Bút in his hell, Satan yearned to associate man; while Prometheus preferred a solitary agony : nay, he even permitted his zeal and tenderness for the peace of others to abstract him from that agony's intenseness.

Aeschylus felt the force of his own portraiture : he never removes his Prometheus from the spectator's sight. The readers of Aeschylus feel it : they are impatient at Io's long narrations; not because those narrations are otherwise than beautiful, but because they would hear Prometheus speak again : they are impatient even at Prometheus's prophetic replies to Io, because they would hear him speak only of Prometheus. From the moment of the first dawning of his character upon their minds, its effect is electrifying. He is silent : he disdains as much to answer the impotent and selfish compassion of Vulcan, as to murmur beneath the brutal cruelty of Strength. It was not thus that *he* pitied in his days of joy : it was not thus that *he* acted in his days of power : and his spirit is above them, and recks not of them; and when their pity and their scoffs pollute his ears no more, he pours out his impassioned sorrows to the air, and winds, and waters, and earth, and sun, whom he had never visited with benefits, and 'taxed not with unkindness.' The striking nature of these, our first ideas of Prometheus, is not enfeebled by any subsequent ones. We see him daring and unflinching beneath the torturing and dishonouring hand, yet keenly alive to the torture and dishonour; for himself fearless and rash, yet for others considerate and wary; himself unpitied, yet to others pitiful. And when, at the last, he calls no longer upon the sun, and earth, and waters, from whom the Avenger is secluding him; but demands of Aether, who is rolling light to all eyes excepting his, whether he beholds how he suffers by injustice ;—our hearts rise up within us, and bear witness that the suffering is indeed unjust.

It is apparent with what bitter feeling the conceiver of this character must have regarded the transferred praise and love of Athens—of his country. 'Are you not ashamed,' said Menander to Philemon, 'to conquer me in comedy?' Such a reproach might Aeschylus have used to his dramatic rival, and extracted as deep a blush as ever stained Philemon's cheek. But he did not. Silent as his own Prometheus, he left for ever the Athens on whom he had conferred the immortality of his name and works; and went to Sicily, to die. In that place of exile he wrote his epitaph instead of tragedies, calling with his dying voice on the grove of Marathon [1] and the conquered Persians, as the only witnesses of his glory. 'If thorns be in thy path,' said Marcus Antoninus [2], 'turn aside.' But where should *he* turn, who would avoid the ingratitude and changefulness of man?

Among those who have passed judgement upon Aeschylus, it is remarkable how many have passed a similar one to that of the Athenians, when, according to Suidas, they 'broke down the benches' previous to his departure for Sicily ;—a phrase interpreted by Scaliger to signify a final condemnation of his work. He is 'damned by faint praise'; by an alternate acknowledgement of his genius, and censure of his taste ; and by an invidious opposition to Sophocles and Euripides. Of the three great critics of antiquity,—Longinus, Dionysius of Halicarnassus, and Quintilian,—Dionysius alone does not measure his criticism to twice the length of his commendation. Quintilian calls him 'rudis in plerisque et incompositus,' which

my sense of justice almost gives me courage to call a false criticism. Longinus —Longinus !! uses similar language :— ἐνίοτε μέντοι ἀκατεργάστους καὶ οἰονεὶ ποκοειδεῖς τὰς ἐννοίας καὶ ἀμαλάκτους φέροντος. Now there are, undeniably, some things in Aeschylus, which, like the expressions of Callisthenes, would properly fall under the censure of Longinus, as being οὐχ ὑψηλά, ἀλλὰ μετέωρα. But according to every principle by which he himself could urge his immortal claim upon posterity, the Homer of criticism should have named with less of coldness and more of rapture, the Homer of dramatic poetry.

With regard to the execution of this attempt, it is not necessary for me to say many words. I have rendered the iambics into blank verse, their nearest parallel ; and the choral odes and other lyric intermixtures, into English lyrics, irregular and rimed. Irregularity I imagined to be indispensable to the conveyance of any part of the effect of the original measure, of which little seems to be understood by modern critics, than that it is irregular. To the literal sense I have endeavoured to bend myself as closely as was poetically possible : but if, after all,—and it is too surely the case,—'quantum mutatus !' must be applied ; may the reader say so rather sorrowfully than severely, and forgive my English for not being Greek, and myself for not being Aeschylus.

And will Aeschylus forgive, among my many other offences against him, the grave offence of profaning his Prometheus, by attaching to it some miscellaneous poems by its translator [3]? Will he not rather retort upon me, his chorus's strongly expressed disapprobation of *unequal unions*? And how can I defend myself? ἀπόλεμος ὅδε γ' ὁ πόλεμος.

---

[1] See the epitaph which is attributed to him.
[2] Lib. viii. cap. 5.

[3] Printed in this edition among the 'Early Poems,' pp. 60-77.

PROMETHEUS BOUND

PERSONS OF THE DRAMA

PROMETHEUS.   HEPHAESTUS.
OCEANUS.   Io, daughter of Inachus.
HERMES.   STRENGTH and FORCE.
          CHORUS of Ocean Nymphs.

SCENE.—STRENGTH *and* FORCE, HEPHAESTUS *and* PROMETHEUS, *at the Rocks.*

Strength. We reach the utmost limit
     of the earth,
The Scythian track, the desert without
     man.
And now. Hephaestus, thou must needs
     fulfil
The mandate of our Father, and with links
Indissoluble of adamantine chains,
Fasten against this beetling precipice
This guilty god. Because he filched away
Thine own bright flower, the glory of
     plastic fire,
And gifted mortals with it,—such a sin
It doth behove he expiate to the gods,
Learning to accept the empery of Zeus
And leave off his old trick of loving man.
     Hephaestus. O Strength and Force,—
          for you, our Zeus's will
Presents a deed for doing, no more !—
     but *I,*
I lack your daring, up this storm-rent
     chasm
To fix with violent hands a kindred god,—
Howbeit necessity compels me so
That I must dare it—and our Zeus com-
     mands
With a most inevitable word. Ho, thou !
High-thoughted son of Themis who is
     sage !
Thee loath, I loath must rivet fast in chains
Against this rocky height unclomb by
     man,
Where never human voice nor face shall
     find
Out thee who lov'st them, and thy
     beauty's flower,
Scorched in the sun's clear heat, shall
     fade away.
Night shall come up with garniture of
     stars

To comfort thee with shadow, and the
     sun
Disperse with retrickt beams the morning-
     frosts,
But through all changes, sense of present
     woe
Shall vex thee sore, because with none
     of them
There comes a hand to free.   Such fruit
     is plucked
From love of man !—and in that thou, a
     god,
Didst brave the wrath of gods and give
     away
Undue respect to mortals, for that crime
Thou art adjudged to guard this joyless
     rock,
Erect, unslumbering, bending not the
     knee,
And many a cry and unavailing moan
To utter on the air.   For Zeus is stern,
And new-made kings are cruel.
     Strength.   Be it so.
Why loiter in vain pity ? Why not hate
A god the gods hate ?—one too who be-
     trayed
Thy glory unto men ?
     Hephaestus.   An awful thing
Is kinship joined to friendship.
     Strength.   Grant it be ;
Is disobedience to the Father's word
A possible thing ? Dost quail not more
     for that ?
     Hephaestus. Thou, at least, art a stern
          one ! ever bold.
     Strength. Why, if I wept, it were no
          remedy.
And do not *thou* spend labour on the air
To bootless uses.
     Hephaestus.   Cursed handicraft !

I curse and hate thee, O my craft!

Strength.   Why hate
Thy craft most plainly innocent of all
These pending ills?

Hephaestus.   I would some other hand
Were here to work it!

Strength.   All work hath its pain,
Except to rule the gods.   There is none
    free
Except King Zeus.

Hephaestus.   I know it very well :
I argue not against it.

Strength.   Why not, then,
Make haste and lock the fetters over HIM,
Lest Zeus behold thee lagging?

Hephaestus.   Here be chains.
Zeus may behold these.

Strength.   Seize him,—strike amain !
Strike with the hammer on each side his
    hands—
Rivet him to the rock.

Hephaestus.   The work is done,
And thoroughly done.

Strength.   Still faster grapple him,—
Wedge him in deeper,—leave no inch
    to stir !
He's terrible for finding a way out
From the irremediable.

Hephaestus.   Here's an arm, at least,
Grappled past freeing.

Strength.   Now, then, buckle me
The other securely.   Let this wise one
    learn
He's duller than our Zeus.

Hephaestus.   Oh, none but he
Accuse me justly !

Strength.   Now, straight through
    the chest,
Take him and bite him with the clenching
    tooth
Of the adamantine wedge, and rivet him.

Hephaestus. Alas, Prometheus, what
    thou sufferest here
I sorrow over.

Strength.   Dost thou flinch again,
And breathe groans for the enemies of
    Zeus ?
Beware lest thine own pity find thee out.

Hephaestus. Thou dost behold a spec-
    tacle that turns
The sight o' the eyes to pity.

Strength.   I behold
A sinner suffer his sin's penalty.

But lash the thongs about his sides.

Hephaestus.   So much
I must do.   Urge no farther than I must.

Strength. Aye, but I *will* urge !—and,
    with shout on shout,
Will hound thee at this quarry.   Get
    thee down
And ring amain the iron round his legs.

Hephaestus. That work was not long
    doing.

Strength.   Heavily now
Let fall the strokes upon the perforant
    gyves :
For He who rates the work has a heavy
    hand.

Hephaestus. Thy speech is savage as
    thy shape.

Strength.   Be thou
Gentle and tender ! but revile not me
For the firm will and the untruckling
    hate.

Hephaestus. Let us go.   He is netted
    round with chains.

Strength. Here, now, taunt on ! and
    having spoiled the gods
Of honours, crown withal thy mortal men
Who live a whole day out.   Why how
    could *they*
Draw off from thee one single of thy
    griefs ?
Methinks the Daemons gave thee a wrong
    name,
Prometheus, which means Providence,—
    because
Thou dost thyself need providence to see
Thy roll and ruin from the top of doom.

Prometheus (*alone*). O holy Aether,
    and swift-wingèd Winds,
And River-wells, and laughter innumer-
    ous
Of yon sea waves !   Earth, mother of us
    all,
And all-viewing cyclic Sun, I cry on
    you,—
Behold me a god, what I endure from
    gods !
    Behold, with throe on throe,
    How, wasted by this woe,
I wrestle down the myriad years of time !
    Behold, how fast around me,
The new King of the happy ones sublime
Has flung the chain he forged, has shamed
    and bound me !

Woe, woe! to-day's woe and the coming
　　morrow's,
I cover with one groan. And where is
　　found me
　　　A limit to these sorrows?
And yet what word do I say? I have
　　foreknown
Clearly all things that should be; nothing
　　done
Comes sudden to my soul—and I must
　　bear
What is ordained with patience, being
　　aware
Necessity doth front the universe
With an invincible gesture. Yet this curse
Which strikes me now, I find it hard to
　　brave
In silence or in speech. Because I gave
Honour to mortals, I have yoked my soul
To this compelling fate. Because I stole
The secret fount of fire, whose bubbles
　　went
Over the ferule's brim, and manward sent
Art's mighty means and perfect rudiment,
That sin I expiate in this agony,
Hung here in fetters, 'neath the blanching
　　sky.
　　　Ah, ah me! what a sound,
What a fragrance sweeps up from a
　　pinion unseen
Of a god, or a mortal, or nature between,
Sweeping up to this rock where the earth
　　has her bound,
To have sight of my pangs, or some
　　guerdon obtain—
Lo, a god in the anguish, a god in the
　　chain!
　　　The god, Zeus hateth sore
　　　And his gods hate again,
As many as tread on his glorified floor,
Because I loved mortals too much ever-
　　more.
Alas me! what a murmur and motion I
　　hear,
　　　As of birds flying near!
　　　And the air undersings
　　　The light stroke of their wings—
And all life that approaches I wait for
　　in fear.

Chorus of Sea Nymphs, first strophe.

　　Fear nothing! our troop
　　Floats lovingly up

　　With a quick-oaring stroke
　　Of wings steered to the rock,
Having softened the soul of our father
　　below!
For the gales of swift-bearing have sent
　　me a sound,
And the clank of the iron, the malleted
　　blow,
　　Smote down the profound
　　Of my caverns of old,
And struck the red light in a blush from
　　my brow,—
Till I sprang up unsandalled, in haste to
　　behold,
And rushed forth on my chariot of wings
　　manifold.

Prometheus. Alas me!—alas me!
Ye offspring of Tethys who bore at her
　　breast
Many children, and eke of Oceanus,—he,
Coiling still around earth with perpetual
　　unrest!
　　　Behold me and see
　　　How transfixed with the fang
　　　Of a fetter I hang
On the high-jutting rocks of this fissure,
　　and keep
An uncoveted watch o'er the world and
　　the deep.

Chorus, first antistrophe.

I behold thee, Prometheus—yet now,
　　yet now,
A terrible cloud whose rain is tears
Sweeps over mine eyes that witness how
　　　Thy body appears
Hung awaste on the rocks by infrangible
　　chains!
For new is the Hand and the rudder that
　　steers
The ship of Olympus through surge and
　　wind—
And of old things passed, no track is
　　behind.

Prometheus. Under earth, under Hades
　　Where the home of the shade is,
All into the deep, deep Tartarus,
　　I would he had hurled me adown!
I would he had plunged me, fastened thus
In the knotted chain with the savage
　　clang,

All into the dark, where there should be
    none,
Neither god nor another, to laugh and
    see !
But now the winds sing through and
    shake
The hurtling chains wherein I hang,—
And I, in my naked sorrows, make
    Much mirth for my enemy.

Chorus, second strophe.

Nay ! who of the gods hath a heart so
    stern
    As to use thy woe for a mock and mirth?
Who would not turn more mild to learn
    Thy sorrows ? who of the heaven and
        earth,
    Save Zeus ? But he
    Right wrathfully
Bears on his sceptral soul unbent,
And rules thereby the heavenly seed,
Nor will he pause till he content
His thirsty heart in a finished deed ;
Or till Another shall appear,
To win by fraud, to seize by fear
The hard-to-be-captured government.

Prometheus. Yet even of *me* he shall
    have need,
That monarch of the blessed seed,
Of me, of me, who now am cursed
    By his fetters dire,—
To wring my secret out withal
    And learn by whom his sceptre shall
Be filched from him—as was, at first,
        His heavenly fire.
But he never shall enchant me
    With his honey-lipped persuasion !
Never, never shall he daunt me
    With the oath and threat of passion,
Into speaking as they want me,
Till he loose this savage chain,
    And accept the expiation
Of my sorrow, in his pain.

Chorus, second antistrophe.

Thou art, sooth, a brave god,
    And, for all thou hast borne
From the stroke of the rod,
    Nought relaxest from scorn !
But thou speakest unto me
    Too free and unworn ;
And a terror strikes through me

And festers my soul
    And I fear, in the roll
Of the storm, for thy fate
    In the ship far from shore !
Since the son of Saturnius is hard in
    his hate
And unmoved in his heart evermore.

Prometheus. I know that Zeus is stern.
I know he metes his justice by his will.
And yet, his soul shall learn
More softness when once broken by this
    ill,—
And curbing his unconquerable vaunt
He shall rush on in fear to meet with me
Who rush to meet with him in agony,
To issues of harmonious covenant.
Chorus. Remove the veil from all
    things and relate
The story to us,—of what crime accused,
Zeus smites thee with dishonourable
    pangs.
Speak ! if to teach us do not grieve thy-
    self.
    Prometheus. The utterance of these
        things is torture to me,
But so, too, is their silence ! each way lies
Woe strong as fate.
        When gods began with wrath,
And war rose up between their starry
    brows,
Some choosing to cast Chronos from his
    throne
That Zeus might king it there, and some
    in haste
With opposite oaths that they would
    have no Zeus
To rule the gods for ever,—I, who brought
The counsel I thought meetest, could not
    move
The Titans, children of the Heaven and
    Earth,
What time, disdaining in their rugged
    souls
My subtle machinations, they assumed
It was an easy thing for force to take
The mastery of fate. My mother, then,
Who is called not only Themis but Earth
    too,
(Her single beauty joys in many names)
Did teach me with reiterant prophecy
What future should be,—and how con-
    quering gods

Should not prevail by strength and violence,
But by guile only. When I told them so,
They would not deign to contemplate the truth
On all sides round,—whereat I deemed it best
To lead my willing mother upwardly,
And set my Themis face to face with Zeus
As willing to receive her. Tartarus,
With its abysmal cloister of the Dark,
Because I gave that counsel, covers up
The antique Chronos and his siding hosts,
And, by that counsel helped, the king of gods
Hath recompensed me with these bitter pangs!
For kingship wears a cancer at the heart,—
Distrust in friendship. Do ye also ask,
What crime it is for which he tortures me—
That shall be clear before you. When at first
He filled his father's throne, he instantly
Made various gifts of glory to the gods,
And dealt the empire out. Alone of men,
Of miserable men, he took no count,
But yearned to sweep their track off from the world,
And plant a newer race there. Not a god
Resisted such desire except myself!
I dared it! *I* drew mortals back to light,
From meditated ruin deep as hell!—
For which wrong, I am bent down in these pangs
Dreadful to suffer, mournful to behold,—
And I, who pitied man, am thought myself
Unworthy of pity,—while I render out
Deep rhythms of anguish 'neath the harping hand
That strikes me thus!—a sight to shame your Zeus!

Chorus. Hard as thy chains, and cold as all these rocks,
Is he, Prometheus, who withholds his heart
From joining in thy woe. I yearned before
To fly this sight—and, now I gaze on it,
I sicken inwards.

Prometheus. To my friends, indeed,
I must be a sad sight.

Chorus. And didst thou sin
No more than so?

Prometheus. I did restrain besides
My mortals from premeditating death.

Chorus. How didst thou medicine the plague-fear of death?

Prometheus. I set blind Hopes to inhabit in their house.

Chorus. By that gift, thou didst help thy mortals well.

Prometheus. I gave them also,—fire.

Chorus. And have they now,
Those creatures of a day, the red-eyed fire?

Prometheus. They have! and shall learn by it, many arts.

Chorus. And, truly, for such sins Zeus tortures thee,
And will remit no anguish? Is there set
No limit before thee to thine agony?

Prometheus. No other! only what seems good to HIM.

Chorus. And how will it seem good?
what hope remains?
Seest thou not that thou hast sinned?
But that thou hast sinned
It glads me not to speak of, and grieves thee—
Then let it pass from both! and seek thyself
Some outlet from distress.

Prometheus. It is in truth
An easy thing to stand aloof from pain
And lavish exhortation and advice
On one vexed sorely by it. I have known
All in prevision. By my choice, my choice,
I freely sinned—I will confess my sin—
And helping mortals, found mine own despair.
I did not think indeed that I should pine
Beneath such pangs against such skyey rocks,
Doomed to this drear hill and no neighbouring
Of any life!—but mourn not ye for griefs
I bear to-day!—hear rather, dropping down
To the plain, how other woes creep on to me,

And learn the consummation of my doom.
Beseech you, nymphs, beseech you,
    grieve for me
Who now am grieving!—for Grief walks
    the earth,
And sits down at the foot of each by turns.
    Chorus. We hear the deep clash of thy
        words,
    Prometheus, and obey!
And I spring with a rapid foot away
From the rushing car and the holy air,
    The track of birds—
And I drop to the rugged ground and
    there
    Await the tale of thy despair.

Enter OCEANUS.

Oceanus. I reach the bourne of my weary
    road
    Where I may see and answer thee,
    Prometheus, in thine agony!
On the back of the quick-winged bird I
    glode,
    And I bridled him in
    With the will of a god!
Behold, thy sorrow aches in me,
    Constrained by the force of kin.
Nay, though that tie were all undone,
For the life of none beneath the sun
Would I seek a larger benison
    Than I seek for thine!
And thou shalt learn my words are
    truth,—
That no fair parlance of the mouth
    Grows falsely out of mine.
Now give me a deed to prove my faith,—
For no faster friend is named in breath
    Than I, Oceanus, am thine.
    Prometheus. Ha! what has brought
        thee? Hast thou also come
To look upon my woe? How hast thou
    dared
To leave the depths called after thee,
    the caves
Self-hewn and self-roofed with spon-
    taneous rock,
To visit earth, the mother of my chain?
Hast come indeed to view my doom and
    mourn
That I should sorrow thus? Gaze on,
    and see
How I, the fast friend of your Zeus,—
    how I,

The erector of the empire in his hand,—
Am bent beneath that hand, in this de-
    spair!
    Oceanus. Prometheus, I behold,—and
        I would fain
Exhort thee, though already subtle
    enough,
To a better wisdom. Titan, know thyself,
And take new softness to thy manners
    since
A new king rules the gods. If words
    like these,
Harsh words and trenchant, thou wilt
    fling abroad,
Zeus haply, though he sit so far and high,
May hear thee do it, and so this wrath
    of his,
Which now affects thee fiercely, shall
    appear
A mere child's sport at vengeance.
    Wretched god,
Rather dismiss the passion which thou
    hast,
And seek a change from grief. Perhaps
    I seem
To address thee with old saws and out-
    worn sense,—
Yet such a curse, Prometheus, surely
    waits
On lips that speak too proudly!—thou,
    meantime,
Art none the meeker, nor dost yield a jot
To evil circumstance, preparing still
To swell the account of grief with other
    griefs
Than what are borne. Beseech thee,
    use me then
For counsel! do not spurn against the
    pricks,—
Seeing that who reigns, reigns by cruelty
Instead of right. And now, I go from
    hence,
And will endeavour if a power of mine
Can break thy fetters through. For thee,
    —be calm,
And smooth thy words from passion.
    Knowest thou not
Of perfect knowledge, thou who knowest
    too much,
That where the tongue wags, ruin never
    lags?
    Prometheus. I gratulate thee who hast
        shared and dared

All things with me, except their penalty!
Enough so! leave these thoughts. It
    cannot be
That thou shouldst move HIM. HE may
    not be moved ;
And *thou*, beware of sorrow on this road.
    Oceanus. Aye! ever wiser for another's
    use
Than thine! the event, and not the
    prophecy,
Attests it to me. Yet where now I rush,
Thy wisdom hath no power to drag me
    back ;
Because I glory, glory, to go hence
And win for thee deliverance from thy
    pangs,
As a free gift from Zeus.
    Prometheus. Why there, again,
I give thee gratulation and applause !
Thou lackest no goodwill. But, as for
    deeds,
Do nought! 'twere all done vainly ;
    helping nought,
Whatever thou wouldst do. Rather take
    rest,
And keep thyself from evil. If I grieve,
I do not therefore wish to multiply
The griefs of others. Verily, not so !
For still my brother's doom doth vex
    my soul,—
My brother Atlas, standing in the west,
Shouldering the column of the heaven
    and earth,
A difficult burden ! I have also seen,
And pitied as I saw, the earth-born one,
The inhabitant of old Cilician caves,
The great war-monster of the hundred
    heads
(All taken and bowed beneath the violent
    Hand),
Typhon the fierce, who did resist the
    gods,
And, hissing slaughter from his dreadful
    jaws,
Flash out ferocious glory from his eyes,
As if to storm the throne of Zeus!
    Whereat,
The sleepless arrow of Zeus flew straight
    at him,—
The headlong bolt of thunder breathing
    flame,
And struck him downward from his
    eminence

Of exultation! Through the very soul
It struck him, and his strength was
    withered up
To ashes, thunder-blasted. Now, he lies
A helpless trunk supinely, at full length
Beside the strait of ocean, spurred into
By roots of Aetna—high upon whose tops
Hephaestus sits and strikes the flashing
    ore.
From thence the rivers of fire shall burst
    away
Hereafter, and devour with savage jaws
The equal plains of fruitful Sicily,
Such passion he shall boil back in hot darts
Of an insatiate fury and sough of flame,
Fallen Typhon,—howsoever struck and
    charred
By Zeus's bolted thunder ! But for thee,
Thou art not so unlearned as to need
My teaching—let thy knowledge save
    thyself.
I quaff the full cup of a present doom,
And wait till Zeus hath quenched his
    will in wrath.
    Oceanus. Prometheus, art thou igno-
    rant of this,—
That words do medicine anger ?
    Prometheus. If the word
With seasonable softness touch the soul,
And, where the parts are ulcerous, sear
    them not
By any rudeness.
    Oceanus. With a noble aim
To dare as nobly—is there harm in *that* ?
Dost thou discern it? Teach me.
    Prometheus. I discern
Vain aspiration,—unresultive work.
    Oceanus. Then suffer me to bear the
    brunt of this !
Since it is profitable that one who is
    wise
Should seem not wise at all.
    Prometheus. And such would seem
My very crime.
    Oceanus. In truth thine argument
Sends me back home.
    Prometheus. Lest any lament for me
Should cast thee down to hate.
    Oceanus. The hate of Him,
Who sits a new king on the absolute
    throne ?
    Prometheus. Beware of him,—lest
    thine heart grieve by him.

Oceanus. Thy doom, Prometheus, be
　　my teacher!
Prometheus.　　Go!
Depart—beware!—and keep the mind
　　thou hast.
Oceanus. Thy words drive after, as I
　　rush before—
Lo! my four-footed Bird sweeps smooth
　　and wide
The flats of air with balanced pinions,
　　glad
To bend his knee at home in the ocean-
　　stall.

　　　　　　　　　[*Exit* OCEANUS.

Chorus, first strophe.

I moan thy fate, I moan for thee,
　　Prometheus! From my eyes too tender,
Drop after drop incessantly
　　The tears of my heart's pity render
My cheeks wet from their fountains
　　free,—
Because that Zeus, the stern and cold,
　　Whose law is taken from his breast,
　　Uplifts his sceptre manifest
　　　　Over the gods of old.

First antistrophe.

　　All the land is moaning
With a murmured plaint to-day ;
　　All the mortal nations,
　　Having habitations
　　In the holy Asia,
　　Are a dirge intoning
For thine honour and thy brothers',
　　Once majestic beyond others
　　　In the old belief,—
Now are groaning in the groaning
　　Of thy deep-voiced grief.

Second strophe.

Mourn the maids inhabitant
　　Of the Colchian land,
Who with white, calm bosoms, stand
　　In the battle's roar !
Mourn the Scythian tribes that haunt
The verge of earth, Maeotis' shore.

Second antistrophe.

Yea ! Arabia's battle crown,
And dwellers in the beetling town

Mount Caucasus sublimely nears,—
An iron squadron, thundering down
　　With the sharp-prowed spears.

But one other before, have I seen to
　　remain,
　　By invincible pain
Bound and vanquished,—one Titan !—
　　'twas Atlas, who bears
In a curse from the gods, by that
　　strength of his own
Which he evermore wears,
The weight of the heaven on his
　　shoulder alone,
While he sighs up the stars !
And the tides of the ocean wail bursting
　　their bars,—
　　Murmurs still the profound,—
And black Hades roars up through the
　　chasm of the ground,—
And the fountains of pure-running rivers
　　moan low
　　In a pathos of woe.

Prometheus. Beseech you, think not
　　I am silent thus
Through pride or scorn ! I only gnaw
　　my heart
With meditation, seeing myself so
　　wronged.
For so—their honours to these new-
　　made gods,
What other gave but I,—and dealt them
　　out
With distribution ? Aye—but here I am
　　dumb !
For here, I should repeat your know-
　　ledge to you,
If I spake aught.　List rather to the deeds
I did for mortals !—how, being fools
　　before,
I made them wise and true in aim of soul.
And let me tell you—not as taunting men,
But teaching you the intention of my gifts,
How, first beholding, they beheld in vain,
And hearing, heard not, but, like shapes
　　in dreams,
Mixed all things wildly down the tedious
　　time,
Nor knew to build a house against the
　　sun
With wicketed sides, nor any woodcraft
　　knew,

But lived, like silly ants, beneath the
ground
In hollow caves unsunned. There, came
to them
No steadfast sign of winter, nor of spring
Flower-perfumed, nor of summer full
of fruit,
But blindly and lawlessly they did all
things,
Until I taught them how the stars do rise
And set in mystery, and devised for them
Number, the inducer of philosophies,
The synthesis of Letters, and, beside,
The artificer of all things, Memory,
That sweet Muse-mother. I was first
to yoke
The servile beasts in couples, carrying
An heirdom of man's burdens on their
backs.
I joined to chariots, steeds, that love the
bit
They champ at—the chief pomp of golden
ease!
And none but I originated ships,
The seaman's chariots, wandering on
the brine
With linen wings. And I—oh, miser-
able!—
Who did devise for mortals all these arts.
Have no device left now to save myself
From the woe I suffer.
   Chorus.   Most unseemly woe
Thou sufferest, and dost stagger from
the sense,
Bewildered! Like a bad leech falling sick
Thou art faint at soul, and canst not find
the drugs
Required to save thyself.
   Prometheus.   Hearken the rest,
And marvel further—what more arts
and means
I did invent,—this, greatest!—if a man
Fell sick, there was no cure, nor esculent
Nor chrism nor liquid, but for lack of
drugs
Men pined and wasted, till I showed
them all
Those mixtures of emollient remedies
Whereby they might be rescued from
disease.
I fixed the various rules of mantic art,
Discerned the vision from the common
dream,

Instructed them in vocal auguries
Hard to interpret, and defined as plain
The wayside omens,—flights of crook-
clawed birds,—
Showed which are, by their nature,
fortunate,
And which not so, and what the food of
each,
And what the hates, affections, social
needs,
Of all to one another,—taught what sign
Of visceral lightness, coloured to a shade,
May charm the genial gods, and what
fair spots
Commend the lung and liver. Burning so
The limbs encased in fat, and the long
chine,
I led my mortals on to an art abstruse,
And cleared their eyes to the image in
the fire,
Erst filmed in dark. Enough said now
of this.
For the other helps of man hid under-
ground,
The iron and the brass, silver and gold,
Can any dare affirm he found them out
Before me? none, I know! unless he
choose
To lie in his vaunt. In one word learn
the whole,—
That all arts came to mortals from
Prometheus.
   Chorus. Give mortals now no inex-
pedient help,
Neglecting thine own sorrow! I have
hope still
To see thee, breaking from the fetter
here,
Stand up as strong as Zeus.
   Prometheus.   This ends not thus,
The oracular Fate ordains. I must be
bowed
By infinite woes and pangs, to escape
this chain.
Necessity is stronger than mine art.
   Chorus. Who holds the helm of that
Necessity?
   Prometheus. The threefold Fates and
the unforgetting Furies.
   Chorus. Is Zeus less absolute than
these are?
   Prometheus.   Yea,
And therefore cannot fly what is ordained.

Chorus. What is ordained for Zeus,
　　except to be
A king for ever ?
　　Prometheus.　　'Tis too early yet
For thee to learn it : ask no more.
　　Chorus.　　　　　　Perhaps
Thy secret may be something holy ?
　　Prometheus.　　　　　　Turn
To another matter ! this, it is not time
To speak abroad, but utterly to veil
In silence.　For by that same secret kept,
I 'scape this chain's dishonour and its
　　woe.

Chorus, first strophe.

Never, oh never,
　　May Zeus, the all-giver,
Wrestle down from his throne
　　In that might of his own
To antagonize mine !
　　Nor let me delay
As I bend on my way
Toward the gods of the shrine,
Where the altar is full
Of the blood of the bull,
Near the tossing brine
Of Ocean my father !
May no sin be sped in the word that is
　　said,
　　But my vow be rather
　　　Consummated,
Nor evermore fail, nor evermore pine.

First antistrophe.

'Tis sweet to have
　　Life lengthened out
With hopes proved brave
　　By the very doubt,
Till the spirit enfold
Those manifest joys which were foretold !
　　But I thrill to behold
　　　Thee, victim doomed,
By the countless cares
And the drear despairs,
　　For ever consumed, —
And all because thou, who art fearless
　　now
　　Of Zeus above,
Didst overflow for mankind below
　　With a free-souled, reverent love.

Ah friend, behold and see !
What 's all the beauty of humanity ?
　　Can it be fair ?

What 's all the strength ?—is it strong ?
　　And what hope can they bear,
These dying livers—living one day long ?
　　Ah. seest thou not, my friend,
　　　How feeble and slow
　　And like a dream, doth go
This poor blind manhood, drifted from
　　its end ?
　　And how no mortal wranglings can
　　　confuse
　　　The harmony of Zeus ?

Prometheus, I have learnt these things
　　From the sorrow in thy face.
　　Another song did fold its wings
Upon my lips in other days,
When round the bath and round the bed
The hymeneal chant instead
　　I sang for thee, and smiled,—
And thou didst lead, with gifts and
　　vows,
　　Hesione, my father's child,
　　To be thy wedded spouse.

Io *enters.*

Io. What land is this ? what people is
　　here ?
And who is he that writhes, I see,
　　In the rock-hung chain ?
Now what is the crime that hath brought
　　thee to pain ?
Now what is the land—make answer
　　free—
Which I wander through, in my wrong
　　and fear ?
　　Ah ! ah ! ah me !
The gad-fly stingeth to agony !
O Earth, keep off that phantasm pale
Of earth-born Argus !—ah !—I quail
　　When my soul descries
That herdsman with the myriad eyes
Which seem, as he comes, one crafty eye.
Graves hide him not, though he should
　　die,
But he doggeth me in my misery
From the roots of death, on high—on
　　high—
And along the sands of the siding deep,
All famine-worn, he follows me,
And his waxen reed doth undersound
　　The waters round,
And giveth a measure that giveth sleep.

Woe, woe, woe!
Where shall my weary course be done?—
What wouldst thou with me, Saturn's
  son?
And in what have I sinned, that I should
  go
Thus yoked to grief by thine hand for
  ever?
Ah! ah! dost vex me so
  That I madden and shiver,
  Stung through with dread?
Flash the fire down, to burn me!
Heave the earth up, to cover me!
Or plunge me in the deep, with the salt
  waves over me,
  That the sea-beasts may be fed!
O king, do not spurn me
  In my prayer!
For this wandering everlonger, ever-
  more,
  Hath overworn me,—
And I know not on what shore
I may rest from my despair.

Chorus. Hearest thou what the ox-
  horned maiden saith?
Prometheus. How could I choose but
  hearken what she saith,
The frenzied maiden? — Inachus's
  child?—
Who love-warms Zeus's heart, and now
  is lashed
By Heré's hate along the unending ways?

Io. Who taught thee to articulate that
  name,—
My father's? Speak to his child,
By grief and shame defiled!
Who art thou, victim, thou—who dost
  acclaim
Mine anguish in true words, on the wide
  air?
And callest too by name the curse that
  came
  From Heré unaware,
To waste and pierce me with its mad-
  dening goad?
Ah—ah—I leap
With the pang of the hungry—I bound
  on the road—
I am driven by my doom—
I am overcome

By the wrath of an enemy strong and
  deep!
Are any of those who have tasted pain,
  Alas! as wretched as I?
Now tell me plain, doth aught remain
For my soul to endure beneath the sky?
Is there any help to be holpen by?
If knowledge be in thee, let it be said!
  Cry aloud—cry
To the wandering, woful maid.

Prometheus. Whatever thou wouldst
  learn I will declare,—
No riddle upon my lips, but such straight
  words
As friends should use to each other
  when they talk.
Thou seest Prometheus, who gave
  mortals fire.
  Io. O common Help of all men, known
    of all,
O miserable Prometheus, — for what
  cause
Dost thou endure thus?
  Prometheus. I have done with wail
For my own griefs—but lately.
  Io. Wilt thou not
Vouchsafe the boon to me?
  Prometheus. Say what thou wilt,
For I vouchsafe all.
  Io. Speak then, and reveal
Who shut thee in this chasm.
  Prometheus. The will of Zeus,
The hand of his Hephaestus.
  Io. And what crime,
Dost expiate so?
  Prometheus. Enough for thee I have
    told,
In so much only.
  Io. Nay—but show besides
The limit of my wandering, and the time
Which yet is lacking to fulfil my grief.
  Prometheus. Why, not to know were
    better than to know,
For such as thou.
  Io. Beseech thee, blind me not
To that which I must suffer.
  Prometheus. If I do,
The reason is not that I grudge a boon.
  Io. What reason, then, prevents thy
    speaking out?
  Prometheus. No grudging! but a fear
    to break thine heart.

Io. Less care for me, I pray thee!
    Certainty,
I count for advantage.
  Prometheus.   Thou wilt have it so,
And, therefore, I must speak. Now
    hear—
  Chorus.   Not yet.
Give half the guerdon my way. Let us
    learn
First, what the curse is that befell the
    maid,—
Her own voice telling her own wasting
    woes :
The sequence of that anguish shall await
The teaching of thy lips.
  Prometheus.   It doth behove
That thou, Maid Io, shouldst vouchsafe
    to these
The grace they pray,—the more, be-
    cause they are called
Thy father's sisters! since to open out
And mourn out grief where it is possible
To draw a tear from the audience, is a
    work
That pays its own price well.
  Io.   I cannot choose
But trust you, nymphs, and tell you all
    ye ask,
In clear words—though I sob amid my
    speech
In speaking of the storm-curse sent from
    Zeus,
And of my beauty, from which height
    it took
Its swoop on me, poor wretch! left thus
    deformed
And monstrous to your eyes. For ever-
    more
Around my virgin-chamber, wandering
    went
The nightly visions which entreated
    me
With syllabled smooth sweetness.—
    ' Blessed maid,
Why lengthen out thy maiden hours
    when fate
Permits the noblest spousal in the world?
When Zeus burns with the arrow of thy
    love,
And fain would touch thy beauty?—
    Maiden, thou
Despise not Zeus! depart to Lerné's
    mead

That's green around thy father's flocks
    and stalls,
Until the passion of the heavenly Eye
Be quenched in sight.' Such dreams
    did all night long
Constrain me—me, unhappy!—till I
    dared
To tell my father how they trod the dark
With visionary steps. Whereat he sent
His frequent heralds to the Pythian fane,
And also to Dodona, and inquired
How best, by act or speech, to please
    the gods.
The same returning, brought back oracles
Of doubtful sense, indefinite response,
Dark to interpret ; but at last there came
To Inachus an answer that was clear,—
Thrown straight as any bolt, and spoken
    out—
This—'he should drive me from my
    home and land,
And bid me wander to the extreme
    verge
Of all the earth—or, if he willed it not,
Should have a thunder with a fiery eye,
Leap straight from Zeus to burn up all
    his race
To the last root of it.' By which Loxian
    word
Subdued, he drove me forth, and shut
    me out,
He loath, me loath,—but Zeus's violent bit
Compelled him to the deed!—when
    instantly
My body and soul were changèd and
    distraught,
And, hornèd as ye see, and spurred along
By the fanged insect, with a maniac leap
I rushed on to Cerchnea's limpid stream
And Lerné's fountain-water. There,
    the earth-born,
The herdsman Argus, most immitigable
Of wrath, did find me out, and track me
    out
With countless eyes, set staring at my
    steps!—
And though an unexpected sudden doom
Drew him from life—I, curse-tormented
    still,
Am driven from land to land before the
    scourge
The gods hold o'er me. So, thou hast
    heard the past,

And if a bitter future thou canst tell,
Speak on! I charge thee, do not flatter me
Through pity, with false words; for, in
    my mind,
Deceiving works more shame than tor-
    turing doth.

Chorus.

Ah! silence here!
Nevermore, nevermore,
Would I languish for
The stranger's word
To thrill in mine ear!—
Nevermore for the wrong and the woe
    and the fear
So hard to behold,
So cruel to bear,
Piercing my soul with a double-edged
    sword
Of a sliding cold!
Ah Fate!—ah me!—
I shudder to see
This wandering maid in her agony.

Prometheus. Grief is too quick in thee,
    and fear too full.
Be patient till thou hast learnt the rest.
Chorus.   Speak—teach!
To those who are sad already, it seems
    sweet,
By clear foreknowledge to make perfect,
    pain.
Prometheus. The boon ye asked me
    first was lightly won,—
For first ye asked the story of this maid's
    grief
As her own lips might tell it. Now
    remains
To list what other sorrows she so young
Must bear from Heré!—Inachus's child,
O thou!—drop down thy soul my
    weighty words,
And measure out the landmarks which
    are set
To end thy wandering. Toward the
    orient sun
First turn thy face from mine, and jour-
    ney on
Along the desert flats, till thou shalt come
Where Scythia's shepherd peoples dwell
    aloft,
Perched in wheeled wagons under
    woven roofs,

And twang the rapid arrow past the
    bow—
Approach them not; but siding in thy
    course,
The rugged shore-rocks resonant to the
    sea,
Depart that country. On the left hand
    dwell
The iron-workers, called the Chalybes,
Of whom beware, for certes they are
    uncouth,
And nowise bland to strangers. Reach-
    ing so
The stream Hybristes (well the *scorner*
    called),
Attempt no passage,—it is hard to pass,—
Or ere thou come to Caucasus itself,
That highest of mountains, where the
    river leaps
The precipice in his strength!—thou
    must toil up
Those mountain-tops that neighbour
    with the stars,
And tread the south way, and draw
    near, at last,
The Amazonian host that hateth man,
Inhabitants of Themiscyra, close
Upon Thermodon, where the sea's rough
    jaw
Doth gnash at Salmydessa and provide
A cruel host to seamen, and to ships
A stepdame. They with unreluctant hand
Shall lead thee on and on, till thou arrive
Just where the ocean-gates show nar-
    rowest
On the Cimmerian isthmus. Leaving
    which,
Behoves thee swim with fortitude of
    soul
The strait Maeotis. Aye! and evermore
That traverse shall be famous on men's
    lips,
That strait, called Bosphorus, the horned
    one's road,
So named because of thee, who so wilt
    pass
From Europe's plain to Asia's continent.
How think ye, nymphs? the king of
    gods appears
Impartial in ferocious deeds? Behold!
The god desirous of this mortal's love
Hath cursed her with these wanderings.
        Ah, fair child,

Thou hast met a bitter groom for bridal
    troth !
For all thou yet hast heard, can only prove
The incompleted prelude of thy doom.
    Io. Ah, Ah !
    Prometheus. Is't thy turn, now, to
        shriek and moan ?
How wilt thou, when thou hast hearkened
    what remains ?
    Chorus. Besides the grief thou hast
        told, can aught remain ?
    Prometheus. A sea—of foredoomed evil
        worked to storm.
    Io. What boots my life, then ? why
        not cast myself
Down headlong from this miserable rock,
That, dashed against the flats, I may
    redeem
My soul from sorrow ? Better once to die,
Than day by day to suffer.
    Prometheus.   Verily,
It would be hard for thee to bear my woe
For whom it is appointed not to die.
Death frees from woe : but I before me see
In all my far prevision, not a bound
To all I suffer, ere that Zeus shall fall
From being a king.
    Io.   And can it ever be
That Zeus shall fall from empire ?
    Prometheus.   *Thou*, methinks,
Wouldst take some joy to see it.
    Io.   Could I choose ?
I, who endure such pangs, now, by that
    god !
    Prometheus. Learn from me, therefore,
        that the event shall be.
    Io. By whom shall his imperial scep-
        tred hand
Be emptied so ?
    Prometheus. Himself shall spoil him-
        self,
Through his idiotic counsels.
    Io.   How ? declare !
Unless the word bring evil.
    Prometheus.   He shall wed—
And in the marriage-bond be joined to
    grief.
    Io. A heavenly bride — or human ?
        Speak it out,
If it be utterable.
    Prometheus. Why should I say which ?
It ought not to be uttered, verily.
    Io.   Then

It is his wife shall tear him from his
    throne ?
    Prometheus. It is his wife shall bear
        a son to him,
More mighty than the father.
    Io.   From this doom
Hath he no refuge ?
    Prometheus.   None—or ere that I,
Loosed from these fetters—
    Io.   Yea—but who shall loose,
While Zeus is adverse ?
    Prometheus.   One who is born
        of thee,—
It is ordained so.
    Io.   What is this thou sayest ?
A son of mine shall liberate thee from
    woe ?
    Prometheus. After ten generations,
        count three more,
And find him in the third.
    Io.   The oracle
Remains obscure.
    Prometheus. And search it not to learn
Thine own griefs from it.
    Io.   Point me not to a good,
To leave me straight bereaved.
    Prometheus.   I am prepared
To grant thee one of two things.
    Io.   But which two ?
Set them before me—grant me power
    to choose.
    Prometheus. I grant it—choose now !
        shall I name aloud
What griefs remain to wound thee, or
    what hand
Shall save me out of mine ?
    Chorus.   Vouchsafe, O god,
The one grace of the twain to her who
    prays,
The next to me—and turn back neither
    prayer
Dishonour'd by denial.   To herself
Recount the future wandering of her
    feet ;
Then point me to the looser of thy chain,
Because I yearn to know him.
    Prometheus.   Since ye will,
Of absolute will, this knowledge, I will
    set
No contrary against it, nor keep back
A word of all ye ask for. Io, first
To thee I must relate thy wandering
    course

Far winding. As I tell it, write it down
In thy soul's book of memories. When
    thou hast past
The refluent bound that parts two
    continents,
Track on the footsteps of the orient sun
In his own fire—across the roar of seas,—
Fly till thou hast reached the Gorgonaean
    flats
Beside Cisthene. There, the Phorcides,
Three ancient maidens, live, with shape
    of swan,
One tooth between them, and one com-
    mon eye,
On whom the sun doth never look at all
With all his rays, nor evermore the moon,
When she looks through the night!
    Anear to whom
Are the Gorgon sisters three, enclothed
    with wings,
With twisted snakes for ringlets, man-
    abhorred—
There is no mortal gazes in their face,
And gazing can breathe on. I speak of
    such
To guard thee from their horror. Aye!
    and list
Another tale of a dreadful sight! beware
The Griffins, those unbarking dogs of
    Zeus,
Those sharp-mouthed dogs!—and the
    Arimaspian host
Of one-eyed horsemen, habiting beside
The river of Pluto that runs bright with
    gold.
Approach them not, beseech thee.
    Presently
Thou 'lt come to a distant land, a dusky
    tribe
Of dwellers at the fountain of the Sun,
Whence flows the river Aethiops ; wind
    along
Its banks and turn off at the cataracts,
Just as the Nile pours from the Bybline
    hills
His holy and sweet wave!—his course
    shall guide
Thine own to that triangular Nile-ground
Where, Io, is ordained for thee and
    thine,
A lengthened exile. Have I said, in this,
Aught darkly or incompletely?—now
    repeat

The question, make the knowledge fuller!
    Lo,
I have more leisure than I covet, here.
  Chorus. If thou canst tell us aught
    that's left untold,
Or loosely told, of her most dreary flight,
Declare it straight! but if thou hast
    uttered all,
Grant us that latter grace for which we
    prayed,
Remembering how we prayed it.
  Prometheus.   She has heard
The uttermost of her wandering. There
    it ends.
But that she may be certain not to have
    heard
All vainly, I will speak what she endured
Ere coming hither, and invoke the past
To prove my prescience true. And
    so—to leave
A multitude of words, and pass at once
To the subject of thy course!—When
    thou hadst gone
To those Molossian plains which sweep
    around
Dodona shouldering Heaven, whereby
    the fane
Of Zeus Thesprotian keepeth oracle,
And, wonder past belief, where oaks do
    wave
Articulate adjurations—(aye, the same
Saluted thee in no perplexèd phrase
But clear with glory, noble wife of Zeus
That shouldst be, there,—some sweet-
    ness took thy sense !)
Thou didst rush further onward,—stung
    along
The ocean-shore, toward Rhea's mighty
    bay,
And, tost back from it, was tost to it again
In stormy evolution !—and, know well,
In coming time that hollow of the sea
Shall bear the name Ionian, and present
A monument of Io's passage through,
Unto all mortals. Be these words the
    signs
Of my soul's power to look beyond the veil
Of visible things. The rest, to you and
    her,
I will declare in common audience,
    nymphs,
Returning thither where my speech
    brake off.

There is a town Canobus, built upon
The earth's fair margin, at the mouth of
　　　Nile,
And on the mound washed up by it!—
　　　Io, there
Shall Zeus give back to thee thy perfect
　　　mind,
And only by the pressure and the touch
Of a hand not terrible; and thou to Zeus
Shalt bear a dusky son who shall be called
Thence, Epaphus, Touched! That son
　　　shall pluck the fruit
Of all that land wide-watered by the flow
Of Nile; but after him, when counting out
As far as the fifth full generation, then
Full fifty maidens, a fair woman-race,
Shall back to Argos turn reluctantly,
To fly the proffered nuptials of their kin,
Their father's brothers. These being
　　　passion-struck,
Like falcons bearing hard on flying doves,
Shall follow, hunting at a quarry of love
They should not hunt—till envious
　　　Heaven maintain
A curse betwixt that beauty and their
　　　desire,
And Greece receive them, to be overcome
In murtherous woman-war, by fierce
　　　red hands
Kept savage by the night. For every
　　　wife
Shall slay a husband, dyeing deep in blood
The sword of a double edge!—(I wish
　　　indeed
As fair a marriage-joy to all my foes!)
One bride alone shall fail to smite to death
The head upon her pillow, touched with
　　　love,
Made impotent of purpose, and impelled
To choose the lesser evil,—shame on
　　　her cheeks,
To blood-guilt on her hands. Which
　　　bride shall bear
A royal race in Argos. Tedious speech
Were needed to relate particulars
Of these things—'tis enough that, from
　　　her seed,
Shall spring the strong He, famous with
　　　the bow,
Whose arm shall break my fetters off.
　　　Behold,
My mother Themis, that old Titaness,
Delivered to me such an oracle,—

But how and when, I should be long to
　　　speak,
And thou, in hearing, wouldst not gain
　　　at all.

　　Io. Eleleu, eleleu!
　　How the spasm and the pain
　　And the fire on the brain
　　　Strike, burning me through!
How the sting of the curse, all aflame
　　　as it flew,
　　Pricks me onward again!
How my heart, in its terror, is spurning
　　　my breast,
And my eyes, like the wheels of a chariot,
　　　roll round!
I am whirled from my course, to the
　　　east, to the west,
In the whirlwind of frenzy all madly
　　　inwound—
And my mouth is unbridled for anguish
　　　and hate,
And my words beat in vain, in wild
　　　storms of unrest,
　　On the sea of my desolate fate.
　　　　　　　　　　[Io rushes out.

　　　　Chorus. Strophe.

Oh, wise was he, oh, wise was he,
Who first within his spirit knew
And with his tongue declared it true,
That love comes best that comes unto
　　The equal of degree!
And that the poor and that the low
Should seek no love from those above
Whose souls are fluttered with the flow
Of airs about their golden height,
Or proud because they see arow
　　Ancestral crowns of light.

　　　　Antistrophe.

Oh, never, never, may ye, Fates,
　　Behold me with your awful eyes
　　Lift mine too fondly up the skies
Where Zeus upon the purple waits!—
　　Nor let me step too near—too near—
To any suitor, bright from heaven!
　　Because I see—because I fear
This loveless maiden vexed and laden
By this fell curse of Heré, driven
　　On wanderings dread and drear.

　　　　Epode.

Nay, grant an equal troth instead
　　Of nuptial love, to bind me by!—

It will not hurt—I shall not dread
  To meet it in reply.
But let not love from those above
Revert and fix me, as I said,
  With that inevitable Eye!
I have no sword to fight that fight—
I have no strength to tread that path—
I know not if my nature hath
The power to bear,—I cannot see
Whither, from Zeus's infinite,
I have the power to flee.

Prometheus. Yet Zeus albeit most absolute of will,
Shall turn to meekness—such a marriage rite
He holds in preparation, which anon
Shall thrust him headlong from his gerent seat
Adown the abysmal void, and so the curse
His father Chronos muttered in his fall,
As he fell from his ancient throne and cursed,
Shall be accomplished wholly. No escape
From all that ruin shall the filial Zeus
Find granted to him from any of his gods,
Unless I teach him. I, the refuge, know,
And I, the means.—Now, therefore, let him sit
And brave the imminent doom, and fix his faith
On his supernal noises, hurtling on
With restless hand the bolt that breathes out fire—
For these things shall not help him, none of them,
Nor hinder his perdition when he falls
To shame, and lower than patience.—
  Such a foe
He doth himself prepare against himself,
A wonder of unconquerable Hate,
An organizer of sublimer fire
Than glares in lightnings, and of grander sound
Than aught the thunder rolls, out-thundering it,
With power to shatter in Poseidon's fist
The trident-spear, which, while it plagues the sea,
Doth shake the shores around it. Aye, and Zeus,
Precipitated thus, shall learn at length

The difference betwixt rule and servitude.
  Chorus. Thou makest threats for Zeus of thy desires.
  Prometheus. I tell you, all these things shall be fulfilled,
Even so as I desire them.
  Chorus. Must we then
Look out for one shall come to master Zeus?
  Prometheus. These chains weigh lighter than his sorrows shall.
  Chorus. How art thou not afraid to utter such words?
  Prometheus. What should *I* fear, who cannot die?
  Chorus. But *he*
Can visit thee with dreader woe than death's.
  Prometheus. Why let him do it!—I am here, prepared
For all things and their pangs.
  Chorus. The wise are they
Who reverence Adrasteia.
  Prometheus. Reverence thou.
Adore thou, flatter thou, whomever reigns,
Whenever reigning! but for me, your Zeus
Is less than nothing. Let him act and reign
His brief hour out according to his will—
He will not, therefore, rule the gods too long.
But lo! I see that courier-god of Zeus,
That new-made menial of the new-crowned king.
He doubtless comes to announce to us something new.

HERMES *enters.*

  Hermes. I speak to thee, the sophist, the talker down
Of scorn by scorn, the sinner against gods,
The reverencer of men, the thief of fire,—
I speak to thee and adjure thee! Zeus requires
Thy declaration of what marriage rite
Thus moves thy vaunt and shall hereafter cause
His fall from empire. Do not wrap thy speech
In riddles, but speak clearly! Never cast

Ambiguous paths, Prometheus, for my feet,
Since Zeus, thou may'st perceive, is scarcely won
To mercy by such means.
  Prometheus. A speech well-mouthed
In the utterance, and full-minded in the sense,
As doth befit a servant of the gods!
New gods, ye newly reign, and think forsooth
Ye dwell in towers too high for any dart
To carry a wound there!—have I not stood by
While two kings fell from thence? and shall I not
Behold the third, the same who rules you now,
Fall, shamed to sudden ruin?—Do I seem
To tremble and quail before your modern gods?
Far be it from me!—For thyself, depart,
Re-tread thy steps in haste. To all thou hast asked
I answer nothing.
  Hermes. Such a wind of pride
Impelled thee of yore full sail upon these rocks.
  Prometheus. I would not barter—learn thou soothly that!—
My suffering for thy service. I maintain
It is a nobler thing to serve these rocks
Than live a faithful slave to father Zeus.
Thus upon scorners I retort their scorn.
  Hermes. It seems that thou dost glory in thy despair.
  Prometheus. I glory? would my foes did glory so,
And I stood by to see them!—Naming whom
Thou art not unremembered.
  Hermes. Dost thou charge
Me also with the blame of thy mischance?
  Prometheus. I tell thee I loathe the universal gods,
Who for the good I gave them rendered back
The ill of their injustice.
  Hermes. Thou art mad—
Thou art raving, Titan, at the fever-height.
  Prometheus. If it be madness to abhor my foes,

May I be mad!
  Hermes. If thou wert prosperous,
Thou wouldst be unendurable.
  Prometheus. Alas!
  Hermes. Zeus knows not that word.
  Prometheus. But maturing Time
Teaches all things.
  Hermes. Howbeit, thou hast not learnt
The wisdom yet thou needest.
  Prometheus. If I had,
I should not talk thus with a slave like thee.
  Hermes. No answer thou vouchsafest, I believe,
To the great Sire's requirement.
  Prometheus. Verily
I owe him grateful service,—and should pay it.
  Hermes. Why, thou dost mock me, Titan, as I stood
A child before thy face.
  Prometheus. No child, forsooth,
But yet more foolish than a foolish child,
If thou expect that I should answer aught
Thy Zeus can ask. No torture from his hand
Nor any machination in the world
Shall force mine utterance, ere he loose, himself,
These cankerous fetters from me! For the rest,
Let him now hurl his blanching light-nings down,
And with his white-winged snows and mutterings deep
Of subterranean thunders, mix all things,
Confound them in disorder. None of this
Shall bend my sturdy will, and make me speak
The name of his dethroner who shall come.
  Hermes. Can this avail thee? Look to it!
  Prometheus. Long ago
It was looked forward to—precounselled of.
  Hermes. Vain god, take righteous courage!—dare for once
To apprehend and front thine agonies
With a just prudence.
  Prometheus. Vainly dost thou chafe
My soul with exhortation, as yonder sea

Goes beating on the rock. Oh! think
no more
That I, fear-struck by Zeus to a woman's
mind,
Will supplicate him, loathèd as he is,
With feminine upliftings of my hands,
To break these chains. Far from me be
the thought!
Hermes. I have indeed, methinks, said
much in vain,—
For still thy heart, beneath my showers
of prayers,
Lies dry and hard,—nay, leaps like
a young horse
Who bites against the new bit in his teeth,
And tugs and struggles against the new-
tried rein,—
Still fiercest in the feeblest thing of all,
Which sophism is,—since absolute will
disjoined
From perfect mind is worse than weak.
Behold,
Unless my words persuade thee, what
a blast
And whirlwind of inevitable woe
Must sweep persuasion through thee!
For at first
The Father will split up this jut of rock
With the great thunder and the bolted
flame,
And hide thy body where a hinge of stone
Shall catch it like an arm ;—and when
thou hast passed
A long black time within, thou shalt
come out
To front the sun while Zeus's winged
hound,
The strong carnivorous eagle, shall
wheel down
To meet thee, self-called to a daily feast,
And set his fierce beak in thee, and tear off
The long rags of thy flesh, and batten deep
Upon thy dusky liver. Do not look
For any end moreover to this curse,
Or ere some god appear, to accept thy
pangs
On his own head vicarious, and descend
With unreluctant step the darks of hell
And gloomy abysses around Tartarus.
Then ponder this !—this threat is not a
growth
Of vain invention ; it is spoken and meant!
King Zeus's mouth is impotent to lie,

Consummating the utterance by the act—
So, look to it, thou !—take heed,—and
nevermore
Forget good counsel, to indulge self-will.
Chorus. Our Hermes suits his reasons
to the times ;
At least I think so,—since he bids thee
drop
Self-will for prudent counsel. Yield to
him !
When the wise err, their wisdom makes
their shame.
Prometheus. Unto me the foreknower,
this mandate of power
He cries, to reveal it.
What's strange in my fate, if I suffer
from hate
At the hour that I feel it?
Let the locks of the lightning, all bristling
and whitening,
Flash, coiling me round,
While the ether goes surging 'neath
thunder and scourging
Of wild winds unbound !
Let the blast of the firmament whirl
from its place
The earth rooted below,
And the brine of the ocean, in rapid
emotion,
Be it driven in the face
Of the stars up in heaven, as they walk
to and fro !
Let him hurl me anon, into Tartarus—
on—
To the blackest degree,
With Necessity's vortices strangling me
down ;
But he cannot join death to a fate meant
for *me!*
Hermes. Why the words that he speaks
and the thoughts that he thinks
Are maniacal !—add,
If the Fate who hath bound him, should
loose not the links,
He were utterly mad.
Then depart ye who groan with him,
Leaving to moan with him,—
Go in haste ! lest the roar of the thunder
anearing
Should blast you to idiocy, living and
hearing.
Chorus. Change thy speech for an-
other, thy thought for a new,

If to move me and teach me indeed
  be thy care!
For thy words swerve so far from the
  loyal and true
  That the thunder of Zeus seems more
    easy to bear.
How! couldst teach me to venture such
    vileness? behold!
  I *choose*, with this victim, this anguish
    foretold!
I recoil from the traitor in hate and
  disdain,—
And I know that the curse of the
  treason is worse
  Than the pang of the chain.
Hermes. Then remember, O nymphs,
  what I tell you before,
  Nor, when pierced by the arrows that
    Até will throw you,
Cast blame on your fate, and declare
  evermore
  That Zeus thrust you on anguish he
    did not foreshow you.
Nay, verily, nay! for ye perish anon
  For your deed—by your choice!—by
    no blindness of doubt,
No abruptness of doom!—but by mad-
  ness alone,

In the great net of Até, whence none
  cometh out,
  Ye are wound and undone!
Prometheus. Aye! in act, now—in
  word, now, no more,
  Earth is rocking in space!
And the thunders crash up with a roar
  upon roar,
And the eddying lightnings flash fire
  in my face,
And the whirlwinds are whirling the
  dust round and round,
  And the blasts of the winds universal,
    leap free
And blow each upon each with a passion
  of sound,
  And ether goes mingling in storm
    with the sea!
Such a curse on my head, in a manifest
  dread,
  From the hand of your Zeus has been
    hurtled along.
O my mother's fair glory! O Aether,
  enringing
All eyes with the sweet common light
  of thy bringing,
  Dost see how I suffer this wrong?

A LAMENT FOR ADONIS

FROM THE GREEK OF BION

I mourn for Adonis—Adonis is dead,
  Fair Adonis is dead, and the Loves
  are lamenting.
Sleep, Cypris, no more on thy purple-
  strewed bed!
  Arise, wretch stoled in black,—beat
  thy breast unrelenting,
And shriek to the worlds, 'Fair Adonis
  is dead.'

II

I mourn for Adonis—the Loves are
  lamenting.
  He lies on the hills in his beauty and
  death,—

The white tusk of a boar has trans-
  pierced his white thigh.
Cytherea grows mad at his thin
  gasping breath,
While the black blood drips down on
  the pale ivory,
And his eye-balls lie quenched with
  the weight of his brows,
The rose fades from his lips, and upon
  them just parted
The kiss dies the goddess consents
  not to lose,
Though the kiss of the Dead cannot
  make her glad-hearted:
  He knows not who kisses him dead
  in the dews.

III

I mourn for Adonis—the Loves are
lamenting.
Deep, deep in the thigh, is Adonis's
wound,
But a deeper, is Cypris's bosom pre-
senting.
The youth lieth dead while his dogs
howl around,
And the nymphs weep aloud from the
mists of the hill,
And the poor Aphrodité, with tresses
unbound,
All dishevelled, unsandalled, shrieks
mournful and shrill
Through the dusk of the groves. The
thorns, tearing her feet,
Gather up the red flower of her blood
which is holy,
Each footstep she takes,—and the
valleys repeat
The sharp cry she utters, and draw it
out slowly.
She calls on her spouse, her Assyrian,
on him
Her own youth, while the dark blood
spreads over his body,
The chest taking hue from the gash
in the limb,
And the bosom once ivory, turning to
ruddy.

IV

Ah, ah, Cytherea! the Loves are
lamenting.
She lost her fair spouse, and so lost
her fair smile—
When he lived she was fair by the
whole world's consenting,
Whose fairness is dead with him!
woe worth the while!
All the mountains above and the oak-
lands below
Murmur, ah, ah Adonis! the streams
overflow
Aphrodité's deep wail,—river-fountains
in pity
Weep soft in the hills, and the flowers
as they blow
Redden outward with sorrow, while all
hear her go
With the song of her sadness through
mountain and city.

V

Ah, ah, Cytherea! Adonis is dead,
Fair Adonis is dead—Echo answers,
Adonis!
Who weeps not for Cypris, when
bowing her head
She stares at the wound where it
gapes and astonies?
—When, ah, ah!—she saw how the
blood ran away
And empurpled the thigh, and, with
wild hands flung out,
Said with sobs, 'Stay, Adonis! unhappy
one, stay,
Let me feel thee once more—let me
ring thee about
With the clasp of my arms, and press
kiss into kiss!
Wait a little, Adonis, and kiss me
again,
For the last time, beloved,—and but so
much of this
That the kiss may learn life from the
warmth of the strain!
—Till thy breath shall exude from thy
soul to my mouth,
To my heart,—and the love-charm I,
once more receiving,
May drink thy love in it, and keep of
a truth
That one kiss in the place of Adonis
the living.
Thou fliest me, mournful one, fliest me far,
My Adonis, and seekest the Acheron
portal,—
To Hell's cruel King goest down with
a scar,
While I weep and live on like a
wretched immortal,
And follow no step!—O Persephoné,
take him,
My husband!—thou'rt better and
brighter than I,
So all beauty flows down to thee!
I cannot make him
Look up at my grief,—there's despair
in my cry,
Since I wail for Adonis who died to
me . . . died to me . . .
—Then, I fear thee!—Art thou dead,
my Adored?
Passion ends like a dream in the sleep
that's denied to me,—

Cypris is widowed,—the Loves seek
their lord
All the house through in vain! Charm
of cestus has ceased
With thy clasp!—oh, too bold in the
hunt past preventing,
Aye, mad, thou so fair . . . to have strife
with a beast!'—
Thus the goddess wailed on—and the
Loves are lamenting.

VI

Ah, ah, Cytherea! Adonis is dead.
She wept tear after tear, with the
blood which was shed,—
And both turned into flowers for the
earth's garden-close,
Her tears, to the wind flower,—his
blood, to the rose.

VII

I mourn for Adonis—Adonis is dead.
Weep no more in the woods, Cytherea,
thy lover!
So, well! make a place for his corse in
thy bed,
With the purples thou sleepest in,
under and over.
He's fair, though a corse—a fair corse...
like a sleeper.
Lay him soft in the silks he had
pleasure to fold,
When, beside thee at night, holy
dreams deep and deeper
Enclosed his young life on the couch
made of gold.
Love him still, poor Adonis! cast on
him together
The crowns and the flowers! since he
died from the place,
Why let all die with him—let the
blossoms go wither,
Rain myrtles and olive-buds down on
his face!
Rain the myrrh down, let all that is
best fall a-pining,
Since the myrrh of his life from thy
keeping is swept!—

—Pale he lay, thine Adonis, in purples
reclining,—
The Loves raised their voices around
him and wept.
They have shorn their bright curls off
to cast on Adonis;
One treads on his bow,—on his arrows,
another,—
One breaks up a well-feathered quiver,
and one is
Bent low at a sandal, untying the
strings,
And one carries the vases of gold
from the springs,
While one washes the wound,—and
behind them a brother
Fans down on the body sweet air
with his wings.

VIII

Cytherea herself, now, the Loves are
lamenting.
Each torch at the door Hymenaeus
blew out;
And, the marriage-wreath dropping its
leaves as repenting.
No more 'Hymen, Hymen,' is
chanted about,
But the *ai ai* instead — 'ai alas' is
begun
For Adonis, and then follows 'ai
Hymenaeus!'
The Graces are weeping for Cinyris'
son,
Sobbing low, each to each, 'His fair
eyes cannot see us!'—
Their wail strikes more shrill than the
sadder Dioné's.
The Fates mourn aloud for Adonis,
Adonis,
Deep chanting; he hears not a word
that they say.
He *would* hear, but Persephoné has
him in keeping.
—Cease moan, Cytherea—leave pomps
for to-day,
And weep new when a new year
refits thee for weeping.

A VISION OF POETS

O Sacred Essence, lighting me this hour,
How may I lightly stile thy great power?
Echo.   Power.
Power! but of whence? under the greenwood spraye?
Or liv'st in Heaven? saye.
Echo.   In Heavens aye.
In Heavens aye! tell, may I it obtayne
By alms, by fasting, prayer,—by paine?
Echo.   By paine.
Show me the paine, it shall be undergone:
I to mine end will still go on.
Echo.   Go on.
                                Britannia's Pastorals.

A POET could not sleep aright,
For his soul kept up too much light
Under his eyelids for the night.

And thus he rose disquieted
With sweet rimes ringing through his
        head,
And in the forest wandered,

Where, sloping up the darkest glades,
The moon had drawn long colonnades,
Upon whose floor the verdure fades

To a faint silver,—pavement fair
The antique wood-nymphs scarce would
        dare
To footprint o'er, had such been there,

And rather sit by breathlessly,
With fear in their large eyes, to see
The consecrated sight.   But HE

The poet, who with spirit-kiss
Familiar, had long claimed for his
Whatever earthly beauty is,—

Who also in his spirit bore
A Beauty passing the earth's store,
Walked calmly onward evermore.

His aimless thoughts in metre went,
Like a babe's hand without intent
Drawn down a seven-stringed instru-
        ment.

Nor jarred it with his humour as,
With a faint stirring of the grass,
An apparition fair did pass.

He might have feared another time,
But all things fair and strange did chime
With his thoughts then, as rime to
        rime.

An angel had not startled him,
Alighted from Heaven's burning rim
To breathe from glory in the Dim ;

Much less a lady riding slow
Upon a palfrey white as snow,
And smooth as a snow-cloud could go.

Full upon his she turned her face,—
' What, ho, sir poet ! dost thou pace
Our woods at night, in ghostly chace

' Of some fair Dryad of old tales,
Who chaunts between the nightingales,
And over sleep by song prevails ?'

She smiled ; but he could see arise
Her soul from far adown her eyes,
Prepared as if for sacrifice.

She looked a queen who seemeth gay
From royal grace alone.   ' Now, nay,'
He answered,—' slumber passed away

' Compelled by instincts in my head
That I should see to-night, instead
Of a fair nymph, some fairer Dread.

She looked up quickly to the sky
And spake :—' The moon's regality
Will hear no praise ! she is as I.

' She is in heaven, and I on earth ;
This is my kingdom—I come forth
To crown all poets to their worth.'

He brake in with a voice that mourned:
'To their worth, lady? They are scorned
By men they sing for, till inurned.

'To their worth? Beauty in the mind
Leaves the hearth cold,—and love-refined
Ambitions make the world unkind.

'The boor who ploughs the daisy down,
The chief whose mortgage of renown
Fixed upon graves, has bought a crown—

'Both these are happier, more approved
Than poets!—why should I be moved
In saying . . . both are more beloved?'

'The south can judge not of the north,'
She resumed calmly; 'I come forth
To crown all poets to their worth.

'Yea, verily, to anoint them all
With blessed oils which surely shall
Smell sweeter as the ages fall.'

'As sweet,' the poet said, and rung
A low sad laugh, 'as flowers are, sprung
Out of their graves when they die young.

'As sweet as window eglantine,
Some bough of which, as they decline,
The hired nurse gathers at their sign.

'As sweet, in short, as perfumed shroud
Which the gay Roman maidens sewed
For English Keats, singing aloud.'

The lady answered, 'Yea, as sweet!
The things thou namest, being complete
In fragrance as I measure it.

'Since sweet the death-clothes and the
        knell
Of him who having lived, dies well,—
And holy sweet the asphodel

'Stirred softly by that foot of his,
When he treads brave on all that is,
Into the world of souls, from this.

'Since sweet the tears, dropped at the
        door
Of tearless Death,—and even before.
Sweet, consecrated evermore.

'What, dost thou judge it a strange thing,
That poets, crowned for vanquishing,
Should bear some dust from out the ring?

'Come on with me, come on with me,
And learn in coming! let me free
Thy spirit into verity.'

She ceased: her palfrey's paces sent
No separate noises as she went;
'Twas a bee's hum, a little spent.

And while the poet seemed to tread
Along the drowsy noise so made,
The forest heaved up overhead

Its billowy foliage through the air,
And the calm stars did far and spare
O'erswim the masses everywhere;

Save when the overtopping pines
Did bar their tremulous light with lines
All fixed and black. Now the moon shines

A broader glory. You may see
The trees grow rarer presently:
The air blows up more fresh and free.

Until they come from dark to light,
And from the forest to the sight
Of the large Heaven-heart, bare with
        night,—

A fiery throb in every star,
Those burning arteries that are
The conduits of God's life afar!

A wild brown moorland underneath,
And four pools breaking up the heath
With white low gleamings, blank as
        death.

Beside the first pool, near the wood,
A dead tree in set horror stood,
Peeled and disjointed, stark as rood,

Since thunder-stricken, years ago,
Fixed in the spectral strain and throe
Wherewith it struggled from the blow:

A monumental tree, alone,
That will not bend in storms, nor groan,
But break off sudden like a stone.

Its lifeless shadow lies oblique
Upon the pool,—where, javelin-like,
The star-rays quiver while they strike.

'Drink,' said the lady, very still—
'Be holy and cold.' He did her will,
And drank the starry water chill.

The next pool they came near unto
Was bare of trees : there, only grew
Straight flags and lilies, just a few,

Which sullen on the water sate
And leant their faces on the flat,
As weary of the starlight-state.

'Drink,' said the lady, grave and slow,
' *World's use* behoveth thee to know.'
He drank the bitter wave below.

The third pool, girt with thorny bushes,
And flaunting weeds, and reeds and
rushes
That winds sang through in mournful
gushes,

Was whitely smeared in many a round
By a slow slime : the starlight swound
Over the ghastly light it found.

'Drink,' said the lady, sad and slow,
' *World's love* behoveth thee to know.'
He looked to her, commanding so.

Her brow was troubled, but her eye
Struck clear to his soul. For all reply
He drank the water suddenly,—

Then, with a deathly sickness, passed
Beside the fourth pool and the last,
Where weights of shadow were down-
cast

From yew and alder, and rank trails
Of nightshade clasping the trunk-scales,
And flung across the intervals

From yew to yew. Who dares to stoop
Where those dank branches overdroop,
Into his heart the chill strikes up ;

He hears a silent gliding coil,
The snakes strain hard against the soil,
His foot slips in their slimy oil,

And toads seem crawling on his hand,
And clinging bats, but dimly scanned,
Full in his face their wings expand.

A paleness took the poet's cheek :
' Must I drink *here* ?' he seemed to seek
The lady's will with utterance meek.

' Aye, aye,' she said, ' it so must be '
(And this time she spake cheerfully)
' Behoves thee know *World's cruelty.*'

He bowed his forehead till his mouth
Curved in the wave, and drank unloath,
As if from rivers of the south.

His lips sobbed through the water rank,
His heart paused in him while he drank,
His brain beat heart-like, rose and sank,

And he swooned backward to a dream,
Wherein he lay 'twixt gloom and gleam,
With Death and Life at each extreme.

And spiritual thunders, born of soul
Not cloud, did leap from mystic pole
And o'er him roll and counter-roll,

Crushing their echoes reboant
With their own wheels. Did Heaven
so grant
His spirit a sign of covenant ?

At last came silence. A slow kiss
Did crown his forehead after this :
His eyelids flew back for the bliss.

The lady stood beside his head,
Smiling a thought, with hair dispread.
The moonshine seemed dishevellèd

In her sleek tresses manifold,
Like Danae's in the rain of old,
That dripped with melancholy gold.

But SHE was holy, pale, and high,
As one who saw an ecstasy
Beyond a foretold agony.

' Rise up !' said she, with voice where
song
Eddied through speech—' rise up ! be
strong !
And learn how right avenges wrong.'

The poet rose up on his feet :
He stood before an altar set
For sacrament, with vessels meet ;

And mystic altar-lights which shine
As if their flames were crystalline
Carved flames, that would not shrink or
pine.

The altar filled the central place
Of a great church, and toward its face
Long aisles did shoot and interlace,

And from it a continuous mist
Of incense (round the edges kissed
By a yellow light of amethyst)

Wound upward slowly and throbbingly,
Cloud within cloud, right silverly,
Cloud above cloud, victoriously,—

Broke full against the archèd roof,
And, thence refracting, eddied off,
And floated through the marble woof

Of many a fine-wrought architrave,
Then, poising its white masses brave,
Swept solemnly down aisle and nave;

Where now in dark, and now in light,
The countless columns, glimmering
    white.
Seemed leading out to the Infinite.

Plunged half-way up the shaft they
    showed,
In that pale shifting incense-cloud,
Which flowed them by, and overflowed,

Till mist and marble seemed to blend,
And the whole temple, at the end,
With its own incense to distend,—

The arches, like a giant's bow,
To bend and slacken,—and below,
The nichèd saints to come and go.

Alone, amid the shifting scene,
That central altar stood serene
In its clear steadfast taper-sheen.

Then first, the poet was aware
Of a chief angel standing there
Before that altar, in the glare.

His eyes were dreadful, for you saw
That *they* saw God—his lips and jaw,
Grand-made and strong, as Sinai's Law

They could enunciate and refrain
From vibratory after-pain,
And his brow's height was sovereign.

On the vast background of his wings
Rises his image, and he flings,
From each plumed arc, pale glitterings

And fiery flakes (as beateth more
Or less, the angel-heart) before
And round him, upon roof and floor,

Edging with fire the shifting fumes;
While at his side, 'twixt lights and
    glooms,
The phantasm of an organ booms.

Extending from which instrument
And angel, right and left-way bent,
The poet's sight grew sentient

Of a strange company around
And toward the altar,—pale and bound
With bay above the eyes profound.

Deathful their faces were, and yet
The power of life was in them set—
Never forgot, nor to forget.

Sublime significance of mouth,
Dilated nostril full of youth,
And forehead royal with the truth.

These faces were not multiplied
Beyond your count, but side by side
Did front the altar, glorified.

Still as a vision, yet exprest
Full as an action—look and geste
Of buried saint in risen rest.

The poet knew them.   Faint and dim
His spirits seemed to sink in him,
Then, like a dolphin, change and swim

The current.   These were poets true,
Who died for Beauty, as martyrs do
For Truth—the ends being scarcely two.

God's prophets of the Beautiful
These poets were; of iron rule,
The rugged cilix, serge of wool.

Here, Homer, with the broad suspense
Of thunderous brows, and lips intense
Of garrulous god-innocence.

There, Shakespeare, on whose forehead
    climb
The crowns o' the world. Oh, eyes
    sublime,
With tears and laughters for all time!

Here, Aeschylus, the women swooned
To see so awful, when he frowned
As the gods did!—he standeth crowned.

Euripides, with close and mild
Scholastic lips,—that could be wild,
And laugh or sob out like a child

Even in the classes. Sophocles,
With that king's look which, down the
    trees,
Followed the dark effigies

Of the lost Theban.   Hesiod old,
Who, somewhat blind and deaf and cold,
Cared most for gods and bulls.   And bold

Electric Pindar, quick as fear,
With race-dust on his cheeks, and clear
Slant startled eyes that seem to hear

The chariot rounding the last goal,
To hurtle past it in his soul.
And Sappho, with that gloriole

Of ebon hair on calmèd brows.
O poet-woman ! none forgoes
The leap, attaining the repose !

Theocritus, with glittering locks
Dropt sideway, as betwixt the rocks
He watched the visionary flocks.

And Aristophanes, who took
The world with mirth, and laughter-
      struck
The hollow caves of Thought and woke

The infinite echoes hid in each.
And Virgil : shade of Mantuan beech
Did help the shade of bay to reach

And knit around his forehead high :
For his gods wore less majesty
Than his brown bees hummed death-
      lessly.

Lucretius—nobler than his mood ;
Who dropped his plummet down the
      broad
Deep universe, and said ' No God,'

Finding no bottom : he denied
Divinely the divine, and died
Chief poet on the Tiber-side

By grace of God ! his face is stern,
As one compelled, in spite of scorn,
To teach a truth he would not learn.

And Ossian, dimly seen or guessed ˙
Once counted greater than the rest,
When mountain-winds blew out his vest.

And Spenser drooped his dreaming head
(With languid sleep-smile you had said
From his own verse engenderèd)

On Ariosto's, till they ran
Their curls in one.—The Italian
Shot nimbler heat of bolder man

From his fine lids.   And Dante stern
And sweet, whose spirit was an urn
For wine and milk poured out in turn.

Hard-souled Alfieri ; and fancy-willed
Boiardo,—who with laughter filled
The pauses of the jostled shield.

And Berni, with a hand stretched out
To sleek that storm.   And, not without
The wreath he died in, and the doubt

He died by, Tasso ! bard and lover,
Whose visions were too thin to cover
The face of a false woman over.

And soft Racine,—and grave Corneille,
The orator of rimes, whose wail
Scarce shook his purple.   And Petrarch
      pale,

From whose brainlighted heart were
      thrown
A thousand thoughts beneath the sun,
Each lucid with the name of One.

And Camoens, with that look he had,
Compelling India's Genius sad
From the wave through the Lusiad,—

The murmurs of the storm-cape ocean
Indrawn in vibrative emotion
Along the verse.   And, while devotion

In his wild eyes fantastic shone
Under the tonsure blown upon
By airs celestial,—Calderon.

And bold De Vega,—who breathed quick
Verse after verse, till death's old trick
Put pause to life and rhetoric.

And Goethe—with that reaching eye
His soul reached out from, far and high,
And fell from inner entity.

And Schiller, with heroic front,
Worthy of Plutarch's kiss upon 't,
Too large for wreath of modern wont.

And Chaucer, with his infantine
Familiar clasp oft hings divine :
That mark upon his lip is wine.

Here, Milton's eyes strike piercing-dim :
The shapes of suns and stars did swim
Like clouds from them, and granted him

God for sole vision. Cowley, there;
Whose active fancy debonair
Drew straws like amber—foul to fair.

Drayton and Browne,—with smiles they
   drew
From outward nature, still kept new
From their own inward nature true.

And Marlowe, Webster, Fletcher, Ben—
Whose fire-hearts sowed our furrows
   when
The world was worthy of such men.

And Burns, with pungent passionings
Set in his eyes. Deep lyric springs
Are of the fire-mount's issuings.

And Shelley, in his white ideal,
All statue-blind! And Keats the real
Adonis, with the hymeneal

Fresh vernal buds half sunk between
His youthful curls, kissed straight and
   sheen
In his Rome-grave, by Venus queen.

And poor, proud Byron,—sad as grave,
And salt as life : forlornly brave,
And quivering with the dart he drave.

And visionary Coleridge, who
Did sweep his thoughts as angels do
Their wings, with cadence up the Blue.

These poets faced, and many more,
The lighted altar looming o'er
The clouds of incense dim and hoar :

And all their faces, in the lull
Of natural things, looked wonderful
With life and death and deathless rule.

All, still as stone, and yet intense ;
As if by spirit's vehemence
That stone were carved, and not by sense.

But where the heart of each should beat,
There seemed a wound instead of it,
From whence the blood dropped to their
   feet,

Drop after drop—dropped heavily,
As century follows century
Into the deep eternity.

Then said the lady—and her word
Came distant, as wide waves were stirred
Between her and the ear that heard,

' *World's use* is cold, *world's love* is vain,
World's cruelty is bitter bane,
But pain is not the fruit of pain.

' Hearken, O poet, whom I led
From the dark wood. Dismissing dread,
Now hear this angel in my stead.

' His organ's clavier strikes along
These poets' hearts, sonorous, strong,
They gave him without count of wrong,—

' A diapason whence to guide
Up to God's feet, from these who died,
An anthem fully glorified.

' Whereat God's blessing . . . IBARAK
   (ברך)
Breathes back this music—folds it back
About the earth in vapoury rack,

' And men walk in it, crying " Lo,
The world is wider, and we know
The very heavens look brighter so.

" The stars move statelier round the edge
Of the silver spheres, and give in pledge
Their light for nobler privilege.

" No little flower but joys or grieves,
Full life is rustling in the sheaves,
Full spirit sweeps the forest-leaves."

' So works this music on the earth,
God so admits it, sends it forth,
To add another worth to worth—

' A new creation-bloom that rounds
The old creation, and expounds
His Beautiful in tuneful sounds.

' Now hearken!' Then the poet gazed
Upon the angel glorious-faced,
Whose hand, majestically raised,

Floated across the organ-keys,
Like a pale moon o'er murmuring seas,
With no touch but with influences.

Then rose and fell (with swell and swound
Of shapeless noises wandering round
A concord which at last they found)

Those mystic keys—the tones were
   mixed,
Dim, faint, and thrilled and throbbed
   betwixt
The incomplete and the unfixed :

And therein mighty minds were heard
In mighty musings, inly stirred,
And struggling outward for a word.

Until these surges, having run
This way and that, gave out as one
An Aphroditè of sweet tune,—

A Harmony, that, finding vent,
Upward in grand ascension went,
Winged to a heavenly argument—

Up, upward! like a saint who strips
The shroud back from his eyes and lips,
And rises in apocalypse.

A harmony sublime and plain,
Which cleft (as flying swan, the rain,—
Throwing the drops off with a strain

Of her white wing) those undertones
Of perplext chords, and soared at once
And struck out from the starry thrones

Their several silver octaves as
It passed to God. The music was
Of divine stature—strong to pass.

And those who heard it, understood
Something of life in spirit and blood—
Something of nature's fair and good.

And while it sounded, those great souls
Did thrill as racers at the goals,
And burn in all their aureoles.

But she, the lady, as vapour-bound,
Stood calmly in the joy of sound,—
Like Nature with the showers around.

And when it ceased, the blood which fell,
Again, alone grew audible,
Tolling the silence as a bell.

The sovran angel lifted high
His hand, and spake out sovranly :
'Tried poets, hearken and reply !

'Give me true answers. If we grant
That not to suffer, is to want
The conscience of the jubilant,—

'If ignorance of anguish is
But ignorance,—and mortals miss
Far prospects, by a level bliss,—

'If, as two colours must be viewed
In a visible image, mortals should
Need good and evil, to see good,—

'If to speak nobly, comprehends
To feel profoundly—if the ends
Of power and suffering, Nature blends,—

'If poets on the tripod must
Writhe like the Pythian, to make just
Their oracles, and merit trust,—

'If every vatic word that sweeps
To change the world, must pale their lips,
And leave their own souls in eclipse,—

'If to search deep the universe
Must pierce the searcher with the curse,—
Because that bolt (in man's reverse)

'Was shot to the heart o' the wood, and lies
Wedged deepest in the best,—if eyes
That look for visions and surprise

'From influent angels, must shut down
Their lids first, upon sun and moon,
The head asleep upon a stone,—

'If ONE who did redeem you back,
By His own loss, from final wrack,
Did consecrate by touch and track

'Those temporal sorrows, till the taste
Of brackish waters of the waste
Is salt with tears He dropt too fast,—

'If all the crowns of earth must wound
With prickings of the thorns He found,—
If saddest sighs swell sweetest sound,—

'What say ye unto this ?—refuse
This baptism in salt water ?—choose
Calm breasts, mute lips, and labour loose?

'Or, oh ye gifted givers ! ye
Who give your liberal hearts to me,
To make the world this harmony,

'Are ye resigned that they be spent
To such world's help ?'—
                    The Spirits bent
Their awful brows and said—'Content.'

Content ! it sounded like *amen*,
Said by a choir of mourning men ;
An affirmation full of pain

And patience,—aye, of glorying
And adoration,—as a king
Might seal an oath for governing.

Then said the angel—and his face
Lightened abroad, until the place
Grew larger for a moment's space,—

The long aisles flashing out in light,
And nave and transept, columns white
And arches crossed, being clear to sight

As if the roof were off, and all
Stood in the noon-sun,—' Lo ! I call
To other hearts as liberal.

' This pedal strikes out in the air :
My instrument has room to bear
Still fuller strains and perfecter.

' Herein is room, and shall be room
While Time lasts, for new hearts to come
Consummating while they consume.

' What living man will bring a gift
Of his own heart, and help to lift
The tune ?—The race is to the swift.'

So asked the angel.   Straight the while,
A company came up the aisle
With measured step and sorted smile ;

Cleaving the incense-clouds that rise,
With winking unaccustomed eyes,
And love-locks smelling sweet of spice.

One bore his head above the rest,
As if the world were dispossessed ;
And One did pillow chin on breast,

Right languid—an as he should faint.
One shook his curls across his paint,
And moralized on worldly taint.

One, slanting up his face, did wink
The salt rheum to the eyelid's brink,
To think—O gods ! or—not to think !

Some trod out stealthily and slow,
As if the sun would fall in snow
If they walked to instead of fro.

And some, with conscious ambling free,
Did shake their bells right daintily
On hand and foot, for harmony.

And some, composing sudden sighs
In attitudes of point-device,
Rehearsed impromptu agonies.

And when this company drew near
The spirits crowned, it might appear,
Submitted to a ghastly fear.

As a sane eye in master-passion
Constrains a maniac to the fashion
Of hideous maniac imitation

In the least geste—the dropping low
O' the lid, the wrinkling of the brow,
Exaggerate with mock and mow,—

So mastered was that company
By the crowned vision utterly,
Swayed to a maniac mockery.

One dulled his eyeballs, as they ached
With Homer's forehead, though he lacked
An inch of any.   And one racked

His lower lip with restless tooth,
As Pindar's rushing words forsooth
Were pent behind it.   One, his smooth

Pink cheeks, did rumple passionate,
Like Aeschylus—and tried to prate
On trolling tongue, of fate and fate.

One set her eyes like Sappho's—or
Any light woman's ! one forbore
Like Dante, or any man as poor

In mirth, to let a smile undo
His hard-shut lips.   And one that drew
Sour humours from his mother, blew

His sunken cheeks out to the size
Of most unnatural jollities,
Because Anacreon looked jest-wise.

So with the rest.—It was a sight
A great world-laughter would requite,
Or great world-wrath, with equal right.

Out came a speaker from that crowd
To speak for all—in sleek and proud
Exordial periods, while he bowed

His knee before the angel.—'Thus,
O angel who hast called for us,
We bring thee service emulous,—

' Fit service from sufficient soul,
Hand-service, to receive world's dole,
Lip-service, in world's ear to roll

' Adjusted concords—soft enow
To hear the wine-cups passing, through,
And not too grave to spoil the show.

' Thou, certes, when thou askest more,
O sapient angel, leanest o'er
The window-sill of metaphor.

' To give our hearts up ! fie !—that rage
Barbaric antedates the age :
It is not done on any stage.

' Because your scald or gleeman went
With seven or nine-stringed instrument
Upon his back—must ours be bent ?

' We are not pilgrims, by your leave ;
No, nor yet martyrs ! if we grieve,
It is to rime to . . . summer eve.

' And if we labour, it shall be,
As suiteth best with our degree,
In after-dinner reverie.'

More yet that speaker would have said,
Poising, between his smiles fair-fed,
Each separate phrase till finishèd.

But all the foreheads of those born
And dead true poets flashed with scorn
Betwixt the bay leaves round them
        worn—

Aye, jetted such brave fire, that they,
The new-come, shrank and paled away,
Like leaden ashes when the day

Strikes on the hearth.   A spirit-blast,
A presence known by power, at last
Took them up mutely—they had passed.

And *he*, our pilgrim-poet, saw
Only their places, in deep awe,—
What time the angel's smile did draw

His gazing upward.   Smiling on,
The angel in the angel shone,
Revealing glory in benison.

Till, ripened in the light which shut
The poet in, his spirit mute
Dropped sudden, as a perfect fruit.

He fell before the angel's feet,
Saying—' If what is true is sweet,
In something I may compass it.

' For, where my worthiness is poor,
My will stands richly at the door,
To pay shortcomings evermore.

' Accept me therefore.   Not for price,
And not for pride, my sacrifice
Is tendered ! for my soul is nice

' And will beat down those dusty seeds
Of bearded corn, if she succeeds
In soaring while the covey feeds.

' I soar—I am drawn up like the lark
To its white cloud.   So high my mark,
Albeit my wing is small and dark.

' I ask no wages—seek no fame.
Sew me, for shroud round face and name,
God's banner of the oriflamme.

' I only would have leave to loose
(In tears and blood, if so He choose)
Mine inward music out to use,

' I only would be spent—in pain
And loss, perchance—but not in vain,
Upon the sweetness of that strain !

' Only project, beyond the bound
Of mine own life, so lost and found,
My voice, and live on in its sound !

' Only embrace and be embraced
By fiery ends,—whereby to waste,
And light God's future with my past.'

The angel's smile grew more divine,
The mortal speaking—aye, its shine
Swelled fuller, like a choir-note fine,

Till the broad glory round his brow
Did vibrate with the light below ;
But what he said, I do not know.

Nor know I if the man who prayed,
Rose up accepted, unforbade,
From the church-floor where he was
        laid,—

Nor if a listening life did run
Through the king-poets, one by one
Rejoicing in a worthy son.

My soul, which might have seen, grew
        blind
By what it looked on : I can find
No certain count of things behind.

I saw alone, dim, white, and grand
As in a dream, the angel's hand
Stretched forth in gesture of command

Straight through the haze.   And so, as
        erst,
A strain more noble than the first
Mused in the organ, and outburst.

With giant march, from floor to roof
Rose the full notes,—now parted off
In pauses massively aloof

Like measured thunders,—now rejoined
In concords of mysterious kind
Which fused together sense and mind,—

Now flashing sharp on sharp along
Exultant, in a mounting throng,—
Now dying off to a low song

Fed upon minors!—wavelike sounds
Re-eddying into silver rounds,
Enlarging liberty with bounds.

And every rhythm that seemed to close
Survived in confluent underflows
Symphonious with the next that rose.

Thus the whole strain being multiplied
And greatened,—with its glorified
Wings shot abroad from side to side,—

Waved backward (as a wind might wave
A Brocken mist, and with as brave
Wild roaring) arch and architrave,

Aisle, transept, column, marble wall,—
Then swelling outward, prodigal
Of aspiration beyond thrall,

Soared,—and drew up with it the whole
Of this said vision—as a soul
Is raised by a thought.   And as a scroll

Of bright devices is unrolled
Still upward, with a gradual gold,—
So rose the vision manifold,

Angel and organ, and the round
Of spirits, solemnized and crowned,—
While the freed clouds of incense wound

Ascending, following in their track,
And glimmering faintly, like the rack
O' the moon in her own light cast back.

And as that solemn Dream withdrew,
The lady's kiss did fall anew
Cold on the poet's brow as dew.

And that same kiss which bound him
    first
Beyond the senses, now reversed
Its own law, and most subtly pierced

His spirit with the sense of things
Sensual and present.   Vanishings
Of glory, with Aeolian wings

Struck him and passed : the lady's face
Did melt back in the chrysopras
Of the orient morning sky that was

Yet clear of lark,—and there and so
She melted, as a star might do,
Still smiling as she melted—slow.

Smiling so slow, he seemed to see
Her smile the last thing, gloriously,
Beyond her—far as memory.

Then he looked round : he was alone.
He lay before the breaking sun,
As Jacob at the Bethel stone.

And thought's entangled skein being
    wound,
He knew the moorland of his swound,
And the pale pools that smeared the
    ground ;

The far wood-pines, like offing ships—
The fourth pool's yew anear him drips,
World's cruelty attaints his lips,

And still he tastes it—bitter still—
Through all that glorious possible
He had the sight of present ill.

Yet rising calmly up and slowly
With such a cheer as scorneth folly,
A mild delightsome melancholy,

He journeyed homeward through the
    wood,
And prayed along the solitude,
Betwixt the pines,—' O God, my God!'

The golden morning's open flowings
Did sway the trees to murmurous bow-
    ings,
In metric chant of blessed poems.

And passing homeward through the
    wood,
He prayed along the solitude,—
'Thou, Poet-God, art great and good!

' And though we must have, and have had
Right reason to be earthly sad,—
Thou, Poet-God, art great and glad!'

CONCLUSION

Life treads on life, and heart on heart :
We press too close in church and mart
To keep a dream or grave apart.

And I was 'ware of walking down
That same green forest where had gone
The poet-pilgrim.   One by one

I traced his footsteps.   From the east
A red and tender radiance pressed
Through the near trees, until I guessed

The sun behind shone full and round ;
While up the leafiness profound
A wind scarce old enough for sound

Stood ready to blow on me when
I turned that way ; and now and then
The birds sang and brake off again

To shake their pretty feathers dry
Of the dew sliding droppingly
From the leaf-edges, and apply

Back to their song.   'Twixt dew and
          bird
So sweet a silence ministered,
God seemed to use it for a word.

Yet morning souls did leap and run
In all things, as the least had won
A joyous insight of the sun.

And no one looking round the wood
Could help confessing as he stood,
This Poet-God is glad and good.

But hark ! a distant sound that grows !
A heaving, sinking of the boughs—
A rustling murmur, not of those !

A breezy noise, which is not breeze !
And white-clad children by degrees
Steal out in troops among the trees,

Fair little children, morning-bright,
With faces grave, yet soft to sight,
Expressive of restrained delight.

Some plucked the palm-boughs within
          reach,
And others leapt up high to catch
The upper boughs, and shake from each

A rain of dew, till, wetted so,
The child who held the branch let go,
And it swang backward with a flow

Of faster drippings.   Then I knew
The children laughed—but the laugh flew
From its own chirrup, as might do

A frightened song-bird ; and a child
Who seemed the chief, said very mild,
' Hush ! keep this morning undefiled.'

His eyes rebuked them from calm
          spheres ;
His soul upon his brow appears
In waiting for more holy years.

I called the child to me, and said,
' What are your palms for ?'—'To be
          spread,'
He answered, ' on a poet dead.

' The poet died last month, and now
The world which had been somewhat
          slow
In honouring his living brow,

' Commands the palms—they must be
          strown
On his new marble very soon,
In a procession of the town.'

I sighed and said, ' Did he foresee
Any such honour ?'   ' Verily
I cannot tell you,' answered he.

' But this I know.—I fain would lay
Mine own head down, another day,
As *he* did,—with the fame away.

' A lily, a friend's hand had plucked,
Lay by his death-bed, which he looked
As deep down as a bee had sucked,

' Then, turning to the lattice, gazed
O'er hill and river, and upraised
His eyes illumined and amazed

' With the world's beauty, up to God,
Re-offering on their iris broad
The images of things bestowed

' By the chief Poet.—" God ! " he cried,
" Be praised for anguish, which has
          tried ;
For beauty, which has satisfied :—

" For this world's presence, half within
And half without me—thought and
    scene—
This sense of Being and Having been.

" I thank Thee that my soul hath room
For Thy grand world. Both guests
    may come—
Beauty, to soul—Body, to tomb.

" I am content to be so weak :
Put strength into the words I speak,
And I am strong in what I seek.

" I am content to be so bare
Before the archers, everywhere
My wounds being stroked by heavenly
    air.

" I laid my soul before Thy feet,
That Images of fair and sweet
Should walk to other men on it.

" I am content to feel the step
Of each pure Image !—let those keep
To mandragore who care to sleep.

" I am content to touch the brink
Of the other goblet, and I think
My bitter drink a wholesome drink.

" Because my portion was assigned
Wholesome and bitter—Thou art kind,
And I am blessèd to my mind.

" Gifted for giving, I receive
The maythorn, and its scent outgive :
I grieve not that I once did grieve.

" In my large joy of sight and touch
Beyond what others count for such,
I am content to suffer much.

" *I know*—is all the mourner saith,
Knowledge by suffering entereth ;
And Life is perfected by Death." '

The child spake nobly. Strange to hear,
His infantine soft accents clear
Charged with high meanings, did appear ;

And fair to see, his form and face,
Winged out with whiteness and pure
    grace
From the green darkness of the place.

Behind his head a palm-tree grew :
An orient beam which pierced it through
Transversely on his forehead drew

The figure of a palm-branch brown
Traced on its brightness up and down
In fine fair lines,—a shadow-crown.

Guido might paint his angels so—
A little angel, taught to go
With holy words to saints below.

Such innocence of action yet
Significance of object met
In his whole bearing strong and sweet.

And all the children, the whole band,
Did round in rosy reverence stand,
Each with a palm-bough in his hand.

' And so he died,' I whispered.—' Nay,
Not *so*,' the childish voice did say —
' That poet turned him, first, to pray

' In silence, and God heard the rest
'Twixt the sun's footsteps down the west.
Then he called one who loved him best,

· Yea, he called softly through the room
(His voice was weak yet tender)—
    " Come,"
He said, " come nearer ! Let the bloom

" Of Life grow over, undenied,
This bridge of Death, which is not wide—
I shall be soon at the other side.

" Come, kiss me !" So the one in truth
Who loved him best—in love, not ruth,
Bowed down and kissed him mouth to
    mouth.

' And, in that kiss of Love, was won
Life's manumission. All was done—
The mouth that kissed last, kissed *alone*.

' But in the former, confluent kiss,
The same was sealed, I think, by His,
To words of truth and uprightness.'

The child's voice trembled—his lips shook
Like a rose leaning o'er a brook,
Which vibrates though it is not struck.

' And who,' I asked, a little moved
Yet curious-eyed, ' was this that loved
And kissed him last, as it behoved ?'

' *I*,' softly said the child ; and then,
' *I*,' said he louder, once again ;
' *His* son,—my rank is among men.

'And now that men exalt his name
I come to gather palms with them,
That holy Love may hallow Fame.

'He did not die alone, nor should
His memory live so, 'mid these rude
World-praisers—a worse solitude.

'Me, a voice calleth to that tomb
Where these are strewing branch and
    bloom,
Saying, *come nearer!*—and I come.

'Glory to God!' resumèd he,
And his eyes smiled for victory
O'er their own tears which I could see

Fallen on the palm, down cheek and
    chin—
'That poet now has entered in
The place of rest which is not sin.

'And while he rests, his songs in troops
Walk up and down our earthly slopes,
Companioned by diviner Hopes.'

'But *thou*,' I murmured,—to engage
The child's speech farther—'hast an age
Too tender for this orphanage.'

'Glory to God—to God!' he saith,
'KNOWLEDGE BY SUFFERING ENTERETH,
AND LIFE IS PERFECTED BY DEATH.'

THE POET'S VOW

O be wiser thou,
Instructed that true knowledge leads to love.—WORDSWORTH.

PART THE FIRST

SHOWING WHEREFORE THE VOW WAS MADE

I

EVE is a twofold mystery;
    The stillness Earth doth keep,—
The motion wherewith human hearts
    Do each to either leap,
As if all souls between the poles,
    Felt 'Parting comes in sleep.'

II

The rowers lift their oars to view
    Each other in the sea;
The landsmen watch the rocking boats
    In a pleasant company;
While up the hill go gladlier still
    Dear friends by two and three.

III

The peasant's wife hath looked without
    Her cottage door and smiled,
For there the peasant drops his spade
    To clasp his youngest child
Which hath no speech, but its hands
    can reach
    And stroke his forehead mild.

IV

A poet sate that eventide
    Within his hall alone,
As silent as its ancient lords
    In the coffined place of stone,
When the bat hath shrunk from the
    praying monk,
    And the praying monk is gone.

V

Nor wore the dead a stiller face
    Beneath the cerement's roll:
His lips refusing out in words
    Their mystic thoughts to dole,
His steadfast eye burnt inwardly,
    As burning out his soul.

VI

You would not think that brow cou'd
    e'er
    Ungentle moods express,
Yet seemed it, in this troubled world,
    Too calm for gentleness;
When the very star that shines from
    far
    Shines trembling ne'ertheless.

VII

It lacked, all need, the softening light
  Which other brows supply ;
We should conjoin the scathèd trunks
  Of our humanity,
That each leafless spray entwining may
  Look softer 'gainst the sky.

VIII

None gazed within the poet's face,
  The poet gazed in none ;
He threw a lonely shadow straight
  Before the moon and sun,
Affronting nature's heaven-dwelling
    creatures
  With wrong to nature done.

IX

Because this poet daringly—
  The nature at his heart,
And that quick tune along his veins
  He could not change by art—
Had vowed his blood of brotherhood
  To a stagnant place apart.

X

He did not vow in fear, or wrath,
  Or grief's fantastic whim,—
But, weights and shows of sensual things
  Too closely crossing him,
On his soul's eyelid the pressure slid
  And made its vision dim.

XI

And darkening in the dark he strove
  'Twixt earth and sea and sky,
To lose in shadow, wave, and cloud,
  His brother's haunting cry.
The winds were welcome as they swept,
God's five-day work he would accept,
  But let the rest go by.

XII

He cried—'O touching, patient Earth,
  That weepest in thy glee,
Whom God created very good,
  And very mournful, we !
Thy voice of moan doth reach His throne,
  As Abel's rose from thee.

XIII

'Poor crystal sky, with stars astray !
  Mad winds, that howling go
From east to west ! perplexèd seas,
  That stagger from their blow !

O motion wild ! O wave defiled !
  Our curse hath made you so.

XIV

'*We!* and *our* curse ! do *I* partake
  The desiccating sin ?
Have *I* the apple at my lips ?
  The money-lust within ?
Do *I* human stand with the wounding
    hand,
  To the blasting heart akin ?

XV

'Thou solemn pathos of all things,
  For solemn joy designed !
Behold, submissive to your cause
  A holy wrath I find,
And, for your sake, the bondage break
  That knits me to my kind.

XVI

'Hear me forswear man's sympathies,
  His pleasant yea and no,
His riot on the piteous earth
  Whereon his thistles grow !
His changing love—with stars above !
  His pride—with graves below !

XVII

'Hear me forswear his roof by night,
  His bread and salt by day,
His talkings at the wood-fire hearth,
  His greetings by the way,
His answering looks, his systemed books,
  All man, for ay and ay.

XVIII

'That so my purged, once human heart,
  From all the human rent,
May gather strength to pledge and drink
  Your wine of wonderment,
While you pardon me, all blessingly,
  The woe mine Adam sent.

XIX

'And I shall feel your unseen looks
  Innumerous, constant, deep,
And soft as haunted Adam once,
  Though sadder, round me creep,—
As slumbering men have mystic ken
  Of watchers on their sleep.

XX

'And ever, when I lift my brow
  At evening to the sun,
No voice of woman or of child
  Recording "Day is done,"
Your silences shall a love express,
  More deep than such an one.'

PART THE SECOND

SHOWING TO WHOM THE VOW WAS DECLARED

I

THE poet's vow was inly sworn,
  The poet's vow was told:
He shared among his crowding friends
  The silver and the gold,
They clasping bland his gift,—his hand
  In a somewhat slacker hold.

II

They wended forth, the crowding friends,
  With farewells smooth and kind:
They wended forth, the solaced friends,
  And left but twain behind:
One loved him true as brothers do,
  And one was Rosalind.

III

He said—'My friends have wended forth
  With farewells smooth and kind;
Mine oldest friend, my plighted bride,
  Ye need not stay behind.
Friend, wed my fair bride for my sake,
And let my lands ancestral make
  A dower for Rosalind.

IV

'And when beside your wassail board
  Ye bless your social lot,
I charge you that the giver be
  In all his gifts forgot,
Or alone of all his words recall
  The last,—Lament me not.'

V

She looked upon him silently,
  With her large, doubting eyes,
Like a child that never knew but love,
  Whom words of wrath surprise,
Till the rose did break from either cheek,
  And the sudden tears did rise.

VI

She looked upon him mournfully,
  While her large eyes were grown
Yet larger with the steady tears,
  Till, all his purpose known,
She turnèd slow, as she would go—
  The tears were shaken down.

VII

She turnèd slow, as she would go,
  Then quickly turned again,
And gazing in his face to seek
  Some little touch of pain—
'I thought,' she said,—but shook her
    head,—
  She tried that speech in vain.

VIII

'I thought—but I am half a child,
  And very sage art thou—
The teachings of the heaven and earth
  Should keep us soft and low:
They have drawn *my* tears in early years,
  Or ere I wept—as now.

IX

'But now that in thy face I read
  Their cruel homily,
Before their beauty I would fain
  Untouched, unsoftened be,—
If *I* indeed could look on even
The senseless, loveless earth and heaven
  As *thou* canst look on *me!*

X

'And couldest thou as coldly view
  Thy childhood's far abode,
Where little feet kept time with thine
  Along the dewy sod,
And thy mother's look from holy book,
  Rose, like a thought of God?

XI

'O brother,—called so, ere her last
  Betrothing words were said!
O fellow-watcher in her room,
  With hushèd voice and tread!
Rememberest thou how, hand in hand
O friend, O lover, we did stand,
  And knew that she was dead?

XII

'I will not live Sir Roland's bride,—
  That dower I will not hold!
I tread below my feet that go,
  These parchments bought and sold.
The tears I weep are mine to keep,
  And worthier than thy gold.'

XIII

The poet and Sir Roland stood
  Alone, each turned to each,
Till Roland brake the silence left
  By that soft-throbbing speech—
'Poor heart!' he cried, 'it vainly tried
  The distant heart to reach.

XIV

'And thou, O distant, sinful heart,
  That climbest up so high,
To wrap and blind thee with the snows
  That cause to dream and die—
What blessing can, from lips of man,
  Approach thee with his sigh?

XV

'Aye, what from earth—create for man,
  And moaning in his moan?
Aye, what from stars—revealed to man,
  And man-named, one by one?
Aye, more! what blessing can be given,
Where the Spirits seven do show in
    heaven
A MAN upon the throne?—

XVI

'A man on earth HE wandered once,
  All meek and undefiled,
And those who loved Him, said "He
    wept"—
  None ever said He smiled;
Yet there might have been a smile unseen,
When He bowed His holy face, I ween,
  To bless that happy child.

XVII

'And now HE pleadeth up in heaven
  For our humanities,
Till the ruddy light on seraphs' wings
  In pale emotion dies.
They can better bear His Godhead's glare
  Than the pathos of His eyes.

XVIII

'I will go pray our God to-day
  To teach thee how to scan
His work divine, for human use
  Since earth on axle ran!

To teach thee to discern as plain
His grief divine—the blood-drop's stain
  He left there, MAN for man.

XIX

'So, for the blood's sake, shed by Him
  Whom angels God declare,
Tears, like it, moist and warm with love,
  Thy reverent eyes shall wear,
To see i' the face of Adam's race
  The nature God doth share.'

XX

'I heard,' the poet said, ' thy voice
  As dimly as thy breath:
The sound was like the noise of life
  To one anear his death,—
Or of waves that fail to stir the pale
  Sere leaf they roll beneath.

XXI

'And still between the sound and me
  White creatures like a mist
Did interfloat confusedly,—
  Mysterious shapes unwist!
Across my heart and across my brow
I felt them droop like wreaths of snow,
  To still the pulse they kist.

XXII

'The castle and its lands are thine—
  The poor's—it shall be done.
Go, *man*, to love! I go to live
  In Courland hall, alone.
The bats along the ceilings cling,
The lizards in the floors do run,
And storms and years have worn and reft
The stain by human builders left
  In working at the stone.'

PART THE THIRD

SHOWING HOW THE VOW WAS KEPT

I

HE dwelt alone, and sun and moon
  Were witness that he made
Rejection of his humanness
  Until they seemed to fade:
His face did so; for he did grow
  Of his own soul afraid.

II

The self-poised God may dwell alone
  With inward glorying,
But God's chief angel waiteth for
  A brother's voice, to sing ;
And a lonely creature of sinful nature—
  It is an awful thing.

III

An awful thing that feared itself
  While many years did roll,
A lonely man, a feeble man,
  A part beneath the whole—
He bore by day, he bore by night
That pressure of God's infinite
  Upon his finite soul.

IV

The poet at his lattice sate,
  And downward lookèd he ;
Three Christians wended by to prayers,
  With mute ones in their ee :
Each turned above a face of love,
  And called him to the far chapèlle
With voice more tuneful than its bell—
  But still they wended three.

V

There journeyed by a bridal pomp,
  A bridegroom and his dame :
He speaketh low for happiness,
  She blusheth red for shame ;
But never a tone of benison
  From out the lattice came.

VI

A little child with inward song,
  No louder noise to dare,
Stood near the wall to see at play
  The lizards green and rare—
Unblessed the while for his childish smile
  Which cometh unaware.

PART THE FOURTH

SHOWING HOW ROSALIND FARED BY
  THE KEEPING OF THE VOW

I

In death-sheets lieth Rosalind,
  As white and still as they ;
And the old nurse that watched her bed,
  Rose up with 'Well-a-day ! '

And oped the casement to let in
The sun, and that sweet doubtful din
Which droppeth from the grass and bough
Sans wind and bird, none knoweth how—
  To cheer her as she lay.

II

The old nurse started when she saw
  Her sudden look of woe ;
But the quick wan tremblings round her
    mouth
  In a meek smile did go,
And calm she said, 'When I am dead,
  Dear nurse, it shall be so.

III

'Till then, shut out those sights and
    sounds,
  And pray God pardon me,
That I without this pain no more
  His blessèd works can see !
And lean beside me, loving nurse,
That thou mayst hear, ere I am worse,
  What thy last love should be.'

IV

The loving nurse leant over her,
  As white she lay beneath ;
The old eyes searching, dim with life,
  The young ones dim with death,
To read their look if sound forsook
  The trying, trembling breath.

V

'When all this feeble breath is done,
  And I on bier am laid,
My tresses smoothed for never a feast,
  My body in shroud arrayed,
Uplift each palm in a saintly calm,
  As if that still I prayed.

VI

'And heap beneath mine head the flowers
  You stoop so low to pull,—
The little white flowers from the wood,
  Which grow there in the cool,
Which *he* and I, in childhood's games,
Went plucking, knowing not their names,
  And filled thine apron full.

VII

'Weep not ! *I* weep not. Death is
    strong,
  The eyes of Death are dry !
But lay this scroll upon my breast,
  When hushed its heavings lie,

And wait awhile for the corpse's smile
  Which shineth presently.

VIII

' And when it shineth, straightway call
  Thy youngest children dear,
And bid them gently carry me
  All barefaced on the bier—
But bid them pass my kirkyard grass
  That waveth long anear.

IX

'And up the bank where I used to sit
  And dream what life would be,
Along the brook, with its sunny look
  Akin to living glee,—
O'er the windy hill, through the forest
    still,
  Let them gently carry me.

X

' And through the piney forest still,
  And down the open moorland—
Round where the sea beats mistily
  And blindly on the foreland;
And let them chant that hymn I know,
Bearing me soft, bearing me slow,
  To the ancient hall of Courland.

XI

' And when withal they near the hall,
  In silence let them lay
My bier before the bolted door,
  And leave it for a day.
For I have vowed, though I am proud,
To go there as a guest in shroud,
  And not be turned away.'

XII

The old nurse looked within her eyes,
  Whose mutual look was gone ;
The old nurse stooped upon her mouth,
  Whose answering voice was done ;
And nought she heard, till a little bird
  Upon   the   casement's   woodbine
      swinging,
Broke out into a loud sweet singing
  For joy o' the summer sun.
' Alack ! alack ! ' — she watched no
    more—
  With head on knee she wailèd sore ;
And the little bird sang o'er and o'er
  For joy o' the summer sun.

PART THE FIFTH

SHOWING HOW THE VOW WAS BROKEN

I

THE poet oped his bolted door,
  The midnight sky to view :
A spirit-feel was in the air
Which seemed to touch his spirit bare
  Whenever his breath he drew ;
And the stars a liquid softness had,
As alone their holiness forbade
  Their falling with the dew.

II

They shine upon the steadfast hills,
  Upon the swinging tide,
Upon the narrow track of beach,
  And the murmuring pebbles pied ;
They shine on every lovely place,
They shine upon the corpse's face,
  As *it* were fair beside.

III

It lay before him, humanlike,
  Yet so unlike a thing !
More awful in its shrouded pomp
  Than any crownèd king—
All calm and cold, as it did hold
  Some secret, glorying.

IV

A heavier weight than of its clay
  Clung to his heart and knee :
As if those folded palms could strike,
  He staggered groaningly,
And then o'erhung, without a groan,
The meek close mouth that smiled alone,
  Whose speech the scroll must be.

THE WORDS OF ROSALIND'S SCROLL

' I LEFT thee last, a child at heart,
  A woman scarce in years :
I come to thee, a solemn corpse,
  Which neither feels nor fears.
I have no breath to use in sighs ;
They laid the death-weights on mine
    eyes,
  To seal them safe from tears.

' Look on me with thine own calm look—
  I meet it calm as thou !
No look of thine can change *this* smile,
  Or break thy sinful vow.

I tell thee that my poor scorned heart
Is of thine earth . . . thine earth, a part—
    It cannot vex thee now.

' But out, alas! these words are writ
    By a living, loving One,
Adown whose cheeks, the proofs of life,
    The warm quick tears do run.
Ah, let the unloving corpse control
Thy scorn back from the loving soul
    Whose place of rest is won.

' I have prayed for thee with bursting sobs,
    When passion's course was free.
I have prayed for thee with silent lips,
    In the anguish none could see.
They whispered oft, " She sleepeth
        soft "—
    But I only prayed for thee.

' Go to! I pray for thee no more—
    The corpse's tongue is still:
Its folded fingers point to heaven,
    But point there stiff and chill.
No farther wrong, no farther woe
Hath licence from the sin below
    Its tranquil heart to thrill.

' I charge thee, by the living's prayer,
    And the dead's silentness,
To wring from out thy soul a cry
    Which God shall hear and bless!
Lest Heaven's own palm droop in my
        hand,
And pale among the saints I stand,
    A saint companionless.'

v

Bow lower down before the throne,
    Triumphant Rosalind!
He boweth on thy corpse his face,
    And weepeth as the blind.
'Twas a dread sight to see them so—
For the senseless corpse rocked to and fro
    With the wail of his living mind.

vi

But dreader sight, could such be seen,
    His inward mind did lie,
Whose long-subjected humanness
    Gave out its lion cry,
And fiercely rent its tenement
    In a mortal agony.

vii

I tell you, friends, had you heard his wail,
    'Twould haunt you in court and mart,
And in merry feast, until you set
    Your cup down to depart—
That weeping wild of a reckless child
    From a proud man's broken heart.

viii

O broken heart, O broken vow,
    That wore so proud a feature!
God, grasping as a thunderbolt
    The man's rejected nature,
Smote him therewith, i' the presence
        high
Of his so worshipped earth and sky
    That looked on all indifferently—
    A wailing human creature.

ix

A human creature found too weak
    To bear his human pain!
(May Heaven's dear grace have spoken
        peace
    To his dying heart and brain!)
For when they came at dawn of day
To lift the lady's corpse away,
    Her bier was holding twain.

x

They dug beneath the kirkyard grass,
    For both, one dwelling deep,
To which, when years had mossed the
        stone,
Sir Roland brought his little son
    To watch the funeral heap.
    And when the happy boy would rather
Turn upward his blithe eyes to see
The wood-doves nodding from the tree—
    ' Nay, boy, look downward,' said his
        father,
' Upon this human dust asleep.
And hold it in thy constant ken
That God's own unity compresses
    (One into one) the human many,
And that his everlastingness is
    The bond which is not loosed by any!—
    That thou and I this law must keep,
If not in love, in sorrow then!
Though smiling not like other men,
    Still, like them, we must weep.'

MISCELLANEOUS POEMS

THE ROMAUNT OF MARGRET

Can my affections find out nothing best,
But still and still remove?
                    QUARLES.

I

I PLANT a tree whose leaf
    The yew-tree leaf will suit ;
But when its shade is o'er you laid,
    Turn round and pluck the fruit.
Now reach my harp from off the wall
    Where shines the sun aslant !
The sun may shine and we be cold—
O hearken, loving hearts and bold,
    Unto my wild romaunt,
                Margret, Margret.

II

Sitteth the fair ladye
    Close to the river side,
Which runneth on with a merry tone
    Her merry thoughts to guide.
It runneth through the trees,
    It runneth by the hill,
Nathless the lady's thoughts have found
    A way more pleasant still.
                Margret, Margret.

III

The night is in her hair
    And giveth shade to shade,
And the pale moonlight on her forehead
        white
    Like a spirit's hand is laid ;
Her lips part with a smile
    Instead of speakings done :
I ween, she thinketh of a voice,
    Albeit uttering none.
                Margret, Margret.

IV

All little birds do sit
    With heads beneath their wings :
Nature doth seem in a mystic dream,
    Absorbed from her living things.

That dream by that ladye
    Is certes unpartook,
For she looketh to the high cold stars
    With a tender human look.
                Margret, Margret.

V

The lady's shadow lies
    Upon the running river ;
It lieth no less in its quietness,
    For that which resteth never :
Most like a trusting heart
    Upon a passing faith,—
Or as, upon the course of life,
    The steadfast doom of death.
                Margret, Margret.

VI

The lady doth not move,
    The lady doth not dream,
Yet she seeth her shade no longer laid
    In rest upon the stream.
It shaketh without wind,
    It parteth from the tide,
It standeth upright in the cleft moonlight,
    It sitteth at her side.
                Margret, Margret.

VII

Look in its face, ladye,
    And keep thee from thy swound !
With a spirit bold, thy pulses hold,
    And hear its voice's sound.
For so will sound thy voice,
    When thy face is to the wall ;
And such will be thy face, ladye,
    When the maidens work thy pall.
                Margret, Margret.

VIII

' Am I not like to thee ? '—
    The voice was calm and low ;
And between each word you might have
        heard
    The silent forests grow.
' *The like may sway the like,*'
    By which mysterious law
Mine eyes from thine and my lips from
        thine
    The light and breath may draw.
                Margret, Margret.

IX

'My lips do need thy breath,
  My lips do need thy smile,
And my pallid eyne, that light in thine
  Which met the stars erewhile.
Yet go with light and life,
  If that thou lovest one
In all the earth, who loveth thee
  As truly as the sun,
        Margret, Margret.'

X

Her cheek had waxèd white
  Like cloud at fall of snow ;
Then like to one at set of sun
  It waxèd red alsò ;
For love's name maketh bold,
  As if the loved were near.
And then she sighed the deep long sigh
  Which cometh after fear.
        Margret, Margret.

XI

'Now, sooth, I fear thee not—
  Shall never fear thee now !'
(And a noble sight was the sudden light
  Which lit her lifted brow.)
'Can earth be dry of streams ?
  Or hearts, of love ?' she said ;
'Who doubteth love, can know not love :
  He is already dead.'
        Margret, Margret.

XII

'I have' . . . and here her lips
  Some word in pause did keep,
And gave the while a quiet smile,
  As if they paused in sleep,—
'I have . . . a brother dear,
  A knight of knightly fame !
I broidered him a knightly scarf
  With letters of my name.
        Margret, Margret.

XIII

'I fed his grey goss-hawk,
  I kissed his fierce bloodhound,
I sate at home when he might come
  And caught his horn's far sound :
I sang him hunters' songs,
  I poured him the red wine—
He looked across the cup and said,
  I love thee, sister mine.'
        Margret, Margret.

XIV

IT trembled on the grass,
  With a low, shadowy laughter ;
The sounding river which rolled for ever,
  Stood dumb and stagnant after.
'Brave knight thy brother is !
  But better loveth he
Thy chaliced wine than thy chanted song,
  And better both, than thee,
        Margret, Margret.'

XV

The lady did not heed
  The river's silence while
Her own thoughts still ran at their will,
  And calm was still her smile.
'My little sister wears
  The look our mother wore :
I smooth her locks with a golden comb,
  I bless her evermore.'
        Margret, Margret.

XVI

'I gave her my first bird,
  When first my voice it knew ;
I made her share my posies rare,
  And told her where they grew.
I taught her God's dear name
  With prayer and praise, to tell—
She looked from heaven into my face,
  And said, *I love thee well.*'
        Margret, Margret.

XVII

IT trembled on the grass
  With a low, shadowy laughter :
You could see each bird as it woke and
    stared
  Through the shrivelled foliage after.
'Fair child thy sister is !
  But better loveth she
Thy golden comb than thy gathered
    flowers,
  And better both, than thee,
        Margret, Margret.'

XVIII

The lady did not heed
  The withering on the bough :
Still calm her smile, albeit the while
  A little pale her brow.

'I have a father old,
    The lord of ancient halls ;
An hundred friends are in his court,
    Yet only me he calls.
            Margret, Margret.

XIX

'An hundred knights are in his court,
    Yet read I by his knee ;
And when forth they go to the tourney
        show,
    I rise not up to see.
'Tis a weary book to read,
    My tryst 's at set of sun,
But loving and dear beneath the stars
    Is his blessing when I've done.'
            Margret, Margret.

XX

IT trembled on the grass
    With a low, shadowy laughter ;
And moon and star, though bright and far,
    Did shrink and darken after.
'High lord thy father is !
    But better loveth he
His ancient halls than his hundred friends,
    His ancient halls, than thee.
            Margret, Margret.'

XXI

The lady did not heed
    That the far stars did fail :
Still calm her smile, albeit the while . . .
    Nay, but she is not pale !
I have a more than friend
    Across the mountains dim :
No other's voice is soft to me,
    Unless it nameth *him*.'
            Margret, Margret.

XXII

' Though louder beats mine heart
    I know his tread again,
And his far plume ay, unless turned
        away,
    For the tears do blind me then.
We brake no gold, a sign
    Of stronger faith to be,—
But I wear his last look in my soul,
    Which said, *I love but thee!*'
            Margret, Margret.

XXIII

IT trembled on the grass
    With a low, shadowy laughter ;
And the wind did toll, as a passing soul
    Were sped by church-bell after ;
And shadows, 'stead of light,
    Fell from the stars above,
In flakes of darkness on her face
    Still bright with trusting love.
            Margret, Margret.

XXIV

' He *loved* but only thee !
    That love is transient too :
The wild hawk's bill doth dabble still
    I' the mouth that vowed thee true.
Will he open his dull eyes,
    When tears fall on his brow ?
Behold, the death-worm to his heart
    Is a nearer thing than *thou*,
            Margret, Margret.'

XXV

Her face was on the ground—
    None saw the agony,
But the men at sea did that night agree
    They heard a drowning cry ;
And when the morning brake,
    Fast rolled the river's tide,
With the green trees waving overhead,
    And a white corse laid beside.
            Margret, Margret.

XXVI

A knight's bloodhound and he
    The funeral watch did keep ;
With a thought o' the chase he stroked
        its face
    As it howled to see him weep.
A fair child kissed the dead,
    But shrank before its cold ;
And alone yet proudly in his hall
    Did stand a baron old.
            Margret, Margret.

XXVII

Hang up my harp again !
    I have no voice for song :
Not song, but wail, and mourners pale,
    Not bards, to love belong.
O failing human love !
    O light, by darkness known !
O false, the while thou treadest earth !
    O deaf beneath the stone !
            Margret, Margret.

ISOBEL'S CHILD

So find we profit,
By losing of our prayers.
SHAKESPEARE.

I

To rest the weary nurse has gone.
  An eight-day watch had watchèd she,
Still rocking beneath sun and moon
  The baby on her knee,
Till Isobel its mother said,
' The fever waneth—wend to bed,
  For now the watch comes round to me.'

II

Then wearily the nurse did throw
Her pallet in the darkest place
  Of that sick room, and slept and
    dreamed :
  For, as the gusty wind did blow
  The night-lamp's flare across her face,
She saw, or seemed to see, but dreamed,
  That the poplars tall on the opposite
    hill,
  The seven tall poplars on the hill,
  Did clasp the setting sun until
  His rays dropped from him, pined and
    still
      As blossoms in frost !
Till he waned and paled, so weirdly
    crossed,
To the colour of moonlight which doth
    pass
Over the dank ridged churchyard grass.
  The poplars held the sun, and he
The eyes of the nurse that they should
    not see,
Not for a moment, the babe on her knee,
Though she shuddered to feel that it
    grew to be
  Too chill, and lay too heavily.

III

She only dreamed ; for all the while
'Twas Lady Isobel that kept
The little baby,—and it slept
Fast, warm, as if its mother's smile,
Laden with love's dewy weight,
And red as rose of Harpocrate
Dropt upon its eyelids, pressed
Lashes to cheek in a sealèd rest.

IV

And more and more smiled Isobel
To see the baby sleep so well—
  She knew not that she smiled.
Against the lattice, dull and wild
Drive the heavy droning drops,
Drop by drop, the sound being one—
As momently time's segments fall
On the ear of God, who hears through all
  Eternity's unbroken monotone.
And more and more smiled Isobel
To see the baby sleep so well—
  She knew not that she smiled.
The wind in intermission stops
Down in the beechen forest,
  Then cries aloud
  As one at the sorest,
  Self-stung, self-driven.
And rises up to its very tops,
Stiffening erect the branches bowed,
Dilating with a tempest-soul
The trees that with their dark hands break
Through their own outline and heavily roll
Shadows as massive as clouds in heaven,
Across the castle lake.
And more and more smiled Isobel
To see the baby sleep so well ;
She knew not that she smiled ;
She knew not that the storm was wild.
Through the uproar drear she could not
  hear
The castle clock which struck anear—
She heard the low, light breathing of her
  child.

V

O sight for wondering look !
While the external nature broke
Into such abandonment,
While the very mist heart-rent
By the lightning, seemed to eddy
Against nature, with a din,
A sense of silence and of steady
Natural calm appeared to come
From things without, and enter in
  The human creature's room.

VI

So motionless she sate,
The babe asleep upon her knees,
You might have dreamed their souls had
  gone
Away to things inanimate,

In such to live, in such to moan ;
And that their bodies had ta'en back,
In mystic change, all silences
That cross the sky in cloudy rack,
Or dwell beneath the reedy ground
In waters safe from their own sound.
    Only she wore
The deepening smile I named before,
And *that* a deepening love expressed ;
And who at once can love and rest ?

VII

In sooth the smile that then was keeping
Watch upon the baby sleeping,
Floated with its tender light
Downward, from the drooping eyes,
Upward, from the lips apart,
Over cheeks which had grown white
    With an eight-day weeping.
All smiles come in such a wise,
Where tears shall fall or have of old—
Like northern lights that fill the heart
    Of heaven in sign of cold.

VIII

    Motionless she sate.
Her hair had fallen by its weight
On each side of her smile, and lay
Very blackly on the arm
Where the baby nestled warm,
Pale as baby carved in stone
    Seen by glimpses of the moon
    Up a dark cathedral aisle.
But, through the storm, no moonbeam fell
Upon the child of Isobel—
Perhaps you saw it by the ray
    Alone of her still smile.

IX

A solemn thing it is to me
To look upon a babe that sleeps ;
Wearing in its spirit-deeps
The undeveloped mystery
Of our Adam's taint and woe,
Which, when they developed be,
Will not let it slumber so !
Lying new in life beneath
The shadow of the coming death,
With that soft, low, quiet breath,
    As if it felt the sun !
Knowing all things by their blooms,
Not their roots, yea, sun and sky,
Only by the warmth that comes
Out of each,—earth, only by

The pleasant hues that o'er it run,—
And human love, by drops of sweet
White nourishment still hanging round
The little mouth so slumber-bound.
All which broken sentiency
And conclusion incomplete,
Will gather and unite and climb
    To an immortality
Good or evil, each sublime,
Through life and death to life again.
O little lids, now folded fast,
Must ye learn to drop at last
Our large and burning tears ?
O warm quick body, must thou lie,
When the time comes round to die,
Still, from all the whirl of years,
Bare of all the joy and pain ?—
O small frail being, wilt thou stand
    At God's right hand,
Lifting up those sleeping eyes
Dilated by great destinies,
To an endless waking ? thrones and
    seraphim,
Through the long ranks of their solem-
    nities,
Sunning thee with calm looks of Heaven's
    surprise,
    But thine alone on Him ?—
Or else, self-willed, to tread the Godless
    place
(God keep thy will !), feel thine own
    energies
Cold, strong, objectless, like a dead
    man's clasp,
The sleepless deathless life within thee,
    grasp,—
While myriad faces, like one changeless
    face,
With woe *not love*'s, shall glass thee
    everywhere,
And overcome thee with thine own
    despair ?

More soft, less solemn images
Drifted o'er the lady's heart,
    Silently as snow.
She had seen eight days depart
Hour by hour, on bended knees,
With pale-wrung hands and prayings low
And broken, through which came the
    sound
Of tears that fell against the ground,

Making sad stops :—' Dear Lord, dear
    Lord!'
She still had prayed (the heavenly
    word,
Broken by an earthly sigh),
—' Thou, who didst not erst deny
The mother-joy to Mary mild,
Blessèd in the blessèd child,
Which hearkened in meek babyhood
Her cradle-hymn, albeit used
To all that music interfused
In breasts of angels high and good!
Oh, take not, Lord, my babe away—
Oh, take not to Thy songful heaven
The pretty baby Thou hast given,
Or ere that I have seen him play
Around his father's knees and known
That *he* knew how my love has gone
    From all the world to him.
Think, God among the cherubim,
How I shall shiver every day
In Thy June sunshine, knowing where
The grave-grass keeps it from his fair
Still cheeks! and feel at every tread
His little body which is dead
And hidden in the turfy fold,
Doth make thy whole warm earth a-cold!
O God, I am so young, so young—
I am not used to tears at nights
Instead of slumber—nor to prayer
With sobbing lips and hands out-wrung!
Thou knowest all my prayings were
"I bless Thee, God, for past delights—
Thank God!" I am not used to bear
Hard thoughts of death ; the earth doth
    cover
No face from me of friend or lover.
And must the first who teaches me
The form of shrouds and funerals, be
Mine own first-born belovèd? he
Who taught me first this mother-love?
Dear Lord, who spreadest out above
Thy loving, transpierced hands to meet
All lifted hearts with blessing sweet,—
Pierce not my heart, my tender heart,
Thou madest tender! Thou who art
So happy in Thy heaven alway!
Take not mine only bliss away!'

XI

She so had prayed : and God, who hears
Through seraph-songs the sound of tears,

From that belovèd babe had ta'en
The fever and the beating pain.
And more and more smiled Isobel
To see the baby sleep so well
(She knew not that she smiled, I wis),
Until the pleasant gradual thought
Which near her heart the smile en-
    wrought,
Now soft and slow, itself, did seem
To float along a happy dream,
    Beyond it into speech like this.

XII

' I prayed for thee, my little child,
And God has heard my prayer !
And when thy babyhood is gone,
We two together, undefiled
By men's repinings, will kneel down
Upon His earth which will be fair
(Not covering thee, sweet !) to us twain,
And give Him thankful praise.'

XIII

Dully and wildly drives the rain :
Against the lattices drives the rain.

XIV

' I thank Him now, that I can think
    Of those same future days,
Nor from the harmless image shrink
    Of what I there might see—
Strange babies on their mothers' knee,
Whose innocent soft faces might
From off mine eyelids strike the light,
    With looks not meant for me !'

XV

Gustily blows the wind through the rain,
As against the lattices drives the rain.

XVI

' But now, O baby mine, together
We turn this hope of ours again
To many an hour of summer weather,
When we shall sit and intertwine
Our spirits, and instruct each other
In the pure loves of child and mother !
Two human loves make one divine.'

XVII

The thunder tears through the wind and
    the rain,
As full on the lattices drives the rain.

XVIII

' My little child, what wilt thou choose?
Now let me look at thee and ponder.
What gladness, from the gladnesses
Futurity is spreading under
Thy gladsome sight? Beneath the trees
Wilt thou lean all day, and lose
Thy spirit with the river seen
Intermittently between
The winding beechen alleys,—
Half in labour, half repose.
Like a shepherd keeping sheep.
Thou, with only thoughts to keep
Which never a bound will overpass,
And which are innocent as those
That feed among Arcadian valleys
      Upon the dewy grass?'

XIX

The large white owl that with age is
      blind,
That hath sate for years in the old tree
      hollow,
Is carried away in a gust of wind!
His wings could bear him not as fast
As he goeth now the lattice past—
He is borne by the winds; the rains do
      follow:
His white wings to the blast out-flowing,
      He hooteth in going,
And still, in the lightnings, coldly glitter
      His round unblinking eyes.

XX

' Or, baby, wilt thou think it fitter
To be eloquent and wise,—
One upon whose lips the air
Turns to solemn verities,
For men to breathe anew, and win
A deeper-seated life within?
Wilt be a philosopher,
By whose voice the earth and skies
Shall speak to the unborn?
Or a poet, broadly spreading
The golden immortalities
Of thy soul on natures lorn
And poor of such, them all to guard
From their decay,—beneath thy treading,
Earth's flowers recovering hues of
      Eden,—
And stars, drawn downward by thy looks,
To shine ascendant in thy books?'

XXI

The tame hawk in the castle-yard,
How it screams to the lightning, with
      its wet
Jagged plumes overhanging the parapet!
And at the lady's door the hound
      Scratches with a crying sound.

XXII

' But, O my babe, thy lids are laid
      Close, fast upon thy cheek,—
And not a dream of power and sheen
Can make a passage up between;
Thy heart is of thy mother's made,
      Thy looks are very meek;
And it will be their chosen place
To rest on some belovèd face,
As these on thine—and let the noise
Of the whole world go on, nor drown
      The tender silence of thy joys!
Or when that silence shall have grown
Too tender for itself, the same
Yearning for sound,—to look above
And utter its one meaning, LOVE,
      That *He* may hear His name!'

XXIII

No wind, no rain, no thunder!
The waters had trickled not slowly,
The thunder was not spent,
Nor the wind near finishing.
Who would have said that the storm
      was diminishing?
No wind, no rain, no thunder!
Their noises dropped asunder
From the earth and the firmament,
From the towers and the lattices,
Abrupt and echoless
As ripe fruits on the ground unshaken
      wholly,—
      As life in death!
And sudden and solemn the silence fell,
Startling the heart of Isobel
      As the tempest could not.
Against the door went panting the breath
Of the lady's hound whose cry was still,
And she, constrained howe'er she would
      not,
Lifted her eyes, and saw the moon
Looking out of heaven alone
      Upon the poplared hill,—
      A calm of God, made visible
      That men might bless it at their will.

XXIV

The moonshine on the baby's face
  Falleth clear and cold.
The mother's looks have fallen back
  To the same place ;
Because no moon with silver rack,
Nor broad sunrise in jasper skies,
    Has power to hold
    Our loving eyes,
Which still revert, as ever must
Wonder and Hope, to gaze on the dust.

XXV

The moonshine on the baby's face
  Cold and clear remaineth :
The mother's looks do shrink away,—
The mother's looks return to stay,
  As charmèd by what paineth.
Is any glamour in the case ?
Is it dream or is it sight ?
Hath the change upon the wild
Elements, that signs the night,
  Passed upon the child ?
It is not dream, but sight !—

XXVI

The babe has awakened from sleep,
And unto the gaze of its mother
Bent over it, lifted another !
Not the baby-looks that go
Unaimingly to and fro,
But an earnest gazing deep,
Such as soul gives soul at length,
When, by work and wail of years,
It winneth a solemn strength,
  And mourneth as it wears.
A strong man could not brook
With pulse unhurried by fears
To meet that baby's look
O'erglazed by manhood's tears—
The tears of a man full grown,
With a power to wring our own,
In the eyes all undefiled
Of a little three-months' child !
To see that babe-brow wrought
By the witnessing of thought,
To judgement's prodigy !
And the small soft mouth unweaned,
By mother's kiss o'erleaned
(Putting the sound of loving
Where no sound else was moving,
  Except the speechless cry),

Quickened to mind's expression,
  Shaped to articulation,
Yea, uttering words—yea, naming woe,
In tones that with it strangely went,
Because so baby-innocent,
As the child spake out to the mother so.—

XXVII

' O mother, mother, loose thy prayer !
  Christ's name hath made it strong.
It bindeth me, it holdeth me
With its most loving cruelty,
From floating my new soul along
  The happy heavenly air.
It bindeth me, it holdeth me
In all this dark, upon this dull
Low earth, by only weepers trod !—
It bindeth me, it holdeth me !—
Mine angel looketh sorrowful
  Upon the face of God[1].

XXVIII

' Mother, mother, can I dream
Beneath your earthly trees ?
I had a vision and a gleam—
I heard a sound more sweet than these
  When rippled by the wind.
Did you see the Dove with wings
Bathed in golden glisterings
From a sunless light behind,
Dropping on me from the sky
Soft as mother's kiss, until
I seemed to leap, and yet was still ?
Saw you how His love-large eye
Looked upon me mystic calms,
Till the power of His divine
Vision was indrawn to mine ?

XXIX

' Oh, the dream within the dream !
I saw celestial places even.
Oh, the vistas of high palms,
Making finites of delight
Through the heavenly infinite—
Lifting up their green still tops
  To the heaven of Heaven !
Oh, the sweet life-tree that drops
Shade like light across the river
Glorified in its for-ever
  Flowing from the Throne !

[1] For I say unto you, That in heaven their
angels do always behold the face of my Father
which is in heaven.—*Matt.* xviii. 10.

Oh, the shining holinesses
Of the thousand, thousand faces
God-sunned by the thronèd ONE!
And made intense with such a love,
That though I saw them turned above,
Each loving seemed for also me!
And, oh, the Unspeakable, the HE,
The manifest in secrecies,
Yet of mine own heart partaker,—
With the overcoming look
Of One who hath been once forsook,
  And blesseth the forsaker.
Mother, mother, let me go
Toward the Face that looketh so.
Through the mystic, wingèd Four
Whose are inward, outward eyes
Dark with light of mysteries,
And the restless evermore
" Holy, holy, holy,"—through
The sevenfold Lamps that burn in view
Of cherubim and seraphim,—
Through the four-and-twenty crowned
Stately elders, white around,
Suffer me to go to Him !

XXX

' Is your wisdom very wise,
Mother, on the narrow earth,
Very happy, very worth
That I should stay to learn ?
Are these air-corrupting sighs
Fashioned by unlearnèd breath ?
Do the students' lamps that burn
All night, illumine death ?
Mother, albeit this be so,
Loose thy prayer and let me go
Where that bright chief angel stands
Apart from all his brother bands,
Too glad for smiling, having bent
In angelic wilderment
O'er the depths of God, and brought
Reeling thence, one only thought
To fill his whole eternity.
He the teacher is for me !—
He can teach what I would know—
Mother, mother, let me go !

XXXI

' Can your poet make an Eden
  No winter will undo,
And light a starry fire while heeding
  His hearth's is burning too ?
Drown in music the earth's din,

And keep his own wild soul within
The law of his own harmony ?—
Mother, albeit this be so,
Let me to my Heavèn go !
A little harp me waits thereby—
A harp whose strings are golden all,
And tuned to music spherical,
Hanging on the green life-tree
Where no willows ever be.
Shall I miss that harp of mine?
Mother, no !—the Eye divine
Turned upon it, makes it shine ;
And when I touch it, poems sweet
Like separate souls shall fly from it,
Each to an immortal fytte.
We shall all be poets there,
Gazing on the chiefest Fair.

XXXII

' Love ! earth's love ! and *can* we love
Fixedly where all things move ?
Can the sinning love each other ?
    Mother, mother,
I tremble in thy close embrace,
I feel thy tears adown my face.
Thy prayers do keep me out of bliss—
    O dreary earthly love !
Loose thy prayer and let me go
To the place which loving is
Yet not sad ; and when is given
Escape to *thee* from this below,
Thou shalt behold me that I wait
For thee beside the happy Gate,
And silence shall be up in heaven
    To hear our greeting kiss.'

XXXIII

The nurse awakes in the morning sun,
And starts to see beside her bed
The lady with a grandeur spread
Like pathos o'er her face,—as one
God-satisfied and earth-undone.
  The babe upon her arm was dead !
And the nurse could utter forth no cry,—
She was awed by the calm in the mother's
    eye.

XXXIV

' Wake, nurse !' the lady said ;
' *We* are waking—he and I—
I, on earth, and he, in sky !
And thou must help me to o'erlay
With garment white, this little clay
Which needs no more our lullaby.

XXXV

'I changed the cruel prayer I made,
And bowed my meekened face, and
 prayed
That God would do His will! and thus
He did it, nurse! He parted *us*.
And His sun shows victorious
The dead calm face,—and *I* am calm,
And Heaven is hearkening a new psalm.

XXXVI

'This earthly noise is too anear,
Too loud, and will not let me hear
The little harp.   My death will soon
Make silence.'

                    And a sense of tune,
A satisfied love meanwhile
Which nothing earthly could despoil,
Sang on within her soul.

XXXVII

                    Oh you,
Earth's tender and impassioned few,
Take courage to entrust your love
To Him so named, who guards above
 Its ends and shall fulfil!
Breaking the narrow prayers that may
Befit your narrow hearts, away
 In His broad, loving will.

THE ROMAUNT OF THE PAGE

I

A KNIGHT of gallant deeds
 And a young page at his side,
From the holy war in Palestine
 Did slow and thoughtful ride,
As each were a palmer and told for beads
 The dews of the eventide.

II

'O young page,' said the knight,
 'A noble page art thou!
Thou fearest not to steep in blood
 The curls upon thy brow;
And once in the tent, and twice in the
 fight,
 Didst ward me a mortal blow.'

III

'O brave knight,' said the page,
 'Or ere we hither came,
We talked in tent, we talked in field,
 Of the bloody battle-game;
But here, below this greenwood bough,
 I cannot speak the same.

IV

'Our troop is far behind,
 The woodland calm is new;
Our steeds, with slow grass-muffled
 hoofs,
 Tread deep the shadows through;
And in my mind some blessing kind
 Is dropping with the dew.

V

'The woodland calm is pure—
 I cannot choose but have
A thought from these, o' the beechen-
 trees
 Which in our England wave,
And of the little finches fine
Which sang there, while in Palestine
 The warrior-hilt we drave.

VI

'Methinks, a moment gone,
 I heard my mother pray!
I heard, sir knight, the prayer for *me*
 Wherein she passed away;
And I know the heavens are leaning
 down
 To hear what I shall say.'

VII

The page spake calm and high,
 As of no mean degree;
Perhaps he felt in nature's broad
 Full heart, his own was free:
And the knight looked up to his lifted eye.
 Then answered smilingly :—

VIII

'Sir page, I pray your grace!
 Certes, I meant not so
To cross your pastoral mood, sir page,
 With the crook of the battle-bow:
But a knight may speak of a lady's face,
I ween, in any mood or place,
 If the grasses die or grow.

IX

'And this I meant to say,—
  My lady's face shall shine
As ladies' faces use, to greet
  My page from Palestine;
Or, speak she fair or prank she gay,
  She is no lady of mine.

X

'And this I meant to fear,—
  Her bower may suit thee ill!
For, sooth, in that same field and tent,
  Thy *talk* was somewhat still;
And fitter thy hand for my knightly spear,
  Than thy tongue for my lady's will.'

XI

Slowly and thankfully
  The young page bowed his head:
His large eyes seemed to muse a smile,
  Until he blushed instead,
And no lady in her bower, pardiè,
  Could blush more sudden red.
'Sir Knight,—thy lady's bower to me
  Is suited well,' he said.

XII

Beati, beati, mortui!
From the convent on the sea,
  One mile off, or scarce as nigh,
Swells the dirge as clear and high
As if that, over brake and lea,
Bodily the wind did carry
The great altar of Saint Mary,
And the fifty tapers burning o'er it,
And the lady Abbess dead before it,
And the chanting nuns whom yester-
  week
Her voice did charge and bless,—
Chanting steady, chanting meek,
Chanting with a solemn breath
Because that they are thinking less
Upon the Dead than upon death!
Beati, beati, mortui!
Now the vision in the sound
Wheeleth on the wind around.
Now it sleepeth back, away—
The uplands will not let it stay
To dark the western sun.
Mortui!—away at last,—
Or ere the page's blush is past!
And the knight heard all, and the page
  heard none.

XIII

'A boon, thou noble knight,
  If ever I servèd thee!
Though thou art a knight and I am a page,
  Now grant a boon to me;
And tell me sooth, if dark or bright,
  If little loved or loved aright
    Be the face of thy ladye.'

XIV

Gloomily looked the knight;—
  'As a son thou hast servèd me,
And would to none I had granted boon
  Except to only thee!
For haply then I should love aright,
For then I should know if dark or bright
  Were the face of my ladye.

XV

'Yet ill it suits my knightly tongue
  To grudge that granted boon!
That heavy price from heart and life
  I paid in silence down.
The hand that claimed it, cleared in fine
My father's fame: I swear by mine,
  That price was nobly won.

XVI

'Earl Walter was a brave old earl,—
  He was my father's friend;
And while I rode the lists at court
  And little guessed the end,
My noble father in his shroud,
Against a slanderer lying loud,
  He rose up to defend.

XVII

'Oh, calm, below the marble grey
  My father's dust was strown!
Oh, meek, above the marble grey
  His image prayed alone!
The slanderer lied—the wretch was
  brave,—
For, looking up the minster-nave,
He saw my father's knightly glaive
  Was changed from steel to stone.

XVIII

'Earl Walter's glaive was steel,
  With a brave old hand to wear it,
And dashed the lie back in the mouth
Which lied against the godly truth
  And against the knightly merit!

The slanderer, 'neath the avenger's heel,
Struck up the dagger in appeal
From stealthy lie to brutal force—
And out upon the traitor's corse
  Was yielded the true spirit.

XIX

'I would mine hand had fought that fight
  And justified my father!
I would mine heart had caught that wound
  And slept beside him rather!
I think it were a better thing
Than murthered friend and marriage-ring
  Forced on my life together.

XX

'Wail shook Earl Walter's house;
  His true wife shed no tear;
She lay upon her bed as mute
  As the earl did on his bier:
Till—"Ride, ride fast," she said at last,
"And bring the avengèd's son anear!
Ride fast—ride free, as a dart can flee,
For white of blee with waiting for me
  Is the corse in the next chambère."

XXI

'I came—I knelt beside her bed—
  Her calm was worse than strife;
"My husband, for thy father dear,
Gave freely, when thou wert not here,
  His own and eke my life.
A boon! Of that sweet child we make
An orphan for thy father's sake,
  Make thou, for ours, a wife."

XXII

'I said, "My steed neighs in the court,
  My bark rocks on the brine,
And the warrior's vow I am under now
  To free the pilgrim's shrine;
But fetch the ring and fetch the priest
And call that daughter of thine,
And rule she wide from my castle on Nyde
  While I am in Palestine."

XXIII

'In the dark chambère, if the bride was
    fair,
  Ye wis, I could not see,
But the steed thrice neighed, and the
    priest fast prayed,
  And wedded fast were we.

Her mother smiled upon her bed
As at its side we knelt to wed,
  And the bride rose from her knee
And kissed the smile of her mother dead,
  Or ever she kissed me.

XXIV

'My page, my page, what grieves thee so,
  That the tears run down thy face?'—
'Alas, alas! mine own sistèr
  Was in thy lady's case!
But *she* laid down the silks she wore
And followed him she wed before,
Disguised as his true servitor,
  To the very battle-place.'

XXV

And wept the page, but laughed the
    knight,—
  A careless laugh laughed he:
'Well done it were for thy sistèr,
  But not for my ladye!
My love, so please you, shall requite
No woman, whether dark or bright,
  Unwomaned if she be.'

XXVI

The page stopped weeping and smiled
    cold—
  'Your wisdom may declare
That womanhood is proved the best
By golden brooch and glossy vest
  The mincing ladies wear;
Yet is it proved, and was of old,
Anear as well, I dare to hold,
  By truth, or by despair.'

XXVII

He smiled no more, he wept no more,
  But passionate he spake,—
'Oh, womanly she prayed in tent,
  When none beside did wake!
Oh, womanly she paled in fight,
  For one belovèd's sake!—
And her little hand defiled with blood,
Her tender tears of womanhood
  Most woman-pure did make!'

XXVIII

—'Well done it were for thy sistèr,
  Thou tellest well her tale!
But for my lady, she shall pray
  I' the kirk of Nydesdale.

Not dread for me but love for me
  Shall make my lady pale ;
No casque shall hide her woman's tear—
It shall have room to trickle clear
  Behind her woman's veil.'

XXIX

—'But what if she mistook thy mind
  And followed thee to strife,
Then kneeling, did entreat thy love,
  As Paynims ask for life ?'
—'I would forgive, and evermore
Would love her as my servitor,
  But little as my wife.

XXX

'Look up—there is a small bright cloud
  Alone amid the skies !
So high, so pure, and so apart,
  A woman's honour lies.
The page looked up—the cloud was
    sheen—
A sadder cloud did rush, I ween,
  Betwixt it and his eyes :

XXXI

Then dimly dropped his eyes away
  From welkin unto hill—
Ha ! who rides there ?—the page is 'ware,
  Though the cry at his heart is still !
And the page seeth all and the knight
    seeth none,
Though banner and spear do fleck the
    sun,
  And the Saracens ride at will.

XXXII

He speaketh calm, he speaketh low,—
  ' Ride fast, my master, ride,
Or ere within the broadening dark
  The narrow shadows hide.'
' Yea, fast, my page, I will do so,
  And keep thou at my side.'

XXXIII

' Now nay, now nay, ride on thy way,
  Thy faithful page precede,
For I must loose on saddle-bow
My battle-casque that galls, I trow,
  The shoulder of my steed ;
And I must pray, as I did vow,
  For one in bitter need.

XXXIV

' Ere night I shall be near to thee,—
  Now ride, my master, ride !
Ere night, as parted spirits cleave
To mortals too beloved to leave,
  I shall be at thy side.'
The knight smiled free at the fantasy,
  And adown the dell did ride.

XXXV

Had the knight looked up to the page's
    face,
  No smile the word had won :
Had the knight looked up to the page's
    face,
  I ween he had never gone :
Had the knight looked back to the page's
    geste,
  I ween he had turned anon !
For dread was the woe in the face so
    young,
And wild was the silent geste that flung
Casque, sword to earth—as the boy down-
    sprung,
  And stood—alone, alone.

XXXVI

He clenched his hands as if to hold
  His soul's great agony—
' Have I renounced my womanhood,
  For wifehood unto *thee*,
And is this the last, last look of thine
  That ever I shall see ?

XXXVII

' Yet God thee save, and mayst thou have
  A lady to thy mind,
More woman-proud and half as true
  As one thou leav'st behind !
And God me take with HIM to dwell—
For HIM I cannot love too well,
  As I have loved my kind.'

XXXVIII

SHE looketh up, in earth's despair,
  The hopeful heavens to seek :
That little cloud still floateth there,
  Whereof her loved did speak.
How bright the little cloud appears !
Her eyelids fall upon the tears,
  And the tears down either cheek.

XXXIX

The tramp of hoof, the flash of steel—
  The Paynims round her coming!
The sound and sight have made her
    calm,—
  False page, but truthful woman!
She stands amid them all unmoved:
A heart once broken by the loved
  Is strong to meet the foeman.

XL

'Ho, Christian page! art keeping sheep,
  From pouring wine-cups resting?'—
'I keep my master's noble name,
  For warring, not for feasting;
And if that here Sir Hubert were,
My master brave, my master dear,
  Ye would not stay to question.'

XLI

'Where is thy master, scornful page,
  That we may slay or bind him?'—
'Now search the lea and search the wood,
  And see if ye can find him!
Nathless, as hath been often tried,
Your Paynim heroes faster ride
  Before him than behind him.'

XLII

'Give smoother answers, lying page,
  Or perish in the lying.'—
'I trow that if the warrior brand
Beside my foot, were in my hand,
  'Twere better at replying.'
They cursed her deep, they smote her low,
They cleft her golden ringlets through;
  The Loving is the Dying.

XLIII

She felt the scimitar gleam down,
  And met it from beneath
With smile more bright in victory
  Than any sword from sheath,—
Which flashed across her lip serene,
Most like the spirit-light between
  The darks of life and death.

XLIV

Ingemisco, ingemisco!
From the convent on the sea,
Now it sweepeth solemnly!
As over wood and over lea

Bodily the wind did carry
The great altar of Saint Mary,
And the fifty tapers paling o'er it,
And the Lady Abbess stark before it,
And the weary nuns with hearts that
    faintly
Beat along their voices saintly—
  Ingemisco, ingemisco!
Dirge for abbess laid in shroud
Sweepeth o'er the shroudless dead,
Page or lady, as we said,
With the dews upon her head,
All as sad if not as loud.
  Ingemisco, ingemisco!
Is ever a lament begun
By any mourner under sun,
Which, ere it endeth, suits but *one?*

THE LAY OF THE BROWN ROSARY

FIRST PART

'Onora, Onora,'—her mother is calling,
She sits at the lattice and hears the dew
    falling
Drop after drop from the sycamores
    laden
With dew as with blossom, and calls
    home the maiden,
    'Night cometh, Onora.'

She looks down the garden-walk cav-
    erned with trees,
To the limes at the end where the green
    arbour is—
'Some sweet thought or other may keep
    where it found her,
While forgot or unseen in the dreamlight
    around her
    Night cometh—Onora!'

She looks up the forest whose alleys
    shoot on
Like the mute minster-aisles when the
    anthem is done,
And the choristers sitting with faces
    aslant
Feel the silence to consecrate more than
    the chant—
    'Onora, Onora!'

And forward she looketh across the
   brown heath—
'Onora, art coming?'—what is it she
   seeth?
Nought, nought, but the grey border-
   stone that is wist
To dilate and assume a wild shape in
   the mist—
   'My daughter!'—Then over

The casement she leaneth, and as she
   doth so,
She is 'ware of her little son playing
   below:
'Now where is Onora?'—He hung
   down his head
And spake not, then answering blushed
   scarlet-red,—
   'At the tryst with her lover.'

But his mother was wroth. In a stern-
   ness quoth she,
'As thou play'st at the ball, art thou
   playing with me?
When we know that her lover to battle
   is gone,
And the saints know above that she
   loveth but one
   And will ne'er wed another?'

Then the boy wept aloud. 'Twas a fair
   sight yet sad
To see the tears run down the sweet
   blooms he had:
He stamped with his foot, said—'The
   saints know I lied
Because truth that is wicked is fittest to
   hide!
   Must I utter it, mother?'

In his vehement childhood he hurried
   within,
And knelt at her feet as in prayer
   against sin;
But a child at a prayer never sobbeth as
   he—
'Oh! she sits with the nun of the brown
   rosary,
   At nights in the ruin!

'The old convent ruin the ivy rots off,
Where the owl hoots by day, and the
   toad is sun-proof;

Where no singing-birds build, and the
   trees gaunt and grey
As in stormy sea-coasts appear blasted
   one way—
   But is *this* the wind's doing?

'A nun in the east wall was buried alive,
Who mocked at the priest when he
   called her to shrive,—
And shrieked such a curse, as the stone
   took her breath,
The old abbess fell backward and
   swooned unto death
   With an Ave half-spoken.

'I tried once to pass it, myself and my
   hound,
Till, as fearing the lash, down he
   shivered to ground.
A brave hound, my mother! a brave
   hound, ye wot!
And the wolf thought the same with his
   fangs at her throat
   In the pass of the Brocken.

'At dawn and at eve, mother, who
   sitteth there,
With the brown rosary never used for
   a prayer?
Stoop low, mother, low! If we went
   there to see,
What an ugly great hole in that east wall
   must be
   At dawn and at even!

'Who meet there, my mother, at dawn
   and at even?
Who meet by that wall, never looking
   to heaven?
O sweetest my sister, what doeth with
   thee,
The ghost of a nun with a brown rosary
   And a face turned from heaven?

'Saint Agnes o'erwatcheth my dreams,
   and erewhile
I have felt through mine eyelids the
   warmth of her smile;
But last night, as a sadness like pity
   came o'er her,
She whispered—"Say *two* prayers at
   dawn for Onora!
   The Tempted is sinning."'

'Onora, Onora!' they heard her not coming—
Not a step on the grass, not a voice through the gloaming;
But her mother looked up, and she stood on the floor
Fair and still as the moonlight that came there before,
    And a smile just beginning.

It touches her lips—but it dares not arise
To the height of the mystical sphere of her eyes;
And the large musing eyes, neither joyous nor sorry,
Sing on like the angels in separate glory
    Between clouds of amber.

For the hair droops in clouds amber-coloured, till stirred
Into gold by the gesture that comes with a word;
While—O soft!—her speaking is so interwound
Of the dim and the sweet, 'tis a twilight of sound
    And floats through the chamber.

'Since thou shrivest my brother, fair mother,' said she,
'I count on thy priesthood for marrying of me;
And I know by the hills that the battle is done—
That my lover rides on—will be here with the sun,
    'Neath the eyes that behold thee.'

Her mother sate silent—too tender, I wis,
Of the smile her dead father smiled dying to kiss;
But the boy started up pale with tears, passion-wrought,—
'O wicked fair sister, the hills utter nought!
    If he cometh, who told thee?'

'I know by the hills,' she resumed, calm and clear,
'By the beauty upon them, that HE is anear:

Did they ever look so since he bade me adieu?
Oh, love in the waking, sweet brother, is true
    As Saint Agnes in sleeping.'

Half-ashamed and half-softened the boy did not speak,
And the blush met the lashes which fell on his cheek:
She bowed down to kiss him—dear saints, did he see
Or feel on her bosom the BROWN ROSARY,
    That he shrank away weeping!

SECOND PART

A bed.—ONORA *sleeping.* Angels, *but not near.*

First Angel.
    Must we stand so far, and she
    So very fair?
Second Angel.   As bodies be.
First Angel.
    And she so mild?
Second Angel.   As spirits when
    They meeken, not to God, but men.
First Angel.
    And she so young,—that I who bring
    Good dreams for saintly children, might
    Mistake that small soft face to-night,
    And fetch her such a blessèd thing,
    That at her waking she would weep
    For childhood lost anew in sleep.
    How hath she sinned?
Second Angel.   In bartering love;
    God's love—for man's.
First Angel.   We may reprove
    The world for this, not only her.
    Let me approach to breathe away
    This dust o' the heart with holy air.
Second Angel.
    Stand off! She sleeps, and did not pray.
First Angel.
    Did none pray for her?
Second Angel.   Aye, a child,—
    Who never, praying, wept before :
    While, in a mother undefiled
    Prayer goeth on in sleep, as true
    And pauseless as the pulses do.

First Angel.
Then I approach.
Second Angel.   It is not WILLED.
First Angel.
One word : is she redeemed ?
Second Angel.   No more !
The place is filled. [*Angels vanish.*
Evil Spirit in a Nun's garb by the bed.
Forbear that dream—forbear that dream !
    too near to Heaven it leaned.
Onora in sleep.
Nay, leave me this—but only this ! 'tis
    but a dream, sweet fiend !
Evil Spirit.
It is a *thought.*
Onora in sleep.
A sleeping thought—most innocent of
    good.
It doth the Devil no harm, sweet fiend !
    it cannot, if it would.
I say in it no holy hymn, I do no holy work,
I scarcely hear the sabbath-bell that
    chimeth from the kirk.
Evil Spirit.
Forbear that dream—forbear that dream !
Onora in sleep.
            Nay, let me dream at least.
That far-off bell, it may be took for viol
    at a feast.
I only walk among the fields, beneath
    the autumn-sun,
With my dead father, hand in hand, as
    I have often done.
Evil Spirit.
Forbear that dream—forbear that dream !
Onora in sleep.
            Nay, sweet fiend, let me go.
I never more can walk with *him,* oh,
    never more but so.
For they have tied my father's feet
    beneath the kirkyard stone,
Oh, deep and straight, oh, very straight !
    they move at nights alone :
And then he calleth through my dreams,
    he calleth tenderly,
' Come forth, my daughter, my beloved,
    and walk the fields with me ! '
Evil Spirit.
Forbear that dream, or else disprove its
    pureness by a sign.
Onora in sleep.
Speak on, thou shalt be satisfied ! my
    word shall answer thine.

I heard a bird which used to sing
    when I a child was praying,
I see the poppies in the corn I used to
    sport away in.—
What shall I do — tread down the
    dew, and pull the blossoms blow-
    ing ?
Or clap my wicked hands to fright the
    finches from the rowan ?
Evil Spirit.
Thou shalt do something harder still.
    Stand up where thou dost stand
Among the fields of Dreamland with thy
    father hand in hand,
And clear and slow, repeat the vow—
    declare its cause and kind,
Which, not to break, in sleep or wake,
    thou bearest on thy mind.
Onora in sleep.
I bear a vow of sinful kind, a vow for
    mournful cause :
I vowed it deep, I vowed it strong—the
    spirits laughed applause :
The spirits trailed along the pines low
    laughter like a breeze,
While, high atween their swinging tops,
    the stars appeared to freeze.
Evil Spirit.
More calm and free,—speak out to me,
    why such a vow was made.
Onora in sleep.
Because that God decreed my death,
    and I shrank back afraid.
Have patience, O dead father mine !
    I did not fear to die ;—
I wish I were a young dead child, and
    had thy company !
I wish I lay beside thy feet, a buried
    three-year child,
And wearing only a kiss of thine upon
    my lips that smiled !
The linden-tree that covers thee might
    so have shadowed twain,
For death itself I did not fear—'tis love
    that makes the pain.
Love feareth death.   I was no child—
    I was betrothed that day ;
I wore a troth-kiss on my lips I could
    not give away.
How could I bear to lie content and still
    beneath a stone,
And feel mine own betrothed go by—
    alas ! no more mine own,—

Go leading by in wedding pomp some
  lovely lady brave,
With cheeks that blushed as red as rose,
  while mine were white in grave?
How could I bear to sit in Heaven, on
  e'er so high a throne,
And hear him say to her—to *her!* that
  else he loveth none?
Though e'er so high I sate above, though
  e'er so low he spake,
As clear as thunder I should hear the
  new oath he might take,
That hers, forsooth, were heavenly
  eyes—ah, me! while very dim
Some heavenly eyes (indeed of Heaven!)
  would darken down to *him.*
    Evil Spirit.
Who told thee thou wast called to death?
    Onora in sleep.
            I sate all night beside thee—
The grey owl on the ruined wall shut
  both his eyes to hide thee,
And ever he flapped his heavy wing all
  brokenly and weak,
And the long grass waved against the
  sky, around his gasping beak.
I sate beside thee all the night, while
  the moonlight lay forlorn,
Strewn round us like a dead world's
  shroud, in ghastly fragments torn.
And through the night, and through
  the hush, and over the flapping
  wing,
We heard beside the Heavenly Gate the
  angels murmuring :—
We heard them say, ' Put day to day,
  and count the days to seven,
And God will draw Onora up the
  golden stairs of Heaven ;
And yet the Evil ones have leave that
  purpose to defer,
For if she has no need of HIM, He has
  no need of her.'—
    Evil Spirit.
Speak out to me, speak bold and free.
    Onora in sleep.
            And then I heard thee say,
'I count upon my rosary brown the
  hours thou hast to stay !
Yet God permits us Evil ones to put by
  that decree,
Since if thou hast no need of HIM, He
  has no need of thee—

And if thou wilt forgo the sight of
  angels, verily
Thy true love gazing on thy face, shall
  guess what angels be ;
Nor bride shall pass, save thee ' . . .
    Alas !—my father's hand 's acold,
The meadows seem—
    Evil Spirit.
            Forbear the dream, or let the
  vow be told !
    Onora in sleep.
I vowed upon thy rosary brown, this
  string of antique beads,
By charnel lichens overgrown, and dank
  among the weeds,
This rosary brown, which is thine own,—
  lost soul of buried nun,
Who, lost by vow, wouldst render now
  all souls alike undone,—
I vowed upon thy rosary brown,—and,
  till such vow should break,
A pledge always of living days, 'twas
  hung around my neck—
I vowed to thee on rosary (dead father,
  look not so !),
*I would not thank God in my weal, nor
  seek God in my woe.*
    Evil Spirit.
And canst thou prove—
    Onora in sleep.
            O love—my love !
    I felt him near again !
I saw his steed on mountain-head, I
  heard it on the plain !
Was this no weal for me to feel ?—is
  greater weal than this?
Yet when he came, I wept his name—
  and the angels heard but *his.*
    Evil Spirit.
Well done, well done !
    Onora in sleep.
Aye me ! the sun . . . the dreamlight 'gins
  to pine,
Aye me ! how dread can look the Dead !—
    Aroint thee, father mine !

She starteth from slumber, she sitteth
  upright,
And her breath comes in sobs while she
  stares through the night.
There is nought. The great willow, her
  lattice before,

Large-drawn in the moon, lieth calm on
  the floor.
But her hands tremble fast as their pulses,
  and, free
From the death-clasp, close over—the
  BROWN ROSARY.

THIRD PART

'Tis a morn for a bridal; the merry
  bride-bell
Rings clear through the green-wood
  that skirts the chapelle,
And the priest at the altar awaiteth the
  bride,
And the sacristans slyly are jesting aside
  At the work shall be doing;

While down through the wood rides that
  fair company,
The youths with the courtship, the
  maids with the glee,
Till the chapel-cross opens to sight, and
  at once
All the maids sigh demurely and think
  for the nonce,
    'And so endeth a wooing!'

And the bride and the bridegroom are
  leading the way,
With his hand on her rein, and a word
  yet to say:
Her dropt eyelids suggest the soft
  answers beneath,
And the little quick smiles come and go
  with her breath,
    When she sigheth or speaketh.

And the tender bride-mother breaks off
  unaware
From an Ave, to think that her daughter
  is fair,
Till in nearing the chapel and glancing
  before
She seeth her little son stand at the
  door:
    Is it play that he seeketh?

Is it play? when his eyes wander
  innocent-wild,
And sublimed with a sadness unfitting a
  child?

He trembles not, weeps not—the passion
  is done,
And calmly he kneels in their midst,
  with the sun
    On his head like a glory.

'O fair-featured maids, ye are many!'
  he cried,—
'But, in fairness and vileness, who
  matcheth the bride?
O brave-hearted youths, ye are many!
  but whom,
For the courage and woe, can ye match
  with the groom,
    As ye see them before ye?'

Out spake the bride's mother, 'The
  vileness is thine,
If thou shame thine own sister, a bride
  at the shrine!'
Out spake the bride's lover, 'The vile-
  ness be mine,
If he shame mine own wife at the hearth
  or the shrine,
    And the charge be unprovèd.

'Bring the charge, prove the charge,
  brother! speak it aloud:
Let thy father and hers, hear it deep in
  his shroud!'—
—'O father, thou seest—for dead eyes
  can see—
How she wears on her bosom *a brown
  rosary*,
    O my father belovèd!'

Then outlaughed the bridegroom, and
  outlaughed withal
Both maidens and youths, by the old
  chapel-wall.
'So she weareth no love-gift, kind
  brother,' quoth he,
'She may wear an she listeth a brown
  rosary,
    Like a pure-hearted lady.'

Then swept through the chapel the long
  bridal train.
Though he spake to the bride she replied
  not again:
On, as one in a dream, pale and stately
  she went
Where the altar-lights burn o'er the
  great sacrament,
    Faint with daylight, but steady.

But her brother had passed in between
    them and her,
And calmly knelt down on the high-altar
    stair—
Of an infantine aspect so stern to the
    view
That the priest could not smile on the
    child's eyes of blue
    As he would for another.

He knelt like a child marble-sculptured
    and white,
That seems kneeling to pray on the tomb
    of a knight,
With a look taken up to each iris of stone
From the greatness and death where he
    kneeleth, but none
    From the face of a mother.

'In your chapel, O priest, ye have
    wedded and shriven
Fair wives for the hearth, and fair
    sinners for Heaven!
But this fairest my sister, ye think now
    to wed,
Bid her kneel where she standeth, and
    shrive her instead:
    O shrive her and wed not!'

In tears, the bride's mother,—'Sir priest,
    unto thee
Would he lie, as he lied to this fair
    company.'
In wrath, the bride's lover,—'The lie
    shall be clear!
Speak it out, boy! the saints in their
    niches shall hear:
    Be the charge proved or said not.'

Then serene in his childhood he lifted
    his face,
And his voice sounded holy and fit for
    the place:
'Look down from your niches, ye still
    saints, and see
How she wears on her bosom *a brown
    rosary!*
    Is it used for the praying?'

The youths looked aside—to laugh there
    were a sin—
And the maidens' lips trembled from
    smiles shut within.

Quoth the priest, 'Thou art wild, pretty
    boy! Blessed she
Who prefers at her bridal a brown rosary
    To a worldly arraying!'

The bridegroom spake low and led
    onward the bride,
And before the high altar they stood
    side by side:
The rite-book is opened, the rite is begun,
They have knelt down together to rise
    up as one.
    Who laughed by the altar?

The maidens looked forward, the youths
    looked around,
The bridegroom's eye flashed from his
    prayer at the sound;
And each saw the bride, as if no bride
    she were,
Gazing cold at the priest without gesture
    of prayer,
    As he read from the psalter.

The priest never knew that she did so,
    but still
He felt a power on him too strong for
    his will,
And whenever the Great Name was
    there to be read,
His voice sank to silence—THAT could
    not be said,
    Or the air could not hold it.

'I have sinnèd,' quoth he, 'I have
    sinnèd, I wot'—
And the tears ran adown his old cheeks
    at the thought.
They dropped fast on the book, but he
    read on the same,
And ay was the silence where should
    be the NAME,—
    As the choristers told it.

The rite-book is closed, and the rite
    being done
They who knelt down together arise
    up as one.
Fair riseth the bride—oh, a fair bride
    is she,
But, for all (think the maidens) that
    brown rosary,
    No saint at her praying!

What aileth the bridegroom ? He glares
    blank and wide—
Then suddenly turning he kisseth the
    bride—
His lip stung her with cold ; she glanced
    upwardly mute :
' Mine own wife,' he said, and fell stark
    at her foot
    In the word he was saying.

They have lifted him up,—but his head
    sinks away,
And his face showeth bleak in the
    sunshine and grey.
Leave him now where he lieth—for oh,
    never more
Will he kneel at an altar or stand on a
    floor !
    Let his bride gaze upon him.

Long and still was her gaze, while they
    chafèd him there
And breathed in the mouth whose last
    life had kissed her,
But when they stood up—only *they!*
    with a start
The shriek from her soul struck her
    pale lips apart—
    She has lived, and forgone him !

And low on his body she droppeth
    adown—
' Didst call me thine own wife, belovèd—
    thine own ?
Then take thine own with thee ! thy
    coldness is warm
To the world's cold without thee ! Come,
    keep me from harm
    In a calm of thy teaching.'

She looked in his face earnest-long, as
    in sooth
There were hope of an answer,—and
    then kissed his mouth,
And with head on his bosom, wept,
    wept bitterly,—
' Now, O God, take pity—take pity on
    me !—
    God, hear my beseeching !'

She was 'ware of a shadow that crossed
    where she lay,
She was 'ware of a presence that withered
    the day—

Wild she sprang to her feet,—' I sur-
    render to *thee*
The broken vow's pledge,—the accursed
    rosary,—
    I am ready for dying !'

She dashed it in scorn to the marble-
    paved ground
Where it fell mute as snow, and a weird
    music-sound
Crept up, like a chill, up the aisles long
    and dim,—
As the fiends tried to mock at the
    choristers' hymn
    And moaned in the trying.

FOURTH PART

ONORA looketh listlessly adown the
    garden walk :
' I am weary, O my mother, of thy
    tender talk ;
I am weary of the trees a-waving to and
    fro,
Of the steadfast skies above, the running
    brooks below.
All things are the same but I,—only I
    am dreary,
And, mother, of my dreariness behold
    me very weary.

' Mother, brother, pull the flowers I
    planted in the spring
And smiled to think I should smile more
    upon their gathering :
The bees will find out other flowers—
    oh, pull them, dearest mine,
And carry them and carry me before
    Saint Agnes' shrine.'
—Whereat they pulled the summer
    flowers she planted in the spring,
And her and them all mournfully to
    Agnes' shrine did bring.

She looked up to the pictured saint and
    gently shook her head—
' The picture is too calm for *me*—too
    calm for *me*,' she said :
' The little flowers we brought with us,
    before it we may lay,
For those are used to look at heaven,—
    but *I* must turn away,

Because no sinner under sun can dare
or bear to gaze
On God's or angel's holiness, except in
Jesu's face.'

She spoke with passion after pause—
'And were it wisely done,
If we who cannot gaze above, should
walk the earth alone?
If we whose virtue is so weak, should
have a will so strong,
And stand blind on the rocks, to choose
the right path from the wrong?
To choose perhaps a love-lit hearth,
instead of love and Heaven,—
A single rose, for a rose-tree, which
beareth seven times seven?
A rose that droppeth from the hand,
that fadeth in the breast,—
Until, in grieving for the worst, we
learn what is the best!'
Then breaking into tears,—'Dear God,'
she cried, 'and must we see
All blissful things depart from us, or ere
we go to THEE?
We cannot guess Thee in the wood, or
hear Thee in the wind?
Our cedars must fall round us, ere we
see the light behind?
Aye sooth, we feel too strong in weal,
to need Thee on that road,
But woe being come, the soul is dumb
that crieth not on "God."'

Her mother could not speak for tears;
she ever musèd thus,
'*The bees will find out other flowers,*—
but what is left for *us*?'
But her young brother stayed his sobs
and knelt beside her knee,
—'Thou sweetest sister in the world,
hast never a word for me?'
She passed her hand across his face,
she pressed it on his cheek,
So tenderly, so tenderly—she needed
not to speak.

The wreath which lay on shrine that day,
at vespers bloomed no more:
The woman fair who placed it there had
died an hour before.

Both perished mute, for lack of root,
earth's nourishment to reach.
O reader, breathe (the ballad saith)
some sweetness out of each!

A ROMANCE OF THE GANGES

I

SEVEN maidens 'neath the midnight
Stand near the river-sea,
Whose water sweepeth white around
The shadow of the tree.
The moon and earth are face to face,
And earth is slumbering deep;
The wave-voice seems the voice of dreams
That wander through her sleep.
The river floweth on.

II

What bring they 'neath the midnight,
Beside the river-sea?
They bring the human heart wherein
No nightly calm can be,—
That droppeth never with the wind,
Nor drieth with the dew:
Oh, calm it, God! Thy calm is broad
To cover spirits, too.
The river floweth on.

III

The maidens lean them over
The waters, side by side,
And shun each other's deepening eyes,
And gaze adown the tide;
For each within a little boat
A little lamp hath put,
And heaped for freight some lily's weight
Or scarlet rose half shut.
The river floweth on.

IV

Of shell of coco carven,
Each little boat is made:
Each carries a lamp, and carries a flower,
And carries a hope unsaid;
And when the boat hath carried the lamp
Unquenched, till out of sight,
The maiden is sure that love will en-
dure,—
But love will fail with light.
The river floweth on.

v

Why, all the stars are ready
 To symbolize the soul,
The stars untroubled by the wind,
 Unwearied as they roll;
And yet the soul by instinct sad
 Reverts to symbols low—
To that small flame, whose very name
 Breathed o'er it, shakes it so!
 The river floweth on.

vi

Six boats are on the river,
 Seven maidens on the shore,
While still above them steadfastly
 The stars shine evermore.
Go, little boats, go soft and safe,
 And guard the symbol spark !—
The boats aright go safe and bright
 Across the waters dark.
 The river floweth on.

vii

The maiden Luti watcheth
 Where onwardly they float :
That look in her dilating eyes
 Might seem to drive her boat!
Her eyes still mark the constant fire,
 And kindling unawares
That hopeful while, she lets a smile
 Creep silent through her prayers.
 The river floweth on.

viii

The smile—where hath it wandered?
 She riseth from her knee,
She holds her dark, wet locks away—
 There is no light to see !
She cries a quick and bitter cry—
 'Nuleeni, launch me thine !
We must have light abroad to-night,
 For all the wreck of mine.'
 The river floweth on.

ix

'I do remember watching
 Beside this river-bed,
When on my childish knee was laid
 My dying father's head ;
I turned mine own, to keep the tears
 From falling on his face :
What doth it prove when Death and Love
 Choose out the self-same place ?'
 The river floweth on.

x

'They say the dead are joyful
 The death-change here receiving :
Who say—ah, me !—who dare to say
 Where joy comes to the living ?
Thy boat, Nuleeni ! look not sad—
 Light up the waters rather !
I weep no faithless lover where
 I wept a loving father.'
 The river floweth on

xi

' My heart foretold his falsehood
 Ere my little boat grew dim :
And though I closed mine eyes to dream
 That one last dream of *him*,
They shall not now be wet to see
 The shining vision go :
From earth's cold love I look above
 To the holy house of snow[1].'
 The river floweth on.

xii

'Come thou—thou never knewest
 A grief, that thou shouldst fear one !
Thou wearest still the happy look
 That shines beneath a dear one ;
Thy humming-bird is in the sun[2],
 Thy cuckoo in the grove,
And all the three broad worlds, for thee
 Are full of wandering love.'
 The river floweth on.

xiii

'Why, maiden, dost thou loiter ?
 What secret wouldst thou cover ?
That peepul cannot hide thy boat,
 And I can guess thy lover.
I heard thee sob his name in sleep . . .
 It was a name I knew ;
Come, little maid, be not afraid,
 But let us prove him true !'
 The river floweth on.

[1] The Hindoo heaven is localized on the sum-
mit of Mount Meru—one of the mountains of
Himalaya or Himmaleh, which signifies, I be-
lieve, in Sanscrit, the abode of snow, winter, or
coldness.
[2] Himadeva, the Indian god of love, is
imagined to wander through the three worlds,
accompanied by the humming-bird, cuckoo,
and gentle breezes.

XIV

The little maiden cometh,
  She cometh shy and slow,
I ween she seeth through her lids,
  They drop adown so low ;
Her tresses meet her small bare feet —
  She stands and speaketh nought,
Yet blusheth red, as if she said
  The name she only thought.
      The river floweth on.

XV

She knelt beside the water,
  She lighted up the flame,
And o'er her youthful forehead's calm
  The fitful radiance came :—
' Go, little boat, go, soft and safe,
  And guard the symbol spark ! '
Soft, safe, doth float the little boat
  Across the waters dark.
      The river floweth on.

XVI

Glad tears her eyes have blinded,
  The light they cannot reach ;
She turneth with that sudden smile
  She learnt before her speech—
' I do not hear his voice ! the tears
  Have dimmed my light away !
But the symbol light will last to-night,
  The love will last for ay.'
      The river floweth on.

XVII

Then Luti spake behind her,
  Outspake she bitterly,
' By the symbol light that lasts to-night,
  Wilt vow a vow to me ? '—
Nuleeni gazeth up her face,
  Soft answer maketh she :
' By loves that last when lights are past,
  I vow that vow to thee ! '
      The river floweth on.

XVIII

An earthly look had Luti
  Though her voice was deep as prayer :
' The rice is gathered from the plains
  To cast upon thine hair [1].

[1] The casting of rice upon the head, and the fixing of the band or tali about the neck, are parts of the Hindoo marriage ceremonial.

But when *he* comes, his marriage-band
  Around thy neck to throw,
Thy bride-smile raise to meet his gaze,
  And whisper,— *There is one betrays,*
  While Luti suffers woe.'
      The river floweth on.

XIX

' And when in seasons after,
  Thy little bright-faced son
Shall lean against thy knee and ask
  What deeds his sire hath done,
Press deeper down thy mother-smile
  His glossy curls among—
View deep his pretty childish eyes,
  And whisper,— *There is none denies,*
  While Luti speaks of wrong.'
      The river floweth on.

XX

Nuleeni looked in wonder,
  Yet softly answered she :
' By loves that last when lights are past,
  I vowed that vow to thee.
But why glads it thee that a bride-day be
  By a word of *woe* defiled ?
That a word of *wrong* take the cradle-song
  From the ear of a sinless child ? '—
' Why ? ' Luti said, and her laugh was
    dread,
  And her eyes dilated wild—
' That the fair new love may her bride-
    groom prove,
  And the father shame the child.'
      The river floweth on.

XXI

' Thou flowest still, O river,
  Thou flowest 'neath the moon !
Thy lily hath not changed a leaf [1],
  Thy charmèd lute a tune !
He mixed his voice with thine—and *his*
  Was all I heard around ;
But now, beside his chosen bride,
  I hear the river's sound.'
      The river floweth on.

XXII

' I gaze upon her beauty
  Through the tresses that enwreathe it;
The light above thy wave, is hers—
  My rest, alone beneath it.

[1] The Ganges is represented as a white woman, with a water-lily in her right hand, and in her left a lute.

Oh, give me back the dying look
　My father gave thy water !
Give back !—and let a little love
　O'erwatch his weary daughter ! '
　　　　The river floweth on.

XXIII

' Give back ! ' she hath departed—
　The word is wandering with her ;
And the stricken maidens hear afar
　The step and cry together.
Frail symbols ?　None are frail enow
　For mortal joys to borrow !—
While bright doth float Nuleeni's boat,
　She weepeth, dark with sorrow.
　　　　The river floweth on.

RIME OF THE DUCHESS MAY

I

To the belfry, one by one, went the
　ringers from the sun,
　　　Toll slowly.
And the oldest ringer said, 'Ours is
　music for the Dead,
　When the rebecks are all done.'

II

Six abeles i' the churchyard grow on the
　northside in a row,
　　　Toll slowly.
And the shadows of their tops rock across
　the little slopes
　Of the grassy graves below.

III

On the south side and the west, a small
　river runs in haste,
　　　Toll slowly.
And between the river flowing and the
　fair green trees a-growing
　Do the dead lie at their rest.

IV

On the east I sate that day, up against
　a willow grey.
　　　Toll slowly.
Through the rain of willow-branches, I
　could see the low hill-ranges,
　And the river on its way.

V

There I sate beneath the tree, and the
　bell tolled solemnly,
　　　Toll slowly.
While the trees' and river's voices flowed
　between the solemn noises,—
　Yet death seemed more loud to me.

VI

There, I read this ancient rime, while
　the bell did all the time
　　　Toll slowly.
And the solemn knell fell in with the tale
　of life and sin,
　Like a rhythmic fate sublime.

THE RIME

I

Broad the forests stood (I read) on the
　hills of Linteged—
　　　Toll slowly.
And three hundred years had stood mute
　adown each hoary wood,
　Like a full heart having prayed.

II

And the little birds sang east, and the
　little birds sang west,
　　　Toll slowly.
And but little thought was theirs of the
　silent antique years,
　In the building of their nest.

III

Down the sun dropt large and red, on
　the towers of Linteged,—
　　　Toll slowly.
Lance and spear upon the height,
　bristling strange in fiery light,
　While the castle stood in shade.

IV

There, the castle stood up black, with
　the red sun at its back,—
　　　Toll slowly.
Like a sullen smouldering pyre, with a
　top that flickers fire
　When the wind is on its track.

V

And five hundred archers tall did besiege
  the castle wall,
    Toll slowly.
And the castle, seethed in blood, fourteen
  days and nights had stood,
  And to-night was near its fall.

VI

Yet thereunto, blind to doom, three
  months since, a bride did come,—
    Toll slowly.
One who proudly trod the floors, and
  softly whispered in the doors,
  ' May good angels bless our home.'

VII

Oh, a bride of queenly eyes, with a front
  of constancies !
    Toll slowly.
Oh, a bride of cordial mouth,—where the
  untired smile of youth
  Did light outward its own sighs.

VIII

'Twas a Duke's fair orphan-girl, and her
  uncle's ward, the Earl ;
    Toll slowly.
Who betrothed her, twelve years old, for
  the sake of dowry gold,
  To his son Lord Leigh, the churl.

IX

But what time she had made good all her
  years of womanhood,
    Toll slowly.
Unto both those lords of Leigh, spake
  she out right sovranly,
  ' My will runneth as my blood.

X

'And while this same blood makes red
  this same right hand's veins,' she
  said,—
    Toll slowly.
' 'Tis my will as lady free, not to wed
  a lord of Leigh,
  But Sir Guy of Linteged.'

XI

The old Earl he smilèd smooth, then he
  sighed for wilful youth,—
    Toll slowly.

' Good my niece, that hand withal looketh
  somewhat soft and small
  For so large a will, in sooth.'

XII

She, too, smiled by that same sign,—but
  her smile was cold and fine,—
    Toll slowly.
' Little hand clasps muckle gold, or it
  were not worth the hold
  Of thy son, good uncle mine !'

XIII

Then the young lord jerked his breath,
  and sware thickly in his teeth,
    Toll slowly.
' He would wed his own betrothed, an
  she loved him an she loathed,
  Let the life come or the death.'

XIV

Up she rose with scornful eyes, as her
  father's child might rise,—
    Toll slowly.
' Thy hound's blood, my lord of Leigh,
  stains thy knightly heel,' quoth
  she,
  ' And he moans not where he lies.

XV

' But a woman's will dies hard, in the
  hall or on the sward ! '—
    Toll slowly.
' By that grave, my lords, which made me
  orphaned girl and dowered lady,
  I deny you wife and ward.'

XVI

Unto each she bowed her head, and
  swept past with lofty tread.
    Toll slowly.
Ere the midnight-bell had ceased, in the
  chapel had the priest
  Blessed her, bride of Linteged.

XVII

Fast and fain the bridal train along the
  night-storm rode amain.
    Toll slowly.
Hard the steeds of lord and serf struck
  their hoofs out on the turf,
  In the pauses of the rain.

XVIII

Fast and fain the kinsmen's train along
    the storm pursued amain—
      Toll slowly.
Steed on steed-track, dashing off—
    thickening, doubling, hoof on hoof,
In the pauses of the rain.

XIX

And the bridegroom led the flight on his
    red-roan steed of might,
      Toll slowly.
And the bride lay on his arm, still, as if
    she feared no harm,
Smiling out into the night.

XX

'Dost thou fear?' he said at last.—'Nay,'
    she answered him in haste,—
      Toll slowly.
'Not such death as we could find—only
    life with one behind—
Ride on fast as fear—ride fast!'

XXI

Up the mountain wheeled the steed—
    girth to ground, and fetlocks
    spread,—
      Toll slowly.
Headlong bounds, and rocking flanks,—
    down he staggered, down the
    banks,
To the towers of Linteged.

XXII

High and low the serfs looked out, red
    the flambeaus tossed about,—
      Toll slowly.
In the courtyard rose the cry—'Live the
    Duchess and Sir Guy!'
But she never heard them shout.

XXIII

On the steed she dropt her cheek, kissed
    his mane and kissed his neck.—
      Toll slowly.
'I had happier died by thee, than lived
    on, a Lady Leigh,'
Were the first words she did speak.

XXIV

But a three months' joyaunce lay 'twixt
    that moment and to-day,
      Toll slowly.

When five hundred archers tall stand
    beside the castle wall,
To recapture Duchess May.

XXV

And the castle standeth black, with the
    red sun at its back,—
      Toll slowly.
And a fortnight's siege is done—and,
    except the duchess, none
Can misdoubt the coming wrack.

XXVI

Then the captain, young Lord Leigh, with
    his eyes so grey of blee,
      Toll slowly.
And thin lips that scarcely sheath the cold
    white gnashing of his teeth,
Gnashed in smiling, absently,

XXVII

Cried aloud, 'So goes the day, bridegroom
    fair of Duchess May!'—
      Toll slowly.
'Look thy last upon that sun! if thou
    seest to-morrow's one,
'Twill be through a foot of clay.

XXVIII

'Ha, fair bride! dost hear no sound, save
    that moaning of the hound?'—
      Toll slowly.
'Thou and I have parted troth,—yet
    I keep my vengeance-oath,
And the other may come round.

XXIX

'Ha! thy will is brave to dare, and thy
    new love past compare,'—
      Toll slowly.
'Yet thine old love's faulchion brave is
    as strong a thing to have
As the will of lady fair.

XXX

'Peck on blindly, netted dove!—If a
    wife's name thee behove,'
      Toll slowly.
'Thou shalt wear the same to-morrow,
    ere the grave has hid the sorrow
Of thy last ill-mated love.

XXXI

'O'er his fixed and silent mouth, thou
and I will call back troth.'
Toll slowly.
'He shall altar be and priest,—and he
will not cry at least
  "I forbid you—I am loath!"'

XXXII

'I will wring thy fingers pale in the
gauntlet of my mail.'
Toll slowly.
'"Little hand and muckle gold" close
shall lie within my hold,
  As the sword did, to prevail.'

XXXIII

Oh, the little birds sang east, and the
little birds sang west,
Toll slowly.
Oh, and laughed the Duchess May, and
her soul did put away
  All his boasting, for a jest.

XXXIV

In her chamber did she sit, laughing low
to think of it,—
Toll slowly.
'Tower is strong and will is free—thou
'canst boast, my lord of Leigh,
  But thou boastest little wit.'

XXXV

In her tire-glass gazèd she, and she
blushed right womanly.
Toll slowly.
She blushed half from her disdain—half,
her beauty was so plain,
  —'Oath for oath, my lord of Leigh!'

XXXVI

Straight she called her maidens in—
  'Since ye gave me blame herein,'
Toll slowly.
'That a bridal such as mine should lack
gauds to make it fine,
  Come and shrive me from that sin.

XXXVII

'It is three months gone to-day since
I gave mine hand away.'
Toll slowly.

'Bring the gold and bring the gem, we
will keep bride-state in them,
  While we keep the foe at bay.

XXXVIII

'On your arms I loose mine hair!—comb
it smooth and crown it fair.'
Toll slowly.
'I would look in purple pall from this
lattice down the wall,
  And throw scorn to one that's
there!'

XXXIX

Oh, the little birds sang east, and the
little birds sang west.
Toll slowly.
On the tower the castle's lord leant in
silence on his sword,
  With an anguish in his breast.

XL

With a spirit-laden weight, did he lean
down passionate.
Toll slowly.
They have almost sapped the wall,—they
will enter therewithal,
  With no knocking at the gate.

XLI

Then the sword he leant upon, shivered,
snapped upon the stone,—
Toll slowly.
'Sword,' he thought, with inward laugh,
'ill thou servest for a staff
  When thy nobler use is done!

XLII

'Sword, thy nobler use is done!—tower
is lost, and shame begun!'—
Toll slowly.
'If we met them in the breach, hilt to
hilt or speech to speech,
  We should die there, each for one.

XLIII

'If we met them at the wall, we should
singly, vainly fall,'—
Toll slowly.
'But if *I* die here alone,—then I die,
who am but one,
  And die nobly for them all.

XLIV

'Five true friends lie for my sake, in the
   moat and in the brake,'—
     Toll slowly.
'Thirteen warriors lie at rest, with a
   black wound in the breast,
   And not one of these will wake.

XLV

'So no more of this shall be!—heart-blood
   weighs too heavily,'—
     Toll slowly.
'And I could not sleep in grave, with the
   faithful and the brave
   Heaped around and over me.

XLVI

'Since young Clare a mother hath, and
   young Ralph a plighted faith,'—
     Toll slowly.
'Since my pale young sister's cheeks
   blush like rose when Ronald
   speaks,
   Albeit never a word she saith—

XLVII

'These shall never die for me—life-blood
   falls too heavily : '
     Toll slowly.
'And if *I* die here apart,—o'er my dead
   and silent heart
   They shall pass out safe and free.

XLVIII

'When the foe hath heard it said—
   "Death holds Guy of Linteged,"'
     Toll slowly.
'That new corse new peace shall bring,
   and a blessèd, blessèd thing
   Shall the stone be at its head.

XLIX

'Then my friends shall pass out free, and
   shall bear my memory,'—
     Toll slowly.
'Then my foes shall sleek their pride,
   soothing fair my widowed bride,
   Whose sole sin was love of me.

L

'With their words all smooth and sweet,
   they will front her and entreat,'
     Toll slowly.

'And their purple pall will spread under-
   neath her fainting head
   While her tears drop over it.

LI

'She will weep her woman's tears, she
   will pray her woman's prayers,'—
     Toll slowly.
'But her heart is young in pain, and her
   hopes will spring again
   By the suntime of her years.

LII

'Ah, sweet May! ah, sweetest grief!—
   once I vowed thee my belief,'
     Toll slowly.
'That thy name expressed thy sweetness,
   —May of poets, in completeness!
   Now my May-day seemeth brief.'

LII

All these silent thoughts did swim o'er
   his eyes grown strange and dim,—
     Toll slowly.
Till his true men in the place, wished
   they stood there face to face
   With the foe instead of him.

LIV

'One last oath, my friends that wear
   faithful hearts to do and dare !'—
     Toll slowly.
'Tower must fall, and bride be lost !—
   swear me service worth the cost!'
   —Bold they stood around to swear.

LV

'Each man clasp my hand and swear, by
   the deed we failed in there,'
     Toll slowly.
'Not for vengeance, not for right, will
   ye strike one blow to-night !'
   —Pale they stood around to swear.

LVI

'One last boon, young Ralph and Clare !
   faithful hearts to do and dare !'—
     Toll slowly.
'Bring that steed up from his stall, which
   she kissed before you all !
   Guide him up the turret-stair.

LVII

'Ye shall harness him aright, and lead
    upward to this height.'
    Toll slowly.
'Once in love and twice in war hath he
    borne me strong and far :
He shall bear me far to-night.'

LVIII

Then his men looked to and fro, when
    they heard him speaking so.
    Toll slowly.
—''Las! the noble heart,' they thought,—
    'he in sooth is grief-distraught :
Would we stood here with the foe !'

LIX

But a fire flashed from his eye, 'twixt
    their thought and their reply,—
    Toll slowly.
'Have ye so much time to waste ? We
    who ride here, must ride fast,
As we wish our foes to fly.'

LX

They have fetched the steed with care,
    in the harness he did wear,
    Toll slowly.
Past the court, and through the doors,
    across the rushes of the floors,
But they goad him up the stair.

LXI

Then from out her bower chambère, did
    the Duchess May repair.
    Toll slowly.
'Tell me now what is your need,' said
    the lady, 'of this steed,
That ye goad him up the stair ?'

LXII

Calm she stood; unbodkined through, fell
    her dark hair to her shoe,—
    Toll slowly.
And the smile upon her face, ere she
    left the tiring-glass,
Had not time enough to go.

LXIII

'Get thee back, sweet Duchess May!
    hope is gone like yesterday,'—
    Toll slowly.

'One half-hour completes the breach ;
    and thy lord grows wild of speech !
Get thee in, sweet lady, and pray.

LXIV

'In the east tower, high'st of all, loud
    he cries for steed from stall.'
    Toll slowly.
'He would ride as far,' quoth he, 'as
    for love and victory,
Though he rides the castle-wall.'

LXV

'And we fetch the steed from stall, up
    where never a hoof did fall.'—
    Toll slowly.
'Wifely prayer meets deathly need !
    may the sweet Heavens hear thee
    plead
If he rides the castle-wall.'

LXVI

Low she dropt her head, and lower, till
    her hair coiled on the floor,—
    Toll slowly.
And tear after tear you heard fall dis-
    tinct as any word
Which you might be listening for.

LXVII

'Get thee in, thou soft ladye !—here is
    never a place for thee !'—
    Toll slowly.
'Braid thine hair and clasp thy gown,
    that thy beauty in its moan
May find grace with Leigh of Leigh.'

LXVIII

She stood up in bitter case, with a pale
    yet steady face,
    Toll slowly.
Like a statue thunderstruck, which,
    though quivering, seems to look
Right against the thunder-place.

LXIX

And her foot trod in, with pride, her
    own tears i' the stone beside.—
    Toll slowly.
'Go to, faithful friends, go to !—judge
    no more what ladies do,—
No, nor how their lords may ride !'

LXX

Then the good steed's rein she took, and
  his neck did kiss and stroke :
      Toll slowly.
Soft he neighed to answer her, and then
  followed up the stair,
For the love of her sweet look.

LXXI

Oh, and steeply, steeply wound up the
  narrow stair around !
      Toll slowly.
Oh, and closely, closely speeding, step
  by step beside her treading,
Did he follow, meek as hound.

LXXII

On the east tower, high'st of all,—there,
  where never a hoof did fall,—
      Toll slowly.
Out they swept, a vision steady,—noble
  steed and lovely lady,
Calm as if in bower or stall.

LXXIII

Down she knelt at her lord's knee, and
  she looked up silently,—
      Toll slowly.
And he kissed her twice and thrice, for
  that look within her eyes
Which he could not bear to see.

LXXIV

Quoth he, 'Get thee from this strife,—
  and the sweet saints bless thy
  life !'—
      Toll slowly.
'In this hour, I stand in need of my
  noble red-roan steed,
But no more of my noble wife.'

LXXV

Quoth she, 'Meekly have I done all thy
  biddings under sun ;'
      Toll slowly.
'But by all my womanhood, which is
  proved so, true and good,
I will never do this one.

LXXVI

'Now by womanhood's degree, and by
  wifehood's verity,'
      Toll slowly.

'In this hour if thou hast need of thy
  noble red-roan steed,
Thou hast also need of *me*.

LXXVII

'By this golden ring ye see on this
  lifted hand, pardiè,'
      Toll slowly.
'If, this hour, on castle-wall, can be
  room for steed from stall,
Shall be also room for *me*.

LXXVIII

'So the sweet saints with me be' (did
  she utter solemnly)
      Toll slowly.
'If a man, this eventide, on this castle
  wall will ride,
He shall ride the same with *me*.'

LXXIX

Oh, he sprang up in the selle, and he
  laughed out bitter-well,—
      Toll slowly.
'Wouldst thou ride among the leaves,
  as we used on other eves,
To hear chime a vesper-bell ?'

LXXX

She clang closer to his knee—'Aye, be-
  neath the cypress-tree !'—
      Toll slowly.
'Mock me not, for otherwhere than along
  the greenwood fair
Have I ridden fast with thee.

LXXXI

'Fast I rode with new-made vows, from
  my angry kinsman's house.'
      Toll slowly.
'What, and would you men should reck
  that I dared more for love's sake
As a bride than as a spouse ?

LXXXII

'What, and would you it should fall, as
  a proverb, before all,'
      Toll slowly.
'That a bride may keep your side while
  through castle-gate you ride,
Yet eschew the castle-wall ?'

LXXXIII

Ho ! the breach yawns into ruin, and
    roars up against her suing,
        Toll slowly.
With the inarticulate din, and the
    dreadful falling in—
    Shrieks of doing and undoing !

LXXXIV

Twice he wrung her hands in twain,
    but the small hands closed again.
        Toll slowly.
Back he reined the steed—back, back !
    but she trailed along his track
With a frantic clasp and strain.

LXXXV

Evermore the foemen pour through the
    crash of window and door,—
        Toll slowly.
And the shouts of Leigh and Leigh, and
    the shrieks of ' kill !' and ' flee !'
Strike up clear amid the roar.

LXXXVI

Thrice he wrung her hands in twain,—
    but they closed and clung again,—
        Toll slowly.
Wild she clung, as one, withstood,
    clasps a Christ upon the rood,
In a spasm of deathly pain.

LXXXVII

She clung wild and she clung mute,
    with her shuddering lips half-shut.
        Toll slowly.
Her head fallen as half in swound,—
    hair and knee swept on the ground,
She clung wild to stirrup and foot.

LXXXVIII

Back he reined his steed back-thrown
    on the slippery coping-stone :
        Toll slowly.
Back the iron hoofs did grind on the
    battlement behind
Whence a hundred feet went down.

LXXXIX

And his heel did press and goad on the
    quivering flank bestrode,—
        Toll slowly.

' Friends and brothers, save my wife !—
    Pardon, sweet, in change for
    life,—
    But I ride alone to God.'

XC

Straight as if the Holy name had up-
    breathed her like a flame,
        Toll slowly.
She upsprang, she rose upright,—in his
    selle she sate in sight,
By her love she overcame.

XCI

And her head was on his breast, where
    she smiled as one at rest,—
        Toll slowly.
' Ring,' she cried, ' O vesper-bell, in the
    beechwood's old chapelle !
But the passing-bell rings best.'

XCII

They have caught out at the rein, which
    Sir Guy threw loose—in vain,—
        Toll slowly.
For the horse in stark despair, with his
    front hoofs poised in air,
On the last verge rears amain.

XCIII

Now he hangs, he rocks between, and
    his nostrils curdle in !—
        Toll slowly.
Now he shivers head and hoof—and he
    flakes of foam fall off,
And his face grows fierce and thin !

XCIV

And a look of human woe from his
    staring eyes did go,
        Toll slowly.
And a sharp cry uttered he, in a foretold
    agony
    Of the headlong death below,—

XCV

And, ' Ring, ring, thou passing-bell,'
    still she cried, ' i' the old chap-
    elle !'—
        Toll slowly.
Then back-toppling, crashing back—
    a dead weight flung out to wrack,
Horse and riders overfell.

I

Oh, the little birds sang east, and the
little birds sang west,
  Toll slowly.
And I read this ancient Rime, in the
churchyard, while the chime
Slowly tolled for one at rest.

II

The abeles moved in the sun, and the
river smooth did run,
  Toll slowly.
And the ancient Rime rang strange,
with its passion and its change,
Here, where all done lay undone.

III

And beneath a willow tree, I a little
grave did see,
  Toll slowly.
Where was graved,—HERE UNDEFILED,
LIETH MAUD, A THREE-YEAR CHILD,
EIGHTEEN HUNDRED, FORTY-THREE.

IV

Then, O spirits, did I say, ye who rode
so fast that day,—
  Toll slowly.
Did star-wheels and angel wings, with
their holy winnowings,
Keep beside you all the way?

V

Though in passion ye would dash, with
a blind and heavy crash,
  Toll slowly.
Up against the thick-bossed shield of
God's judgement in the field,—
Though your heart and brain were
rash,—

VI

Now, your will is all unwilled—now,
your pulses are all stilled!
  Toll slowly.
Now, ye lie as meek and mild (whereso
laid) as Maud the child,
Whose small grave was lately filled.

VII

Beating heart and burning brow, ye are
very patient now,
  Toll slowly.

And the children might be bold to pluck
the kingcups from your mould
Ere a month had let them grow.

VIII

And you let the goldfinch sing in the alder
near in spring,
  Toll slowly.
Let her build her nest and sit all the
three weeks out on it,
Murmuring not at anything.

IX

In your patience ye are strong; cold
and heat ye take not wrong.
  Toll slowly.
When the trumpet of the angel blows
eternity's evangel,
Time will seem to you not long.

X

Oh, the little birds sang east, and the
little birds sang west,
  Toll slowly.
And I said in underbreath,—All our life
is mixed with death,
And who knoweth which is best?

XI

Oh, the little birds sang east, and the
little birds sang west,
  Toll slowly.
And I smiled to think God's greatness
flowed around our incomplete-
ness,—
Round our restlessness, His rest.

THE ROMANCE OF THE
SWAN'S NEST

So the dreams depart,
So the fading phantoms flee,
And the sharp reality
Now must act its part.
  WESTWOOD'S *Beads from a Rosary.*

I

LITTLE Ellie sits alone
'Mid the beeches of a meadow,
  By a stream-side on the grass,
And the trees are showering down
Doubles of their leaves in shadow,
  On her shining hair and face.

II

She has thrown her bonnet by,
And her feet she has been dipping
In the shallow water's flow ;
Now she holds them nakedly
In her hands, all sleek and dripping,
While she rocketh to and fro.

III

Little Ellie sits alone,
And the smile she softly uses,
Fills the silence like a speech,
While she thinks what shall be done,—
And the sweetest pleasure chooses
For her future within reach.

IV

Little Ellie in her smile
Chooses . . . 'I will have a lover,
Riding on a steed of steeds !
He shall love me without guile,
And to *him* I will discover
The swan's nest among the reeds.

V

' And the steed shall be red-roan,
And the lover shall be noble,
With an eye that takes the breath ;
And the lute he plays upon,
Shall strike ladies into trouble,
As his sword strikes men to death.

VI

' And the steed it shall be shod
All in silver, housed in azure,
And the mane shall swim the wind ;
And the hoofs along the sod
Shall flash onward and keep measure,
Till the shepherds look behind.

VII

' But my lover will not prize
All the glory that he rides in,
When he gazes in my face.
He will say, " O Love, thine eyes
Build the shrine my soul abides in,
And I kneel here for thy grace.'

VIII

' Then, aye, then—he shall kneel low,
With the red-roan steed anear him,
Which shall seem to understand—
Till I answer, " Rise and go !
For the world must love and fear him
Whom I gift with heart and hand."

IX

' Then he will arise so pale,
I shall feel my own lips tremble
With a *yes* I must not say,
Nathless maiden-brave, " Farewell,"
I will utter, and dissemble—
" Light to-morrow with to-day."

X

' Then he'll ride among the hills
To the wide world past the river,
There to put away all wrong,
To make straight distorted wills,
And to empty the broad quiver
Which the wicked bear along.

XI

' Three times shall a young foot-page
Swim the stream and climb the mountain
And kneel down beside my feet—
" Lo, my master sends this gage,
Lady, for thy pity's counting !
What wilt thou exchange for it ? "

XII

' And the first time, I will send
A white rosebud for a guerdon,—
And the second time, a glove ;
But the third time—I may bend
From my pride, and answer—" Pardon,
If he comes to take my love."

XIII

' Then the young foot-page will run—
Then my lover will ride faster,
Till he kneeleth at my knee :
" I am a duke's eldest son !
Thousand serfs do call me master,—
But, O Love, I love but *thee !* "

XIV

' He will kiss me on the mouth
Then, and lead me as a lover
Through the crowds that praise his deeds :
And, when soul-tied by one troth,
Unto *him* I will discover
That swan's nest among the reeds.'

XV

Little Ellie, with her smile
Not yet ended, rose up gaily,

Tied the bonnet, donned the shoe,
And went homeward, round a mile,
Just to see, as she did daily,
    What more eggs were with the two.

XVI

Pushing through the elm-tree copse,
Winding up the stream, light-hearted,
    Where the osier pathway leads—
    Past the boughs she stoops—and stops.
Lo, the wild swan had deserted,
    And a rat had gnawed the reeds.

XVII

Ellie went home sad and slow.
If she found the lover ever,
    With his red-roan steed of steeds,
    Sooth I know not! but I know
She could never show him—never,
    That swan's nest among the reeds!

BERTHA IN THE LANE

I

Put the broidery-frame away,
    For my sewing is all done:
The last thread is used to-day:
    And I need not join it on.
    Though the clock stands at the noon
I am weary.   I have sewn,
    Sweet, for thee, a wedding-gown.

II

Sister, help me to the bed,
    And stand near me, Dearest-sweet.
Do not shrink nor be afraid,
    Blushing with a sudden heat!
    No one standeth in the street?—
By God's love I go to meet,
    Love I thee with love complete.

III

Lean thy face down! drop it in
    These two hands, that I may hold
'Twixt their palms thy cheek and chin,
    Stroking back the curls of gold.
    'Tis a fair, fair face, in sooth—
    Larger eyes and redder mouth
Than mine were in my first youth.

IV

Thou art younger by seven years—
    Ah !—so bashful at my gaze,
That the lashes, hung with tears,
    Grow too heavy to upraise ?
    I would wound thee by no touch
    Which thy shyness feels as such :
Dost thou mind me, Dear, so much ?

V

Have I not been nigh a mother
    To thy sweetness—tell me, Dear ?
Have we not loved one another
    Tenderly, from year to year,
    Since our dying mother mild
    Said with accents undefiled,
    'Child, be mother to this child !'

VI

Mother, mother, up in heaven,
    Stand up on the jasper sea,
And be witness I have given
    All the gifts required of me,—
    Hope that blessed me, bliss that
        crowned,
    Love, that left me with a wound,
    Life itself, that turneth round !

VII

Mother, mother, thou art kind,
    Thou art standing in the room,
In a molten glory shrined,
    That rays off into the gloom !
    But thy smile is bright and bleak
    Like cold waves—I cannot speak,
I sob in it, and grow weak.

VIII

Ghostly mother, keep aloof
    One hour longer from my soul—
For I still am thinking of
    Earth's warm-beating joy and dole!
    On my finger is a ring
    Which I still see glittering,
    When the night hides everything.

IX

Little sister, thou art pale !
    Ah, I have a wandering brain—
But I lose that fever-bale,
    And my thoughts grow calm again.
    Lean down closer—closer still !
    I have words thine ear to fill,—
    And would kiss thee at my will.

X

Dear, I heard thee in the spring,
  Thee and Robert—through the trees,—
When we all went gathering
  Boughs of May-bloom for the bees.
Do not start so! think instead
How the sunshine overhead
Seemed to trickle through the shade.

XI

What a day it was, that day!
  Hills and vales did openly
Seem to heave and throb away
  At the sight of the great sky;
And the Silence, as it stood
In the Glory's golden flood,
Audibly did bud—and bud.

XII

Through the winding hedgerows green,
  How we wandered, I and you,—
With the bowery tops shut in,
  And the gates that showed the view!
How we talked there! thrushes soft
Sang our praises out—or oft
Bleatings took them from the croft:

XIII

Till the pleasure grown too strong
  Left me muter evermore,
And, the winding road being long,
  I walked out of sight, before,
And so, wrapt in musings fond,
Issued (past the wayside pond)
On the meadow-lands beyond.

XIV

I sate down beneath the beech
  Which leans over to the lane,
And the far sound of your speech
  Did not promise any pain;
And I blessed you full and free,
With a smile stooped tenderly
O'er the May-flowers on my knee.

XV

But the sound grew into word
  As the speakers drew more near—
Sweet, forgive me that I heard
  What you wished me not to hear.
Do not weep so—do not shake—
Oh,—I heard thee, Bertha, make
Good true answers for my sake.

XVI

Yes, and HE too! let him stand
  In thy thoughts, untouched by blame.
Could he help it, if my hand
  He had claimed with hasty claim?
That was wrong perhaps—but then
Such things be—and will, again.
Women cannot judge for men.

XVII

Had he seen thee, when he swore
  He would love but me alone?
Thou wert absent—sent before
  To our kin in Sidmouth town.
When he saw thee who art best
Past compare, and loveliest,
He but judged thee as the rest.

XVIII

Could we blame him with grave words,
  Thou and I, Dear, if we might?
Thy brown eyes have looks like birds,
  Flying straightway to the light:
Mine are older.—Hush!—look out—
Up the street! Is none without?
How the poplar swings about.

XIX

And that hour—beneath the beech,
  When I listened in a dream,
And he said in his deep speech,
  That he owed me all *esteem*,—
Each word swam in on my brain
With a dim, dilating pain,
Till it burst with that last strain.

XX

I fell flooded with a dark,
  In the silence of a swoon.
When I rose, still cold and stark,
  There was night,—I saw the moon.
And the stars, each in its place,
And the May-blooms on the grass,
Seemed to wonder what I was.

XXI

And I walked as if apart
  From myself, when I could stand—
And I pitied my own heart,
  As if I held it in my hand,
Somewhat coldly,—with a sense
Of fulfilled benevolence,
And a 'Poor thing' negligence.

XXII

And I answered coldly too,
  When you met me at the door;
And I only *heard* the dew
  Dripping from me to the floor;
  And the flowers I bade you see
  Were too withered for the bee,—
  As my life, henceforth, for me.

XXIII

Do not weep so—Dear—heart-warm!
  All was best as it befell:
If I say he did me harm,
  I speak wild,—I am not well.
  All his words were kind and good—
  He esteemed me! Only, blood
  Runs so faint in womanhood.

XXIV

Then I always was too grave,—
  Liked the saddest ballad sung,—
With that look, besides, we have
  In our faces, who die young.
  I had died, Dear, all the same;
  Life's long, joyous, jostling game
  Is too loud for my meek shame.

XXV

We are so unlike each other,
  Thou and I, that none could guess
We were children of one mother,
  But for mutual tenderness.
  Thou art rose-lined from the cold,
  And meant, verily, to hold
  Life's pure pleasures manifold.

XXVI

I am pale as crocus grows
  Close beside a rose-tree's root;
Whosoe'er would reach the rose,
  Treads the crocus underfoot.
  I, like May-bloom on thorn-tree—
  Thou, like merry summer-bee!
  Fit, that I be plucked for thee.

XXVII

Yet who plucks me?—no one mourns,
  I have lived my season out,
And now die of my own thorns
  Which I could not live without.
  Sweet, be merry! How the light
  Comes and goes! If it be night,
  Keep the candles in my sight.

XXVIII

Are there footsteps at the door?
  Look out quickly. Yea, or nay?
Some one might be waiting for
  Some last word that I might say.
  Nay! So best!—so angels would
  Stand off clear from deathly road,
  Not to cross the sight of God.

XXIX

Colder grow my hands and feet.
  When I wear the shroud I made,
Let the folds lie straight and neat,
  And the rosemary be spread,
  That if any friend should come
  (To see *thee*, sweet!) all the room
  May be lifted out of gloom.

XXX

And, dear Bertha, let me keep
  On my hand this little ring,
Which at nights, when others sleep,
  I can still see glittering:
  Let me wear it out of sight,
  In the grave,—where it will light
  All the dark up, day and night.

XXXI

On that grave, drop not a tear!
  Else, though fathom-deep the place,
Through the woollen shroud I wear
  I shall feel it on my face.
  Rather smile there, blessèd one,
  Thinking of me in the sun,
  Or forget me—smiling on!

XXXII

Art thou near me? nearer? so!
  Kiss me close upon the eyes,
That the earthly light may go
  Sweetly, as it used to rise,
  When I watched the morning-grey
  Strike, betwixt the hills, the way
  He was sure to come that day.

XXXIII

So,—no more vain words be said!—
  The hosannas nearer roll.
Mother, smile now on thy Dead,
  I am death-strong in my soul.
  Mystic Dove alit on cross,
  Guide the poor bird of the snows
  Through the snow-wind above loss!

XXXIV

Jesus, Victim, comprehending
    Love's divine self-abnegation,
Cleanse my love in its self-spending,
    And absorb the poor libation!
Wind my thread of life up higher,
Up, through angels' hands of fire!—
    I aspire while I expire.

LADY GERALDINE'S COURTSHIP

A ROMANCE OF THE AGE

A poet writes to his friend. PLACE—*A
room in Wycombe Hall.* TIME—*Late
in the evening.*

DEAR my friend and fellow student,
    I would lean my spirit o'er you!
Down the purple of this chamber, tears
    should scarcely run at will.
I am humbled who was humble. Friend,
    —I bow my head before you.
You should lead me to my peasants,—
    but their faces are too still.

There's a lady—an earl's daughter,—
    she is proud and she is noble,
And she treads the crimson carpet, and
    she breathes the perfumed air,
And a kingly blood sends glances up her
    princely eye to trouble,
And the shadow of a monarch's crown
    is softened in her hair.

She has halls among the woodlands,
    she has castles by the breakers,
She has farms and she has manors, she
    can threaten and command,
And the palpitating engines snort in
    steam across her acres,
As they mark upon the blasted heaven
    the measure of the land.

There are none of England's daughters
    who can show a prouder presence;
Upon princely suitors praying, she has
    looked in her disdain.
She was sprung of English nobles,
    I was born of English peasants;
What was *I* that I should love her—
    save for competence to pain?

I was only a poor poet, made for singing
    at her casement,
As the finches or the thrushes, while
    she thought of other things.
Oh, she walked so high above me, she
    appeared to my abasement,
In her lovely silken murmur, like an
    angel clad in wings!

Many vassals bow before her as her
    carriage sweeps their doorways;
She has blest their little children,—as a
    priest or queen were she.
Far too tender, or too cruel far, her
    smile upon the poor was,
For I thought it was the same smile
    which she used to smile on *me.*

She has voters in the Commons, she has
    lovers in the palace;
And of all the fair court-ladies, few have
    jewels half as fine;
Oft the prince has named her beauty
    'twixt the red wine and the chalice.
Oh, and what was *I* to love her? my
    beloved, my Geraldine!

Yet I could not choose but love her.
    I was born to poet-uses,
To love all things set above me, all of
    good and all of fair:
Nymphs of mountain, not of valley, we
    are wont to call the Muses
And in nympholeptic climbing, poets
    pass from mount to star.

And because I was a poet, and because
    the public praised me,
With a critical deduction for the modern
    writer's fault,
I could sit at rich men's tables,—though
    the courtesies that raised me,
Still suggested clear between us the
    pale spectrum of the salt.

And they praised me in her presence;
    —'Will your book appear this
    summer?'
Then returning to each other—'Yes,
    our plans are for the moors.'
Then with whisper dropped behind me
    —'There he is! the latest comer!
Oh, she only likes his verses! what is
    over, she endures.

' Quite low-born ! self-educated ! some-
    what gifted though by nature,—
And we make a point of asking him,—
    of being very kind.
You may speak, he does not hear you !
    and besides, he writes no satire,—
All these serpents kept by charmers
    leave the natural sting behind.'

I grew scornfuller, grew colder, as I
    stood up there among them,
Till as frost intense will burn you, the
    cold scorning scorched my brow ;
When a sudden silver speaking, gravely
    cadenced, over-rung them,
And a sudden silken stirring touched
    my inner nature through.

I looked upward and beheld her. With
    a calm and regnant spirit,
Slowly round she swept her eyelids,
    and said clear before them all—
' Have you such superfluous honour, sir,
    that able to confer it
You will come down, Mister Bertram,
    as my guest to Wycombe Hall ? '

Here she paused,—she had been paler
    at the first word of her speaking,
But because a silence followed it,
    blushed somewhat, as for shame,
Then, as scorning her own feeling,
    resumed calmly—' I am seeking
More distinction than these gentlemen
    think worthy of my claim.

' Ne'ertheless, you see, I seek it—not
    because I am a woman '
(Here her smile sprang like a fountain,
    and, so, overflowed her mouth),
' But because my woods in Sussex have
    some purple shades at gloaming
Which are worthy of a king in state, or
    poet in his youth.

' I invite you, Mister Bertram, to no
    scene for worldly speeches—
Sir, I scarce should dare—but only where
    God asked the thrushes first—
And if *you* will sing beside them, in the
    covert of my beeches,
I will thank you for the woodlands, . . .
    for the human world, at worst.'

Then she smiled around right childly,
    then she gazed around right
    queenly,
And I bowed—I could not answer ;
    alternated light and gloom—
While as one who quells the lions, with
    a steady eye serenely,
She, with level fronting eyelids, passed
    out stately from the room.

Oh, the blessèd woods of Sussex, I can
    hear them still around me,
With their leafy tide of greenery still
    rippling up the wind.
Oh, the cursèd woods of Sussex ! where
    the hunter's arrow found me,
When a fair face and a tender voice had
    made me mad and blind !

In that ancient hall of Wycombe, thronged
    the numerous guests invited,
And the lovely London ladies trod the
    floors with gliding feet ;
And their voices low with fashion, not
    with feeling, softly freighted
All the air about the windows, with
    elastic laughters sweet.

For at eve, the open windows flung their
    light out on the terrace,
Which the floating orbs of curtains did
    with gradual shadow sweep,
While the swans upon the river, fed at
    morning by the heiress,
Trembled downward through their
    snowy wings at music in their
    sleep.

And there evermore was music, both of
    instrument and singing,
Till the finches of the shrubberies grew
    restless in the dark ;
But the cedars stood up motionless,
    each in a moonlight ringing,
And the deer, half in the glimmer,
    strewed the hollows of the park.

And though sometimes she would bind me
    with her silver-corded speeches
To commix my words and laughter with
    the converse and the jest,
Oft I sate apart, and gazing on the river
    through the beeches,
Heard, as pure the swans swam down
    it, her pure voice o'erfloat the rest.

In the morning, horn of huntsman, hoof
    of steed, and laugh of rider,
Spread out cheery from the court-yard
    till we lost them in the hills,
While herself and other ladies, and her
    suitors left beside her,
Went a-wandering up the gardens
    through the laurels and abeles.

Thus, her foot upon the new-mown grass,
    bareheaded, with the flowing
Of the virginal white vesture gathered
    closely to her throat,—
And the golden ringlets in her neck
    just quickened by her going,
And appearing to breathe sun for air,
    and doubting if to float,—

With a branch of dewy maple, which
    her right hand held above her,
And which trembled a green shadow in
    betwixt her and the skies,
As she turned her face in going, thus,
    she drew me on to love her,
And to worship the divineness of the
    smile hid in her eyes.

For her eyes alone smile constantly :
    her lips have serious sweetness,
And her front is calm—the dimple rarely
    ripples on the cheek ;
But her deep blue eyes smile constantly,
    as if they in discreetness
Kept the secret of a happy dream she
    did not care to speak.

Thus she drew me the first morning,
    out across into the garden,
And I walked among her noble friends
    and could not keep behind.
Spake she unto all and unto me—
    ' Behold, I am the warden
Of the song-birds in these lindens,
    which are cages to their mind.

' But within this swarded circle, into
    which the lime-walk brings us,
Whence the beeches, rounded greenly,
    stand away in reverent fear,
I will let no music enter, saving what
    the fountain sings us,
Which the lilies round the basin may
    seem pure enough to hear.

' The live air that waves the lilies waves
    the slender jet of water
Like a holy thought sent feebly up from
    soul of fasting saint :
Whereby lies a marble Silence, sleeping!
    (Lough the sculptor wrought her)
So asleep she is forgetting to say Hush !
    —a fancy quaint.

' Mark how heavy white her eyelids !
    not a dream between them lingers,
And the left hand's index droppeth from
    the lips upon the cheek ;
While the right hand,—with the sym-
    bol rose held slack within the
    fingers,—
Has fallen backward in the basin—yet
    this Silence will not speak !

' That the essential meaning growing
    may exceed the special symbol,
Is the thought as I conceive it : it applies
    more high and low.
Our true noblemen will often through
    right nobleness grow humble,
And assert an inward honour by
    denying outward show.'

' Nay, your Silence,' said I, ' truly, holds
    her symbol rose but slackly,
Yet *she holds it*—or would scarcely be a
    Silence to our ken ;
And your nobles wear their ermine on
    the outside, or walk blackly
In the presence of the social law as
    mere ignoble men.

' Let the poets dream such dreaming !
    madam, in these British islands
'Tis the substance that wanes ever, 'tis
    the symbol that exceeds.
Soon we shall have nought but symbol !
    and, for statues like this Silence,
Shall accept the rose's image—in another
    case, the weed's.'

' Not so quickly,' she retorted,—' I con-
    fess, where'er you go, you
Find for things, names—shows for
    actions, and pure gold for honour
    clear ;
But when all is run to symbol in the
    Social, I will throw you
The world's book which now reads dryly,
    and sit down with Silence here.'

Half in playfulness she spoke, I thought,
  and half in indignation ;
Friends who listened, laughed her words
  off, while her lovers deemed her
  fair :
A fair woman, flushed with feeling, in
  her noble-lighted station
Near the statue's white reposing—and
  both bathed in sunny air !—

With the trees round, not so distant but
  you heard their vernal murmur,
And beheld in light and shadow the
  leaves in and outward move,
And the little fountain leaping toward
  the sun-heart to be warmer,
Then recoiling in a tremble from the
  too much light above.

'Tis a picture for remembrance. And
  thus, morning after morning,
Did I follow as she drew me by the
  spirit to her feet.
Why, her greyhound followed also !
  dogs—we both were dogs for
  scorning—
To be sent back when she pleased it and
  her path lay through the wheat.

And thus, morning after morning, spite
  of vows and spite of sorrow,
Did I follow at her drawing, while the
  week-days passed along,
Just to feed the swans this noontide, or
  to see the fawns to-morrow,
Or to teach the hill-side echo some
  sweet Tuscan in a song.

Aye, for sometimes on the hill-side, while
  we sate down in the gowans,
With the forest green behind us, and
  its shadow cast before,
And the river running under, and across
  it from the rowans
A brown partridge whirring near us,
  till we felt the air it bore,—

There, obedient to her praying, did I
  read aloud the poems
Made to Tuscan flutes, or instruments
  more various of our own ;

Read the pastoral parts of Spenser—or
  the subtle interflowings
Found in Petrarch's sonnets—here 's the
  book—the leaf is folded down !

Or at times a modern volume,— Words-
  worth's solemn-thoughted idyl,
Howitt's ballad-verse, or Tennyson's
  enchanted reverie,—
Or from Browning some ' Pomegranate,'
  which, if cut deep down the
  middle,
Shows a heart within blood-tinctured,
  of a veined humanity.

Or at times I read there, hoarsely, some
  new poem of my making :
Poets ever fail in reading their own
  verses to their worth,—
For the echo in you breaks upon the
  words which you are speaking,
And the chariot-wheels jar in the gate
  through which you drive them
  forth.

After, when we were grown tired of
  books, the silence round us fling-
  ing
A slow arm of sweet compression, felt
  with beatings at the breast,
She would break out, on a sudden, in
  a gush of woodland singing,
Like a child's emotion in a god—a naiad
  tired of rest.

Oh, to see or hear her singing ! scarce
  I know which is divinest—
For her looks sing too—she modulates
  her gestures on the tune ;
And her mouth stirs with the song, like
  song : and when the notes are
  finest,
'Tis the eyes that shoot out vocal light
  and seem to swell them on.

Then we talked—oh, how we talked ! her
  voice, so cadenced in the talking,
Made another singing—of the soul !
  a music without bars ;
While the leafy sounds of woodlands,
  humming round where we were
  walking,
Brought interposition worthy-sweet,—
  as skies about the stars.

And she spake such good thoughts
natural, as if she always thought
them ;
She had sympathies so rapid, open, free
as bird on branch,
Just as ready to fly east as west, which-
ever way besought them,
In the birchen-wood a chirrup, or a
cock-crow in the grange.

In her utmost lightness there is truth—
and often she speaks lightly,
Has a grace in being gay, which even
mournful souls approve,
For the root of some grave earnest
thought is understruck so rightly
As to justify the foliage and the waving
flowers above.

And she talked on—we talked, rather !
upon all things, substance, shadow,
Of the sheep that browsed the grasses,
of the reapers in the corn,
Of the little children from the schools,
seen winding through the
meadow—
Of the poor rich world beyond them, still
kept poorer by its scorn.

So, of men, and so, of letters—books are
men of higher stature,
And the only men that speak aloud for
future times to hear ;
So, of mankind in the abstract, which
grows slowly into nature,
Yet will lift the cry of ' progress,' as it
trod from sphere to sphere.

And her custom was to praise me when
I said,—' The Age culls simples,
With a broad clown's back turned
broadly to the glory of the stars.
We are gods by our own reck'ning, and
may well shut up the temples,
And wield on, amid the incense-steam,
the thunder of our cars.

' For we throw out acclamations of self-
thanking, self-admiring,
With, at every mile run faster,—" O the
wondrous wondrous age,"
Little thinking if we work our SOULS as
nobly as our iron,
Or if angels will commend us at the goal
of pilgrimage.

' Why, what is this patient entrance
into nature's deep resources,
But the child's most gradual learning to
walk upright without bane ?
When we drive out, from the cloud of
steam, majestical white horses,
Are we greater than the first men who
led black ones by the mane ?

' If we trod the deeps of ocean, if we
struck the stars in rising,
If we wrapped the globe intensely with
one hot electric breath,
'Twere but power within our tether, no
new spirit-power comprising,
And in life we were not greater men,
nor bolder men in death.'

She was patient with my talking ; and
I loved her, loved her, certes,
As I loved all heavenly objects, with
uplifted eyes and hands !
As I loved pure inspirations, loved the
graces, loved the virtues,
In a Love content with writing his own
name on desert sands.

Or at least I thought so, purely !—thought
no idiot Hope was raising
Any crown to crown Love's silence—
silent Love that sate alone.
Out, alas ! the stag is like me—he, that
tries to go on grazing
With the great deep gun-wound in his
neck, then reels with sudden
moan.

It was thus I reeled. I told you that her
hand had many suitors ;
But she smiles them down imperially,
as Venus did the waves,
And with such a gracious coldness, that
they cannot press their futures
On the present of her courtesy, which
yieldingly enslaves.

And this morning, as I sate alone within
the inner chamber,
With the great saloon beyond it, lost in
pleasant thought serene,
For I had been reading Camöens—that
poem you remember,
Which his lady's eyes are praised in, as
the sweetest ever seen.

And the book lay open, and my thought
    flew from it, taking from it
A vibration and impulsion to an end
    beyond its own,
As the branch of a green osier, when a
    child would overcome it,
Springs up freely from his clasping and
    goes swinging in the sun.

As I mused I heard a murmur,—it grew
    deep as it grew longer—
Speakers using earnest language—
    ' Lady Geraldine, you *would* ! '
And I heard a voice that pleaded ever
    on, in accents stronger
As a sense of reason gave it power to
    make its rhetoric good.

Well I knew that voice—it was an earl's,
    of soul that matched his station,
Soul completed into lordship—might and
    right read on his brow ;
Very finely courteous—far too proud to
    doubt his domination
Of the common people, he atones for
    grandeur by a bow.

High straight forehead, nose of eagle,
    cold blue eyes, of less expression
Than resistance, coldly casting off the
    looks of other men,
As steel, arrows,—unelastic lips, which
    seem to taste possession,
And be cautious lest the common air
    should injure or distrain.

For the rest, accomplished, upright,—
    aye, and standing by his order
With a bearing not ungraceful ; fond of
    art and letters too ;
Just a good man made a proud man,—as
    the sandy rocks that border
A wild coast, by circumstances, in a
    regnant ebb and flow.

Thus, I knew that voice—I heard it, and
    I could not help the hearkening.
In the room I stood up blindly, and my
    burning heart within
Seemed to seethe and fuse my senses, till
    they ran on all sides darkening,
And scorched, weighed, like melted metal
    round my feet that stood therein.

And that voice, I heard it pleading, for
    love's sake, for wealth, position,
For the sake of liberal uses, and great
    actions to be done—
And she interrupted gently, ' Nay, my
    lord, the old tradition
Of your Normans, by some worthier hand
    than mine is, should be won.'

' Ah, that white hand ! ' he said quickly,—
    and in his he either drew it
Or attempted—for with gravity and
    instance she replied,
' Nay, indeed, my lord, this talk is vain,
    and we had best eschew it,
And pass on, like friends, to other points
    less easy to decide.'

What he said again, I know not.   It is
    likely that his trouble
Worked his pride up to the surface, for
    she answered in slow scorn,
' And your lordship judges rightly.
    Whom I marry, shall be noble,
Aye, and wealthy.   I shall never blush
    to think how he was born.'

There, I maddened ! her words stung me.
    Life swept through me into fever,
And my soul sprang up astonished,
    sprang, full-statured in an hour.
Know you what it is when anguish, with
    apocalyptic NEVER,
To a Pythian height dilates you,—and
    despair sublimes to power ?

From my brain, the soul-wings budded,—
    waved a flame about my body,
Whence conventions coiled to ashes.
    I felt self-drawn out, as man,
From amalgamate false natures, and I
    saw the skies grow ruddy
With the deepening feet of angels, and
    I knew what spirits can.

I was mad—inspired—say either !
    (anguish worketh inspiration)
Was a man, or beast—perhaps so, for
    the tiger roars, when speared ;
And I walked on, step by step, along
    the level of my passion—
Oh my soul ! and passed the doorway
    to her face, and never feared.

He had left her, peradventure, when my
    footstep proved my coming—
But for *her*—she half arose, then sate—
    grew scarlet and grew pale.
Oh, she trembled !—'tis so always with
    a worldly man or woman
In the presence of true spirits—what else
    can they do but quail ?

Oh, she fluttered like a tame bird, in
    among its forest-brothers
Far too strong for it ; then drooping,
    bowed her face upon her hands—
And I spake out wildly, fiercely, brutal
    truths of her and others :
I, she planted in the desert, swathed her,
    windlike, with my sands.

I plucked up her social fictions, bloody-
    rooted though leaf-verdant,—
Trod them down with words of shaming,
    —all the purple and the gold,
All the 'landed stakes' and lordships,
    all, that spirits pure and ardent
Are cast out of love and honour because
    chancing not to hold.

'For myself I do not argue,' said I,
    'though I love you, madam,
But for better souls that nearer to the
    height of yours have trod :
And this age shows, to my thinking, still
    more infidels to Adam,
Than directly, by profession, simple in-
    fidels to God.

'Yet, O God,' I said, 'O grave,' I said,
    'O mother's heart and bosom,
With whom first and last are equal,
    saint and corpse and little child !
We are fools to your deductions, in these
    figments of heart-closing ;
We are traitors to your causes, in these
    sympathies defiled.

'Learn more reverence, madam, not for
    rank or wealth—*that* needs no
    learning,
That comes quickly—quick as sin does,
    aye, and culminates to sin ;
But for Adam's seed, MAN ! Trust me,
    'tis a clay above your scorning,
With God's image stamped upon it, and
    God's kindling breath within.

'What right have you, madam. gazing in
    your palace mirror daily,
Getting so by heart your beauty which
    all others must adore,
While you draw the golden ringlets down
    your fingers, to vow gaily
You will wed no man that 's only good to
    God, and nothing more ?

'Why, what right have you, made fair
    by that same God—the sweetest
    woman
Of all women He has fashioned—with
    your lovely spirit-face,
Which would seem too near to vanish if
    its smile were not so human,
And your voice of holy sweetness, turn-
    ing common words to grace,

'What right *can* you have, God's other
    works to scorn, despise, revile
    them
In the gross, as mere men, broadly—not
    as *noble* men, forsooth,—
As mere Parias of the outer world, for-
    bidden to assoil them
In the hope of living, dying, near that
    sweetness of your mouth ?

'Have you any answer, madam ? If my
    spirit were less earthly,
If its instrument were gifted with a better
    silver string,
I would kneel down where I stand, and
    say—Behold me ! I am worthy
Of thy loving, for I love thee ! I am
    worthy as a king.

'As it is—your ermined pride, I swear,
    shall feel this stain upon her,
That *I*, poor, weak, tost with passion,
    scorned by me and you again,
Love you, madam—dare to love you—to
    my grief and your dishonour,
To my endless desolation, and your
    impotent disdain ! '

More mad words like these—mere mad-
    ness ! friend, I need not write
    them fuller,
For I hear my hot soul dropping on the
    lines in showers of tears.

Oh, a woman! friend, a woman! why,
    a beast had scarce been duller
Than roar bestial loud complaints against
    the shining of the spheres.

But at last there came a pause.   I stood
    all vibrating with thunder
Which my soul had used.   The silence
    drew her face up like a call.
Could you guess what word she uttered?
    She looked up, as if in wonder,
With tears beaded on her lashes, and
    said 'Bertram!'—it was all.

If she had cursed me, and she might have
    —or if even, with queenly bearing
Which at need is used by women, she
    had risen up and said,
'Sir, you are my guest, and therefore I
    have given you a full hearing,
Now, beseech you, choose a name exact-
    ing somewhat less, instead,'—

I had borne it!—but that 'Bertram'—
    why it lies there on the paper
A mere word, without her accent,—and
    you cannot judge the weight
Of the calm which crushed my passion:
    I seemed drowning in a vapour,—
And her gentleness destroyed me whom
    her scorn made desolate.

So, struck backward and exhausted by
    that inward flow of passion
Which had rushed on, sparing nothing,
    into forms of abstract truth,
By a logic agonizing through unseemly
    demonstration,
And by youth's own anguish turning
    grimly grey the hairs of youth,—

By the sense accursed and instant, that
    if even I spake wisely
I spake basely—using truth, if what I
    spake, indeed was true,
To avenge wrong on a woman—her, who
    sate there weighing nicely
A poor manhood's worth, found guilty of
    such deeds as I could do!—

By such wrong and woe exhausted—
    what I suffered and occasioned,—
As a wild horse through a city runs with
    lightning in his eyes,

And then dashing at a church's cold and
    passive wall, impassioned,
Strikes the death into his burning brain,
    and blindly drops and dies—

So I fell, struck down before her! do
    you blame me, friend, for weak-
    ness?
'Twas my strength of passion slew me!
    —fell before her like a stone.
Fast the dreadful world rolled from me,
    on its roaring wheels of black-
    ness—
When the light came, I was lying in this
    chamber, and alone.

Oh, of course, she charged her lacqueys
    to bear out the sickly burden,
And to cast it from her scornful sight—
    but not *beyond* the gate;
She is too kind to be cruel, and too
    haughty not to pardon
Such a man as I—'twere something to
    be level to her hate.

But for me—you now are conscious
    why, my friend, I write this letter,
How my life is read all backward, and
    the charm of life undone:
I shall leave her house at dawn; I would
    to-night, if I were better—
And I charge my soul to hold my body
    strengthened for the sun.

When the sun has dyed the oriel, I depart,
    with no last gazes,
No weak moanings (one word only, left
    in writing for her hands),
Out of reach of all derision, and some
    unavailing praises,
To make front against this anguish in the
    far and foreign lands.

Blame me not.   I would not squander
    life in grief—I am abstemious:
I but nurse my spirit's falcon, that its
    wing may soar again.
There's no room for tears of weakness in
    the blind eyes of a Phemius!
Into work the poet kneads them,—and
    he does not die *till then*.

CONCLUSION

Bertram finished the last pages, while
along the silence ever
Still in hot and heavy splashes, fell the
tears on every leaf:
Having ended he leans backward in his
chair, with lips that quiver
From the deep unspoken, aye, and deep
unwritten thoughts of grief.

Soh! how still the lady standeth! 'tis a
dream—a dream of mercies!
'Twixt the purple lattice-curtains, how
she standeth still and pale!
'Tis a vision, sure, of mercies, sent to
soften his self-curses—
Sent to sweep a patient quiet o'er the
tossing of his wail.

'Eyes,' he said, 'now throbbing through
me! are ye eyes that did undo me?
Shining eyes, like antique jewels set in
Parian statue-stone!
Underneath that calm white forehead, are
ye ever burning torrid
O'er the desolate sand-desert of my heart
and life undone?'

With a murmurous stir uncertain, in the
air, the purple curtain
Swelleth in and swelleth out around her
motionless pale brows,
While the gliding of the river sends a
rippling noise for ever
Through the open casement whitened by
the moonlight's slant repose.

Said he—'Vision of a lady! stand there
silent, stand there steady!
Now I see it plainly, plainly; now I
cannot hope or doubt—
There, the brows of mild repression—
there, the lips of silent passion,
Curvèd like an archer's bow to send the
bitter arrows out.'

Ever, evermore the while in a slow
silence she kept smiling,
And approached him slowly, slowly, in
a gliding measured pace;
With her two white hands extended, as
if praying one offended,
And a look of supplication, gazing earnest
in his face.

Said he—'Wake me by no gesture,—
sound of breath, or stir of vesture!
Let the blessèd apparition melt not yet
to its divine!
No approaching—hush, no breathing! or
my heart must swoon to death in
The too utter life thou bringest—O thou
dream of Geraldine!'

Ever, evermore the while in a slow
silence she kept smiling—
But the tears ran over lightly from her
eyes, and tenderly;
'Dost thou, Bertram, truly love me?
Is no woman far above me
Found more worthy of thy poet heart
than such a one as I?'

Said he—'I would dream so ever, like
the flowing of that river,
Flowing ever in a shadow greenly onward
to the sea!
So, thou vision of all sweetness—princely
to a full completeness,—
Would my heart and life flow onward—
deathward—through this dream
of THEE!'

Ever, evermore the while in a slow
silence she kept smiling,
While the silver tears ran faster down
the blushing of her cheeks;
Then with both her hands enfolding both
of his, she softly told him,
'Bertram, if I say I love thee, . . . 'tis
the vision only speaks.'

Softened, quickened to adore her, on his
knee he fell before her—
And she whispered low in triumph, 'It
shall be as I have sworn!
Very rich he is in virtues,—very noble—
noble, certes;
And I shall not blush in knowing that
men call him lowly born.'

THE RUNAWAY SLAVE AT PILGRIM'S POINT

I

I STAND on the mark beside the shore
    Of the first white pilgrim's bended
      knee,
Where exile turned to ancestor,
    And God was thanked for liberty ;
I have run through the night, my skin
    is as dark,
I bend my knee down on this mark . . .
    I look on the sky and the sea.

II

O pilgrim-souls, I speak to you !
    I see you come out proud and slow
From the land of the spirits pale as dew,
    And round me and round me ye go !
O pilgrims, I have gasped and run
All night long from the whips of one
    Who in your names works sin and woe.

III

And thus I thought that I would come
    And kneel here where ye knelt before,
And feel your souls around me hum
    In undertone to the ocean's roar ;
And lift my black face, my black hand,
Here, in your names, to curse this land
    Ye blessed in freedom's, evermore.

IV

I am black, I am black !
    And yet God made me, they say ;
But if He did so, smiling back
    He must have cast His work away
Under the feet of His white creatures,
With a look of scorn,—that the dusky
    features
    Might be trodden again to clay.

V

And yet He has made dark things
    To be glad and merry as light :
There's a little dark bird sits and sings :
    There's a dark stream ripples out of
      sight ;

And the dark frogs chant in the safe
    morass,
And the sweetest stars are made to pass
    O'er the face of the darkest night.

VI

But *we* who are dark, we are dark !
    Ah God, we have no stars !
About our souls in care and cark
    Our blackness shuts like prison-bars ;
The poor souls crouch so far behind
That never a comfort can they find
    By reaching through the prison-bars.

VII

Indeed we live beneath the sky,
    That great smooth Hand of God
      stretched out
On all His children fatherly,
    To save them from the dread and doubt
Which would be, if, from this low place,
All opened straight up to His face
    Into the grand eternity.

VIII

And still God's sunshine and His frost,
    They make us hot, they make us cold,
As if we were not black and lost :
    And the beasts and birds, in wood and
      fold,
Do fear and take us for very men !
Could the whip-poor-will or the cat of
    the glen
    Look into my eyes and be bold ?

IX

I am black, I am black !—
    But, once, I laughed in girlish glee,
For one of my colour stood in the track
    Where the drivers drove, and looked
      at me,
And tender and full was the look he
    gave—
Could a slave look *so* at another slave ?—
    I look at the sky and the sea.

X

And from that hour our spirits grew
    As free as if unsold, unbought :
Oh, strong enough, since we were two,
    To conquer the world, we thought !
The drivers drove us day by day ;
We did not mind, we went one way,
    And no better a freedom sought.

XI

In the sunny ground between the canes,
  He said 'I love you' as he passed :
When the shingle-roof rang sharp with
    the rains,
I heard how he vowed it fast ;
While others shook he smiled in the hut,
As he carved me a bowl of the coco-nut
  Through the roar of the hurricanes.

XII

I sang his name instead of a song,
  Over and over I sang his name—
Upward and downward I drew it along
  My various notes,—the same, the same!
I sang it low, that the slave-girls near
Might never guess from aught they could
    hear,
  It was only a name—a name.

XIII

I look on the sky and the sea.
  We were two to love, and two to
    pray,—
Yes, two, O God, who cried to Thee,
  Though nothing didst Thou say.
Coldly Thou sat'st behind the sun !
And now I cry who am but one,
  Thou wilt not speak to-day.—

XIV

We were black, we were black,
  We had no claim to love and bliss,
What marvel, if each went to wrack ?
  They wrung my cold hands out of his,—
They dragged him . . . where? . . I
    crawled to touch
His blood's mark in the dust ! . . not much,
  Ye pilgrim-souls, . . though plain as
    this !

XV

Wrong, followed by a deeper wrong !
  Mere grief 's too good for such as I ;
So the white men brought the shame
    ere long
  To strangle the sob of my agony.
They would not leave me for my dull
Wet eyes !—it was too merciful
  To let me weep pure tears and die.

XVI

I am black, I am black !
  I wore a child upon my breast . . .
An amulet that hung too slack,
  And, in my unrest, could not rest.
Thus we went moaning, child and mother,
One to another, one to another,
  Until all ended for the best.

XVII

For hark ! I will tell you low . . . low . . .
  I am black, you see,—
And the babe who lay on my bosom so,
  Was far too white . . . too white for me ;
As white as the ladies who scorned to pray
Beside me at church but yesterday,
  Though my tears had washed a place
    for my knee.

XVIII

My own, own child ! I could not bear
  To look in his face, it was so white ;
I covered him up with a kerchief there ;
  I covered his face in close and tight :
And he moaned and struggled, as well
    might be,
For the white child wanted his liberty—
  Ha, ha ! he wanted the master-right.

XIX

He moaned and beat with his head and
    feet,
  His little feet that never grew—
He struck them out, as it was meet,
  Against my heart to break it through.
I might have sung and made him mild—
But I dared not sing to the white-faced
    child
  The only song I knew.

XX

I pulled the kerchief very close :
  He could not see the sun, I swear,
More, then, alive, than now he does
  From between the roots of the mango
    . . . where ?
. . . I know where. Close ! a child and
    mother
Do wrong to look at one another,
  When one is black and one is fair.

XXI

Why, in that single glance I had
    Of my child's face, . . I tell you all,
I saw a look that made me mad !
    The *master's* look, that used to fall
On my soul like his lash . . . or worse !—
And so, to save it from my curse,
    I twisted it round in my shawl.

XXII

And he moaned and trembled from foot
        to head,
    He shivered from head to foot ;
Till, after a time, he lay instead
    Too suddenly still and mute.
I felt, beside, a stiffening cold :
I dared to lift up just a fold, . .
    As in lifting a leaf of the mango-fruit.

XXIII

But *my* fruit . . . ha, ha !—there, had been
    (I laugh to think on 't at this hour !)
Your fine white angels (who have seen
    Nearest the secret of God's power)
And plucked my fruit to make them wine,
And sucked the soul of that child of mine,
    As the humming-bird sucks the soul
        of the flower.

XXIV

Ha, ha, the trick of the angels white !
    They freed the white child's spirit so.
I said not a word, but, day and night,
    I carried the body to and fro,
And it lay on my heart like a stone . . .
        as chill.
—The sun may shine out as much as he
        will :
    I am cold, though it happened a month
        ago.

XXV

From the white man's house, and the
        black man's hut,
    I carried the little body on ;
The forest's arms did round us shut,
    And silence through the trees did run.
They asked no question as I went,—
They stood too high for astonishment,—
    They could see God sit on His throne

XXVI

My little body, kerchiefed fast.
    I bore it on through the forest . . . on ;
And when I felt it was tired at last,
    I scooped a hole beneath the moon.
Through the forest-tops the angels far,
With a white sharp finger from every star,
    Did point and mock at what was done.

XXVII

Yet when it was all done aright, . .
    Earth, 'twixt me and my baby,
        strewed, . .
All, changed to black earth, . . nothing
        white, . .
    A dark child in the dark !—ensued
Some comfort, and my heart grew young ;
I sate down smiling there and sung
    The song I learnt in my maidenhood.

XXVIII

And thus we two were reconciled,
    The white child and black mother, thus ;
For, as I sang it soft and wild,
    The same song, more melodious,
Rose from the grave whereon I sate :
It was the dead child singing that,
    To join the souls of both of us.

XXIX

I look on the sea and the sky !
    Where the pilgrims' ships first anchored
        lay
The free sun rideth gloriously,
    But the pilgrim-ghosts have slid away
Through the earliest streaks of the morn :
My face is black, but it glares with a scorn
    Which they dare not meet by day.

XXX

Ah !—in their 'stead, their hunter sons !
    Ah, ah ! they are on me—they hunt in
        a ring—
Keep off ! I brave you all at once—
    I throw off your eyes like snakes that
        sting !
You have killed the black eagle at nest,
        I think :
Did you never stand still in your triumph,
        and shrink
    From the stroke of her wounded wing ?

XXXI

(Man, drop that stone you dared to
      lift!—)
  I wish you who stand there five
      a-breast,
Each, for his own wife's joy and gift,
  A little corpse as safely at rest
As mine in the mangos!—Yes, but *she*
May keep live babies on her knee,
  And sing the song she likes the best.

XXXII

I am not mad: I am black.
  I see you staring in my face—
I know you staring, shrinking back,
  Ye are born of the Washington-race,
And this land is the free America,
And this mark on my wrist .. (I prove
      what I say)
  Ropes tied me up here to the flogging-
      place.

XXXIII

You think I shrieked then? Not a sound!
  I hung, as a gourd hangs in the sun;
I only cursed them all around
  As softly as I might have done
My very own child.—From these sands
Up to the mountains, lift your hands,
  O slaves, and end what I begun!

XXXIV

Whips, curses; these must answer those!
  For in this UNION you have set
Two kinds of men in adverse rows,
  Each loathing each: and all forget
The seven wounds in Christ's body fair,
While HE sees gaping everywhere
  Our countless wounds that pay no debt.

XXXV

Our wounds are different.   Your white
      men
  Are, after all, not gods indeed,
Nor able to make Christs again
  Do good with bleeding. *We* who bleed
(Stand off!) we help not in our loss!
We are too heavy for our cross,
  And fall and crush you and your seed.

XXXVI

I fall, I swoon! I look at the sky:
  The clouds are breaking on my brain:
I am floated along, as if I should die
  Of liberty's exquisite pain.
In the name of the white child waiting
      for me
In the death-dark where we may kiss
      and agree,
White men, I leave you all curse-free
  In my broken heart's disdain!

THE CRY OF THE CHILDREN

Φεῦ, φεῦ· τί προσδέρκεσθέ μ' ὅμμασιν, τέκνα;
                                        Medea.

I

Do ye hear the children weeping, O my
      brothers,
  Ere the sorrow comes with years?
They are leaning their young heads
      against their mothers,
  And *that* cannot stop their tears.
The young lambs are bleating in the
      meadows,
  The young birds are chirping in the
      nest,
The young fawns are playing with the
      shadows,
  The young flowers are blowing toward
      the west—
But the young, young children, O my
      brothers,
  They are weeping bitterly!
They are weeping in the playtime of the
      others,
  In the country of the free.

II

Do you question the young children in
      the sorrow,
  Why their tears are falling so?
The old man may weep for his to-morrow
  Which is lost in Long Ago;
The old tree is leafless in the forest,
  The old year is ending in the frost,
The old wound, if stricken, is the sorest,
  The old hope is hardest to be lost.

But the young, young children, O my
    brothers,
  Do you ask them why they stand
Weeping sore before the bosoms of their
    mothers,
  In our happy Fatherland?

III

They look up with their pale and sunken
    faces,
  And their looks are sad to see,
For the man's hoary anguish draws and
    presses
  Down the cheeks of infancy.
'Your old earth,' they say, 'is very dreary;
  Our young feet,' they say, 'are very
    weak!
Few paces have we taken, yet are
    weary—
  Our grave-rest is very far to seek.
Ask the aged why they weep, and not
    the children;
  For the outside earth is cold;
And we young ones stand without, in
    our bewildering,
  And the graves are for the old.'

IV

'True,' say the children, 'it may happen
  That we die before our time;
Little Alice died last year—her grave is
    shapen
  Like a snowball, in the rime.
We looked into the pit prepared to take
    her:
  Was no room for any work in the close
    clay!
From the sleep wherein she lieth none
    will wake her,
  Crying, "Get up, little Alice! it is day."
If you listen by that grave, in sun and
    shower,
  With your ear down, little Alice never
    cries;
Could we see her face, be sure we should
    not know her,
  For the smile has time for growing in
    her eyes:
And merry go her moments, lulled and
    stilled in
  The shroud by the kirk-chime!
It is good when it happens,' say the
    children,
  'That we die before our time.'

V

Alas, alas, the children! they are seeking
  Death in life, as best to have;
They are binding up their hearts away
    from breaking,
  With a cerement from the grave.
Go out, children, from the mine and from
    the city,
  Sing out, children, as the little thrushes
    do;
Pluck you handfuls of the meadow cow-
    slips pretty,
  Laugh aloud, to feel your fingers let
    them through!
But they answer, 'Are your cowslips of
    the meadows
  Like our weeds anear the mine?
Leave us quiet in the dark of the coal-
    shadows,
  From your pleasures fair and fine!

VI

'For oh,' say the children, 'we are weary,
  And we cannot run or leap;
If we cared for any meadows, it were
    merely
  To drop down in them and sleep.
Our knees tremble sorely in the stooping,
  We fall upon our faces, trying to go;
And, underneath our heavy eyelids droop-
    ing,
  The reddest flower would look as pale
    as snow;
For, all day, we drag our burden tiring
  Through the coal-dark, under-
    ground—
Or, all day, we drive the wheels of iron
  In the factories, round and round.

VII

'For, all day, the wheels are droning,
    turning,—
  Their wind comes in our faces,—
Till our hearts turn,—our head, with
    pulses burning,
  And the walls turn in their places:
Turns the sky in the high window blank
    and reeling,
  Turns the long light that drops adown
    the wall,
Turn the black flies that crawl along the
    ceiling,
  All are turning, all the day, and we
    with all.

And all day, the iron wheels are droning,
    And sometimes we could pray,
"O ye wheels" (breaking out in a mad
    moaning),
    "Stop! be silent for to-day!"'

VIII

Aye! be silent! Let them hear each other
    breathing
    For a moment, mouth to mouth!
Let them touch each other's hands, in
    a fresh wreathing
    Of their tender human youth!
Let them feel that this cold metallic
    motion
    Is not all the life God fashions or
       reveals:
Let them prove their living souls against
    the notion
    That they live in you, or under you,
       O wheels!—
Still, all day, the iron wheels go onward,
    Grinding life down from its mark;
And the children's souls, which God is
    calling sunward,
    Spin on blindly in the dark.

IX

Now tell the poor young children, O my
    brothers,
    To look up to Him and pray;
So the blessèd One who blesseth all the
    others,
    Will bless them another day.
They answer, 'Who is God that He
    should hear us,
    While the rushing of the iron wheels
       is stirred?
When we sob aloud, the human creatures
    near us
    Pass by, hearing not, or answer not
       a word.
And *we* hear not (for the wheels in their
    resounding)
    Strangers speaking at the door:
Is it likely God, with angels singing
    round Him,
    Hears our weeping any more?

X

'Two words, indeed, of praying we
    remember,
    And at midnight's hour of harm,

"Our Father," looking upward in the
    chamber,
    We say softly for a charm[1].
We know no other words, except "Our
    Father,"
    And we think that, in some pause of
       angels' song,
God may pluck them with the silence
    sweet to gather,
    And hold both within His right hand
       which is strong.
"Our Father!" If He heard us, He
    would surely
    (For they call Him good and mild)
Answer, smiling down the steep world
    very purely,
    "Come and rest with Me, My child."

XI

'But, no!' say the children, weeping
    faster,
    'He is speechless as a stone;
And they tell us, of His image is the master
    Who commands us to work on.
Go to!' say the children,—'up in Heaven,
    Dark, wheel-like, turning clouds are
       all we find.
Do not mock us; grief has made us un-
    believing—
    We look up for God, but tears have
       made us blind.'
Do you hear the children weeping and
    disproving,
    O my brothers, what ye preach?
For God's possible is taught by His
    world's loving,
    And the children doubt of each.

XII

And well may the children weep before
    you!
    They are weary ere they run;
They have never seen the sunshine, nor
    the glory
    Which is brighter than the sun.

---

[1] A fact rendered pathetically historical by
Mr. Horne's report of his Commission. The
name of the poet of *Orion* and *Cosmo de'
Medici* has, however, a change of associations,
and comes in time to remind me that we have
some noble poetic heat of literature still,—
however open to the reproach of being somewhat
gelid in our humanity. [1844.]

They know the grief of man, without its
        wisdom ;
    They sink in man's despair, without
        its calm ;
Are slaves, without the liberty in Christ-
        dom,
    Are martyrs, by the pang without the
        palm,—
Are worn, as if with age, yet unretriev-
        ingly
        The harvest of its memories cannot
            reap,—
Are orphans of the earthly love and
        heavenly.
        Let them weep ! let them weep !

XIII

They look up, with their pale and sunken
        faces,
    And their look is dread to see,
For they mind you of their angels in
        high places,
    With eyes turned on Deity !—
'How long,' they say, 'how long, O cruel
        nation,
    Will you stand, to move the world, on
        a child's heart,—
Stifle down with a mailed heel its palpita-
        tion,
    And tread onward to your throne amid
        the mart ?
Our blood splashes upward, O gold-
        heaper,
    And your purple shows your path !
But the child's sob in the silence curses
        deeper
    Than the strong man in his wrath.'

A CHILD ASLEEP

I

How he sleepeth, having drunken
    Weary childhood's mandragore !
From his pretty eyes have sunken
    Pleasures to make room for more—
Sleeping near the withered nosegay
    which he pulled the day before.

II

Nosegays ! leave them for the waking ;
    Throw them earthward where they
        grew ;
Dim are such, beside the breaking
    Amaranths he looks unto :
Folded eyes see brighter colours than
    the open ever do.

III

Heaven-flowers, rayed by shadows
        golden
    From the palms they sprang beneath,
Now perhaps divinely holden,
    Swing against him in a wreath :
We may think so from the quickening
    of his bloom and of his breath.

IV

Vision unto vision calleth,
    While the young child dreameth on ;
Fair, O dreamer, thee befalleth
    With the glory thou hast won !
Darker wert thou in the garden, yester-
    morn by summer sun.

V

We should see the spirits ringing
    Round thee, were the clouds away ;
'Tis the child-heart draws them,
        singing
    In the silent-seeming clay :
Singing !—stars that seem the mutest,
    go in music all the way.

VI

As the moths around a taper,
    As the bees around a rose,
As the gnats around a vapour,
    So the spirits group and close
Round about a holy childhood, as if
    drinking its repose.

VII

Shapes of brightness overlean thee,
    Flash their diadems of youth
On the ringlets which half screen thee,
    While thou smilest . . . not in sooth
Thy smile, but the overfair one, dropt
    from some ethereal mouth.

VIII

Haply it is angels' duty,
  During slumber, shade by shade
To fine down this childish beauty
  To the thing it must be made,
Ere the world shall bring it praises, or
  the tomb shall see it fade.

IX

Softly, softly! make no noises!
  Now he lieth dead and dumb;
Now he hears the angels' voices
  Folding silence in the room;
Now he muses deep the meaning of the
  Heaven-words as they come.

X

Speak not! he is consecrated;
  Breathe no breath across his eyes:
Lifted up and separated
  On the hand of God he lies,
In a sweetness beyond touching,—held
  in cloistral sanctities.

XI

Could ye bless him—father—mother,
  Bless the dimple in his cheek?
Dare ye look at one another,
  And the benediction speak?
Would ye not break out in weeping, and
  confess yourselves too weak?

XII

He is harmless—ye are sinful;
  Ye are troubled—he, at ease;
From his slumber, virtue winful
  Floweth outward with increase.
Dare not bless him! but be blessèd by
  his peace—and go in peace.

THE FOURFOLD ASPECT

I

When ye stood up in the house
  With your little childish feet,
And, in touching Life's first shows,
  First the touch of Love did meet,—
Love and Nearness seeming one,
  By the heartlight cast before,
And, of all Belovèds, none
  Standing farther than the door!

Not a name being dear to thought,
  With its owner beyond call;
Nor a face, unless it brought
  Its own shadow to the wall;
When the worst recorded change
  Was of apple dropt from bough,
When love's sorrow seemed more
    strange
  Than love's treason can seem now,—
Then, the Loving took you up
  Soft, upon their elder knees,—
Telling why the statues droop
  Underneath the churchyard trees,
And how ye must lie beneath them
  Through the winters long and deep,
Till the last trump overbreathe them,
  And ye smile out of your sleep . . .
Oh, ye lifted up your head, and it seemed
    as if they said
A tale of fairy ships
  With a swan-wing for a sail!—
Oh, ye kissed their loving lips
  For the merry, merry tale!—
So carelessly ye thought upon the Dead.

II

Soon ye read in solemn stories
  Of the men of long ago—
Of the pale bewildering glories
  Shining farther than we know;
Of the heroes with the laurel,
  Of the poets with the bay,
Of the two worlds' earnest quarrel
  For that beauteous Helena;
How Achilles at the portal
  Of the tent, heard footsteps nigh,
And his strong heart, half-immortal
  Met the *keitai* with a cry;
How Ulysses left the sunlight
  For the pale eidola race
Blank and passive through the dun
    light,
  Staring blindly in his face;
How that true wife said to Paetus,
  With calm smile and wounded heart,
'Sweet, it hurts not!'—how Admetus
  Saw his blessed one depart;
How King Arthur proved his mission,
  And Sir Roland wound his horn,
And at Sangreal's moony vision
  Swords did bristle round like corn.
Oh, ye lifted up your head, and it seemed
  the while ye read,

That this Death, then, must be found
A Valhalla for the crowned,
The heroic who prevail :
None, be sure, can enter in
Far below a paladin
Of a noble, noble tale !—
So awfully ye thought upon the Dead.

III

Aye, but soon ye woke up shrieking,—
　As a child that wakes at night
From a dream of sisters speaking
　In a garden's summer-light,—
That wakes, starting up and bounding,
　In a lonely, lonely bed,
With a wall of darkness round him,
　Stifling black about his head !—
And the full sense of your mortal
　Rushed upon you deep and loud,
And ye heard the thunder hurtle
　From the silence of the cloud !
Funeral-torches at your gateway
　Threw a dreadful light within.
All things changed ! you rose up
　straightway,
　And saluted Death and Sin.
Since,—your outward man has rallied,
　And your eye and voice grown
　bold—
Yet the Sphinx of Life stands pallid,
　With her saddest secret told.
Happy places have grown holy :
　If ye went where once ye went,
Only tears would fall down slowly,
　As at solemn sacrament.
Merry books, once read for pastime,
　If ye dared to read again,
Only memories of the last time
　Would swim darkly up the brain.
Household names, which used to flutter
　Through your laughter unawares,—
God's Divinest ye could utter
　With less trembling in your prayers!
Ye have dropt adown your head, and it
　seems as if ye tread
On your own hearts in the path
Ye are called to in His wrath,—
And your prayers go up in wail !
—' Dost Thou see, then, all our loss,
O Thou agonized on cross ?
Art thou reading all its tale ?'
So mournfully ye think upon the Dead.

IV

Pray, pray, thou who also weepest,
　And the drops will slacken so.
Weep, weep,—and the watch thou
　keepest
　With a quicker count will go.
Think.—the shadow on the dial
　For the nature most undone,
Marks the passing of the trial,
　Proves the presence of the sun.
Look, look up, in starry passion,
　To the throne above the spheres !
Learn,—the spirit's gravitation
　Still must differ from the tear's.
Hope,—with all the strength thou usest
　In embracing thy despair.
Love,—the earthly love thou losest
　Shall return to thee more fair.
Work,—make clear the forest-tangles
　Of the wildest stranger-land.
Trust,—the blessèd deathly angels
　Whisper, ' Sabbath hours at hand !'
By the heart's wound when most gory,
　By the longest agony,
Smile !—Behold, in sudden glory
　The TRANSFIGURED smiles on *thee!*
And ye lifted up your head, and it seemed
　as if He said,
' My Belovèd, is it so ?
Have ye tasted of my woe ?
Of my Heaven ye shall not fail !'—
He stands brightly where the shade is,
With the keys of Death and Hades,
And there, ends the mournful tale.—
So hopefully ye think upon the Dead.

NIGHT AND THE MERRY MAN

NIGHT

'NEATH my moon what doest thou,
With a somewhat paler brow
Than she giveth to the ocean ?
He, without a pulse or motion,
Muttering low before her stands,
Lifting his invoking hands,
Like a seer before a sprite,
To catch her oracles of light.
But thy soul out-trembles now
Many pulses on thy brow !
Where be all thy laughters clear,
Others laughed alone to hear ?

Where, thy quaint jests, said for fame?
Where, thy dances, mixed with game?
Where, thy festive companies,
Moonèd o'er with ladies' eyes,
All more bright for thee, I trow?
'Neath my moon, what doest thou?

THE MERRY MAN

I am digging my warm heart,
Till I find its coldest part;
I am digging wide and low,
Further than a spade will go;
Till that, when the pit is deep
And large enough, I there may heap
All my present pain and past
Joy, dead things that look aghast
By the daylight.—Now 'tis done.
Throw them in, by one and one!
I must laugh, at rising sun.

Memories—of fancy's golden
Treasures which my hands have holden,
Till the chillness made them ache;
Of childhood's hopes, that used to wake
If birds were in a singing strain,
And for less cause, sleep again;
Of the moss-seat in the wood,
Where I trysted solitude;
Of the hill-top, where the wind
Used to follow me behind,
Then in sudden rush to blind
Both my glad eyes with my hair,
Taken gladly in the snare;
Of the climbing up the rocks,—
Of the playing neath the oaks,
Which retain beneath them now
Only shadow of the bough;
Of the lying on the grass
While the clouds did overpass,
Only they, so lightly driven,
Seeming betwixt me and Heaven!
Of the little prayers serene,
Murmuring of earth and sin;
Of large-leaved philosophy
Leaning from my childish knee;
Of poetic book sublime,
Soul-kissed for the first dear time,—
Greek or English,—ere I knew
Life was not a poem too.
Throw them in, by one and one!
I must laugh, at rising sun.

Of the glorious ambitions,
Yet unquenched by their fruitions;
Of the reading out the nights;
Of the straining at mad heights;
Of achievements, less descried
By a dear few, than magnified;
Of praises, from the many earned,
When praise from love was undiscerned;
Of the sweet reflecting gladness,
Softened by itself to sadness—
Throw them in, by one and one!
I must laugh, at rising sun.

What are these? more, more than these!
Throw in, dearer memories!—
Of voices—whereof but to speak,
Makes mine own all sunk and weak;
Of smiles, the thought of which is
        sweeping
All my soul to floods of weeping;
Of looks, whose absence fain would weigh
My looks to the ground for ay;
Of clasping hands—ah me! I wring
Mine, and in a tremble fling
Downward, downward, all this paining!
Partings, with the sting remaining;
Meetings, with a deeper throe,
Since the joy is ruined so;
Changes, with a fiery burning—
(Shadows upon all the turning);
Thoughts of—with a storm they came—
Them, I have not breath to name.
Downward, downward, be they cast
In the pit! and now at last
My work beneath the moon is done,
And I shall laugh, at rising sun.

But let me pause or ere I cover
All my treasures darkly over.
I will speak not in thine ears,
Only tell my beaded tears
Silently, most silently!
When the last is calmly told,
Let that same moist rosary
With the rest sepulchred be.
Finished now. The darksome mould
Sealeth up the darksome pit.
I will lay no stone on it:
Grasses I will sow instead,
Fit for Queen Titania's tread;
Flowers, encoloured with the sun,
And αι αι written upon none.

Thus, whenever saileth by
The Lady World of dainty eye,
Not a grief shall here remain,
Silken shoon to damp or stain ;
And while she lisps, 'I have not seen
Any place more smooth and clean ' . . .
Here she cometh !—Ha, ha !—who
Laughs as loud as I can do ?

EARTH AND HER PRAISERS

I

THE Earth is old ;
Six thousand winters make her heart a-
    cold ;
The sceptre slanteth from her palsied hold.
She saith, ' 'Las me !—God's word that
    I was '' good ''
Is taken back to heaven,
From whence when any sound comes, I
    am riven
By some sharp bolt.   And now no angel
    would
Descend with sweet dew-silence on my
    mountains,
To glorify the lovely river-fountains
    That gush along their side.
I see, O weary change ! I see instead
    This human wrath and pride,
These thrones, and tombs, judicial wrong,
    and blood,
And bitter words are poured upon mine
    head—
'' O Earth ! thou art a stage for tricks
    unholy,
A church for most remorseful melancholy !
Thou art so spoilt, we should forget we had
An Eden in thee,—wert thou not so sad.''
Sweet children, I am old ! ye, every one,
Do keep me from a portion of my sun.
    Give praise in change for brightness !
That I may shake my hills in infiniteness
Of breezy laughter, as in youthful mirth,
To hear Earth's sons and daughters
    praising Earth.'

II

Whereupon a child began,
With spirit running up to man,
As by angel's shining ladder
(May he find no cloud above !),

Seeming he had ne'er been sadder
    All his days than now,—
Sitting in the chestnut grove,
With that joyous overflow
Of smiling from his mouth, o'er brow
And cheek and chin, as if the breeze
Leaning tricksy from the trees
To part his golden hairs, had blown
Into an hundred smiles that one.

III

' O rare, rare Earth ! ' he saith,
    ' I will praise thee presently ;
Not to-day ; I have no breath !
    I have hunted squirrels three—
Two ran down in the furzy hollow,
Where I could not see nor follow ;
One sits at the top of the filbert-tree,
With a yellow nut, and a mock at me :
    Presently it shall be done.
When I see which way those two
    have run ;
When the mocking one at the filbert top
Shall leap a-down, and beside me stop :
    Then, rare Earth, rare Earth,
Will I pause, having known thy worth,
    To say all good of thee ! '

IV

Next a lover, with a dream
'Neath his waking eyelids hidden,
And a frequent sigh unbidden,
And an idlesse all the day
Beside a wandering stream,
And a silence that is made
Of a word he dares not say,—
Shakes slow his pensive head.
    ' Earth, Earth ! ' saith he,
' If spirits, like thy roses, grew
On one stalk, and winds austere
Could but only blow them near,
    To share each other's dew !
If, when summer rains agree
To beautify thy hills, I knew
Looking off them I might see
    Some one very beauteous too,—
    Then Earth,' saith he,
' I would praise . . . nay, nay—not thee.'

V

Will the pedant name her next ?
Crabbèd with a crabbèd text,
Sits he in his study nook,
With his elbow on a book,

And with stately crossèd knees,
And a wrinkle deeply thrid
Through his lowering brow,
Caused by making proofs enow
That Plato in 'Parmenides'
Meant the same Spinosa did,—
Or, that an hundred of the groping
Like himself, had made one Homer,
Homeros being a misnomer.
What hath *he* to do with praise
Of Earth, or aught? Whene'er the
      sloping
Sunbeams through his window daze
His eyes off from the learned phrase,
Straightway he draws close the curtain.
May abstraction keep him dumb!
Were h's lips to ope, 'tis certain
Derivatum est would come.

VI

Then a mourner moveth pale
In a silence full of wail,
Raising not his sunken head
Because he wandered last that way
With that one beneath the clay:
Weeping not, because that one,
The only one who would have said,
' Cease to weep, beloved ! ' has gone
Whence returneth comfort none.
The silence breaketh suddenly,—
' Earth, I praise thee ! ' crieth he,
' Thou hast a grave for also *me*.'

VII

Ha, a poet! know him by
The ecstasy-dilated eye,
Not uncharged with tears that ran
Upward from his heart of man;
By the cheek, from hour to hour,
Kindled bright or sunken power;
With a sense of lonely power;
By the brow uplifted higher
Than others, for more low declining;
By the lip which words of fire
Overboiling have burned white,
While they gave the nations light!
Aye, in every time and place
Ye may know the poet's face
      By the shade, or shining.

VIII

'Neath a golden cloud he stands,
Spreading his impassioned hands.

' O God's Earth ! ' he saith, ' the sign
From the Father-soul to mine
Of all beauteous mysteries,
Of all perfect images,
Which, divine in His divine,
In my human only are
Very excellent and fair !—
Think not, Earth, that I would raise
Weary forehead in thy praise
(Weary, that I cannot go
Farther from thy region low)
If were struck no richer meanings
From thee than thyself. The leanings
Of the close trees o'er the brim
Of a sunshine-haunted stream,
Have a sound beneath their leaves,
      Not of wind, not of wind,
Which the poet's voice achieves :
The faint mountains, heaped behind,
Have a falling on their tops,
      Not of dew, not of dew,
Which the poet's fancy drops :
Viewless things his eyes can view ;
Driftings of his dream do light
All the skies by day and night,
And the seas that deepest roll
Carry murmurs of his soul.
Earth, I praise thee! praise thou *me!*
God perfecteth His creation
With this recipient poet-passion,
And makes the beautiful to be.
I praise thee, O belovèd sign,
From the God-soul unto mine !
Praise me, that I cast on thee
The cunning sweet interpretation,
The help and glory and dilation
      Of mine immortality ! '

IX

There was silence. None did dare
To use again the spoken air
Of that far-charming voice, until
A Christian resting on the hill,
With a thoughtful smile subdued
(Seeming learnt in solitude)
Which a weeper might have viewed
Without new tears, did softly say,
And looked up unto heaven alway
While he praised the Earth—
                              ' O Earth,
I count the praises thou art worth,
By thy waves that move aloud,
By thy hills against the cloud,

By thy valleys warm and green,
By the copses' elms between,
By their birds which, like a sprite
Scattered by a strong delight
Into fragments musical,
Stir and sing in every bush ;
By thy silver founts that fall,
As if to entice the stars at night
To thine heart; by grass and rush,
And little weeds the children pull,
Mistook for flowers !
                    —Oh, beautiful
Art thou, Earth, albeit worse
Than in heaven is callèd good !
Good to us, that we may know
Meekly from thy good to go ;
While the holy, crying Blood,
Puts its music kind and low
'Twixt such ears as are not dull,
And thine ancient curse !

                    x

' Praisèd be the mosses soft
In thy forest pathways oft,
And the thorns, which make us think
Of the thornless river-brink,
    Where the ransomed tread ;
Praisèd be thy sunny gleams,
And the storm, that worketh dreams
    Of calm unfinishèd ;
Praisèd be thine active days,
And thy night-time's solemn need,
When in God's dear book we read
    No night shall be therein ;
Praisèd be thy dwellings warm
By household faggot's cheerful blaze,
Where, to hear of pardoned sin,
Pauseth oft the merry din,
Save the babe's upon the arm,
Who croweth to the crackling wood ;
Yea,—and, better understood,
Praisèd be thy dwellings cold,
Hid beneath the churchyard mould,
Where the bodies of the saints,
Separate from earthly taints,
Lie asleep, in blessing bound,
Waiting for the trumpet's sound
To free them into blessing ;—none
Weeping more beneath the sun,
Though dangerous words of human
    love
Be graven very near, above.

                    xi

' Earth, we Christians praise thee thus,
Even for the change that comes,
With a grief, from thee to us !
For thy cradles and thy tombs,
For the pleasant corn and wine,
And summer-heat ; and also for
The frost upon the sycamore,
    And hail upon the vine ! '

THE VIRGIN MARY TO THE
CHILD JESUS

But see the Virgin blest
Hath laid her babe to rest.
            MILTON'S *Hymn on the Nativity.*

Sleep, sleep, mine Holy One !
My flesh, my Lord !—what name ? I do
    not know
A name that seemeth not too high or low,
    Too far from me or heaven.
My Jesus, *that* is best ! that word being
    given
By the majestic angel whose command
Was softly as a man's beseeching said,
When I and all the earth appeared to stand
    In the great overflow
Of light celestial from his wings and head.
    Sleep, sleep, my saving One !

                    II

And art Thou come for saving, baby-
    browed
And speechless Being—art Thou come
    for saving ?
The palm that grows beside our door is
    bowed
By treadings of the low wind from the
    south,
A restless shadow through the chamber
    waving :
Upon its bough a bird sings in the sun ;
But Thou, with that close slumber on
    Thy mouth,
Dost seem of wind and sun already weary.
Art come for saving. O my weary One !

                    III

Perchance this sleep that shutteth out
    the dreary
Earth-sounds and motions, opens on Thy
    soul
    High dreams on fire with God ;

High songs that make the pathways
    where they roll
More bright than stars do theirs ; and
    visions new
Of Thine eternal Nature's old abode.
    Suffer this mother's kiss,
    Best thing that earthly is,
To glide the music and the glory through,
Nor narrow in Thy dream the broad up-
    liftings
    Of any seraph wing.
Thus noiseless, thus. Sleep, sleep, my
    dreaming One !

IV

The slumber of His lips meseems to run
Through *my* lips to mine heart,—to all
    its shiftings
Of sensual life, bringing contrariousness
In a great calm. I feel I could lie
    down
As Moses did, and die [1],—and then live
    most.
I am 'ware of you, heavenly Presences,
That stand with your peculiar light un-
    lost,
Each forehead with a high thought for
    a crown,
Unsunned i' the sunshine ! I am 'ware.
    Ye throw
No shade against the wall ! How motion-
    less
Ye round me with your living statuary,
While through your whiteness, in and
    outwardly,
Continual thoughts of God appear to go,
Like light's soul in itself. I bear, I bear,
To look upon the dropt lids of your eyes,
Though their external shining testifies
To that beatitude within, which were
Enough to blast an eagle at his sun.
I fall not on my sad clay face before ye,—
    I look on His. I know
My spirit which dilateth with the woe
    Of His mortality
    May well contain your glory.
    Yea, drop your lids more low.
Ye are but fellow-worshippers with me !
    Sleep, sleep, my worshipped One !

[1] It is a Jewish tradition that Moses died of
the kisses of God's lips.

V

We sate among the stalls at Bethlehem.
The dumb kine from their fodder turn-
    ing them,
    Softened their hornèd faces
    To almost human gazes
    Toward the newly Born :
The simple shepherds from the star-lit
    brooks
    Brought visionary looks,
As yet in their astonied hearing rung
    The strange, sweet angel-tongue :
The magi of the East, in sandals worn,
    Knelt reverent, sweeping round,
With long pale beards, their gifts upon the
    ground,
    The incense, myrrh, and gold
These baby hands were impotent to hold.
So, let all earthlies and celestials wait
    Upon Thy royal state.
    Sleep, sleep, my kingly One !

VI

I am not proud—meek angels, ye invest
New meeknesses to hear such utterance
    rest
On mortal lips,—'I am not proud'—*not
    proud !*
Albeit in my flesh God sent His Son,
Albeit over Him my head is bowed
As others bow before Him, still mine
    heart
Bows lower than their knees. O centuries
That roll, in vision, your futurities
    My future grave athwart,—
Whose murmurs seem to reach me while
    I keep
    Watch o'er this sleep,—
Say of me as the Heavenly said—'Thou
    art
The blessedest of women !'—blessedest,
Not holiest, not noblest—no high name,
Whose height misplaced may pierce me
    like a shame,
When I sit meek in heaven !
            For me, for me,
God knows that I am feeble like the
    rest !—
I often wandered forth, more child than
    maiden,
Among the midnight hills of Galilee
    Whose summits looked heaven-laden,

Listening to silence as it seemed to be
God's voice, so soft yet strong—so fain to
    press
Upon my heart as heaven did on the
    height,
And waken up its shadows by a light,
And show its vileness by a holiness.
Then I knelt down most silent like the
    night,
    Too self-renounced for fears,
Raising my small face to the boundless
    blue
Whose stars did mix and tremble in my
    tears :
God heard *them* falling after—with His
  \ dew.

VII

So, seeing my corruption, can I see
This Incorruptible now born of me,
This fair new Innocence no sun did chance
To shine on (for even Adam was no child),
Created from my nature all defiled,
This mystery, from out mine ignorance,—
Nor feel the blindness, stain, corruption,
    more
Than others do, or *I* did heretofore ?—
Can hands wherein such burden pure has
    been,
Not open with the cry ' unclean, unclean,'
More oft than any else beneath the skies ?
    Ah King, ah Christ, ah son !
The kine, the shepherds, the abasèd wise,
    Must all less lowly wait
    Than I, upon thy state.—
    Sleep, sleep, my kingly One !

VIII

Art Thou a King, then ? Come, His
    universe,
    Come, crown me Him a King !
Pluck rays from all such stars as never fling
    Their light where fell a curse,
And make a crowning for this kingly
    brow !—
What is my word ?—Each empyreal star
    Sits in a sphere afar
    In shining ambuscade.
    The child-brow, crowned by none,
    Keeps its unchildlike shade.
    Sleep, sleep, my crownless One !

IX

Unchildlike shade !—No other babe doth
    wear
An aspect very sorrowful, as Thou.—
No small babe-smiles, my watching heart
    has seen,
To float like speech the speechless lips
    between :
No dovelike cooing in the golden air,
No quick short joys of leaping babyhood.
Alas, our earthly good
In heaven thought evil, seems too good for
    Thee :
    Yet, sleep, my weary One !

X

And then the drear sharp tongue of
    prophecy,
With the dread sense of things which shall
    be done,
Doth smite me inly, like a sword ! a
    sword ?—
(*That* ' smites the Shepherd.') Then, I
    think aloud
The words ' despised,'—' rejected,'—
    every word
Recoiling into darkness as I view
    The DARLING on my knee.
Bright angels,—move not !—lest ye stir
    the cloud
Betwixt my soul and His futurity !
I must not die, with mother's work
    to do,
    And could not live—and see.

XI

    It is enough to bear
    This image still and fair—
    This holier in sleep,
    Than a saint at prayer ;
    This aspect of a child
    Who never sinned or smiled ;
    This Presence in an infant's face,
    This sadness most like love,
    This love than love more deep,
    This weakness like omnipotence
    It is so strong to move.
    Awful is this watching place,
    Awful what I see from hence—
    A king, without regalia,
    A God, without the thunder,

A child, without the heart for play ;
Aye, a Creator, rent asunder
From His first glory and cast away
On His own world, for me alone
To hold in hands created, crying—Son !

XII

That tear fell not on Thee,
Beloved, yet Thou stirrest in Thy slumber !
Thou, stirring not for glad sounds out of number
Which through the vibratory palm-trees run
From summer wind and bird,
So quickly hast Thou heard
A tear fall silently?
Wak'st Thou, O loving One?

AN ISLAND

All goeth but Goddis will.—OLD POET.

I

My dream is of an island place
Which distant seas keep lonely,
A little island, on whose face
The stars are watchers only.
Those bright still stars! they need not seem
Brighter or stiller in my dream.

II

An island full of hills and dells,
All rumpled and uneven
With green recesses, sudden swells,
And odorous valleys driven
So deep and straight, that always there
The wind is cradled to soft air.

III

Hills running up to heaven for light
Through woods that half-way ran !
As if the wild earth mimicked right
The wilder heart of man :
Only it shall be greener far
And gladder than hearts ever are.

IV

More like, perhaps, that mountain piece
Of Dante's paradise,
Disrupt to an hundred hills like these,
In falling from the skies ;
Bringing within it, all the roots
Of heavenly trees and flowers and fruits.

V

For saving where the grey rocks strike
Their javelins up the azure,
Or where deep fissures, miser-like,
Hoard up some fountain treasure
(And e'en in them—stoop down and hear—
Leaf sounds with water in your ear !),

VI

The place is all awave with trees,
Limes, myrtles purple-beaded,
Acacias having drunk the lees
Of the night-dew, faint-headed,
And wan, grey olive-woods, which seem
The fittest foliage for a dream.

VII

Trees, trees on all sides! they combine
Their plumy shades to throw ;
Through whose clear fruit and blossom fine
Whene'er the sun may go,
The ground beneath he deeply stains,
As passing through cathedral-panes.

VIII

But little needs this earth of ours
That shining from above her,
When many Pleiades of flowers
(Not one lost) star her over,
The rays of their unnumbered hues
Being all refracted by the dews.

IX

Wide-petalled plants, that boldly drink
The Amreeta of the sky ;
Shut bells, that dull with rapture sink ;
And lolling buds, half shy :
I cannot count them, but between,
Is room for grass and mosses green,

X

And brooks, that glass in different strengths
All colours in disorder,
Or gathering up their silver lengths
Beside their winding border,
Sleep, haunted through the slumber hidden,
By lilies white as dreams in Eden.

XI

Nor think each archèd tree with each
  Too closely interlaces,
To admit of vistas out of reach,
  And broad moon-lighted places,
Upon whose sward the antlered deer
May view their double image clear.

XII

For all this island's creature-full
  (Kept happy not by halves),
Mild cows, that at the vine-wreaths pull,
  Then low back at their calves
With tender lowings, to approve
The warm mouths milking them for love.

XIII

Free gamesome horses, antelopes,
  And harmless leaping leopards,
And buffaloes upon the slopes,
  And sheep unruled by shepherds ;
Hares, lizards, hedgehogs, badgers, mice,
Snakes, squirrels, frogs, and butterflies.

XIV

And birds that live there in a crowd,
  Horned owls, rapt nightingales,
Larks bold with heaven, and peacocks
    proud,
  Self-sphered in those grand tails;
All creatures glad and safe, I deem.
No guns nor springes in my dream !

XV

The island's edges are a-wing
  With trees that overbranch
The sea with song-birds welcoming
  The curlews to green change;
And doves from half-closed lids espy
The red and purple fish go by.

XVI

One dove is answering in trust
  The water every minute,
Thinking so soft a murmur must
  Have her mate's cooing in it :
So softly doth earth's beauty round
Infuse itself in ocean's sound.

XVII

My sanguine soul bounds forwarder
  To meet the bounding waves ;
Beside them straightway I repair,
  To live within the caves ;

And near me two or three may dwell
Whom dreams fantastic please as well.

XVIII

Long winding caverns, glittering far
  Into a crystal distance !
Through clefts of which, shall many a star
  Shine clear without resistance,
And carry down its rays the smell
Of flowers above invisible.

XIX

I said that two or three might choose
  Their dwelling near mine own :
Those who would change man's voice
    and use,
  For Nature's way and tone—
Man's veering heart and careless eyes,
For Nature's steadfast sympathies.

XX

Ourselves, to meet her faithfulness,
  Shall play a faithful part :
Her beautiful shall ne'er address
  The monstrous at our heart ;
Her musical shall ever touch
Something within us also such.

XXI

Yet shall she not our mistress live,
  As doth the moon of ocean,
Though gently as the moon she give
  Our thoughts a light and motion :
More like a harp of many lays,
Moving its master while he plays.

XXII

No sod in all that island doth
  Yawn open for the dead ;
No wind hath borne a traitor's oath ;
  No earth, a mourner's tread :
We cannot say by stream or shade,
' I suffered *here*,—was *here* betrayed.'

XXIII

Our only 'farewell' we shall laugh
  To shifting cloud or hour,
And use our only epitaph
  To some bud turned a flower :
Our only tears shall serve to prove
Excess in pleasure or in love.

XXIV

Our fancies shall their plumage catch
    From fairest island birds,
Whose eggs let young ones out at hatch,
    Born singing! then our words
Unconsciously shall take the dyes
Of those prodigious fantasies.

XXV

Yea, soon, no consonant unsmooth
    Our smile-tuned lips shall reach ;
Sounds sweet as Hellas spake in youth
    Shall glide into our speech.
(What music, certes, can you find
As soft as voices which are kind ?)

XXVI

And often, by the joy without
    And in us, overcome,
We, through our musing, shall let float
    Such poems,—sitting dumb,—
As Pindar might have writ, if he
Had tended sheep in Arcady ;

XXVII

Or Aeschylus—the pleasant fields
    He died in, longer knowing ;
Or Homer, had men's sins and shields
    Been lost in Meles flowing ;
Or Poet Plato, had the undim
Unsetting Godlight broke on him.

XXVIII

Choose me the cave most worthy choice
    To make a place for prayer,
And I will choose a praying voice
    To pour our spirits there.
How silverly the echoes run—
Thy will be done,—Thy will be done.

XXIX

Gently yet strangely uttered words !—
    They lift me from my dream :
The island fadeth with its swards
    That did no more than seem :
The streams are dry, no sun could find—
The fruits are fallen, without wind.

XXX

So oft the doing of God's will
    Our foolish wills undoeth !
And yet what idle dream breaks ill
    Which morning-light subdueth ?
And who would murmur and misdoubt
When God's great sunrise finds him out ?

THE SOUL'S TRAVELLING

*Ἤδη νοεροὺς
Πετάσαι ταρσούς.*—SYNESIUS.

I

I DWELL amid the city ever.
The great humanity which beats
Its life along the stony streets,
Like a strong and unsunned river
    In a self-made course,
I sit and hearken while it rolls.
Very sad and very hoarse,
Certes, is the flow of souls :
Infinitest tendencies
By the finite prest and pent,
In the finite, turbulent,
How we tremble in surprise,
When sometimes, with an awful sound,
God's great plummet strikes the ground !

II

The champ of the steeds on the silver
        bit.
As they whirl the rich man's carriage by;
The beggar's whine as he looks at it,—
But it goes too fast for charity ;
The trail on the street of the poor man's
        broom,
That the lady who walks to her palace-
        home,
On her silken skirt may catch no dust ;
The tread of the business-men who must
Count their per-cents by the paces they
        take ;
The cry of the babe unheard of its mother
Though it lie on her breast, while she
        thinks of the other
Laid yesterday where it will not wake ;
The flower-girl's prayer to buy roses
        and pinks,
Held out in the smoke, like stars by day ;
The gin-door's oath that hollowly chinks
Guilt upon grief and wrong upon hate ;
The cabman's cry to get out of the way
The dustman's call down the area-grate,
The young maid's jest, and the old wife's
        scold,
The haggling talk of the boys at a stall,
The fight in the street which is backed
        for gold,

The plea of the lawyers in Westminster
    Hall ;
The drop on the stones of the blind
    man's staff
As he trades in his own grief's sacredness ;
The brothel shriek, and the Newgate
    laugh,
The hum upon 'Change, and the organ's
    grinding—
The grinder's face being nevertheless
Dry and vacant of even woe,
While the children's hearts are leaping so
At the merry music's winding ;
The black-plumed funeral's creeping train,
Long and slow (and yet they will go
As fast as Life, though it hurry and strain),
Creeping the populous houses through,
And nodding their plumes at either side,—
At many a house where an infant, new
To the sunshiny world, has just struggled
    and cried,—
At many a house, where sitteth a bride
Trying to-morrow's coronals
With a scarlet blush to-day :
    Slowly creep the funerals,
As none should hear the noise and say,
'The living, the living, must go away
    To multiply the dead.'
Hark ! an upward shout is sent !
In grave strong joy from tower to steeple
    The bells ring out—
The trumpets sound, the people shout,
The young queen goes to her Parliament.
She turneth round her large blue eyes,
More bright with childish memories
Than royal hopes, upon the people :
On either side she bows her head
    Lowly, with a queenly grace,
And smile most trusting-innocent,
As if she smiled upon her mother ;
The thousands press before each other
    To bless her to her face ;
And booms the deep majestic voice
Through trump and drum,—' May the
    queen rejoice
    In the people's liberties ! '—

III

I dwell amid the city,
And hear the flow of souls in act and
    speech,
For pomp or trade, for merrymake or
    folly ;

I hear the confluence and sum of each,
    And that is melancholy !—
Thy voice is a complaint, O crownèd city,
The blue sky covering thee like God's
    great pity.

IV

O blue sky ! it mindeth me
Of places where I used to see
Its vast unbroken circle thrown
From the far pale-peakèd hill
Out to the last verge of ocean,
As by God's arm it were done
Then for the first time, with the emotion
Of that first impulse on it still.
Oh, we spirits fly at will,
Faster than the wingèd steed
Whereof in old book we read,
With the sunlight foaming back
From his flanks to a misty wrack,
And his nostril reddening proud
As he breasteth the steep thundercloud,—
Smoother than Sabrina's chair
Gliding up from wave to air,
While she smileth debonair
Yet holy, coldly and yet brightly,
Like her own mooned waters nightly,
    Through her dripping hair.

V

Very fast and smooth we fly,
Spirits, though the flesh be by.
All looks feed not from the eye,
Nor all hearings from the ear ;
We can hearken and espy
Without either ; we can journey
Bold and gay as knight to tourney,
And though we wear no visor down
To dark our countenance, the foe
Shall never chafe us as we go.

VI

I am gone from peopled town !
It passeth its street-thunder round
My body which yet hears no sound :
For now another sound, another
Vision, my soul's senses have—
O'er a hundred valleys deep,
Where the hills' green shadows sleep
Scarce known (because the valley-trees
Cross those upland images),
O'er a hundred hills, each other
Watching to the western wave,

I have travelled,—I have found
The silent, lone, remembered ground.

VII

I have found a grassy niche
Hollowed in a seaside hill,
As if the ocean-grandeur which
Is aspectable from the place
Had struck the hill as with a mace
Sudden and cleaving.   You might fill
That little nook with the little cloud
Which sometimes lieth by the moon
To beautify a night of June.
A cavelike nook, which, opening all
To the wide sea, is disallowed
From its own earth's sweet pastoral;
Cavelike, but roofless overhead,
And made of verdant banks instead
Of any rocks, with flowerets spread,
Instead of spar and stalactite,
Cowslips and daisies, gold and white;
Such pretty flowers on such green sward,
You think the sea they look toward
Doth serve them for another sky
As warm and blue as that on high.

VIII

And in this hollow is a seat,
And when you shall have crept to it,
Slipping down the banks too steep
To be o'erbrowsèd by the sheep,
Do not think—though at your feet
The cliff's disrupt—you shall behold
The line where earth and ocean meet.
You sit too much above to view
The solemn confluence of the two:
You can hear them as they greet;
You can hear that evermore
Distance-softened noise, more old
Than Nereid's singing,—the tide spent
Joining soft issues with the shore
In harmony of discontent,—
And when you hearken to the grave
Lamenting of the underwave,
You must believe in earth's communion,
Albeit you witness not the union.

IX

Except that sound, the place is full
Of silences, which when you cull
By any word, it thrills you so
That presently you let them grow

To meditation's fullest length
Across your soul with a soul's strength:
And as they touch your soul, they borrow
Both of its grandeur and its sorrow,
That deathly odour which the clay
Leaves on its deathlessness alway.

X

Alway! alway? must this be?
Rapid Soul from city gone,
Dost thou carry inwardly
What doth make the city's moan?
Must this deep sigh of thine own
Haunt thee with humanity?
Green-visioned banks that are too steep
To be o'erbrowsèd by the sheep,
May all sad thoughts adown you creep
Without a shepherd?—Mighty sea,
Can we dwarf thy magnitude,
And fit it to our straitest mood?—
O fair, fair Nature! are we thus
Impotent and querulous
Among thy workings glorious,
Wealth and sanctities,—that still
Leave us vacant and defiled,
And wailing like a soft-kissed child,
Kissed soft against his will?

XI

God, God!
With a child's voice I cry,
Weak, sad, confidingly—
God, God!
Thou knowest, eyelids, raised not
always up
Unto Thy love (as none of ours are), droop
As ours, o'er many a tear!
Thou knowest, though Thy universe is
broad,
Two little tears suffice to cover all:
Thou knowest, thou, who art so prodigal
Of beauty, we are oft but stricken deer
Expiring in the woods—that care for none
Of those delightsome flowers they die
upon.

XII

O blissful Mouth which breathed the
mournful breath
We name our souls, self-spoilt!—by
that strong passion
Which paled Thee once with sighs,—by
that strong death

Which made Thee once unbreathing—
　　from the wrack
Themselves have called around them,
　　call them back,
Back to Thee in continuous aspiration !
　　For here, O Lord,
For here they travel vainly,—vainly pass
From city pavement to untrodden sward,
Where the lark finds her deep nest in
　　the grass
Cold with the earth's last dew. Yea,
　　very vain
The greatest speed of all these souls of
　　men,
Unless they travel upward to the throne,
Where sittest THOU, the satisfying ONE,
With help for sins and holy perfectings
For all requirements—while the arch-
　　angel, raising
Unto Thy face his full ecstatic gazing,
Forgets the rush and rapture of his wings.

TO BETTINE

THE CHILD-FRIEND OF GOETHE

I have the second sight, Goethe!
　　　　Letters of a Child.

I

BETTINE, friend of Goethe,
Hadst thou the second sight—
Upturning worship and delight
　　With such a loving duty
To his grand face, as women will,
The childhood 'neath thine eyelids still ?

II

Before his shrine to doom thee,
Using the same child's smile
That heaven and earth, beheld erewhile
　　For the first time, won from thee,
Ere star and flower grew dim and dead,
Save at his feet and o'er his head ?

III

Digging thine heart and throwing
Away its childhood's gold,
That so its woman-depth might hold
　　His spirit's overflowing ?

For surging souls, no worlds can bound,
Their channel in the heart have found.

IV

O child, to change appointed,
Thou hadst not second sight !
What eyes the future view aright,
　　Unless by tears anointed ?
Yea, only tears themselves can show
The burning ones that have to flow.

V

O woman, deeply loving,
Thou hadst not second sight !
The star is very high and bright,
　　And none can see it moving.
Love looks around, below, above,
Yet all his prophecy is—love.

VI

The bird thy childhood's playing
Sent onward o'er the sea,
Thy dove of hope came back to thee
　　Without a leaf. Art laying
Its wet cold wing no sun can dry,
Still in thy bosom secretly ?

VII

Our Goethe's friend, Bettine,
I have the second sight !
The stone upon his grave is white,
　　The funeral stone between ye ;
And in thy mirror thou hast viewed
Some change as hardly understood.

VIII

Where's childhood ? where is Goethe ?
The tears are in thine eyes.
Nay, thou shalt yet reorganize
　　Thy maidenhood of beauty
In his own glory, which is smooth
Of wrinkles and sublime in youth.

IX

The poet's arms have wound thee,
He breathes upon thy brow,
He lifts thee upward in the glow
　　Of his great genius round thee,—
The childlike poet undefiled
Preserving evermore THE CHILD.

MAN AND NATURE

A SAD man on a summer day
Did look upon the earth and say—

'Purple cloud, the hill-top binding,
Folded hills, the valleys wind in,
Valleys, with fresh streams among you,
Streams, with bosky trees along you,
Trees, with many birds and blossoms,
Birds, with music-trembling bosoms,
Blossoms, dropping dews that wreathe
    you
To your fellow flowers beneath you,
Flowers, that constellate on earth,
Earth, that shakest to the mirth
Of the merry Titan ocean,
All his shining hair in motion !
Why am I thus the only one
Who can be dark beneath the sun ?'

But when the summer day was past,
He looked to heaven and smiled at last,
Self-answered so—
        'Because, O cloud,
Pressing with thy crumpled shroud
Heavily on mountain top,—
Hills, that almost seem to drop,
Stricken with a misty death
To the valleys underneath,—
Valleys, sighing with the torrent,—
Waters, streaked with branches hor-
    rent,—
Branchless trees, that shake your head
Wildly o'er your blossoms spread
Where the common flowers are found,—
Flowers, with foreheads to the ground,—
Ground, that shriekest while the sea
With his iron smiteth thee—
I am, besides, the only one
Who can be bright *without* the sun.'

A SEASIDE WALK

I

WE walked beside the sea
After a day which perished silently
Of its own glory—like the princess weird
Who, combating the Genius, scorched
    and seared,
Uttered with burning breath, 'Ho !
    victory !'
And sank adown a heap of ashes pale.
So runs the Arab tale.

II

The sky above us showed
A universal and unmoving cloud,
On which the cliffs permitted us to see
Only the outline of their majesty,
As master-minds when gazed at by the
    crowd !
And, shining with a gloom, the water grey
    Swang in its moon-taught way.

III

Nor moon nor stars were out :
They did not dare to tread so soon about,
Though trembling, in the footsteps of
    the sun ;
The light was neither night's nor day's,
    but one
Which, life-like, had a beauty in its doubt,
And Silence's impassioned breathings
    round
    Seemed wandering into sound.

IV

O solemn-beating heart
Of nature ! I have knowledge that thou art
Bound unto man's by cords he cannot
    sever—
And, what time they are slackened by
    him ever,
So to attest his own supernal part,
Still runneth thy vibration fast and strong
    The slackened cord along.

V

For though we never spoke
Of the grey water and the shaded rock,
Dark wave and stone unconsciously were
    fused
Into the plaintive speaking that we used
Of absent friends and memories unfor-
    sook ;
And, had we seen each other's face, we
    had
    Seen haply, each was sad.

THE SEA-MEW

AFFECTIONATELY INSCRIBED TO
M. E. H.

I

How joyously the young sea-mew
Lay dreaming on the waters blue,
Whereon our little bark had thrown
A little shade, the only one,—
But shadows ever man pursue.

II

Familiar with the waves and free
As if their own white foam were he,
His heart upon the heart of ocean
Lay learning all its mystic motion,
And throbbing to the throbbing sea.

III

And such a brightness in his eye,
As if the ocean and the sky
Within him had lit up and nurst
A soul God gave him not at first,
To comprehend their majesty.

IV

We were not cruel, yet did sunder
His white wing from the blue waves
under,
And bound it, while his fearless eyes
Shone up to ours in calm surprise,
As deeming us some ocean wonder !

V

We bore our ocean bird unto
A grassy place, where he might view
The flowers that curtsy to the bees,
The waving of the tall green trees,
The falling of the silver dew.

VI

But flowers of earth were pale to him
Who had seen the rainbow fishes swim;
And when earth's dew around him lay
He thought of ocean's wingèd spray,
And his eye waxèd sad and dim.

VII

The green trees round him only made
A prison with their darksome shade ;
And drooped his wing, and mournèd he
For his own boundless glittering sea—
Albeit he knew not they could fade.

VIII

Then One her gladsome face did bring,
Her gentle voice's murmuring,
In ocean's stead his heart to move
And teach him what was human love—
He thought it a strange, mournful thing.

IX

He lay down in his grief to die
(First looking to the sea-like sky
That hath no waves !), because, alas !
Our human touch did on him pass,
And with our touch, our agony.

FELICIA HEMANS

TO L. E. L.[1], REFERRING TO HER
MONODY ON THE POETESS [2]

I

Thou bay-crowned living One that o'er
the bay-crowned Dead art bowing,
And o'er the shadeless moveless brow
the vital shadow throwing,
And o'er the sighless songless lips the
wail and music wedding,
And dropping o'er the tranquil eyes,
the tears not of their shedding !—

II

Take music from the silent Dead, whose
meaning is completer,
Reserve thy tears for living brows,
where all such tears are meeter,
And leave the violets in the grass to
brighten where thou treadest !
No flowers for her ! no need of flowers—
albeit 'bring flowers,' thou saidest.

III

Yes, flowers, to crown the 'cup and
lute !' since both may come to
breaking;
Or flowers, to greet the 'bride !' the
heart's own beating works its
aching ;
Or flowers, to soothe the 'captive's'
sight, from earth's free bosom
gathered,
Reminding of his earthly hope, then
withering as it withered.

[1] Letitia Elizabeth Landon, 1802–38.
[2] Mrs. Hemans died 1835.

IV

But bring not near the solemn corse,
    a type of human seeming,
Lay only dust's stern verity upon the
    dust undreaming ;
And while the calm perpetual stars shall
    look upon it solely,
Her spherèd soul shall look on *them*,
    with eyes more bright and holy.

V

Nor mourn, O living One, because her
    part in life was mourning.
Would she have lost the poet's fire for
    anguish of the burning ?—
The minstrel harp, for the strained string?
    the tripod, for the afflated
Woe? or the vision, for those tears in
    which it shone dilated?

VI

Perhaps she shuddered while the world's
    cold hand her brow was wreathing.
But never wronged that mystic breath
    which breathed in all her breath-
    ing,
Which drew from rocky earth and man,
    abstractions high and moving,
Beauty, if not the beautiful, and love, if
    not the loving.

VII

Such visionings have paled in sight ;
    the Saviour she descrieth.
And little recks *who* wreathed the brow
    which on His bosom lieth :
The whiteness of His innocence o'er all
    her garments, flowing,
There, learneth she the sweet ' new song,'
    she will not mourn in knowing.

VIII

Be happy, crowned and living One !
    and, as thy dust decayeth,
May thine own England say for thee,
    what now for Her it sayeth—
' Albeit softly in our ears her silver song
    was ringing,
The footfall of her parting soul is softer
    than her singing !'

L. E. L.'S LAST QUESTION

Do you think of me as I think of you?
    From her poem written during the
    voyage to the Cape.

I

' Do you think of me as I think of you,
My friends, my friends?'—She said it
    from the sea,
The English minstrel in her minstrelsy,
While, under brighter skies than erst
    she knew,
Her heart grew dark, and groped there,
    as the blind,
To reach across the waves friends left
    behind—
' Do you think of me as I think of you?'

II

It seemed not much to ask—as *I* of *you?*
We all do ask the same. No eyelids cover
Within the meekest eyes, that question
    over.
And little in the world the Loving do
But sit (among the rocks?) and listen for
The echo of their own love evermore—
' Do you think of me as I think of you?'

III

Love-learnèd she had sung of love and
    love,—
And like a child that, sleeping with
    dropt head
Upon the fairy-book he lately read,
Whatever household noises round him
    move,
Hears in his dream some elfin turbu-
    lence,—
Even so, suggestive to her inward sense,
All sounds of life assumed one tune of love.

IV

And when the glory of her dream with-
    drew,
When knightly gestes and courtly
    pageantries
Were broken in her visionary eyes
By tears the solemn seas attested true.—
Forgetting that sweet lute beside her hand
She asked not, ' Do you praise me, O
    my land?'—
But, ' Think ye of me, friends, as I of
    you?'

v

Hers was the hand that played for many
    a year
Love's silver phrase for England,—
    smooth and well.
Would God, her heart's more inward
    oracle
In that lone moment might confirm her
    dear !
For when her questioned friends in agony
Made passionate response, 'We think of
    thee,'
Her place was in the dust, too deep to
    hear.

vi

Could she not wait to catch their answer-
    ing breath ?
Was she content, content, with ocean's
    sound,
Which dashed its mocking infinite around
One thirsty for a little love ?—beneath
Those stars content, where last her song
    had gone,—
They mute and cold in radiant life,—as
    soon
Their singer was to be, in darksome
    death [1] ?

vii

Bring your vain answers—cry, 'We
    think of thee !'
How think ye of her ? warm in long ago
Delights ?—or crowned with budding
    bays ? Not so.
None smile and none are crowned where
    lieth she,
With all her visions unfulfilled save one,
Her childhood's—of the palm-trees in
    the sun—
And lo ! their shadow on her sepulchre !

viii

' Do ye think of me as I think of you ?'—
O friends, O kindred, O dear brotherhood
Of all the world ! what are we, that we
    should
For covenants of long affection sue ?
Why press so near each other when the
    touch
Is barred by graves ? Not much, and yet
    too much,
Is this 'Think of me as I think of you.'

[1] Her lyric on the polar star came home with
her latest papers.

ix

But while on mortal lips I shape anew
A sigh to mortal issues,—verily
Above the unshaken stars that see us
    die,
A vocal pathos rolls ; and HE who drew
All life from dust, and for all, tasted
    death,
By death and life and love, appealing,
    saith,
Do you think of Me as I think of you ?

CROWNED AND WEDDED

i

WHEN last before her people's face her
    own fair face she bent,
Within the meek projection of that
    shade she was content
To erase the child-smile from her lips,
    which seemed as if it might
Be still kept holy from the world to
    childhood still in sight—
To erase it with a solemn vow,—a
    princely vow—to rule ;
A priestly vow—to rule by grace of God
    the pitiful ;
A very godlike vow—to rule in right and
    righteousness,
And with the law and for the land !—so
    God the vower bless !

ii

The minster was alight that day, but
    not with fire, I ween,
And long-drawn glitterings swept adown
    that mighty aislèd scene;
The priests stood stolèd in their pomp,
    the sworded chiefs in theirs,
And so, the collared knights, and so, the
    civil ministers,
And so, the waiting lords and dames—
    and little pages best
At holding trains—and legates so, from
    countries east and west.
So, alien princes, native peers, and high-
    born ladies bright,
Along whose brows the Queen's, new
    crowned, flashed coronets to light.

And so, the people at the gates, with priestly hands on high,
Which bring the first anointing to all legal majesty.
And so the DEAD—who lie in rows beneath the minster floor,
There, verily an awful state maintaining evermore;
The statesman whose clean palm will kiss no bribe, whate'er it be,
The courtier who, for no fair queen, will rise up to his knee;
The court-dame who, for no court-tire, will leave her shroud behind;
The laureate who no courtlier rime than 'dust to dust' can find;
The kings and queens who having made that vow and worn that crown,
Descended unto lower thrones and darker, deep adown!
Dieu et mon droit—what is 't to them?— what meaning can it have?—
The King of kings, the right of death— God's judgement and the grave.
And when betwixt the quick and dead, the young fair queen had vowed,
The living shouted 'May she live! Victoria, live!' aloud.
And as the loyal shouts went up, true spirits prayed between,
'The blessings happy monarchs have, be thine, O crownèd queen!'

III

But now before her people's face she bendeth her's anew,
And calls them, while she vows, to be her witness thereunto.
She vowed to rule, and, in that oath, her childhood put away:
She doth maintain her womanhood, in vowing love to-day.
O lovely lady!—let her vow!—such lips become such vows,
And fairer goeth bridal wreath than crown with vernal brows.
O lovely lady!—let her vow!—yea, let her vow to love!—
And though she be no less a queen— with purples hung above,

The pageant of a court behind, the royal kin around,
And woven gold to catch her looks turned maidenly to ground,
Yet may the bride-veil hide from her a little of that state,
While loving hopes, for retinues, about her sweetness wait.
SHE vows to love who vowed to rule— (the chosen at her side)
Let none say, 'God preserve the queen!' —but rather, 'Bless the bride!'
None blow the trump, none bend the knee, none violate the dream
Wherein no monarch but a wife, she to herself may seem.
Or if ye say, 'Preserve the queen!'— oh, breathe it inward low—
She is a *woman*, and *beloved!*—and 'tis enough but so.
Count it enough, thou noble prince, who tak'st her by the hand,
And claimest for thy lady-love, our lady of the land!
And since, Prince Albert, men have called thy spirit high and rare,
And true to truth and brave for truth, as some at Augsburg were,—
We charge thee by thy lofty thoughts, and by thy poet-mind
Which not by glory and degree takes measure of mankind,
Esteem that wedded hand less dear for sceptre than for ring,
And hold her uncrowned womanhood to be the royal thing.

IV

And now, upon our queen's last vow, what blessings shall we pray?
None, straitened to a shallow crown, will suit our lips to-day.
Behold, they must be free as love—they must be broad as free,
Even to the borders of heaven's light and earth's humanity.
Long live she!—send up loyal shouts— and true hearts pray between,—
'The blessings happy PEASANTS have, be thine, O crownèd queen!'

CROWNED AND BURIED

I

NAPOLEON!—years ago, and that great word
Compàct of human breath in hate and dread
And exultation, skied us overhead—
An atmosphere whose lightning was the sword
Scathing the cedars of the world,—drawn down
In burnings, by the metal of a crown.

II

Napoleon! nations, while they cursed that name,
Shook at their own curse; and while others bore
Its sound, as of a trumpet, on before,
Brass-fronted legions justified its fame;
And dying men, on trampled battle-sods,
Near their last silence, uttered it for God's.

III

Napoleon! sages, with high foreheads drooped,
Did use it for a problem : children small
Leapt up to greet it, as at manhood's call :
Priests blessed it from their altars overstooped
By meek-eyed Christs,—and widows with a moan
Spake it, when questioned why they sate alone.

IV

That name consumed the silence of the snows
In Alpine keeping, holy and cloud-hid;
The mimic eagles dared what Nature's did,
And over-rushed her mountainous repose
In search of eyries; and the Egyptian river
Mingled the same word with its grand 'For ever.'

V

That name was shouted near the pyramidal
Nilotic tombs, whose mummied habitants,
Packed to humanity's significance,
Motioned it back with stillness! shouts as idle
As hireling artists' work of myrrh and spice
Which swathed last glories round the Ptolemies.

VI

The world's face changed to hear it. Kingly men
Came down in chidden babes' bewilderment
From autocratic places, each content
With sprinkled ashes for anointing.—Then
The people laughed, or wondered for the nonce,
To see one throne a composite of thrones.

VII

Napoleon! even the torrid vastitude
Of India felt in throbbings of the air
That name which scattered by disastrous blare
All Europe's bound-lines,—drawn afresh in blood.
Napoleon—from the Russias, west to Spain!
And Austria trembled—till ye heard her chain.

VIII

And Germany was 'ware; and Italy
Oblivious of old fames—her laurel-locked,
High-ghosted Caesars passing unin-voked—
Did crumble her own ruins with her knee,
To serve a newer.—Aye! but Frenchmen cast
A future from them nobler than her past.

IX

For, verily, though France augustly rose
With that raised NAME, and did assume by such
The purple of the world, none gave so much
As she, in purchase—to speak plain, in loss—

Whose hands, toward freedom stretched,
    dropped paralysed
To wield a sword or fit an undersized

X

King's crown to a great man's head. And
    though along
Her Paris' streets, did float on frequent
    streams
Of triumph, pictured or emmarbled
    dreams
Dreamt right by genius in a world gone
    wrong,—
No dream, of all so won, was fair to see
As the lost vision of her liberty.

XI

Napoleon! 'twas a high name lifted high!
It met at last God's thunder sent to clear
Our compassing and covering atmosphere
And open a clear sight beyond the sky
Of supreme empire; this of earth's was
    done—
And kings crept out again to feel the sun.

XII

The kings crept out—the peoples sate at
    home,
And finding the long-invocated peace
(A pall embroidered with worn images
Of rights divine) too scant to cover doom
Such as they suffered,—cursed the corn
    that grew
Rankly, to bitter bread, on Waterloo.

XIII

A deep gloom centred in the deep repose;
The nations stood up mute to count their
    dead.
And *he* who owned the NAME which
    vibrated
Through silence,—trusting to his noblest
    foes
When earth was all too grey for chivalry,
Died of their mercies 'mid the desert sea.

XIV

O wild St. Helen! very still she kept him,
With a green willow for all pyramid,—
Which stirred a little if the low wind did,
A little more, if pilgrims overwept him,
Disparting the little boughs to see the clay
Which seemed to cover his for judgement-
    day.

XV

Nay, not so long!—France kept her old
    affection
As deeply as the sepulchre the corse,
Until, dilated by such love's remorse
To a new angel of the resurrection,
She cried, 'Behold, thou England! I
    would have
The dead whereof thou wottest, from
    that grave.'

XVI

And England answered in the courtesy
Which, ancient foes turned lovers, may
    befit,—
'Take back thy dead! and when thou
    buriest it,
Throw in all former strifes 'twixt thee
    and me.'
Amen, mine England! 'tis a courteous
    claim—
But ask a little room too... for thy shame!

XVII

Because it was not well, it was not well,
Nor tuneful with thy lofty-chanted part
Among the Oceanides,—that Heart
To bind and bare and vex with vulture fell.
I would, my noble England! men might
    seek
All crimson stains upon thy breast—not
    cheek!

XVIII

I would that hostile fleets had scarred
    Torbay,
Instead of the lone ship which waited
    moored
Until thy princely purpose was assured,
Then left a shadow, not to pass away—
Not for to-night's moon, nor to-
    morrow's sun!
Green watching hills, ye witnessed what
    was done[1]!

XIX

But since it *was* done,—in sepulchral dust
We fain would pay back something of
    our debt
To France, if not to honour, and forget
How through much fear we falsified the
    trust
Of a fallen foe and exile.—We return
Orestes to Electra... in his urn.

[1] Written at Torquay.

XX

A little urn—a little dust inside,
Which once outbalanced the large earth, albeit
To-day a four-years child might carry it
Sleek-browed and smiling, 'Let the burden 'bide!'
Orestes to Electra!—O fair town
Of Paris, how the wild tears will run down

XXI

And run back in the chariot-marks of time,
When all the people shall come forth to meet
The passive victor, death-still in the street
He rode through 'mid the shouting and bell-chime
And martial music, under eagles which
Dyed their rapacious beaks at Austerlitz.

XXII

Napoleon! he hath come again—borne home
Upon the popular ebbing heart,—a sea
Which gathers its own wrecks perpetually,
Majestically moaning. Give him room!—
Room for the dead in Paris! welcome solemn
And grave-deep, 'neath the cannon-moulded column [1]!

XXIII

There, weapon spent and warrior spent may rest
From roar of fields,—provided Jupiter
Dare trust Saturnus to lie down so near
His bolts!—and this he may. For, dispossessed
Of any godship lies the godlike arm—
The goat, Jove sucked, as likely to do harm.

XXIV

And yet . . . Napoleon!—the recovered name
Shakes the old casements of the world! and we
Look out upon the passing pageantry,
Attesting that the Dead makes good his claim

[1] It was the first intention to bury him under the column.

To a French grave,—another kingdom won,
The last, of few spans—by Napoleon.

XXV

Blood fell like dew beneath his sunrise—sooth;
But glittered dew-like in the covenanted
Meridian light. He was a despot—granted!
But the αὐτός of his autocratic mouth
Said yea i' the people's French; he magnified
The image of the freedom he denied.

XXVI

And if they asked for rights, he made reply
'Ye have my glory!'—and so, drawing round them
His ample purple, glorified and bound them
In an embrace that seemed identity.
He ruled them like a tyrant—true! but none
Were ruled like slaves: each felt Napoleon.

XXVII

I do not praise this man: the man was flawed
For Adam—much more, Christ!—his knee unbent,
His hand unclean, his aspiration pent
Within a sword-sweep—pshaw!—but since he had
The genius to be loved, why, let him have
The justice to be honoured in his grave.

XXVIII

I think this nation's tears thus poured together
Better than shouts. I think this funeral
Grander than crownings, though a Pope bless all.
I think this grave stronger than thrones. But whether
The crowned Napoleon or the buried clay
Be worthier, I discern not. Angels may.

TO FLUSH, MY DOG

I

Loving friend, the gift of one
Who her own true faith has run
 Through thy lower nature [1],
Be my benediction said
With my hand upon thy head,
 Gentle fellow creature!

II

Like a lady's ringlets brown,
Flow thy silken ears adown
 Either side demurely
Of thy silver-suited breast,
Shining out from all the rest
 Of thy body purely.

III

Darkly brown thy body is,
Till the sunshine striking this
 Alchemize its dullness,
When the sleek curls manifold
Flash all over into gold,
 With a burnished fullness.

IV

Underneath my stroking hand,
Startled eyes of hazel bland
 Kindling, growing larger,
Up thou leapest with a spring,
Full of prank and curveting,
 Leaping like a charger.

V

Leap! thy broad tail waves a light;
Leap! thy slender feet are bright,
 Canopied in fringes;
Leap—those tasselled ears of thine
Flicker strangely, fair and fine,
 Down their golden inches.

VI

Yet, my pretty, sportive friend,
Little is 't to such an end
 That I praise thy rareness!
Other dogs may be thy peers
Haply in these drooping ears,
 And this glossy fairness.

[1] This dog was the gift of my dear and admired friend, Miss Mitford, and belongs to the beautiful race she has rendered celebrated among English and American readers. The Flushes have their laurels as well as the Caesars,—the chief difference (at least the very head and front of it) consisting, perhaps, in the bald head of the latter under the crown. [1844.]

VII

But of *thee* it shall be said,
This dog watched beside a bed
 Day and night unweary,—
Watched within a curtained room,
Where no sunbeam brake the gloom
 Round the sick and dreary.

VIII

Roses, gathered for a vase,
In that chamber died apace,
 Beam and breeze resigning;
This dog only, waited on,
Knowing that when light is gone
 Love remains for shining.

IX

Other dogs in thymy dew
Tracked the hares and followed through
 Sunny moor or meadow;
This dog only, crept and crept
Next a languid cheek that slept,
 Sharing in the shadow.

X

Other dogs of loyal cheer
Bounded at the whistle clear,
 Up the woodside hieing;
This dog only, watched in reach
Of a faintly uttered speech,
 Or a louder sighing.

XI

And if one or two quick tears
Dropped upon his glossy ears,
 Or a sigh came double,—
Up he sprang in eager haste,
Fawning, fondling, breathing fast,
 In a tender trouble.

XII

And this dog was satisfied
If a pale thin hand would glide
 Down his dewlaps sloping,—
Which he pushed his nose within,
After,—platforming his chin
 On the palm left open.

XIII

This dog, if a friendly voice
Call him now to blyther choice
 Than such chamber-keeping,
'Come out!' praying from the door,—
Presseth backward as before,
 Up against me leaping.

XIV

Therefore to this dog will I,
Tenderly not scornfully,
    Render praise and favour :
With my hand upon his head,
Is my benediction said
    Therefore, and for ever.

XV

And because he loves me so,
Better than his kind will do
    Often, man or woman,
Give I back more love again
Than dogs often take of men,
    Leaning from my Human.

XVI

Blessings on thee, dog of mine,
Pretty collars make thee fine,
    Sugared milk make fat thee !
Pleasures wag on in thy tail,
Hands of gentle motion fail
    Nevermore, to pat thee !

XVII

Downy pillow take thy head,
Silken coverlid bestead,
    Sunshine help thy sleeping !
No fly's buzzing wake thee up,
No man break thy purple cup,
    Set for drinking deep in.

XVIII

Whiskered cats arointed flee,
Sturdy stoppers keep from thee
    Cologne distillations ;
Nuts lie in thy path for stones,
And thy feast-day macaroons
    Turn to daily rations !

XIX

Mock I thee, in wishing weal ?—
Tears are in my eyes to feel
    Thou art made so straitly,
Blessing needs must straiten too,—
Little canst thou joy or do,
    Thou who lovest *greatly*.

XX

Yet be blessèd to the height
Of all good and all delight
    Pervious to thy nature ;
Only *loved* beyond that line,
With a love that answers thine,
    Loving fellow creature !

THE DESERTED GARDEN

I MIND me in the days departed,
How often underneath the sun
With childish bounds I used to run
    To a garden long deserted.

The beds and walks were vanished quite;
And wheresoe'er had struck the spade,
The greenest grasses Nature laid,
    To sanctify her right.

I called the place my wilderness,
For no one entered there but I ;
The sheep looked in, the grass to espy,
    And passed it ne'ertheless.

The trees were interwoven wild,
And spread their boughs enough about
To keep both sheep and shepherd out,
    But not a happy child.

Adventurous joy it was for me !
I crept beneath the boughs, and found
A circle smooth of mossy ground
    Beneath a poplar tree.

Old garden rose-trees hedged it in,
Bedropt with roses waxen-white
Well satisfied with dew and light
    And careless to be seen.

Long years ago it might befall,
When all the garden flowers were trim,
The grave old gardener prided him
    On these the most of all.

Some lady, stately overmuch,
Here moving with a silken noise,
Has blushed beside them at the voice
    That likened her to such.

And these, to make a diadem,
She often may have plucked and twined,
Half-smiling as it came to mind
    That few would look at *them*.

Oh, little thought that lady proud,
A child would watch her fair white rose,
When buried lay her whiter brows,
    And silk was changed for shroud !—

Nor thought that gardener (full of scorns
For men unlearned and simple phrase),
A child would bring it all its praise
   By creeping through the thorns !

To me upon my low moss seat,
Though never a dream the roses sent
Of science or love's compliment,
   I ween they smelt as sweet.

It did not move my grief to see
The trace of human step departed :
Because the garden was deserted,
   The blither place for me !

Friends, blame me not ! a narrow ken
Has childhood 'twixt the sun and sward :
We draw the moral afterward—
   We feel the gladness then.

And gladdest hours for me did glide
In silence at the rose-tree wall ;
A thrush made gladness musical
   Upon the other side.

Nor he nor I did e'er incline
To peck or pluck the blossoms white ;
How should I know but roses might
   Lead lives as glad as mine ?

To make my hermit-home complete,
I brought clear water from the spring
Praised in its own low murmuring,—
   And cresses glossy wet.

And so, I thought, my likeness grew
(Without the melancholy tale)
To ' gentle hermit of the dale,'
   And Angelina too.

For oft I read within my nook
Such minstrel stories ; till the breeze
Made sounds poetic in the trees,—
   And then I shut the book.

If I shut this wherein I write
I hear no more the wind athwart
Those trees,—nor feel that childish heart
   Delighting in delight.

My childhood from my life is parted,
My footstep from the moss which drew
Its fairy circle round : anew
   The garden is deserted.

Another thrush may there rehearse
The madrigals which sweetest are ;
No more for me !—myself afar
   Do sing a sadder verse.

Ah me, ah me ! when erst I lay
In that child's-nest so greenly wrought,
I laughed unto myself and thought
   ' The time will pass away.'

And still I laughed, and did not fear
But that, whene'er was past away
The childish time, some happier play
   My womanhood would cheer.

I knew the time would pass away,
And yet, beside the rose-tree wall,
Dear God, how seldom, if at all,
   Did I look up to pray !

The time is past ;—and now that grows
The cypress high among the trees,
And I behold white sepulchres
   As well as the white rose,—

When graver, meeker thoughts are given,
And I have learnt to lift my face,
Reminded how earth's greenest place
   The colour draws from heaven,—

It something saith for earthly pain,
But more for Heavenly promise free,
That I who was, would shrink to be
   That happy child again.

MY DOVES

O Weisheit ! Du red'st wie eine Taube!
                GOETHE.

My little doves have left a nest
   Upon an Indian tree,
Whose leaves fantastic take their rest
   Or motion from the sea ;
For, ever there, the sea-winds go
With sunlit paces to and fro.

The tropic flowers looked up to it,
   The tropic stars looked down,
And there my little doves did sit,
   With feathers softly brown,
And glittering eyes that showed their
     right
To general Nature's deep delight.

And God them taught, at every close
  Of murmuring waves beyond,
And green leaves round, to interpose
  Their choral voices fond,
Interpreting that love must be
The meaning of the earth and sea.

Fit ministers! Of living loves,
  Theirs hath the calmest fashion,
Their living voice the likest moves
  To lifeless intonation.
The lovely monotone of springs
And winds, and such insensate things.

My little doves were ta'en away
  From that glad nest of theirs,
Across an ocean rolling grey,
  And tempest-clouded airs :
My little doves,—who lately knew
The sky and wave by warmth and blue!

And now, within the city prison,
  In mist and chillness pent,
With sudden upward look they listen
  For sounds of past content—
For lapse of water, swell of breeze,
Or nut-fruit falling from the trees.

The stir without the glow of passion,
  The triumph of the mart,
The gold and silver as they clash on
  Man's cold metallic heart—
The roar of wheels, the cry for bread,—
These only sounds are heard instead.

Yet still, as on my human hand
  Their fearless heads they lean,
And almost seem to understand
  What human musings mean,
(Their eyes, with such a plaintive shine,
Are fastened upwardly to mine !)

Soft falls their chant as on the nest
  Beneath the sunny zone ;
For love that stirred it in their breast
  Has not aweary grown,
And 'neath the city's shade can keep
The well of music clear and deep.

And love that keeps the music, fills
  With pastoral memories :
All echoings from out the hills,
  All droppings from the skies,
All flowings from the wave and wind,
Remembered in their chant, I find.

So teach ye me the wisest part,
  My little doves ! to move
Along the city-ways with heart
  Assured by holy love,
And vocal with such songs as own
A fountain to the world unknown.

'Twas hard to sing by Babel's stream—
  More hard, in Babel's street !
But if the soulless creatures deem
  Their music not unmeet
For sunless walls—let *us* begin,
Who wear immortal wings within !

To me, fair memories belong
  Of scenes that used to bless,
For no regret, but present song,
  And lasting thankfulness,
And very soon to break away,
Like types, in purer things than they.

I will have hopes that cannot fade,
  For flowers the valley yields !
I will have humble thoughts instead
  Of silent, dewy fields !
My spirit and my God shall be
My seaward hill, my boundless sea.

HECTOR IN THE GARDEN

I

Nine years old ! The first of any
  Seem the happiest years that come :
Yet when *I* was nine, I said
  No such word !—I thought instead
That the Greeks had used as many
  In besieging Ilium.

II

Nine green years had scarcely brought me
  To my childhood's haunted spring :
I had life, like flowers and bees,
  In betwixt the country trees,
And the sun the pleasure taught me
  Which he teacheth every thing.

III

If the rain fell, there was sorrow,
  Little head leant on the pane,
Little finger drawing down it
  The long trailing drops upon it,
And the ' Rain, rain, come to-morrow,'
  Said for charm against the rain.

IV

Such a charm was right Canidian,
  Though you meet it with a jeer!
  If I said it long enough,
  Then the rain hummed dimly off,
And the thrush with his pure Lydian
  Was left only to the ear ;

V

And the sun and I together
  Went a-rushing out of doors !
  We, our tender spirits, drew
  Over hill and dale in view,
Glimmering hither, glimmering thither,
  In the footsteps of the showers.

VI

Underneath the chestnuts dripping,
  Through the grasses wet and fair,
  Straight I sought my garden-ground
  With the laurel on the mound,
And the pear-tree oversweeping
  A side-shadow of green air.

VII

In the garden lay supinely
  A huge giant wrought of spade !
  Arms and legs were stretched at length
  In a passive giant strength,—
The fine meadow turf, cut finely,
  Round them laid and interlaid.

VIII

Call him Hector, son of Priam !
  Such his title and degree :
  With my rake I smoothed his brow,
  Both his cheeks I weeded through,
But a rimer such as I am
  Scarce can sing his dignity.

IX

Eyes of gentianellas azure,
  Staring, winking at the skies ;
  Nose of gillyflowers and box ;
  Scented grasses put for locks,
Which a little breeze, at pleasure,
  Set a-waving round his eyes.

X

Brazen helm of daffodillies,
  With a glitter toward the light ;
  Purple violets for the mouth,
  Breathing perfumes west and south ;
And a sword of flashing lilies,
  Holden ready for the fight.

XI

And a breastplate made of daisies,
  Closely fitting, leaf on leaf ;
  Periwinkles interlaced
  Drawn for belt about the waist ;
While the brown bees, humming praises,
  Shot their arrows round the chief.

XII

And who knows (I sometimes wondered)
  If the disembodied soul
  Of old Hector, once of Troy,
  Might not take a dreary joy
Here to enter—if it thundered,
  Rolling up the thunder-roll ?

XIII

Rolling this way from Troy-ruin,
  In this body rude and rife
  Just to enter, and take rest
  'Neath the daisies of the breast—
They, with tender roots, renewing
  His heroic heart to life ?

XIV

Who could know ? I sometimes started
  At a motion or a sound !
  Did his mouth speak—naming Troy,
  With an ὀτοτοτοτοῖ ?
Did the pulse of the Strong-hearted
  Make the daisies tremble round ?

XV

It was hard to answer, often :
  But the birds sang in the tree—
  But the little birds sang bold
  In the pear-tree green and old,
And my terror seemed to soften
  Through the courage of their glee.

XVI

Oh, the birds, the tree, the ruddy
  And white blossoms, sleek with rain !
  Oh, my garden, rich with pansies !
  Oh, my childhood's bright romances !
All revive, like Hector's body,
  And I see them stir again !

XVII

And despite life's changes—chances,
  And despite the deathbell's toll,
  They press on me in full seeming !
  Help, some angel ! stay this dreaming !
As the birds sang in the branches,
  Sing God's patience through my soul !

XVIII

That no dreamer, no neglecter
    Of the present's work unsped,
    I may wake up and be doing,
    Life's heroic ends pursuing,
Though my past is dead as Hector,
    And though Hector is twice dead.

SLEEPING AND WATCHING

I

SLEEP on, baby, on the floor,
    Tired of all the playing!
Sleep with smile the sweeter for
    That, you dropped away in!
On your curls' full roundness, stand
    Golden lights serenely;
One cheek, pushed out by the hand,
    Folds the dimple inly.
Little head and little foot
    Heavy laid for pleasure,
Underneath the lids half shut,
    Slants the shining azure.—
Open-soul in noonday sun,
    So, you lie and slumber!
Nothing evil having done,
    Nothing can encumber.

II

I, who cannot sleep as well,
    Shall I sigh to view you?
Or sigh further to foretell
    All that may undo you?
Nay, keep smiling, little child,
    Ere the sorrow neareth:
I will smile too! patience mild
    Pleasure's token weareth.
Nay, keep sleeping before loss:
    I shall sleep though losing!
As by cradle, so by cross,
    Sure is the reposing.

III

And God knows who sees us twain,
    Child at childish leisure,
I am near as tired of pain
    As you seem of pleasure.
Very soon too, by His grace
    Gently wrapt around me,
Shall I show as calm a face,
    Shall I sleep as soundly.

Differing in this, that you
    Clasp your playthings, sleeping,
While my hand shall drop the few
    Given to my keeping:
Differing in this, that I
    Sleeping shall be colder,
And in waking presently,
    Brighter to beholder:
Differing in this beside
    (Sleeper, have you heard me?
Do you move, and open wide
    Eyes of wonder toward me?)—
That while you, I thus recall
    From your sleep, I solely,
Me from mine an angel shall,
    With reveillie holy.

SOUNDS

Ἤκουσας ἢ οὐκ ἤκουσας;
                    AESCHYLUS.

I

HEARKEN, hearken!
The rapid river carrieth
Many noises underneath
    The hoary ocean:
Teaching his solemnity
Sounds of inland life and glee,
Learnt beside the waving tree,
When the winds in summer prank
Toss the shades from bank to bank,
And the quick rains, in emotion
Which rather gladdens earth than grieves,
Count and visibly rehearse
The pulses of the universe
Upon the summer leaves—
Learnt among the lilies straight,
When they bow them to the weight
Of many bees whose hidden hum
Seemeth from themselves to come—
Learnt among the grasses green,
Where the rustling mice are seen
By the gleaming, as they run,
Of their quick eyes in the sun;
And lazy sheep are browsing through,
With their noses trailed in dew;
And the squirrel leaps adown,
Holding fast the filbert brown;
And the lark, with more of mirth
In his song than suits the earth,

Droppeth some in soaring high,
To pour the rest out in the sky ;
While the woodland doves, apart
In the copse's leafy heart,
Solitary, not ascetic,
Hidden and yet vocal, seem
Joining, in a lovely psalm,
Man's despondence, nature's calm,
Half mystical and half pathetic,
Like a sighing in a dream [1].
All these sounds the river telleth,
Softened to an undertone
Which ever and anon he swelleth
By a burden of his own,
     In the ocean's ear.
Aye ! and Ocean seems to hear
With an inward gentle scorn,
Smiling to his caverns worn.

                    II

   Hearken, hearken !
The child is shouting at his play
Just in the tramping funeral's way;
The widow moans as she turns aside
To shun the face of the blushing bride,
While, shaking the tower of the ancient
        church,
The marriage bells do swing ;
And in the shadow of the porch
An idiot sits, with his lean hands full
Of hedgerow flowers and a poet's skull,
Laughing loud and gibbering,
Because it is so brown a thing,
While he sticketh the gaudy poppies red
In and out the senseless head
Where all sweet fancies grew instead.
And you may hear, at the self-same time,
Another poet who reads his rime,
Low as a brook in the summer air,—

[1] While floating up bright forms ideal,
     Mistress, or friend, around me stream ;
   Half sense-supplied, and half unreal,
     Like music mingling with a dream.
                         JOHN KENYON.

   I do not doubt that the 'music' of the two
concluding lines mingled, though very uncon-
sciously, with my own ' dream,' and gave their
form and pressure to the above distich. The
ideas however being sufficiently distinct, I am
satisfied with sending this note to the press after
my verses, and with acknowledging another
obligation to the valued friend to whom I
already owe so many. [1844.]

Save when he droppeth his voice adown,
To dream of the amaranthine crown
His mortal brows shall wear ;
And a baby cries with a feeble sound
'Neath the weary weight of the life
        new-found ;
And an old man groans,—with his
        testament
Only half-signed,—for the life that's
        spent ;
And lovers twain do softly say,
As they sit on a grave, 'For ay, for ay' ;
And foemen twain, while Earth their
        mother
Looks greenly upward, curse each other.
A schoolboy drones his task, with looks
Cast over the page to the elm-tree rooks ;
A lonely student cries aloud
Eureka ! clasping at his shroud ;
A beldame's age-cracked voice doth sing
To a little infant slumbering ;
A maid forgotten weeps alone,
Muffling her sobs on the trysting stone ;
A sick man wakes at his own mouth's wail,
A gossip coughs in her thrice-told tale,
A muttering gamester shakes the dice,
A reaper foretells good luck from the skies,
A monarch vows as he lifts his hand to
        them ;
A patriot leaving his native land to them,
Cries to the world against perjured state,
A priest disserts upon linen skirts,
A sinner screams for one hope more,
A dancer's feet do palpitate
A piper's music out on the floor.
And nigh to the awful Dead, the living
Low speech and stealthy steps are giving,
Because he cannot hear !
And *he* who on that narrow bier
Has room enough, is closely wound
In a silence piercing more than sound.

                    III

   Hearken, hearken !
   God speaketh to thy soul,
Using the supreme voice which doth
        confound
All life with consciousness of Deity,
     All senses into one,—
As the seer-saint of Patmos, loving John
   (For whom did backward roll
The cloud-gate of the future) turned to *see*
The Voice which spake. It speaketh now,

Through the regular breath of the calm
  creation,
Through the moan of the creature's
  desolation
Striking, and in its stroke, resembling
The memory of a solemn vow,
Which pierceth the din of a festival
To one in the midst,—and he letteth fall
  The cup, with a sudden trembling.

IV

Hearken, hearken!
  God speaketh in thy soul,
  Saying, 'O thou that movest
With feeble steps across this earth of
  Mine,
To break beside the fount thy golden bowl
  And spill its purple wine,—
Look up to heaven and see how, like
  a scroll,
My right hand hath thine immortality
In an eternal grasping! thou, that lovest
The songful birds and grasses underfoot,
And also what change mars and tombs
  pollute—
I am the end of love!—give love to *Me!*
O thou that sinnest, grace doth more
  abound
Than all thy sin! sit still beneath My
  rood,
And count the droppings of My victim-
  blood,
  And seek none other sound!'

V

Hearken, hearken!
Shall we hear the lapsing river
And our brother's sighing ever,
  And not the voice of God?

THE LOST BOWER

I

In the pleasant orchard closes,
' God bless all our gains,' say we;
But ' May God bless all our losses,'
  Better suits with our degree.
Listen, gentle—aye, and simple! listen,
  children on the knee!

II

Green the land is where my daily
Steps in jocund childhood played,
Dimpled close with hill and valley,
Dappled very close with shade;
Summer-snow of apple blossoms running
  up from glade to glade.

III

There is one hill I see nearer
In my vision of the rest;
And a little wood seems clearer
As it climbeth from the west,
Sideway from the tree-locked valley, to
  the airy upland crest.

IV

Small the wood is, green with hazels,
And, completing the ascent,
Where the wind blows and sun dazzles
Thrills in leafy tremblement,
Like a heart that, after climbing, beateth
  quickly through content.

V

Not a step the wood advances
O'er the open hill-top's bound;
There, in green arrest, the branches
See their image on the ground:
You may walk beneath them smiling,
  glad with sight and glad with
  sound.

VI

For you hearken on your right hand,
How the birds do leap and call
In the greenwood, out of sight and
Out of reach and fear of all;
And the squirrels crack the filberts
  through their cheerful madrigal.

VII

On your left, the sheep are cropping
The slant grass and daisies pale,
And five apple-trees stand dropping
Separate shadows toward the vale,
Over which, in choral silence, the hills
  look you their ' All hail!'

VIII

Far out, kindled by each other,
Shining hills on hills arise,
Close as brother leans to brother
When they press beneath the eyes
Of some father praying blessings from
  the gifts of paradise.

IX

While beyond, above them mounted,
And above their woods alsò,
Malvern hills, for mountains counted
Not unduly, loom a-row—
Keepers of Piers Plowman's visions
  through the sunshine and the
  snow [1].

X

Yet, in childhood, little prized I
That fair walk and far survey :
'Twas a straight walk unadvised by
The least mischief worth a nay ;
Up and down—as dull as grammar on
  the eve of holiday.

XI

But the wood, all close and clenching
Bough in bough and root in root,—
No more sky (for over-branching)
At your head than at your foot,—
Oh, the wood drew me within it, by a
  glamour past dispute.

XII

Few and broken paths showed through
  it,
Where the sheep had tried to run,—
Forced with snowy wool to strew it
Round the thickets, when anon
They, with silly thorn-pricked noses,
  bleated back into the sun.

XIII

But my childish heart beat stronger
Than those thickets dared to grow :
I could pierce them ! I could longer
Travel on, methought, than so.
Sheep for sheep-paths ! braver children
  climb and creep where they would
  go.

XIV

And the poets wander, said I,
Over places all as rude :
Bold Rinaldo's lovely lady
Sate to meet him in a wood :
Rosalinda, like a fountain, laughed out
  pure with solitude.

[1] The Malvern Hills of Worcestershire are the scene of Langland's Visions, and thus present the earliest classic ground of English poetry.

XV

And if Chaucer had not travelled
Through a forest by a well,
He had never dreamt nor marvelled
At those ladies fair and fell
Who lived smiling without loving in their
  island-citadel.

XVI

Thus I thought of the old singers,
And took courage from their song,
Till my little struggling fingers
Tore asunder gyve and thong
Of the brambles which entrapped me, and
  the barrier branches strong.

XVII

On a day, such pastime keeping,
With a fawn's heart debonair,
Under-crawling, overleaping
Thorns that prick and boughs that bear,
I stood suddenly astonied—I was glad-
  dened unaware.

XVIII

From the place I stood in, floated
Back the covert dim and close,
And the open ground was coated
Carpet-smooth with grass and moss,
And the blue-bell's purple presence signed
  it worthily across.

XIX

Here a linden-tree stood, bright'ning
All adown its silver rind ;
For as some trees draw the lightning,
So this tree, unto my mind,
Drew to earth the blessed sunshine from
  the sky where it was shrined.

XX

Tall the linden-tree, and near it
An old hawthorn also grew ;
And wood-ivy like a spirit
Hovered dimly round the two,
Shaping thence that bower of beauty
  which I sing of thus to you.

XXI

'Twas a bower for garden fitter
Than for any woodland wide ;
Though a fresh and dewy glitter
Struck it through from side to side,
Shaped and shaven was the freshness,
  as by garden-cunning plied.

XXII

Oh, a lady might have come there,
Hooded fairly like her hawk,
With a book or lute in summer,
And a hope of sweeter talk,—
Listening less to her own music than for
    footsteps on the walk.

XXIII

But that bower appeared a marvel
In the wildness of the place ;
With such seeming art and travail,
Finely fixed and fitted was
Leaf to leaf, the dark-green ivy, to the
    summit from the base.

XXIV

And the ivy veined and glossy
Was enwrought with eglantine ;
And the wild hop fibred closely,
And the large-leaved columbine,
Arch of door and window mullion, did
    right sylvanly entwine.

XXV

Rose-trees either side the door were
Growing lithe and growing tall,
Each one set a summer warder
For the keeping of the hall,—
With a red rose and a white rose, lean-
    ing, nodding at the wall.

XXVI

As I entered—mosses hushing
Stole all noises from my foot ;
And a green elastic cushion,
Clasped within the linden's root,
Took me in a chair of silence very rare
    and absolute.

XXVII

All the floor was paved with glory,
Greenly, silently inlaid
(Through quick motions made before
    me),
With fair counterparts in shade
Of the fair serrated ivy-leaves which
    slanted overhead.

XXVIII

' Is such pavement in a palace ? '
So I questioned in my thought.
The sun, shining through the chalice
Of the red rose hung without,
Threw within a red libation, like an
    answer to my doubt.

XXIX

At the same time, on the linen
Of my childish lap there fell
Two white may-leaves, downward
    winning
Through the ceiling's miracle,
From a blossom, like an angel, out of
    sight yet blessing well.

XXX

Down to floor and up to ceiling
Quick I turned my childish face,
With an innocent appealing
For the secret of the place
To the trees, which surely knew it, in
    partaking of the grace.

XXXI

Where 's no foot of human creature,
How could reach a human hand ?
And if this be work of nature,
Why has nature turned so bland,
Breaking off from other wild work ?   It
    was hard to understand.

XXXII

Was she weary of rough-doing,—
Of the bramble and the thorn ?
Did she pause in tender rueing
Here of all her sylvan scorn ?
Or, in mock of art's deceiving, was the
    sudden mildness worn ?

XXXIII

Or could this same bower (I fancied)
Be the work of Dryad strong,
Who, surviving all that chancèd
In the world's old pagan wrong,
Lay hid, feeding in the woodland on the
    last true poet's song ?

XXXIV

Or was this the house of fairies,
Left, because of the rough ways,
Unassoiled by Ave Marys
Which the passing pilgrim prays,
And beyond Saint Catherine's chiming
    on the blessèd Sabbath days ?

XXXV

So, young muser, I sate listening
To my fancy's wildest word.
On a sudden, through the glistening
Leaves around, a little stirred,
Came a sound, a sense of music, which
    was rather felt than heard.

XXXVI

Softly, finely, it enwound me;
From the world it shut me in,—
Like a fountain, falling round me,
Which with silver waters thin
Clips a little water Naiad sitting smilingly
within.

XXXVII

Whence the music came, who knoweth?
I know nothing. But indeed
Pan or Faunus never bloweth
So much sweetness from a reed
Which has sucked the milk of waters
at the oldest river-head.

XXXVIII

Never lark the sun can waken
With such sweetness! when the lark,
The high planets overtaking
In the half-evanished Dark,
Casts his singing to their singing, like
an arrow to the mark.

XXXIX

Never nightingale so singeth:
Oh, she leans on thorny tree,
And her poet-song she flingeth
Over pain to victory!
Yet she never sings such music,—or
she sings it not to me.

XL

Never blackbirds, never thrushes,
Nor small finches sing as sweet,
When the sun strikes through the
bushes
To their crimson clinging feet,
And their pretty eyes look sideways to
the summer heavens complete.

XLI

If it *were* a bird, it seemèd,
Most like Chaucer's, which, in sooth,
He of green and azure dreamèd,
While it sate in spirit-ruth
On that bier of a crowned lady, singing
nigh her silent mouth.

XLII

If it *were* a bird!—ah, sceptic,
Give me 'yea' or give me 'nay'—
Though my soul were nympholeptic,
As I heard that virèlay,
You may stoop your pride to pardon.
for my sin is far away.

XLIII

I rose up in exaltation
And an inward trembling heat,
And (it seemed) in geste of passion
Dropped the music to my feet
Like a garment rustling downwards!—
such a silence followed it.

XLIV

Heart and head beat through the quiet
Full and heavily, though slower.
In the song, I think, and by it,
Mystic Presences of power
Had up-snatched me to the Timeless,
then returned me to the Hour.

XLV

In a child-abstraction lifted,
Straightway from the bower I past,
Foot and soul being dimly drifted
Through the greenwood, till, at last,
In the hill-top's open sunshine I all
consciously was cast.

XLVI

Face to face with the true mountains
I stood silently and still,
Drawing strength from fancy's dauntings,
From the air about the hill,
And from Nature's open mercies, and
most debonair goodwill.

XLVII

Oh, the golden-hearted daisies
Witnessed there, before my youth,
To the truth of things, with praises
Of the beauty of the truth,
And I woke to Nature's real, laughing
joyfully for both.

XLVIII

And I said within me, laughing,
I have found a bower to-day,
A green lusus—fashioned half in
Chance, and half in Nature's play—
And a little bird sings nigh it, I will
nevermore missay.

XLIX

Henceforth, *I* will be the fairy
Of this bower not built by one ;
I will go there, sad or merry,
With each morning's benison,
And the bird shall be my harper in the
     dream-hall I have won.

L

So I said.   But the next morning,
(—Child, look up into my face—
'Ware, O sceptic, of your scorning !
This is truth in its pure grace !)
The next morning, all had vanished, or
     my wandering missed the place.

LI

Bring an oath most sylvan holy,
And upon it swear me true —
By the wind-bells swinging slowly
Their mute curfews in the dew,
By the advent of the snowdrop, by the
     rosemary and rue,—

LII

I affirm by all or any,
Let the cause be charm or chance,
That my wandering searches many
Missed the bower of my romance—
That I nevermore, upon it, turned my
     mortal countenance.

LIII

I affirm that, since I lost it,
Never bower has seemed so fair ;
Never garden-creeper crossed it
With so deft and brave an air—
Never bird sung in the summer, as I
     saw and heard them there.

LIV

Day by day, with new desire,
Toward my wood I ran in faith,
Under leaf and over brier,
Through the thickets, out of breath—
Like the prince who rescued Beauty
     from the sleep as long as death.

LV

But his sword of mettle clashèd,
And his arm smote strong, I ween,
And her dreaming spirit flashèd
Through her body's fair white screen,
And the light thereof might guide him
     up the cedar alleys green.

LVI

But for me, I saw no splendour—
All my sword was my child-heart ;
And the wood refused surrender
Of that bower it held apart,
Safe as Oedipus's grave-place, 'mid
     Colonos' olives swart.

LVII

As Aladdin sought the basements
His fair palace rose upon,
And the four-and-twenty casements
Which gave answers to the sun ;
So, in wilderment of gazing I looked up,
     and I looked down.

LVIII

Years have vanished since as wholly
As the little bower did then ;
And you call it tender folly
That such thoughts should come again ?
Ah, I cannot change this sighing for
     your smiling, brother men !

LIX

For this loss it did prefigure
Other loss of better good,
When my soul, in spirit-vigour,
And in ripened womanhood,
Fell from visions of more beauty than
     an arbour in a wood.

LX

I have lost—oh, many a pleasure,
Many a hope, and many a power—
Studious health, and merry leisure,
The first dew on the first flower !
But the first of all my losses was the
     losing of the bower.

LXI

I have lost the dream of Doing,
And the other dream of Done,
The first spring in the pursuing,
The first pride in the Begun,—
First recoil from incompletion, in the
     face of what is won—

LXII

Exaltations in the far light
Where some cottage only is ;
Mild dejections in the starlight,
Which the sadder-hearted miss ;
And the child-cheek blushing scarlet for
the very shame of bliss.

LXIII

I have lost the sound child-sleeping
Which the thunder could not break ;
Something too of the strong leaping
Of the staglike heart awake,
Which the pale is low for keeping in
the road it ought to take.

LXIV

Some respect to social fictions
Has been also lost by me ;
And some generous genuflexions,
Which my spirit offered free
To the pleasant old conventions of our
false humanity.

LXV

All my losses did I tell you,
Ye, perchance, would look away ;—
Ye would answer me, ' Farewell ! you
Make sad company to-day,
And your tears are falling faster than
the bitter words you say.'

LXVI

For God placed me like a dial
In the open ground with power,
And my heart had for its trial
All the sun and all the shower !
And I suffered many losses,— and my
first was of the bower.

LXVII

Laugh you ? If that loss of mine be
Of no heavy-seeming weight—
When the cone falls from the pine-tree
The young children laugh thereat ;
Yet the wind that struck it, riseth, and
the tempest shall be great.

LXVIII

One who knew me in my childhood
In the glamour and the game,
Looking on me long and mild, would
Never know me for the same.
Come, unchanging recollections, where
those changes overcame.

LXIX

By this couch I weakly lie on,
While I count my memories,—
Through the fingers which, still sigh-
ing,
I press closely on mine eyes,—
Clear as once beneath the sunshine,
I behold the bower arise.

LXX

Springs the linden-tree as greenly,
Stroked with light adown its rind ;
And the ivy-leaves serenely
Each in either intertwined ;
And the rose-trees at the doorway, they
have neither grown nor pined.

LXXI

From those overblown faint roses
Not a leaf appeareth shed,
And that little bud discloses
Not a thorn's-breadth more of red
For the winters and the summers which
have passed me overhead.

LXXII

And that music overfloweth,
Sudden sweet, the sylvan eaves :
Thrush or nightingale—who knoweth ?
Fay or Faunus—who believes ?
But my heart still trembles in me to the
trembling of the leaves.

LXXIII

Is the bower lost, then ? who sayeth
That the bower indeed is lost ?
Hark ! my spirit in it prayeth
Through the sunshine and the frost,—
And the prayer preserves it greenly, to
the last and uttermost.

LXXIV

Till another open for me
In God's Eden-land unknown,
With an angel at the doorway,
White with gazing at His Throne,
And a saint's voice in the palm-trees,
singing—' All is lost . . . and *won !* '

A SONG AGAINST SINGING

TO E. J. H.

I

THEY bid me sing to thee,
Thou golden-haired and silver-voicèd
child,—
With lips by no worse sigh than sleep's
defiled,
With eyes unknowing how tears dim
the sight,
And feet all trembling at the new delight,
Treaders of earth to be!

II

Ah no! the lark may bring
A song to thee from out the morning cloud,
The merry river from its lilies bowed,
The brisk rain from the trees, the lucky
wind,
That half doth make its music, half doth
find,—
But I—I may not sing.

III

How could I think it right,
New-comer on our earth as, Sweet,
thou art,
To bring a verse from out a human heart
Made heavy with accumulated tears,
And cross with such amount of weary
years
Thy day-sum of delight?

IV

Even if the verse were said,
Thou, who wouldst clap thy tiny hands
to hear
The wind or rain, gay bird or river clear,
Wouldst, at that sound of sad humanities,
Upturn thy bright uncomprehending
eyes
And bid me play instead.

V

Therefore no song of mine,—
But prayer in place of singing; prayer
that would
Commend thee to the new-creating God,
Whose gift is childhood's heart without
its stain
Of weakness, ignorance, and changing
vain—
That gift of God be thine!

VI

So wilt thou ay be young,
In lovelier childhood than thy shining
brow
And pretty winning accents make thee
now:
Yea, sweeter than this scarce articulate
sound
(How sweet!) of 'father,' 'mother,'
shall be found
The ABBA on thy tongue.

VII

And so, as years shall chase
Each other's shadows, thou wilt less
resemble
Thy fellows of the earth who toil and
tremble,
Than him thou seest not, thine angel bold
Yet meek, whose ever-lifted eyes behold
The Ever-loving's face.

WINE OF CYPRUS

GIVEN TO ME BY H. S. BOYD, AUTHOR
OF 'SELECT PASSAGES FROM THE
GREEK FATHERS,' ETC., TO WHOM
THESE STANZAS ARE ADDRESSED

I

IF old Bacchus were the speaker
He would tell you with a sigh,
Of the Cyprus in this beaker
I am sipping like a fly,—
Like a fly or gnat on Ida
At the hour of goblet-pledge,
By queen Juno brushed aside, a
Full white arm-sweep, from the edge.

II

Sooth, the drinking should be ampler
When the drink is so divine,
And some deep-mouthed Greek exampler
Would become your Cyprus wine:
Cyclops' mouth might plunge aright in,
While his one eye over-leered—
Nor too large were mouth of Titan,
Drinking rivers down his beard.

III

Pan might dip his head so deep in
  That his ears alone pricked out,
Fauns around him, pressing, leaping,
  Each one pointing to his throat :
While the Naiads, like Bacchantes,
  Wild, with urns thrown out to waste,
Cry,—'O earth, that thou wouldst grant
    us
  Springs to keep, of such a taste !'

IV

But for me, I am not worthy
  After gods and Greeks to drink,
And my lips are pale and earthy
  To go bathing from this brink :
Since you heard them speak the last time
  They have faded from their blooms,
And the laughter of my pastime
  Has learnt silence at the tombs.

V

Ah, my friend ! the antique drinkers
  Crowned the cup and crowned the
    brow.
Can I answer the old thinkers
  In the forms they thought of, now ?
Who will fetch from garden-closes
  Some new garlands while I speak,
That the forehead, crowned with roses,
  May strike scarlet down the cheek ?

VI

Do not mock me ! with my mortal
  Suits no wreath again, indeed ;
I am sad-voiced as the turtle
  Which Anacreon used to feed :
Yet as that same bird demurely
  Wet her beak in cup of his,
So, without a garland, surely
  I may touch the brim of this.

VII

Go,—let others praise the Chian !—
  This is soft as Muses' string,
This is tawny as Rhea's lion,
  This is rapid as his spring,
Bright as Paphia's eyes e'er met us,
  Light as ever trod her feet !
And the brown bees of Hymettus
  Make their honey not so sweet.

VIII

Very copious are my praises,
  Though I sip it like a fly !—
Ah—but, sipping,—times and places
  Change before me suddenly :
As Ulysses' old libation
  Drew the ghosts from every part,
So your Cyprus wine, dear Grecian,
  Stirs the Hades of my heart.

IX

And I think of those long mornings
  Which my thought goes far to seek,
When, betwixt the folio's turnings,
  Solemn flowed the rhythmic Greek :
Past the pane the mountain spreading,
  Swept the sheep-bell's tinkling noise,
While a girlish voice was reading,
  Somewhat low for $\alpha\iota$'s and $o\iota$'s.

X

Then, what golden hours were for us !—
  While we sate together there,
How the white vests of the chorus
  Seemed to wave up a live air !
How the cothurns trod majestic
  Down the deep iambic lines,
And the rolling anapaestic
  Curled like vapour over shrines !

XI

Oh, our Aeschylus, the thunderous !
  How he drove the bolted breath
Through the cloud, to wedge it ponderous
  In the gnarlèd oak beneath.
Oh, our Sophocles, the royal,
  Who was born to monarch's place,
And who made the whole world loyal,
  Less by kingly power than grace.

XII

Our Euripides, the human,
  With his droppings of warm tears,
And his touches of things common
  Till they rose to touch the spheres !
Our Theocritus, our Bion,
  And our Pindar's shining goals !—
These were cup-bearers undying,
  Of the wine that 's meant for souls :

XIII

And my Plato, the divine one,
　　If men know the gods aright
By their motions as they shine on
　　With a glorious trail of light !—
And your noble Christian bishops,
　　Who mouthed grandly the last Greek !
Though the sponges on their hyssops
　　Were distent with wine—too weak.

XIV

Yet, your Chrysostom, you praised him
　　As a liberal mouth of gold ;
And your Basil, you upraised him
　　To the height of speakers old.
And we both praised Heliodorus
　　For his secret of pure lies,—
Who forged first his linkèd stories
　　In the heat of lady's eyes.

XV

And we both praised your Synesius
　　For the fire shot up his odes,
Though the Church was scarce propitious
　　As he whistled dogs and gods.
And we both praised Nazianzen
　　For the fervid heart and speech :
Only I eschewed his glancing
　　At the lyre hung out of reach.

XVI

Do you mind that deed of Atè
　　Which you bound me to so fast,—
Reading ' De Virginitate,'
　　From the first line to the last ?
How I said at ending, solemn,
　　As I turned and looked at you,
That Saint Simeon on the column
　　Had had somewhat less to do ?

XVII

For we sometimes gently wrangled,
　　Very gently, be it said,
Since our thoughts were disentangled
　　By no breaking of the thread !
And I charged you with extortions
　　On the nobler fames of old—
Aye, and sometimes thought your Porsons
　　Stained the purple they would fold.

XVIII

For the rest—a mystic moaning
　　Kept Cassandra at the gate,
With wild eyes the vision shone in,
　　And wide nostrils scenting fate.
And Prometheus, bound in passion
　　By brute Force to the blind stone,
Showed us looks of invocation
　　Turned to ocean and the sun.

XIX

And Medea we saw burning
　　At her nature's planted stake :
And proud Oedipus fate-scorning
　　While the cloud came on to break—
While the cloud came on slow—slower,
　　Till he stood discrowned, resigned !—
But the reader's voice dropped lower
　　When the poet called him BLIND.

XX

Ah, my gossip ! you were older,
　　And more learned, and a man !—
Yet that shadow, the enfolder
　　Of your quiet eyelids, ran
Both our spirits to one level,
　　And I turned from hill and lea
And the summer-sun's green revel,
　　To your eyes that could not see.

XXI

Now Christ bless you with the one light
　　Which goes shining night and day !
May the flowers which grow in sunlight
　　Shed their fragrance in your way !
Is it not right to remember
　　All your kindness, friend of mine,
When we two sate in the chamber,
　　And the poets poured us wine ?

XXII

So, to come back to the drinking
　　Of this Cyprus,—it is well,
But those memories, to my thinking,
　　Make a better oenomel ;
And whoever be the speaker,
　　None can murmur with a sigh,
That, in drinking from *that* beaker,
　　I am sipping like a fly.

A RHAPSODY OF LIFE'S
PROGRESS

Fill all the stops of life with tuneful breath.
CORNELIUS MATHEWS, *Poems of Man* [1].

I

WE are borne into life—it is sweet, it is
strange.
We lie still on the knee of a mild Mystery,
Which smiles with a change !
But we doubt not of changes, we know
not of spaces,
The Heavens seem as near as our own
mother's face is,
And we think we could touch all the
stars that we see ;
And the milk of our mother is white on
our mouth ;
And, with small childish hands, we are
turning around
The apple of Life which another has
found ;
It is warm with our touch, not with sun
of the south,
And we count, as we turn it, the red
side for four.
   O Life, O Beyond,
  Thou art sweet, thou art strange ever-
more!

II

Then all things look strange in the pure
golden ether :
We walk through the gardens with hands
linked together,
  And the lilies look large as the trees;
And as loud as the birds sing the bloom-
loving bees,
And the birds sing like angels, so
mystical-fine,
And the cedars are brushing the arch-
angels' feet,
And time is eternity, love is divine,
  And the world is complete.
Now, God bless the child,—father,
mother, respond !
   O Life, O Beyond,
  Thou art strange, thou art sweet.

[1] A small volume, by an American poet—
as remarkable in thought and manner for a
vital sinewy vigour as the right arm of 'Path-
finder.' [1844.]

III

Then we leap on the earth with the
armour of youth,
  And the earth rings again,
And we breathe out, ' O beauty,'—we
cry out, ' O truth,'
And the bloom of our lips drops with wine,
And our blood runs amazed 'neath the
calm hyaline,
The earth cleaves to the foot, the sun
burns to the brain,—
What is this exultation ? and what this
despair ?—
The strong pleasure is smiting the nerves
into pain,
And we drop from the Fair as we climb
to the Fair,
  And we lie in a trance at its feet ;
And the breath of an angel cold-piercing
the air
Breathes fresh on our faces in swoon,
And we think him so near he is this side
the sun,
And we wake to a whisper self-murmured
and fond,
   O Life, O Beyond,
  Thou art strange, thou art sweet !

IV

And the winds and the waters in pastoral
measures
Go winding around us, with roll upon roll,
Till the soul lies within in a circle of
pleasures
  Which hideth the soul.
And we run with the stag, and we leap
with the horse,
And we swim with the fish through the
broad water-course,
And we strike with the falcon, and hunt
with the hound,
And the joy which is in us flies out by
a wound.
And we shout so aloud, ' We exult, we
rejoice,'
That we lose the low moan of our
brothers around ;
And we shout so a deep down creation's
profound,
  We are deaf to God's voice.
And we bind the rose-garland on fore-
head and ears

Yet we are not ashamed,
And the dew of the roses that runneth
　　unblamed
　Down our cheeks, is not taken for tears.
Help us, God, trust us, man, love us,
　　woman !　'I hold
Thy small head in my hands,—with its
　　grapelets of gold
Growing bright through my fingers,—
　　like altar for oath,
'Neath the vast golden spaces like wit-
　　nessing faces
That watch the eternity strong in the
　　troth—
　　I love thee, I leave thee,
　　Live for thee, die for thee !
　　I prove thee, deceive thee,
　　Undo evermore thee !
Help me, God, slay me, man !— one is
　　mourning for both.'
And we stand up, though young, near the
　　funeral-sheet
Which covers the Caesar and old Phara-
　　mond,
And death is so nigh us, life cools from
　　its heat.
　　　O Life, O Beyond,
　　　Art thou fair,—*art* thou sweet ?

V

Then we act to a purpose—we spring up
　　erect:
We will tame the wild mouths of the
　　wilderness-steeds,
We will plough up the deep in the ships
　　double-decked,
We will build the great cities, and do
　　the great deeds,
Strike the steel upon steel, strike the
　　soul upon soul,
Strike the dole on the weal, overcoming
　　the dole,
Let the cloud meet the cloud in a grand
　　thunder-roll !
' While the eagle of Thought rides the
　　tempest in scorn,
Who cares if the lightning is burning
　　the corn?
　　Let us sit on the thrones
　　In a purple sublimity,
　　And grind down men's bones
　　To a pale unanimity.

Speed me, God !—serve me, man !—I am
　　god over men ;
When I speak in my cloud, none shall
　　answer again.
　'Neath the stripe and the bond,
　　Lie and mourn at my feet ! '—
　O thou Life, O Beyond,
　　Thou art strange, thou art sweet !

VI

Then we grow into thought,—and with
　　inward ascensions
Touch the bounds of our Being.
We lie in the dark here, swathed doubly
　　around
With our sensual relations and social
　　conventions,
Yet are 'ware of a sight, yet are 'ware
　　of a sound
　　Beyond Hearing and Seeing,—
Are aware that a Hades rolls deep on all
　　sides
　　With its infinite tides
About and above us,—until the strong
　　arch
Of our life creaks and bends as if ready
　　for falling,
And through the dim rolling we hear
　　the sweet calling
Of spirits that speak in a soft under-tongue
　　The sense of the mystical march.
And we cry to them softly, ' Come
　　nearer, come nearer,
And lift up the lap of this Dark, and
　　speak clearer,
　　And teach us the song that ye sung.'
And we smile in our thought if they
　　answer or no,
For to dream of a sweetness is sweet as
　　to know.
　　Wonders breathe in our face
　　And we ask not their name ;
　　Love takes all the blame
　　Of the world's prison-place.
And we sing back the songs as we guess
　　them, aloud ;
And we send up the lark of our music
　　that cuts
　　Untired through the cloud,
To beat with its wings at the lattice
　　Heaven shuts ;
Yet the angels look down and the mortals
　　look up

As the little wings beat,
And the poet is blessed with their pity
    or hope.
'Twixt the heavens and the earth *can* a
    poet despond?
        O Life, O Beyond,
    Thou art strange, thou art sweet!

VII

Then we wring from our souls their
    applicative strength,
And bend to the cord the strong bow of
    our ken,
And bringing our lives to the level of
    others
Hold the cup we have filled, to their
    uses at length.
'Help me, God! love me, man! I am
    man among men,
        And my life is a pledge
        Of the ease of another's!'
From the fire and the water we drive
    out the steam
With a rush and a roar and the speed of
    a dream;
And the car without horses, the car with-
    out wings,
        Roars onward and flies
        On its grey iron edge,
'Neath the heat of a Thought sitting still
    in our eyes:
And our hand knots in air, with the
    bridge that it flings,
Two peaks far disrupted by ocean and
    skies,
And, lifting a fold of the smooth-flowing
    Thames,
Draws under the world with its turmoils
    and pothers,
While the swans float on softly, un-
    touched in their calms
By humanity's hum at the root of the
    springs.
And with reachings of Thought we reach
    down to the deeps
        Of the souls of our brothers,—
We teach them full words with our slow-
    moving lips,
'God,' 'Liberty,' 'Truth,'—which they
    hearken and think
And work into harmony, link upon link,

Till the silver meets round the earth gelid
    and dense,
Shedding sparks of electric responding
    intense
        On the dark of eclipse.
Then we hear through the silence and
    glory afar,
        As from shores of a star
In aphelion, the new generations that cry
Disenthralled by our voice to harmonious
    reply,
        'God,' 'Liberty,' 'Truth!'
        We are glorious forsooth—
        And our name has a seat,
Though the shroud should be donned.
        O Life, O Beyond,
    Thou art strange, thou art sweet!

VIII

Help me, God—help me, man! I am low,
    I am weak—
Death loosens my sinews and creeps in
    .my veins:
My body is cleft by these wedges of pains
    From my spirit's serene,
And I feel the externe and insensate
    creep in
        On my organized clay.
        I sob not, nor shriek,
        Yet I faint fast away!
I am strong in the spirit, — deep-
    thoughted, clear-eyed,—
I could walk, step for step, with an
    angel beside,
        On the heaven-heights of truth
        Oh. the soul keeps its youth,
But the body faints sore, it is tired in
    the race,
It sinks from the chariot ere reaching
    the goal,
        It is weak, it is cold,
        The rein drops from its hold—
It sinks back, with the death in its face.
        On, chariot—on, soul,
        Ye are all the more fleet—
        Be alone at the goal
        Of the strange and the sweet!

IX

Love us, God, love us, man! we believe,
    we achieve—
        Let us love, let us live,

For the acts correspond ;
We are glorious—and DIE !
And again on the knee of a mild Mystery
That smiles with a change,
Here we lie.
O DEATH, O BEYOND,
Thou art sweet, thou art strange !

A LAY OF THE EARLY ROSE

—— discordance that can accord.
Romaunt of the Rose.

A ROSE once grew within
A garden April-green,
In her loneness, in her loneness,
And the fairer for that oneness.

A white rose delicate
On a tall bough and straight :
Early comer, early comer,
Never waiting for the summer.

Her pretty gestes did win
South winds to let her in,
In her loneness, in her loneness,
All the fairer for that oneness.

' For if I wait,' said she,
' Till time for roses be,—
For the moss-rose and the musk-rose,
Maiden-blush and royal-dusk rose,—

' What glory then for me
In such a company ?—
Roses plenty, roses plenty,
And one nightingale for twenty ?

' Nay, let me in,' said she,
' Before the rest are free,—
In my loneness, in my loneness,
All the fairer for that oneness.

' For I would lonely stand
Uplifting my white hand,
On a mission, on a mission,
To declare the coming vision.

' Upon which lifted sign,
What worship will be mine ?
What addressing, what caressing,
And what thanks and praise and blessing !

' A windlike joy will rush
Through every tree and bush,
Bending softly in affection
And spontaneous benediction.

' Insects, that only may
Live in a sunbright ray,
To my whiteness, to my whiteness,
Shall be drawn, as to a brightness,—

' And every moth and bee,
Approach me reverently,
Wheeling o'er me, wheeling o'er me
Coronals of motioned glory.

' Three larks shall leave a cloud,
To my whiter beauty vowed,
Singing gladly all the moontide,
Never waiting for the suntide.

' Ten nightingales shall flee
Their woods for love of me,
Singing sadly all the suntide,
Never waiting for the moontide.

' I ween the very skies
Will look down with surprise,
When low on earth they see me
With my starry aspect dreamy.

' And earth will call her flowers
To hasten out of doors ;
By their curtsies and sweet-smelling
To give grace to my foretelling.'

So praying, did she win
South winds to let her in,
In her loneness, in her loneness,
And the fairer for that oneness.

But ah,—alas for her !
No thing did minister
To her praises, to her praises,
More than might unto a daisy's.

No tree nor bush was seen
To boast a perfect green,
Scarcely having, scarcely having
One leaf broad enough for waving.

The little flies did crawl
Along the southern wall,
Faintly shifting, faintly shifting
Wings scarce long enough for lifting.

The lark, too high or low,
I ween, did miss her so,
With his nest down in the gorses,
And his song in the star-courses.

The nightingale did please
To loiter beyond seas:
Guess him in the Happy Islands,
Learning music from the silence.

Only the bee, forsooth,
Came in the place of both,
Doing honour, doing honour
To the honey-dews upon her.

The skies looked coldly down
As on a royal crown ;
Then with drop for drop, at leisure,
They began to rain for pleasure.

Whereat the Earth did seem
To waken from a dream,
Winter-frozen, winter-frozen,
Her unquiet eyes unclosing—

Said to the Rose, ' Ha, Snow !
And art thou fallen so ?
Thou, who wast enthronèd stately
All along my mountains lately ?

' Holla, thou world-wide snow !
And art thou wasted so ?
With a little bough to catch thee,
And a little bee to watch thee ? '

—Poor Rose, to be misknown !
Would she had ne'er been blown,
In her loneness, in her loneness,
All the sadder for that oneness !

Some word she tried to say,
Some no . . . . ah, wellaway !
But the passion did o'ercome her,
And the fair frail leaves dropped from her.

Dropped from her, fair and mute,
Close to a poet's foot,
Who beheld them, smiling slowly,
As at something sad yet holy,—

Said, ' Verily and thus
It chances too with us
Poets, singing sweetest snatches
While that deaf men keep the watches :

' Vaunting to come before
Our own age evermore,
In a loneness, in a loneness,
And the nobler for that oneness.

' Holy in voice and heart,
To high ends, set apart !
All unmated, all unmated,
Just because so consecrated.

' But if alone we be,
Where is our empery ?
And if none can reach our stature,
Who can mete our lofty nature ?

' What bell will yield a tone,
Swung in the air alone ?
If no brazen clapper bringing,
Who can hear the chimèd ringing ?

' What angel, but would seem
To sensual eyes, ghost-dim ?
And without assimilation,
Vain is interpenetration.

' And thus, what can we do,
Poor rose and poet too,
Who both antedate our mission
In an unprepared season ?

' Drop leaf—be silent song !
Cold things we come among :
We must warm them, we must warm them,
Ere we ever hope to charm them.

' Howbeit ' (here his face
Lightened around the place,—
So to mark the outward turning
Of his spirit's inward burning)

' Something it is, to hold
In God's worlds manifold,
First revealed to creature-duty,
Some new form of His mild Beauty.

' Whether that form respect
The sense or intellect,
Holy be, in mood or meadow,
The Chief Beauty's sign and shadow !

' Holy, in me and thee,
Rose fallen from the tree,—
Though the world stand dumb around us,
All unable to expound us.

'Though none us deign to bless,
  Blessèd are we, nathless;
Blessèd still and consecrated,
In that, rose, we were created.

'Oh, shame to poet's lays,
  Sung for the dole of praise,—
Hoarsely sung upon the highway
With that *obolum da mihi!*

'Shame, shame to poet's soul
  Pining for such a dole,
When Heaven-chosen to inherit
The high throne of a chief spirit!

'Sit still upon your thrones,
  O ye poetic ones!
And if, sooth, the world decry you,
Let it pass unchallenged by you!

'Ye to yourselves suffice,
  Without its flatteries.
Self-contentedly approve you
Unto HIM who sits above you,—

'In prayers—that upward mount
  Like to a fair-sunned fount
Which, in gushing back upon you,
Hath an upper music won you.

'In faith—that still perceives
  No rose can shed her leaves,
Far less, poet fall from mission,
With an unfulfilled fruition.

'In hope—that apprehends
  An end beyond these ends,
And great uses rendered duly
By the meanest song sung truly.

'In thanks—for all the good
  By poets understood—
For the sound of seraphs moving
Down the hidden depths of loving,—

'For sights of things away
  Through fissures of the clay,
Promised things which *shall* be given
And sung over, up in Heaven,—

'For life, so lovely-vain,
  For death, which breaks the chain,—
For this sense of present sweetness.—
And this yearning to completeness!'

THE POET AND THE BIRD

A FABLE

I

SAID a people to a poet—'Go out from
    among us straightway!
While we are thinking earthly things,
    thou singest of divine.
There's a little fair brown nightingale,
    who, sitting in the gateway,
  Makes fitter music to our ear than any
    song of thine!'

II

The poet went out weeping—the nightin-
    gale ceased chanting,
  'Now, wherefore, O thou nightingale,
    is all thy sweetness done?'
—'I cannot sing my earthly things, the
    heavenly poet wanting,
  Whose highest harmony includes the
    lowest under sun.'

III

The poet went out weeping,—and died
    abroad, bereft there:
  The bird flew to his grave and died
    amid a thousand wails.
And, when I last came by the place,
    I swear the music left there
  Was only of the poet's song, and not
    the nightingale's.

THE CRY OF THE HUMAN

I

'THERE is no God,' the foolish saith,
  But none 'There is no sorrow,'
And nature oft the cry of faith
  In bitter need will borrow:
Eyes, which the preacher could not
    school,
  By wayside graves are raisèd,
And lips say 'God be pitiful,'
  Who ne'er said 'God be praisèd.'
        Be pitiful, O God

II

The tempest stretches from the steep
  The shadow of its coming,
The beasts grow tame, and near us creep,
  As help were in the human;
Yet, while the cloud-wheels roll and grind,
  We spirits tremble under!—
The hills have echoes, but we find
  No answer for the thunder.
          Be pitiful, O God!

III

The battle hurtles on the plains,
  Earth feels new scythes upon her;
We reap our brothers for the wains,
  And call the harvest—honour;
Draw face to face, front line to line,
  One image all inherit,—
Then kill, curse on, by that same sign,
  Clay, clay,—and spirit, spirit.
          Be pitiful, O God!

IV

The plague runs festering through the town,
  And never a bell is tolling,
And corpses, jostled 'neath the moon,
  Nod to the dead-cart's rolling.
The young child calleth for the cup,
  The strong man brings it weeping;
The mother from her babe looks up,
  And shrieks away its sleeping.
          Be pitiful, O God!

V

The plague of gold strikes far and near,
  And deep and strong it enters;
This purple chimar which we wear
  Makes madder than the centaur's:
Our thoughts grow blank, our words grow strange,
We cheer the pale gold-diggers—
Each soul is worth so much on 'Change,
  And marked, like sheep, with figures.
          Be pitiful, O God!

VI

The curse of gold upon the land
  The lack of bread enforces;
The rail-cars snort from strand to strand,
  Like more of Death's white horses!
The rich preach 'rights' and future days,
  And hear no angel scoffing,—
The poor die mute—with starving gaze
  On corn-ships in the offing.
          Be pitiful, O God!

VII

We meet together at the feast,
  To private mirth betake us;
We stare down in the winecup, lest
  Some vacant chair should shake us.
We name delight, and pledge it round—
  'It shall be ours to-morrow!'
God's seraphs, do your voices sound
  As sad in naming sorrow?
          Be pitiful, O God!

VIII

We sit together, with the skies,
  The steadfast skies, above us,
We look into each other's eyes,
  'And how long will you love us?'—
The eyes grow dim with prophecy,
  The voices, low and breathless,—
'Till death us part!'—O words, to be
  Our best, for love the deathless!
          Be pitiful, O God!

IX

We tremble by the harmless bed
  Of one loved and departed:
Our tears drop on the lips that said
  Last night, 'Be stronger-hearted!'
O God,—to clasp those fingers close,
  And yet to feel so lonely!—
To see a light upon such brows,
  Which is the daylight only!
          Be pitiful, O God!

X

The happy children come to us,
  And look up in our faces:
They ask us—Was it thus, and thus,
  When we were in their places?—
We cannot speak;—we see anew
  The hills we used to live in,
And feel our mother's smile press through
  The kisses she is giving.
          Be pitiful, O God!

XI

We pray together at the kirk,
  For mercy, mercy, solely:
Hands weary with the evil work,
  We lift them to the Holy.

The corpse is calm below our knee,
  Its spirit, bright before Thee—
Between them, worse than either, we—
  Without the rest of glory !
          Be pitiful, O God !

XII

We leave the communing of men,
  The murmur of the passions,
And live alone, to live again
  With endless generations.
Are we so brave ?—The sea and sky
In silence lift their mirrors,
And, glassed therein, our spirits high
  Recoil from their own terrors.
          Be pitiful, O God !

XIII

We sit on hills our childhood wist,
  Woods, hamlets, streams, beholding :
The sun strikes through the farthest mist,
  The city's spire to golden.
The city's golden spire it was,
When hope and health were strongest,
But now it is the churchyard grass
  We look upon the longest.
          Be pitiful, O God !

XIV

And soon all vision waxeth dull—
  Men whisper, ' He is dying ':
We cry no more ' Be pitiful !'
  We have no strength for crying.
No strength, no need. Then, soul of mine,
  Look up and triumph rather—
Lo, in the depth of God's Divine,
  The Son adjures the Father,
          BE PITIFUL, O GOD !

A PORTRAIT

One name is Elizabeth.—BEN JONSON.

I WILL paint her as I see her.
  Ten times have the lilies blown,
  Since she looked upon the sun.

And her face is lily-clear,
  Lily-shaped, and dropped in duty
  To the law of its own beauty.

Oval cheeks encoloured faintly,
  Which a trail of golden hair
  Keeps from fading off to air :

And a forehead fair and saintly,
  Which two blue eyes undershine,
  Like meek prayers before a shrine.

Face and figure of a child,—
  Though too calm, you think, and tender,
  For the childhood you would lend her.

Yet child-simple, undefiled,
  Frank, obedient,—waiting still
  On the turnings of your will.

Moving light, as all young things,
  As young birds, or early wheat,
  When the wind blows over it.

Only, free from flutterings
  Of loud mirth that scorneth measure—
  Taking love for her chief pleasure.

Choosing pleasures, for the rest,
  Which come softly—just as she,
  When she nestles at your knee.

Quiet talk she liketh best,
  In a bower of gentle looks,—
  Watering flowers, or reading books.

And her voice, it murmurs lowly,
  As a silver stream may run,
  Which yet feels, you feel, the sun.

And her smile, it seems half holy,
  As if drawn from thoughts more far
  Than our common jestings are.

And if any poet knew her,
  He would sing of her with falls
  Used in lovely madrigals.

And if any painter drew her,
  He would paint her unaware
  With a halo round the hair.

And if reader read the poem,
  He would whisper—' You have done a
  Consecrated little Una.'

And a dreamer (did you show him
  That same picture) would exclaim,
  ' Tis my angel, with a name !'

And a stranger, when he sees her
  In the street even—smileth stilly,
  Just as you would at a lily.

And all voices that address her,
  Soften, sleeken every word,
  As if speaking to a bird.

And all fancies yearn to cover
  The hard earth whereon she passes,
  With the thymy scented grasses.

And all hearts do pray, ' God love her !'—
  Aye, and always, in good sooth,
  We may all be sure HE DOTH.

CONFESSIONS

I

FACE to face in my chamber, my silent
    chamber, I saw her :
God and she and I only, . . there, I sate
    down to draw her
Soul through the clefts of confession. . .
    Speak, I am holding thee fast,
As the angels of resurrection shall do it
    at the last.
    ' My cup is blood-red
      With my sin,' she said,
  ' And I pour it out to the bitter lees,
As if the angels of judgement stood over
    me strong at the last,
    Or as thou wert as these !'

II

When God smote His hands together,
    and struck out thy soul as a spark
Into the organized glory of things, from
    deeps of the dark,—
Say, didst thou shine, didst thou burn,
    didst thou honour the power in
    the form,
As the star does at night, or the fire-fly,
    or even the little ground-worm ?
    ' I have sinned,' she said,
    ' For my seed-light shed
  Has smouldered away from His first
    decrees !
The cypress praiseth the fire-fly, the
    ground-leaf   praiseth   the
    worm,—
  I am viler than these !'

III

When God on that sin had pity, and
    did not trample thee straight
With His wild rains beating and drench-
    ing thy light found inadequate ;

When He only sent thee the north-
    winds, a little searching and chill,
To quicken thy flame . . didst thou kindle
    and flash to the heights of His
    will ?
    ' I have sinned,' she said,
    ' Unquickened, unspread
  My fire dropt down, and I wept on
    my knees !
I only said of His winds of the north as
    I shrank from their chill, . .
    What delight is in these ?'

IV

When God on that sin had pity, and did
    not meet it as such,
But tempered the wind to thy uses, and
    softened the world to thy touch,
At least thou wast moved in thy soul,
    though unable to prove it afar,
Thou couldst carry thy light like a jewel,
    not giving it out like a star ?
    ' I have sinned,' she said,
    ' And not merited
  The gift He gives, by the grace He sees !
The mine-cave praiseth the jewel, the
    hillside praiseth the star ;
    I am viler than these.'

V

Then I cried aloud in my passion, . .
    Unthankful and impotent crea-
    ture,
To throw up thy scorn unto God through
    the rents in thy beggarly nature !
If He, the all-giving and loving, is
    served so unduly, what then
Hast thou done to the weak and the false,
    and the changing, . . thy fellows
    of men ?
    ' I have *loved*,' she said,
    (Words bowing her head
  As the wind the wet acacia-trees !)
' I saw God sitting above me,—but I . . .
    I sate among men,
    And I have loved these.'

VI

Again with a lifted voice, like a choral
    trumpet that takes
The lowest note of a viol that trembles,
    and triumphing breaks

On the air with it solemn and clear,—
   'Behold! I have sinned not in
     this!
Where I loved, I have loved much and
    well,—I have verily loved not
    amiss.
   Let the living,' she said,
   'Inquire of the Dead,
In the house of the pale-fronted Images:
My own true dead will answer for me,
    that I have not loved amiss
   In my love for all these.

VII

'The least touch of their hands in the
    morning, I keep it by day and
    by night;
Their least step on the stair, at the door,
    still throbs through me, if ever
    so light;
Their least gift, which they left to my
    childhood, far off, in the long-
    ago years,
Is now turned from a toy to a relic, and
    seen through the crystals of
    tears.
   Dig the snow,' she said,
   'For my churchyard bed,
Yet I, as I sleep, shall not fear to freeze,
If one only of these my beloveds, shall
    love me with heart-warm tears,
   As I have loved these!

VIII

'If I angered any among them, from
    thenceforth my own life was
    sore;
If I fell by chance from their presence,
    I clung to their memory more.
Their tender I often felt holy, their
    bitter I sometimes called sweet;
And whenever their heart has refused
    me, I fell down straight at
    their feet.
   I have loved,' she said,—
   'Man is weak, God is dread,
Yet the weak man dies with his spirit
    at ease,
Having poured such an unguent of love
    but once on the Saviour's feet,
   As I lavished for these.'

IX

'Go,' I cried, 'thou hast chosen the
    Human, and left the Divine!
Then, at least, have the Human shared
    with thee their wild berry-wine?
Have they loved back thy love, and
    when strangers approached
    thee with blame,
Have they covered thy fault with their
    kisses, and loved thee the same?'
   But she shrunk and said,
   'God, over my head,
Must sweep in the wrath of his judge-
    ment-seas,
If *He* shall deal with me sinning, but
    only indeed the same
   And no gentler than these.'

LOVED ONCE

I

I CLASSED, appraising once,
Earth's lamentable sounds,—the wella-
    day,
   The jarring yea and nay,
The fall of kisses on unanswering clay,
The sobbed farewell, the welcome
    mournfuller,—
But all did leaven the air
With a less bitter leaven of sure despair
Than these words—'I loved ONCE.'

II

   And who saith 'I loved ONCE'?
Not angels,—whose clear eyes, love,
    love foresee,
   Love, through eternity,
And by To Love do apprehend To Be.
Not God, called LOVE, His noble crown-
    name, casting
   A light too broad for blasting!
The great God changing not from ever-
    lasting,
   Saith never 'I loved ONCE.'

III

   Oh, never is 'Loved ONCE'
Thy word, thou Victim-Christ, misprizèd
    friend!
   Thy cross and curse may rend,
But having loved Thou lovest to the end.

This is man's saying—man's. Too weak
   to move
   One spherèd star above,
Man desecrates the eternal God-word
   Love
   By his No More, and Once.

IV

How say ye ' We loved once,'
Blasphemers ? Is your earth not cold
   enow,
   Mourners, without that snow ?
Ah, friends ! and would ye wrong each
   other so ?
And could ye say of some whose love is
   known,
   Whose prayers have met your own,
Whose tears have fallen for you, whose
   smiles have shone
   So long,—'We loved them ONCE' ?

V

Could ye ' We loved her once '
Say calm of me, sweet friends, when
   out of sight ?
   When hearts of better right
Stand in between me and your happy
   light ?
Or when, as flowers kept too long in
   the shade,
   Ye find my colours fade,
And all that is not love in me, decayed?
   Such words—Ye loved me ONCE !

VI

Could ye ' We loved her once '
Say cold of me when further put away
   In earth's sepulchral clay,—
When mute the lips which deprecate
   to-day ?
Not so ! not then—least then. When
   life is shriven,
   And death's full joy is given,—
Of those who sit and love you up in
   heaven,
   Say not ' We loved them once.'

VII

Say never, ye loved ONCE.
God is too near above, the grave, beneath,
   And all our moments breathe
Too quick in mysteries of life and death,

For such a word. The eternities avenge
   Affections light of range.
There comes no change to justify that
   change,
   Whatever comes—Loved ONCE !

VIII

And yet that same word ONCE
Is humanly acceptive. Kings have said,
   Shaking a discrowned head,
' We ruled once,'—dotards, ' We once
   taught and led.'
Cripples once danced i' the vines—and
   bards approved
   Were once by scornings moved :
But love strikes one hour—LOVE ! those
   never loved
   Who dream that they loved ONCE.

THE HOUSE OF CLOUDS

I

I WOULD build a cloudy House
   For my thoughts to live in,
When for earth too fancy-loose,
   And too low for heaven.
Hush ! I talk my dream aloud ;
   I build it bright to see,—
I build it on the moonlit cloud
   To which I looked with *thee*.

II

Cloud-walls of the morning's grey,
   Faced with amber column,
Crowned with crimson cupola
   From a sunset solemn :
May-mists, for the casements, fetch,
   Pale and glimmering,
With a sunbeam hid in each,
   And a smell of spring.

III

Build the entrance high and proud,
   Darkening and then brightening,
Of a riven thunder-cloud,
   Veinèd by the lightning :
Use one with an iris-stain
   For the door within,
Turning to a sound like rain
   As I enter in.

IV

Build a spacious hall thereby,
    Boldly, never fearing;
Use the blue place of the sky
    Which the wind is clearing;
Branched with corridors sublime,
    Flecked with winding stairs,
Such as children wish to climb,
    Following their own prayers.

V

In the mutest of the house,
    I will have my chamber:
Silence at the door shall use
    Evening's light of amber;
Solemnizing every mood,
    Softening in degree,
Turning sadness into good
    As I turn the key.

VI

Be my chamber tapestried
    With the showers of summer,
Close, but soundless,—glorified
    When the sunbeams come here;
Wandering harpers, harping on
    Waters stringed for such,
Drawing colour, for a tune,
    With a vibrant touch.

VII

Bring a shadow green and still
    From the chestnut forest,
Bring a purple from the hill,
    When the heat is sorest;
Spread them out from wall to wall,
    Carpet-wove around,
Whereupon the foot shall fall
    In light instead of sound.

VIII

Bring fantastic cloudlets home
    From the noontide zenith,
Ranged for sculptures round the room,
    Named as Fancy weeneth.
Some be Junos, without eyes,
    Naiads, without sources;
Some be birds of paradise,
    Some, Olympian horses.

IX

Bring the dews the birds shake off,
    Waking in the hedges,—
Those too, perfumed, for a proof,
    From the lilies' edges;
From our England's field and moor,
    Bring them calm and white in,
Whence to form a mirror pure
    For Love's self-delighting.

X

Bring a grey cloud from the east
    Where the lark is singing
(Something of the song at least
    Unlost in the bringing):
That shall be a morning chair
    Poet-dream may sit in,
When it leans out on the air,
    Unrimed and unwritten.

XI

Bring the red cloud from the sun!
    While he sinketh, catch it:
That shall be a couch,—with one
    Sidelong star to watch it,—
Fit for Poet's finest thought
    At the curfew-sounding;
Things unseen being nearer brought
    Than the seen, around him.

XII

Poet's thought,—not poet's sigh.
    'Las, they come together!
Cloudy walls divide and fly,
    As in April weather!
Cupola and column proud,
    Structure bright to see.
Gone! except that moonlit cloud
    To which I looked with *thee*.

XIII

Let them.   Wipe such visionings
    From the fancy's cartel:
Love secures some fairer things,
    Dowered with his immortal.
The sun may darken, heaven be bowed,
    But still unchanged shall be,—
Here, in my soul,—that moonlit cloud,
    To which I looked with THEE!

A SABBATH MORNING AT SEA

I

THE ship went on with solemn face ;
  To meet the darkness on the deep,
  The solemn ship went onward.
I bowed down weary in the place,
  For parting tears and present sleep
    Had weighed mine eyelids down-
      ward.

II

Thick sleep which shut all dreams from
    me,
  And kept my inner self apart
  And quiet from emotion,
Then brake away and left me free,
  Made conscious of a human heart
    Betwixt the heaven and ocean.

III

The new sight, the new wondrous sight!
  The waters round me, turbulent,—
  The skies impassive o'er me,
Calm, in a moonless, sunless light,
  Half glorified by that intent
    Of holding the day-glory !

IV

Two pale thin clouds did stand upon
  The meeting line of sea and sky,
  With aspect still and mystic.
I think they did foresee the sun,
  And rested on their prophecy
    In quietude majestic,

V

Then flushed to radiance where they
    stood,
  Like statues by the open tomb
  Of shining saints half risen.—
The sun !—he came up to be viewed,
  And sky and sea made mighty room
    To inaugurate the vision.

VI

I oft had seen the dawnlight run,
  As red wine, through the hills, and
    break
    Through many a mist's inurning ;

But, here, no earth profaned the sun !
  Heaven, ocean, did alone partake
    The sacrament of morning.

VII

Away with thoughts fantastical !
  I would be humble to my worth,
  Self-guarded as self-doubted :
Though here no earthly shadows fall,
  I, joying, grieving without earth,
    May desecrate without it.

VIII

God's sabbath morning sweeps the
    waves ;
  I would not praise the pageant high,
  Yet miss the dedicature.
I, carried toward the sunless graves
  By force of natural things,—should I
    Exult in only nature ?

IX

And could I bear to sit alone
  'Mid nature's fixed benignities,
  While my warm pulse was moving ?
Too dark thou art, O glittering sun,
  Too strait ye are, capacious seas,
    To satisfy the loving !

X

It seems a better lot than so,
  To sit with friends beneath the beech,
  And feel them dear and dearer ;
Or follow children as they go
  In pretty pairs, with softened speech,
    As the church-bells ring nearer.

XI

Love me, sweet friends, this sabbath day !
  The sea sings round me while ye roll
    Afar the hymn unaltered,
And kneel, where once I knelt to pray,
  And bless me deeper in the soul,
    Because the voice has faltered.

XII

And though this sabbath comes to me
  Without the stolèd minister
  Or chanting congregation,
God's Spirit brings communion, HE
  Who brooded soft on waters drear,
    Creator on creation.

XIII

Himself, I think, shall draw me higher,
  Where keep the saints with harp and
    song
    An endless sabbath morning,
And on that sea commixed with fire
  Oft drop their eyelids, raised too long
    To the full Godhead's burning.

A FLOWER IN A LETTER

I

My lonely chamber next the sea
Is full of many flowers set free
  By summer's earliest duty :
Dear friends upon the garden-walk
Might stop amid their fondest talk
  To pull the least in beauty.

II

A thousand flowers—each seeming one
That learnt by gazing on the sun
  To counterfeit his shining :
Within whose leaves the holy dew
That falls from heaven, has won anew
  A glory, in declining.

III

Red roses, used to praises long,
Contented with the poet's song,
  The nightingale's being over ;
And lilies white, prepared to touch
The whitest thought, nor soil it much,
  Of dreamer turned to lover.

IV

Deep violets, you liken to
The kindest eyes that look on you,
  Without a thought disloyal ;
And cactuses a queen might don,
If weary of a golden crown,
  And still appear as royal.

V

Pansies for ladies all—(I wis
That none who wear such brooches, miss
  A jewel in the mirror) ;
And tulips, children love to stretch
Their fingers down, to feel in each
  Its beauty's secret nearer.

VI

Love's language may be talked with
    these ;
To work out choicest sentences
  No blossoms can be meeter ;
And, such being used in Eastern bowers,
Young maids may wonder if the flowers
  Or meanings be the sweeter.

VII

And such being strewn before a bride,
Her little foot may turn aside,
  Their longer bloom decreeing,
Unless some voice's whispered sound
Should make her gaze upon the ground
  Too earnestly—for seeing.

VIII

And such being scattered on a grave,
Whoever mourneth there, may have
  A type which seemeth worthy
Of that fair body hid below,
Which bloomed on earth a time ago,
  Then perished as the earthy.

IX

And such being wreathed for worldly
    feast,
Across the brimming cup some guest
  Their rainbow colours viewing,
May feel them, with a silent start,
The covenant, his childish heart
  With nature made,—renewing.

X

No flowers our gardened England hath
To match with these, in bloom and breath,
  Which from the world are hiding,
In sunny Devon moist with rills,—
A nunnery of cloistered hills,
  The elements presiding.

XI

By Loddon's stream the flowers are fair
That meet one gifted lady's care
  With prodigal rewarding
(For Beauty is too used to run
To Mitford's bower—to want the sun
  To light her through the garden).

XII

But, here, all summers are comprised—
The nightly frosts shrink exorcised
  Before the priestly moonshine ;
And every wind with stolèd feet,
In wandering down the alleys sweet,
  Steps lightly on the sunshine,

XIII

And (having promised Harpocrate
Among the nodding roses, that
  No harm shall touch his daughters)
Gives quite away the rushing sound,
He dares not use upon such ground,
  To ever-trickling waters.

XIV

Yet, sun and wind ! what can ye do
But make the leaves more brightly show
  In posies newly gathered ?
I look away from all your best,
To one poor flower unlike the rest,
  A little flower half-withered.

XV

I do not think it ever was
A pretty flower,—to make the grass
  Look greener where it reddened ;
And now it seems ashamed to be
Alone, in all this company,
  Of aspect shrunk and saddened.

XVI

A chamber-window was the spot
It grew in, from a garden-pot,
  Among the city shadows.
If any, tending it, might seem
To smile, 'twas only in a dream
  Of nature in the meadows.

XVII

How coldly on its head did fall
The sunshine, from the city wall
  In pale refraction driven !
How sadly, plashed upon its leaves,
The raindrops, losing in the eaves
  The first sweet news of heaven !

XVIII

And those who planted, gathered it
In gamesome or in loving fit,
  And sent it as a token
Of what their city pleasures be,—
For one, in Devon by the sea
  And garden-blooms, to look on.

XIX

But SHE, for whom the jest was meant,
With a grave passion innocent
  Receiving what was given,—
Oh, if her face she turnèd then,
Let none say 'twas to gaze again
  Upon the flowers of Devon !

XX

Because, whatever virtue dwells
In genial skies, warm oracles
  For gardens brightly springing,—
The flower which grew beneath your
    eyes,
Belovèd friends, to mine supplies
  A beauty worthier singing !

THE MASK

I

I HAVE a smiling face, she said,
  I have a jest for all I meet,
I have a garland for my head
  And all its flowers are sweet,—
And so you call me gay, she said.

II

Grief taught to me this smile, she said,
  And Wrong did teach this jesting bold ;
These flowers were plucked from garden-
    bed
  While a death-chime was tolled.
And what now will you say ?—she said.

III

Behind no prison-grate, she said,
  Which slurs the sunshine half a mile,
Live captives so uncomforted
  As souls behind a smile.
God's pity let us pray, she said.

IV

I know my face is bright, she said,—
  Such brightness, dying suns diffuse ;
I bear upon my forehead shed
  The sign of what I lose,—
The ending of my day, she said.

V

If I dared leave this smile, she said,
  And take a moan upon my mouth,
And tie a cypress round my head,
  And let my tears run smooth,—
It were the happier way, she said.

VI

And since that must not be, she said,
  I fain your bitter world would leave.
How calmly, calmly, smile the Dead,
  Who do not, therefore, grieve !
The yea of Heaven is yea, she said.

VII

But in your bitter world, she said,
  Face-joy's a costly mask to wear.
'Tis bought with pangs long nourishèd,
  And rounded to despair.
Grief's earnest makes life's play, she said.

VIII

Ye weep for those who weep? she said—
  Ah fools ! I bid you pass them by.
Go, weep for those whose hearts have
    bled
  What time their eyes were dry.
Whom sadder can I say ? she said.

CALLS ON THE HEART

I

FREE Heart, that singest to-day,
Like a bird on the first green spray,
Wilt thou go forth to the world,
Where the hawk hath his wing un-
    furled
To follow, perhaps, thy way ?
Where the tamer, thine own will bind,
And, to make thee sing, will blind,
While the little hip grows for the free
    behind ?
    Heart, wilt thou go ?
    —' No, no!
  Free hearts are better so.'

II

The world, thou hast heard it told,
Has counted its robber-gold,
And the pieces stick to the hand.
The world goes riding it fair and grand,
  While the truth is bought and sold !
World-voices east, world-voices west,
They call thee, Heart, from thine early
    rest,
' Come hither, come hither and be our
    guest.'
    Heart, wilt thou go ?
    —' No, no!
  Good hearts are calmer so.'

III

Who calleth thee, Heart ? World's
    Strife,
With a golden heft to his knife ;
World's Mirth, with a finger fine
That draws on a board in wine
  Her blood-red plans of life ;
World's Gain, with a brow knit down ;
World's Fame, with a laurel crown,
Which rustles most as the leaves turn
    brown—
    Heart, wilt thou go ?
    —' No, no!
  Calm hearts are wiser so.'

IV

Hast heard that Proserpina
(Once fooling) was snatched away,
To partake the dark king's seat,—
And that the tears ran fast on her feet
  To think how the sun shone yester-
    day ?
With her ankles sunken in asphodel
She wept for the roses of earth which
    fell
From her lap when the wild car drave
    to hell.
    Heart, wilt thou go ?
    —' No, no!
  Wise hearts are warmer so.'

V

And what is this place not seen,
Where Hearts may hide serene ?
' 'Tis a fair still house well-kept,
Which humble thoughts have swept,
  And holy prayers made clean.
There, I sit with Love in the sun,
And we two never have done
Singing sweeter songs than are guessed
    by one.'
    Heart, wilt thou go ?
    —' No, no!
  Warm hearts are fuller so.'

VI

O Heart, O Love,—I fear
That Love may be kept too near.
Hast heard, O Heart, that tale,
How Love may be false and frail
  To a heart once holden dear ?
—' But this true Love of mine
Clings fast as the clinging vine,

And mingles pure as the grapes in wine.'
   Heart, wilt thou go?
     —'No, no!
   Full hearts beat higher so.'

VII

O Heart, O Love, beware!—
Look up, and boast not there.
For who has twirled at the pin?
'Tis the World, between Death and
     Sin,—
  The World, and the world's
     Despair!
And Death has quickened his pace
To the hearth, with a mocking face,
Familiar as Love, in Love's own place—
   Heart, wilt thou go?
     —'Still, no!
   High hearts must grieve even so.'

VIII

The house is waste to-day,—
The leaf has dropt from the spray,
The thorn, prickt through to the song.
If summer doeth no wrong
   The winter will, they say.
Sing, Heart! what heart replies?
In vain we were calm and wise,
If the tears unkissed stand on in our eyes.
   Heart, wilt thou go?
     —'Ah, no!
   Grieved hearts must break even so.'

IX

Howbeit all is not lost.
The warm noon ends in frost,
And worldly tongues of promise,
Like sheep-bells, die off from us
   On the desert hills cloud-crossed!
Yet, through the silence, shall
Pierce the death-angel's call,
And 'Come up hither,' recover all.
   Heart, wilt thou go?
     —'I go!
   Broken hearts triumph so.'

WISDOM UNAPPLIED

I

IF I were thou, O butterfly,
And poised my purple wing to spy
The sweetest flowers that live and die,

II

I would not waste my strength on those,
As thou,—for summer has a close,
And pansies bloom not in the snows.

III

If I were thou, O working bee,
And all that honey-gold I see
Could delve from roses easily,

IV

I would not hive it at man's door,
As thou,—that heirdom of my store
Should make him rich, and leave me poor.

V

If I were thou, O eagle proud,
And screamed the thunder back aloud,
And faced the lightning from the cloud,

VI

I would not build my eyrie-throne,
As thou,—upon a crumbling stone,
Which the next storm may trample down.

VII

If I were thou, O gallant steed,
With pawing hoof, and dancing head,
And eye outrunning thine own speed,

VIII

I would not meeken to the rein,
As thou,—nor smooth my nostril plain
From the glad desert's snort and strain.

IX

If I were thou, red-breasted bird,
With song at shut-up window heard,
Like Love's sweet yes too long deferred,

X

I would not overstay delight,
As thou,—but take a swallow-flight,
Till the new spring returned to sight.

XI

While yet I spake, a touch was laid
Upon my brow, whose pride did fade
As thus, methought, an angel said,—

XII

'If I were thou who sing'st this song,
Most wise for others, and most strong
In seeing right while doing wrong,

XIII

'I would not waste my cares, and choose,
As *thou*,—to seek what thou must lose,
Such gains as perish in the use.

XIV

'I would not work where none can win,
As *thou*,—half way 'twixt grief and sin,
But look above, and judge within.

XV

'I would not let my pulse beat high,
As *thou*,—towards fame's regality,
Nor yet in love's great jeopardy.

XVI

'I would not champ the hard cold bit,
As *thou*,—of what the world thinks fit,
But take God's freedom, using it.

XVII

'I would not play earth's winter out,
As *thou*,—but gird my soul about,
And live for life past death and doubt.

XVIII

'Then sing, O singer!—but allow,
Beast, fly, and bird, called foolish now,
Are wise (for all thy scorn) as thou!'

MEMORY AND HOPE

I

BACK-LOOKING Memory
And prophet Hope both sprang from out
    the ground;
One, where the flashing of Cherubic
    sword
    Fell sad, in Eden's ward,—
And one, from Eden earth, within the
    sound
Of the four rivers lapsing pleasantly,
What time the promise after curse was
    said—
    'Thy seed shall bruise his head.'

II

Poor Memory's brain is wild,
As moonstruck by that flaming atmo-
    sphere
When she was born. Her deep eyes
    shine and shone
    With light that conquereth sun

And stars to wanner paleness year by
    year.
With odorous gums, she mixeth things
    defiled :
She trampleth down earth's grasses green
    and sweet,
    With her far-wandering feet.

III

She plucketh many flowers,
Their beauty on her bosom's coldness
    killing :
She teacheth every melancholy sound
    To winds and waters round :
She droppeth tears with seed where man
    is tilling
The rugged soil in his exhausted hours :
She smileth—ah me! in her smile doth go
    A mood of deeper woe.

IV

Hope tripped on out of sight,
Crowned with an Eden wreath she saw
    not wither,
And went a-nodding through the wilder-
    ness
    With brow that shone no less
Than a sea-gull's wing, brought nearer
    by rough weather ;
Searching the treeless rock for fruits of
    light ;
Her fair quick feet being armed from
    stones and cold
    By slippers of pure gold.

V

Memory did Hope much wrong
And, while she dreamed, her slippers
    stole away ;
But still she wended on with mirth un-
    heeding,
    Although her feet were bleeding,
Till Memory tracked her on a certain day,
And with most evil eyes did search her
    long
And cruelly, whereat she sank to ground
    In a stark deadly swound.

VI

And so my Hope were slain,
Had it not been that THOU wast standing
    near,
O Thou, who saidest 'live,' to creatures
    lying
    In their own blood and dying!

For Thou her forehead to Thine heart didst
    rear
And make its silent pulses sing again,—
Pouring a new light o'er her darkened
    eyne,
    With tender tears from Thine !

VII

Therefore my Hope arose
From out her swound and gazed upon
    Thy face,
And, meeting there that soft subduing
    look
Which Peter's spirit shook,
Sank downward in a rapture to embrace
Thy piercèd hands and feet with kisses
    close,
And prayed Thee to assist her evermore
    To 'reach the things before.'

VIII

Then gavest Thou the smile
Whence angel-wings thrill quick like
    summer lightning,
Vouchsafing rest beside Thee, where she
    never
From Love and Faith may sever.—
Whereat the Eden crown she saw not
    whitening
A time ago, though whitening all the
    while,
Reddened with life, to hear the Voice
    which talked
    To Adam as He walked.

HUMAN LIFE'S MYSTERY

I

WE sow the glebe, we reap the corn,
    We build the house where we may
    rest,
And then, at moments, suddenly,
We look up to the great wide sky,
Inquiring wherefore we were born . . .
    For earnest, or for jest ?

II

The senses folding thick and dark
    About the stifled soul within,

We guess diviner things beyond,
And yearn to them with yearning fond ;
We strike out blindly to a mark
    Believed in, but not seen.

III

We vibrate to the pant and thrill
    Wherewith Eternity has curled
In serpent-twine about God's seat ;
While, freshening upward to His feet,
In gradual growth His full-leaved will
    Expands from world to world.

IV

And, in the tumult and excess
    Of act and passion under sun,
We sometimes hear—oh, soft and far,
As silver star did touch with star,
The kiss of Peace and Righteousness
    Through all things that are done.

V

God keeps His holy mysteries
    Just on the outside of man's dream.
In diapason slow, we think
To hear their pinions rise and sink,
While they float pure beneath His eyes,
    Like swans adown a stream.

VI

Abstractions, are they, from the forms
    Of His great beauty ?—exaltations
From His great glory ?—strong previsions
Of what we shall be ?—intuitions
Of what we are—in calms and storms,
    Beyond our peace and passions ?

VII

Things nameless ! which, in passing so,
    Do stroke us with a subtle grace.
We say, 'Who passes?'—they are dumb.
We cannot see them go or come :
Their touches fall soft—cold—as snow
    Upon a blind man's face.

VIII

Yet, touching so, they draw above
    Our common thoughts to Heaven's
    unknown ;
Our daily joy and pain, advance
To a divine significance,—
Our human love—O mortal love,
    That light is not its own !

IX

And, sometimes, horror chills our blood
    To be so near such mystic Things,
And we wrap round us, for defence,
Our purple manners, moods of sense—
As angels, from the face of God,
    Stand hidden in their wings.

X

And, sometimes, through life's heavy
        swound
    We grope for them !—with strangled
        breath
We stretch our hands abroad and try
To reach them in our agony,—
And widen, so, the broad life-wound
    Which soon is large enough for death.

A CHILD'S THOUGHT OF GOD

I

THEY say that God lives very high :
    But if you look above the pines
You cannot see our God ; and why ?

II

And if you dig down in the mines
    You never see Him in the gold ;
Though, from Him, all that 's glory shines.

III

God is so good, He wears a fold
    Of heaven and earth across His face—
Like secrets kept, for love, untold.

IV

But still I feel that His embrace
    Slides down by thrills, through all
        things made,
Through sight and sound of every place.

V

As if my tender mother laid
    On my shut lids her kisses' pressure,
Half-waking me at night, and said
    'Who kissed you through the dark,
        dear guesser ?'

THE CLAIM

I

GRIEF sate upon a rock and sighed one
        day,
    (Sighing is all her rest !)
'Wellaway, wellaway, ah, wellaway !'
As ocean beat the stone, did she her
        breast,
'Ah, wellaway ! . . ah me ! alas, ah me !'
    Such sighing uttered she.

II

A Cloud spake out of heaven, as soft as
        rain
    That falls on water,—' Lo,
The Winds have wandered from me !
        I remain
Alone in the sky-waste, and cannot go
To lean my whiteness on the mountain
        blue
    Till wanted for more dew.

III

'The Sun has struck my brain to weary
        peace,
    Whereby constrained and pale
I spin for him a larger golden fleece
Than Jason's, yearning for as full a sail.
Sweet Grief, when thou hast sighèd to
        thy mind,
    Give me a sigh for wind,

IV

'And let it carry me adown the west.'
    But Love, who, pròstrated,
Lay at Grief's foot, his lifted eyes
        possessed
Of her full image, answered in her stead :
' Now nay, now nay ! she shall not give
        away
What is my wealth, for any Cloud that
        flieth.
    Where Grief makes moan,
    Love claims his own !
And therefore do I lie here night and day,
And eke my life out with the breath she
        sigheth.'

SONG OF THE ROSE

ATTRIBUTED TO SAPPHO

(*From Achilles Tatius*)

IF Zeus chose us a King of the flowers
    in his mirth,
  He would call to the rose and would
    royally crown it,
For the rose, ho, the rose! is the grace
    of the earth,
  Is the light of the plants that are
    growing upon it.
For the rose, ho, the rose! is the eye of
    the flowers,
  Is the blush of the meadows that feel
    themselves fair,—
Is the lightning of beauty, that strikes
    through the bowers
  On pale lovers who sit in the glow
    unaware.
Ho, the rose breathes of love! ho, the
    rose lifts the cup
  To the red lips of Cypris invoked for
    a guest!
Ho, the rose, having curled its sweet
    eaves for the world,
  Takes delight in the motion its petals
    keep up,
As they laugh to the Wind as it laughs
    from the west.

A DEAD ROSE

I

O ROSE, who dares to name thee?
No longer roseate now, nor soft, nor
    sweet,
But pale, and hard, and dry, as stubble-
    wheat,—
  Kept seven years in a drawer—thy
    titles shame thee.

II

The breeze that used to blow thee
Between the hedgerow thorns, and take
    away
An odour up the lane to last all day,—
  If breathing now, — unsweetened
    would forgo thee.

III

The sun that used to smite thee,
And mix his glory in thy gorgeous urn
Till beam appeared to bloom, and flower
    to burn,—
  If shining now,—with not a hue
    would light thee.

IV

The dew that used to wet thee,
And, white first, grow incarnadined,
    because
It lay upon thee where the crimson
    was,—
  If dropping now,—would darken,
    where it met thee.

V

The fly that 'lit upon thee,
To stretch the tendrils of its tiny feet
Along thy leaf's pure edges after heat,—
  If 'lighting now,—would coldly over-
    run thee.

VI

The bee that once did suck thee,
And build thy perfumed ambers up his
    hive,
And swoon in thee for joy, till scarce
    alive,—
  If passing now,—would blindly over-
    look thee.

VII

The heart doth recognize thee,
Alone, alone! the heart doth smell thee
    sweet,
Doth view thee fair, doth judge thee
    most complete,
  Perceiving all those changes that dis-
    guise thee.

VIII

Yes, and the heart doth owe thee
More love, dead rose, than to any roses
    bold
Which Julia wears at dances, smiling
    cold!—
  Lie still upon this heart—which
    breaks below thee!

THE EXILE'S RETURN

I

WHEN from thee, weeping I removed,
  And from my land for years,
I thought not to return, Beloved,
  With those same parting tears.
I come again to hill and lea,
  Weeping for thee.

II

I clasped thine hand, when standing last
  Upon the shore in sight.
The land is green, the ship is fast,
  I shall be there to-night :
I shall be there—no longer *we*—
  No more with thee !

III

Had I beheld thee dead and still,
  I might more clearly know,
How heart of thine could turn as chill
  As hearts by nature so ;
How change could touch the falsehood-
    free
  And changeless *thee*.

IV

But now thy fervid looks last-seen
  Within my soul remain ;
'Tis hard to think that *they* have been,
  To be no more again !
That I shall vainly wait—ah me !
  A word from thee.

V

I could not bear to look upon
  That mound of funeral clay,
Where one sweet voice is silence,—one
  Ethereal brow decay ;
Where all thy mortal I may see,
  But never thee.

VI

For thou art where all friends are gone
  Whose parting pain is o'er ;
And I, who love and weep alone,
  Where thou wilt weep no more,
Weep bitterly and selfishly,
  For *me*, not *thee*.

VII

I know, Beloved, thou canst not know
  That I endure this pain ;
For saints in heaven, the Scriptures show,
  Can never grieve again —
And grief known mine, even there,
    would be
  Still shared by thee.

THE SLEEP

He giveth His beloved sleep.—*Ps.* cxxvii. 2.

I

OF all the thoughts of God that are
Borne inward unto souls afar,
Along the Psalmist's music deep,
Now tell me if that any is,
For gift or grace, surpassing this—
' He giveth His belovèd, sleep ?'

II

What would we give to our beloved?
The hero's heart, to be unmoved,
The poet's star-tuned harp, to sweep,
The patriot's voice, to teach and rouse,
The monarch's crown, to light the
    brows ?—
He giveth His belovèd, sleep.

III

What do we give to our beloved ?
A little faith all undisproved,
A little dust to overweep,
And bitter memories to make
The whole earth blasted for our sake.
He giveth His belovèd, sleep.

IV

' Sleep soft, beloved !' we sometimes say,
But have no tune to charm away
Sad dreams that through the eyelids
    creep.
But never doleful dream again
Shall break the happy slumber when
He giveth His belovèd, sleep.

V

O earth, so full of dreary noises !
O men, with wailing in your voices !
O delvèd gold, the wailers heap !
O strife, O curse, that o'er it fall !
God strikes a silence through you all,
And giveth His belovèd, sleep.

VI

His dews drop mutely on the hill ;
His cloud above it saileth still,
Though on its slope men sow and reap.
More softly than the dew is shed,
Or cloud is floated overhead,
He giveth His belovèd, sleep.

VII

Aye, men may wonder while they scan
A living, thinking, feeling man
Confirmed in such a rest to keep ;
But angels say, and through the word
I think their happy smile is *heard*—
' He giveth His belovèd, sleep.'

VIII

For me, my heart that erst did go
Most like a tired child at a show,
That sees through tears the mummers
　　leap,
Would now its wearied vision close,
Would childlike on His love repose,
Who giveth His belovèd, sleep.

IX

And, friends, dear friends,—when it
　　shall be
That this low breath is gone from me,
And round my bier ye come to weep,
Let One, most loving of you all,
Say, ' Not a tear must o'er her fall ;
He giveth His belovèd, sleep.'

THE MEASURE

He comprehended the dust of the earth in a
measure (שָׁלִישׁ).—*Isaiah* xl. 12.

Thou givest them tears to drink in a measure
(שָׁלִישׁ)[1].—*Psalm* lxxx. 5.

I

God, the Creator, with a pulseless hand
Of unoriginated power, hath weighed
The dust of earth and tears of man in one
　　Measure, and by one weight.
　　So saith His holy book.

II

Shall we, then, who have issued from
　　the dust,
And there return,—shall we, who toil
　　for dust,

[1] I believe that the word occurs in no other
part of the Hebrew Scriptures.

And wrap our winnings in this dusty life,
　　Say, ' No more tears, Lord God !
　　The measure runneth o'er ' ?

III

Oh, Holder of the balance, laughest Thou?
Nay, Lord ! be gentler to our foolishness,
For His sake who assumed our dust and
　　turns
　　On Thee pathetic eyes
　　Still moistened with our tears.

IV

And teach us, O our Father, while we
　　weep,
To look in patience upon earth and
　　learn—
Waiting, in that meek gesture, till at last
　　These tearful eyes be filled
　　With the dry dust of death.

COWPER'S GRAVE

I

It is a place where poets crowned may
　　feel the heart's decaying ;
It is a place where happy saints may
　　weep amid their praying.
Yet let the grief and humbleness, as low
　　as silence, languish :
Earth surely now may give her calm to
　　whom she gave her anguish.

II

O poets, from a maniac's tongue was
　　poured the deathless singing ;
O Christians, at your cross of hope, a
　　hopeless hand was clinging !
O men, this man in brotherhood your
　　weary paths beguiling,
Groaned inly while he taught you peace,
　　and died while ye were smiling !

III

And now, what time ye all may read
　　through dimming tears his story,
How discord on the music fell, and dark-
　　ness on the glory,
And how when, one by one, sweet sounds
　　and wandering lights departed,
He wore no less a loving face because so
　　broken-hearted,

IV

He shall be strong to sanctify the poet's
    high vocation,
And bow the meekest Christian down in
    meeker adoration ;
Nor ever shall he be, in praise, by wise
    or good forsaken,
Named softly as the household name of
    one whom God hath taken.

V

With quiet sadness and no gloom I learn
    to think upon him,—
With meekness that is gratefulness to
    God whose heaven hath won him,
Who suffered once the madness-cloud to
    His own love to blind him,
But gently led the blind along where
    breath and bird could find him ;

VI

And wrought within his shattered brain
    such quick poetic senses
As hills have language for, and stars,
    harmonious influences.
The pulse of dew upon the grass, kept
    his within its number,
And silent shadows from the trees re-
    freshed him like a slumber.

VII

Wild timid hares were drawn from woods
    to share his home-caresses,
Uplooking to his human eyes with sylvan
    tendernesses.
The very world, by God's constraint,
    from falsehood's ways removing,
Its women and its men became, beside
    him, true and loving.

VIII

And though, in blindness, he remained
    unconscious of that guiding,
And things provided came without the
    sweet sense of providing,
He testified this solemn truth, while
    frenzy desolated,
—Nor man nor nature satisfy whom only
    God created.

IX

Like a sick child that knoweth not his
    mother while she blesses
And drops upon his burning brow the
    coolness of her kisses,—

That turns his fevered eyes around—'My
    mother ! where's my mother ?'—
As if such tender words and deeds could
    come from any other !—

X

The fever gone, with leaps of heart he
    sees her bending o'er him,
Her face all pale from watchful love, the
    unweary love she bore him !—
Thus, woke the poet from the dream his
    life's long fever gave him,
Beneath those deep pathetic Eyes, which
    closed in death to save him.

XI

Thus ? oh, not *thus !* no type of earth can
    image that awaking,
Wherein he scarcely heard the chant of
    seraphs, round him breaking,
Or felt the new immortal throb of soul
    from body parted,
But felt those eyes alone, and knew,—
    '*My* Saviour ! *not* deserted !'

XII

Deserted ! Who hath dreamt that when
    the cross in darkness rested,
Upon the Victim's hidden face, no love
    was manifested ?
What frantic hands outstretched have
    e'er the atoning drops averted ?
What tears have washed them from the
    soul, that *one* should be deserted ?

XIII

Deserted ! God could separate from His
    own essence rather ;
And Adam's sins *have* swept between the
    righteous Son and Father.
Yea, once, Immanuel's orphaned cry His
    universe hath shaken —
It went up single, echoless, 'My God, I
    am forsaken !'

XIV

It went up from the Holy's lips amid His
    lost creation,
That, of the lost, no son should use those
    words of desolation !
That earth's worst frenzies, marring
    hope, should mar not hope's
    fruition,
And I, on Cowper's grave, should see
    his rapture in a vision.

THE WEAKEST THING

I

WHICH is the weakest thing of all
  Mine heart can ponder?
The sun, a little cloud can pall
  With darkness yonder?
The cloud, a little wind can move
  Where'er it listeth?
The wind, a little leaf above,
  Though sere, resisteth?

II

What time that yellow leaf was green,
  My days were gladder;
But now, whatever Spring may mean,
  I must grow sadder.
Ah me! a *leaf* with sighs can wring
  My lips asunder?
Then is mine heart the weakest thing
  Itself can ponder.

III

Yet, Heart, when sun and cloud are pined
  And drop together,
And at a blast which is not wind
  The forests wither,
Thou, from the darkening deathly curse,
  To glory breakest,—
The Strongest of the universe
  Guarding the weakest!

THE PET-NAME

—— the name
Which from THEIR lips seemed a caress.
  MISS MITFORD'S *Dramatic Scenes.*

I

I HAVE a name, a little name,
  Uncadenced for the ear,
Unhonoured by ancestral claim,
Unsanctified by prayer and psalm
  The solemn font anear.

II

It never did, to pages wove
  For gay romance, belong;
It never dedicate did move
As 'Sacharissa,' unto love—
  'Orinda,' unto song.

III

Though I write books it will be read
  Upon the leaves of none,
And afterward, when I am dead,
Will ne'er be graved for sight or tread,
  Across my funeral-stone.

IV

This name, whoever chance to call,
  Perhaps your smile may win.
Nay, do not smile! mine eyelids fall
Over mine eyes, and feel withal
  The sudden tears within.

V

Is there a leaf that greenly grows
  Where summer meadows bloom,
But gathereth the winter snows,
And changeth to the hue of those,
  If lasting till they come?

VI

Is there a word, or jest, or game,
  But time encrusteth round
With sad associate thoughts the same?
And so to me my very name
  Assumes a mournful sound.

VII

My brother gave that name to me
  When we were children twain,—
When names acquired baptismally
Were hard to utter, as to see
  That life had any pain.

VIII

No shade was on us then, save one
  Of chestnuts from the hill—
And through the word our laugh did run
As part thereof. The mirth being done,
  He calls me by it still.

IX

Nay, do not smile! I hear in it
  What none of you can hear,—
The talk upon the willow seat,
The bird and wind that did repeat
  Around, our human cheer.

X

I hear the birthday's noisy bliss,
  My sisters' woodland glee,—
My father's praise, I did not miss,
When stooping down he cared to kiss
  The poet at his knee,—

XI

And voices, which, to name me, ay
   Their tenderest tones were keeping—
To some I never more can say
An answer, till God wipes away
   In heaven these drops of weeping.

XII

My name to me a sadness wears,
   No murmurs cross my mind.
Now God be thanked for these thick tears,
Which show, of those departed years,
   Sweet memories left behind.

XIII

Now God be thanked for years enwrought
   With love which softens yet.
Now God be thanked for every thought
Which is so tender it has caught
   Earth's guerdon of regret.

XIV

Earth saddens, never shall remove
   Affections purely given ;
And e'en that mortal grief shall prove
The immortality of love,
   And heighten it with Heaven.

THE MOURNING MOTHER

OF THE DEAD BLIND

I

Dost thou weep, mourning mother,
   For thy blind boy in grave ?
That no more with each other
   Sweet counsel ye can have ?—
That he, left dark by nature,
   Can never more be led
By thee, maternal creature,
   Along smooth paths instead ?
That thou canst no more show him
   The sunshine, by the heat ;
The river's silver flowing,
   By murmurs at his feet ?
The foliage, by its coolness ;
   The roses, by their smell ;
And all creation's fullness,
   By Love's invisible ?

Weepest thou to behold not
   His meek blind eyes again,—
Closed doorways which were folded,
   And prayed against in vain—
And under which sate smiling
   The child-mouth evermore,
As one who watcheth, wiling
   The time by, at a door ?
And weepest thou to feel not
   His clinging hand on thine—
Which now, at dream-time, will not
   Its cold touch disentwine ?
And weepest thou still ofter,
   Oh, never more to mark
His low soft words, made softer
   By speaking in the dark ?
Weep on, thou mourning mother !

II

But since to him when living
   Thou wast both sun and moon,
Look o'er his grave, surviving,
   From a high sphere alone.
Sustain that exaltation,
   Expand that tender light,
And hold in mother-passion
   Thy Blessèd in thy sight.
See how he went out straightway
   From the dark world he knew,—
No twilight in the gateway
   To mediate 'twixt the two,—
Into the sudden glory,
   Out of the dark he trod,
Departing from before thee
   At once to light and GOD !—
For the first face, beholding
   The Christ's in its divine,
For the first place, the golden
   And tideless hyaline ;
With trees, at lasting summer,
   That rock to songful sound,
While angels, the new-comer,
   Wrap a still smile around.
Oh, in the blessed psalm now,
   His happy voice he tries,
Spreading a thicker palm-bough,
   Than others, o'er his eyes !
Yet still, in all the singing,
   Thinks haply of thy song
Which, in his life's first springing,
   Sang to him all night long ;

And wishes it beside him,
  With kissing lips that cool
And soft did overglide him,
  To make the sweetness full.
Look up, O mourning mother,
  Thy blind boy walks in light!
Ye wait for one another,
  Before God's infinite.
But thou art now the darkest,
  Thou mother left below—
Thou, the sole blind,—thou markest,
  Content that it be so,—
Until ye two have meeting
  Where Heaven's pearl-gate is,
And *he* shall lead thy feet in,
  As once thou leddest *his*.
Wait on, thou mourning mother.

A VALEDICTION

I

God be with thee, my belovèd—God be
    with thee!
  Else alone thou goest forth,
  Thy face unto the north,
Moor and pleasance all around thee and
    beneath thee,
  Looking equal in one snow;
  While I who try to reach thee,
  Vainly follow, vainly follow,
  With the farewell and the hollo,
  And cannot reach thee so.
  Alas, I can but teach thee!
God be with thee, my belovèd—God be
    with thee.

II

Can I teach thee, my belovèd—can I
    teach thee?
  If I said, 'Go left or right,'
  The counsel would be light,
The wisdom, poor of all that could enrich
    thee.
  My right would show like left;
  My raising would depress thee,
  My choice of light would blind thee,
  Of way, would leave behind thee,
  Of end, would leave bereft.
  Alas, I can but bless thee!
May God teach thee, my belovèd—may
    God teach thee.

III

Can I bless thee, my belovèd—can I
    bless thee?
  What blessing word can I,
  From mine own tears, keep dry?
What flowers grow in my field where-
    with to dress thee?
  My good reverts to ill;
  My calmnesses would move thee,
  My softnesses would prick thee,
  My bindings up would break thee,
  My crownings, curse and kill.
  Alas, I can but love thee!
May God bless thee, my belovèd—may
    God bless thee.

IV

Can I love thee, my belovèd—can I love
    thee?
  And is *this* like love, to stand
  With no help in my hand,
When strong as death I fain would watch
    above thee?
  My love-kiss can deny
  No tear that falls beneath it;
  Mine oath of love can swear thee
  From no ill that comes near thee,—
  And thou diest while I breathe it,
  And I—I can but die!
May God love thee, my belovèd—may
    God love thee.

LESSONS FROM THE GORSE

To win the secret of a weed's plain heart.
                                    LOWELL.

I

Mountain gorses, ever-golden,
Cankered not the whole year long!
Do ye teach us to be strong,
Howsoever pricked and holden
Like your thorny blooms, and so
Trodden on by rain and snow,
Up the hillside of this life, as bleak as
    where ye grow?

II

Mountain blossoms, shining blos-
    soms,
Do ye teach us to be glad
When no summer can be had,
Blooming in our inward bosoms?

Ye, whom God preserveth still,—
Set as lights upon a hill,
Tokens to the wintry earth that Beauty
    liveth still!

III

Mountain gorses, do ye teach us
From that academic chair,
Canopied with azure air,
That the wisest word man reaches
Is the humblest he can speak?
Ye, who live on mountain peak,
Yet live low along the ground, beside
    the grasses meek!

IV

Mountain gorses, since Linnaeus
Knelt beside you on the sod,
For your beauty thanking God,—
For your teaching, ye should see us
Bowing in prostration new!
Whence arisen,—if one or two
Drops be on our cheeks—O world, they
    are not tears but dew.

THE LADY'S YES

I

'Yes,' I answered you last night;
  'No,' this morning, sir, I say.
Colours seen by candle-light
  Will not look the same by day.

II

When the viols played their best,
  Lamps above, and laughs below,
Love me sounded like a jest,
  Fit for *yes* or fit for *no*.

III

Call me false or call me free—
  Vow, whatever light may shine,
No man on your face shall see
  Any grief, for change on mine.

IV

Yet the sin is on us both;
  Time to dance is not to woo;
Wooing light makes fickle troth,
  Scorn of *me* recoils on *you*.

V

Learn to win a lady's faith
  Nobly, as the thing is high,
Bravely, as for life and death—
  With a loyal gravity.

VI

Lead her from the festive boards,
  Point her to the starry skies,
Guard her, by your truthful words,
  Pure from courtship's flatteries.

VII

By your truth she shall be true,
  Ever true, as wives of yore;
And her *yes*, once said to you,
  Shall be Yes for evermore.

A WOMAN'S SHORTCOMINGS

I

She has laughed as softly as if she sighed,
  She has counted six, and over,
Of a purse well filled, and a heart well
    tried—
  Oh, each a worthy lover!
They 'give her time'; for her soul must
    slip
  Where the world has set the grooving.
She will lie to none with her fair red
    lip—
  But love seeks truer loving.

II

She trembles her fan in a sweetness dumb,
  As her thoughts were beyond recalling,
With a glance for *one*, and a glance for
    some,
  From her eyelids rising and falling;
Speaks common words with a blushful air,
  Hears bold words, unreproving;
But her silence says—what she never
    will swear—
  And love seeks better loving.

III

Go, lady, lean to the night-guitar,
  And drop a smile to the bringer,
Then smile as sweetly, when he is far,
  At the voice of an indoor singer.
Bask tenderly beneath tender eyes;
  Glance lightly, on their removing;
And join new vows to old perjuries—
  But dare not call it loving.

IV

Unless you can think, when the song is done,
No other is soft in the rhythm;
Unless you can feel, when left by One,
That all men else go with him;
Unless you can know, when upraised by his breath,
That your beauty itself wants proving;
Unless you can swear, 'For life, for death!'—
Oh, fear to call it loving!

V

Unless you can muse in a crowd all day
On the absent face that fixed you;
Unless you can love, as the angels may,
With the breadth of heaven betwixt you;
Unless you can dream that his faith is fast,
Through behoving and unbehoving;
Unless you can *die* when the dream is past—
Oh, never call it loving!

A MAN'S REQUIREMENTS

I

Love me, sweet, with all thou art,
Feeling, thinking, seeing,—
Love me in the lightest part,
Love me in full being.

II

Love me with thine open youth
In its frank surrender;
With the vowing of thy mouth,
With its silence tender.

III

Love me with thine azure eyes,
Made for earnest granting!
Taking colour from the skies,
Can Heaven's truth be wanting?

IV

Love me with their lids, that fall
Snow-like at first meeting;
Love me with thine heart, that all
The neighbours then see beating.

V

Love me with thine hand stretched out
Freely—open-minded;
Love me with thy loitering foot,—
Hearing one behind it.

VI

Love me with thy voice, that turns
Sudden faint above me;
Love me with thy blush that burns
When I murmur, *Love me!*

VII

Love me with thy thinking soul—
Break it to love-sighing;
Love me with thy thoughts that roll
On through living—dying.

VIII

Love me in thy gorgeous airs,
When the world has crowned thee!
Love me, kneeling at thy prayers,
With the angels round thee.

IX

Love me pure, as musers do,
Up the woodlands shady;
Love me gaily, fast, and true,
As a winsome lady.

X

Through all hopes that keep us brave,
Further off or nigher,
Love me for the house and grave,—
And for something higher.

XI

Thus, if thou wilt prove me, dear,
Woman's love no fable,
I will love *thee*—half-a-year—
As a man is able.

A YEAR'S SPINNING

I

HE listened at the porch that day,
To hear the wheel go on, and on;
And then it stopped—ran back away—
While through the door he brough the sun.
But now my spinning is all done.

II

He sate beside me, with an oath
  That love ne'er ended, once begun.
I smiled—believing for us both,
    What was the truth for only one.
  And now my spinning is all done.

III

My mother cursed me that I heard
  A young man's wooing as I spun.
Thanks, cruel mother, for that word,—
    For I have, since, a harder known!
  And now my spinning is all done.

IV

I thought—O God!—my first-born's cry
  Both voices to mine ear would drown.
I listened in mine agony—
    It was the *silence* made me groan!
  And now my spinning is all done.

V

Bury me 'twixt my mother's grave
  (Who cursed me on her death-bed lone)
And my dead baby's (God it save!),
    Who, not to bless me, would not moan.
  And now my spinning is all done.

VI

A stone upon my heart and head,
  But no name written on the stone!
Sweet neighbours, whisper low instead,
    'This sinner was a loving one—
  And now her spinning is all done.'

VII

And let the door ajar remain,
  In case he should pass by anon;
And leave the wheel out very plain,—
    That HE, when passing in the sun,
  May see the spinning is all done.

CHANGE UPON CHANGE

I

FIVE months ago the stream did flow,
  The lilies bloomed within the sedge,
And we were lingering to and fro,
Where none will track thee in this snow,
  Along the stream, beside the hedge.
Ah, sweet, be free to love and go!

For if I do not hear thy foot,
  The frozen river is as mute,
  The flowers have dried down to the
    root.
And why, since these be changed
    since May,
  Shouldst *thou* change less than *they?*

II

And slow, slow, as the winter snow,
  The tears have drifted to mine eyes;
And my poor cheeks, five months ago,
Set blushing at thy praises so,
  Put paleness on for a disguise.
Ah, sweet, be free to praise and go!
  For if my face is turned too pale,
  It was thine oath that first did fail,—
  It was thy love proved false and frail!
  And why, since these be changed enow,
  Should *I* change less than *thou?*

THAT DAY

I

I STAND by the river where both of us
    stood,
And there is but one shadow to darken
    the flood;
And the path leading to it, where both
    used to pass,
Has the step but of one, to take dew
    from the grass,—
        One forlorn since that day.

II

The flowers of the margin are many to
    see;
None stoops at my bidding to pluck
    them for me.
The bird in the alder sings loudly and
    long,—
My low sound of weeping disturbs not
    his song,
        As thy vow did that day.

III

I stand by the river—I think of the vow—
Oh, calm as the place is, vow-breaker,
    be thou!
I leave the flower growing, the bird,
    unreproved;—
Would I trouble *thee* rather than *them,*
    my beloved,
        And my lover that day?

IV

Go, be sure of my love—by that treason
   forgiven ;
Of my prayers—by the blessings they
   win thee from Heaven ;
Of my grief—(guess the length of the
   sword by the sheath's)
By the silence of life, more pathetic
   than death's !
       Go,—be clear of that day !

A REED

I

I AM no trumpet, but a reed :
No flattering breath shall from me lead
   A silver sound, a hollow sound :
I will not ring, for priest or king,
   One blast that in re-echoing
      Would leave a bondsman faster bound.

II

I am no trumpet, but a reed,—
A broken reed, the wind indeed
   Left flat upon a dismal shore ;
Yet if a little maid, or child,
Should sigh within it, earnest-mild,
   This reed will answer evermore.

III

I am no trumpet, but a reed.
Go, tell the fishers, as they spread
   Their nets along the river's edge,
I will not tear their nets at all,
Nor pierce their hands, if they should fall ;
   Then let them leave me in the sedge.

THE DEAD PAN

Excited by Schiller's *Götter Griechenlands*,
and partly founded on a well-known tradition
mentioned in a treatise of Plutarch (*De Oracu-
lorum Defectu*), according to which, at the hour
of the Saviour's agony, a cry of ' Great Pan is
dead ! ' swept across the waves in the hearing
of certain mariners,—and the oracles ceased.

It is in all veneration to the memory of the
deathless Schiller that I oppose a doctrine still
more dishonouring to poetry than to Christi-
anity.

As Mr. Kenyon's graceful and harmonious
paraphrase of the German poem was the first
occasion of the turning of my thoughts in this
direction, I take advantage of the pretence to
indulge my feelings (which overflow on other
grounds) by inscribing my lyric to that dear
friend and relative, with the earnestness of ap-
preciating esteem as well as of affectionate
gratitude. [1844.]

I

GODS of Hellas, gods of Hellas,
Can ye listen in your silence ?
Can your mystic voices tell us
Where ye hide ? In floating islands,
With a wind that evermore
Keeps you out of sight of shore ?
       Pan, Pan is dead.

II

In what revels are ye sunken,
In old Aethiopia ?
Have the Pygmies made you drunken,
Bathing in mandragora
Your divine pale lips, that shiver
Like the lotus in the river ?
       Pan, Pan is dead.

III

Do ye sit there still in slumber,
In gigantic Alpine rows ?
The black poppies out of number
Nodding, dripping from your brows
To the red lees of your wine,
And so kept alive and fine ?
       Pan, Pan is dead.

IV

Or lie crushed your stagnant corses
Where the silver spheres roll on,
Stung to life by centric forces
Thrown like rays out from the sun ?—
While the smoke of your old altars
Is the shroud that round you welters ?
       Great Pan is dead.

V

' Gods of Hellas, gods of Hellas,'
Said the old Hellenic tongue !
Said the hero-oaths, as well as
Poets' songs the sweetest sung !
Have ye grown deaf in a day ?
Can ye speak not yea or nay—
       Since Pan is dead ?

VI

Do ye leave your rivers flowing
All alone, O Naiades,
While your drenchèd locks dry slow in
This cold feeble sun and breeze ?—
Not a word the Naiads say,
Though the rivers run for ay.
                    For Pan is dead.

VII

From the gloaming of the oak-wood,
O ye Dryads, could ye flee ?
At the rushing thunderstroke, would
No sob tremble through the tree ?—
Not a word the Dryads say,
Though the forests wave for ay.
                    For Pan is dead.

VIII

Have ye left the mountain places,
Oreads wild, for other tryst ?
Shall we see no sudden faces
Strike a glory through the mist ?
Not a sound the silence thrills
Of the everlasting hills.
                    Pan, Pan is dead.

IX

O twelve gods of Plato's vision,
Crowned to starry wanderings,—
With your chariots in procession,
And your silver clash of wings !
Very pale ye seem to rise,
Ghosts of Grecian deities,—
                    Now Pan is dead !

X

Jove, that right hand is unloaded,
Whence the thunder did prevail,
While in idiocy of godhead
Thou art staring the stars pale !
And thine eagle, blind and old,
Roughs his feathers in the cold.
                    Pan, Pan is dead.

XI

Where, O Juno, is the glory
Of thy regal look and tread ?
Will they lay, for evermore, thee,
On thy dim, straight, golden bed ?
Will thy queendom all lie hid
Meekly under either lid ?
                    Pan, Pan is dead.

XII

Ha, Apollo ! floats his golden
Hair all mist-like where he stands,
While the Muses hang enfolding
Knee and foot with faint wild hands ?
'Neath the clanging of thy bow,
Niobe looked lost as thou !
                    Pan, Pan is dead.

XIII

Shall the casque with its brown iron,
Pallas' broad blue eyes, eclipse,
And no hero take inspiring
From the god-Greek of her lips ?
'Neath her olive dost thou sit,
Mars the mighty, cursing it ?
                    Pan, Pan is dead.

XIV

Bacchus, Bacchus ! on the panther
He swoons,—bound with his own vines ;
And his Maenads slowly saunter,
Head aside, among the pines,
While they murmur dreamingly,
' Evohe—ah—evohe—! '
                    Ah, Pan is dead !

XV

Neptune lies beside the trident,
Dull and senseless as a stone ;
And old Pluto deaf and silent
Is cast out into the sun :
Ceres smileth stern thereat,
' We *all* now are desolate—
                    Now Pan is dead.'

XVI

Aphrodite ! dead and driven
As thy native foam, thou art ;
With the cestus long done heaving
On the white calm of thine heart !
Ai Adonis! at that shriek,
Not a tear runs down her cheek—
                    Pan, Pan is dead.

XVII

And the Loves, we used to know from
One another, huddled lie,
Frore as taken in a snow-storm,
Close beside her tenderly,—
As if each had weakly tried
Once to kiss her as he died.
                    Pan, Pan is dead.

XVIII

What, and Hermes? Time enthralleth
All thy cunning, Hermes, thus,—
And the ivy blindly crawleth
Round thy brave caduceus?
Hast thou no new message for us,
Full of thunder and Jove-glories?
    Nay, Pan is dead.

XIX

Crownèd Cybele's great turret
Rocks and crumbles on her head;
Roar the lions of her chariot
Toward the wilderness, unfed.
Scornful children are not mute,—
'Mother, mother, walk afoot—
    Since Pan is dead.'

XX

In the fiery-hearted centre
Of the solemn universe,
Ancient Vesta,—who could enter
To consume thee with this curse?
Drop thy grey chin on thy knee,
O thou palsied Mystery!
    For Pan is dead.

XXI

Gods, we vainly do adjure you,—
Ye return nor voice nor sign!
Not a votary could secure you
Even a grave for your Divine!
Not a grave, to show thereby,
Here these grey old gods do lie.
    Pan, Pan is dead.

XXII

Even that Greece who took your wages
Calls the obolus outworn;
And the hoarse deep-throated ages
Laugh your godships unto scorn;
And the poets do disclaim you,
Or grow colder if they name you—
    And Pan is dead.

XXIII

Gods bereavèd, gods belated,
With your purples rent asunder!
Gods discrowned and desecrated,
Disinherited of thunder!
Now, the goats may climb and crop
The soft grass on Ida's top—
    Now, Pan is dead.

XXIV

Calm, of old, the bark went onward,
When a cry more loud than wind
Rose up, deepened, and swept sunward,
From the pilèd Dark behind;
And the sun shrank and grew pale,
Breathed against by the great wail—
    'Pan, Pan is dead.'

XXV

And the rowers from the benches
Fell,—each shuddering on his face—
While departing Influences
Struck a cold back through the place;
And the shadow of the ship
Reeled along the passive deep—
    'Pan, Pan is dead.'

XXVI

And that dismal cry rose slowly
And sank slowly through the air,
Full of spirit's melancholy
And eternity's despair!
And they heard the words it said—
'PAN IS DEAD—GREAT PAN IS DEAD—
    PAN, PAN IS DEAD.'

XXVII

'Twas the hour when One in Sion
Hung for love's sake on a cross;
When His brow was chill with dying,
And His soul was faint with loss;
When His priestly blood dropped down-
  ward,
And His kingly eyes looked throne-
  ward—
    Then, Pan was dead.

XXVIII

By the love He stood alone in
His sole Godhead rose complete,
And the false gods fell down moaning,
Each from off his golden seat;
All the false gods with a cry
Rendered up their deity—
    Pan, Pan was dead.

XXIX

Wailing wide across the islands,
They rent, vest-like, their Divine!
And a darkness and a silence
Quenched the light of every shrine;
And Dodona's oak swang lonely
Henceforth, to the tempest only,
    Pan, Pan was dead.

XXX

Pythia staggered,—feeling o'er her,
Her lost god's forsaking look ;
Straight her eyeballs filmed with horror,
And her crispy fillets shook,
And her lips gasped through their foam
For a word that did not come.
           Pan, Pan was dead.

XXXI

O ye vain false gods of Hellas,
Ye are silent evermore !
And I dash down this old chalice,
Whence libations ran of yore.
See, the wine crawls in the dust
Wormlike—as your glories must,
           Since Pan is dead.

XXXII

Get to dust, as common mortals,
By a common doom and track !
Let no Schiller from the portals
Of that Hades call you back,
Or instruct us to weep all
At your antique funeral.
           Pan, Pan is dead.

XXXIII

By your beauty, which confesses
Some chief Beauty conquering you,—
By our grand heroic guesses,
Through your falsehood, at the True,—
We will weep *not* . . ! earth shall roll
Heir to each god's aureole—
           And Pan is dead.

XXXIV

Earth outgrows the mythic fancies
Sung beside her in her youth ;
And those debonair romances
Sound but dull beside the truth.
Phoebus' chariot-course is run :
Look up, poets, to the sun !
           Pan, Pan is dead.

XXXV

Christ hath sent us down the angels ;
And the whole earth and the skies
Are illumed by altar-candles
Lit for blessèd mysteries ;
And a Priest's hand, through creation,
Waveth calm and consecration—
           And Pan is dead.

XXXVI

Truth is fair : should we forgo it ?
Can we sigh right for a wrong ?
God Himself is the best Poet,
And the Real is His song.
Sing His truth out fair and full,
And secure His beautiful.
           Let Pan be dead.

XXXVII

Truth is large. Our aspiration
Scarce embraces half we be :
Shame, to stand in His creation,
And doubt truth's sufficiency !—
To think God's song unexcelling
The poor tales of our own telling—
           When Pan is dead.

XXXVIII

What is true and just and honest,
What is lovely, what is pure—
All of praise that hath admonisht,
All of virtue, shall endure,—
These are themes for poets' uses,
Stirring nobler than the Muses,
           Ere Pan was dead.

XXXIX

O brave poets, keep back nothing,
Nor mix falsehood with the whole :
Look up Godward ; speak the truth in
Worthy song from earnest soul !
Hold, in high poetic duty,
Truest Truth the fairest Beauty.
           Pan, Pan is dead.

A CHILD'S GRAVE AT FLORENCE

A. A. E. C. BORN JULY 1848. DIED
NOVEMBER 1849

I

Of English blood, of Tuscan birth, . .
    What country should we give her?
Instead of any on the earth,
    The civic Heavens receive her.

II

And here, among the English tombs,
    In Tuscan ground we lay her,
While the blue Tuscan sky endomes
    Our English words of prayer.

III

A little child !—how long she lived,
  By months, not years, is reckoned :
Born in one July, she survived
  Alone to see a second.

IV

Bright-featured, as the July sun
  Her little face still played in,
And splendours, with her birth begun,
  Had had no time for fading.

V

So, LILY, from those July hours,
  No wonder we should call her ;
She looked such kinship to the flowers,
  Was but a little taller.

VI

A Tuscan Lily,—only white,
  As Dante, in abhorrence
Of red corruption, wished aright
  The lilies of his Florence.

VII

We could not wish her whiter,—her
  Who perfumed with pure blossom
The house !—a lovely thing to wear
  Upon a mother's bosom !

VIII

This July creature thought perhaps
  Our speech not worth assuming ;
She sate upon her parents' laps,
  And mimicked the gnat's humming ;

IX

Said 'father,' 'mother'—then, left off,
  For tongues celestial, fitter ;
Her hair had grown just long enough
  To catch heaven's jasper-glitter.

X

Babes ! Love could always hear and see
  Behind the cloud that hid them.
'Let little children come to Me,
  And do not thou forbid them.'

XI

So, unforbidding, have we met,
  And gently here have laid her,
Though winter is no time to get
  The flowers that should o'erspread
    her.

XII

We should bring pansies quick with
    spring,
  Rose, violet, daffodilly,
And also, above everything,
  White lilies for our Lily.

XIII

Nay, more than flowers, this grave
    exacts,—
  Glad, grateful attestations
Of her sweet eyes and pretty acts,
  With calm renunciations.

XIV

Her very mother with light feet
  Should leave the place too earthy,
Saying, 'The angels have thee, Sweet,
  Because we are not worthy.'

XV

But winter kills the orange buds,
  The gardens in the frost are,
And all the heart dissolves in floods,
  Remembering we have lost her !

XVI

Poor earth, poor heart,—too weak, too
    weak,
  To miss the July shining !
Poor heart !—what bitter words we speak
  When God speaks of resigning !

XVII

Sustain this heart in us that faints,
  Thou God, the self-existent !
We catch up wild at parting saints,
  And feel Thy Heaven too distant.

XVIII

The wind that swept them out of sin
  Has ruffled all our vesture :
On the shut door that let them in,
  We beat with frantic gesture,—

XIX

To us, us also—open straight !
  The outer life is chilly—
Are we too, like the earth, to wait
  Till next year for our Lily?

XX

—Oh, my own baby on my knees,
  My leaping, dimpled treasure,
At every word I write like these,
  Clasped close, with stronger pressure !

XXI

Too well my own heart understands,—
  At every word beats fuller—
My little feet, my little hands,
  And hair of Lily's colour!

XXII

—But God gives patience, Love learns
    strength,
  And Faith remembers promise,
And Hope itself can smile at length
  On other hopes gone from us.

XXIII

Love, strong as Death, shall conquer
    Death,
  Through struggle, made more glorious.
This mother stills her sobbing breath,
  Renouncing, yet victorious.

XXIV

Arms, empty of her child, she lifts,
  With spirit unbereaven,—
'God will not all take back His gifts;
  My Lily's mine in heaven!

XXV

'Still mine! maternal rights serene
  Not given to another!
The crystal bars shine faint between
  The souls of child and mother.

XXVI

'Meanwhile,' the mother cries, 'content!
  Our love was well divided.
Its sweetness following where she went,
  Its anguish stayed where I did.

XXVII

'Well done of God, to halve the lot,
  And give her all the sweetness;
To us, the empty room and cot,—
  To her, the Heaven's completeness.

XXVIII

'To us, this grave—to her, the rows
  The mystic palm-trees spring in;
To us, the silence in the house,—
  To her, the choral singing.

XXIX

'For her, to gladden in God's view,—
  For us, to hope and bear on!—
Grow, Lily, in thy garden new
  Beside the rose of Sharon.

XXX

'Grow fast in heaven, sweet Lily clipped,
  In love more calm than this is,—
And may the angels dewy-lipped
  Remind thee of our kisses!

XXXI

'While none shall tell thee of our tears,
  These human tears now falling,
Till, after a few patient years,
  One home shall take us all in.

XXXII

'Child, father, mother—who, left out?
  Not mother, and not father!—
And when, our dying couch about,
  The natural mists shall gather,

XXXIII

'Some smiling angel close shall stand
  In old Correggio's fashion,
And bear a LILY in his hand,
  For death's ANNUNCIATION.'

CATARINA TO CAMOENS

DYING IN HIS ABSENCE ABROAD, AND
REFERRING TO THE POEM IN WHICH
HE RECORDED THE SWEETNESS OF
HER EYES

I

ON the door you will not enter,
  I have gazed too long—adieu!
Hope withdraws her peradventure—
  Death is near me,—and not *you.*
    Come, O lover,
    Close and cover
These poor eyes, you called, I ween,
'Sweetest eyes, were ever seen.'

II

When I heard you sing that burden
  In my vernal days and bowers,
Other praises disregarding,
  I but hearkened that of yours—
    Only saying
    In heart-playing,
'Blessed eyes mine eyes have been,
If the sweetest, HIS have seen!'

III

But all changes.   At this vesper,
　　Cold the sun shines down the door.
If you stood there, would you whisper
　　'Love, I love you,' as before,—
　　　　Death pervading
　　　　Now, and shading
Eyes you sang of, that yestreen,
As the sweetest ever seen?

IV

Yes, I think, were you beside them,
　　Near the bed I die upon,—
Though their beauty you denied them,
　　As you stood there, looking down,
　　　　You would truly
　　　　Call them duly,
For the love's sake found therein,—
'Sweetest eyes, were ever seen.'

V

And if *you* looked down upon them,
　　And if *they* looked up to *you*,
All the light which has foregone them
　　Would be gathered back anew.
　　　　They would truly
　　　　Be as duly
Love-transformed to beauty's sheen,—
'Sweetest eyes, were ever seen.'

VI

But, ah me! you only see me,
　　In your thoughts of loving man,
Smiling soft perhaps and dreamy
　　Through the wavings of my fan,—
　　　　And unweeting
　　　　Go repeating,
In your reverie serene,
'Sweetest eyes, were ever seen.'

VII

While my spirit leans and reaches
　　From my body still and pale,
Fain to hear what tender speech is
　　In your love to help my bale—
　　　　O my poet,
　　　　Come and show it!
Come, of latest love, to glean
'Sweetest eyes, were ever seen.'

VIII

O my poet, O my prophet,
　　When you praised their sweetness so,
Did you think, in singing of it,
　　That it might be near to go?
　　　　Had you fancies
　　　　From their glances,
That the grave would quickly screen
'Sweetest eyes, were ever seen'?

IX

No reply! the fountain's warble
　　In the court-yard sounds alone.
As the water to the marble
　　So my heart falls with a moan
　　　　From love-sighing
　　　　To this dying.
Death forerunneth Love to win
'Sweetest eyes, were ever seen.'

X

Will you come?   When I'm departed
　　Where all sweetnesses are hid;
Where thy voice, my tender-hearted,
　　Will not lift up either lid.
　　　　Cry, O lover,
　　　　Love is over!
Cry beneath the cypress green—
'Sweetest eyes, were ever seen.'

XI

When the angelus is ringing,
　　Near the convent will you walk,
And recall the choral singing
　　Which brought angels down our talk?
　　　　Spirit-shriven
　　　　I viewed Heaven,
Till you smiled—'Is earth unclean,
Sweetest eyes, were ever seen?'

XII

When beneath the palace-lattice,
　　You ride slow as you have done,
And you see a face there—that is
　　Not the old familiar one,—
　　　　Will you oftly
　　　　Murmur softly,
'Here, ye watched me morn and e'en,
Sweetest eyes, were ever seen'?

XIII

When the palace-ladies, sitting
  Round your gittern, shall have said,
'Poet, sing those verses written
  For the lady who is dead,'
    Will you tremble,
    Yet dissemble,—
Or sing hoarse, with tears between,
'Sweetest eyes, were ever seen'?

XIV

'Sweetest eyes!' how sweet in flowings
  The repeated cadence is!
Though you sang a hundred poems,
  Still the best one would be this.
    I can hear it
    'Twixt my spirit
And the earth-noise intervene—
'Sweetest eyes, were ever seen!'

XV

But the priest waits for the praying,
  And the choir are on their knees,
And the soul must pass away in
  Strains more solemn high than these.
    Miserere
    For the weary!
Oh, no longer for Catrine,
'Sweetest eyes, were ever seen!'

XVI

Keep my ribbon, take and keep it
  (I have loosed it from my hair)[1],
Feeling, while you overweep it,
  Not alone in your despair,
    Since with saintly
    Watch unfaintly
Out of heaven shall o'er you lean
'Sweetest eyes, were ever seen.'

XVII

But—but *now*—yet unremovèd
  Up to Heaven, they glisten fast.
You may cast away, Belovèd,
  In your future all my past.
    Such old phrases
    May be praises
For some fairer bosom-queen—
'Sweetest eyes, were ever seen!'

[1] She left him the ribbon from her hair.

XVIII

Eyes of mine, what are ye doing?
  Faithless, faithless,—praised amiss
If a tear be of your showing,
  Dropt for any hope of HIS!
    Death has boldness
    Besides coldness,
If unworthy tears demean
'Sweetest eyes, were ever seen.'

XIX

I will look out to his future;
  I will bless it till it shine.
Should he ever be a suitor
  Unto sweeter eyes than mine,
    Sunshine gild them,
    Angels shield them,
Whatsoever eyes terrene
Be the sweetest HIS have seen!

LIFE AND LOVE

I

FAST this Life of mine was dying,
  Blind already and calm as death,
Snowflakes on her bosom lying
  Scarcely heaving with her breath.

II

Love came by, and having known her
  In a dream of fabled lands,
Gently stooped, and laid upon her
  Mystic chrism of holy hands;

III

Drew his smile across her folded
  Eyelids, as the swallow dips:
Breathed as finely as the cold did,
  Through the locking of her lips.

IV

So, when Life looked upward, being
  Warmed and breathed on from above,
What sight could she have for seeing,
  Evermore . . . but only LOVE?

A DENIAL

I

We have met late—it is too late to meet,
  O friend, not more than friend!
Death's forecome shroud is tangled
  round my feet,
And if I step or stir, I touch the end.
  In this last jeopardy
Can I approach thee, I, who cannot move?
How shall I answer thy request for love?
  Look in my face and see.

II

I love thee not, I dare not love thee! go
  In silence; drop my hand.
If thou seek roses, seek them where
  they blow
In garden-alleys, not in desert-sand.
  Can life and death agree,
That thou shouldst stoop thy song to
  my complaint?
I cannot love thee. If the word is faint,
  Look in my face and see.

III

I might have loved thee in some former
  days.
  Oh, then, my spirits had leapt
As now they sink, at hearing thy love-
  praise.
Before these faded cheeks were over-
  wept,
  Had this been asked of me,
To love thee with my whole strong
  heart and head,—
I should have said still . . . yes, but
  smiled and said,
  'Look in my face and see!'

IV

But now . . . God sees me, God, who
  took my heart
  And drowned it in life's surge.
In all your wide warm earth I have no
  part—
A light song overcomes me like a dirge.
  Could Love's great harmony
The saints keep step to when their
  bonds are loose,
Not weigh me down? am *I* a wife to
  choose?
  Look in my face and see.

V

While I behold, as plain as one who
  dreams,
  Some woman of full worth,
Whose voice, as cadenced as a silver
  stream's,
Shall prove the fountain-soul which
  sends it forth;
  One younger, more thought-free
And fair and gay, than I, thou must forget,
With brighter eyes than these . . . which
  are not wet . . .
  Look in my face and see!

VI

So farewell thou, whom I have known
  too late
  To let thee come so near.
Be counted happy while men call thee
  great,
And one belovèd woman feels thee
  dear!—
  Not I!—that cannot be.
I am lost, I am changed,—I must go
  farther, where
The change shall take me worse, and
  no one dare
  Look in my face to see.

VII

Meantime I bless thee. By these
  thoughts of mine
  I bless thee from all such!
I bless thy lamp to oil, thy cup to wine,
Thy hearth to joy, thy hand to an equal
  touch
  Of loyal troth. For me,
I love thee not, I love thee not!—away!
Here's no more courage in my soul to say
  'Look in my face and see.'

PROOF AND DISPROOF

I

Dost thou love me, my belovèd?
  Who shall answer yes or no?
What is provèd or disprovèd
  When my soul inquireth so,
Dost thou love me, my belovèd?

II

I have seen thy heart to-day,
　　Never open to the crowd,
While to love me ay and ay
　　Was the vow as it was vowed
By thine eyes of steadfast grey.

III

Now I sit alone, alone—
　　And the hot tears break and burn.
Now, Belovèd, thou art gone,
　　Doubt and terror have their turn.
Is it love that I have known?

IV

I have known some bitter things,—
　　Anguish, anger, solitude.
Year by year an evil brings,
　　Year by year denies a good;
March winds violate my springs.

V

I have known how sickness bends,
　　I have known how sorrow breaks,—
How quick hopes have sudden ends,
　　How the heart thinks till it aches
Of the smile of buried friends.

VI

Last, I have known *thee*, my brave
　　Noble thinker, lover, doer!
The best knowledge last I have.
　　But thou comest as the thrower
Of fresh flowers upon a grave.

VII

Count what feelings used to move me!
　　Can this love assort with those?
Thou, who art so far above me,
　　Wilt thou stoop so, for repose?
Is it true that thou canst love me?

VIII

Do not blame me if I doubt thee.
　　I can call love by its name
When thine arm is wrapt about me;
　　But even love seems not the same,
When I sit alone, without thee.

IX

In thy clear eyes I descried
　　Many a proof of love, to-day;
But to-night, those unbelied
　　Speechful eyes being gone away,
There's the proof to seek, beside.

X

Dost thou love me, my belovèd?
　　Only *thou* canst answer yes!
And, thou gone, the proof's disprovèd,
　　And the cry rings answerless—
Dost thou love me, my belovèd?

QUESTION AND ANSWER

I

LOVE you seek for, presupposes
　　Summer heat and sunny glow.
Tell me, do you find moss-roses
　　Budding, blooming in the snow?
Snow might kill the rose-tree's root—
Shake it quickly from your foot,
　　Lest it harm you as you go.

II

From the ivy where it dapples
　　A grey ruin, stone by stone,—
Do you look for grapes or apples,
　　Or for sad green leaves alone?
Pluck the leaves off, two or three—
Keep them for morality
　　When you shall be safe and gone.

INCLUSIONS

I

OH, wilt thou have my hand, Dear, to
　　lie along in thine?
As a little stone in a running stream, it
　　seems to lie and pine.
Now drop the poor pale hand, Dear, . .
　　unfit to plight with thine.

II

Oh, wilt thou have my cheek, Dear,
　　drawn closer to thine own?
My cheek is white, my cheek is worn,
　　by many a tear run down.
Now leave a little space, Dear, . . lest it
　　should wet thine own.

III

Oh, must thou have my soul, Dear, com-
　　mingled with thy soul?—
Red grows the cheek, and warm the
　　hand, . . the part is in the whole!
Nor hands nor cheeks keep separate,
　　when soul is joined to soul.

INSUFFICIENCY

I

There is no one beside thee and no one
    above thee,
  Thou standest alone as the nightingale
    sings!
And my words that would praise thee
    are impotent things,
For none can express thee though all
    should approve thee.
  I love thee so, Dear, that I only can
    love thee.

II

Say, what can I do for thee? weary
    thee, grieve thee?
  Lean on thy shoulder, new burdens
    to add?
  Weep my tears over thee, making thee
    sad?
Oh, hold me not—love me not! let me
    retrieve thee.
  I love thee so, Dear, that I only can
    leave thee.

THE LITTLE FRIEND [1]

WRITTEN IN THE BOOK WHICH SHE
MADE AND SENT TO ME

τὸ δ' ἤδη ἐξ ὀφθαλμῶν ἀπελήλυθεν.
                    MARCUS ANTONINUS.

The book thou givest, dear as such,
  Shall bear thy dearer name;
And many a word the leaves shall touch,
  For thee who form'dst the same!
And on them many a thought shall grow
  'Neath memory's rain and sun,
Of thee, glad child, who dost not know
  That thought and pain are one!

Yes! thoughts of thee, who satest oft,
  A while since, at my side—
So wild to tame,—to move so soft,
  So very hard to chide:
The childish vision at thine heart,
  The lesson on the knee;
The wandering looks which *would* depart,
  Like gulls, across the sea!

[1] This and the following eight Poems first
appeared in 1838, but were omitted in the
Collected Editions of 1850 and 1856.

The laughter, which no half-belief
  In wrath could all suppress :
The falling tears, which looked like grief,
  And were but gentleness :
The fancies sent, for bliss, abroad,
  As Eden's were not done—
Mistaking still the cherub's sword
  For shining of the sun!

The sportive speech with wisdom in 't—
  The question strange and bold—
The childish fingers in the print
  Of God's creative hold :
The praying words in whispers said,
  The sin with sobs confest;
The leaning of the young meek head
  Upon the Saviour's breast!

The gentle consciousness of praise,
  With hues that went and came;
The brighter blush, a word could raise,
  Were *that*—a father's name!
The shadow on thy smile for each
  That on his face could fall!
So quick hath love been, *thee* to teach,
  What soon it teacheth all.

Sit still as erst beside his feet!
  The future days are dim,—
But those will seem to thee most sweet
  Which keep thee nearest *him!*
Sit at his feet in quiet mirth,
  And let him see arise
A clearer sun and greener earth
  Within thy loving eyes!—

Ah, loving eyes! that used to lift
  Your childhood to my face—
That leave a memory on the gift
  I look on in your place—
May bright-eyed hosts your guardians be
  From all but thankful tears,—
While, brightly as ye turned on *me*,
  Ye meet th' advancing years!

THE STUDENT

Τι οὖν τοῦτο πρὸς σέ; καὶ οὐδὲν λέγω ὅτι πρὸς
τὸν τεθνηκότα, ἀλλὰ πρὸς τὸν ζῶντα, τί ὁ ἔπαινος;
                    MARCUS ANTONINUS.

'My midnight lamp is weary as my soul,
And, being unimmortal, has gone out.
And now alone yon moony lamp of
    heaven,
Which God lit and not man, illuminates

These volumes, others wrote in weari-
    ness
As I have read them ; and this cheek
    and brow,
Whose paleness, burnèd in with heats
    of thought,
Would make an angel smile to see how
    ill
Clay thrust from Paradise consorts with
    mind—
If angels could, like men, smile bitterly.

'Yet must my brow be paler! I have
    vowed
To clip it with the crown which cannot
    fade,
When *it* is faded.   Not in vain ye cry,
O glorious voices that survive the tongues
From whence was drawn your separate
    sovereignty—
For I would reign beside you ! I would
    melt
The golden treasures of my health and
    life
Into that name ! My lips are vowed apart
From cheerful words ; mine ears, from
    pleasant sounds ;
Mine eyes, from sights God made so
    beautiful,—
My feet, from wanderings under shady
    trees ;
Mine hands, from clasping of dear-loving
    friends,—
My very heart, from feelings which
    move soft !
Vowed am I from the day's delightsome-
    ness,
And dreams of night ! and when the
    house is dumb
In sleep, which is the pause 'twixt life
    and life,
I live and waken thus ; and pluck away
Slumber's sleek poppies from my painèd
    lids—
Goading my mind with thongs wrought
    by herself,
To toil and struggle along this mountain-
    path
Which hath no mountain-airs ; until she
    sweat
Like Adam's brow, and gasp, and rend
    away
In agony, her garment of the flesh !'

And so his midnight lamp was lit anew,
And burned till morning.   But his lamp
    of life
Till morning burned not ! He was found
    embraced,
Close, cold, and stiff, by Death's com-
    pelling sleep ;
His breast and brow supported on a page
Charàctered over with a praise of *fame*,
Of its divineness and beatitude—
Words which had often caused that heart
    to throb,
That cheek to burn ; though silent lay
    they now,
Without a single beating in the pulse,
And all the fever gone !

                            I saw a bay
Spring verdant from a newly-fashioned
    grave.
The grass upon the grave was verdanter,
That being watered by the eyes of One
Who bore not to look up toward the tree !
Others looked on it—some, with passing
    glance,
Because the light wind stirrèd in its
    leaves ;
And some, with sudden lighting of the soul
In admiration's ecstasy !—Aye ! some
Did wag their heads like oracles, and say,
''Tis very well !'—but none rememberèd
The heart which housed the root, except
    that ONE
Whose sight was lost in weeping !

                            Is it thus,
Ambition, idol of thè intellect ?
Shall we drink aconite, alone to use
Thy golden bowl? and sleep ourselves
    to death—
To dream thy visions about life? O Power
That art a very feebleness !—before
Thy clayey feet we bend our knees of clay,
And round thy senseless brow bind
    diadems
With paralytic hands, and shout 'a god,'
With voices mortal hoarse ! Who can
    discern
Th' infirmities they share in? Being blind,
We cannot see thy blindness: being weak,
We cannot feel thy weakness: being low,
We cannot mete thy baseness : being
    unwise,
We cannot understand thy idiocy !

STANZAS

I MAY sing ; but minstrel's singing
Ever ceaseth with his playing.
I may smile ; but time is bringing
Thoughts for smiles to wear away in.
I may view thee, mutely loving ;
But *shall* view thee so in dying !
I may sigh ; but life 's removing,
And with breathing endeth sighing !
    Be it so !

When no song of mine comes near thee,
Will its memory fail to soften ?
When no smile of mine can cheer thee,
Will thy smile be used as often ?
When my looks the darkness boundeth,
Will thine own be lighted after ?
When my sigh no longer soundeth,
Wilt thou list another's laughter ?
    Be it so !

THE YOUNG QUEEN

This awful responsibility is imposed upon me
so suddenly and at so early a period of my life,
that I should feel myself utterly oppressed by
the burden, were I not sustained by the hope that
Divine Providence, which has called me to this
work, will give me strength for the performance
of it.—*The Queen's Declaration in Council.*

THE shroud is yet unspread
To wrap our crownèd dead ;
His soul hath scarcely hearkened for the
 thrilling word of doom ;
And Death, that makes serene
Even brows where crowns have been,
Hath scarcely time to meeten his for
 silence of the tomb.

Saint Paul's king-dirging note
The city's heart hath smote—
The city's heart is struck with thought
 more solemn than the tone !
A shadow sweeps apace
Before the nation's face,
Confusing in a shapeless blot the sepul-
 chre and throne.

The palace sounds with wail—
The courtly dames are pale—
A widow o'er the purple bows, and
 weeps its splendour dim :
And we who hold the boon,
A king for freedom won,
Do feel eternity rise up between our
 thanks and him.

And while all things express
All glory's nothingness,
A royal maiden treadeth firm where *that*
 departed trod !
The deathly scented crown
Weighs her shining ringlets down ;
But calm she lifts her trusting face, and
 calleth upon God.

Her thoughts are deep within her :
No outward pageants win her
From memories that in her soul are
 rolling wave on wave—
Her palace walls enring
The dust that was a king—
And very cold beneath her feet, she feels
 her father's grave.

And One, as fair as she,
Can scarce forgotten be,—
Who clasped a little infant dead, for all
 a kingdom's worth !
The mournèd, blessèd One,
Who views Jehovah's throne,
Ay smiling to the angels, that she lost
 a throne on earth.

Perhaps our youthful Queen
Remembers what has been—
Her childhood's rest by loving heart, and
 sport on grassy sod—
Alas ! can others wear
A mother's heart for her ?
But calm she lifts her trusting face, and
 calleth upon God.

Yea ! call on God, thou maiden
Of spirit nobly laden,
And leave such happy days behind, for
 happy-making years !
A nation looks to thee
For steadfast sympathy :
Make room within thy bright clear eyes
 for all its gathered tears.

And so the grateful isles
Shall give thee back their smiles,
And as thy mother joys in thee, in them
 shalt *thou* rejoice ;
Rejoice to meekly bow
A somewhat paler brow,
While the King of kings shall bless thee
 by the British people's voice !

VICTORIA'S TEARS

Hark! the reiterated clangour sounds!
Now murmurs, like the sea or like the storm,
Or like the flames on forests, move and mount
From rank to rank, and loud and louder roll,
Till all the people is one vast applause.
                    LANDOR'S *Gebir*.

'O MAIDEN! heir of kings!
  A king has left his place!
The majesty of Death has swept
  All other from his face!
And thou upon thy mother's breast
  No longer lean adown,
But take the glory for the rest,
And rule the land that loves thee best!'
    She heard, and wept—
    She wept, to wear a crown!

They decked her courtly halls;
  They reined her hundred steeds;
They shouted at her palace gate,
  'A noble Queen succeeds!'
Her name has stirred the mountain's
    sleep,
  Her praise has filled the town!
And mourners God had stricken deep,
Looked hearkening up, and did not weep.
    Alone she wept,
    Who wept, to wear a crown!

She saw no purples shine,
  For tears had dimmed her eyes;
She only knew her childhood's flowers
  Were happier pageantries!
And while her heralds played the part,
  For million shouts to drown—
'God save the Queen' from hill to mart,—
She heard through all her beating heart,
    And turned and wept—
    She wept, to wear a crown!

God save thee, weeping Queen!
  Thou shalt be well beloved!
The tyrant's sceptre cannot move,
  As those pure tears have moved!
The nature in thine eyes we see,
  That tyrants cannot own—
The love that guardeth liberties!
Strange blessing on the nation lies,
    Whose Sovereign wept—
    Yea! wept, to wear its crown!

God bless thee, weeping Queen,
  With blessing more divine!
And fill with happier love than earth's
  That tender heart of thine!
That when the thrones of earth shall be
  As low as graves brought down,
A piercèd Hand may give to thee
The crown which angels shout to see!
    Thou wilt not *weep*
    To wear that heavenly crown!

VANITIES

From fading things, fond men, lift your desire.
                    DRUMMOND.

COULD ye be very blest in hearkening
  Youth's often danced-to melodies—
Hearing it piped, the midnight darkening
  Doth come to show the starry skies,—
To freshen garden-flowers, the rain?—
  It is in vain, it is in vain!

Could ye be very blest in urging
  A captive nation's strength to thunder
Out into foam, and with its surging
  The Xerxean fetters break asunder?
The storm is cruel as the chain!—
  It is in vain, it is in vain!

Could ye be very blest in paling
  Your brows with studious nights and
    days,
When like your lamps your life is fading,
  And sighs, not breath, are wrought from
    praise?
Your tombs, not ye, that praise retain—
  It is in vain, it is in vain!

Yea! but ye *could* be very blest,
  If some ye nearest love were nearest!
Must *they* not love when lovèd best?
  Must *ye* not happiest love when dearest?
Alas! how hard to feel again,—
  It is in vain, it is in vain!

For those ye love are not unsighing,—
  They are unchanging least of all:
And ye the loved—ah! no denying,
  Will leave your lips beneath the pall,
When passioned ones have o'er it sain—
  'It is in vain, it is in vain!'

A SUPPLICATION FOR LOVE

HYMN I

The Lord Jesus, although gone to the Father, and we see Him no more, is still present with His Church; and in His heavenly glory expends upon her as intense a love, as in the agony of the garden, and the crucifixion of the tree. Those eyes that wept, still gaze upon her.— *Recalled words of an extempore Discourse, preached at Sidmouth*, 1833.

God, namèd Love, whose fount Thou art,
   Thy crownless Church before Thee
     stands,
With too much hating in her heart,
   And too much striving in her hands!

O loving Lord! O slain for love!
   Thy blood upon Thy garments came—
Inwrap their folds our brows above,
   Before we tell Thee all our shame!

'Love as I loved you,' was the sound
   That on Thy lips expiring sate!
Sweet words, in bitter strivings drowned!
   We hated as the worldly hate.

The spear that pierced for love Thy side,
   We dared for wrathful use to crave;
And with our cruel noise denied
   Its silence to Thy blood-red grave!

Ah, blood! that speaketh more of love
   Than Abel's—could we speak like Cain,
And grieve and scare that holy Dove,
   The parting love-gift of the Slain?

Yet, Lord, Thy wrongèd love fulfil!
   Thy Church, though fallen, before
     Thee stands—
Behold, the voice is Jacob's still,
   Albeit the hands are Esau's hands!

Hast Thou no tears, like those besprent
   Upon Thy Zion's ancient part?
No moving looks, like those which sent
   Their softness through a traitor's heart?

No touching tale of anguish dear;
   Whereby like children we may creep,
All trembling, to each other near,
   And view each other's face, and weep?

Oh, move us—Thou hast power to
     move—
   One in the one Beloved to be!
Teach us the heights and depths of love—
   Give Thine—that we may love like
     Thee!

THE MEDIATOR

HYMN II

As the greatest of all sacrifices was required, we may be assured that no other would have sufficed.—Boyd's *Essay on the Atonement*.

How high Thou art! our songs can
     own
   No music Thou couldst stoop to hear!
But still the Son's expiring groan
   Is vocal in the Father's ear.

How pure Thou art! our hands are dyed
   With curses, red with murder's hue—
But He hath stretched His hands to hide
   The sins that pierced them from Thy
     view.

How strong Thou art! we tremble lest
   The thunders of Thine arm be moved—
But He is lying on Thy breast,
   And Thou must clasp Thy best Beloved!

How kind Thou art! Thou didst not
     choose
   To joy in Him for ever so;
But that embrace Thou wilt not loose
   For vengeance, didst for love forgo!

High God, and pure, and strong, and
     kind!
   The low, the foul, the feeble, spare!
Thy brightness in His face we find—
   Behold our darkness only *there!*

THE WEEPING SAVIOUR

HYMN III

         —— tell
Whether His countenance can thee affright,
Tears in His eyes quench the amazing light.
         Donne.

When Jesus' friend had ceased to be,
   Still Jesus' heart its friendship kept—
'Where have ye laid him?'—'Come and
     see!'
But ere His eyes could see, they wept.

Lord! not in sepulchres alone,
  Corruption's worm is rank and free;
The shroud of death our bosoms own—
  The shades of sorrow! Come and see!

Come, Lord! God's image cannot shine
  Where sin's funereal darkness
    lowers—
Come! turn those weeping eyes of Thine
  Upon these sinning souls of ours!

And let those eyes, with shepherd
    care,
  Their moving watch above us keep;
Till love the strength of sorrow wear,
  And as thou weepedst, *we* may weep!

For surely we may weep to know,
  So dark and deep our spirit's stain;
That had Thy blood refused to flow,
  Thy very tears had flowed in vain.

SONNETS FROM THE PORTUGUESE

I

I THOUGHT once how Theocritus had sung
Of the sweet years, the dear and wished-
    for years,
Who each one in a gracious hand appears
To bear a gift for mortals, old or young:
And, as I mused it in his antique tongue,
I saw, in gradual vision through my tears,
The sweet, sad years, the melancholy
    years,
Those of my own life, who by turns had
    flung
A shadow across me. Straightway I
    was 'ware,
So weeping, how a mystic Shape did
    move
Behind me, and drew me backward by
    the hair,
And a voice said in mastery while I
    strove, . .
'Guess now who holds thee?'—'Death,'
    I said. But, there,
The silver answer rang, . . 'Not Death,
    but Love.'

II

BUT only three in all God's universe
Have heard this word thou hast said,—
    Himself, beside
Thee speaking, and me listening! and
    replied
One of us . . . *that* was God, . . and laid
    the curse
So darkly on my eyelids, as to amerce
My sight from seeing thee,—that if
    I had died,

The deathweights, placed there, would
    have signified
Less absolute exclusion. 'Nay' is worse
From God than from all others, O my
    friend!
Men could not part us with their worldly
    jars,
Nor the seas change us, nor the tem-
    pests bend;
Our hands would touch for all the
    mountain-bars,—
And, heaven being rolled between us at
    the end,
We should but vow the faster for the stars.

III

UNLIKE are we, unlike, O princely
    Heart!
Unlike our uses and our destinies.
Our ministering two angels look surprise
On one another, as they strike athwart
Their wings in passing. Thou, bethink
    thee, art
A guest for queens to social pageantries,
With gages from a hundred brighter eyes
Than tears even can make mine, to ply
    thy part
Of chief musician. What hast *thou* to do
With looking from the lattice-lights at me,
A poor, tired, wandering singer, . . sing-
    ing through
The dark, and leaning up a cypress tree?
The chrism is on thine head,—on mine,
    the dew,—
And Death must dig the level where
    these agree.

IV

Thou hast thy calling to some palace-
      floor,
Most gracious singer of high poems!
      where
The dancers will break footing, from
      the care
Of watching up thy pregnant lips for
      more.
And dost thou lift this house's latch too
      poor
For hand of thine? and canst thou think
      and bear
To let thy music drop here unaware
In folds of golden fullness at my door?
Look up and see the casement broken in,
The bats and owlets builders in the roof!
My cricket chirps against thy mandolin.
Hush, call no echo up in further proof
Of desolation! there's a voice within
That weeps . . . as thou must sing . . .
      alone, aloof.

V

I lift my heavy heart up solemnly,
As once Electra her sepulchral urn,
And, looking in thine eyes, I overturn
The ashes at thy feet. Behold and see
What a great heap of grief lay hid in me,
And how the red wild sparkles dimly
      burn
Through the ashen greyness. If thy
      foot in scorn
Could tread them out to darkness utterly,
It might be well perhaps. But if instead
Thou wait beside me for the wind to
      blow
The grey dust up, . . those laurels on
      thine head,
O my Belovèd, will not shield thee so,
That none of all the fires shall scorch
      and shred
The hair beneath. Stand farther off
      then! go.

VI

Go from me. Yet I feel that I shall stand
Henceforward in thy shadow. Never-
      more
Alone upon the threshold of my door
Of individual life, I shall command
The uses of my soul, nor lift my hand

Serenely in the sunshine as before,
Without the sense of that which I
      forbore, . .
Thy touch upon the palm. The widest
      land
Doom takes to part us, leaves thy heart
      in mine
With pulses that beat double. What I do
And what I dream include thee, as the
      wine
Must taste of its own grapes. And
      when I sue
God for myself, He hears that name of
      thine,
And sees within my eyes the tears of two.

VII

The face of all the world is changed,
      I think,
Since first I heard the footsteps of thy soul
Move still, oh, still, beside me, as they
      stole
Betwixt me and the dreadful outer brink
Of obvious death, where I, who thought
      to sink,
Was caught up into love, and taught
      the whole
Of life in a new rhythm. The cup of dole
God gave for baptism, I am fain to drink,
And praise its sweetness, Sweet, with
      thee anear.
The names of country, heaven, are
      changed away
For where thou art or shalt be, there or
      here;
And this . . . this lute and song . . .
      loved yesterday
(The singing angels know) are only dear,
Because thy name moves right in what
      they say.

VIII

What can I give thee back, O liberal
And princely giver, who hast brought
      the gold
And purple of thine heart, unstained,
      untold,
And laid them on the outside of the wall
For such as I to take or leave withal,
In unexpected largesse? am I cold,
Ungrateful, that for these most manifold
High gifts, I render nothing back at all?
Not so; not cold,—but very poor instead.

Ask God who knows. For frequent tears
    have run
The colours from my life, and left so dead
And pale a stuff, it were not fitly done
To give the same as pillow to thy head.
Go farther! let it serve to trample on.

IX

CAN it be right to give what I can give?
To let thee sit beneath the fall of tears
As salt as mine, and hear the sighing
    years
Re-sighing on my lips renunciative
Through those infrequent smiles which
    fail to live
For all thy adjurations? O my fears,
That this can scarce be right! We are
    not peers,
So to be lovers; and I own, and grieve,
That givers of such gifts as mine are, must
Be counted with the ungenerous. Out,
    alas!
I will not soil thy purple with my dust,
Nor breathe my poison on thy Venice-
    glass,
Nor give thee any love . . . which were
    unjust.
Beloved, I only love thee! let it pass.

X

YET, love, mere love, is beautiful indeed
And worthy of acceptation. Fire is bright,
Let temple burn, or flax. An equal light
Leaps in the flame from cedar-plank or
    weed.
And love is fire; and when I say at need
I love thee . . mark! . . *I love thee!* . . in
    thy sight
I stand transfigured, glorified aright,
With conscience of the new rays that
    proceed
Out of my face toward thine. There's
    nothing low
In love, when love the lowest: meanest
    creatures
Who love God, God accepts while
    loving so.
And what I *feel*, across the inferior
    features
Of what I *am*, doth flash itself, and show
How that great work of Love enhances
    Nature's.

XI

AND therefore if to love can be desert,
I am not all unworthy. Cheeks as pale
As these you see, and trembling knees
    that fail
To bear the burden of a heavy heart,—
This weary minstrel-life that once was
    girt
To climb Aornus, and can scarce avail
To pipe now 'gainst the valley nightingale
A melancholy music,—why advert
To these things? O Belovèd, it is plain
I am not of thy worth nor for thy place!
And yet, because I love thee, I obtain
From that same love this vindicating
    grace,
To live on still in love, and yet in vain, . .
To bless thee, yet renounce thee to thy
    face.

XII

INDEED this very love which is my boast,
And which, when rising up from breast
    to brow,
Doth crown me with a ruby large enow
To draw men's eyes and prove the
    inner cost, . .
This love even, all my worth, to the
    uttermost,
I should not love withal, unless that thou
Hadst set me an example, shown me how,
When first thine earnest eyes with mine
    were crossed,
And love called love. And thus, I
    cannot speak
Of love even, as a good thing of my own.
Thy soul hath snatched up mine all
    faint and weak,
And placed it by thee on a golden
    throne,—
And that I love (O soul, we must be
    meek!)
Is by thee only, whom I love alone.

XIII

AND wilt thou have me fashion into speech
The love I bear thee, finding words
    enough,
And hold the torch out, while the winds
    are rough,
Between our faces, to cast light on
    each?—
I drop it at thy feet. I cannot teach

My hand to hold my spirit so far off
From myself ... me ... that I should
   bring thee proof
In words, of love hid in me out of reach.
Nay, let the silence of my womanhood
Commend my woman-love to thy belief,—
Seeing that I stand unwon, however
   wooed,
And rend the garment of my life, in brief,
By a most dauntless, voiceless fortitude,
Lest one touch of this heart convey its
   grief.

XIV

IF thou must love me, let it be for nought
Except for love's sake only. Do not say
' I love her for her smile ... her look ...
   her way
Of speaking gently, . . for a trick of
   thought
That falls in well with mine, and certes
   brought
A sense of pleasant ease on such a day '—
For these things in themselves, Belovèd,
   may
Be changed, or change for thee,—and
   love, so wrought,
May be unwrought so. Neither love
   me for
Thine own dear pity's wiping my cheeks
   dry,—
A creature might forget to weep, who
   bore
Thy comfort long, and lose thy love
   thereby!
But love me for love's sake, that evermore
Thou mayst love on, through love's
   eternity.

XV

ACCUSE me not, beseech thee, that I wear
Too calm and sad a face in front of thine ;
For we two look two ways, and cannot
   shine
With the same sunlight on our brow
   and hair.
On me thou lookest, with no doubting
   care,
As on a bee shut in a crystalline,—
Since sorrow hath shut me safe in love's
   divine,
And to spread wing and fly in the
   outer air
Were most impossible failure, if I strove

To fail so. But I look on thee ... on thee ...
Beholding, besides love, the end of love,
Hearing oblivion beyond memory !
As one who sits and gazes from above,
Over the rivers to the bitter sea.

XVI

AND yet, because thou overcomest so,
Because thou art more noble and like
   a king,
Thou canst prevail against my fears and
   fling
Thy purple round me, till my heart
   shall grow
Too close against thine heart, henceforth
   to know
How it shook when alone. Why,
   conquering
May prove as lordly and complete
   a thing
In lifting upward, as in crushing low !
And as a vanquished soldier yields his
   sword
To one who lifts him from the bloody
   earth,—
Even so, Belovèd, I at last record,
Here ends my strife. If thou invite me
   forth,
I rise above abasement at the word.
Make thy love larger to enlarge my worth.

XVII

MY poet, thou canst touch on all the notes
God set between His After and Before,
And strike up and strike off the general
   roar
Of the rushing worlds, a melody that floats
In a serene air purely. Antidotes
Of medicated music, answering for
Mankind's forlornest uses, thou canst
   pour
From thence into their ears. God's
   will devotes
Thine to such ends, and mine to wait
   on thine.
How, Dearest, wilt thou have me for
   most use ?
A hope, to sing by gladly ? . . or a fine
Sad memory, with thy songs to interfuse?
A shade, in which to sing ... of palm
   or pine ?
A grave, on which to rest from singing? . .
   Choose.

XVIII

I NEVER gave a lock of hair away
To a man, dearest, except this to thee,
Which now upon my fingers thoughtfully
I ring out to the full brown length and say
'Take it.'   My day of youth went
    yesterday ;
My hair no longer bounds to my foot's glee,
Nor plant I it from rose or myrtle-tree,
As girls do, any more.   It only may
Now shade on two pale cheeks, the
    mark of tears,
Taught drooping from the head that
    hangs aside
Through sorrow's trick.   I thought the
    funeral-shears
Would take this first, but Love is
    justified,—
Take it, thou, . . finding pure, from all
    those years,
The kiss my mother left here when she
    died.

XIX

THE soul's Rialto hath its merchandise ;
I barter curl for curl upon that mart,
And from my poet's forehead to my heart,
Receive this lock which outweighs
    argosies,—
As purply black, as erst, to Pindar's eyes,
The dim purpureal tresses gloomed
    athwart
The nine white Muse-brows.   For this
    counterpart, . .
Thy bay-crown's shade, Belovèd, I
    surmise,
Still lingers on thy curl, it is so black !
Thus, with a fillet of smooth-kissing
    breath,
I tie the shadow safe from gliding back,
And lay the gift where nothing hindereth,
Here on my heart, as on thy brow, to lack
No natural heat till mine grows cold in
    death.

XX

BELOVÈD, my Belovèd, when I think
That thou wast in the world a year ago,
What time I sate alone here in the snow
And saw no footprint, heard the silence
    sink
No moment at thy voice, . . but, link by link,
Went counting all my chains, as if that so
They never could fall off at any blow

Struck by thy possible hand . . . why,
    thus I drink
Of life's great cup of wonder ! Wonderful,
Never to feel thee thrill the day or night
With personal act or speech,—nor ever
    cull
Some prescience of thee with the
    blossoms white
Thou sawest growing !   Atheists are as
    dull,
Who cannot guess God's presence out
    of sight.

XXI

SAY over again, and yet once over again,
That thou dost love me.   Though the
    word repeated
Should seem 'a cuckoo-song,' as thou
    dost treat it,
Remember, never to the hill or plain,
Valley and wood, without her cuckoo-
    strain,
Comes the fresh Spring in all her green
    completed.
Belovèd, I, amid the darkness greeted
By a doubtful spirit-voice, in that doubt's
    pain
Cry . . . 'Speak once more . . . thou
    lovest !'   Who can fear
Too many stars, though each in heaven
    shall roll—
Too many flowers, though each shall
    crown the year ?
Say thou dost love me, love me, love
    me—toll
The silver iterance !—only minding, dear,
To love me also in silence, with thy soul.

XXII

WHEN our two souls stand up erect and
    strong,
Face to face, silent, drawing nigh and
    nigher,
Until the lengthening wings break into
    fire
At either curvèd point,—what bitter
    wrong
Can the earth do to us, that we should
    not long
Be here contented ? Think.   In mounting
    higher,
The angels would press on us, and aspire
To drop some golden orb of perfect song
Into our deep, dear silence.   Let us stay

Rather on earth, Belovèd,—where the
    unfit
Contrarious moods of men recoil away
And isolate pure spirits, and permit
A place to stand and love in for a day,
With darkness and the death-hour
    rounding it.

XXIII

Is it indeed so ? If I lay here dead,
Wouldst thou miss any life in losing mine ?
And would the sun for thee more coldly
    shine,
Because of grave-damps falling round
    my head ?
I marvelled, my Belovèd, when I read
Thy thoughts so in the letter.   I am thine—
But . . . so much to thee ?   Can I pour
    thy wine
While my hands tremble ?   Then my
    soul, instead
Of dreams of death, resumes life's lower
    range.
Then, love me, Love ! look on me . . .
    breathe on me !
As brighter ladies do not count it strange,
For love, to give up acres and degree,
I yield the grave for thy sake, and ex-
    change
My near sweet view of Heaven, for
    earth with thee !

XXIV

LET the world's sharpness like a clasping
    knife
Shut in upon itself and do no harm
In this close hand of Love, now soft and
    warm,
And let us hear no sound of human strife
After the click of the shutting.   Life to
    life—
I lean upon thee, dear, without alarm,
And feel as safe as guarded by a charm
Against the stab of worldlings, who if rife
Are weak to injure.   Very whitely still
The lilies of our lives may reassure
Their blossoms from their roots, acces-
    sible
Alone to heavenly dews that drop not
    fewer :
Growing straight, out of man's reach, on
    the hill.
God only, who made us rich, can make
    us poor.

XXV

A HEAVY heart, Belovèd, have I borne
From year to year until I saw thy face,
And sorrow after sorrow took the place
Of all those natural joys as lightly worn
As the stringed pearls . . . each lifted in
    its turn
By a beating heart at dance-time.
    Hopes apace
Were changed to long despairs, till God's
    own grace
Could scarcely lift above the world forlorn
My heavy heart.   Then *thou* didst bid
    me bring
And let it drop adown thy calmly great
Deep being !   Fast it sinketh, as a thing
Which its own nature doth precipitate,
While thine doth close above it, mediating
Betwixt the stars and the unaccomplished
    fate.

XXVI

I LIVED with visions for my company,
Instead of men and women, years ago,
And found them gentle mates, nor
    thought to know
A sweeter music than they played to me.
But soon their trailing purple was not
    free
Of this world's dust,—their lutes did
    silent grow,
And I myself grew faint and blind below
Their vanishing eyes.   Then THOU didst
    come . . . to be,
Belovèd, what they seemed.   Their
    shining fronts,
Their songs, their splendours (better,
    yet the same,
As river-water hallowed into fonts),
Met in thee, and from out thee overcame
My soul with satisfaction of all wants—
Because God's gifts put man's best
    dreams to shame.

XXVII

MY own Belovèd, who hast lifted me
From this drear flat of earth where I was
    thrown,
And, in betwixt the languid ringlets,
    blown
A life-breath, till the forehead hopefully
Shines out again, as all the angels see,

Before thy saving kiss! My own, my own,
Who camest to me when the world was
    gone,
And I who looked for only God, found
    thee !
I find thee ; I am safe, and strong, and glad.
As one who stands in dewless asphodel,
Looks backward on the tedious time he
    had
In the upper life,—so I, with bosom-swell,
Make witness. here, between the good
    and bad,
That Love, as strong as Death, retrieves
    as well.

XXVIII

My letters ! all dead paper, . . mute and
    white !—
And yet they seem alive and quivering
Against my tremulous hands which loose
    the string
And let them drop down on my knee
    to-night.
This said, . . he wished to have me in
    his sight
Once, as a friend : this fixed a day in spring
To come and touch my hand...a simple
    thing,
Yet I wept for it !—this, . . the paper's
    light . . .
Said, *Dear, I love thee ;* and I sank and
    quailed
As if God's future thundered on my past.
This said, *I am thine*—and so its ink has
    paled
With lying at my heart that beat too fast.
And this . . . O Love, thy words have ill
    availed,
If, what this said, I dared repeat at last !

XXIX

I THINK of thee !—my thoughts do twine
    and bud
About thee, as wild vines, about a tree,
Put out broad leaves, and soon there 's
    nought to see
Except the straggling green which hides
    the wood.
Yet, O my palm-tree, be it understood
I will not have my thoughts instead of thee
Who art dearer, better ! rather instantly
Renew thy presence. As a strong tree
    should,

Rustle thy boughs and set thy trunk all
    bare,
And let these bands of greenery which
    insphere thee,
Drop heavily down, . . burst, shattered,
    everywhere !
Because, in this deep joy to see and hear
    thee
And breathe within thy shadow a new air,
I do not think of thee—I am too near thee.

XXX

I SEE thine image through my tears to-
    night,
And yet to-day I saw thee smiling. How
Refer the cause ?—Belovèd, is it thou
Or I, who makes me sad ? The acolyte
Amid the chanted joy and thankful rite,
May so fall flat, with pale insensate brow,
On the altar-stair. I hear thy voice and
    vow
Perplexed, uncertain, since thou art out
    of sight,
As he, in his swooning ears, the choir's
    amen.
Belovèd, dost thou love ? or did I see all
The glory as I dreamed, and fainted when
Too vehement light dilated my ideal,
For my soul's eyes ? Will that light
    come again,
As now these tears come. . . falling hot
    and real ?

XXXI

THOU comest ! all is said without a word.
I sit beneath thy looks, as children do
In the noon-sun, with souls that tremble
    through
Their happy eyelids from an unaverred
Yet prodigal inward joy. Behold, I erred
In that last doubt ! and yet I cannot rue
The sin most, but the occasion . . . that
    we two
Should for a moment stand unministered
By a mutual presence. Ah, keep near
    and close,
Thou dovelike help ! and, when my fears
    would rise,
With thy broad heart serenely interpose.
Brood down with thy divine sufficiencies
These thoughts which tremble when
    bereft of those,
Like callow birds left desert to the skies.

XXXII

THE first time that the sun rose on thine
      oath
To love me, I looked forward to the moon
To slacken all those bonds which seemed
      too soon
And quickly tied to make a lasting troth.
Quick-loving hearts, I thought, may
      quickly loathe ;
And, looking on myself, I seemed not one
For such man's love !—more like an out
      of tune
Worn viol, a good singer would be wroth
To spoil his song with, and which,
      snatched in haste,
Is laid down at the first ill-sounding note.
I did not wrong myself so, but I placed
A wrong on *thee*. For perfect strains
      may float
'Neath master-hands, from instruments
      defaced,—
And great souls, at one stroke, may do
      and dote.

XXXIII

YES, call me by my pet-name ! let me hear
The name I used to run at, when a child,
From innocent play, and leave the cow-
      slips piled,
To glance up in some face that proved
      me dear
With the look of its eyes. I miss the clear
Fond voices, which, being drawn and
      reconciled
Into the music of Heaven's undefiled,
Call me no longer. Silence on the bier,
While I call God . . . call God !—So let
      thy mouth
Be heir to those who are now exanimate.
Gather the north flowers to complete the
      south,
And catch the early love up in the late.
Yes, call me by that name,—and I, in
      truth,
With the same heart, will answer, and
      not wait.

XXXIV

WITH the same heart, I said, I'll answer
      thee
As those, when thou shalt call me by my
      name—
Lo, the vain promise ! is the same, the
      same,

Perplexed and ruffled by life's strategy ?
When called before, I told how hastily
I dropped my flowers or brake off from
      a game,
To run and answer with the smile that
      came
At play last moment, and went on with me
Through my obedience. When I answer
      now,
I drop a grave thought—break from
      solitude ;
Yet still my heart goes to thee . . . ponder
      how . . .
Not as to a single good, but all my good !
Lay thy hand on it, best one, and allow
That no child's foot could run fast as this
      blood.

XXXV

IF I leave all for thee, wilt thou exchange
And be all to me ? Shall I never miss
Home-talk and blessing and the common
      kiss
That comes to each in turn, nor count it
      strange,
When I look up, to drop on a new range
Of walls and floors . . . another home
      than this ?
Nay, wilt thou fill that place by me
      which is
Filled by dead eyes too tender to know
      change ?
That's hardest. If to conquer love, has
      tried,
To conquer grief, tries more . . . as all
      things prove ;
For grief indeed is love and grief beside.
Alas, I have grieved so I am hard to love.
Yet love me—wilt thou ? Open thine
      heart wide,
And fold within, the wet wings of thy
      dove.

XXXVI

WHEN we met first and loved, I did not
      build
Upon the event with marble. Could it
      mean
To last, a love set pendulous between
Sorrow and sorrow ? Nay, I rather
      thrilled,
Distrusting every light that seemed to
      gild

The onward path, and feared to overlean
A finger even. And, though I have
    grown serene
And strong since then, I think that God
    has willed
A still renewable fear . . . O love,
    O troth . . .
Lest these enclaspèd hands should never
    hold,
This mutual kiss drop down between us
    both
As an unowned thing, once the lips being
    cold.
And Love, be false! if *he*, to keep one oath,
Must lose one joy, by his life's star
    foretold.

XXXVII

PARDON, oh, pardon, that my soul should
    make
Of all that strong divineness which I
    know
For thine and thee, an image only so
Formed of the sand, and fit to shift and
    break.
It is that distant years which did not take
Thy sovranty, recoiling with a blow,
Have forced my swimming brain to
    undergo
Their doubt and dread, and blindly to
    forsake
The purity of likeness, and distort
Thy worthiest love to a worthless
    counterfeit.
As if a shipwrecked Pagan, safe in port,
His guardian sea-god to commemorate.
Should set a sculptured porpoise, gills
    a-snort
And vibrant tail, within the temple-gate.

XXXVIII

FIRST time he kissed me, he but only
    kissed
The fingers of this hand wherewith I
    write;
And, ever since, it grew more clean and
    white, . .
Slow to world-greetings . . . quick with
    its ' Oh, list,'
When the angels speak. A ring of
    amethyst
I could not wear here, plainer to my sight,
Than that first kiss. The second passed
    in height

The first, and sought the forehead, and
    half missed,
Half falling on the hair. Oh, beyond
    meed!
That was the chrism of love, which love's
    own crown,
With sanctifying sweetness, did precede.
The third upon my lips was folded down
In perfect, purple state; since when,
    indeed,
I have been proud and said, ' My love,
    my own.'

XXXIX

BECAUSE thou hast the power and own'st
    the grace
To look through and behind this mask
    of me
(Against which years have beat thus
    blanchingly
With their rains) and behold my soul's
    true face,
The dim and weary witness of life's
    race!—
Because thou hast the faith and love to see,
Through that same soul's distracting
    lethargy,
The patient angel waiting for a place
In the new heavens! because nor sin
    nor woe,
Nor God's infliction, nor death's neigh-
    bourhood,
Nor all which others viewing, turn to
    go, . .
Nor all which makes me tired of all,
    self-viewed, . .
Nothing repels thee, . . dearest, teach
    me so
To pour out gratitude, as thou dost, good.

XL

OH, yes! they love through all this world
    of ours!
I will not gainsay love, called love for-
    sooth.
I have heard love talked in my early youth,
And since, not so long back but that the
    flowers
Then gathered, smell still. Mussulmans
    and Giaours
Throw kerchiefs at a smile, and have no
    ruth
For any weeping. Polypheme's white
    tooth

Slips on the nut, if, after frequent showers,
The shell is over-smooth,—and not so
     much
Will turn the thing called love, aside to
     hate,
Or else to oblivion. But thou art not such
A lover, my Belovèd! thou canst wait
Through sorrow and sickness, to bring
     souls to touch,
And think it soon when others cry 'Too
     late.'

XLI

I THANK all who have loved me in their
     hearts,
With thanks and love from mine. Deep
     thanks to all
Who paused a little near the prison-wall,
To hear my music in its louder parts,
Ere they went onward, each one to the
     mart's
Or temple's occupation, beyond call.
But thou, who, in my voice's sink and fall,
When the sob took it, thy divinest Art's
Own instrument didst drop down at thy
     foot,
To hearken what I said between my
     tears, . .
Instruct me how to thank thee!—Oh, to
     shoot
My soul's full meaning into future years,
That *they* should lend it utterance, and
     salute
Love that endures, from Life that dis-
     appears!

XLII

' *My future will not copy fair my past* '—
I wrote that once ; and thinking at my side
My ministering life-angel justified
The word by his appealing look upcast
To the white throne of God, I turned at
     last,
And there, instead, saw thee, not un-
     allied
To angels in thy soul! Then I, long tried
By natural ills, received the comfort fast,
While budding, at thy sight, my pilgrim's
     staff
Gave out green leaves with morning
     dews impearled.
I seek no copy now of life's first half :
Leave here the pages with long musing
     curled,

And write me new my future's epigraph,
New angel mine, unhoped for in the
     world !

XLIII

How do I love thee ? Let me count the
     ways.
I love thee to the depth and breadth and
     height
My soul can reach, when feeling out of
     sight
For the ends of Being and ideal Grace.
I love thee to the level of every day's
Most quiet need, by sun and candlelight.
I love thee freely, as men strive for Right ;
I love thee purely, as they turn from
     Praise.
I love thee with the passion put to use
In my old griefs, and with my childhood's
     faith.
I love thee with a love I seemed to lose
With my lost saints,—I love thee with
     the breath,
Smiles, tears, of all my life !—and, if God
     choose,
I shall but love thee better after death.

XLIV

BELOVÈD, thou hast brought me many
     flowers
Plucked in the garden, all the summer
     through
And winter, and it seemed as if they grew
In this close room, nor missed the sun
     and showers.
So, in the like name of that love of ours,
Take back these thoughts which here
     unfolded too,
And which on warm and cold days I
     withdrew
From my heart's ground. Indeed, those
     beds and bowers
Be overgrown with bitter weeds and rue,
And wait thy weeding ; yet here's
     eglantine,
Here's ivy !—take them, as I used to do
Thy flowers, and keep them where they
     shall not pine.
Instruct thine eyes to keep their colours
     true,
And tell thy soul, their roots are left in
     mine.

SONNETS

THE SOUL'S EXPRESSION

WITH stammering lips and insufficient
   sound
I strive and struggle to deliver right
That music of my nature, day and night
With dream and thought and feeling
   interwound,
And inly answering all the senses round
With octaves of a mystic depth and
   height
Which step out grandly to the infinite
From the dark edges of the sensual
   ground !
This song of soul I struggle to outbear
Through portals of the sense, sublime
   and whole,
And utter all myself into the air.
But if I did it,—as the thunder-roll
Breaks its own cloud, my flesh would
   perish there,
Before that dread apocalypse of soul.

THE SERAPH AND POET

THE seraph sings before the manifest
God-One, and in the burning of the
   Seven,
And with the full life of consummate
   Heaven
Heaving beneath him, like a mother's
   breast
Warm with her first-born's slumber in
   that nest.
The poet sings upon the earth grave-
   riven,
Before the naughty world, soon self-
   forgiven
For wronging him,—and in the darkness
   prest
From his own soul by worldly weights.
   Even so,
Sing, seraph with the glory ! heaven is
   high.
Sing, poet with the sorrow ! earth is low.
The universe's inward voices cry
' Amen ' to either song of joy and woe.
Sing, seraph,—poet,—sing on equally !

BEREAVEMENT

WHEN some Belovèds, 'neath whose
   eyelids lay
The sweet lights of my childhood, one
   by one
Did leave me dark before the natural sun,
And I astonied fell and could not
   pray,—
A thought within me to myself did say,
' Is God less God, that *thou* art left un-
   done ?
Rise, worship, bless Him, in this sack-
   cloth spun,
As in that purple !'—But I answered,
   Nay !
What child his filial heart in words can
   loose,
If he behold his tender father raise
The hand that chastens sorely ? can he
   choose
But sob in silence with an upward
   gaze ?—
And *my* great Father, thinking fit to
   bruise,
Discerns in speechless tears both prayer
   and praise.

CONSOLATION

ALL are not taken ; there are left behind
Living Belovèds, tender looks to bring,
And make the daylight still a happy thing,
And tender voices, to make soft the wind.
But if it were not so—if I could find
No love in all the world for comforting,
Nor any path but hollowly did ring,
Where ' dust to dust ' the love from life
   disjoined,
And if, before those sepulchres unmoving,
I stood alone (as some forsaken lamb
Goes bleating up the moors in weary
   dearth),
Crying ' Where are ye, O my loved and
   loving ? ' . . .
I know a Voice would sound, ' Daughter,
   I AM.
Can I suffice for HEAVEN, and not for
   earth ? '

TO MARY RUSSELL MITFORD
IN HER GARDEN

WHAT time I lay these rimes anear thy
　　feet,
Benignant friend, I will not proudly say
As better poets use, ' These *flowers* I lay,'
Because I would not wrong thy roses
　　sweet,
Blaspheming so their name.   And yet,
　　repeat,
Thou, overleaning them this springtime
　　day,
With heart as open to love as theirs to
　　May,
—' Low-rooted verse may reach some
　　heavenly heat,
Even like my blossoms, if as nature-true,
Though not as precious.'   Thou art un-
　　perplext,
Dear friend, in whose dear writings
　　drops the dew
And blow the natural airs,—thou, who
　　art next
To nature's self in cheering the world's
　　view,—
To preach a sermon on so known a text!

ON A PORTRAIT OF WORDS-
WORTH BY B. R. HAYDON

WORDSWORTH upon Helvellyn! Let the
　　cloud
Ebb audibly along the mountain-wind,
Then break against the rock, and show
　　behind
The lowland valleys floating up to crowd
The sense with beauty.   He with fore-
　　head bowed
And humble-lidded eyes, as one inclined
Before the sovran thought of his own
　　mind
And very meek with inspirations proud,
Takes here his rightful place as poet-
　　priest
By the high altar, singing prayer and
　　prayer
To the higher Heavens.   A noble vision
　　free
Our Haydon's hand has flung out from
　　the mist!
No portrait this, with Academic air!
This is the poet and his poetry.

PAST AND FUTURE

My future will not copy fair my past
On any leaf but Heaven's.   Be fully
　　done,
Supernal Will! I would not fain be one
Who, satisfying thirst and breaking fast
Upon the fullness of the heart, at last
Says no grace after meat.   My wine has
　　run
Indeed out of my cup, and there is none
To gather up the bread of my repast
Scattered and trampled,—yet I find some
　　good
In earth's green herbs, and streams that
　　bubble up
Clear from the darkling ground,—con-
　　tent until
I sit with angels before better food.
Dear Christ! when Thy new vintage fills
　　my cup,
This hand shall shake no more, nor that
　　wine spill.

IRREPARABLENESS

I HAVE been in the meadows all the day
And gathered there the nosegay that
　　you see,
Singing within myself as a bird or bee
When such do field-work on a morn of
　　May.
But now I look upon my flowers, decay
Has met them in my hands more fatally
Because more warmly clasped,—and
　　sobs are free
To come instead of songs.   What do
　　you say,
Sweet counsellors, dear friends? that I
　　should go
Back straightway to the fields, and
　　gather more?
Another, sooth, may do it,—but not I!
My heart is very tired, my strength is
　　low,
My hands are full of blossoms plucked
　　before,
Held dead within them till myself shall
　　die.

TEARS

Thank God, bless God, all ye who
    suffer not
More grief than ye can weep for. That
    is well—
That is light grieving! lighter, none
    befell
Since Adam forfeited the primal lot.
Tears! what are tears? The babe weeps
    in its cot,
The mother singing,—at her marriage-
    bell
The bride weeps,—and before the oracle
Of high-faned hills, the poet has forgot
Such moisture on his cheeks. Thank
    God for grace,
Ye who weep only! If, as some have
    done,
Ye grope tear-blinded in a desert place
And touch but tombs,—look up! those
    tears will run
Soon in long rivers down the lifted
    face,
And leave the vision clear for stars and
    sun.

SUBSTITUTION

When some belovèd voice that was to you
Both sound and sweetness, faileth sud-
    denly,
And silence, against which you dare not
    cry,
Aches round you like a strong disease
    and new—
What hope? what help? what music
    will undo
That silence to your sense? Not friend-
    ship's sigh.
Not reason's subtle count. Not melody
Of viols, nor of pipes that Faunus blew.
Not songs of poets, nor of nightingales,
Whose hearts leap upward through the
    cypress trees
To the clear moon! nor yet the spheric
    laws
Self-chanted,—nor the angels' sweet
    All hails,
Met in the smile of God. Nay, none of
    these.
Speak Thou, availing Christ!—and fill
    this pause.

GRIEF

I tell you, hopeless grief is passion-
    less;
That only men incredulous of despair,
Half-taught in anguish, through the
    midnight air
Beat upward to God's throne in loud
    access
Of shrieking and reproach. Full desert-
    ness
In souls, as countries, lieth silent-bare
Under the blanching, vertical eye-glare
Of the absolute Heavens. Deep-hearted
    man, express
Grief for thy Dead in silence like to
    death:—
Most like a monumental statue set
In everlasting watch and moveless woe,
Till itself crumble to the dust beneath.
Touch it: the marble eyelids are not
    wet;
If it could weep, it could arise and go.

COMFORT

Speak low to me, my Saviour, low and
    sweet
From out the hallelujahs, sweet and low,
Lest I should fear and fall, and miss
    Thee so
Who art not missed by any that entreat.
Speak to me as to Mary at Thy feet!
And if no precious gums my hands
    bestow,
Let my tears drop like amber, while
    I go
In reach of Thy divinest voice complete
In humanest affection—thus, in sooth,
To lose the sense of losing. As a child,
Whose song-bird seeks the wood for
    evermore,
Is sung to in its stead by mother's
    mouth,
Till, sinking on her breast, love-recon-
    ciled,
He sleeps the faster that he wept before.

PERPLEXED MUSIC

AFFECTIONATELY INSCRIBED TO E. J.

EXPERIENCE, like a pale musician, holds
A dulcimer of patience in his hand,
Whence harmonies we cannot under-
stand,
Of God's will in His worlds, the strain
unfolds
In sad, perplexed minors. Deathly colds
Fall on us while we hear and counter-
mand
Our sanguine heart back from the fancy-
land
With nightingales in visionary wolds.
We murmur,—' Where is any certain
tune
Or measured music, in such notes as
these ?'—
But angels, leaning from the golden seat,
Are not so minded ; their fine ear hath
won
The issue of completed cadences,
And, smiling down the stars, they
whisper—SWEET.

WORK

WHAT are we set on earth for? Say, to
toil ;
Nor seek to leave thy tending of the vines,
For all the heat o' the day, till it declines,
And Death's mild curfew shall from
work assoil.
God did anoint thee with His odorous oil,
To wrestle, not to reign ; and He assigns
All thy tears over, like pure crystallines,
For younger fellow workers of the soil
To wear for amulets. So others shall
Take patience, labour, to their heart
and hand,
From thy hand, and thy heart, and thy
brave cheer,
And God's grace fructify through thee
to all.
The least flower, with a brimming cup,
may stand,
And share its dewdrop with another
near.

FUTURITY

AND, O belovèd voices, upon which
Ours passionately call, because ere long
Ye brake off in the middle of that song
We sang together softly, to enrich
The poor world with the sense of love,
and witch
The heart out of things evil,—I am
strong,
Knowing ye are not lost for ay among
The hills, with last year's thrush. God
keeps a niche
In Heaven, to hold our idols : and albeit
He brake them to our faces, and denied
That our close kisses should impair their
white,—
I know we shall behold them raised,
complete,
The dust swept from their beauty,—
glorified
New Memnons singing in the great
God-light.

THE TWO SAYINGS

Two sayings of the Holy Scriptures beat
Like pulses in the Church's brow and
breast !
And by them we find rest in our unrest,
And, heart-deep in salt tears, do yet
entreat
God's fellowship, as if on heavenly seat.
The first is JESUS WEPT,—whereon is
prest
Full many a sobbing face that drops its
best
And sweetest waters on the record
sweet.
And one is, where the Christ, denied
and scorned,
LOOKED UPON PETER. Oh, to render
plain,
By help of having loved a little and
mourned,
That look of sovran love and sovran
pain
Which HE, who could not sin yet
suffered, turned
On him who could reject but not sustain !

THE LOOK

The Saviour looked on Peter. Aye, no word,
No gesture of reproach! the Heavens serene,
Though heavy with armed justice, did not lean
Their thunders that way! the forsaken Lord
Looked only, on the traitor. None record
What that look was, none guess; for those who have seen
Wronged lovers loving through a death-pang keen,
Or pale-cheeked martyrs smiling to a sword,
Have missed Jehovah at the judgement-call.
And Peter, from the height of blasphemy—
'I never knew this man'—did quail and fall,
As knowing straight THAT GOD,—and turnèd free
And went out speechless from the face of all,
And filled the silence, weeping bitterly.

THE MEANING OF THE LOOK

I THINK that look of Christ might seem to say—
'Thou Peter! art thou then a common stone
Which I at last must break My heart upon,
For all God's charge to His high angels may
Guard My foot better? Did I yesterday
Wash *thy* feet, My beloved, that they should run
Quick to deny Me 'neath the morning sun?
And do thy kisses, like the rest, betray?
The cock crows coldly.— Go, and manifest
A late contrition, but no bootless fear!
For when thy final need is dreariest,
Thou shalt not be denied, as I am here—
My voice, to God and angels, shall attest,
Because I KNOW *this man, let him be clear*.'

A THOUGHT FOR A LONELY DEATH-BED

INSCRIBED TO MY FRIEND E. C.

If God compel thee to this destiny,
To die alone,—with none beside thy bed
To ruffle round with sobs thy last word said,
And mark with tears the pulses ebb from thee,—
Pray then alone—' O Christ, come tenderly!
By Thy forsaken Sonship in the red
Drear wine-press,—by the wilderness outspread,—
And the lone garden where Thine agony
Fell bloody from Thy brow,—by all of those
Permitted desolations, comfort mine!
No earthly friend being near me, interpose
No deathly angel 'twixt my face and Thine,
But stoop Thyself to gather my life's rose,
And smile away my mortal to Divine.'

WORK AND CONTEMPLATION

The woman singeth at her spinning-wheel
A pleasant chant, ballad, or barcarole:
She thinketh of her song, upon the whole,
Far more than of her flax; and yet the reel
Is full, and artfully her fingers feel
With quick adjustment, provident control,
The lines, too subtly twisted to unroll,
Out to a perfect thread. I hence appeal
To the dear Christian Church—that we may do
Our Father's business in these temples mirk,
Thus swift and steadfast,—thus, intent and strong;
While, thus, apart from toil, our souls pursue
Some high, calm, spheric tune, and prove our work
The better for the sweetness of our song.

PAIN IN PLEASURE

A Thought lay like a flower upon mine
    heart,
And drew around it other thoughts like
    bees
For multitude and thirst of sweet-
    nesses,—
Whereat rejoicing, I desired the art
Of the Greek whistler, who to wharf
    and mart
Could lure those insect swarms from
    orange-trees,
That I might hive with me such thoughts,
    and please
My soul so, always. Foolish counterpart
Of a weak man's vain wishes! While I
    spoke,
The thought I called a flower, grew
    nettle-rough—
The thoughts, called bees, stung me to
    festering.
Oh, entertain (cried Reason, as she
    woke)
Your best and gladdest thoughts but long
    enough,
And they will all prove sad enough to
    sting.

FLUSH OR FAUNUS

You see this dog. It was but yesterday
I mused forgetful of his presence here
Till thought on thought drew downward
    tear on tear,
When from the pillow, where wet-
    cheeked I lay,
A head as hairy as Faunus, thrust its way
Right sudden against my face,—two
    golden-clear
Great eyes astonished mine,—a drooping
    ear
Did flap me on either cheek to dry the
    spray!
I started first, as some Arcadian,
Amazed by goatly god in twilight grove;
But, as the bearded vision closelier ran
My tears off, I knew Flush, and rose
    above
Surprise and sadness,—thanking the true
    Pan,
Who, by low creatures, leads to heights
    of love.

FINITE AND INFINITE

The wind sounds only in opposing
    straits,
The sea, beside the shore; man's spirit
    rends
Its quiet only up against the ends
Of wants and oppositions, loves and
    hates,
Where, worked and worn by passionate
    debates,
And losing by the loss it apprehends,
The flesh rocks round, and every breath
    it sends
Is ravelled to a sigh. All tortured states
Suppose a straitened place. Jehovah
    Lord,
Make room for rest, around me! out of
    sight
Now float me, of the vexing land ab-
    horred,
Till in deep calms of space my soul may
    right
Her nature,—shoot large sail on length-
    ening cord,
And rush exultant on the Infinite.

AN APPREHENSION

If all the gentlest-hearted friends I know
Concentred in one heart their gentle-
    ness,
That still grew gentler, till its pulse was
    less
For life than pity,—I should yet be slow
To bring my own heart nakedly below
The palm of such a friend, that he should
    press
Motive, condition, means, appliances,
My false ideal joy and fickle woe,
Out full to light and knowledge; I should
    fear
Some plait between the brows—some
    rougher chime
In the free voice . . . O angels, let your
    flood
Of bitter scorn dash on me! do ye hear
What *I* say, who bear calmly all the time
This everlasting face to face with God?

DISCONTENT

Light human nature is too lightly tost
And ruffled without cause,—complaining
on,
Restless with rest—until, being over-
thrown,
It learneth to lie quiet. Let a frost
Or a small wasp have crept to the inner-
most
Of our ripe peach, or let the wilful sun
Shine westward of our window,—straight
we run
A furlong's sigh, as if the world were lost.
But what time through the heart and
through the brain
God hath transfixed us,—we, so moved
before,
Attain to a calm. Aye, shouldering
weights of pain,
We anchor in deep waters, safe from
shore,
And hear, submissive, o'er the stormy
main,
God's chartered judgements walk for
evermore.

PATIENCE TAUGHT BY NATURE

' O dreary life,' we cry, ' O dreary life ! '
And still the generations of the birds
Sing through our sighing, and the flocks
and herds
Serenely live while we are keeping strife
With Heaven's true purpose in us, as
a knife
Against which we may struggle ! ocean
girds
Unslackened the dry land, savannah-
swards
Unweary sweep,—hills watch, unworn ;
and rife
Meek leaves drop yearly from the forest-
trees,
To show above the unwasted stars that
pass
In their old glory. O thou God of old,
Grant me some smaller grace than comes
to these !—
But so much patience as a blade of grass
Grows by, contented through the heat
and cold.

CHEERFULNESS TAUGHT BY REASON

I think we are too ready with complaint
In this fair world of God's. Had we no
hope
Indeed beyond the zenith and the slope
Of yon grey blank of sky, we might
grow faint
To muse upon eternity's constraint
Round our aspirant souls ; but since
the scope
Must widen early is it well to droop,
For a few days consumed in loss and
taint ?
O pusillanimous Heart, be comforted,—
And, like a cheerful traveller, take the
road,
Singing beside the hedge. What if the
bread
Be bitter in thine inn, and thou unshod
To meet the flints ?—At least it may be
said,
' Because the way is *short*, I thank Thee,
God ! '

EXAGGERATION

We overstate the ills of life, and take
Imagination (given us to bring down
The choirs of singing angels overshone
By God's clear glory) down our earth
to rake
The dismal snows instead,—flake follow-
ing flake,
To cover all the corn. We walk upon
The shadow of hills across a level
thrown,
And pant like climbers. Near the alder-
brake
We sigh so loud, the nightingale within
Refuses to sing loud, as else she would.
O brothers ! let us leave the shame and
sin
Of taking vainly, in a plaintive mood,
The holy name of Grief ! – holy herein,
That by the grief of One came all our
good.

ADEQUACY

Now by the verdure on thy thousand hills,
Belovèd England,—doth the earth ap-
    pear
Quite good enough for men to overbear
The will of God in, with rebellious
    wills!
We cannot say the morning-sun fulfils
Ingloriously its course, nor that the clear
Strong stars without significance in-
    sphere
Our habitation.   We, meantime, our ills
Heap up against this good, and lift a cry
Against this work-day world, this ill-
    spread feast,
As if ourselves were better certainly
Than what we come to.   Maker and
    High Priest,
I ask Thee not my joys to multiply,—
Only to make me worthier of the least.

TO GEORGE SAND

A DESIRE

Thou large-brained woman and large-
    hearted man,
Self-called George Sand! whose soul,
    amid the lions
Of thy tumultuous senses, moans defiance,
And answers roar for roar, as spirits can!
I would some mild miraculous thunder ran
Above the applauded circus, in appliance
Of thine own nobler nature's strength
    and science,
Drawing two pinions, white as wings
    of swan,
From thy strong shoulders, to amaze the
    place
With holier light! that thou to woman's
    claim,
And man's, mightst join beside the
    angel's grace
Of a pure genius sanctified from blame,—
Till child and maiden pressed to thine
    embrace,
To kiss upon thy lips a stainless fame.

TO GEORGE SAND

A RECOGNITION

True genius, but true woman! dost deny
Thy woman's nature with a manly scorn,
And break away the gauds and armlets
    worn
By weaker women in captivity?
Ah, vain denial! that revolted cry
Is sobbed in by a woman's voice for-
    lorn!—
Thy woman's hair, my sister, all unshorn,
Floats back dishevelled strength in agony,
Disproving thy man's name! and while
    before
The world thou burnest in a poet-fire,
We see thy woman-heart beat evermore
Through the large flame.   Beat purer,
    heart, and higher,
Till God unsex thee on the heavenly
    shore,
Where unincarnate spirits purely aspire.

THE PRISONER

I count the dismal time by months and
    years,
Since last I felt the green sward under
    foot,
And the great breath of all things
    summer-mute
Met mine upon my lips.   Now earth
    appears
As strange to me as dreams of distant
    spheres,
Or thoughts of Heaven we weep at.
    Nature's lute
Sounds on behind this door so closely shut,
A strange, wild music to the prisoner's
    ears,
Dilated by the distance, till the brain
Grows dim with fancies which it feels
    too fine,
While ever, with a visionary pain,
Past the precluded senses, sweep and
    shine
Streams, forests, glades,— and many a
    golden train
Of sunlit hills, transfigured to Divine.

INSUFFICIENCY

WHEN I attain to utter forth in verse
Some inward thought, my soul throbs
        audibly
Along my pulses, yearning to be free
And something farther, fuller, higher,
        rehearse,
To the individual, true, and the universe,
In consummation of right harmony.
But, like a wind-exposed, distorted tree,
We are blown against for ever by the curse
Which breathes through nature. Oh, the
        world is weak—
The effluence of each is false to all,
And what we best conceive, we fail to
        speak.
Wait, soul, until thine ashen garments
        fall,
And then resume thy broken strains, and
        seek
Fit peroration without let or thrall.

TWO SKETCHES

I. H. B.

THE shadow of her face upon the wall
May take your memory to the perfect
        Greek,
But when you front her, you would call
        the cheek
Too full, sir, for your models, if withal
That bloom it wears could leave you
        critical,
And that smile reaching toward the rosy
        streak;
For one who smiles so, has no need to
        speak
To lead your thoughts along, as steed to
        stall.
A smile that turns the sunny side o' the
        heart
On all the world, as if herself did win
By what she lavished on an open mart!
Let no man call the liberal sweetness,
        sin,—
For friends may whisper, as they stand
        apart,
'Methinks there 's still some warmer
        place within.'

II. A. B.

HER azure eyes, dark lashes hold in fee;
Her fair superfluous ringlets, without
        check,
Drop after one another down her neck,
As many to each cheek as you might see
Green leaves to a wild rose! this sign
        outwardly,
And a like woman-covering seems to
        deck
Her inner nature. For she will not fleck
World's sunshine with a finger. Sym-
        pathy
Must call her in Love's name! and then,
        I know,
She rises up, and brightens as she
        should,
And lights her smile for comfort, and is
        slow
In nothing of high-hearted fortitude.
To smell this flower, come near it! such
        can grow
In that sole garden where Christ's brow
        dropped blood.

MOUNTAINEER AND POET

THE simple goatherd, between Alp and
        sky,
Seeing his shadow, in that awful tryst,
Dilated to a giant's on the mist,
Esteems not his own stature larger by
The apparent image, but more patiently
Strikes his staff down beneath his clench-
        ing fist,
While the snow-mountains lift their
        amethyst
And sapphire crowns of splendour, far
        and nigh,
Into the air around him. Learn from
        hence
Meek morals, all ye poets that pursue
Your way still onward up to eminence!
Ye are not great because creation drew
Large revelations round your earliest
        sense,
Nor bright because God's glory shines
        for you.

THE POET

THE poet hath the child's sight in his
    breast,
And sees all *new*. What oftenest he has
    viewed,
He views with the first glory. Fair and
    good
Pall never on him. at the fairest, best,
But stand before him holy and undressed
In week-day false conventions, such as
    would
Drag other men down from the altitude
Of primal types, too early dispossessed.
Why, God would tire of all His heavens,
    as soon
As thou, O godlike. childlike poet, didst,
Of daily and nightly sights of sun and
    moon!
And therefore hath He set thee in the
    midst,
Where men may hear thy wonder's
    ceaseless tune,
And praise His world for ever, as thou
    bidst.

HIRAM POWERS' GREEK SLAVE

THEY say Ideal beauty cannot enter
The house of anguish. On the threshold
    stands
An alien Image with enshackled hands,
Called the Greek Slave! as if the artist
    meant her
(That passionless perfection which he
    lent her,
Shadowed not darkened where the sill
    expands)
To, so, confront man's crimes in different
    lands
With man's ideal sense. Pierce to the
    centre,
Art's fiery finger!—and break up ere long
The serfdom of this world! appeal, fair
    stone,
From God's pure heights of beauty
    against man's wrong!
Catch up in thy divine face, not alone
East griefs but west,—and strike and
    shame the strong,
By thunders of white silence, over-
    thrown.

LIFE

EACH creature holds an insular point in
    space ;
Yet what man stirs a finger, breathes
    a sound,
But all the multitudinous beings round
In all the countless worlds, with time
    and place
For their conditions, down to the central
    base,
Thrill, haply, in vibration and rebound,
Life answering life across the vast
    profound,
In full antiphony, by a common grace?
I think, this sudden joyaunce which
    illumes
A child's mouth sleeping, unaware may
    run
From some soul newly loosened from
    earth's tombs.
I think, this passionate sigh, which
    half-begun
I stifle back. may reach and stir the
    plumes
Of God's calm angel standing in the sun.

LOVE

WE cannot live, except thus mutually
We alternate, aware or unaware,
The reflex act of life ; and when we bear
Our virtue outward most impulsively,
Most full of invocation, and to be
Most instantly compellant, certes, there
We live most life, whoever breathes
    most air,
And counts his dying years by sun and
    sea.
But when a soul, by choice and con-
    science, doth
Throw out her full force on another soul,
The conscience and the concentration
    both
Make mere life, Love. For Life in
    perfect whole
And aim consummated, is Love in sooth,
As nature's magnet-heat rounds pole
    with pole.

HEAVEN AND EARTH

And there was silence in heaven about the space of half an hour.—Revelation viii. 1.

GOD, who, with thunders and great
    voices kept
Beneath Thy throne, and stars most
    silver-paced
Along the inferior gyres, and open-faced
Melodious angels round,—canst inter-
    cept
Music with music,—yet, at will, hast
    swept
All back, all back (said he in Patmos
    placed),
To fill the heavens with silence of the
    waste
Which lasted half an hour!—lo, I who
    have wept
All day and night, beseech Thee by my
    tears,
And by that dread response of curse
    and groan
Men alternate across these hemispheres,
Vouchsafe us such a half-hour's hush
    alone,
In compensation for our stormy years !
As heaven has paused from song, let
    earth, from moan.

THE PROSPECT

METHINKS we do as fretful children do,
Leaning their faces on the window-pane
To sigh the glass dim with their own
    breath's stain,
And shut the sky and landscape from
    their view.
And thus, alas ! since God the maker
    drew
A mystic separation 'twixt those twain,
The life beyond us, and our souls in pain,
We miss the prospect which we are
    called unto
By grief we are fools to use. Be still
    and strong,
O man, my brother ! hold thy sobbing
    breath,
And keep thy soul's large window pure
    from wrong,—
That so, as life's appointment issueth,
Thy vision may be clear to watch along
The sunset consummation-lights of death.

HUGH STUART BOYD [1]

HIS BLINDNESS

GOD would not let the spheric Lights accost
This God-loved man, and bade the earth
    stand off
With all her beckoning hills, whose
    golden stuff
Under the feet of the royal sun is crossed.
Yet such things were to him not wholly
    lost,—
Permitted, with his wandering eyes
    light-proof,
To catch fair visions, rendered full enough
By many a ministrant accomplished
    ghost,—
Still seeing, to sounds of softly-turned
    book-leaves,
Sappho's crown-rose, and Meleager's
    spring,
And Gregory's starlight on Greek-bur-
    nished eves !
Till Sensuous and Unsensuous seemed
    one thing,
Viewed from one level,—earth's reapers
    at the sheaves
Scarce plainer than Heaven's angels on
    the wing !

HUGH STUART BOYD

HIS DEATH, 1848

BELOVÈD friend, who living many years
With sightless eyes raised vainly to the
    sun,
Didst learn to keep thy patient soul in tune
To visible nature's elemental cheers !
God has not caught thee to new hemi-
    spheres
Because thou wast aweary of this one ;—
I think thine angel's patience first was
    done,

[1] To whom was inscribed, in grateful affec-
tion, my poem of ' Cyprus Wine.' There comes
a moment in life when even gratitude and
affection turn to pain, as they do now with me.
This excellent and learned man, enthusiastic for
the good and the beautiful, and one of the most
simple and upright of human beings, passed
out of his long darkness through death in the
summer of 1848, Dr. Adam Clarke's daughter
and biographer, Mrs. Smith (happier, in this
than the absent), fulfilling a doubly filial duty as
she sate by the death-bed of her father's friend
and hers.

And that he spake out with celestial tears,
'Is it enough, dear God? then lighten so
This soul that smiles in darkness!'
                                    Steadfast friend,
Who never didst my heart or life mis-
    know,
Nor either's faults too keenly appre-
    hend,—
How can I wonder when I see thee go
To join the Dead found faithful to the end?

HUGH STUART BOYD

LEGACIES

THREE gifts the Dying left me,—
    Aeschylus,
And Gregory Nazianzen, and a clock,
Chiming the gradual hours out like a flock

Of stars whose motion is melodious.
The books were those I used to read from,
    thus
Assisting my dear teacher's soul to un-
    lock
The darkness of his eyes.   Now, mine
    they mock,
Blinded in turn, by tears! now, mur-
    murous
Sad echoes of my young voice, years
    agone
Intoning from these leaves the Grecian
    phrase,
Return and choke my utterance.   Books,
    lie down
In silence on the shelf there, within gaze;
And thou, clock, striking the hour's
    pulses on,
Chime in the day which ends these
    parting days!

CASA GUIDI WINDOWS

A POEM, IN TWO PARTS

ADVERTISEMENT TO THE FIRST EDITION

THIS poem contains the impressions of the writer upon events in Tuscany of which she was a witness. 'From a window,' the critic may demur. She bows to the objection in the very title of her work. No continuous narrative nor exposition of political philosophy is attempted by her. It is a simple story of personal impressions, whose only value is in the intensity with which they were received, as proving her warm affection for a beautiful and unfortunate country, and the sincerity with which they are related, as indicating her own good faith and freedom from partisanship.

Of the two parts of this poem, the first was written nearly three years ago, while the second resumes the actual situation of 1851. The discrepancy between the two parts is a sufficient guarantee to the public of the truthfulness of the writer, who, though she certainly escaped the epidemic 'falling sickness' of enthusiasm for Pio Nono, takes shame upon herself that she believed, like a woman, some royal oaths, and lost sight of the probable consequences of some obvious popular defects. If the discrepancy should be painful to the reader, let him understand that to the writer it has been more so. But such discrepancies we are called upon to accept at every hour by the conditions of our nature, implying the interval between aspiration and performance, between faith and dis-illusion, between hope and fact.

> O trusted broken prophecy,
> O richest fortune sourly crost,
> Born for the future, to the future lost !

Nay, not lost to the future in this case.
The future of Italy shall not be disinherited.

FLORENCE, 1851.

CASA GUIDI WINDOWS

PART I

I HEARD last night a little child go singing
'Neath Casa Guidi windows, by the
    church,
O bella libertà, O bella ! stringing
    The same words still on notes he went
      in search
So high for, you concluded the upspring-
      ing
Of such a nimble bird to sky from perch
Must leave the whole bush in a tremble
    green,
    And that the heart of Italy must beat,
While such a voice had leave to rise
    serene

'Twixt church and palace of a Florence
    street !
A little child, too, who not long had been
    By mother's finger steadied on his
      feet,
And still *O bella libertà* he sang.

Then I thought, musing, of the innume-
    rous
    Sweet songs which still for Italy out-
      rang
From older singers' lips, who sang not
    thus
    Exultingly and purely, yet, with pang
Fast sheathed in music, touched the heart
    of us

So finely, that the pity scarcely pained.
I thought how Filicaja led on others,
  Bewailers for their Italy enchained,
And how they called her childless among
    mothers,
  Widow of empires, aye, and scarce
    refrained
Cursing her beauty to her face, as
    brothers
  Might a shamed sister's,—' Had she
    been less fair
She were less wretched,'—how, evoking
    so
  From congregated wrong and heaped
    despair
Of men and women writhing under
    blow,
  Harrowed and hideous in a filthy lair,
Some personating Image, wherein woe
  Was wrapt in beauty from offending
    much,
They called it Cybele, or Niobe,
  Or laid it corpse-like on a bier for such,
Where all the world might drop for
    Italy
  Those cadenced tears which burn not
    where they touch,—
' Juliet of nations, canst thou die as we ?
  And was the violet crown that crowned
    thy head
So over-large, though new buds made it
    rough,
  It slipped down and across thine eye-
    lids dead,
O sweet, fair Juliet?' Of such songs
    enough,
  Too many of such complaints! behold,
    instead,
Void at Verona, Juliet's marble trough¹.
  As void as that is, are all images
Men set between themselves and actual
    wrong,
  To catch the weight of pity, meet the
    stress
Of conscience,—since 'tis easier to gaze
    long
  On mournful masks, and sad effigies,
Than on real, live, weak creatures
    crushed by strong.

  For me who stand in Italy to-day

¹ They show at Verona, as the tomb of Juliet,
an empty trough of stone.

Where worthier poets stood and sang
    before,
  I kiss their footsteps, yet their words
    gainsay.
I can but muse in hope upon this shore
  Of golden Arno as it shoots away
Through Florence' heart beneath her
    bridges four !
  Bent bridges, seeming to strain off like
    bows,
And tremble while the arrowy undertide
  Shoots on and cleaves the marble as it
    goes,
And strikes up palace-walls on either
    side,
  And froths the cornice out in glittering
    rows,
With doors and windows quaintly multi-
    plied,
  And terrace-sweeps, and gazers upon
    all,
By whom if flower or kerchief were
    thrown out
  From any lattice there, the same would
    fall
Into the river underneath no doubt,
  It runs so close and fast 'twixt wall
    and wall.
How beautiful! the mountains from with-
    out
  In silence listen for the word said next.
What word will men say,—here where
    Giotto planted
  His campanile, like an unperplexed
Fine question Heaven-ward, touching
    the things granted
  A noble people who, being greatly
    vexed
In act, in aspiration keep undaunted ?
  What word will God say ? Michel's
    Night and Day
And Dawn and Twilight wait in marble
    scorn ²,
  Like dogs upon a dunghill, couched on
    clay
From whence the Medicean stamp's out-
    worn,
  The final putting off of all such sway

² These famous statues recline in the Sagrestia
Nuova, on the tombs of Giuliano de' Medici,
third son of Lorenzo the Magnificent, and
Lorenzo of Urbino, his grandson. Strozzi's
epigram on the Night, with Michel Angelo's
rejoinder, is well known.

By all such hands, and freeing of the
  unborn
  In Florence and the great world out-
    side Florence.
Three hundred years his patient statues
  wait
  In that small chapel of the dim St.
    Lawrence.
Day's eyes are breaking bold and passion-
  ate
  Over his shoulder, and will flash abhor-
    rence
On darkness and with level looks meet
  fate,
  When once loose from that marble
    film of theirs ;
The Night has wild dreams in her sleep,
  the Dawn
  Is haggard as the sleepless Twilight
    wears
A sort of horror ; as the veil withdrawn
  'Twixt the artist's soul and works had
    left them heirs
Of speechless thoughts which would not
  quail nor fawn,
  Of angers and contempts, of hope and
    love ;
For not without a meaning did he place
  The princely Urbino on the seat above
With everlasting shadow on his face;
  While the slow dawns and twilights
    disapprove
The ashes of his long-extinguished race,
  Which never more shall clog the feet
    of men.
I do believe, divinest Angelo,
  That winter-hour, in Via Larga, when
They bade thee build a statue up in snow [1],
  And straight that marvel of thine art
    again
Dissolved beneath the sun's Italian glow,
  Thine eyes, dilated with the plastic
    passion,
Thawing too, in drops of wounded man-
  hood, since,
  To mock alike thine art and indig-
    nation,
Laughed at the palace-window the new
  prince,—
  ('Aha ! this genius needs for exalta-
    tion,

[1] This mocking task was set by Pietro, the
unworthy successor of Lorenzo the Magnificent.

When all 's said, and howe'er the proud
  may wince,
  A little marble from our princely
    mines ! ')
I do believe that hour thou laughedst too,
  For the whole sad world and for thy
    Florentines,
After those few tears—which were only
  few !
  That as, beneath the sun, the grand
    white lines
Of thy snow-statue trembled and with-
  drew,—
  The head, erect as Jove's, being
    palsied first,
The eyelids flattened, the full brow
  turned blank,—
  The right hand, raised but now as if
    it cursed,
Dropt, a mere snowball (till the people
  sank
  Their voices, though a louder laughter
    burst
From the royal window), thou couldst
  proudly thank
  God and the prince for promise and
    presage,
And laugh the laugh back, I think verily,
  Thine eyes being purged by tears of
    righteous rage
To read a wrong into a prophecy,
  And measure a true great man's
    heritage
Against a mere great duke's posterity.
  I think thy soul said then, ' I do not need
A princedom and its quarries, after all ;
  For if I write, paint, carve a word,
    indeed,
On book or board or dust, on floor or
  wall,
  The same is kept of God, who taketh
    heed
That not a letter of the meaning fall
  Or ere it touch and teach His world's
    deep heart,
Outlasting, therefore, all your lordships,
  sir !
So keep your stone, beseech you, for
  your part,
  To cover up your grave-place and refer
The proper titles ; *I* live by my art.
  The thought I threw into this snow
    shall stir

This gazing people when their gaze
        is done ;
And the tradition of your act and mine,
    When all the snow is melted in the sun,
Shall gather up, for unborn men, a sign
Of what is the true princedom,—aye,
        and none
Shall laugh that day, except the drunk
        with wine.'

Amen, great Angelo ! the day's at hand.
If many laugh not on it, shall we weep?
    Much more we must not, let us
        understand.
Through rimers sonneteering in their
        sleep,
    And archaists mumbling dry bones up
        the land,
And sketchers lauding ruined towns
        a-heap,—
    Through all that drowsy hum of voices
        smooth,
The hopeful bird mounts carolling from
        brake,
    The hopeful child, with leaps to catch
        his growth,
Sings open-eyed for liberty's sweet sake!
And I, a singer also, from my youth,
Prefer to sing with these who are awake,
    With birds, with babes, ▲with men
        who will not fear
The baptism of the holy morning dew
    (And many of such wakers now are
        here,
Complete in their anointed manhood, who
    Will greatly dare and greatlier perse-
        vere),
Than join those old thin voices with my
        new,
    And sigh for Italy with some safe sigh
Cooped up in music'twixt an oh and ah,—
    Nay, hand in hand with that young
        child, will I
Go singing rather, ' Bella libertà,'
    Than, with those poets, croon the
        dead or cry
' Se tu men bella fossi, Italia ! '

' Less wretched if less fair.' Perhaps
        a truth
Is so far plain in this—that Italy,
    Long trammelled with the purple of
        her youth

Against her age's ripe activity,
    Sits still upon her tombs, without
        death's ruth,
But also without life's brave energy.
    ' Now tell us what is Italy?' men
        ask :
And others answer, ' Virgil, Cicero,
    Catullus, Caesar.' What beside? to
        task
The memory closer—' Why, Boccaccio,
    Dante, Petrarca,' — and if still the
        flask
Appears to yield its wine by drops too
        slow,—
    ' Angelo, Raffael, Pergolese,'—all
Whose strong hearts beat through stone,
        or charged again
    The paints with fire of souls electrical,
Or broke up heaven for music. What
        more then ?
    Why, then, no more. The chaplet's
        last beads fall
In naming the last saintship within ken,
    And, after that, none prayeth in the
        land.
Alas, this Italy has too long swept
    Heroic ashes up for hour-glass sand ;
Of her own past, impassioned nympho-
        lept !
    Consenting to be nailed here by the
        hand
To the very bay-tree under which she
        stepped
    A queen of old, and plucked a leafy
        branch.
And, licensing the world too long indeed
    To use her broad phylacteries to
        staunch
And stop her bloody lips, she takes no
        heed
    How one clear word would draw an
        avalanche
Of living sons around her, to succeed
    The vanished generations. Can she
        count
These oil-eaters, with large, live, mobile
        mouths
    Agape for macaroni, in the amount
Of consecrated heroes of her south's
    Bright rosary? The pitcher at the
        fount,
The gift of gods, being broken, she
        much loathes

To let the ground-leaves of the place
    confer
A natural bowl. So henceforth she
    would seem
No nation, but the poet's pensioner,
With alms from every land of song and
    dream,
    While ay her pipers sadly pipe of
      her,
Until their proper breaths, in that
    extreme
    Of sighing, split the reed on which
      they played !
Of which, no more. But never say 'no
    more'
    To Italy's life ! Her memories undis-
      mayed
Still argue 'evermore,'—her graves
    implore
    Her future to be strong and not
      afraid ;
Her very statues send their looks before.

We do not serve the dead—the past
    is past !
God lives, and lifts His glorious mornings
    up
    Before the eyes of men, awake at last,
Who put away the meats they used to
    sup,
    And down upon the dust of earth
      outcast
The dregs remaining of the ancient cup,
    Then turn to wakeful prayer and
      worthy act.
The dead, upon their awful 'vantage
    ground,
    The sun not in their faces,—shall
      abstract
No more our strength : we will not be
    discrowned
    As guardians of their crowns ; nor
      deign transact
A barter of the present, for a sound
    Of good, so counted in the foregone
      days.
O Dead, ye shall no longer cling to us
    With rigid hands of desiccating praise,
And drag us backward by the garment
    thus,
    To stand and laud you in long-drawn
      virelays !
We will not henceforth be oblivious

Of our own lives, because ye lived
    before,
Nor of our acts, because ye acted well.
    We thank you that ye first unlatched
      the door,
But will not make it inaccessible
    By thankings on the threshold any
      more.
We hurry onward to extinguish hell
    With our fresh souls, our younger
      hope, and God's
Maturity of purpose. Soon shall we
    Die also ! and, that then our periods
Of life may round themselves to memory,
    As smoothly as on our graves the
      burial-sods,
We now must look to it to excel as ye,
    And bear our age as far, unlimited
By the last mind-mark ! so, to be in-
    voked
    By future generations, as their Dead.

'Tis true that when the dust of death
    has choked
    A great man's voice, the common
      words he said
Turn oracles,—the common thoughts
    he yoked
    Like horses, draw like griffins !—this
      is true
And acceptable. I, too, should desire,
    When men make record, with the
      flowers they strew,
'Savonarola's soul went out in fire
    Upon our Grand-duke's piazza[1], and
      burned through
A moment first, or ere he did expire,
    The veil betwixt the right and wrong,
      and showed
How near God sate and judged the
    judges there,—'
    Upon the self-same pavement over-
      strewed,
To cast my violets with as reverent
    care,
    And prove that all the winters which
      have snowed

[1] Savonarola was burnt for his testimony
against papal corruptions as early as March,
1498 : and, as late as our own day, it has been
a custom in Florence to strew with violets the
pavement where he suffered, in grateful recog-
nition of the anniversary.

Cannot snow out the scent from stones
    and air,
    Of a sincere man's virtues.   This
        was he,
Savonarola, who, while Peter sank
    With his whole boat-load, called
        courageously
'Wake Christ, wake Christ!'—Who,
        having tried the tank
Of old church-waters used for baptistry
Ere Luther came to spill them, swore
        they stank!
    Who also by a princely deathbed cried,
'Loose Florence, or God will not loose
        thy soul!'
    Then fell back the Magnificent and
        died
Beneath the star-look, shooting from
        the cowl,
    Which turned to wormwood bitterness
        the wide
Deep sea of his ambitions.   It were foul
    To grudge Savonarola and the rest
Their violets! rather pay them quick
        and fresh!
The emphasis of death makes manifest
The eloquence of action in our flesh ;
    And men who, living, were but dimly
        guessed,
When once free from their life's en-
        tangled mesh,
    Show their full length in graves, or
        oft indeed
Exaggerate their stature, in the flat,
    To noble admirations which exceed
Most nobly, yet will calculate in that
    But accurately. We, who are the
        seed
Of buried creatures, if we turned and
        spat
Upon our antecedents, we were vile.
Bring violets rather! If these had not
        walked
    Their furlong, could we hope to walk
        our mile?
Therefore bring violets.   Yet if we,
        self-baulked,
    Stand still, a-strewing violets all the
        while,
These moved in vain, of whom we have
        vainly talked.
    So rise up henceforth with a cheerful
        smile,

And having strewn the violets, reap the
        corn,
    And having reaped and garnered,
        bring the plough
And draw new furrows 'neath the
        healthy morn,
    And plant the great Hereafter in this
        Now.

Of old 'twas so.   How step by step
        was worn,
    As each man gained on each, se-
        curely!—how
Each by his own strength sought his
        own ideal,—
    The ultimate Perfection leaning bright
From out the sun and stars, to bless the
        leal
    And earnest search of all for Fair and
        Right,
Through doubtful forms, by earth ac-
        counted real!
    Because old Jubal blew into delight
The souls of men, with clear-piped
        melodies,
    If youthful Asaph were content at
        most
To draw from Jubal's grave, with
        listening eyes,
    Traditionary music's floating ghost
Into the grass-grown silence, were it
        wise?
    And was't not wiser, Jubal's breath
        being lost,
That Miriam clashed her cymbals to
        surprise
    The sun between her white arms
        flung apart,
With new, glad, golden sounds? that
        David's strings
    O'erflowed his hand with music from
        his heart?
So harmony grows full from many
        springs,
    And happy accident turns holy art.

You enter, in your Florence wanderings,
    The church of St. Maria Novella. Pass
The left stair, where at plague-time
        Macchiavel [1]
    Saw One with set fair face as in a glass,

---

[1] See his description of the plague in Florence.

Dressed out against the fear of death
and hell,
　Rustling her silks in pauses of the
mass,
To keep the thought off how her hus-
band fell,
　When she left home, stark dead across
her feet,—
The stair leads up to what the Orgagnas
save
　Of Dante's demons: you, in pass-
ing it,
Ascend the right stair from the farther
nave,
　To muse in a small chapel scarcely lit
By Cimabue's Virgin. Bright and brave,
　That picture was accounted, mark, of
old.
A king stood bare before its sovran
grace [1],
　A reverent people shouted to behold
The picture, not the king, and even the
place
　Containing such a miracle, grew bold,
Named the Glad Borgo from that beau-
teous face,—
　Which thrilled the artist, after work,
to think
His own ideal Mary-smile should stand
　So very near him,—he, within the
brink
Of all that glory, let in by his hand
　With too divine a rashness! Yet none
shrink
Who come to gaze here now—albeit
'twas planned
　Sublimely in the thought's simplicity.
The Lady, throned in empyreal state,
　Minds only the young babe upon her
knee,
While sidelong angels bear the royal
weight,
　Prostrated meekly, smiling tenderly
Oblivion of their wings; the Child
thereat

Stretching its hand like God. If any
should,
Because of some stiff draperies and
loose joints,
Gaze scorn down from the heights of
Raffaelhood,
On Cimabue's picture,—Heaven anoints
　The head of no such critic, and his
blood
The poet's curse strikes full on and
appoints
　To ague and cold spasms for ever-
more.
A noble picture ! worthy of the shout
　Wherewith along the streets the
people bore
Its cherub faces, which the sun threw
out
　Until they stooped and entered the
church door !—
Yet rightly was young Giotto talked
about,
　Whom Cimabue found among the
sheep [2],
And knew, as gods know gods, and
carried home
　To paint the things he had painted,
with a deep
And fuller insight, and so overcome
　His chapel-lady with a heavenlier
sweep
Of light. For thus we mount into the
sum
　Of great things known or acted. I
hold, too,
That Cimabue smiled upon the lad,
　At the first stroke which passed what
he could do,—
Or else his Virgin's smile had never had
　Such sweetness in 't. All great men
who foreknew
Their heirs in art, for art's sake have
been glad,
　And bent their old white heads as if
uncrowned,
Fanatics of their pure ideals still
　Far more than of their triumphs, which
were found

[1] Charles of Anjou, in his passage through
Florence, was permitted to see this picture while
yet in Cimabue's 'bottega.' The populace fol-
lowed the royal visitor, and, from the universal
delight and admiration, the quarter of the city
in which the artist lived was called 'Borgo
Allegri.' The picture was carried in triumph to
the church, and deposited there.

[2] How Cimabue found Giotto, the shepherd-
boy, sketching a ram of his flock upon a stone,
is prettily told by Vasari,—who also relates that
the elder artist Margheritone died 'infastidito'
of the successes of the new school.

With some less vehement struggle of the
    will.
If old Margheritone trembled, swooned,
And died despairing at the open sill
    Of other men's achievements (who
        achieved,
By loving art beyond the master!), he
    Was old Margheritone, and conceived
Never, at first youth and most ecstasy,
    A Virgin like that dream of one, which
        heaved
The death-sigh from his heart. If wistfully
    Margheritone sickened at the smell
Of Cimabue's laurel, let him go!—
    For Cimabue stood up very well
In spite of Giotto's—and Angelico,
    The artist-saint, kept smiling in his cell
The smile with which he welcomed the
        sweet slow
    Inbreak of angels (whitening through
        the dim
That he might paint them!), while the
        sudden sense
Of Raffael's future was revealed to him
By force of his own fair works' com-
        petence.
The same blue waters where the dol-
        phins swim
Suggest the tritons. Through the blue
        Immense,
    Strike out, all swimmers! cling not in
        the way
Of one another, so to sink ; but learn
    The strong man's impulse, catch the
        fresh'ning spray
He throws up in his motions, and discern
    By his clear, westering eye, the time
        of day.
Thou, God, hast set us worthy gifts to
        earn,
    Besides Thy heaven and Thee! and
        when I say
There's room here for the weakest man
        alive
    To live and die,—there's room too,
        I repeat,
For all the strongest to live well, and strive
    Their own way, by their individual
        heat,—
Like some new bee-swarm leaving the
        old hive,
    Despite the wax which tempts so
        violet-sweet.

Then let the living live, the dead retain
    Their grave-cold flowers!—though
        honour's best supplied
By bringing actions, to prove theirs not
    vain.

Cold graves, we say? it shall be testified
That living men who burn in heart and
    brain,
Without the dead, were colder. If we
    tried
To sink the past beneath our feet, be sure
    The future would not stand. Precipi-
        tate
This old roof from the shrine—and,
        insecure,
    The nesting swallows fly off, mate from
        mate.
How scant the gardens, if the graves
        were fewer !
    The tall green poplars grew no longer
        straight,
Whose tops not looked to Troy. Would
        any fight
    For Athens, and not swear by Mara-
        thon ?
Who dared build temples, without tombs
        in sight ?
    Or live, without some dead man's
        benison ?
Or seek truth, hope for good, and strive
        for right,
If, looking up, he saw not in the sun
Some angel of the martyrs all day long
    Standing and waiting? Your last
        rhythm will need.
Your earliest key-note. Could I sing
        this song,
    If my dead masters had not taken
        heed
To help the heavens and earth to make
        me strong,
    As the wind ever will find out some
        reed,
And touch it to such issues as belong
    To such a frail thing? None may
        grudge the dead
Libations from full cups. Unless we
        choose
    To look back to the hills behind us
        spread,
The plains before us sadden and confuse;
If orphaned, we are disinherited.

I would but turn these lachrymals to use,
And pour fresh oil in from the olive
grove,
To furnish them as new lamps. Shall I
say
What made my heart beat with exulting
love,
A few weeks back?—
. . . . The day was such a day
As Florence owes the sun. The sky
above,
Its weight upon the mountains seemed to
lay,
And palpitate in glory, like a dove
Who has flown too fast, full-hearted!—
take away
The image! for the heart of man beat
higher
That day in Florence, flooding all her
streets
And piazzas with a tumult and desire.
The people, with accumulated heats,
And faces turned one way, as if one
fire
Both drew and flushed them, left their
ancient beats,
And went up toward the palace-Pitti
wall,
To thank their Grand-duke, who, not
quite of course,
Had graciously permitted, at their call,
The citizens to use their civic force
To guard their civic homes. So, one
and all,
The Tuscan cities streamed up to the
source
Of this new good, at Florence, taking it
As good so far, presageful of more good,—
The first torch of Italian freedom, lit
To toss in the next tiger's face who
should
Approach too near them in a greedy
fit,—
The first pulse of an even flow of blood,
To prove the level of Italian veins
Toward rights perceived and granted.
How we gazed
From Casa Guidi windows, while, in
trains
Of orderly procession—banners raised,
And intermittent bursts of martial
strains
Which died upon the shout, as if amazed

By gladness beyond music—they
passed on!
The Magistracy, with insignia, passed,—
And all the people shouted in the
sun,
And all the thousand windows which
had cast
A ripple of silks, in blue and scarlet,
down
(As if the houses overflowed at last),
Seemed growing larger with fair heads
and eyes.
The Lawyers passed,—and still arose
the shout,
And hands broke from the windows
to surprise
Those grave calm brows with bay-tree
leaves thrown out.
The Priesthood passed,—the friars
with worldly-wise
Keen sidelong glances from their beards
about
The street to see who shouted! many
a monk
Who takes a long rope in the waist,
was there!
Whereat the popular exultation drunk
With indrawn 'vivas' the whole sunny
air,
While, through the murmuring win-
dows, rose and sunk
A cloud of kerchiefed hands,—'The
Church makes fair
Her welcome in the new Pope's name.'
Ensued
The black sign of the 'Martyrs!' (name
no name,
But count the graves in silence). Next,
were viewed
The Artists; next, the Trades; and after
came
The People,—flag and sign, and rights
as good,—
And very loud the shout was for that
same
Motto, 'Il popolo.' IL POPOLO,—
The word means dukedom, empire,
majesty,
And kings in such an hour might read
it so.
And next, with banners, each in his
degree,
Deputed representatives a-row

Of every separate state of Tuscany.
Siena's she-wolf, bristling on the fold
Of the first flag, preceded Pisa's hare,
And Massa's lion floated calm in gold,
Pienza's following with his silver stare.
Arezzo's steed pranced clear from
bridle-hold,—
And well might shout our Florence,
greeting there
These, and more brethren. Last, the
world had sent
The various children of her teeming
flanks—
Greeks, English, French—as if to a
parliament
Of lovers of her Italy in ranks,
Each bearing its land's symbol reverent.
At which the stones seemed breaking
into thanks
And rattling up the sky, such sounds
in proof
Arose; the very house-walls seemed to
bend;
The very windows, up from door to
roof,
Flashed out a rapture of bright heads, to
mend
With passionate looks, the gesture's
whirling off
A hurricane of leaves. Three hours did
end
While all these passed; and ever in
the crowd,
Rude men, unconscious of the tears that
kept
Their beards moist, shouted; some few
laughed aloud,
And none asked any why they laughed
and wept.
Friends kissed each other's cheeks,
and foes long vowed
More warmly did it,—two-months' babies
leapt
Right upward in their mothers' arms,
whose black,
Wide, glittering eyes looked elsewhere;
lovers pressed
Each before either, neither glancing
back;
And peasant maidens, smoothly 'tired
and tressed,
Forgot to finger on their throats the
slack

Great pearl-strings; while old blind men
would not rest,
But pattered with their staves and slid
their shoes
Along the stones, and smiled as if they
saw.
O heaven, I think that day had noble use
Among God's days. So near stood Right
and Law,
Both mutually forborne! Law would
not bruise,
Nor Right deny, and each in reverent awe
Honoured the other. And if, ne'er-
theless,
That good day's sun delivered to the vines
No charta, and the liberal Duke's
excess
Did scarce exceed a Guelf's or Ghibel-
line's
In any special actual righteousness
Of what that day he granted, still the signs
Are good and full of promise, we must
say,
When multitudes approach their kings
with prayers
And kings concede their people's right
to pray,
Both in one sunshine. Griefs are not
despairs,
So uttered, nor can royal claims dismay
When men from humble homes and ducal
chairs
Hate wrong together. It was well to
view
Those banners ruffled in a ruler's face
Inscribed, 'Live freedom, union, and
all true
Brave patriots who are aided by God's
grace!'
Nor was it ill, when Leopoldo drew
His little children to the window-place
He stood in at the Pitti, to suggest
They too should govern as the people
willed.
What a cry rose then! some, who saw
the best,
Declared his eyes filled up and overfilled
With good warm human tears which
unrepressed
Ran down. I like his face; the fore-
head's build
Has no capacious genius, yet perhaps
Sufficient comprehension,—mild and sad,

And careful nobly,—not with care that
wraps
Self-loving hearts, to stifle and make mad,
But careful with the care that shuns a
lapse
Of faith and duty, studious not to add
A burden in the gathering of a gain.
And so, God save the Duke, I say with
those
Who that day shouted it, and while
dukes reign,
May all wear in the visible overflows
Of spirit, such a look of careful pain !
For God must love it better than repose.

And all the people who went up to let
Their hearts out to that Duke, as has
been told—
Where guess ye that the living people
met,
Kept tryst, formed ranks, chose
leaders, first unrolled
Their banners?
In the Loggia? where is set
Cellini's godlike Perseus, bronze—or
gold—
(How name the metal, when the statue
flings
Its soul so in your eyes?) with brow
and sword
Superbly calm, as all opposing things,
Slain with the Gorgon, were no more
abhorred
Since ended?
No, the people sought no wings
From Perseus in the Loggia, nor im-
plored
An inspiration in the place beside,
From that dim bust of Brutus, jagged
and grand,
Where Buonarroti passionately tried
From out the close-clenched marble
to demand
The head of Rome's sublimest homi-
cide,—
Then dropt the quivering mallet from
his hand,
Despairing he could find no model-stuff
Of Brutus, in all Florence, where he
found
The gods and gladiators thick enough.
Nor there! the people chose still holier
ground !

The people, who are simple, blind, and
rough,
Know their own angels, after looking
round.
Whom chose they then? where met they?

On the stone
Called Dante's,—a plain flat stone,
scarce discerned
From others in the pavement,—where-
upon
He used to bring his quiet chair out,
turned
To Brunelleschi's church, and pour alone
The lava of his spirit when it burned.
It is not cold to-day. O passionate
Poor Dante, who, a banished Floren-
tine,
Didst sit austere at banquets of the
great,
And muse upon this far-off stone of
thine,
And think how oft some passer used to
wait
A moment, in the golden day's decline,
With 'Good night, dearest Dante ! '—
well, good night !
I muse now, Dante, and think, verily,
Though chapelled in the by-way, out of
sight,
Ravenna's bones would thrill with
ecstasy,
Couldst know thy favourite stone's
elected right
As tryst-place for thy Tuscans to fore-
see
Their earliest chartas from. Good night,
good morn,
Henceforward, Dante ! now my soul
is sure
That thine is better comforted of scorn,
And looks down earthward in com-
pleter cure,
Than when, in Santa Croce church for-
lorn
Of any corpse, the architect and hewer
Did pile the empty marbles as thy
tomb [1].

[1] The Florentines, to whom the Ravennese
refused the body of Dante (demanded of them
'in a late remorse of love '), have given a ceno-
taph in this church to their divine poet. Some-
thing less than a grave !

For now thou art no longer exiled,
    now
Best honoured!—we salute thee who art
    come
    Back to the old stone with a softer
    brow
Than Giotto drew upon the wall, for some
    Good lovers of our age to track and
    plough [1]
Their way to, through time's ordures
    stratified,
    And startle broad awake into the dull
Bargello chamber! now, thou 'rt milder
    eyed,—
Now Beatrix may leap up glad to cull
Thy first smile, even in heaven and at
    her side,
    Like that which, nine years old, looked
    beautiful
At May-game. What do I say? I only
    meant
    That tender Dante loved his Florence
    well,
While Florence, now, to love him is
    content;
    And, mark ye, that the piercingest
    sweet smell
Of love's dear incense by the living sent
To find the dead, is not accessible
To lazy livers! no narcotic,—not
    Swung in a censer to a sleepy tune,—
But trod out in the morning air, by hot
    Quick spirits, who tread firm to ends
    foreshown,
And use the name of greatness unforgot,
    To meditate what greatness may be
    done.

For Dante sits in heaven, and ye stand
    here,
    And more remains for doing, all must
    feel,
Than trysting on his stone from year to
    year
    To shift processions, civic toe to heel,
The town's thanks to the Pitti. Are ye
    freer
    For what was felt that day? a chariot-
    wheel
May spin fast, yet the chariot never roll.

[1] In allusion to Mr. Kirkup's discovery of
Giotto's fresco-portrait of Dante.

But if that day suggested something
    good,
And bettered, with one purpose, soul by
    soul,—
    Better means freer. A land's brother-
    hood
Is most puissant: men, upon the whole,
    Are what they can be,—nations, what
    they would.

Will, therefore, to be strong, thou Italy!
    Will to be noble! Austrian Metternich
Can fix no yoke unless the neck agree;
    And thine is like the lion's when the
    thick
Dews shudder from it, and no man
    would be
    The stroker of his mane, much less
    would prick
His nostril with a reed. When nations
    roar
Like lions, who shall tame them, and
    defraud
Of the due pasture by the river-shore?
    Roar, therefore! shake your dew-laps
    dry abroad.
The amphitheatre with open door
    Leads back upon the benchers, who
    applaud
The last spear-thruster.

                    Yet the Heavens forbid
That we should call on passion to con-
    front
The brutal with the brutal, and, amid
    This ripening world, suggest a lion's-
    hunt
And lion's-vengeance for the wrongs
    men did
    And do now, though the spears are
    getting blunt.
We only call, because the sight and
    proof
    Of lion-strength hurts nothing; and to
    show
A lion-heart, and measure paw with
    hoof,
    Helps something, even, and will in-
    struct a foe
As well as the onslaught, how to stand
    aloof!
    Or else the world gets past the mere
    brute blow

Or given or taken.   Children use the fist
  Until they are of age to use the brain ;
And so we needed Caesars to assist
  Man's justice, and Napoleons to ex-
    plain
God's counsel, when a point was nearly
    missed,
  Until our generations should attain
Christ's stature nearer.   Not that we,
    alas,
  Attain already ; but a single inch
Will raise to look down on the swords-
    man's pass,
  As knightly Roland on the coward's
    flinch :
And, after chloroform and ether-gas,
  We find out slowly what the bee and
    finch .
Have ready found, through Nature's lamp
    in each,
  How to our races we may justify
Our individual claims, and, as we reach
  Our own grapes, bend the top vines
    to supply
The children's uses,—how to fill a breach
  With olive branches,—how to quench
    a lie
With truth, and smite a foe upon the
    cheek
  With Christ's most conquering kiss.
    Why, these are things
Worth a great nation's finding, to prove
    weak
  The 'glorious arms' of military kings.
And so with wide embrace, my England,
    seek
  To stifle the bad heat and flickerings
Of this world's false and nearly expended
    fire !
  Draw palpitating arrows to the wood,
And twang abroad thy high hopes, and
    thy higher
  Resolves, from that most virtuous
    altitude !
Till nations shall unconsciously aspire
  By looking up to thee, and learn that
    good
And glory are not different.   Announce
    law
  By freedom ; exalt chivalry by peace ;
Instruct how clear calm eyes can overawe,
  And how pure hands, stretched simply
    to release

A bond-slave, will not need a sword to
    draw
  To be held dreadful.   O my England,
    crease
Thy purple with no alien agonies !
  No struggles toward encroachment, no
    vile war !
Disband thy captains, change thy vic-
    tories,
  Be henceforth prosperous as the angels
    are,
Helping, not humbling.

                        Drums and battle cries
  Go out in music of the morning star—
And soon we shall have thinkers in the
    place
  Of fighters, each found able as a man
To strike electric influence through a
    race,
  Unstayed by city-wall and barbican.
The poet shall look grander in the face
  Than even of old (when he of Greece
    began
To sing 'that Achillean wrath which slew
  So many heroes'),—seeing he shall
    treat
The deeds of souls heroic toward the
    true—
  The oracles of life—previsions sweet
And awful, like divine swans gliding
    through
  White arms of Ledas, which will leave
    the heat
Of their escaping godship to endue
  The human medium with a heavenly
    flush.

Meanwhile, in this same Italy we want
  Not popular passion, to arise and
    crush,
But popular conscience, which may
    covenant
  For what it knows.   Concede without
    a blush,
To grant the 'civic guard' is not to grant
  The civic spirit, living and awake.
Those lappets on your shoulders, citizens,
  Your eyes strain after sideways till
    they ache,
(While still, in admirations and amens,
  The crowd comes up on festa-days, to
    take

The great sight in)—are not intelligence,
Not courage even—alas, if not the sign
Of something very noble, they are
    nought ;
For every day ye dress your sallow kine
With fringes down their cheeks, though
    unbesought
    They loll their heavy heads and drag
        the wine,
And bear the wooden yoke as they were
    taught
    The first day.   What ye want is
        light—indeed
Not sunlight—(ye may well look up
    surprised
    To those unfathomable heavens that
        feed
Your purple hills!)—but God's light
    organized
    In some high soul, crowned capable
        to lead
The conscious people, conscious and
    advised,—
    For if we lift a people like mere clay,
It falls the same.   We want thee, O
    unfound
    And sovran teacher!—if thy beard be
        grey
Or black, we bid thee rise up from the
    ground
    And speak the word God giveth thee
        to say,
Inspiring into all this people round,
    Instead of passion, thought, which
        pioneers
All generous passion, purifies from sin,
    And strikes the hour for.   Rise up
        teacher! here 's
A crowd to make a nation !—best begin
By making each a man, till all be peers
Of earth's true patriots and pure martyrs
    in
    Knowing and daring.   Best unbar the
        doors
Which Peter's heirs keep locked so
    overclose
    They only let the mice across the
        floors,
While every churchman dangles, as he
    goes,
    The great key at his girdle, and abhors
In Christ's name, meekly.   Open wide
    the house,

Concede the entrance with Christ's
    liberal mind,
And set the tables with His wine and
    bread.
    What ! 'commune in both kinds?'
        In every kind—
Wine, wafer, love, hope, truth, un-
    limited,
Nothing kept back.   For when a man
    is blind
To starlight, will he see the rose is
    red ?
A bondsman shivering at a Jesuit's
    foot—
'Vae ! meâ culpâ !' is not like to stand
    A freedman at a despot's, and dispute
His titles by the balance in his hand,
    Weighing them 'suo jure.' Tend the
        root
If careful of the branches, and expand
    The inner souls of men before you
        strive
For civic heroes.

                        But the teacher, where ?
From all these crowded faces, all alive,
Eyes, of their own lids flashing them-
    selves bare,
    And brows that with a mobile life
        contrive
A deeper shadow,—may we in no wise
    dare
To put a finger out, and touch a man,
And cry 'this is the leader?' What,
    all these !—
    Broad heads, black eyes,—yet not
        a soul that ran
From God down with a message? all,
    to please
    The donna waving measures with her
        fan,
And not the judgement-angel on his knees
    (The trumpet just an inch off from his
        lips),
Who when he breathes next, will put
    out the sun ?

Yet mankind's self were foundered in
    eclipse,
If lacking doers, with great works to be
    done;
    And lo, the startled earth already dips
Back into light—a better day's begun—

And soon this leader, teacher, will
　　stand plain,
And build the golden pipes and synthesize
This people-organ for a holy strain.
We hold this hope, and still in all these
　　eyes,
　　Go sounding for the deep look which
　　　shall drain
Suffused thought into channelled enter-
　　prise.
　　Where is the teacher? What now
　　　may he do,
Who shall do greatly? Doth he gird
　　his waist
　　With a monk's rope, like Luther? or
　　　pursue
The goat, like Tell? or dry his nets in
　　haste,
　　Like Masaniello when the sky was
　　　blue?
Keep house, like other peasants, with
　　inlaced,
　　Bare, brawny arms about a favourite
　　　child,
And meditative looks beyond the door,
　　(But not to mark the kidling's teeth
　　　have filed
The green shoots of his vine which last
　　year bore
　　Full twenty bunches,) or, on triple-
　　　piled
Throne-velvets sit at ease, to bless the
　　poor,
　　Like other pontiffs, in the Poorest's
　　　name?
The old tiara keeps itself aslope
　　Upon his steady brows, which, all the
　　　same,
Bend mildly to permit the people's hope?

Whatever hand shall grasp this ori-
　　flamme,
Whatever man (last peasant or first
　　pope
　　Seeking to free his country!) shall
　　　appear,
Teach, lead, strike fire into the masses, fill
　　These empty bladders with fine air,
　　　insphere
These wills into a unity of will,
　　And make of Italy a nation—dear
And blessed be that man! the Heavens
　　shall kill

No leaf the earth lets grow for him,
　　and Death
Shall cast him back upon the lap of Life
　　To live more surely, in a clarion-
　　　breath
Of hero-music. Brutus, with the knife,
　　Rienzi, with the fasces, throb beneath
Rome's stones,—and more,—who threw
　　away joy's fife
　　Like Pallas, that the beauty of their
　　　souls
Might ever shine untroubled and entire.
　　But if it can be true that he who
　　　rolls
The Church's thunders, will reserve her
　　fire
　　For only light, — from eucharistic
　　　bowls
Will pour new life for nations that ex-
　　pire,
　　And rend the scarlet of his papal vest
To gird the weak loins of his country-
　　men—
I hold that he surpasses all the rest
Of Romans, heroes, patriots,—and that
　　when
　　He sate down on the throne, he dis-
　　　possessed
The first graves of some glory. See
　　again,
　　This country-saving is a glorious thing,
And if a common man achieved it?
　　well.
　　Say, a rich man did? excellent. A
　　　king?
That grows sublime. A priest? im-
　　probable.
　　A pope? Ah, there we stop, and
　　　cannot bring
Our faith up to the leap, with history's
　　bell
　　So heavy round the neck of it—albeit
We fain would grant the possibility,
　　For *thy* sake, Pio Nono!

　　　　　　　　　　Stretch thy feet
In that case—I will kiss them reverently
　　As any pilgrim to the papal seat!
And, such proved possible, thy throne
　　to me
　　Shall seem as holy a place as Pellico's
Venetian dungeon, or as Spielberg's
　　grate,

At which the Lombard woman hung
the rose
Of her sweet soul, by its own dewy
weight,
To feel the dungeon round her sun-
shine close,
And pining so, died early, yet too late
For what she suffered. Yea, I will
not choose
Betwixt thy throne, Pope Pius, and the
spot
Marked red for ever, spite of rains
and dews,
Where two fell riddled by the Aus-
trian's shot,
The brothers Bandiera, who accuse,
With one same mother-voice and face
(that what
They speak may be invincible) the sins
Of earth's tormentors before God the
just,
Until the unconscious thunder-bolt
begins
To loosen in His grasp.

And yet we must
Beware, and mark the natural kiths
and kins
Of circumstance and office, and distrust
The rich man reasoning in a poor
man's hut,
The poet who neglects pure truth to
prove
Statistic fact, the child who leaves a rut
For a smoother road, the priest who
vows his glove
Exhales no grace, the prince who
walks a-foot,
The woman who has sworn she will
not love,
And this Ninth Pius in Seventh
Gregory's chair,
With Andrea Doria's forehead!

Count what goes
To making up a pope, before he
wear
That triple crown. We pass the world-
wide throes
Which went to make the popedom,—
the despair
Of free men, good men, wise men; the
dread shows

Of women's faces, by the faggot's flash,
Tossed out, to the minutest stir and throb
O' the white lips, the least tremble
of a lash,
To glut the red stare of a licensed mob;
The short mad cries down oubliettes,
and plash
So horribly far off; priests, trained to rob,
And kings that, like encouraged
nightmares, sate
On nations' hearts most heavily distressed
With monstrous sights and apoph-
thegms of fate!—
We pass these things,—because 'the
times' are prest
With necessary charges of the weight
Of all this sin, and 'Calvin, for the rest,
Made bold to burn Servetus—Ah, men
err!'—
And, so do *churches!* which is all we mean
To bring to proof in any register
Of theological fat kine and lean—
So drive them back into the pens! refer
Old sins (with pourpoint, 'quotha' and
'I ween')
Entirely to the old times, the old times;
Nor ever ask why this preponderant,
Infallible, pure Church could set her
chimes
Most loudly then, just then,—most ju-
bilant,
Precisely then—when mankind stood
in crimes
Full heart-deep, and Heaven's judge-
ments were not scant.
Inquire still less, what signifies a
church
Of perfect inspiration and pure laws,
Who burns the first man with a
brimstone-torch,
And grinds the second, bone by bone,
because
The times, forsooth, are used to rack
and scorch!
What *is* a holy Church, unless she awes
The times down from their sins? Did
Christ select
Such amiable times, to come and teach
Love to, and mercy? The whole
world were wrecked,
If every mere great man, who lives to
reach
A little leaf of popular respect,

Attained not simply by some special breach
 In the age's customs, by some precedence
In thought and act, which, having proved him higher
 Than those he lived with, proved his competence
In helping them to wonder and aspire.

My words are guiltless of the bigot's sense.
My soul has fire to mingle with the fire
 Of all these souls, within or out of doors
Of Rome's church or another. I believe
 In one Priest, and one temple, with its floors
Of shining jasper gloom'd at morn and eve
 By countless knees of earnest auditors,
And crystal walls, too lucid to perceive,
 That none may take the measure of the place
And say, 'So far the porphyry, then, the flint—
 To this mark, mercy goes, and there, ends grace,'
Though still the permeable crystals hint
 At some white starry distance, bathed in space.
I feel how nature's ice-crusts keep the dint
 Of undersprings of silent Deity.
I hold the articulated gospels, which
 Show Christ among us, crucified on tree.
I love all who love truth, if poor or rich
 In what they have won of truth possessively.
No altars and no hands defiled with pitch
 Shall scare me off, but I will pray and eat
With all these—taking leave to choose my ewers
 And say at last, 'Your visible churches cheat
Their inward types,—and, if a church assures
 Of standing without failure and defeat,
The same both fails and lies.'

    To leave which lures
Of wider subject through past years, —behold,
We come back from the popedom to the pope,
 To ponder what he *must* be, ere we are bold
For what he *may* be, with our heavy hope
 To trust upon his soul. So, fold by fold,
Explore this mummy in the priestly cope,
 Transmitted through the darks of time, to catch
The man within the wrappage, and discern
 How he, an honest man, upon the watch
Full fifty years, for what a man may learn,
 Contrived to get just there; with what a snatch
Of old-world oboli he had to earn
 The passage through; with what a drowsy sop,
To drench the busy barkings of his brain;
 What ghosts of pale tradition, wreathed with hop
'Gainst wakeful thought, he had to entertain
 For heavenly visions; and consent to stop
The clock at noon, and let the hour remain
 (Without vain windings up) inviolate,
Against all chimings from the belfry. Lo,
 From every given pope you must abate,
Albeit you love him, some things—good, you know—
 Which every given heretic you hate,
Assumes for his, as being plainly so.
 A pope must hold by popes a little,—yes,
By councils,—from Nicaea up to Trent,—
 By hierocratic empire, more or less
Irresponsible to men,—he must resent
 Each man's particular conscience, and repress
Inquiry, meditation, argument,
 As tyrants faction. Also, he must not
Love truth too dangerously, but prefer
 'The interests of the Church' (because a blot

Is better than a rent, in miniver),
  Submit to see the people swallow hot
Husk-porridge, which his chartered
    churchmen stir
  Quoting the only true God's epigraph,
'Feed my lambs, Peter!'—must consent
    to sit
  Attesting with his pastoral ring and
    staff,
To such a picture of our Lady, hit
  Off well by artist angels (though not
    half
As fair as Giotto would have painted it)—
  To such a vial, where a dead man's
    blood
Runs yearly warm beneath a church-
    man's finger ;
  To such a holy house of stone and
    wood,
Whereof a cloud of angels was the
    bringer
  From Bethlehem to Loreto.—Were
    it good
For any pope on earth to be a flinger
  Of stones against these high-niched
    counterfeits ?
Apostates only are iconoclasts.
  He dares not say, while this false
    thing abets
That true thing, 'this is false.' He
    keeps his fasts
  And prayers, as prayer and fast were
    silver frets
To change a note upon a string that
    lasts,
  And make a lie a virtue. Now, if he
Did more than this, higher hoped, and
    braver dared,
  I think he were a pope in jeopardy,
Or no pope rather, for his truth had
    barred
  The vaulting of his life,—and certainly,
If he do only this, mankind's regard
  Moves on from him at once, to seek
    some new
Teacher and leader. He is good and
    great
  According to the deeds a pope can do ;
Most liberal, save those bonds ; affection-
    ate,
  As princes may be, and, as priests
    are, true ;
But only the ninth Pius after eight,

When all 's praised most. At best and
    hopefullest,
He 's pope—we want a man ! his heart
    beats warm,
  But, like the prince enchanted to the
    waist,
He sits in stone, and hardens by a charm
  Into the marble of his throne high-
    placed.
Mild benediction, waves his saintly arm—
  So, good ! but what we want 's a per-
    fect man,
Complete and all alive : half travertine
  Half suits our need, and ill subserves
    our plan.
Feet, knees, nerves, sinews, energies
    divine
  Were never yet too much for men
    who ran
In such hard ways as must be this of thine,
  Deliverer whom we seek, whoe'er thou
    art,
Pope, prince, or peasant ! If, indeed,
    the first,
  The noblest, therefore ! since the
    heroic heart
Within thee must be great enough to burst
  Those trammels buckling to the baser
    part
Thy saintly peers in Rome, who crossed
    and cursed
  With the same finger.

               Come, appear, be found,
If pope or peasant, come ! we hear the
    cock,
  The courtier of the mountains when
    first crowned
With golden dawn ; and orient glories
    flock
  To meet the sun upon the highest
    ground.
Take voice and work ! we wait to hear
    thee knock
  At some one of our Florentine nine
    gates,
On each of which was imaged a sublime
  Face of a Tuscan genius, which, for
    hate's
And love's sake, both, our Florence in
    her prime
  Turned boldly on all comers to her
    states,

As heroes turned their shields in antique
  time,
  Emblazoned with honourable acts.
    And though
The gates are blank now of such images,
  And Petrarch looks no more from
    Nicolo
Toward dear Arezzo, 'twixt the acacia
  trees,
  Nor Dante, from gate Gallo—still we
    know,
Despite the razing of the blazonries,
  Remains the consecration of the shield!
The dead heroic faces will start out
  On all these gates, if foes should take
    the field,
And blend sublimely, at the earliest shout,
  With living heroes who will scorn to
    yield
A hair's-breadth even, when, gazing
  round about,
  They find in what a glorious company
They fight the foes of Florence. Who
  will grudge
  His one poor life, when that great
    man we see
Has given five hundred years, the world
  being judge,
  To help the glory of his Italy?
Who, born the fair side of the Alps, will
  budge,
  When Dante stays, when Ariosto stays,
When Petrarch stays for ever? Ye bring
  swords,
  My Tuscans? Aye, if wanted in this
    haze,
Bring swords. But first bring souls!—
  bring thoughts and words,
  Unrusted by a tear of yesterday's,
Yet awful by its wrong,—and cut these
  cords,
  And mow this green lush falseness to
    the roots,
And shut the mouth of hell below the
  swathe!
  And, if ye can bring songs too, let the
    lute's
Recoverable music softly bathe
  Some poet's hand, that, through all
    bursts and bruits
Of popular passion, all unripe and rathe
  Convictions of the popular intellect,
Ye may not lack a finger up the air,

Annunciative, reproving, pure, erect,
To show which way your first Ideal bare
  The whiteness of its wings, when
    (sorely pecked
By falcons on your wrists) it unaware
  Arose up overhead, and out of sight.

Meanwhile, let all the far ends of the
  world
  Breathe back the deep breath of their
    old delight,
To swell the Italian banner just unfurled.
  Help, lands of Europe! for, if Austria
    fight,
The drums will bar your slumber. Had
  ye curled
  The laurel for your thousand artists'
    brows,
If these Italian hands had planted none?
  Can any sit down idle in the house,
Nor hear appeals from Buonarroti's stone
  And Raffael's canvas, rousing and to
    rouse?
Where's Poussin's master? Gallic
  Avignon
  Bred Laura, and Vaucluse's fount has
    stirred
The heart of France too strongly, as it lets
  Its little stream out (like a wizard's
    bird
Which bounds upon its emerald wing
  and wets
  The rocks on each side), that she should
    not gird
Her loins with Charlemagne's sword
  when foes beset
  The country of her Petrarch. Spain
    may well
Be minded how from Italy she caught,
  To mingle with her tinkling Moorish
    bell,
A fuller cadence and a subtler thought.
  And even the New World, the recep-
    tacle
Of freemen, may send glad men, as it
  ought,
  To greet Vespucci Amerigo's door.
While England claims, by trump of
  poetry,
  Verona, Venice, the Ravenna-shore,
And dearer holds John Milton's Fiesole
  Than Langland's Malvern with the
    stars in flower.

And Vallombrosa, we two went to see
  Last June, beloved companion,—
    where sublime
The mountains live in holy families,
  And the slow pinewoods ever climb
    and climb
Half up their breasts, just stagger as they
    seize
  Some grey crag, drop back with it
    many a time,
And straggle blindly down the precipice !
  The Vallombrosan brooks were strewn
    as thick
That June-day, knee-deep, with dead
    beechen leaves,
  As Milton saw them, ere his heart
    grew sick
And his eyes blind. I think the monks
    and beeves
  Are all the same too. Scarce they have
    changed the wick
On good St. Gualbert's altar, which re-
    ceives
  The convent's pilgrims,—and the pool
    in front
(Wherein the hill-stream trout are cast,
    to wait
  The beatific vision and the grunt
Used at refectory) keeps its weedy state,
  To baffle saintly abbots who would
    count
The fish across their breviary nor 'bate
  The measure of their steps. O water-
    falls
And forests ! sound and silence ! moun-
    tains bare,
  That leap up peak by peak, and catch
    the palls
Of purple and silver mist to rend and
    share
  With one another, at electric calls
Of life in the sunbeams,—till we cannot
    dare
  Fix your shapes, count your number !
    we must think
Your beauty and your glory helped to fill
  The cup of Milton's soul so to the brink,
He never more was thirsty, when God's
    will
  Had shattered to his sense the last
    chain-link
By which he had drawn from Nature's
    visible

The fresh well-water. Satisfied by this,
He sang of Adam's paradise and smiled,
  Remembering Vallombrosa. There-
    fore is
The place divine to English man and
    child,
  And pilgrims leave their souls here in
    a kiss.

For Italy's the whole earth's treasury,
    piled
  With reveries of gentle ladies, flung
Aside, like ravelled silk, from life's worn
    stuff ;
  With coins of scholars' fancy, which,
    being rung
On work-day counter, still sound silver-
    proof ;
  In short, with all the dreams of
    dreamers young,
Before their heads have time for slipping
    off
  Hope's pillow to the ground. How
    oft, indeed,
We've sent our souls out from the rigid
    north,
  On bare white feet which would not
    print nor bleed,
To climb the Alpine passes and look forth,
  Where booming low the Lombard
    rivers lead
To gardens, vineyards, all a dream is
    worth,—
  Sights, thou and I, Love, have seen
    afterward
From Tuscan Bellosguardo, wide awake[1],
  When, standing on the actual blessed
    sward
Where Galileo stood at nights to take
  The vision of the stars, we have found it
    hard,
Gazing upon the earth and heaven, to make
  A choice of beauty.

                         Therefore let us all
Refreshed in England or in other land,
  By visions, with their fountain-rise and
    fall,
Of this earth's darling,—we, who under-
    stand
  A little how the Tuscan musical

[1] Galileo's villa, close to Florence, is built on
an eminence called Bellosguardo.

Vowels do round themselves as if they
  planned
    Eternities of separate sweetness,—
      we,
Who loved Sorrento vines in picture-
  book,
    Or ere in wine-cup we pledged faith
      or glee,—
Who loved Rome's wolf, with demi-gods
  at suck,
    Or ere we loved truth's own divi-
      nity,—
Who loved, in brief, the classic hill and
  brook,
    And Ovid's dreaming tales, and
      Petrarch's song,
Or ere we loved Love's self even !—let
  us give
    The blessing of our souls, (and wish
      them strong
To bear it to the height where prayers
  arrive,
    When faithful spirits pray against a
      wrong,)
To this great cause of southern men,
  who strive
    In God's name for man's rights, and
      shall not fail !

Behold, they shall not fail. The shouts
  ascend
    Above the shrieks, in Naples, and
      prevail.
Rows of shot corpses, waiting for the
  end
    Of burial, seem to smile up straight
      and pale
Into the azure air and apprehend
    That final gun-flash from Palermo's
      coast
Which lightens their apocalypse of
  death.
    So let them die ! The world shows
      nothing lost ;
Therefore, not blood. Above or under-
  neath,
    What matter, brothers, if ye keep your
      post
On duty's side ? As sword returns to
  sheath,
    So dust to grave, but souls find place
      in Heaven.
Heroic daring is the true success,

The eucharistic bread requires no
  leaven ;
And though your ends were hopeless,
  we should bless
Your cause as holy. Strive—and,
  having striven,
Take, for God's recompense, that
  righteousness !

PART II

I WROTE a meditation and a dream,
    Hearing a little child sing in the street.
I leant upon his music as a theme,
    Till it gave way beneath my heart's
      full beat,
Which tried at an exultant prophecy
    But dropped before the measure was
      complete—
Alas, for songs and hearts ! O Tuscany,
    O Dante's Florence, is the type too
      plain ?
Didst thou, too, only sing of liberty,
    As little children take up a high strain
With unintentioned voices, and break off
    To sleep upon their mothers' knees
      again ?
Couldst thou not watch one hour ? then,
  sleep enough—
    That sleep may hasten manhood, and
      sustain
The faint pale spirit with some muscular
  stuff.

But we, who cannot slumber as thou
  dost,
We thinkers, who have thought for thee
  and failed,
    We hopers, who have hoped for thee
      and lost,
We poets, wandered round by dreams [1],
  who hailed
    From this Atrides' roof (with lintel-
      post
Which still drips blood,—the worse part
  hath prevailed)
    The fire-voice of the beacons, to declare
Troy taken, sorrow ended,—cozened
  through

[1] See the opening passage of the Agamemnon
of Aeschylus.

A crimson sunset in a misty air,—
What now remains for such as we, to do?
   God's judgements, peradventure, will He bare
To the roots of thunder, if we kneel and sue?

   From Casa Guidi windows I looked forth,
And saw ten thousand eyes of Florentines
   Flash back the triumph of the Lombard north,—
Saw fifty banners, freighted with the signs
And exultations of the awakened earth,
Float on above the multitude in lines,
   Straight to the Pitti. So, the vision went.
And so, between those populous rough hands
   Raised in the sun, Duke Leopold outleant,
And took the patriot's oath, which henceforth stands
Among the oaths of perjurers, eminent
To catch the lightnings ripened for these lands.

   Why swear at all, thou alse Duke Leopold?
What need to swear? What need to boast thy blood
   Unspoilt of Austria, and thy heart unsold
Away from Florence? It was understood
   God made thee not too vigorous or too bold ;
And men had patience with thy quiet mood,
And women, pity, as they saw thee pace
Their festive streets with premature grey hairs.
   We turned the mild dejection of thy face
To princely meanings, took thy wrinkling cares
   For ruffling hopes, and called thee weak, not base.
Nay, better light the torches for more prayers
   And smoke the pale Madonnas at the shrine,
Being still 'our poor Grand-duke, our good Grand-duke,

   Who cannot help the Austrian in his line,'—
Than write an oath upon a nation's book
   For men to spit at with scorn's blurring brine !
Who dares forgive what none can overlook ?

   For me, I do repent me in this dust
Of towns and temples, which makes Italy,—
   I sigh amid the sighs which breathe a gust
Of dying century to century
   Around us on the uneven crater-crust
Of these old worlds,—I bow my soul and knee !
   Absolve me, patriots, of my woman's fault
That ever I believed the man was true !—
   These sceptred strangers shun the common salt,
And, therefore, when the general board's in view,
   And they stand up to carve for blind and halt,
The wise suspect the viands which ensue.
   I much repent that, in this time and place,
Where many corpse-lights of experience burn
   From Caesar's and Lorenzo's festering race,
To enlighten groping reasoners, I could learn
   No better counsel for a simple case,
Than to put faith in princes, in my turn.
   Had all the death-piles of the ancient years
Flared up in vain before me ? knew I not
   What stench arises from some purple gears?
And how the sceptres witness whence they got
   Their briar-wood, crackling through the atmosphere's
Foul smoke, by princely perjuries, kept hot ?
   Forgive me, ghosts of patriots,—Brutus, thou,
Who trailest downhill into life again

Thy blood-weighed cloak, to indict
me with thy slow
Reproachful eyes!—for being taught in
vain
That, while the illegitimate Caesars
show
Of meaner stature than the first full strain
(Confessed incompetent to conquer
Gaul),
They swoon as feebly and cross Rubicons
As rashly as any Julius of them all!
Forgive, that I forgot the mind which runs
Through absolute races, too un-
sceptical!
I saw the man among his little sons,
His lips were warm with kisses while
he swore,—
And I, because I am a woman, I,
Who felt my own child's coming life
before
The prescience of my soul, and held
faith high,—
I could not bear to think, whoever bore,
That lips, so warmed, could shape so cold
a lie.

From Casa Guidi windows I looked out,
Again looked, and beheld a different sight.
The Duke had fled before the people's
shout
'Long live the Duke!' A people, to
speak right,
Must speak as soft as courtiers, lest a
doubt
Should curdle brows of gracious sove-
reigns, white.
Moreover that same dangerous shout-
ing meant
Some gratitude for future favours, which
Were only promised, the Constituent
Implied, the whole being subject to the
hitch
In 'motu proprios,' very incident
To all these Czars, from Paul to Paulo-
vitch.
Whereat the people rose up in the dust
Of the ruler's flying feet, and shouted still
And loudly, only, this time, as was just,
Not 'Live the Duke,' who had fled, for
good or ill,
But 'Live the People,' who remained
and must,
The unrenounced and unrenounceable.

Long live the people! How they
lived! and boiled
And bubbled in the cauldron of the street.
How the young blustered, nor the old
recoiled,—
And what a thunderous stir of tongues
and feet
Trod flat the palpitating bells, and foiled
The joy-guns of their echo, shattering it!
How down they pulled the Duke's
arms everywhere!
How up they set new café-signs, to show
Where patriots might sip ices in pure
air—
(The fresh paint smelling somewhat). To and fro
How marched the civic guard, and
stopped to stare
When boys broke windows in a civic
glow.
How rebel songs were sung to loyal
tunes,
And bishops cursed in ecclesiastic metres.
How all the Circoli grew large as
moons,
And all the speakers, moonstruck,—
thankful greeters
Of prospects which struck poor the
ducal boons, . .
A mere free press, and chambers!—
frank repeaters
Of great Guerazzi's praises. . . .
'There 's a man,
The father of the land!—who, truly
great,
Takes off that national disgrace and ban,
The farthing tax upon our Florence-gate,
And saves Italia as he only can.'
How all the nobles fled, and would not
wait,
Because they were most noble,—
which being so,
How liberals vowed to burn their palaces,
Because free Tuscans were not free
to go.
How grown men raged at Austria's
wickedness,
And smoked,—while fifty striplings in
a row
Marched straight to Piedmont for the
wrong's redress!
You say we failed in duty, we who
wore

Black velvet like Italian democrats,
  Who slashed our sleeves like patriots,
    nor forswore
The true republic in the form of hats?
  We chased the archbishop from the
    Duomo door—
We chalked the walls with bloody caveats
  Against all tyrants. If we did not
    fight
Exactly, we fired muskets up the air,
  To show that victory was ours of
    right.
We met, had free discussion every-
    where
  (Except perhaps i' the Chambers) day
    and night.
We proved the poor should be em-
    ployed, . . . that's fair,—
  And yet the rich not worked for any-
    wise,—
Pay certified, yet payers abrogated,—
  Full work secured, yet liabilities
To over-work excluded,—not one bated
  Of all our holidays, that still, at twice
Or thrice a-week, are moderately rated.
  We proved that Austria was dislodged,
    or would
Or should be, and that Tuscany in arms
  Should, would, dislodge her, ending
    the old feud ;
And yet, to leave our piazzas, shops, and
    farms,
  For the simple sake of fighting, was
    not good—
We proved that also. 'Did we carry
    charms
  Against being killed ourselves, that
    we should rush
On killing others? what! desert here-
    with
  Our wives and mothers?—was that
    duty? tush!'
At which we shook the sword within
    the sheath,
  Like heroes—only louder ; and the
    flush
Ran up the cheek to meet the future
    wreath.
  Nay, what we proved, we shouted—
    how we shouted
(Especially the boys did), boldly planting
  That tree of liberty, whose fruit is
    doubted,

Because the roots are not of nature's
    granting.
  A tree of good and evil!—none, with-
    out it,
Grow gods!—alas, and, with it, men are
    wanting!

O holy knowledge, holy liberty,
O holy rights of nations! If i speak
  These bitter things against the jugglery
Of days that in your names proved blind
    and weak,
  It is that tears are bitter. When we see
The brown skulls grin at death in church-
    yards bleak,
  We do not cry, 'This Yorick is too
    light,'
For death grows deathlier with that
    mouth he makes.
  So with my mocking. Bitter things
    I write,
Because my soul is bitter for your sakes,
  O freedom! O my Florence!

                              Men who might
Do greatly in a universe that breaks
  And burns, must ever *know* before
    they do.
Courage and patience are but sacrifice ;
  And sacrifice is offered for and to
Something conceived of. Each man pays
    a price
  For what himself counts precious,
    whether true
Or false the appreciation it implies.
  But here,—no knowledge, no con-
    ception, nought!
Desire was absent, that provides great
    deeds
  From out the greatness of prevenient
    thought.
And action, action, like a flame that needs
  A steady breath and fuel, being caught
Up, like a burning reed from other reeds,
  Flashed in the empty and uncertain air,
Then wavered, then went out. Behold,
    who blames
  A crookèd course, when not a goal is
    there,
To round the fervid striving of the games?
  An ignorance of means may minister
To greatness, but an ignorance of aims
  Makes it impossible to be great at all.

So, with our Tuscans! Let none dare
    to say,
  'Here virtue never can be national.
Here fortitude can never cut a way
    Between the Austrian muskets, out
    of thrall.'
I tell you rather, that, whoever may
    Discern true ends here, shall grow
    pure enough
To love them, brave enough to strive for
    them,
    And strong to reach them, though the
    roads be rough!
That having learnt—by no mere apoph-
    thegm—
    Not just the draping of a graceful stuff
About a statue, broidered at the hem,—
    Not just the trilling on an opera stage,
Of 'libertà' to bravos—(a fair word,
    Yet too allied to inarticulate rage
And breathless sobs, for singing, though
    the chord
    Were deeper than they struck it!) but
    the gauge
Of civil wants sustained, and wrongs
    abhorred,—
    The serious, sacred meaning and full
    use
Of freedom for a nation,—then, indeed,
    Our Tuscans, underneath the bloody
    dews
Of some new morning, rising up agreed
    And bold, will want no Saxon souls
    or thews,
To sweep their piazzas clear of Austria's
    breed.

Alas, alas! it was not so this time.
Conviction was not, courage failed, and
    truth
    Was something to be doubted of. The
    mime
Changed masks, because a mime. The
    tide as smooth
    In running in as out, no sense of
    crime
Because no sense of virtue, sudden ruth
    Seized on the people.—They would
    have again
Their good Grand-duke, and leave
    Guerazzi, though
    He took that tax from Florence.
    'Much in vain

He takes it from the market-carts, we
    trow,
    While urgent that no market-men
    remain,
But all march off and leave the spade
    and plough,
    To die among the Lombards. Was
    it thus
The dear paternal Duke did? Live the
    Duke!'
    At which the joy-bells multitudinous,
Swept by an opposite wind, as loudly
    shook.
    Call back the mild archbishop to his
    house,
To bless the people with his frightened
    look,—
    He shall not yet be hanged, you com-
    prehend.
Seize on Guerazzi; guard him in full view,
    Or else we stab him in the back, to end.
Rub out those chalked devices! set up
    new!
    The Duke's arms! doff your Phrygian
    caps; and mend
The pavement of the piazzas broke into
    By barren poles of freedom! smooth
    the way
For the ducal carriage, lest his highness
    sigh
    'Here trees of liberty grew yesterday.'
'Long live the Duke!'—How roared the
    cannonry,
    How rocked the bell-towers, and
    through thickening spray
Of nosegays, wreaths, and kerchiefs
    tossed on high,
    How marched the civic guard, the
    people still
Being good at shouts,—especially the
    boys.
Alas, poor people, of an unfledged will
Most fitly expressed by such a callow
    voice!
Alas, still poorer Duke, incapable
Of being worthy even of so much noise!

You think he came back instantly,
    with thanks
And tears in his faint eyes, and hands
    extended
    To stretch the franchise through their
    utmost ranks?

That having, like a father, apprehended,
   He came to pardon fatherly those
      pranks
Played out, and now in filial service
      ended?—
   That some love-token, like a prince,
      he threw,
To meet the people's love-call, in return?
   Well, how he came I will relate to you;
And if your hearts should burn, why,
      hearts *must* burn,
   To make the ashes which things old
      and new
Shall be washed clean in—as this Duke
      will learn.

   From Casa Guidi windows, gazing,
      then,
I saw and witness how the Duke came
      back.
   The regular tramp of horse and tread
      of men
Did smite the silence like an anvil black
   And sparkless. With her wide eyes
      at full strain,
Our Tuscan nurse exclaimed, 'Alack,
      alack,
   Signora! these shall be the Austrians.'
   'Nay,
Be still,' I answered, 'do not wake the
      child!'
—For so, my two-months' baby sleeping
      lay
In milky dreams upon the bed and smiled,
   And I thought, 'he shall sleep on,
      while he may,
Through the world's baseness. Not
      being yet defiled,
   Why should he be disturbed by what
      is done?'
Then, gazing, I beheld the long-drawn
      street
   Live out, from end to end, full in the sun,
With Austria's thousands. Sword and
      bayonet,
   Horse, foot, artillery,—cannons roll-
      ing on,
Like blind slow storm-clouds gestant
      with the heat
   Of undeveloped lightnings, each be-
      strode
By a single man, dust white from head
      to heel,

Indifferent as the dreadful thing he
      rode,
Like a sculptured Fate serene and
      terrible.
As some smooth river which has
      overflowed,
Will slow and silent down its current
      wheel
   A loosened forest, all the pines erect,—
So, swept, in mute significance of storm,
   The marshalled thousands,—not an
      eye deflect
To left or right, to catch a novel form
   Of Florence city adorned by architect
And carver, or of Beauties live and
      warm
   Scared at the casements!—all, straight-
      forward eyes
And faces, held as steadfast as their
      swords,
   And cognizant of acts, not imageries.
The key, O Tuscans, too well fits the
      wards!
   Ye asked for mimes,—these bring
      you tragedies;
For purple,—these shall wear it as your
      lords.
   Ye played like children,—die like
      innocents.
Ye mimicked lightnings with a torch,—
      the crack
   Of the actual bolt, your pastime,
      circumvents.
Ye called up ghosts, believing they were
      slack
   To follow any voice from Gilbca's
      tents, . .
Here's Samuel!—and, so, Grand-dukes
      come back!

And yet, they are no prophets though
      they come.
That awful mantle, they are drawing
      close,
   Shall be searched, one day, by the
      shafts of Doom
Through double folds now hoodwinking
      the brows.
   Resuscitated monarchs disentomb
Grave-reptiles with them, in their new
      life-throes.
   Let such beware. Behold, the people
      waits,

Like God. As He, in His serene of
might,
So they, in their endurance of long
straits.
Ye stamp no nation out, though day
and night
Ye tread them with that absolute heel
which grates
And grinds them flat from all attempted
height.
You kill worms sooner with a garden-
spade
Than you kill peoples : peoples will not
die ;
The tail curls stronger when you lop
the head ;
They writhe at every wound and
multiply,
And shudder into a heap of life that 's
made
Thus vital from God's own vitality.
'Tis hard to shrivel back a day of
God's
Once fixed for judgement : 'tis as hard to
change
The people's, when they rise beneath
their loads
And heave them from their backs with
violent wrench,
To crush the oppressor !—for that
judgement-rod's
The measure of this popular revenge.

Meantime, from Casa Guidi windows,
we
Beheld the armament of Austria flow
Into the drowning heart of Tuscany.
And yet none wept, none cursed, or, if
'twas so,
They wept and cursed in silence.
Silently
Our noisy Tuscans watched the invading
foe ;
They had learnt silence. Pressed
against the wall,
And grouped upon the church-steps
opposite,
A few pale men and women stared at all!
God knows what they were feeling,
with their white
Constrainèd faces, they, so prodigal
Of cry and gesture when the world goes
right,

Or wrong indeed. But here, was
depth of wrong,
And here, still water ; they were silent
here ;
And through that sentient silence,
struck along
That measured tramp from which it
stood out clear,
Distinct the sound and silence, like
a gong
At midnight, each by the other awfuller,—
While every soldier in his cap displayed
A leaf of olive. Dusty, bitter thing !
Was such plucked at Novara, is it said ?

A cry is up in England, which doth ring
The hollow world through, that for
ends of trade
And virtue, and God's better wor-
shipping,
We henceforth should exalt the name
of Peace,
And leave those rusty wars that eat the
soul,—
Besides their clippings at our golden
fleece.
I, too, have loved peace, and from bole
to bole
Of immemorial, undeciduous trees,
Would write, as lovers use, upon a scroll,
The holy name of Peace, and set it high
Where none could pluck it down. On
trees, I say,—
Not upon gibbets !—With the greenery
Of dewy branches and the flowery May,
Sweet mediation betwixt earth and sky
Providing, for the shepherd's holiday.
Not upon gibbets !—though the vulture
leaves
The bones to quiet, which he first
picked bare.
Not upon dungeons ! though the
wretch who grieves
And groans within, less stirs the outer air
Than any little field-mouse stirs the
sheaves.
Not upon chain-bolts ! though the slave's
despair
Has dulled his helpless, miserable
brain,
And left him blank beneath the freeman's
whip,
To sing and laugh out idiocies of pain.

Nor yet on starving homes! where
  many a lip
  Has sobbed itself asleep through
    curses vain.
I love no peace which is not fellowship,
  And which includes not mercy. I
    would have
Rather, the raking of the guns across
  The world, and shrieks against
    Heaven's architrave ;
Rather, the struggle in the slippery
    fosse
  Of dying men and horses, and the
    wave
Blood-bubbling. . . . Enough said !—
    by Christ's own cross,
  And by this faint heart of my woman-
    hood,
Such things are better than a Peace
    that sits
  Beside a hearth in self-commended
    mood,
And takes no thought how wind and
    rain by fits
  Are howling out of doors against the
    good
Of the poor wanderer. What! your
    peace admits
  Of outside anguish while it keeps at
    home?
I loathe to take its name upon my
    tongue.
  'Tis nowise peace. 'Tis treason, stiff
    with doom,—
'Tis gagged despair, and inarticulate
    wrong,
  Annihilated Poland, stifled Rome,
Dazed Naples, Hungary fainting 'neath
    the thong,
  And Austria wearing a smooth olive-
    leaf
On her brute forehead, while her hoofs
    outpress
  The life from these Italian souls, in
    brief.
O Lord of Peace, who art Lord of
    Righteousness,
  Constrain the anguished worlds from
    sin and grief,
Pierce them with conscience, purge them
    with redress,
  And give us peace which is no counter-
    feit !

But wherefore should we look out any
    more
  From Casa Guidi windows? Shut them
    straight,
And let us sit down by the folded door,
  And veil our saddened faces, and, so,
    wait
What next the judgement-heavens make
    ready for.
  I have grown too weary of these
    windows. Sights
Come thick enough and clear enough in
    thought,
  Without the sunshine ; souls have
    inner lights.
And since the Grand-duke has come back
    and brought
  This army of the North which thus
    requites
His filial South, we leave him to be
    taught.
  His South, too, has learnt something
    certainly,
Whereof the practice will bring profit
    soon ;
  And peradventure other eyes may see,
From Casa Guidi windows, what is done
  Or undone. Whatsoever deeds they
    be,
Pope Pius will be glorified in none.

Record that gain, Mazzini !—it shall
    top
Some heights of sorrow. Peter's rock,
    so named,
Shall lure no vessel any more to drop
Among the breakers. Peter's chair is
    shamed
  Like any vulgar throne, the nations
    lop
To pieces for their firewood unre-
    claimed,—
  And, when it burns too, we shall see
    as well
In Italy as elsewhere. Let it burn.
  The cross, accounted still adorable,
Is Christ's cross only !—if the thief's
    would earn
  Some stealthy genuflexions, we rebel ;
And here the impenitent thief's has had
    its turn,
  As God knows ; and the people on
    their knees

Scoff and toss back the croziers, stretched
    like yokes
  To press their heads down lower by
    degrees.
So Italy, by means of these last strokes,
  Escapes the danger which preceded
    these,
Of leaving captured hands in cloven
    oaks,—
  Of leaving very souls within the buckle
Whence bodies struggled outward,—of
    supposing
  That freemen may, like bondsmen,
    kneel and truckle.
And then stand up as usual, without losing
  An inch of stature.

        Those whom she-wolves suckle
Will bite as wolves do in the grapple-
    closing
  Of adverse interests. This, at last, is
    known
(Thank Pius for the lesson), that albeit
  Among the popedom's hundred heads
    of stone
Which blink down on you from the roof's
    retreat
  In Siena's tiger-striped cathedral, Joan
And Borgia 'mid their fellows you may
    greet,
  A harlot and a devil,—you will see
Not a man, still less angel, grandly set
  With open soul to render man more
    free.
The fishers are still thinking of the net,
  And, if not thinking of the hook too, we
Are counted somewhat deeply in their
    debt ;
  But that's a rare case—so, by hook
    and crook
They take the advantage, agonizing
    Christ
  By rustier nails than those of Cedron's
    brook,
I' the people's body very cheaply
    priced,—
  And quote high priesthood out of Holy
    book,
While buying death-fields with the
    sacrificed.

    Priests, priests,—there's no such
      name !—God's own, except

Ye take most vainly.   Through heaven's
    lifted gate
  The priestly ephod in sole glory swept,
When Christ ascended, entered in, and
    sate
  (With victor face sublimely overwept)
At Deity's right hand, to mediate
  He alone, He for ever.   On his breast
The Urim and the Thummim, fed with
    fire
  From the full Godhead, flicker with
    the unrest
Of human, pitiful heartbeats. Come up
    higher,
  All Christians ! Levi's tribe is dispos-
    sest.
That solitary alb ye shall admire,
  But not cast lots for. The last chrism,
    poured right,
Was on that Head, and poured for burial,
  And not for domination in men's sight.
What *are* these churches ? The old
    temple wall
  Doth overlook them juggling with the
    sleight
Of surplice, candlestick, and altar-pall ;
  East church and west church, aye,
    north church and south,
Rome's church and England's,—let them
    all repent,
  And make concordats 'twixt their soul
    and mouth,
Succeed St. Paul by working at the tent,
  Become infallible guides by speaking
    truth,
And excommunicate their pride that bent
  And cramped the souls of men.

            Why, even here,
Priestcraft burns out, the twinèd linen
    blazes ;
  Not, like asbestos, to grow white and
    clear,
But all to perish !—while the fire-smell
    raises
  To life some swooning spirits, who,
    last year,
Lost breath and heart in these church-
    stifled places.
  Why, almost, through this Pius, we
    believed
The priesthood could be an honest thing,
    he smiled

So saintly while our corn was being
      sheaved
For his own granaries. Showing now
      defiled
   His hireling hands, a better help 's
      achieved
Than if they blessed us shepherd-like
      and mild.
   False doctrine, strangled by its own
      amen,
Dies in the throat of all this nation. Who
   Will speak a pope's name, as they rise
      again ?
What woman or what child will count
      him true ?
   What dreamer, praise him with the
      voice or pen ?
What man, fight for him ?—Pius takes
      his due.

   Record that gain, Mazzini !—Yes, but
      first
Set down thy people's faults ;—set down
      the want
   Of soul-conviction ; set down aims
      dispersed,
And incoherent means, and valour scant
   Because of scanty faith, and schisms
      accursed,
That wrench these brother-hearts from
      covenant
   With freedom and each other. Set
      down this,
And this, and see to overcome it when
   The seasons bring the fruits thou wilt
      not miss
If wary. Let no cry of patriot men
   Distract thee from the stern analysis
Of masses who cry only ! keep thy ken
   Clear as thy soul is virtuous. Heroes'
      blood
Splashed up against thy noble brow in
      Rome,—
   Let such not blind thee to an interlude
Which was not also holy, yet did come
   'Twixt sacramental actions,—brother-
      hood,
Despised even there, and something of
      the doom
   Of Remus, in the trenches. Listen
      now—
Rossi died silent near where Caesar died.
   He did not say, ' My Brutus, is it thou ?'

But Italy unquestioned testified,
   'I killed him !—I am Brutus.—I
      avow.'
At which the whole world's laugh of
      scorn replied,
   ' A poor maimed copy of Brutus !'
                              Too much like,
Indeed, to be so unlike ! too un-
      skilled
   At Philippi and the honest battle-
      pike,
To be so skilful where a man is killed
   Near Pompey's statue, and the daggers
      strike
At unawares i' the throat. Was thus
      fulfilled
   An omen once of Michel Angelo ?—
When Marcus Brutus he conceived com-
      plete,
   And strove to hurl him out by blow
      on blow
Upon the marble, at Art's thunderheat,
   Till haply (some pre-shadow rising
      slow,
Of what his Italy would fancy meet
   To be called BRUTUS) straight his
      plastic hand
Fell back before his prophet-soul, and
      left
   A fragment, a maimed Brutus,—but
      more grand
Than this, so named at Rome, was !
                              Let thy weft
   Present one woof and warp, Mazzini !—
      stand
With no man hankering for a dagger's
      heft,—
   No, not for Italy !—nor stand apart,
No, not for the republic !—from those
      pure
   Brave men who hold the level of thy
      heart
In patriot truth, as lover and as doer,
   Albeit they will not follow where thou
      art
As extreme theorist. Trust and distrust
      fewer ;
   And so bind strong and keep unstained
      the cause
Which (God's sign granted) war-trumps
      newly blown
   Shall yet annunciate to the world's
      applause.

But now, the world is busy; it has grown
    A Fair-going world. Imperial England
    draws
The flowing ends of the earth, from Fez,
    Canton,
    Delhi and Stockholm, Athens and
    Madrid,
The Russias and the vast Americas,
    As if a queen drew in her robes amid
Her golden cincture,—isles, peninsulas,
    Capes, continents, far inland countries
    hid
By jasper-sands and hills of chrysopras,
    All trailing in their splendours through
    the door
Of the gorgeous Crystal Palace. Every
    nation,
    To every other nation strange of yore,
Gives face to face the civic salutation,
    And holds up in a proud right hand
    before
That congress, the best work which she
    can fashion
    By her best means. 'These corals,
    will you please
To match against your oaks? They grow
    as fast
    Within my wilderness of purple seas.'—
'This diamond stared upon me as I passed
    (As a live god's eye from a marble
    frieze)
Along a dark of diamonds. Is it classed?'—
    ' I wove these stuffs so subtly that the
    gold
Swims to the surface of the silk like cream,
    And curdles to fair patterns. Ye be-
    hold!'—
'These delicatest muslins rather seem
    Than be, you think? Nay, touch them
    and be bold,
Though such veiled Chakhi's face in
    Hafiz' dream.'—
    ' These carpets—you walk slow on
    them like kings,
Inaudible like spirits, while your foot
    Dips deep in velvet roses and such
    things.'—
' Even Apollonius might commend this
    flute [1].

[1] Philostratus relates of Apollonius how he
objected to the musical instrument of Linus the
Rhodian, that it could not enrich or beautify.
The history of music in our day would satisfy
the philosopher on one point at least.

The music, winding through the stops,
    upsprings
To make the player very rich! com-
    pute.'—
    'Here's goblet-glass, to take in with
    your wine
The very sun its grapes were ripened
    under!
Drink light and juice together, and
    each fine.'—
' This model of a steam-ship moves your
    wonder?
You should behold it crushing down
    the brine,
Like a blind Jove, who feels his way
    with thunder.'—
    'Here's sculpture! Ah, *we* live too!
    why not throw
Our life into our marbles? Art has place
    For other artists after Angelo.'—
'I tried to paint out here a natural face;
    For nature includes Raffael, as we
    know,
Not Raffael nature. Will it help my
    case?'—
    'Methinks you will not match this
    steel of ours!'—
' Nor you this porcelain! One might
    dream the clay
Retained in it the larvae of the flowers,
They bud so, round the cup, the old
    spring way.'—
    ' Nor you these carven woods, where
    birds in bowers
With twisting snakes and climbing
    cupids, play.'

O Magi of the east and of the west,
Your incense, gold, and myrrh are ex-
    cellent!—
    What gifts for Christ, then, bring ye
    with the rest?
Your hands have worked well. Is your
    courage spent
    In handwork only? Have you nothing
    best,
Which generous souls may perfect and
    present,
    And He shall thank the givers for?
    no light
Of teaching, liberal nations, for the poor,
    Who sit in darkness when it is not
    night?

No cure for wicked children? Christ,—
    no cure!
No help for women, sobbing out of sight
Because men made the laws? no brothel-
    lure
    Burnt out by popular lightnings?—
    Hast thou found
No remedy, my England, for such woes?
    No outlet, Austria, for the scourged
    and bound,
No entrance for the exiled? no repose,
    Russia, for knouted Poles worked
    underground,
And gentle ladies bleached among the
    snows?—
    No mercy for the slave, America?—
No hope for Rome, free France, chivalric
    France?—
    Alas, great nations have great shames,
    I say.
No pity, O world, no tender utterance
    Of benediction, and prayers stretched
    this way
For poor Italia, baffled by mischance?—
    O gracious nations, give some ear to me!
You all go to your Fair, and I am one
    Who at the roadside of humanity
Beseech your alms,—God's justice to be
    done.
    So, prosper!

        In the name of Italy,
Meantime, her patriot dead have benison.
    They only have done well,—and,
    what they did
Being perfect, it shall triumph. Let
    them slumber.
No king of Egypt in a pyramid
Is safer from oblivion, though he number
    Full seventy cerements for a coverlid.
These Dead be seeds of life, and shall
    encumber
The sad heart of the land, until it loose
The clammy clods and let out the spring-
    growth
    In beatific green through every bruise.
The tyrant should take heed to what he
    doth,
    Since every victim-carrion turns to use,
And drives a chariot, like a god made
    wroth,
    Against each piled injustice. Aye,
    the least,

Dead for Italia, not in vain has died,
Though many vainly, ere life's struggle
    ceased,
To mad dissimilar ends have swerved
    aside;
    Each grave her nationality has pieced
By its own majestic breadth, and fortified
    And pinned it deeper to the soil. For-
    lorn
Of thanks, be, therefore, no one of these
    graves!
    Not Hers,—who, at her husband's
    side, in scorn,
Outfaced the whistling shot and hissing
    waves,
    Until she felt her little babe unborn
Recoil, within her, from the violent staves
    And bloodhounds of the world,—at
    which, her life
Dropt inwards from her eyes and
    followed it
    Beyond the hunters. Garibaldi's wife
And child died so. And now, the
    sea-weeds fit
    Her body, like a proper shroud and
    coif,
And murmurously the ebbing waters grit
    The little pebbles while she lies in-
    terred
In the sea-sand. Perhaps, ere dying
    thus,
    She looked up in his face (which
    never stirred
From its clenched anguish) as to make
    excuse
    For leaving him for his, if so she
    erred.
He well remembers that she could not
    choose.
A memorable grave! Another is
At Genoa. There, a king may fitly lie,
    Who, bursting that heroic heart of his
At lost Novara, that he could not die
    (Though thrice into the cannon's eyes
    for this
He plunged his shuddering steed, and
    felt the sky
    Reel back between the fire-shocks),
    stripped away
The ancestral ermine ere the smoke had
    cleared,
    And, naked to the soul, that none
    might say

His kingship covered what was base
and bleared
  With treason, went out straight an
exile, yea,
An exiled patriot. Let him be revered.

Yea, verily, Charles Albert has died
well ;
And if he lived not all so, as one spoke,
  The sin pass softly with the passing
bell.
For he was shriven, I think, in cannon-
smoke,
  And, taking off his crown, made visible
A hero's forehead. Shaking Austria's
yoke
  He shattered his own hand and heart.
'So best,'
His last words were upon his lonely bed,
  'I do not end like popes and dukes at
least—
Thank God for it.' And now that he
is dead,
  Admitting it is proved and manifest
That he was worthy, with a discrowned
head,
  To measure heights with patriots, let
them stand
Beside the man in his Oporto shroud,
  And each vouchsafe to take him by
the hand,
And kiss him on the cheek, and say
aloud,—
  'Thou, too, hast suffered for our
native land !
My brother, thou art one of us ! be
proud.'

Still, graves, when Italy is talked upon.
Still, still, the patriot's tomb, the
stranger's hate.
  Still Niobe ! still fainting in the sun,
By whose most dazzling arrows violate
  Her beauteous offspring perished !
has she won
Nothing but garlands for the graves,
from Fate ?
  Nothing but death-songs ?—Yes, be it
understood
Life throbs in noble Piedmont ! while
the feet
  Of Rome's clay image, dabbled soft
in blood,

Grow flat with dissolution, and, as meet,
  Will soon be shovelled off like other
mud,
To leave the passage free in church and
street.
  And I, who first took hope up in this
song,
Because a child was singing one . . .
behold,
  The hope and omen were not, haply,
wrong !
Poets are soothsayers still, like those
of old
  Who studied flights of doves,—and
creatures young
And tender, mighty meanings may un-
fold.

The sun strikes, through the windows,
up the floor ;
  Stand out in it, my own young Florentine,
Not two years old, and let me see
thee more !
  It grows along thy amber curls, to
shine
Brighter than elsewhere. Now, look
straight before,
  And fix thy brave blue English eyes on
mine,
And from my soul, which fronts the
future so,
  With unabashed and unabated gaze,
Teach me to hope for, what the angels
know
  When they smile clear as thou dost.
Down God's ways
With just alighted feet, between the
snow
  And snowdrops, where a little lamb may
graze,
Thou hast no fear, my lamb, about the
road,
  Albeit in our vain-glory we assume
That, less than we have, thou hast
learnt of God.
  Stand out, my blue-eyed prophet !—thou,
to whom
The earliest world-day light that ever
flowed,
  Through Casa Guidi windows, chanced
to come !
Now shake the glittering nimbus of
thy hair,

And be God's witness that the elemental
New springs of life are gushing every-
where
To cleanse the water-courses, and pre-
vent all
Concrete obstructions which infest the
air!
That earth's alive, and gentle or ungentle
Motions within her, signify but
growth!—
The ground swells greenest o'er the
labouring moles.

Howe'er the uneasy world is vexed
and wroth,
Young children, lifted high on parent
souls,
Look round them with a smile upon
the mouth,
And take for music every bell that tolls;

(Who said we should be better if like
these?)
But *we* sit murmuring for the future though
Posterity is smiling on our knees,
Convicting us of folly.   Let us go—
We will trust God.   The blank inter-
stices
Men take for ruins, He will build into
With pillared marbles rare, or knit
across
With generous arches, till the fane's
complete.
This world has no perdition, if some
loss.

Such cheer I gather from thy smiling,
Sweet!
The self-same cherub-faces which em-
boss
The Vail, lean inward to the Mercy-seat.

AURORA LEIGH

A POEM, IN NINE BOOKS.

DEDICATION TO JOHN KENYON, ESQ.

THE words 'cousin' and 'friend' are constantly recurring in this poem, the last pages of which have been finished under the hospitality of your roof, my own dearest cousin and friend;—cousin and friend, in a sense of less equality and greater disinterestedness than ' Romney ' 's.

Ending, therefore, and preparing once more to quit England, I venture to leave in your hands this book, the most mature of my works, and the one into which my highest convictions upon Life and Art have entered; that as, through my various efforts in literature and steps in life, you have believed in me, borne with me, and been generous to me, far beyond the common uses of mere relationship or sympathy of mind, so you may kindly accept, in sight of the public, this poor sign of esteem, gratitude, and affection from

Your unforgetting

E. B. B.

39 DEVONSHIRE PLACE,
October 17, 1856.

AURORA LEIGH

FIRST BOOK

OF writing many books there is no end;
And I who have written much in prose
and verse
For others' uses, will write now for
mine,—
Will write my story for my better self
As when you paint your portrait for a
friend,
Who keeps it in a drawer and looks at it
Long after he has ceased to love you, just
To hold together what he was and is.

I, writing thus, am still what men call
young,
I have not so far left the coasts of life
To travel inland, that I cannot hear
That murmur of the outer Infinite
Which unweaned babies smile at in their
sleep
When wondered at for smiling; not so
far,
But still I catch my mother at her post
Beside the nursery-door, with finger up,
'Hush, hush—here 's too much noise!'
while her sweet eyes

Leap forward, taking part against her
word
In the child's riot. Still I sit and feel
My father's slow hand, when she had
left us both,
Stroke out my childish curls across his
knee,
And hear Assunta's daily jest (she knew
He liked it better than a better jest)
Inquire how many golden scudi went
To make such ringlets. O my father's
hand,
Stroke heavily, heavily the poor hair
down,
Draw, press the child's head closer to
thy knee!
I'm still too young, too young, to sit
alone.

I write. My mother was a Florentine,
Whose rare blue eyes were shut from
seeing me
When scarcely I was four years old, my
life
A poor spark snatched up from a failing
lamp

Which went out therefore. She was
  weak and frail;
She could not bear the joy of giving life,
The mother's rapture slew her. If her
  kiss
Had left a longer weight upon my lips
It might have steadied the uneasy breath,
And reconciled and fraternized my soul
With the new order. As it was, indeed,
I felt a mother-want about the world,
And still went seeking, like a bleating
  lamb
Left out at night in shutting up the fold,—
As restless as a nest-deserted bird
Grown chill through something being
  away, though what
It knows not. I, Aurora Leigh, was born
To make my father sadder, and myself
Not overjoyous, truly. Women know
The way to rear up children (to be just),
They know a simple, merry, tender
  knack
Of tying sashes, fitting baby-shoes,
And stringing pretty words that make
  no sense,
And kissing full sense into empty words,
Which things are corals to cut life upon,
Although such trifles : children learn by
  such,
Love's holy earnest in a pretty play
And get not over-early solemnized,
But seeing, as in a rose-bush, Love's
  Divine
Which burns and hurts not,—not a
  single bloom,—
Become aware and unafraid of Love.
Such good do mothers. Fathers love as
  well
—Mine did, I know,—but still with
  heavier brains,
And wills more consciously responsible,
And not as wisely, since less foolishly ;
So mothers have God's licence to be
  missed.

My father was an austere Englishman,
Who, after a dry lifetime spent at home
In college-learning, law, and parish talk,
Was flooded with a passion unaware,
His whole provisioned and complacent
  past
Drowned out from him that moment.
  As he stood

In Florence, where he had come to spend
  a month
And note the secret of Da Vinci's drains,
He musing somewhat absently perhaps
Some English question . . whether men
  should pay
The unpopular but necessary tax
With left or right hand—in the alien sun
In that great square of the Santissima
There drifted past him (scarcely marked
  enough
To move his comfortable island scorn)
A train of priestly banners, cross and
  psalm,
The white-veiled rose-crowned maidens
  holding up
Tall tapers, weighty for such wrists,
  aslant
To the blue luminous tremor of the air,
And letting drop the white wax as they
  went
To eat the bishop's wafer at the church ;
From which long trail of chanting priests
  and girls,
A face flashed like a cymbal on his face
And shook with silent clangour brain
  and heart,
Transfiguring him to music. Thus, even
  thus,
He too received his sacramental gift
With eucharistic meanings ; for he loved.

And thus beloved, she died. I've heard
  it said
That but to see him in the first surprise
Of widower and father, nursing me,
Unmothered little child of four years old,
His large man's hands afraid to touch
  my curls,
As if the gold would tarnish,—his grave
  lips
Contriving such a miserable smile
As if he knew needs must, or I should die,
And yet 'twas hard,—would almost make
  the stones
Cry out for pity. There's a verse he set
In Santa Croce to her memory,—
'Weep for an infant too young to weep
  much
When death removed this mother'—stops
  the mirth
To-day on women's faces when they
  walk

With rosy children hanging on their
    gowns,
Under the cloister to escape the sun
That scorches in the piazza. After which
He left our Florence and made haste to
    hide
Himself, his prattling child, and silent
    grief,
Among the mountains above Pelago ;
Because unmothered babes, he thought,
    had need
Of mother nature more than others use,
And Pan's white goats, with udders
    warm and full
Of mystic contemplations, come to feed
Poor milkless lips of orphans like his
    own—
Such scholar-scraps he talked, I've heard
    from friends,
For even prosaic men who wear grief
    long
Will get to wear it as a hat aside
With a flower stuck in 't. Father, then,
    and child,
We lived among the mountains many
    years,
God's silence on the outside of the house,
And we who did not speak too loud
    within,
And old Assunta to make up the fire,
Crossing herself whene'er a sudden
    flame
Which lightened from the firewood, made
    alive
That picture of my mother on the wall.

The painter drew it after she was dead,
And when the face was finished, throat
    and hands,
Her cameriera carried him, in hate
Of the English-fashioned shroud, the last
    brocade
She dressed in at the Pitti ; 'he should
    paint
No sadder thing than that,' she swore,
    ' to wrong
Her poor signora.' Therefore very
    strange
The effect was. I, a little child, would
    crouch
For hours upon the floor with knees
    drawn up,
And gaze across them, half in terror, half

In adoration, at the picture there,—
That swan-like supernatural white life
Just sailing upward from the red stiff silk
Which seemed to have no part in it nor
    power
To keep it from quite breaking out of
    bounds,
For hours I sate and stared. Assunta's
    awe
And my poor father's melancholy eyes
Still pointed that way. That way went
    my thoughts
When wandering beyond sight. And
    as I grew
In years, I mixed, confused, uncon-
    sciously,
Whatever I last read or heard or dreamed,
Abhorrent, admirable, beautiful,
Pathetical, or ghastly, or grotesque,
With still that face . . . which did not
    therefore change,
But kept the mystic level of all forms,
Hates, fears, and admirations, was by
    turns
Ghost, fiend, and angel, fairy, witch,
    and sprite,
A dauntless Muse who eyes a dreadful
    Fate,
A loving Psyche who loses sight of Love,
A still Medusa with mild milky brows
All curdled and all clothed upon with
    snakes
Whose slime falls fast as sweat will ; or
    anon
Our Lady of the Passion, stabbed with
    swords
Where the Babe sucked ; or Lamia in
    her first
Moonlighted pallor, ere she shrunk and
    blinked
And shuddering wriggled down to the
    unclean ;
Or my own mother, leaving her last smile
In her last kiss upon the baby-mouth
My father pushed down on the bed for
    that,—
Or my dead mother, without smile or
    kiss.
Buried at Florence. All which images,
Concentred on the picture, glassed them-
    selves
Before my meditative childhood, as
The incoherencies of change and death

Are represented fully, mixed and merged,
In the smooth fair mystery of perpetual
    Life.

And while I stared away my childish
    wits
Upon my mother's picture (ah, poor
    child!)
My father, who through love had suddenly
Thrown off the old conventions, broken
    loose
From chin-bands of the soul, like Lazarus,
Yet had no time to learn to talk and walk
Or grow anew familiar with the sun,—
Who had reached to freedom, not to
    action, lived,
But lived as one entranced, with thoughts,
    not aims,—
Whom love had unmade from a common
    man
But not completed to an uncommon
    man,—
My father taught me what he had learnt
    the best
Before he died and left me,—grief and
    love.
And, seeing we had books among the
    hills,
Strong words of counselling souls confederate
With vocal pines and waters,—out of
    books
He taught me all the ignorance of men,
And how God laughs in heaven when any
    man
Says 'Here I'm learned; this, I understand;
In that, I am never caught at fault or
    doubt.'
He sent the schools to school, demonstrating
A fool will pass for such through one
    mistake,
While a philosopher will pass for such,
Through said mistakes being ventured
    in the gross
And heaped up to a system.
                                    I am like,
They tell me, my dear father. Broader
    brows
Howbeit, upon a slenderer undergrowth
Of delicate features,—paler, near as
    grave;

But then my mother's smile breaks up the
    whole,
And makes it better sometimes than itself.

So, nine full years, our days were hid
    with God
Among His mountains: I was just thirteen,
Still growing like the plants from unseen
    roots
In tongue-tied Springs,—and suddenly
    awoke
To full life and life's needs and agonies
With an intense, strong, struggling
    heart beside
A stone-dead father. Life, struck sharp
    on death,
Makes awful lightning. His last word
    was, 'Love'—
'Love, my child, love, love!'—(then he
    had done with grief)
'Love, my child.' Ere I answered he
    was gone,
And none was left to love in all the world.

There, ended childhood. What succeeded next
I recollect as, after fevers, men
Thread back the passage of delirium,
Missing the turn still, baffled by the door;
Smooth endless days, notched here and
    there with knives;
A weary, wormy darkness, spurred i'
    the flank
With flame, that it should eat and end
    itself
Like some tormented scorpion. Then
    at last
I do remember clearly, how there came
A stranger with authority, not right
(I thought not), who commanded, caught
    me up
From old Assunta's neck; how, with a
    shriek,
She let me go,—while I, with ears too full
Of my father's silence to shriek back
    a word,
In all a child's astonishment at grief
Stared at the wharf-edge where she
    stood and moaned,
My poor Assunta, where she stood and
    moaned!
The white walls, the blue hills, my Italy,

Drawn backward from the shuddering
    steamer-deck,
Like one in anger drawing back her
    skirts
Which suppliants catch at. Then the
    bitter sea
Inexorably pushed between us both,
And sweeping up the ship with my
    despair
Threw us out as a pasture to the stars.

Ten nights and days we voyaged on the
    deep;
Ten nights and days without the common
    face
Of any day or night; the moon and sun
Cut off from the green reconciling earth,
To starve into a blind ferocity
And glare unnatural; the very sky
(Dropping its bell-net down upon the sea
As if no human heart should 'scape alive,)
Bedraggled with the desolating salt,
Until it seemed no more that holy heaven
To which my father went. All new
    and strange;
The universe turned stranger, for a child.

Then, land!—then, England! oh, the
    frosty cliffs
Looked cold upon me. Could I find a
    home
Among those mean red houses through
    the fog?
And when I heard my father's language
    first
From alien lips which had no kiss for mine
I wept aloud, then laughed, then wept,
    then wept,
And some one near me said the child
    was mad
Through much sea-sickness. The train
    swept us on.
Was this my father's England? the great
    isle?
The ground seemed cut up from the
    fellowship
Of verdure, field from field, as man from
    man;
The skies themselves looked low and
    positive,
As almost you could touch them with
    a hand,
And dared to do it they were so far off

From God's celestial crystals; all things
    blurred
And dull and vague. Did Shakespeare
    and his mates.
Absorb the light here?—not a hill or stone
With heart to strike a radiant colour up
Or active outline on the indifferent air.

I think I see my father's sister stand
Upon the hall-step of her country-house
To give me welcome. She stood straight
    and calm,
Her somewhat narrow forehead braided
    tight
As if for taming accidental thoughts
From possible pulses; brown hair
    pricked with grey
By frigid use of life (she was not old
Although my father's elder by a year),
A nose drawn sharply, yet in delicate
    lines;
A close mild mouth, a little soured about
The ends, through speaking unrequited
    loves
Or peradventure niggardly half-truths;
Eyes of no colour,—once they might
    have smiled,
But never, never have forgot themselves
In smiling; cheeks, in which was yet
    a rose
Of perished summers, like a rose in a
    book,
Kept more for ruth than pleasure,—if
    past bloom,
Past fading also.

               She had lived, we'll say,
A harmless life, she called a virtuous life,
A quiet life, which was not life at all
(But that, she had not lived enough to
    know),
Between the vicar and the county squires,
The lord-lieutenant looking down some-
    times
From the empyrean to assure their souls
Against chance-vulgarisms, and, in the
    abyss
The apothecary, looked on once a year
To prove their soundness of humility.
The poor-club exercised her Christian
    gifts
Of knitting stockings, stitching petticoats,
Because we are of one flesh after all
And need one flannel (with a proper sense

Of difference in the quality)—and still
The book-club, guarded from your
  modern trick
Of shaking dangerous questions from the
  crease,
Preserved her intellectual. She had lived
A sort of cage-bird life, born in a cage,
Accounting that to leap from perch to
  perch
Was act and joy enough for any bird.
Dear heaven, how silly are the things
  that live
In thickets, and eat berries !
                              I, alas,
A wild bird scarcely fledged, was brought
  to her cage,
And she was there to meet me. Very kind.
Bring the clean water, give out the fresh
  seed.

She stood upon the steps to welcome me,
Calm, in black garb. I clung about her
  neck,—
Young babes, who catch at every shred
  of wool
To draw the new light closer, catch and
  cling
Less blindly. In my ears, my father's
  word
Hummed ignorantly, as the sea in shells,
' Love, love, my child.' She, black there
  with my grief,
Might feel my love— she was his sister
  once,
I clung to her. A moment she seemed
  moved,
Kissed me with cold lips, suffered me
  to cling,
And drew me feebly through the hall into
The room she sate in.
        There, with some strange spasm
Of pain and passion, she wrung loose
  my hands
Imperiously, and held me at arm's length,
And with two grey-steel naked-bladed
  eyes
Searched through my face,—aye, stabbed
  it through and through,
Through brows and cheeks and chin, as
  if to find
A wicked murderer in my innocent face,
If not here, there perhaps. Then,
  drawing breath,

She struggled for her ordinary calm
And missed it rather,—told me not to
  shrink,
As if she had told me not to lie or swear,—
' She loved my father and would love
  me too
As long as I deserved it.' Very kind.

I understood her meaning afterward ;
She thought to find my mother in my face,
And questioned it for that. For she,
  my aunt,
Had loved my father truly, as she could,
And hated, with the gall of gentle souls,
My Tuscan mother who had fooled away
A wise man from wise courses, a good man
From obvious duties, and, depriving her,
His sister, of the household precedence,
Had wronged his tenants, robbed his
  native land,
And made him mad, alike by life and death,
In love and sorrow. She had pored for
  years
What sort of woman could be suitable
To her sort of hate, to entertain it with,
And so, her very curiosity
Became hate too, and all the idealism
She ever used in life, was used for hate,
Till hate, so nourished, did exceed at last
The love from which it grew, in strength
  and heat,
And wrinkled her smooth conscience
  with a sense
Of disputable virtue (say not, sin)
When Christian doctrine was enforced
  at church.

And thus my father's sister was to me
My mother's hater. From that day, she did
Her duty to me (I appreciate it
In her own word as spoken to herself),
Her duty, in large measure, well-pressed
  out,
But measured always. She was generous,
  bland,
More courteous than was tender, gave
  me still
The first place,—as if fearful that God's
  saints
Would look down suddenly and say,
      ' Herein
You missed a point, I think, through
  lack of love.'

Alas, a mother never is afraid
Of speaking angerly to any child,
Since love, she knows, is justified of love.

And I, I was a good child on the whole,
A meek and manageable child. Why not?
I did not live, to have the faults of life:
There seemed more true life in my
    father's grave
Than in all England. Since *that* threw
    me off
Who fain would cleave (his latest will,
    they say,
Consigned me to his land), I only thought
Of lying quiet there where I was thrown
Like sea-weed on the rocks, and suffer-
    ing her
To prick me to a pattern with her pin
Fibre from fibre, delicate leaf from leaf,
And dry out from my drowned anatomy
The last sea-salt left in me.
                 So it was.
I broke the copious curls upon my head
In braids, because she liked smooth-
    ordered hair.
I left off saying my sweet Tuscan words
Which still at any stirring of the heart
Came up to float across the English phrase
As lilies (*Bene* or *Che che*), because
She liked my father's child to speak his
    tongue.
I learnt the collects and the catechism,
The creeds, from Athanasius back to Nice,
The Articles, the Tracts *against* the times
(By no means Buonaventure's 'Prick of
    Love'),
And various popular synopses of
Inhuman doctrines never taught by John,
Because she liked instructed piety.
I learnt my complement of classic French
(Kept pure of Balzac and neologism)
And German also, since she liked a range
Of liberal education,—tongues, not books.
I learnt a little algebra, a little
Of the mathematics,—brushed with
    extreme flounce
The circle of the sciences, because
She misliked women who are frivolous.
I learnt the royal genealogies
Of Oviedo, the internal laws
Of the Burmese empire,—by how many
    feet
Mount Chimborazo outsoars Teneriffe,

What navigable river joins itself
To Lara, and what census of the year
    five
Was taken at Klagenfurt,—because she
    liked
A general insight into useful facts.
I learnt much music,—such as would
    have been
As quite impossible in Johnson's day
As still it might be wished—fine sleights
    of hand
And unimagined fingering, shuffling off
The hearer's soul through hurricanes of
    notes
To a noisy Tophet; and I drew . . .
From French engravings, nereids neatly
    draped,
(With smirks of simmering godship)—
    I washed in
Landscapes from nature (rather say,
    washed out).
I danced the polka and Cellarius,
Spun glass, stuffed birds, and modelled
    flowers in wax,
Because she liked accomplishments in
    girls.
I read a score of books on womanhood
To prove, if women do not think at all,
They may teach thinking (to a maiden-
    aunt
Or else the author),—books that boldly
    assert
Their right of comprehending husband's
    talk
When not too deep, and even of answering
With pretty 'may it please you,' or 'so
    it is,'—
Their rapid insight and fine aptitude,
Particular worth and general missionari-
    ness,
As long as they keep quiet by the fire
And never say 'no' when the world
    says 'aye,'
For that is fatal,—their angelic reach
Of virtue, chiefly used to sit and darn,
And fatten household sinners,—their, in
    brief,
Potential faculty in everything
Of abdicating power in it: she owned
She liked a woman to be womanly,
And English women, she thanked God
    and sighed

(Some people always sigh in thanking
    God),
Were models to the universe. And last
I learnt cross-stitch, because she did not
    like
To see me wear the night with empty
    hands
A-doing nothing. So, my shepherdess
Was something after all (the pastoral
    saints
Be praised for 't), leaning lovelorn with
    pink eyes
To match her shoes, when I mistook the
    silks ;
Her head uncrushed by that round
    weight of hat
So strangely similar to the tortoise-shell
Which slew the tragic poet.
                 By the way,
The works of women are symbolical.
We sew, sew, prick our fingers, dull
    our sight,
Producing what ? A pair of slippers, sir,
To put on when you're weary—or a stool
To stumble over and vex you .. 'curse
    that stool !'
Or else at best, a cushion, where you lean
And sleep, and dream of something we
    are not
But would be for your sake. Alas, alas !
This hurts most, this—that, after all, we
    are paid
The worth of our work, perhaps.
               In looking down
Those years of education (to return)
I wonder if Brinvilliers suffered more
In the water-torture, .. flood succeeding
    flood
To drench the incapable throat and split
    the veins.
Than I did. Certain of your feebler souls
Go out in such a process ; many pine
To a sick, inodorous light ; my own
    endured :
I had relations in the Unseen, and drew
The elemental nutriment and heat
From nature, as earth feels the sun at
    nights,
Or as a babe sucks surely in the dark.
I kept the life thrust on me, on the outside
Of the inner life with all its ample room
For heart and lungs, for will and intellect,
Inviolable by conventions. God,

I thank thee for that grace of thine !
               At first
I felt no life which was not patience,—did
The thing she bade me, without heed
    to a thing
Beyond it, sate in just the chair she placed,
With back against the window, to exclude
The sight of the great lime-tree on the
    lawn,
Which seemed to have come on purpose
    from the woods
To bring the house a message,—aye, and
    walked
Demurely in her carpeted low rooms,
As if I should not, hearkening my own
    steps,
Misdoubt I was alive. I read her books,
Was civil to her cousin, Romney Leigh,
Gave ear to her vicar, tea to her visitors,
And heard them whisper, when I
    changed a cup
(I blushed for joy at that),—' The Italian
    child,
For all her blue eyes and her quiet ways,
Thrives ill in England : she is paler yet
Than when we came the last time ; she
    will die.'

' Will die.' My cousin, Romney Leigh,
    blushed too,
With sudden anger, and approaching me
Said low between his teeth, ' You're
    wicked now ?
You wish to die and leave the world
    a-dusk
For others, with your naughty light
    blown out ?'
I looked into his face defyingly ;
He might have known that, being what
    I was,
'Twas natural to like to get away
As far as dead folk can : and then indeed
Some people make no trouble when
    they die.
He turned and went abruptly, slammed
    the door
And shut his dog out.
             Romney, Romney Leigh.
I have not named my cousin hitherto,
And yet I used him as a sort of friend ;
My elder by few years, but cold and shy
And absent .. tender, when he thought
    of it,

Which scarcely was imperative, grave
    betimes,
As well as early master of Leigh Hall,
Whereof the nightmare sate upon his
    youth
Repressing all its seasonable delights
And agonizing with a ghastly sense
Of universal hideous want and wrong
To incriminate possession. When he
    came
From college to the country, very oft
He crossed the hill on visits to my aunt,
With gifts of blue grapes from the hot-
    houses,
A book in one hand,—mere statistics (if
I chanced to lift the cover), count of all
The goats whose beards grow sprouting
    down toward hell
Against God's separative judgement-hour.
And she, she almost loved him,—even
    allowed
That sometimes he should seem to sigh
    my way ;
It made him easier to be pitiful,
And sighing was his gift. So, undisturbed
At whiles she let him shut my music up
And push my needles down, and lead
    me out
To see in that south angle of the house
The figs grow black as if by a Tuscan rock,
On some light pretext.   She would
    turn her head
At other moments, go to fetch a thing,
And leave me breath enough to speak
    with him,
For his sake ; it was simple.
                Sometimes too
He would have saved me utterly, it
    seemed,
He stood and looked so.
              Once, he stood so near
He dropped a sudden hand upon my head
Bent down on woman's work, as soft
    as rain —
But then I rose and shook it off as fire,
The stranger's touch that took my
    father's place
Yet dared seem soft.
          I used him for a friend
Before I ever knew him for a friend.
'Twas better, 'twas worse also, afterward :
We came so close, we saw our differences
Too intimately. Always Romney Leigh

Was looking for the worms, I for the
    gods.
A godlike nature his ; the gods look down,
Incurious of themselves ; and certainly
'Tis well I should remember, how, those
    days,
I was a worm too and he looked on me.

A little by his act perhaps, yet more
By something in me, surely not my will,
I did not die. But slowly, as one in
    swoon,
To whom life creeps back in the form of
    death,
With a sense of separation, a blind pain
Of blank obstruction, and a roar i' the ears
Of visionary chariots which retreat
As earth grows clearer . . slowly, by
    degrees,
I woke, rose up . . where was I ? in the
    world ;
For uses therefore I must count worth
    while.

I had a little chamber in the house,
As green as any privet-hedge a bird
Might choose to build in, though the
    nest itself
Could show but dead-brown sticks and
    straws ; the walls
Were green, the carpet was pure green,
    the straight
Small bed was curtained greenly, and
    the folds
Hung green about the window which
    let in
The outdoor world with all its greenery.
You could not push your head out and
    escape
A dash of dawn-dew from the honey-
    suckle,
But so you were baptized into the grace
And privilege of seeing. . .
              First, the lime
(I had enough there, of the lime, be sure,—
My morning-dream was often hummed
    away
By the bees in it), past the lime, the
    lawn,
Which, after sweeping broadly round
    the house,
Went trickling through the shrubberies
    in a stream

Of tender turf, and wore and lost itself
Among the acacias, over which you saw
The irregular line of elms by the deep lane
Which stopped the grounds and dammed
   the overflow
Of arbutus and laurel. Out of sight
The lane was ; sunk so deep, no foreign
   tramp
Nor drover of wild ponies out of Wales
Could guess if lady's hall or tenant's
   lodge
Dispensed such odours,—though his
   stick well-crooked
Might reach the lowest trail of blossom-
   ing brier
Which dipped upon the wall. Behind
   the elms,
And through their tops, you saw the
   folded hills
Striped up and down with hedges
   (burly oaks
Projecting from the line to show them-
   selves),
Through which my cousin Romney's
   chimneys smoked
As still as when a silent mouth in frost
Breathes, showing where the woodlands
   hid Leigh Hall ;
While, far above, a jut of table-land,
A promontory without water, stretch-
   ed,—
You could not catch it if the days were
   thick,
Or took it for a cloud ; but, otherwise,
The vigorous sun would catch it up at eve
And use it for an anvil till he had filled
The shelves of heaven with burning
   thunderbolts,
Protesting against night and darkness :—
   then,
When all his setting trouble was resolved
To a trance of passive glory, you might see
In apparition on the golden sky
(Alas, my Giotto's background !) the
   sheep run
Along the fine clear outline, small as mice
That run along a witch's scarlet thread.

Not a grand nature. Not my chestnut-
   woods
Of Vallombrosa, cleaving by the spurs
To the precipices. Not my headlong leaps
Of waters, that cry out for joy or fear

In leaping through the palpitating pines,
Like a white soul tossed out to eternity
With thrills of time upon it. Not indeed
My multitudinous mountains, sitting in
The magic circle, with the mutual touch
Electric, panting from their full deep
   hearts
Beneath the influent heavens, and
   waiting for
Communion and commission. Italy
Is one thing, England one.
           On English ground
You understand the letter,—ere the fall
How Adam lived in a garden. All the
   fields
Are tied up fast with hedges, nosegay-
   like ;
The hills are crumpled plains, the plains
   parterres,
The trees, round, woolly, ready to be
   clipped,
And if you seek for any wilderness
You find, at best, a park. A nature tamed
And grown domestic like a barn-door
   fowl,
Which does not awe you with its claws
   and beak
Nor tempt you to an eyrie too high up,
But which, in cackling, sets you
   thinking of
Your eggs to-morrow at breakfast, in
   the pause
Of finer meditation.
           Rather say,
A sweet familiar nature, stealing in
As a dog might, or child, to touch your
   hand
Or pluck your gown, and humbly mind
   you so
Of presence and affection, excellent
For inner uses, from the things without.

I could not be unthankful, I who was
Entreated thus and holpen. In the room
I speak of, ere the house was well awake,
And also after it was well asleep,
I sate alone, and drew the blessing in
Of all that nature. With a gradual step,
A stir among the leaves, a breath, a ray,
It came in softly, while the angels made
A place for it beside me. The moon came,
And swept my chamber clean of foolish
   thoughts.

The sun came, saying, 'Shall I lift this
    light
Against the lime-tree, and you will not
    look?
I make the birds sing—listen! but, for
    you,
God never hears your voice, excepting
    when
You lie upon the bed at nights and weep.'

Then, something moved me. Then,
    I wakened up
More slowly than I verily write now,
But wholly, at last, I wakened, opened
    wide
The window and my soul, and let the airs
And outdoor sights sweep gradual
    gospels in,
Regenerating what I was. O Life,
How oft we throw it off and think,—
    'Enough,
Enough of life in so much!—here's a
    cause
For rupture;—herein we must break
    with Life,
Or be ourselves unworthy; here we are
    wronged,
Maimed, spoiled for aspiration: farewell
    Life!'
And so, as froward babes, we hide our eyes
And think all ended.—Then, Life calls
    to us
In some transformed, apocalyptic voice,
Above us, or below us, or around:
Perhaps we name it Nature's voice, or
    Love's,
Tricking ourselves, because we are
    more ashamed
To own our compensations than our
    griefs:
Still, Life's voice!—still, we make our
    peace with Life.

And I, so young then, was not sullen.
    Soon
I used to get up early, just to sit
And watch the morning quicken in the
    grey,
And hear the silence open like a flower
Leaf after leaf,—and stroke with listless
    hand
The woodbine through the window, till
    at last

I came to do it with a sort of love,
At foolish unaware: whereat I smiled,—
A melancholy smile, to catch myself
Smiling for joy.
                    Capacity for joy
Admits temptation. It seemed, next,
    worth while
To dodge the sharp sword set against
    my life;
To slip downstairs through all the
    sleepy house,
As mute as any dream there, and escape
As a soul from the body, out of doors,
Glide through the shrubberies, drop
    into the lane,
And wander on the hills an hour or two,
Then back again before the house should
    stir.

Or else I sate on in my chamber green,
And lived my life, and thought my
    thoughts, and prayed
My prayers without the vicar; read my
    books,
Without considering whether they were
    fit
To do me good. Mark, there. We
    get no good
By being ungenerous, even to a book,
And calculating profits,—so much help
By so much reading. It is rather when
We gloriously forget ourselves and
    plunge
Soul-forward, headlong, into a book's
    profound,
Impassioned for its beauty and salt of
    truth—
'Tis then we get the right good from
    a book.

I read much. What my father taught
    before
From many a volume, Love re-empha-
    sized
Upon the self-same pages: Theophrast
Grew tender with the memory of his eyes,
And Aelian made mine wet. The trick
    of Greek
And Latin, he had taught me, as he would
Have taught me wrestling or the game
    of fives
If such he had known,—most like a
    shipwrecked man

Who heaps his single platter with goats'
    cheese
And scarlet berries ; or like any man
Who loves but one, and so gives all at once,
Because he has it, rather than because
He counts it worthy. Thus, my father
    gave ;
And thus, as did the women formerly
By young Achilles, when they pinned
    a veil
Across the boy's audacious front, and
    swept
With tuneful laughs the silver-fretted
    rocks,
He wrapt his little daughter in his large
Man's doublet, careless did it fit or no.

But, after I had read for memory,
I read for hope. The path my father's foot
Had trod me out (which suddenly broke
    off
What time he dropped the wallet of the
    flesh
And passed) alone I carried on, and set
My child-heart 'gainst the thorny under-
    wood,
To reach the grassy shelter of the trees.
Ah babe i' the wood, without a brother-
    babe !
My own self-pity, like the red-breast bird,
Flies back to cover all that past with
    leaves.

Sublimest danger, over which none
    weeps,
When any young wayfaring soul goes
    forth
Alone, unconscious of the perilous road,
The day-sun dazzling in his limpid eyes,
To thrust his own way, he an alien,
    through
The world of books! Ah, you!—you
    think it fine,
You clap hands—'A fair day!'—you
    cheer him on,
As if the worst, could happen, were to rest
Too long beside a fountain. Yet, behold,
Behold!—the world of books is still the
    world,
And worldlings in it are less merciful
And more puissant. For the wicked there
Are winged like angels ; every knife
    that strikes

Is edged from elemental fire to assail
A spiritual life ; the beautiful seems right
By force of beauty, and the feeble wrong
Because of weakness ; power is justified
Though armed against Saint Michael ;
    many a crown
Covers bald foreheads. In the book-
    world, true,
There's no lack, neither, of God's saints
    and kings,
That shake the ashes of the grave aside
From their calm locks and undiscomfited
Look steadfast truths against Time's
    changing mask.
True, many a prophet teaches in the
    roads ;
True, many a seer pulls down the
    flaming heavens
Upon his own head in strong martyrdom
In order to light men a moment's space.
But stay !—who judges?—who dis-
    tinguishes
'Twixt Saul and Nahash justly, at first
    sight,
And leaves king Saul precisely at the sin,
To serve king David? who discerns at
    once
The sound of the trumpets, when the
    trumpets blow
For Alaric as well as Charlemagne?
Who judges wizards, and can tell true
    seers
From conjurors? the child, there?
    Would you leave
That child to wander in a battle-field
And push his innocent smile against the
    guns ;
Or even in a catacomb,—his torch
Grown ragged in the fluttering air, and
    all
The dark a-mutter round him ? not a child.

I read books bad and good—some bad
    and good
At once (good aims not always make
    good books :
Well-tempered spades turn up ill-
    smelling soils
In digging vineyards even) ; books that
    prove
God's being so definitely, that man's
    doubt
Grows self-defined the other side the line,

Made atheist by suggestion; moral books,
Exasperating to licence ; genial books,
Discounting from the human dignity ;
And merry books, which set you weep-
    ing when
The sun shines,—aye, and melancholy
    books,
Which make you laugh that any one
    should weep
In this disjointed life for one wrong more.

The world of books is still the world,
    I write,
And both worlds have God's providence,
    thank God,
To keep and hearten: with some struggle,
    indeed,
Among the breakers, some hard swim-
    ming through
The deeps—I lost breath in my soul
    sometimes
And cried, ' God save me if there 's any
    God,'
But, even so, God saved me ; and, being
    dashed
From error on to error, every turn
Still brought me nearer to the central
    truth.

I thought so. All this anguish in the
    thick
Of men's opinions .. press and counter-
    press,
Now up, now down, now underfoot, and
    now
Emergent .. all the best of it, perhaps,
But throws you back upon a noble trust
And use of your own instinct,—merely
    proves
Pure reason stronger than bare inference
At strongest. Try it,—fix against heaven's
    wall
The scaling-ladders of school logic—
    mount
Step by step !—sight goes faster ; that
    still ray
Which strikes out from you, how, you
    cannot tell,
And why, you know not (did you elim-
    inate,
That such as you indeed should analyse ?),
Goes straight and fast as light, and high
    as God.

The cygnet finds the water, but the man
Is born in ignorance of his element
And feels out blind at first, disorganized
By sin i' the blood,—his spirit-insight
    dulled
And crossed by his sensations. Presently
He feels it quicken in the dark sometimes,
When, mark, be reverent, be obedient,
For such dumb motions of imperfect life
Are oracles of vital Deity
Attesting the Hereafter. Let who says
' The soul's a clean white paper,' rather
    say,
A palimpsest, a prophet's holograph
Defiled, erased and covered by a monk's,—
The apocalypse, by a Longus ! poring on
Which obscene text, we may discern
    perhaps
Some fair, fine trace of what was written
    once,
Some upstroke of an alpha and omega
Expressing the old scripture.
                    Books, books, books !
I had found the secret of a garret-room
Piled high with cases in my father's name,
Piled high, packed large,—where, creep-
    ing in and out
Among the giant fossils of my past,
Like some small nimble mouse between
    the ribs
Of a mastodon, I nibbled here and there
At this or that box, pulling through the
    gap,
In heats of terror, haste, victorious joy,
The first book first. And how I felt it beat
Under my pillow, in the morning's dark,
An hour before the sun would let me read !
My books ! At last because the time was
    ripe,
I chanced upon the poets.
                    As the earth
Plunges in fury, when the internal fires
Have reached and pricked her heart, and,
    throwing flat
The marts and temples, the triumphal
    gates
And towers of observation, clears herself
To elemental freedom—thus, my soul,
At poetry's divine first finger-touch,
Let go conventions and sprang up sur-
    prised,
Convicted of the great eternities
Before two worlds.

What's this, Aurora Leigh,
You write so of the poets, and not laugh?
Those virtuous liars, dreamers after dark,
Exaggerators of the sun and moon,
And soothsayers in a tea-cup?
            I write so
Of the only truth-tellers now left to God,
The only speakers of essential truth,
Opposed to relative, comparative,
And temporal truths; the only holders by
His sun-skirts, through conventional
        grey glooms;
The only teachers who instruct mankind
From just a shadow on a charnel-wall
To find man's veritable stature out
Erect, sublime,—the measure of a man,
And that's the measure of an angel, says
The apostle. Aye, and while your com-
        mon men
Lay telegraphs, gauge railroads, reign,
        reap, dine,
And dust the flaunty carpets of the world
For kings to walk on, or our president,
The poet suddenly will catch them up
With his voice like a thunder,—'This is
        soul,
This is life, this word is being said in
        heaven,
Here's God down on us! what are you
        about?'
How all those workers start amid their
        work,
Look round, look up, and feel, a mo-
        ment's space,
That carpet-dusting, though a pretty
        trade,
Is not the imperative labour after all.

My own best poets, am I one with you,
That thus I love you,—or but one
        through love?
Does all this smell of thyme about my feet
Conclude my visit to your holy hill
In personal presence, or but testify
The rustling of your vesture through my
        dreams
With influent odours? When my joy
        and pain,
My thought and aspiration, like the stops
Of pipe or flute, are absolutely dumb
Unless melodious, do you play on me
My pipers,—and if, sooth, you did not
        blow,

Would no sound come? or is the music
        mine,
As a man's voice or breath is called his
        own,
Inbreathed by the Life-breather? There's
        a doubt
For cloudy seasons!
            But the sun was high
When first I felt my pulses set themselves
For concord; when the rhythmic turbu-
        lence
Of blood and brain swept outward upon
        words,
As wind upon the alders, blanching them
By turning up their under-natures till
They trembled in dilation. O delight
And triumph of the poet, who would say
A man's mere 'yes,' a woman's common
        'no,'
A little human hope of that or this,
And says the word so that it burns you
        through
With a special revelation, shakes the
        heart
Of all the men and women in the world,
As if one came back from the dead and
        spoke,
With eyes too happy, a familiar thing
Become divine i' the utterance! while
        for him
The poet, speaker, he expands with joy;
The palpitating angel in his flesh
Thrills inly with consenting fellowship
To those innumerous spirits who sun
        themselves
Outside of time.
            O life, O poetry,
—Which means life in life! cognizant of
        life
Beyond this blood-beat, passionate for
        truth
Beyond these senses!—poetry, my life,
My eagle, with both grappling feet still
        hot
From Zeus's thunder, who hast ravished
        me
Away from all the shepherds, sheep, and
        dogs,
And set me in the Olympian roar and
        round
Of luminous faces for a cup-bearer,
To keep the mouths of all the godheads
        moist

For everlasting laughters,—I myself
Half drunk across the beaker with their
        eyes!
How those gods look!
                Enough so, Ganymede,
We shall not bear above a round or two.
We drop the golden cup at Here's foot
And swoon back to the earth,—and find
        ourselves
Face-down among the pine-cones, cold
        with dew,
While the dogs bark, and many a shep-
        herd scoffs,
'What's come now to the youth?' Such
        ups and downs
Have poets.
                Am I such indeed? The name
Is royal, and to sign it like a queen,
Is what I dare not,—though some royal
        blood
Would seem to tingle in me now and then,
With sense of power and ache,—with
        imposthumes
And manias usual to the race. Howbeit
I dare not : 'tis too easy to go mad
And ape a Bourbon in a crown of straws;
The thing's too common.
                Many fervent souls
Strike rime on rime, who would strike
        steel on steel
If steel had offered, in a restless heat
Of doing something. Many tender souls
Have strung their losses on a riming
        thread,
As children, cowslips :—the more pains
        they take,
The work more withers. Young men,
        aye, and maids,
Too often sow their wild oats in tame
        verse,
Before they sit down under their own vine
And live for use. Alas, near all the birds
Will sing at dawn,—and yet we do not
        take
The chaffering swallow for the holy lark.

In those days, though, I never analysed,
Not even myself. Analysis comes late.
You catch a sight of Nature, earliest,
In full front sun-face, and your eyelids
        wink
And drop before the wonder of 't ; you
        miss

The form, through seeing the light. I lived,
        those days,
And wrote because I lived—unlicensed
        else ;
My heart beat in my brain. Life's violent
        flood
Abolished bounds,—and, which my
        neighbour's field,
Which mine, what mattered? it is thus
        in youth !
We play at leap-frog over the god Term ;
The love within us and the love without
Are mixed, confounded ; if we are loved
        or love,
We scarce distinguish : thus, with other
        power ;
Being acted on and acting seem the same :
In that first onrush of life's chariot-
        wheels,
We know not if the forests move or we.

And so, like most young poets, in a flush
Of individual life I poured myself
Along the veins of others, and achieved
Mere lifeless imitations of live verse,
And made the living answer for the dead,
Profaning nature. 'Touch not, do not
        taste,
Nor handle,'—we're too legal, who write
        young :
We beat the phorminx till we hurt our
        thumbs,
As if still ignorant of counterpoint ;
We call the Muse,—'O Muse, benignant
        Muse,'—
As if we had seen her purple-braided
        head,
With the eyes in it, start between the
        boughs
As often as a stag's. What make-believe,
With so much earnest ! what effete results
From virile efforts ! what cold wire-
        drawn odes,
From such white heats !—bucolics, where
        the cows
Would scare the writer if they splashed
        the mud
In lashing off the flies,—didactics, driven
Against the heels of what the master said ;
And counterfeiting epics, shrill with
        trumps
A babe might blow between two straining
        cheeks

Of bubbled rose, to make his mother
    laugh ;
And elegiac griefs, and songs of love,
Like cast-off nosegays picked up on the
    road,
The worse for being warm : all these
    things, writ
On happy mornings, with a morning
    heart,
That leaps for love, is active for resolve,
Weak for art only. Oft, the ancient
    forms
Will thrill, indeed, in carrying the young
    blood.
The wine-skins, now and then, a little
    warped,
Will crack even, as the new wine gurgles
    in.
Spare the old bottles !—spill not the new
    wine.

By Keats's soul, the man who never
    stepped
In gradual progress like another man,
But, turning grandly on his central self,
Ensphered himself in twenty perfect
    years
And died, not young (the life of a long
    life
Distilled to a mere drop, falling like a tear
Upon the world's cold cheek to make it
    burn
For ever) ; by that strong excepted soul,
I count it strange and hard to understand
That nearly all young poets should write
    old,
That Pope was sexagenary at sixteen,
And beardless Byron academical,
And so with others. It may be perhaps
Such have not settled long and deep
    enough
In trance, to attain to clairvoyance,—
    and still
The memory mixes with the vision, spoils,
And works it turbid.
                    Or perhaps, again,
In order to discover the Muse-Sphinx,
The melancholy desert must sweep round,
Behind you as before.—
                    For me, I wrote
False poems, like the rest, and thought
    them true
Because myself was true in writing them.

I peradventure have writ true ones since
With less complacence.
                    But I could not hide
My quickening inner life from those at
    watch.
They saw a light at a window now and
    then,
They had not set there : who had set it
    there ?
My father's sister started when she caught
My soul agaze in my eyes. She could
    not say
I had no business with a sort of soul,
But plainly she objected,—and demurred
That souls were dangerous things to carry
    straight
Through all the spilt saltpetre of the
    world.
She said sometimes, 'Aurora, have you
    done
Your task this morning ? have you read
    that book ?
And are you ready for the crochet
    here ?'—
As if she said, 'I know there 's some-
    thing wrong ;
I know I have not ground you down
    enough
To flatten and bake you to a wholesome
    crust
For household uses and proprieties,
Before the rain has got into my barn
And set the grains a-sprouting. What,
    you're green
With outdoor impudence ? you almost
    grow ?'
To which I answered, 'Would she hear
    my task,
And verify my abstract of the book ?
Or should I sit down to the crochet work?
Was such her pleasure ?' Then I sate
    and teased
The patient needle till it spilt the thread,
Which oozed off from it in meandering
    lace
From hour to hour. I was not, there-
    fore, sad ;
My soul was singing at a work apart
Behind the wall of sense, as safe from
    harm
As sings the lark when sucked up out of
    sight
In vortices of glory and blue air.

And so, through forced work and spon-
   taneous work,
The inner life informed the outer life,
Reduced the irregular blood to a settled
   rhythm,
Made cool the forehead with fresh-
   sprinkling dreams,
And, rounding to the spheric soul the
   thin,
Pined body, struck a colour up the cheeks,
Though somewhat faint. I clenched my
   brows across
My blue eyes greatening in the looking-
   glass,
And said, ' We'll live, Aurora ! we'll be
   strong.
The dogs are on us—but we will not die.'

Whoever lives true life, will love true
   love.
I learnt to love that England. Very oft,
Before the day was born, or otherwise
Through secret windings of the after-
   noons,
I threw my hunters off and plunged
   myself
Among the deep hills, as a hunted stag
Will take the waters, shivering with the
   fear
And passion of the course. And when
   at last
Escaped, so many a green slope built on
   slope
Betwixt me and the enemy's house be-
   hind,
I dared to rest, or wander, in a rest
Made sweeter for the step upon the grass,
And view the ground's most gentle dim-
   plement
(As if God's finger touched but did not
   press
In making England), such an up and down
Of verdure,—nothing too much up or
   down,
A ripple of land ; such little hills, the sky
Can stoop to tenderly and the wheat-
   fields climb ;
Such nooks of valleys lined with orchises,
Fed full of noises by invisible streams ;
And open pastures where you scarcely
   tell
White daisies from white dew,—at in-
   tervals

The mythic oaks and elm-trees standing
   out
Self-poised upon their prodigy of shade,—
I thought my father's land was worthy
   too
Of being my Shakespeare's.
                    Very oft alone,
Unlicensed ; not unfrequently with leave
To walk the third with Romney and his
   friend
The rising painter, Vincent Carrington,
Whom men judge hardly as bee-bon-
   neted,
Because he holds that, paint a body well,
You paint a soul by implication, like
The grand first Master. Pleasant walks !
   for if
He said, ' When I was last in Italy,'
It sounded as an instrument that's played
Too far off for the tune—and yet it's fine
To listen.
              Often we walked only two,
If cousin Romney pleased to walk with
   me.
We read, or talked, or quarrelled, as it
   chanced.
We were not lovers, nor even friends
   well-matched :
Say rather, scholars upon different
   tracks,
And thinkers disagreed ; he, overfull
Of what is, and I, haply, overbold
For what might be.
                    But then the thrushes sang,
And shook my pulses and the elms' new
   leaves ;
At which I turned, and held my finger up,
And bade him mark that, howsoe'er the
   world
Went ill, as he related, certainly
The thrushes still sang in it. At the
   word
His brow would soften,—and he bore
   with me
In melancholy patience, not unkind,
While breaking into voluble ecstasy
I flattered all the beauteous country
   round,
As poets use, the skies, the clouds, the
   fields,
The happy violets hiding from the roads
The primroses run down to, carrying
   gold ;

The tangled hedgerows, where the cows push out
Impatient horns and tolerant churning mouths
'Twixt dripping ash-boughs, — hedgerows all alive
With birds and gnats and large white butterflies
Which look as if the May-flower had caught life
And palpitated forth upon the wind ;
Hills, vales, woods, netted in a silver mist,
Farms, granges, doubled up among the hills ;
And cattle grazing in the watered vales,
And cottage-chimneys smoking from the woods,
And cottage-gardens smelling everywhere,
Confused with smell of orchards. 'See,' I said,
'And see ! is God not with us on the earth ?
And shall we put Him down by aught we do ?
Who says there's nothing for the poor and vile
Save poverty and wickedness ? behold !'
And ankle-deep in English grass I leaped
And clapped my hands, and called all very fair.

In the beginning when God called all good,
Even then was evil near us, it is writ;
But we indeed who call things good and fair,
The evil is upon us while we speak ;
Deliver us from evil, let us pray.

SECOND BOOK

TIMES followed one another. Came a morn
I stood upon the brink of twenty years,
And looked before and after, as I stood
Woman and artist,—either incomplete,
Both credulous of completion. There I held
The whole creation in my little cup,
And smiled with thirsty lips before I drank
'Good health to you and me, sweet neighbour mine,
And all these peoples.'
                    I was glad, that day ;
The June was in me, with its multitudes
Of nightingales all singing in the dark,
And rosebuds reddening where the calyx split.
I felt so young, so strong, so sure of God !
So glad, I could not choose be very wise !
And, old at twenty, was inclined to pull
My childhood backward in a childish jest
To see the face of 't once more, and farewell !
In which fantastic mood I bounded forth
At early morning,—would not wait so long
As even to snatch my bonnet by the strings,
But, brushing a green trail across the lawn
With my gown in the dew, took will and way
Among the acacias of the shrubberies,
To fly my fancies in the open air
And keep my birthday, till my aunt awoke
To stop good dreams.   Meanwhile I murmured on
As honeyed bees keep humming to themselves,
'The worthiest poets have remained uncrowned
Till death has bleached their foreheads to the bone ;
And so with me it must be unless I prove
Unworthy of the grand adversity,
And certainly I would not fail so much.
What, therefore, if I crown myself to-day
In sport, not pride, to learn the feel of it,
Before my brows be numbed as Dante's own
To all the tender pricking of such leaves ?
Such leaves ! what leaves ?'
                    I pulled the branches down
To choose from.
                    'Not the bay ! I choose no bay
(The fates deny us if we are overbold),
Nor myrtle—which means chiefly love ; and love
Is something awful which one dares not touch

So early o' mornings. This verbena
  strains
The point of passionate fragrance; and
  hard by,
This guelder-rose, at far too slight a beck
Of the wind, will toss about her flower-
  apples.
Ah—there's my choice,—that ivy on the
  wall,
That headlong ivy! not a leaf will grow
But thinking of a wreath. Large leaves,
  smooth leaves,
Serrated like my vines, and half as green.
I like such ivy, bold to leap a height
'Twas strong to climb; as good to grow
  on graves
As twist about a thyrsus; pretty too
(And that's not ill) when twisted round
  a comb.'

Thus speaking to myself, half singing it,
Because some thoughts are fashioned
  like a bell
To ring with once being touched, I drew
  a wreath
Drenched, blinding me with dew, across
  my brow,
And fastening it behind so, turning faced
. . My public!—cousin Romney—with
  a mouth
Twice graver than his eyes.
                    I stood there fixed,—
My arms up, like the caryatid, sole
Of some abolished temple, helplessly
Persistent in a gesture which derides
A former purpose. Yet my blush was
  flame,
As if from flax, not stone.
                    'Aurora Leigh,
The earliest of Auroras!'
                    Hand stretched out
I clasped, as shipwrecked men will clasp
  a hand,
Indifferent to the sort of palm. The tide
Had caught me at my pastime, writing
  down
My foolish name too near upon the sea
Which drowned me with a blush as
  foolish. 'You,
My cousin!'
          The smile died out in his eyes
And dropped upon his lips, a cold dead
  weight,

For just a moment, 'Here's a book I
  found!
No name writ on it—poems, by the
  form!
Some Greek upon the margin,—lady's
  Greek
Without the accents. Read it? Not
  a word.
I saw at once the thing had witchcraft
  in 't,
Whereof the reading calls up dangerous
  spirits :
I rather bring it to the witch.'
                    'My book.
You found it' . .
                'In the hollow by the stream
That beech leans down into—of which
  you said
The Oread in it has a Naiad's heart
And pines for waters.'
                    'Thank you.'
                    'Thanks to you,
My cousin! that I have seen you not
  too much
Witch, scholar, poet, dreamer, and the
  rest,
To be a woman also.'
                    With a glance
The smile rose in his eyes again and
  touched
The ivy on my forehead, light as air.
I answered gravely, 'Poets needs must be
Or men or women—more 's the pity.'
                    'Ah,
But men, and still less women, happily,
Scarce need be poets. Keep to the
  green wreath,
Since even dreaming of the stone and
  bronze
Brings headaches, pretty cousin, and
  defiles
The clean white morning dresses.'
                    'So you judge!
Because I love the beautiful I must
Love pleasure chiefly, and be over-
  charged
For ease and whiteness! well, you know
  the world,
And only miss your cousin, 'tis not much.
But learn this; I would rather take my
  part
With God's Dead, who afford to walk
  in white

Yet spread His glory, than keep quiet
 here
And gather up my feet from even a step
For fear to soil my gown in so much dust.
I choose to walk at all risks.—Here, if
 heads
That hold a rhythmic thought must
 ache perforce,
For my part I choose headaches,—and
 to-day's
My birthday.'
   'Dear Aurora, choose instead
To cure them. You have balsams.'
       'I perceive.
The headache is too noble for my sex.
You think the heartache would sound
 decenter,
Since that's the woman's special, proper
 ache,
And altogether tolerable, except
To a woman.'
  Saying which, I loosed my wreath,
And swinging it beside me as I walked,
Half petulant, half playful, as we walked,
I sent a sidelong look to find his
 thought,—
As falcon set on falconer's finger may,
With sidelong head, and startled, brav-
 ing eye,
Which means, 'You'll see—you'll see!
 I'll soon take flight,
You shall not hinder.' He, as shaking
 out
His hand and answering 'Fly then,' did
 not speak,
Except by such a gesture. Silently
We paced, until, just coming into sight
Of the house-windows, he abruptly
 caught
At one end of the swinging wreath, and
 said
'Aurora!' There I stopped short,
 breath and all.

'Aurora, let's be serious, and throw by
This game of head and heart. Life
 means, be sure,
Both heart and head,—both active, both
 complete,
And both in earnest. Men and women
 make
The world, as head and heart make
 human life.

Work man, work woman, since there's
 work to do
In this beleaguered earth, for head and
 heart,
And thought can never do the work of
 love:
But work for ends, I mean for uses, not
For such sleek fringes (do you call them
 ends,
Still less God's glory?) as we sew
 ourselves
Upon the velvet of those baldaquins
Held 'twixt us and the sun. That book
 of yours,
I have not read a page of; but I toss
A rose up—it falls calyx down, you see!
The chances are that, being a woman,
 young
And pure, with such a pair of large,
 calm eyes,
You write as well . . and ill . . upon the
 whole,
As other women. If as well, what then?
If even a little better, . . still, what
 then?
We want the Best in art now, or no art.
The time is done for facile settings up
Of minnow gods, nymphs here and
 tritons there;
The polytheists have gone out in God,
That unity of Bests. No best, no God!
And so with art, we say. Give art's
 divine,
Direct, indubitable, real as grief,
Or leave us to the grief we grow ourselves
Divine by overcoming with mere hope
And most prosaic patience. You, you
 are young
As Eve with nature's daybreak on her
 face,
But this same world you are come to,
 dearest coz,
Has done with keeping birthdays, saves
 her wreaths
To hang upon her ruins,—and forgets
To rime the cry with which she still
 beats back
Those savage, hungry dogs that hunt
 her down
To the empty grave of Christ. The
 world's hard pressed;
The sweat of labour in the early curse
Has (turning acrid in six thousand years)

Become the sweat of torture.   Who has
    time,
An hour's time . . think!—to sit upon
    a bank
And hear the cymbal tinkle in white
    hands?
When Egypt's slain, I say, let Miriam
    sing!—
Before—where's Moses?'
                    'Ah, exactly that.
Where's Moses?—is a Moses to be found?
You'll seek him vainly in the bulrushes,
While I in vain touch cymbals.   Yet
    concede,
Such sounding brass has done some
    actual good
(The application in a woman's hand,
If that were credible, being scarcely
    spoilt)
In colonizing beehives.'
                    'There it is!—
You play beside a death-bed like a child,
Yet measure to yourself a prophet's place
To teach the living.   None of all these
    things
Can women understand.   You generalize
—Oh, nothing,—not even grief!   Your
    quick-breathed hearts,
So sympathetic to the personal pang,
Close on each separate knife-stroke,
    yielding up
A whole life at each wound, incapable
Of deepening, widening a large lap of life
To hold the world-full woe.   The human
    race
To you means, such a child, or such a man,
You saw one morning waiting in the
    cold,
Beside that gate, perhaps.   You gather up
A few such cases, and when strong
    sometimes
Will write of factories and of slaves, as if
Your father were a negro, and your son
A spinner in the mills.   All's yours and
    you,
All, coloured with your blood, or other-
    wise
Just nothing to you.   Why, I call you hard
To general suffering.   Here's the world
    half blind
With intellectual light, half brutalized
With civilization, having caught the
    plague

In silks from Tarsus, shrieking east and
    west
Along a thousand railroads, mad with pain
And sin too!..does one woman of you all
(You who weep easily) grow pale to see
This tiger shake his cage?—does one of
    you
Stand still from dancing, stop from
    stringing pearls,
And pine and die because of the great sum
Of universal anguish?—Show me a tear
Wet as Cordelia's, in eyes bright as yours,
Because the world is mad.   You cannot
    count,
That you should weep for this account,
    not you!
You weep for what you know.   A red-
    haired child
Sick in a fever, if you touch him once,
Though but so little as with a finger-tip,
Will set you weeping; but a million
    sick . .
You could as soon weep for the rule of
    three
Or compound fractions.   Therefore this
    same world,
Uncomprehended by you, must remain
Uninfluenced by you.—Women as you
    are,
Mere women, personal and passionate,
You give us doting mothers, and perfect
    wives,
Sublime Madonnas, and enduring saints!
We get no Christ from you,—and verily
We shall not get a poet, in my mind.'

'With which conclusion you conclude'..
                    'But this:
That you, Aurora, with the large live brow
And steady eyelids, cannot condescend
To play at art, as children play at swords,
To show a pretty spirit, chiefly admired
Because true action is impossible.
You never can be satisfied with praise
Which men give women when they
    judge a book
Not as mere work but as mere woman's
    work,
Expressing the comparative respect
Which means the absolute scorn.   "Oh,
    excellent!
What grace, what facile turns, what
    fluent sweeps,

What delicate discernment . . almost
    thought !
The book does honour to the sex, we
    hold.
Among our female authors we make room
For this fair writer, and congratulate
The country that produces in these times
Such women, competent to . . spell.'' '
                ' Stop there.'
I answered, burning through his thread
    of talk
With a quick flame of emotion,—' You
    have read
My soul, if not my book, and argue well.
I would not condescend . . we will not
    say
To such a kind of praise (a worthless end
Is praise of all kinds), but to such a use
Of holy art and golden life. I am young,
And peradventure weak—you tell me
    so—
Through being a woman. And, for all
    the rest,
Take thanks for justice. I would rather
    dance
At fairs on tight-rope, till the babies
    dropped
Their gingerbread for joy,—than shift
    the types
For tolerable verse, intolerable
To men who act and suffer. Better far
Pursue a frivolous trade by serious means,
Than a sublime art frivolously.'
                  ' You,
Choose nobler work than either, O moist
    eyes
And hurrying lips and heaving heart !
    We are young,
Aurora, you and I. The world,—look
    round,—
The world, we're come to late, is
    swollen hard
With perished generations and their sins :
The civilizer's spade grinds horribly
On dead men's bones, and cannot turn
    up soil
That 's otherwise than fetid. All success
Proves partial failure ; all advance im-
    plies
What 's left behind ; all triumph, some-
    thing crushed
At the chariot-wheels ; all government,
    some wrong :

And rich men make the poor, who curse
    the rich,
Who agonize together, rich and poor,
Under and over, in the social spasm
And crisis of the ages. Here 's an age
That makes its own vocation ! here we
    have stepped
Across the bounds of time ! here 's nought
    to see,
But just the rich man and just Lazarus,
And both in torments, with a mediate
    gulf,
Though not a hint of Abraham's bosom.
             Who
Being man, Aurora, can stand calmly by
And view these things, and never tease
    his soul
For some great cure ? No physic for
    this grief,
In all the earth and heavens too ?'
                 ' You believe
In God, for your part ?—aye ? that He
    who makes,
Can make good things from ill things,
    best from worst,
As men plant tulips upon dunghills when
They wish them finest ?'
             ' True. A death-heat is
The same as life-heat, to be accurate,
And in all nature is no death at all,
As men account of death, so long as God
Stands witnessing for life perpetually,
By being just God. That 's abstract
    truth, I know,
Philosophy, or sympathy with God :
But I, I sympathize with man, not God
(I think I was a man for chiefly this),
And when I stand beside a dying bed,
'Tis death to me. Observe,—it had
    not much
Consoled the race of mastodons to know,
Before they went to fossil, that anon
Their place would quicken with the
    elephant :
They were not elephants but mastodons ;
And I, a man, as men are now, and not
As men may be hereafter, feel with men
In the agonizing present.'
                ' Is it so,'
I said, ' my cousin ? is the world so bad,
While I hear nothing of it through the
    trees ?
The world was always evil,—but so bad?'

'So bad, Aurora. Dear, my soul is grey
With poring over the long sum of ill ;
So much for vice, so much for discontent,
So much for the necessities of power,
So much for the connivances of fear,
Coherent in statistical despairs
With such a total of distracted life, . .
To see it down in figures on a page,
Plain, silent, clear, as God sees through
        the earth
The sense of all the graves,—that 's
        terrible
For one who is not God, and cannot right
The wrong he looks on.   May I choose
        indeed
But vow away my years, my means,
        my aims,
Among the helpers, if there 's any help
In such a social strait ?   The common
        blood
That swings along my veins is strong
        enough
To draw me to this duty.'
                        Then I spoke.
'I have not stood long on the strand of
        life,
And these salt waters have had scarcely
        time
To creep so high up as to wet my feet :
I cannot judge these tides—I shall,
        perhaps.
A woman's always younger than a man
At equal years, because she is disallowed
Maturing by the outdoor sun and air,
And kept in long-clothes past the age
        to walk.
Ah well, I know you men judge other-
        wise !
You think a woman ripens as a peach,
In the cheeks, chiefly.   Pass it to me
        now ;
I'm young in age, and younger still,
        I think,
As a woman.   But a child may say amen
To a bishop's prayer and feel the way it
        goes,
And I, incapable to loose the knot
Of social questions, can approve, applaud
August compassion, Christian thoughts
        that shoot
Beyond the vulgar white of personal aims.
Accept my reverence.'
                There he glowed on me

With all his face and eyes.   'No other
        help ?'
Said he—'no more than so ?'
                        'What help ?' I asked.
'You'd scorn my help,—as Nature's
        self, you say,
Has scorned to put her music in my mouth
Because a woman's.   Do you now turn
        round
And ask for what a woman cannot give ?'

'For what she only can, I turn and ask,'
He answered, catching up my hands in
        his,
And dropping on me from his high-eaved
        brow
The full weight of his soul,—'I ask for
        love,
And that, she can ; for life in fellowship
Through bitter duties—that, I know she
        can ;
For wifehood—will she ?'
                'Now,' I said, 'may God
Be witness 'twixt us two !' and with
        the word,
Meseemed I floated into a sudden light
Above his stature,—'am I proved too
        weak
To stand alone, yet strong enough to bear
Such leaners on my shoulder ? poor
        to think,
Yet rich enough to sympathize with
        thought ?
Incompetent to sing, as blackbirds can,
Yet competent to love, like HIM ?'
                        I paused ;
Perhaps I darkened, as the lighthouse
        will
That turns upon the sea.   'It 's always so.
Anything does for a wife.'
                        'Aurora, dear,
And dearly honoured,'—he pressed in
        at once
With eager utterance,—' you translate
        me ill.
I do not contradict my thought of you
Which is most reverent, with another
        thought
Found less so.   If your sex is weak for art
(And I who said so, did but honour you
By using truth in courtship), it is strong
For life and duty.   Place your fecund
        heart

In mine, and let us blossom for the world
That wants love's colour in the grey of
    time.
My talk, meanwhile, is arid to you, aye,
Since all my talk can only set you where
You look down coldly on the arena-heaps
Of headless bodies, shapeless, indistinct !
The Judgement-Angel scarce would find
    his way
Through such a heap of generalized dis-
    tress
To the individual man with lips and eyes,
Much less Aurora. Ah, my sweet, come
    down,
And hand in hand we'll go where yours
    shall touch
These victims, one by one ! till, one by
    one,
The formless, nameless trunk of every
    man
Shall seem to wear a head with hair
    you know,
And every woman catch your mother's
    face
To melt you into passion.'
                'I am a girl,'
I answered slowly ; 'you do well to name
My mother's face. Though far too early,
    alas,
God's hand did interpose 'twixt it and
    me,
I know so much of love as used to shine
In that face and another. Just so much ;
No more indeed at all. I have not seen
So much love since, I pray you pardon me,
As answers even to make a marriage with
In this cold land of England. What
    you love,
Is not a woman, Romney, but a cause :
You want a helpmate, not a mistress, sir.
A wife to help your ends,—in her no end !
Your cause is noble, your ends excellent,
But I, being most unworthy of these
    and that,
Do otherwise conceive of love. Farewell.'

'Farewell, Aurora ? you reject me thus?'
He said.
        'Sir, you were married long ago.
You have a wife already whom you love,
Your social theory. Bless you both, I say.
For my part, I am scarcely meek enough
To be the handmaid of a lawful spouse.

Do I look a Hagar, think you ?'
                'So you jest.'

'Nay, so, I speak in earnest,' I replied.
'You treat of marriage too much like,
    at least,
A chief apostle : you would bear with you
A wife .. a sister .. shall we speak it out?
A sister of charity.'
              'Then, must it be
Indeed farewell ? And was I so far wrong
In hope and in illusion, when I took
The woman to be nobler than the man,
Yourself the noblest woman, in the use
And comprehension of what love is,—
    love,
That generates the likeness of itself
Through all heroic duties ? so far wrong,
In saying bluntly, venturing truth on
    love,
"Come, human creature, love and work
    with me,"—
Instead of, "Lady, thou art wondrous fair,
And, where the Graces walk before,
    the Muse
Will follow at the lightning of their eyes,
And where the Muse walks, lovers need
    to creep :
Turn round and love me, or I die of love."'

With quiet indignation I broke in.
'You misconceive the question like a man,
Who sees a woman as the complement
Of his sex merely. You forget too much
That every creature, female as the male,
Stands single in responsible act and
    thought
As also in birth and death. Whoever says
To a loyal woman, "Love and work
    with me,"
Will get fair answers if the work and love,
Being good themselves, are good for
    her—the best
She was born for. Women of a softer
    mood,
Surprised by men when scarcely awake
    to life,
Will sometimes only hear the first word,
    love,
And catch up with it any kind of work,
Indifferent, so that dear love go with it.
I do not blame such women, though,
    for love,

They pick much oakum ; earth's fanatics make
Too frequently heaven's saints. But *me* your work
Is not the best for,—nor your love the best,
Nor able to commend the kind of work
For love's sake merely. Ah, you force me, sir,
To be over-bold in speaking of myself :
I too have my vocation,—work to do,
The heavens and earth have set me since I changed
My father's face for theirs, and, though your world
Were twice as wretched as you represent,
Most serious work, most necessary work
As any of the economists'. Reform,
Make trade a Christian possibility,
And individual right no general wrong ;
Wipe out earth's furrows of the Thine and Mine,
And leave one green for men to play at bowls,
With innings for them all ! . . what then, indeed,
If mortals are not greater by the head
Than any of their prosperities? what then,
Unless the artist keep up open roads
Betwixt the seen and unseen,—bursting through
The best of your conventions with his best,
The speakable, imaginable best
God bids him speak, to prove what lies beyond
Both speech and imagination ? A starved man
Exceeds a fat beast : we'll not barter, sir,
The beautiful for barley.—And, even so,
I hold you will not compass your poor ends
Of barley-feeding and material ease,
Without a poet's individualism
To work your universal. It takes a soul
To move a body : it takes a high-souled man
To move the masses, even to a cleaner sty :
It takes the ideal to blow a hair's-breadth off

The dust of the actual.—Ah, your Fouriers failed,
Because not poets enough to understand
That life develops from within.——For me,
Perhaps I am not worthy, as you say,
Of work like this : perhaps a woman's soul
Aspires, and not creates : yet we aspire,
And yet I'll try out your perhapses, sir ;
And if I fail . . why, burn me up my straw
Like other false works—I'll not ask for grace ;
Your scorn is better, cousin Romney. I,
Who love my art, would never wish it lower
To suit my stature. I may love my art.
You'll grant that even a woman may love art,
Seeing that to waste true love on anything
Is womanly, past question.'
         I retain
The very last word which I said that day,
As you the creaking of the door, years past,
Which let upon you such disabling news
You ever after have been graver. He,
His eyes, the motions in his silent mouth,
Were fiery points on which my words were caught,
Transfixed for ever in my memory
For his sake, not their own. And yet I know
I did not love him . . nor he me . . that's sure . .
And what I said is unrepented of,
As truth is always. Yet . . a princely man !—
If hard to me, heroic for himself !
He bears down on me through the slanting years,
The stronger for the distance. If he had loved,
Aye, loved me, with that retributive face, . .
I might have been a common woman now
And happier, less known and less left alone,
Perhaps a better woman after all,
With chubby children hanging on my neck
To keep me low and wise. Ah me, the vines

That bear such fruit are proud to stoop
    with it.
The palm stands upright in a realm of
    sand.

And I, who spoke the truth then, stand
    upright,
Still worthy of having spoken out the
    truth ;
By being content I spoke it, though it set
Him there, me here.—O woman's vile
    remorse,
To hanker after a mere name, a show,
A supposition, a potential love !
Does every man who names love in our
    lives,
Become a power for that ? Is love's true
    thing
So much best to us, that what personates
    love
Is next best ? A potential love, forsooth !
I'm not so vile.   No, no—he cleaves,
    I think,
This man, this image,—chiefly for the
    wrong
And shock he gave my life, in finding me
Precisely where the devil of my youth
Had set me, on those mountain-peaks of
    hope
All glittering with the dawn-dew, all
    erect
And famished for the noon,— exclaiming,
    while
I looked for empire and much tribute,
    'Come,
I have some worthy work for thee below.
Come, sweep my barns and keep my
    hospitals,
And I will pay thee with a current coin
Which men give women.'
                As we spoke, the grass
Was trod in haste beside us, and my
    aunt,
With smile distorted by the sun,—face,
    voice
As much at issue with the summer-day
As if you brought a candle out of doors,—
Broke in with, 'Romney, here !—My
    child, entreat
Your cousin to the house, and have
    your talk,
If girls must talk upon their birthdays.
    Come.'

He answered for me calmly, with pale lips
That seemed to motion for a smile in vain,
'The talk is ended, madam, where we
    stand.
Your brother's daughter has dismissed
    me here ;
And all my answer can be better said
Beneath the trees, than wrong by such
    a word
Your house's hospitalities.   Farewell.'

With that he vanished.   I could hear
    his heel
Ring bluntly in the lane, as down he leapt
The short way from us.—Then a mea-
    sured speech
Withdrew me.   'What means this,
    Aurora Leigh ?
My brother's daughter has dismissed
    my guests ?'

The lion in me felt the keeper's voice
Through all its quivering dewlaps ;
    I was quelled
Before her,—meekened to the child she
    knew :
I prayed her pardon, said, 'I had little
    thought
To give dismissal to a guest of hers,
In letting go a friend of mine who came
To take me into service as a wife,—
No more than that, indeed.'
                'No more, no more ?
Pray Heaven,' she answered, 'that
    I was not mad.
I could not mean to tell her to her face
That Romney Leigh had asked me for
    a wife,
And I refused him ?'
                'Did he ask ?' I said ;
'I think he rather stooped to take me up
For certain uses which he found to do
For something called a wife.   He never
    asked.'

'What stuff !' she answered; 'are they
    queens, these girls?
They must have mantles, stitched with
    twenty silks,
Spread out upon the ground, before
    they'll step
One footstep for the noblest lover born.'

'But I am born,' I said with firmness, 'I,
To walk another way than his, dear aunt.'

'You walk, you walk! A babe at
    thirteen months
Will walk as well as you,' she cried in
    haste,
'Without a steadying finger. Why,
    you child,
God help you, you are groping in the dark,
For all this sunlight. You suppose,
    perhaps,
That you, sole offspring of an opulent man,
Are rich and free to choose a way to walk?
You think, and it's a reasonable thought,
That I, beside, being well to do in life,
Will leave my handful in my niece's hand
When death shall paralyse these fingers?
    Pray,
Pray, child, albeit I know you love me not,
As if you loved me, that I may not die!
For when I die and leave you, out you go
(Unless I make room for you in my grave),
Unhoused, unfed, my dear, poor brother's
    lamb
(Ah _ heaven,—that pains!)—without
    a right to crop
A single blade of grass beneath these trees,
Or cast a lamb's small shadow on the lawn,
Unfed, unfolded! Ah, my brother, here's
The fruit you planted in your foreign
    loves!—
Aye, there's the fruit he planted! never
    look
Astonished at me with your mother's
    eyes,
For it was they who set you where you are,
An undowered orphan. Child, your
    father's choice
Of that said mother, disinherited
His daughter, his and hers. Men do
    not think
Of sons and daughters, when they fall
    in love,
So much more than of sisters; otherwise
He would have paused to ponder what
    he did,
And shrunk before that clause in the entail
Excluding offspring by a foreign wife
(The clause set up a hundred years ago
By a Leigh who wedded a French
    dancing-girl
And had his heart danced over in return);

But this man shrank at nothing, never
    thought
Of you, Aurora, any more than me—
Your mother must have been a pretty
    thing,
For all the coarse Italian blacks and
    browns,
To make a good man, which my brother
    was,
Unchary of the duties to his house;
But so it fell indeed. Our cousin Vane,
Vane Leigh, the father of this Romney,
    wrote
Directly on your birth, to Italy,
"I ask your baby daughter for my son
In whom the entail now merges by the
    law.
Betroth her to us out of love, instead
Of colder reasons, and she shall not lose
By love or law from henceforth"—so he
    wrote;
A generous cousin, was my cousin Vane.
Remember how he drew you to his knee
The year you came here, just before he
    died,
And hollowed out his hands to hold
    your cheeks,
And wished them redder,—you re-
    member Vane?
And now his son who represents our
    house
And holds the fiefs and manors in his
    place,
To whom reverts my pittance when
    I die
(Except a few books and a pair of shawls),
The boy is generous like him, and pre-
    pared
To carry out his kindest word and thought
To you, Aurora. Yes, a fine young man
Is Romney Leigh; although the sun of
    youth
Has shone too straight upon his brain,
    I know,
And fevered him with dreams of doing
    good
To good-for-nothing people. But a wife
Will put all right, and stroke his temples
    cool
With healthy touches'..

                    I broke in at that.
I could not lift my heavy heart to breathe
Till then, but then I raised it, and it fell

In broken words like these—' No need
    to wait ;
The dream of doing good to .. me, at
    least,
Is ended, without waiting for a wife
To cool the fever for him. We've es-
    caped
That danger,—thank Heaven for it.'
                    ' You,' she cried,
' Have got a fever. What, I talk and
    talk
An hour long to you,—I instruct you how
You cannot eat or drink or stand or sit
Or even die, like any decent wretch
In all this unroofed and unfurnished
    world,
Without your cousin,—and you still
    maintain
There 's room 'twixt him and you, for
    flirting fans
And running knots in eyebrows ? You
    must have
A pattern lover sighing on his knee ?
You do not count enough, a noble heart
(Above book-patterns) which this very
    morn
Unclosed itself in two dear fathers' names
To embrace your orphaned life ? fie, fie !
    But stay,
I write a word, and counteract this sin.'

She would have turned to leave me, but
    I clung.
' O sweet my father's sister, hear my
    word
Before you write yours. Cousin Vane
    did well,
And cousin Romney well,—and I well
    too,
In casting back with all my strength
    and will
The good they meant me. O my God,
    my God !
God meant me good, too, when he
    hindered me
From saying "yes" this morning. If
    you write
A word, it shall be " no." I say no, no!
I tie up " no " upon His altar-horns,
Quite out of reach of perjury ! At least
My soul is not a pauper ; I can live
At least my soul's life, without alms
    from men ;

And if it must be in heaven instead of
    earth,
Let heaven look to it,—I am not afraid.'

She seized my hands with both hers,
    strained them fast,
And drew her probing and unscrupulous
    eyes
Right through me, body and heart.
    ' Yet, foolish Sweet,
You love this man. I've watched you
    when he came,
And when he went, and when we've
    talked of him :
I am not old for nothing ; I can tell
The weather-signs of love : you love
    this man.'

Girls blush sometimes because they are
    alive,
Half wishing they were dead to save
    the shame.
The sudden blush devours them, neck
    and brow ;
They have drawn too near the fire of
    life, like gnats,
And flare up bodily, wings and all.
    What then ?
Who 's sorry for a gnat .. or girl ?
                            I blushed.
I feel the brand upon my forehead now
Strike hot, sear deep, as guiltless men
    may feel
The felon's iron, say, and scorn the mark
Of what they are not. Most illogical
Irrational nature of our womanhood,
That blushes one way, feels another
    way,
And prays, perhaps, another ! After all,
We cannot be the equal of the male
Who rules his blood a little.
                        For although
I blushed indeed, as if I loved the man,
And her incisive smile, accrediting
That treason of false witness in my blush,
Did bow me downward like a swathe
    of grass
Below its level that struck me,—I attest
The conscious skies and all their daily
    suns,
I think I loved him not,—nor then, nor
    since,
Nor ever. Do we love the schoolmaster,

Being busy in the woods? much less,
  being poor,
The overseer of the parish? Do we keep
Our love to pay our debts with?
                  White and cold
I grew next moment. As my blood
  recoiled
From that imputed ignominy, I made
My heart great with it. Then, at last,
  I spoke,
Spoke veritable words but passionate,
Too passionate perhaps . . ground up
  with sobs
To shapeless endings. She let fall my
  hands
And took her smile off, in sedate disgust,
As peradventure she had touched a
  snake,—
A dead snake, mind!—and turning
  round, replied,
'We'll leave Italian manners, if you
  please.
I think you had an English father, child,
And ought to find it possible to speak
A quiet "yes" or "no," like English girls,
Without convulsions. In another month
We'll take another answer—no, or yes.'
With that, she left me in the garden-
  walk.

I had a father! yes, but long ago—
How long it seemed that moment. Oh,
  how far,
How far and safe, God, dost Thou keep
  Thy saints
When once gone from us! We may
  call against
The lighted windows of Thy fair June-
  heaven
Where all the souls are happy,—and
  not one,
Not even my father, look from work
  or play
To ask, 'Who is it that cries after us,
Below there, in the dusk?' Yet formerly
He turned his face upon me quick enough,
If I said 'father.' Now I might cry loud;
The little lark reached higher with his
  song
Than I with crying. Oh, alone, alone,—
Not troubling any in heaven, nor any
  on earth,
I stood there in the garden, and looked up

The deaf blue sky that brings the roses
  out
On such June mornings.
                  You who keep account
Of crisis and transition in this life,
Set down the first time Nature says
  plain 'no'
To some 'yes' in you, and walks over you
In gorgeous sweeps of scorn. We all
  begin
By singing with the birds, and running
  fast
With June-days, hand in hand: but
  once, for all,
The birds must sing against us, and the sun
Strike down upon us like a friend's
  sword caught
By an enemy to slay us, while we read
The dear name on the blade which bites
  at us!—
That's bitter and convincing: after that,
We seldom doubt that something in the
  large
Smooth order of creation, though no
  more
Than haply a man's footstep, has gone
  wrong.

Some tears fell down my cheeks, and
  then I smiled,
As those smile who have no face in the
  world
To smile back to them. I had lost a friend
In Romney Leigh; the thing was sure—
  a friend,
Who had looked at me most gently now
  and then,
And spoken of my favourite books, 'our
  books,'
With such a voice! Well, voice and
  look were now
More utterly shut out from me, I felt,
Than even my father's. Romney now
  was turned
To a benefactor, to a generous man,
Who had tied himself to marry . . me,
  instead
Of such a woman, with low timorous lids
He lifted with a sudden word one day,
And left, perhaps, for my sake.—Ah,
  self-tied
By a contract, male Iphigenia bound
At a fatal Aulis for the winds to change

(But loose him, they'll not change), he
    well might seem
A little cold and dominant in love!
He had a right to be dogmatical,
This poor, good Romney. Love, to him,
    was made
A simple law-clause. If I married him,
I should not dare to call my soul my own
Which so he had bought and paid for:
    every thought
And every heart-beat down there in the
    bill;
Not one found honestly deductible
From any use that pleased him! He
    might cut
My body into coins to give away
Among his other paupers; change my
    sons,
While I stood dumb as Griseld, for black
    babes
Or piteous foundlings; might unques-
    tioned set
My right hand teaching in the Ragged
    Schools,
My left hand washing in the Public Baths,
What time my angel of the Ideal stretched
Both his to me in vain. I could not claim
The poor right of a mouse in a trap, to
    squeal,
And take so much as pity from myself.

Farewell, good Romney! if I loved you
    even,
I could but ill afford to let you be
So generous to me. Farewell, friend,
    since friend
Betwixt us two, forsooth, must be a
    word
So heavily overladen. And, since help
Must come to me from those who love
    me not,
Farewell, all helpers—I must help my-
    self,
And am alone from henceforth.—Then
    I stooped
And lifted the soiled garland from the
    earth,
And set it on my head as bitterly
As when the Spanish monarch crowned
    the bones
Of his dead love. So be it. I preserve
That crown still,—in the drawer there!
    'twas the first.

The rest are like it;—those Olympian
    crowns,
We run for, till we lose sight of the sun
In the dust of the racing chariots!
              After that,
Before the evening fell, I had a note,
Which ran,—'Aurora, sweet Chaldean,
    you read
My meaning backward like your eastern
    books,
While I am from the west, dear. Read
    me now
A little plainer. Did you hate me quite
But yesterday? I loved you for my part;
I love you. If I spoke untenderly
This morning, my belovèd, pardon it;
And comprehend me that I loved you so
I set you on the level of my soul,
And overwashed you with the bitter
    brine
Of some habitual thoughts. Henceforth,
    my flower,
Be planted out of reach of any such,
And lean the side you please, with all
    your leaves!
Write woman's verses and dream wo-
    man's dreams;
But let me feel your perfume in my home
To make my sabbath after working-days.
Bloom out your youth beside me,—be
    my wife.'

I wrote in answer—'We Chaldeans
    discern
Still farther than we read. I know your
    heart,
And shut it like the holy book it is,
Reserved for mild-eyed saints to pore
    upon
Betwixt their prayers at vespers. Well,
    you're right,
I did not surely hate you yesterday;
And yet I do not love you enough to-day
To wed you, cousin Romney. Take this
    word,
And let it stop you as a generous man
From speaking farther. You may tease,
    indeed,
And blow about my feelings, or my leaves,
And here's my aunt will help you with
    east winds
And break a stalk, perhaps, tormenting
    me;

But certain flowers grow near as deep
  as trees,
And, cousin, you'll not move my root,
  not you,
With all your confluent storms. Then
  let me grow
Within my wayside hedge, and pass
  your way !
This flower has never as much to say to you
As the antique tomb which said to travel-
  lers, " Pause,"
"Siste, viator." ' Ending thus, I signed.

The next week passed in silence, so the
  next,
And several after : Romney did not come
Nor my aunt chide me. I lived on and on,
As if my heart were kept beneath a glass,
And everybody stood, all eyes and ears,
To see and hear it tick. I could not sit,
Nor walk, nor take a book, nor lay it
  down,
Nor sew on steadily, nor drop a stitch,
And a sigh with it, but I felt her looks
Still cleaving to me, like the sucking asp
To Cleopatra's breast, persistently
Through the intermittent pantings. Be-
  ing observed,
When observation is not sympathy,
Is just being tortured. If she said a word,
A 'thank you,' or an 'if it please you, dear,'
She meant a commination, or, at best,
An exorcism against the devildom
Which plainly held me. So with all the
  house.
Susannah could not stand and twist my
  hair,
Without such glancing at the looking-
  glass
To see my face there, that she missed
  the plait.
And John,—I never sent my plate for
  soup,
Or did not send it, but the foolish John
Resolved the problem, 'twixt his nap-
  kined thumbs,
Of what was signified by taking soup
Or choosing mackerel. Neighbours who
  dropped in
On morning visits, feeling a joint wrong,
Smiled admonition, sate uneasily,
And talked with measured, emphasized
  reserve,

Of parish news, like doctors to the sick,
When not called in,—as if, with leave
  to speak,
They might say something. Nay, the
  very dog
Would watch me from his sun-patch on
  the floor,
In alternation with the large black fly
Not yet in reach of snapping. So I lived.

A Roman died so ; smeared with honey,
  teased
By insects, stared to torture by the noon:
And many patient souls 'neath English
  roofs
Have died like Romans. I, in looking
  back,
Wish only, now, I had borne the plague
  of all
With meeker spirits than were rife at
  Rome.

For, on the sixth week, the dead sea
  broke up,
Dashed suddenly through beneath the
  heel of Him
Who stands upon the sea and earth and
  swears
Time shall be nevermore. The clock
  struck nine
That morning too,—no lark was out of
  tune,
The hidden farms among the hills
  breathed straight
Their smoke toward heaven, the lime-
  tree scarcely stirred
Beneath the blue weight of the cloudless
  sky,
Though still the July air came floating
  through
The woodbine at my window, in and out,
With touches of the outdoor country-
  news
For a bending forehead. There I sate,
  and wished
That morning-truce of God would last
  till eve,
Or longer. 'Sleep,' I thought, 'late
  sleepers,—sleep,
And spare me yet the burden of your eyes.'

Then, suddenly, a single ghastly shriek
Tore upward from the bottom of the house.

Like one who wakens in a grave and
 shrieks,
The still house seemed to shriek itself
 alive,
And shudder through its passages and
 stairs
With slam of doors and clash of bells.—
 I sprang,
I stood up in the middle of the room,
And there confronted at my chamber-
 door,
A white face,—shivering, ineffectual lips.

'Come, come,' they tried to utter, and
 I went:
As if a ghost had drawn me at the point
Of a fiery finger through the uneven
 dark,
I went with reeling footsteps down the
 stair,
Nor asked a question.
                    There she sate, my aunt,—
Bolt upright in the chair beside her bed,
Whose pillow had no dint! she had used
 no bed
For that night's sleeping, yet slept well.
 My God,
The dumb derision of that grey, peaked
 face
Concluded something grave against the
 sun,
Which filled the chamber with its July
 burst
When Susan drew the curtains ignorant
Of who sate open-eyed behind her. There
She sate . . it sate . . we said 'she'
 yesterday . .
And held a letter with unbroken seal
As Susan gave it to her hand last night:
All night she had held it. If its news
 referred
To duchies or to dunghills, not an inch
She'd budge, 'twas obvious, for such
 worthless odds :
Nor, though the stars were suns and
 overburned
Their spheric limitations, swallowing up
Like wax the azure spaces, could they
 force
Those open eyes to wink once. What
 last sight
Had left them blank and flat so,—draw-
 ing out

The faculty of vision from the roots,
As nothing more, worth seeing, remained
 behind?

Were those the eyes that watched me,
 worried me?
That dogged me up and down the hours
 and days,
A beaten, breathless, miserable soul?
And did I pray, a half-hour back, but so,
To escape the burden of those eyes . .
 those eyes?
'Sleep late,' I said ?—
               Why now, indeed, they sleep.
God answers sharp and sudden on some
 prayers,
And thrusts the thing we have prayed
 for in our face,
A gauntlet with a gift in 't. Every wish
Is like a prayer, with God.
                         I had my wish,
To read and meditate the thing I would,
To fashion all my life upon my thought,
And marry or not marry. Henceforth
 none
Could disapprove me, vex me, hamper me.
Full ground-room, in this desert newly
 made,
For Babylon or Balbec,—when the
 breath,
Now choked with sand, returns for build-
 ing towns.

The heir came over on the funeral day,
And we two cousins met before the dead,
With two pale faces. Was it death or life
That moved us? When the will was read
 and done,
The official guests and witnesses with-
 drawn,
We rose up in a silence almost hard,
And looked at one another. Then I said,
'Farewell, my cousin.'
               But he touched, just touched
My hatstrings tied for going (at the door
The carriage stood to take me), and said
 low,
His voice a little unsteady through his
 smile,
'Siste, viator.'
               'Is there time,' I asked,
'In these last days of railroads, to stop
 short

Like Caesar's chariot (weighing half a ton)
On the Appian road for morals?'
        'There is time,'
He answered grave, 'for necessary
    words,
Inclusive, trust me, of no epitaph
On man or act, my cousin. We have read
A will, which gives you all the personal
    goods
And funded moneys of your aunt.'
        'I thank
Her memory for it. With three hundred
    pounds
We buy in England even, clear standing-
    room
To stand and work in. Only two hours
    since,
I fancied I was poor.'
        'And, cousin, still
You're richer than you fancy. The will
    says,
Three hundred pounds, and any other sum
Of which the said testatrix dies possessed.
I say she died possessed of other sums.'

'Dear Romney, need we chronicle the
    pence?
I'm richer than I thought—that's evident.
Enough so.'
        'Listen rather. You've to do
With business and a cousin,' he resumed,
'And both, I fear, need patience. Here's
    the fact.
The other sum (there *is* another sum,
Unspecified in any will which dates
After possession, yet bequeathed as
    much
And clearly as those said three hundred
    pounds)
Is thirty thousand. You will have it paid
When? . . where? My duty troubles
    you with words.'

He struck the iron when the bar was hot;
No wonder if my eyes sent out some
    sparks.
'Pause there! I thank you. You are
    delicate
In glosing gifts;—but I, who share your
    blood,
Am rather made for giving, like yourself,
Than taking, like your pensioners. Fare-
    well.'

He stopped me with a gesture of calm
    pride.
'A Leigh,' he said, 'gives largesse and
    gives love,
But gloses never: if a Leigh could glose,
He would not do it, moreover, to a Leigh,
With blood trained up along nine cen-
    turies
To hound and hate a lie from eyes like
    yours.
And now we'll make the rest as clear;
    your aunt
Possessed these moneys.'
        'You will make it clear,
My cousin, as the honour of us both,
Or one of us speaks vainly! that's not I.
My aunt possessed this sum,—inherited
From whom, and when? bring docu-
    ments, prove dates.'

'Why now indeed you throw your
    bonnet off
As if you had time left for a logarithm!
The faith's the want. Dear cousin, give
    me faith,
And you shall walk this road with silken
    shoes,
As clean as any lady of our house
Supposed the proudest. Oh, I com-
    prehend
The whole position from your point of
    sight.
I oust you from your father's halls and
    lands
And make you poor by getting rich—
    that's law;
Considering which, in common circum-
    stance,
You would not scruple to accept from me
Some compensation, some sufficiency
Of income—that were justice; but, alas,
I love you,—that's mere nature; you
    reject
My love,—that's nature also; and at once
You cannot, from a suitor disallowed,
A hand thrown back as mine is, into yours
Receive a doit, a farthing,—not for the
    world!
That's woman's etiquette, and obviously
Exceeds the claim of nature, law, and right,
Unanswerable to all. I grant, you see,
The case as you conceive it,—leave you
    room

To sweep your ample skirts of woman-
hood,
While, standing humbly squeezed against
the wall,
I own myself excluded from being just,
Restrained from paying indubitable
debts,
Because denied from giving you my
soul.
That's my misfortune!—I submit to it
As if, in some more reasonable age,
'Twould not be less inevitable. Enough.
You'll trust me, cousin, as a gentleman,
To keep your honour, as you count it,
pure,
Your scruples (just as if I thought them
wise)
Safe and inviolate from gifts of mine.'

I answered mild but earnest. 'I believe
In no one's honour which another keeps,
Nor man's nor woman's. As I keep,
myself,
My truth and my religion, I depute
No father, though I had one this side
death,
Nor brother, though I had twenty, much
less you,
Though twice my cousin, and once
Romney Leigh,
To keep my honour pure. You face,
to-day,
A man who wants instruction, mark me,
not
A woman who wants protection. As to
a man,
Show manhood, speak out plainly, be
precise
With facts and dates. My aunt inherited
This sum, you say—'
'I said she died possessed
Of this, dear cousin.'
'Not by heritage.
Thank you : we're getting to the facts
at last.
Perhaps she played at commerce with
a ship
Which came in heavy with Australian
gold?
Or touched a lottery with her finger-end,
Which tumbled on a sudden into her lap
Some old Rhine tower or principality?
Perhaps she had to do with a marine

Sub-transatlantic railroad, which pre-
pays
As well as pre-supposes? or perhaps
Some stale ancestral debt was after-paid
By a hundred years, and took her by
surprise?—
You shake your head, my cousin; I guess
ill.'

'You need not guess, Aurora, nor de-
ride ;
The truth is not afraid of hurting you.
You'll find no cause, in all your scruples,
why
Your aunt should cavil at a deed of gift
'Twixt her and me.'
'I thought so—ah ! a gift.'

'You naturally thought so,' he resumed.
'A very natural gift.'
'A gift, a gift !
Her individual life being stranded high
Above all want, approaching opulence,
Too haughty was she to accept a gift
Without some ultimate aim : ah, ah,
I see,—
A gift intended plainly for her heirs,
And so accepted . . if accepted . . ah,
Indeed that might be; I am snared
perhaps
Just so. But, cousin, shall I pardon you,
If thus you have caught me with a cruel
springe ?'

He answered gently, ' Need you tremble
and pant
Like a netted lioness? is't my fault, mine,
That you're a grand wild creature of the
woods
And hate the stall built for you? Any way,
Though triply netted, need you glare at
me ?
I do not hold the cords of such a net ;
You're free from me, Aurora !'
'Now may God
Deliver me from this strait ! This gift
of yours
Was tendered . . when? accepted . .
when?' I asked.
'A month . . a fortnight since? Six
weeks ago
It was not tendered; by a word she
dropped

I know it was not tendered nor received.
When was it ? bring your dates.'
           ' What matters when?
A half-hour ere she died, or a half-year,
Secured the gift, maintains the heritage
Inviolable with law. As easy pluck
The golden stars from heaven's em-
     broidered stole
To pin them on the grey side of this earth,
As make you poor again, thank God.'
                 ' Not poor
Nor clean again from henceforth, you
     thank God ?
Well, sir—I ask you—I insist at need,—
Vouchsafe the special date, the special
     date.'

' The day before her death-day,' he
     replied,
' The gift was in her hands. We'll
     find that deed,
And certify that date to you.'
                 As one
Who has climbed a mountain-height and
     carried up
His own heart climbing, panting in his
     throat
With the toil of the ascent, takes breath
     at last,
Looks back in triumph—so I stood and
     looked.
' Dear cousin Romney, we have reached
     the top
Of this steep question, and may rest,
     I think.
But first,—I pray you pardon, that the
     shock
And surge of natural feeling and event
Has made me oblivious of acquainting you
That this, this letter (unread, mark, still
     sealed),
Was found enfolded in the poor dead
     hand :
That spirit of hers had gone beyond the
     address,
Which could not find her though you
     wrote it clear,—
I know your writing, Romney,—recog-
     nize
The open-hearted *A*, the liberal sweep
Of the *G*. Now listen,—let us under-
     stand :
You will not find that famous deed of gift,

Unless you find it in the letter here,
Which, not being mine, I give you
     back.—Refuse
To take the letter ? well then—you and I,
As writer and as heiress, open it
Together, by your leave.——Exactly so :
The words in which the noble offering's
     made
Are nobler still, my cousin ; and, I own,
The proudest and most delicate heart
     alive,
Distracted from the measure of the gift
By such a grace in giving, might accept
Your largesse without thinking any more
Of the burthen of it, than King Solomon
Considered, when he wore his holy ring
Charactered over with the ineffable spell,
How many carats of fine gold made up
Its money-value : so, Leigh gives to
     Leigh !
Or rather, might have given, observe,—
     for that 's
The point we come to. Here 's a proof
     of gift,
But here 's no proof, sir, of acceptancy,
But rather, disproof. Death's black dust,
     being blown,
Infiltrated through every secret fold
Of this sealed letter by a puff of fate,
Dried up for ever the fresh-written ink,
Annulled the gift, disutilized the grace,
And left these fragments.'
            As I spoke, I tore
The paper up and down, and down and up
And crosswise, till it fluttered from my
     hands,
As forest-leaves, stripped suddenly and
     rapt
By a whirlwind on Valdarno, drop again,
Drop slow, and strew the melancholy
     ground
Before the amazèd hills . . . why, so,
     indeed,
I'm writing like a poet, somewhat large
In the type of the image, and exaggerate
A small thing with a great thing,
     topping it :—
But then I'm thinking how his eyes
     looked, his,
With what despondent and surprised
     reproach !
I think the tears were in them as he
     looked ;

I think the manly mouth just trembled.
 Then
He broke the silence.
             ' I may ask, perhaps,
Although no stranger . . only Romney
  Leigh,
Which means still less . . than Vincent
  Carrington,
Your plans in going hence, and where
  you go.
This cannot be a secret.'
                  ' All my life
Is open to you, cousin. I go hence
To London, to the gathering-place of
  souls,
To live mine straight out, vocally, in
  books ;
Harmoniously for others, if indeed
A woman's soul, like man's, be wide
  enough
To carry the whole octave (that 's to
  prove)
Or, if I fail, still purely for myself.
Pray God be with me, Romney.'
                  ' Ah, poor child,
Who fight against the mother's 'tiring
  hand,
And choose the headsman's ! May God
  change His world
For your sake, sweet, and make it mild
  as heaven,
And juster than I have found you.'
                  But I paused.
' And you, my cousin ?'—
            ' I,' he said,— ' you ask ?
You care to ask ? Well, girls have
  curious minds
And fain would know the end of every-
  thing,
Of cousins therefore with the rest. For
  me,
Aurora, I've my work ; you know my
  work ;
And, having missed this year some
  personal hope,
I must beware the rather that I miss
No reasonable duty. While you sing
Your happy pastorals of the meads and
  trees,
Bethink you that I go to impress and
  prove
On stifled brains and deafened ears,
  stunned deaf,

Crushed dull with grief, that nature
  sings itself,
And needs no mediate poet, lute or voice,
To make it vocal. While you ask of men
Your audience, I may get their leave
  perhaps
For hungry orphans to say audibly
" We're hungry, see,"—for beaten and
  bullied wives
To hold their unweaned babies up in sight,
Whom orphanage would better, and for
  all
To speak and claim their portion . . by
  no means
Of the soil, . . but of the sweat in tilling it ;
Since this is nowadays turned privilege,
To have only God's curse on us, and
  not man's.
Such work I have for doing, elbow-deep
In social problems,—as you tie your
  rimes,
To draw my uses to cohere with needs
And bring the uneven world back to its
  round,
Or, failing so much, fill up, bridge at
  least
To smoother issues some abysmal cracks
And feuds of earth, intestine heats have
  made
To keep men separate,—using sorry shifts
Of hospitals, almshouses, infant schools,
And other practical stuff of partial good
You lovers of the beautiful and whole
Despise by system.'
                  ' I despise ? The scorn
Is yours, my cousin. Poets become such
Through scorning nothing. You decry
  them for
The good of beauty sung and taught by
  them,
While they respect your practical partial
  good
As being a part of beauty's self. Adieu !
When God helps all the workers for His
  world,
The singers shall have help of Him,
  not last.'

He smiled as men smile when they will
  not speak
Because of something bitter in the
  thought ;
And still I feel his melancholy eyes

Look judgement on me. It is seven
    years since :
I know not if 'twas pity or 'twas scorn
Has made them so far-reaching : judge
    it ye
Who have had to do with pity more
    than love
And scorn than hatred. I am used,
    since then,
To other ways, from equal men. But so,
Even so, we let go hands, my cousin and I,
And, in between us, rushed the torrent-
    world
To blanch our faces like divided rocks,
And bar for ever mutual sight and touch
Except through swirl of spray and all
    that roar.

THIRD BOOK

' To-DAY thou girdest up thy loins thyself
And goest where thou wouldest :
    presently
Others shall gird thee,' said the Lord,
    ' to go
Where thou wouldst not.' He spoke
    to Peter thus,
To signify the death which he should die
When crucified head downward.
                If He spoke
To Peter then, He speaks to us the same;
The word suits many different martyr-
    doms,
And signifies a multiform of death,
Although we scarcely die apostles, we,
And have mislaid the keys of heaven
    and earth.

For 'tis not in mere death that men
    die most,
And, after our first girding of the loins
In youth's fine linen and fair broidery
To run up hill and meet the rising sun,
We are apt to sit tired, patient as a fool,
While others gird us with the violent
    bands
Of social figments, feints, and formalisms,
Reversing our straight nature, lifting up
Our base needs, keeping down our lofty
    thoughts,
Head downward on the cross-sticks of
    the world.

Yet He can pluck us from that shameful
    cross.
God, set our feet low and our forehead
    high,
And show us how a man was made to
    walk !

Leave the lamp, Susan, and go up to bed.
The room does very well ; I have to
    write
Beyond the stroke of midnight. Get
    away ;
Your steps, for ever buzzing in the room,
Tease me like gnats. Ah, letters ! throw
    them down
At once, as I must have them, to be
    sure,
Whether I bid you never bring me such
At such an hour, or bid you. No excuse ;
You choose to bring them, as I choose
    perhaps
To throw them in the fire. Now get
    to bed,
And dream, if possible, I am not cross.

Why what a pettish, petty thing I grow,—
A mere, mere woman, a mere flaccid
    nerve,
A kerchief left out all night in the rain,
Turned soft so,—overtasked and over-
    strained
And overlived in this close London life !
And yet I should be stronger.
                Never burn
Your letters, poor Aurora ! for they stare
With red seals from the table, saying
    each,
' Here 's something that you know not.'
    Out alas,
'Tis scarcely that the world's more good
    and wise
Or even straighter and more consequent
Since yesterday at this time—yet, again,
If but one angel spoke from Ararat
I should be very sorry not to hear :
So open all the letters ! let me read.
Blanche Ord, the writer in the ' Lady's
    Fan,'
Requests my judgement on . . that,
    afterwards.
Kate Ward desires the model of my cloak,
And signs, ' Elisha to you.' Pringle
    Sharpe

Presents his work on 'Social Conduct,'
craves
A little money for his pressing debts . .
From me, who scarce have money for
my needs;
Art's fiery chariot which we journey in
Being apt to singe our singing-robes to
holes
Although you ask me for my cloak,
Kate Ward!
Here's Rudgely knows it,—editor and
scribe;
He's 'forced to marry where his heart
is not,
Because the purse lacks where he lost
his heart.'
Ah,——lost it because no one picked
it up;
That's really loss,—(and passable impu-
dence.)
My critic Hammond flatters prettily,
And wants another volume like the last.
My critic Belfair wants another book
Entirely different, which will sell (and
live?),
A striking book, yet not a startling book,
The public blames originalities
(You must not pump spring-water
unawares
Upon a gracious public full of nerves),
Good things, not subtle, new yet
orthodox,
As easy reading as the dog-eared page
That's fingered by said public fifty years,
Since first taught spelling by its grand-
mother,
And yet a revelation in some sort:
That's hard, my critic Belfair. So—
what next?
My critic Stokes objects to abstract
thoughts;
'Call a man, John, a woman, Joan,' says
he,
'And do not prate so of *humanities*:'
Whereat I call my critic simply, Stokes.
My critic Jobson recommends more mirth
Because a cheerful genius suits the times,
And all true poets laugh unquenchably
Like Shakespeare and the gods. That's
very hard.
The gods may laugh, and Shakespeare;
Dante smiled
With such a needy heart on two pale lips,

We cry, 'Weep rather, Dante.' Poems
are
Men, if true poems: and who dares
exclaim
At any man's door, 'Here, 'tis understood
The thunder fell last week and killed
a wife
And scared a sickly husband—what of
that?
Get up, be merry, shout and clap your
hands,
Because a cheerful genius suits the
times—'?
None says so to the man, and why indeed
Should any to the poem? A ninth seal;
The apocalypse is drawing to a close.
Ha,—this from Vincent Carrington,—
'Dear friend,
I want good counsel. Will you lend
me wings
To raise me to the subject, in a sketch
I'll bring to-morrow—may I? at eleven?
A poet's only born to turn to use:
So save you! for the world . . and Car-
rington.'
'(Writ after.) Have you heard of
Romney Leigh,
Beyond what's said of him in newspapers,
His phalansteries there, his speeches
here,
His pamphlets, pleas, and statements,
everywhere?
He dropped *me* long ago, but no one
drops
A golden apple—though indeed one day
You hinted that, but jested. Well, at least
You know Lord Howe who sees him . .
whom he sees
And *you* see and I hate to see,—for Howe
Stands high upon the brink of theories,
Observes the swimmers and cries "Very
fine,"
But keeps dry linen equally,—unlike
That gallant breaster, Romney. Strange
it is,
Such sudden madness seizing a young man
To make earth over again,—while I'm
content
To make the pictures. Let me bring the
sketch.
A tiptoe Danae, overbold and hot,
Both arms a-flame to meet her wishing
Jove

Half-way, and burn him faster down;
the face
And breasts upturned and straining, the
loose locks
All glowing with the anticipated gold.
Or here's another on the self-same theme.
She lies here—flat upon her prison-floor,
The long hair swathed about her to the
heel
Like wet sea-weed. You dimly see her
through
The glittering haze of that prodigious rain,
Half blotted out of nature by a love
As heavy as fate. I'll bring you either
sketch.
I think, myself, the second indicates
More passion.'
                    Surely. Self is put away,
And calm with abdication. She is Jove,
And no more Danae—greater thus.
    Perhaps
The painter symbolizes unaware
Two states of the recipient artist-soul,
One, forward, personal, wanting rever-
ence,
Because aspiring only. We'll be calm,
And know that, when indeed our Joves
come down,
We all turn stiller than we have ever
been.

Kind Vincent Carrington. I'll let him
come.
He talks of Florence,—and may say a
word
Of something as it chanced seven years
ago,
A hedgehog in the path, or a lame bird,
In those green country walks, in that
good time
When certainly I was so miserable . .
I seem to have missed a blessing ever
since.

The music soars within the little lark,
And the lark soars. It is not thus with
men.
We do not make our places with our
strains,—
Content, while they rise, to remain be-
hind
Alone on earth instead of so in heaven.
No matter ; I bear on my broken tale.

When Romney Leigh and I had parted
thus,
I took a chamber up three flights of stairs
Not far from being as steep as some larks
climb,
And there, in a certain house in Kensing-
ton,
Three years I lived and worked. Get
leave to work
In this world—'tis the best you get at all;
For God, in cursing, gives us better gifts
Than men in benediction. God says,
    ' Sweat
For foreheads,' men say ' crowns,' and
so we are crowned,
Aye, gashed by some tormenting circle
of steel
Which snaps with a secret spring. Get
work, get work ;
Be sure 'tis better than what you work
to get.

Serene and unafraid of solitude
I worked the short days out,—and
watched the sun
On lurid morns or monstrous afternoons
(Like some Druidic idol's fiery brass
With fixed unflickering outline of dead
heat,
From which the blood of wretches pent
inside
Seems oozing forth to incarnadine the air)
Push out through fog with his dilated disk,
And startle the slant roofs and chimney-
pots
With splashes of fierce colour. Or I saw
Fog only, the great tawny weltering fog
Involve the passive city, strangle it
Alive, and draw it off into the void,
Spires, bridges, streets, and squares, as
if a sponge
Had wiped out London,—or as noon and
night
Had clapped together and utterly struck
out
The intermediate time, undoing them-
selves
In the act. Your city poets see such things
Not despicable. Mountains of the south,
When drunk and mad with elemental
wines
They rend the seamless mist and stand
up bare,

Make fewer singers, haply. No one sings,
Descending Sinai : on Parnassus-mount
You take a mule to climb and not a muse
Except in fable and figure : forests chant
Their anthems to themselves, and leave
    you dumb.
But sit in London at the day's decline,
And view the city perish in the mist
Like Pharaoh's armaments in the deep
    Red Sea,
The chariots, horsemen, footmen, all the
    host,
Sucked down and choked to silence—
    then, surprised
By a sudden sense of vision and of tune,
You feel as conquerors though you did
    not fight,
And you and Israel's other singing girls,
Aye, Miriam with them, sing the song
    you chose.

I worked with patience, which means
    almost power :
I did some excellent things indifferently,
Some bad things excellently. Both
    were praised,
The latter loudest. And by such a time
That I myself had set them down as
    sins
Scarce worth the price of sackcloth,
    week by week
Arrived some letter through the sedulous
    post,
Like these I've read, and yet dissimilar,
With pretty maiden seals,—initials
    twined
Of lilies, or a heart marked *Emily*
(Convicting Emily of being all heart) ;
Or rarer tokens from young bachelors,
Who wrote from college with the same
    goosequill,
Suppose, they had just been plucked of,
    and a snatch
From Horace, ' Collegisse juvat,' set
Upon the first page. Many a letter, signed
Or unsigned, showing the writers at
    eighteen
Had lived too long, although a muse
    should help
Their dawn by holding candles,—com-
    pliments
To smile or sigh at. Such could pass
    with me

No more than coins from Moscow cir-
    culate
At Paris : would ten roubles buy a tag
Of ribbon on the boulevard, worth a sou ?
I smiled that all this youth should love
    me,—sighed
That such a love could scarcely raise
    them up
To love what was more worthy than
    myself ;
Then sighed again, again, less generously,
To think the very love they lavished so
Proved me inferior. The strong loved
    me not,
And he . . my cousin Romney . . did
    not write.
I felt the silent finger of his scorn
Prick every bubble of my frivolous fame
As my breath blew it, and resolve it back
To the air it came from. Oh, I justified
The measure he had taken of my height :
The thing was plain—he was not wrong
    a line ;
I played at art, made thrusts with a toy-
    sword,
Amused the lads and maidens.
                   Came a sigh
Deep, hoarse with resolution,—I would
    work
To better ends, or play in earnest.
    ' Heavens,
I think I should be almost popular
If this went on !'—I ripped my verses up,
And found no blood upon the rapier's
    point ;
The heart in them was just an embryo's
    heart
Which never yet had beat, that it should
    die ;
Just gasps of make-believe galvanic life ;
Mere tones, inorganized to any tune.

And yet I felt it in me where it burnt,
Like those hot fire-seeds of creation held
In Jove's clenched palm before the worlds
    were sown,—
But I—I was not Juno even ! my hand
Was shut in weak convulsion, woman's
    ill,
And when I yearned to loose a finger—lo,
The nerve revolted. 'Tis the same even
    now :
This hand may never, haply, open large,

Before the spark is quenched, or the
  palm charred,
To prove the power not else than by the
  pain.

It burns, it burnt—my whole life burnt
  with it,
And light, not sunlight and not torch-
  light, flashed
My steps out through the slow and
  difficult road.
I had grown distrustful of too forward
  Springs,
The season's books in drear significance
Of morals, dropping round me.   Lively
  books?
The ash has livelier verdure than the yew;
And yet the yew's green longer, and alone
Found worthy of the holy Christmas time:
We'll plant more yews if possible, albeit
We plant the graveyards with them.
                      Day and night
I worked my rhythmic thought, and
  furrowed up
Both watch and slumber with long lines
  of life
Which did not suit their season.   The
  rose fell
From either cheek, my eyes globed
  luminous
Through orbits of blue shadow, and my
  pulse
Would shudder along the purple-veinèd
  wrist
Like a shot bird.   Youth's stern, set
  face to face
With youth's ideal: and when people
  came
And said, ' You work too much, you are
  looking ill,'
I smiled for pity of them who pitied me,
And thought I should be better soon
  perhaps
For those ill looks.   Observe—' I,'
  means in youth
Just I, the conscious and eternal soul
With all its ends, and not the outside life,
The parcel-man, the doublet of the flesh,
The so much liver, lung, integument,
Which make the sum of ' I ' hereafter
  when
World-talkers talk of doing well or ill.
I prosper if I gain a step, although

A nail then pierced my foot : although
  my brain
Embracing any truth froze paralysed,
I prosper : I but change my instrument ;
I break the spade off, digging deep for
  gold,
And catch the mattock up.
                      I worked on, on.
Through all the bristling fence of nights
  and days
Which hedges time in from the eternities,
I struggled,—never stopped to note the
  stakes
Which hurt me in my course.   The mid-
  night oil
Would stink sometimes ; there came
  some vulgar needs :
I had to live that therefore I might work,
And, being but poor, I was constrained,
  for life,
To work with one hand for the booksellers
While working with the other for myself
And art: you swim with feet as well as
  hands,
Or make small way.   I apprehended
  this,—
In England no one lives by verse that lives;
And, apprehending, I resolved by prose
To make a space to sphere my living verse.
I wrote for cyclopaedias, magazines,
And weekly papers, holding up my name
To keep it from the mud.   I learnt the use
Of the editorial ' we ' in a review
As courtly ladies the fine trick of trains,
And swept it grandly through the open
  doors
As if one could not pass through doors at all
Save so encumbered.   I wrote tales beside,
Carved many an article on cherry-stones
To suit light readers,—something in the
  lines
Revealing, it was said, the mallet-hand,
But that, I'll never vouch for : what you
  do
For bread, will taste of common grain,
  not grapes,
Although you have a vineyard in Cham-
  pagne ;
Much less in Nephelococcygia
As mine was, peradventure.
                      Having bread
For just so many days, just breathing-
  room

For body and verse, I stood up straight
    and worked
My veritable work.   And as the soul
Which grows within a child makes the
    child grow,—
Or as the fiery sap, the touch from God,
Careering through a tree, dilates the bark
And roughs with scale and knob, before
    it strikes
The summer foliage out in a green
    flame—
So life, in deepening with me, deepened
    all
The course I took, the work I did.   Indeed
The academic law convinced of sin ;
The critics cried out on the falling off,
Regretting the first manner.   But I felt
My heart's life throbbing in my verse to
    show
It lived, it also—certes incomplete,
Disordered with all Adam in the blood,
But even its very tumours, warts and wens
Still organized by and implying life.

A lady called upon me on such a day.
She had the low voice of your English
    dames,
Unused, it seems, to need rise half a note
To catch attention,—and their quiet
    mood,
As if they lived too high above the earth
For that to put them out in anything :
So gentle, because verily so proud ;
So wary and afraid of hurting you,
By no means that you are not really vile,
But that they would not touch you with
    their foot
To push you to your place ; so self-
    possessed
Yet gracious and conciliating, it takes
An effort in their presence to speak
    truth :
You know the sort of woman,—brilliant
    stuff,
And out of nature.   'Lady Waldemar.'
She said her name quite simply, as if it
    meant
Not much indeed, but something,—took
    my hands,
And smiled as if her smile could help my
    case,
And dropped her eyes on me and let
    them melt.

'Is this,' she said, ' the Muse ?'
                        ' No sibyl even,'
I answered, ' since she fails to guess the
    cause
Which taxed you with this visit, madam.'
                        ' Good,'
She said, 'I value what's sincere at once.
Perhaps if I had found a literal Muse,
The visit might have taxed me.   As it is,
You wear your blue so chiefly in your
    eyes,
My fair Aurora, in a frank good way,
It comforts me entirely for your fame,
As well as for the trouble of ascent
To this Olympus.'
                        There, a silver laugh
Ran rippling through her quickened
    little breaths
The steep stair somewhat justified.
                        ' But still
Your ladyship has left me curious why
You dared the risk of finding the said
    Muse ?'

'Ah,—keep me, notwithstanding, to the
    point,
Like any pedant ?   Is the blue in eyes
As awful as in stockings after all,
I wonder, that you'd have my business
    out
Before I breathe—exact the epic plunge
In spite of gasps ?   Well, naturally you
    think
I've come here, as the lion-hunters go
To deserts, to secure you with a trap
For exhibition in my drawing-rooms
On zoologic soirées ? not in the least.
Roar softly at me ; I am frivolous,
I dare say ; I have played at wild-beast
    shows
Like other women of my class,—but
    now
I meet my lion simply as Androcles
Met his . . when at his mercy.'
                        So, she bent
Her head, as queens may mock,—then
    lifting up
Her eyelids with a real grave queenly
    look,
Which ruled and would not spare, not
    even herself,—
' I think you have a cousin :—Romney
    Leigh.'

'You bring a word from *him*?'—my
    eyes leapt up
To the very height of hers,—' a word
    from *him*?'

'I bring a word about him, actually.
But first' (she pressed me with her
    urgent eyes),
'You do not love him,—you?'
                    'You're frank at least
In putting questions, madam,' I replied;
'I love my cousin cousinly—no more.'

'I guessed as much. I'm ready to be
    frank
In answering also, if you'll question me,
Or even for something less. You stand
    outside,
You artist women, of the common sex;
You share not with us, and exceed us so
Perhaps by what you're mulcted in,
    your hearts
Being starved to make your heads: so
    run the old
Traditions of you. I can therefore speak
Without the natural shame which crea-
    tures feel
When speaking on their level, to their
    like.
There's many a papist she, would rather
    die
Than own to her maid she put a ribbon on
To catch the indifferent eye of such a
    man,
Who yet would count adulteries on her
    beads
At holy Mary's shrine and never blush;
Because the saints are so far off, we lose
All modesty before them. Thus, to-day.
'Tis *I*, love Romney Leigh.'
                    'Forbear,' I cried.
' If here's no muse, still less is any saint;
Nor even a friend, that Lady Waldemar
Should make confessions'..
                    'That's unkindly said.
If no friend, what forbids to make a friend
To join to our confession ere we have
    done?
I love your cousin. If it seems unwise
To say so, it's still foolisher (we're
    frank)
To feel so. My first husband left me
    young,

And pretty enough, so please you, and
    rich enough,
To keep my booth in May-fair with the
    rest
To happy issues. There are marquises
Would serve seven years to call me
    wife, I know,
And, after seven, I might consider it,
For there's some comfort in a marquisate
When all's said,—yes, but after the
    seven years;
I, now, love Romney. You put up your
    lip,
So like a Leigh! so like him!—Pardon
    me,
I'm well aware I do not derogate
In loving Romney Leigh. The name is
    good,
The means are excellent, but the man,
    the man—
Heaven help us both,—I am near as
    mad as he,
In loving such an one.'
                    She slowly swung
Her heavy ringlets till they touched her
    smile,
As reasonably sorry for herself,
And thus continued.
                    'Of a truth, Miss Leigh,
I have not, without struggle, come to this.
I took a master in the German tongue,
I gamed a little, went to Paris twice;
But, after all, this love!... you eat of
    love,
And do as vile a thing as if you ate
Of garlic—which, whatever else you eat,
Tastes uniformly acrid, till your peach
Reminds you of your onion. Am I
    coarse?
Well, love's coarse, nature's coarse—
    ah, there's the rub!
We fair fine ladies, who park out our lives
From common sheep-paths, cannot help
    the crows
From flying over,—we're as natural still
As Blowsalinda. Drape us perfectly
In Lyons' velvet,—we are not, for that,
Lay-figures, look you: we have hearts
    within,
Warm, live, improvident, indecent
    hearts,
As ready for outrageous ends and acts
As any distressed sempstress of them all

That Romney groans and toils for. We
    catch love
And other fevers, in the vulgar way :
Love will not be outwitted by our wit,
Nor outrun by our equipages :—mine
Persisted, spite of efforts. All my cards
Turned up but Romney Leigh ; my
    German stopped
At germane Wertherism ; my Paris
    rounds
Returned me from the Champs Elysées
    just
A ghost, and sighing like Dido's. I
    came home
Uncured,—convicted rather to myself
Of being in love . . . in love ! That's
    coarse, you'll say.
I'm talking garlic.'
              Coldly I replied.
' Apologize for atheism, not love !
For me, I do believe in love, and God.
I know my cousin : Lady Waldemar
I know not : yet I say as much as this ;
Whoever loves him, let her not excuse
But cleanse herself, that, loving such
    a man,
She may not do it with such unworthy
    love
He cannot stoop and take it.'
              'That is said
Austerely, like a youthful prophetess,
Who knits her brows across her pretty
    eyes
To keep them back from following the
    grey flight
Of doves between the temple-columns.
    Dear,
Be kinder with me ; let us two be friends.
I'm a mere woman,—the more weak
    perhaps
Through being so proud ; you're better ;
    as for him,
He's best. Indeed he builds his good-
    ness up
So high, it topples down to the other side
And makes a sort of badness ; there's
    the worst
I have to say against your cousin's best !
And so be mild, Aurora, with my worst
For his sake, if not mine.'
             'I own myself
Incredulous of confidence like this
Availing him or you.'

             'And I, myself,
Of being worthy of him with any love :
In your sense I am not so—let it pass.
And yet I save him if I marry him ;
Let that pass too.'
          'Pass, pass ! we play police
Upon my cousin's life, to indicate
What may or may not pass ?' I cried.
    ' He knows
What 's worthy of him ; the choice re-
    mains with *him* ;
And what he chooses, act or wife, I think
I shall not call unworthy, I, for one.'

' 'Tis somewhat rashly said,' she an-
    swered slow ;
' Now let 's talk reason, though we talk
    of love.
Your cousin Romney Leigh 's a monster ;
    there,
The word 's out fairly, let me prove the
    fact.
We'll take, say, that most perfect of
    antiques
They call the Genius of the Vatican,
(Which seems too beauteous to endure
    itself
In this mixed world,) and fasten it for
    once
Upon the torso of the Dancing Fawn,
(Who might limp surely, if he did not
    dance,)
Instead of Buonarroti's mask : what then ?
We show the sort of monster Romney is,
With god-like virtues and heroic aims
Subjoined to limping possibilities
Of mismade human nature. Grant the
    man
Twice godlike, twice heroic,—still he
    limps,
And here 's the point we come to.'
               ' Pardon me,
But, Lady Waldemar, the point 's the
    thing
We never come to.'
              ' Caustic, insolent
At need ! I like you '—(there, she took
    my hands)
' And now my lioness, help Androcles,
For all your roaring. Help me ! for
    myself
I would not say so—but for him. He
    limps

So certainly, he'll fall into the pit
A week hence,—so I lose him—so he is
    lost !
For when he's fairly married, he a Leigh,
To a girl of doubtful life, undoubtful birth,
Starved out in London till her coarse-
    grained hands
Are whiter than her morals,—even you
May call his choice unworthy.'
                        'Married ! lost !
He, . . . Romney !'
    'Ah, you're moved at last,' she said.
'These monsters, set out in the open sun,
Of course throw monstrous shadows :
    those who think
Awry, will scarce act straightly.   Who
    but he ?
And who but you can wonder ?   He
    has been mad,
The whole world knows, since first,
    a nominal man,
He soured the proctors, tried the gowns-
    men's wits,
With equal scorn of triangles and wine,
And took no honours, yet was honourable.
They'll tell you he lost count of Homer's
    ships
In Melbourne's poor-bills, Ashley's fac-
    tory bills,—
Ignored the Aspasia we all dare to praise,
For other women, dear, we could not
    name
Because we're decent.   Well, he had
    some right
On his side probably ; men always have,
Who go absurdly wrong.   The living boor
Who brews your ale, exceeds in vital
    worth
Dead Caesar who "stops bungholes" in
    the cask ;
And also, to do good is excellent,
For persons of his income, even to boors :
I sympathize with all such things.   But he
Went mad upon them . . madder and
    more mad
From college times to these,—as, going
    down hill,
The faster still, the farther.   You must
    know
Your Leigh by heart : he has sown his
    black young curls
With bleaching cares of half a million men
Already.   If you do not starve, or sin,

You're nothing to him : pay the income-
    tax
And break your heart upon 't, he'll
    scarce be touched ;
But come upon the parish, qualified
For the parish stocks, and Romney will
    be there
To call you brother, sister, or perhaps
A tenderer name still.   Had I any chance
With Mister Leigh, who am Lady
    Waldemar
And never committed felony ?'
                        'You speak
Too bitterly,' I said, 'for the literal truth.'

' The truth is bitter.   Here's a man who
    looks
For ever on the ground ! you must be low,
Or else a pictured ceiling overhead,
Good painting thrown away.   For me,
    I've done
What women may, we're somewhat
    limited,
We modest women, but I've done my
    best.
—How men are perjured when they
    swear our eyes
Have meaning in them ! they're just
    blue or brown,
They just can drop their lids a little.
    And yet
Mine did more, for I read half Fourier
    through,
Proudhon, Considérant, and Louis Blanc,
With various others of his socialists,
And, if I had been a fathom less in love,
Had cured myself with gaping.   As it was,
I quoted from them prettily enough
Perhaps, to make them sound half
    rational
To a saner man than he whene'er we
    talked
(For which I dodged occasion)—learnt
    by heart
His speeches in the Commons and else-
    where
Upon the social question ; heaped reports
Of wicked women and penitentiaries
On all my tables (with a place for Sue),
And gave my name to swell subscription-
    lists
Toward keeping up the sun at nights in
    heaven,

And other possible ends. All things
I did,
Except the impossible . . such as
wearing gowns
Provided by the Ten Hours' movement :
there,
I stopped—we must stop somewhere.
He, meanwhile,
Unmoved as the Indian tortoise 'neath
the world,
Let all that noise go on upon his back :
He would not disconcert or throw me
out,
'Twas well to see a woman of my class
With such a dawn of conscience. For
the heart,
Made firewood for his sake, and flaming
up
To his face,—he merely warmed his
feet at it :
Just deigned to let my carriage stop him
short
In park or street,—he leaning on the door
With news of the committee which sate
last
On pickpockets at suck.'

      'You jest—you jest.'

' As martyrs jest, dear (if you read
their lives),
Upon the axe which kills them. When
all 's done
By me, . . for him—you'll ask him
presently
The colour of my hair—he cannot tell,
Or answers "dark" at random ; while,
be sure,
He 's absolute on the figure, five or ten,
Of my last subscription. Is it bearable,
And I a woman ?'
      ' Is it reparable,
Though I were a man ?'
      ' I know not. That 's to prove.
But first, this shameful marriage ?'
      ' Aye ?' I cried,
' Then really there 's a marriage ?'
      ' Yesterday
I held him fast upon it. " Mister Leigh,"
Said I, " shut up a thing, it makes more
noise.
The boiling town keeps secrets ill ;
I 've known

Yours since last week. Forgive my
knowledge so :
You feel I'm not the woman of the world
The world thinks ; you have borne
with me before,
And used me in your noble work, our
work,
And now you shall not cast me off because
You're at the difficult point, the *join.*
'Tis true
Even I can scarce admit the cogency
Of such a marriage . . where you do
not love
(Except the class), yet marry and throw
your name
Down to the gutter, for a fire-escape
To future generations ! 'tis sublime,
A great example, a true Genesis
Of the opening social era. But take heed,
This virtuous act must have a patent
weight,
Or loses half its virtue. Make it tell,
Interpret it, and set it in the light,
And do not muffle it in a winter-cloak
As a vulgar bit of shame,—as if, at best,
A Leigh had made a misalliance and
blushed
A Howard should know it." Then,
I pressed him more :
" He would not choose," I said, "that
even his kin, . .
Aurora Leigh, even . . should conceive
his act
Less sacrifice, more fantasy." At which
He grew so pale, dear, . . to the lips,
I knew
I had touched him. " Do you know her,"
he inquired,
" My cousin Aurora ?" " Yes," I said,
and lied,
(But truly we all know you by your books)
And so I offered to come straight to you,
Explain the subject, justify the cause,
And take you with me to St. Margaret's
Court
To see this miracle, this Marian Erle,
This drover's daughter (she 's not pretty,
he swears)
Upon whose finger, exquisitely pricked
By a hundred needles, we're to hang
the tie
'Twixt class and class in England,—thus
indeed

By such a presence, yours and mine, to lift
The match up from the doubtful place. At once
He thanked me sighing, murmured to himself
"She'll do it perhaps, she's noble,"—thanked me twice,
And promised, as my guerdon, to put off
His marriage for a month.'
                    I answered then.
'I understand your drift imperfectly.
You wish to lead me to my cousin's betrothed,
To touch her hand if worthy, and hold her hand
If feeble, thus to justify his match.
So be it then. But how this serves your ends,
And how the strange confession of your love
Serves this, I have to learn—I cannot see.'

She knit her restless forehead. 'Then, despite,
Aurora, that most radiant morning name,
You're dull as any London afternoon.
I wanted time, and gained it,—wanted *you*,
And gain you! you will come and see the girl
In whose most prodigal eyes the lineal pearl
And pride of all your lofty race of Leighs
Is destined to solution. Authorized
By sight and knowledge, then, you'll speak your mind,
And prove to Romney, in your brilliant way,
He'll wrong the people and posterity,
(Say such a thing is bad for me and you,
And you fail utterly,) by concluding thus
An execrable marriage. Break it up,
Disroot it—peradventure presently
We'll plant a better fortune in its place.
Be good to me, Aurora, scorn me less
For saying the thing I should not. Well I know
I should not. I have kept, as others have,

The iron rule of womanly reserve
In lip and life, till now : I wept a week
Before I came here.'—Ending, she was pale ;
The last words, haughtily said, were tremulous.
This palfrey pranced in harness, arched her neck,
And, only by the foam upon the bit,
You saw she champed against it.
                    Then I rose.
'I love love : truth's no cleaner thing than love.
I comprehend a love so fiery hot
It burns its natural veil of august shame,
And stands sublimely in the nude, as chaste
As Medicean Venus. But I know,
A love that burns through veils will burn through masks
And shrivel up treachery. What, love and lie !
Nay—go to the opera ! your love's curable.'

'I love and lie ?' she said—'I lie, forsooth ?'
And beat her taper foot upon the floor,
And smiled against the shoe,—' You're hard, Miss Leigh,
Unversed in current phrases.—Bowling-greens
Of poets are fresher than the world's highways :
Forgive me that I rashly blew the dust,
Which dims our hedges even, in your eyes,
And vexed you so much. You find, probably,
No evil in this marriage,—rather good
Of innocence, to pastoralize in song :
You'll give the bond your signature, perhaps,
Beneath the lady's mark,—indifferent
That Romney chose a wife could write her name,
In witnessing he loved her.'
                    'Loved !' I cried ;
'Who tells you that he wants a wife to love ?
He gets a horse to use, not love, I think :
There's work for wives as well,—and after, straw,

When men are liberal. For myself, you
  err
Supposing power in me to break this
  match.
I could not do it, to save Romney's life,
And would not, to save mine.'
            'You take it so,'
She said, 'farewell, then. Write your
  books in peace,
As far as may be for some secret stir
Now obvious to me,—for, most obviously,
In coming hither I mistook the way.'
Whereat she touched my hand and bent
  her head,
And floated from me like a silent cloud
That leaves the sense of thunder.
            I drew breath,
Oppressed in my deliverance. After all
This woman breaks her social system up
For love, so counted—the love possible
To such,—and lilies are still lilies, pulled
By smutty hands, though spotted from
  their white ;
And thus she is better haply, of her kind,
Than Romney Leigh, who lives by dia-
  grams,
And crosses out the spontaneities
Of all his individual, personal life
With formal universals. As if man
Were set upon a high stool at a desk
To keep God's books for Him in red
  and black,
And feel by millions ! What, if even God
Were chiefly God by living out Himself
To an individualism of the Infinite,
Eterne, intense, profuse,—still throwing
  up
The golden spray of multitudinous worlds
In measure to the proclive weight and
  rush
Of His inner nature,—the spontaneous
  love
Still proof and outflow of spontaneous
  life ?
Then live, Aurora.
         Two hours afterward,
Within St. Margaret's Court I stood
  alone,
Close-veiled. A sick child, from an ague-
  fit,
Whose wasted right hand gambled
  'gainst his left
With an old brass button in a blot of sun,

Jeered weakly at me as I passed across
The uneven pavement ; while a woman,
  rouged
Upon the angular cheek-bones, kerchief
  torn,
Thin dangling locks, and flat lascivious
  mouth,
Cursed at a window both ways, in and out,
By turns some bed-rid creature and my-
  self,—
'Lie still there, mother ! liker the dead
  dog
You'll be to-morrow. What, we pick
  our way,
Fine madam, with those damnable small
  feet !
We cover up our face from doing good,
As if it were our purse ! What brings
  you here,
My lady ? is 't to find my gentleman
Who visits his tame pigeon in the eaves?
Our cholera catch you with its cramps
  and spasms,
And tumble up your good clothes, veil
  and all,
And turn your whiteness dead-blue.'
        I looked up;
I think I could have walked through hell
  that day,
And never flinched. 'The dear Christ
  comfort you,'
I said, 'you must have been most miser-
  able,
To be so cruel,'—and I emptied out
My purse upon the stones : when, as I
  had cast
The last charm in the cauldron, the
  whole court
Went boiling, bubbling up, from all its
  doors
And windows, with a hideous wail of
  laughs
And roar of oaths, and blows perhaps ..
  I passed
Too quickly for distinguishing .. and
  pushed
A little side-door hanging on a hinge,
And plunged into the dark, and groped
  and climbed
The long, steep, narrow stair 'twixt
  broken rail
And mildewed wall that let the plaster
  drop

To startle me in the blackness. Still,
     up, up!
So high lived Romney's bride. I paused
     at last
Before a low door in the roof, and
     knocked;
There came an answer like a hurried
     dove—
'So soon? can that be Mister Leigh?
     so soon?'
And, as I entered, an ineffable face
Met mine upon the threshold. 'Oh,
     not you,
Not you!'—the dropping of the voice
     implied,
'Then, if not you, for me not any one.'
I looked her in the eyes, and held her
     hands,
And said, 'I am his cousin,—Romney
     Leigh's;
And here I come to see my cousin too.'
She touched me with her face and with
     her voice,
This daughter of the people. Such soft
     flowers,
From such rough roots? the people,
     under there,
Can sin so, curse so, look so, smell so . . .
     faugh!
Yet have such daughters?
                    Nowise beautiful
Was Marian Erle. She was not white
     nor brown,
But could look either, like a mist that
     changed
According to being shone on more or less:
The hair, too, ran its opulence of curls
In doubt 'twixt dark and bright, nor left
     you clear
To name the colour. Too much hair
     perhaps
(I'll name a fault here) for so small a head,
Which seemed to droop on that side and
     on this,
As a full-blown rose uneasy with its
     weight
Though not a wind should trouble it.
     Again,
The dimple in the cheek had better gone
With redder, fuller rounds; and some-
     what large
The mouth was, though the milky little
     teeth

Dissolved it to so infantine a smile.
For soon it smiled at me; the eyes
     smiled too,
But 'twas as if remembering they had
     wept,
And knowing they should, some day,
     weep again.

We talked. She told me all her story out,
Which I'll re-tell with fuller utterance,
As coloured and confirmed in aftertimes
By others and herself too. Marian Erle
Was born upon the ledge of Malvern Hill
To eastward, in a hut built up at night
To evade the landlord's eye, of mud and
     turf,
Still liable, if once he looked that way,
To being straight levelled, scattered by
     his foot,
Like any other anthill. Born, I say;
God sent her to His world, commissioned
     right,
Her human testimonials fully signed,
Not scant in soul—complete in linea-
     ments;
But others had to swindle her a place
To wail in when she had come. No
     place for her,
By man's law! born an outlaw, was
     this babe;
Her first cry in our strange and strang-
     ling air,
When cast in spasms out by the shud-
     dering womb,
Was wrong against the social code,—
     forced wrong :—
What business had the baby to cry there?

I tell her story and grow passionate.
She, Marian, did not tell it so, but used
Meek words that made no wonder of
     herself
For being so sad a creature. 'Mister
     Leigh
Considered truly that such things should
     change.
They *will*, in heaven—but meantime, on
     the earth,
There's none can like a nettle as a pink,
Except himself. We're nettles, some
     of us,
And give offence by the act of spring-
     ing up;

And, if we leave the damp side of the wall,
The hoes, of course, are on us.' So she said.
Her father earned his life by random jobs
Despised by steadier workmen—keeping swine
On commons, picking hops, or hurrying on
The harvest at wet seasons, or, at need,
Assisting the Welsh drovers, when a drove
Of startled horses plunged into the mist
Below the mountain-road, and sowed the wind
With wandering neighings. In between the gaps
Of such irregular work, he drank and slept,
And cursed his wife because, the pence being out,
She could not buy more drink. At which she turned
(The worm), and beat her baby in revenge
For her own broken heart. There's not a crime
But takes its proper change out still in crime
If once rung on the counter of this world:
Let sinners look to it.
                    Yet the outcast child,
For whom the very mother's face fore-went
The mother's special patience, lived and grew;
Learnt early to cry low, and walk alone,
With that pathetic vacillating roll
Of the infant body on the uncertain feet
(The earth being felt unstable ground so soon),
At which most women's arms unclose at once
With irrepressive instinct. Thus, at three,
This poor weaned kid would run off from the fold,
This babe would steal off from the mother's chair,
And, creeping through the golden walls of gorse,
Would find some keyhole toward the secrecy

Of Heaven's high blue, and, nestling down, peer out—
Oh, not to catch the angels at their games,
She had never heard of angels,—but to gaze
She knew not why, to see she knew not what,
A-hungering outward from the barren earth
For something like a joy. She liked, she said,
To dazzle black her sight against the sky.
For then, it seemed, some grand blind Love came down,
And groped her out, and clasped her with a kiss;
She learnt God that way, and was beat for it
Whenever she went home,—yet came again,
As surely as the trapped hare, getting free,
Returns to his form. This grand blind Love, she said,
This skyey father and mother both in one,
Instructed her and civilized her more
Than even Sunday-school did afterward.
To which a lady sent her to learn books
And sit upon a long bench in a row
With other children. Well, she laughed sometimes
To see them laugh and laugh and maul their texts;
But ofter she was sorrowful with noise
And wondered if their mothers beat them hard
That ever they should laugh so. There was one
She loved indeed,—Rose Bell, a seven years' child
So pretty and clever, who read syllables
When Marian was at letters; *she* would laugh
At nothing—hold your finger up, she laughed,
Then shook her curls down over eyes and mouth
To hide her make-mirth from the school-master:
And Rose's pelting glee, as frank as rain
On cherry-blossoms, brightened Marian too,
To see another merry whom she loved.

She whispered once (the children side
    by side,
With mutual arms entwined about their
    necks)
' Your mother lets you laugh so?' 'Aye,'
    said Rose,
' She lets me. She was dug into the
    ground
Six years since, I being but a yearling
    wean.
Such mothers let us play and lose our
    time,
And never scold nor beat us ! don't you
    wish
You had one like that ?' There, Marian
    breaking off
Looked suddenly in my face. ' Poor
    Rose,' said she,
' I heard her laugh last night in Oxford
    Street.
I'd pour out half my blood to stop that
    laugh.
Poor Rose, poor Rose !' said Marian.
              She resumed.
It tried her, when she had learnt at
    Sunday-school
What God was, what He wanted from
    us all,
And how in choosing sin we vexed the
    Christ,
To go straight home and hear her father
    pull
The Name down on us from the thunder-
    shelf,
Then drink away his soul into the
    dark
From seeing judgement. Father, mother,
    home,
Were God and heaven reversed to her :
    the more
She knew of Right, the more she guessed
    their wrong ;
Her price paid down for knowledge,
    was to know
The vileness of her kindred : through
    her heart,
Her filial and tormented heart, hence-
    forth,
They struck their blows at virtue. Oh,
    'tis hard
To learn you have a father up in heaven
By a gathering certain sense of being,
    on earth,

Still worse than orphaned : 'tis too heavy
    a grief,
The having to thank God for such a joy !
And so passed Marian's life from year
    to year.
Her parents took her with them when
    they tramped,
Dodged lanes and heaths, frequented
    towns and fairs,
And once went farther and saw Man-
    chester,
And once the sea, that blue end of the
    world,
That fair scroll-finis of a wicked book,—
And twice a prison,—back at intervals,
Returning to the hills. Hills draw like
    heaven,
And stronger sometimes, holding out
    their hands
To pull you from the vile flats up to them.
And though perhaps these strollers still
    strolled back,
As sheep do, simply that they knew the
    way,
They certainly felt bettered unaware
Emerging from the social smut of towns
To wipe their feet clean on the mountain
    turf.
In which long wanderings, Marian lived
    and learned,
Endured and learned. The people on
    the roads
Would stop and ask her why her eyes
    outgrew
Her cheeks, and if she meant to lodge
    the birds
In all that hair ; and then they lifted her,
The miller in his cart, a mile or twain,
The butcher's boy on horseback. Often too
The pedlar stopped, and tapped her on
    the head
With absolute forefinger, brown and
    ringed,
And asked if peradventure she could read,
And when she answered ' aye,' would
    toss her down
Some stray odd volume from his heavy
    pack,
A Thomson's Seasons, mulcted of the
    Spring,
Or half a play of Shakespeare's, torn
    across,

(She had to guess the bottom of a page
By just the top sometimes,—as difficult,
As, sitting on the moon, to guess the
    earth!)
Or else a sheaf of leaves (for that small
    Ruth's
Small gleanings) torn out from the heart
    of books,
From Churchyard Elegies and Edens
    Lost,
From Burns, and Bunyan, Selkirk, and
    Tom Jones,—
'Twas somewhat hard to keep the things
    distinct,
And oft the jangling influence jarred the
    child
Like looking at a sunset full of grace
Through a pothouse window while the
    drunken oaths
Went on behind her. But she weeded out
Her book-leaves, threw away the leaves
    that hurt
(First tore them small, that none should
    find a word),
And made a nosegay of the sweet and
    good
To fold within her breast, and pore upon
At broken moments of the noontide glare,
When leave was given her to untie her
    cloak
And rest upon the dusty highway's bank
From the road's dust : or oft, the journey
    done,
Some city friend would lead her by the
    hand
To hear a lecture at an institute.
And thus she had grown, this Marian
    Erle of ours,
To no book-learning,—she was ignorant
Of authors,—not in earshot of the things
Outspoken o'er the heads of common men
By men who are uncommon,—but within
The cadenced hum of such, and capable
Of catching from the fringes of the wind
Some fragmentary phrases, here and
    there,
Of that fine music, which, being carried in
To her soul, had reproduced itself afresh
In finer motions of the lips and lids.

She said, in speaking of it, 'If a flower
Were thrown you out of heaven at in-
    tervals,

You'd soon attain to a trick of looking
    up,—
And so with her.' She counted me her
    years,
Till *I* felt old ; and then she counted me
Her sorrowful pleasures, till I felt
    ashamed.
She told me she was fortunate and calm
On such and such a season, sate and
    sewed,
With no one to break up her crystal
    thoughts,
While rimes from lovely poems span
    around
Their ringing circles of ecstatic tune,
Beneath the moistened finger of the Hour.
Her parents called her a strange, sickly
    child,
Not good for much, and given to sulk and
    stare,
And smile into the hedges and the clouds,
And tremble if one shook her from her fit
By any blow, or word even. Outdoor jobs
Went ill with her, and household quiet
    work
She was not born to. Had they kept
    the north,
They might have had their pennyworth
    out of her
Like other parents, in the factories,
(Your children work for you, not you
    for them,
Or else they better had been choked
    with air
The first breath drawn ;) but, in this
    trampling life,
Was nothing to be done with such a child
But tramp and tramp. And yet she
    knitted hose
Not ill, and was not dull at needlework ;
And all the country people gave her pence
For darning stockings past their natural
    age,
And patching petticoats from old to new,
And other light work done for thrifty
    wives.

One day, said Marian,—the sun shone
    that day—
Her mother had been badly beat, and felt
The bruises sore about her wretched soul
(That must have been) : she came in
    suddenly,

And snatching in a sort of breathless rage
Her daughter's headgear comb, let down
    the hair
Upon her like a sudden waterfall,
Then drew her drenched and passive by
    the arm
Outside the hut they lived in. When
    the child
Could clear her blinded face from all that
    stream
Of tresses . . there, a man stood, with
    beast's eyes
That seemed as they would swallow her
    alive
Complete in body and spirit, hair and
    all,—
And burning stertorous breath that hurt
    her cheek,
He breathed so near. The mother held
    her tight,
Saying hard between her teeth—'Why
    wench, why wench,
The squire speaks to you now—the
    squire's too good ;
He means to set you up, and comfort us.
Be mannerly at least.' The child turned
    round
And looked up piteous in the mother's
    face
(Be sure that mother's death-bed will
    not want
Another devil to damn, than such a look),
'Oh, mother !' then, with desperate
    glance to heaven,
'God, free me from my mother,' she
    shrieked out,
'These mothers are too dreadful.' And,
    with force
As passionate as fear, she tore her hands
Like lilies from the rocks, from hers and
    his,
And sprang down, bounded headlong
    down the steep,
Away from both—away, if possible,
As far as God,—away! They yelled at her,
As famished hounds at a hare. She
    heard them yell ;
She felt her name hiss after her from the
    hills,
Like shot from guns. On, on. And now
    she had cast
The voices off with the uplands. On.
    Mad fear

Was running in her feet and killing the
    ground ;
The white roads curled as if she burnt
    them up,
The green fields melted, wayside trees
    fell back
To make room for her. Then her head
    grew vexed ;
Trees, fields, turned on her and ran
    after her ;
She heard the quick pants of the hills
    behind,
Their keen air pricked her neck : she
    had lost her feet,
Could run no more, yet somehow went
    as fast,
The horizon red 'twixt steeples in the east
So sucked her forward, forward, while
    her heart
Kept swelling, swelling, till it swelled
    so big
It seemed to fill her body,—when it burst
And overflowed the world and swamped
    the light ;
'And now I am dead and safe,' thought
    Marian Erle—
She had dropped, she had fainted.
           As the sense returned,
The night had passed—not life's night.
    She was 'ware
Of heavy tumbling motions, creaking
    wheels,
The driver shouting to the lazy team
That swung their rankling bells against
    her brain,
While, through the wagon's coverture
    and chinks,
The cruel yellow morning pecked at her
Alive or dead upon the straw inside,—
At which her soul ached back into the
    dark
And prayed, 'no more of that.' A
    wagoner
Had found her in a ditch beneath the
    moon,
As white as moonshine save for the
    oozing blood.
At first he thought her dead ; but when
    he had wiped
The mouth and heard it sigh, he raised
    her up,
And laid her in his wagon in the straw,
And so conveyed her to the distant town

To which his business called himself,
  and left
That heap of misery at the hospital.

She stirred ;—the place seemed new and
  strange as death.
The white strait bed, with others strait
  and white,
Like graves dug side by side at measured
  lengths,
And quiet people walking in and out
With wonderful low voices and soft steps
And apparitional equal care for each,
Astonished her with order, silence, law.
And when a gentle hand held out a cup,
She took it, as you do at sacrament,
Half awed, half melted,—not being used,
  indeed,
To so much love as makes the form of love
And courtesy of manners. Delicate drinks
And rare white bread, to which some
  dying eyes
Were turned in observation. O my God,
How sick we must be, ere we make men
  just!
I think it frets the saints in heaven to see
How many desolate creatures on the earth
Have learnt the simple dues of fellowship
And social comfort, in a hospital,
As Marian did. She lay there, stunned,
  half tranced,
And wished, at intervals of growing
  sense,
She might be sicker yet, if sickness made
The world so marvellous kind, the air
  so hushed,
And all her wake-time quiet as a sleep ;
For now she understood (as such things
  were)
How sickness ended very oft in heaven
Among the unspoken raptures :—yet
  more sick,
And surelier happy. Then she dropped
  her lids,
And, folding up her hands as flowers at
  night,
Would lose no moment of the blessed
  time.

She lay and seethed in fever many weeks,
But youth was strong and overcame the
  test ;
Revolted soul and flesh were reconciled

And fetched back to the necessary day
And daylight duties. She could creep
  about
The long bare rooms, and stare out
  drearily
From any narrow window on the street,
Till some one who had nursed her as
  a friend
Said coldly to her, as an enemy,
' She had leave to go next week, being
  well enough,'
(While only her heart ached). 'Go
  next week,' thought she,
' Next week ! how would it be with her
  next week,
Let out into that terrible street alone
Among the pushing people, . . to go . .
  where ? '

One day, the last before the dreaded last,
Among the convalescents, like herself
Prepared to go next morning, she sate
  dumb,
And heard half absently the women
  talk,—
How one was famished for her baby's
  cheeks,
' The little wretch would know her !
  a year old
And lively, like his father !'—one was
  keen
To get to work, and fill some clamorous
  mouths ;
And one was tender for her dear goodman
Who had missed her sorely,—and one,
  querulous . .
' Would pay backbiting neighbours who
  had dared
To talk about her as already dead,'—
And one was proud . . 'and if her
  sweetheart Luke
Had left her for a ruddier face than hers
(The gossip would be seen through at a
  glance)
Sweet riddance of such sweethearts—
  let him hang !
'Twere good to have been sick for such
  an end.'

And while they talked, and Marian felt
  the worse
For having missed the worst of all their
  wrongs,

A visitor was ushered through the wards
And paused among the talkers. 'When
    he looked
It was as if he spoke, and when he spoke
He sang perhaps,' said Marian; 'could
    she tell?
She only knew' (so much she had
    chronicled,
As seraphs might the making of the sun)
'That he who came and spake, was
    Romney Leigh,
And then and there she saw and heard
    him first.'

And when it was her turn to have the
    face
Upon her, all those buzzing pallid lips
Being satisfied with comfort—when he
    changed
To Marian, saying 'And you? you're
    going, where?'—
She, moveless as a worm beneath a stone
Which some one's stumbling foot has
    spurned aside,
Writhed suddenly, astonished with the
    light,
And breaking into sobs cried, 'Where
    I go?
None asked me till this moment. Can
    I say
Where I go,—when it has not seemed
    worth while
To God Himself, who thinks of every one,
To think of me and fix where I shall go?'

'So young,' he gently asked her, 'you
    have lost
Your father and your mother?'
                    'Both,' she said,
'Both lost! my father was burnt up
    with gin
Or ever I sucked milk, and so is lost.
My mother sold me to a man last month,
And so my mother's lost, 'tis manifest.
And I, who fled from her for miles and
    miles,
As if I had caught sight of the fire of hell
Through some wild gap (she was my
    mother, sir),
It seems I shall be lost too, presently,
And so we end, all three of us.'
                    'Poor child,'
He said,—with such a pity in his voice,

It soothed her more than her own
    tears,—'poor child!
'Tis simple that betrayal by mother's love
Should bring despair of God's too.
    Yet be taught,
He 's better to us than many mothers are,
And children cannot wander beyond
    reach
Of the sweep of His white raiment.
    Touch and hold!
And if you weep still, weep where John
    was laid
While Jesus loved him.'
                    'She could say the words,'
She told me, 'exactly as he uttered them
A year back, since in any doubt or dark
They came out like the stars, and shone
    on her
With just their comfort. Common words,
    perhaps;
The ministers in church might say the
    same;
But he, he made the church with what
    he spoke,—
The difference was the miracle,' said she.

Then catching up her smile to ravishment,
She added quickly, 'I repeat his words,
But not his tones: can any one repeat
The music of an organ, out of church?
And when he said "poor child," I shut
    my eyes
To feel how tenderly his voice broke
    through,
As the ointment-box broke on the Holy
    feet
To let out the rich medicative nard.'

She told me how he had raised and
    rescued her
With reverent pity, as, in touching grief,
He touched the wounds of Christ,—and
    made her feel
More self-respecting. Hope, he called,
    belief
In God,—work, worship,—therefore let
    us pray!
And thus, to snatch her soul from atheism,
And keep it stainless from her mother's
    face,
He sent her to a famous sempstress-house
Far off in London, there to work and
    hope.

With that, they parted. She kept sight
of Heaven,
But not of Romney. He had good to do
To others: through the days and through
the nights
She sewed and sewed and sewed. She
drooped sometimes,
And wondered, while along the tawny
light
She struck the new thread into her
needle's eye,
How people without mothers on the hills
Could choose the town to live in!—then
she drew
The stitch, and mused how Romney's
face would look,
And if 'twere likely he'd remember hers
When they two had their meeting after
death.

FOURTH BOOK

THEY met still sooner. 'Twas a year
from thence
That Lucy Gresham, the sick sempstress
girl,
Who sewed by Marian's chair so still
and quick,
And leant her head upon its back to cough
More freely, when, the mistress turning
round,
The others took occasion to laugh out,
Gave up at last. Among the workers,
spoke
A bold girl with black eyebrows and red
lips;
'You know the news? Who's dying,
do you think?
Our Lucy Gresham. I expected it
As little as Nell Hart's wedding. Blush
not, Nell,
Thy curls be red enough without thy
cheeks,
And, some day, there'll be found a man
to dote
On red curls.—Lucy Gresham swooned
last night,
Dropped sudden in the street while
going home;
And now the baker says, who took her up
And laid her by her grandmother in bed,

He'll give her a week to die in. Pass
the silk.
Let's hope he gave her a loaf too, within
reach,
For otherwise they'll starve before they
die,
That funny pair of bedfellows! Miss
Bell,
I'll thank you for the scissors. The old
crone
Is paralytic—that's the reason why
Our Lucy's thread went faster than her
breath,
Which went too quick, we all know.
Marian Erle!
Why, Marian Erle, you're not the fool
to cry?
Your tears spoil Lady Waldemar's new
dress,
You piece of pity!'
                    Marian rose up straight,
And, breaking through the talk and
through the work,
Went outward, in the face of their
surprise,
To Lucy's home, to nurse her back to life
Or down to death. She knew, by such
an act,
All place and grace were forfeit in the
house,
Whose mistress would supply the miss-
ing hand
With necessary, not inhuman haste,
And take no blame. But pity, too, had
dues:
She could not leave a solitary soul
To founder in the dark, while she sate
still
And lavished stitches on a lady's hem
As if no other work were paramount.
'Why, God,' thought Marian, 'has
a missing hand
This moment; Lucy wants a drink,
perhaps.
Let others miss me! never miss me, God!'

So Marian sate by Lucy's bed, content
With duty, and was strong, for recom-
pense,
To hold the lamp of human love arm-high
To catch the death-strained eyes and
comfort them,
Until the angels, on the luminous side

Of death, had got theirs ready. And
  she said,
If Lucy thanked her sometimes, called
  her kind,
It touched her strangely. 'Marian
  Erle, called kind!
What, Marian, beaten and sold, who
  could not die!
'Tis verily good fortune to be kind.
Ah you,' she said, 'who are born to such
  a grace,
Be sorry for the unlicensed class, the poor,
Reduced to think the best good fortune
  means
That others, simply, should be kind to
  them.'

From sleep to sleep when Lucy had
  slid away
So gently, like the light upon a hill,
Of which none names the moment that
  it goes
Though all see when 'tis gone,—a man
  came in
And stood beside the bed. The old
  idiot wretch
Screamed feebly, like a baby overlain,
'Sir, sir, you won't mistake me for the
  corpse?
Don't look at *me*, sir! never bury *me!*
Although I lie here I'm alive as you,
Except my legs and arms,—I eat and drink
And understand, — (that you're the
  gentleman
Who fits the funerals up, Heaven speed
  you, sir,)
And certainly I should be livelier still
If Lucy here .. sir, Lucy is the corpse ..
Had worked more properly to buy me
  wine ;
But Lucy, sir, was always slow at work,
I shan't lose much by Lucy. Marian
  Erle,
Speak up and show the gentleman the
  corpse.'

And then a voice said, 'Marian Erle.'
  She rose ;
It was the hour for angels—there, stood
  hers !
She scarcely marvelled to see Romney
  Leigh.
As light November snows to empty nests,

As grass to graves, as moss to mildewed
  stones,
As July suns to ruins, through the rents,
As ministering spirits to mourners,
  through a loss,
As Heaven itself to men, through pangs
  of death,
He came uncalled wherever grief had
  come.
'And so,' said Marian Erle, 'we met
  anew,'
And added softly, 'so, we shall not part.'

He was not angry that she had left the
  house
Wherein he placed her. Well—she
  had feared it might
Have vexed him. Also, when he found
  her set
On keeping, though the dead was out
  of sight,
That half-dead, half-live body left behind
With cankerous heart and flesh, which
  took your best
And cursed you for the little good it did,
(Could any leave the bed-rid wretch
  alone,
So joyless she was thankless even to
  God,
Much more to you?) he did not say
  'twas well,
Yet Marian thought he did not take it ill,—
Since day by day he came, and every day
She felt within his utterance and his eyes
A closer, tenderer presence of the soul,
Until at last he said, 'We shall not part.'

On that same day, was Marian's work
  complete :
She had smoothed the empty bed, and
  swept the floor
Of coffin sawdust, set the chairs anew
The dead had ended gossip in, and stood
In that poor room so cold and orderly,
The door-key in her hand, prepared to go
As *they* had, howbeit not their way.
  He spoke.

'Dear Marian, of one clay God made
  us all,
And though men push and poke and
  paddle in't
(As children play at fashioning dirt-pies)
And call their fancies by the name of facts,

Assuming difference, lordship, privilege,
When all's plain dirt,—they come back
    to it at last,
The first grave-digger proves it with
    a spade,
And pats all even. Need we wait for this,
You, Marian, and I, Romney?'
              She, at that,
Looked blindly in his face, as when one
    looks
Through driving autumn-rains to find
    the sky.
He went on speaking.
          'Marian, I being born
What men call noble, and you, issued
    from
The noble people,—though the tyrannous
    sword
Which pierced Christ's heart, has cleft
    the world in twain
'Twixt class and class, opposing rich to
    poor,
Shall *we* keep parted? Not so. Let us lean
And strain together rather, each to each,
Compress the red lips of this gaping
    wound
As far as two souls can,—aye, lean and
    league,
I from my superabundance,—from your
    want
You,—joining in a protest 'gainst the
    wrong
On both sides.'
          All the rest, he held her hand
In speaking, which confused the sense
    of much.
Her heart beat against his words beat out so
    thick,
They might as well be written on the dust
Where some poor bird, escaping from
    hawk's beak,
Has dropped and beats its shuddering
    wings,—the lines
Are rubbed so,—yet 'twas something
    like to this,
—'That they two, standing at the two
    extremes
Of social classes, had received one seal,
Been dedicate and drawn beyond them-
    selves
To mercy and ministration,—he, indeed,
Through what he knew, and she,
    through what she felt,

He, by man's conscience, she, by
    woman's heart,
Relinquishing their several 'vantage
    posts
Of wealthy ease and honourable toil,
To work with God at love. And since
    God willed
That putting out his hand to touch this ark
He found a woman's hand there, he'd
    accept
The sign too, hold the tender fingers fast,
And say, "My fellow-worker, be my
    wife!"'

She told the tale with simple, rustic
    turns,—
Strong leaps of meaning in her sudden
    eyes
That took the gaps of any imperfect
    phrase
Of the unschooled speaker; I have
    rather writ
The thing I understood so, than the thing
I heard so. And I cannot render right
Her quick gesticulation, wild yet soft,
Self-startled from the habitual mood she
    used,
Half sad, half languid,—like dumb
    creatures (now
A rustling bird, and now a wandering
    deer,
Or squirrel 'gainst the oak-gloom
    flashing up
His sidelong burnished head, in just her
    way
Of savage spontaneity), that stir
Abruptly the green silence of the woods,
And make it stranger, holier, more
    profound;
As Nature's general heart confessed it-
    self
Of life, and then fell backward on repose.

I kissed the lips that ended.—'So indeed
He loves you, Marian?'
            'Loves me!' She looked up
With a child's wonder when you ask
    him first
Who made the sun—a puzzled blush,
    that grew,
Then broke off in a rapid radiant smile
Of sure solution. 'Loves me! he loves
    all,—

And me, of course. He had not asked
     me else
To work with him for ever and be his wife.'

Her words reproved me. This perhaps
     was love—
To have its hands too full of gifts to give,
For putting out a hand to take a gift ;
To love so much, the perfect round of love
Includes, in strict conclusion, being
     loved ;
As Eden-dew went up and fell again,
Enough for watering Eden. Obviously
She had not thought about his love at all :
The cataracts of her soul had poured
     themselves,
And risen self-crowned in rainbow :
     would she ask
Who crowned her ?—it sufficed that she
     was crowned.
With women of my class 'tis otherwise :
We haggle for the small change of our
     gold,
And so much love accord for so much love,
Rialto-prices. Are we therefore wrong ?
If marriage be a contract, look to it then,
Contracting parties should be equal, just,
But if, a simple fealty on one side,
A mere religion,—right to give, is all,
And certain brides of Europe duly ask
To mount the pile as Indian widows do,
The spices of their tender youth heaped
     up,
The jewels of their gracious virtues worn,
More gems, more glory,—to consume
     entire
For a living husband : as the man's alive,
Not dead, the woman's duty by so much
Advanced in England beyond Hindostan.

I sate there musing, till she touched my
     hand
With hers, as softly as a strange white bird
She feared to startle in touching. ' You
     are kind.
But are you, peradventure, vexed at heart
Because your cousin takes me for a wife ?
I know I am not worthy—nay, in truth,
I'm glad on 't, since, for that, he
     chooses me.
He likes the poor things of the world
     the best ;
I would not therefore, if I could, be rich.

It pleasures him to stoop for buttercups ;
I would not be a rose upon the wall
A queen might stop at, near the palace-
     door,
To say to a courtier, " Pluck that rose
     for me,
It 's prettier than the rest." O Romney
     Leigh !
I'd rather far be trodden by his foot,
Than lie in a great queen's bosom.'
                    Out of breath
She paused.
          ' Sweet Marian, do you disavow
The roses with that face ?'
               She dropt her head
As if the wind had caught that flower
     of her
And bent it in the garden,—then looked up
With grave assurance. ' Well, you
     think me bold !
But so we all are, when we're praying
     God.
And if I'm bold—yet, lady, credit me,
That, since I know myself for what I am,
Much fitter for his handmaid than his wife,
I'll prove the handmaid and the wife at
     once,
Serve tenderly, and love obediently,
And be a worthier mate, perhaps, than
     some
Who are wooed in silk among their
     learned books ;
While I shall set myself to read his eyes,
Till such grow plainer to me than the
     French
To wisest ladies. Do you think I'll miss
A letter, in the spelling of his mind ?
No more than they do when they sit
     and write
Their flying words with flickering wild-
     fowl tails,
Nor ever pause to ask how many *t*s,
Should that be *y*, or *i*, they know 't so well :
I've seen them writing, when I brought
     a dress
And waited,—floating out their soft
     white hands
On shining paper. But they're hard
     sometimes,
For all those hands !—we've used out
     many nights,
And worn the yellow daylight into
     shreds

Which flapped and shivered down our
    aching eyes
Till night appeared more tolerable, just
That pretty ladies might look beautiful,
Who said at last . . "You're lazy in
    that house !
You're slow in sending home the
    work,—I count
I've waited near an hour for 't."
    Pardon me,
I do not blame them, madam, nor
    misprize ;
They are fair and gracious ; aye, but not
    like you,
Since none but you has Mister Leigh's
    own blood
Both noble and gentle,—and, without
    it . . well,
They are fair, I said ; so fair, it scarce
    seems strange
That, flashing out in any looking-glass
The wonder of their glorious brows
    and breasts,
They're charmed so, they forget to
    look behind
And mark how pale we've grown, we
    pitiful
Remainders of the world. And so perhaps
If Mister Leigh had chosen a wife from
    these,
She might, although he 's better than
    her best
And dearly she would know it, steal
    a thought
Which should be all his, an eye-glance
    from his face,
To plunge into the mirror opposite
In search of her own beauty's pearl;
    while I . .
Ah, dearest lady, serge will outweigh
    silk
For winter-wear when bodies feel a-cold,
And I'll be a true wife to your cousin
    Leigh.'

Before I answered he was there himself.
I think he had been standing in the room
And listened probably to half her talk,
Arrested, turned to stone,—as white
    as stone.
Will tender sayings make men look so
    white ?
He loves her then profoundly.

                                'You are here,
Aurora ?   Here I meet you !'—We
    clasped hands.

'Even so, dear Romney. Lady Waldemar
Has sent me in haste to find a cousin of
    mine
Who shall be.'

                    ' Lady Waldemar is good.'

'Here's one, at least, who is good,'
    I sighed, and touched
Poor Marian's happy head, as doglike she,
Most passionately patient, waited on,
A-tremble for her turn of greeting words ;
'I've sate a full hour with your Marian
    Erle,
And learnt the thing by heart,—and
    from my heart
Am therefore competent to give you
    thanks
For such a cousin.'

                    'You accept at last
A gift from me, Aurora, without scorn?
At last I please you ?'—How his voice
    was changed.

'You cannot please a woman against
    her will,
And once you vexed me. Shall we
    speak of that ?
We'll say, then, you were noble in it all
And I not ignorant—let it pass. And now
You please me, Romney, when you
    please yourself ;
So, please you, be fanatical in love,
And I'm well pleased. Ah, cousin !
    at the old hall,
Among the gallery portraits of our Leighs,
We shall not find a sweeter signory
Than this pure forehead's.'

                        Not a word he said.
How arrogant men are !—Even philan-
    thropists,
Who try to take a wife up in the way
They put down a subscription-cheque,—
    if once
She turns and says, ' I will not tax you so,
Most charitable sir,'—feel ill at ease
As though she had wronged them some-
    how.   I suppose
We women should remember what we
    are,

And not throw back an obolus inscribed
With Caesar's image, lightly. I resumed.

'It strikes me, some of those sublime
        Vandykes
Were not too proud to make good saints
        in heaven ;
And if so, then they're not too proud
        to-day,
To bow down (now the ruffs are off
        their necks)
And own this good, true, noble Marian,
        yours,
And mine, I'll say !—For poets (bear
        the word),
Half-poets even, are still whole demo-
        crats,—
Oh, not that we're disloyal to the high,
But loyal to the low, and cognizant
Of the less scrutable majesties. For me,
I comprehend your choice, I justify
Your right in choosing.'
                'No, no, no,' he sighed,
With a sort of melancholy impatient
        scorn,
As some grown man who never had
        a child
Puts by some child who plays at being
        a man,
'You did not, do not, cannot comprehend
My choice, my ends, my motives, nor
        myself :
No matter now ; we'll let it pass, you
        say.
I thank you for your generous cousinship
Which helps this present ; I accept for her
Your favourable thoughts. We're fallen
        on days,
We two who are not poets, when to wed
Requires less mutual love than common
        love
For two together to bear out at once
Upon the loveless many. Work in pairs,
In galley-couplings or in marriage-rings,
The difference lies in the honour, not
        the work,—
And such we're bound to, I and she.
        But love
(You poets are benighted in this age,
The hour's too late for catching even
        moths,
You've gnats instead), love !—love's
        fool-paradise

Is out of date, like Adam's. Set a swan
To swim the Trenton, rather than true
        love
To float its fabulous plumage safely down
The cataracts of this loud transition-
        time,—
Whose roar for ever henceforth in my
        ears
Must keep me deaf to music.'
                        There, I turned
And kissed poor Marian, out of dis-
        content.
The man had baffled, chafed me, till
        I flung
For refuge to the woman,—as, sometimes,
Impatient of some crowded room's close
        smell,
You throw a window open and lean out
To breathe a long breath in the dewy night
And cool your angry forehead. She,
        at least,
Was not built up as walls are, brick by
        brick,
Each fancy squared, each feeling ranged
        by line,
The very heat of burning youth applied
To indurate form and system ! excellent
        bricks,
A well-built wall,—which stops you on
        the road,
And, into which, you cannot see an inch
Although you beat your head against
        it—pshaw !

'Adieu,' I said, 'for this time, cousins
        both,
And, cousin Romney, pardon me the
        word,
Be happy !—oh, in some esoteric sense
Of course !—I mean no harm in wishing
        well.
Adieu, my Marian :—may she come to me,
Dear Romney, and be married from my
        house ?
It is not part of your philosophy
To keep your bird upon the blackthorn ?'

                                'Aye,'
He answered, 'but it is. I take my wife
Directly from the people,—and she
        comes,
As Austria's daughter to imperial France,
Betwixt her eagles, blinking not her race,

From Margaret's Court at garret-height,
to meet
And wed me at St. James's, nor put off
Her gown of serge for that. The things
we do,
We do : we'll wear no mask, as if we
blushed.'

'Dear Romney, you're the poet,'
I replied.
But felt my smile too mournful for my
word,
And turned and went. Aye, masks,
I thought,—beware
Of tragic masks we tie before the glass,
Uplifted on the cothurn half a yard
Above the natural stature! we would play
Heroic parts to ourselves,—and end,
perhaps,
As impotently as Athenian wives
Who shrieked in fits at the Eumenides.

His foot pursued me down the stair.
'At least
You'll suffer me to walk with you beyond
These hideous streets, these graves,
where men alive
Packed close with earthworms, burr
unconsciously
About the plague that slew them ; let
me go.
The very women pelt their souls in mud
At any woman who walks here alone.
How came you here alone?—you are
ignorant.'

We had a strange and melancholy walk :
The night came drizzling downward in
dark rain,
And, as we walked, the colour of the
time,
The act, the presence, my hand upon
his arm,
His voice in my ear, and mine to my
own sense,
Appeared unnatural. We talked modern
books
And daily papers, Spanish marriage-
schemes
And English climate—was't so cold
last year?
And will the wind change by to-morrow
morn?

Can Guizot stand? is London full?
is trade
Competitive? has Dickens turned his
hinge
A-pinch upon the fingers of the great?
And are potatoes to grow mythical
Like moly? will the apple die out too?
Which way is the wind to-night? south-
east? due east?
We talked on fast, while every common
word
Seemed tangled with the thunder at one
end,
And ready to pull down upon our heads
A terror out of sight. And yet to pause
Were surelier mortal : we tore greedily
up
All silence, all the innocent breathing-
points,
As if, like pale conspirators in haste,
We tore up papers where our signatures
Imperilled us to an ugly shame or death.

I cannot tell you why it was. 'Tis plain
We had not loved nor hated : wherefore
dread
To spill gunpowder on ground safe from
fire?
Perhaps we had lived too closely, to
diverge
So absolutely : leave two clocks, they
say,
Wound up to different hours, upon one
shelf,
And slowly, through the interior wheels
of each,
The blind mechanic motion sets itself
A-throb to feel out for the mutual time.
It was not so with us, indeed : while he
Struck midnight, I kept striking six at
dawn,
While he marked judgement, I, redemp-
tion-day ;
And such exception to a general law
Imperious upon inert matter even,
Might make us, each to either, insecure,
A beckoning mystery or a troubling fear.

I mind me, when we parted at the door,
How strange his good-night sounded,—
like good-night
Beside a deathbed, where the morrow's
sun

Is sure to come too late for more good-
    days :
And all that night I thought . . ' " Good-
    night," said he.'

And so, a month passed. Let me set
    it down
At once,—I have been wrong, I have
    been wrong.
We are wrong always when we think
    too much
Of what we think or are : albeit our
    thoughts
Be verily bitter as self-sacrifice,
We're no less selfish. If we sleep on
    rocks
Or roses, sleeping past the hour of noon
We're lazy. This I write against my-
    self.
I had done a duty in the visit paid
To Marian, and was ready otherwise
To give the witness of my presence and
    name
Whenever she should marry.—Which,
    I thought,
Sufficed. I even had cast into the scale
An overweight of justice toward the
    match ;
The Lady Waldemar had missed her tool,
Had broken it in the lock as being too
    straight
For a crooked purpose, while poor
    Marian Erle
Missed nothing in my accents or my
    acts :
I had not been ungenerous on the whole,
Nor yet untender ; so, enough. I felt
Tired, overworked : this marriage some-
    what jarred ;
Or, if it did not, all the bridal noise,
The pricking of the map of life with pins,
In schemes of . . ' Here we'll go,' and
    ' There we'll stay,'
And ' Everywhere we'll prosper in our
    love,'
Was scarce my business : let them
    order it ;
Who else should care ? I threw myself
    aside,
As one who had done her work and
    shuts her eyes
To rest the better.
              I, who should have known,

Forereckoned mischief! Where we
    disavow
Being keeper to our brother we're his
    Cain.

I might have held that poor child to my
    heart
A little longer ! 'twould have hurt me
    much
To have hastened by its beats the
    marriage day,
And kept her safe meantime from
    tampering hands
Or, peradventure, traps. What drew
    me back
From telling Romney plainly the designs
Of Lady Waldemar, as spoken out
To me . . me ? had I any right, aye, right,
With womanly compassion and reserve
To break the fall of woman's impu-
    dence ?—
To stand by calmly, knowing what
    I knew,
And hear him call her *good ?*
             Distrust that word.
' There is none good save God,' said
    Jesus Christ.
If He once, in the first creation-week,
Called creatures good,—for ever, after-
    ward,
The Devil only has done it, and his heirs,
The knaves who win so, and the fools
    who lose ;
The word 's grown dangerous. In the
    middle age,
I think they called malignant fays and
    imps
Good people. A good neighbour, even
    in this,
Is fatal sometimes,—cuts your morning up
To mince-meat of the very smallest talk,
Then helps to sugar her bohea at night
With your reputation. I have known
    good wives,
As chaste, or nearly so, as Potiphar's ;
And good, good mothers, who would
    use a child
To better an intrigue ; good friends,
    beside
(Very good), who hung succinctly round
    your neck
And sucked your breath, as cats are
    fabled to do

By sleeping infants. And we all have
    known
Good critics who have stamped out
    poet's hopes,
Good statesmen who pulled ruin on the
    state,
Good patriots who for a theory risked
    a cause,
Good kings who disembowelled for a
    tax,
Good popes who brought all good to
    jeopardy,
Good Christians who sate still in easy
    chairs
And damned the general world for
    standing up.—
Now may the good God pardon all
    good men !

How bitterly I speak,—how certainly
The innocent white milk in us is turned,
By much persistent shining of the sun !—
Shake up the sweetest in us long enough
With men, it drops to foolish curd, too sour
To feed the most untender of Christ's
    lambs.

I should have thought,—a woman of the
    world
Like her I'm meaning, centre to herself,
Who has wheeled on her own pivot half
    a life
In isolated self-love and self-will,
As a windmill seen at distance radiating
Its delicate white vans against the sky,
So soft and soundless, simply beautiful,
Seen nearer,—what a roar and tear it
    makes,
How it grinds and bruises !—if she loves
    at last,
Her love's a readjustment of self-love,
No more,—a need felt of another's use
To her one advantage, as the mill wants
    grain,
The fire wants fuel, the very wolf wants
    prey,
And none of these is more unscrupulous
Than such a charming woman when she
    loves.
She'll not be thwarted by an obstacle
So trifling as . . her soul is, . . much less
    yours !—
Is God a consideration ?—she loves you,

Not God ; she will not flinch for Him
    indeed :
She did not for the Marchioness of Perth,
When wanting tickets for the fancy ball.
She loves you, sir, with passion, to lunacy,
She loves you like her diamonds . .
    almost.
                                    Well,
A month passed so, and then the notice
    came,
On such a day the marriage at the church.
I was not backward.
                    Half Saint Giles in frieze
Was bidden to meet Saint James in
    cloth of gold,
And, after contract at the altar, pass
To eat a marriage-feast on Hampstead
    Heath.
Of course the people came in un-
    compelled,
Lame, blind, and worse—sick, sorrowful,
    and worse,
The humours of the peccant social wound
All pressed out, poured down upon
    Pimlico,
Exasperating the unaccustomed air
With a hideous interfusion. You'd
    suppose
A finished generation, dead of plague,
Swept outward from their graves into the
    sun,
The moil of death upon them. What a
    sight !
A holiday of miserable men
Is sadder than a burial-day of kings.

They clogged the streets, they oozed
    into the church
In a dark slow stream, like blood. To
    see that sight,
The noble ladies stood up in their pews,
Some pale for fear, a few as red for hate,
Some simply curious, some just insolent,
And some in wondering scorn,—' What
    next ? what next ? '
These crushed their delicate rose-lips
    from the smile
That misbecame them in a holy place,
With broidered hems of perfumed hand-
    kerchiefs ;
Those passed the salts, with confidence
    of eyes
And simultaneous shiver of moiré silk :

While all the aisles, alive and black with
    heads,
Crawled slowly toward the altar from
    the street,
As bruised snakes crawl and hiss out of
    a hole
With shuddering involution, swaying
    slow
From right to left, and then from left to
    right,
In pants and pauses. What an ugly crest
Of faces rose upon you everywhere
From that crammed mass ! you did not
    usually
See faces like them in the open day :
They hide in cellars, not to make you mad
As Romney Leigh is.—Faces !—O my
    God,
We call those, faces? men's and women's
    . . aye,
And children's ;—babies, hanging like a
    rag
Forgotten on their mother's neck,—poor
    mouths,
Wiped clean of mother's milk by mother's
    blow
Before they are taught her cursing.
    Faces? . . phew,
We'll call them vices, festering to
    despairs,
Or sorrows, petrifying to vices : not
A finger-touch of God left whole on them,
All ruined, lost—the countenance worn
    out
As the garment, the will dissolute as the
    act,
The passions loose and draggling in the
    dirt
To trip a foot up at the first free step !
Those, faces? 'twas as if you had stirred
    up hell
To heave its lowest dreg-fiends upper-
    most
In fiery swirls of slime,—such strangled
    fronts,
Such obdurate jaws were thrown up
    constantly
To twit you with your race, corrupt
    your blood,
And grind to devilish colours all your
    dreams
Henceforth,—though, haply, you should
    drop asleep

By clink of silver waters, in a muse
On Raffael's mild Madonna of the Bird.

I've waked and slept through many
    nights and days
Since then,—but still that day will catch
    my breath
Like a nightmare.   There are fatal days,
    indeed,
In which the fibrous years have taken root
So deeply, that they quiver to their tops
Whene'er you stir the dust of such a day.

My cousin met me with his eyes and hand,
And then, with just a word, . . that
    ' Marian Erle
Was coming with her bridesmaids
    presently,'
Made haste to place me by the altar-stair
Where he and other noble gentlemen
And high-born ladies, waited for the
    bride.

We waited. It was early : there was time
For greeting and the morning's com-
    pliment,
And gradually a ripple of women's talk
Arose and fell and tossed about a spray
Of English ss, soft as a silent hush,
And, notwithstanding, quite as audible
As louder phrases thrown out by the men.
—' Yes, really, if we need to wait in church
We need to talk there.'—' She? 'tis
    Lady Ayr,
In blue—not purple! that's the dowager.'
—' She looks as young '—' She flirts as
    young, you mean.
Why if you had seen her upon Thursday
    night,
You'd call Miss Norris modest.'—' *You*
    again !
I waltzed with you three hours back.
    Up at six,
Up still at ten ; scarce time to change
    one's shoes :
I feel as white and sulky as a ghost,
So pray don't speak to me, Lord
    Belcher.'—' No,
I'll look at you instead, and it 's enough
While you have that face.' ' In church,
    my lord ! fie, fie ! '
—' Adair, you stayed for the Division ? '
    —' Lost

By one.' 'The devil it is! I'm sorry for't.
And if I had not promised Mistress
    Grove' . .
'You might have kept your word to
    Liverpool.'
—'Constituents must remember, after all,
We're mortal.'—'We remind them of
    it.'—'Hark,
The bride comes! here she comes, in a
    stream of milk!'
—'There? Dear, you are asleep still;
    don't you know
The five Miss Granvilles? always dressed
    in white
To show they're ready to be married.'
        —'Lower!
The aunt is at your elbow.'—'Lady Maud,
Did Lady Waldemar tell you she had seen
This girl of Leigh's?' 'No,—wait!
    'twas Mistress Brookes,
Who told me Lady Waldemar told her—
No, 'twasn't Mistress Brookes.'—'She's
    pretty?'—'Who?
Mistress Brookes? Lady Waldemar?'
        —'How hot!
Pray is't the law to-day we're not to
    breathe?
You're treading on my shawl—I thank
    you, sir.'
—'They say the bride's a mere child,
    who can't read,
But knows the things she shouldn't, with
    wide-awake
Great eyes. I'd go through fire to look
    at her.'
—'You do, I think.'—'And Lady
    Waldemar
(You see her; sitting close to Romney
    Leigh.
How beautiful she looks, a little flushed!)
Has taken up the girl, and methodized
Leigh's folly. Should I have come here,
    you suppose,
Except she'd asked me?'—'She'd have
    served him more
By marrying him herself.'
        'Ah—there she comes,
The bride, at last!'
        'Indeed, no. Past eleven.
She puts off her patched petticoat to-day
And puts on May-fair manners, so begins
By setting us to wait.'—'Yes, yes, this
    Leigh

Was always odd; it's in the blood, I think;
His father's uncle's cousin's second son
Was, was . . you understand me; and
    for him,
He's stark,—has turned quite lunatic upon
This modern question of the poor—the
    poor.
An excellent subject when you're
    moderate;
You've seen Prince Albert's model
    lodging-house?
Does honour to his Royal Highness.
    Good!
But would he stop his carriage in Cheap-
    side
To shake a common fellow by the fist
Whose name was . . Shakespeare? no.
    We draw a line,
And if we stand not by our order, we
In England, we fall headlong. Here's
    a sight,—
A hideous sight, a most indecent sight!
My wife would come, sir, or I had kept
    her back.
By heaven, sir, when poor Damiens'
    trunk and limbs
Were torn by horses, women of the court
Stood by and stared, exactly as to-day
On this dismembering of society,
With pretty, troubled faces.'
        'Now, at last
She comes now.'
        'Where? who sees? you
    push me, sir,
Beyond the point of what is mannerly.
You're standing, madam, on my second
    flounce.
I do beseech you . . .'
        'No—it's not the bride.
Half-past eleven. How late. The bride-
    groom, mark,
Gets anxious and goes out.'
        'And as I said.
These Leighs! our best blood running
    in the rut!
It's something awful. We had pardoned
    him
A simple misalliance got up aside
For a pair of sky-blue eyes; the House
    of Lords
Has winked at such things, and we've
    all been young.
But here's an intermarriage reasoned out,

A contract (carried boldly to the light
To challenge observation, pioneer
Good acts by a great example) 'twixt
    the extremes
Of martyrized society,—on the left
The well-born, on the right the merest
    mob,
To treat as equals !—'tis anarchical ;
It means more than it says ; 'tis damnable.
Why, sir, we can't have even our coffee
    good,
Unless we strain it.'
            'Here, Miss Leigh !'
                    'Lord Howe,
You're Romney's friend.   What 's all
    this waiting for ? '

'I cannot tell. The bride has lost her head
(And way, perhaps !) to prove her
    sympathy
With the bridegroom.'
        'What,—you also, disapprove ! '

'Oh, I approve of nothing in the world,'
He answered, 'not of you, still less of
    me,
Nor even of Romney, though he 's worth
    us both.
We're all gone wrong.   The tune in us
    is lost ;
And whistling down back alleys to the
    moon
Will never catch it.'
            Let me draw Lord Howe.
A born aristocrat, bred radical,
And educated socialist, who still
Goes floating, on traditions of his kind,
Across the theoretic flood from France,
Though, like a drenched Noah on a
    rotten deck,
Scarce safer for his place there.   He,
    at least,
Will never land on Ararat, he knows,
To recommence the world on the new
    plan :
Indeed, he thinks, said world had better
    end,
He sympathizes rather with the fish
Outside, than with the drowned paired
    beasts within
Who cannot couple again or multiply,—
And that 's the sort of Noah he is,
    Lord Howe.

He never could be anything complete,
Except a loyal, upright gentleman,
A liberal landlord, graceful diner-out,
And entertainer more than hospitable,
Whom authors dine with and forget the
    hock.
Whatever he believes, and it is much,
But nowise certain, now here and now
    there,
He still has sympathies beyond his creed
Diverting him from action. In the House,
No party counts upon him, while for all
His speeches have a noticeable weight.
Men like his books too (he has written
    books),
Which, safe to lie beside a bishop's chair,
At times outreach themselves with jets
    of fire
At which the foremost of the progressists
May warm audacious hands in passing by.
Of stature over-tall, lounging for ease ;
Light hair, that seems to carry a wind
    in it,
And eyes that, when they look on you,
    will lean
Their whole weight, half in indolence
    and half
In wishing you unmitigated good,
Until you know not if to flinch from him
Or thank him.—'Tis Lord Howe.
                'We're all gone wrong,'
Said he, ' and Romney, that dear friend
    of ours,
Is nowise right.   There 's one true
    thing on earth,
That 's love ! he takes it up, and dresses it,
And acts a play with it, as Hamlet did,
To show what cruel uncles we have been,
And how we should be uneasy in our
    minds
While he, Prince Hamlet, weds a pretty
    maid
(Who keeps us too long waiting, we'll
    confess)
By symbol, to instruct us formally
To fill the ditches up 'twixt class and class,
And live together in phalansteries.
What then ?—he 's mad, our Hamlet ! clap his play,
And bind him.'
            'Ah, Lord Howe, this spectacle
Pulls stronger at us than the Dane's.
    See there !

The crammed aisles heave and strain
    and steam with life.
Dear Heaven, what life!'
        'Why, yes,—a poet sees ;
Which makes him different from a
    common man.
I, too, see somewhat, though I cannot
    sing ;
I should have been a poet, only that
My mother took fright at the ugly world,
And bore me tongue-tied. If you'll
    grant me now
That Romney gives us a fine actor-piece
To make us merry on his marriage-morn,
The fable's worse than Hamlet's I'll
    concede.
The terrible people, old and poor and
    blind,
Their eyes eat out with plague and
    poverty
From seeing beautiful and cheerful
    sights,
We'll liken to a brutalized King Lear,
Led out,—by no means to clear scores
    with wrongs—
His wrongs are so far back, he has forgot
(All's past like youth) ; but just to
    witness here
A simple contract,—he, upon his side,
And Regan with her sister Goneril
And all the dappled courtiers and
    court-fools
On their side. Not that any of these
    would say
They're sorry, neither. What is done,
    is done,
And violence is now turned privilege,
As cream turns cheese, if buried long
    enough.
What could such lovely ladies have to do
With the old man there, in those ill-
    odorous rags,
Except to keep the wind-side of him ?
    Lear
Is flat and quiet, as a decent grave ;
He does not curse his daughters in the
    least :
Be these his daughters ? Lear is thinking of
His porridge chiefly . . is it getting cold
At Hampstead ? will the ale be served
    in pots ?
Poor Lear, poor daughters ! Bravo,
    Romney's play.'

A murmur and a movement drew around,
A naked whisper touched us. Some-
    thing wrong.
What's wrong ? The black crowd, as
    an overstrained
Cord, quivered in vibration, and I saw . .
Was that *his* face I saw ? . . his . .
    Romney Leigh's . .
Which tossed a sudden horror like
    a sponge
Into all eyes,—while himself stood
    white upon
The topmost altar-stair and tried to speak,
And failed, and lifted higher above his
    head
A letter, . . as a man who drowns and
    gasps.

'My brothers, bear with me ! I am very
    weak.
I meant but only good. Perhaps I meant
Too proudly, and God snatched the
    circumstance
And changed it therefore. There's no
    marriage—none.
She leaves me,—she departs,—she
    disappears,
I lose her. Yet I never forced her "aye."
To have her "no" so cast into my teeth
In manner of an accusation, thus.
My friends, you are dismissed. Go,
    eat and drink
According to the programme,—and
    farewell !'

He ended. There was silence in the
    church.
We heard a baby sucking in its sleep
At the farthest end of the aisle. Then
    spoke a man,
'Now, look to it, coves, that all the
    beef and drink
Be not filched from us like the other fun,
For beer's spilt easier than a woman's
    lost !
This gentry is not honest with the poor ;
They bring us up, to trick us.'—' Go it,
    Jim,'
A woman screamed back,—' I'm a tender
    soul,
I never banged a child at two years old
And drew blood from him, but I sobbed
    for it

Next moment,—and I've had a plague
    of seven.
I'm tender; I've no stomach even for beef,
Until I know about the girl that's lost,
That's killed, mayhap. I did misdoubt,
    at first,
The fine lord meant no good by her or us.
He, maybe, got the upper hand of her
By holding up a wedding-ring, and then . .
A choking finger on her throat last night,
And just a clever tale to keep us still,
As she is, poor lost innocent. "Disap-
    pear!"
Who ever disappears except a ghost?
And who believes a story of a ghost?
I ask you,—would a girl go off, instead
Of staying to be married? a fine tale!
A wicked man, I say, a wicked man!
For my part I would rather starve on gin
Than make my dinner on his beef and
    beer.'—
At which a cry rose up—'We'll have
    our rights.
We'll have the girl, the girl! Your
    ladies there
Are married safely and smoothly every
    day,
And *she* shall not drop through into a trap
Because she's poor and of the people:
    shame!
We'll have no tricks played off by
    gentlefolks ;
We'll see her righted.'
                Through the rage and roar
I heard the broken words which Romney
    flung
Among the turbulent masses, from the
    ground
He held still with his masterful pale
    face,—
As huntsmen throw the ration to the pack,
Who, falling on it headlong, dog on dog
In heaps of fury, rend it, swallow it up
With yelling hound-jaws,—his indignant
    words,
His suppliant words, his most pathetic
    words,
Whereof I caught the meaning here and
    there
By his gesture . . torn in morsels, yelled
    across,
And so devoured. From end to end,
    the church

Rocked round us like the sea in storm,
    and then
Broke up like the earth in earthquake.
    Men cried out
' Police '—and women stood and shrieked
    for God,
Or dropt and swooned ; or, like a herd
    of deer
(For whom the black woods suddenly
    grow alive,
Unleashing their wild shadows down
    the wind
To hunt the creatures into corners. back
And forward), madly fled, or blindly fell,
Trod screeching underneath the feet of
    those
Who fled and screeched.
                The last sight left to me
Was Romney's terrible calm face above
The tumult !—the last sound was ' Pull
    him down !
Strike—kill him !' Stretching my un-
    reasoning arms,
As men in dreams, who vainly interpose
'Twixt gods and their undoing, with
    a cry
I struggled to precipitate myself
Head-foremost to the rescue of my soul
In that white face, . . till some one
    caught me back,
And so the world went out,—I felt no
    more.

What followed was told after by Lord
    Howe,
Who bore me senseless from the
    strangling crowd
In church and street, and then returned
    alone
To see the tumult quelled. The men of
    law
Had fallen as thunder on a roaring fire,
And made all silent,—while the people's
    smoke
Passed eddying slowly from the emptied
    aisles.

Here's Marian's letter, which a ragged
    child
Brought running, just as Romney at the
    porch
Looked out expectant of the bride. He
    sent

The letter to me by his friend Lord Howe
Some two hours after, folded in a sheet
On which his well-known hand had
    left a word.
Here 's Marian's letter.
            · ' Noble friend, dear saint,
Be patient with me. Never think me vile,
Who might to-morrow morning be your
    wife
But that I loved you more than such
    a name.
Farewell, my Romney. Let me write
    it once,—
My Romney.
        'Tis so pretty a coupled word,
I have no heart to pluck it with a blot.
We say " my God " sometimes, upon our
    knees,
Who is not therefore vexed : so bear
    with it . .
And me. I know I'm foolish, weak,
    and vain ;
Yet most of all I'm angry with myself
For losing your last footstep on the stair
That last time of your coming,—
    yesterday !
The very first time I lost step of yours
(Its sweetness comes the next to what
    you speak),
But yesterday sobs took me by the throat
And cut me off from music.
            ' Mister Leigh,
You'll set me down as wrong in many
    things.
You've praised me, sir, for truth,—and
    now you'll learn
I had not courage to be rightly true.
I once began to tell you how she came,
The woman . . and you stared upon the
    floor
In one of your fixed thoughts . . which
    put me out
For that day. After, some one spoke
    of me,
So wisely, and of you, so tenderly,
Persuading me to silence for your sake ...
Well, well ! it seems this moment I was
    wrong
In keeping back from telling you the truth :
There might be truth betwixt us two, at
    least,
If nothing else. And yet 'twas dangerous.
Suppose a real angel came from heaven

To live with men and women ! he'd go
    mad,
If no considerate hand should tie a blind
Across his piercing eyes. 'Tis thus
    with you :
You see us too much in your heavenly
    light;
I always thought so, angel,—and indeed
There 's danger that you beat yoursel
    to death
Against the edges of this alien world,
In some divine and fluttering pity.
            ' Yes,
It would be dreadful for a friend of yours,
To see all England thrust you out of doors
And mock you from the windows.
    You might say,
Or think (that 's worse), " There 's some
    one in the house
I miss and love still." Dreadful !
            ' Very kind,
I pray you mark, was Lady Waldemar.
She came to see me nine times, rather
    ten—
So beautiful, she hurts one like the day
Let suddenly on sick eyes.
            ' Most kind of all,
Your cousin !—ah, most like you ! Ere
    you came
She kissed me mouth to mouth : I felt
    her soul
Dip through her serious lips in holy fire.
God help me, but it made me arrogant ;
I almost told her that you would not lose
By taking me to wife : though ever since
I've pondered much a certain thing she
    asked . .
" He loves you, Marian ? " . . in a sort of
    mild
Derisive sadness . . as a mother asks
Her babe, " You'll touch that star, you
    think ? "
            ' Farewell !
I know I never touched it.
            ' This is worst :
Babes grow and lose the hope of things
    above ;
A silver threepence sets them leaping
    high—
But no more stars ! mark' that.
            ' I've writ all night
Yet told you nothing. God, if I could die,
And let this letter break off innocent

Just here! But no—for your sake . .
         'Here's the last :
I never could be happy as your wife,
I never could be harmless as your friend,
I never will look more into your face
Till God says, " Look ! " I charge you,
      seek me not,
Nor vex yourself with lamentable
      thoughts
That peradventure I have come to grief ;
Be sure I'm well, I'm merry, I'm at ease,
But such a long way, long way, long
      way off,
I think you'll find me sooner in my grave,
And that 's my choice, observe. For
      what remains,
An over-generous friend will care for me
And keep me happy . . happier . .
         ' There's a blot!
This ink runs thick . . we light girls
      lightly weep . . .
And keep me happier . . was the thing
      to say,
Than as your wife I could be.—O, my star,
My saint, my soul ! for surely you're
      my soul,
Through whom God touched me ! I am
      not so lost
I cannot thank you for the good you did,
The tears you stopped, which fell down
      bitterly,
Like these—the times you made me
      weep for joy
At hoping I should learn to write your
      notes
And save the tiring of your eyes, at night ;
And most for that sweet thrice you
      kissed my lips
Saying, " Dear Marian."
         ' 'Twould be hard to read,
This letter, for a reader half as learn'd ;
But you'll be sure to master it in spite
Of ups and downs. My hand shakes,
      I am blind ;
I'm poor at writing at the best,—and yet
I tried to make my gs the way you
      showed.
Farewell.   Christ love you.—Say " poor
      Marian " now.'

Poor Marian !—wanton Marian !—was it
      so,
Or so ? For days, her touching, foolish lines

We mused on with conjectural fantasy,
As if some riddle of a summer-cloud
On which one tries unlike similitudes
Of now a spotted Hydra-skin cast off,
And now a screen of carven ivory
That shuts the heavens' conventual
      secrets up
From mortals over-bold. We sought
      the sense :
She loved him so perhaps (such words
      mean love),
That, worked on by some shrewd per-
      fidious tongue
(And then I thought of Lady Waldemar),
She left him, not to hurt him ; or perhaps
She loved one in her class,—or did not
      love,
But mused upon her wild bad tramping life
Until the free blood fluttered at her heart,
And black bread eaten by the roadside
      hedge
Seemed sweeter than being put to
      Romney's school
Of philanthropical self-sacrifice
Irrevocably.—Girls are girls, beside,
Thought I, and like a wedding by one rule.
You seldom catch these birds except
      with chaff :
They feel it almost an immoral thing
To go out and be married in broad day,
Unless some winning special flattery
      should
Excuse them to themselves for 't, . .
         ' No one parts
Her hair with such a silver line as you,
One moonbeam from the forehead to the
      crown ! '
Or else. . ' You bite your lip in such a way,
It spoils me for the smiling of the rest,'
And so on. Then a worthless gaud or two
To keep for love,—a ribbon for the neck,
Or some glass pin,—they have their
      weight with girls.

And Romney sought her many days
      and weeks :
He sifted all the refuse of the town,
Explored the trains, inquired among the
      ships,
And felt the country through from end
      to end ;
No Marian !—Though I hinted what I
      knew,—

A friend of his had reasons of her own
For throwing back the match—he would
    not hear :
The lady had been ailing ever since,
The shock had harmed her.   Something
    in his tone
Repressed me ; something in me shamed
    my doubt
To a sigh repressed too.   He went on
    to say
That, putting questions where his Marian
    lodged,
He found she had received for visitors,
Besides himself and Lady Waldemar
And, that once, me—a dubious woman
    dressed
Beyond us both : the rings upon her
    hands
Had dazed the children when she threw
    them pence ;
'She wore her bonnet as the queen
    might hers,
To show the crown,' they said,—'a
    scarlet crown
Of roses that had never been in bud.'

When Romney told me that,—for now
    and then
He came to tell me how the search
    advanced,
His voice dropped : I bent forward for
    the rest :
The woman had been with her, it
    appeared,
At first from week to week, then day
    by day,
And last, 'twas sure . .
            I looked upon the ground
To escape the anguish of his eyes, and
    asked
As low as when you speak to mourners
    new
Of those they cannot bear yet to call dead,
' If Marian had as much as named to him
A certain Rose, an early friend of hers,
A ruined creature.'
            'Never.'—Starting up
He strode from side to side about the
    room,
Most like some prisoned lion sprung
    awake,
Who has felt the desert sting him
    through his dreams.

' What was I to her, that she should tell
    me aught ?
A friend ! was I a friend ? I see all clear.
Such devils would pull angels out of
    heaven,
Provided they could reach them ; 'tis
    their pride ;
And that's the odds 'twixt soul and
    body-plague !
The veriest slave who drops in Cairo's
    street,
Cries, " Stand off from me," to the
    passengers ;
While these blotched souls are eager to
    infect,
And blow their bad breath in a sister's
    face
As if they got some ease by it.'
            I broke through.
' Some natures catch no plagues.   I've
    read of babes
Found whole and sleeping by the spotted
    breast
Of one a full day dead.   I hold it true,
As I'm a woman and know womanhood,
That Marian Erle, however lured from
    place,
Deceived in way, keeps pure in aim and
    heart
As snow that's drifted from the garden-
    bank
To the open road.'
            'Twas hard to hear him laugh.
' The figure's happy.   Well—a dozen
    carts
And trampers will secure you presently
A fine white snow-drift.   Leave it there,
    your snow !
'Twill pass for soot ere sunset.   Pure
    in aim ?
She's pure in aim, I grant you,—like
    myself,
Who thought to take the world upon
    my back
To carry it o'er a chasm of social ill,
And end by letting slip through impotence
A single soul, a child's weight in a soul,
Straight down the pit of hell ! yes, I and
    she
Have reason to be proud of our pure aims.'
Then softly, as the last repenting drops
Of a thunder-shower, he added, ' The
    poor child,

Poor Marian! 'twas a luckless day for her,
When first she chanced on my philan-
   thropy.'

He drew a chair beside me, and sate
   down ;
And I, instinctively, as women use
Before a sweet friend's grief,—when,
   in his ear,
They hum the tune of comfort though
   themselves
Most ignorant of the special words of
   such,
And quiet so and fortify his brain
And give it time and strength for feeling
   out
To reach the availing sense beyond that
   sound,—
Went murmuring to him what, if written
   here,
Would seem not much, yet fetched him
   better help
Than peradventure if it had been more.

I've known the pregnant thinkers of our
   time,
And stood by breathless, hanging on
   their lips,
When some chromatic sequence of fine
   thought
In learned modulation phrased itself
To an unconjectured harmony of truth :
And yet I've been more moved, more
   raised, I say,
By a simple word . . a broken easy thing
A three-years infant might at need re-
   peat,
A look, a sigh, a touch upon the palm,
Which meant less than ' I love you,'
   than by all
The full-voiced rhetoric of those master-
   mouths.

' Ah, dear Aurora,' he began at last,
His pale lips fumbling for a sort of smile,
' Your printer's devils have not spoilt
   your heart :
That 's well. And who knows but, long
   years ago
When you and I talked, you were some-
   what right
In being so peevish with me ? You, at
   least.

Have ruined no one through your
   dreams. Instead,
You've helped the facile youth to live
   youth's day
With innocent distraction, still perhaps
Suggestive of things better than your
   rimes.
Tne little shepherd-maiden, eight years
   old,
I've seen upon the mountains of Vaucluse,
Asleep i' the sun, her head upon her
   knees,
The flocks all scattered,—is more laudable
Than any sheep-dog trained imper-
   fectly,
Who bites the kids through too much zeal.'
                              ' I look
As if I had slept, then ?'
                     He was touched at once
By something in my face. Indeed
   'twas sure
That he and I,— despite a year or two
Of younger life on my side, and on his
The heaping of the years' work on the
   days,
The three-hour speeches from the
   member's seat,
The hot committees in and out of doors,
The pamphlets, 'Arguments,' 'Col-
   lective Views,'
Tossed out as straw before sick houses,
   just
To show one 's sick and so be trod to dirt
And no more use,—through this world's
   underground
The burrowing, groping effort, whence
   the arm
And heart come torn,—'twas sure that
   he and I
Were, after all, unequally fatigued ;
That he, in his developed manhood, stood
A little sunburnt by the glare of life,
While I . . it seemed no sun had shone
   on me,
So many seasons I had missed my
   Springs.
My cheeks had pined and perished from
   their orbs,
And all the youth-blood in them had
   grown white
As dew on autumn cyclamens : alone
My eyes and forehead answered for my
   face.

He said, 'Aurora, you are changed—
    are ill!'

'Not so, my cousin,—only not asleep,'
I answered, smiling gently.   'Let it be.
You scarcely found the poet of Vaucluse
As drowsy as the shepherds. What is art
But life upon the larger scale, the higher,
When, graduating up in a spiral line
Of still expanding and ascending gyres,
It pushes toward the intense significance
Of all things, hungry for the Infinite?
Art's life,—and where we live, we
    suffer and toil.'

He seemed to sift me with his painful
    eyes.
'You take it gravely, cousin; you refuse
Your dreamland's right of common, and
    green rest.
You break the mythic turf where danced
    the nymphs,
With crooked ploughs of actual life,—
    let in
The axes to the legendary woods,
To pay the poll-tax. You are fallen
    indeed
On evil days, you poets, if yourselves
Can praise that art of yours no otherwise;
And, if you cannot, . . better take a trade
And be of use: 'twere cheaper for your
    youth.'

'Of use!' I softly echoed, 'there's the
    point
We sweep about for ever in argument,
Like swallows which the exasperate,
    dying year
Sets spinning in black circles, round
    and round,
Preparing for far flights o'er unknown seas.
And we, where tend we?'
        'Where?' he said, and sighed.
'The whole creation, from the hour we
    are born,
Perplexes us with questions. Not a
    stone
But cries behind us, every weary step,
"Where, where?" I leave stones to reply
    to stones.
Enough for me and for my fleshly heart
To hearken the invocations of my kind,
When men catch hold upon my
    shuddering nerves

And shriek, "What help? what hope?
    what bread i' the house,
What fire i' the frost?" There must
    be some response,
Though mine fail utterly. This social
    Sphinx
Who sits between the sepulchres and
    stews,
Makes mock and mow against the crystal
    heavens,
And bullies God,—exacts a word at least
From each man standing on the side of
    God,
However paying a sphinx-price for it.
We pay it also if we hold our peace,
In pangs and pity. Let me speak and die.
Alas, you'll say I speak and kill instead.'

I pressed in there. 'The best men,
    doing their best,
Know peradventure least of what they do:
Men usefullest i' the world are simply
    used;
The nail that holds the wood, must
    pierce it first,
And He alone who wields the hammer
    sees
The work advanced by the earliest blow.
    Take heart.'

'Ah, if I could have taken yours!' he said,
'But that's past now.' Then rising,—
        'I will take
At least your kindness and encourage-
    ment.
I thank you. Dear, be happy. Sing
    your songs,
If that's your way! but sometimes
    slumber too,
Nor tire too much with following, out
    of breath,
The rimes upon your mountains of
    Delight.
Reflect, if Art be in truth the higher life,
You need the lower life to stand upon
In order to reach up unto that higher;
And none can stand a-tiptoe in the place
He cannot stand in with two stable feet.
Remember then!—for Art's sake, hold
    your life.'

We parted so. I held him in respect.
I comprehended what he was in heart
And sacrificial greatness. Aye, but he

Supposed me a thing too small, to deign
  to know :
He blew me, plainly, from the crucible
As some intruding, interrupting fly,
Not worth the pains of his analysis
Absorbed on nobler subjects. Hurt a fly !
He would not for the world : he 's pitiful
To flies even. 'Sing,' says he, 'and
  tease me still,
If that 's your way, poor insect.' That 's
  your way !

FIFTH BOOK

Aurora Leigh, be humble. Shall I hope
To speak my poems in mysterious tune
With man and nature ?—with the lava-
  lymph
That trickles from successive galaxies
Still drop by drop adown the finger of God
In still new worlds ?—with summer-
  days in this
That scarce dare breathe they are so
  beautiful ?
With spring's delicious trouble in the
  ground,
Tormented by the quickened blood of
  roots,
And softly pricked by golden crocus-
  sheaves
In token of the harvest-time of flowers ?
With winters and with autumns,—and
  beyond
With the human heart's large seasons,
  when it hopes
And fears, joys, grieves, and loves ?—
  with all that strain
Of sexual passion, which devours the flesh
In a sacrament of souls ? with mother's
  breasts
Which, round the new-made creatures
  hanging there,
Throb luminous and harmonious like
  pure spheres ?—
With multitudinous life, and finally
With the great escapings of ecstatic
  souls,
Who, in a rush of too long prisoned flame,
Their radiant faces upward, burn away
This dark of the body, issuing on a world
Beyond our mortal ?—can I speak my
  verse

So plainly in tune to these things and
  the rest,
That men shall feel it catch them on the
  quick,
As having the same warrant over them
To hold and move them if they will or
  no,
Alike imperious as the primal rhythm
Of that theurgic nature ?—I must fail,
Who fail at the beginning to hold and
  move
One man,—and he my cousin, and he
  my friend,
And he born tender, made intelligent,
Inclined to ponder the precipitous sides
Of difficult questions ; yet, obtuse to *me*,
Of *me*, incurious ! likes me very well,
And wishes me a paradise of good,
Good looks, good means, and good
  digestion,—aye,
But otherwise evades me, puts me off
With kindness, with a tolerant gentle-
  ness,—
Too light a book for a grave man's
  reading ! Go,
Aurora Leigh : be humble.
                          There it is,
We women are too apt to look to one,
Which proves a certain impotence in
  art.
We strain our natures at doing some-
  thing great,
Far less because it 's something great
  to do,
Than haply that we, so, commend
  ourselves
As being not small, and more appreci-
  able
To some one friend. We must have
  mediators
Betwixt our highest conscience and the
  judge ;
Some sweet saint's blood must quicken
  in our palms,
Or all the life in heaven seems slow and
  cold :
Good only being perceived as the end
  of good,
And God alone pleased,—that 's too
  poor, we think,
And not enough for us by any means.
Aye—Romney, I remember, told me
  once

We miss the abstract when we compre-
hend.
We miss it most when we aspire,—and
fail.

Yet, so, I will not.—This vile woman's
way
Of trailing garments, shall not trip me up:
I'll have no traffic with the personal
thought
In art's pure temple. Must I work in vain,
Without the approbation of a man ?
It cannot be ; it shall not. Fame itself,
That approbation of the general race,
Presents a poor end (though the arrow
speed,
Shot straight with vigorous finger to
the white),
And the highest fame was never reached
except
By what was aimed above it. Art for art,
And good for God Himself, the essential
Good !
We'll keep our aims sublime, our eyes
erect,
Although our woman-hands should shake
and fail ;
And if we fail . . . But must we ?—
                    Shall I fail ?
The Greeks said grandly in their tragic
phrase,
' Let no one be called happy till his
death.'
To which I add,—Let no one till his
death
Be called unhappy. Measure not the
work
Until the day 's out and the labour done,
Then bring your gauges. If the day's
work 's scant,
Why, call it scant ; affect no compromise ;
And, in that we have nobly striven
at least,
Deal with us nobly, women though we be,
And honour us with truth if not with
praise.

My ballads prospered ; but the ballad's
race
Is rapid for a poet who bears weights
Of thought and golden image. He can
stand
Like Atlas, in the sonnet,—and support

His own heavens pregnant with dynastic
stars ;
But then he must stand still, nor take a
step.

In that descriptive poem called ' The
Hills,'
The prospects were too far and in-
distinct.
'Tis true my critics said, ' A fine view,
that ! '
The public scarcely cared to climb my
book
For even the finest, and the public 's
right ;
A tree 's mere firewood, unless human-
ized,—
Which well the Greeks knew when they
stirred its bark
With close-pressed bosoms of subsiding
nymphs,
And made the forest-rivers garrulous
With babble of gods. For us, we are
called to mark
A still more intimate humanity
In this inferior nature, or ourselves
Must fall like dead leaves trodden under-
foot
By veritable artists. Earth (shut up
By Adam, like a fakir in a box
Left too long buried) remained stiff and
dry,
A mere dumb corpse, till Christ the Lord
came down,
Unlocked the doors, forced open the
blank eyes,
And used his kingly chrism to straighten
out
The leathery tongue turned back into
the throat ;
Since when, she lives, remembers, pal-
pitates
In every limb, aspires in every breath,
Embraces infinite relations. Now
We want no half-gods, Panomphaean
Joves,
Fauns, Naiads, Tritons, Oreads and the
rest,
To take possession of a senseless world
To unnatural vampire-uses. See the
earth,
The body of our body, the green earth,
Indubitably human like this flesh

And these articulated veins through
  which
Our heart drives blood.   There's not a
  flower of spring
That dies ere June, but vaunts itself
  allied
By issue and symbol, by significance
And correspondence, to that spirit-world
Outside the limits of our space and time,
Whereto we are bound.   Let poets give
  it voice
With human meanings,—else they miss
  the thought,
And henceforth step down lower, stand
  confessed
Instructed poorly for interpreters,
Thrown out by an easy cowslip in the
  text.

Even so my pastoral failed: it was a book
Of surface-pictures—pretty, cold, and
  false
With literal transcript,—the worse done,
  I think,
For being not ill-done : let me set my
  mark
Against such doings, and do otherwise.
This strikes me.—If the public whom we
  know
Could catch me at such admissions, I
  should pass
For being right modest.   Yet how proud
  we are,
In daring to look down upon ourselves !

The critics say that epics have died out
With Agamemnon and the goat-nursed
  gods ;
I'll not believe it.   I could never deem
As Payne Knight did (the mythic
  mountaineer
Who travelled higher than he was born
  to live,
And showed sometimes the goitre in his
  throat
Discoursing of an image seen through
  fog),
That Homer's heroes measured twelve
  feet high.
They were but men :—his Helen's hair
  turned grey
Like any plain Miss Smith's who wears
  a front ;

And Hector's infant whimpered at a
  plume
As yours last Friday at a turkey-cock.
All actual heroes are essential men,
And all men possible heroes : every age,
Heroic in proportions, double-faced,
Looks backward and before, expects a
  morn
And claims an epos.
                    Aye, but every age
Appears to souls who live in 't (ask
  Carlyle)
Most unheroic.   Ours, for instance, ours :
The thinkers scout it, and the poets
  abound
Who scorn to touch it with a finger-tip :
A pewter age,—mixed metal, silver-
  washed ;
An age of scum, spooned off the richer
  past,
An age of patches for old gaberdines,
An age of mere transition, meaning
  nought
Except that what succeeds must shame
  it quite
If God please.   That 's wrong thinking,
  to my mind,
And wrong thoughts make poor poems.
                              Every age,
Through being beheld too close, is ill-
  discerned
By those who have not lived past it.
  We'll suppose
Mount Athos carved, as Alexander
  schemed,
To some colossal statue of a man.
The peasants, gathering brushwood in
  his ear,
Had guessed as little as the browsing
  goats
Of form or feature of humanity
Up there,—in fact, had travelled five
  miles off
Or ere the giant image broke on them,
Full human profile, nose and chin distinct,
Mouth, muttering rhythms of silence up
  the sky
And fed at evening with the blood of suns ;
Grand torso,—hand, that flung perpetu-
  ally
The largesse of a silver river down
To all the country pastures. 'Tis even thus
With times we live in,—evermore too great

To be apprehended near.
               But poets should
Exert a double vision; should have
   eyes
To see near things as comprehensively
As if afar they took their point of sight,
And distant things as intimately deep
As if they touched them.   Let us strive
   for this.
I do distrust the poet who discerns
No character or glory in his times,
And trundles back his soul five hundred
   years,
Past moat and drawbridge, into a castle-
   court,
To sing—oh, not of lizard or of toad
Alive i' the ditch there,—'twere excus-
   able,
But of some black chief, half knight, half
   sheep-lifter,
Some beauteous dame, half chattel and
   half queen,
As dead as must be, for the greater part,
The poems made on their chivalric bones;
And that's no wonder: death inherits
   death.

Nay, if there's room for poets in this
   world
A little overgrown (I think there is),
Their sole work is to represent the age,
Their age, not Charlemagne's,—this live,
   throbbing age,
That brawls, cheats, maddens, calculates,
   aspires,
And spends more passion, more heroic
   heat,
Betwixt the mirrors of its drawing-
   rooms,
Than Roland with his knights at Ronces-
   valles.
To flinch from modern varnish, coat or
   flounce,
Cry out for togas and the picturesque,
Is fatal,—foolish too.   King Arthur's self
Was commonplace to Lady Guenever;
And Camelot to minstrels seemed as flat
As Fleet Street to our poets.
               Never flinch,
But still, unscrupulously epic, catch
Upon the burning lava of a song
The full-veined, heaving, double-breasted
   Age:

That, when the next shall come, the men
   of that
May touch the impress with reverent
   hand, and say
'Behold,—behold the paps we all have
   sucked!
This bosom seems to beat still, or at least
It sets ours beating: this is living art,
Which thus presents and thus records
   true life.'

What form is best for poems?   Let me
   think
Of forms less, and the external.   Trust
   the spirit,
As sovran nature does, to make the form;
For otherwise we only imprison spirit
And not embody.   Inward evermore
To outward,—so in life, and so in art
Which still is life.
               Five acts to make a play.
And why not fifteen? why not ten? or
   seven?
What matter for the number of the leaves,
Supposing the tree lives and grows? exact
The literal unities of time and place,
When 'tis the essence of passion to
   ignore
Both time and place?   Absurd.   Keep
   up the fire,
And leave the generous flames to shape
   themselves.

'Tis true the stage requires obsequious-
   ness
To this or that convention; 'exit' here
And 'enter' there; the points for clap-
   ping, fixed,
Like Jacob's white-peeled rods before
   the rams,
And all the close-curled imagery clipped
In manner of their fleece at shearing-time.
Forget to prick the galleries to the heart
Precisely at the fourth act,—culminate
Our five pyramidal acts with one act
   more,—
We're lost so: Shakespeare's ghost
   could scarcely plead
Against our just damnation.   Stand aside;
We'll muse for comfort that, last century,
On this same tragic stage on which we
   have failed,
A wigless Hamlet would have failed the
   same.

And whosoever writes good poetry,
Looks just to art.   He does not write
  for you
Or me,—for London or for Edinburgh ;
He will not suffer the best critic known
To step into his sunshine of free thought
And self-absorbed conception and exact
An inch-long swerving of the holy lines.
If virtue done for popularity
Defiles like vice, can art, for praise or hire,
Still keep its splendour and remain pure
  art ?
Eschew such serfdom.   What the poet
  writes,
He writes : mankind accepts it if it suits,
And that 's success : if not, the poem 's
  passed
From hand to hand, and yet from hand
  to hand,
Until the unborn snatch it, crying out
In pity on their fathers' being so dull,
And that 's success too.
           I will write no plays ;
Because the drama, less sublime in this,
Makes lower appeals, submits more
  menially,
Adopts the standard of the public taste
To chalk its height on, wears a dog-
  chain round
Its regal neck, and learns to carry and
  fetch
The fashions of the day to please the day,
Fawns close on pit and boxes, who clap
  hands
Commending chiefly its docility
And humour in stage-tricks,—or else
  indeed
Gets hissed at, howled at, stamped at
  like a dog,
Or worse, we'll say.   For dogs, unjustly
  kicked,
Yell, bite at need ; but if your dramatist
(Being wronged by some five hundred
  nobodies
Because their grosser brains most natur-
  ally
Misjudge the fineness of his subtle wit)
Shows teeth an almond's breadth, pro-
  tests the length
Of a modest phrase,—' My gentle
  countrymen,
' There 's something in it haply of your
  fault,'—

Why then, besides five hundred nobodies,
He'll have five thousand and five thou-
  sand more
Against him,—the whole public,—all
  the hoofs
Of King Saul's father's asses, in full
  drove,
And obviously deserve it.   He appealed
To these,—and why say more if they
  condemn,
Than if they praise him ?—Weep, my
  Aeschylus,
But low and far, upon Sicilian shores !
For since 'twas Athens (so I read the
  myth)
Who gave commission to that fatal weight
The tortoise, cold and hard, to drop on
  thee
And crush thee,—better cover thy bald
  head ;
She'll hear the softest hum of Hyblan bee
Before thy loudest protestation !
                          Then
The risk 's still worse upon the modern
  stage :
I could not, for so little, accept success,
Nor would I risk so much, in ease and
  calm,
For manifester gains : let those who
  prize,
Pursue them : I stand off.   And yet,
  forbid,
That any irreverent fancy or conceit
Should litter in the Drama's throne-room
  where
The rulers of our art, in whose full veins
Dynastic glories mingle, sit in strength
And do their kingly work,—conceive,
  command,
And, from the imagination's crucial heat,
Catch up their men and women all aflame
For action, all alive and forced to prove
Their life by living out heart, brain, and
  nerve,
Until mankind makes witness, ' These
  be men
As we are,' and vouchsafes the greeting
  due
To Imogen and Juliet—sweetest kin
On art's side.
             'Tis that, honouring to its worth
The drama, I would fear to keep it
  down

To the level of the footlights. Dies no
more
The sacrificial goat, for Bacchus slain,
His filmed eyes fluttered by the whirling
white
Of choral vestures,—troubled in his
blood,
While tragic voices that clanged keen
as swords,
Leapt high together with the altar-flame
And made the blue air wink. The waxen
mask,
Which set the grand still front of Themis'
son
Upon the puckered visage of a player,—
The buskin, which he rose upon and
moved,
As some tall ship first conscious of the
wind
Sweeps slowly past the piers,—the
mouthpiece, where
The mere man's voice with all its breaths
and breaks
Went sheathed in brass, and clashed on
even heights
Its phrasèd thunders,—these things are
no more,
Which once were. And concluding,
which is clear,
The growing drama has outgrown such
toys
Of simulated stature, face, and speech,
It also peradventure may outgrow
The simulation of the painted scene,
Boards, actors, prompters, gaslight,
and costume,
And take for a worthier stage the soul
itself,
Its shifting fancies and celestial lights,
With all its grand orchestral silences
To keep the pauses of its rhythmic
sounds.

Alas, I still see something to be done,
And what I do, falls short of what I see,
Though I waste myself on doing. Long
green days,
Worn bare of grass and sunshine,—
long calm nights,
From which the silken sleeps were
fretted out,
Be witness for me, with no amateur's
Irreverent haste and busy idleness

I set myself to art! What then? what's
done?
What's done, at last?
Behold, at last, a book.
If life-blood's necessary, which it is
(By that blue vein athrob on Mahomet's
brow,
Each prophet-poet's book must show
man's blood !),—
If life-blood's fertilizing, I wrung mine
On every leaf of this,—unless the drops
Slid heavily on one side and left it dry.
That chances often : many a fervid man
Writes books as cold and flat as grave-
yard stones
From which the lichen's scraped ; and
if Saint Preux
Had written his own letters, as he might,
We had never wept to think of the
little mole
'Neath Julie's drooping eyelid. Passion is
But something suffered, after all.
While Art
Sets action on the top of suffering :
The artist's part is both to be and do,
Transfixing with a special, central power
The flat experience of the common man,
And turning outward, with a sudden
wrench,
Half agony, half ecstasy, the thing
He feels the inmost,—never felt the less
Because he sings it. Does a torch less
burn
For burning next reflectors of blue steel,
That *he* should be the colder for his place
'Twixt two incessant fires,—his personal
life's
And that intense refraction which
burns back
Perpetually against him from the round
Of crystal conscience he was born into
If artist-born ? O sorrowful great gift
Conferred on poets, of a twofold life,
When one life has been found enough
for pain !
We, staggering 'neath our burden as
mere men,
Being called to stand up straight as
demi-gods,
Support the intolerable strain and stress
Of the universal, and send clearly up
With voices broken by the human sob,
Our poems to find rimes among the stars!

But soft,—a ' poet ' is a word soon said,
A book 's a thing soon written. Nay,
  indeed,
The more the poet shall be questionable,
The more unquestionably comes his
  book.
And this of mine—well, granting to
  myself
Some passion in it,—furrowing up the
  flats,
Mere passion will not prove a volume
  worth
Its gall and rags even. Bubbles round
  a keel
Mean nought, excepting that the vessel
  moves.
There 's more than passion goes to make
  a man
Or book, which is a man too.
                    I am sad.
I wonder if Pygmalion had these doubts
And, feeling the hard marble first relent,
Grow supple to the straining of his arms,
And tingle through its cold to his
  burning lip,
Supposed his senses mocked, supposed
  the toil
Of stretching past the known and seen
  to reach
The archetypal Beauty out of sight,
Had made his heart beat fast enough
  for two,
And with his own life dazed and blinded
  him!
Not so ; Pygmalion loved,—and whoso
  loves
Believes the impossible.
                    But I am sad :
I cannot thoroughly love a work of mine,
Since none seems worthy of my thought
  and hope
More highly mated. He has shot them
  down,
My Phoebus Apollo, soul within my soul,
Who judges, by the attempted, what 's
  attained,
And with the silver arrow from his height
Has struck down all my works before
  my face
While I said nothing. Is there aught
  to say ?
I called the artist but a greatened man.
He may be childless also, like a man.

I laboured on alone. The wind and
  dust
And sun of the world beat blistering
  in my face ;
And hope, now for me, now against me,
  dragged
My spirits onward, as some fallen balloon,
Which, whether caught by blossoming
  tree or bare,
Is torn alike. I sometimes touched my
  aim,
Or seemed,—and generous souls cried
  out, ' Be strong,
Take courage ; now you're on our
  level,—now !
The next step saves you !' I was
  flushed with praise,
But, pausing just a moment to draw
  breath,
I could not choose but murmur to myself
' Is this all ? all that 's done ? and all
  that 's gained ?
If this then be success, 'tis dismaller
Than any failure.'
                    O my God, my God,
O supreme Artist, who as sole return
For all the cosmic wonder of Thy work,
Demandest of us just a word . . a name,
' My Father !' Thou hast knowledge,
  only Thou,
How dreary 'tis for women to sit still.
On winter nights by solitary fires
And hear the nations praising them
  far off,
Too far ! aye, praising our quick sense
  of love,
Our very heart of passionate womanhood,
Which could not beat so in the verse
  without
Being present also in the unkissed lips
And eyes undried because there 's
  none to ask
The reason they grew moist.
                    To sit alone
And think for comfort how, that very
  night,
Affianced lovers, leaning face to face
With sweet half-listenings for each
  other's breath,
Are reading haply from a page of ours,
To pause with a thrill (as if their cheeks
  had touched)
When such a stanza, level to their mood,

Seems floating their own thought out—
'So I feel
For thee,'—'And I, for thee: this poet
knows
What everlasting love is!'—how, that
night,
Some father, issuing from the misty roads
Upon the luminous round of lamp and
hearth
And happy children, having caught up
first
The youngest there until it shrink and
shriek
To feel the cold chin prick its dimples
through
With winter from the hills, may throw
i' the lap
Of the eldest (who has learnt to drop
her lids
To hide some sweetness newer than
last year's),
Our book and cry, . . 'Ah you, you
care for rimes ;
So here be rimes to pore on under trees,
When April comes to let you! I've
been told
They are not idle as so many are,
But set hearts beating pure as well as fast.
'Tis yours, the book ; I'll write your
name in it,
That so you may not lose, however lost
In poet's lore and charming reverie,
The thought of how your father thought
of *you*
In riding from the town.'

        To have our books
Appraised by love, associated with love,
While *we* sit loveless! is it hard, you
think ?
At least 'tis mournful. Fame, indeed,
'twas said,
Means simply love. It was a man said
that :
And then, there's love and love: the
love of all
(To risk in turn a woman's paradox),
Is but a small thing to the love of one.
You bid a hungry child be satisfied
With a heritage of many cornfields : nay,
He says he's hungry,—he would rather
have
That little barley-cake you keep from
him

While reckoning up his harvests. So
with us
(Here, Romney, too, we fail to
generalize !) ;
We're hungry.
        Hungry! but it's pitiful
To wail like unweaned babes and suck
our thumbs
Because we're hungry. Who, in all
this world
(Wherein we are haply set to pray and
fast,
And learn what good is by its opposite),
Has never hungered? Woe to him who
has found
The meal enough ! if Ugolino's full,
His teeth have crunched some foul
unnatural thing :
For here satiety proves penury
More utterly irremediable. And since
We needs must hunger,—better, for
man's love,
Than God's truth ! better, for companions
sweet,
Than great convictions ! let us bear our
weights,
Preferring dreary hearths to desert souls.
Well, well! they say we're envious,
we who rime ;
But I, because I am a woman perhaps
And so rime ill, am ill at envying.
I never envied Graham his breadth of
style,
Which gives you, with a random smutch
or two,
(Near-sighted critics analyse to smutch)
Such delicate perspectives of full life :
Nor Belmore, for the unity of aim
To which he cuts his cedarn poems, fine
As sketchers do their pencils : nor
Mark Gage,
For that caressing colour and trancing
tone
Whereby you're swept away and
melted in
The sensual element, which with a back
wave
Restores you to the level of pure souls
And leaves you with Plotinus. None
of these,
For native gifts or popular applause,
I've envied ; but for this,—that when
by chance

Says some one,—'There goes Belmore
a great man !
He leaves clean work behind him, and
requires
No sweeper-up of the chips,' . . a girl
I know,
Who answers nothing, save with her
brown eyes,
Smiles unaware as if a guardian saint
Smiled in her :—for this, too,—that
Gage comes home
And lays his last book's prodigal review
Upon his mother's knee, where, years
ago,
He laid his childish spelling-book and
learned
To chirp and peck the letters from her
mouth,
As young birds must. 'Well done,'
she murmured then ;
She will not say it now more wonder-
ingly :
And yet the last ' Well done ' will touch
him more,
As catching up to-day and yesterday
In a perfect chord of love : and so, Mark
Gage,
I envy you your mother !—and you,
Graham,
Because you have a wife who loves you
so,
She half forgets, at moments, to be proud
Of being Graham's wife, until a friend
observes,
'The boy here, has his father's massive
brow,
Done small in wax . . if we push back
the curls.'

Who loves me ? Dearest father,—mother
sweet,—
I speak the names out sometimes by
myself,
And make the silence shiver. They
sound strange,
As Hindostanee to an Ind-born man
Accustomed many years to English
speech ;
Or lovely poet-words grown obsolete,
Which will not leave off singing. Up
in heaven
I have my father,—with my mother's
face

Beside him in a blotch of heavenly light ;
No more for earth's familiar, household
use,
No more. The best verse written by
this hand,
Can never reach them where they sit, to
seem
Well-done to *them*. Death quite un-
fellows us,
Sets dreadful odds betwixt the live and
dead,
And makes us part as those at Babel did
Through sudden ignorance of a common
tongue.
A living Caesar would not dare to play
At bowls with such as my dead father is.

And yet this may be less so than ap-
pears,
This change and separation. Sparrows
five
For just two farthings, and God cares
for each.
If God is not too great for little cares,
Is any creature, because gone to God ?
I've seen some men, veracious, nowise
mad,
Who have thought or dreamed, declared
and testified,
They heard the Dead a-ticking like
a clock
Which strikes the hours of the eternities,
Beside them, with their natural ears,—
and known
That human spirits feel the human way
And hate the unreasoning awe which
waves them off
From possible communion. It may be.

At least, earth separates as well as
heaven.
For instance, I have not seen Romney
Leigh
Full eighteen months . . add six, you
get two years.
They say he 's very busy with good
works,—
Has parted Leigh Hall into almshouses.
He made one day an almshouse of his
heart,
Which ever since is loose upon the latch
For those who pull the string.—I never
did.

It always makes me sad to go abroad,
And now I'm sadder that I went to-night
Among the lights and talkers at Lord
    Howe's.
His wife is gracious, with her glossy
    braids,
And even voice, and gorgeous eyeballs,
    calm
As her other jewels. If she's somewhat
    cold,
Who wonders, when her blood has
    stood so long
In the ducal reservoir she calls her line
By no means arrogantly? she's not
    proud ;
Not prouder than the swan is of the lake
He has always swum in ;—'tis her
    element ;
And so she takes it with a natural
    grace,
Ignoring tadpoles. She just knows,
    perhaps,
There *are* who travel without outriders,
Which isn't her fault. Ah, to watch her
    face,
When good Lord Howe expounds his
    theories
Of social justice and equality!
'Tis curious, what a tender, tolerant bend
Her neck takes : for she loves him,
    likes his talk,
'Such clever talk—that dear, odd
    Algernon !'
She listens on, exactly as if he talked
Some Scandinavian myth of Lemures,
Too pretty to dispute, and too absurd.

She's gracious to me as her husband's
    friend,
And would be gracious, were I not
    a Leigh,
Being used to smile just so, without her
    eyes,
On Joseph Strangways, the Leeds
    mesmerist,
And Delia Dobbs, the lecturer from
    'the States'
Upon the 'Woman's question.' Then,
    for him,
I like him ; he's my friend. And all
    the rooms
Were full of crinkling silks that swept
    about

The fine dust of most subtle courtesies.
What then ?—why then, we come home
    to be sad.

How lovely, One I love not looked to-
    night!
She's very pretty, Lady Waldemar.
Her maid must use both hands to twist
    that coil
Of tresses, then be careful lest the rich
Bronze rounds should slip :—she missed,
    though, a grey hair,
A single one,—I saw it ; otherwise
The woman looked immortal. How
    they told,
Those alabaster shoulders and bare
    breasts,
On which the pearls, drowned out of
    sight in milk,
Were lost, excepting for the ruby-clasp!
They split the amaranth velvet-bodice
    down
To the waist or nearly, with the
    audacious press
Of full-breathed beauty. If the heart
    within
Were half as white !—but, if it were,
    perhaps
The breast were closer covered and the
    sight
Less aspectable, by half, too.

                      I heard
The young man with the German
    student's look—
A sharp face, like a knife in a cleft stick,
Which shot up straight against the
    parting line
So equally dividing the long hair,—
Say softly to his neighbour (thirty-five
And mediaeval), 'Look that way, Sir
    Blaise.
She's Lady Waldemar—to the left,—
    in red—
Whom Romney Leigh, our ablest man
    just now,
Is soon about to marry.'
                    Then replied
Sir Blaise Delorme, with quiet, priest-
    like voice,
Too used to syllable damnations round
To make a natural emphasis worth while :
'Is Leigh your ablest man ? the same,
    I think,

Once jilted by a recreant pretty maid
Adopted from the people? Now, in
    change,
He seems to have plucked a flower from
    the other side
Of the social hedge.'
        'A flower, a flower,' exclaimed
My German student,—his own eyes
    full-blown
Bent on her. He was twenty, certainly.

Sir Blaise resumed with gentle arrogance,
As if he had dropped his alms into a hat
And gained the right to counsel,—'My
    young friend,
I doubt your ablest man's ability
To get the least good or help meet for
    him,
For pagan phalanstery or Christian home,
From such a flowery creature.'
                'Beautiful!'
My student murmured rapt,—'Mark
    how she stirs!
Just waves her head, as if a flower
    indeed,
Touched far off by the vain breath of
    our talk.'

At which that bilious Grimwald (he
    who writes
For the Renovator), who had seemed
    absorbed
Upon the table-book of autographs
(I dare say mentally he crunched the
    bones
Of all those writers, wishing them alive
To feel his tooth in earnest), turned
    short round
With low carnivorous laugh,—'A flower,
    of course!
She neither sews nor spins,—and takes
    no thought
Of her garments . . falling off.'
            The student flinched;
Sir Blaise, the same; then both, draw-
    ing back their chairs
As if they spied black-beetles on the floor,
Pursued their talk, without a word
    being thrown
To the critic.
        Good Sir Blaise's brow is high
And noticeably narrow : a strong wind,
You fancy, might unroof him suddenly,

And blow that great top attic off his
    head
So piled with feudal relics. You admire
His nose in profile, though you miss
    his chin ;
But, though you miss his chin, you
    seldom miss
His ebon cross worn innermostly
    (carved
For penance by a saintly Styrian monk
Whose flesh was too much with him),
    slipping through
Some unaware unbuttoned casualty
Of the under-waistcoat. With an absent
    air
Sir Blaise sate fingering it and speaking
    low,
While I, upon the sofa, heard it all.

'My dear young friend, if we could
    bear our eyes,
Like blessedest Saint Lucy, on a plate,
They would not trick us into choosing
    wives,
As doublets, by the colour. Otherwise
Our fathers chose,—and therefore,
    when they had hung
Their household keys about a lady's
    waist,
The sense of duty gave her dignity ;
She kept her bosom holy to her babes,
And, if a moralist reproved her dress,
'Twas, "Too much starch!"—and not,
    "Too little lawn!"

'Now, pshaw!' returned the other in
    a heat,
A little fretted by being called 'young
    friend,'
Or so I took it,—'for Saint Lucy's sake,
If she's the saint to swear by, let us
    leave
Our fathers,—plagued enough about our
    sons!'
(He stroked his beardless chin), 'yes,
    plagued, sir, plagued :
The future generations lie on us
As heavy as the nightmare of a seer ;
Our meat and drink grow painful
    prophecy :
I ask you,—have we leisure, if we liked,
To hollow out our weary hands to keep
Your intermittent rushlight of the past

From draughts in lobbies ? Prejudice of
    sex
And marriage-law . . the socket drops
    them through
While we two speak,—however may
    protest
Some over-delicate nostrils like your
    own,
'Gainst odours thence arising.'
              ' You are young,'
Sir Blaise objected.
              ' If I am,' he said
With fire,—' though somewhat less so
    than I seem,
The young run on before, and see the
    thing
That 's coming. Reverence for the
    young, I cry.
In that new church for which the world's
    near ripe,
You'll have the younger in the Elder's
    chair,
Presiding with his ivory front of hope
O'er foreheads clawed by cruel carrion-
    birds
Of life's experience.'
         ' Pray your blessing, sir,'
Sir Blaise replied good-humouredly,—
    ' I plucked
A silver hair this morning from my beard,
Which left me your inferior. Would
    I were
Eighteen and worthy to admonish you !
If young men of your order run before
To see such sights as sexual prejudice
And marriage-law dissolved,—in plainer
    words,
A general concubinage expressed
In a universal pruriency,—the thing
Is scarce worth running fast for, and
    you'd gain
By loitering with your elders.'
             ' Ah,' he said,
' Who, getting to the top of Pisgah-hill,
Can talk with one at bottom of the
    view,
To make it comprehensible ? Why, Leigh
Himself, although our ablest man, I
    said,
Is scarce advanced to see as far as this,
Which some are : he takes up imperfectly
The social question—by one handle—
    leaves

The rest to trail. A Christian socialist
Is Romney Leigh, you understand.'
                 ' Not I.
I disbelieve in Christian-pagans, much
As you in women-fishes. If we mix
Two colours, we lose both, and make
    a third
Distinct from either. Mark you ! to
    mistake
A colour is the sign of a sick brain,
And mine, I thank the saints, is clear
    and cool :
A neutral tint is here impossible.
The church,—and by the church,
    I mean of course
The catholic, apostolic, mother-church,—
Draws lines as plain and straight as her
    own wall ;
Inside of which, are Christians, obviously,
And outside . . dogs.'
         ' We thank you. Well I know
The ancient mother-church would fain
    still bite,
For all her toothless gums,—as Leigh
    himself
Would fain be a Christian still, for all
    his wit.
Pass that ; you two may settle it, for me.
You're slow in England. In a month
    I learnt
At Göttingen enough philosophy
To stock your English schools for fifty
    years ;
Pass that, too. Here alone, I stop you
    short,
—Supposing a true man like Leigh
    could stand
Unequal in the stature of his life
To the height of his opinions. Choose
    a wife
Because of a smooth skin?—not he,
    not he !
He'd rail at Venus' self for creaking
    shoes,
Unless she walked his way of righteous-
    ness :
And if he takes a Venus Meretrix
(No imputation on the lady there),
Be sure that, by some sleight of
    Christian art,
He has metamorphosed and converted her
To a Blessed Virgin.'
         ' Soft ! ' Sir Blaise drew breath

As if it hurt him,—' Soft! no blasphemy,
I pray you!'
    ' The first Christians did the thing:
Why not the last?' asked he of Göttingen,
With just that shade of sneering on the
    lip,
Compensates for the lagging of the
    beard,—
' And so the case is. If that fairest fair
Is talked of as the future wife of Leigh,
She 's talked of too, at least as certainly,
As Leigh's disciple. You may find her
    name
On all his missions and commissions,
    schools,
Asylums, hospitals,—he had her down,
With other ladies whom her starry lead
Persuaded from their spheres, to his
    country-place
In Shropshire, to the famed phalanstery
At Leigh Hall, christianized from
    Fourier's own
(In which he has planted out his sapling
    stocks
Of knowledge into social nurseries),
And there, they say, she has tarried
    half a week,
And milked the cows, and churned, and
    pressed the curd,
And said " my sister " to the lowest drab
Of all the assembled castaways ; such
    girls !
Aye, sided with them at the washing-
    tub—
Conceive, Sir Blaise, those naked
    perfect arms,
Round glittering arms, plunged elbow-
    deep in suds,
Like wild swans hid in lilies all a-shake.'

Lord Howe came up. ' What, talking
    poetry
So near the image of the unfavouring
    Muse?
That 's you, Miss Leigh : I've watched
    you half an hour,
Precisely as I watched the statue called
A Pallas in the Vatican ;—you mind
The face, Sir Blaise?—intensely calm
    and sad,
As wisdom cut it off from fellowship,—
But *that* spoke louder. Not a word
    from *you* !

And these two gentlemen were bold,
    I marked,
And unabashed by even your silence.'
                       ' Ah,'
Said I, ' my dear Lord Howe, you shall
    not speak
To a printing woman who has lost her
    place
(The sweet safe corner of the household
    fire
Behind the heads of children), compli-
    ments,
As if she were a woman. We who
    have clipt
The curls before our eyes, may see at
    least
As plain as men do. Speak out, man
    to man ;
No compliments, beseech you '
              ' Friend to friend,
Let that be. We are sad to-night, I
    saw
(—Good night, Sir Blaise ! ah, Smith—
    he has slipped away),
I saw you across the room, and stayed,
    Miss Leigh,
To keep a crowd of lion-hunters off,
With faces toward your jungle. There
    were three ;
A spacious lady, five feet ten and fat,
Who has the devil in her (and there 's
    room),
For walking to and fro upon the earth,
From Chipewa to China ; she requires
Your autograph upon a tinted leaf
'Twixt Queen Pomare's and Emperor
    Soulouque's.
Pray give it ; she has energies, though fat:
For me, I'd rather see a rick on fire
Than such a woman angry. Then
    a youth
Fresh from the backwoods, green as
    the underboughs,
Asks modestly, Miss Leigh, to kiss your
    shoe,
And adds, he has an epic in twelve parts,
Which when you've read, you'll do it
    for his boot :
All which I saved you, and absorb next
    week
Both manuscript and man,—because a
    lord
Is still more potent than a poetess

With any extreme republican. Ah, ah,
You smile, at last, then.'
                              'Thank you.'
                        'Leave the smile.
I'll lose the thanks for 't,—aye, and
        throw you in
My transatlantic girl, with golden eyes,
That draw you to her splendid whiteness
        as
The pistil of a water-lily draws,
Adust with gold. Those girls across the
        sea
Are tyrannously pretty,—and I swore
(She seemed to me an innocent, frank girl)
To bring her to you for a woman's kiss,
Not now, but on some other day or week:
—We'll call it perjury ; I give her up.'

' No, bring her.'
                ' Now,' said he, ' you make it hard
To touch such goodness with a grimy
        palm.
I thought to tease you well, and fret you
        cross,
And steel myself, when rightly vexed
        with you,
For telling you a thing to tease you more.'

' Of Romney ?'
                ' No, no ; nothing worse,' he cried,
' Of Romney Leigh than what is buzzed
        about,—
That he is taken in an eye-trap too,
Like many half as wise. The thing I mean
Refers to you, not him.'
                              ' Refers to me.'

He echoed,—' Me ! You sound it like a
        stone
Dropped down a dry well very listlessly
By one who never thinks about the toad
Alive at the bottom. Presently perhaps
You'll sound your " me" more proudly—
        till I shrink.'

' Lord Howe 's the toad, then, in this
        question ?'
                                    ' Brief,
We'll take it graver. Give me sofa-room,
And quiet hearing. You know Eglinton,
John Eglinton, of Eglinton in Kent ?'

' Is he the toad? — he 's rather like the
        snail,

Known chiefly for the house upon his
        back :
Divide the man and house—you kill the
        man ;
That's Eglinton of Eglinton, Lord
        Howe.'

He answered grave. ' A reputable man,
An excellent landlord of the olden stamp
If somewhat slack in new philanthro-
        pies,
Who keeps his birthdays with a tenants'
        dance,
Is hard upon them when they miss the
        church
Or hold their children back from
        catechism,
But not ungentle when the aged poor
Pick sticks at hedge-sides : nay, I've
        heard him say,
" The old dame has a twinge because she
        stoops ;
That 's punishment enough for felony." '
' O tender-hearted landlord ! may I take
My long lease with him, when the time
        arrives
For gathering winter-faggots !'
                                    ' He likes art,
Buys books and pictures . . of a certain
        kind ;
Neglects no patent duty ; a good son ' ...

' To a most obedient mother. Born to
        wear
His father's shoes, he wears her hus-
        band's too :
Indeed I've heard it 's touching. Dear
        Lord Howe,
You shall not praise me so against your
        heart,
When I'm at worst for praise and faggots.'
                                              ' Be
Less bitter with me, for . . in short,' he
        said,
' I have a letter, which he urged me so
To bring you . . . I could scarcely choose
        but yield ;
Insisting that a new love, passing through
The hand of an old friendship, caught
        from it
Some reconciling odour.'
                              ' Love, you say !
My lord, I cannot love : I only find

The rime for love,—and that 's not love,
        my lord.
Take back your letter.'
            ' Pause : you'll read it first ? '

' I will not read it : it is stereotyped ;
The same he wrote to,—anybody's name,
Anne Blythe the actress, when she died
        so true,
A duchess fainted in a private box :
Pauline the dancer, after the great *pas*
In which her little feet winked overhead
Like other fire-flies, and amazed the pit :
Or Baldinacci, when her F in alt
Had touched the silver tops of heaven
        itself
With such a pungent spirit-dart, the
        Queen
Laid softly, each to each, her white-
        gloved palms,
And sighed for joy : or else (I thank
        your friend)
Aurora Leigh,—when some indifferent
        rimes,
Like those the boys sang round the holy ox
On Memphis-highway, chance perhaps
        to set
Our Apis-public lowing.   Oh, he wants,
Instead of any worthy wife at home,
A star upon his stage of Eglinton ?
Advise him that he is not overshrewd
In being so little modest : a dropped star
Makes bitter waters, says a Book I've
        read,—
And there 's his unread letter.'
                ' My dear friend,'
Lord Howe began . .

            In haste I tore the phrase.
' You mean your friend of Eglinton, or
        me ? '

' I mean you, you,' he answered with
        some fire.
' A happy life means prudent compromise ;
The tare runs through the farmer's
        garnered sheaves,
And though the gleaner's apron holds
        pure wheat
We count her poorer.   Tare with wheat,
        we cry,
And good with drawbacks.   You, you
        love your art,

And, certain of vocation, set your soul
On utterance.   Only, in this world we
        have made
(They say God made it first, but if He did
'Twas so long since, and, since, we have
        spoiled it so,
He scarce would know it, if He looked
        this way,
From hells we preach of, with the flames
        blown out),
—In this bad, twisted, topsy-turvy world
Where all the heaviest wrongs get
        uppermost,—
In this uneven, unfostering England here,
Where ledger-strokes and sword-strokes
        count indeed,
But soul-strokes merely tell upon the flesh
They strike from,— it is hard to stand
        for art,
Unless some golden tripod from the sea
Be fished up, by Apollo's divine chance,
To throne such feet as yours, my
        prophetess,
At Delphi.   Think,—the god comes
        down as fierce
As twenty bloodhounds, shakes you,
        strangles you,
Until the oracular shriek shall ooze in
        froth !
At best 'tis not all ease,—at worst too
        hard :
A place to stand on is a 'vantage gained,
And here 's your tripod.   To be plain,
        dear friend,
You're poor, except in what you richly
        give ;
You labour for your own bread painfully,
Or ere you pour our wine.   For art's
        sake, pause.'

I answered slow,—as some wayfaring
        man,
Who feels himself at night too far from
        home
Makes steadfast face against the bitter
        wind.
' Is art so less a thing than virtue is,
That artists first must cater for their
        ease
Or ever they make issue past themselves
To generous use ? alas, and is it so,
That we, who would be somewhat clean,
        must sweep

Our ways as well as walk them, and no
  friend
Confirm us nobly,—"Leave results to
  God,
But you, be clean?" What! "prudent
  compromise
Makes acceptable life," you say instead,
You, you, Lord Howe?—in things in-
  different, well.
For instance, compromise the wheaten
  bread
For rye, the meat for lentils, silk for serge,
And sleep on down, if needs, for sleep
  on straw ;
But there, end compromise. I will not
  bate
One artist-dream on straw or down, my
  lord,
Nor pinch my liberal soul, though I be
  poor,
Nor cease to love high, though I live
  thus low.'

So speaking, with less anger in my voice
Than sorrow, I rose quickly to depart ;
While he, thrown back upon the noble
  shame
Of such high-stumbling natures, mur-
  mured words,
The right words after wrong ones. Ah,
  the man
Is worthy, but so given to entertain
Impossible plans of superhuman life,—
He sets his virtues on so raised a shelf,
To keep them at the grand millennial
  height,
He has to mount a stool to get at them;
And, meantime, lives on quite the common
  way,
With everybody's morals.
                    As we passed,
Lord Howe insisting that his friendly arm
Should oar me across the sparkling
  brawling stream
Which swept from room to room,—we
  fell at once
On Lady Waldemar. 'Miss Leigh,' she
  said,
And gave me such a smile, so cold and
  bright,
As if she tried it in a 'tiring glass
And liked it ; 'all to-night I've strained
  at you

As babes at baubles held up out of reach
By spiteful nurses ("Never snatch," they
  say),
And there you sate, most perfectly shut in
By good Sir Blaise and clever Mister
  Smith
And then our dear Lord Howe! at last
  indeed
I almost snatched. I have a world to speak
About your cousin's place in Shropshire,
  where
I've been to see his work . . . our work,
  —you heard
I went ? . . . and of a letter yesterday,
In which if I should read a page or two
You might feel interest, though you're
  locked of course
In literary toil.—You'll like to hear
Your last book lies at the phalanstery,
As judged innocuous for the elder girls
And younger women who still care for
  books.
We all must read, you see, before we
  live,
Till slowly the ineffable light comes up
And, as it deepens, drowns the written
  word,—
So said your cousin, while we stood and
  felt
A sunset from his favourite beech-tree
  seat.
He might have been a poet if he would,
But then he saw the higher thing at once
And climbed to it. I think he looks
  well now,
Has quite got over that unfortunate . .
Ah, ah . . I know it moved you. Tender-
  heart!
You took a liking to the wretched girl.
Perhaps you thought the marriage suit-
  able,
Who knows? a poet hankers for romance,
And so on. As for Romney Leigh, 'tis
  sure
He never loved her,—never. By the way,
You have not heard of her . . ? quite out
  of sight,
And out of saving? lost in every sense?'

She might have gone on talking half an
  hour
And I stood still, and cold, and pale, I
  think,

As a garden-statue a child pelts with snow
For pretty pastime. Every now and
  then
I put in 'yes' or 'no,' I scarce knew why;
The blind man walks wherever the dog
  pulls,
And so I answered. Till Lord Howe
  broke in;
'What penance takes the wretch who
  interrupts
The talk of charming women? I, at last,
Must brave it. Pardon, Lady Waldemar!
The lady on my arm is tired, unwell,
And loyally I've promised she shall say
No harder word this evening, than . .
  good night;
The rest her face speaks for her.'—Then
  we went.

And I breathe large at home. I drop
  my cloak,
Unclasp my girdle, loose the band that ties
My hair . . . now could I but unloose my
  soul!
We are sepulchred alive in this close
  world,
And want more room.
              The charming woman there—
This reckoning up and writing down her
  talk
Affects me singularly. How she talked
To pain me! woman's spite.—You wear
  steel-mail;
A woman takes a housewife from her
  breast
And plucks the delicatest needle out
As 'twere a rose, and pricks you carefully
'Neath nails, 'neath eyelids, in your
  nostrils,—say,
A beast would roar so tortured,—but
  a man,
A human creature, must not, shall not
  flinch,
No, not for shame.
              What vexes, after all,
Is just that such as she, with such as I,
Knows how to vex. Sweet heaven, she
  takes me up
As if she had fingered me and dog-eared
  me
And spelled me by the fireside half a life!
She knows my turns, my feeble points.
              —What then?

The knowledge of a thing implies the
  thing;
Of course, she found *that* in me, she saw
  that,
Her pencil underscored *this* for a fault,
And I, still ignorant. Shut the book
  up,—close!
And crush that beetle in the leaves.
                          O heart,
At last we shall grow hard too, like the
  rest,
And call it self-defence because we are
  soft.

And after all, now, . . why should I be
  pained
That Romney Leigh, my cousin, should
  espouse
This Lady Waldemar? And, say, she held
Her newly-blossomed gladness in my
  face, . . .
'Twas natural surely, if not generous,
Considering how, when winter held her
  fast,
I helped the frost with mine, and pained
  her more
Than she pains me. Pains me!—but
  wherefore pained?
'Tis clear my cousin Romney wants
  a wife,—
So, good!—The man's need of the wo-
  man, here,
Is greater than the woman's of the man,
And easier served; for where the man
  discerns
A sex (ah, ah, the man can generalize,
Said he), we see but one, ideally
And really: where we yearn to lose
  ourselves
And melt like white pearls in another's
  wine,
He seeks to double himself by what he
  loves,
And make his drink more costly by our
  pearls.
At board, at bed, at work and holiday,
It is not good for man to be alone,
And that's his way of thinking, first and
  last,
And thus my cousin Romney wants a wife.

But then my cousin sets his dignity
On personal virtue. If he understands

By love, like others, self-aggrandizement,
It is that he may verily be great
By doing rightly and kindly. Once he
      thought,
For charitable ends set duly forth
In Heaven's white judgement-book, to
      marry . . ah,
We'll call her name Aurora Leigh, al-
      though
She 's changed since then!—and once,
      for social ends,
Poor Marian Erle, my sister Marian Erle,
My woodland sister, sweet maid Marian,
Whose memory moans on in me like the
      wind
Through ill-shut casements, making me
      more sad
Than ever I find reasons for. Alas,
Poor pretty plaintive face, embodied
      ghost!
He finds it easy then, to clap thee off
From pulling at his sleeve and book and
      pen,—
He locks thee out at night into the cold
Away from butting with thy horny eyes
Against his crystal dreams, that now
      he 's strong
To love anew? that Lady Waldemar
Succeeds my Marian?
                    After all, why not?
He loved not Marian, more than once he
      loved
Aurora. If he loves at last that Third,
Albeit she prove as slippery as spilt oil
On marble floors, I will not augur him
Ill-luck for that. Good love, howe'er
      ill-placed,
Is better for a man's soul in the end,
Than if he loved ill what deserves love
      well.
A pagan, kissing for a step of Pan
The wild-goat's hoof-print on the loamy
      down,
Exceeds our modern thinker who turns
      back
The strata . . granite, limestone, coal,
      and clay,
Concluding coldly with, 'Here 's law!
      where 's God?'

And then at worse,—if Romney loves
      her not,—
At worst,—if he 's incapable of love,

Which may be—then indeed, for such
      a man
Incapable of love, she 's good enough;
For she, at worst too, is a woman still
And loves him . . as the sort of woman
      can.

My loose long hair began to burn and
      creep,
Alive to the very ends, about my knees:
I swept it backward as the wind sweeps
      flame,
With the passion of my hands. Ah,
      Romney laughed
One day . . (how full the memories come
      up!)
'—Your Florence fire-flies live on in
      your hair,'
He said, ' it gleams so.' Well, I wrung
      them out,
My fire-flies; made a knot as hard as life
Of those loose, soft, impracticable curls,
And then sat down and thought . . ' She
      shall not think
Her thought of me,'—and drew my desk
      and wrote.

' Dear Lady Waldemar, I could not speak
With people round me, nor can sleep
      to-night
And not speak, after the great news
      I heard
Of you and of my cousin. May you be
Most happy; and the good he meant the
      world,
Replenish his own life. Say what I say,
And let my word be sweeter for your
      mouth,
As you are you . . I only Aurora Leigh.'

That 's quiet, guarded: though she hold
      it up
Against the light, she'll not see through
      it more
Than lies there to be seen. So much
      for pride;
And now for peace, a little. Let me stop
All writing back . . ' Sweet thanks, my
      sweetest friend,
You 've made more joyful my great joy
      itself.'
—No, that 's too simple! she would
      twist it thus,

'My joy would still be as sweet as thyme
    in drawers,
However shut up in the dark and dry ;
But violets, aired and dewed by love like
    yours,
Out-smell all thyme : we keep that in our
    clothes,
But drop the other down our bosoms till
They smell like' . . ah, I see her writing
    back
Just so.   She'll make a nosegay of her
    words,
And tie it with blue ribbons at the end
To suit a poet ;—pshaw !
                And then we'll have
The call to church, the broken, sad, bad
    dream
Dreamed out at last, the marriage-vow
    complete
With the marriage breakfast ; praying in
    white gloves,
Drawn off in haste for drinking pagan
    toasts
In somewhat stronger wine than any
    sipped
By gods since Bacchus had his way with
    grapes.

A postscript stops all that and rescues me.
'You need not write. I have been over-
    worked,
And think of leaving London, England
    even,
And hastening to get nearer to the sun
Where men sleep better. So, adieu.'—
    I fold
And seal,——and now I'm out of all the
    coil ;
I breathe now, I spring upward like
    a branch
The ten-years schoolboy with a crooked
    stick
May pull down to his level in search of
    nuts,
But cannot hold a moment. How we
    twang
Back on the blue sky, and assert our
    height,
While he stares after ! Now, the wonder
    seems
That I could wrong myself by such
    a doubt.
We poets always have uneasy hearts,

Because our hearts, large-rounded as the
    globe,
Can turn but one side to the sun at once.
We are used to dip our artist-hands in gall
And potash, trying potentialities
Of alternated colour, till at last
We get confused, and wonder for our skin
How nature tinged it first. Well—here's
    the true
Good flesh-colour; I recognize my hand,—
Which Romney Leigh may clasp as just
    a friend's,
And keep his clean.
                And now, my Italy.
Alas, if we could ride with naked souls
And make no noise and pay no price at all,
I would have seen thee sooner, Italy,
For still I have heard thee crying through
    my life,
Thou piercing silence of ecstatic graves,
Men call that name !

                But even a witch to-day
Must melt down golden pieces in the nard
Wherewith to anoint her broomstick ere
    she rides ;
And poets evermore are scant of gold,
And if they find a piece behind the door
It turns by sunset to a withered leaf.
The Devil himself scarce trusts his
    patented
Gold-making art to any who make rimes,
But culls his Faustus from philosophers
And not from poets. 'Leave my Job,'
    said God ;
And so the Devil leaves him without
    pence,
And poverty proves plainly special grace.
In these new, just, administrative times
Men clamour for an order of merit : why ?
Here's black bread on the table and no
    wine !

At least I am a poet in being poor,
Thank God. I wonder if the manuscript
Of my long poem, if 'twere sold outright,
Would fetch enough to buy me shoes to go
Afoot (thrown in, the necessary patch
For the other side the Alps) ? It cannot be.
I fear that I must sell this residue
Of my father's books, although the Elze-
    virs
Have fly-leaves over-written by his hand

In faded notes as thick and fine and brown
As cobwebs on a tawny monument
Of the old Greeks—*conferenda haec cum his*—
Corruptè citat—lege potiùs,
And so on, in the scholar's regal way
Of giving judgement on the parts of speech,
As if he sate on all twelve thrones up-
    piled,
Arraigning Israel. Aye, but books and
    notes
Must go together. And this Proclus too,
In these dear quaint contracted Grecian
    types,
Fantastically crumpled like his thoughts
Which would not seem too plain ; you
    go round twice
For one step forward, then you take it
    back
Because you're somewhat giddy; there's
    the rule
For Proclus. Ah, I stained this middle
    leaf
With pressing in 't my Florence iris-bell,
Long stalk and all : my father chided me
For that stain of blue blood,—I recollect
The peevish turn his voice took,—'Silly
    girls,
Who plant their flowers in our philo-
    sophy
To make it fine, and only spoil the book!
No more of it, Aurora.' Yes—no more!
Ah, blame of love, that's sweeter than
    all praise
Of those who love not! 'tis so lost to
    me,
I cannot, in such beggared life, afford
To lose my Proclus,—not for Florence
    even.

The kissing Judas, Wolff, shall go in
    stead,
Who builds us such a royal book as this
To honour a chief-poet, folio-built,
And writes above, 'The house of No-
    body!'
Who floats in cream, as rich as any
    sucked
From Juno's breasts, the broad Homeric
    lines,
And, while with their spondaic prodigi-
    ous mouths
They lap the lucent margins as babe-gods,

Proclaims them bastards. Wolff's an
    atheist ;
And if the Iliad fell out, as he says,
By mere fortuitous concourse of old
    songs,
Conclude as much too for the universe.

That Wolff, those Platos : sweep the
    upper shelves
As clean as this, and so I am almost rich,
Which means, not forced to think of
    being poor
In sight of ends. To-morrow : no delay.
I'll wait in Paris till good Carrington
Dispose of such and, having chaffered for
My book's price with the publisher, direct
All proceeds to me. Just a line to ask
His help.
          And now I come, my Italy,
My own hills ! Are you 'ware of me, my
    hills,
How I burn toward you? do you feel
    to-night
The urgency and yearning of my soul,
As sleeping mothers feel the sucking babe
And smile ?— Nay, not so much as when
    in heat
Vain lightnings catch at your inviolate
    tops
And tremble while ye are steadfast. Still
    ye go
Your own determined, calm, indifferent
    way
Toward sunrise, shade by shade, and
    light by light,
Of all the grand progression nought left
    out,
As if God verily made you for yourselves
And would not interrupt your life with
    ours.

SIXTH BOOK

THE English have a scornful insular way
Of calling the French light. The levity
Is in the judgement only, which yet stands,
For say a foolish thing but oft enough
(And here's the secret of a hundred
    creeds,
Men get opinions as boys learn to spell,
By reiteration chiefly), the same thing
Shall pass at last for absolutely wise,

And not with fools exclusively.   And so
We say the French are light, as if we said
The cat mews or the milch-cow gives us
    milk :
Say rather, cats are milked and milch-
    cows mew ;
For what is lightness but inconsequence,
Vague fluctuation 'twixt effect and cause
Compelled by neither? Is a bullet light,
That dashes from the gun-mouth, while
    the eye
Winks and the heart beats one, to flatten
    itself
To a wafer on the white speck on a wall
A hundred paces off? Even so direct,
So sternly undivertible of aim,
Is this French people.
                              All, idealists
Too absolute and earnest, with them all
The idea of a knife cuts real flesh ;
And still, devouring the safe interval
Which Nature placed between the
    thought and act
With those too fiery and impatient souls,
They threaten conflagration to the world,
And rush with most unscrupulous logic on
Impossible practice.   Set your orators
To blow upon them with loud windy
    mouths
Through watchword phrases, jest or
    sentiment,
Which drive our burly brutal English
    mobs
Like so much chaff, whichever way they
    blow,—
This light French people will not thus
    be driven.
They turn indeed,—but then they turn
    upon
Some central pivot of their thought and
    choice,
And veer out by the force of holding fast.
That's hard to understand, for English-
    men
Unused to abstract questions, and un-
    trained
To trace the involutions, valve by valve,
In each orbed bulb-root of a general truth,
And mark what subtly fine integument
Divides opposed compartments.   Free-
    dom's self
Comes concrete to us, to be understood,
Fixed in a feudal form incarnately

To suit our ways of thought and reverence,
The special form, with us, being still the
    thing.
With us, I say, though I'm of Italy
By mother's birth and grave, by father's
    grave
And memory ; let it be ;—a poet's heart
Can swell to a pair of nationalities,
However ill-lodged in a woman's breast.

And so I am strong to love this noble
    France,
This poet of the nations, who dreams on
And wails on (while the household goes
    to wreck)
For ever, after some ideal good,—
Some equal poise of sex, some unvowed
    love
Inviolate, some spontaneous brother-
    hood,
Some wealth that leaves none poor and
    finds none tired,
Some freedom of the many that respects
The wisdom of the few.   Heroic dreams !
Sublime, to dream so ; natural, to wake :
And sad, to use such lofty scaffoldings,
Erected for the building of a church,
To build instead a brothel or a prison—
May God save France !
                              And if at last she sighs
Her great soul up into a great man's face,
To flush his temples out so gloriously
That few dare carp at Caesar for being bald,
What then ?—this Caesar represents, not
    reigns,
And is no despot, though twice absolute :
This Head has all the people for a heart;
This purple's lined with the democracy,—
Now let him see to it ! for a rent within
Would leave irreparable rags without.

A serious riddle : find such anywhere
Except in France ; and when 'tis found
    in France,
Be sure to read it rightly.   So, I mused
Up and down, up and down, the terraced
    streets,
The glittering boulevards, the white
    colonnades
Of fair fantastic Paris who wears trees
Like plumes, as if man made them,
    spire and tower
As if they had grown by nature, tossing up

Her fountains in the sunshine of the
 squares,
As if in beauty's game she tossed the dice,
Or blew the silver down-balls of her
 dreams
To sow futurity with seeds of thought
And count the passage of her festive hours.

The city swims in verdure, beautiful
As Venice on the waters, the sea-swan.
What bosky gardens dropped in close-
 walled courts
Like plums in ladies' laps who start and
 laugh :
What miles of streets that run on after
 trees,
Still carrying all the necessary shops,
Those open caskets with the jewels seen !
And trade is art, and art 's philosophy,
In Paris. There 's a silk for instance,
 there,
As worth an artist's study for the folds,
As that bronze opposite ! nay, the bronze
 has faults,
Art 's here too artful,—conscious as a maid
Who leans to mark her shadow on the wall
Until she lose a 'vantage in her step.
Yet Art walks forward, and knows
 where to walk ;
The artists also are idealists,
Too absolute for nature, logical
To austerity in the application of
The special theory,—not a soul content
To paint a crooked pollard and an ass,
As the English will because they find
 it so
And like it somehow.—There the old
 Tuileries
Is pulling its high cap down on its eyes,
Confounded, conscience-stricken, and
 amazed
By the apparition of a new fair face
In those devouring mirrors. Through
 the grate
Within the gardens, what a heap of babes,
Swept up like leaves beneath the
 chestnut-trees
From every street and alley of the town,
By ghosts perhaps that blow too bleak
 this way
A-looking for their heads ! dear pretty
 babes,
I wish them luck to have their ball-play out

Before the next change. Here the air
 is thronged
With statues poised upon their columns
 fine
As if to stand a moment were a feat,
Against that blue ! What squares,—
 what breathing-room
For a nation that runs fast,—aye, runs
 against
The dentist's teeth at the corner in pale
 rows,
Which grin at progress in an epigram.

I walked the day out, listening to the
 chink
Of the first Napoleon's dry bones in his
 second grave,
By victories guarded 'neath the golden
 dome
That caps all Paris like a bubble. 'Shall
These dry bones live,' thought Louis
 Philippe once,
And lived to know. Herein is argument
For kings and politicians, but still more
For poets, who bear buckets to the well
Of ampler draught.
            These crowds are very good
For meditation (when we are very strong),
Though love of beauty makes us timorous,
And draws us backward from the coarse
 town-sights
To count the daisies upon dappled fields
And hear the streams bleat on among
 the hills
In innocent and indolent repose,
While still with silken elegiac thoughts
We wind out from us the distracting
 world
And die into the chrysalis of a man,
And leave the best that may, to come of us,
In some brown moth. I would be bold
 and bear
To look into the swarthiest face of things,
For God's sake who has made them.

                    Six days' work ;
The last day shutting 'twixt its dawn
 and eve
The whole work bettered of the previous
 five !
Since God collected and resumed in man
The firmaments, the strata, and the
 lights,

Fish, fowl, and beast, and insect,—all
    their trains
Of various life caught back upon His arm,
Reorganized, and constituted MAN,
The microcosm, the adding up of works,—
Within whose fluttering nostrils, then
    at last
Consummating Himself the Maker sighed,
As some strong winner at the foot-race
    sighs
Touching the goal.
                Humanity is great ;
And, if I would not rather pore upon
An ounce of common, ugly, human dust,
An artisan's palm or a peasant's brow,
Unsmooth, ignoble, save to me and
    God,
Than track old Nilus to his silver roots,
Or wait on all the changes of the moon
Among the mountain-peaks of Thessaly
(Until her magic crystal round itself
For many a witch to see in)—set it down
As weakness,—strength by no means.
    How is this
That men of science, osteo'ogists
And surgeons, beat some poets in respect
For nature,—count nought common or
    unclean,
Spend raptures upon perfect specimens
Of indurated veins, distorted joints,
Or beautiful new cases of curved spine,
While we, we are shocked at nature's
    falling off,
We dare to shrink back from her warts
    and blains,
We will not, when she sneezes, look at
    her,
Not even to say 'God bless her'? That's
    our wrong ;
For that, she will not trust us often with
Her larger sense of beauty and desire,
But tethers us to a lily or a rose
And bids us diet on the dew inside,
Left ignorant that the hungry beggar-boy
(Who stares unseen against our absent
    eyes,
And wonders at the gods that we must be,
To pass so careless for the oranges !)
Bears yet a breastful of a fellow-world
To this world, undisparaged, undespoiled,
And (while we scorn him for a flower
    or two,
As being, Heaven help us, less poetical)

Contains himself both flowers and firma-
    ments
And surging seas and aspectable stars,
And all that we would push him out of
    sight
In order to see nearer. Let us pray
God's grace to keep God's image in repute,
That so, the poet and philanthropist
(Even I and Romney) may stand side
    by side,
Because we both stand face to face with
    men,
Contemplating the people in the rough,
Yet each so follow a vocation, his
And mine.
        I walked on, musing with myself
On life and art, and whether after all
A larger metaphysics might not help
Our physics, a completer poetry
Adjust our daily life and vulgar wants
More fully than the special outside plans,
Phalansteries, material institutes,
The civil conscriptions and lay monas-
    teries
Preferred by modern thinkers, as they
    thought
The bread of man indeed made all his life,
And washing seven times in the 'People's
    Baths '
Were sovereign for a people's leprosy,
Still leaving out the essential prophet's
    word
That comes in power. On which, we
    thunder down,
We prophets, poets,—Virtue 's in the
    word !
The maker burnt the darkness up with
    His,
To inaugurate the use of vocal life ;
And, plant a poet's word even, deep
    enough
In any man's breast, looking presently
For offshoots, you have done more for
    the man
Than if you dressed him in a broadcloth
    coat
And warmed his Sunday potage at your
    fire.
Yet Romney leaves me . . .
                God ! what face is that ?
O Romney, O Marian !
                Walking on the quays
And pulling thoughts to pieces leisurely,

As if I caught at grasses in a field
And bit them slow between my absent lips
And shred them with my hands . .
          What face is that ?
What a face, what a look, what a like-
    ness ! Full on mine
The sudden blow of it came down, till all
My blood swam, my eyes dazzled. Then
    I sprang . .

It was as if a meditative man
Were dreaming out a summer afternoon
And watching gnats a-prick upon a pond,
When something floats up suddenly,
    out there,
Turns over . . a dead face, known once
    alive . .
So old, so new ! it would be dreadful now
To lose the sight and keep the doubt of
    this :
He plunges—ha ! he has lost it in the
    splash.

I plunged—I tore the crowd up, either
    side,
And rushed on, forward, forward, after
    her.
Her ? whom ?
    A woman sauntered slow in front,
Munching an apple,—she left off amazed
As if I had snatched it : that 's not she,
    at least.
A man walked arm-linked with a lady
    veiled,
Both heads dropped closer than the need
    of talk :
They started ; he forgot her with his face,
And she, herself, and clung to him as if
My look were fatal. Such a stream of folk,
And all with cares and business of their
    own !
I ran the whole quay down against their
    eyes ;
No Marian ; nowhere Marian. Almost,
    now,
I could call Marian, Marian, with the
    shriek
Of desperate creatures calling for the
    Dead.
Where is she, was she ? was she any-
    where ?
I stood still, breathless, gazing, straining
    out

In every uncertain distance, till at last
A gentleman abstracted as myself
Came full against me, then resolved the
    clash
In voluble excuses,—obviously
Some learned member of the Institute
Upon his way there, walking, for his
    health,
While meditating on the last ' Discourse ';
Pinching the empty air 'twixt finger and
    thumb,
From which the snuff being ousted by
    that shock
Defiled his snow-white waistcoat duly
    pricked
At the button-hole with honourable red ;
' Madame, your pardon,'—there he
    swerved from me
A metre, as confounded as he had heard
That Dumas would be chosen to fill up
The next chair vacant, by his ' men *in us*.'
Since when was genius found respect-
    able ?
It passes in its place, indeed,—which
    means
The seventh floor back, or else the
    hospital :
Revolving pistols are ingenious things,
But prudent men (Academicians are)
Scarce keep them in the cupboard next
    the prunes.

And so, abandoned to a bitter mirth,
I loitered to my inn. O world, O world,
O jurists, rimers, dreamers, what you
    please,
We play a weary game of hide-and-seek !
We shape a figure of our fantasy,
Call nothing something, and run after it
And lose it, lose ourselves too in the
    search,
Till clash against us comes a somebody
Who also has lost something and is lost,
Philosopher against philanthropist,
Academician against poet, man
Against woman, against the living the
    dead,—
Then home, with a bad headache and
    worse jest !

To change the water for my heliotropes
And yellow roses. Paris has such flowers.
But England, also. 'Twas a yellow rose,

By that south window of the little house,
My cousin Romney gathered with his
    hand
On all my birthdays for me, save the
    last ;
And then I shook the tree too rough,
    too rough,
For roses to stay after.
                        Now, my maps.
I must not linger here from Italy
Till the last nightingale is tired of song,
And the last fire-fly dies off in the maize.
My soul 's in haste to leap into the sun
And scorch and seethe itself to a finer
    mood,
Which here, in this chill north, is apt
    to stand
Too stiffly in former moulds.
                        That face persists.
It floats up, it turns over in my mind,
As like to Marian, as one dead is like
The same alive. In very deed a face
And not a fancy, though it vanished so ;
The small fair face between the darks
    of hair,
I used to liken, when I saw her first,
To a point of moonlit water down a well :
The low brow, the frank space between
    the eyes,
Which always had the brown pathetic
    look
Of a dumb creature who had been
    beaten once
And never since was easy with the world.
Ah, ah,—now I remember perfectly
Those eyes, to-day,—how overlarge
    they seemed,
As if some patient passionate despair
(Like a coal dropt and forgot on tapestry,
Which slowly burns a widening circle
    out)
Had burnt them larger, larger. And
    those eyes
To-day, I do remember, saw me too,
As I saw them, with conscious lids
    astrain
In recognition. Now a fantasy,
A simple shade or image of the brain,
Is merely passive, does not retro-act,
Is seen, but sees not.
                        'Twas a real face,
Perhaps a real Marian.
                        Which being so,

I ought to write to Romney, 'Marian 's
    here ;
Be comforted for Marian.'
                        My pen fell,
My hands struck sharp together, as
    hands do
Which hold at nothing. Can I write to
    him
A half-truth ? can I keep my own soul
    blind
To the other half, . . the worse ? What
    are our souls,
If still, to run on straight a sober pace
Nor start at every pebble or dead leaf,
They must wear blinkers, ignore facts,
    suppress
Six tenths of the road ? Confront the
    truth, my soul !
And oh, as truly as that was Marian's face,
The arms of that same Marian clasped
    a thing
. . Not hid so well beneath the scanty
    shawl,
I cannot name it now for what it was.

A child. Small business has a castaway
Like Marian with that crown of prosper-
    ous wives
At which the gentlest she grows arrogant
And says, ' my child.' Who finds an
    emerald ring
On a beggar's middle finger and requires
More testimony to convict a thief ?
A child 's too costly for so mere a wretch ;
She filched it somewhere, and it means,
    with her,
Instead of honour, blessing, merely
    shame.

I cannot write to Romney, ' Here she is,
Here 's Marian found ! I 'll set you on
    her track :
I saw her here, in Paris, . . and her
    child.
She put away your love two years ago,
But, plainly, not to starve. You
    suffered then ;
And, now that you've forgot her utterly
As any last year's annual, in whose place
You've planted a thick flowering ever-
    green,
I choose, being kind, to write and tell
    you this

To make you wholly easy—she 's not
dead,
But only .. damned.'
            Stop there : I go too fast ;
I'm cruel like the rest,—in haste to take
The first stir in the arras for a rat,
And set my barking, biting thoughts
    upon 't.
—A child! what then? Suppose a
    neighbour 's sick
And asked her, 'Marian, carry out my
    child
In this Spring air,'—I punish her for that?
Or say, the child should hold her round
    the neck
For good child-reasons, that he liked it so
And would not leave her—she had
    winning ways—
I brand her therefore that she took the
    child?
Not so.
    I will not write to Romney Leigh.
For now he 's happy,—and she may
    indeed
Be guilty,—and the knowledge of her
    fault
Would draggle his smooth time. But
    I, whose days
Are not so fine they cannot bear the rain,
And who moreover having seen her face
Must see it again, .. will see it, by my
    hopes
Of one day seeing heaven too. The police
Shall track her, hound her, ferret their
    own soil ;
We'll dig this Paris to its catacombs
But certainly we'll find her, have her out,
And save her, if she will or will not—
    child
Or no child,—if a child, then one to save !

The long weeks passed on without con-
    sequence.
As easy find a footstep on the sand
The morning after spring-tide, as the
    trace
Of Marian's feet between the incessant
    surfs
Of this live flood. She may have moved
    this way,—
But so the star-fish does, and crosses out
The dent of her small shoe. The foiled
    police

Renounced me. 'Could they find a girl
    and child,
No other signalment but girl and child ?
No data shown but noticeable eyes
And hair in masses, low upon the brow,
As if it were an iron crown and pressed?
Friends heighten, and suppose they
    specify :
Why, girls with hair and eyes are every-
    where
In Paris ; they had turned me up in vain
No Marian Erle indeed, but certainly
Mathildes, Justines, Victoires, .. or, if
    I sought
The English, Betsies, Saras, by the score.
They might as well go out into the fields
To find a speckled bean, that 's somehow
    specked,
And somewhere in the pod.'—They left
    me so.
Shall I leave Marian ? have I dreamed
    a dream ?

—I thank God I have found her ! I must
    say
'Thank God,' for finding her, although
    'tis true
I find the world more sad and wicked
    for 't.
But she—
        I'll write about her, presently.
My hand 's a-tremble, as I had just caught
    up
My heart to write with, in the place of it.
At least you 'd take these letters to be writ
At sea, in storm !—wait now ..
            A simple chance
Did all. I could not sleep last night,
    and, tired
Of turning on my pillow and harder
    thoughts,
Went out at early morning, when the air
Is delicate with some last starry touch,
To wander through the Market-place of
    Flowers
(The prettiest haunt in Paris), and make
    sure
At worst that there were roses in the
    world.
So wandering, musing, with the artist's
    eye,
That keeps the shade-side of the thing it
    loves,

Half-absent, whole-observing, while the
crowd
Of young vivacious and black-braided
heads
Dipped, quick as finches in a blossomed
tree,
Among the nosegays, cheapening this
and that
In such a cheerful twitter of rapid
speech,—
My heart leapt in me, startled by a voice
That slowly, faintly, with long breaths
that marked
The interval between the wish and
word,
Inquired in stranger's French, 'Would
that be much,
That branch of flowering mountain-
gorse?'—'So much?
Too much for me, then!' turning the
face round
So close upon me that I felt the sigh
It turned with.
 'Marian, Marian!'—face to face—
'Marian! I find you. Shall I let you go?'
I held her two slight wrists with both
my hands;
'Ah, Marian, Marian, can I let you go?'
—She fluttered from me like a cyclamen,
As white, which taken in a sudden wind
Beats on against the palisade.—'Let
pass,'
She said at last. 'I will not,' I replied;
'I lost my sister Marian many days,
And sought her ever in my walks and
prayers,
And, now I find her . . . do we throw
away
The bread we worked and prayed for,—
crumble it
And drop it, . . to do even so by thee
Whom still I've hungered after more
than bread,
My sister Marian?—can I hurt thee, dear?
Then why distrust me? Never tremble so.
Come with me rather where we'll talk
and live
And none shall vex us. I've a home
for you
And me and no one else' . . .
   She shook her head.
'A home for you and me and no one else
Ill-suits one of us : I prefer to such,

A roof of grass on which a flower might
spring,
Less costly to me than the cheapest
here;
And yet I could not, at this hour, afford
A like home even. That you offer yours,
I thank you. You are good as heaven
itself—
As good as one I knew before . . Fare-
well.'

I loosed her hands,—'In *his* name, no
farewell!'
(She stood as if I held her.) 'For his
sake,
For his sake, Romney's! by the good he
meant,
Aye, always! by the love he pressed for
once,—
And by the grief, reproach, abandon-
ment,
He took in change' . .
   'He Romney! who grieved *him*?
Who had the heart for 't? what reproach
touched *him*?
Be merciful,—speak quickly.'
    'Therefore come,'
I answered with authority.—'I think
We dare to speak such things and name
such names
In the open squares of Paris!'
     Not a word
She said, but in a gentle humbled way
(As one who had forgot herself in grief)
Turned round and followed closely where
I went,
As if I led her by a narrow plank
Across devouring waters, step by step;
And so in silence we walked on a mile.

And then she stopped: her face was
white as wax.
'We go much farther?'
    'You are ill,' I asked,
'Or tired?'
  She looked the whiter for her smile.
'There's one at home,' she said, 'has
need of me
By this time,—and I must not let him
wait.'

'Not even,' I asked, 'to hear of Romney
Leigh?'

'Not even,' she said, 'to hear of Mister
    Leigh.'

'In that case,' I resumed, 'I go with
    you,
And we can talk the same thing there
    as here.
None waits for me: I have my day to
    spend.'

IIer lips moved in a spasm without a
    sound,—
But then she spoke. 'It shall be as you
    please;
And better so—'tis shorter seen than
    told:
And though you will not find me worth
    your pains,
That, even, may be worth some pains to
    know
For one as good as you are.'
                Then she led
The way, and I, as by a narrow plank
Across devouring waters, followed her,
Stepping by her footsteps, breathing by
    her breath,
And holding her with eyes that would
    not slip;
And so, without a word, we walked a mile,
And so, another mile, without a word.

Until the peopled streets being all dis-
    missed,
House-rows and groups all scattered like
    a flock,
The market-gardens thickened, and the
    long
White walls beyond, like spiders' outside
    threads,
Stretched, feeling blindly toward the
    country-fields
Through half-built habitations and half-
    dug
Foundations,—intervals of trenchant
    chalk
That bit betwixt the grassy uneven turfs
Where goats (vine-tendrils trailing from
    their mouths)
Stood perched on edges of the cellarage
Which should be, staring as about to
    leap
To find their coming Bacchus. All the
    place

Seemed less a cultivation than a waste.
Men work here, only,—scarce begin to
    live:
All's sad, the country struggling with
    the town,
Like an untamed hawk upon a strong
    man's fist,
That beats its wings and tries to get away,
And cannot choose be satisfied so soon
To hop through court-yards with its
    right foot tied,
The vintage plains and pastoral hills in
    sight.

We stopped beside a house too high and
    slim
To stand there by itself, but waiting till
Five others, two on this side, three on
    that,
Should grow up from the sullen second
    floor
They pause at now, to build it to a row.
The upper windows partly were unglazed
Meantime,—a meagre, unripe house: a
    line
Of rigid poplars elbowed it behind,
And, just in front, beyond the lime and
    bricks
That wronged the grass between it and
    the road,
A great acacia with its slender trunk
And overpoise of multitudinous leaves
(In which a hundred fields might spill
    their dew
And intense verdure, yet find room
    enough)
Stood reconciling all the place with green.

I followed up the stair upon her step.
She hurried upward, shot across a face,
A woman's, on the landing,—'How now,
    now!
Is no one to have holidays but you?
You said an hour, and stay three hours,
    I think,
And Julie waiting for your betters here?
Why if he had waked he might have
    waked, for me.'
—Just murmuring an excusing word she
    passed
And shut the rest out with the chamber-
    door,
Myself shut in beside her.

'Twas a room
Scarce larger than a grave, and near as
  bare ;
Two stools, a pallet-bed ; I saw the room :
A mouse could find no sort of shelter in 't,
Much less a greater secret ; curtainless,—
The window fixed you with its torturing
  eye,
Defying you to take a step apart
If peradventure you would hide a thing.
I saw the whole room, I and Marian there
Alone.
      Alone ? She threw her bonnet off,
Then, sighing as 'twere sighing the last
  time,
Approached the bed, and drew a shawl
  away :
You could not peel a fruit you fear to
  bruise
More calmly and more carefully than so,—
Nor would you find within, a rosier flushed
Pomegranate—
            There he lay upon his back,
The yearling creature, warm and moist
  with life
To the bottom of his dimples,—to the ends
Of the lovely tumbled curls about his face ;
For since he had been covered over-much
To keep him from the light-glare, both
  his cheeks
Were hot and scarlet as the first I've rose
The shepherd's heart-blood ebbed away
  into
The faster for his love. And love was here
As instant ; in the pretty baby-mouth,
Shut close as if for dreaming that it
  sucked,
The little naked feet, drawn up the way
Of nestled birdlings ; everything so soft
And tender,—to the tiny holdfast hands,
Which, closing on a finger into sleep,
Had kept the mould of 't.
            While we stood there dumb,
For oh, that it should take such innocence
To prove just guilt, I thought, and stood
  there dumb,—
The light upon his eyelids pricked them
  wide,
And, staring out at us with all their blue,
As half perplexed between the angelhood
He had been away to visit in his sleep,
And our most mortal presence, gradually
He saw his mother's face, accepting it

In change for heaven itself with such a
  smile
As might have well been learnt there,—
  never moved,
But smiled on, in a drowse of ecstasy,
So happy (half with her and half with
  heaven)
He could not have the trouble to be stirred,
But smiled and lay there. Like a rose,
  I said ?
As red and still indeed as any rose,
That blows in all the silence of its leaves,
Content in blowing to fulfil its life.

She leaned above him (drinking him as
  wine)
In that extremity of love, 'twill pass
For agony or rapture, seeing that love
Includes the whole of nature, rounding it
To love . . no more,—since more can
  never be
Than just love. Self-forgot, cast out of
  self,
And drowning in the transport of the
  sight,
Her whole pale passionate face, mouth,
  forehead, eyes,
One gaze, she stood : then, slowly as he
  smiled
She smiled too, slowly, smiling unaware,
And drawing from his countenance to
  hers
A fainter red, as if she watched a flame
And stood in it a-glow. ' How beautiful,'
Said she.
            I answered, trying to be cold.
(Must sin have compensations, was my
  thought,
As if it were a holy thing like grief ?
And is a woman to be fooled aside
From putting vice down, with that
  woman's toy
A baby ?)—' Aye ! the child is well
  enough,'
I answered. ' If his mother's palms are
  clean
They need be glad of course in clasping
  such ;
But if not, I would rather lay my hand,
Were I she, on God's brazen altar-bars
Red-hot with burning sacrificial lambs,
Than touch the sacred curls of such a
  child.'

She plunged her fingers in his clustering
locks,
As one who would not be afraid of fire;
And then with indrawn steady utterance
said,
'My lamb, my lamb! although, through
such as thou,
The most unclean got courage and
approach
To God, once,—now they cannot, even
with men,
Find grace enough for pity and gentle
words.'

'My Marian,' I made answer, grave and
sad,
'The priest who stole a lamb to offer him,
Was still a thief. And if a woman steals
(Through God's own barrier-hedges of
true love,
Which fence out licence in securing love)
A child like this, that smiles so in her face,
She is no mother but a kidnapper,
And he's a dismal orphan, not a son,
Whom all her kisses cannot feed so full
He will not miss hereafter a pure home
To live in, a pure heart to lean against,
A pure good mother's name and memory
To hope by, when the world grows thick
and bad
And he feels out for virtue.'
                        'Oh,' she smiled
With bitter patience, 'the child takes
his chance;
Not much worse off in being fatherless
Than I was, fathered. He will say, belike,
His mother was the saddest creature
born;
He'll say his mother lived so contrary
To joy, that even the kindest, seeing her,
Grew sometimes almost cruel: he'll not
say
She flew contrarious in the face of God
With bat-wings of her vices. Stole my
child,—
My flower of earth, my only flower on
earth,
My sweet, my beauty!' . . Up she
snatched the child,
And, breaking on him in a storm of tears,
Drew out her long sobs from their
shivering roots,
Until he took it for a game, and stretched

His feet and flapped his eager arms like
wings
And crowed and gurgled through his
infant laugh:
'Mine, mine,' she said. 'I have as sure
a right
As any glad proud mother in the world,
Who sets her darling down to cut his teeth
Upon her church-ring. If she talks of law,
I talk of law! I claim my mother-dues
By law,—the law which now is para-
mount,—
The common law, by which the poor and
weak
Are trodden underfoot by vicious men,
And loathed for ever after by the good.
Let pass! I did not filch,—I found the
child.'

'You found him, Marian?'
                        'Aye, I found him where
I found my curse,—in the gutter, with
my shame!
What have you, any of you, to say to that,
Who all are happy, and sit safe and high,
And never spoke before to arraign my
right
To grief itself? What, what, . . being
beaten down
By hoofs of maddened oxen into a ditch,
Half-dead, whole mangled, when a girl
at last
Breathes, sees . . and finds there, bedded
in her flesh
Because of the extremity of the shock,
Some coin of price! . . and when a good
man comes
(That's God! the best men are not
quite as good)
And says, "I dropped the coin there:
take it you,
And keep it,—it shall pay you for the
loss,"—
You all put up your finger—"See the
thief!
Observe what precious thing she has
come to filch.
How bad those girls are!" Oh, my
flower, my pet,
I dare forget I have you in my arms
And fly off to be angry with the world,
And fright you, hurt you with my
tempers, till

You double up your lip? Why, that indeed
Is bad : a naughty mother ! '
                       ' You mistake,'
I interrupted ; 'if I loved you not,
I should not, Marian, certainly be here.'

'Alas,' she said, 'you are so very good ;
And yet I wish indeed you had never come
To make me sob until I vex the child.
It is not wholesome for these pleasure-
    plats
To be so early watered by our brine.
And then, who knows ? he may not like
    me now
As well, perhaps, as ere he saw me fret,—
One's ugly fretting ! he has eyes the
    same
As angels, but he cannot see as deep,
And so I've kept for ever in his sight
A sort of smile to please him,—as you
    place
A green thing from the garden in a cup,
To make believe it grows there.   Look,
    my sweet,
My cowslip-ball ! we've done with that
    cross face,
And here's the face come back you used
    to like.
Ah, ah ! he laughs ! he likes me.   Ah,
    Miss Leigh,
You're great and pure ; but were you
    purer still,—
As if you had walked, we'll say, no
    otherwhere
Than up and down the new Jerusalem,
And held your trailing lutestring up
    yourself
From brushing the twelve stones, for fear
    of some
Small speck as little as a needle-prick,
White stitched on white,—the child
    would keep to *me*,
Would choose his poor lost Marian, like
    me best,
And, though you stretched your arms,
    cry back and cling,
As we do when God says it's time to die
And bids us go up higher.   Leave us, then;
We two are happy.   Does *he* push me off?
He's satisfied with me, as I with him.'

'So soft to one, so hard to others !   Nay,'
I cried, more angry that she melted me,

'We make henceforth a cushion of our
    faults
To sit and practise easy virtues on ?
I thought a child was given to sanctify
A woman,—set her in the sight of all
The clear-eyed heavens, a chosen
    minister
To do their business and lead spirits up
The difficult blue heights.   A woman
    lives,
Not bettered, quickened toward the truth
    and good
Through being a mother ? . . then she's
    none ! although
She damps her baby's cheeks by kissing
    them,
As we kill roses.'
                 ' Kill !   O Christ,' she said,
And turned her wild sad face from side
    to side
With most despairing wonder in it,
    ' What,
What have you in your souls against me
    then,
All of you ?   am I wicked, do you think?
God knows me, trusts me with the child ;
    but you,
You think me really wicked ? '
                       ' Complaisant,'
I answered softly, ' to a wrong you've
    done,
Because of certain profits,—which is
    wrong
Beyond the first wrong, Marian.   When
    you left
The pure place and the noble heart, to
    take
The hand of a seducer' . .
                ' Whom ? whose hand ?
I took the hand of ' . .
                Springing up erect
And lifting up the child at full arm's
    length,
As if to bear him like an oriflamme
Unconquerable to armies of reproach,—
' By *him*,' she said, ' my child's head
    and its curls,
By these blue eyes no woman born could
    dare
A perjury on, I make my mother's oath,
That if I left that Heart, to lighten it,
The blood of mine was still, except for
    grief !

No cleaner maid than I was, took a step
To a sadder end,—no matron-mother
now
Looks backward to her early maidenhood
Through chaster pulses. I speak steadily;
And if I lie so, . . if, being fouled in will
And paltered with in soul by devil's lust,
I dared to bid this angel take my part, . .
Would God sit quiet, let us think, in
heaven,
Nor strike me dumb with thunder? Yet
I speak:
He clears me therefore. What,
" seduced " 's your word?
Do wolves seduce a wandering fawn in
France?
Do eagles, who have pinched a lamb
with claws,
Seduce it into carrion? So with me.
I was not ever, as you say, seduced,
But simply, murdered.'
There she paused, and sighed,
With such a sigh as drops from agony
To exhaustion,—sighing while she let
the babe
Slide down upon her bosom from her
arms,
And all her face's light fell after him
Like a torch quenched in falling. Down
she sank,
And sate upon the bedside with the child.

But I, convicted, broken utterly,
With woman's passion clung about her
waist
And kissed her hair and eyes,—' I have
been wrong,
Sweet Marian ' . . (weeping in a tender
rage)
' Sweet holy Marian! And now, Marian,
now,
I'll use your oath although my lips are
hard,
And by the child, my Marian, by the child,
I swear his mother shall be innocent
Before my conscience, as in the open
Book
Of Him who reads for judgement. Inno-
cent,
My sister! let the night be ne'er so dark
The moon is surely somewhere in the
sky;
So surely is your whiteness to be found

Through all dark facts. But pardon,
pardon me,
And smile a little, Marian,—for the child,
If not for me, my sister.'
                              The poor lip
Just motioned for the smile and let it go:
And then, with scarce a stirring of the
mouth,
As if a statue spoke that could not
breathe,
But spoke on calm between its marble
lips,—
' I'm glad, I'm very glad you clear me so.
I should be sorry that you set me down
With harlots, or with even a better name
Which misbecomes his mother. For the
rest,
I am not on a level with your love,
Nor ever was, you know,—but now am
worse,
Because that world of yours has dealt
with me
As when the hard sea bites and chews
a stone
And changes the first form of it. I've
marked
A shore of pebbles bitten to one shape
From all the various life of madrepores;
And so, that little stone, called Marian
Erle,
Picked up and dropped by you and
another friend,
Was ground and tortured by the inces-
sant sea
And bruised from what she was,—
changed! death 's a change,
And she, I said, was murdered; Marian 's
dead.
What can you do with people when they
are dead,
But, if you are pious, sing a hymn and go,
Or, if you are tender, heave a sigh and go,
But go by all means,—and permit the
grass
To keep its green feud up 'twixt them
and you?
Then leave me,—let me rest. I'm dead,
I say,
And if, to save the child from death as
well,
The mother in me has survived the rest,
Why, that 's God's miracle you must
not tax,

I'm not less dead for that : I'm nothing
    more
But just a mother. Only for the child
I'm warm, and cold, and hungry, and
    afraid,
And smell the flowers a little and see
    the sun,
And speak still, and am silent,—just for
    him!
I pray you therefore to mistake me not
And treat me haply as I were alive ;
For though you ran a pin into my soul,
I think it would not hurt nor trouble me.
Here's proof, dear lady,—in the market-
    place
But now, you promised me to say a word
About . . a friend, who once, long years
    ago,
Took God's place toward me, when He
    leans and loves
And does not thunder, . . whom at last
    I left,
As all of us leave God. You thought
    perhaps
I seemed to care for hearing of that
    friend ?
Now, judge me! we have sate here
    half an hour
And talked together of the child and me,
And I not asked as much as, "What's
    the thing
You had to tell me of the friend . . the
    friend ?"
He's sad, I think you said,—he's sick
    perhaps?
'Tis nought to Marian if he's sad or sick.
Another would have crawled beside
    your foot
And prayed your words out. Why,
    a beast, a dog,
A starved cat, if he had fed it once with
    milk,
Would show less hardness. But I'm
    dead, you see,
And that explains it.'
          Poor, poor thing, she spoke
And shook her head, as white and calm
    as frost
On days too cold for raining any more,
But still with such a face, so much alive,
I could not choose but take it on my arm
And stroke the placid patience of its
    cheeks,—

Then told my story out, of Romney Leigh,
How, having lost her, sought her, missed
    her still,
He. broken-hearted for himself and her,
Had drawn the curtains of the world
    awhile
As if he had done with morning.
    There I stopped,
For when she gasped, and pressed me
    with her eyes,
'And now . . how is it with him? tell
    me now,'
I felt the shame of compensated grief,
And chose my words with scruple—
    slowly stepped
Upon the slippery stones set here and
    there
Across the sliding water. ' Certainly,
As evening empties morning into night,
Another morning takes the evening up
With healthful, providential interchange ;
And, though he thought still of her,'—
          ' Yes, she knew,
She understood : she had supposed in-
    deed
That. as one stops a hole upon a flute,
At which a new note comes and shapes
    the tune,
Excluding her would bring a worthier in,
And, long ere this, that Lady Waldemar
He loved so ' . .
    ' Loved,' I started,—'loved her so !
Now tell me' . .
    'I will tell you,' she replied :
' But, since we're taking oaths, you'll
    promise first
That he in England, he, shall never learn
In what a dreadful trap his creature here,
Round whose unworthy neck he had
    meant to tie
The honourable ribbon of his name,
Fell unaware and came to butchery :
Because,—I know him,—as he takes to
    heart
The grief of every stranger, he's not like
To banish mine as far as I should choose
In wishing him most happy. Now he
    leaves
To think of me, perverse, who went my
    way,
Unkind, and left him,—but if once he
    knew . .
Ah, then, the sharp nail of my cruel wrong

Would fasten me for ever in his sight,
Like some poor curious bird, through
  each spread wing
Nailed high up over a fierce hunter's fire,
To spoil the dinner of all tenderer folk
Come in by chance. Nay, since your
  Marian's dead,
You shall not hang her up, but dig a hole
And bury her in silence! ring no bells.'

I answered gaily, though my whole
  voice wept,
'We'll ring the joy-bells, not the
  funeral-bells,
Because we have her back, dead or alive.'

She never answered that, but shook her
  head;
Then low and calm, as one who, safe in
  heaven,
Shall tell a story of his lower life,
Unmoved by shame or anger,—so she
  spoke.
She told me she had loved upon her knees,
As others pray, more perfectly absorbed
In the act and inspiration. She felt his
For just his uses, not her own at all,
His stool, to sit on or put up his foot,
His cup, to fill with wine or vinegar,
Whichever drink might please him at
  the chance
For that should please her always: let
  him write
His name upon her . . it seemed natural;
It was most precious, standing on his
  shelf,
To wait until he chose to lift his hand.
Well, well,—I saw her then, and must
  have seen
How bright her life went floating on
  her love,
Like wicks the housewives send afloat
  on oil
Which feeds them to a flame that lasts
  the night.

To do good seemed so much his business,
That, having done it, she was fain to think,
Must fill up his capacity for joy.
At first she never mooted with herself
If *he* was happy, since he made her so,
Or if he loved her, being so much beloved.
Who thinks of asking if the sun is light,

Observing that it lightens? who's so bold,
To question God of His felicity?
Still less. And thus she took for granted
  first
What first of all she should have put to
  proof,
And sinned against him so, but only so.
'What could you hope,' she said, 'of
  such as she?
You take a kid you like, and turn it out
In some fair garden: though the creature's
  fond
And gentle, it will leap upon the beds
And break your tulips, bite your tender
  trees;
The wonder would be if such innocence
Spoiled less: a garden is no place for kids.'

And, by degrees, when he who had
  chosen her
Brought in his courteous and benignant
  friends
To spend their goodness on her, which
  she took
So very gladly, as a part of his,—
By slow degrees it broke on her slow sense
That she too in that Eden of delight
Was out of place, and, like the silly kid,
Still did most mischief where she meant
  most love.
A thought enough to make a woman mad
(No beast in this but she may well go mad),
That saying 'I am thine to love and use'
May blow the plague in her protesting
  breath
To the very man for whom she claims
  to die,—
That, clinging round his neck, she pulls
  him down
And drowns him,—and that, lavishing
  her soul,
She hales perdition on him. 'So, being
  mad,'
Said Marian . .
                'Ah—who stirred such
  thoughts, you ask?
Whose fault it was, that she should have
  such thoughts?
None's fault, none's fault. The light
  comes, and we see:
But if it were not truly for our eyes,
There would be nothing seen, for all the
  light.

And so with Marian: if she saw at last,
The sense was in her,—Lady Waldemar
Had spoken all in vain else.'
                              ' O my heart,
O prophet in my heart,' I cried aloud,
' Then Lady Waldemar spoke ! '
                              ' *Did* she speak,'
Mused Marian softly, ' or did she only
    sign ?
Or did she put a word into her face
And look, and so impress you with the
    word ?
Or leave it in the foldings of her gown,
Like rosemary smells a movement will
    shake out
When no one's conscious ? who shall
    say, or guess ?
One thing alone was certain—from the
    day
The gracious lady paid a visit first,
She, Marian, saw things different,—felt
    distrust
Of all that sheltering roof of circumstance
Her hopes were building into with clay
    nests :
Her heart was restless, pacing up and
    down
And fluttering, like dumb creatures before
    storms,
Not knowing wherefore she was ill at
    ease.'

' And still the lady came,' said Marian
    Erle,
' Much oftener than *he* knew it, Mister
    Leigh.
She bade me never tell him she had come,
She liked to love me better than he knew,
So very kind was Lady Waldemar :
And every time she brought with her
    more light,
And every light made sorrow clearer . .
    Well,
Ah, well ! we cannot give her blame for
    that ;
'Twould be the same thing if an angel
    came,
Whose right should prove our wrong.
    And every time
The lady came, she looked more beautiful
And spoke more like a flute among green
    trees,
Until at last, as one, whose heart being sad

On hearing lovely music, suddenly
Dissolves in weeping, I brake out in tears
Before her, asked her counsel,—" Had
    I erred
In being too happy ? would she set me
    straight ?
For she, being wise and good and born
    above
The flats I had never climbed from, could
    perceive
If such as I, might grow upon the hills ;
And whether such poor herb sufficed to
    grow,
For Romney Leigh to break his fast
    upon 't,—
Or would he pine on such, or haply
    starve ? "
She wrapt me in her generous arms at
    once,
And let me dream a moment how it feels
To have a real mother, like some girls :
But when I looked, her face was
    younger . . aye,
Youth's too bright not to be a little hard,
And beauty keeps itself still uppermost,
That's true !—Though Lady Waldemar
    was kind
She hurt me, hurt, as if the morning-sun
Should smite us on the eyelids when we
    sleep,
And wake us up with headache. Aye,
    and soon
Was light enough to make my heart
    ache too :
She told me truths I asked for,—'twas
    my fault,—
" That Romney could not love me, if he
    would,
As men call loving : there are bloods
    that flow
Together like some rivers and not mix,
Through contraries of nature. He indeed
Was set to wed me, to espouse my class,
Act out a rash opinion,—and, once wed,
So just a man and gentle could not choose
But make my life as smooth as marriage-
    ring,
Bespeak me mildly, keep me a cheerful
    house,
With servants, brooches, all the flowers
    I liked,
And pretty dresses, silk the whole year
    round " . .

At which I stopped her,—"This for me.
 And now
For *him*."—She hesitated,—truth grew
 hard ;
She owned, "'Twas plain a man like
 Romney Leigh
Required a wife more level to himself.
If day by day he had to bend his height
To pick up sympathies, opinions,
 thoughts,
And interchange the common talk of life
Which helps a man to live as well as talk,
His days were heavily taxed. Who buys
 a staff
To fit the hand, that reaches but the knee?
He'd feel it bitter to be forced to miss
The perfect joy of married suited pairs,
Who, bursting through the separating
 hedge
Of personal dues with that sweet eglan-
 tine
Of equal love, keep saying, ' So *we* think,
It strikes *us*,—that's *our* fancy.' "—When
 I asked
If earnest will, devoted love, employed
In youth like mine, would fail to raise
 me up
As two strong arms will always raise a
 child
To a fruit hung overhead, she sighed and
 sighed . .
"That could not be," she feared. "You
 take a pink,
You dig about its roots and water it
And so improve it to a garden-pink,
But will not change it to a heliotrope,
The kind remains. And then, the harder
 truth—
This Romney Leigh, so rash to leap a pale,
So bold for conscience, quick for martyr-
 dom,
Would suffer steadily and never flinch,
But suffer surely and keenly, when his
 class
Turned shoulder on him for a shameful
 match,
And set him up as ninepin in their talk
To bowl him down with jestings."—
 There, she paused ;
And when I used the pause in doubting
 that
We wronged him after all in what we
 feared—

"Suppose such things could never touch
 him more
In his high conscience (if the things
 should be)
Than, when the queen sits in an upper
 room,
The horses in the street can spatter
 her !"—
A moment, hope came,—but the lady
 closed
That door and nicked the lock and shut
 it out,
Observing wisely that, "the tender heart
Which made him over-soft to a lower
 class,
Would scarcely fail to make him sensitive
To a higher,—how they thought and
 what they felt."

' Alas, alas,' said Marian, rocking slow
The pretty baby who was near asleep,
The eyelids creeping over the blue
 balls,—
' She made it clear, too clear—I saw the
 whole !
And yet who knows if I had seen my way
Straight out of it by looking, though
 'twas clear,
Unless the generous lady, 'ware of this,
Had set her own house all afire for me
To light me forwards ? Leaning on my
 face
Her heavy agate eyes which crushed
 my will,
She told me tenderly (as when men
 come
To a bedside to tell people they must die),
" She knew of knowledge,—aye, of
 knowledge knew,
That Romney Leigh had loved *her*
 formerly.
And *she* loved *him*, she might say, now
 the chance
Was past,—but that, of course, he never
 guessed,—
For something came between them,
 something thin
As a cobweb, catching every fly of doubt
To hold it buzzing at the window-pane
And help to dim the daylight. Ah,
 man's pride
Or woman's—which is greatest ? most
 averse

To brushing cobwebs? Well, but she
   and he
Remained fast friends; it seemed not
   more than so,
Because he had bound his hands and
   could not stir.
An honourable man, if somewhat rash;
And she, not even for Romney, would
   she spill
A blot .. as little even as a tear ..
Upon his marriage-contract,—not to gain
A better joy for two than came by that:
For, though I stood between her heart
   and heaven,
She loved me wholly."'
          Did I laugh or curse?
I think I sate there silent, hearing all,
Aye, hearing double,—Marian's tale, at
   once,
And Romney's marriage-vow, '*I'll keep
to* THEE,'
Which means that woman-serpent. Is
   it time
For church now?
       'Lady Waldemar spoke more,'
Continued Marian, ' but, as when a soul
Will pass out through the sweetness of
   a song
Beyond it, voyaging the uphill road,
Even so mine wandered from the things
   I heard
To those I suffered. It was afterward
I shaped the resolution to the act.
For many hours we talked. What need
   to talk?
The fate was clear and close; it touched
   my eyes;
But still the generous lady tried to keep
The case afloat, and would not let it go,
And argued, struggled upon Marian's
   side,
Which was not Romney's! though she
   little knew
What ugly monster would take up the
   end,—
What griping death within the drowning
   death
Was ready to complete my sum of death.'

I thought,—Perhaps he's sliding now
   the ring
Upon that woman's finger ..
          She went on:

' The lady, failing to prevail her way,
Up-gathered my torn wishes from the
   ground
And pieced them with her strong
   benevolence;
And, as I thought I could breathe freer
   air
Away from England, going without pause,
Without farewell, just breaking with a
   jerk
The blossomed offshoot from my thorny
   life,—
She promised kindly to provide the
   means,
With instant passage to the colonies
And full protection,—" would commit
   me straight
To one who once had been her waiting-
   maid
And had the customs of the world, intent
On changing England for Australia
Herself, to carry out her fortune so."
For which I thanked the Lady Waldemar,
As men upon their death-beds thank
   last friends
Who lay the pillow straight: it is not
   much,
And yet 'tis all of which they are capable,
This lying smoothly in a bed to die.
And so, 'twas fixed;—and so, from day
   to day,
The woman named came in to visit me.'

Just then the girl stopped speaking,—
   sate erect,
And stared at me as if I had been a ghost
(Perhaps I looked as white as any ghost)
With large-eyed horror. ' Does God
   make,' she said,
' All sorts of creatures really, do you
   think?
Or is it that the Devil slavers them
So excellently, that we come to doubt
Who's stronger, He who makes, or he
   who mars?
I never liked the woman's face or voice
Or ways: it made me blush to look at her;
It made me tremble if she touched my
   hand;
And when she spoke a fondling word
   I shrank
As if one hated me who had power to
   hurt;

And, every time she came, my veins ran
    cold
As somebody were walking on my grave.
At last I spoke to Lady Waldemar:
" Could such an one be good to trust?"
    I asked.
Whereat the lady stroked my cheek and
    laughed
Her silver-laugh (one must be born to
    laugh,
To put such music in it),—" Foolish girl,
Your scattered wits are gathering wool
    beyond
The sheep-walk reaches!—leave the
    thing to me."
And therefore, half in trust, and half in
    scorn
That I had heart still for another fear
In such a safe despair, I left the thing.

' The rest is short. I was obedient:
I wrote my letter which delivered *him*
From Marian to his own prosperities,
And followed that bad guide. The
    lady?—hush,
I never blame the lady. Ladies who
Sit high, however willing to look down,
Will scarce see lower than their dainty
    feet;
And Lady Waldemar saw less than I,
With what a Devil's daughter I went forth
Along the swine's road, down the pre-
    cipice,
In such a curl of hell-foam caught and
    choked,
No shriek of soul in anguish could pierce
    through
To fetch some help. They say there's
    help in heaven
For all such cries. But if one cries from
    hell . .
What then?—the heavens are deaf upon
    that side.

' A woman . . hear me, let me make it
    plain, . .
A woman . . not a monster . . both her
    breasts
Made right to suckle babes . . she took
    me off
A woman also, young and ignorant
And heavy with my grief, my two poor
    eyes

Near washed away with weeping, till
    the trees,
The blessed unaccustomed trees and fields
Ran either side the train like stranger
    dogs
Unworthy of any notice,—took me off
So dull, so blind, so only half alive,
Not seeing by what road, nor by what
    ship,
Nor toward what place, nor to what end
    of all.
Men carry a corpse thus,—past the
    doorway, past
The garden-gate, the children's play-
    ground, up
The green lane,—then they leave it in
    the pit,
To sleep and find corruption, cheek to
    cheek
With him who stinks since Friday.
               ' But suppose;
To go down with one's soul into the grave,
To go down half dead, half alive, I say,
And wake up with corruption, . . cheek
    to cheek
With him who stinks since Friday!
    There it is,
And that's the horror of 't, Miss Leigh.
               ' You feel?
You understand?—no, do not look at me,
But understand. The blank, blind,
    weary way,
Which led, where'er it led, away at
    least;
The shifted ship, to Sydney or to France,
Still bound, wherever else, to another
    land;
The swooning sickness on the dismal sea,
The foreign shore, the shameful house,
    the night,
The feeble blood, the heavy-headed
    grief, . .
No need to bring their damnable drugged
    cup,
And yet they brought it. Hell's so
    prodigal
Of devil's gifts, hunts liberally in packs,
Will kill no poor small creature of the
    wilds
But fifty red wide throats must smoke
    at it,
As HIS at me . . when waking up at last . .
I told you that I waked up in the grave.

'Enough so!—it is plain enough so. True,
We wretches cannot tell out all our wrong
Without offence to decent happy folk.
I know that we must scrupulously hint
With half-words, delicate reserves, the
    thing
Which no one scrupled we should feel
    in full.
Let pass the rest, then; only leave my
    oath
Upon this sleeping child,—man's vio-
    lence,
Not man's seduction, made me what I am,
As lost as . . I told *him* I should be lost.
When mothers fail us, can we help our-
    selves?
That's fatal!—And you call it being lost,
That down came next day's noon and
    caught me there
Half gibbering and half raving on the
    floor,
And wondering what had happened up
    in heaven,
That suns should dare to shine when
    God Himself
Was certainly abolished.
                            ' I was mad,
How many weeks, I know not,—many
    weeks.
I think they let me go when I was mad,
They feared my eyes and loosed me, as
    boys might
A mad dog which they had tortured.
    Up and down
I went, by road and village, over tracts
Of open foreign country, large and
    strange,
Crossed everywhere by long thin poplar-
    lines
Like fingers of some ghastly skeleton
    Hand
Through sunlight and through moonlight
    evermore
Pushed out from hell itself to pluck me
    back,
And resolute to get me, slow and sure;
While every roadside Christ upon his
    cross
Hung reddening through his gory wounds
    at me,
And shook his nails in anger, and came
    down
To follow a mile after, wading up

The low vines and green wheat, crying
    " Take the girl !
She 's none of mine from henceforth."
    Then I knew
(But this is somewhat dimmer than the
    rest)
The charitable peasants gave me bread
And leave to sleep in straw : and twice
    they tied,
At parting, Mary's image round my
    neck—
How heavy it seemed ! as heavy as a
    stone ;
A woman has been strangled with less
    weight :
I threw it in a ditch to keep it clean
And ease my breath a little, when none
    looked ;
I did not need such safeguards :—brutal
    men
Stopped short, Miss Leigh, in insult,
    when they had seen
My face,—I must have had an awful
    look.
And so I lived : the weeks passed on,—
    I lived.
'Twas living my old tramp-life o'er again,
But, this time, in a dream, and hunted
    round
By some prodigious Dream-fear at my
    back,
Which ended yet : my brain cleared
    presently ;
And there I sate, one evening, by the road,
I, Marian Erle, myself, alone, undone,
Facing a sunset low upon the flats
As if it were the finish of all time,
The great red stone upon my sepulchre,
Which angels were too weak to roll away.

SEVENTH BOOK

'The woman's motive ? shall we daub
    ourselves
With finding roots for nettles ? 'tis soft
    clay
And easily explored. She had the means,
The moneys, by the lady's liberal grace,
In trust for that Australian scheme and
    me,
Which so, that she might clutch with
    both her hands

And chink to her naughty uses undis-
    turbed,
She served me (after all it was not strange,
'Twas only what my mother would have
    done)
A motherly, right damnable good turn.

'Well, after. There are nettles every-
    where,
But smooth green grasses are more
    common still ;
The blue of heaven is larger than the
    cloud ;
A miller's wife at Clichy took me in
And spent her pity on me,—made me calm
And merely very reasonably sad.
She found me a servant's place in Paris,
    where
I tried to take the cast-off life again,
And stood as quiet as a beaten ass
Who, having fallen through overloads,
    stands up
To let them charge him with another
    pack.

'A few months, so. My mistress, young
    and light,
Was easy with me, less for kindness than
Because she led, herself, an easy time
Betwixt her lover and her looking-glass,
Scarce knowing which way she was
    praised the most.
She felt so pretty and so pleased all day
She could not take the trouble to be cross,
But sometimes, as I stooped to tie her
    shoe,
Would tap me softly with her slender foot
Still restless with the last night's dancing
    in 't,
And say, "Fie, pale-face! are you English
    girls
All grave and silent? mass-book still,
    and Lent?
And first-communion pallor on your
    cheeks,
Worn past the time for 't? little fool, be
    gay!"
At which she vanished like a fairy,
    through
A gap of silver laughter.
                        'Came an hour
When all went otherwise. She did not
    speak,

But clenched her brows, and clipped me
    with her eyes
As if a viper with a pair of tongs,
Too far for any touch, yet near enough
To view the writhing creature,—then at
    last,
"Stand still there, in the holy Virgin's
    name,
Thou Marian ; thou'rt no reputable girl,
Although sufficient dull for twenty saints !
I think thou mock'st me and my house,"
    she said ;
"Confess thou'lt be a mother in a month,
Thou mask of saintship."
                        'Could I answer her ?
The light broke in so. It meant *that*
    then, *that* ?
I had not thought of that, in all my
    thoughts,
Through all the cold, numb aching of
    my brow,
Through all the heaving of impatient life
Which threw me on death at intervals,—
    through all
The upbreak of the fountains of my heart
The rains had swelled too large : it
    could mean *that* ?
Did God make mothers out of victims,
    then,
And set such pure amens to hideous
    deeds ?
Why not ? He overblows an ugly grave
With violets which blossom in the spring.
And *I* could be a mother in a month ?
I hope it was not wicked to be glad.
I lifted up my voice and wept, and
    laughed,
To heaven, not her, until it tore my throat.
"Confess, confess !"—what was there
    to confess,
Except man's cruelty, except my wrong ?
Except this anguish, or this ecstasy ?
This shame or glory ? The light woman
    there
Was small to take it in : an acorn-cup
Would take the sea in sooner.
                        ' "Good," she cried ;
"Unmarried and a mother, and she
    laughs !
These unchaste girls are always impu-
    dent.
Get out, intriguer ! leave my house and
    trot.

I wonder you should look me in the face,
With such a filthy secret."
             'Then I rolled
My scanty bundle up and went my way,
Washed white with weeping, shuddering
    head and foot
With blind hysteric passion, staggering
    forth
Beyond those doors. 'Twas natural of
    course
She should not ask me where I meant
    to sleep ;
I might sleep well beneath the heavy
    Seine,
Like others of my sort ; the bed was laid
For us. But any woman, womanly,
Had thought of him who should be in
    a month,
The sinless babe that should be in a month,
And if by chance he might be warmer
    housed
Than underneath such dreary dripping
    eaves.'

I broke on Marian there. 'Yet she
    herself,
A wife, I think, had scandals of her own,
A lover not her husband.'
             'Aye,' she said,
' But gold and meal are measured other-
    wise ;
I learnt so much at school,' said Marian
    Erle.

' O crooked world,' I cried, ' ridiculous
If not so lamentable ! 'Tis the way
With these light women of a thrifty vice,
My Marian,—always hard upon the rent
In any sister's virtue ! while they keep
Their own so darned and patched with
    perfidy,
That, though a rag itself, it looks as well
Across a street, in balcony or coach,
As any perfect stuff might. For my part,
I'd rather take the wind-side of the stews
Than touch such women with my finger-
    end !
They top the poor street-walker by
    their lie
And look the better for being so much
    worse :
The devil 's most devilish when respect-
    able.

But you, dear, and your story.'
                'All the rest
Is here,' she said, and signed upon the
    child.
'I found a mistress-sempstress who was
    kind
And let me sew in peace among her girls.
And what was better than to draw the
    threads
All day and half the night for him and him ?
And so I lived for him, and so he lives,
And so I know, by this time, God lives
    too.'

She smiled beyond the sun and ended so,
And all my soul rose up to take her part
Against the world's successes, virtues,
    fames.
' Come with me, sweetest sister,' I re-
    turned,
'And sit within my house and do me good
From henceforth, thou and thine ! ye
    are my own
From henceforth. I am lonely in the
    world,
And thou art lonely, and the child is half
An orphan. Come,—and henceforth
    thou and I
Being still together will not miss a friend,
Nor he a father, since two mothers shall
Make that up to him. I am journeying
    south,
And in my Tuscan home I'll find a niche
And set thee there, my saint, the child
    and thee,
And burn the lights of love before thy face,
And ever at thy sweet look cross myself
From mixing with the world's prosperi-
    ties ;
That so, in gravity and holy calm,
We two may live on toward the truer
    life.'

She looked me in the face and answered
    not,
Nor signed she was unworthy, nor gave
    thanks,
But took the sleeping child and held it out
To meet my kiss, as if requiting me
And trusting me at once. And thus, at
    once,
I carried him and her to where I live ;
She 's there now, in the little room, asleep,

I hear the soft child-breathing through
    the door,
And all three of us, at to-morrow's break,
Pass onward, homeward, to our Italy.
Oh, Romney Leigh, I have your debts
    to pay,
And I'll be just and pay them.
                        But yourself!
To pay your debts is scarcely difficult,
To buy your life is nearly impossible,
Being sold away to Lamia. My head
    aches,
I cannot see my road along this dark ;
Nor can I creep and grope, as fits the dark,
For these foot-catching robes of woman-
    hood :
A man might walk a little . . but I !—
    He loves
The Lamia-woman,—and I, write to him
What stops his marriage, and destroys
    his peace,—
Or what perhaps shall simply trouble him,
Until she only need to touch his sleeve
With just a finger's tremulous white flame,
Saying, 'Ah,—Aurora Leigh ! a pretty
    tale,
A very pretty poet ! I can guess
The motive '—then, to catch his eyes
    in hers
And vow she does not wonder,—and
    they two
To break in laughter as the sea along
A melancholy coast, and float up higher,
In such a laugh, their fatal weeds of love !
Aye, fatal, aye. And who shall answer me
Fate has not hurried tides,—and if to-
    night
My letter would not be a night too late,
An arrow shot into a man that 's dead,
To prove a vain intention ? Would I show
The new wife vile, to make the husband
    mad ?
No, Lamia ! shut the shutters, bar the
    doors
From every glimmer on thy serpent-skin !
I will not let thy hideous secret out
To agonize the man I love—I mean
The friend I love . . as friends love.
                        It is strange,
To-day while Marian told her story like
To absorb most listeners, how I listened
    chief
To a voice not hers, nor yet that enemy's,

Nor God's in wrath, . . but one that
    mixed with mine
Long years ago among the garden-trees,
And said to *me*, to *me* too, ' Be my wife,
Aurora.' It is strange with what a swell
Of yearning passion, as a snow of ghosts
Might beat against the impervious door
    of heaven,
I thought, ' Now, if I had been a woman,
    such
As God made women, to save men by
    love,—
By just my love I might have saved this
    man,
And made a nobler poem for the world
Than all I have failed in.' But I failed
    besides
In this ; and now he 's lost ! through me
    alone !
And, by my only fault, his empty house
Sucks in, at this same hour, a wind from
    hell
To keep his hearth cold, make his case-
    ments creak
For ever to the tune of plague and sin—
O Romney, O my Romney, O my friend,
My cousin and friend ! my helper, when
    I would,
My love, that might be ! mine !
                        Why, how one weeps
When one 's too weary ! Were a wit-
    ness by,
He'd say some folly . . that I loved the
    man,
Who knows ? . . and make me laugh
    again for scorn.
At strongest, women are as weak in flesh,
As men, at weakest, vilest are in soul :
So, hard for women to keep pace with
    men !
As well give up at once, sit down at once,
And weep as I do. Tears, tears ! *why*
    we weep ?
'Tis worth inquiry ?—that we've shamed
    a life,
Or lost a love, or missed a world, perhaps ?
By no means. Simply, that we've
    walked too far,
Or talked too much, or felt the wind i'
    the east,—
And so we weep, as if both body and soul
Broke up in water—this way.
                        Poor mixed rags

Forsooth we're made of, like those other
    dolls
That lean with pretty faces into fairs.
It seems as if I had a man in me,
Despising such a woman.
                              Yet indeed,
To see a wrong or suffering moves us all
To undo it though we should undo our-
    selves,
Aye, all the more, that we undo ourselves;
That's womanly, past doubt, and not ill-
    moved.
A natural movement therefore, on my
    part,
To fill the chair up of my cousin's wife,
And save him from a devil's company!
We're all so,—made so —'tis our woman's
    trade
To suffer torment for another's ease.
The world's male chivalry has perished
    out,
But women are knights-errant to the last;
And if Cervantes had been Shakespeare
    too,
He had made his Don a Donna.
                              So it clears,
And so we rain our skies blue.
                              Put away
This weakness. If, as I have just now said,
A man's within me,—let him act himself,
Ignoring the poor conscious trouble of
    blood
That's called the woman merely.   I will
    write
Plain words to England,—if too late,
    too late,
If ill-accounted, then accounted ill;
We'll trust the heavens with something.
                              'Dear Lord Howe,
You'll find a story on another leaf
Of Marian Erle,—what noble friend of
    yours
She trusted once, through what flagitious
    means,
To what disastrous ends;—the story's
    true.
I found her wandering on the Paris quays,
A babe upon her breast,—unnatural,
Unseasonable outcast on such snow
Unthawed to this time.   I will tax in this
Your friendship, friend, if that convicted
    She
Be not his wife yet, to denounce the facts

To himself,—but, otherwise, to let them
    pass
On tip-toe like escaping murderers,
And tell my cousin merely—Marian lives,
Is found, and finds her home with such
    a friend,
Myself, Aurora.   Which good news,
    "She's found,"
Will help to make him merry in his love:
I send it, tell him, for my marriage-gift,
As good as orange-water for the nerves,
Or perfumed gloves for headache,—
    though aware
That he, except of love, is scarcely sick:
I mean the new love this time, . . since
    last year.
Such quick forgetting on the part of men!
Is any shrewder trick upon the cards
To enrich them? pray instruct me how
    'tis done :
First, clubs,—and while you look at
    clubs, 'tis spades ;
That's prodigy.   The lightning strikes
    a man,
And when we think to find him dead
    and charred . .
Why, there he is on a sudden, playing
    pipes
Beneath the splintered elm-tree ! Crime
    and shame
And all their hoggery trample your
    smooth world,
Nor leave more footmarks than Apollo's
    kine
Whose hoofs were muffled by the thiev-
    ing god
In tamarisk-leaves and myrtle.   I'm so
    sad,
So weary and sad to-night, I'm some-
    what sour,—
Forgive me. To be blue and shrew at once,
Exceeds all toleration except yours,
But yours, I know, is infinite. Farewell.
To-morrow we take train for Italy.
Speak gently of me to your gracious wife,
As one, however far, shall yet be near
In loving wishes to your house.'
                              I sign.
And now I loose my heart upon a page,
This —
            'Lady Waldemar, I'm very glad
I never liked you ; which you knew so
    well

You spared me, in your turn, to like me
   much :
Your liking surely had done worse for
   me
Than has your loathing, though the last
   appears
Sufficiently unscrupulous to hurt,
And not afraid of judgement. Now, there's
   space
Between our faces,—I stand off, as if
I judged a stranger's portrait and pro-
   nounced
Indifferently the type was good or bad.
What matter to me that the lines are
   false,
I ask you ? did I ever ink my lips
By drawing your name through them as
   a friend's,
Or touch your hands as lovers do ?
   Thank God
I never did : and since you're proved so
   vile,
Aye, vile, I say,—we'll show it pre-
   sently,—
I'm not obliged to nurse my friend in
   you,
Or wash out my own blots, in counting
   yours,
Or even excuse myself to honest souls
Who seek to press my lip or clasp my
   palm,—
"Alas, but Lady Waldemar came first ! "

"'Tis true, by this time you may near
   me so
That you're my cousin's wife. You've
   gambled deep
As Lucifer, and won the morning-star
In that case,—and the noble house of
   Leigh
Must henceforth with its good roof shelter
   you :
I cannot speak and burn you up between
Those rafters, I who am born a Leigh,—
   nor speak
And pierce your breast through Rom-
   ney's, I who live
His friend and cousin,—so, you're safe.
   You two
Must grow together like the tares and
   wheat
Till God's great fire.—But make the
   best of time.

'And hide this letter : let it speak no
   more
Than I shall, how you tricked poor
   Marian Erle,
And set her own love digging its own
   grave
Within her green hope's pretty garden-
   ground,—
Aye, sent her forth with some one of
   your sort
To a wicked house in France, from
   which she fled
With curses in her eyes and ears and
   throat,
Her whole soul choked with curses,—
   mad in short,
And madly scouring up and down for
   weeks
The foreign hedgeless country, lone and
   lost,—
So innocent, male-fiends might slink
   within
Remote hell-corners, seeing her so de-
   filed.

'But you,—you are a woman and more
   bold.
To do you justice, you'd not shrink to
   face . .
We'll say, the unfledged life in the other
   room,
Which, treading down God's corn, you
   trod in sight
Of all the dogs, in reach of all the
   guns,—
Aye, Marian's babe, her poor unfathered
   child,
Her yearling babe !—you'd face him
   when he wakes
And opens up his wonderful blue eyes :
You'd meet them and not wink perhaps,
   nor fear
God's triumph in them and supreme
   revenge
When righting His creation's balance-
   scale
(You pulled as low as Tophet) to the top
Of most celestial innocence. For me
Who am not as bold, I own those infant
   eyes
Have set me praying.
            'While they look at heaven,
No need of protestation in my words

Against the place you've made them!
    let them look.
They'll do your business with the
    heavens, be sure:
I spare you common curses.
                    'Ponder this;
If haply you're the wife of Romney
    Leigh
(For which inheritance beyond your birth
You sold that poisonous porridge called
    your soul),
I charge you, be his faithful and true wife!
Keep warm his hearth and clean his
    board, and, when
He speaks, be quick with your obedience;
Still grind your paltry wants and low
    desires
To dust beneath his heel; though, even
    thus,
The ground must hurt him,—it was writ
    of old,
"Ye shall not yoke together ox and ass,"
The nobler and ignobler. Aye, but you
Shall do your part as well as such ill
    things
Can do aught good. You shall not vex
    him,—mark,
You shall not vex him, jar him when
    he's sad,
Or cross him when he's eager. Under-
    stand
To trick him with apparent sympathies,
Nor let him see thee in the face too near
And unlearn thy sweet seeming. Pay
    the price
Of lies, by being constrained to lie on
    still:
'Tis easy for thy sort: a million more
Will scarcely damn thee deeper.
                    'Doing which
You are very safe from Marian and myself;
We'll breathe as softly as the infant here,
And stir no dangerous embers. Fail
    a point,
And show our Romney wounded, ill-
    content,
Tormented in his home, we open mouth,
And such a noise will follow, the last
    trump's
Will scarcely seem more dreadful, even
    to you;
You'll have no pipers after: Romney will
(I know him) push you forth as none of his,

All other men declaring it well done,
While women, even the worst, your
    like, will draw
Their skirts back, not to brush you in
    the street,
And so I warn you. I'm . . . Aurora
    Leigh.'

The letter written I felt satisfied.
The ashes, smouldering in me, were
    thrown out
By handfuls from me: I had writ my heart
And wept my tears, and now was cool
    and calm;
And, going straightway to the neigh-
    bouring room,
I lifted up the curtains of the bed
Where Marian Erle, the babe upon her
    arm,
Both faces leaned together like a pair
Of folded innocences self-complete,
Each smiling from the other, smiled and
    slept.
There seemed no sin, no shame, no
    wrath, no grief.
I felt she too had spoken words that night,
But softer certainly, and said to God,
Who laughs in heaven perhaps that such
    as I
Should make ado for such as she.—
    'Defiled'
I wrote? 'defiled' I thought her? Stoop,
Stoop lower, Aurora! get the angels'
    leave
To creep in somewhere, humbly, on your
    knees,
Within this round of sequestration white
In which they have wrapt earth's found-
    lings, heaven's elect.

The next day we took train to Italy
And fled on southward in the roar of
    steam.
The marriage-bells of Romney must be
    loud,
To sound so clear through all: I was not
    well,
And truly, though the truth is like a jest,
I could not choose but fancy, half the way,
I stood alone i' the belfry, fifty bells
Of naked iron, mad with merriment
(As one who laughs and cannot stop
    himself),

All clanking at me, in me, over me,
Until I shrieked a shriek I could not hear,
And swooned with noise,—but still, along
  my swoon,
Was 'ware the baffled changes backward
  rang,
Prepared, at each emerging sense, to beat
And crash it out with clangour.   I was
  weak ;
I struggled for the posture of my soul
In upright consciousness of place and
  time,
But evermore, 'twixt waking and asleep,
Slipped somehow, staggered, caught at
  Marian's eyes
A moment (it is very good for strength
To know that some one needs you to be
  strong),
And so recovered what I called myself,
For that time.
          I just knew it when we swept
Above the old roofs of Dijon ; Lyons
  dropped
A spark into the night, half trodden out
Unseen.   But presently the winding
  Rhone
Washed out the moonlight large along
  his banks
Which strained their yielding curves out
  clear and clean
To hold it,—shadow of town and castle
  blurred
Upon the hurrying river.   Such an air
Blew thence upon the forehead,—half
  an air
And half a water,—that I leaned and
  looked,
Then, turning back on Marian, smiled
  to mark
That she looked only on her child, who
  slept,
His face toward the moon too.
                    So we passed
The liberal open country and the close,
And shot through tunnels, like a lightning-
  wedge
By great Thor-hammers driven through
  the rock,
Which, quivering through the intestine
  blackness, splits,
And lets it in at once : the train swept in
Athrob with effort, trembling with
  resolve,

The fierce denouncing whistle wailing on
And dying off smothered in the shudder-
  ing dark,
While we, self-awed, drew troubled
  breath, oppressed
As other Titans underneath the pile
And nightmare of the mountains.   Out,
  at last,
To catch the dawn afloat upon the land !
—Hills, slung forth broadly and gauntly
  everywhere,
Not crampt in their foundations, pushing
  wide
Rich outspreads of the vineyards and the
  corn
(As if they entertained i' the name of
  France),
While, down their straining sides,
  streamed manifest
A soil as red as Charlemagne's knightly
  blood,
To consecrate the verdure.   Some one
  said,
'Marseilles!'   And lo, the city of
  Marseilles,
With all her ships behind her, and be-
  yond,
The scimitar of ever-shining sea
For right-hand use, bared blue against
  the sky !

That night we spent between the purple
  heaven
And purple water : I think Marian slept ;
But I, as a dog a-watch for his master's
  foot,
Who cannot sleep or eat before he hears,
I sate upon the deck and watched the night
And listened through the stars for Italy.
Those marriage-bells I spoke of, sounded
  far,
As some child's go-cart in the street
  beneath
To a dying man who will not pass the day,
And knows it, holding by a hand he loves.
I too sate quiet, satisfied with death,
Sate silent : I could hear my own soul
  speak,
And had my friend,—for Nature comes
  sometimes
And says, 'I am ambassador for God.'
I felt the wind soft from the land of
  souls;

The old miraculous mountains heaved in
sight,
One straining past another along the
shore,
The way of grand dull Odyssean ghosts,
Athirst to drink the cool blue wine of seas
And stare on voyagers. Peak pushing
peak
They stood : I watched, beyond that
Tyrian belt
Of intense sea betwixt them and the ship,
Down all their sides the misty olive-
woods
Dissolving in the weak congenial moon
And still disclosing some brown convent-
tower
That seems as if it grew from some
brown rock,
Or many a little lighted village, dropt
Like a fallen star upon so high a point,
You wonder what can keep it in its place
From sliding headlong with the waterfalls
Which powder all the myrtle and orange
groves
With spray of silver. Thus my Italy
Was stealing on us. Genoa broke with
day,
The Doria's long pale palace striking out,
From green hills in advance of the white
town,
A marble finger dominant to ships,
Seen glimmering through the uncertain
grey of dawn.

And then I did not think, 'my Italy,'
I thought, 'my father!' O my father's
house,
Without his presence !—Places are too
much
Or else too little, for immortal man,—
Too little, when love's May o'ergrows
the ground,
Too much, when that luxuriant robe of
green
Is rustling to our ankles in dead leaves.
'Tis only good to be or here or there,
Because we had a dream on such a stone,
Or this or that,—but, once being wholly
waked
And come back to the stone without the
dream,
We trip upon 't,—alas, and hurt our-
selves ;

Or else it falls on us and grinds us flat,
The heaviest grave-stone on this burying
earth.
—But while I stood and mused, a quiet
touch
Fell light upon my arm, and turning
round,
A pair of moistened eyes convicted mine.
'What, Marian ! is the babe astir so
soon ?'
'He sleeps,' she answered ; 'I have
crept up thrice,
And seen you sitting, standing, still at
watch.
I thought it did you good till now, but
now ' ..
'But now,' I said, 'you leave the child
alone.'
'And you're alone,' she answered,—and
she looked
As if I too were something. Sweet the
help
Of one we have helped ! Thanks,
Marian, for such help.

I found a house at Florence on the hill
Of Bellosguardo. 'Tis a tower which
keeps
A post of double-observation o'er
That valley of Arno (holding as a hand
The outspread city) straight toward
Fiesole
And Mount Morello and the setting sun,
The Vallombrosan mountains opposite,
Which sunrise fills as full as crystal cups
Turned red to the brim because their
wine is red.
No sun could die nor yet be born unseen
By dwellers at my villa : morn and eve
Were magnified before us in the pure
Illimitable space and pause of sky,
Intense as angels' garments blanched
with God,
Less blue than radiant. From the outer
wall
Of the garden drops the mystic floating
grey
Of olive trees (with interruptions green
From maize and vine), until 'tis caught
and torn
Upon the abrupt black line of cypresses
Which signs the way to Florence.
Beautiful

The city lies along the ample vale,
Cathedral, tower and palace, piazza and
street,
The river trailing like a silver cord
Through all, and curling loosely, both
before
And after, over the whole stretch of
land
Sown whitely up and down its opposite
slopes
With farms and villas.
Many weeks had passed,
No word was granted.—Last, a letter
came
From Vincent Carrington :—' My dear
Miss Leigh,
You've been as silent as a poet should,
When any other man is sure to speak.
If sick, if vexed, if dumb, a silver piece
Will split a man's tongue,—straight he
speaks and says,
" Received that cheque." But you! ..
I send you funds
To Paris, and you make no sign at all.
Remember I'm responsible and wait
A sign of you, Miss Leigh.
' Meantime your book
Is eloquent as if you were not dumb ;
And common critics, ordinarily deaf
To such fine meanings, and, like deaf
men, loath
To seem deaf, answering chance-wise,
yes or no,
" It must be " or " it must not " (most
pronounced
When least convinced), pronounce for
once aright :
You'd think they really heard,—and so
they do ..
The burr of three or four who really hear
And praise your book aright : Fame's
smallest trump
Is a great ear-trumpet for the deaf as
posts,
No other being effective. Fear not,
friend ;
We think here you have written a good
book,
And you, a woman ! It was in you—yes,
I felt 'twas in you : yet I doubted half
If that od-force of German Reichenbach,
Which still from female finger-tips burns
blue,

Could strike out as our masculine white
heats
To quicken a man. Forgive me. All my
heart
Is quick with yours since, just a fort-
night since,
I read your book and loved it.
' Will you love
My wife, too ? Here 's my secret I
might keep
A month more rom you ! but I yield
it up
Because I know you'll write the sooner
for 't,
Most women (of your height even) count-
ing love
Life's only serious business. Who 's
my wife
That shall be in a month, you ask ? nor
guess ?
Remember what a pair of topaz eyes
You once detected, turned against the
wall,
That morning in my London painting-
room ;
The face half-sketched, and slurred ;
the eyes alone !
But you . . you caught them up with
yours, and said
" Kate Ward's eyes, surely."—Now I
own the truth :
I had thrown them there to keep them
safe from Jove,
They would so naughtily find out their
way
To both the heads of both my Danaës
Where just it made me mad to look at
them.
Such eyes ! I could not paint or think
of eyes
But those,—and so I flung them into
paint
And turned them to the wall's care.
Aye, but now
I've let them out, my Kate's : I've
painted her,
(I change my style and leave mythologies)
The whole sweet face ; it looks upon
my soul
Like a face on water, to beget itself.
A half-length portrait, in a hanging cloak
Like one you wore once ; 'tis a little
frayed,—

I pressed too for the nude harmonious
arm—
But she, she'd have her way, and have
her cloak;
She said she could be like you only so,
And would not miss the fortune. Ah,
my friend,
You'll write and say she shall not miss
your love
Through meeting mine? in faith, she
would not change.
She has your books by heart more than
my words,
And quotes you up against me till I'm
pushed
Where, three months since, her eyes
were : nay, in fact,
Nought satisfied her but to make me paint
Your last book folded in her dimpled
hands
Instead of my brown palette as I wished,
And, grant me, the presentment had been
newer;
She'd grant me nothing : I compounded
for
The naming of the wedding-day next
month,
And gladly too. 'Tis pretty, to remark
How women can love women of your
sort,
And tie their hearts with love-knots to
your feet,
Grow insolent about you against men
And put us down by putting up the lip,
As if a man,—there *are* such, let us own,
Who write not ill,—remains a man,
poor wretch,
While you——! Write weaker than
Aurora Leigh,
And there'll be women who believe of you
(Besides my Kate) that if you walked
on sand
You would not leave a footprint.
                          'Are you put
To wonder by my marriage, like poor
Leigh?
"Kate Ward!" he said. "Kate Ward!"
he said anew.
"I thought . ." he said, and stopped,—
    " I did not think . ."
And then he dropped to silence.
                          'Ah, he's changed.
I had not seen him, you're aware, for long,

But went of course. I have not touched
on this
Through all this letter,—conscious of
your heart,
And writing lightlier for the heavy fact,
As clocks are voluble with lead.
                          'How poor,
To say I'm sorry! dear Leigh, dearest
Leigh.
In those old days of Shropshire,—pardon
me,—
When he and you fought many a field of
gold
On what you should do, or you should
not do,
Make bread or verses (it just came to
that),
I thought you'd one day draw a silken
peace
Through a golden ring. I thought so :
foolishly,
The event proved,—for you went more
opposite
To each other, month by month, and
year by year,
Until this happened. God knows best,
we say,
But hoarsely. When the fever took him
first,
Just after I had writ to you in France,
They tell me Lady Waldemar mixed
drinks
And counted grains, like any salaried
nurse,
Excepting that she wept too. Then
Lord Howe,
You're right about Lord Howe, Lord
Howe's a trump,
And yet, with such in his hand, a man
like Leigh
May lose as *he* does. There's an end to all,
Yes, even this letter, though this second
sheet
May find you doubtful. Write a word
for Kate :
She reads my letters always, like a wife,
And if she sees her name I'll see her smile
And share the luck. So, bless you,
friend of two !
I will not ask you what your feeling is
At Florence with my pictures; I can hear
Your heart a-flutter over the snow-hills:
And, just to pace the Pitti with you once,

I'd give a half-hour of to-morrow's walk
With Kate . . I think so.   Vincent Car-
    rington.'

The noon was hot; the air scorched
    like the sun
And was shut out.   The closed persiani
    threw
Their long-scored shadows on my villa-
    floor,
And interlined the golden atmosphere
Straight, still,—across the pictures on
    the wall,
The statuette on the console (of young
    Love
And Psyche made one marble by a kiss),
The low couch where I leaned, the
    table near,
The vase of lilies Marian pulled last night
(Each green leaf and each white leaf
    ruled in black
As if for writing some new text of fate),
And the open letter, rested on my knee,
But there the lines swerved, trembled,
    though I sate
Untroubled, plainly, reading it again
And three times.   Well, he's married;
    that is clear.
No wonder that he's married, nor much
    more
That Vincent's therefore 'sorry.' Why,
    of course
The lady nursed him when he was not
    well,
Mixed drinks,—unless nepenthe was the
    drink
'Twas scarce worth telling.   But a man
    in love
Will see the whole sex in his mistress'
    hood,
The prettier for its lining of fair rose,
Although he catches back and says at
    last,
'I'm sorry.' Sorry. Lady Waldemar
At prettiest, under the said hood, pre-
    served
From such a light as I could hold to her face
To flare its ugly wrinkles out to shame,
Is scarce a wife for Romney, as friends
    judge,
Aurora Leigh or Vincent Carrington,
That's plain.   And if he's 'conscious
    of my heart' . .

It may be natural, though the phrase is
    strong
(One's apt to use strong phrases, being
    in love);
And even that stuff of 'fields of gold,'
    'gold rings,'
And what he 'thought,' poor Vincent,
    what he 'thought,'
May never mean enough to ruffle me.
—Why, this room stifles.   Better burn
    than choke;
Best have air, air, although it comes
    with fire,—
Throw open blinds and windows to the
    noon
And take a blister on my brow instead
Of this dead weight! best, perfectly be
    stunned
By those insufferable cicale, sick
And hoarse with rapture of the summer-
    heat,
That sing, like poets, till their hearts
    break,—sing
Till men say, 'It's too tedious.'
                    Books succeed,
And lives fail.   Do I feel it so, at last?
Kate loves a worn-out cloak for being
    like mine,
While I live self-despised for being my-
    self,
And yearn toward some one else, who
    yearns away
From what he is, in his turn. Strain a step
For ever, yet gain no step? Are we such,
We cannot, with our admirations even,
Our tip-toe aspirations, touch a thing
That's higher than we? is all a dismal flat,
And God alone above each, as the sun
O'er level lagunes, to make them shine
    and stink,—
Laying stress upon us with immediate
    flame,
While we respond with our miasmal fog
And call it mounting higher because we
    grow
More highly fatal?
                    Tush, Aurora Leigh!
You wear your sackcloth looped in
    Caesar's way
And brag your failings as mankind's.
    Be still.
There *is* what's higher, in this very
    world,

Than you can live, or catch at.   Stand
    aside,
And look at others—instance little Kate!
She'll make a perfect wife for Carrington.
She always has been looking round the
    earth
For something good and green to alight
    upon
And nestle into, with those soft-winged
    eyes,
Subsiding now beneath his manly hand
'Twixt trembling lids of inexpressive joy.
I will not scorn her, after all, too much,
That so much she should love me :
    a wise man
Can pluck a leaf, and find a lecture in 't;
And I, too, .. God has made me,—I've
    a heart
That 's capable of worship, love, and loss;
We say the same of Shakespeare's.
    I'll be meek
And learn to reverence, even this poor
    myself.

The book, too—pass it. 'A good book,'
    says he,
'And you a woman.' I had laughed
    at that,
But long since. I'm a woman,—it is true;
Alas, and woe to us, when we feel it most!
Then, least care have we for the crowns
    and goals
And compliments on writing our good
    books.

The book has some truth in it, I believe,
And truth outlives pain, as the soul does
    life.
I know we talk our Phaedons to the end,
Through all the dismal faces that we make,
O'er-wrinkled with dishonouring agony
From decomposing drugs.   I have
    written truth,
And I a woman,—feebly, partially,
Inaptly in presentation, Romney'll add,
Because a woman.   For the truth itself,
That 's neither man's nor woman's, but
    just God's,
None else has reason to be proud of truth:
Himself will see it sifted, disenthralled,
And kept upon the height and in the
    light,
As far as and no farther than 'tis truth;

For, now He has left off calling firma-
    ments
And strata, flowers and creatures, very
    good,
He says it still of truth, which is His own.

Truth, so far, in my book ;—the truth
    which draws
Through all things upwards,— that a
    twofold world
Must go to a perfect cosmos.   Natural
    things
And spiritual,—who separates those two
In art, in morals, or the social drift,
Tears up the bond of nature and brings
    death,
Paints futile pictures, writes unreal verse,
Leads vulgar days, deals ignorantly
    with men,
Is wrong, in short, at all points.   We
    divide
This apple of life, and cut it through the
    pips,—
The perfect round which fitted Venus'
    hand
Has perished as utterly as if we ate
Both halves.   Without the spiritual,
    observe,
The natural's impossible,—no form,
No motion : without sensuous, spiritual
Is inappreciable,—no beauty or power :
And in this twofold sphere the twofold
    man
(For still the artist is intensely a man)
Holds firmly by the natural, to reach
The spiritual beyond it,—fixes still
The type with mortal vision, to pierce
    through,
With eyes immortal, to the antetype
Some call the ideal,—better called the
    real,
And certain to be called so presently
When things shall have their names.
    Look long enough
On any peasant's face here, coarse and
    lined,
You'll catch Antinous somewhere in
    that clay,
As perfect featured as he yearns at Rome
From marble pale with beauty ; then
    persist,
And, if your apprehension 's competent,
You'll find some fairer angel at his back,

As much exceeding him as he the boor,
And pushing him with empyreal disdain
For ever out of sight. Aye, Carrington
Is glad of such a creed : an artist must,
Who paints a tree, a leaf, a common
    stone
With just his hand, and finds it suddenly
A-piece with and conterminous to his
    soul.
Why else do these things move him,
    leaf, or stone?
The bird's not moved, that pecks at
    a spring-shoot ;
Nor yet the horse, before a quarry
    a-graze :
But man, the twofold creature, appre-
    hends
The twofold manner, in and outwardly,
And nothing in the world comes single
    to him,
A mere itself,—cup, column, or candle-
    stick,
All patterns of what shall be in the
    Mount ;
The whole temporal show related royally,
And built up to eterne significance
Through the open arms of God.
    ' There's nothing great
Nor small,' has said a poet of our day,
Whose voice will ring beyond the
    curfew of eve
And not be thrown out by the matin's
    bell :
And truly, I reiterate, nothing's small !
No lily-muffled hum of a summer-bee,
But finds some coupling with the
    spinning stars ;
No pebble at your foot, but proves
    a sphere ;
No chaffinch, but implies the cherubim ;
And (glancing on my own thin, veinèd
    wrist),
In such a little tremor of the blood
The whole strong clamour of a vehement
    soul
Doth utter itself distinct. Earth's
    crammed with heaven,
And every common bush afire with God ;
But only he who sees, takes off his shoes,
The rest sit round it and pluck black-
    berries,
And daub their natural faces unaware
More and more from the first similitude.

Truth, so far, in my book ! a truth
    which draws
From all things upward. I, Aurora, still
Have felt it hound me through the
    wastes of life
As Jove did Io ; and, until that Hand
Shall overtake me wholly and on my head
Lay down its large unfluctuating peace,
The feverish gad-fly pricks me up and
    down.
It must be. Art's the witness of what Is
Behind this show. If this world's show
    were all,
Then imitation would be all in Art ;
There, Jove's hand gripes us !—For we
    stand here, we,
If genuine artists, witnessing for God's
Complete, consummate, undivided work ;
—That every natural flower which
    grows on earth
Implies a flower upon the spiritual side,
Substantial, archetypal, all a-glow
With blossoming causes,—not so far
    away,
But we, whose spirit-sense is somewhat
    cleared,
May catch at something of the bloom
    and breath,—
Too vaguely apprehended, though in-
    deed
Still apprehended, consciously or not,
And still transferred to picture, music,
    verse,
For thrilling audient and beholding souls
By signs and touches which are known
    to souls.
How known, they know not,—why,
    they cannot find,
So straight call out on genius, say, 'A man
Produced this,' when much rather they
    should say,
' 'Tis insight and he saw this.'
                          Thus is Art
Self-magnified in magnifying a truth
Which, fully recognized, would change
    the world
And shift its morals. If a man could feel,
Not one day, in the artist's ecstasy,
But every day, feast, fast, or working-day,
The spiritual significance burn through
The hieroglyphic of material shows,
Henceforward he would paint the globe
    with wings,

And reverence fish and fowl, the bull,
    the tree,
And even his very body as a man,—
Which now he counts so vile, that all
    the towns
Make offal of their daughters for its use,
On summer-nights, when God is sad in
    heaven
To think what goes on in His recreant
    world
He made quite other; while that moon
    He made
To shine there, at the first love's covenant,
Shines still, convictive as a marriage-ring
Before adulterous eyes.
                How sure it is,
That, if we say a true word, instantly
We feel 'tis God's, not ours, and pass it on
Like bread at sacrament we taste and pass
Nor handle for a moment, as indeed
We dared to set up any claim to such!
And I—my poem,—let my readers talk.
I'm closer to it—I can speak as well:
I'll say with Romney, that the book is
    weak,
The range uneven, the points of sight
    obscure,
The music interrupted.
              Let us go.
The end of woman (or of man, I think)
Is not a book. Alas, the best of books
Is but a word in Art, which soon grows
    cramped,
Stiff, dubious-statured with the weight of
    years,
And drops an accent or digamma down
Some cranny of unfathomable time,
Beyond the critic's reaching. Art itself,
We've called the larger life, must feel
    the soul
Live past it. For more's felt than is
    perceived,
And more's perceived than can be in-
    terpreted,
And Love strikes higher with his lambent
    flame
Than Art can pile the faggots.
              Is it so?
When Jove's hand meets us with com-
    posing touch,
And when at last we are hushed and
    satisfied,
Then Io does not call it truth, but love?

Well, well! my father was an English-
    man:
My mother's blood in me is not so strong
That I should bear this stress of Tuscan
    noon
And keep my wits. The town, there,
    seems to seethe
In this Medaean boil-pot of the sun,
And all the patient hills are bubbling
    round
As if a prick would leave them flat.
    Does heaven
Keep far off, not to set us in a blaze?
Not so,—let drag your fiery fringes,
    heaven,
And burn us up to quiet. Ah, we know
Too much here, not to know what's
    best for peace;
We have too much light here, not to
    want more fire
To purify and end us. We talk, talk,
Conclude upon divine philosophies,
And get the thanks of men for hopeful
    books,
Whereat we take our own life up, and ..
    pshaw!
Unless we piece it with another's life
(A yard of silk to carry out our lawn)
As well suppose my little handkerchief
Would cover Samminiato, church and
    all,
If out I threw it past the cypresses,
As, in this ragged, narrow life of mine,
Contain my own conclusions.
              But at least
We'll shut up the persiani and sit down,
And when my head's done aching, in
    the cool,
Write just a word to Kate and Carrington.
May joy be with them! she has chosen
    well,
And he not ill.
           I should be glad, I think,
Except for Romney. Had *he* married
    Kate,
I surely, surely, should be very glad.
This Florence sits upon me easily,
With native air and tongue. My graves
    are calm,
And do not too much hurt me. Marian's
    good,
Gentle and loving,—lets me hold the
    child,

Or drags him up the hills to find me
   flowers
And fill these vases ere I'm quite
   awake,—
My grandiose red tulips, which grow
   wild,
Or Dante's purple lilies, which he blew
To a larger bubble with his prophet
   breath,
Or one of those tall flowering reeds that
   stand
In Arno, like a sheaf of sceptres left
By some remote dynasty of dead gods
To suck the stream for ages and get green,
And blossom wheresoe'er a hand divine
Had warmed the place with ichor. Such
   I find
At early morning laid across my bed,
And wake up pelted with a childish laugh
Which even Marian's low precipitous
   'hush'
Has vainly interposed to put away,—
While I, with shut eyes, smile and
   motion for
The dewy kiss that's very sure to come
From mouth and cheeks, the whole
   child's face at once
Dissolved on mine,—as if a nosegay burst
Its string with the weight of roses over-
   blown,
And dropt upon me. Surely I should
   be glad.
The little creature almost loves me now,
And calls my name, 'Alola,' stripping off
The *r*s like thorns, to make it smooth
   enough
To take between his dainty, milk-fed lips,
God love him! I should certainly be glad,
Except, God help me, that I'm sorrowful
Because of Romney.
       Romney, Romney! Well,
This grows absurd!—too like a tune that
   runs
I' the head, and forces all things in the
   world,
Wind, rain, the creaking gnat, or stut-
   tering fly,
To sing itself and vex you,—yet perhaps
A paltry tune you never fairly liked,
Some 'I'd be a butterfly,' or 'C'est
   l'amour':
We're made so,—not such tyrants to
   ourselves

But still we are slaves to nature. Some
   of us
Are turned, too, overmuch like some poor
   verse
With a trick of ritournelle: the same
   thing goes
And comes back ever.
          Vincent Carrington
Is 'sorry,' and I'm sorry; but *he*'s strong
To mount from sorrow to his heaven of
   love,
And when he says at moments, 'Poor,
   poor Leigh,
Who'll never call his own so true a heart,
So fair a face even,'—he must quickly lose
The pain of pity, in the blush he makes
By his very pitying eyes. The snow,
   for him,
Has fallen in May and finds the whole
   earth warm,
And melts at the first touch of the green
   grass.

But Romney,—he has chosen, after all.
I think he had as excellent a sun
To see by, as most others, and perhaps
Has scarce seen really worse than some
   of us
When all's said. Let him pass. I'm
   not too much
A woman, not to be a man for once
And bury all my Dead like Alaric,
Depositing the treasures of my soul
In this drained water-course, then letting
   flow
The river of life again with commerce-
   ships
And pleasure-barges full of silks and
   songs.
Blow, winds, and help us.
         Ah, we mock ourselves
With talking of the winds; perhaps as
   much
With other resolutions. How it weighs,
This hot, sick air! and how I covet here
The Dead's provision on the river-couch,
With silver curtains drawn on tinkling
   rings!
Or else their rest in quiet crypts,—laid by
From heat and noise;—from those cicale,
   say,
And this more vexing heart-beat.
             So it is:

We covet for the soul, the body's part,
To die and rot. Even so, Aurόra, ends
Our aspiration who bespoke our place
So far in the east. The occidental flats
Had fed us fatter, therefore? we have
    climbed
Where herbage ends? we want the
    beast's part now,
And tire of the angel's?—Men define a
    man,
The creature who stands front-ward to
    the stars,
The creature who looks inward to him-
    self,
The tool-wright, laughing creature. 'Tis
    enough:
We'll say instead, the inconsequent
    creature, man,
For that 's his specialty. What creature
    else
Conceives the circle, and then walks the
    square?
Loves things proved bad, and leaves a
    thing proved good?
You think the bee makes honey half a
    year,
To loathe the comb in winter and desire
The little ant's food rather? But a man—
Note men!—they are but women after all,
As women are but Auroras!—there are
    men
Born tender, apt to pale at a trodden
    worm,
Who paint for pastime, in their favourite
    dream,
Spruce auto-vestments flowered with
    crocus-flames.
There are, too, who believe in hell, and lie;
There are, too, who believe in heaven,
    and fear:
There are, who waste their souls in
    working out
Life's problem on these sands betwixt
    two tides,
Concluding,—' Give us the oyster's part,
    in death.'

Alas, long-suffering and most patient
    God,
Thou needst be surelier God to bear
    with us
Than even to have made us! Thou aspire,
    aspire

From henceforth for me! Thou who hast
    Thyself
Endured this fleshhood, knowing how
    as a soaked
And sucking vesture it can drag us down
And choke us in the melancholy Deep,
Sustain me, that with Thee I walk these
    waves,
Resisting!—breathe me upward, Thou
    in me
Aspiring who art the way, the truth, the
    life,—
That no truth henceforth seem indifferent,
No way to truth laborious, and no life,
Not even this life I live, intolerable!

The days went by. I took up the old days,
With all their Tuscan pleasures worn
    and spoiled,
Like some lost book we dropped in the
    long grass
On such a happy summer-afternoon
When last we read it with a loving friend,
And find in autumn when the friend is
    gone,
The grass cut short, the weather changed,
    too late,
And stare at, as at something wonderful
For sorrow,—thinking how two hands
    before
Had held up what is left to only one,
And how we smiled when such a vehe-
    ment nail
Impressed the tiny dint here which
    presents
This verse in fire for ever. Tenderly
And mournfully I lived. I knew the birds
And insects,—which looked fathered by
    the flowers
And emulous of their hues: I recognized
The moths, with that great overpoise of
    wings
Which make a mystery of them how at all
They can stop flying: butterflies, that
    bear
Upon their blue wings such red embers
    round,
They seem to scorch the blue air into holes
Each flight they take: and fire-flies, that
    suspire
In short soft lapses of transported flame
Across the tingling Dark, while overhead
The constant and inviolable stars

Outburn those light-of-love : melodious
    owls
(If music had but one note and was sad,
'Twould sound just so); and all the
    silent swirl
Of bats that seem to follow in the air
Some grand circumference of a shadowy
    dome
To which we are blind : and then the
    nightingales,
Which pluck our heart across a garden-
    wall
(When walking in the town) and carry it
So high into the bowery almond-trees
We tremble and are afraid, and feel as if
The golden flood of moonlight unaware
Dissolved the pillars of the steady earth
And made it less substantial. And I
    knew
The harmless opal snakes, the large-
    mouthed frogs
(Those noisy vaunters of their shallow
    streams);
And lizards, the green lightnings of the
    wall,
Which, if you sit down quiet, nor sigh
    loud,
Will flatter you and take you for a stone,
And flash familiarly about your feet
With such prodigious eyes in such small
    heads !—
I knew them (though they had some-
    what dwindled from
My childish imagery), and kept in mind
How last I sate among them equally,
In fellowship and mateship, as a child
Feels equal still toward insect, beast,
    and bird,
Before the Adam in him has forgone
All privilege of Eden,—making friends
And talk with such a bird or such a goat,
And buying many a two-inch-wide rush-
    cage
To let out the caged cricket on a tree,
Saying, ' Oh, my dear grillino, were you
    cramped ?
And are you happy with the ilex-leaves ?
And do you love me who have let you go ?
Say *yes* in singing, and I'll understand.'

But now the creatures all seemed farther
    off,
No longer mine, nor like me, only *there*,

A gulf between us. I could yearn
    indeed,
Like other rich men, for a drop of dew
To cool this heat,—a drop of the early
    dew,
The irrecoverable child-innocence
(Before the heart took fire and withered
    life)
When childhood might pair equally with
    birds ;
But now . . the birds were grown too
    proud for us !
Alas, the very sun forbids the dew.

And I, I had come back to an empty nest,
Which every bird's too wise for. How
    I heard
My father's step on that deserted ground,
His voice along that silence, as he told
The names of bird and insect, tree and
    flower,
And all the presentations of the stars
Across Valdarno, interposing still
' My child,' ' my child.' When fathers
    say ' my child,'
'Tis easier to conceive the universe,
And life's transitions down the steps of
    law.

I rode once to the little mountain-house
As fast as if to find my father there,
But, when in sight of 't, within fifty yards,
I dropped my horse's bridle on his neck
And paused upon his flank. The house's
    front
Was cased with lingots of ripe Indian
    corn
In tesselated order and device
Of golden patterns, not a stone of wall
Uncovered—not an inch of room to grow
A vine-leaf. The old porch had dis-
    appeared ;
And right in the open doorway sate a girl
At plaiting straws, her black hair strained
    away
To a scarlet kerchief caught beneath her
    chin
In Tuscan fashion,—her full ebon eyes,
Which looked too heavy to be lifted so,
Still dropped and lifted toward the mul-
    berry-tree
On which the lads were busy with their
    staves

In shout and laughter, stripping every
    bough
As bare as winter, of those summer leaves
My father had not changed for all the silk
In which the ugly silkworms hide them-
    selves.
Enough. My horse recoiled before my
    heart ;
I turned the rein abruptly. Back we went
As fast, to Florence.
           That was trial enough
Of graves. I would not visit, if I could,
My father's, or my mother's any more,
To see if stone-cutter or lichen beat
So early in the race, or throw my flowers,
Which could not out-smell heaven or
    sweeten earth.
They live too far above, that I should
    look
So far below to find them : let me think
That rather they are visiting my grave,
Called life here (undeveloped yet to life),
And that they drop upon me, now and
    then,
For token or for solace, some small weed
Least odorous of the growths of paradise,
To spare such pungent scents as kill with
    joy.

My old Assunta, too, was dead, was
    dead—
O land of all men's past ! for me alone,
It would not mix its tenses. I was past,
It seemed, like others,—only not in
    heaven.
And many a Tuscan eve I wandered down
The cypress alley like a restless ghost
That tries its feeble ineffectual breath
Upon its own charred funeral-brands
    put out
Too soon, where black and stiff stood
    up the trees
Against the broad vermilion of the skies.
Such skies !—all clouds abolished in a
    sweep
Of God's skirt, with a dazzle to ghosts
    and men,
As down I went, saluting on the bridge
The hem of such before 'twas caught away
Beyond the peaks of Lucca. Underneath,
The river, just escaping from the weight
Of that intolerable glory, ran
In acquiescent shadow murmurously ;

While, up beside it, streamed the festa-
    folk
With fellow-murmurs from their feet
    and fans,
And *issimo* and *ino* and sweet poise
Of vowels in their pleasant scandalous
    talk ;
Returning from the grand-duke's dairy-
    farm
Before the trees grew dangerous at eight
(For, 'trust no tree by moonlight,'
    Tuscans say),
To eat their ice at Donay's tenderly,—
Each lovely lady close to a cavalier
Who holds her dear fan while she feeds
    her smile
On meditative spoonfuls of vanille
And listens to his hot-breathed vows of
    love
Enough to thaw her cream and scorch
    his beard.

'Twas little matter. I could pass them by
Indifferently, not fearing to be known.
No danger of being wrecked upon a friend,
And forced to take an iceberg for an isle !
The very English, here, must wait and
    learn
To hang the cobweb of their gossip out
To catch a fly. I'm happy. It's sublime,
This perfect solitude of foreign lands !
To be, as if you had not been till then,
And were then, simply that you chose
    to be :
To spring up, not be brought forth from
    the ground,
Like grasshoppers at Athens, and skip
    thrice
Before a woman makes a pounce on you
And plants you in her hair !—possess,
    yourself,
A new world all alive with creatures new,
New sun, new moon, new flowers, new
    people—ah,
And be possessed by none of them ! no
    right
In one, to call your name, inquire your
    where,
Or what you think of Mister Some-one's
    book,
Or Mister Other's marriage or decease,
Or how's the headache which you had
    last week,

Or why you look so pale still, since it 's
   gone?
—Such most surprising riddance of one's
   life
Comes next one's death; 'tis disem-
   bodiment
Without the pang. I marvel, people
   choose
To stand stock-still like fakirs, till the
   moss
Grows on them and they cry out, self-
   admired,
'How verdant and how virtuous!'
   Well, I'm glad :
Or should be, if grown foreign to myself
As surely as to others.
             Musing so,
I walked the narrow unrecognizing
   streets,
Where many a palace-front peers
   gloomily
Through stony vizors iron-barred (pre-
   pared
Alike, should foe or lover pass that way,
For guest or victim), and came wandering
   out
Upon the churches with mild open doors
And plaintive wail of vespers, where a
   few,
Those chiefly women, sprinkled round
   in blots
Upon the dusky pavement, knelt and
   prayed
Toward the altar's silver glory. Oft a ray
(I liked to sit and watch) would tremble
   out,
Just touch some face more lifted, more
   in need
(Of course a woman's),—while I dreamed
   a tale
To fit its fortunes. There was one who
   looked
As if the earth had suddenly grown too
   large
For such a little humpbacked thing as she ;
The pitiful black kerchief round her neck
Sole proof she had had a mother. One,
   again,
Looked sick for love,—seemed praying
   some soft saint
To put more virtue in the new fine scarf
She spent a fortnight's meals on, yester-
   day,

That cruel Gigi might return his eyes
From Giuliana. There was one, so old,
So old, to kneel grew easier than to
   stand,—
So solitary, she accepts at last
Our Lady for her gossip, and frets on
Against the sinful world which goes its
   rounds
In marrying and being married, just the
   same
As when 'twas almost good and had
   the right
(Her Gian alive, and she herself eighteen).
'And yet, now even, if Madonna willed,
She'd win a tern in Thursday's lottery
And better all things. Did she dream
   for nought,
That, boiling cabbage for the fast-day's
   soup,
It smelt like blessed entrails ? such a
   dream
For nought ? would sweetest Mary cheat
   her so,
And lose that certain candle, straight
   and white
As any fair grand-duchess in her teens,
Which otherwise should flare here in
   a week ?
Benigna sis, thou beauteous Queen of
   heaven!'

I sate there musing, and imagining
Such utterance from such faces : poor
   blind souls
That writhe toward heaven along the
   devil's trail,—
Who knows, I thought, but He may
   stretch His hand
And pick them up ? 'tis written in the
   Book
He heareth the young ravens when they
   cry,
And yet they cry for carrion.—O my
   God,
And we, who make excuses for the rest,
We do it in our measure. Then I knelt,
And dropped my head upon the pave-
   ment too,
And prayed, since I was foolish in desire
Like other creatures, craving offal-food,
That He would stop His ears to what
   I said,
And only listen to the run and beat

Of this poor, passionate, helpless blood—
                      And then
I lay, and spoke not: but He heard in
   heaven.

So many Tuscan evenings passed the
   same.
I could not lose a sunset on the bridge,
And would not miss a vigil in the church,
And liked to mingle with the outdoor
   crowd
So strange and gay and ignorant of my
   face,
For men you know not, are as good as
   trees.
And only once, at the Santissima,
I almost chanced upon a man I knew,
Sir Blaise Delorme. He saw me
   certainly,
And somewhat hurried, as he crossed
   himself,
The smoothness of the action,—then
   half bowed,
But only half, and merely to my shade,
I slipped so quick behind the porphyry
   plinth
And left him dubious if 'twas really I
Or peradventure Satan's usual trick
To keep a mounting saint uncanonized.
But he was safe for that time, and I too ;
The argent angels in the altar-flare
Absorbed his soul next moment. The
   good man !
In England we were scarce acquain-
   tances,
That here in Florence he should keep
   my thought
Beyond the image on his eye, which came
And went : and yet his thought dis-
   turbed my life :
For, after that, I oftener sate at home
On evenings, watching how they fined
   themselves
With gradual conscience to a perfect
   night,
Until the moon, diminished to a curve,
Lay out there like a sickle for His hand
Who cometh down at last to reap the
   earth.
At such times, ended seemed my trade
   of verse ;
I feared to jingle bells upon my robe
Before the four-faced silent cherubim :

With God so near me, could I sing of God ?
I did not write, nor read, nor even think,
But sate absorbed amid the quickening
   glooms,
Most like some passive broken lump of salt
Dropped in by chance to a bowl of
   oenomel,
To spoil the drink a little and lose itself,
Dissolving slowly, slowly, until lost.

EIGHTH BOOK

ONE eve it happened, when I sate alone,
Alone, upon the terrace of my tower,
A book upon my knees to counterfeit
The reading that I never read at all,
While Marian, in the garden down below,
Knelt by the fountain I could just hear
   thrill
The drowsy silence of the exhausted day,
And peeled a new fig from that purple
   heap
In the grass beside her, turning out the
   red
To feed her eager child (who sucked at it
With vehement lips across a gap of air
As he stood opposite, face and curls a-
   flame
With that last sun-ray, crying, ' give me,
   give,'
And stamping with imperious baby-feet,
We're all born princes) — something
   startled me,—
The laugh of sad and innocent souls,
   that breaks
Abruptly, as if frightened at itself.
'Twas Marian laughed. I saw her
   glance above
In sudden shame that I should hear her
   laugh,
And straightway dropped my eyes upon
   my book,
And knew, the first time, 'twas Boc-
   caccio's tale,
The Falcon's, of the lover who for love
Destroyed the best that loved him.
   Some of us
Do it still, and then we sit and laugh
   no more.
Laugh *you*, sweet Marian,—you've the
   right to laugh,

Since God Himself is for you, and a child!
For me there's somewhat less,—and so
   I sigh.

The heavens were making room to hold
   the night,
The sevenfold heavens unfolding all their
   gates
To let the stars out slowly (prophesied
In close-approaching advent, not dis-
   cerned),
While still the cue-owls from the cy-
   presses
Of the Poggio called and counted every
   pulse
Of the skyey palpitation. Gradually
The purple and transparent shadows slow
Had filled up the whole valley to the brim,
And flooded all the city, which you saw
As some drowned city in some enchanted
   sea,
Cut off from nature,—drawing you who
   gaze,
With passionate desire, to leap and
   plunge
And find a sea-king with a voice of waves,
And treacherous soft eyes, and slippery
   locks
You cannot kiss but you shall bring away
Their salt upon your lips. The duomo-
   bell
Strikes ten, as if it struck ten fathoms
   down,
So deep ; and twenty churches answer it
The same, with twenty various instances.
Some gaslights tremble along squares
   and streets :
The Pitti's palace-front is drawn in fire ;
And, past the quays, Maria Novella Place,
In which the mystic obelisks stand up
Triangular, pyramidal, each based
Upon its four-square brazen tortoises,
To guard that fair church, Buonarroti's
   Bride,
That stares out from her large blind
   dial-eyes
(Her quadrant and armillary dials, black
With rhythms of many suns and moons),
   in vain
Inquiry for so rich a soul as his.
Methinks I have plunged, I see it all so
   clear . .
And, O my heart, . . the sea-king !

                In my ears
The sound of waters. There he stood,
   my king !

I felt him, rather than beheld him. Up
I rose, as if he were my king indeed,
And then sate down, in trouble at myself,
And struggling for my woman's empery.
'Tis pitiful ; but women are so made :
We'll die for you perhaps,—'tis prob-
   able ;
But we'll not spare you an inch of our
   full height :
We'll have our whole just stature,—five
   feet four,
Though laid out in our coffins : pitiful.
—' You, Romney !——Lady Waldemar
   is here ?'

He answered in a voice which was not
   his.
' I have her letter ; you shall read it soon.
But first, I must be heard a little, I,
Who have waited long and travelled far
   for that,
Although you thought to have shut
   a tedious book
And farewell. Ah, you dog-eared such
   a page,
And here you find me.'
            Did he touch my hand,
Or but my sleeve ? I trembled, hand
   and foot,—
He must have touched me.—' Will you
   sit ?' I asked,
And motioned to a chair ; but down he
   sate,
A little slowly, as a man in doubt,
Upon the couch beside me,—couch and
   chair
Being wheeled upon the terrace.
              ' You are come,
My cousin Romney ?—this is wonderful.
But all is wonder on such summer-nights ;
And nothing should surprise us any more,
Who see that miracle of stars. Behold.'

I signed above, where all the stars
   were out,
As if an urgent heat had started there
A secret writing from a sombre page,
A blank, last moment, crowded suddenly
With hurrying splendours.

'Then you do not know'—
He murmured.
    'Yes, I know,' I said, ' I know.
I had the news from Vincent Carrington.
And yet I did not think you'd leave the
    work
In England, for so much even,—though
    of course
You'll make a work-day of your holiday,
And turn it to our Tuscan people's
    use,—
Who much need helping since the
    Austrian boar
(So bold to cross the Alp to Lombardy
And dash his brute front unabashed
    against
The steep snow-bosses of that shield of
    God
Who soon shall rise in wrath and shake
    it clear),
Came hither also, raking up our grape
And olive-gardens with his tyrannous
    tusk,
And rolling on our maize with all his
    swine.'

'You had the news from Vincent
    Carrington,'
He echoed,—picking up the phrase
    beyond,
As if he knew the rest was merely talk
To fill a gap and keep out a strong
    wind ;
'You had, then, Vincent's personal
    news ?'
                'His own,'
I answered. 'All that ruined world of
    yours
Seems crumbling into marriage. Car-
    rington
Has chosen wisely.'
            'Do you take it so ?'
He cried, ' and is it possible at last ' . .
He paused there,—and then, inward to
    himself,
'Too much at last, too late !—yet
    certainly' . .
(And there his voice swayed as an
    Alpine plank
That feels a passionate torrent under-
    neath)
'The knowledge, had I known it first
    or last,

Could scarce have changed the actual
    case for *me*.
And best for *her* at this time.'
              Nay, I thought,
He loves Kate Ward, it seems, now,
    like a man,
Because he has married Lady Waldemar!
Ah, Vincent's letter said how Leigh
    was moved
To hear that Vincent was betrothed to
    Kate.
With what cracked pitchers go we to
    deep wells
In this world ! Then I spoke,—'I did
    not think,
My cousin, you had ever known Kate
    Ward.'

' In fact I never knew her. 'Tis enough
That Vincent did, and therefore chose
    his wife
For other reasons than those topaz eyes
We've heard of. Not to undervalue them,
For all that. One takes up the world
    with eyes.'

—Including Romney Leigh, I thought
    again,
Albeit he knows them only by repute.
How vile must all men be, since *he* 's
    a man.

His deep pathetic voice, as if he guessed
I did not surely love him, took the word ;
' You never got a letter from Lord Howe
A month back, dear Aurora ?'

              'None,' I said.

'I felt it was so,' he replied : 'yet,
    strange !
Sir Blaise Delorme has passed through
    Florence ?'
                'Aye,
By chance I saw him in Our Lady's
    church
(I saw him, mark you, but he saw not me),
Clean-washed in holy water from the
    count
Of things terrestrial,—letters, and the
    rest ;
He had crossed us out together with
    his sins.

Aye, strange; but only strange that good
  Lord Howe
Preferred him to the post because of
  pauls.
For me I'm sworn to never trust a man—
At least with letters.'

                    'There were facts to tell,
To smooth with eye and accent. Howe
  supposed . .
Well, well, no matter! there was dubious
  need ;
You heard the news from Vincent
  Carrington.
And yet perhaps you had been startled
  less
To see me, dear Aurora, if you had read
That letter.'
            —Now he sets me down as vexed.
I think I've draped myself in woman's
  pride
To a perfect purpose. Oh, I'm vexed,
  it seems !
My friend Lord Howe deputes his friend
  Sir Blaise
To break as softly as a sparrow's egg
That lets a bird tenderly, the news
Of Romney's marriage to a certain saint ;
To *smooth with eye and accent,*—indicate
His possible presence. Excellently well
You've played your part, my Lady
  Waldemar,—
As I've played mine.
              ' Dear Romney,' I began,
' You did not use, of old, to be so like
A Greek king coming from a taken Troy,
'Twas needful that precursors spread
  your path
With three-piled carpets, to receive your
  foot
And dull the sound of 't. For myself,
  be sure,
Although it frankly grinds the gravel here,
I still can bear it. Yet I'm sorry too
To lose this famous letter, which Sir
  Blaise
Has twisted to a lighter absently
To fire some holy taper: dear Lord Howe
Writes letters good for all things but to
  lose ;
And many a flower of London gossipry
Has dropped wherever such a stem broke
  off.

Of course I feel that, lonely among my
  vines,
Where nothing's talked of, save the
  blight again,
And no more Chianti ! Still the letter's use
As preparation . . Did I start indeed?
Last night I started at a cockchafer,
And shook a half-hour after. Have you
  learnt
No more of women, 'spite of privilege,
Than still to take account too seriously
Of such weak flutterings ? Why, we
  like it, sir,
We get our powers and our effects that
  way :
The trees stand stiff and still at time of
  frost,
If no wind tears them ; but, let summer
  come,
When trees are happy,—and a breath
  avails
To set them trembling through a million
  leaves
In luxury of emotion. Something less
It takes to move a woman : let her start
And shake at pleasure,—nor conclude at
  yours,
The winter's bitter,—but the summer's
  green.'

He answered, ' Be the summer ever green
With you, Aurora !—though you sweep
  your sex
With somewhat bitter gusts from where
  you live
Above them,—whirling downward from
  your heights
Your very own pine-cones, in a grand
  disdain
Of the lowland burrs with which you
  scatter them.
So high and cold to others and yourself,
A little less to Romney were unjust,
And thus, I would not have you. Let
  it pass:
I feel content so. You can bear indeed
My sudden step beside you : but for me,
'Twould move me sore to hear your
  softened voice,—
Aurora's voice,—if softened unaware
In pity of what I am.'
                    Ah, friend, I thought,
As husband of the Lady Waldemar

You're granted very sorely pitiable!
And yet Aurora Leigh must guard her
    voice
From softening in the pity of your case,
As if from lie or licence. Certainly
We'll soak up all the slush and soil of
    life
With softened voices, ere we come to
    you.

At which I interrupted my own thought
And spoke out calmly. 'Let us ponder,
    friend,
Whate'er our state we must have made
    it first ;
And though the thing displease us, aye,
    perhaps
Displease us warrantably, never doubt
That other states, thought possible once,
    and then
Rejected by the instinct of our lives,
If then adopted had displeased us more
Than this in which the choice, the will,
    the love,
Has stamped the honour of a patent act
From henceforth. What we choose
    may not be good,
But, that we choose it, proves it good
    for *us*
Potentially, fantastically, now
Or last year, rather than a thing we
    saw,
And saw no need for choosing. Moths
    will burn
Their wings,—which proves that light is
    good for moths,
Who else had flown not where they
    agonize.'

'Aye, light is good,' he echoed, and there
    paused ;
And then abruptly,.. 'Marian. Marian's
    well ?'

I bowed my head but found no word.
    'Twas hard
To speak of *her* to Lady Waldemar's
New husband. How much did he know,
    at last ?
How much ? how little ? —— He would
    take no sign,
But straight repeated,—' Marian. Is
    she well ?'

'She's well,' I answered.

              She was there in sight
An hour back, but the night had drawn
    her home,
Where still I heard her in an upper room,
Her low voice singing to the child in bed,
Who restless with the summer-heat and
    play
And slumber snatched at noon, was long
    sometimes
In falling off, and took a score of songs
And mother-hushes ere she saw him
    sound.

'She's well,' I answered.
                 'Here ?' he asked.
                 'Yes, here.'

He stopped and sighed. 'That shall be
    presently,
But now this must be. I have words to
    say,
And would be alone to say them, I with
    you,
And no third troubling.'
            'Speak then,' I returned,
'She will not vex you.'

                   At which, suddenly,
He turned his face upon me with its smile
As if to crush me. 'I have read your
    book,
Aurora.'
         'You have read it,' I replied,
'And I have writ it,—we have done
    with it.
And now the rest ?'
            'The rest is like the first,'
He answered,—'for the book is in my
    heart,
Lives in me, wakes in me, and dreams
    in me :
My daily bread tastes of it,—and my wine
Which has no smack of it, I pour it out,
It seems unnatural drinking.'
                Bitterly
I took the word up ; 'Never waste your
    wine.
The book lived in me ere it lived in you ;
I know it closer than another does,
And how it's foolish, feeble, and afraid,
And all unworthy so much compliment.

Beseech you, keep your wine,—and,
    when you drink,
Still wish some happier fortune to a
    friend,
Than even to have written a far better
    book.'

He answered gently, 'That is con-
    sequent :
The poet looks beyond the book he has
    made,
Or else he had not made it. If a man
Could make a man, he'd henceforth be
    a god
In feeling what a little thing is man :
It is not my case. And this special book,
I did not make it, to make light of it :
It stands above my knowledge, draws
    me up ;
'Tis high to me. It may be that the book
Is not so high, but I so low, instead ;
Still high to me. I mean no compliment :
I will not say there are not, young or old,
Male writers, aye, or female, let it pass,
Who'll write us richer and completer
    books.
A man may love a woman perfectly,
And yet by no means ignorantly maintain
A thousand women have not larger eyes :
Enough that she alone has looked at him
With eyes that, large or small, have won
    his soul.
And so, this book, Aurora,—so, your
    book.'

'Alas,' I answered, 'is it so, indeed?'
And then was silent.

                        'Is it so, indeed,'
He echoed, 'that *alas* is all your word?'
I said,—'I'm thinking of a far-off June,
When you and I, upon my birthday once,
Discoursed of life and art, with both
    untried.
I'm thinking, Romney, how 'twas
    morning then,
And now 'tis night.'
        'And now,' he said, ''tis night.'

'I'm thinking,' I resumed, ''tis some-
    what sad,
That if I had known, that morning in
    the dew,

My cousin Romney would have said
    such words
On such a night at close of many years,
In speaking of a future book of mine,
It would have pleased me better as a hope,
Than as an actual grace it can at all :
That 's sad, I'm thinking.'
                'Aye,' he said, ''tis night.'

'And there,' I added lightly, 'are the
    stairs !
And here, we'll talk of stars and not of
    books.'

'You have the stars,' he murmured,—
    'it is well :
Be like them ! shine, Aurora, on my dark,
Though high and cold and only like a star,
And for this short night only,—you,
    who keep
The same Aurora of the bright June day
That withered up the flowers before my
    face,
And turned me from the garden evermore
Because I was not worthy. Oh, de-
    served,
Deserved ! that I, who verily had not
    learnt
God's lesson half, attaining as a dunce
To obliterate good words with fractious
    thumbs
And cheat myself of the context,—*I*
    should push
Aside, with male ferocious impudence,
The world's Aurora who had conned
    her part
On the other side the leaf ! ignore her so,
Because she was a woman and a queen,
And had no beard to bristle through her
    song,
My teacher, who has taught me with a
    book,
My Miriam, whose sweet mouth, when
    nearly drowned
I still heard singing on the shore ! De-
    served,
That here I should look up into the stars
And miss the glory' . .
                'Can I understand?'
I broke in. 'You speak wildly, Romney
    Leigh,
Or I hear wildly. In that morning-time
We recollect, the roses were too red,

The trees too green, reproach too natural
If one should see not what the other saw:
And now, it's night, remember; we have
  shades
In place of colours; we are now grown
  cold,
And old, my cousin Romney.   Pardon
  me,—
I'm very happy that you like my book,
And very sorry that I quoted back
A ten years' birthday.   'Twas so mad
  a thing
In any woman, I scarce marvel much
You took it for a venturous piece of spite,
Provoking such excuses as indeed
I cannot call you slack in.'
                 'Understand,'
He answered sadly, 'something, if but so.
This night is softer than an English day,
And men may well come hither when
  they're sick,
To draw in easier breath from larger air.
'Tis thus with me; I come to you,—to
  you,
My Italy of women, just to breathe
My soul out once before you, ere I go,
As humble as God makes me at the last
(I thank Him), quite out of the way of men
And yours, Aurora,—like a punished
  child,
His cheeks all blurred with tears and
  naughtiness,
To silence in a corner.   I am come
To speak, beloved' . .
          'Wisely, cousin Leigh,
And worthily of us both!'
              'Yes, worthily;
For this time I must speak out and confess
That I, so truculent in assumption once,
So absolute in dogma, proud in aim,
And fierce in expectation,—I, who felt
The whole world tugging at my skirts
  for help,
As if no other man than I, could pull,
Nor woman, but I led her by the hand,
Nor cloth hold, but I had it in my coat,
Do know myself to-night for what I was
On that June-day, Aurora.   Poor bright
  day,
Which meant the best . . a woman and
  a rose,
And which I smote upon the cheek with
  words

Until it turned and rent me!   Young
  you were,
That birthday, poet, but you talked the
  right:
While I, . . I built up follies like a wall
To intercept the sunshine and your face.
Your face! that's worse.'
          'Speak wisely, cousin Leigh.'

'Yes, wisely, dear Aurora, though too
  late:
But then, not wisely.   I was heavy then,
And stupid, and distracted with the cries
Of tortured prisoners in the polished brass
Of that Phalarian bull, society,
Which seems to bellow bravely like ten
  bulls
But, if you listen, moans and cries instead
Despairingly, like victims tossed and
  gored
And trampled by their hoofs.   I heard
  the cries
Too close: I could not hear the angels
  lift
A fold of rustling air, nor what they said
To help my pity.   I beheld the world
As one great famishing carnivorous
  mouth,—
A huge, deserted, callow, blind bird
  Thing,
With piteous open beak that hurt my
  heart,
Till down upon the filthy ground I
  dropped,
And tore the violets up to get the worms.
Worms, worms, was all my cry: an
  open mouth,
A gross want, bread to fill it to the lips,
No more.   That poor men narrowed
  their demands
To such an end, was virtue, I supposed,
Adjudicating that to see it so
Was reason.   Oh, I did not push the case
Up higher, and ponder how it answers
  when
The rich take up the same cry for them-
  selves,
Professing equally,—" An open mouth,
A gross need, food to fill us, and no more."
Why that's so far from virtue, only vice
Can find excuse for 't! that makes
  libertines,
And slurs our cruel streets from end to end

With eighty thousand women in one
smile,
Who only smile at night beneath the gas.
The body's satisfaction and no more,
Is used for argument against the soul's,
Here too; the want, here too, implies
the right.
—How dark I stood that morning in the
sun,
My best Aurora (though I saw your eyes),
When first you told me . . oh, I recollect
The sound, and how you lifted your
small hand,
And how your white dress and your
burnished curls
Went greatening round you in the still
blue air,
As if an inspiration from within
Had blown them all out when you spoke
the words,
Even these,—"You will not compass
your poor ends
Of barley-feeding and material ease,
Without the poet's individualism
To work your universal. It takes a soul,
To move a body,—it takes a high-
souled man,
To move the masses, even to a cleaner
sty :
It takes the ideal, to blow an inch inside
The dust of the actual : and your
Fouriers failed,
Because not poets enough to understand
That life develops from within." I say
Your words,—I could say other words
of yours,
For none of all your words will let me
go ;
Like sweet verbena which, being brushed
against,
Will hold us three hours after by the smell
In spite of long walks upon windy hills.
But these words dealt in sharper per-
fume,—these
Were ever on me, stinging through my
dreams,
And saying themselves for ever o'er my
acts
Like some unhappy verdict. That I
failed,
Is certain. Sty or no sty, to contrive
The swine's propulsion toward the
precipice,

Proved easy and plain. I subtly organized
And ordered, built the cards up high
and higher,
Till, some one breathing, all fell flat
again ;
In setting right society's wide wrong,
Mere life's so fatal. So I failed in-
deed,
Once, twice, and oftener,—hearing
through the rents
Of obstinate purpose, still those words
of yours,
" You will not compass your poor ends,
not you ! "
But harder than you said them ; every
time
Still farther from your voice, until they
came
To overcrow me with triumphant scorn
Which vexed me to resistance. Set
down this
For condemnation,—I was guilty here ;
I stood upon my deed and fought my
doubt,
As men will,—for I doubted,—till at last
My deed gave way beneath me suddenly
And left me what I am :—the curtain
dropped,
My part quite ended, all the footlights
quenched,
My own soul hissing at me through the
dark,
I ready for confession,—I was wrong,
I've sorely failed, I've slipped the ends
of life,
I yield, you have conquered.'
          'Stay,' I answered him ;
'I've something for your hearing, also. I
Have failed too.'
     'You ! ' he said, 'you're very great ;
The sadness of your greatness fits you
well :
As if the plume upon a hero's casque
Should nod a shadow upon his victor
face.'

I took him up austerely,—'You have
read
My book, but not my heart ; for recollect,
'Tis writ in Sanscrit which you bungle
at.
I've surely failed, I know, if failure
means

To look back sadly on work gladly
    done,—
To wander on my mountains of Delight,
So called (I can remember a friend's
    words
As well as you, sir), weary and in want
Of even a sheep-path, thinking bitterly . .
Well, well! no matter. I but say so
    much,
To keep you, Romney Leigh, from
    saying more,
And let you feel I am not so high indeed,
That I can bear to have you at my foot,—
Or safe, that I can help you. That
    June-day,
Too deeply sunk in craterous sunsets now
For you or me to dig it up alive,—
To pluck it out all bleeding with spent
    flame
At the roots, before those moralizing
    stars
We have got instead,—that poor lost
    day, you said
Some words as truthful as the thing of
    mine
You cared to keep in memory; and
    I hold
If I, that day, and, being the girl I was,
Had shown a gentler spirit, less
    arrogance,
It had not hurt me. You will scarce
    mistake
The point here: I but only think, you see,
More justly, that's more humbly, of
    myself,
Than when I tried a crown on and
    supposed . .
Nay, laugh, sir,—I'll laugh with you!—
    pray you, laugh.
I've had so many birthdays since that day
I've learnt to prize mirth's opportunities,
Which come too seldom. Was it you
    who said
I was not changed? the same Aurora? Ah,
We could laugh there, too! Why,
    Ulysses' dog
Knew *him*, and wagged his tail and
    died: but if
I had owned a dog, I too, before my Troy,
And if you brought him here, . . I
    warrant you
He'd look into my face, bark lustily,
And live on stoutly, as the creatures will

Whose spirits are not troubled by long
    loves.
A dog would never know me, I'm so
    changed,
Much less a friend . . except that you're
    misled
By the colour of the hair, the trick of
    the voice,
Like that Aurora Leigh's.'
                'Sweet trick of voice!
I would be a dog for this, to know it at last,
And die upon the falls of it. O love,
O best Aurora! are you then so sad
You scarcely had been sadder as my wife?'

'Your wife, sir! I must certainly be
    changed,
If I, Aurora, can have said a thing
So light, it catches at the knightly spurs
Of a noble gentleman like Romney Leigh
And trips him from his honourable sense
Of what befits' . .
                'You wholly misconceive,'
He answered.
            I returned,—' I'm glad of it.
But keep from misconception, too,
    yourself:
I am not humbled to so low a point,
Nor so far saddened. If I am sad at all,
Ten layers of birthdays on a woman's
    head
Are apt to fossilize her girlish mirth,
Though ne'er so merry: I'm perforce
    more wise,
And that, in truth, means sadder. For
    the rest,
Look here, sir: I was right upon the
    whole
That birthday morning. 'Tis impossible
To get at men excepting through their
    souls,
However open their carnivorous jaws;
And poets get directlier at the soul,
Than any of your economists:—for which
You must not overlook the poet's work
When scheming for the world's ne-
    cessities.
The soul's the way. Not even Christ
    Himself
Can save man else than as He holds
    man's soul;
And therefore did He come into our
    flesh,

As some wise hunter creeping on his
    knees
With a torch, into the blackness of
    a cave,
To face and quell the beast there,—take
    the soul,
And so possess the whole man, body
    and soul.
I said, so far, right, yes; not farther,
    though :
We both were wrong that June-day,—
    both as wrong
As an east wind had been. I who
    talked of art,
And you who grieved for all men's
    griefs . . what then ?
We surely made too small a part for
    God
In these things. What we are, imports
    us more
Than what we eat; and life, you've
    granted me,
Develops from within. But innermost
Of the inmost, most interior of the interne,
God claims His own, Divine humanity
Renewing nature,—or the piercingest
    verse,
Pressed in by subtlest poet, still must keep
As much upon the outside of a man
As the very bowl in which he dips his
    beard.
—And then, . . the rest ; I cannot
    surely speak :
Perhaps I doubt more than you doubted
    then,
If I, the poet's veritable charge,
Have borne upon my forehead. If I have,
It might feel somewhat liker to a crown,
The foolish green one even.—Ah,
    I think,
And chiefly when the sun shines, that
    I've failed.
But what then, Romney? Though we
    fail indeed,
You . . I . . a score of such weak
    workers, . . He
Fails never. If He cannot work by us,
He will work over us. Does He want
    a man,
Much less a woman, think you ? Every
    time
The star winks there, so many souls
    are born,

Who all shall work too. Let our own
    be calm.
We should be ashamed to sit beneath
    those stars,
Impatient that we're nothing.'
                ' Could we sit
Just so for ever, sweetest friend,' he said,
' My failure would seem better than
    success.
And yet indeed your book has dealt with
    me
More gently, cousin, than you ever will!
Your book brought down entire the
    bright June-day,
And set me wandering in the garden-
    walks,
And let me watch the garland in a place
You blushed so . . nay, forgive me, do
    not stir,—
I only thank the book for what it taught,
And what permitted. Poet, doubt your-
    self,
But never doubt that you're a poet to me
From henceforth. You have written
    poems, sweet,
Which moved me in secret, as the sap is
    moved
In still March-branches, signless as a
    stone :
But this last book o'ercame me like soft
    rain
Which falls at midnight, when the tight-
    ened bark
Breaks out into unhesitating buds
And sudden protestations of the spring.
In all your other books, I saw but *you* :
A man may see the moon so, in a pond,
And not be nearer therefore to the moon,
Nor use the sight . . except to drown
    himself :
And so I forced my heart back from the
    sight,
For what had *I*, I thought, to do with *her*,
Aurora . . Romney ? But, in this last book,
You showed me something separate from
    yourself,
Beyond you, and I bore to take it in
And let it draw me. You have shown
    me truths,
O June-day friend, that help me now at
    night
When June is over ! truths not yours,
    indeed,

But set within my reach by means of you,
Presented by your voice and verse the
way
To take them clearest. Verily I was
wrong ;
And verily many thinkers of this age,
Aye, many Christian teachers, half in
heaven,
Are wrong in just my sense who under-
stood
Our natural world too insularly, as if
No spiritual counterpart completed it,
Consummating its meaning, rounding all
To justice and perfection, line by line,
Form by form, nothing single nor alone,
The great below clenched by the great
above,
Shade here authenticating substance
there,
The body proving spirit, as the effect
The cause : we meantime being too
grossly apt
To hold the natural, as dogs a bone
(Though reason and nature beat us in
the face),
So obstinately, that we'll break our teeth
Or ever we let go. For everywhere
We're too materialistic,—eating clay
(Like men of the west) instead of Adam's
corn
And Noah's wine, clay by handfuls, clay
by lumps,
Until we're filled up to the throat with
clay,
And grow the grimy colour of the ground
On which we are feeding. Aye,
materialist
The age's name is. God Himself, with
some,
Is apprehended as the bare result
Of what His hand materially has made,
Expressed in such an algebraic sign
Called God ;—that is, to put it otherwise.
They add up nature to a nought of God
And cross the quotient. There are many
even,
Whose names are written in the Chris-
tian church
To no dishonour, diet still on mud
And splash the altars with it. You might
think
The clay, Christ laid upon their eyelids
when,

Still blind, He called them to the use of
sight,
Remained there to retard its exercise
With clogging incrustations. Close to
heaven,
They see for mysteries, through the
open doors,
Vague puffs of smoke from pots of
earthenware ;
And fain would enter, when their time
shall come,
With quite another body than Saint Paul
Has promised,—husk and chaff, the
whole barley-corn,
Or where 's the resurrection ? '
                                    ' Thus it is,'
I sighed. And he resumed with mourn-
ful face :
' Beginning so, and filling up with clay
The wards of this great key, the natural
world,
And fumbling vainly therefore at the lock
Of the spiritual, we feel ourselves shut in
With all the wild-beast roar of struggling
life,
The terrors and compunctions of our
souls,
As saints with lions,—we who are not
saints,
And have no heavenly lordship in our
stare
To awe them backward. Aye, we are
forced, so pent,
To judge the whole too partially, . .
confound
Conclusions. Is there any common
phrase
Significant, with the adverb heard alone,
The verb being absent, and the pronoun
out ?
But we, distracted in the roar of life,
Still insolently at God's adverb snatch,
And bruit against Him that His thought
is void,
His meaning hopeless,—cry, that every-
where
The government is slipping from His hand,
Unless some other Christ (say Romney
Leigh)
Come up and toil and moil and change
the world,
Because the First has proved inadequate,
However we talk bigly of His work

And piously of His person. We blas-
pheme
At last, to finish our doxology,
Despairing on the earth for which He
died.'

'So now,' I asked, 'you have more hope
of men?'

'I hope,' he answered. 'I am come to
think
That God will have His work done, as
you said,
And that we need not be disturbed too
much
For Romney Leigh or others having failed
With this or that quack nostrum,—recipes
For keeping summits by annulling depths,
For wrestling with luxurious lounging
sleeves,
And acting heroism without a scratch.
We fail,—what then? Aurora, if I smiled
To see you, in your lovely morning-pride,
Try on the poet's wreath which suits the
noon
(Sweet cousin, walls must get the
weather-stain
Before they grow the ivy!), certainly
I stood myself there worthier of contempt,
Self-rated, in disastrous arrogance,
As competent to sorrow for mankind
And even their odds. A man may well
despair,
Who counts himself so needful to success.
I failed: I throw the remedy back on God,
And sit down here beside you, in good
hope.'

'And yet take heed,' I answered, 'lest
we lean
Too dangerously on the other side,
And so fail twice. Be sure, no earnest
work
Of any honest creature, howbeit weak,
Imperfect, ill-adapted, fails so much,
It is not gathered as a grain of sand
To enlarge the sum of human action used
For carrying out God's end. No creature
works
So ill, observe, that therefore he's
cashiered.
The honest earnest man must stand and
work,

The woman also,—otherwise she drops
At once below the dignity of man,
Accepting serfdom. Free men freely
work.
Whoever fears God, fears to sit at ease.'

He cried, 'True. After Adam, work was
curse;
The natural creature labours, sweats,
and frets.
But, after Christ, work turns to privilege,
And henceforth, one with our humanity,
The Six-day Worker working still in us
Has called us freely to work on with
Him
In high companionship. So, happiest!
I count that Heaven itself is only work
To a surer issue. Let us work, indeed,
But no more work as Adam,—nor as
Leigh
Erewhile, as if the only man on earth,
Responsible for all the thistles blown
And tigers couchant, struggling in amaze
Against disease and winter, snarling on
For ever, that the world's not paradise.
Oh, cousin, let us be content, in work,
To do the thing we can, and not presume
To fret because it's little. 'Twill employ
Seven men, they say, to make a perfect
pin;
Who makes the head, content to miss
the point,
Who makes the point, agreed to leave
the join:
And if a man should cry, " I want a pin,
And I must make it straightway, head
and point,"
His wisdom is not worth the pin he wants.
Seven men to a pin,—and not a man too
much!
Seven generations, haply, to this world,
To right it visibly a finger's breadth,
And mend its rents a little. Oh, to storm
And say, "This world here is intolerable;
I will not eat this corn, nor drink this
wine,
Nor love this woman, flinging her my soul
Without a bond for 't as a lover should,
Nor use the generous leave of happiness
As not too good for using generously "—
(Since virtue kindles at the touch of joy
Like a man's cheek laid on a woman's
hand,

And God, who knows it, looks for quick returns
From joys)—to stand and claim to have a life
Beyond the bounds of the individual man,
And raze all personal cloisters of the soul
To build up public stores and magazines,
As if God's creatures otherwise were lost,
The builder surely saved by any means !
To think,—I have a pattern on my nail,
And I will carve the world new after it
And solve so these hard social questions,
   —nay,
Impossible social questions, since their roots
Strike deep in Evil's own existence here
Which God permits because the question's hard
To abolish evil nor attaint free-will.
Aye, hard to God, but not to Romney Leigh !
For Romney has a pattern on his nail
(Whatever may be lacking on the Mount),
And, not being overnice to separate
What's element from what's convention, hastes
By line on line to draw you out a world,
Without your help indeed, unless you take
His yoke upon you and will learn of Him,
So much He has to teach ! so good a world !
The same, the whole creation's groaning for !
No rich nor poor, no gain nor loss nor stint ;
No potage in it able to exclude
A brother's birthright, and no right of birth,
The potage,—both secured to every man,
And perfect virtue dealt out like the rest
Gratuitously, with the soup at six,
To whoso does not seek it.'
          'Softly, sir,'
I interrupted,—'I had a cousin once
I held in reverence. If he strained too wide,
It was not to take honour but give help ;
The gesture was heroic. If his hand
Accomplished nothing . . (well, it is not proved)
That empty hand thrown impotently out

Were sooner caught, I think, by One in heaven,
Than many a hand that reaped a harvest in
And keeps the scythe's glow on it. Pray you, then,
For my sake merely, use less bitterness
In speaking of my cousin.'
         'Ah,' he said,
'Aurora ! when the prophet beats the ass,
The angel intercedes.' He shook his head—
'And yet to mean so well and fail so foul,
Expresses ne'er another beast than man :
The antithesis is human. Hearken, dear ;
There's too much abstract willing, purposing,
In this poor world. We talk by aggregates,
And think by systems, and, being used to face
Our evils in statistics, are inclined
To cap them with unreal remedies
Drawn out in haste on the other side the slate.'

'That's true,' I answered, fain to throw up thought
And make a game of 't,—'Yes, we generalize
Enough to please you. If we pray at all,
We pray no longer for our daily bread
But next centenary's harvests. If we give,
Our cup of water is not tendered till
We lay down pipes and found a Company
With Branches. Ass or angel, 'tis the same :
A woman cannot do the thing she ought,
Which means whatever perfect thing she can,
In life, in art, in science, but she fears
To let the perfect action take her part,
And rest there : she must prove what she can do
Before she does it, prate of woman's rights,
Of woman's mission, woman's function, till
The men (who are prating too on their side) cry,
"A woman's function plainly is .. to talk."
Poor souls, they are very reasonably vexed ;

They cannot hear each other talk.'
                    ' And you,
An artist, judge so?'
                    ' I, an artist,—yes :
Because, precisely, I'm an artist, sir,
And woman, if another sate in sight,
I'd whisper,—Soft, my sister! not a word!
By speaking we prove only we can speak,
Which he, the man here, never doubted.
    What
He doubts is, whether we can *do* the thing
With decent grace we've not yet done
    at all.
Now, do it; bring your statue,—you
    have room !
He'll see it even by the starlight here ;
And if 'tis e'er so little like the god
Who looks out from the marble silently
Along the track of his own shining dart
Through the dusk of ages, there's no
    need to speak ;
The universe shall henceforth speak for
    you,
And witness, "She who did this thing,
    was born
To do it,—claims her licence in her work."
And so with more works. Whoso cures
    the plague,
Though twice a woman, shall be called
    a leech :
Who rights a land's finances, is excused
For touching coppers, though her hands
    be white,—
But we, we talk !'
                    ' It is the age's mood,'
He said ; ' we boast, and do not. We
    put up
Hostelry signs where'er we lodge a day,
Some red colossal cow with mighty paps
A Cyclops' fingers could not strain to
    milk,—
Then bring out presently our saucerful
Of curds. We want more quiet in our
    works,
More knowledge of the bounds in which
    we work ;
More knowledge that each individual man
Remains an Adam to the general race,
Constrained to see, like Adam, that he
    keep
His personal state's condition honestly,
Or vain all thoughts of his to help the
    world,—

Which still must be developed from its *one*
If bettered in its many. We indeed,
Who think to lay it out new like a park,
We take a work on us which is not man's,
For God alone sits far enough above
To speculate so largely. None of us
(Not Romney Leigh) is mad enough to
    say,
We'll have a grove of oaks upon that slope
And sink the need of acorns. Govern-
    ment,
If veritable and lawful, is not given
By imposition of the foreign hand,
Nor chosen from a pretty pattern-book
Of some domestic idealogue who sits
And coldly chooses empire, where as well
He might republic. Genuine government
Is but the expression of a nation, good
Or less good,—even as all society,
Howe'er unequal, monstrous, crazed,
    and cursed,
Is but the expression of men's single lives,
The loud sum of the silent units. What,
We'd change the aggregate and yet retain
Each separate figure? whom do we cheat
    by that ?
Now, not even Romney.'
                    ' Cousin, you are sad.
Did all your social labour at Leigh Hall
And elsewhere, come to nought then?'
                    ' It *was* nought,'
He answered mildly. 'There is room
    indeed
For statues still, in this large world of
    God's,
But not for vacuums,—so I am not sad ;
Not sadder than is good for what I am.
My vain phalanstery dissolved itself ;
My men and women of disordered lives,
I brought in orderly to dine and sleep,
Broke up those waxen masks I made
    them wear,
With fierce contortions of the natural
    face,—
And cursed me for my tyrannous con-
    straint
In forcing crooked creatures to live
    straight ;
And set the country hounds upon my back
To bite and tear me for my wicked deed
Of trying to do good without the church
Or even the squires, Aurora. Do you
    mind

Your ancient neighbours? The great
book-club teems
With "sketches," "summaries," and
"last tracts" but twelve,
On socialistic troublers of close bonds
Betwixt the generous rich and grateful
poor.
The vicar preached from "Revelations"
(till
The doctor woke), and found me with
"the frogs"
On three successive Sundays; aye, and
stopped
To weep a little (for he's getting old)
That such perdition should o'ertake a man
Of such fair acres,—in the parish, too!
He printed his discourses "by request,"
And if your book shall sell as his did, then
Your verses are less good than I suppose.
The women of the neighbourhood sub-
scribed,
And sent me a copy bound in scarlet silk,
Tooled edges, blazoned with the arms of
Leigh:
I own that touched me.'
        'What, the pretty ones?
Poor Romney!'
    'Otherwise the effect was small:
I had my windows broken once or twice
By liberal peasants naturally incensed
At such a vexer of Arcadian peace,
Who would not let men call their wives
their own
To kick like Britons, and made obstacles
When things went smoothly as a baby
drugged,
Toward freedom and starvation,—bring-
ing down
The wicked London tavern-thieves and
drabs
To affront the blessed hillside drabs and
thieves
With mended morals, quotha,—fine new
lives!—
My windows paid for't. I was shot at,
once,
By an active poacher who had hit a hare
From the other barrel (tired of springeing
game
So long upon my acres, undisturbed,
And restless for the country's virtue,—
yet
He missed me), aye, and pelted very oft

In riding through the village. "There
he goes
Who'd drive away our Christian gentle-
folks,
To catch us undefended in the trap
He baits with poisonous cheese, and
lock us up
In that pernicious prison of Leigh Hall
With all his murderers! Give another
name
And say Leigh Hell, and burn it up
with fire."
And so they did, at last, Aurora.'
        'Did?'

'You never heard it, cousin? Vincent's
news
Came stinted, then.'
    'They did? they burnt Leigh Hall?

'You're sorry, dear Aurora? Yes in-
deed,
They did it perfectly: a thorough work,
And not a failure, this time. Let us grant
'Tis somewhat easier, though, to burn
a house
Than build a system;—yet that's easy,
too,
In a dream. Books, pictures,—aye, the
pictures! what,
You think your dear Vandykes would
give them pause?
Our proud ancestral Leighs, with those
peaked beards,
Or bosoms white as foam thrown up on
rocks
From the old-spent wave. Such calm
defiant looks
They flared up with! now nevermore
to twit
The bones in the family-vault with
ugly death.
Not one was rescued, save the Lady
Maud,
Who threw you down, that morning
you were born,
The undeniable lineal mouth and chin
To wear for ever for her gracious sake,
For which good deed I saved her; the
rest went:
And you, you're sorry, cousin. Well,
for me,
With all my phalansterians safely out

(Poor hearts, they helped the burners, it was said,
And certainly a few clapped hands and yelled),
The ruin did not hurt me as it might,—
As when for instance I was hurt one day
A certain letter being destroyed. In fact,
To see the great house flare so . . oaken floors,
Our fathers made so fine with rushes once
Before our mothers furbished them with trains,
Carved wainscoats, panelled walls, the favourite slide
For draining off a martyr (or a rogue),
The echoing galleries, half a half-mile long,
And all the various stairs that took you up
And took you down, and took you round about
Upon their slippery darkness, recollect,
All helping to keep up one blazing jest!
The flames through all the casements pushing forth
Like red-hot devils crinkled into snakes,
All signifying,—"Look you, Romney Leigh,
We save the people from your saving, here,
Yet so as by fire! we make a pretty show
Besides,—and that's the best you've ever done."
—To see this, almost moved myself to clap!
The "vale et plaude" came too with effect
When, in the roof fell, and the fire that paused,
Stunned momently beneath the stroke of slates
And tumbling rafters, rose at once and roared,
And wrapping the whole house (which disappeared
In a mounting whirlwind of dilated flame),
Blew upward, straight, its drift of fiery chaff
In the face of Heaven, which blenched and ran up higher.'

'Poor Romney!'
          'Sometimes when I dream,' he said,

'I hear the silence after, 'twas so still.
For all those wild beasts, yelling, cursing round,
Were suddenly silent, while you counted five,
So silent, that you heard a young bird fall
From the top-nest in the neighbouring rookery,
Through edging over-rashly toward the light.
The old rooks had already fled too far,
To hear the screech they fled with, though you saw
Some flying still, like scatterings of dead leaves
In autumn-gusts, seen dark against the sky,—
All flying,—ousted, like the House of Leigh.'

'Dear Romney!'
          'Evidently 'twould have been
A fine sight for a poet, sweet, like you,
To make the verse blaze after. I myself,
Even I, felt something in the grand old trees,
Which stood that moment like brute Druid gods
Amazed upon the rim of ruin, where,
As into a blackened socket, the great fire
Had dropped,—still throwing up splinters now and then
To show them grey with all their centuries,
Left there to witness that on such a day
The House went out.'
          'Ah!'
               'While you counted five,
I seemed to feel a little like a Leigh,—
But then it passed, Aurora. A child cried,
And I had enough to think of what to do
With all those houseless wretches in the dark,
And ponder where they'd dance the next time, they
Who had burnt the viol.'
          'Did you think of that?
Who burns his viol will not dance, I know,
To cymbals, Romney.'
          'O my sweet sad voice,'
He cried,—'O voice that speaks and overcomes!
The sun is silent, but Aurora speaks.'

'Alas,' I said, 'I speak I know not what :
I'm back in childhood, thinking as a child,
A foolish fancy—will it make you smile ?
I shall not from the window of my room
Catch sight of those old chimneys any
    more.'

' No more,' he answered. ' If you pushed
    one day
Through all the green hills to our fathers'
    house,
You'd come upon a great charred circle,
    where
The patient earth was singed an acre
    round ;
With one stone-stair, symbolic of my
    life,
Ascending, winding, leading up to
    nought !
'Tis worth a poet's seeing. Will you go ?'

I made no answer. Had I any right
To weep with this man, that I dared to
    speak ?
A woman stood between his soul and
    mine,
And waved us off from touching ever-
    more,
With those unclean white hands of hers.
    Enough.
We had burnt our viols and were silent.
                                    So,
The silence lengthened till it pressed.
    I spoke,
To breathe : ' I think you were ill after-
    ward.'

' More ill,' he answered, ' had been
    scarcely ill.
I hoped this feeble fumbling at life's knot
Might end concisely,—but I failed to die,
As formerly I failed to live, and thus
Grew willing, having tried all other ways,
To try just God's. Humility 's so good,
When pride's impossible. Mark us, how
    .we make
Our virtues, cousin, from our worn-out
    sins,
Which smack of them from henceforth.
    Is it right,
For instance, to wed here while you
    love there ?
And yet because a man sins once, the sin

Cleaves to him, in necessity to sin,
That if he sin not *so*, to damn himself,
He sins *so*, to damn others with himself :
And thus, to wed here, loving there,
    becomes
A duty. Virtue buds a dubious leaf
Round mortal brows ; your ivy 's better,
    dear.

—Yet she, 'tis certain, is my very wife,
The very lamb left mangled by the wolves
Through my own bad shepherding : and
    could I choose
But take her on my shoulder past this
    stretch
Of rough, uneasy wilderness, poor lamb,
Poor child, poor child ?—Aurora, my
    beloved,
I will not vex you any more to-night,
But, having spoken what I came to say,
The rest shall please you. What she
    · can, in me,—
Protection, tender liking, freedom, ease,
She shall have surely, liberally, for her
And hers, Aurora. Small amends they'll
    make
For hideous evils which she had not
    known
Except by me, and for this imminent loss.
This forfeit presence of a gracious friend,
Which also she must forfeit for my sake,
Since, ... drop your hand in mine
    a moment, sweet,
We're parting !——ah, my snowdrop,
    what a touch,
As if the wind had swept it off ! you
    grudge
Your gelid sweetness on my palm but so,
A moment ? angry, that I could not bear
You . . speaking, breathing, living, side
    by side
With some one called my wife . . and
    live, myself ?
Nay, be not cruel—you must understand !
Your lightest footfall on a floor of mine
Would shake the house, my lintel being
    uncrossed
'Gainst angels : henceforth it is night
    with me,
And so, henceforth, I put the shutters up :
Auroras must not come to spoil my dark.'

He smiled so feebly, with an empty
    hand

Stretched sideway from me,—as indeed
   he looked
To any one but me to give him help;
And, while the moon came suddenly out
   full,
The double-rose of our Italian moons,
Sufficient plainly for the heaven and
   earth
(The stars struck dumb and washed away
   in dews
Of golden glory, and the mountains
   steeped
In divine languor), he, the man, appeared
So pale and patient, like the marble man
A sculptor puts his personal sadness in
To join his grandeur of ideal thought,—
As if his mallet struck me from my height
Of passionate indignation, I who had
   risen
Pale, doubting paused, . . . Was Romney
   mad indeed?
Had all this wrong of heart made sick
   the brain?

Then quiet, with a sort of tremulous pride,
'Go, cousin,' I said coldly; 'a farewell
Was sooner spoken 'twixt a pair of
   friends
In those old days, than seems to suit
   you now.
Howbeit, since then, I've writ a book
   or two,
I'm somewhat dull still in the manly art
Of phrase and metaphrase. Why, any
   man
Can carve a score of white Loves out of
   snow,
As Buonarroti in my Florence there,
And set them on the wall in some safe
   shade,
As safe, sir, as your marriage! very good;
Though if a woman took one from the
   ledge
To put it on the table by her flowers
And let it mind her of a certain friend,
'Twould drop at once (so better), would
   not bear
Her nail-mark even, where she took
   it up
A little tenderly,—so best, I say:
For me, I would not touch the fragile
   thing
And risk to spoil it half an hour before

The sun shall shine to melt it : leave it
   there.
I'm plain at speech, direct in purpose:
   when
I speak, you'll take the meaning as it is,
And not allow for puckerings in the silk
By clever stitches :—I'm a woman, sir,
I use the woman's figures naturally,
As you the male licence. So, I wish
   you well.
I'm simply sorry for the griefs you've had,
And not for your sake only, but man-
   kind's.
This race is never grateful: from the
   first,
One fills their cup at supper with pure
   wine,
Which back they give at cross-time on
   a sponge,
In vinegar and gall.'
                ' If gratefuller,'
He murmured, 'by so much less pitiable!
God's self would never have come down
   to die,
Could man have thanked him for it.'
                ' Happily
'Tis patent that, whatever,' I resumed,
' You suffered from this thanklessness of
   men,
You sink no more than Moses' bulrush-
   boat
When once relieved of Moses,—for
   you're light,
You're light, my cousin! which is well
   for you,
And manly. For myself,—now mark
   me, sir,
They burnt Leigh Hall ; but if, consum-
   mated
To devils, heightened beyond Lucifers,
They had burnt instead, a star or two
   of those
We saw above there just a moment back,
Before the moon abolished them,—
   destroyed
And riddled them in ashes through a sieve
On the head of the foundering universe,—
   what then?
If you and I remained still you and I,
It could not shift our places as mere
   friends,
Nor render decent you should toss
   a phrase

Beyond the point of actual feeling!—nay,
You shall not interrupt me : as you said,
We're parting.   Certainly, not once nor
    twice
To-night you've mocked me somewhat,
    or yourself,
And I, at least, have not deserved it so
That I should meet it unsurprised.
    But now,
Enough : we're parting . . parting.
    Cousin Leigh,
I wish you well through all the acts of life
And life's relations, wedlock not the least,
And it shall " please me," in your words,
    to know
You yield your wife, protection, freedom,
    ease,
And very tender liking.   May you live
So happy with her, Romney, that your
    friends
Shall praise her for it.   Meantime some
    of us
Are wholly dull in keeping ignorant
Of what she has suffered by you, and
    what debt
Of sorrow your rich love sits down to pay :
But if 'tis sweet for love to pay its debt,
'Tis sweeter still for love to give its gift,
And you, be liberal in the sweeter way,
You can, I think.   At least, as touches me,
You owe her, cousin Romney, no amends.
She is not used to hold my gown so fast,
You need entreat her now to let it go ;
The lady never was a friend of mine,
Nor capable,—I thought you knew as
    much,—
Of losing for your sake so poor a prize
As such a worthless friendship.   Be
    content,
Good cousin, therefore, both for her
    and you !
I'll never spoil your dark, nor dull your
    noon,
Nor vex you when you're merry, or at
    rest :
You shall not need to put a shutter up
To keep out this Aurora,—though your
    north
Can make Auroras which vex nobody,
Scarce known from night, I fancied ! let
    me add,
My larks fly higher than some windows.
    Well,

You've read your Leighs.   Indeed
    'twould shake a house,
If such as I came in with outstretched
    hand
Still warm and thrilling from the clasp
    of one . .
Of one we know, . . to acknowledge,
    palm to palm,
As mistress there, the Lady Waldemar.'

' Now God be with us ' . . with a sudden
    clash
Of voice he interrupted—' what name's
    that ?
You spoke a name, Aurora.'
                    'Pardon me ;
I would that, Romney, I could name
    your wife
Nor wound you, yet be worthy.'
                    ' Are we mad ?'
He echoed—' wife ! mine ! Lady Wal-
    demar !
I think you said my wife.'   He sprang
    to his feet,
And threw his noble head back toward
    the moon
As one who swims against a stormy sea,
Then laughed with such a helpless,
    hopeless, scorn,
I stood and trembled.
                    ' May God judge me so,'
He said at last,—' I came convicted here,
And humbled sorely if not enough.
    I came,
Because this woman from her crystal
    soul
Had shown me something which a man
    calls light :
Because too, formerly, I sinned by her
As then and ever since I have, by God,
Through arrogance of nature,—though
    I loved . .
Whom best, I need not say, since that
    is writ
Too plainly in the book of my misdeeds :
And thus I came here to abase myself,
And fasten, kneeling, on her regent
    brows
A garland which I startled thence one
    day
Of her beautiful June-youth.   But here
    again
I'm baffled,—fail in my abasement as

My aggrandizement : there's no room
    left for me
At any woman's foot who misconceives
My nature, purpose, possible actions.
    What !
Are you the Aurora who made large
    my dreams
To frame your greatness ? you conceive
    so small ?
You stand so less than woman, through
    being more,
And lose your natural instinct (like
    a beast)
Through intellectual culture ? since in-
    deed
I do not think that any common she
Would dare adopt such monstrous
    forgeries
For the legible life-signature of such
As I, with all my blots,—with all my
    blots !
At last then, peerless cousin, we are
    peers,
At last we're even. Ah, you've left
    your height,
And here upon my level we take hands,
And here I reach you to forgive you,
    sweet,
And that's a fall, Aurora. Long ago
You seldom understood me,—but before,
I could not blame you. Then, you only
    seemed
So high above, you could not see below;
But now I breathe,—but now I pardon!—
    nay,
We're parting. Dearest, men have
    burnt my house,
Maligned my motives,—but not one,
    I swear,
Has wronged my soul as this Aurora
    has,
Who called the Lady Waldemar my
    wife.'

'Not married to her ! yet you said' . .
             'Again?
Nay, read the lines' (he held a letter
    out)
'She sent you through me.'
         By the moonlight there,
I tore the meaning out with passionate
    haste
Much rather than I read it. Thus it ran.

NINTH BOOK

Even thus. I pause to write it out at
    length,
The letter of the Lady Waldemar.

'I prayed your cousin Leigh to take you
    this,
He says he'll do it. After years of love,
Or what is called so, when a woman frets
And fools upon one string of a man's name,
And fingers it for ever till it breaks,—
He may perhaps do for her such a thing,
And she accept it without detriment
Although she should not love him any
    more.
And I, who do not love him, nor love you,
Nor you, Aurora,—choose you shall
    repent
Your most ungracious letter and confess,
Constrained by his convictions (he's
    convinced),
You've wronged me foully. Are you
    made so ill,
You woman—to impute such ill to *me* ?
We both had mothers,—lay in their
    bosom once.
And after all, I thank you, Aurora Leigh,
For proving to myself that there are things
I would not do,—not for my life, nor him,
Though something I have somewhat
    overdone,—
For instance, when I went to see the gods
One morning on Olympus, with a step
That shook the thunder from a certain
    cloud,
Committing myself vilely. Could I think,
The Muse I pulled my heart out from
    my breast
To soften, had herself a sort of heart,
And loved my mortal ? He at least loved
    her,
I heard him say so,—'twas my recom-
    pense,
When, watching at his bedside fourteen
    days,
He broke out ever like a flame at whiles
Between the heats of fever,—" Is it thou?
Breathe closer, sweetest mouth !" and
    when at last
The fever gone, the wasted face extinct,

As if it irked him much to know me there,
He said, " 'Twas kind, 'twas good, 'twas
   womanly "
(And fifty praises to excuse no love),
"But was the picture safe he had
   ventured for ? "
And then, half wandering,—"I have
   loved her well,
Although she could not love me."—
   " Say instead,"
I answered, "she does love you."—
   'Twas my turn
To rave : I would have married him so
   changed,
Although the world had jeered me
   properly
For taking up with Cupid at his worst,
The silver quiver worn off on his hair.
"No, no," he murmured, "no, she loves
   me not ;
Aurora Leigh does better : bring her book
And read it softly, Lady Waldemar,
Until I thank your friendship more for
   that
Than even for harder service." So I read
Your book, Aurora, for an hour that day :
I kept its pauses, marked its emphasis ;
My voice, empaled upon its hooks of rime,
Not once would writhe, nor quiver, nor
   revolt ;
I read on calmly,—calmly shut it up,
Observing, "There 's some merit in the
   book ;
And yet the merit in't is thrown away,
As chances still with women if we write
Or write not : we want string to tie our
   flowers,
So drop them as we walk, which serves
   to show
The way we went. Good morning,
   Mister Leigh ;
You'll find another reader the next time.
A woman who does better than to love,
I hate ; she will do nothing very well :
Male poets are preferable, straining less
And teaching more." I triumphed o'er
   you both,
And left him.
      ' When I saw him afterward
I had read your shameful letter, and my
   heart.
He came with health recovered, strong
   though pale,

Lord Howe and he, a courteous pair of
   friends,
To say what men dare say to women,
   when
Their debtors. But I stopped them with
   a word,
And proved I had never trodden such
   a road
To carry so much dirt upon my shoe.
Then, putting into it something of disdain,
I asked forsooth his pardon, and my own,
For having done no better than to love,
And that not wisely,—though 'twas long
   ago,
And had been mended radically since.
I told him, as I tell you now, Miss Leigh,
And proved, I took some trouble for his
   sake
(Because I knew he did not love the girl)
To spoil my hands with working in the
   stream
Of that poor bubbling nature,—till she
   went,
Consigned to one I trusted, my own maid
Who once had lived full five months in
   my house
(Dressed hair superbly), with a lavish
   purse
To carry to Australia where she had left
A husband, said she. If the creature lied,
The mission failed, we all do fail and lie
More or less—and I'm sorry—which is all
Expected from us when we fail the most
And go to church to own it. What I meant,
Was just the best for him, and me, and
   her . .
Best even for Marian !—I am sorry for 't,
And very sorry. Yet my creature said
She saw her stop to speak in Oxford Street
To one . . no matter ! I had sooner cut
My hand off (though 'twere kissed the
   hour before,
And promised a duke's troth-ring for the
   next)
Than crush her silly head with so much
   wrong.
Poor child ! I would have mended it with
   gold,
Until it gleamed like St. Sophia's dome
When all the faithful troop to morning
   prayer :
But he, he nipped the bud of such a
   thought

With that cold Leigh look which I fancied once,
And broke in, "Henceforth she was called his wife :
His wife required no succour : he was bound
To Florence, to resume this broken bond ;
Enough so. Both were happy, he and Howe,
To acquit me of the heaviest charge of all—"
—At which I shot my tongue against my fly
And struck him ; "Would he carry,—he was just,
A letter from me to Aurora Leigh,
And ratify from his authentic mouth
My answer to her accusation ?"—"Yes,
If such a letter were prepared in time."
—He's just, your cousin,—aye, abhorrently :
He'd wash his hands in blood, to keep them clean.
And so, cold, courteous, a mere gentleman,
He bowed, we parted.
                    'Parted. Face no more,
Voice no more, love no more ! wiped wholly out
Like some ill scholar's scrawl from heart and slate,—
Aye, spit on and so wiped out utterly
By some coarse scholar ! I have been too coarse,
Too human. Have we business, in our rank,
With blood i' the veins ? I will have henceforth none,
Not even to keep the colour at my lip :
A rose is pink and pretty without blood,
Why not a woman ? When we've played in vain
The game, to adore,—we have resources still,
And can play on at leisure, being adored :
Here's Smith already swearing at my feet
That I'm the typic She. Away with Smith !—
Smith smacks of Leigh,—and henceforth I'll admit
No socialist within three crinolines,
To live and have his being. But for you,
Though insolent your letter and absurd,

And though I hate you frankly,—take my Smith !
For when you have seen this famous marriage tied,
A most unspotted Erle to a noble Leigh
(His love astray on one he should not love),
Howbeit you may not want his love, beware,
You'll want some comfort. So I leave you Smith,
Take Smith !—he talks Leigh's subjects, somewhat worse ;
Adopts a thought of Leigh's, and dwindles it ;
Goes leagues beyond, to be no inch behind ;
Will mind you of him, as a shoe-string may
Of a man : and women, when they are made like you,
Grow tender to a shoe-string, footprint even,
Adore averted shoulders in a glass,
And memories of what, present once, was loathed.
And yet, you loathed not Romney,— though you played
At "fox and goose" about him with your soul ;
Pass over fox, you rub out fox,—ignore
A feeling, you eradicate it,—the act's Identical.
              'I wish you joy, Miss Leigh ;
You've made a happy marriage for your friend,
And all the honour, well-assorted love,
Derives from you who love him, whom he loves !
You need not wish me joy to think of it ;
I have so much. Observe, Aurora Leigh,
Your droop of eyelid is the same as his,
And, but for you, I might have won his love,
And, to you, I have shown my naked heart ;
For which three things, I hate, hate, hate you. Hush,
Suppose a fourth !—I cannot choose but think
That, with him, I were virtuouser than you
Without him : so I hate you from this gulf
And hollow of my soul, which opens out

To what, except for you, had been my
    heaven,
And is, instead, a place to curse by! Love.'

An active kind of curse. I stood there
    cursed,
Confounded. I had seized and caught
    the sense
Of the letter, with its twenty stinging
    snakes,
In a moment's sweep of eyesight, and
    I stood
Dazed.—'Ah! not married.'
            'You mistake,' he said,
'I'm married. Is not Marian Erle my
    wife?
As God sees things, I have a wife and
    child ;
And I, as I'm a man who honours God,
Am here to claim them as my child and
    wife.'

I felt it hard to breathe, much less to
    speak.
Nor word of mine was needed. Some
    one else
Was there for answering. 'Romney,'
    she began,
'My great good angel, Romney.'
                    Then at first,
I knew that Marian Erle was beautiful.
She stood there, still and pallid as a saint,
Dilated, like a saint in ecstasy,
As if the floating moonshine interposed
Betwixt her foot and the earth, and raised
    her up
To float upon it. 'I had left my child,
Who sleeps,' she said, 'and having drawn
    this way
I heard you speaking, . . friend!—Con-
    firm me now.
You take this Marian, such as wicked men
Have made her, for your honourable
    wife?'

The thrilling, solemn, proud, pathetic
    voice.
He stretched his arms out toward that
    thrilling voice,
As if to draw it on to his embrace.
—'I take her as God made her, and as men
Must fail to unmake her, for my honoured
    wife.'

She never raised her eyes, nor took a step,
But stood there in her place, and spoke
    again.
—'You take this Marian's child, which
    is her shame
In sight of men and women, for your child,
Of whom you will not ever feel ashamed?'

The thrilling, tender, proud, pathetic
    voice.
He stepped on toward it, still with out-
    stretched arms,
As if to quench upon his breast that voice.
—'May God so father me, as I do him,
And so forsake me, as I let him feel
He's orphaned haply. Here I take the
    child
To share my cup, to slumber on my knee,
To play his loudest gambol at my foot,
To hold my finger in the public ways,
Till none shall need inquire, "Whose
    child is this?"
The gesture saying so tenderly, "My
    own."'

She stood a moment silent in her place ;
Then turning toward me very slow and
    cold,
—'And you,—what say you?—will you
    blame me much,
If, careful for that outcast child of mine,
I catch this hand that's stretched to me
    and him,
Nor dare to leave him friendless in the
    world
Where men have stoned me? Have I
    not the right
To take so mere an aftermath from life,
Else found so wholly bare? Or is it wrong
To let your cousin, for a generous bent,
Put out his ungloved fingers among briers
To set a tumbling bird's-nest somewhat
    straight?
You will not tell him, though we're
    innocent,
We are not harmless, . . and that both
    our harms
Will stick to his good smooth noble life
    like burrs,
Never to drop off though he shakes the
    cloak?
You've been my friend: you will not
    now be his?

You've known him that he's worthy of
  a friend,
And you're his cousin, lady, after all,
And therefore more than free to take his
  part,
Explaining, since the nest is surely spoilt
And Marian what you know her,—though
  a wife,
The world would hardly understand her
  case
Of being just hurt and honest ; while,
  for him,
'Twould ever twit him with his bastard
  child
And married harlot. Speak, while yet
  there's time.
You would not stand and let a good man's
  dog
Turn round and rend him, because his,
  and reared
Of a generous breed,—and will you let
  his act,
Because it's generous? Speak. I'm
  bound to you,
And I'll be bound by only you, in this.'

The thrilling, solemn voice, so passionless,
Sustained, yet low, without a rise or fall,
As one who had authority to speak,
And not as Marian.
                 I looked up to feel
If God stood near me, and beheld His
  heaven
As blue as Aaron's priestly robe appeared
To Aaron when he took it off to die.
And then I spoke—'Accept the gift, I say,
My sister Marian, and be satisfied.
The hand that gives, has still a soul behind
Which will not let it quail for having
  given,
Though foolish worldlings talk they know
  not what
Of what they know not. Romney's
  strong enough
For this : do you be strong to know he's
  strong :
He stands on Right's side ; never flinch
  for him,
As if he stood on the other. You'll be
  bound
By me ? I am a woman of repute ;
No fly-blow gossip ever specked my life ;
My name is clean and open as this hand,

Whose glove there's not a man dares
  blab about
As if he had touched it freely. Here's
  my hand
To clasp your hand, my Marian, owned
  as pure !
As pure,—as I'm a woman and a Leigh !—
And, as I'm both, I'll witness to the
  world
That Romney Leigh is honoured in his
  choice
Who chooses Marian for his honoured
  wife.'

Her broad wild woodland eyes shot out
  a light,
Her smile was wonderful for rapture.
  'Thanks,
My great Aurora.' Forward then she
  sprang,
And dropping her impassioned spaniel
  head
With all its brown abandonment of
  curls
On Romney's feet, we heard the kisses
  drawn
Through sobs upon the foot, upon the
  ground—
'O Romney! O my angel! O unchanged,
Though since we've parted I have past
  the grave !
But Death itself could only better *thee*,
Not change thee !—*Thee* I do not thank
  at all :
I but thank God who made thee what
  thou art,
So wholly godlike.'
                 When he tried in vain
To raise her to his embrace, escaping
  thence
As any leaping fawn from a huntsman's
  grasp,
She bounded off and 'lighted beyond
  reach,
Before him, with a staglike majesty
Of soft, serene defiance,—as she knew
He could not touch her, so was tolerant
He had cared to try. She stood there
  with her great
Drowned eyes, and dripping cheeks, and
  strange sweet smile
That lived through all, as if one held
  a light

Across a waste of waters,—shook her
    head
To keep some thoughts down deeper in
    her soul,—
Then, white and tranquil like a summer-
    cloud
Which, having rained itself to a tardy
    peace,
Stands still in heaven as if it ruled the day,
Spoke out again—'Although, my gener-
    ous friend,
Since last we met and parted you're
    unchanged,
And, having promised faith to Marian
    Erle,
Maintain it, as she were not changed at
    all;
And though that's worthy, though that's
    full of balm
To any conscious spirit of a girl
Who once has loved you as I loved you
    once,—
Yet still it will not make her . . if she's
    dead,
And gone away where none can give or
    take
In marriage,—able to revive, return
And wed you,—will it, Romney? Here's the point,
My friend, we'll see it plainer: you and I
Must never, never, never join hands so.
Nay, let me say it,—for I said it first
To God, and placed it, rounded to an oath,
Far, far above the moon there, at His feet,
As surely as I wept just now at yours,—
We never, never, never join hands so.
And now, be patient with me; do not
    think
I'm speaking from a false humility.
The truth is, I am grown so proud with
    grief,
And He has said so often through His
    nights
And through His mornings, "Weep a
    little still,
Thou foolish Marian, because women
    must,
But do not blush at all except for sin,"—
That I, who felt myself unworthy once
Of virtuous Romney and his high-born
    race,
Have come to learn,—a woman, poor or
    rich,

Despised or honoured, is a human soul,
And what her soul is, that, she is herself,
Although she should be spit upon of men,
As is the pavement of the churches here,
Still good enough to pray in. And
    being chaste
And honest, and inclined to do the right,
And love the truth, and live my life out
    green
And smooth beneath his steps, I should
    not fear
To make him thus a less uneasy time
Than many a happier woman. Very
    proud
You see me. Pardon, that I set a trap
To hear a confirmation in your voice,
Both yours and yours. It is so good to
    know
'Twas really God who said the same
    before;
And thus it is in heaven, that first God
    speaks,
And then His angels. Oh, it does me
    good,
It wipes me clean and sweet from devil's
    dirt,
That Romney Leigh should think me
    worthy still
Of being his true and honourable wife!
Henceforth I need not say, on leaving
    earth,
I had no glory in it. For the rest,
The reason's ready (master, angel, friend,
Be patient with me) wherefore you and I
Can never, never, never join hands so.
I know you'll not be angry like a man
(For *you* are none) when I shall tell the
    truth,
Which is, I do not love you, Romney
    Leigh,
I do not love you. Ah well! catch my
    hands,
Miss Leigh, and burn into my eyes with
    yours,—
I swear I do not love him. Did I once?
'Tis said that women have been bruised
    to death
And yet, if once they loved, that love of
    theirs
Could never be drained out with all their
    blood:
I've heard such things and pondered.
    Did I indeed

Love once; or did I only worship? Yes,
Perhaps, O friend, I set you up so high
Above all actual good or hope of good
Or fear of evil, all that could be mine,
I haply set you above love itself,
And out of reach of these poor woman's
    arms,
Angelic Romney. What was in my
    thought?
To be your slave, your help, your toy,
    your tool.
To be your love . . I never thought of that:
To give you love . . still less. I gave
    you love?
I think I did not give you anything;
I was but only yours,—upon my knees.
All yours, in soul and body, in head and
    heart,
A creature you had taken from the ground
Still crumbling through your fingers to
    your feet
To join the dust she came from. Did
    I love,
Or did I worship? judge, Aurora Leigh!
But, if indeed I loved, 'twas long ago,—
So long! before the sun and moon were
    made,
Before the hells were open,—ah, before
I heard my child cry in the desert night,
And knew he had no father. It may be
I'm not as strong as other women are,
Who, torn and crushed, are not undone
    from love.
It may be I am colder than the dead,
Who, being dead, love always. But for
    me,
Once killed, this ghost of Marian loves
    no more,
No more . . except the child! . . no more
    at all.
I told your cousin, sir, that I was dead;
And now, she thinks I'll get up from my
    grave,
And wear my chin-cloth for a wedding-
    veil,
And glide along the churchyard like a
    bride
While all the dead keep whispering
    through the withes,
"You would be better in your place
    with us,
You pitiful corruption!" At the thought,
The damps break out on me like leprosy

Although I'm clean. Aye, clean as
    Marian Erle!
As Marian Leigh, I know, I were not
    clean:
Nor have I so much life that I should love,
Except the child. Ah God! I could not
    bear
To see my darling on a good man's knees,
And know, by such a look, or such a sigh,
Or such a silence, that he thought some-
    times,
"This child was fathered by some
    cursed wretch" . .
For, Romney,—angels are less tender-
    wise
Than God and mothers: even *you* would
    think
What *we* think never. He is ours, the
    child;
And we would sooner vex a soul in heaven
By coupling with it the dead body's
    thought,
It left behind it in a last month's grave,
Than, in my child, see other than . . my
    child.
We only, never call him fatherless
Who has God and his mother. O my babe,
My pretty, pretty blossom, an ill-wind
Once blew upon my breast! can any
    think
I'd have another,—one called happier,
A fathered child, with father's love and
    race
That's worn as bold and open as a smile,
To vex my darling when he's asked his
    name
And has no answer? What! a happier
    child
Than mine, my best,—who laughed so
    loud to-night
He could not sleep for pastime? Nay,
    I swear
By life and love, that, if I lived like some,
And loved like . . *some*, aye, loved you,
    Romney Leigh,
As some love (eyes that have wept so
    much, see clear),
I've room for no more children in my
    arms,
My kisses are all melted on one mouth,
I would not push my darling to a stool
To dandle babies. Here's a hand shall
    keep

For ever clean without a marriage-ring,
To tend my boy until he cease to need
One steadying finger of it, and desert
(Not miss) his mother's lap, to sit with
    men.
And when I miss him (not he me) I'll come
And say, "Now give me some of
    Romney's work,
To help your outcast orphans of the world
And comfort grief with grief." For you,
    meantime,
Most noble Romney, wed a noble wife,
And open on each other your great
    souls,—
I need not farther bless you. If I dared
But strain and touch her in her upper
    sphere
And say, "Come down to Romney—
    pay my debt!"
I should be joyful with the stream of joy
Sent through me. But the moon is in
    my face . .
I dare not,—though I guess the name he
    loves ;
I'm learned with my studies of old days,
Remembering how he crushed his under-
    lip
When some one came and spoke, or did
    not come :
Aurora, I could touch her with my hand,
And fly because I dare not.'
                        She was gone.
He smiled so sternly that I spoke in haste :
' Forgive her—she sees clearly for her-
    self :
Her instinct 's holy.'
            ' I forgive !' he said,
' I only marvel how she sees so sure,
While others' . . there he paused,—then
    hoarse, abrupt,—
' Aurora ! you forgive us, her and me ?
For her, the thing she sees, poor loyal
    child,
If once corrected by the thing I know,
Had been unspoken, since she loves you
    well,
Has leave to love you :—while for me,
    alas,
If once or twice I let my heart escape
This night, . . remember, where hearts
    slip and fall
They break beside : we're parting,—
    parting,—ah,

You do not love, that you should surely
    know
What that word means. Forgive, be
    tolerant ;
It had not been, but that I felt myself
So safe in impuissance and despair,
I could not hurt you though I tossed my
    arms
And sighed my soul out. The most utter
    wretch
Will choose his postures when he comes
    to die,
However in the presence of a queen ;
And you'll forgive me some unseemly
    spasms
Which meant no more than dying. Do
    you think
I had ever come here in my perfect mind,
Unless I had come here in my settled mind
Bound Marian's, bound to keep the bond
    and give
My name, my house, my hand, the things
    I could,
To Marian ? For even *I* could give as
    much :
Even I, affronting her exalted soul
By a supposition that she wanted these,
Could act the husband's coat and hat set
    up
To creak i' the wind and drive the world-
    crows off
From pecking in her garden. Straw
    can fill
A hole to keep out vermin. Now, at last,
I own heaven's angels round her life
    suffice
To fight the rats of our society,
Without this Romney : I can see it at last ;
And here is ended my pretension which
The most pretended. Over-proud of
    course,
Even so !—but not so stupid . . blind . .
    that I,
Whom thus the great Taskmaster of the
    world
Has set to meditate mistaken work,
My dreary face against a dim blank wall
Throughout man's natural lifetime,—
    could pretend
Or wish . . O love, I have loved you !
    O my soul,
I have lost you !—but I swear by all
    yourself,

And all you might have been to me these
 years
If that June-morning had not failed my
 hope,—
I'm not so bestial, to regret that day
This night,—this night, which still to
 you is fair!
Nay, not so blind, Aurora. I attest
Those stars above us which I cannot
 see . .'

'You cannot' . .
    'That if Heaven itself should stoop,
Remix the lots, and give me another
 chance,
I'd say, "No other!"—I'd record my
 blank.
Aurora never should be wife of mine.'

'Not see the stars?'
            ''Tis worse still, not to see
To find your hand, although we're
 parting, dear.
A moment let me hold it ere we part;
And understand my last words—these,
 at last!
I would not have you thinking when I'm
 gone
That Romney dared to hanker for your
 love
In thought or vision, if attainable
(Which certainly for me it never was),
And wished to use it for a dog to-day
To help the blind man stumbling. God
 forbid!
And now I know He held you in His palm,
And kept you open-eyed to all my faults,
To save you at last from such a dreary end.
Believe me, dear, that, if I had known
 like Him
What loss was coming on me, I had done
As well in this as He has.—Farewell, you
Who are still my light,—farewell! How
 late it is:
I know that, now. You've been too
 patient, sweet.
I will but blow my whistle toward the lane,
And some one comes,—the same who
 brought me here.
Get in—Good-night.'
        'A moment. Heavenly Christ!
A moment. Speak once, Romney. 'Tis
 not true.

I hold your hands, I look into your face—
You see me?'
        'No more than the blessed stars.
Be blessed too, Aurora. Nay, my sweet,
You tremble. Tender-hearted! Do you
 mind
Of yore, dear, how you used to cheat
 old John,
And let the mice out slyly from his traps,
Until he marvelled at the soul in mice
Which took the cheese and left the
 snare? The same
Dear soft heart always! 'Twas for this
 I grieved
Howe's letter never reached you. Ah,
 you had heard
Of illness,—not the issue, not the extent:
My life long sick with tossings up and
 down,
The sudden revulsion in the blazing house,
The strain and struggle both of body and
 soul,
Which left fire running in my veins for
 blood:
Scarce lacked that thunderbolt of the
 falling beam
Which nicked me on the forehead as I
 passed
The gallery-door with a burden. Say
 heaven's bolt,
Not William Erle's, not Marian's father's,
 —tramp
And poacher, whom I found for what he
 was,
And, eager for her sake to rescue him,
Forth swept from the open highway of
 the world,
Road-dust and all,—till, like a woodland
 boar
Most naturally unwilling to be tamed,
He notched me with his tooth. But not
 a word
To Marian! and I do not think, besides,
He turned the tilting of the beam my
 way,—
And if he laughed, as many swear, poor
 wretch,
Nor he nor I supposed the hurt so deep.
We'll hope his next laugh may be merrier,
In a better cause.'
        'Blind, Romney?'
            'Ah, my friend,
You'll learn to say it in a cheerful voice.

I, too, at first desponded.   To be blind,
Turned out of nature, mulcted as a man,
Refused the daily largesse of the sun
To humble creatures ! When the fever's
      heat
Dropped from me, as the flame did from
      my house,
And left me ruined like it, stripped of all
The hues and shapes of aspectable life,
A mere bare blind stone in the blaze of
      day,
A man, upon the outside of the earth,
As dark as ten feet under, in the grave,—
Why that seemed hard.'
                              ' No hope ?'
                    ' A tear ! you weep,
Divine Aurora ? tears upon my hand !
I've seen you weeping for a mouse, a
      bird,—
But, weep for me, Aurora ? Yes, there's
      hope.
Not hope of sight,—I could be learned,
      dear,
And tell you in what Greek and Latin
      name
The visual nerve is withered to the root,
Though the outer eyes appear indifferent,
Unspotted in their crystals. But there's
      hope.
The spirit, from behind this dethroned
      sense,
Sees, waits in patience till the walls
      break up
From which the bas-relief and fresco
      have dropt :
There's hope.   The man here, once so
      arrogant
And restless, so ambitious, for his part,
Of dealing with statistically packed
Disorders (from a pattern on his nail),
And packing such things quite another
      way,—
Is now contented.   From his personal
      loss
He has come to hope for others when
      they lose,
And wear a gladder faith in what we
      gain . .
Through bitter experience, compensation
      sweet,
Like that tear, sweetest.   I am quiet
      now,
As tender surely for the suffering world,

But quiet,—sitting at the wall to learn,
Content henceforth to do the thing I can :
For, though as powerless, said I, as a
      stone,
A stone can still give shelter to a worm,
And it is worth while being a stone for
      that :
There's hope, Aurora.'
                    ' Is there hope for me ?
For me ?—and is there room beneath the
      stone
For such a worm ?—And if I came and
      said . .
What all this weeping scarce will let
      me say,
And yet what women cannot say at all
But weeping bitterly . . (the pride keeps
      up,
Until the heart breaks under it) . . I
      love,—
I love you, Romney' . .
                    ' Silence !' he exclaimed.
' A woman's pity sometimes makes her
      mad.
A man's distraction must not cheat his
      soul
To take advantage of it.   Yet, 'tis hard—
Farewell, Aurora.'
                    ' But I love you, sir ;
And when a woman says she loves a man,
The man must hear her, though he love
      her not,
Which . . hush ! . . he has leave to
      answer in his turn ;
She will not surely blame him.   As for me,
You call it pity,—think I'm generous?
'Twere somewhat easier, for a woman
      proud
As I am, and I'm very vilely proud,
To let it pass as such, and press on you
Love born of pity,—seeing that excellent
      loves
Are born so, often, nor the quicklier
      die,—
And this would set me higher by the head
Than now I stand.   No matter : let the
      truth
Stand high ; Aurora must be humble : no,
My love's not pity merely.   Obviously
I'm not a generous woman, never was,
Or else, of old, I had not looked so near
To weights and measures, grudging you
      the power

To give, as first I scorned your power
    to judge
For me, Aurora. I would have no gifts
Forsooth, but God's,—and I would use
    them too
According to my pleasure and my choice,
As He and I were equals, you below,
Excluded from that level of interchange
Admitting benefaction. You were wrong
In much? you said so. I was wrong
    in most.
Oh, most! You only thought to rescue
    men
By half-means, half-way, seeing half
    their wants,
While thinking nothing of your personal
    gain.
But I who saw the human nature broad
At both sides, comprehending too the
    soul's,
And all the high necessities of Art,
Betrayed the thing I saw, and wronged
    my own life
For which I pleaded. Passioned to exalt
The artist's instinct in me at the cost
Of putting down the woman's, I forgot
No perfect artist is developed here
From any imperfect woman. Flower
    from root,
And spiritual from natural, grade by
    grade
In all our life. A handful of the earth
To make God's image! the despised poor
    earth,
The healthy odorous earth,—I missed
    with it
The divine Breath that blows the nostrils
    out
To ineffable inflatus,—aye, the breath
Which love is. Art is much, but love is
    more.
O Art, my Art, thou'rt much, but Love
    is more!
Art symbolizes heaven, but Love is God
And makes heaven. I, Aurora, fell from
    mine.
I would not be a woman like the rest,
A simple woman who believes in love
And owns the right of love because she
    loves,
And, hearing she 's beloved, is satisfied
With what contents God: I must analyse,
Confront, and question; just as if a fly

Refused to warm itself in any sun
Till such was *in leone* : I must fret
Forsooth because the month was only
    May,
Be faithless of the kind of proffered love,
And captious, lest it miss my dignity,
And scornful, that my lover sought a wife
To use .. to use! O Romney, O my love,
I am changed since then, changed wholly,
    —for indeed
If now you'd stoop so low to take my love
And use it roughly, without stint or spare,
As men use common things with more
    behind
(And, in this, ever would be more behind),
To any mean and ordinary end,—
The joy would set me like a star, in
    heaven,
So high up, I should shine because of
    height
And not of virtue. Yet in one respect,
Just one, beloved, I am in no wise
    changed :
I love you, loved you .. loved you first
    and last,
And love you on for ever. Now I know
I loved you always, Romney. She
    who died
Knew that, and said so ; Lady Waldemar
Knows that ; .. and Marian. I had
    known the same,
Except that I was prouder than I knew,
And not so honest. Aye, and, as I live,
I should have died so, crushing in my hand
This rose of love, the wasp inside and all,
Ignoring ever to my soul and you
Both rose and pain,—except for this
    great loss,
This great despair,—to stand before
    your face
And know you do not see me where
    I stand.
You think, perhaps, I am not changed
    from pride,
And that I chiefly bear to say such words,
Because you cannot shame me with
    your eyes ?
O calm, grand eyes, extinguished in
    a storm,
Blown out like lights o'er melancholy seas,
Though shrieked for by the ship-
    wrecked,—O my Dark,
My Cloud,—to go before me every day

While I go ever toward the wilderness,—
I would that you could see me bare to
the soul!
If this be pity, 'tis so for myself,
And not for Romney! *he* can stand alone;
A man like *him* is never overcome:
No woman like me, counts him pitiable
While saints applaud him. He mistook
the world;
But I mistook my own heart, and that slip
Was fatal. Romney,—will you leave
me here?
So wrong, so proud, so weak, so un-
consoled,
So mere a woman!—and I love you so,
I love you, Romney—'
                    Could I see his face,
I wept so? Did I drop against his breast,
Or did his arms constrain me? were
my cheeks
Hot, overflooded, with my tears, or his?
And which of our two large explosive
hearts
So shook me? That, I know not.
There were words
That broke in utterance . . melted, in
the fire,—
Embrace, that was convulsion, . . then
a kiss
As long and silent as the ecstatic night,
And deep, deep, shuddering breaths,
which meant beyond
Whatever could be told by word or kiss.

But what he said . . I have written day
by day,
With somewhat even writing. Did
I think
That such a passionate rain would
intercept
And dash this last page? What he said,
indeed,
I fain would write it down here like the
rest,
To keep it in my eyes, as in my ears,
The heart's sweet scripture, to be read
at night
When weary, or at morning when afraid,
And lean my heaviest oath on when
I swear
That, when all 's done, all tried, all
counted here,
All great arts, and all good philosophies,

This love just puts its hand out in a dream
And straight outstretches all things.
                              What he said,
I fain would write. But if an angel spoke
In thunder, should we haply know
much more
Than that it thundered? If a cloud came
down
And wrapt us wholly, could we draw
its shape,
As if on the outside and not overcome?
And so he spake. His breath against
my face
Confused his words, yet made them
more intense
(As when the sudden finger of the wind
Will wipe a row of single city-lamps
To a pure white line of flame, more
luminous
Because of obliteration), more intense,
The intimate presence carrying in itself
Complete communication, as with souls
Who, having put the body off, perceive
Through simply being. Thus, 'twas
granted me
To know he loved me to the depth and
height
Of such large natures, ever competent,
With grand horizons by the sea or land,
To love's grand sunrise. Small spheres
hold small fires,
But he loved largely, as a man can love
Who, baffled in his love, dares live his life,
Accept the ends which God loves, for
his own,
And lift a constant aspect.
                              From the day
I brought to England my poor searching
face
(An orphan even of my father's grave)
He had loved me, watched me, watched
his soul in mine,
Which in me grew and heightened into
love.
For he, a boy still, had been told the tale
Of how a fairy bride from Italy
With smells of oleanders in her hair,
Was coming through the vines to touch
his hand;
Whereat the blood of boyhood on the
palm
Made sudden heats. And when at last
I came,

And lived before him, lived, and rarely
    smiled,
He smiled and loved me for the thing
    I was,
As every child will love the year's first
    flower
(Not certainly the fairest of the year,
But, in which, the complete year seems
    to blow),
The poor sad snowdrop,—growing
    between drifts,
Mysterious medium 'twixt the plant and
    frost,
So faint with winter while so quick with
    spring,
And doubtful if to thaw itself away
With that snow near it.   Not that
    Romney Leigh
Had loved me coldly. If I thought so once,
It was as if I had held my hand in fire
And shook for cold.   But now I under-
    stood
For ever, that the very fire and heat
Of troubling passion in him burned him
    clear,
And shaped, to dubious order, word
    and act :
That, just because he loved me over all,
All wealth, all lands, all social privilege,
To which chance made him unexpected
    heir,
And, just because on all these lesser gifts,
Constrained by conscience and the sense
    of wrong
He had stamped with steady hand God's
    arrow-mark
Of dedication to the human need,
He thought it should be so too, with
    his love.
He, passionately loving, would bring
    down
His love, his life, his best (because the
    best),
His bride of dreams, who walked so
    still and high
Through flowery poems as through
    meadow-grass,
The dust of golden lilies on her feet,
That *she* should walk beside him on the
    rocks
In all that clang and hewing out of men,
And help the work of help which was
    his life,

And prove he kept back nothing,—not
    his soul.
And when I failed him,—for I failed
    him, I,
And when it seemed he had missed my
    love, he thought
'Aurora makes room for a working-
    noon,'
And so, self-girded with torn strips of
    hope,
Took up his life as if it were for death
(Just capable of one heroic aim),
And threw it in the thickest of the
    world,—
At which men laughed as if he had
    drowned a dog.
No wonder,—since Aurora failed him
    first !
The morning and the evening made his
    day.

But oh, the night ! oh, bitter-sweet !
    oh, sweet !
O dark, O moon and stars, O ecstasy
Of darkness ! O great mystery of love,
In which absorbed, loss, anguish, trea-
    son's self
Enlarges rapture,—as a pebble dropt
In some full wine-cup over-brims the
    wine !
While we two sate together, leaned
    that night
So close, my very garments crept and
    thrilled
With strange electric life, and both my
    cheeks
Grew red, then pale, with touches from
    my hair
In which his breath was,—while the
    golden moon
Was hung before our faces as the badge
Of some sublime inherited despair,
Since ever to be seen by only one,—
A voice said, low and rapid as a sigh,
Yet breaking, I felt conscious, from a
    smile,
'Thank God, who made me blind, to
    make me see !
Shine on, Aurora, dearest light of souls,
Which rul'st for evermore both day and
    night !
I am happy.'
        I flung closer to his breast,

As sword that, after battle, flings to
    sheath ;
And, in that hurtle of united souls,
The mystic motions which in common
    moods
Are shut beyond our sense, broke in on us,
And, as we sate, we felt the old earth
    spin,
And all the starry turbulence of worlds
Swing round us in their audient circles,
    till,
If that same golden moon were overhead
Or if beneath our feet, we did not know.

And then calm, equal, smooth with
    weights of joy,
His voice rose, as some chief musician's
    song
Amid the old Jewish temple's Selah-
    pause,
And bade me mark how we two met at
    last
Upon this moon-bathed promontory of
    earth,
To give up much on each side, then take
    all.
'Beloved,' it sang, 'we must be here to
    work ;
And men who work can only work for
    men,
And, not to work in vain, must compre-
    hend
Humanity and so work humanly,
And raise men's bodies still by raising
    souls,
As God did first.'
        'But stand upon the earth,'
I said, 'to raise them (this is human too,
There 's nothing high which has not first
    been low,
My humbleness, said One, has made Me
    great !),
As God did last.'
        'And work all silently
And simply,' he returned, 'as God does
    all ;
Distort our nature never for our work,
Nor count our right hands stronger for
    being hoofs.
The man most man, with tenderest
    human hands,
Works best for men,—as God in Naza-
    reth.'

He paused upon the word, and then
    resumed :
'Fewer programmes, we who have no
    prescience.
Fewer systems, we who are held and do
    not hold.
Less mapping out of masses to be saved,
By nations or by sexes. Fourier's void,
And Comte absurd,—and Cabet, puerile.
Subsist no rules of life outside of life,
No perfect manners, without Christian
    souls :
The Christ Himself had been no Lawgiver
Unless He had given the life, too, with
    the law.'

I echoed thoughtfully—'The man, most
    man,
Works best for men, and, if most man
    indeed,
He gets his manhood plainest from his
    soul :
While obviously this stringent soul itself
Obeys the old law of development,
The Spirit ever witnessing in ours,
And Love, the soul of soul, within the
    soul,
Evolving it sublimely. First, God's
    love.'

'And next,' he smiled, 'the love of
    wedded souls,
Which still presents that mystery's
    counterpart.
Sweet shadow-rose, upon the water of
    life,
Of such a mystic substance, Sharon gave
A name to ! human, vital, fructuous rose,
Whose calyx holds the multitude of
    leaves,
Loves filial, loves fraternal, neighbour-
    loves
And civic—all fair petals, all good scents,
All reddened, sweetened from one central
    Heart !'

'Alas,' I cried, 'it was not long ago,
You swore this very social rose smelt ill.'

'Alas,' he answered, 'is it a rose at all ?
The filial 's thankless, the fraternal 's
    hard,
The rest is lost. I do but stand and think,
Across the waters of a troubled life

This Flower of Heaven so vainly over-
hangs,
What perfect counterpart would be in
sight
If tanks were clearer.   Let us clean the
tubes,
And wait for rains. O poet, O my love,
Since *I* was too ambitious in my deed
And thought to distance all men in success
(Till God came on me, marked the place
and said,
"Ill-doer, henceforth keep within this line,
Attempting less than others,"—and I
stand
And work among Christ's little ones,
content),
Come thou, my compensation, my dear
sight,
My morning-star, my morning,—rise and
shine,
And touch my hills with radiance not
their own.
Shine out for two, Aurora, and fulfil
My falling-short that must be ! work for
two,
As I, though thus restrained, for two,
shall love !
Gaze on, with inscient vision toward the
sun,
And, from his visceral heat, pluck out
the roots
Of light beyond him.   Art 's a service,—
mark :
A silver key is given to thy clasp,
And thou shalt stand unwearied, night
and day,
And fix it in the hard, slow-turning wards,
To open, so, that intermediate door
Betwixt the different planes of sensuous
form
And form insensuous, that inferior men
May learn to feel on still through these
to those,
And bless thy ministration.   The world
waits
For help.   Beloved, let us love so well,
Our work shall still be better for our love,
And still our love be sweeter for our work,
And both commended, for the sake of each,
By all true workers and true lovers born.
Now press the clarion on thy woman's lip
(Love's holy kiss shall still keep con-
secrate)

And breathe thy fine keen breath along
the brass,
And blow all class-walls level as Jericho's
Past Jordan,—crying from the top of
souls,
To souls, that, here assembled on earth's
flats,
They get them to some purer eminence
Than any hitherto beheld for clouds !
What height we know not,—but the way
we know,
And how by mounting ever, we attain,
And so climb on. It is the hour for souls,
That bodies, leavened by the will and love,
Be lightened to redemption. The world's
old,
But the old world waits the time to be
renewed,
Toward which, new hearts in individual
growth
Must quicken, and increase to multitude
In new dynasties of the race of men ;
Developed whence, shall grow spontan-
eously
New churches, new economies, new
laws
Admitting freedom, new societies
Excluding falsehood : HE shall make all
new.'

My Romney !—Lifting up my hand in his,
As wheeled by Seeing spirits toward the
east,
He turned instinctively, where, faint and
far,
Along the tingling desert of the sky,
Beyond the circle of the conscious hills,
Were laid in jasper-stone as clear as glass
The first foundations of that new, near
Day
Which should be builded out of heaven
to God.
He stood a moment with erected brows
In silence, as a creature might who
gazed,—
Stood calm, and fed his blind, majestic
eyes
Upon the thought of perfect noon : and
when
I saw his soul saw,—'Jasper first,' I said,
'And second, sapphire ; third, chalce-
dony ;
The rest in order,—last, an amethyst.'

POEMS BEFORE CONGRESS

PREFACE

THESE poems were written under the pressure of the events they indicate, after a residence in Italy of so many years, that the present triumph of great principles is heightened to the writer's feelings by the disastrous issue of the last movement, witnessed from 'Casa Guidi Windows' in 1849. Yet, if the verses should appear to English readers too pungently rendered to admit of a patriotic respect to the English sense of things, I will not excuse myself on such grounds, nor on the ground of my attachment to the Italian people, and my admiration of their heroic constancy and union. What I have written has simply been written because I love truth and justice *quand même*,—'more than Plato' and Plato's country, more than Dante and Dante's country, more even than Shakespeare and Shakespeare's country.

And if patriotism means the flattery of one's nation in every case, then the patriot, take it as you please, is merely a courtier; which I am not, though I have written 'Napoleon III in Italy.' It is time to limit the significance of certain terms, or to enlarge the significance of certain things. Nationality is excellent in its place; and the instinct of self-love is the root of a man, which will develop into sacrificial virtues. But all the virtues are means and uses; and, if we hinder their tendency to growth and expansion, we both destroy them as virtues, and degrade them to that rankest species of corruption reserved for the most noble organizations. For instance,—non-intervention in the affairs of neighbouring states is a high political virtue; but non-intervention does not mean, passing by on the other side when your neighbour falls among thieves,— or Phariseeism would recover it from Christianity. Freedom itself is virtue, as well as privilege; but freedom of the seas does not mean piracy, nor freedom of the land, brigandage; nor freedom of the senate, freedom to cudgel a dissident member, nor freedom of the press, freedom to calumniate and lie. So, if patriotism be a virtue indeed, it cannot mean an exclusive devotion to one's country's interests,—for that is only another form of devotion to personal interests, family interests, or provincial interests, all of which, if not driven past themselves, are vulgar and immoral objects. Let us put away the little Pedlingtonism unworthy of a great nation, and too prevalent among us. If the man who does not look beyond this natural life is of a somewhat narrow order, what must be the man who does not look beyond his own frontier or his own sea?

I confess that I dream of the day when an English statesman shall arise with a heart too large for England, having courage in the face of his countrymen to assert of some suggested policy,—'This is good for your trade: this is necessary for your domination; but it will vex a people hard by; it will hurt a people farther off; it will profit nothing to the general humanity: therefore, away with it!—it is not for you or for me.' When a British minister dares speak so, and when a British public applauds him speaking, then shall the nation be so glorious, that her praise, instead of exploding from within, from loud civic mouths, shall come to her from without, as all worthy praise must, from the alliances she has fostered, and from the populations she has saved.

And poets who write of the events of that time, shall not need to justify themselves in prefaces, for ever so little jarring of the national sentiment, imputable to their rimes.

ROME, *February*, 1860.

POEMS BEFORE CONGRESS

NAPOLEON III IN ITALY

I

EMPEROR, Emperor!
From the centre to the shore,
From the Seine back to the Rhine,
Stood eight millions up and swore
By their manhood's right divine
  So to elect and legislate,
This man should renew the line
Broken in a strain of fate
And leagued kings at Waterloo,
When the people's hands let go.
    Emperor
    Evermore

II

With a universal shout
They took the old regalia out
From an open grave that day;
From a grave that would not close,
Where the first Napoleon lay
  Expectant, in repose,
As still as Merlin, with his conquering face
Turned up in its unquenchable appeal
To men and heroes of the advancing
    race,—
  Prepared to set the seal
Of what has been on what shall be.
    Emperor
    Evermore.

III

  The thinkers stood aside
  To let the nation act.
Some hated the new-constituted fact
Of empire, as pride treading on their
    pride. .
Some quailed, lest what was poisonous
    in the past
Should graft itself in that Druidic bough
  On this green now.
  Some cursed, because at last
The open heavens to which they had
    look'd in vain
For many a golden fall of marvellous rain
  Were closed in brass; and some
Wept on because a gone thing could not
    come;

And some were silent, doubting all things
    for
  That popular conviction,—evermore
Emperor.

IV

That day I did not hate
Nor doubt, nor quail nor curse.
I, reverencing the people, did not bate
My reverence of their deed and oracle,
  Nor vainly prate
  Of better and of worse
Against the great conclusion of their will.
  And yet, O voice and verse,
Which God set in me to acclaim and sing
Conviction, exaltation, aspiration,
We gave no music to the patent thing,
Nor spared a holy rhythm to throb and
    swim
  About the name of him
Translated to the sphere of domination
  By democratic passion!
  I was not used, at least,
  Nor can be, now or then,
  To stroke the ermine beast
  On any kind of throne
(Though builded by a nation for its own),
And swell the surging choir for kings of
    men—
  'Emperor
  Evermore.'

V

  But now, Napoleon, now
That, leaving far behind the purple throng
  Of vulgar monarchs, thou
  Tread'st higher in thy deed
  Than stair of throne can lead,
  To help in the hour of wrong
The broken hearts of nations to be
    strong,—
  Now, lifted as thou art
  To the level of pure song,
We stand to meet thee on these Alpine
    snows!
And while the palpitating peaks break out
Ecstatic from somnambular repose
With answers to the presence and the
    shout,

We, poets of the people, who take part
With elemental justice, natural right,
Join in our echoes also, nor refrain.
We meet thee, O Napoleon, at this height
At last, and find thee great enough to
    praise.
Receive the poet's chrism, which smells
    beyond
    The priest's, and pass thy ways;—
An English poet warns thee to maintain
God's word, not England's:—let His
    truth be true
And all men liars! with His truth respond
To all men's lie. Exalt the sword and
    smite
On that long anvil of the Apennine
Where Austria forged the Italian chain
    in view
Of seven consenting nations, sparks of fine
    Admonitory light,
Till men's eyes wink before convictions
    new.
Flash in God's justice to the world's
    amaze,
Sublime Deliverer!—after many days
Found worthy of the deed thou art come
    to do—
Emperor
Evermore.

VI

But Italy, my Italy,
Can it last, this gleam?
Can she live and be strong,
Or is it another dream
Like the rest we have dreamed so long?
    And shall it, must it be,
That after the battle-cloud has broken
She will die off again
Like the rain,
Or like a poet's song
Sung of her, sad at the end
Because her name is Italy,—
Die and count no friend?
Is it true,—may it be spoken,—
That she who has lain so still,
With a wound in her breast,
And a flower in her hand,
And a gravestone under her head
While every nation at will
Beside her has dared to stand
And flout her with pity and scorn,
Saying, 'She is at rest,

She is fair, she is dead,
And, leaving room in her stead
To Us who are later born,
This is certainly best!'
Saying, 'Alas, she is fair,
Very fair, but dead,
And so we have room for the race.'
—Can it be true, be true,
That she lives anew?
That she rises up at the shout of her sons,
At the trumpet of France,
And lives anew?—is it true
That she has not moved in a trance,
As in Forty-eight?
When her eyes were troubled with blood
Till she knew not friend from foe,
Till her hand was caught in a strait
Of her cerement and baffled so
From doing the deed she would;
And her weak foot stumbled across
The grave of a king,
And down she dropt at heavy loss,
And she gloomily covered her face and
    said,
'We have dreamed the thing;
She is not alive, but dead.'

VII

Now, shall we say
Our Italy lives indeed?
And if it were not for the beat and bray
Of drum and trump of martial men,
Should we feel the underground heave
    and strain,
Where heroes left their dust as a seed
    Sure to emerge one day?
And if it were not for the rhythmic march
Of France and Piedmont's double hosts,
    Should we hear the ghosts
Thrill through ruined aisle and arch,
Throb along the frescoed wall,
Whisper an oath by that divine
They left in picture, book, and stone,
That Italy is not dead at all?
Aye, if it were not for the tears in our eyes,
These tears of a sudden passionate joy,
    Should we see her arise
From the place where the wicked are
    overthrown,
    Italy, Italy? loosed at length
    From the tyrant's thrall,
Pale and calm in her strength?
Pale as the silver cross of Savoy

When the hand that bears the flag is brave,
And not a breath is stirring, save
  What is blown
Over the war-trump's lip of brass,
Ere Garibaldi forces the pass !

VIII

Aye, it is so, even so.
Aye, and it shall be so.
Each broken stone that long ago
She flung behind her as she went
In discouragement and bewilderment
Through the cairns of Time, and missed
    her way
  Between to-day and yesterday,
  Up springs a living man.
And each man stands with his face in
    the light
  Of his own drawn sword,
Ready to do what a hero can.
Wall to sap, or river to ford,
Cannon to front, or foe to pursue,
Still ready to do, and sworn to be true,
  As a man and a patriot can.
Piedmontese, Neapolitan,
Lombard, Tuscan, Romagnole,
Each man's body having a soul,—
Count how many they stand,
All of them sons of the land,
Every live man there
Allied to a dead man below,
And the deadest with blood to spare
To quicken a living hand
In case it should ever be slow.
Count how many they come
To the beat of Piedmont's drum,
With faces keener and grayer
Than swords of the Austrian slayer,
All set against the foe.
    ' Emperor
    Evermore.'

IX

Out of the dust, where they ground them,
Out of the holes, where they dogged them ;
Out of the hulks, where they wound them
In iron, tortured and flogged them ;
Out of the streets, where they chased
    them,
Taxed them and then bayoneted
    them,—
Out of the homes, where they spied on
    them

(Using their daughters and wives),
Out of the church, where they fretted
    them,
Rotted their souls and debased them,
Trained them to answer with knives,
Then cursed them all at their
    prayers!—
Out of cold lands, not theirs,
Where they exiled them, starved them,
    lied on them ;
Back they come like a wind, in vain
Cramped up in the hills, that roars its
    road
The stronger into the open plain ;
Or like a fire that burns the hotter
And longer for the crust of cinder,
Serving better the ends of the potter ;
Or like a restrained word of God,
Fulfilling itself by what seems to
    hinder.
    ' Emperor
    Evermore.'

X

Shout for France and Savoy !
Shout for the helper and doer.
Shout for the good sword's ring,
Shout for the thought still truer.
Shout for the spirits at large
Who passed for the dead this spring,
Whose living glory is sure.
Shout for France and Savoy !
Shout for the council and charge !
Shout for the head of Cavour ;
And shout for the heart of a King
That's great with a nation's joy.
    Shout for France and Savoy !

XI

Take up the child, Macmahon, though
Thy hand be red
From Magenta's dead,
And riding on, in front of the troop,
  In the dust of the whirlwind of
    war
Through the gate of the city of Milan,
    stoop
And take up the child to thy saddle-
    bow,
Nor fear the touch as soft as a flower
  Of his smile as clear as a star !
Thou hast a right to the child, we
    say,

Since the women are weeping for joy as
those
Who, by thy help and from this day,
  Shall be happy mothers indeed.
They are raining flowers from terrace
and roof:
  Take up the flower in the child.
While the shout goes up of a nation freed
  And heroically self-reconciled,
Till the snow on that peaked Alp aloof
Starts, as feeling God's finger anew,
And all those cold white marble fires
Of mounting saints on the Duomo-spires
  Flicker against the Blue.
    'Emperor
    Evermore.'

XII

  Aye, it is He,
Who rides at the King's right hand !
Leave room to his horse and draw to the
side,
Nor press too near in the ecstasy
Of a newly delivered impassioned land:
  He is moved, you see,
  He who has done it all.
They call it a cold stern face ;
  But this is Italy
Who rises up to her place !—
For this he fought in his youth,
Of this he dreamed in the past ;
The lines of the resolute mouth
  Tremble a little at last.
Cry, he has done it all !
    'Emperor
    Evermore.'

XIII

It is not strange that he did it,
Though the deed may seem to strain
To the wonderful, unpermitted,
For such as lead and reign.
But he is strange, this man :
The people's instinct found him
(A wind in the dark that ran
Through a chink where was no door),
And elected him and crowned him
    Emperor
    Evermore.

XIV

Autocrat ? let them scoff,
  Who fail to comprehend
That a ruler incarnate of
  The people, must transcend

All common king-born kings.
These subterranean springs
A sudden outlet winning,
Have special virtues to spend.
The people's blood runs through him,
Dilates from head to foot,
Creates him absolute,
And from this great beginning
Evokes a greater end
To justify and renew him—
    Emperor
    Evermore.

XV

What ! did any maintain
That God or the people (think !)
Could make a marvel in vain ?—
Out of the water-jar there,
Draw wine that none could drink ?
Is this a man like the rest,
This miracle, made unaware
By a rapture of popular air,
And caught to the place that was best ?
You think he could barter and cheat
As vulgar diplomates use,
With the people's heart in his breast ?
Prate a lie into shape
Lest truth should cumber the road ;
Play at the fast and loose
Till the world is strangled with tape ;
Maim the soul's complete
To fit the hole of a toad ;
And filch the dogman's meat
To feed the offspring of God ?

XVI

Nay, but he, this wonder,
He cannot palter nor prate,
Though many around him and under,
With intellects trained to the curve,
Distrust him in spirit and nerve
Because his meaning is straight.
Measure him ere he depart
With those who have governed and led ;
Larger so much by the heart,
Larger so much by the head.
    Emperor
    Evermore.

XVII

He holds that, consenting or dissident,
  Nations must move with the time ;
Assumes that crime with a precedent
  Doubles the guilt of the crime ;

—Denies that a slaver's bond,
  Or a treaty signed by knaves
(*Quorum magna pars* and beyond
Was one of an honest name),
Gives an inexpugnable claim
To abolishing men into slaves.
      Emperor
      Evermore.

XVIII

He will not swagger nor boast
  Of his country's meeds, in a tone
Missuiting a great man most
  If such should speak of his own ;
Nor will he act, on her side,
  From motives baser, indeed,
Than a man of a noble pride
  Can avow for himself at need ;
Never, for lucre or laurels,
  Or custom, though such should be rife,
Adapting the smaller morals
  To measure the larger life.
He, though the merchants persuade,
  And the soldiers are eager for strife,
Finds not his country in quarrels
  Only to find her in trade,—
While still he accords her such honour
  As never to flinch for her sake
Where men put service upon her,
  Found heavy to undertake
And scarcely like to be paid :
  Believing a nation may act
Unselfishly—shiver a lance
(As the least of her sons may, in fact)
  And not for a cause of finance.
    Emperor
    Evermore.

XIX

  Great is he,
Who uses his greatness for all.
His name shall stand perpetually
  As a name to applaud and cherish,
Not only within the civic wall
For the loyal, but also without
  For the generous and free.
  Just is he,
Who is just for the popular due
  As well as the private debt.
The praise of nations ready to perish
  Fall on him,—crown him in view
Of tyrants caught in the net,
And statesmen dizzy with fear and doubt!

And though, because they are many,
  And he is merely one,
And nations selfish and cruel
Heap up the inquisitor's fuel
To kill the body of high intents,
And burn great deeds from their place,
Till this, the greatest of any,
May seem imperfectly done ;
Courage, whoever circumvents !
Courage, courage, whoever is base !
The soul of a high intent, be it known,
Can die no more than any soul
Which God keeps by Him under the
    throne ;
And this, at whatever interim,
Shall live, and be consummated
Into the being of deeds made whole.
Courage, courage! happy is he,
Of whom (himself among the dead
And silent), this word shall be said :
—That he might have had the world with
    him,
But chose to side with suffering men,
And had the world against him when
He came to deliver Italy.
    Emperor
    Evermore.

THE DANCE

I

You remember down at Florence our
    Cascine,
  Where the people on the feast-days
    walk and drive,
And, through the trees, long-drawn in
    many a green way,
  O'er-roofing hum and murmur like a
    hive,
  The river and the mountains look alive?

II

You remember the piazzone there, the
    stand-place
  Of carriages a-brim with Florence
    Beauties,
Who lean and melt to music as the band
    plays,
  Or smile and chat with some one who
    afoot is,
  Or on horseback, in observance of
    male duties?

III

'Tis so pretty, in the afternoons of summer,
  So many gracious faces brought to-
    gether!
Call it rout, or call it concert, they have
    come here,
  In the floating of the fan and of the
    feather,
  To reciprocate with beauty the fine
    weather.

IV

While the flower-girls offer nosegays
    (because *they* too
  Go with other sweets) at every car-
    riage-door;
Here, by shake of a white finger, signed
    away to
  Some next buyer, who sits buying
    score on score,
  Piling roses upon roses evermore.

V

And last season, when the French camp
    had its station
  In the meadow-ground, things quick-
    ened and grew gayer
Through the mingling of the liberating
    nation
  With this people; groups of French-
    men everywhere,
  Strolling, gazing, judging lightly . .
    'who was fair.'

VI

Then the noblest lady present took upon
    her
  To speak nobly from her carriage for
    the rest;
'Pray these officers from France to do us
    honour
  By dancing with us straightway.'—
    The request
  Was gravely apprehended as ad-
    dressed.

VII

And the men of France bareheaded,
    bowing lowly,
  Led out each a proud signora to the
    space
Which the startled crowd had rounded
    for them—slowly,

Just a touch of still emotion in his face,
  Not presuming, through the symbol,
    on the grace.

VIII

There was silence in the people: some
    lips trembled,
  But none jested. Broke the music,
    at a glance:
And the daughters of our princes, thus
    assembled,
  Stepped the measure with the gallant
    sons of France.
  Hush! it might have been a Mass, and
    not a dance.

IX

And they danced there till the blue that
    overskied us
  Swooned with passion, though the
    footing seemed sedate;
And the mountains, heaving mighty
    hearts beside us,
  Sighed a rapture in a shadow, to
    dilate,
  And touch the holy stone where Dante
    sate.

X

Then the sons of France bareheaded,
    lowly bowing,
  Led the ladies back where kinsmen of
    the south
Stood, received them;—till, with burst
    of overflowing
  Feeling . . husbands, brothers, Flor-
    ence's male youth,
  Turned, and kissed the martial
    strangers mouth to mouth.

XI

And a cry went up, a cry 'from all that
    people!
  —You have heard a people cheering,
    you suppose,
For the Member, Mayor . . with chorus
    from the steeple?
  This was different: scarce as loud
    perhaps (who knows?),
  For we saw wet eyes around us ere
    the close.

XII

And we felt as if a nation, too long
    borne in
    By hard wrongers, comprehending in
        such attitude
That God had spoken somewhere since
    the morning,
    That men were somehow brothers,
        by no platitude,
    Cried exultant in great wonder and
        free gratitude.

A TALE OF VILLAFRANCA

TOLD IN TUSCANY

I

My little son, my Florentine,
    Sit down beside my knee,
And I will tell you why the sign
    Of joy which flushed our Italy,
Has faded since but yesternight ;
    And why your Florence of delight
    Is mourning as you see.

II

A great man (who was crowned one day)
    Imagined a great Deed :
He shaped it out of cloud and clay,
    He touched it finely till the seed
Possessed the flower : from heart and
    brain
He fed it with large thoughts humane,
    To help a people's need.

III

He brought it out into the sun—
    They blessed it to his face :
' O great pure Deed, that hast undone
    So many bad and base !
O generous Deed, heroic Deed,
Come forth, be perfected, succeed,
    Deliver by God's grace.'

IV

Then sovereigns, statesmen, north and
    south,
    Rose up in wrath and fear,
And cried, protesting by one mouth,
    ' What monster have we here ?
A great Deed at this hour of day ?
A great just Deed—and not for pay ?
    Absurd,—or insincere.

V

' And if sincere, the heavier blow
    In that case we shall bear,
For where 's our blessed "status quo,"
    Our holy treaties, where,—
Our rights to sell a race, or buy,
Protect and pillage, occupy,
    And civilize despair ?'

VI

Some muttered that the great Deed
    meant
    A great pretext to sin ;
And others, the pretext, so lent,
    Was heinous (to begin).
Volcanic terms of ' great ' and ' just ' ?
Admit such tongues of flame, the crust
    Of time and law falls in.

VII

A great Deed in this world of ours ?
    Unheard of the pretence is :
It threatens plainly the great Powers ;
    Is fatal in all senses.
A just Deed in the world ?—call out
The rifles ! be not slack about
    The national defences.

VIII

And many murmured, ' From this source
    What red blood must be poured !'
And some rejoined, ''Tis even worse ;
    What red tape is ignored !'
All cursed the Doer for an evil
Called here, enlarging on the Devil,—
    There, monkeying the Lord !

IX

Some said, it could not be explained,
    Some, could not be excused ;
And others, ' Leave it unrestrained,
    Gehenna's self is loosed.'
And all cried, ' Crush it, maim it, gag it !
Set dog-toothed lies to tear it ragged,
    Truncated and traduced !'

X

But HE stood sad before the sun
    (The peoples felt their fate).
' The world is many,—I am one ;
    My great Deed was too great.
God's fruit of justice ripens slow :
Men's souls are narrow ; let them grow.
    My brothers, we must wait.'

XI

The tale is ended, child of mine,
　Turned graver at my knee.
They say your eyes, my Florentine,
　Are English : it may be :
And yet I've marked as blue a pair
Following the doves across the square
　At Venice by the sea.

XII

Ah, child ! ah, child ! I cannot say
　A word more.　You conceive
The reason now, why just to-day
　We see our Florence grieve.
Ah, child, look up into the sky !
In this low world, where great Deeds die,
　What matter if we live ?

A COURT LADY

I

HER hair was tawny with gold, her
　eyes with purple were dark,
Her cheeks' pale opal burnt with a red
　and restless spark.

II

Never was lady of Milan nobler in name
　and in race ;
Never was lady of Italy fairer to see in
　the face.

III

Never was lady on earth more true as
　woman and wife,
Larger in judgement and instinct, prouder
　in manners and life.

IV

She stood in the early morning, and
　said to her maidens, ' Bring
That silken robe made ready to wear at
　the court of the king.

V

' Bring me the clasps of diamond, lucid,
　clear of the mote,
Clasp me the large at the waist, and
　clasp me the small at the throat.

VI

' Diamonds to fasten the hair, and
　diamonds to fasten the sleeves,
Laces to drop from their rays, like
　a powder of snow from the eaves.'

VII

Gorgeous she entered the sunlight
　which gathered her up in a flame,
While, straight in her open carriage,
　she to the hospital came.

VIII

In she went at the door, and gazing
　from end to end,
' Many and low are the pallets, but
　each is the place of a friend.'

IX

Up she passed through the wards, and
　stood at a young man's bed :
Bloody the band on his brow, and livid
　the droop of his head.

X

' Art thou a Lombard, my brother ?
　Happy art thou,' she cried,
And smiled like Italy on him : he
　dreamed in her face and died.

XI

Pale with his passing soul, she went on
　still to a second :
He was a grave hard man, whose years
　by dungeons were reckoned.

XII

Wounds in his body were sore, wounds
　in his life were sorer.
' Art thou a Romagnole ? '　Her eyes
　drove lightnings before her.

XIII

' Austrian and priest had joined to double
　and tighten the cord
Able to bind thee, O strong one,—free
　by the stroke of a sword.

XIV

' Now be grave for the rest of us, using
　the life overcast
To ripen our wine of the present, (too
　new,) in glooms of the past.'

XV

Down she stepped to a pallet where lay
 a face like a girl's,
Young, and pathetic with dying,—a deep
 black hole in the curls.

XVI

'Art thou from Tuscany, brother? and
 seest thou, dreaming in pain,
Thy mother stand in the piazza, search-
 ing the List of the slain?'

XVII

Kind as a mother herself, she touched
 his cheeks with her hands :
'Blessed is she who has borne thee,
 although she should weep as she
 stands.'

XVIII

On she passed to a Frenchman, his arm
 carried off by a ball :
Kneeling, . . 'O more than my brother!
 how shall I thank thee for all?

XIX

'Each of the heroes around us has fought
 for his land and line,
But *thou* hast fought for a stranger, in
 hate of a wrong not thine.

XX

'Happy are all free peoples, too strong
 to be dispossessed.
But blessed are those among nations, who
 dare to be strong for the rest!'

XXI

Ever she passed on her way, and came
 to a couch where pined
One with a face from Venetia, white with
 a hope out of mind.

XXII

Long she stood and gazed, and twice she
 tried at the name,
But two great crystal tears were all that
 faltered and came.

XXIII

Only a tear for Venice?—she turned as
 in passion and loss,
And stooped to his forehead and kissed
 it, as if she were kissing the cross.

XXIV

Faint with that strain of heart she moved
 on then to another,
Stern and strong in his death. 'And
 dost thou suffer, my brother?'

XXV

Holding his hands in hers :—'Out of the
 Piedmont lion
Cometh the sweetness of freedom!
 sweetest to live or to die on.'

XXVI

Holding his cold rough hands,—'Well,
 oh, well have ye done
In noble, noble Piedmont, who would
 not be noble alone.'

XXVII

Back he fell while she spoke. She rose
 to her feet with a spring,—
'That was a Piedmontese! and this is
 the Court of the King.'

AN AUGUST VOICE

Una voce augusta.
MONITORE TOSCANO

I

You'll take back your Grand Duke?
 I made the treaty upon it.
Just venture a quiet rebuke ;
 Dall' Ongaro write him a sonnet ;
Ricasoli gently explain
 Some need of the constitution :
He'll swear to it over again,
 Providing an 'easy solution.'
You'll call back the Grand Duke.

II

You'll take back your Grand Duke?
 I promised the Emperor Francis
To argue the case by his book,
 And ask you to meet his advances.
The Ducal cause, we know
 (Whether you or he be the wronger),
Has very strong points ;—although
 Your bayonets, there, have stronger.
You'll call back the Grand Duke.

III

You'll take back your Grand Duke?
  He is not pure altogether.
For instance, the oath which he took
  (In the Forty-eight rough weather)
He'd 'nail your flag to his mast,'
  Then softly scuttled the boat you
Hoped to escape in at last,
  And both by a ' Proprio motu.'
You'll call back the Grand Duke.

IV

You'll take back your Grand Duke?
  The scheme meets nothing to shock it
In this smart letter, look,
  We found in Radetsky's pocket;
Where his Highness in sprightly style
  Of the flower of his Tuscans wrote,
'These heads be the hottest in file;
  Pray shoot them the quickest.' Quote,
And call back the Grand Duke.

V

You'll take back your Grand Duke?
  There *are* some things to object to.
He cheated, betrayed, and forsook,
  Then called in the foe to protect you.
He taxed you for wines and for meats
  Throughout that eight years' pastime
Of Austria's drum in your streets—
  Of course you remember the last time
You called back your Grand Duke.

VI

You'll take back the Grand Duke?
  It is not race he is poor in,
Although he never could brook
  The patriot cousin at Turin.
His love of kin you discern,
  By his hate of your flag and me—
So decidedly apt to turn
  All colours at sight of the Three[1].
You'll call back the Grand Duke.

VII

You'll take back your Grand Duke?
  'Twas weak that he fled from the Pitti;
But consider how little he shook
  At thought of bombarding your city!
And, balancing that with this,

[1] The Italian tricolor: red, green, and white.

  The Christian rule is plain for us;
. . Or the Holy Father's Swiss
  Have shot his Perugians in vain for us.
You'll call back the Grand Duke.

VIII

Pray take back your Grand Duke.
  —I, too, have suffered persuasion.
All Europe, raven and rook,
  Screeched at me armed for your nation.
Your cause in my heart struck spurs;
  I swept such warnings aside for you:
My very child's eyes. and Hers,
  Grew like my brother's who died for
    you.
You'll call back the Grand Duke?

IX

You'll take back your Grand Duke?
  My French fought nobly with reason,—
Left many a Lombardy nook
  Red as with wine out of season.
Little we grudged what was done there,
  Paid freely your ransom of blood:
Our heroes stark in the sun there,
  We would not recall if we could.
You'll call back the Grand Duke?

X

You'll take back your Grand Duke?
  His son rode fast as he got off
That day on the enemy's hook,
  When *I* had an epaulette shot off.
Though splashed (as I saw him afar, no,
  Near) by those ghastly rains,
The mark, when you've washed him in
    Arno,
  Will scarcely be larger than Cain's.
You'll call back the Grand Duke.

XI

You'll take back your Grand Duke?
  'Twill be so simple, quite beautiful:
The shepherd recovers his crook,
  . . If you should be sheep, and dutiful.
I spoke a word worth chalking
  On Milan's wall—but stay,
Here 's Poniatowsky talking,—
  You'll listen to *him* to-day,
And call back the Grand Duke.

XII

You'll take back your Grand Duke?
  Observe, there's no one to force it,—
Unless the Madonna, St. Luke
  Drew for you, choose to endorse it.
I charge you by great St. Martino
  And prodigies quickened by wrong,
Remember your Dead on Ticino ;
  Be worthy, be constant, be strong.
—Bah !—call back the Grand Duke ! !

CHRISTMAS GIFTS

ὡς βασιλεῖ, ὡς θεῷ, ὡς νεκρῷ.
GREGORY NAZIANZEN.

I

THE Pope on Christmas Day
  Sits in St. Peter's chair ;
But the peoples murmur and say,
  'Our souls are sick and forlorn,
And who will show us where
  Is the stable where Christ was born ?'

II

The star is lost in the dark ;
  The manger is lost in the straw ;
The Christ cries faintly . . hark ! . .
  Through bands that swaddle and
    strangle—
But the Pope in the chair of awe
  Looks down the great quadrangle.

III

The magi kneel at his foot,
  Kings of the east and west,
But, instead of the angels (mute
  Is the 'Peace on earth' of their song),
The peoples, perplexed and opprest,
  Are sighing, 'How long, how long?'

IV

And, instead of the kine, bewilder in
  Shadow of aisle and dome,
The bear who tore up the children,
  The fox who burnt up the corn,
And the wolf who suckled at Rome
  Brothers to slay and to scorn.

V

Cardinals left and right of him,
  Worshippers round and beneath,
The silver trumpets at sight of him
  Thrill with a musical blast :
But the people say through their teeth,
  'Trumpets ? we wait for the Last !'

VI

He sits in the place of the Lord,
  And asks for the gifts of the time ;
Gold, for the haft of a sword,
  To win back Romagna averse,
Incense, to sweeten a crime,
  And myrrh, to embitter a curse.

VII

Then a king of the west said, 'Good !—
  I bring thee the gifts of the time ;
Red, for the patriot's blood,
  Green, for the martyr's crown,
White, for the dew and the rime,
  When the morning of God comes
    down.'

VIII

—O mystic tricolor bright !
  The Pope's heart quailed like a man's :
The cardinals froze at the sight,
  Bowing their tonsures hoary :
And the eyes in the peacock-fans
  Winked at the alien glory.

IX

But the peoples exclaimed in hope,
  'Now blessed be he who has brought
These gifts of the time to the Pope,
  When our souls were sick and forlorn.
—And *here* is the star we sought,
  To show us where Christ was born !'

ITALY AND THE WORLD

I

FLORENCE, Bologna, Parma, Modena.
  When you named them a year ago,
So many graves reserved by God, in a
  Day of judgement, you seemed to know,
To open and let out the resurrection.

II

And meantime (you made your reflection
　If you were English), was nought to
　　be done
But sorting sables, in predilection
　For all those martyrs dead and gone,
Till the new earth and heaven made
　　ready ?

III

And if your politics were not heady,
　Violent, . . 'Good,' you added, 'good
In all things ! mourn on sure and steady.
　Churchyard thistles are wholesome
　　food
For our European wandering asses.

IV

'The date of the resurrection passes
　Human foreknowledge : men unborn
Will gain by it (even in the lower
　　classes),
　But none of these. It is not the morn
Because the cock of France is crowing.

V

'Cocks crow at midnight, seldom know-
　　ing
　Starlight from dawn-light : 'tis a mad
Poor creature.' Here you paused, and
　　growing
　Scornful, . . suddenly, let us add,
The trumpet sounded, the graves were
　　open.

VI

Life and life and life ! agrope in
　The dusk of death, warm hands,
　　stretched out
For swords, proved more life still to
　　hope in,
　Beyond and behind. Arise with a
　　shout,
Nation of Italy, slain and buried !

VII

Hill to hill and turret to turret
　Flashing the tricolor,—newly created
Beautiful Italy, calm, unhurried,
　Rise heroic and renovated,
Rise to the final restitution.

VIII

Rise ; prefigure the grand solution
　Of earth's municipal, insular schisms,—
Statesmen draping self-love's conclusion
　In cheap, vernacular patriotisms,
Unable to give up Judaea for Jesus.

IX

Bring us the higher example ; release us
　Into the larger coming time :
And into Christ's broad garment piece us
　Rags of virtue as poor as crime,
National selfishness, civic vaunting.

X

No more Jew nor Greek then,—taunting
　Nor taunted ;—no more England nor
　　France !
But one confederate brotherhood plant-
　　ing
　One flag only, to mark the advance,
Onward and upward, of all humanity.

XI

For civilization perfected
　Is fully developed Christianity.
'Measure the frontier,' shall it be said,
　'Count the ships,' in national vanity ?
—Count the nation's heart-beats sooner.

XII

For, though behind by a cannon or
　　schooner,
　That nation still is predominant,
Whose pulse beats quickest in zeal to
　　oppugn or
　Succour another, in wrong or want,
Passing the frontier in love and abhor-
　　rence.

XIII

Modena, Parma, Bologna, Florence,
　Open us out the wider way !
Dwarf in that chapel of old St. Lawrence
　Your Michel Angelo's giant Day,
With the grandeur of this Day breaking
　　o'er us !

XIV

Ye who, restrained as an ancient chorus,
　Mute while the coryphaeus spake,
Hush your separate voices before us,
　Sink your separate lives for the sake
Of one sole Italy's living for ever !

xv

Givers of coat and cloak too,—never
    Grudging that purple of yours at the
        best,—
By your heroic will and endeavour
    Each sublimely dispossessed,
That all may inherit what each sur-
    renders !

xvi

Earth shall bless you, O noble emenders
    On egotist nations ! Ye shall lead
The plough of the world, and sow new
    splendours
Into the furrow of things, for seed,—
Ever the richer for what ye have given.

xvii

Lead us and teach us, till earth and
    heaven
    Grow larger around us and higher
        above.
Our sacrament-bread has a bitter leaven ;
    We bait our traps with the name of
        love,
Till hate itself has a kinder meaning.

xviii

Oh, this world : this cheating and
    screening
    Of cheats ! this conscience for candle-
        wicks,
Not beacon-fires! this overweening
    Of underhand diplomatical tricks,
Dared for the country while scorned for
    the counter !

xix

Oh, this envy of those who mount here,
    And oh, this malice to make them trip !
Rather quenching the fire there, drying
    the fount here,
    To frozen body and thirsty lip,
Than leave to a neighbour their minis-
    tration.

xx

I cry aloud in my poet-passion,
    Viewing my England o'er Alp and sea.
I loved her more in her ancient fashion :
    She carries her rifles too thick for me,
Who spares them so in the cause of a
    brother.

xxi

Suspicion, panic ? end this pother.
    The sword, kept sheathless at peace-
        time, rusts.
None fears for himself while he feels
    for another :
    The brave man either fights or trusts,
And wears no mail in his private chamber.

xxii

Beautiful Italy ! golden amber
    Warm with the kisses of lover and
        traitor !
Thou who hast drawn us on to remember,
    Draw us to hope now : let us be
        greater
By this new future than that old story.

xxiii

Till truer glory replaces all glory,
    As the torch grows blind at the dawn
        of day ;
And the nations, rising up, their sorry
    And foolish sins shall put away,
As children their toys when the teacher
    enters.

xxiv

Till Love's one centre devour these
    centres
    Of many self-loves ; and the patriot's
        trick
To better his land by egotist ventures,
    Defamed from a virtue, shall make
        men sick,
As the scalp at the belt of some red hero.

xxv

For certain virtues have dropped to zero,
    Left by the sun on the mountain's
        dewy side ;
Churchman's charities, tender as Nero,
    Indian suttee, heathen suicide,
Service to rights divine, proved hollow :

xxvi

And Heptarchy patriotisms must follow.
    —National voices, distinct yet de-
        pendent,
Ensphering each other, as swallow does
    swallow,
    With circles still widening and ever
        ascendant,
In multiform life to united progression,—

XXVII

These shall remain. And when, in the
   session
   Of nations, the separate language is
    heard,
Each shall aspire, in sublime indiscretion,
   To help with a thought or exalt with
    a word
Less her own than her rival's honour.

XXVIII

Each Christian nation shall take upon her
   The law of the Christian man in vast :
The crown of the getter shall fall to the
   donor,
   And last shall be first while first shall
    be last,
And to love best shall still be, to reign
    unsurpassed.

A CURSE FOR A NATION

PROLOGUE

I HEARD an angel speak last night,
    And he said, ' Write !
Write a Nation's curse for me,
And send it over the Western Sea.'

I faltered, taking up the word :
    ' Not so, my lord !
If curses must be, choose another
To send thy curse against my brother.

' For I am bound by gratitude,
    By love and blood,
To brothers of mine across the sea,
Who stretch out kindly hands to me.'

' Therefore,' the voice said, ' shalt thou
    write
    My curse to-night.
From the summits of love a curse is driven,
As lightning is from the tops of heaven.'

' Not so,' I answered. ' Evermore
    My heart is sore
For my own land's sins : for little feet
Of children bleeding along the street :

' For parked-up honours that gainsay
    The right of way :
For almsgiving through a door that is
Not open enough for two friends to kiss :

' For love of freedom which abates
    Beyond the Straits :
For patriot virtue starved to vice on
Self-praise, self-interest, and suspicion :

' For an oligarchic parliament,
    And bribes well-meant.
What curse to another land assign,
When heavy-souled for the sins of mine ?'

' Therefore,' the voice said, ' shalt thou
    write
    My curse to-night.
Because thou hast strength to see and
    hate
A foul thing done *within* thy gate.'

' Not so,' I answered once again.
    ' To curse, choose men.
For I, a woman, have only known
How the heart melts and the tears run
    down.'

' Therefore,' the voice said, ' shalt thou
    write
    My curse to-night.
Some women weep and curse, I say
(And no one marvels), night and day.

' And thou shalt take their part to-night,
    Weep and write.
A curse from the depths of womanhood
Is very salt, and bitter, and good.'

So thus I wrote, and mourned indeed,
    What all may read.
And thus, as was enjoined on me,
I send it over the Western Sea.

THE CURSE

I

BECAUSE ye have broken your own chain
    With the strain
Of brave men climbing a Nation's height,
Yet thence bear down with brand and
    thong
On souls of others,—for this wrong
    This is the curse.   Write.

Because yourselves are standing straight
            In the state
Of Freedom's foremost acolyte,
Yet keep calm footing all the time
On writhing bond-slaves,—for this crime
            This is the curse.   Write.

Because ye prosper in God's name,
            With a claim
To honour in the old world's sight,
Yet do the fiend's work perfectly
In strangling martyrs,—for this lie
            This is the curse.   Write.

II

Ye shall watch while kings conspire
Round the people's smouldering fire,
            And, warm for your part,
Shall never dare—O shame!
To utter the thought into flame
            Which burns at your heart.
            This is the curse.   Write.

Ye shall watch while nations strive
With the bloodhounds, die or survive,
            Drop faint from their jaws,
Or throttle them backward to death,
And only under your breath
            Shall favour the cause.
            This is the curse.   Write.

Ye shall watch while strong men draw
The nets of feudal law
            To strangle the weak,

And, counting the sin for a sin,
Your soul shall be sadder within
            Than the word ye shall speak.
            This is the curse.   Write.

When good men are praying erect
That Christ may avenge His elect
            And deliver the earth,
The prayer in your ears, said low,
Shall sound like the tramp of a foe
            That's driving you forth.
            This is the curse.   Write.

When wise men give you their praise,
They shall pause in the heat of the phrase,
            As if carried too far.
When ye boast your own charters kept
            true,
Ye shall blush ;—for the thing which ye do
            Derides what ye are.
            This is the curse.   Write.

When fools cast taunts at your gate,
Your scorn ye shall somewhat abate
            As ye look o'er the wall,
For your conscience, tradition, and name
Explode with a deadlier blame
            Than the worst of them all.
            This is the curse.   Write.

Go, wherever ill deeds shall be done,
Go, plant your flag in the sun
            Beside the ill-doers !
And recoil from clenching the curse
Of God's witnessing Universe
            With a curse of yours.
            THIS is the curse.   Write.

LAST POEMS

TO 'GRATEFUL FLORENCE'
TO THE MUNICIPALITY, HER REPRESENTATIVE
AND TO TOMMASEO, ITS SPOKESMAN
MOST GRATEFULLY

ADVERTISEMENT TO THE FIRST EDITION

THESE Poems are given as they occur on a list drawn up last June. A few had already been printed in periodicals.

There is hardly such direct warrant for publishing the Translations; which were only intended, many years ago, to accompany and explain certain Engravings after ancient Gems, in the projected work of a friend, by whose kindness they are now recovered: but as two of the original series (the *Adonis* of Bion, and 'Song of the Rose' from Achilles Tatius) have subsequently appeared, it is presumed that the remainder may not improperly follow.

A single recent version is added.

LONDON, *February*, 1862.

LAST POEMS

LITTLE MATTIE

I

DEAD! Thirteen a month ago!
  Short and narrow her life's walk;
Lover's love she could not know
  Even by a dream or talk:
Too young to be glad of youth,
  Missing honour, labour, rest,
And the warmth of a babe's mouth
  At the blossom of her breast.
Must you pity her for this
And for all the loss it is,
You, her mother, with wet face,
Having had all in your case?

II

Just so young but yesternight,
  Now she is as old as death.
Meek, obedient in your sight,
  Gentle to a beck or breath
Only on last Monday! Yours,
  Answering you like silver bells
Lightly touched! An hour matures:
  You can teach her nothing else.
She has seen the mystery hid
Under Egypt's pyramid:
By those eyelids pale and close
Now she knows what Rhamses knows.

III

Cross her quiet hands, and smooth
  Down her patient locks of silk,
Cold and passive as in truth
  You your fingers in spilt milk
Drew along a marble floor;
  But her lips you cannot wring
Into saying a word more,
  'Yes,' or 'No,' or such a thing:
Though you call and beg and wreak
Half your soul out in a shriek,
She will lie there in default
And most innocent revolt.

IV

Aye, and if she spoke, may be
  She would answer like the Son,
'What is now 'twixt thee and me?'
  Dreadful answer! better none.
Yours on Monday, God's to-day!
  Yours, your child, your blood, your
    heart,
Called .. you called her, did you say,
  'Little Mattie' for your part?
Now already it sounds strange,
And you wonder, in this change,
What He calls His angel-creature,
Higher up than you can reach her.

V

'Twas a green and easy world
  As she took it; room to play
(Though one's hair might get uncurled
  At the far end of the day).
What she suffered she shook off
  In the sunshine; what she sinned
She could pray on high enough
  To keep safe above the wind.
If reproved by God or you,
'Twas to better her, she knew;
And if crossed, she gathered still
'Twas to cross out something ill.

VI

You, you had the right, you thought,
  To survey her with sweet scorn,
Poor gay child, who had not caught
  Yet the octave-stretch forlorn
Of your larger wisdom! Nay,
  Now your places are changed so,
In that same superior way
  She regards you dull and low
As you did herself exempt
From life's sorrows. Grand contempt
Of the spirits risen awhile,
Who look back with such a smile!

VII

There's the sting of 't. That, I think,
  Hurts the most a thousandfold!
To feel sudden, at a wink,
  Some dear child we used to scold,
Praise, love both ways, kiss and tease,
  Teach and tumble as our own,
All its curls about our knees,
  Rise up suddenly full-grown.

Who could wonder such a sight
Made a woman mad outright?
Show me Michael with the sword
Rather than such angels, Lord!

A FALSE STEP

I

Sweet, thou hast trod on a heart.
  Pass! there's a world full of men;
And women as fair as thou art
  Must do such things now and then.

II

Thou only hast stepped unaware,—
  Malice, not one can impute;
And why should a heart have been there
  In the way of a fair woman's foot?

III

It was not a stone that could trip,
  Nor was it a thorn that could rend:
Put up thy proud underlip!
  'Twas merely the heart of a friend.

IV

And yet peradventure one day
  Thou, sitting alone at the glass,
Remarking the bloom gone away,
  Where the smile in its dimplement was,

V

And seeking around thee in vain
  From hundreds who flattered before,
Such a word as, 'Oh, not in the main
  Do I hold thee less precious, but
    more!' ..

VI

Thou'lt sigh, very like, on thy part,
  'Of all I have known or can know,
I wish I had only that Heart
  I trod upon ages ago!'

VOID IN LAW

I

Sleep, little babe, on my knee,
  Sleep, for the midnight is chill,
And the moon has died out in the tree,
  And the great human world goeth ill.
Sleep, for the wicked agree:
  Sleep, let them do as they will.
Sleep.

II

Sleep, thou hast drawn from my breast
    The last drop of milk that was good ;
And now, in a dream, suck the rest,
    Lest the real should trouble thy blood.
Suck, little lips dispossessed,
    As we kiss in the air whom we would.
Sleep.

III

O lips of thy father ! the same,
    So like ! Very deeply they swore
When he gave me his ring and his name,
    To take back, I imagined, no more !
And now is all changed like a game,
    Though the old cards are used as of
        yore ?
Sleep.

IV

' Void in law,' said the Courts.   Some-
        thing wrong
    In the forms ?   Yet, ' Till death part
        us two,
I, James, take thee, Jessie,' was strong,
    And ONE witness competent.   True
Such a marriage was worth an old song,
    Heard in Heaven though, as plain as
        the New.
Sleep.

V

Sleep, little child, his and mine !
    Her throat has the antelope curve,
And her cheek just the colour and line
    Which fade not before him nor swerve :
Yet *she* has no child !—the divine
    Seal of right upon loves that deserve.
Sleep.

VI

My child ! though the world take her part,
    Saying, ' She was the woman to choose,
He had eyes, was a man in his heart,'—
    We twain the decision refuse :
We . . weak as I am, as thou art, . .
    Cling on to him, never to loose.
Sleep.

VII

He thinks that, when done with this
        place,
    All 's ended ? he'll new-stamp the ore ?
Yes, Caesar's—but not in our case.
    Let him learn we are waiting before

The grave's mouth, the heaven's gate,
        God's face,
    With implacable love evermore.
Sleep.

VIII

He 's ours, though he kissed her but now ;
    He 's ours, though she kissed in reply ;
He 's ours, though himself disavow,
    And God's universe favour the lie ;
Ours to claim, ours to clasp, ours below,
    Ours above, . . if we live, if we die.
Sleep.

IX

Ah, baby, my baby, too rough
    Is my lullaby ?   What have I said ?
Sleep !   When I've wept long enough
    I shall learn to weep softly instead,
And piece with some alien stuff
    My heart to lie smooth for thy head.
Sleep.

X

Two souls met upon thee, my sweet ;
    Two loves led thee out to the sun :
Alas, pretty hands, pretty feet,
    If the one who remains (only one)
Set her grief at thee, turned in a heat
    To thine enemy,—were it well done ?
Sleep.

XI

May He of the manger stand near
    And love thee !   An infant He came
To His own who rejected Him here,
    But the Magi brought gifts all the same.
I hurry the cross on my Dear !
    My gifts are the griefs I declaim !
Sleep.

LORD WALTER'S WIFE

I

' BUT why do you go,' said the lady,
        while both sate under the yew,
And her eyes were alive in their depth,
        as the kraken beneath the sea-
        blue.

II

' Because I fear you,' he answered ;—
        ' because you are far too fair,
And able to strangle my soul in a mesh
        of your gold-coloured hair.'

III

'Oh, that,' she said, 'is no reason!
    Such knots are quickly undone,
And too much beauty, I reckon, is
    nothing but too much sun.'

IV

'Yet farewell so,' he answered ;—'the
    sunstroke's fatal at times.
I value your husband, Lord Walter,
    whose gallop rings still from the
    limes.'

V

'Oh, that,' she said, 'is no reason.
    You smell a rose through a fence :
If two should smell it, what matter?
    who grumbles, and where's the
    pretence ?'

VI

'But I,' he replied, 'have promised
    another, when love was free,
To love her alone, alone, who alone
    and afar loves me.'

VII

'Why, that,' she said, 'is no reason.
    Love's always free, I am told.
Will you vow to be safe from the head-
    ache on Tuesday, and think it
    will hold?'

VIII

'But you,' he replied, 'have a
    daughter, a young little child,
    who was laid
In your lap to be pure ; so I leave you:
    the angels would make me afraid.'

IX

'Oh, that,' she said, 'is no reason.
    The angels keep out of the way ;
And Dora, the child, observes nothing,
    although you should please me
    and stay.'

X

At which he rose up in his anger,—
    'Why, now, you no longer are
    fair !
Why, now, you no longer are fatal, but
    ugly and hateful, I swear.'

XI

At which she laughed out in her scorn.—
    'These men ! Oh, these men over-
    nice,
Who are shocked if a colour not virtuous,
    is frankly put on by a vice.'

XII

Her eyes blazed upon him—'And *you !*
    You bring us your vices so near
That we smell them ! You think in our
    presence a thought 'twould de-
    fame us to hear !

XIII

'What reason had you, and what right,
    —I appeal to your soul from my
    life,—
To find me too fair as a woman ? Why,
    sir, I am pure, and a wife.

XIV

'Is the day-star too fair up above you?
    It burns you not. Dare you imply
I brushed you more close than the star
    does, when Walter had set me as
    high ?

XV

'If a man finds a woman too fair, he
    means simply adapted too much
To uses unlawful and fatal. The praise !
    — shall I thank you for such ?

XVI

'Too fair ?—not unless you misuse us !
    and surely if, once in a while,
You attain to it, straightway you call us
    no longer too fair, but too vile.

XVII

'A moment,—I pray your attention !—I
    have a poor word in my head
I must utter, though womanly custom
    would set it down better unsaid.

XVIII

'You grew, sir, pale to impertinence,
    once when I showed you a ring.
You kissed my fan when I dropped it.
    No matter !—I've broken the
    thing.

XIX

'You did me the honour, perhaps, to be
    moved at my side now and then
In the senses—a vice, I have heard,
    which is common to beasts and
    some men.

XX

'Love's a virtue for heroes!—as white
    as the snow on high hills,
And immortal as every great soul is that
    struggles, endures, and fulfils.

XXI

'I love my Walter profoundly,—you,
    Maude, though you faltered a
    week,
For the sake of . . what was it? an eye-
    brow? or, less still, a mole on a
    cheek?

XXII

'And since, when all's said, you're too
    noble to stoop to the frivolous cant
About crimes irresistible, virtues that
    swindle, betray and supplant,

XXIII

'I determined to prove to yourself that,
    whate'er you might dream or avow
By illusion, you wanted precisely no
    more of me than you have now.

XXIV

'There! Look me full in the face!—in
    the face. Understand, if you can,
That the eyes of such women as I am,
    are clean as the palm of a man.

XXV

'Drop his hand, you insult him. Avoid
    us for fear we should cost you
    a scar—
You take us for harlots, I tell you, and
    not for the women we are.

XXVI

'You wronged me: but then I con-
    sidered . . . there's Walter! And
    so at the end,
I vowed that he should not be mulcted,
    by me, in the hand of a friend.

XXVII

'Have I hurt you indeed? We are quits
    then. Nay, friend of my Walter,
    be mine!
Come Dora, my darling, my angel, and
    help me to ask him to dine.'

BIANCA AMONG THE NIGHTIN-GALES

I

THE cypress stood up like a church
    That night we felt our love would hold,
And saintly moonlight seemed to search
    And wash the whole world clean as
    gold;
The olives crystallized the vales'
    Broad slopes until the hills grew strong:
The fireflies and the nightingales
    Throbbed each to either, flame and
    song.
The nightingales, the nightingales.

II

Upon the angle of its shade
    The cypress stood, self-balanced high;
Half up, half down, as double-made,
    Along the ground, against the sky.
And we, too! from such soul-height went
    Such leaps of blood, so blindly driven,
We scarce knew if our nature meant
    Most passionate earth or intense
    heaven.
The nightingales, the nightingales.

III

We paled with love, we shook with love,
    We kissed so close we could not vow;
Till Giulio whispered, 'Sweet, above
    God's Ever guarantees this Now.'
And through his words the nightingales
    Drove straight and full their long clear
    call,
Like arrows through heroic mails,
    And love was awful in it all.
The nightingales, the nightingales.

IV

O cold white moonlight of the north,
    Refresh these pulses, quench this hell!
O coverture of death drawn forth
    Across this garden-chamber . . well!

But what have nightingales to do
    In gloomy England, called the free . .
(Yes, free to die in ! . .) when we two
    Are sundered, singing still to me ?
And still they sing, the nightingales.

v

I think I hear him, how he cried
    ' My own soul's life ' between their
        notes.
Each man has but one soul supplied,
    And that 's immortal.   Though his
        throat 's
On fire with passion now, to *her*
    He can't say what to me he said !
And yet he moves her, they aver.
    The nightingales sing through my head,
The nightingales, the nightingales.

vi

He says to *her* what moves her most.
    He would not name his soul within
Her hearing,—rather pays her cost
    With praises to her lips and chin.
Man has but one soul, 'tis ordained,
    And each soul but one love, I add ;
Yet souls are damned and love 's profaned.
    These nightingales will sing me mad !
The nightingales, the nightingales.

vii

I marvel how the birds can sing.
    There 's little difference, in their view,
Betwixt our Tuscan trees that spring
    As vital flames into the blue,
And dull round blots of foliage meant
    Like saturated sponges here
To suck the fogs up.   As content
    Is *he* too in this land, 'tis clear.
And still they sing, the nightingales.

viii

My native Florence ! dear, forgone !
    I see across the Alpine ridge
How the last feast-day of Saint John
    Shot rockets from Carraia bridge.
The luminous city, tall with fire,
    Trod deep down in that river of ours,
While many a boat with lamp and choir
    Skimmed birdlike over glittering
        towers.
I will not hear these nightingales.

ix

I seem to float, *we* seem to float
    Down Arno's stream in festive guise ;
A boat strikes flame into our boat,
    And up that lady seems to rise
As then she rose.   The shock had flashed
    A vision on us !   What a head,
What leaping eyeballs !—beauty dashed
    To splendour by a sudden dread.
And still they sing, the nightingales.

x

Too bold to sin, too weak to die ;
    Such women are so.   As for me,
I would we had drowned there, he and I,
    That moment, loving perfectly.
He had not caught her with her loosed
    Gold ringlets . . rarer in the south . .
Nor heard the ' Grazie tanto ' bruised
    To sweetness by her English mouth.
And still they sing, the nightingales.

xi

She had not reached him at my heart
    With her fine tongue, as snakes indeed
Kill flies ; nor had I, for my part,
    Yearned after, in my desperate need,
And followed him as he did her
    To coasts left bitter by the tide,
Whose very nightingales, elsewhere
    Delighting, torture and deride !
For still they sing, the nightingales.

xii

A worthless woman ! mere cold clay
    As all false things are ! but so fair,
She takes the breath of men away
    Who gaze upon her unaware.
I would not play her larcenous tricks
    To have her looks ! She lied and stole,
And spat into my love's pure pyx
    The rank saliva of her soul.
And still they sing, the nightingales.

xiii

I would not for her white and pink,
    Though such he likes—her grace of
        limb,
Though such he has praised—nor yet,
        I think,
    For life itself, though spent with him,

Commit such sacrilege, affront
  God's nature which is love, intrude
'Twixt two affianced souls, and hunt
  Like spiders, in the altar's wood.
I cannot bear these nightingales.

XIV

If she chose sin, some gentler guise
  She might have sinned in, so it seems :
She might have pricked out both my eyes,
  And I still seen him in my dreams !
—Or drugged me in my soup or wine,
  Nor left me angry afterward :
To die here with his hand in mine
  His breath upon me, were not hard.
(Our Lady hush these nightingales !)

XV

But set a springe for *him*, ' mio ben,'
  My only good, my first last love !—
Though Christ knows well what sin is, when
  He sees some things done they must move
Himself to wonder.   Let her pass.
  I think of her by night and day.
Must *I* too join her . . out, alas ! . .
  With Giulio, in each word I say ?
And evermore the nightingales !

XVI

Giulio, my Giulio !—sing they so,
  And you be silent ?   Do I speak,
And you not hear ?   An arm you throw
  Round some one, and I feel so weak ?
—Oh, owl-like birds ! They sing for spite,
  They sing for hate, they sing for doom !
They'll sing through death who sing through night,
  They'll sing and stun me in the tomb—
The nightingales, the nightingales !

MY KATE

I

SHE was not as pretty as women I know,
And yet all your best made of sunshine and snow
Drop to shade, melt to nought in the long-trodden ways,
While she 's still remembered on warm and cold days—
                    My Kate.

II

Her air had a meaning, her movements a grace ;
You turned from the fairest to gaze on her face :
And when you had once seen her forehead and mouth,
You saw as distinctly her soul and her truth—
                    My Kate.

III

Such a blue inner light from her eyelids outbroke,
You looked at her silence and fancied she spoke :
When she did, so peculiar yet soft was the tone,
Though the loudest spoke also, you heard her alone—
                    My Kate.

IV

I doubt if she said to you much that could act
As a thought or suggestion : she did not attract
In the sense of the brilliant or wise : I infer
'Twas her thinking of others, made you think of her—
                    My Kate.

V

She never found fault with you, never implied
Your wrong by her right ; and yet men at her side
Grew nobler, girls purer, as through the whole town
The children were gladder that pulled at her gown—
                    My Kate.

VI

None knelt at her feet confessed lovers in thrall ;
They knelt more to God than they used, —that was all :
If you praised her as charming, some asked what you meant,
But the charm of her presence was felt when she went—
                    My Kate.

VII

The weak and the gentle, the ribald and
    rude,
She took as she found them, and did
    them all good ;
It always was so with her—see what
    you have !
She has made the grass greener even
    here . . with her grave—
                My Kate.

VIII

My dear one !—when thou wast alive
    with the rest,
I held thee the sweetest and loved thee
    the best :
And now thou art dead, shall I not take
    thy part
As thy smiles used to do for thyself, my
    sweet Heart—
                My Kate ?

A SONG FOR THE RAGGED
SCHOOLS OF LONDON

WRITTEN IN ROME

I

I AM listening here in Rome.
    ' England's strong,' say many speakers,
' If she winks, the Czar must come,
    Prow and topsail, to the breakers.'

II

' England 's rich in coal and oak,'
    Adds a Roman, getting moody,
' If she shakes a travelling cloak,
    Down our Appian roll the scudi.'

III

' England 's righteous,' they rejoin,
    ' Who shall grudge her exaltations,
When her wealth of golden coin
    Works the welfare of the nations ? '

IV

I am listening here in Rome.
    Over Alps a voice is sweeping—
' England 's cruel ! save us some
    Of these victims in her keeping ! '

V

As the cry beneath the wheel
    Of an old triumphal Roman
Cleft the people's shouts like steel,
    While the show was spoilt for no man,

VI

Comes that voice.   Let others shout,
    Other poets praise my land here :
I am sadly sitting out,
    Praying, ' God forgive her grandeur.'

VII

Shall we boast of empire, where
    Time with ruin sits commissioned ?
In God's liberal blue air
    Peter's dome itself looks wizened ;

VIII

And the mountains, in disdain,
    Gather back their lights of opal
From the dumb, despondent plain,
    Heaped with jawbones of a people.

IX

Lordly English, think it o'er,
    Caesar's doing is all undone !
You have cannons on your shore,
    And free parliaments in London,

X

Princes' parks, and merchants' homes,
    Tents for soldiers, ships for seamen,—
Aye, but ruins worse than Rome's
    In your pauper men and women.

XI

Women leering through the gas
    (Just such bosoms used to nurse you),
Men, turned wolves by famine—pass !
    Those can speak themselves, and curse
    you.

XII

But these others—children small,
    Spilt like blots about the city,
Quay, and street, and palace-wall—
    Take them up into your pity !

XIII

Ragged children with bare feet,
    Whom the angels in white raiment
Know the names of, to repeat
    When they come on you for payment.

XIV

Ragged children, hungry-eyed,
    Huddled up out of the coldness
On your doorsteps, side by side,
    Till your footman damns their boldness.

XV

In the alleys, in the squares,
  Begging, lying little rebels ;
In the noisy thoroughfares,
  Struggling on with piteous trebles.

XVI

Patient children—think what pain
  Makes a young child patient—ponder!
Wronged too commonly to strain
  After right, or wish, or wonder.

XVII

Wicked children, with peaked chins,
  And old foreheads ! there are many
With no pleasures except sins,
  Gambling with a stolen penny.

XVIII

Sickly children, that whine low
  To themselves and not their mothers,
From mere habit,—never so
  Hoping help or care from others.

XIX

Healthy children, with those blue
  English eyes, fresh from their Maker,
Fierce and ravenous, staring through
  At the brown loaves of the baker.

XX

I am listening here in Rome,
  And the Romans are confessing,
' English children pass in bloom
  All the prettiest made for blessing.

XXI

' *Angli angeli!* ' (resumed
  From the mediaeval story)
' Such rose angelhoods, emplumed
  In such ringlets of pure glory ! '

XXII

Can we smooth down the bright hair,
  O my sisters, calm, unthrilled in
Our heart's pulses ? Can we bear
  The sweet looks of our own children,

XXIII

While those others, lean and small,
  Scurf and mildew of the city,
Spot our streets, convict us all
  Till we take them into pity ?

XXIV

' Is it our fault ? ' you reply,
  ' When, throughout civilization,
Every nation's empery
  Is asserted by starvation ?

XXV

' All these mouths we cannot feed,
  And we cannot clothe these bodies.'
Well, if man 's so hard indeed,
  Let them learn at least what God is !

XXVI

Little outcasts from life's fold,
  The grave's hope they may be joined in,
By Christ's covenant consoled
  For our social contract's grinding.

XXVII

If no better can be done,
  Let us do but this,—endeavour
That the sun behind the sun
  Shine upon them while they shiver !

XXVIII

On the dismal London flags,
  Through the cruel social juggle,
Put a thought beneath their rags
  To ennoble the heart's struggle.

XXIX

O my sisters, not so much
  Are we asked for—not a blossom
From our children's nosegay, such
  As we gave it from our bosom,—

XXX

Not the milk left in their cup,
  Not the lamp while they are sleeping,
Not the little cloak hung up
  While the coat 's in daily keeping,—

XXXI

But a place in RAGGED SCHOOLS,
  Where the outcasts may to-morrow
Learn by gentle words and rules
  Just the uses of their sorrow.

XXXII

O my sisters ! children small,
  Blue-eyed, wailing through the city—
Our own babes cry in them all :
  Let us take them into pity.

MAY'S LOVE

I

You love all, you say,
  Round, beneath, above me :
Find me then some way
  Better than to love me,
Me, too, dearest May!

II

O world-kissing eyes
  Which the blue heavens melt to !
I, sad, overwise,
  Loathe the sweet looks dealt to
All things—men and flies.

III

You love all, you say :
  Therefore, Dear, abate me
Just your love, I pray !
  Shut your eyes and hate me—
Only *me*—fair May !

AMY'S CRUELTY

I

FAIR Amy of the terraced house,
  Assist me to discover
Why you who would not hurt a mouse
  Can torture so your lover.

II

You give your coffee to the cat,
  You stroke the dog for coming,
And all your face grows kinder at
  The little brown bee's humming.

III

But when *he* haunts your door .. the town
  Marks coming and marks going ..
You seem to have stitched your eyelids
    down
  To that long piece of sewing !

IV

You never give a look, not you,
  Nor drop him a ' Good morning,'
To keep his long day warm and blue,
  So fretted by your scorning.

V

She shook her head—' The mouse and
    bee
  For crumb or flower will linger :
The dog is happy at my knee,
  The cat purrs at my finger.

VI

' But *he* .. to *him*, the least thing given
  Means great things at a distance ;
He wants my world, my sun, my heaven,
  Soul, body, whole existence.

VII

' They say love gives as well as takes ;
  But I'm a simple maiden,—
My mother's first smile when she wakes
  I still have smiled and prayed in.

VIII

' I only know my mother's love
  Which gives all and asks nothing;
And this new loving sets the groove
  Too much the way of loathing.

IX

' Unless he gives me all in change,
  I forfeit all things by him :
The risk is terrible and strange—
  I tremble, doubt, .. deny him.

X

' He's sweetest friend, or hardest foe,
  Best angel, or worst devil ;
I either hate or .. love him so,
  I can't be merely civil !

XI

' You trust a woman who puts forth,
  Her blossoms thick as summer's ?
You think she dreams what love is worth,
  Who casts it to new-comers ?

XII

' Such love 's a cowslip-ball to fling,
  A moment's pretty pastime ;
I give .. all me, if anything,
  The first time and the last time.

XIII

' Dear neighbour of the trellised house,
  A man should murmur never,
Though treated worse than dog and
    mouse,
  Till doted on for ever !'

MY HEART AND I

I

ENOUGH ! we're tired, my heart and I.
  We sit beside the headstone thus,
  And wish that name were carved for us.
The moss reprints more tenderly
  The hard types of the mason's knife,
  As heaven's sweet life renews earth's
    life
With which we're tired, my heart and I.

II

You see we're tired, my heart and I.
  We dealt with books, we trusted men,
  And in our own blood drenched the
    pen,
As if such colours could not fly.
  We walked too straight for fortune's
    end,
  We loved too true to keep a friend ;
At last we're tired, my heart and I.

III

How tired we feel, my heart and I !
  We seem of no use in the world ;
  Our fancies hang grey and uncurled
About men's eyes indifferently ;
  Our voice which thrilled you so, will
    let
  You sleep ; our tears are only wet :
What do we here, my heart and I ?

IV

So tired, so tired, my heart and I !
  It was not thus in that old time
  When Ralph sate with me 'neath the
    lime
To watch the sunset from the sky.
  'Dear love, you're looking tired,' he
    said ;
  I, smiling at him, shook my head :
'Tis now we're tired, my heart and I.

V

So tired, so tired, my heart and I !
  Though now none takes me on his arm
  To fold me close and kiss me warm
Till each quick breath end in a sigh
  Of happy languor. Now, alone,
  We lean upon this graveyard stone,
Uncheered, unkissed, my heart and I.

VI

Tired out we are, my heart and I.
  Suppose the world brought diadems
  To tempt us, crusted with loose gems
Of powers and pleasures ? Let it try.
  We scarcely care to look at even
  A pretty child, or God's blue heaven,
We feel so tired, my heart and I.

VII

Yet who complains ? My heart and I ?
  In this abundant earth no doubt
  Is little room for things worn out :
Disdain them, break them, throw them by.
  And if before the days grew rough
  We *once* were loved, used,—well
    enough,
I think, we've fared, my heart and I.

THE BEST THING IN THE WORLD

WHAT 's the best thing in the world ?
June-rose, by May-dew impearled ;
Sweet south-wind, that means no rain ;
Truth, not cruel to a friend ;
Pleasure, not in haste to end ;
Beauty, not self-decked and curled
Till its pride is over-plain ;
Light, that never makes you wink ;
Memory, that gives no pain ;
Love, when, *so*, you're loved again.
What 's the best thing in the world ?
—Something out of it, I think.

WHERE 'S AGNES ?

I

NAY, if I had come back so,
  And found her dead in her grave,
And if a friend I know
  Had said, ' Be strong, nor rave :
She lies there, dead below :

II

' I saw her, I who speak,
  White, stiff, the face one blank :
The blue shade came to her cheek
  Before they nailed the plank,
For she had been dead a week.'

III

Why, if he had spoken so,
  I might have believed the thing,
Although her look, although
  Her step, laugh, voice's ring
Lived in me still as they do.

IV

But dead that other way,
  Corrupted thus and lost?
That sort of worm in the clay?
  I cannot count the cost,
That I should rise and pay.

V

My Agnes false? such shame?
  She? Rather be it said
That the pure saint of her name
  Has stood there in her stead,
And tricked you to this blame.

VI

Her very gown, her cloak
  Fell chastely: no disguise,
But expression! while she broke
  With her clear grey morning-eyes
Full upon me and then spoke.

VII

She wore her hair away
  From her forehead,—like a cloud
Which a little wind in May
  Peels off finely: disallowed
Though bright enough to stay.

VIII

For the heavens must have the place
  To themselves, to use and shine in
As her soul would have her face
  To press through upon mine, in
That orb of angel grace.

IX

Had she any fault at all,
  'Twas having none, I thought too—
There seemed a sort of thrall;
  As she felt her shadow ought to
Fall straight upon the wall.

X

Her sweetness strained the sense
  Of common life and duty;
And every day's expense
  Of moving in such beauty
Required, almost, defence.

XI

What good, I thought, is done
  By such sweet things, if any?
This world smells ill i' the sun
  Though the garden-flowers are
    many,—
She is only one.

XII

Can a voice so low and soft
  Take open actual part
With Right,—maintain aloft
  Pure truth in life or art,
Vexed always, wounded oft?—

XIII

She fit, with that fair pose
  Which melts from curve to curve,
To stand, run, work with those
  Who wrestle and deserve,
And speak plain without glose?

XIV

But I turned round on my fear
  Defiant, disagreeing—
What if God has set her here
  Less for action than for Being?—
For the eye and for the ear.

XV

Just to show what beauty may,
  Just to prove what music can,—
And then to die away
  From the presence of a man,
Who shall learn, henceforth, to pray?

XVI

As a door, left half ajar
  In heaven, would make him think
How heavenly-different are
  Things glanced at through the chink,
Till he pined from near to far.

XVII

That door could lead to hell?
  That shining merely meant
Damnation? What! She fell
  Like a woman, who was sent
Like an angel, by a spell?

XVIII

She, who scarcely trod the earth,
  Turned mere dirt? My Agnes,—mine!
Called so! felt of too much worth
  To be used so! too divine
To be breathed near, and so forth!

XIX

Why, I dared not name a sin
    In her presence : I went round,
Clipped its name and shut it in
    Some mysterious crystal sound,—
Changed the dagger for the pin.

XX

Now you name herself *that word?*
    O my Agnes! O my saint!
Then the great joys of the Lord
    Do not last? Then all this paint
Runs off nature? leaves a board?

XXI

Who's dead here? No, not she :
    Rather I! or whence this damp
Cold corruption's misery?
    While my very mourners stamp
Closer in the clods on me.

XXII

And my mouth is full of dust
    Till I cannot speak and curse—
Speak and damn him . . 'Blame's
        unjust'?
    Sin blots out the universe,
All because she would and must?

XXIII

She, my white rose, dropping off
    The high rose-tree branch! and not
That the night-wind blew too rough,
    Or the noon-sun burnt too hot,
But, that being a rose—'twas enough!

XXIV

Then henceforth, may earth grow trees!
    No more roses!—hard straight lines
To score lies out! none of these
    Fluctuant curves! but firs and pines,
Poplars, cedars, cypresses!

DE PROFUNDIS

I

THE face which, duly as the sun,
Rose up for me with life begun,
To mark all bright hours of the day
With hourly love, is dimmed away,—
And yet my days go on, go on.

II

The tongue which, like a stream, could run
Smooth music from the roughest stone,
And every morning with 'Good day'
Make each day good, is hushed away,—
And yet my days go on, go on.

III

The heart which, like a staff, was one
For mine to lean and rest upon,
The strongest on the longest day
With steadfast love, is caught away,—
And yet my days go on, go on.

IV

And cold before my summer's done,
And deaf in Nature's general tune,
And fallen too low for special fear,
And here, with hope no longer here,—
While the tears drop, my days go on.

V

The world goes whispering to its own,
'This anguish pierces to the bone';
And tender friends go sighing round,
'What love can ever cure this wound?'
My days go on, my days go on.

VI

The past rolls forward on the sun
And makes all night. O dreams begun,
Not to be ended! Ended bliss,
And life that will not end in this!
My days go on, my days go on.

VII

Breath freezes on my lips to moan :
As one alone, once not alone,
I sit and knock at Nature's door,
Heart-bare, heart-hungry, very poor,
Whose desolated days go on.

VIII

I knock and cry,—Undone, undone!
Is there no help, no comfort,—none?
No gleaning in the wide wheat-plains
Where others drive their loaded wains?
My vacant days go on, go on.

IX

This Nature, though the snows be down,
Thinks kindly of the bird of June :
The little red hip on the tree
Is ripe for such. What is for me,
Whose days so winterly go on?

X

No bird am I, to sing in June,
And dare not ask an equal boon.
Good nests and berries red are Nature's
To give away to better creatures,—
And yet my days go on, go on.

XI

I ask less kindness to be done,—
Only to loose these pilgrim-shoon
(Too early worn and grimed), with sweet
Cool deathly touch to these tired feet,
Till days go out which now go on.

XII

Only to lift the turf unmown
From off the earth where it has grown,
Some cubit-space, and say, ' Behold,
Creep in, poor Heart, beneath that fold,
Forgetting how the days go on.'

XIII

What harm would that do ? Green anon
The sward would quicken, overshone
By skies as blue ; and crickets might
Have leave to chirp there day and night
While my new rest went on, went on.

XIV

From gracious Nature have I won
Such liberal bounty ? may I run
So, lizard-like, within her side,
And there be safe, who now am tried
By days that painfully go on ?

XV

—A Voice reproves me thereupon,
More sweet than Nature's when the drone
Of bees is sweetest, and more deep
Than when the rivers overleap
The shuddering pines, and thunder on.

XVI

God's Voice, not Nature's ! Night and
        noon
He sits upon the great white throne
And listens for the creatures' praise.
What babble we of days and days ?
The Dayspring He, whose days go on.

XVII

He reigns above, He reigns alone ;
Systems burn out and leave His throne :
Fair mists of seraphs melt and fall
Around Him, changeless amid all,—
Ancient of Days, whose days go on.

XVIII

He reigns below, He reigns alone,
And, having life in love forgone
Beneath the crown of sovran thorns,
He reigns the Jealous God. Who
        mourns
Or rules with Him, while days go on ?

XIX

By anguish which made pale the sun,
I hear Him charge His saints that
        none
Among His creatures anywhere
Blaspheme against Him with despair,
However darkly days go on.

XX

Take from my head the thorn-wreath
        brown !
No mortal grief deserves that crown.
O súpreme Love, chief Misery,
The sharp regalia are for THEE
Whose days eternally go on !

XXI

For us,—whatever 's undergone,
Thou knowest, willest what is done.
Grief may be joy misunderstood ;
Only the Good discerns the good.
I trust Thee while my days go on.

XXII

Whatever 's lost, it first was won :
We will not struggle nor impugn.
Perhaps the cup was broken here,
That Heaven's new wine might show
        more clear.
I praise Thee while my days go on.

XXIII

I praise Thee while my days go on ;
I love Thee while my days go on :
Through dark and dearth, through fire
        and frost,
With emptied arms and treasure lost,
I thank Thee while my days go on.

XXIV

And having in Thy life-depth thrown
Being and suffering (which are one),
As a child drops his pebble small
Down some deep well, and hears it fall
Smiling—so I. THY DAYS GO ON.

A MUSICAL INSTRUMENT

I

WHAT was he doing, the great god Pan,
  Down in the reeds by the river?
Spreading ruin and scattering ban,
Splashing and paddling with hoofs of
    a goat,
And breaking the golden lilies afloat
  With the dragon-fly on the river.

II

He tore out a reed, the great god Pan,
  From the deep cool bed of the river:
The limpid water turbidly ran,
And the broken lilies a-dying lay,
And the dragon-fly had fled away,
  Ere he brought it out of the river.

III

High on the shore sate the great god Pan,
  While turbidly flowed the river;
And hacked and hewed as a great god can,
With his hard bleak steel at the patient
    reed,
Till there was not a sign of a leaf indeed
  To prove it fresh from the river.

IV

He cut it short, did the great god Pan
  (How tall it stood in the river!),
Then drew the pith, like the heart of
    a man,
Steadily from the outside ring,
And notched the poor dry empty thing
  In holes, as he sate by the river.

V

'This is the way,' laughed the great
    god Pan
  (Laughed while he sate by the river),
'The only way, since gods began
To make sweet music, they could suc-
    ceed.'
Then, dropping his mouth to a hole in
    the reed,
  He blew in power by the river.

VI

Sweet, sweet, sweet, O Pan!
  Piercing sweet by the river!
Blinding sweet, O great god Pan!
The sun on the hill forgot to die,
And the lilies revived, and the dragon-fly
  Came back to dream on the river.

VII

Yet half a beast is the great god Pan,
  To laugh as he sits by the river,
Making a poet out of a man:
The true gods sigh for the cost and
    pain,—
For the reed which grows nevermore
    again
  As a reed with the reeds in the river.

FIRST NEWS FROM VILLA-FRANCA

I

PEACE, peace, peace, do you say?
  What!—with the enemy's guns in our
    ears?
  With the country's wrong not rendered
    back?
What!—while Austria stands at bay
  In Mantua, and our Venice bears
    The cursed flag of the yellow and black?

II

Peace, peace, peace, do you say?
  And this the Mincio? Where's the fleet,
  And where's the sea? Are we all blind
Or mad with the blood shed yesterday,
  Ignoring Italy under our feet,
  And seeing things before, behind?

III

Peace, peace, peace, do you say?
  What!—uncontested, undenied?
  Because we triumph, we succumb?
A pair of Emperors stand in the way
  (One of whom is a man, beside),
  To sign and seal our cannons dumb?

IV

No, not Napoleon!—he who mused
  At Paris, and at Milan spake,
  And at Solferino led the fight:
Not he we trusted, honoured, used
  Our hopes and hearts for . . till they
    break—
  Even so, you tell us . . in his sight.

V

Peace, peace, is still your word?
  We say you lie then!—that is plain.
  There *is* no peace, and shall be none.

Our very Dead would cry ' Absurd ! '
  And clamour that they died in vain,
  And whine to come back to the sun.

VI

Hush ! more reverence for the Dead !
  They've done the most for Italy
  Evermore since the earth was fair.
Now would that *we* had died instead,
  Still dreaming peace meant liberty,
  And did not, could not mean despair.

VII

Peace, you say ?—yes, peace, in truth !
  But such a peace as the ear can achieve
  'Twixt the rifle's click and the rush of
    the ball,
'Twixt the tiger's spring and the crunch
    of the tooth,
  'Twixt the dying atheist's negative
  And God's Face—waiting, after all !

KING VICTOR EMANUEL ENTER-ING FLORENCE, APRIL, 1860

I

KING of us all, we cried to thee, cried to
    thee,
  Trampled to earth by the beasts impure,
  Dragged by the chariots which shame
    as they roll :
The dust of our torment far and wide to
    thee
  Went up, dark'ning thy royal soul.
    Be witness, Cavour,
That the King was sad for the people in
    thrall,
    This King of us all!

II

King, we cried to thee ! Strong in re-
    plying,
  Thy word and thy sword sprang rapid
    and sure,
  Cleaving our way to a nation's place.
Oh, first soldier of Italy !—crying
  Now grateful, exultant, we look in
    thy face.
    Be witness, Cavour,
That, freedom's first soldier, the freed
    should call
    First King of them all!

III

This is our beautiful Italy's birthday ;
  High-thoughted souls, whether many
    or fewer,
  Bring her the gift, and wish her the
    good,
While Heaven presents on this sunny
    earth-day
  The noble king to the land renewed :
    Be witness, Cavour !
Roar, cannon-mouths ! Proclaim, install
    The King of us all !

IV

Grave he rides through the Florence
    gateway,
  Clenching his face into calm, to im-
    mure
  His struggling heart till it half dis-
    appears ;
If he relaxed for a moment, straightway
  He would break out into passionate
    tears—
    (Be witness, Cavour !)
While rings the cry without interval,
    ' Live, King of us all ! '

V

Cry, free peoples ! Honour the nation
  By crowning the true man—and none
    is truer :
  Pisa is here, and Livorno is here,
And thousands of faces, in wild exulta-
    tion,
  Burn over the windows to feel him
    near—
    (Be witness, Cavour !)
Burn over from terrace, roof, window,
    and wall,
    On this King of us all.

VI

Grave ! A good man 's ever the graver
  For bearing a nation's trust secure ;
  And *he*, he thinks of the Heart, beside,
Which broke for Italy, failing to save her,
  And pining away by Oporto's tide :
    Be witness, Cavour,
That he thinks of his vow on that royal
    pall,
    This King of us all.

VII

Flowers, flowers, from the flowery city!
  Such innocent thanks for a deed so
    pure,
  As, melting away for joy into flowers,
The nation invites him to enter his Pitti
  And evermore reign in this Florence
    of ours.
      Be witness, Cavour!
He'll stand where the reptiles were used
    to crawl,
      This King of us all.

VIII

Grave, as the manner of noble men is—
  Deeds unfinished will weigh on the
    doer :
  And, baring his head to those crape-
    veiled flags,
He bows to the grief of the South and
    Venice.
  Oh, riddle the last of the yellow to rags,
    And swear by Cavour
That the King shall reign where the
    tyrants fall,
      True King of us all !

THE SWORD OF CASTRUCCIO
CASTRACANI

Questa è per me.—KING VICTOR EMANUEL.

I

WHEN Victor Emanuel the King,
  Went down to his Lucca that day,
The people, each vaunting the thing
  As he gave it, gave all things away,—
  In a burst of fierce gratitude, say,
As they tore out their hearts for the king.

II

—Gave the green forest-walk on the
    wall,
  With the Apennine blue through the
    trees ;
Gave the palaces, churches, and all
  The great pictures which burn out of
    these :
  But the eyes of the King seemed to
    freeze
As he glanced upon ceiling and wall.

III

'Good,' said the King as he passed.
  Was he cold to the arts ?—or else coy
To possession ? or crossed, at the last
  (Whispered some), by the vote in
    Savoy ?
Shout! Love him enough for his joy!
'Good,' said the King as he passed.

IV

He, travelling the whole day through
    flowers
  And protesting amenities, found
At Pistoia, betwixt the two showers
  Of red roses, the ' Orphans ' (renowned
  As the heirs of Puccini), who wound
With a sword through the crowd and
    the flowers.

V

' 'Tis the sword of Castruccio, O King,—
  In that strife of intestinal hate,
Very famous! Accept what we bring,
  We who cannot be sons, by our fate,
  Rendered citizens by thee of late,
And endowed with a country and king.

VI

'Read! Puccini has willed that this sword
  (Which once made in an ignorant feud
Many orphans) remain in our ward
  Till some patriot its pure civic blood
  Wipe away in the foe's and make good,
In delivering the land by the sword.'

VII

Then the King exclaimed, 'This is for
    me !'
  And he dashed out his hand on the hilt,
While his blue eye shot fire openly,
  And his heart overboiled till it spilt
  A hot prayer,—'God! the rest as
    Thou wilt !
But grant me this !—*This* is for *me*.'

VIII

O Victor Emanuel, the King,
  The sword be for *thee*, and the deed,
And nought for the alien, next spring,
  Nought for Hapsburg and Bourbon
    agreed—
  But, for us, a great Italy freed,
With a hero to head us,—our King !

SUMMING UP IN ITALY

(INSCRIBED TO INTELLIGENT
PUBLICS OUT OF IT)

I

Observe how it will be at last,
  When our Italy stands at full stature,
A year ago tied down so fast
  That the cord cut the quick of her
    nature!
You'll honour the deed and its scope,
  Then, in logical sequence upon it,
Will use up the remnants of rope
  By hanging the men who have done it.

II

The speech in the Commons, which hits
    you
  A sketch off, how dungeons must feel,—
The official dispatch, which commits you
  From stamping out groans with your
    heel,—
Suggestions in journal or book for
  Good efforts,—are praised as is meet:
But what in this world can men look for,
  Who only achieve and complete?

III

True, you've praise for the fireman who
    sets his
  Brave face to the axe of the flame,
Disappears in the smoke, and then fetches
  A babe down, or idiot that 's lame,—
For the boor even, who rescues through
    pity
  A sheep from the brute who would
    kick it:
But saviours of nations!—'tis pretty,
  And doubtful: they *may* be so wicked:

IV

Azeglio, Farini, Mamiani,
  Ricasoli,—doubt by the dozen!—
    here 's
Pepoli too, and Cipriani,
  Imperial cousins and cozeners—
Arese, Laiatico,—courtly
  Of manners, if stringent of mouth:
Garibaldi! we'll come to him shortly
  (As soon as he *ends* in the South).

V

Napoleon—as strong as ten armies,
  Corrupt as seven devils—a fact
You accede to, then seek where the
    harm is
  Drained off from the man to his act,
And find—a free nation! Suppose
  Some hell-brood in Eden's sweet
    greenery,
Convoked for creating—a rose!
  Would it suit the infernal machinery?

VI

Cavour,—to the despot's desire,
  Who his own thought so craftily
    marries—
What is he but just a thin wire
  For conducting the lightning from
    Paris?
Yes, write down the two as compeers,
  Confessing (you would not permit a
    lie)
He bore up his Piedmont ten years
  Till she suddenly smiled and was Italy.

VII

And the King, with that 'stain on his
    scutcheon [1],'
  Savoy—as the calumny runs
(If it be not his blood,—with his clutch
    on
  The sword, and his face to the guns).
O first, where the battle-storm gathers,
  O loyal of heart on the throne,
Let those keep the 'graves of their
    fathers,'
  Who quail, in a nerve, from their own!

VIII

For *thee*—through the dim Hades-portal
  The dream of a voice—' Blessed thou
Who hast made all thy race twice
    immortal!
  No need of the sepulchres now!
—Left to Bourbons and Hapsburgs,
    who fester
  Above-ground with worm-eaten souls,
While the ghost of some pale feudal
    jester
  Before them strews treaties in holes.'

[1] Blue Book. Diplomatical Correspondence.

IX

But hush!—am I dreaming a poem
　Of Hades, Heaven, Justice? Not I—
I began too far off, in my proem,
　With what men believe and deny:
And on earth, whatsoever the need is
　(To sum up as thoughtful reviewers),
The moral of every great deed is
　The virtue of slandering the doers.

'DIED . . .'

(THE 'TIMES' OBITUARY)

I

WHAT shall we add now? He is dead.
　And I who praise and you who blame,
　With wash of words across his name,
Find suddenly declared instead—
　' *On Sunday, third of August, dead.*'

II

Which stops the whole we talked to-day.
　I, quickened to a plausive glance
　At his large general tolerance
By common people's narrow way,
Stopped short in praising. Dead, they
　say.

III

And you, who had just put in a sort
　Of cold deduction—' rather, large
　Through weakness of the continent
　　marge,
Than greatness of the thing contained '—
Broke off. Dead!—there, you stood
　restrained.

IV

As if we had talked in following one
　Up some long gallery. 'Would you
　　choose
　An air like that? The gait is loose—
Or noble.' Sudden in the sun
An oubliette winks. Where is he? Gone.

V

Dead. Man's 'I was' by God's 'I
　am '—
　All hero-worship comes to that.
　High heart, high thought, high fame,
　　as flat
As a gravestone. Bring your *Jacet jam*—
The epitaph 's an epigram.

VI

Dead. There 's an answer to arrest
　All carping. Dust 's his natural place?
　He'll let the flies buzz round his face
And, though you slander, not protest?
—From such an one, exact the Best?

VII

Opinions gold or brass are null.
　We chuck our flattery or abuse,
　Called Caesar's due, as Charon's dues,
I' the teeth of some dead sage or fool,
To mend the grinning of a skull.

VIII

Be abstinent in praise and blame.
　The man's still mortal, who stands
　　first,
　And mortal only, if last and worst.
Then slowly lift so frail a fame,
Or softly drop so poor a shame.

THE FORCED RECRUIT

SOLFERINO, 1859

I

IN the ranks of the Austrian you found
　him,
　He died with his face to you all ;
Yet bury him here where around him
　You honour your bravest that fall.

II

Venetian, fair-featured and slender,
　He lies shot to death in his youth,
With a smile on his lips over-tender
　For any mere soldier's dead mouth.

III

No stranger, and yet not a traitor,
　Though alien the cloth on his breast,
Underneath it how seldom a greater
　Young heart, has a shot sent to rest !

IV

By your enemy tortured and goaded
　To march with them, stand in their file,
His musket (see) never was loaded,
　He facing your guns with that smile !

V

As orphans yearn on to their mothers,
  He yearned to your patriot bands ;—
'Let me die for our Italy, brothers,
  If not in your ranks, by your hands !

VI

'Aim straightly, fire steadily ! spare me
  A ball in the body which may
Deliver my heart here, and tear me
  This badge of the Austrian away !'

VII

So thought he, so died he this morning.
  What then ? many others have died.
Aye, but easy for men to die scorning
  The death-stroke, who fought side by
    side—

VIII

One tricolor floating above them ;
  Struck down 'mid triumphant acclaims
Of an Italy rescued to love them
  And blazon the brass with their names.

IX

But he,—without witness or honour,
  Mixed, shamed in his country's regard,
With the tyrants who march in upon her,
  Died faithful and passive: 'twas hard.

X

'Twas sublime. In a cruel restriction
  Cut off from the guerdon of sons,
With most filial obedience, conviction,
  His soul kissed the lips of her guns.

XI

That moves you ? Nay, grudge not to
  show it,
  While digging a grave for him here :
The others who died, says your poet,
  Have glory,—let *him* have a tear.

GARIBALDI

I

HE bent his head upon his breast
  Wherein his lion-heart lay sick :—
'Perhaps we are not ill-repaid ;
Perhaps this is not a true test ;
  Perhaps that was not a foul trick ;
  Perhaps none wronged, and none
    betrayed.

II

'Perhaps the people's vote which here
  United, there may disunite,
  And both be lawful as they think ;
Perhaps a patriot statesman, dear
  For chartering nations, can with right
  Disfranchise those who hold the ink.

III

'Perhaps men's wisdom is not craft ;
  Men's greatness, not a selfish greed ;
  Men's justice, not the safer side ;
Perhaps even women, when they
    laughed,
  Wept, thanked us that the land was
    freed,
  Not wholly (though they kissed us)
    lied.

IV

'Perhaps no more than this we meant,
  When up at Austria's guns we flew,
  And quenched them with a cry apiece,
Italia !—Yet a dream was sent . .
  The little house my father knew,
  The olives and the palms of Nice.'

V

He paused, and drew his sword out slow,
  Then pored upon the blade intent,
  As if to read some written thing ;
While many murmured,—'He will go
  In that despairing sentiment
  And break his sword before the King.'

VI

He poring still upon the blade,
  His large lid quivered, something fell.
  'Perhaps,' he said, 'I was not born
With such fine brains to treat and trade,—
  And if a woman knew it well,
  Her falsehood only meant her scorn.

VII

'Yet through Varese's cannon-smoke
  My eye saw clear : men feared this man
  At Como, where this sword could seal
Death's protocol with every stroke :
  And now . . the drop there scarcely can
  Impair the keenness of the steel.

VIII

So man and sword may have their use;
　And if the soil beneath my foot
　In valour's act is forfeited,
I'll strike the harder, take my dues
　Out nobler, and all loss confute
　From ampler heavens above my head.

IX

'My King, King Victor, I am thine!
　So much Nice-dust as what I am
　(To make our Italy) must cleave.
Forgive that.' Forward with a sign
　He went.
　　　　　　You've seen the telegram?
Palermo's taken, we believe.

ONLY A CURL

I

FRIENDS of faces unknown and a land
　Unvisited over the sea,
Who tell me how lonely you stand
　With a single gold curl in the hand
　Held up to be looked at by me,—

II

While you ask me to ponder and say
　What a father and mother can do,
With the bright fellow-locks put away
Out of reach, beyond kiss, in the clay
　Where the violets press nearer than
　you.

III

Shall I speak like a poet, or run
　Into weak woman's tears for relief?
Oh, children!—I never lost one,—
　Yet my arm's round my own little son,
　And Love knows the secret of Grief.

IV

And I feel what it must be and is,
　When God draws a new angel so
Through the house of a man up to His,
　With a murmur of music, you miss,
　And a rapture of light, you forgo.

V

How you think, staring on at the door,
　Where the face of your angel flashed
　in,
That its brightness, familiar before,
Burns off from you ever the more
　For the dark of your sorrow and sin.

VI

'God lent him and takes him,' you sigh;
　—Nay, there let me break with your
　pain:
God's generous in giving, say I,—
And the thing which He gives, I deny
　That He ever can take back again.

VII

He gives what He gives. I appeal
　To all who bear babes—in the hour
When the veil of the body we feel
Rent round us,—while torments reveal
　The motherhood's advent in power,

VIII

And the babe cries!—has each of us
　known
By apocalypse (God being there
Full in nature) the child is our own,
Life of life, love of love, moan of moan,
　Through all changes, all times, every-
　where.

IX

He's ours and for ever. Believe,
　O father!—O mother, look back
To the first love's assurance. To give
Means with God not to tempt or deceive
　With a cup thrust in Benjamin's sack.

X

He gives what He gives. Be content!
　He resumes nothing given,—be sure!
God lend? Where the usurers lent
In His temple, indignant He went
　And scourged away all those impure.

XI

He lends not; but gives to the end,
　As He loves to the end. If it seem
That He draws back a gift, com-
　prehend
'Tis to add to it rather,—amend,
　And finish it up to your dream,—

XII

Or keep,—as a mother will toys
Too costly, though given by herself,
Till the room shall be stiller from noise,
And the children more fit for such joys,
Kept over their heads on the shelf.

XIII

So look up, friends ! you, who indeed
Have possessed in your house a sweet
piece
Of the Heaven which men strive for,
must need
Be more earnest than others are,—speed
Where they loiter, persist where they
cease.

XIV

You know how one angel smiles there.
Then weep not. 'Tis easy for you
To be drawn by a single gold hair
Of that curl, from earth's storm and
despair,
To the safe place above us. Adieu.

A VIEW ACROSS THE ROMAN CAMPAGNA

1861

I

OVER the dumb Campagna-sea,
Out in the offing through mist and
rain,
Saint Peter's Church heaves silently
Like a mighty ship in pain,
Facing the tempest with struggle and
strain.

II

Motionless waifs of ruined towers,
Soundless breakers of desolate land:
The sullen surf of the mist devours
That mountain-range upon either hand,
Eaten away from its outline grand.

III

And over the dumb Campagna-sea
Where the ship of the Church heaves
on to wreck,
Alone and silent as God must be,
The Christ walks. Aye, but Peter's
neck
Is stiff to turn on the foundering deck.

IV

Peter, Peter ! if such be thy name,
Now leave the ship for another to steer,
And proving thy faith evermore the same,
Come forth, tread out through the
dark and drear,
Since He who walks on the sea is here.

V

Peter, Peter ! He does not speak ;
He is not as rash as in old Galilee :
Safer a ship, though it toss and leak,
Than a reeling foot on a rolling sea !
And he 's got to be round in the girth,
thinks he.

VI

Peter, Peter ! He does not stir ;
His nets are heavy with silver fish ;
He reckons his gains, and is keen to infer
—' The broil on the shore, if the Lord
should wish ;
But the sturgeon goes to the Caesar's
dish.'

VII

Peter, Peter ! thou fisher of men,
Fisher of fish wouldst thou live instead ?
Haggling for pence with the other Ten,
Cheating the market at so much a head,
Griping the Bag of the traitor Dead ?

VIII

At the triple crow of the Gallic cock
Thou weep'st not, thou, though thine
eyes be dazed :
What bird comes next in the tempest-
shock ?
—Vultures ! see,—as when Romulus
gazed,—
To inaugurate Rome for a world
amazed !

THE KING'S GIFT

I

TERESA, ah, Teresita !
Now what has the messenger brought her,
Our Garibaldi's young daughter,
To make her stop short in her singing ?
Will she not once more repeat a
Verse from that hymn of our hero's,
Setting the souls of us ringing ?
Break off the song where the tear rose ?
Ah, Teresita !

II

A young thing, mark, is Teresa :
Her eyes have caught fire, to be sure, in
That necklace of jewels from Turin,
 Till blind their regard to us men is.
But still she remembers to raise a
Sly look to her father, and note—
 'Could she sing on as well about
 Venice,
Yet wear such a flame at her throat ?
 Decide for Teresa.'

III

Teresa! ah, Teresita!
His right hand has paused on her head—
'Accept it, my daughter,' he said ;
 'Aye, wear it, true child of thy mother !
Then sing, till all start to their feet, a
New verse ever bolder and freer !
 King Victor's no king like another,
But verily noble as *we* are,
 Child, Teresita !'

PARTING LOVERS

SIENA, 1860

I

I LOVE thee, love thee, Giulio ;
 Some call me cold, and some demure ;
And if thou hast ever guessed that so
 I loved thee .. well, the proof was poor,
 And no one could be sure.

II

Before thy song (with shifted rimes
 To suit my name) did I undo
The persian ? If it stirred sometimes,
 Thou hast not seen a hand push through
 A foolish flower or two.

III

My mother listening to my sleep,
 Heard nothing but a sigh at night,—
The short sigh rippling on the deep,
 When hearts run out of breath and
 sight
 Of men, to God's clear light.

IV

When others named thee,—thought thy
 brows
 Were straight, thy smile was tender,—
 'Here
He comes between the vineyard-rows !'
 - I said not 'Aye,' nor waited, Dear,
 To feel thee step too near.

V

I left such things to bolder girls,—
 Olivia or Clotilda. Nay,
When that Clotilda, through her curls,
 Held both thine eyes in hers one day,
 I marvelled, let me say.

VI

I could not try the woman's trick :
 Between us straightway fell the blush
Which kept me separate, blind and sick.
 A wind came with thee in a flush,
 As blown through Sinai's bush.

VII

But now that Italy invokes
 Her young men to go forth and chase
The foe or perish,—nothing chokes
 My voice, or drives me from the place.
 I look thee in the face.

VIII

I love thee ! It is understood,
 Confest : I do not shrink or start.
No blushes ! all my body's blood
 Has gone to greaten this poor heart,
 That, loving, we may part.

IX

Our Italy invokes the youth
 To die if need be. Still there's room,
Though earth is strained with dead in
 truth :
 Since twice the lilies were in bloom
 They have not grudged a tomb.

X

And many a plighted maid and wife
 And mother, who can say since then
'My country,'—cannot say through life
 'My son,' 'my spouse,' 'my flower
 of men,'
 And not weep dumb again.

XI

Heroic males the country bears,—
But daughters give up more than sons.:
Flags wave, drums beat, and unawares
You flash your souls out with the guns,
And take your Heaven at once.

XII

But we!—we empty heart and home
Of life's life, love! We bear to think
You're gone,—to feel you may not
come,—
To hear the door-latch stir and clink,
Yet no more you! . . nor sink.

XIII

Dear God! when Italy is one,
Complete, content from bound to bound,
Suppose, for my share, earth's undone
By one grave in't!—as one small wound
Will kill a man, 'tis found.

XIV

What then? If love's delight must end,
At least we'll clear its truth from flaws.
I love thee, love thee, sweetest friend!
Now take my sweetest without pause,
And help the nation's cause.

XV

And thus, of noble Italy
We'll both be worthy! Let her show
The future how we made her free,
Not sparing life . . nor Giulio,
Nor this . . this heartbreak! Go.

MOTHER AND POET[1]

TURIN, AFTER NEWS FROM GAETA, 1861

I

DEAD! One of them shot by the sea in
the east,
And one of them shot in the west by
the sea.
Dead! both my boys! When you sit
at the feast
And are wanting a great song for Italy
free,
Let none look at *me*!

[1] This was Laura Savio, of Turin, a poetess
and patriot, whose sons were killed at Ancona
and Gaeta.

II

Yet I was a poetess only last year,
And good at my art, for a woman,
men said;
But *this* woman, *this*, who is agonized
here,
—The east sea and west sea rime
on in her head
For ever instead.

III

What art can a woman be good at? Oh,
vain!
What art *is* she good at, but hurting
her breast
With the milk-teeth of babes, and
a smile at the pain?
Ah, boys, how you hurt! you were
strong as you pressed,
And I proud, by that test.

IV

What art's for a woman! To hold on
her knees
Both darlings! to feel all their arms
round her throat,
Cling, strangle a little! to sew by
degrees
And 'broider the long-clothes and neat
little coat;
To dream and to dote.

V

To teach them . . It stings there! *I*
made them indeed
Speak plain the word *country*. *I*
taught them, no doubt,
That a country's a thing men should die
for at need.
I prated of liberty, rights, and about
The tyrant cast out.

VI

And when their eyes flashed . . O my
beautiful eyes! . .
I exulted; nay, let them go forth at
the wheels
Of the guns, and denied not. But then
the surprise
When one sits quite alone! Then one
weeps, then one kneels!
God, how the house feels!

VII

At first, happy news came, in gay letters moiled
　With my kisses,—of camp-life and glory, and how
They both loved me ; and, soon coming home to be spoiled,
　In return would fan off every fly from my brow
　　With their green laurel-bough.

VIII

Then was triumph at Turin : 'Ancona was free !'
　And some one came out of the cheers in the street,
With a face pale as stone, to say something to me.
　My Guido was dead ! I fell down at his feet,
　　While they cheered in the street.

IX

I bore it ; friends soothed me ; my grief looked sublime
　As the ransom of Italy. One boy remained
To be leant on and walked with, recalling the time
　When the first grew immortal, while both of us strained
　　To the height he had gained.

X

And letters still came, shorter, sadder, more strong,
　Writ now but in one hand, 'I was not to faint,—
One loved me for two—would be with me ere long :
　And *Viva l'Italia !—he* died for, our saint,
　　Who forbids our complaint.'

XI

My Nanni would add, 'he was safe, and aware
　Of a presence that turned off the balls,—was imprest
It was Guido himself, who knew what I could bear,

And how 'twas impossible, quite dispossessed,
　　To live on for the rest.'

XII

On which, without pause, up the telegraph-line
　Swept smoothly the next news from Gaeta :—*Shot.*
Tell his mother. Ah, ah, 'his,' 'their' mother,—not 'mine,'
　No voice says '*My* mother ' again to me. What !
　　You think Guido forgot?

XIII

Are souls straight so happy that, dizzy with Heaven,
　They drop earth's affections, conceive not of woe?
I think not. Themselves were too lately forgiven
　Through THAT Love and Sorrow which reconciled so
　　The Above and Below.

XIV

O Christ of the five wounds, who look'dst through the dark
　To the face of Thy mother ! consider, I pray,
How we common mothers stand desolate, mark,
　Whose sons, not being Christs, die with eyes turned away,
　　And no last word to say !

XV

Both boys dead? but that's out of nature. We all
　Have been patriots, yet each house must always keep one.
'Twere imbecile, hewing out roads to a wall ;
　And, when Italy's made, for what end is it done
　　If we have not a son ?

XVI

Ah, ah, ah! when Gaeta's taken what
then?
When the fair wicked queen sits no
more at her sport
Of the fire-balls of death crashing souls
out of men?
When the guns of Cavalli with final
retort
Have cut the game short?

XVII

When Venice and Rome keep their new
jubilee,
When your flag takes all heaven for
its white, green, and red,
When *you* have your country from
mountain to sea,
When King Victor has Italy's crown
on his head,
(And *I* have my Dead)—

XVIII

What then? Do not mock me. Ah,
ring your bells low,
And burn your lights faintly! *My*
country is *there*,
Above the star pricked by the last peak
of snow:
My Italy 's THERE, with my brave civic
Pair,
To disfranchise despair!

XIX

Forgive me. Some women bear children
in strength,
And bite back the cry of their pain in
self-scorn;
But the birth-pangs of nations will wring
us at length
Into wail such as this—and we sit on
forlorn
When the man-child is born.

XX

Dead! One of them shot by the sea in
the east,
And one of them shot in the west by
the sea.
Both! both my boys! If in keeping
the feast
You want a great song for your Italy
free,
Let none look at *me*!

NATURE'S REMORSES

ROME, 1861

I

HER soul was bred by a throne, and fed
From the sucking-bottle used in her
race
On starch and water (for mother's
milk
Which gives a larger growth instead),
And, out of the natural liberal grace,
Was swaddled away in violet silk.

II

And young and kind, and royally blind,
Forth she stepped from her palace-
door
On three-piled carpet of compli-
ments,
Curtains of incense drawn by the wind
In between her for evermore
And daylight issues of events.

III

On she drew, as a queen might do,
To meet a Dream of Italy,—
Of magical town and musical wave,
Where even a god, his amulet blue
Of shining sea, in an ecstasy
Dropt and forgot in a nereid's cave.

IV

Down she goes, as the soft wind blows,
To live more smoothly than mortals
can,
To love and to reign as queen and
wife,
To wear a crown that smells of a rose,
And still, with a sceptre as light as a
fan,
Beat sweet time to the song of life.

V

What is this? As quick as a kiss
Falls the smile from her girlish mouth!
The lion-people has left its lair,
Roaring along her garden of bliss,
And the fiery underworld of the South
Scorched a way to the upper air.

VI

And a fire-stone ran in the form of a man,
  Burningly, boundingly, fatal and fell,
    Bowling the kingdom down!
    Where was the king?
She had heard somewhat, since life
      began,
  Of terrors on earth and horrors in hell,
  But never, never of such a thing!

VII

You think she dropped when her dream
      was stopped,
  When the blotch of Bourbon blood
      inlay,
    Lividly rank, her new lord's cheek?
Not so. Her high heart overtopped
  The royal part she had come to play.
    Only the men in that hour were
      weak.

VIII

And twice a wife by her ravaged life,
  And twice a queen by her kingdom lost,
    She braved the shock and the
      counter-shock
Of hero and traitor, bullet and knife,
  While Italy pushed, like a vengeful
      ghost,
    That son of the Cursed from Gaeta's
      rock.

IX

What will ye give her, who could not
      deliver,
  German Princesses? A laurel-wreath
  All over-scored with your signatures,
Graces, Serenities, Highnesses ever?
  Mock her not, fresh from the truth of
      Death,
    Conscious of dignities higher than
      yours.

X

What will ye put in your casket shut,
  Ladies of Paris, in sympathy's name?
    Guizot's daughter, what have you
      brought her?
Withered immortelles, long ago cut
  For guilty dynasties perished in shame,
    Putrid to memory, Guizot's daugh-
      ter?

XI

Ah, poor queen! so young and serene!
  What shall we do for her, now hope's
      done,
    Standing at Rome in these ruins
      old,
She too a ruin and no more a queen?
  Leave her that diadem made by the
      sun
    Turning her hair to an innocent gold.

XII

Aye! bring close to her, as 'twere a rose,
      to her,
  Yon free child from an Apennine city
    Singing for Italy,—dumb in the
      place!
Something like solace, let us suppose,
      to her
  Given, in that homage of wonder and
      pity,
    By his pure eyes to her beautiful face.

XIII

Nature, excluded, savagely brooded,
  Ruined all queendom and dogmas of
      state,—
    Then in reaction remorseful and
      mild,
Rescues the womanhood, nearly eluded,
  Shows her what's sweetest in woman-
      ly fate—
    Sunshine from Heaven, and the
      eyes of a child.

THE NORTH AND THE SOUTH

[THE LAST POEM]

ROME, MAY, 1861

I

'Now give us lands where the olives
      grow,'
  Cried the North to the South,
'Where the sun with a golden mouth
      can blow
Blue bubbles of grapes down a vineyard-
      row!'
  Cried the North to the South.

' Now give us men from the sunless plain,'
　　Cried the South to the North,
'By need of work in the snow and the
　　rain,
Made strong, and brave by familiar pain !'
　　Cried the South to the North.

II

' Give lucider hills and intenser seas,'
　　Said the North to the South,
'Since ever by symbols and bright degrees
Art, childlike, climbs to the dear Lord's
　　knees,'
　　Said the North to the South.

'Give strenuous souls for belief and
　　prayer,'
　　Said the South to the North,
'That stand in the dark on the lowest
　　stair,
While affirming of God, " He is certainly
　　there," '
　　Said the South to the North.

III

' Yet oh, for the skies that are softer
　　and higher ! '
　　Sighed the North to the South ;
' For the flowers that blaze, and the trees
　　that aspire,
And the insects made of a song or a fire !'
　　Sighed the North to the South.

'And oh, for a seer to discern the
　　same ! '
　　Sighed the South to the North ;
' For a poet's tongue of baptismal flame,
To call the tree or the flower by its
　　name ! '
　　Sighed the South to the North.

IV

The North sent therefore a man of men
　　As a grace to the South ;
And thus to Rome came Andersen.
—' Alas, but must you take him again ?'
　　Said the South to the North.

TRANSLATIONS

PARAPHRASE ON THEOCRITUS

THE CYCLOPS

IDYLL XI

AND so an easier life our Cyclops drew,
　　The ancient Polyphemus, who in youth
Loved Galatea while the manhood grew
　　Adown his cheeks and darkened round
　　　his mouth.
No jot he cared for apples, olives, roses ;
　　Love made him mad : the whole world
　　　was neglected,
The very sheep went backward to their
　　closes
　　From out the fair green pastures, self-
　　　directed.
　　　And singing Galatea, thus, he wore
　　　The sunrise down along the weedy
　　　　shore,
And pined alone, and felt the cruel wound
　　Beneath his heart, which Cypris' arrow
　　　bore,

With a deep pang ; but, so, the cure was
　　found ;
　　And sitting on a lofty rock he cast
　　His eyes upon the sea, and sang at
　　　last :—

' O whitest Galatea, can it be
　　That thou shouldst spurn me off who
　　　love thee so ?
More white than curds, my girl, thou
　　art to see,
More meek than lambs, more full of leap-
　　ing glee
Than kids, and brighter than the early
　　glow
On grapes that swell to ripen,—sour like
　　thee !
Thou comest to me with the fragrant sleep,
　　And with the fragrant sleep thou goest
　　　from me ;
Thou fliest . . fliest, as a frightened sheep
　　Flies the grey wolf !—yet Love did
　　　overcome me,

So long;—I loved thee, maiden, first of all
  When down the hills (my mother fast
    beside thee)
I saw thee stray to pluck the summer-fall
  Of hyacinth bells, and went myself to
    guide thee:
And since my eyes have seen thee, they
    can leave thee
  No more, from that day's light! But
    thou . . by Zeus,
Thou wilt not care for *that*, to let it grieve
    thee!
  I know thee, fair one, why thou
    springest loose
From my arm round thee. Why? I tell
    thee, Dear!
  One shaggy eyebrow draws its smudg-
    ing road
Straight through my ample front, from
    ear to ear,—
  One eye rolls underneath; and yawn-
    ing, broad
Flat nostrils feel the bulging lips too near.
Yet . . ho, ho!—*I*,—whatever I appear,—
  Do feed a thousand oxen! When I
    have done,
I milk the cows, and drink the milk that 's
    best!
  I lack no cheese, while summer keeps
    the sun;
And after, in the cold, it 's ready prest!
  And then, I know to sing, as there is
    none
Of all the Cyclops can, . . a song of thee,
Sweet apple of my soul, on love's fair tree,
And of myself who love thee . . till the
    West
Forgets the light, and all but I have rest.
I feed for thee, besides, eleven fair does,
  And all in fawn; and four tame whelps
    of bears.
Come to me, Sweet! thou shalt have all
    of those
  In change for love! I will not halve
    the shares.
Leave the blue sea, with pure white arms
    extended
  To the dry shore; and, in my cave's
    recess,
Thou shalt be gladder for the noonlight
    ended,—
  For here be laurels, spiral cypresses,
Dark ivy, and a vine whose leaves enfold

Most luscious grapes; and here is water
    cold,
  The wooded Aetna pours down through
    the trees
From the white snows,—which gods
    were scarce too bold
To drink in turn with nectar. Who
    with these
Would choose the salt wave of the
    lukewarm seas?
Nay, look on me! If I am hairy and
    rough,
  I have an oak's heart in me; there 's
    a fire
In these grey ashes which burns hot
    enough;
  And when I burn for *thee*, I grudge
    the pyre
No fuel . . not my soul, nor this one eye,—
Most precious thing I have, because
    thereby
I see thee, Fairest! Out, alas! I wish
My mother had borne me finnèd like a fish,
That I might plunge down in the ocean
    near thee,
  And kiss thy glittering hand between
    the weeds,
If still thy face were turned; and I would
    bear thee
  Each lily white, and poppy fair that
    bleeds
Its red heart down its leaves!—one gift,
    for hours
  Of summer, . . one, for winter; since,
    to cheer thee,
I could not bring at once all kinds of
    flowers.
Even now, girl, now, I fain would learn
    to swim,
  If stranger in a ship sailed nigh, I wis,—
  That I may know how sweet a thing it is
To live down with you, in the Deep and
    Dim!
Come up, O Galatea, from the ocean,
  And having come, forget again to go!
As I, who sing out here my heart's
    emotion,
  Could sit for ever. Come up from
    below!
Come, keep my flocks beside me, milk
    my kine,—
  Come, press my cheese, distrain my
    whey and curd!

Ah, mother! she alone . . that mother of
  mine . .
  Did wrong me sore! I blame her!—
    Not a word
Of kindly intercession did she address
Thine ear with for my sake ; and ne'er-
  theless
  She saw me wasting, wasting, day by
    day!
  Both head and feet were aching, I will
    say,
All sick for grief, as I myself was sick!
  O Cyclops, Cyclops, whither hast thou
    sent
  Thy soul on fluttering wings? If thou
    wert bent
On turning bowls, or pulling green and
  thick
  The sprouts to give thy lambkins,—
    thou wouldst make thee
  A wiser Cyclops than for what we
    take thee.
Milk dry the present! Why pursue too
  quick
That future which is fugitive aright?
  Thy Galatea thou shalt haply find,—
  Or else a maiden fairer and more kind ;
For many girls do call me through the
  night,
  And, as they call, do laugh out silverly.
  I, too, am something in the world,
    I see!'

While thus the Cyclops love and lambs
  did fold,
Ease came with song, he could not buy
  with gold.

PARAPHRASES ON APULEIUS

PSYCHE GAZING ON CUPID

Metamorph., Lib. IV

THEN Psyche, weak in body and soul,
  put on
  The cruelty of Fate, in place of strength:
She raised the lamp to see what should
  be done,
  And seized the steel, and was a man
    at length

In courage, though a woman! Yes, but
  when
  The light fell on the bed whereby she
    stood
To view the '*beast*' that lay there,—
  certes, then,
  She saw the gentlest, sweetest beast
    in wood—
Even Cupid's self, the beauteous god!
  more beauteous
  For that sweet sleep across his eyelids
    dim!
The light, the lady carried as she viewed,
  Did blush for pleasure as it lighted him,
The dagger trembled from its aim un-
  duteous ;
  And *she* . . oh, *she*—amazed and soul-
    distraught,
And fainting in her whiteness like a veil,
  Slid down upon her knees, and, shud-
    dering, thought
To hide—though in her heart—the dagger
  pale!
She would have done it, but her hands
  did fail
  To hold the guilty steel, they shivered
    so,—
And feeble, exhausted, unawares she took
  To gazing on the god,—till, look by look,
  Her eyes with larger life did fill and
    glow.
She saw his golden head alight with curls:
  She might have guessed their bright-
    ness in the dark
  By that ambrosial smell of heavenly
    mark!
She saw the milky brow, more pure than
  pearls,
  The purple of the cheeks, divinely
    sundered
By the globed ringlets, as they glided free,
Some back, some forwards,—all so
  radiantly,
  That, as she watched them there, she
    never wondered
To see the lamplight, where it touched
  them, tremble :
On the god's shoulders, too, she marked
  his wings
  Shine faintly at the edges and resemble
A flower that's near to blow. The poet
  sings
  And lover sighs, that Love is fugitive ;

And certes, though these pinions lay
  reposing,
  The feathers on them seemed to stir
    and live
As if by instinct, closing and unclosing.
  Meantime the god's fair body slumbered
    deep,
  All worthy of Venus, in his shining
    sleep;
  While at the bed's foot lay the quiver,
    bow,
And darts,—his arms of godhead. Psyche
  gazed
  With eyes that drank the wonders in,
    —said,—' Lo,
Be these my husband's arms?'—and
  straightway raised
  An arrow from the quiver-case, and
    tried
Its point against her finger,—trembling
  till
  She pushed it in too deeply (foolish
    bride !)
And made her blood some dewdrops
  small distil,
And learnt to love Love, of her own
  goodwill.

PSYCHE WAFTED BY ZEPHYRUS

Metamorph., Lib. IV

WHILE Psyche wept upon the rock for-
  saken,
  Alone, despairing, dreading,—gradu-
    ally
By Zephyrus she was enwrapt and taken
  Still trembling,—like the lilies planted
    high,—
Through all her fair white limbs. Her
  vesture spread,
  Her very bosom eddying with sur-
    prise,—
He drew her slowly from the mountain-
  head,
  And bore her down the valleys with
    wet eyes,
And laid her in the lap of a green dell
  As soft with grass and flowers as any
    nest,
With trees beside her, and a limpid well :
  Yet Love was not far off from all that
    Rest.

PSYCHE AND PAN

Metamorph., Lib. V

THE gentle River, in her Cupid's honour,
  Because he used to warm the very
    wave,
Did ripple aside, instead of closing on her,
  And cast up Psyche, with a refluence
    brave,
Upon the flowery bank,—all sad and
  sinning.
Then Pan, the rural god, by chance was
  leaning
  Along the brow of waters as they
    wound,
  Kissing the reed-nymph till she sank
    to ground,
And teaching, without knowledge of the
  meaning,
  To run her voice in music after his
Down many a shifting note (the goats
  around,
  In wandering pasture and most leap-
    ing bliss,
Drawn on to crop the river's flowery hair);
And as the hoary god beheld her there,
  The poor, worn, fainting Psyche !—
    knowing all
  The grief she suffered, he did gently call
Her name, and softly comfort her des-
  pair :—

' O wise, fair lady, I am rough and rude,
And yet experienced through my weary
  age !
  And if I read aright, as soothsayer
    should,
Thy faltering steps of heavy pilgrimage,
  Thy paleness, deep as snow we
    cannot see
The roses through,—thy sighs of quick
  returning,
Thine eyes that seem, themselves, two
  souls in mourning,—
  Thou lovest, girl, too well, and
    bitterly !
But hear me : rush no more to a head-
  long fall :
  Seek no more deaths ! leave wail, lay
    sorrow down,
And pray the sovran god ; and use
  withal

Such prayer as best may suit a tender
youth,
Well-pleased to bend to flatteries from
thy mouth
And feel them stir the myrtle of his
crown.'

—So spake the shepherd-god ; and
answer none
Gave Psyche in return : but silently
She did him homage with a bended
knee,
And took the onward path.—

PSYCHE PROPITIATING CERES

Metamorph., Lib. VI

THEN mother Ceres from afar beheld
her,
While Psyche touched, with reverent
fingers meek,
The temple's scythes ; and with a cry
compelled her :—
' O wretched Psyche, Venus roams to
seek
Thy wandering footsteps round the
weary earth,
Anxious and maddened, and adjures
thee forth
To accept the imputed pang, and let
her wreak
Full vengeance with full force of deity !
Yet *thou*, forsooth, art in my temple
here,
Touching my scythes, assuming my
degree,
And daring to have thoughts that are
not fear !'
—But Psyche clung to her feet, and as
they moved
Rained tears along their track, tear,
dropped on tear,
And drew the dust on in her trailing
locks,
And still, with passionate prayer, the
charge disproved :—
'Now, by thy right hand's gathering
from the shocks
Of golden corn,—and by thy gladsome
rites
Of harvest,—and thy consecrated sights

Shut safe and mute in chests,—and by
the course
Of thy slave-dragons,—and the driving
force
Of ploughs along Sicilian glebes pro-
found,—
By thy swift chariot,—by thy steadfast
ground,—
By all those nuptial torches that departed
With thy lost daughter,—and by
those that shone
Back with her, when she came again
glad-hearted,—
And by all other mysteries which are
done
In silence at Eleusis,—I beseech thee,
O Ceres, take some pity, and abstain
From giving to my soul extremer pain
Who am the wretched Psyche ! Let me
teach thee
A little mercy, and have thy leave to
spend
A few days only in thy garnered corn,
Until that wrathful goddess, at the
end,
Shall feel her hate grow mild, the
longer borne,—
Or till, alas !—this faintness at my breast
Pass from me, and my spirit apprehend
From life-long woe a breath-time hour
of rest !'
—But Ceres answered, ' I am moved in-
deed
By prayers so moist with tears, and
would defend
The poor beseecher from more utter need:
But where old oaths, anterior ties,
commend,
I cannot fail to a sister, lie to a friend,
As Venus is to *me*. Depart with speed !'

PSYCHE AND THE EAGLE

Metamorph., Lib. VI

BUT sovran Jove's rapacious Bird, the
regal
High percher on the lightning, the great
eagle
Drove down with rushing wings ; and,
—thinking how,
By Cupid's help, he bore from Ida's brow

A cup-boy for his master,—he inclined
To yield, in just return, an influence
    kind;
The god being honoured in his lady's
    woe.
And thus the Bird wheeled downward
    from the track,
Gods follow gods in, to the level low
Of that poor face of Psyche left in wrack.
—'Now fie, thou simple girl!' the
    Bird began ;
'For if thou think to steal and carry back
A drop of holiest stream that ever ran,
No simpler thought, methinks, were
    found in man.
What! know'st thou not these Stygian
    waters be
Most holy, even to Jove? that as, on
    earth,
Men swear by gods, and by the thunder's
    worth,
Even so the heavenly gods do utter forth
Their oaths by Styx's flowing majesty?
And yet, one little urnful, I agree
To grant thy need!' Whereat, all
    hastily,
He takes it, fills it from the willing
    wave,
And bears it in his beak, incarnadined
By the last Titan-prey he screamed to
    have ;
And, striking calmly out, against the
    wind,
Vast wings on each side,—there, where
    Psyche stands,
He drops the urn down in her lifted
    hands.

PSYCHE AND CERBERUS

Metamorph., Lib. VI

A MIGHTY dog with three colossal necks,
    And heads in grand proportion ; vast
    as fear,
With jaws that bark the thunder out
    that breaks
    In most innocuous dread for ghosts
    anear,
Who are safe in death from sorrow : he
    reclines
Across the threshold of queen Proser-
    pine's

Dark-sweeping halls, and, there, for
    Pluto's spouse,
Doth guard the entrance of the empty
    house.
When Psyche threw the cake to him,
    once amain
He howled up wildly from his hunger-
    pain,
And was still, after.—

PSYCHE AND PROSERPINE

Metamorph., Lib. VI

THEN Psyche entered in to Proserpine
In the dark house, and straightway did
    decline
With meek denial the luxurious seat,
    The liberal board for welcome stran-
    gers spread,
But sate down lowly at the dark queen's
    feet,
    And told her tale, and brake her
    oaten bread.
And when she had given the pyx in
    humble duty,
    And told how Venus did entreat the
    queen
To fill it up with only one day's beauty
    She used in Hades, star-bright and
    serene,
To beautify the Cyprian, who had been
    All spoilt with grief in nursing her
    sick boy,—
Then Proserpine, in malice and in joy,
    Smiled in the shade, and took the
    pyx, and put
    A secret in it ; and so, filled and
    shut,
Gave it again to Psyche. Could she
    tell
It held no beauty, but a dream of hell?

PSYCHE AND VENUS

Metamorph., Lib. VI

AND Psyche brought to Venus what was
    sent
By Pluto's spouse ; the paler, that she
    went
So low to seek it, down the dark
    descent.

MERCURY CARRIES PSYCHE TO OLYMPUS

Metamorph., Lib. VI

THEN Jove commanded the god Mercury
To float up Psyche from the earth. And she
Sprang at the first word, as the fountain springs,
And shot up bright and rustling through his wings.

MARRIAGE OF PSYCHE AND CUPID

Metamorph., Lib VI

AND Jove's right-hand approached the ambrosial bowl
  To Psyche's lips, that scarce dared yet to smile,—
'Drink, O my daughter, and acquaint thy soul
  With deathless uses, and be glad the while!
No more shall Cupid leave thy lovely side;
  Thy marriage-joy begins for never-ending.'
While yet he spake,—the nuptial feast supplied,—
  The bridegroom on the festive couch was bending
O'er Psyche in his bosom—Jove, the same,
  On Juno, and the other deities,
Alike ranged round. The rural cup-boy came
  And poured Jove's nectar out with shining eyes,
While Bacchus, for the others, did as much,
  And Vulcan spread the meal; and all the Hours
Made all things purple with a sprinkle of flowers,
Or roses chiefly, not to say the touch
  Of their sweet fingers; and the Graces glided
Their balm around, and the Muses, through the air,
  Struck out clear voices, which were still divided

By that divinest song Apollo there
  Intoned to his lute; while Aphroditè fair
Did float her beauty along the tune, and play
  The notes right with her feet. And thus, the day
Through every perfect mood of joy was carried.
The Muses sang their chorus; Satyrus
Did blow his pipes; Pan touched his reed ;—and thus
At last were Cupid and his Psyche married.

PARAPHRASES ON NONNUS

HOW BACCHUS FINDS ARIADNE SLEEPING

Dionysiaca, Lib. XLVII

WHEN Bacchus first beheld the desolate
And sleeping Ariadne, wonder straight
Was mixed with love in his great golden eyes;
He turned to his Bacchantes in surprise,
And said with guarded voice,—'Hush! strike no more
Your brazen cymbals; keep those voices still
Of voice and pipe; and since ye stand before
Queen Cypris, let her slumber as she will!
And yet the cestus is not here in proof.
A Grace, perhaps, whom sleep has stolen aloof:
In which case, as the morning shines in view,
Wake this Aglaia !—yet in Naxos, who
Would veil a Grace so? Hush! And if that she
Were Hebe, which of all the gods can be
The pourer-out of wine? or if we think
She 's like the shining moon by ocean's brink,
The guide of herds,—why, could she sleep without
Endymion's breath on her cheek? or if I doubt

Of silver-footed Thetis, used to tread
These shores,—even *she* (in reverence
    be it said)
Has no such rosy beauty to dress deep
With the blue waves. The Loxian
    goddess might
Repose so from her hunting-toil aright
Beside the sea, since toil gives birth to
    sleep,
But who would find her with her tunic
    loose,
Thus? Stand off, Thracian! stand off!
    Do not leap,
Not this way! Leave that piping, since
    I choose,
O dearest Pan, and let Athenè rest!
And yet if she be Pallas . . truly
    guessed . .
Her lance is—where? her helm and
    aegis—where?'
—As Bacchus closed, the miserable
    Fair
Awoke at last, sprang upward from the
    sands,
And gazing wild on that wild throng
    that stands
Around, around her, and no Theseus
    there!—
Her voice went moaning over shore and
    sea,
Beside the halcyon's cry; she called her
    love;
She named her hero, and raged mad-
    deningly
Against the brine of waters; and
    above,
Sought the ship's track, and cursed the
    hours she slept;
And still the chiefest execration swept
Against queen Paphia, mother of the
    ocean;
And cursed and prayed by times in her
    emotion
The winds all round.   .   .   .

.   .   .   .

Her grief did make her glorious; her
    despair
Adorned her with its weight. Poor
    wailing child!
She looked like Venus when the goddess
    smiled
At liberty of godship, debonair;
Poor Ariadne! and her eyelids fair

Hid looks beneath them lent her by Per-
    suasion
And every Grace, with tears of Love's
    own passion.
She wept long; then she spake:—
    'Sweet sleep did come
While sweetest Theseus went. Oh, glad
    and dumb,
I wish he had left me still! for in my sleep
I saw his Athens, and did gladly keep
My new bride-state within my Theseus'
    hall;
And heard the pomp of Hymen, and the
    call
Of "Ariadne, Ariadne," sung
In choral joy; and there, with joy I hung
Spring-blossoms round love's altar!—
    aye, and wore
A wreath myself; and felt *him* evermore,
Oh, evermore beside me, with his mighty
Grave head bowed down in prayer to
    Aphrodriè!
Why, what a sweet, sweet dream! *He*
    went with it,
And left me here unwedded where I sit!
Persuasion help me! The dark night did
    make me
  A brideship, the fair morning takes
    away;
My Love had left me when the Hour
    did wake me;
  And while I dreamed of marriage, as
    I say,
And blest it well, my blessèd Theseus
    left me:
And thus the sleep, I loved so, has
    bereft me.
Speak to me, rocks, and tell my grief
    to-day,
Who stole my love of Athens?'. . . .

HOW BACCHUS COMFORTS ARIADNE

Dionysiaca, Lib. XLVII

THEN Bacchus' subtle speech her sorrow
    crossed:—
'O maiden, dost thou mourn for having
    lost
The false Athenian heart? and dost thou
    still
Take thought of Theseus, when thou
    mayst at will

Have Bacchus for a husband? Bacchus
   bright!
A god in place of mortal! Yes, and
   though
The mortal youth be charming in thy
   sight,
That man of Athens cannot strive below,
In beauty and valour, with my deity!
Thou'lt tell me of the labyrinthine
   dweller,
The fierce man-bull, he slew: I pray
   thee, be,
Fair Ariadne, the true deed's true teller,
And mention thy clue's help! because,
   forsooth,
Thine armed Athenian hero had not
   found
A power to fight on that prodigious
   ground,
Unless a lady in her rosy youth
Had lingered near him: not to speak
   the truth
Too definitely out till names be known—
Like Paphia's—Love's—and Ariadne's
   own.
Thou wilt not say that Athens can com-
   pare
With Aether, nor that Minos rules like
   Zeus,
Nor yet that Gnossus has such golden
   air
As high Olympus. Ha! for noble use
We came to Naxos! Love has well in-
   tended
To change thy bridegroom! Happy
   thou, defended
From entering in thy Theseus' earthly
   hall,
That thou mayst hear the laughters rise
   and fall
Instead, where Bacchus rules! Or wilt
   thou choose
A still-surpassing glory?—take it all,—
A heavenly house, Kronion's self for
   kin,—
A place where Cassiopea sits within
Inferior light, for all her daughter's
   sake,
Since Perseus, even amid the stars, must
   take
Andromeda in chains ethereal!
But *I* will wreathe *thee*, sweet, an astral
   crown,

And as my queen and spouse thou shalt
   be known—
Mine, the crown-lover's!' Thus, at
   length, he proved
His comfort on her; and the maid was
   moved;
And casting Theseus' memory down the
   brine,
She straight received the troth of her
   divine
Fair Bacchus; Love stood by to close
   the rite:
The marriage-chorus struck up clear and
   light,
Flowers sprouted fast about the chamber
   green,
And with spring-garlands on their heads,
   I ween,
The Orchomenian dancers came along
And danced their rounds in Naxos to
   the song.
A Hamadryad sang a nuptial dit
Right shrilly: and a Naiad sate beside
A fountain, with her bare foot shelving it,
And hymned of Ariadne, beauteous bride,
Whom thus the god of grapes had deified.
Ortygia sang out, louder than her wont,
An ode which Phoebus gave her to be
   tried,
And leapt in chorus, with her steadfast
   front,
While prophet Love, the stars have
   called a brother,
Burnt in his crown, and twined in one
   another
His love-flower with the purple roses,
   given
In type of that new crown assigned in
   heaven.

PARAPHRASE ON HESIOD

BACCHUS AND ARIADNE
Theog. 947

THE golden-hairèd Bacchus did espouse
   That fairest Ariadne, Minos' daughter,
And made her wifehood blossom in the
   house;
   Where such protective gifts Kronion
     brought her,
Nor Death nor Age could find her when
   they sought her.

PARAPHRASE ON EURIPIDES

ANTISTROPHE

Troades, 853 [1]

Love, Love, who once didst pass the
    Dardan portals,
    Because of Heavenly passion!
Who once didst lift up Troy in exultation,
To mingle in thy bond the high Im-
    mortals!—
    Love, turned from his own name
      To Zeus's shame,
    Can help no more at all.
And Eos' self, the fair, white-steeded
    Morning,—
Her light which blesses other lands,
    returning,
    Has changed to a gloomy pall!
She looked across the land with eyes of
    amber,—
    She saw the city's fall,—
    She, who, in pure embraces,
Had held there, in the hymeneal chamber,
Her children's father, bright Tithonus
    old,
Whom the four steeds with starry brows
    and paces
Bore on, snatched upward, on the car of
    gold,
And with him, all the land's full hope
    of joy!
The love-charms of the gods are vain for
    Troy.

PARAPHRASES ON HOMER

HECTOR AND ANDROMACHE

Iliad, Lib. VI

She rushed to meet him: the nurse
    following
Bore on her bosom the unsaddened child,
A simple babe, prince Hector's well-
    loved son,
Like a star shining when the world is dark.
Scamandrius, Hector called him; but
    the rest
Named him Astyanax, the city's prince,
Because that Hector only, had saved
    Troy.

[1] Rendered after Mr. Burges's, reading, in
some respects—not quite all.

He, when he saw his son, smiled silently;
While, dropping tears, Andromache
    pressed on,
And clung to his hand, and spake, and
    named his name.

'Hector, my best one,—thine own
    nobleness
Must needs undo thee. Pity hast thou
    none
For this young child, and this most sad
    myself,
Who soon shall be thy widow—since
    that soon
The Greeks will slay thee in the general
    rush—
And then, for me, what refuge, 'reft of
    thee,
But to go graveward? Then, no comfort
    more
Shall touch me, as in the old sad times
    thou know'st—
Grief only—grief! I have no father now,
No mother mild! Achilles the divine,
He slew my father, sacked his lofty
    Thebes,
Cilicia's populous city, and slew its king,
Eëtion—father!—did not spoil the corse,
Because the Greek revered him in his soul,
But burnt the body with its daedal arms,
And poured the dust out gently. Round
    that tomb
The Oreads, daughters of the goat-nursed
    Zeus,
Tripped in a ring, and planted their
    green elms.
There were seven brothers with me in
    the house,
Who all went down to Hades in one
    day,—
For *he* slew all, Achilles the divine,
Famed for his swift feet,—slain among
    their herds
Of cloven-footed bulls and flocking sheep!
My mother too, who queened it o'er the
    woods
Of Hippoplacia, he, with other spoil,
Seized,—and, for golden ransom, freed
    too late,—
Since, as she went home, arrowy Artemis
Met her and slew her at my father's door.
But—oh, my Hector,—thou art still to
    me

Father and mother!—yes, and brother
    dear,
O thou, who art my sweetest spouse
    beside!
Come now, and take me into pity! Stay
I' the town here with us! Do not make
    thy child
An orphan, nor a widow, thy poor wife!
Call up the people to the fig-tree, where
The city is most accessible, the wall
Most easy of assault!—for thrice thereby
The boldest Greeks have mounted to
    the breach,—
Both Ajaxes, the famed Idomeneus,
Two sons of Atreus, and the noble one
Of Tydeus,—whether taught by some
    wise seer,
Or by their own souls prompted and
    inspired.'

Great Hector answered:—'Lady, for
    these things
It is my part to care. And *I* fear most
My Trojans, and their daughters, and
    their wives,
Who through their long veils would
    glance scorn at me,
If, coward-like, I shunned the open war.
Nor doth my own soul prompt me to
    that end!
I learnt to be a brave man constantly,
And to fight foremost where my Trojans
    fight,
And vindicate my father's glory and
    mine—
Because I know, by instinct and my
    soul,
The day comes that our sacred Troy
    must fall,
And Priam and his people. Knowing
    which,
I have no such grief for all my Trojans'
    sake,
For Hecuba's, for Priam's, our old king,
Not for my brothers', who so many and
    brave
Shall bite the dust before our enemies,—
As, sweet, for *thee!*—to think some
    mailèd Greek
Shall lead thee weeping and deprive thy
    life
Of the free sun-sight—that, when gone
    away

To Argos, thou shalt throw the distaff
    there,
Not for thy uses—or shalt carry instead
Upon thy loathing brow, as heavy as
    doom,
The water of Greek wells—Messeis' own,
Or Hyperea's!—that some stander-by,
Marking thy tears fall, shall say, "This
    is She,
The wife of that same Hector who fought
    best
Of all the Trojans, when all fought for
    Troy—"
Aye!—and, so speaking, shall renew thy
    pang
That,'reft of Him so named, thou shouldst
    survive
To a slave's life! But earth shall hide
    my corse
Ere that shriek sound, wherewith thou
    art dragged from Troy.'

Thus Hector spake, and stretched his
    arms to his child.
Against the nurse's breast, with childly
    cry,
The boy clung back, and shunned his
    father's face,
And feared the glittering brass and
    waving hair
Of the high helmet, nodding horror down.
The father smiled, the mother could not
    choose
But smile too. Then he lifted from his
    brow
The helm, and set it on the ground to
    shine:
Then, kissed his dear child—raised him
    with both arms,
And thus invoked Zeus and the general
    gods:—

'Zeus, and all godships! grant this boy
    of mine
To be the Trojans' help, as I myself,—
To live a brave life and rule well in Troy!
Till men shall say, "The son exceeds the
    sire
By a far glory." Let him bring home spoil
Heroic, and make glad his mother's heart.'

With which prayer, to his wife's extended
    arms

He gave the child ; and she received him
straight
To her bosom's fragrance—smiling up
her tears.
Hector gazed on her till his soul was
moved ;
Then softly touched her with his hand
and spake.
' My best one—'ware of passion and
excess
In any fear. There's no man in the world
Can send me to the grave apart from
fate,—
And no man . . Sweet, I tell thee . . can
fly fate—
No good nor bad man. Doom is self-
fulfilled.
But now, go home, and ply thy woman's
task
Of wheel and distaff ! bid thy maidens
haste
Their occupation. War's a care for
men—
For all men born in Troy, and chief for me.'

Thus spake the noble Hector, and re-
sumed
His crested helmet, while his spouse
went home ;
But as she went, still looked back lovingly,
Dropping the tears from her reverted face.

THE DAUGHTERS OF PANDARUS

Odyss. Lib. XX

AND so these daughters fair of Pandarus,
The whirlwinds took. The gods had
slain their kin :
They were left orphans in their father's
house.
And Aphroditè came to comfort them
With incense, luscious honey, and fra-
grant wine ;
And Herè gave them beauty of face and
soul
Beyond all women ; purest Artemis
Endowed them with her stature and
white grace ;
And Pallas taught their hands to flash
along
Her famous looms. Then, bright with
deity,

Toward far Olympus, Aphroditè went
To ask of Zeus (who has his thunder-joys
And his full knowledge of man's mingled
fate)
How best to crown those other gifts
with love
And worthy marriage : but, what time
she went,
The ravishing Harpies snatched the
maids away,
And gave them up, for all their loving
eyes,
To serve the Furies who hate constantly.

ANOTHER VERSION

So the storms bore the daughters of
Pandarus out into thrall—
The gods slew their parents ; the orphans
were left in the hall.
And there, came, to feed their young
lives, Aphroditè divine,
With the incense, the sweet-tasting
honey, the sweet-smelling wine ;
Herè brought them her wit above
woman's, and beauty of face ;
And pure Artemis gave them her stature,
that form might have grace :
And Athenè instructed their hands in
her works of renown ;
Then, afar to Olympus, divine Aphroditè
moved on :
To complete other gifts, by uniting each
girl to a mate,
She sought Zeus, who has joy in the
thunder and knowledge of fate,
Whether mortals have good chance or
ill ! But the Harpies alate
In the storm came, and swept off the
maidens, and gave them to wait,
With that love in their eyes, on the
Furies who constantly hate.

PARAPHRASE ON ANACREON

ODE TO THE SWALLOW

THOU indeed, little Swallow,
A sweet yearly comer,
Art building a hollow
New nest every summer,
And straight dost depart
Where no gazing can follow,

Past Memphis, down Nile!
Ah! but Love all the while
Builds his nest in my heart,
Through the cold winter-weeks :
And as one Love takes flight,
Comes another, O Swallow,
In an egg warm and white,
And another is callow.
And the large gaping beaks
Chirp all day and all night :
And the Loves who are older
Help the young and the poor Loves,
And the young Loves grown bolder
Increase by the score Loves—
Why, what can be done?
If a noise comes from one,
Can I bear all this rout of a hundred and
    more Loves ?

PARAPHRASES ON HEINE

[THE LAST TRANSLATION]

ROME, 1860

I

I

OUT of my own great woe
I make my little songs,
Which rustle their feathers in throngs
And beat on her heart even so.

II

They found the way, for their part,
Yet come again, and complain,
Complain, and are not fain
To say what they saw in her heart.

II

I

ART thou indeed so adverse ?
Art thou so changed indeed?
Against the woman who wrongs me
I cry to the world in my need.

II

O recreant lips unthankful,
How could ye speak evil, say,
Of the man who so well has kissed you
On many a fortunate day ?

III

I

MY child, we were two children,
Small, merry by childhood's law ;
We used to crawl to the hen-house
And hide ourselves in the straw.

II

We crowed like cocks, and whenever
The passers near us drew—
Cock-a-doodle! they thought
'Twas a real cock that crew.

III

The boxes about our courtyard
We carpeted to our mind,
And lived there both together—
Kept house in a noble kind.

IV

The neighbour's old cat often
Came to pay us a visit ;
We made her a bow and curtsey,
Each with a compliment in it.

V

After her health we asked,
Our care and regard to evince—
(We have made the very same speeches
To many an old cat since).

VI

We also sate and wisely
Discoursed, as old folks do,
Complaining how all went better
In those good times we knew,—

VII

How love and truth and believing
Had left the world to itself,
And how so dear was the coffee,
And how so rare was the pelf.

VIII

The children's games are over,
The rest is over with youth—
The world, the good games, the good
    times,
The belief, and the love, and the truth.

IV

I

Thou lovest me not, thou lovest me not!
　'Tis scarcely worth a sigh :
Let me look in thy face, and no king in
　　his place
　Is a gladder man than I.

II

Thou hatest me well, thou hatest me
　　well—
　Thy little red mouth has told :
Let it reach me a kiss, and, however it is,
　My child, I am well consoled.

V

I

My own sweet Love, if thou in the
　　grave,
　The darksome grave, wilt be,
Then will I go down by the side, and
　　crave
　Love-room for thee and me.

II

I kiss and caress and press thee wild,
　Thou still, thou cold, thou white !
I wail, I tremble, and weeping mild,
　Turn to a corpse at the right.

III

The Dead stand up, the midnight
　　calls,
　They dance in airy swarms—
We two keep still where the grave-
　　shade falls,
　And I lie on in thine arms.

IV

The Dead stand up, the Judgement-
　　day
　Bids such to weal or woe—
But nought shall trouble us where we
　　stay
　Embraced and embracing below.

VI

I

The years they come and go,
The races drop in the grave,
Yet never the love doth so,
Which here in my heart I have.

II

Could I see thee but once, one day,
And sink down so on my knee,
And die in thy sight while I say,
' Lady, I love but thee ! '

SOME ACCOUNT OF THE GREEK CHRISTIAN POETS [1]

I

THE Greek language was a strong intellectual life, stronger than any similar one which has lived in the breath of 'articulately speaking men,' and survived it. No other language has lived so long and died so hard,—pang by pang, each with a dolphin colour—yielding reluctantly to that doom of death and silence which must come at last to the speaker and the speech. Wonderful it is to look back fathoms down the great past, thousands of years away—where whole generations lie unmade to dust—where the sounding of their trumpets, and the rushing of their scythed chariots, and that great shout which brought down the birds stone dead from beside the sun, are more silent than the dog breathing at our feet, or the fly's paces on our window-pane ; and yet, from the heart of which silence, to feel *words* rise up like a smoke—words of men, even words of women, uttered at first, perhaps, in 'excellent low voices,' but audible and distinct to our times, through 'the dreadful pother' of life and death, the hissing of the steam-engine and the cracking of the cerement ! It is wonderful to look back and listen. Blind Homer spoke this Greek after blind Demodocus, with a quenchless light about his brows, which he felt through his blindness. Pindar rolled his chariots in it, prolonging the clamour of the games. Sappho's heart beat through it, and heaved up the world's. Aeschylus strained it to the stature of his high thoughts. Plato crowned it with his divine peradventures. Aristophanes made it drunk with the wine of his fantastic merriment. The later Platonists wove their souls away in it, out of sight of other souls. The first Christians heard in it God's new revelation, and confessed their Christ in it from the suppliant's knee, and presently from the bishop's throne. To all times, and their transitions, the language lent itself. Through the long summer of above two thousand years, from the grasshopper Homer sang of, to that grasshopper of Manuel Phile, which might indeed have been 'a burden,' we can in nowise mistake the chirping of the bloodless, deathless, wondrous creature. It chirps on in Greek still. At the close of that long summer, though Greece lay withered to her root, her academic groves and philosophic gardens all leafless and bare, still from the depth of the desolation rose up the voice—

> O cuckoo, shall I call thee bird,
> Or but a wandering voice ?

which did not grow hoarse, like other cuckoos, but sang not unsweetly, if more faintly than before. Strangely vital was this Greek language—

Some straggling spirits were behind, to be
Laid out with most thrift on its memory

It seemed as if nature could not part with so lovely a tune, as if she felt it ringing on still in her head—or as if she hummed it to herself, as the watchman used to do, with 'night wandering round ' him, when he watched wearily on the palace roof of the doomed house of Atreus.

But, although it is impossible to touch with a thought the last estate of Greek poetical literature without the wonder occurring of its being still Greek, still

[1] Originally printed in the *Athenaeum*, February and March, 1842.

poetry,—though we are startled by the phenomenon of lifelike sounds coming up from the ashes of a mighty people— at the aspect of an Alcestis returned from the dead, *veiled* but identical,—we are forced to admit, after the first pause of admiration, that a change has passed upon the great thing we recognize, a change proportionate to the greatness, and involving a caducity. Therefore, in adventuring some imperfect account of the Greek ecclesiastical poets, it is right to premise it with the full and frank admission, that they are not accomplished poets—that they do not, in fact, reach with their highest lifted hand, the lowest foot of those whom the world has honoured as Greek poets, but who have honoured the world more by their poetry. The instrument of the Greek tongue was, at the Christian era, an antique instrument, somewhat worn, somewhat stiff in the playing, somewhat deficient in notes which it had once, somewhat feeble and uncertain in such as it retained. The subtlety of the ancient music, the variety of its cadences, the intersections of sweetness in the rise and fall of melodies, rounded and contained in the unity of its harmony, are as utterly lost to this later period as the digamma was to an earlier one. We must not seek for them; we shall not find them; their place knows them no more. Not only was there a lack in the instrument—there was also a deficiency in the players. Thrown aside, after the old flute-story, by a goddess, it was taken up by a mortal hand—by the hand of men gifted and noble in their generation, but belonging to it intellectually, even by their gifts and their nobleness. Another immortal, a true genius, might —nay, would—have asserted himself, and wrung a poem of almost the ancient force from the infirm instrument. It is easy to fancy, and to wish that it had been so—that some martyr or bishop, when bishops were martyrs, and the earth was still warm with the Sacrificial blood, had been called to the utterance of his soul's devotion, with the emphasis of a great poet's power. No one, how-

ever, was so called. Of all the names which shall presently be reckoned, and of which it is the object of this sketch to give some account, beseeching its readers to hold several in honourable remembrance, not one can be crowned with a steady hand as a true complete poet's name. Such a crown is a sacred dignity, and, as it should not be touched idly, it must not be used here. A born Warwick could find, here, no head for a crown.

Yet we shall reckon names 'for remembrance,' and speak of things not ignoble—of meek heroic Christians, and heavenward faces washed serene by tears—strong knees bending humbly for the very strength's sake—bright intellects burning often to the winds in fantastic shapes, but oftener still with an honest inward heat, vehement on heart and brain—most eloquent fallible lips that convince us less than they persuade —a divine loquacity of human falsities— poetical souls, that are not souls of poets! Surely not ignoble things! And the reader will perceive at once that the writer's heart is not laid beneath the wheels of a cumbrous ecclesiastical antiquity—that its intent is to love what is lovable, to honour what is honourable, and to kiss both through the dust of centuries, but by no means to recognize a *hierarchy*, whether in the church or in literature.

If, indeed, an opinion on the former relation might be regarded here, it would be well to suggest that to these 'Fathers,' as we call them filially, with heads turned away, we owe more reverence for the greyness of their beards than theological gratitude for the outstretching of their hands. Devoted and disinterested as many among them were, they themselves were at most times evidently and consciously surer of their *love*, in a theologic sense, than of their knowledge in any. It is no place for a reference to religious controversy; and if it were, we are about to consider them simply as poets, without trenching on the very wide ground of their prose works and ecclesiastical opinions. Still, one passing remark may be admissible, since the fact *is* so remarkable—how any body of Christian men can profess to derive their opinions from 'the opinions of the Fathers,' when *all* bodies might do so equally. These fatherly opinions are, in truth, multiform, and multitudinous as the fatherly 'sublime grey hairs.' There is not only a father apiece for every child, but, not to speak it unfilially, a piece of every father for' every child. Justin Martyr would, of himself, set up a wilderness of sects, besides 'something over,' for the future ramifications of each several one. What then should be done with our 'Fathers'? Leave them to perish by the time-Ganges, as old men innocent and decrepit, and worthy of no use or honour? Surely not. We may learn of them, if God will let us, *love*, and love is much— we may learn devotedness of them and warm our hearts by theirs; and this, although we rather distrust them as commentators, and utterly refuse them the reverence of our souls, in the capacity of theological oracles.

Their place in literature, which we have to do with to-day, may be found, perhaps, by a like moderation. That place is not, it has been admitted, of the highest; and that it is not of the lowest the proof will presently be attempted. There is a mid-air kingdom of the birds called Nephelococcygia, of which Aristophanes tells us something; and we might stand there a moment so as to measure the local adaptitude, putting up the Promethean umbrella to hide us from the 'Gods,' if it were not for the 'men and columns' lower down. But as it is, the very suggestion, if persisted in, would sink all the ecclesiastical antiquity it is desirable to find favour for, to all eternity, in the estimation of the kindest reader. No! the mid-air kingdom of the birds will not serve the wished-for purpose even illustratively, and by grace of the nightingale. 'May the sweet saints pardon us' for wronging them by an approach to such a sense, which, if attained and determined, would have consigned them so certainly to what St. Augustine called—when *he* was moderate too—*mitissima damnatio*, a very mild species of damnation.

It would be, in fact, a rank injustice to the beauty we are here to recognize, to place these writers in the rank of mediocrities, supposing the harsh sense. They may be called mediocrities as poets among poets, but not so as no poets at all. Some of them may sing before gods and men, and in front of any column, from Trajan's to that projected one in Trafalgar Square, to which is promised the miraculous distinction of making the National Gallery sink lower than we see it now. They may, as a body, sing exultingly, holding the relation of column to gallery, in front of the whole 'corpus' of Latin ecclesiastical poetry, and claim the world's ear and the poet's palm. That the modern Latin poets have been more read by scholars, and are better known by reputation to the general reader, is unhappily true: but the truth involves no good reason why it should be so, nor much marvel that it is so. Besides the greater accessibility of Latin literature, the vicissitude of life is extended to posthumous fame, and Time, who is Justice to the poet, is sometimes too busy in pulverizing bones to give the due weight to memories. The modern Latin poets, 'elegant'—which is the critic's word to spend upon them— elegant as they are occasionally, polished and accurate as they are comparatively, stand cold and lifeless, with statue-eyes, near these good, fervid, faulty Greeks of ours—and we do not care to look again. Our Greeks do, in their degree, claim their ancestral advantage, not the mere advantage of language,—nay, least the advantage of language, a comparative elegance and accuracy of expression being ceded to the Latins,—but that higher distinction inherent in brain and breast, of vivid thought and quick sensibility. What if we swamp for a moment the Tertullians and Prudentiuses, and touch, by a permitted anachronism, with one hand Vida, with the other Gregory Nazianzen, what then? What though the Italian poet be smooth as the Italian Canova—working like him out of stone—smooth and cold, disdaining to ruffle his dactyls with the beating of his pulses—what then? Would we change for him our sensitive Gregory, with all his defects in the glorious *scientia metrica*? We would not—perhaps we should not, even if those defects were not attributable, as Mr. Boyd, in the preface to his work on the Fathers, most justly intimates, to the changes incident to a declining language.

It is, too, as religious poets that we are called upon to estimate those neglected Greeks—as religious poets, of whom the universal church and the world's literature would gladly embrace more names than can be counted to either. For it is strange that, although Wilhelm Meister's uplooking and downlooking aspects,—the reverence to things above and things below, the religious all-clasping spirit—be, and must be, in degree and measure, the grand necessity of every true poet's soul, of religious poets, strictly so called, the earth is very bare. Religious 'parcel-poets' we have, indeed, more than enough; writers of hymns, translators of Scripture into prose, or of prose generally into rimes, of whose heart-devotion a higher faculty were worthy. Also there have been poets, not a few, singing as if earth were still Eden; and poets, many, singing as if in the first hour of exile, when the echo of the curse was louder than the whisper of the promise. But the right 'genius of Christianism' has done little up to this moment, even for Chateaubriand. We want the touch of Christ's hand upon our literature, as it touched other dead things—we want the sense of the saturation of Christ's blood upon the souls of our poets, that it may cry *through* them in answer to the ceaseless wail of the Sphinx of our humanity, expounding agony into renovation. Something of this has been perceived in art when its glory was at the fullest. Something of a yearning after this may be seen among the Greek Christian poets, something which would have been *much* with a stronger faculty.

It will not harm us in any case, as lovers of literature and honest judges, if we breathe away, or peradventure *besom* away, the thick dust which lies upon their heavy folios, and besom away, or peradventure *breathe* away, the inward intellectual dust, which must be confessed to lie thickly, too, upon the heavy poems, and make our way softly and meekly into the heart of such hidden beauties (hidden and scattered), as our good luck, or good patience, or, to speak more reverently, the intrinsic goodness of the Fathers of Christian Poetry, shall permit us to discover. May gentle readers favour the endeavour, with 'gentle airs,' if any!—readers not too proud to sleep, were it only for Homer's sake; nor too passionate, at their worst displeasure, to do worse than growl in their sleeves, after the manner of 'most delicate monsters.' It is not intended to crush this forbearing class with folios, nor even with a folio; only to set down briefly in their sight what shall appear to the writer the characteristics of each poet, and to illustrate the opinion by the translation of a few detached passages, or, in certain possible cases, of short entire poems. And so much has been premised, simply that too much be not expected.

It has the look of an incongruity, to begin an account of the Greek Christian poets with a Jew; and Ezekiel is a Jew in his very name, and a 'poet of the Jews' by profession. Moreover, he is wrapt in such a mystery of chronology that nobody can be quite sure of his not having lived before the Christian era—and one whole whisper establishes him as a unit of the famous seventy or seventy-two, under Ptolemy Philadelphus. Let us waive the chronology in favour of the mystery. He is brought out into light by Clemens Alexandrinus; and being associated with Greek poets, and a writer himself of Greek verses, we may receive him in virtue of the τοτοτοτοτοτοτοτοτοτοτιγξ, with little fear, in his case, of implying an injustice in that middle bird-locality of Nephelococcygia. The reader must beware of confounding him with the prophet; and the circumstance of the latter's inspiration is sufficiently distinguishing. Our Greek Ezekiel is, indeed, whatever his chronology may be, no *vates* in the ancient sense. A Greek tragedy (and some fragments of a tragedy are all that we hold of him), by a Jew, and on a Jewish subject, *The Exodus from Egypt,* may startle the most serene of us into curiosity—with which curiosity begins and ends the only strong feeling we can bring to bear upon the work; since, if the execution of it is somewhat curious too, there is a gentle collateral dullness which effectually secures us from feverish excitement. Moses prologizes after the worst manner of Euripides (worse than the worse), compendiously relating his adventures among the bulrushes and in Pharaoh's household, concluded by his slaying an Egyptian, *because nobody was looking.* So saith the poet. Then follows an interview between the Israelite and Zipporah, and her companions, wherein he puts to her certain geographical questions, and she (as far as we can make out through fragmentary cracks) rather *brusquely* proposes their mutual marriage: on which subject he does not venture an opinion; but we find him next confiding his dreams in a family fashion to her father, who considers them satisfactory. Here occurs a broad crack down the tragedy—and we are suddenly called to the revelation from the bush by an extraordinarily ordinary dialogue between Deity and Moses. It is a surprising specimen of the kind of composition adverted to some lines ago, as the translation of Scripture into prose; and the sublime simplicity of the scriptural narrative being thus done (away) into Greek for a certain time, the following reciprocation—to which our old moralities can scarcely do more, or less, than furnish a parallel—prays for an English—exposure. The Divine Being is supposed to address Moses :—

But what is this thou holdest in thine
    hand ?—
Let thy reply be sudden.

    Moses.   'Tis my rod—
I chasten with it quadrupeds and men.
    Voice from the Bush. Cast it upon the
        ground—and straight recoil ;
For it shall be, to move thy wonder-
    ment,
A terrible serpent.
    Moses.   It is cast. But THOU,
Be gracious to me, Lord. How terrible !
How monstrous ! Oh, be pitiful to me !
I shudder to behold it, my limbs shake.

The reader is already consoled for the destiny which mutilated the tragedy, without requiring the last words of the analysis. Happily characteristic of the 'meekest of men' is Moses's naïve admission of the uses of his rod—to beat men and animals withal—of course 'when nobody is looking.'

Clemens Alexandrinus, to whom we owe whatever gratitude is due for our fragmentary Ezekiel, was originally an Athenian philosopher, afterwards a converted Christian, a Presbyter of the Church at Alexandria, and preceptor of the famous Origen. Clemens flourished at the close of the second century. As a prose writer—and we have no prose writings of his, except such as were produced subsequently to his conversion —he is learned and various. His 'Pedagogue' is a wanderer, to universal intents and purposes; and his 'Tapestry,' if the *Stromata* may be called so, is embroidered in all cross-stitches of philosophy, with not much scruple as to the shading of colours. In the midst of all is something, ycleped a dithyrambic ode, addressed to the Saviour, composite of fantastic epithets in the mode of the old litanies, and almost as bald of merit as the Jew-Greek drama, though Clemens himself (worthier in worthier places) be the poet. Here is the opening, which is less fanciful than what follows it :—

    Curb for wild horses,
    Wing for bird-courses
      Never yet flown !
    Helm, safe for weak ones,
    Shepherd, bespeak once,
      The young lambs thine own.
    Rouse up the youth,
    Shepherd and feeder,

So let them bless thee,
Praise and confess thee,—
Pure words on pure mouth,—
Christ, the child-leader !
Oh, the saints' Lord,
All-dominant word !
Holding, by Christdom,
God's highest wisdom !
Column in place
When sorrows seize us,—
Endless in grace
Unto man's race,
Saving one, Jesus !
Pastor and ploughman,
Helm, curb, together,—
Pinion that now can
(Heavenly of feather)
Raise and release us !
Fisher who catcheth
Those whom he watcheth. . .

It goes on ; but we need not do so.
'By the pricking of our thumbs,' we
know that the reader has had enough
of it.

II

PASSING rapidly into the fourth century,
we would offer our earliest homage to
Gregory Nazianzen.

That name must ever be to us a friend,

when the two Apolinarii cross our path
and intercept the 'all hail.' Apolinarius
the grammarian, formerly of Alexandria,
held the office of presbyter in the church
of Laodicaea, and his son Apolinarius,
an accomplished rhetorician, that of
reader, an ancient ecclesiastical office,
in the same church. This younger
Apolinarius was a man of indomitable
energies and most practical inferences ;
and when the edict of Julian forbade to
the Christians the study of Grecian
letters, he, assisted perhaps by his
father's hope and hand, stood strong in
the gap, not in the attitude of supplica-
tion, not with the gesture of consolation,
but in power and sufficiency to fill up
the void and baffle the tyrant. Both
father and son were in the work, by
some testimony ; the younger Apoli-
narius standing out, by all, as the chief
worker, and only one in any extensive

sense. ' Does Julian deny us Homer ?'
said the brave man in his armed soul—
' I am Homer !' and straightway he
turned the whole Biblical history, down
to Saul's accession, into Homeric hexa-
meters—dividing the work, so as to
clench the identity of first and second
Homers, into twenty-four books, each
superscribed by a letter of the alphabet,
and the whole acceptable, according to
the expression of Sozomen, ἀντὶ τῆς
Ὁμήρου ποιήσεως, in the place of Homer's
poetry. ' Does Julian deny us Euri-
pides ?' said Apolinarius again—' I am
Euripides !' and up he sprang—as good
a Euripides (who can doubt it ?) as he
ever was a Homer. ' Does Julian forbid
us Menander ?—Pindar ?—Plato ?—I am
Menander !—I am Pindar !—I am Plato !'
And comedies, lyrics, philosophics,
flowed fast at the word ; and the gospels
and epistles adapted themselves naturally
to the rules of Socratic disputation.
A brave man, forsooth, was our Apoli-
narius of Laodicaea, and literally a man
of men—for observe, says Sozomen,
with a venerable innocence, at which
the gravest may smile gravely—as at
a doublet worn awry at the Council of
Nice—that the old authors did each man
his own work, whereas this Apolinarius
did every man's work in addition to his
own ; and so admirably—intimates the
ecclesiastical critic—that if it were not
for the common prejudice in favour of
antiquity, no ancient could be missed
in the all-comprehensive representative-
ness of the Laodicaean writer. So
excellent was his ability to ' outbrave
the stars in several kinds of light,'
besides the Caesar ! Whether Julian,
naturally mortified to witness this ger-
mination of illustrious heads under the
very iron of his searing, vowed vengeance
against the Hydra-spirit, by the sacred
memory of the animation of his own
beard, we do not exactly know. To
embitter the wrong, Apolinarius sent
him a treatise upon truth—a confutation
of the pagan doctrine, apart from the
scriptural argument — the Emperor's
notice of which is both worthy of his
Caesarship, and a good model-notice

for all sorts of critical dignities. Ἀνέγνων
ἔγνων κατέγνων, is the Greek of it ; so
that, turning from the letter to catch
something of the point, we may write it
down—'I have perused, I have mused,
I have abused': which provoked as
imperious a retort—'Thou mayest have
perused, but thou hast not mused—for
hadst thou mused, thou wouldst not have
abused.' Brave Laodicaean !

Apolinarius's laudable *double* of Greek
literature has perished, the reader will
be concerned to hear, from the face of the
earth, being, like other *lusus*, or marvels,
or monsters, brief of days. One only
tragedy remains, with which the memory
of Gregory Nazianzen has been right
tragically affronted, and which Gregory
—εἴ τις αἴσθησις, as he said of Con-
stantine—would cast off with the scorn
and anger befitting an Apolinarian heresy.
For Apolinarius, besides being an epoist,
dramatist, lyrist, philosopher, and rhe-
torician, was, we are sorry to add, in
the eternal bustle of his soul, a heretic—
possibly for the advantage of something
additional to do. He not only intruded
into the churches hymns which were
not authorized, being his own composi-
tion—so that reverend brows grew dark
to hear women with musical voices sing
them softly to the turning of their distaff,
—but he fell into the heresy of denying
a human soul to the perfect MAN, and of
leaving the Divinity in bare combination
with the Adamic dust. No wonder that
a head so beset with many thoughts and
individualities should at last turn round !
—that eyes rolling in fifty fine frenzies
of twenty-five fine poets should at last
turn blind !—that a determination to rival
all geniuses should be followed by a
disposition more baleful in its exercise,
to understand 'all mysteries' ! Nothing
can be plainer than the step after step
whereby, through excess of vainglory
and morbid mental activity, Apolinarius,
the vice-poet of Greece, subsided into
Apolinarius the chief heretic of Christen-
dom.

To go back sighingly to the tragedy,
where we shall have to sigh again—the
only tragedy left to us of all the tragic

works of Apolinarius (but we do not
sigh for *that*!)—let no voice evermore
attribute it to Gregory Nazianzen. How
could Mr. Alford do so, however hesitat-
ingly, in his *Chapters*, attaching to it,
without the hesitation, a charge upon
the writer, whether Gregory or another
man, that *he*, whoever he was, had, of
his own free will and choice, destroyed
the old Greek originals out of which his
tragedy was constructed, and left it
a monument of their sacrifice as of the
blood on his barbarian hand ? The
charge passes, not only before a breath,
but before its own breath. The tragedy
is, in fact, a specimen of *centoism*, which
is the adaptation of the phraseology of
one work to the construction of another ;
and we have only to glance at it to
perceive the *Medaea* of Euripides dislo-
cated into the *Christus Patiens*. Instead
of the ancient opening—

Oh, would ship Argo had not sailed away
To Colchos by the rough Symplegades !
Nor ever had been felled in Pelion's grove
The pine, hewn for her side ! . . .
　　　　　So she, my queen
Medaea, had not touched this fatal shore,
Soul-struck by love of Jason !

Apolinarius opens it thus—

Oh, would the serpent had not glode along
To Eden's garden-land,—nor ever had
The crafty dragon planted in that grove
A slimy snare ! So she, rib-born of man,
The wretched misled mother of our race,
Had dared not to dare on beyond worst
　　　　　daring,
Soul-struck by love of—apples !

' Let us alone for keeping our counte-
nance '—and at any rate we are bound
to ask gravely of Mr. Alford, *is the
Medaea destroyed ?*—and if not, did the
author of the *Christus Patiens* destroy
his originals ?—and if not, may we not
say of Mr. Alford's charge against that
author, ' Oh, would he had not made
it ! ' So far from Apolinarius being
guilty of destroying his originals, it was
his reverence for them which struggled
with the edict of the persecutor, and
accomplished this dramatic adventure ;—
and this adventure, the only remaining

specimen of his adventurousness, may help us to the secret of his wonderful fertility and omnirepresentativeness, which is probably this—that the great majority of his works, tragic, comic, lyric, and philosophic, consisted simply of *centos*. Yet we pray for justice to Apolinarius : we pray for honour to his motives and energies. Without pausing to inquire whether it had been better and wiser to let poetry and literature depart at once before the tyranny of the edict, than to drag them back by the hair into attitudes grotesquely ridiculous —better and wiser for the Greek Christian schools to let them forgo altogether the poems of their Euripides, than adapt to the meek sorrows of the tender Virgin-mother the bold, bad, cruel frenzy of Medaea, in such verses as these—

She howls out ancient oaths, invokes the faith
Of pledged right-hands, and calls for wit-
    ness, God !

—we pray straightforwardly for justice and honour to the motives and ener-gies of Apolinarius. ' Oh, would that ' many lived *now*, as appreciative of the influences of poetry on our schools and country, as impatient of their contrac-tion, as self-devoted in the great work of extending them ! There remains of his poetical labours, besides the tragedy, a translation of David's Psalms into ' heroic verse,' which the writer of these remarks has not seen,—and of which those critics who desire to deal gently with Apolinarius seem to begin their indulgence by doubting the authenticity.

It is pleasant to turn shortly round, and find ourselves face to face, not with the author of *Christus Patiens*, but with one antagonistical both to his poetry and his heresy, Gregory Nazi-anzen. A noble and tender man was this Gregory, and so tender, because so noble ; a man to lose no cubit of his stature for being looked at steadfastly, or struck at reproachfully. ' You may cast me down,' he said, ' from my bishop's throne, but you cannot banish me from before God's.' And bishop as

he was, his saintly crown stood higher than his tiara, and his loving martyr-smile, the crown of a nature more benign than his fortune, shone up to-ward both. Son of the Bishop of Nazianzen, and holder of the diocese which was his birthplace, previous to his elevation to the level of the storm in the bishopric of Constantinople, little did he care for bishoprics or high places of any kind—the desire of his soul being for solitude, quietude, and that silent religion which should ' rather *be* than *seem*.' But his father's head bent whitely before him, even in the chamber of his brother's death,—and Basil, his beloved friend, the ' half of his soul,' pressed on him with the weight of love ; and Gregory, feeling their tears upon his cheeks, did not count his own, but took up the priestly office. Poor Gregory ! not merely as a priest, but as a man, he had a sighing life of it. His student days at Athens, where he and Basil read together poems and philosophies and holier things, or talked low and *misopogonistically* of their fellow student Julian's bearded boding smile, were his happiest days. He says of himself,

As many stones
Were thrown at *me*, as other men had
    flowers.

Nor was persecution the worst evil ; for friend after friend, beloved after beloved, passed away from before his face, and the voice which charmed them living spoke brokenly beside their graves—his funeral orations marked severally the wounds of his heart,—and his genius served, as genius often does, to lay an emphasis on his grief. The passage we shall venture to translate is rather a cry than a song :—

Where are my wingèd words ? Dissolved
    in air.
Where is my flower of youth ? All withered.
        Where
My glory ? Vanished ! Where the strength
        I knew
From comely limbs ? Disease hath changed
    it too,

And bent them. Where the riches and the
  lands?
GOD HATH THEM! Yea, and sinners' snatch-
  ing hands
Have grudged the rest. Where is my
  father, mother,
And where my blessed sister, my sweet
  brother?—
Gone to the grave!—There did remain for
  me
Alone my fatherland, till destiny,
Malignly stirring a black tempest, drove
My foot from that last rest. And now I rove
Estranged and desolate a foreign shore,
And drag my mournful life and age all
  hoar
Throneless and cityless, and childless save
This father-care for children, which I have,
Living from day to day on wandering feet.
Where shall I cast this body? What will
  greet
My sorrows with an end? What gentle
  ground
And hospitable grave will wrap me round?
Who last my dying eyelids stoop to close—
Some saint, the Saviour's friend? or one of
  those
Who do not know Him?—The air interpose,
And scatter these words too.

The return upon the first thought is
highly pathetic, and there is a restless-
ness of anguish about the whole passage
which consecrates it with the cross of
nature. His happy Athenian associa-
tions gave a colour, unwashed out by
tears, to his mind and works. Half
apostolical he was, and half scholastical;
and while he mused, on his bishop's
throne, upon the mystic tree of twelve
fruits, and the shining of the river of
life, he carried, as Milton did, with
a gentle and not ungraceful distraction,
both hands full of green trailing branches
from the banks of the Cephissus, nay,
from the very plane-tree which Socrates
sat under with Phaedrus, when they two
talked about beauty to the rising and
falling of its leaves. As an orator, he
was greater, all must feel if some do not
think, than his contemporaries; and
the 'golden mouth' might confess it
meekly. Erasmus compares him to
Isocrates, but the *un*likeness is obvious:
Gregory was not excellent at an artful
blowing of the pipes. He spoke grandly,

as the wind does, in *gusts*; and as in
a mighty wind, which combines unequal
noises, the creaking of trees and rude
swinging of doors, as well as the sublime
sovereign rush along the valleys, we
gather the idea from his eloquence less
of music than of power. Not that he is
cold as the wind is—the metaphor goes
no further: Gregory cannot be cold,
even by disfavour of his antithetic points.
He is various in his oratory, full and
rapid in allusion, briefly graphic in
metaphor, equally sufficient for indig-
nation or pathos, and gifted peradventure
with a keener dagger of sarcasm than
should hang in a saint's girdle. His
orations against Julian have all these
characteristics, but they are not poetry,
and we must pass down lower, and
quite over his beautiful letters, to
Gregory the poet.

He wrote *thirty thousand verses*,
among which are several long poems,
severally defective in a defect common
but not necessary to short occasional
poems, and lamentable anywhere, a
want of unity and completeness. The
excellences of his prose are trans-
cribed, with whatever faintness, in his
poetry—the exaltation, the devotion, the
sweetness, the pathos, even to the play-
ing of satirical power about the graver
meanings. But although noble thoughts
break up the dullness of the groundwork
—although, with the instinct of greater
poets, he bares his heart in his poetry,
and the heart is worth baring, still mono-
tony of construction without unity of
intention is the most wearisome of mono-
tonies, and, except in the case of a few
short poems, we find it everywhere in
Gregory. The lack of variety is extended
to the cadences, and the pauses fall stiffly
come corpo morto cade. Melodious lines
we have often: harmonious passages
scarcely ever—the music turning heavily
on its own axle, as inadequate to living
evolution. The poem on his own life
(*De Vitâ suâ*) is, in many places, interest-
ing and affecting, yet faulty with all these
faults. The poem on Celibacy, which
state is commended by Gregory as
becometh a bishop, has occasionally

graphic touches, but is dull enough generally to suit the fairest spinster's view of that melancholy subject. If Hercules could have read it, he must have rested in the middle—from which the reader is entreated to forbear the inference that the poem has not been read through by the writer of the present remarks, seeing that that writer marked the grand concluding moment with a white stone, and laid up the memory of it among the chief triumphs, to say nothing of the fortunate deliverances, *vitae suae*. In Gregory's elegiac poems our ears, at least, are better contented, because the sequence of pentameter to hexameter *necessarily* excludes the various cadence which they yearn for under other circumstances. His anacreontics are sometimes nobly written, with a certain brave recklessness as if the thoughts despised the measure ; and we select from this class a specimen of his poetry, both because three of his hymns have already appeared in the *Athenaeum*, and because the anacreontic in question includes to a remarkable extent the various qualities we have attributed to Gregory, not omitting that play of satirical humour with which he delights to ripple the abundant flow of his thoughts. The writer, though also a translator, feels less misgiving than usual in offering to the reader, in such English as is possible, this spirited and beautiful poem.

SOUL AND BODY

What wilt thou possess or be ?
O my soul, I ask of thee.
What of great, or what of small,
Counted precious therewithal ?
Be it only rare, and want it.
I am ready, soul, to grant it.
Wilt thou choose to have and hold
Lydian Gyges' charm of old,
So to rule us with a ring,
Turning round the jewelled thing,
Hidden by its face concealed,
And revealed by its revealed ?—
Or preferrest Midas' fate—
He who died in golden state,
All things being changed to gold ?
Of a golden hunger dying,
Through a surfeit of ' would I ' -ing !

Wilt have jewels brightly cold ?
Or may fertile acres please ?
Or the sheep of many a fold,
Camels, oxen, for the wold ?
Nay !—I will not give thee these !
These to take thou hast not will—
These to give I have not skill—
Since I cast earth's cares abroad,
That day when I turned to God.

Wouldst a throne—a crown sublime,
Bubble blown upon the time ?
So thou mayest sit to-morrow
Looking downward in meek sorrow,
Some one walking by thee scorning,
Who adored thee yester morning,
Some malign one ?—Wilt be bound
Fast in marriage ? (joy unsound !)
And be turnèd round and round
As the time turns ? Wilt thou catch it,
That sweet sickness? and to match it
Have babies by the hearth, bewildering ?
And if I tell thee the best children
Are none—what answer ?
          Wilt thou thunder
Thy rhetorics—move the people under ?
Covetest to sell the laws
With no justice in thy cause,
And bear on, or else be borne,
Before tribunals worthy scorn ?
Wilt thou shake a javelin rather
Breathing war ? or wilt thou gather
Garlands from the wrestler's ring ?
Or kill beasts for glorying ?
Covetest the city's shout,
And to be in brass struck out ?
Cravest thou that shade of dreaming,
Passing air of shifting seeming,
Rushing of a printless arrow,
Clapping echo of a hand ?
What to those who understand
Are to-day's enjoyments narrow,
Which to-morrow go again,—
Which are shared with evil men,—
And of which no man in his dying
Taketh aught for softer lying ?
What then wouldst thou, if thy mood
Choose not these ? what wilt thou be,
O my soul ? a deity ?
A God before the face of God,
Standing glorious in His glories,
Choral in His angels' chorus ?

Go ! upon thy wing arise,
Plumèd by quick energies,
Mount in circles up the skies :
And I will bless thy wingèd passion,
Help with words thine exaltation,

And, like a bird of rapid feather,
Outlaunch thee, Soul, upon the aether.

But *thou*, O fleshly nature, say,
Thou with odours from the clay,
Since thy presence I must have
As a lady with a slave,
What wouldst *thou* possess or be,
That thy breath may stay with thee?
Nay! I owe thee nought beside,
Though thine hands be open wide.
Would a table suit thy wishes,
Fragrant with sweet oils and dishes
Wrought to subtle niceness? where
Stringèd music strokes the air,
And blithe hand-clappings, and the smooth
Fine postures of the tender youth
And virgins wheeling through the dance
With an unveiled countenance, —
Joys for drinkers, who love shame,
And the maddening wine-cup's flame?—
Wilt thou such, howe'er decried?—
Take them,—and *a rope beside!*

Nay! this boon I give instead,
Unto friend insatiated,—
May some rocky house receive thee,
Self-rooted, to conceal thee chiefly;
Or if labour there must lurk,
Be it by a short day's work!
And for garment, camel's hair,
As the righteous clothèd were,
Clothe thee! or the bestial skin
Adam's bareness hid within,—
Or some green thing from the way,
Leaf of herb, or branch of vine,
Swelling, purpling as it may,
Fearless to be drunk for wine!
Spread a table there beneath thee,
Which a sweetness shall upbreathe thee,
And which the dearest earth is giving,
Simple present to all living!
When that we have placed thee near it,
We will feed thee with glad spirit.
Wilt thou eat? soft, take the bread,
Oaten cake, if that bestead—
Salt will season all aright,
And thine own good appetite,
Which we measure not, nor fetter:
'Tis an uncooked condiment,
Famine's self the only better.
Wilt thou drink? why, here doth bubble
Water from a cup unspent,
Followed by no tipsy trouble,
Pleasure sacred from the grape!
Wilt thou have it in some shape
More like luxury? we are
No grudgers of wine-vinegar!
But if all will not suffice thee,

And thou covetest to draw
In that pitcher with a flaw,
Brimful pleasures heaven denies thee!
Go, and seek out, by that sign,
Other help than this of mine!
For me, I have not leisure so
To warm thee, sweet, my household foe,
Until, like a serpent frozen,
New-maddened with the heat, thou loosen
Thy rescued fang within mine heart!

Wilt have measureless delights
Of gold-roofed palaces, and sights
From pictured or from sculptured art,
With motion near their life; and splendour
Of bas-relief, with tracery tender,
And varied and contrasted hues?
Wilt thou have, as nobles use,
Broidered robes to flow about thee?
Jewelled fingers? Need we doubt thee?
Gauds for which the wise will flout thee?
I most, who of all beauty know
It must be inward, to be so!

And thus I speak to mortals low,
Living for the hour, and o'er
Its shadow, seeing nothing more!
But for those of nobler bearing,
Who live more worthily of wearing
A portion of the heavenly nature—
To low estate of clayey creature,
See, I bring the beggar's meed,
Nutriment beyond the need!
Oh, beholder of the Lord,
Prove on me the flaming sword!
Be mine husbandman, to nourish
Holy plants, that words may flourish
Of which mine enemy would spoil me,
Using pleasurehood to foil me!
Lead me closer to the tree
Of all life's eternity;
Which, as I have pondered, is
The knowledge of God's greatnesses:
Light of One, and shine of Three,
Unto whom all things that be
Flow and tend!
          In such a guise,
Whoever on the earth is wise
Will speak unto himself,—and who
Such inner converse would eschew,
We say perforce of that poor wight,
'He lived in vain!' and if *aright*,
It is not the worst word we might.

Amphilochius, Bishop of Iconium, was
beloved and much appreciated by Gre-
gory, and often mentioned in his writ-
ings. Few of the works of Amphilochius

are extant, and of these only one is a poem. It is a didactic epistle to Seleucus, *On the Right Direction of his Studies and Life*, and has been attributed to Gregory Nazianzen by some writers, upon very inadequate evidence,—that adduced (the similar phraseology which conveys, in this poem and a poem of Gregory's, the catalogue of canonical scriptures) being as easily explained by the imitation of one poet, as by the identity of two. They differ, moreover, upon ground more important than phraseology: Amphilochius appearing to reject, or, at least, to receive doubtfully, Jude's epistle, and the Second of Peter. And there is a harsh force in the whole poem, which does not remind us of our Nazianzen, while it becomes, in the course of dissuading Seleucus from the amusements of the amphitheatre, graphic and effective. We hear, through the description, the grinding of the tigers' teeth, the sympathy of the people with the tigers showing still more savage.

They sit unknowing of these agonies,
Spectators at a show. When a man flies
From a beast's jaw, they groan, as if at least
They missed the ravenous pleasure, like the beast,
And sate there vainly. When, in the next spring,
The victim is attained, and, uttering
The deep roar or quick shriek between the fangs,
Beats on the dust the passion of his pangs,
All pity dieth in their glaring look—
They clap to see the blood run like a brook ;
They stare with hungry eyes, which tears should fill,
And cheer the beasts on with their soul's good will ;
And wish more victims to their maw, and urge
And lash their fury, as they shared the surge,
Gnashing their teeth, like beasts, on flesh of men.

There is an appalling reality in this picture. The epistle consists of 333 lines, which we mention specifically, because the poet takes advantage of the circumstance to illustrate or enforce an important theological doctrine :—

Three hundred lines, three decads, monads three,
Comprise my poem. *Love the Trinity.*

It would be almost a pain, and quite a regret, to pass from this fourth century without speaking a word which belongs to it—a word which rises to our lips, a word worthy of honour—Heliodorus. Though a bishop and an imaginative writer, his *Aethiopica* has no claim on our attention, either by right of Christianity or poetry ; and yet we may be pardoned on our part for love's sake, and on account of the false position into which, by negligence of readers or insufficiency of translators, his beautiful romance has fallen, if we praise it heartily and faithfully even here. Our tears praised it long ago—our recollection does so now—and its own pathetic eloquence and picturesque descriptiveness are ripe for any praise. It has, besides, a vivid Arabian Night charm, almost as charming as Scheherazade herself, suggestive of an Arabian Night story drawn out 'in many a winding bout,' and not merely on the ground of extemporaneous loving and methodical (must we say it?) *lying*. In good sooth—no, not in good sooth, but in evil leasing—every hero and heroine of them all, from Abou Hassan to 'the divine Chariclaea,' does lie most vehemently and abundantly by gift of nature and choice of author, whether bishop or sultana. 'It is,' as Pepys observes philosophically of the comparative destruction of gin-shops and churches in the Great Fire of London, 'pretty to observe' how they all lie. And although the dearest of story-tellers, our own Chaucer, has told us that 'some leasing is, of which there cometh none advauntage to no wight,' even that species is used by them magnanimously in its turn, for the bare glory's sake, and without caring for the 'advauntage.' With equal liberality, but more truth, we write down the Bishop of Tricca's romance *charming*, and wish the charm of it (however we may be out of place in naming him among poets) upon any poet who has not yet felt it, and whose eyes, giving honour, may wander over these remarks. The poor bishop thought as well of his book as we do, perhaps better; for when commanded, under ecclesiastical censure, to burn it or give up his bishopric, he gave up the bishopric. And who blames Heliodorus? He thought well of his romance; he was angry with those who did not; he was weak with the love of it. Let whosoever blames, speak low. Romance-writers are not educated for martyrs, and the exacted martyrdom was very very hard. Think of that English bishop who burnt his hand by an act of volition—only his hand, and which was sure to be burnt afterwards; and how he was praised for it! Heliodorus had to do with a dearer thing—handwriting, not hands. Authors will pardon him, if bishops do not.

Nonnus of Panopolis, the poet of the *Dionysiaca*, a work of some twenty-two thousand verses, on some twenty-two thousand subjects shaken together, *flourished*, as people say of many a dry-rooted soul, at the commencement of the fifth century. He was converted from paganism, but we are sorry to make the melancholy addition that he was never converted from the *Dionysiaca*. The only Christian poem we owe to him—a paraphrase, in hexameters, of the apostle John's Gospel—does all that a bald verbosity and an obscure tautology can do or undo, to quench the divinity of that divine narrative. The two well-known words, bearing on their brief vibration the whole passion of a world saved through pain from pain, are thus traduced:—

They answered him
' Come and behold.' *Then Jesus himself groaned,*
Dropping strange tears from eyes unused to weep.

'Unused to weep!' *Was* it so of the Man of sorrows? Oh, obtuse poet! We had translated the opening passage of the Paraphrase, and laid it by for transcription, but are repelled. Enough is said. Nonnus was never converted from the *Dionysiaca*.

III

SYNESIUS, of Cyrene, learnt Plato's philosophy so well of Hypatia of Alexandria at the commencement of the fifth century, or rather before, that, to the obvious honour of that fair and learned teacher, he never, as Bishop of Ptolemais, could attain to unlearning it. He did not wish to be Bishop of Ptolemais; he had divers objections to the throne and the domination. He loved his dogs, he loved his wife; he loved Hypatia and Plato as well as he loved truth; and he loved beyond all things, under the womanly instruction of the former, to have his own way. He was a poet, too; the chief poet, we do not hesitate to record our opinion—the chief, for true and natural gifts, of all our Greek Christian poets; and it was his choice to pray lyrically between the dew and the cloud rather than preach dogmatically between the doxies. If Gregory shrank from the episcopal office through a meek self-distrust and a yearning for solitude, Synesius repulsed the invitation to it through an impatience of control over heart and life, and for the earnest joy's sake of thinking out his own thought in the hunting-grounds, with no deacon or disciple astuter than his dog to watch the thought in his face, and trace it backward or forward, as the case might be, into something more or less than what was orthodox. Therefore he, a man of many and wandering thoughts, refused the bishopric—not weepingly, indeed, as Gregory did, nor feigning madness with another of the *nolentes episcopari* of that earnest period, but with a sturdy enunciation of resolve, more likely to be effectual, of keeping his wife by his side as long as he lived, and of doubting as long as he pleased to doubt upon the resurrection of the body. But Synesius was a man of genius, and of all such true energies as are taken for granted in the name; and the very sullenness of his nay being expressive to grave judges of the faithfulness of his 'yea and amen,' he was considered too noble a man not to be made a bishop of in his own despite and on his own terms. The fact proves the latitude of discipline, and even of doctrine, permitted to the churches of that age ; and it does not appear that the church at Ptolemais suffered any wrong as its result, seeing that Synesius, recovering from the shock militant of his ordination, in the course of which his ecclesiastical friends had 'laid hands upon him' in the roughest sense of the word, performed his new duties willingly—was no sporting bishop otherwise than as a 'fisher of men'—sent his bow to the dogs, and his dogs to Jericho, that nearest Coventry to Ptolemais, silencing his 'staunch hound's authentic voice' as soon as ever any importance became attached to the authenticity of his own. And if, according to the bond, he retained his wife and his Platonisms, we may honour him by the inference that he did so for conscience' sake still more than love's, since the love was inoperative in other matters. For spiritual fervour and exaltation he has honour among men and angels ; and however intent upon spiritualizing away the most glorified material body from 'the heaven of his invention,' he held fast and earnestly, as anybody's clenched hand could a horn of the altar, the Homoousion doctrine of the Christian heaven, and other chief doctrines emphasizing the divine sacrifice. But this poet has a higher place among poets than this bishop among bishops ; the highest, we must repeat our conviction, of all yet named or to be named by us as 'Greek Christian poets.' Little, indeed, of his poetry has reached us, but this little is great in a nobler sense than that of quantity ; and when of his odes, anacreontic for the most part, we cannot say praisefully that 'they smell of Anacreon,' it is because their fragrance is holier and more abiding—it is because the human soul burning in the censer effaces from our spiritual perceptions the attar of a thousand rose-trees whose roots are in Teos. These odes have, in fact, a wonderful rapture and ecstasy.

And if we find in them the phraseology of Plato or Plotinus, for he leant lovingly to the later Platonists—nay, if we find in them oblique references to the outworn mythology of paganism, even so have we beheld the mixed multitude of unconnected motes wheeling, rising in a great sunshine, as the sunshine were a motive energy,—and even so the burning, adoring poet-spirit sweeps upward the motes of world-fancies (as if being in the world their tendency was Godward) upward in a strong stream of sunny light, while she rushes into the presence of 'the Alone.' We say the *spirit* significantly in speaking of this poet's aspiration. His is an ecstasy of abstract intellect, of pure spirit, cold though impetuous ; the heart does not beat in it, nor is the human voice heard ; the poet is true to the heresy of the ecclesiastic, and there is no resurrection of the body. We shall attempt a translation of the ninth ode, closer if less graceful and polished than Mr. Boyd's, helping our hand to courage by the persuasion that the genius of its poetry must look through the thickest blanket of our dark.

Well-beloved and glory-laden,
Born of Solyma's pure maiden !
I would hymn Thee, blessed Warden,
Driving from Thy Father's garden
Blinking serpent's crafty lust,
With his bruised head in the dust !
Down Thou camest, low as earth,
Bound to those of mortal birth ;
Down Thou camest, low as hell,
Where shepherd-Death did tend and keep
A thousand nations like to sheep,
While weak with age old Hades fell
Shivering through his dark to view Thee,
And the Dog did backward yell
With jaws all gory to let through Thee !
So, redeeming from their pain
Choirs of disembodied ones,
Thou didst lead whom Thou didst gather,
Upward in ascent again,
With a great hymn to the Father,
Upward to the pure white thrones !
King, the daemon tribes of air
Shuddered back to feel Thee there !
And the holy stars stood breathless,
Trembling in their chorus deathless ;

A low laughter fillèd ether—
Harmony's most subtle sire
From the seven strings of his lyre
Stroked a measured music hither—
Io paean ! victory !
Smiled the star of morning—he
Who smileth to foreshow the day !
Smilèd Hesperus the golden,
Who smileth soft for Venus gay !
While that hornèd glory holden
Brimful from the fount of fire,
The white moon, was leading higher
In a gentle pastoral wise
All the nightly deities !
Yea, and Titan threw abroad
The far shining of his hair
'Neath Thy footsteps holy-fair,
Owning Thee the Son of God ;
The Mind artificer of all,
And his own fire's original !

And THOU upon Thy wing of will
Mounting,—Thy God-foot uptill
The neck of the blue firmament,—
Soaring, didst alight content
Where the spirit-spheres were singing,
And the fount of good was springing,
In the silent heaven !
Where Time is not with his tide
Ever running, never weary,
Drawing earth-born things aside
Against the rocks : nor yet are given
The plagues death-bold that ride the dreary
Tost matter-depths.   Eternity
Assumes the places which they yield !
Not aged, howsoe'er she held
Her crown from everlastingly—
At once of youth, at once of eld,
While in that mansion which is hers
To God and gods she ministers !

How the poet rises in his 'singing
clothes' embroidered all over with the
mythos and the philosophy ! Yet his
eye is to the Throne : and we must not
call him half a heathen by reason of a
Platonic idiosyncrasy, seeing that the
esoteric of the most suspicious turnings
of his phraseology is 'Glory to the true
God.'   For another ode Paris should be
here to choose it—we are puzzled among
the beautiful. Here is one with a
thought in it from Gregory's prose,
which belongs to Synesius by right of
conquest :—

O my deathless, O my blessèd,
Maid-born, glorious son confessèd,

O my Christ of Solyma !
I who earliest learnt to play
This measure for Thee, fain would bring
Its new sweet tune to cittern-string—
Be propitious, O my King !
Take this music which is mine,
Anthem'd from the songs divine !

We will sing Thee, deathless One,
God Himself, and God's great Son—
Of sire of endless generations,
Son of manifold creations !
Nature mutually endued,
Wisdom in infinitude !
God, before the angels burning—
Corpse, among the mortals mourning !
What time Thou wert pourèd mild
From an earthy vase defiled,
Magi with fair arts besprent,
At Thy new star's orient,
Trembled inly, wondered wild,
Questioned with their thoughts abroad—
' What then is the new-born child ?
WHO the hidden God ?'
God, or corpse, or King ?—
Bring your gifts, oh hither bring
Myrrh for rite—for tribute, gold—
Frankincense for sacrifice !
God ! Thine incense take and hold !
King ! I bring Thee gold of price !
Myrrh with tomb will harmonize !

For Thou, entombed, hast purified
Earthly ground and rolling tide,
And the path of daemon nations,
And the free air's fluctuations,
And the depth below the deep !
Thou God, helper of the dead,
Low as Hades didst Thou tread !
Thou King, gracious aspect keep !
Take this music which is mine,
Anthem'd from the songs divine.

Eudocia—in the twenty-first year of
the fifth century—wife of Theodosius,
and empress of the world, thought good
to extend her sceptre—

(Hac claritate gemina
O gloriosa foemina !)

over Homer's poems, and cento-ize them
into an epic on the Saviour's life. She
was the third fair woman accused of
sacrificing a world for an apple, having
moved her husband to wrath by giving
away his imperial gift of a large one to
her own philosophic friend Paulinus ;
and being unhappily more learned than

her two predecessors in the sin, in the course of her exile to Jerusalem she took ghostly comfort by separating Homer's εἴδωλον from his φρένες. There she sat among the ruins of the holy city, addressing herself most unholily, with whatever good intentions and delicate fingers, to pulling Homer's gold to pieces bit by bit, even as the ladies of France devoted what remained to them of virtuous energy *pour parfiler* under the benignant gaze of Louis Quinze. She, too, who had no right of the purple to literary ineptitude—she, born no empress of Rome, but daughter of Leontius the Athenian, what had she to do with Homer, *parfilant*? Was it not enough for Homer that he was turned once, like her own cast imperial mantle, by Apolinarius into a Jewish epic, but that he must be unpicked again by Eudocia for a Christian epic? The reader, who has heard enough of centos, will not care to hear how she did it. That she did it was too much; and the deed recoiled. For mark the poetical justice of her destiny; let all readers mark it; and all writers, especially female writers, who may be half as learned, and not half as fair—that although she wrote many poems, one *On the Persian War*, whose title and merit are recorded, not one, except this cento, has survived. The obliterative sponge we hear of in Aeschylus has washed out every verse except this cento's 'damned spot.' This remains. This is called Eudocia! this stands for the daughter of Leontius, and this only in the world! O fair mischief! she is punished by her hand.

And yet, are we born critics any more than she was born an empress, that we should not have a heart? and is our heart stone, that it should not wax soft within us while the vision is stirred 'between our eyelids and our eyes,' of this beautiful Athenais, baptized once by Christian waters, and once by human tears, into Eudocia, the imperial mourner?—this learned pupil of a learned father, crowned once by her golden hair, and once by her golden crown,

yet praised more for poetry and learning than for beauty and greatness by such grave writers as Socrates and Evagrius, the ecclesiastical historians?—this world's empress, pale with the purple of her palaces, an exile even on the throne from her Athens, and soon twice an exile, from father's grave and husband's bosom? We relent before such a vision. And what if, relentingly, we declare her innocent of the Homeric cento?—what if we find her 'a whipping boy' to take the blame?—what if we write down a certain Proba *improba*, and bid her bear it? For Eudocia having been once a mark to slander may have been so again; and Falconia Proba having committed cento-ism upon Virgil must have been capable of anything. The Homeric cento has been actually attributed to her by certain critics, with whom we would join in all earnestness our most sour voices, gladly, for Eudocia's sake, who is closely dear to us, and not malignly for Proba's, who was *improba* without our help. So shall we impute evil to only one woman, and she not an Athenian; while our worst wish, even to her, assumes this innoxious shape, that she had used a distaff rather than a stylus, though herself and the yet more 'Sleeping Beauty' had owned one horoscope between them! Amen to our wish! A busy distaff and a sound sleep to Proba!

And now that golden-haired, golden-crowned daughter of Leontius, for whom neither the much learning nor the much sorrow drove Hesperus from her sovran eyes—let her pass on unblenched. Be it said of her, softly as she goes, by all gentle readers—'She is innocent, whether for centos or for apples! She wrote only such Christian Greek poems as Christians and poets might rejoice to read, but which perished with her beauty, as being of one seed with it.'

Midway in the sixth century we encounter Paul Silentiarius, called so in virtue of the office held by him in the court of Justinian, and chiefly esteemed for his descriptive poem on the Byzantine church of St. Sophia, which, after the Arian conflagration, was rebuilt gorgeously by the emperor. This church was not dedicated to a female saint, according to the supposition of many persons, but to the second person of the Trinity, the ἁγία σοφία—holy wisdom; while the poem being recited in the imperial presence, and the poet's gaze often forgetting to rise higher than the imperial smile, Paul Silentiarius dwelt less on the divine dedication and the spiritual uses of the place, than on the glory of the dedicator and the beauty of the structure. We hesitate, moreover, to grant to his poem the praise which has been freely granted to it by more capable critics, of its power to realize this beauty of structure to the eyes of the reader. It is highly elaborate and artistic; but the elaboration and art appear to us architectural far more than picturesque. There is no sequency, no congruity, no keeping, no light and shade. The description has reference to the working as well as to the work, to the materials as well as to the working. The eyes of the reader are suffered to approach the whole only in analysis, or rather in analysis analysed. Every part, part by part, is recounted to him excellently well—is brought close till he may touch it with his eyelashes; but when he seeks for the general effect it is in pieces—there is none of it. Byron shows him more in the passing words,

I have beheld Sophia's bright roofs swell
    Their glittering mass i' the sun,

than Silentiarius in all his poem. Yet the poem has abundant merit in diction and harmony; and besides higher noblenesses, the pauses are modulated with an artfulness not commonly attained by these later Greeks, and the ear exults in an unaccustomed rhythmetic pomp which the inward critical sense is inclined to murmur at, as an expletive verbosity.

Whoever looketh with a mortal eye
To heaven's emblazoned forms, not steadfastly

With unreverted neck can bear to measure
That meadow-round of star-apparelled pleasure,
But drops his eyelids to the verdant hill,
Yearning to see the river run at will,
With flowers on each side,—and the ripening corn,
And grove thick set with trees, and flocks at morn
Leaping against the dews,—and olives twined,
And green vine-branches trailingly inclined,—
And the blue calmness skimmed by dripping oar
Along the Golden Horn.
                    But if he bring
His foot across this threshold, never more
Would he withdraw it; fain, with wandering
Moist eyes, and ever-turning head, to stay,
Since all satiety is driven away
Beyond the noble structure. Such a fane
Of blameless beauty hath our Caesar raised
By God's perfective grace, and not in vain!
O emperor, these labours we have praised,
Draw down the glorious Christ's perpetual smile:
For thou, the high-peaked Ossa didst not pile
Upon Olympus' head, nor Pelion throw
Upon the neck of Ossa, opening so
The aether to the steps of mortals! no!
Having achieved a work more high than hope,
Thou dost not need these mountains as a slope
Whereby to scale the heaven! Wings take thee thither
From purest piety to highest aether.

The following passage, from the same 'Description,' is hard to turn into English, through the accumulative riches of the epithets. Greek words atone for their vainglorious redundancy by their beauty, but we cannot think so of these our own pebbles.

Who will unclose me Homer's sounding lips,
And sing the marble mead that oversweeps
The mighty walls and pavements spread around
Of this tall temple, which the sun has crowned?
The hammer with its iron tooth was loosed
Into Carystus' summit green, and bruised
The Phrygian shoulder of the daedal stone;—

This marble, coloured after roses fused
In a white air, and that, with flowers thereon
Both purple and silver, shining tenderly !
And that which in the broad fair Nile sank
    low
The barges to their edge, the porphyry's
    glow
Sown thick with little stars ! and thou mayst
    see
The green stone of Laconia glitter free !
And all the Carian hill's deep bosom brings,
Streaked bow-wise, with a livid white and
    red,—
And all the Lydian chasm keeps covered,—
A hueless blossom with a ruddier one
Soft mingled ! all, besides, the Libyan sun
Warms with his golden splendour, till he
    make
A golden yellow glory for his sake,
Along the roots of the Maurusian height !
And all the Celtic mountains give to sight
From crystal clefts : black marbles dappled
    fair
With milky distillations here and there !
And all the onyx yields in metal-shine
Of precious greenness !—all that land of
    thine,
Aetolia, hath on even plains engendered
But not on mountain-tops,—a marble
    rendered
Here nigh to green, of tints which emeralds
    use,
Here with a sombre purple in the hues !
Some marbles are like new-dropt snow, and
    some
Alight with blackness !—Beauty's rays have
    come,
So congregate, beneath this holy dome !

And thus the poet takes us away from
the church and dashes our senses and
admirations down these marble quarries!
Yet it is right for us to admit the miracle
of a poem made out of stones! and when
he spoke of unclosing Homer's lips on
such a subject he was probably thinking
of Homer's ships, and meant to intimate
that one catalogue was as good for him
as another.

John Geometra arose in no propitious
orient probably with the seventh cen-
tury, although the time of his 'elevation'
appears to be uncertain within a hundred
years.

He riseth slowly, as his sullen car
Had all the weights of sleep and death hung
    on it.

Plato, refusing his divine fellowship
to any one who was not a geometrician
or who was a poet, might have kissed
our Johannes, who was not divine, upon
both cheeks, in virtue of his other name
and in vice of his verses. He was the
author of certain hymns to the Virgin
Mary, as accumulative of epithets and
admirations as ten of her litanies, in-
clusive of a pious compliment, which,
however geometrically exact in its pro-
portions, sounds strangely.

Oh health to thee ! new living car of the sky,
Afire on the wheels of four virtues at once !
Oh health to thee ! Seat, than the cherubs
    more high,
More pure than the seraphs, *more broad
    than the thrones*.

Towards the close of the last hymn,
the exhausted poet empties back some-
thing of the ascription into his own lap
by a remarkable *mihi quoque.*

Oh health to me, royal one ! if there belong
Any grace to my singing, that grace is from
    thee.
Oh health to me, royal one ! if in my song
Thou hast pleasure—oh, thine is the grace
    of the glee !

We may mark the time of George
Pisida, about thirty years deep in the
seventh century. He has been con-
founded with the rhetorical Archbishop
of Nicomedia, but held the office of
scaevophylax, only lower than the high-
est, in the metropolitan church of St.
Sophia, and was a poet, singing half in
the church and half in the court, and
considerably nearer to the feet of the
Emperor Heraclius than can please us
in any measure. Hoping all things,
however, in our poetical charity, we are
willing to hope even this—that the man
whom Heraclius carried about with him
as a singing-man when he went to fight
the Persians, and who sang and recited
accordingly, and provided notes of ad-
miration for all the imperial notes of
interrogation, and gave his admiring
poems the appropriate and suggestive
name of *acroases*—auscultations, things
intended to be heard,—might neverthe-
less love Heraclius the fighting-man,

not slave-wise or flatterer-wise, but man-wise or dog-wise, in good truth, and up to the brim of his praise ; and so hoping, we do not dash the praise down as a libation to the infernal task-masters. Still it is an impotent conclusion to a free-hearted poet's musing on the *Six Days' Work*, to wish God's creation under the sceptre of his particular friend ! It looks as if the particular friend had an ear like Dionysius, and the poet— ah, the poet !—a mark as of a chain upon his brow in the shadow of his court laurel.

We shall not revive the question agitated among his contemporaries, whether Euripides or George Pisida wrote the best iambics ; but that our George knew the secret of beauty, and that, having noble thoughts, he could utter them nobly, is clear, despite of Heraclius. That he is, besides, unequal; often coldly perplexed when he means to be ingenious, only violent when he seeks to be inspired; that he premeditates ecstasies, and is inclined to the attitudes of the orators ; in brief, that he 'not only' and not seldom sleeps but *snores*—are facts as true of him as the praise is. His Hexaëmeron, to which we referred as his chief work, is rather a meditation or rhythmetical speech upon the finished creation, than a retrospection of the six days —and also there is more of Plato in it than of Moses. It has many fine things, and whole passages of no ordinary eloquence, though difficult to separate and select.

Whatever eyes seek God to view His Light,
As far as they behold Him close in night !
Whoever searcheth with insatiate balls
Th' abysmal glare, or gazeth on Heaven's walls
Against the fire-disk of the sun, the same
According to the vision he may claim,
Is dazzled from his sense. What soul of flame
Is called sufficient to view onward thus
The way whereby the sun's light came to us ?

O distant Presence in fixed motion ! Known
To all men, and inscrutable to one :
Perceived—uncomprehended ! unexplained
To all the spirits, yet by each attained,

Because its God-sight is Thy work ! O Presence,
Whatever holy greatness of Thine essence
Lie virtue-hidden—Thou hast given our eyes
The vision of Thy plastic energies ;—
Not shown in angels only (those create
All fiery-hearted, in a mystic state
Of bodiless body), but, if order be
Of natures more sublime than they or we,
In highest Heaven, or mediate aether, or
This world now seen, or one that came before
Or one to come—quick in Thy purpose—there !
Working in fire and water, earth and air—
In every tuneful star, and tree, and bird—
In all the swimming, creeping life unheard,
In all green herbs, and chief of all, in MAN.

There are other poems of inferior length, *On the Persian War*, in three books, or, alas, 'auscultations'— *The Heracliad*, again on the Persian war, and in two (of course) auscultations again,—*Against Severus, On the Vanity of Life, The War of the Huns*, and others. From the *Vanity of Life*, which has much beauty and force, we shall take a last specimen :—

Some yearn to rule the state, to sit above,
And touch the cares of hate as near as love—
Some their own reason for tribunal take,
And for all thrones the humblest prayers they make !
Some love the orator's vainglorious art,—
The wise love silence and the hush of heart,—
Some to ambition's spirit-curse are fain,
That golden apple with a bloody stain ;
While some do battle in her face (more rife
Of noble ends) and conquer strife with strife !
And while your groaning tables gladden these,
Satiety's quick chariot to disease,
Hunger the wise man helps, to water, bread,
And light wings to the dreams about his head.

The truth becomes presently obvious, that—

The sage o'er all the world his sceptre waves,
And earth is common ground to thrones and graves.

John Damascenus, to whom we should not give by any private impulse of admiration the title of Chrysorrhoas accorded to him by his times, lived at Damascus, his native city, early in the eighth century, holding an unsheathed sword of controversy until the point drew down the lightning. He retired before the affront rather than the injury; and in company with his beloved friend and fellow poet, Cosmas of Jerusalem (whose poetical remains the writer of these remarks has vainly sought the sight of, and therefore can only, as by hearsay, ascribe some value to them), hid the remnant of his life in the monastery of Saba, where Phocas of the twelfth century looked upon the tomb of either poet. John Damascenus wrote several acrostics on the chief festivals of the churches, which are not much better, although very much longer, than acrostics need be. When he writes out of his heart, without looking to the first letters of his verses—as, indeed, in his anacreontic his eyes are too dim for iota hunting—he is another man, and almost a strong man; for the heart being sufficient to speak we want no Delphic oracle—'Pan is NOT dead.' In our selection from the anacreontic hymn the tears seem to trickle audibly—we welcome them as a Castalia, or, rather, 'as Siloa's brook,' flowing by an oracle more divine than any Grecian one :—

From my lips in their defilement,
From my heart in its beguilement,
From my tongue which speaks not fair,
From my soul stained everywhere,
O my Jesus, take my prayer !

Spurn me not for all it says,
Not for words and not for ways,—
Not for shamelessness endued !
Make me brave to speak my mood,
O my Jesus, as I would !
Or teach me, which I rather seek,
What to do and what to speak.

I have sinned more than she,
Who learning where to meet with Thee,
And bringing myrrh, the highest priced,
Anointed bravely, from her knee,
Thy blessed feet accordingly—
My God, my Lord, my Christ !—
As Thou saidest not ' Depart '
To that suppliant from her heart,
Scorn me not, O Word, that art

The gentlest one of all words said !
But give Thy feet to me instead
That tenderly I may them kiss
And clasp them close, and never miss
With over-dropping tears, as free
And precious as that myrrh could be,
T' anoint them bravely from my knee !

Wash me with Thy tears : draw nigh me,
That their salt may purify me :
THOU remit my sins who knowest
All the sinning, to the lowest—
Knowest all my wounds, and seest
All the stripes Thyself decreest ;
Yea, but knowest all my faith,
Seest all my force to death,—
Hearest all my wailings low,
That mine evil should be so !
Nothing hidden but appears
In Thy knowledge, O Divine,
O Creator, Saviour mine—
Not a drop of falling tears,
Not a breath of inward moan,
Not a heart-beat . . . which is gone !—

After this deep pathos of Christianity we dare not say a word—we dare not even praise it as poetry : our heart is stirred, and not ' idly.' The only sound which can fitly succeed the cry of the contrite soul is that of Divine condonation or of angelic rejoicing. Let us who are sorrowful still, be silent too.

IV

ALTHOUGH doubts, as broad as four hundred years, separate the earliest and latest period talked of as the age of Simeon Metaphrastes by those *viri illustrissimi* the classical critics, we may set him down, without much peril to himself or us, at the close of the tenth century, or very early in the eleventh. He is chiefly known for his *Lives of the Saints*, which have been lifted up as a mark both for honour and dishonour; which Psellus hints at as a favourite literature of the angels, which Leo Allatius exalts as chafing the temper of the heretics, and respecting which we, in an exemplary serenity, shall straightway accede to one-half of the opinion of Bellarmine—that the work speaketh not as things actually happened, but as they might have happened—'*non ut res gestae fuerant, sed ut geri potuerant.*' Our half of this weighty opinion is the first clause—we demur upon '*ut geri potuerant,*'—and we need not go further than the former to win a light of commentary for the term 'metaphrases,' applied to the saintly biographies in otherwise a doubtful sense, and worn obliquely upon the sleeve of the biographer Metaphrastes, in no doubtful token of his skill in metamorphosing things as they were into things as they might have been. And Simeon having received from Constantinople the honour of his birth within her walls, and returning to her the better honour of the distinctions and usefulness of his life,—so writeth Psellus, his encomiast, with a graceful turn of thought,—expired in an 'odour of sanctity,' befitting the biographer of all the saints—breathing out from his breathless remains such an incense of celestial sweetness, that if it had not been for the maladroitness of certain unfragrant persons whose desecration of the next tomb acted instantly as a stopper, the whole earth might at this day be *metaphrased* to our nostrils, as steeped in an attar-gul of Eden or Ede!—we might be dwelling in a phoenix nest at this day. Through the maladroitness, however, in question, there is lost to us every sweeter influence from the life and death of Simeon Metaphrastes than may result from the lives and deaths of his saints, and from other works of his, whether commentaries, orations, or poems; and we cannot add that the aroma from his writings bears any proportion in value to the fragrance from his sepulchre. Little of his poetry has reached us, and we are satisfied with the limit. There were three Simeons, who did precede our Simeon, as the world knoweth, and whose titles were Stylitae or Columnarii, because it pleased them in their saintly volition to take the highest place and live out their natural lives supernaturally, each upon the top of a column. Peradventure the columns which our Simeon refused to live upon conspired against his poetry: peradventure it is on their account that we find ourselves between two alphabetic acrostics, written solemnly by his hand, and take up one wherein every alternate line begins with a letter of the alphabet; its companion in the couplet being left to run behind it, out of livery and sometimes out of breath. Will the public care to look upon such a curiosity? Will our verse-writers care to understand what harm may be done by a conspiration of columns—gods and men quite on one side? And will candid readers care to confess at last, that there is an earnestness in the poem, acrostic as it is— a leaning to beauty's side—which is above the acrosticism? Let us try:—

Ah, tears upon mine eyelids, sorrow on
 mine heart!
I bring Thee soul-repentance, Creator as
 Thou art.
Bounding joyous actions, deep as arrows
 go—
Pleasures self-revolving, issue into woe
Creatures of our mortal, headlong rush to
 sin—
I have seen them;—of them—ah me,—I
 have been!
Duly pitying Spirits, from your spirit-frame,
Bring your cloud of weeping,—worthy of
 the same!
Else I would be bolder—If that light of
 Thine,
Jesus, quell the evil, let it on me shine.
Fail me truth, is living, less than death for-
 lorn,
When the sinner readeth—'better be un-
 born'?
God, I raise toward Thee both eyes of my
 heart,
With a sharp cry—'Help me!'—while
 mine hopes depart.
Help me! Death is bitter, all hearts com-
 prehend;
But I fear beyond it—end beyond the
 end!
Inwardly behold me, how my soul is black—
 Sympathize in gazing, do not spurn me
 back!
Knowing that Thy pleasure is not to destroy,
 That Thou fain wouldst save me—this is
 all my joy.
Lo, the lion, hunting spirits in their deep,
 (Stand beside me!) roareth—(help me!)
 nears to leap.

Mayst Thou help me, Master! Thou art
pure alone—
   Thou alone art sinless—one Christ on
   a throne.
Nightly deeds I loved them—hated day's
instead—
   Hence this soul-involving darkness on
   mine head!
O Word, who constrainest things estranged
and curst,
   If Thy hand can save me, that work were
   the first!
Pensive o'er my sinning, counting all its
ways,
   Terrors shake me, waiting adequate dis-
   mays.
Quenchless glories many, hast Thou—
many a rod—
   Thou, too, hast Thy measures—Can I
   bear Thee, God?
Rend away my counting from my soul's
decline,
   Show me of the portion of those saved of
   Thine!
Slow drops of my weeping to Thy mercy
run—
   Let its rivers wash me, by that mercy
   won.
Tell me what is worthy, in our dreary
now,
   As the future glory? (madness!) what,
   as Thou?
Union, oh, vouchsafe me to Thy fold be-
neath,
   Lest the wolf across me gnash his gory
   teeth!
View me, judge me gently! spare me,
Master bland,—
   Brightly lift Thine eyelids, kindly stretch
   Thine hand!
Winged and choral angels! 'twixt my
spirit lone,
   And all deathly visions, interpose your
   own!
Yea, my Soul, remember death and woe
inwrought—
   After-death affliction, wringing earth's to
   nought.
Zone me, Lord, with graces! Be founda-
tions built
   Underneath me; save me! as Thou
   know'st and wilt!

The omission of our X (in any case
too sullen a letter to be employed in
the service of an acrostic) has permitted
us to write line for line with the Greek;
and we are able to infer, to the honour
of the Greek poet, that, although he did
not live upon a column, he was not far
below one, in the virtue of self-mortifi-
cation. We are tempted to accord
him some more gracious and serious
justice, by breaking away a passage
from his *Planctus Mariae*, the lament of
Mary on embracing the Lord's body;
and giving a moment's insight into
a remarkable composition, which, how-
ever deprived of its poetical right of
measure, is, in fact, nearer to a poem,
both in purpose and achievement, than
any versified matter we have looked
upon from this metaphrastic hand :—

'O uncovered corse, yet Word of the
Living One! self-doomed to be uplifted
on the cross for the drawing of all men
unto Thee, — what member of Thine
hath no wound? O my blessed brows,
embraced by the thorn-wreath which is
pricking at my heart! O beautiful and
priestly One, who hadst not where to
lay Thine head and rest, and now wilt
lay it only in the tomb, resting *there*—
sleeping, as Jacob said, a lion's sleep!
O cheeks turned to the smiter! O lips,
new hive for bees, yet fresh from the
sharpness of vinegar and bitterness of
gall! O mouth, wherein was no guile,
yet betrayed by the traitor's kiss!
O hand, creative of man, yet nailed to
the cross, and since, stretched out unto
Hades, with help for the first trans-
gressor! O feet, once walking on the
deep to hallow the waters of nature!
O me, my son! . . . Where is thy
chorus of sick ones?—those whom Thou
didst cure of their diseases, and bring
back from the dead? Is none here, but
only Nicodemus, to draw the nails from
those hands and feet?—none here, but
only Nicodemus, to lift Thee from the
cross, heavily, heavily, and lay Thee in
these mother-arms, which bore Thee
long ago, in Thy babyhood, and were
glad *then*? These hands, which swaddled
Thee then, let them bind Thy grave-
clothes now. And yet,—O bitter
funerals!——O Giver of life from the
dead, liest Thou dead before mine eyes?
Must *I*, who said "hush" beside Thy
cradle, wail this passion upon Thy

grave? *I*, who washed Thee in Thy first bath, must I drop on Thee these hotter tears? I, who raised Thee high in my maternal arms,—but *then* Thou leapedst,—*then* Thou springedst up in Thy child-play. . . .'

It is better to write so than to stand upon a column. And, although the passage does, both generally and specifically, in certain of its ideas, recall the antithetic eloquence of that Gregory Nazianzen before whom this Simeon must be dumb, we have touched his 'oration' so called, nearer than our subject could permit us to do any of Gregory's, because the *Planctus* involves an imagined situation, is poetical in its design. Moreover, we must prepare to look downwards; the poets were descending from the gorgeous majesty of the hexameter and the severe simplicity of iambics, down through the mediate *versus politici*, a loose metre, adapted to the popular ear, to the lowest deep of a 'measured prose,'—which has been likened (but which *we* will not liken) to the blank verse of our times. Presently we may offer an example from Psellus of a prose acrostic —the reader being delighted with the prospect! 'A whole silver threepence, mistress.'

Michael Psellus lived midway in the eleventh century, and appears to have been a man of much aspiration towards the higher places of the earth. A senator of no ordinary influence, preceptor of the Emperor Michael previous to that accession, he is supposed to have included in his instructions the advantages of sovereignty, and in his precepts the most subtle means of securing them. We were about to add that his acquirements as a scholar were scarcely less imperial than those of his pupil as a prince; but the expression might have been inappropriate. There are cases not infrequent—not entirely opposite to the present case, and worthy always of all meditation by such intelligent men as affect extensive acquisition —when acquirements are not ruled by the man, but rule him. Whatever

originates from the mind cannot obstruct her individual faculty; nay, whatever she receives inwardly and marks her power over by creating out of it a *tertium quid*, according to the law of the perpetual generation of spiritual verities, is not obstructive but impulsive to the evolution of faculty; but the erudition, whether it be erudition as the world showed it formerly, or miscellaneous literature, as the world shows it now, the accumulated acquirement of whatever character, which remains *extraneous* to the mind, is and must be in the same degree an obstruction and deformity. How many are there from Psellus to Bayle, bound hand and foot intellectually with the rolls of their own papyrus—men whose erudition has grown stronger than their souls! How many whom we would gladly see washed in the clean waters of a little ignorance, and take our own part in their refreshment! Not that knowledge is bad, but that wisdom is better; and that it is better and wiser in the sight of the angels of knowledge to think out one true thought with a thrush's song and a green light for all lexicon—or to think it without the light and without the song, because truth is beautiful, where they are not seen or heard—than to mummy our benumbed souls with the circumvolutions of twenty thousand books. And so Michael Psellus was a learned man.

We have sought earnestly, yet in vain—and the fact may account for our ill-humour—a sight of certain iambics upon vices and virtues, and Tantalus and Sphinx, which are attributed to this writer, and cannot be in the moon after all: earnestly, yet with no fairer encouragement to our desire than what befalls it from his *poems* (!) *On the Councils*, the first of which, and only the first, through the softness of our charities, we bring to confront the reader :—

Know the holy councils, King, to their utmost number,
Such as roused the impious ones from their world-wide slumber!

Seven in all those councils were—Nice the
first containing,
When the godly master-soul Constantine
was reigning,
What time at Byzantium, hallowed with the
hyssop,
In heart and word, Metrophanes presided
as archbishop !
It cut away Arius' tongue's maniacal de-
lusion,
Which cut off from he Trinity the blessed
Homoousion—
Blasphemed (O miserable man !) the maker
of the creature,
And low beneath the Father cast the equal
Filial nature.

The prose acrostic, contained in an
office written by Psellus to the honour
of Simeon, is elaborated on the words
'I sing thee who didst write the
metaphrases'; every sentence being
insulated, and beginning with a charmed
letter.

Say in a dance how we shall go,
Who never could a measure know ?

why thus—(and yet Psellus, who did
know everything, wrote a synopsis of
the metres !)—why thus :—
'Inspire me, Word of God, with
a rhythmic chant, for I am borne onward
to praise Simeon Metaphrastes, and
Logothetes, as he is fitly called, the
man worthy of admiration.
'Solemnly from the heavenly heights
did the Blessed Ghost descend on thee,
wise one, and finding thine heart pure,
rested there, there verily in the body !'
Surely we need not write any more.
But Michael Psellus was a very learned
man.
John of Euchaita, or Euchania, or
Theodoropolis—the three names do
appear through the twilight to belong to
one city—was a bishop, probably con-
temporary with Psellus—is only a poet
now. We turn to see the voice which
speaks to us. It is a voice with a soul
in it, clear and sweet and living; and we
who have walked long in the desert,
leap up to its sound as to the dim
flowing of a stream, and would take
a deep breath by its side both for the
weariness which is gone and the repose
which is coming. But it is a rarer

thing than a stream in the desert: it is
a voice in the desert—the only voice
of a city. The city may have three
names, as we have said, or the three
names may more fitly appertain to three
cities—scholars knit their brows and
wax doubtful as they talk ; but a city
denuded of its multitudes it surely is,
ruined even of its ruins it surely is : no
exhalation arises from its tombs—the
foxes have lost their way to it—the
bittern's cry is as dumb as the vanished
population—only the Voice remains.
John Mauropus, of Euchaita, Euchania,
Theodoropolis ! one living man among
many dead, as the Arabian tale goes of
the city of enchantment !—one speech-
ful voice among the silent, sole survivor
of the breath which maketh words,
effluence of the soul replacing the
bittern's cry—speak to us ! And thou
shalt be to us as a poet—we will salute
thee by that high name. For have we
not stood face to face with Michael
Psellus and him of the metaphrases?
Surely as a poet may we salute *thee* !
His poetry has, as if in contrast to
the scenery of circumstances in which
we find it, or to the fatality of circum-
stances in which it has *not* been found
(and even Mr. Clarke in his learned
work upon Sacred Literature, which is,
however, incommunicative generally
upon sacred poetry, appears unconscious
of his being and his bishopric)—his
poetry has a character singularly vital,
fresh, and serene. There is nothing in
it of the rapture of inspiration, little of
the operativeness of art—nothing of
imagination in a high sense, or of ear-
service in any : he is not, he says, of
those—

Who rain hard with redundancies of words,
And thunder and lighten out of eloquence.

His Greek being opposed to that of the
Silentiarii and the Pisidae by a peculiar
simplicity and ease of collocation which
the reader feels lightly in a moment,
the thoughts move through its trans-
parency with a certain calm nobleness
and sweet living earnestness, with holy
upturned eyes and human tears beneath

the lids, till the reader feels lovingly too. We startle him from his reverie with an octave note on a favourite literary fashion of the living London, drawn from the voice of the lost city ; discovering by that sound the first serial illustrator of pictures by poems, in the person of our Johannes. Here is a specimen from an annual of Euchaita, or Euchania, or Theodoropolis—we may say 'annual' although the pictures were certainly not in a book, but were probably ornaments of the beautiful temple in the midst of the city, concerning which there is a tradition. Here is a specimen selected for love's sake, because it 'illustrates' a portrait of Gregory Nazianzen :—

What meditates thy thoughtful gaze, my
    father ?
To tell me some new truth ? Thou canst
    not so !
For all that mortal hands are weak to gather
Thy blessed books unfolded long ago.

These are striking verses, upon the Blessed among women, weeping :—

O Lady of the passion, dost thou weep ?
What help can we then through our tears
    survey,
If such as thou a cause for wailing keep ?
What help, what hope, for us, sweet Lady,
    say ?
'Good man, it doth befit thine heart to lay
More courage next it, having seen me so.
All other hearts find other balm to-day—
The whole world's consolation is my woe !'

Would any hear what can be said of a Transfiguration before Raffael's :—

Tremble, spectator, at the vision won thee—
Stand afar off, look downward from the
    height,—
Lest Christ too nearly seen should lighten
    on thee,
And from thy fleshly eyeballs strike the sight,
As Paul fell ruined by that glory white,—
Lo, the disciples prostrate, each apart,
Each impotent to bear the lamping light !
And all that Moses and Elias might,
The darkness caught the grace upon her
    heart
And gave them strength for ! *Thou*, if ever-
    more
A God-voice pierce thy dark,—rejoice,
    adore !

Our poet was as unwilling a bishop as the most sturdy of the *nolentes* ; and there are poems written both in depreciation of, and in retrospective regret for, the ordaining dignity, marked by noble and holy beauties which we are unwilling to pass without extraction. Still we are constrained for space, and must come at last to his chief individual characteristic—to the gentle humanities which, strange to say, preponderate in the solitary voice—to the familiar smiles and sighs which go up and down in it to our ear. We will take the poem *To his Old House*, and see how the house survives by his good help, when the sun shines no more on the golden statue of Constantine :—

Oh, be not angry with me, gentle house,
That I have left thee empty and deserted !
Since thou thyself that evil didst arouse,
In being to thy masters so false-hearted—
In loving none of those who did possess
    thee—
In minist'ring to no one to an end—
In no one's service caring to confess thee,
But loving still the change of friend for
    friend,
And sending the last, plague-wise, to the
    door !
And so, or ere thou canst betray and leave
    me,
I, a wise lord, dismiss thee, servitor,
And antedate the wrong thou mayst achieve
    me
Against my will, by what my will allows,
Yet not without some sorrow, gentle house !

For oh, beloved house ! what time I render
My last look back on thee I grow more
    tender !
Pleasant possession, hearth for father's age,
Dear gift of buried hands, sole heritage !
My blood is stirred—and love, that learnt
    its play
From all sweet customs, moves mine heart
    thy way !
For thou wert all my nurse and helpful
    creature—
For thou wert all my tutor and my teacher—
In thee through lengthening toils I struggled
    deep—
In thee I watched all night without its sleep—
In thee I worked the wearier daytime out,
Exalting truth, or trying by a doubt.

. . . .

And oh, my father's roof! the memory leaves
Such pangs as break mine heart,` beloved
 eaves;
But God's word conquers all! . .

He is forced to a strange land, revert-
ing with this benediction to the 'dearest
house':—

Farewell, farewell, mine own familiar one,
Estranged for evermore from this day's sun,
Fare-thee-well so! Farewell, O second
 mother,
O nurse and help,—remains there not an-
 other!
My bringing-up to some sublimer measure
Of holy childhood and perfected pleasure!
Now other spirits must thou tend and teach,
And minister thy quiet unto each,
For reasoning uses, if they love such use,
But nevermore to me! God keep thee, house,
God keep thee, faithful corner, where I drew
So calm a breath of life! And God keep you,
Kind neighbours! Though I leave you by
 His grace,
Let no grief bring a shadow to your face,
Because whate'er He willeth to be done
His will makes easy, makes the distant one,
And soon brings all embraced before His
 throne!

We pass Philip Solitarius, who lived
at the close of this eleventh century,
even as we have passed one or two
besides of his fellow poets: because they,
having hidden themselves beyond the
reach of our eyes and the endeavour of
our hands, and we being careful to
speak by knowledge rather than by
testimony, nothing remains to us but
this same silent passing—this regretful
one, as our care to do better must
testify—albeit our fancy will not, by any
means, account them, with all their
advantages of absence, 'the best part of
the solemnity.'

Early in the twelfth century we are
called to the recognition of Theodore
Prodromus, theologian, philosopher,
and poet. His poems are unequal, con-
sisting principally of a series of
tetrastichs—Greek epigrams for lack of
point, French epigrams for lack of
poetry—upon the Old and New Testa-
ments, and the Life of Chrysostom,—
all nearly as bare of the rags of literary
merit as might be expected from the

design; and three didactic poems upon
Love, Providence, and against Bareus
the heretic, into which the poet has cast
the recollected life of his soul. The
soul deports herself as a soul should,
with a vivacity and energy which work
outward and upward into eloquence.
The sentiments are lofty, the expression
free; there is an instinct to a middle
and an end. Music we miss, even to
the elementary melody: the poet thinks
his thoughts, and speaks them; not
indeed what all poets, so called, do
esteem a necessary effort, and indeed
what we should thank him for doing;
but he *sings* them in nowise, and they
are not of that divine order which are
crowned by right of their divinity with
an inseparable aureole of sweet sound.
His poem upon Love—φιλία says the
Greek word, but friendship does not
answer to it—is a dialogue between the
personification and a stranger. It opens
thus dramatically, the stranger speak-
ing:—

Love! Lady diademed with honour, whence
And whither goest thou? Thy look presents
Tears to the lid—thy mien is vext and low—
Thy locks fall wildly from thy drooping
 brow—
Thy blushes are all pale—thy garb is fit
For mourning in, and shoon and zone are
 loose!
So changed thou art to sadness every whit,
And all that pomp and purple thou didst use,
That seemly sweet—that new rose on the
 mouth—
Those fair-smoothed tresses, and that grace-
 ful zone,
Bright sandals, and the rest thou haddest on,
Are all departed, gone to nought together!
And now thou walkest mournful in the train
Of mourning women!—where and whence,
 again?
 Love. From earth to God my Father.
 Stranger.   Dost thou say
That earth of Love is desolated?
 Love.   Yea!
It so much scorned me.
 Stranger.   Scorned?
 Love.   And cast me out
From its door.
 Stranger. From its door?
 Love.   As if without
I had my lot to die!

Love consents to give her confidence to the wondering stranger; whereupon, as they sit in the shadow of a tall pine, she tells a Platonic story of all the good she had done in heaven before the stars, and the angels, and the throned Triad, and of all her subsequent sufferings on the melancholy and ungrateful earth. The poem, which includes much beauty, ends with a quaint sweetness in the troth-plighting of the stranger and the lady. Mayst thou have been faithful to that oath, O Theodore Prodromus! but thou didst swear 'too much to be believed—so *much*.'

The poems *On Providence* and *Against Bareus* exceed the *Love*, perhaps, in power and eloquence to the full measure of the degree in which they fall short of the interest of the latter's design. Whereupon we dedicate the following selection from the *Providence* to Mr. Carlyle's 'gigmen' and all 'respectable persons':—

Ah me! what tears mine eyes are welling forth,
To witness in this synagogue of earth
Wise men speak wisely while the scoffers sing,
And rich men folly, for much honouring!
Melitus trifles,—Socrates decrees
Our further knowledge! Death to Socrates,
And long life to Melitus!

. . . . .

Chiefdom of evil, gold! blind child of clay,
Gnawing with fixèd tooth earth's heart away!
Go! perish from us! objurgation vain
To soulless nature, powerless to contain
One ill unthrust upon it! Rather perish
That turpitude of crowds, by which they cherish
Bad men for their good fortune, or condemn,
Because of evil fortune, virtuous men!

. . . . .

Oh, for a trumpet-mouth! an iron tongue
Sufficient for all speech! foundations hung
High on Parnassus' top to bear my feet—
So from that watch-tower, words which shall be meet,
I may out-thunder to the nations near me—
'Ye worshippers of gold, poor rich men, hear me!
Where do ye wander?—for what object stand?
That gold is earth's ye carry in your hand,

And floweth earthward! bad men have its curse
The most profusely: would yourselves be worse
So to be richer?—better in your purse?
Your royal purple—'twas a dog that found it!
Your pearl of price—a sickened oyster owned it!
Your glittering gems are pebbles, dust-astray—
Your palace pomp was wrought of wood and clay,
Smoothed rock and moulded plinth! earth's clay! earth's wood!
Earth's common-hearted stones! Is this your mood,
To honour *earth*, to worship *earth* . . . nor blush?'—
What dost thou murmur, savage mouth? Hush, hush!
Thy wrath is vainly breathed. The depth to tread
Of God's deep judgements, was not Paul's, he said.

The 'savage mouth' speaks in power, with whatever harshness: and we are tempted to contrast with this vehement utterance another short poem by the same poet, a little quaint withal, but light, soft, almost tuneful—as written for a *Book of Beauty*, and that not of Euchaita! The subject is *Life*.

Oh, take me, thou mortal, . . . thy LIFE for thy praiser!
Thou hast met, found, and seized me, and know'st what my ways are.
Nor leave me for slackness, nor yield me for pleasure,
Nor look up too saintly, nor muse beyond measure!
There's the veil from my head—see the worst of my mourning!
There are wheels to my feet—have a dread of their turning!
There are wings round my waist—I may flatter and flee thee!
There are yokes on my hands—fear the chains I decree thee!
Hold *me*! hold a shadow, the winds as they quiver;
Hold *me*! hold a dream, smoke, a track on the river.
Oh, take me, thou mortal, . . . thy Life for thy praiser,
Thou hast met not and seized not—nor know'st what my ways are!

Nay, frown not, and shrink not—nor call
  me an aspen ;
There's the veil from my head ! I have
  dropped from thy clasping !
A fall-back within it I soon may afford
  thee ;
There are wheels to my feet—I may roll
  back toward thee—
There are wings round my waist—I may
  flee back and clip thee—
There are yokes on my hands—I may *soon*
  cease to whip thee !
Take courage ! I rather would hearten than
  hip thee !

John Tzetza divides the twelfth century
with his name, which is not a great one.
In addition to an iambic fragment upon
education, he has written indefatigably
in the metre *politicus*, what must be read,
if read at all, with a corresponding
energy,—thirteen ' Chiliads,' of *variae
historiae*, so called after Aelian's—
Aelian's without the ' honey-tongue,'—
very various histories indeed, about
crocodiles and flies, and Plato's philo-
sophy and Cleopatra's nails, and Samson
and Phidias, and the resurrection from
the dead, and the Calydonian boar—
' everything under the sun ' being, in
fact, their imperfect epitome. The
omission is simply POETRY ! there is no
apparent consciousness of her entity in
the mind of this versifier ; no aspiration
towards her presence, not so much as
a sigh upon her absence. We do not,
indeed, become aware, in the whole
course of this laborious work, of much
unfolding of faculty ; take it lower than
the poetical ; of nothing much beyond
an occasional dry, sly, somewhat boorish
humour, which being good humour be-
sides, would not be a bad thing were its
traces only more extended. But the
general level of the work is a dull talka-
tiveness, a prosy adversity, who is no
' Daughter of Jove,' and a slumberous-
ness without a dream. We adjudge to
our reader the instructive history of the
Phoenix.

A phoenix is a single bird and synchronous
    with nature,
The peacock cannot equal him in beauty or
    in stature !

In radiance he outshines the gold ; the
    world in wonder yieldeth ;
His nest he fixeth in the trees, and all of
    spices buildeth.
And when he dies, a little worm, from out
    his body twining,
Doth generate him back again whene'er
    the sun is shining ;
He lives in Aegypt, and he dies in Aethiopia
    only, as
Asserts Philostratus, who wrote the Life of
    Apollonius.
And as the wise Aegyptian scribe, the holy
    scribe Choeremon,
Hath entered on these Institutes, all centre
    their esteem on,
Seven thousand years and six of age, this
    phoenix of the story,
Expireth from the fair Nile side, whereby
    he had his glory !

In the early part of the fourteenth
century, Manuel Phile, pricked emulously
to the heart by the successful labours of
Tzetza, embraced into identity with him-
self the remaining half of Aelian, and
developed in his poetical treatise *On
the Properties of Animals*, to which
Isachimus Camerarius provided a con-
clusion—the Natural History of that
industrious and amusing Greek-Roman.
The Natural History is translated into
verse, but by no means glorified ; and
yet the poet of animals, Phile, has carried
away far more of the Aelian honey
clinging to the edges of his *patera* than
the poet of the Chiliads did ever wot of.
What we find in him is not beauty, what
we hear in him is not music, but there
is an open feeling for the beautiful which
stirs at a word, and we have a scarcely
confessed contentment in hearkening to
those twice-told stories of birds and
beasts and fishes, measured out to us in
the low monotony of his chanting voice.
Our selections shall say nothing of the
live grasshopper, called, with the first
breath of these papers, an emblem of
the vital Greek tongue ; because the
space left to us closes within our sight,
and the science of the age does not thirst
to receive, through our hands, the history
of grasshoppers, according to Aelian or
Phile either. Everybody knows what
Phile tells us here, that grasshoppers

live upon morning dew, and cannot sing when it is dry. Everybody knows that the lady grasshopper sings not at all. And if the moral, drawn by Phile from this latter fact, of the advantage of silence in the female sex generally, be true and important, it is also too obvious to exact our enforcement of it. Therefore we pass by the grasshopper, and the nightingale too, for all her fantastic song, and hasten to introduce to European naturalists a Philhellenic species of *heron*, which has escaped the researches of Cuvier, and the peculiarities of which may account to the philosophic reader for that instinct of the 'wisdom of our forefathers,' which established an English university in approximation with the fens. It is earnestly to be hoped that the nice ear in question for the Attic dialect may still be preserved among the herons of Cambridgeshire.

A Grecian island nourisheth to bless
A race of herons in all nobleness.
If some barbarian bark approach the shore,
They hate, they flee,—no eagle can outsoar!
But if by chance an Attic voice be wist,
They grow softhearted straight, philhellenist;
Press on in earnest flocks along the strand,
And stretch their wings out to the comer's hand.
Perhaps he nears them with a gentle mind,—
They love his love, though foreign to their kind!
For so the island giveth wingèd teachers,
In true love lessons, to all wingless creatures.

He has written, besides, *A Dialogue between Mind and Phile*, and other poems; and we cannot part without taking from him a more solemn tone, which may sound as an 'Amen!' to the good we have said of him. The following address to the Holy Spirit is concentrated in expression:—

O living Spirit, O falling of God-dew,
O Grace which dost console us and renew;
O vital light, O breath of angelhood,
O generous ministration of things good—
Creator of the visible, and best
Upholder of the great unmanifest
Power infinitely wise, new boon sublime,
Of science and of art, constraining might;
In whom I breathe, live, speak, rejoice, and write,
Be with us in all places, for all time!

'And now,' saith the patientest reader of all, 'you have done. Now we have watched out the whole night of the world with you, by no better light than these poetical rushlights, and the wicks fail, and the clock of the universal hour is near upon the stroke of the seventeenth century, and you have surely done!' Surely *not*, we answer; for we see a hand which the reader sees not, which beckons us over to Crete, and clasps within its shadowy fingers a roll of hymns anacreontical, written by Maximus Margunius! and not for the last of our readers would we lose this last of the Greeks, owing him salutation. Yet the hymns have, for the true anacreontic fragrance, a musty odour, and we have scant praise for them in our nostrils. Their inspiration is from Gregory Nazianzen, whose *Soul and Body* are renewed in them by a double species of transmigration; and although we kiss the feet of Gregory's high excellences, we cannot admit any one of them to be a safe conductor of poetical inspiration. And in union with Margunius's plagiaristic tendencies there is a wearisome lengthiness, harder to bear. He will knit you to the whole length of an *Honi soit qui mal y pense*, till you fall asleep to the humming of the stitches what time you should be reading the 'moral.' We ourselves once dropped into a 'distraction,' as the French say,—for nothing could be more different from what the English say, than our serene state of self-abnegation—at the beginning of a house-building by this Maximus Margunius: when, reading on some hundred lines with our bare bodily eyes, and our soul starting up on a sudden to demand a measure of the progress, behold, he was building it still, with a trowel in the same hand: it was not forwarder by a brick. The swallows had time to hatch two nestfuls in a chimney while he finished the chimney-pot! Nevertheless he has moments of earnestness, and they leave beauties in their trace. Let us listen to this extract from his fifth hymn:—

Take me as a hermit lone
With a desert life and moan ;
Only Thou anear to mete
Slow or quick my pulse's beat ;
Only Thou, the night to chase
With the sunlight in Thy face !
Pleasure to the eyes may come
From a glory seen afar,
But if life concentre gloom
Scattered by no little star,
Then, how feeble, God, we are !
Nay, whatever bird there be,
(Aether by his flying stirred,)
He, in this thing, must be free—
And I, Saviour, am Thy bird,
Pricking with an open beak
At the words that Thou dost speak
Leave a breath upon my wings,
That above these nether things
I may rise to where Thou art,—
I may flutter next Thine heart !
For if a light within me burn,
It must be darkness in an urn,
Unless within its crystalline,
That unbeginning light of Thine
Shine !—oh, Saviour, *let* it shine !

He is the last of our Greeks. The light from Troy city, with which all Greek glory began, 'threw three times six,' said Aeschylus, that man with a soul,—beacon after beacon, into the heart of Greece. 'Three times six,' too, threw the light from Greece, when her own heart-light had gone out like Troy's, onward along the ridges of time. Three times six—but what faint beacons are the last !—sometimes only a red brand ; sometimes only a small trembling flame ; sometimes only a white glimmer, as of ashes breathed on by the wind ; faint beacons and far ! How far ! We have watched them along the cloudy tops of the great centuries, through the ages dark but for them,—and now stand looking with eyes of farewell upon the last pale sign on the last mist-bound hill. But it is the sixteenth century. Beyond the ashes on the hill a red light is gathering—above the falling of the dews a great sun is rising : there is a rushing of life and song upward ; let it still be UPWARD !—Shakespeare is in the world ! And the Genius of English Poetry, she who only of all the earth is worthy (Goethe's spirit may hear us say so, and smile), stooping, with a royal gesture, to kiss the dead lips of the Genius of Greece, stands up her successor in the universe, by virtue of that chrism, and in right of her own crown.

THE BOOK OF THE POETS[1]

I

THE voice of the turtle is heard in the land. The green book of the earth is open, and the four winds are turning the leaves, while Nature, chief secretary to the creative Word, sits busy at her inditing of many a lovely poem—her *Flower and the Leaf* on this side, her *Cuckoo and the Nightingale* on that; her *Paradise of Dainty Devices* in and out among the valleys, her *Polyolbion* away across the hills, her *Britannia's Pastorals* on the home meadows, her sonnets of tufted primroses, her lyrical outgushings of May blossoming, her epical and didactic solemnities of light and shadow—and many an illustrative picture to garnish the universal annual. What book shall we open side by side with Nature's? First, the book of God. *The Book of the Poets* may well come next—even this book, if it deserve indeed the nobility of its name.

But this book, which is not Campbell's *Selection from the British Poets*, nor Southey's, nor different from either by being better, resembles many others of the nobly named, whether princes or hereditary legislators, in bearing a name too noble for its desert. This book, consisting of short extracts from the books of the poets, beginning with Chaucer, ending with Beattie, and missing sundry by the way—we call it indefinitely 'A book of the poets,' and leave it thankful. The extracts from Chaucer are topsy-turvy—one from the *Canterbury Tales'* prologue thrown in between two from the Knight's Tale; while Gower may blame 'his fortune'—

(And some men hold opinion
That it is constellation,)

[1] Originally published as a review in the *Athenaeum*, June—August, 1842, in a series of five papers, on a selection entitled *The Book of the Poets.*

for the dry specimen crumbled off from his man-mountainism. Of Lydgate there is scarcely a page; of Occleve, Hawes, and Skelton—the two last especially interesting in poetical history,—of Sackville, and the whole generation of dramatists, not a word. 'The table is not full,' and the ringing on it of Phillips's *Splendid Shilling* will not bribe us to endurance. What! place for Pomfret's platitudes, and no place for Shakespeare's divine sonnets? and no place for Jonson's and Fletcher's lyrics! Do lyrics and sonnets perish out of place whenever their poets make tragedies too, quenched by the entity of tragedy? We suggest that Shakespeare has nearly as much claim to place in any possible book of the poets (though also a book of the poetasters) as ever can have John Hughes, who 'as a poet, is chiefly known,' saith the critical editor, 'by his tragedy of the *Siege of Damascus.*' Let this book therefore accept our boon, and remain a book of the poets, thankfully if not gloriously,—while we, on our own side, may be thankful too, that in the present days of the millennium of Jeremy Bentham—a more literally golden age than the laureates of Saturnus dreamed withal—any memory of the poets should linger with the booksellers, and 'come up this way' with the spring. The thing is good, in that it is at all. Send a little child into a garden, and he will be sure to bring you a nosegay worth having, though the red weed in it should 'side the lily,' and sundry of the prettiest flowers be held stalk upwards. Flowers are flowers and poets are poets, and 'A book of the poets' must be right welcome at every hour of the clock.

For the preliminary essay, which is very moderately well done, we embrace it, with our fingers at least, in taking up the volume. It pleases us better on the solitary point of the devotional poets than Mr. Campbell's beautiful treatise, doing, as it seems to us, more frank justice to the Witherses, the Quarleses, and the Crashaws. Otherwise the criticism and philosophy to be found in it are scarcely of the happiest—although even the first astonishing paragraph which justifies the utility of poetry on the ground of its being an attractive variety of language, a persuasive medium for abstract ideas (as reasonable were the justification of a seraph's essence deduced from the cloud beneath his foot!), shall not provoke us back to discontent from the vision of the poets of England suggested by the title of this 'Book,' and stretching along gloriously to our survey.

Our poetry has an heroic genealogy. It arose, where the sun rises, in the far East. It came out from Arabia, and was tilted on the lance-heads of the Saracens into the heart of Europe, Armorica catching it in rebound from Spain, and England from Armorica. It issued in its first breath from Georgia, wrapt in the gathering cry of Persian Odin: and passing from the orient of the sun to the antagonistic snows of Iceland, and oversweeping the black pines of Germany and the jutting shores of Scandinavia, and embodying in itself all wayside sounds, even to the rude shouts of the brazen-throated Cimbri— so modified, multiplied, resonant in a thousand Runic echoes, it rushed abroad like a blast into Britain. In Britain, the Arabic Saracenic Armorican and the Georgian Gothic Scandinavian mixed sound at last; and the dying suspirations of the Grecian and Latin literatures, the last low stir of the *Gesta Romanorum*, with the apocryphal personations of lost authentic voices, breathed up together through the fissures of the rent universe, to help the new intonation and accomplish the cadence. Genius was thrust onward to a new slope of the world. And soon, when simpler minstrels had sat there long enough to tune the ear of the time—when Layamon and his successors had hummed long enough, like wild bees, upon the lips of our

infant poetry predestined to eloquence,— then Robert Langland, the monk, walking for cloister 'by a wode's syde,' on the Malvern hills, took counsel with his holy 'Plowman,' and sang of other visions than their highest ridge can show. While we write, the woods upon those beautiful hills are obsolete, even as Langland's verses; scarcely a shrub grows upon the hills! but it is well for the thinkers of England to remember reverently, while taking thought of her poetry they stand among the gorse, that if we may boast now of more honoured localities, of Shakespeare's 'rocky Avon,' and Spenser's 'soft-streaming Thames,' and Wordsworth's 'Rydal Mere,' still our first holy poet-ground is there.

But it is in Chaucer we touch the true height, and look abroad into the kingdoms and glories of our poetical literature—it is with Chaucer that we begin our 'Books of the Poets,' our collections and selections, our pride of place and name. And the genius of the poet shares the character of his position: he was made for an early poet, and the metaphors of dawn and spring doubly become him. A morning-star, a lark's exaltation, cannot usher in a glory better. The 'cheerful morning face,' 'the breezy call of incense-breathing morn,' you recognize in his countenance and voice: it is a voice full of promise and prophecy. He is the good omen of our poetry, the 'good bird,' according to the Romans, 'the best good angel of the spring,' the nightingale, according to his own creed of good luck, heard before the cuckoo.

Up rose the sunne, and uprose Emilie,

and uprose her poet, the first of a line of kings, conscious of futurity in his smile. He is a king and inherits the earth, and expands his great soul smilingly to embrace his great heritage. Nothing is too high for him to touch with a thought, nothing too low to dower with an affection. As a complete creature cognate of life and death, he cries upon God: as a sympathetic creature he singles out a daisy from the universe ('si douce est la marguerite'), to lie down by half a summer's day and bless it for fellowship. His senses are open and delicate, like a young child's—his sensibilities capacious of supersensual relations, like an experienced thinker's. Child-like, too, his tears and smiles lie at the edge of his eyes, and he is one proof more among the many, that the deepest pathos and the quickest gaieties hide together in the same nature. He is too wakeful and curious to lose the stirring of a leaf, yet not too wide awake to see visions of green and white ladies between the branches; and a fair house of fame and a noble court of love are built and holden in the winking of his eyelash. And because his imagination is neither too 'high fantastical' to refuse proudly the gravitation of the earth, nor too 'light of love' to lose it carelessly, he can create as well as dream, and work with clay as well as cloud—and when his men and women stand close by the actual ones, your stop-watch shall reckon no difference in the beating of their hearts. He knew the secret of nature and art—that truth is beauty,—and saying 'I will make "A Wife of Bath" as well as Emilie, and you shall remember her as long,' we do remember her as long. And he sent us a train of pilgrims, each with a distinct individuality apart from the pilgrimage, all the way from Southwark and the Tabard Inn, to Canterbury and Becket's shrine : and their laughter comes never to an end, and their talk goes on with the stars, and all the railroads which may intersect the spoilt earth for ever cannot hush the 'tramp, tramp' of their horses' feet.

Controversy is provocative. We cannot help observing, because certain critics observe otherwise, that Chaucer utters as true music as ever came from poet or musician; that some of the sweetest cadences in all our English are extant in his—'swete upon his tongue' in completest modulation. Let 'Denham's strength, and Waller's sweetness join' the Io Paean of a later age, the

eurekamen of Pope and his generation. Not one of the 'Queen Anne's men,' measuring out tuneful breath upon their fingers, like ribbons for topknots, did know the art of versification as the old rude Chaucer knew it. Call him rude for the picturesqueness of the epithet ; but his verse has, at least, as much regularity in the sense of true art, and more manifestly in proportion to our increasing acquaintance with his dialect and pronunciation, as can be discovered or dreamed in the French school. Critics indeed have set up a system based upon the crushed atoms of first principles, maintaining that poor Chaucer wrote by accent only! Grant to them that he counted no verses on his fingers ; grant that he never disciplined his highest thoughts to walk up and down in a paddock—ten paces and a turn ; grant that his singing is not after the likeness of their sing-song—but there end your admissions. It is our ineffaceable impression, in fact, that the whole theory of accent and quantity held in relation to ancient and modern poetry stands upon a fallacy, totters rather than stands; and that when considered in connexion with such old moderns as our Chaucer the fallaciousness is especially apparent. Chaucer wrote by quantity, just as Homer did before him, just as Goethe did after him, just as all poets must. Rules differ, principles are identical. All rhythm presupposes quantity. Organ-pipe or harp, the musician plays by time. Greek or English, Chaucer or Pope, the poet sings by time. What is this accent but a stroke, an emphasis, with a successive pause to make complete the time ? And what is the difference between this accent and quantity but the difference between a harp-note and an organ-note ? otherwise, quantity expressed in different ways ? It is as easy for matter to subsist out of space, as music out of time.

Side by side with Chaucer comes Gower, who is ungratefully disregarded too often, because side by side with Chaucer. He who rides in the king's chariot will miss the people's *hic est*. Could Gower be considered apart, there might be found signs in him of an independent royalty, however his fate may seem to lie in waiting for ever in his brother's antechamber, like Napoleon's tame kings. To speak our mind, he has been much undervalued. He is nailed to a comparative degree; and everybody seems to make it a condition of speaking of him, that something be called inferior within him, and something superior out of him. He is laid down flat, as a dark background for 'throwing out' Chaucer's lights—he is used as a ποῦ στῶ for leaping up into the empyrean of Chaucer's praise. This is not just nor worthy. His principal poem, the *Confessio Amantis*, preceded the *Canterbury Tales*, and proves an abundant fancy, a full head and full heart, and neither ineloquent. We do not praise its design—in which the father-confessor is set up as a storyteller, like the Bishop of Tricca, 'avec l'âme,' like the Cardinal de Retz, 'la moins ecclésiastique du monde,'—while we admit that he tells his stories as if born to the manner of it, and that they are not much the graver, nor, peradventure, the holier either, for the circumstance of the confessorship. They are indeed told gracefully and pleasantly enough, and if with no superfluous life and gesture, with an active sense of beauty in some sort, and as flowing a rhythm as may bear comparison with many octosyllabics of our day; Chaucer himself having done more honour to their worth as stories than we can do in our praise, by adopting and crowning several of their number for king's sons within his own palaces. And this recalls that, at the opening of one glorious felony, the Man of Lawes Tale, he has written, a little unlawfully and ungratefully considering the connexion, some lines of harsh significance upon poor Gower—whence has been conjectured by the grey gossips of criticism, a literary jealousy, an unholy enmity, nothing less than a soul-chasm between the contemporary poets. We believe nothing of it; no, nor of the Shakespeare and Jonson feud after it—

> To alle such cursed stories we saie fy.

That Chaucer wrote in irritation is clear: that he was angry seriously and lastingly, or beyond the pastime of passion spent in a verse as provoked by a verse, there appears to us no reason for crediting. But our idea of the nature of the irritation will expound itself in our idea of the offence, which is here in Dan Gower's proper words, as extracted from the Ladie Venus's speech in the *Confessio Amantis*.

> And grete well Chaucer whan ye mete,
> As my disciple and poëte !—
>
> .   .   .   .
>
> Forthy now in his daiës old,
> Thou shalt him tellë this message,
> That he upon his latter age,
> To sette an ende of alle his werke
> As he who is mine ownë clerke,
> Do make his testament of love.

We would not slander Chaucer's temper,—we believe, on the contrary, that he had the sweetest temper in the world,—and still it is our conviction, none the weaker, that he was far from being entirely pleased by this 'message.' We are sure he did not like the message, and not many poets would. His 'elvish countenance' might well grow dark, and 'his sugred mouth' speak somewhat sourly, in response to such a message. Decidedly, in our own opinion, it was an impertinent message, a provocative message, a most inexcusable and odious message! Waxing hotter ourselves the longer we think of it, there is the more excuse for Chaucer. For, consider, gentle reader! this indecorous message preceded the appearance of the *Canterbury Tales*, and proceeded from a rival poet in the act of completing his principal work—its plain significance being 'I have done my poem, and you cannot do yours because you are superannuated.' And this, while the great poet addressed was looking forward farther than the visible horizon, his eyes dilated with a mighty purpose. And to be counselled by this, to shut them forsooth, and take his crook and dog and place in the valleys like a grey shepherd of the Pyrenees—he, who felt his foot strong upon the heights! he, with no wrinkle on his forehead deep enough to touch the outermost of inward smooth dreams—he, in the divine youth of his healthy soul, in the quenchless love of his embracing sympathies, in the untired working of his perpetual energies—to 'make an ende of alle his werke' and be old, as if he were not a poet! 'Go to, O vain man'—we do not reckon the age of the poet's soul by the shadow on the dial! Enough that it falls upon his grave.

Occleve and Lydgate both breathed the air of the world while Chaucer breathed it, although surviving him so long as rather to take standing as his successors than contemporaries. Both called him 'master' with a faithful reverting tenderness, and, however we are bound to distinguish Lydgate as the higher poet of the two, Occleve's 'Alas' may become the other's lips—

Alas, that thou thine excellent prudence
In thy bed mortell mightest not bequeath!

For, alas! it was not bequeathed. Lydgate's *Thebaid*, attached by its introduction to the *Canterbury Tales*, gives or enforces the occasion for sighing comparisons with the master's picturesque vivacity, while equally in delicacy and intenseness we admit no progress in the disciple. He does, in fact, appear to us so much overrated by the critics, that we are tempted to extend to his poetry his own admission on his monkish dress—

I wear a habit of perfection
Although my life agree not with that same—

and to opine concerning the praise and poetry taken together, that the latter agrees not with that same. An elegant poet—*poeta elegans*—was he called by the courteous Pits,—a questionable compliment in most cases, while the application in the particular one agrees

not with that same. An improver of the language he is granted to be by all —and a voluminous writer of respectable faculties in his position could scarcely help being so,—he has flashes of genius, but they are not prolonged to the point of warming the soul,—can strike a bold note, but fails to hold it on,—attains to moments of power and pathos, but wears, for working days, no habit of perfection.

These are our thoughts of Lydgate; and yet when he ceased his singing, none sang better; there was silence in the land. In Scotland, indeed, poet-tongues were not all mute; the air across the borders 'gave delight and hurt not.' Here in the south it was otherwise : and unless we embrace in our desolation such *poems* as the riming chronicles of Harding and Fabian, we must hearken for music to the clashing of 'Bilboa blades,' and be content that the wars of the red and white roses should silence the warbling of the nightingales. That figure dropped to our pen's point, and the reader may accept it as a figure—as no more. To illustrate by figures the times and the seasons of poetical manifestation and decay, is at once easier and more reasonable than to attempt to account for them by causes. We do not believe that poets multiply in peace-time like sheep and sheaves, nor that they fly, like partridges, at the first beating of the drum; and we do believe, having a previous faith in the pneumatic character of their gift, that the period of its bestowment is not subject to the calculations of our philosophy. Let, therefore, the long silence from Chaucer and his disciples down to the sixteenth century be left standing as a fact undisturbed by any good reasons for its existence, or by any other company than some harmless metaphor—harmless and ineffectual as a glow-worm's glitter at the foot of a colossal statue of Harpocrates. Call it, if you please, as Warton does, 'a nipping frost succeeding a premature spring'; or call it, because we would not think our

Chaucer premature, or the silence cruel —the trance of English Poetry! her breath, once emitted creatively, indrawn and retained—herself sinking into deep sleep, like the mother of Apollonius before the glory of a vision. to awaken, to leap up (ἐξέθορε says Philostratus, the narrator) in a flowery meadow, at the clapping of the white wings of a chorus of encircling swans. We shall endeavour to realize this awaking.

II

Is Hawes a swan? a black (letter) swan? since we promised to speak of swans in connexion with the sixteenth century. Certain voices will 'say nay, say nay'; and already, and without our provocation, he seems to us unjustly depreciated. Warton was called 'the indulgent historian of our poetry' for being so kind as to discover 'one fine line' in him! What name must the overkind have, in whose susceptible memories whole passages stand up erect, claiming the epithet or the like of the epithet—and that, less as the *largesse* of the indulgent than the debt of the just? Yet Langland's *Piers Plowman*, and Chaucer's *House of Fame*, and Lydgate's *Temple of Glasse*, and the *Pastyme of Plesure*, by Stephen Hawes, are the four columnar marbles, the four allegorical poems, on whose foundation is exalted into light the great allegorical poem of the world, Spenser's *Faery Queen*. There was a force of suggestion which preceded Sackville's, and Hawes uttered it. His work is very grave for a pastime, being a course of instruction upon the seven sciences, the trivium and quadrivium of the schools ; whereby Grand Amour, scholar and hero, wooing and winning Belle Pucelle, marries her according to the *lex ecclesiae*, is happy 'all the rest of his life' by the *lex* of all matrimonial romances—and, at leisure and in old age, dies by the *lex naturae*. He tells his own story quite to an end, including the particulars of his funeral and epitaph ; and is considerate enough to leave the reader in full assurance of

his posthumous reputation. And now let those who smile at the design dismiss their levity before the poet's utterance :—

O mortall folke, you may beholde and see
Howe I lye here, sometime a mighty knight,
The ende of joye and all prosperitie
Is death at last thorough his course and
        might.
After the day there cometh the dark night,
For though the day appear ever so long,
At last the bell ringeth to even song.

—it 'ringeth' in our ear with a soft and solemn music to which the soul is prodigal of echoes. We may answer for the poetic faculty of its 'maker.' He is, in fact, not merely ingenious and fanciful, but *abounds*—the word, with an allowance for the unhappiness of his subject, is scarcely too strong—with passages of thoughtful sweetness and cheerful tenderness, at which we are constrained to smile and sigh, and both for 'pastyme.'

Was never payne but it had joye at last
In the fayre morrow.

There is a lovely cadence ! And then Amour's courtship of his 'swete ladie' —a 'cynosure' before Milton's !—conducted as simply, yet touchingly, as if he were innocent of the seven deadly sciences, and knew no more of 'the Ladye Grammere' than might become a troubadour :—

O swete ladie, the true and perfect star
Of my true heart ! Oh, take ye now pitie !
Think on my payne which am tofore you
        here,—
With your swete eyes behold you me, and
        see
How thought and woe by great extremitie,
Hath changed my colour into pale and wan !
It was not so when I to love began.

The date assigned to this *Pastyme of Plesure* is 1506, some fifty years before the birth of Spenser. Whether it was written in vain for Spenser, judge ye. To the present generation it is covered deep with the dust of more than three centuries, and few tongues ask above the place—'What lies here?'

Barclay is our next swan—and verily might be mistaken, in any sort taken, by naturalists, for a crow. He is our first writer of eclogues, the translator of the *Ship of Fools*, and a thinker of his own thoughts with sufficient intrepidity.

Skelton 'floats double, swan and shadow,' as poet laureate of the University of Oxford, and 'royal orator' of Henry VII. He presents a strange specimen of a court-poet, and if, as Erasmus says, 'Britannicarum literarum lumen' at the same time—the light is a pitchy torchlight, wild and rough. Yet we do not despise Skelton: despise him? it were easier to hate. The man is very strong—he triumphs, foams, is rabid, in the sense of strength; he mesmerizes our souls with the sense of strength—it is as easy to despise a wild beast in a forest as John Skelton, poet laureate. He is as like a wild beast as a poet laureate can be. In his wonderful dominion over language he tears it, as with teeth and paws, ravenously, savagely: devastating rather than creating, dominant rather for liberty than for dignity. It is the very *sans-culottism* of eloquence—the oratory of a Silenus drunk with anger only! Mark him as the satyr of poets! fear him as the Juvenal of satyrs! and watch him with his rugged, rapid, picturesque savageness, his 'breathless rimes,' to use the fit phrase of the satirist Hall, or—

His rimes all ragged,
Tattered, and jagged,

to use his own,—climbing the high trees of Delphi, and pelting from thence his victim underneath, whether priest or cardinal, with rough-rinded apples! And then ask, could he write otherwise than so? The answer is this opening to his poem of the *Bouge of Court*, and the impression inevitable, of the serious sense of beauty and harmony to which it gives evidence :—

In autumn when the sun *in virgine*,
By radiant heat enripened hath our corne,
When Luna, full of mutabilitie,
As empëress, the diadem hath worne
Of our pole Arctic, smiling as in scorn
At our folie and our unstedfastnesse.—

But our last word of Skelton must be, that we do not doubt his influence for good upon our language. He was a writer singularly fitted for beating out the knots of the cordage, and straining the lengths to extension ; a rough worker at rough work. Strong, rough Skelton! We can no more deride him than my good lord cardinal could. If our critical eyebrows must motion contempt at somebody of the period, we choose Tusser, and his *Five Hundred Points of Good Husbandry and Housewifery*. Whatever we say of Tusser, no fear of harming a poet,—

Make ready a bin
For chaff to lie in,—

and there may be room *therein*, in compliment to the author of the proposition, for his own verses.

Lord Surrey passes as the tuner of our English nearly up to its present pitch of delicacy and smoothness; and we admit that he had a melody in his thoughts which they dared not disobey. That he is, as has been alleged by a chief critic, 'our first metrical writer,' lies not in our creed ; and even Turberville's more measured praise,—

Our mother tongue by him hath got such lyght,
That ruder speche thereby is banisht qwyht,—

we have difficulty in accepting. We venture to be of opinion that he did not belong to that order of master-minds with whom transitions originate, although qualified, by the quickness of a yielding grace, to assist effectually a transitional movement. There are names which catch the proverbs of praise as a hedge-thorn catches sheep's wool, by position and approximation rather than adaptitude : and this name is of them. Yet it is a high name. His poetry makes the ear lean to it, it is so sweet and low ; the English he made it of being ready to be sweet, and falling ripe in sweetness into other hands than his. For the poems of his friend, Sir Thomas Wyatt, have more thought, freedom, and variety, more general earnestness, more of the attributes of masterdom, than Lord Surrey's ; while it were vain to reproach for lack of melody the writer of that loveliest lyric, ' My lute, be still.' And Wyatt is various in metres, and the first song-writer (that praise we must secure to him) of his generation. For the rest, there is an inequality in the structure of his verses which is very striking and observable in Surrey himself : as if the language, consciously insecure in her position, were balancing her accentual being and the forms of her pronunciation, half giddily, on the very turning point of transition. Take from Wyatt such a stanza as this, for instance,—

The long love that in my thoughts I harbour,
And in my heart doth keep his residence,
Into my face presseth with bold pretence,
And there campeth, displaying his banner.—

and oppose to it the next example, polished as Pope,—

But I am here in Kent and Christendom,
Among the Muses where I read and rime ;
Where, if thou list, mine own John Poins,
    to come,
Thou shalt be judge how I do spend my time.

It is well to mark Wyatt as a leader in the art of didactic poetic composition under the epistolary form, ' sternly milde' (as Surrey said of his countenance) in the leaning toward satire. It is very well to mark many of his songs as of exceeding beauty, and as preserving clear their touching simplicity from that plague of over-curious conceits which infest his writings generally. That was the plague of Italian literature transmitted by contagion, together with better things—together with the love of love-lore, and the sonnet structure, the summer-bower for one fair thought, delighted in and naturalized in England by Wyatt and Surrey. For the latter,—

From Tuscane came his ladye's worthy race :

and his Muse as well as Geraldine. Drops from Plato's cup, passing through Petrarch's, not merely perfumed and coloured but diluted by the medium, we find in Surrey's cup also. We must not underpraise Surrey to balance the overpraise we murmur at. Denying him supremacy as a reformer, the denial of his poetic nobleness is far from us. We attribute to him the chivalry of the *light* ages—we call him a scholastic troubadour. The longest and most beautiful of his poems (' describing the lover's whole state ') was a memory in the mind of Milton when he wrote his *Allegro*. He has that measure of pathos whose expression is no gesture of passion, but the skilful fingering on a well-tuned lute. He affects us at worst not painfully, and

With easie sighs such as folks draw in love.

He wrote the first English blank verse, in his translation of two books of the *Aeneid*. He leads, in seeming, to the ear of the world, and by predestination of ' popular breath,' that little choral swan-chant which, swelled by Wyatt, Vaux, Bryan, and others, brake the common air in the days of the eighth Henry. And he fulfilled in sorrow his awarded fate as a poet,—his sun going down at noon !—and the cleft head, with its fair youthful curls. testifying like that fabled head of Orpheus to the music of the living tongue !

Sackville, Lord Dorset, takes up the new blank verse from the lips of Surrey, and turns it to its right use of tragedy. We cannot say that he does for it much more. His *Gorboduc*, with some twenty years between it and Shakespeare, is farther from the true drama in versification and all the rest than *Gammer Gurton* is from *Gorboduc*. Sackville's blank verse, like Lord Surrey's before him, is only heroic verse without rime ; and we must say so in relation to Gascoigne, who wrote the second blank-verse tragedy, the *Jocasta*, and the first blank-verse original poem, *The Stele Glass*. The secret of the blank verse of Shakespeare, and Fletcher, and Milton, did not dwell with them ! the arched cadence, with its artistic key-stone and under-flood of broad continuous sound, was never achieved nor attempted by its first builders. We sometimes whisper in our silence that Marlowe's 'brave sublunary' instincts should have groped that way. But no! Chaucer had more sense of music in the pause than Marlowe had. Marlowe's rhythm is not, indeed, hard and stiff and uniform, like the sentences of *Gorboduc*, as if the pattern one had been cut in boxwood; there is a difference between uniformity and monotony, and he found it; his cadence revolves like a wheel, progressively, if slowly and heavily, and with an orbicular grandeur of unbroken and unvaried music.

It remains to us to speak of the work by which Sackville is better known than by *Gorboduc* — the *Mirror for Magistrates*. The design of it has been strangely praised, seeing that whatever that peculiar merit were, Lydgate's *Fall of Princes* certainly cast the shadow before. But Sackville's commencement of the execution proved the master's hand; and that the great canvas fell abandoned to the blurring brushes of inadequate disciples was an ill-fortune compensated adequately by the honour attributed to the Induction—of inducing a nobler genius than his own, even Spenser's, to a nobler labour. We cannot doubt the influence of that Induction. Its colossal figures, in high allegorical relief, were exactly adapted to impress the outspread fancy of the most sensitive of poets. A yew-tree cannot stand at noon in an open pleasaunce without throwing the outline of its branches on the broad and sunny grass. Still, admitting the suggestion in its fullness, nothing can differ more than the allegorical results of the several geniuses of Lord Dorset and Spenser. Teardrop and dewdrop respond more similarly to analysis—or morbid grief and ideal joy. Sackville stands close wrapt in the 'blanket of his dark,' and will not drop his mantle for the sun. Spenser's business is with the lights of the world, and the lights beyond the world.

But this Sackville, this Earl of Dorset ('Oh, a fair earl was he!'), stands too low for admeasurement with Spenser:

and we must look back, if covetous of comparisons, to some one of a loftier and more kingly stature. We must look back far, and stop at Chaucer. Spenser and Chaucer do naturally remind us of each other, they two being the most cheerful-hearted of the poets—with whom cheerfulness, as an attribute of poetry, is scarcely a common gift. But the world will be upon us! The world moralizes of late, and in its fashion, upon the immorality of mournful poems, upon the criminality of 'melodious tears,' upon the morbidness of the sorrows of poets—because Lord Byron was morbidly sorrowful, and because a crowd of his ephemeral imitators hung their heads all on one side and were insincerely sorrowful. The fact, however, has been, apart from Lord Byron and his disciples, that the '$a\iota$ $a\iota$' of Apollo's flower is vocally sad in the prevailing majority of poetical compositions. The philosophy is, perhaps, that the poetic temperament, halfway between the light of the ideal and the darkness of the real, and rendered by each more sensitive to the other, and unable, without a struggle, to pass out clear and calm into either, bears the impress of the necessary conflict in dust and blood! The philosophy may be, that only the stronger spirits do accomplish this victory, having lordship over their own genius—whether they accomplish it by looking bravely to the good ends of evil things, which is the practical ideal, and possible to all men in a measure—or by abstracting the inward sense from sensual things and their influences, which is subjectivity perfected—or by glorifying sensual things with the inward sense, which is objectivity transfigured—or by attaining to the highest vision of the idealist, which is subjectivity turned outward into an actual objectivity.

To the last triumph Shakespeare attained; but Chaucer and Spenser fulfilled their destiny and grew to their mutual likeness as cheerful poets by certain of the former processes. They two are alike in their cheerfulness, yet are their cheerfulnesses most unlike.

Each poet laughs : yet their laughters ring with as far a difference as the sheep-bell on the hill and the joy-bell in the city. Each is earnest in his gladness : each active in persuading you of it. You are persuaded, and hold each for a cheerful man. The whole difference is, that Chaucer has a cheerful humanity : Spenser, a cheerful ideality. One rejoices walking on the sunny side of the street : the other, walking out of the street in a way of his own, kept green by a blessed vision. One uses the adroitness of his fancy by distilling out of the visible universe her occult smiles : the other, by fleeing beyond the possible frown, the occasions of natural ills, to that 'cave of cloud' where he may smile safely to himself. One holds festival with men—seldom so coarse and loud indeed as to startle the deer from their green covert at Woodstock—or with homely Nature and her 'douce Marguerite' low in the grasses : the other adopts for his playfellows imaginary or spiritual existences, and will not say a word to Nature herself, unless it please her to dress for his masque and speak daintily sweet and rare like a spirit. The human heart of one utters oracles—the imagination of the other speaks for his heart, and we miss no prophecy. For music, we praised Chaucer's, and not only as Dryden did, for ' a Scotch tune.' But never issued there from lip or instrument, or the tuned causes of Nature, more lovely sound than we gather from our Spenser's art. His mouth is vowed away from the very possibilities of harshness. Right leans to wrong in its excess. His rhythm is the continuity of melody, not harmony, because too smooth for modulation—because ' by his vow ' he dares not touch a discord for the sake of consummating a harmony. It is the singing of an angel in a dream : it has not enough of contrary for waking music. Of his great poem we may say, that we miss no humanity in it, because we make a new humanity out of it and are satisfied in our human hearts—a new humanity vivified by the poet's life, moving in

happy measure to the chanting of his thoughts, and upon ground supernaturally beautified by his sense of the beautiful. As an allegory, it enchants us away from its own purposes. Una is Una to us ; and Sans Foy is a traitor, and Errour is 'an ugly monster,' with a 'tayle' ; and we thank nobody in the world, not even Spenser, for trying to prove it otherwise. Do we dispraise an allegorical poem by throwing off its allegory? we trow not. Probably, certainly to our impression, the highest triumph of an allegory, from this of the *Faery Queen* down to the *Pilgrim's Progress*, is the abnegation of itself.

Oh those days of Elizabeth ! We call them the days of Elizabeth, but the glory fell over the ridge, in illumination of the half-century beyond ! those days of Elizabeth ! Full were they of poets as the summer-days are of birds,—

No branch on which a fine bird did not sit,
No bird but his sweet song did shrilly sing,
No song but did contayne a lovely dit.

We hear of the dramatists, and shall speak of them presently ; but the lyric singers were yet more numerous,—there were singers in every class. Never since the first nightingale brake voice in Eden arose such a jubilee-concert—never before nor since has such a crowd of true poets uttered true poetic speech in one day ! Not in England evermore ! Not in Greece, that we know. Not in Rome, by what we know. Talk of their Augustan era—we will not talk of it, lest we desecrate our own of Elizabeth. The latter was rightly prefigured by our figure of the chorus of swans. It was besides the Milky Way of poetry : it was the miracle-age of poetical history. We may fancy that the master-souls of Shakespeare and Spenser, breathing, stirring in divine emotion, shot vibratory life through other souls in electric association ! we may hear, in fancy, one wind moving every leaf in a forest—one voice responded to by a thousand rock-echoes. Why, a common man walking through the earth in those days grew a poet by position—even as a child's shadow cast upon a mountain slope is dilated to the aspect of a giant's.

If we, for our own parts, did enact a Briareus, we might count these poets on the fingers of our hundred hands, after the fashion of the poets of Queen Anne's time, counting their syllables. We do not talk of them as 'faultless monsters,' however wonderful in the multitude and verity of their gifts : their faults were numerous, too. Many poets of an excellent sweetness, thinking of poetry that, like love,

It was to be all made of fantasy !

fell poetry-sick, as they might fall love-sick, and knotted associations, far and free enough to girdle the earth withal, into true love-knots of quaintest devices. Many poets affected novelty rather than truth ; and many attained to novelty rather by attitude than altitude, whether of thought or word. Worst of all, many were incompetent to Sir Philip Sidney's ordeal—the translation of their verses into prose—and would have perished utterly by that hot ploughshare. Still, the natural healthy eye turns toward the light, and the true calling of criticism remains the distinguishing of beauty. Love and honour to the poets of Elizabeth—honour and love to them all ! Honour even to the fellow workers with Sackville in the *Mirror for Magistrates*, to Ferrers, Churchyard, and others, who had their hand upon the ore if they did not clasp it !—and to Warner, the poet of *Albion's England*, singing snatches of ballad pathos, while he worked, for the most part heavily, too, with a bowed back as at a stiff soil—and to Gascoigne, reflecting beauty and light from his *Stele Glass*, though his *Fruites of War* are scarcely fruits from Parnassus—and to Daniel, tender and noble, and teaching, in his *Musophilus*, the chivalry of poets, though in his *Civil Wars* somewhat too historical, as Drayton has written of him—and to Drayton, generous in the *Polyolbion* of his poet-blessing on every hill and river through this fair England, and not in-eloquent in his *Heroical Epistles*, though

somewhat tame and level in his *Barons' Wars*—and to the two brother Fletchers, Giles and Phineas, authors of *Christ's Victory* and *The Purple Island*, for whom the Muse's kiss followed close upon the mother's, gifting their lips with no vulgar music and their house with that noble kinsman, Fletcher the dramatist ! Honour, too, to Davies, who 'reasoned in verse' with a strong mind and strong enunciation, though he wrote one poem on the Soul and another on Dancing, and concentrated the diverging rays of intellect and folly in his sonnets on the reigning Astraea—and to Fulke Greville, Lord Brooke, who had deep thoughts enough to accomplish ten poets of these degenerate days, though because of some obscurity in their expression you would find some twenty critics ' full of oaths ' by the pyramids, that they all meant nought—and to Chamberlayne, picturesque, imaginative, earnest (by no means dramatic) in his poetic romance of *Pharonnida*, though accumulative to excess of figures, and pedantic in such verbal learning as ' entheon charms,' the ' catagraph ' of a picture, the exagitations and congestions of elements, *et sic omnia!*—to Chalkhill, wrapt, even bound, 'in soft Lydian airs,' till himself, as well as his Clearchus and Thealma, fall asleep in involutions of harmony—and to Browne, something languid in his *Britannia's Pastorals*, by sitting in the sun with Guarini and Marini, and 'perplext in the extreme' by a thousand images and sounds of beauty calling him across the dewy fields—and to Wither, author of the *Shepherd's Hunting*, and how much else ? Wither, who wrote of poetry like a poet, and in return has been dishonoured and mis-prised by some of his own kind !— a true sincere poet of blessed oracles ! Honour, love, and praise to him and all ! May pardon come to us from the un-named.

Honour also to the translators of poems —to such as Chapman and Sylvester— great hearts, interpreters of great hearts, and afterwards worthily thanked by the Miltons, and Popes, and Keatses, for their gift of greatness to the language of their England.

Honour to the satirists!—to Marston, who struck boldly and coarsely at an offence from the same level with the offender—to Hall, preserving his own elevation, and flashing downwardly those thick lightnings in which we smell the sulphur—and to Donne, whose instinct to beauty overcame the resolution of his satiric humour.

Honour, again, to the singers of brief poems, to the lyrists and sonneteers! O Shakespeare, let thy name rest gently among them, perfuming the place. We 'swear' that these sonnets and songs do verily breathe, 'not of themselves, but *thee*'; and we recognize and bless them as short sighs from thy large poetic heart, burdened with diviner inspiration! O rare Ben Jonson, let us have thy songs, rounded each with a spherical thought, and the lyrics from thy masques alive with learned fantasy, and thine epigrams keen and quaint, and thy noble epitaphs, under which the dead seem stirring! Fletcher, thou shalt be with us—prophet of *Comus* and *Penseroso*! giddy with inhalation from the fount of the beautiful, speaking out wildly thought upon thought, measure upon measure, as the bird sings, because his own voice is lovely to him. Sidney, true knight and fantastic poet, whose soul did too curiously inquire the fashion of the beautiful—the fashion rather than the secret!—but left us in one line the completest *Ars Poetica* extant,—

Foole, sayde my Muse to mee, looke in thine heart, and write.

Thy name be famous in all England and Arcadia! And Raleigh, tender and strong, of voice sweet enough to answer that 'Passionate Shepherd,' yet trumpet-shrill to speak the 'Soul's errand' thrilling the depths of our own! having honour and suffering as became a poet, from the foot of the Lady of England light upon his cloak, to the cloak of his executioner wrapping redly his breathless corpse. Marlowe, we must not forget his 'Shepherd' in his tragedies:

and 'Come live with me' sounds passionately still through the dead cold centuries. And Drummond, the over-praised and under-praised—a passive poet, if we may use the phraseology—who was not careful to achieve greatness, but whose natural pulses beat music, and with whom the consciousness of life was the sentiment of beauty. And Lyly, shriven from the sins of his *Euphues*, with a quaint grace in his songs; and Donne, who takes his place naturally in this new class, having a dumb *angel*, and knowing more noble poetry than he articulates. Herrick, the Ariel of poets, sucking 'where the bee sucks' from the rose-heart of Nature, and reproducing the fragrance idealized; and Carew, using all such fragrance as a courtly essence, with less of self-abandonment and more of artificial application; and Herbert, with his face as the face of a spirit, dimly bright; and fantastic Quarles, in rude and graphic gesticulation, expounding verity and glory; and Breton, and Turberville, and Lodge, and Hall (not the satirist), and all the hundred swans, nameless, or too numerous to be named, of that Cayster of the rolling time.

Then, high in the miraculous climax, come the dramatists—from whose sinews was knit the overcoming strength of our literature over all the nations of the world. 'The drama is the executive of literature,' said De Staël: and the Greek's 'action, action, action' we shall not miss in our drama. Honour to the dramatists, as honour *from* them! Shakespeare is our security that we shall say so less briefly soon.

III

WE must take a few steps backward for position's sake, and then be satisfied with a rapid glance at the Drama. From the days of Norman William, the representations called Mysteries and Moralities had come and gone without a visible poet; and Skelton appears before us almost the first English claimant of a dramatic reputation, with the authorship of the interludes of *Magnificence* and the *Nigromansir.* The latter is chiefly famous for Warton's affirmation of having held it in his hands, giving courteous occasion to Ritson's denial of its existence: and our own palms having never been crossed by the silver of either, we cannot prophesy on the degree of individual honour involved in the literary claim. Bale, one of the eighth Henry's bishops, was an active composer of Moralities ; and John Heywood, his royal jester and 'author of that very merry interlude' called *The Four P's,* united in his merriment that caustic sense with that lively ease which have not been too common since in his accomplished dramatic posterity. Yet those who in the bewilderment of their admirations (or senses) attribute to John Heywood the *Pinner of Wakefield* are more obviously—we are sorely tempted to add, more ridiculously—wrong, than those who attribute it to Shakespeare. The Canon of Windsor's *Ralph Royster Doyster,* and the Bishop of Bath and Wells's *Gammer Gurton,* followed each other close into light, the earliest modern comedies, by the force of the *âme ecclésiastique.* A little after came Ferrys, memorialized by Puttenham as 'the principall man of his profession ' (of poetry), and 'of no lesse myrthe and felicitie than John Heywood, but of much more skille and magnificence in his meter.' But seeing that even Oblivion forgot Ferrys, leaving his name and Puttenham's praise when she defaced his works, and seeing, too, the broad farcedom of the earlier, however episcopal, writers, we find ourselves in an unwilling posture of recognition before Edwards, as the first extant regular dramatist of England. It is a pitiful beginning. *The Four P's* would be a more welcome A to us. They express more power with their inarticulate roughness than does this *Damon and Pythias,* with its rimed, loitering frigidity, or even than this *Palamon and Arcite,* in which the sound of the hunting horn cast into ecstasy the too gracious soul of Queen Elizabeth. But Sir John Davies's

divine Astraea was, at that grey dawn of her day, ignorant of greater poets ; and we ('happy in this') go on toward them. After Edwards, behold Sackville with that *Gorboduc* we have named, the first blank-verse tragedy we can name, praised by Sidney for its exemplary preservation of the unities and for 'climbing to the height of Seneca his stile,'—tight-fitting praise, considering that the composition is high enough to account for its snow, and cold enough to emulate the Roman's. And after Sackville behold the first dramatic geniuses, in juxtaposition with the first dramatists—Peele, and Kyd, mad as his own Hieronimo (we will grant it to such critics as are too utterly in their senses), only—

> When he is mad,
> Then, methinks, he is a brave fellow !

and then, methinks, and by such madness, the possibility of a Shakespeare was revealed. Kyd's blank verse is probably the first breaking of the true soil ; and certainly far better and more dramatic than Marlowe's is—crowned poet as the latter stands before us—poet of the English Faustus, which we will not talk of against the German, nor set up its grand, luxurious, melancholy devil against Goethe's subtle, biting, Voltairish devil, each being devil after its kind,—the poet of the Jew which Shakespeare drew (not), yet a true Jew, 'with a berde,'—and the poet of the first historical drama,—since the *Gorboduc* scarcely can be called one. Marlowe was more essentially a poet than a dramatist ; and if the remark appear self-evident and universally applicable, we will take its reverse in Kyd, who was more essentially, with all his dramatic faults, a dramatist than a poet. Passing from the sound of the elemental monotonies of the rhythm of Marlowe, we cannot pause before Nash and Greene to distinguish their characteristics. It is enough to name these names of gifted dramatists, who lived, or at least wrote, rather before Shakespeare than with him, and helped to make him credible.

Through them, like a lens, we behold his light. Of them we conjecture—these are the blind elements working before the earthquake ;—before the great 'Shakescene,' as Greene said when he was cross ! And we may say when we are fanciful, these are the experiments of Nature, made in her solution of the problem of how much deathless poetry will agree with how much mortal clay ! —these are the potsherd vessels half filled, and failing at last,—until up to the edge of *one* the liquid inspiration rose and bubbled in hot beads to quench the thirsty lips of the world.

It is hard to speak of Shakespeare—these measures of the statures of common poets fall from our hands when we seek to measure him : it is harder to praise him. Like the tall plane-tree which Xerxes found standing in the midst of an open country, and honoured inappropriately with his ' barbaric pomp,' with bracelets and chains and rings suspended on its branches, so has it been with Shakespeare. A thousand critics have commended him with praises as unsuitable as a gold ring to a plane-tree. A thousand hearts have gone out to him, carrying necklaces. Some have discovered that he individualized, and some that he generalized, and some that he subtilized—almost *trans*-transcendentally. Some would have it that he was a wild genius, sowing wild oats and stealing deer to the end, with no more judgement forsooth than ' youth the hare' ; and some, that his very pulses beat by that critical law of art in which he was blameless !—some, that all his study was in his horn-book, and not much of that ; and some, that he was as learned a polyglot as ever had been dull but for Babel !—some, that his own ideal burned steadfastly within his own fixed contemplations, unstirred by breath from without ; and some, that he wrote for the gold on his palm and the 'rank popular breath' in his nostrils, apart from consciousness of greatness and desire of remembrance. If the opinions prove nothing, their contradictions prove the exaltation of the object ;

their contradictions are praise. For men differ about things above their reach, not within it—about the mountains in the moon, not Primrose Hill : and more than seven cities of men have differed in their talk about Homer also ! Homer, also, was convicted of indiscreet nodding ; and Homer, also, had no manner of judgement ! and the *Ars Poetica* people could not abide his bad taste ! And we find another analogy. We, who have no leaning to the popular cant of Romanticism and Classicism, and believe the old Greek BEAUTY to be both new and old, and as alive and not more grey in Webster's *Duchess of Malfy* than in Aeschylus's *Eumenides*, do reverence this Homer and this Shakespeare as the colossal borderers of the two intellectual departments of the world's age—do behold from their feet the antique and modern literatures sweep outwardly away, and conclude, that whereas the Greek bore in his depth the seed and prophecy of all the Hellenic and Roman poets, so did Shakespeare, ' whose seed was in himself' also, those of a later generation !

For the rest we must speak briefly of Shakespeare, and very weakly too, except for love. That he was a great natural genius nobody, we believe, has doubted—the fact has passed with the cheer of mankind ; but that he was a great artist the majority has doubted. Yet Nature and Art cannot be reasoned apart into antagonistic principles. Nature is God's art—the accomplishment of a spiritual significance hidden in a sensible symbol. Poetic art (man's) looks past the symbol with a divine guess and reach of soul into the mystery of the significance—disclosing from the analysis of the visible things the synthesis or unity of the ideal—and expounds like symbol and like significance out of the infinite of God's doing into the finite of man's comprehending. Art lives by Nature, and not the bare mimetic life generally attributed to Art : she does not imitate, she expounds. *Interpres naturae*—is the poet-artist ; and the poet wisest in Nature is the most artistic poet! and thus our Shakespeare passes to the presidency unquestioned, as the greatest artist in the world. We believe in his judgement as in his genius. We believe in his learning, both of books and men, and hills and valleys: in his grammars and dictionaries we do not believe. In his philosophy of language we believe absolutely—in his Babel-learning, not at all. We believe reverently in the miracle of his variety; and it is observable that we become aware of it less by the numerousness of his persons and their positions than by the *depth* of the least of either—by the sense of visibility beyond what we see, as in Nature. Our creed goes on to declare him most passionate and most rational—of an emotion which casts us into thought, of a reason which leaves us open to emotion! most grave and most gay—while we scarcely can guess that the man Shakespeare is grave or gay, because he interposes between ourselves and his personality the whole breadth and length of his ideality. His associative faculty—the wit's faculty besides the poet's—for him who was both wit and poet, shed sparks like an electric wire. He was wise in the world, having studied it in his heart; what is called 'the knowledge of the world' being just the knowledge of one heart, and certain exterior symbols. What else? What otherwise could he, the young transgressor of Sir Thomas Lucy's fences, new from Stratford and the Avon, close in theatric London, have seen, or touched, or handled of the Hamlets and Lears and Othellos, that he should draw them? 'How can I take portraits,' said Marmontel, in a similar inexperience, 'before I have beheld faces?' Voltaire embraced him, in reply. Well applauded, Voltaire. It was a *mot* for Marmontel's utterance, and Voltaire's praise—for Marmontel, not ror Shakespeare. Every being is his own centre to the universe, and in himself must one root of the compasses be fixed to attain to any measurement—nay, every being is his own mirror to the universe. Shakespeare wrote from

within—the beautiful; and we recognize from within—the true. He is universal, because he is individual. And, without any prejudice of admiration, we may go on to account his faults to be the proofs of his power—the cloud of dust cast up by the multitude of the chariots. The activity of his associative faculty is occasionally morbid: in the abundance of his winged thoughts the locust flies with the bee, and the ground is dark with the shadow of them. Take faults, take excellences, it is impossible to characterize this Shakespeare by an epithet—have we heard the remark before, that it should sound so obvious? We say of Corneille, the noble; of Racine, the tender; of Aeschylus, the terrible; of Sophocles, the perfect; but not one of these words, not one appropriately descriptive epithet, can we attach to Shakespeare without a conscious recoil. Shakespeare! the name is the description.

He is the most wonderful artist in blank verse of all in England, and almost the earliest. We do not say that he first broke the enchaining monotony, of which the Sackvilles and the Marlowes left us complaining; because the versification of *Hieronimo* ran at its own strong will, and the *Pinner of Wakefield* may have preceded his first plays. We do not even say, what we might, that his hand first proved the compass and infinite modulation of the new instrument; but we do say, that it never answered another hand as it answered his. We do say, this fingering was never learned of himself by another. From Massinger's more resonant majesty, from even Fletcher's more numerous and artful cadences, we turn back to his artlessness of art, to his singular and supreme estate as a versificator. Often when he is at the sweetest, his words are poor monosyllables, his pauses frequent to brokenness, and the structure oi the several lines less varied than was taught after Fletcher's masterdom; but the whole results in an ineffable charming of the ear which we acquiesce in without seeking its cause, a happy mystery of music.

This is little for Shakespeare; yet so much for the place, that we are forced into brevities for our observations which succeed. We chronicle only the names of Chapman, Dekker, Webster, Tourneur, Randolph, Middleton, and Thomas Heywood, although great names, and worthy, it is not too much to add, of Shakespeare's brotherhood. Many besides lean from our memory to the paper, but we put them away reverently. It was the age of the dramatists—the age of strong passionate men, scattering on every side their good and evil oracles of vehement humanity, and extenuating no thought in its word : and in that age 'to write like a man' was a deed accomplished by many besides him of whom it was spoken, Jonson's ' son Cartwright.'

At Jonson's name we stop perforce, and do salutation in the dust to the impress of that ' learned sock.' He was a learned man, as everybody knows ; and, as everybody does not believe, not the worse for his learning. His material, brought laboriously from east and west, is wrapped in a flame of his own. If the elasticity and abandonment of Shakespeare and of certain of Shakespeare's brothers are not found in his writings, the reason of the defects need not be sought out in his readings. His genius, high and verdant as it grew, yet belonged to the hard woods : it was lance-wood rather than bow-wood—a genius rather noble than graceful—eloquent, with a certain severity and emphasis of enunciation. It would have been the same if he, too, had known ' little Latin and lesse Greek.' There was a dash of the rhetorical in his dramatic. Not that we deny him empire over the passions : his heart had rhetoric as well as his understanding, and he wrote us a *Sad Shepherd* as well as a *Catiline*. His versification heaves heavily with thought. For his comic powers, let *Volpone* and *The Alchymist* attest them with that unextinguishable laughter which is the laughter of gods or poets still more than of the wits' coffee-house. Was it ' done at the Mermaid '—was it ever fancied there, that ' rare Ben Jonson ' should be called a pedantic poet ? Nay, but only a scholastic one.

And Beaumont and Fletcher, the Castor and Pollux of this starry poetic sphere *(lucida sidera !)*, our silence shall not cover them ; nor will we put asunder, in our speech, the names which friendship and poetry joined together, nor distinguish by a laboured analysis the vivacity of one from the solidity of the other ; seeing that men who, according to tradition, lived in one house, and wore one cloak, and wrote on one page, may well, by the sanctity of that one grave they have also in common, maintain for ever beyond it the unity they coveted. The characteristics of these writers stand out in a softened light from the deep tragic background of the times. We may liken them to Shakespeare in one mood of his mind, because there are few classes of beauty the type or likeness of which is not discoverable in Shakespeare. From the rest they stand out contrastingly, as the Apollo of the later Greek sculpture-school,—too graceful for divinity and too vivacious for marble,—placed in a company of the antiquer statues with their grand blind look of the almightiness of repose. We cannot say of these poets as of the rest, ' they write all like men ' ; we cannot think they write like women either—perhaps they write a little like centaurs. We are of opinion in any way that the grace is more obvious than the strength ; and there may be something centauresque and of twofold nature in their rushing mutabilities, and changes on passion and weakness. Clearest of all is that they wrote like poets, and in a versification most surpassingly musical though liberal, as if music served them for love's sake, unbound ! They had an excellent genius, but not a strong enough invention to include judgement ; judgement being the consistency of invention, and consistency always, whether in morals or literature, depending upon strength. We do not, in fact, find in them any perfect and covenanted whole—we do not find it in character, or in plot, or in composition ; and lamenting the defect on many grounds we do so on this chief one, that their good is just good, their evil just evil, unredeemed into good like Shakespeare's and Nature's evil by unity of design, but lying apart, a willingly chosen, through and through evil—and ' *by this time it stinketh.*' If other results are less lamentable they are no less fatal. The mirror which these poets held up to us is vexed with a thousand cracks, and everything visible is in fragments. Their conceptions all tremble on a per-adventure—' peradventure they shall do well ': there is no royal absolute will that they should do well—the poets are less kings than workmen. And being workmen they are weak—the moulds fall from their hands—are clutched with a spasm or fall with a faintness. After which querulousness we shall leave the question as to whether their tragic or comic powers be put to more exquisite use—not for solution, nor for doubt (since we hold fast an opinion), but for praise the most rarely appropriate or possible.

One passing word of Ford, the pathetic —for he may wear on his sleeve the epithet of Euripides, and no daw peck there. Most tender is he, yet not to feebleness—most mournful, yet not to languor; yet we like to hear the war-horse leaps of Dekker on the same tragic ground with him, producing at once contrast and completeness. Ungrateful thought!—the *Witch of Edmonton* be-witched us to it. Ford can fill the ear and soul singly with the trumpet-note of his pathos ; and in its pauses you shall hear the murmuring voices of Nature—such a nightingale, for instance, as never sang on a common night. Then that death scene in the *Broken Heart*! who has equalled *that*? It is single in the drama—the tragic of tragedy, and the sublime of grief. A word, too, of Massinger, who writes all like a giant— a dry-eyed giant. He is too ostentatiously strong for flexibility, and too heavy for rapidity, and monotonous through his perpetual final trochee ; his gesture and enunciation are slow and majestic. And another word of Shirley, an inferior writer, though touched, to our fancy,

with something of a finer ray, and closing, in worthy purple, the proces-sion of the Elizabethan men. Shirley is the last dramatist. *Valete et plaudite, o posteri.*

Standing in his traces, and looking backward and before, we become aware of the distinct demarcations of five eras of English poetry : the first, the Chau-cerian, although we might call it *Chaucer*; the second, the Elizabethan ; the third, which culminates in Cowley ; the fourth, in Dryden and the French school ; the fifth, the return to nature in Cowper and his successors of our day. These five rings mark the age of the fair and sting-less serpent we are impelled, like the ancient mariner, to bless—but not ' un-aware.' *Ah benedicite!* we bless her so, out of our Chaucer's rubric, softly, but with a plaintiveness of pleasure ! For when the last echo of the Elizabethan harmonies had died away with Shirley's footsteps, in the twilight of that golden day ; when Habington and Lovelace, and every last bird before nightfall was dumb, and Crashaw's fine rapture, holy as a summer sense of silence, left us to the stars—the first voices startling the thinker from his reverting thoughts are verily of another spirit. The voices are eloquent enough, thoughtful enough, fanciful enough ; but something is de-fective. Can any one suffer, as an experimental reader, the transition be-tween the second and third periods, without feeling that something is de-fective ? What is so ? And who dares to guess that it may be INSPIRATION ?

IV

' POETRY is of too spiritual a nature,' Mr. Campbell has observed, ' to admit of its authors being exactly grouped by a Linnaean system of classification.' Nevertheless, from those subtle influ-ences which poets render and receive, and from other causes less obvious but no less operative, it has resulted, even to ourselves in this slight survey of the poets of our country, that the signs used by us simply as signs of historical demarcation have naturally fallen or risen into signs of poetical classification. The five eras we spoke of in our last paper have each a characteristic as clear in poetry as in chronology; and a deeper gulf than an *Anno Domini* yawns betwixt an Elizabethan man and a man of that third era upon which we are entering. The change of the poetical characteristic was not, indeed, without gradation. The hands of the clock had been moving silently for a whole hour before the new one struck—and even in Davies, even in Drayton, we felt the cold foreshadow of a change. The word 'sweetness,' which presses into our sentences against the will of our rhetoric whenever we speak of Shakespeare ('sweetest Shakespeare') or his kin, we lose the taste of in the later waters—they are brackish with another age.

In what did the change consist? Practically and partially in the idol-worship of *rime*. Among the elder poets, the rime was only a felicitous adjunct, a musical accompaniment, the tinkling of a cymbal through the choral harmonies. You heard it across the changes of the pause, as an undertone of the chant, marking the time with an audible indistinctness, and catching occasionally and reflecting the full light of the emphasis of the sense in mutual elucidation. But the new practice endeavoured to identify in all possible cases the rime and what may be called the sentimental emphasis; securing the latter to the tenth riming *syllable*, and so dishonouring the emphasis of the sentiment into the base use of the marking of the time. And not only by this unnatural provision did the emphasis minister to the rime, but the pause did so also. 'Away with all pauses,' said the reformers, 'except the legitimate pause at the tenth riming syllable. O rime, live for ever! Rime alone take the incense from our altars—tinkling cymbal alone be our music!'—And so arose, in dread insignificance, 'the heart and impart men.'

Moreover, the corruption of the versification was but a type of the change in the poetry itself, and sufficiently ex-pressive. The accession to the throne of the poets, of the *wits* in the new current sense of the term, or of the *beaux esprits*—a term to be used the more readily because descriptive of the actual pestilential influence of French literature—was accompanied by the substitution of elegant thoughts for poetic conceptions ('elegant,' alas! beginning to be the critical pass-word), of adroit illustrations for beautiful images, of ingenuity for genius. Yet this third era is only the preparation for the fourth consummating one—the hesitation before the crime—we smell the blood through it in the bath-room. And our fancy grows hysterical, like poor Octavia, while the dismal extent of the *quantum mutatus* develops itself in detail.

'Waller's sweetness!' it is a needy antithesis to Denham's strength—and, if anything beside, a sweetness as far removed from that which we have lately recognized, as the saccharine of the palate from the melodious of the ear. Will Saccharissa frown at our comparison from the high sphere of his verse? or will she, a happy 'lady who can sleep when she pleases,' please to oversleep our offence? It is certain that we but walk in her footsteps in our disdain of her poet, even if we disdain him—and most seriously we disown any such partaking of her 'crueltie.' Escaping from the first astonishment of an unhappy transition, and from what is still more vexing, those 'base, common, and popular' critical voices, which, in and out of various 'arts of poetry,' have been pleased to fix upon this same transitional epoch as the genesis of excellence to our language and versification, we do not, we hope it of ourselves, undervalue Waller. There is a certain grace 'beyond the reach of art,' or rather beyond the destructive reach of his ideas of art, to which, we opine, if he had not been a courtier and a renegade, the Lady Dorothea might have bent her courtly head unabashed, even as the Penshurst beeches did. We gladly acknowledge in him, as in Denham and other poets of the transition, an occasional remorseful recurrence by half lines and whole lines, or even a few lines together, to the poetic past. We will do anything but agree with Mr. Hallam, who, in his excellent and learned work on *The Literature of Europe*, has passed some singular judgements upon the poets, and none more startling than his comparison of Waller to Milton, on the ground of the sustenance of power. The crying truth is louder than Mr. Hallam, and cries, in spite of fame, with whom poor Waller was an *enfant trouvé*, an heir by chance, rather than merit—that he is feeble poetically quite as surely as morally and politically, and that, so far from being an equal and sustained poet, he has not strength for unity even in his images, nor for continuity in his thoughts, nor for adequacy in his expression, nor for harmony in his versification. This is at least our strong and sustained impression of Edmund Waller.

With a less natural gift of poetry than Waller, Denham has not only more strength of purpose and language (an easy superiority), but some strength in the abstract: he puts forth rather a sinewy hand to the new structure of English versification. It is true, indeed, that in his only poem which survives to any competent popularity—his *Cooper's Hill*—we may find him again and again, by an instinct to a better principle, receding to the old habit of the medial pause, instead of the would-be sufficiency of the final one. But, generally, he is true to his modern sect of the Pharisees; and he helps their prosperity otherwise by adopting that pharisaic fashion of setting forth,* vaingloriously, a little virtue of thought and poetry in pointed and antithetic expression, which all the wits delighted in, from himself, a chief originator, to Pope, the perfecter. The famous lines, inheriting by entail a thousand critical admirations—

Strong without rage, without o'erflowing full,

and, as Sydney Smith might put it,

'a great many other things, without a great many other things,' contain the germ and prophecy of the whole Queen Anne's generation. For the rest, we will be brief in our melancholy, and say no more of Denham than that he was a Dryden *in small*.

The genius of the new school was its anomaly, even Abraham Cowley. We have said nothing of 'the metaphysical poets' because we disclaim the classification, and believe with Mr. Leigh Hunt that every poet, inasmuch as he is a poet, is a metaphysician. In taking note, therefore, of this Cowley, who stands on the very vibratory soil of the transition, and stretches his faltering and protesting hands on either side to the old and to the new, let no one brand him for 'metaphysics.' He was a true poet, both by natural constitution and cultivation, but without the poet's heart. His admirers have compared him to Pindar—and, taking Pindar out of his rapture, they may do so still : he was a Pindar writing by *métier* rather than by *verve*. In rapidity and subtlety of the associative faculty, which, however, with him, moved circularly rather than onward, he was sufficiently Pindaric : but, as it is a fault in the Greek lyrist to leave his buoyancy to the tumultuous rush of his associations too unmisgivingly and entirely for the right reverence of Unity in Beauty, so is it the crime of the English poet to commit coldly what the other permitted passively, and with a conscious volition, quick yet calm, calm when quickest, to command from the ends of the universe the associations of material sciences and spiritual philosophies. Quickness of the associative or suggestive faculty is common, we have had occasion to observe, to the wit (in the modern sense) and the poet—its application only being of a reverse difference. Cowley confounded the application, and became a witty poet. The Elizabethan writers were inclined to a too curious illuminating of thought by imagery. Cowley was coarsely curious : he went to the shambles for his chambers of imagery, and very often through the mud. All which faults appear to us attributable to his coldness of temperament, and his defectiveness in the instinct towards Beauty; to having the intellect only of a great poet, not the sensibility. His *Davideis*, our first epic in point of time, has fine things in it. His translations (or rather paraphrases) of Anacreon are absolutely the most perfect of any English composition of their order. His other poems contain profuse material, in image and reflection, for the accomplishment of three poets, each greater than himself. He approached the beautiful and the true as closely as mere Fancy could; but that very same Fancy, unfixed by feeling, too often, in the next breath, approximated him to the hideous and the false. Noble thoughts are in Cowley—we say noble, and we might say sublime; but, while we speak, he falls below the first praise. Yet his influence was for good rather than for evil, by inciting to a struggle backward, a delay in the revolutionary movement: and this, although a wide gulf yawned between him and the former age, and his heart's impulse was not strong enough to cast him across it. For his actual influence, he lifts us up and casts us down—charms. and goes nigh to disgust us—does all but make us love and weep.

And then came 'glorious John,' with the whole fourth era in his arms—and eloquent above the sons of men, to talk down, thunder down poetry as if it were an exhalation. Do we speak as if he were not a poet? nay, but we speak of the character of his influences! nay, but he was a poet—an excellent poet—in marble! and Phidias, with the sculpturesque ideal separated from his working tool, might have carved him. He was a poet without passion, just as Cowley was—but, then, Cowley lived by fancy, and that would have been poor living for John Dryden. Unlike Cowley, too, he had an earnestness which of itself was influential. He was inspired in his understanding and his senses only; but to the point of dis-

enchanting the world most marvellously. He had a large soul for a man, containing sundry Queen Anne's men, one within another, like quartetto tables; but it was not a large soul for a poet, and it entertained the universe by potato patches. He established finally the reign of the literati for the reign of the poets—and the critics clapped their hands. He established finally the despotism of the final emphasis—and no one dared, in affecting criticism, to speak any more at all against a tinkling cymbal. And so, in distinctive succession to poetry and inspiration, began the new system of harmony 'as by law established '—and so he translated Virgil not only into English but into Dryden; and so he was kind enough to translate Chaucer too, as an example—made him a much finer speaker, and not, according to our doxy, so good a versifier—and cured the readers of the old 'Knight's Tale' of sundry of their tears!—and so he reasoned powerfully in verse—and threw into verse, besides, the whole force of his strong sensual being; and so he wrote what has been called from generation to generation, down to the threshold of our days, 'the best ode in the English language.' To complete which successes he thrust out nature with a fork; and for a long time, and in spite of Horace's prophecy, she never came back again. Do we deny our gratitude and his glory to glorious John because we speak thus? In nowise would we do it. He was a man greatly endowed; and our language and our literature remain, in certain respects, the greater for his greatness—more practical, more rapid, and with an air of mixed freedom and adroitness which we welcome as an addition to the various powers of either. With regard to his influence—and he was most influential upon POETRY—we have spoken; and have the whole of the opening era from which to prove.

While we return upon our steps for a breathing moment, and pause before Milton, the consideration occurs to us that a person of historical ignorance in respect to this divine poet would hesitate and be at a loss to which era of our poetry to attach him through the internal evidence of his works. He has not the tread of a contemporary of Dryden, and Rochester's *nothingness* is a strange accompaniment to the voice of his greatness. Neither can it be quite predicated of him that he walks an Elizabethan man —there is a certain fine bloom or farina, rather felt than seen, upon the old poems, unrecognized upon his. But the love of his genius leant backward to those olden oracles : and it is pleasant to think that he was actually born before Shakespeare's death ; that they too looked upwardly to the same daylight and stars ; and that he might have stretched his baby arms (*animosus infans*) to the faint hazel eyes of the poet of poets. Let us think in any wise that he drew in some living subtle Shakespearian benediction, providing for greatness.

The Italian poets had 'rained influence' on the Elizabethan 'field of the cloth of gold' ; and from the Italian poets, as well as the classical sources and the elder English ones, did Milton accomplish his soul. Yet the poet Milton was not made by what he received ; not even by what he loved. High above the current of poetical influences he held his own grand personality ; and there never lived poet in any age (unless we assume ignorantly of Homer) more isolated in the contemporaneous world than he. He was not worked upon from out of it, nor did he work outwardly upon it. As Cromwell's secretary and Salmasius's antagonist, he had indeed an audience ; but as a poet, a scant one ; his music, like the spherical tune, being inaudible because too fine and high. It is almost awful to think of him issuing from the arena of controversy victorious and *blind*—putting away from his dark brows the bloody laurel—left alone after the heat of the day by those for whom he had combated ; and originating in that enforced dark quietude his epic vision for the inward sight of the unborn ; so to avenge himself on the world's neglect by exacting

from it an eternal future of reminiscence. The circumstances of the production of his great work are worthy in majesty of the poem itself ; and the writer is the ideal to us of the majestic personality of a poet. He is the student, the deep thinker, the patriot, the believer, the thorough brave man — breathing freely for truth and freedom under the leaden weights of his adversities, never reproaching God for his griefs by his despair, working in the chain, praying without ceasing in the serenity of his sightless eyes ; and, because the whole visible universe was swept away from betwixt them and the Creator, contemplating more intently the invisible infinite, and shaping all his thoughts to it in grander proportion ! O noble Christian poet ! Which is hardest ? self-renunciation, and the sackcloth and the cave ? or grief-renunciation, and the working on, on, under the stripe ? He did what was hardest. He was Agonistes building up, instead of pulling down ; and his high religious fortitude gave a character to his works. He stood in the midst of those whom we are forced to consider the corrupt versificators of his day, an iconoclast of their idol rime, and protesting practically against the sequestration of pauses. His lyrical poems, move they ever so softly, step loftily, and with something of an epic air. His sonnets are the first sonnets of a free rhythm— and this although Shakespeare and Spenser were sonneteers. His *Comus*, and *Samson*, and *Lycidas*—how are we to praise them ? His epic is the second to Homer's, and the first in sublime effects—a sense as of divine benediction flowing through it from end to end. Not that we compare, for a moment, Milton's genius with Homer's ; but that Christianity is in the poem besides Milton. If we hazard a remark which is not admiration, it shall be this—that with all his heights and breadths (which we may measure geometrically if we please from the *Davideis* of Cowley), with all his rapt devotions and exaltations towards the highest of all, we do miss something—we, at least, who are writing, miss something—of what may be called, but rather metaphysically than theologically, *spirituality*. His spiritual personages are vast enough, but not rarefied enough. They are humanities, enlarged, uplifted, transfigured—but no more. In the most spiritual of his spirits there is a conscious, obvious, even ponderous materialism. And hence comes the celestial gunpowder, and hence the clashing with swords, and hence the more continuous evil which we feel better than we describe, the thick atmosphere clouding the heights of the subject. And if anybody should retort, that complaining so we complain of Milton's humanity—we shake our heads. For Shakespeare also was a *man*; and our creed is, that the *Midsummer Night's Dream* displays more of the fairyhood of fairies than the *Paradise Lost* does of the angelhood of angels. The example may serve the purpose of explaining our objection; both leaving us room for the one remark more—that Ben Jonson and John Milton, the most scholastic of our poets, brought out of their scholarship different gifts to our language; that Jonson brought more Greek, and Milton more Latin—while the influences of the latter and greater poet were at once more slowly and more extensively effectual.

Butler was the contemporary of Milton: we confess a sort of continuous 'innocent surprise' in the thought of it, however the craziness of our imagination may be in fault. We have stood by as witnesses while the great poet sanctified the visible earth with the oracle of his blindness; and are startled that a profane voice should be hardy enough to break the echo, and jest in the new consecrated temple. But this is rather a roundheaded than a longheaded way of adverting to poor Butler; who, for all his gross injustice to the purer religionists, in the course of 'flattering the vices and daubing the iniquities' of King Charles's court, does scarcely deserve at our hands, either to be treated as a poet or punished for being

a contemporary of the poet Milton. Butler's business is the business of desecration, the exact reverse of a poet's: and by the admission of all the world his business is well done. His learning is various and extensive, and his fancy communicates to it its mobility. His wit has a gesture of authority, as if it might, if it pleased, be wisdom. His power over language, 'tattered and ragged' like Skelton's, is as wonderful as his power over images. And if nobody can commend the design of his *Hudibras*, which is the English counterpart of *Don Quixote*—a more objectionable servility than an adaptation from a serious composition, in which case that humorous effect would have been increased by the travesty, which is actually injured, and precisely in an inverse ratio, by the burlesque copy of the burlesque—everybody must admit the force of the execution. When Prior attempted afterwards the same line of composition with his peculiar grace and airiness of diction—when Swift ground society into jests with a rougher turning of the wheel—still, then and since, has this Butler stood alone. He is the genius of his class—a natural enemy to poetry under the form of a poet: not a great man, but a powerful man.

V

WE return to the generation of Dryden and to Pope his inheritor— Pope, the perfecter, as we have already taken occasion to call him—who stood in the presence of his father Dryden, before that energetic soul, weary with its long literary work which was not always clean and noble, had uttered its last wisdom or foolishness through the organs of the body. Unfortunately, Pope had his advisers apart from his muses; and their counsel was 'be correct.' To be correct, therefore, to be great through correctness, was the end of his ambition, an aspiration scarcely more calculated for the production of noble poems than the philosophy of utilitarianism is for that of lofty virtues. Yet correctness seemed a virtue rare in the land; Dr. Johnson having crowned Lord Roscommon over Shakespeare's head, 'the only correct writer before Addison'! The same critic predicated of Milton, that he could not cut figures upon cherry-stones— Pope glorified correctness, and dedicated himself to cherry-stones from first to last. A cherry-stone was the apple of his eye.

Now we are not about to take up any popular cry against Pope; he has been over-praised and is under-praised; and, in the silence of our poetical experience, ourselves may confess personally to the guiltiness of either extremity. He was not a great poet; he meant to be a correct poet, and he was what he meant to be, according to his construction of the thing meant—there are few amongst us who fulfil so literally their ambitions. Moreover, we will admit to our reader in the confessional, that, however convinced in our innermost opinion of the superiority of Dryden's genius, we have more pleasure in reading Pope than we ever could enjoy or imagine under Pope's master. We incline to believe that Dryden being the greatest poet-power, Pope is the best poet-manual; and that whatever Dryden has done— we do not say conceived, we do not say suggested, but DONE—Pope has done that thing better. For translations, we hold up Pope's Homer against Dryden's Virgil and the world. Both translations are utterly and equally contrary to the antique, both bad with the same sort of excellence; but Pope's faults are Dryden's faults, while Dryden's are not Pope's. We say the like of the poems from Chaucer; we say the like of the philosophic and satirical poems: the art of reasoning in verse is admirably attained by either poet, but practised with more grace and point by the later one. To be sure, there is the *Alexander's Feast* ode, called, until people half believed what they said, the greatest ode in the language! But here is, to make the scales even again, the *Eloisa*, with tears on it—faulty but tender—of a sensibility which glorious

John was not born with a heart for. To be sure, it was not necessary that John Dryden should keep a Bolingbroke to him for him: but to be sure again, it is something to be born with a heart, particularly for a poet. We recognize besides, in Pope, a delicate fineness of tact, of which the precise contrary is unpleasantly obvious in his great master; Horace Walpole's description of Selwyn, *une bête inspirée*, with a restriction of *bête* to the animal sense, fitting glorious John like his crown. Now there is nothing of this coarseness of the senses about Pope; the little pale Queen Anne's valetudinarian had a nature fine enough to stand erect upon the point of a needle like a schoolman's angel; and whatever he wrote coarsely, he did not write from inward impulse, but from external conventionality, from a bad social Swift-sympathy. For the rest, he carries out his master's principles into most excellent and delicate perfection: he is rich in his degree. And there is, indeed, something charming even to an enemy's ear in this exquisite balancing of sounds and phrases, these 'shining rows' of oppositions and appositions, this glorifying of commonplaces by antithetic processes, this catching, in the rebound, of emphasis upon rime and rime; all, in short, of this Indian jugglery and Indian carving upon . . . cherry-stones!—'and she herself' (that is, poetry)—

And she herself one fair Antithesis.

When Voltaire threw his *Henriade* into the fire and Hénault rescued it, 'Souvenez-vous,' said the president to the poet, 'that I burnt my lace ruffles for the sake of your epic.' It was about as much as the epic was worth. For our own part, we would sacrifice not only our point, but the prosperity of our very fingers, to save from a similar catastrophe these works of Pope; and this, although the most perfect and original of all of them, *The Rape of the Lock*, had its fortune in a fire-safe. They are the works of a master. A great poet?—oh no! A true poet?—perhaps not. Yet a man, be it remembered, of such mixed gracefulness and power, that Lady Mary Wortley deigned to coquet with him, and Dennis shook before him in his shoes.

Nature, as we have observed, had been expelled by a fork, under the hand of Pope's progenitors; and if in him and around him we see no sign of her return, we do not blame Pope for what is, both in spirit and in form, the sin of his school. Still less would we 'play at bowles' with Byron, and praise his right use of the right poetry of Art. Our views of Nature and of Art have been sufficiently explained to leave our opinion obvious of the controversy in question, in which, as in a domestic broil, 'there were faults on both sides.' Let a poet never write the words 'tree,' 'hill,' 'river,' and he may still be true to nature. Most untrue, on the other hand, most narrow, is the poetical sectarianism, and essentially most unpoetical, which stands among the woods and fields announcing with didactic phlegm, 'Here only is nature.' Nature is where God is! Poetry is where God is! Can you go up or down or around and not find Him? In the loudest hum of your machinery, in the dunnest volume of your steam, in the foulest street of your city—there, as surely as in the Brocken pine-woods and the watery thunders of Niagara—there, as surely as He is above all, lie Nature and Poetry in full life. Speak, and they will answer! Nature is a large meaning! Let us make column-room for it in the comprehension of our love! for the coral rock built up by the insect and the marble erected by the man.

In this age of England, however, pet-named the Augustan, there was no room either for Nature or Art : Art and Nature (for we will not separate their names) were at least maimed and dejected and sickening day by day—

Quoth she, I grieve to see your leg
Stuck in a hole here, like a peg ;

and even so, or like the peg of a top humming drowsily, our poetry stood still. There was an abundance of 'correct writers,' yes, and of 'elegant writers': there was Parnell, for instance, who would be called besides a pleasing writer by any pleasing critic ; and Addison, a proverb for the 'virtuousest, discreetest, best' with all the world. Or if, after the Scotch mode of Monk-barns, we call our poets by their pos-sessions, not so wronging their charac-teristics, there was *The Dispensary*, the *Art of Preserving Health*, the *Art of Cookery*,—and *Trivia*, or the *Fan*—take Gay by either of those names ! and *Cider*, or the *Splendid Shilling*—take Phillips, Milton's imitator, by either of these ! and there was Pomfret, not our 'choice,' the concentrate essence of namby-pam-byism ; and Prior, a brother spirit of the French Gresset—a half-brother, of an inferior race, yet to be praised by us for one instinct obvious in him, a blind stretching of the hand to a sweeter order of versification than was current. Of Young we could write much : he was the very genius of antithesis; a genius breaking from 'the system,' with its broken chain upon his limbs, and frown-ing darkly through the grey monotony —a grander writer by spasms than by volitions. Blair was of his class, but rougher ; a brawny contemplative Orson. And how many of our readers may be unaware of the underground existence of another *Excursion* than the deathless one of our days, and in blank verse, too, and in several cantos ; and how nobody will thank us for digging at these fossil remains ! It is better to remember Mallet by his touching ballad of the *William and Margaret*, a word taken from diviner lips to becoming purpose; only we must not be thrown back upon the 'Ballads,' lest we wish to live with them for ever. Our literature is rich in ballads, a form epitomical of the epic and dramatic, and often vocal when no other music is astir ; and to give a particular account of which would take us far across our borders.

As it is, we are across them ; we are benighted in our wandering and strait-ened for room. We glance back vainly to the lights of the later drama, and see Dryden, who had the heart to write rimed plays after Shakespeare, and but little heart for anything else,—and Congreve, and Lillo, and Southerne, and Rowe, all gifted writers, and Otway, master of tears, who starved in our streets for his last tragedy—a poet most effective in broad touches; rather moving, as it appears to us, by scenes than by words.

Returning to the general poets, we meet, with bent faces toward hillside Nature, Thomson and Dyer; in writing which names together we do not depreciate Thomson's, however we may a little exalt Dyer's. We praise neither of these writers for being descriptive poets; but for that faithful transcript of their own impressions, which is a common subject of praise in both—Dyer being more distinct, perhaps, in his images, and Thomson more impressive in his general effect. Both are faulty in their blankverse diction; the latter too florid and verbose, the former (although *Grongar Hill* is simple almost to baldness) too pedantic and *constructive*—far too 'saponaceous' and 'pomaceous.' We offer pastoral salutation also to Shenstone and Hammond; pairing them like Polyphemus's sheep; fain to be courteous if we could: and we *could* if we were *Phillida*. Surely it is an accomplishment to utter a pretty thought so simply that the world is forced to remember it; and that gift was Shenstone's, and he the most poetical of country gentlemen. May every shrub on the lawn of Leasowes be evergreen to his brow. And next, O most patient reader, pressed to a conclusion and in a pairing humour, we come to Gray and Akenside together—yes, together! because if Gray had written a philosophic poem he would have written it like the *Pleasures of Imagination*, and because Akenside would have written odes like Gray, if he could have commanded a rapture. Gray, studious and sitting in the cold, learnt the secret of a simulated and innocent fire (the Greek fire he might have *called* it), which burns beautifully to the eye, but never would have harmed M. Hénault's ruffles. Collins had twenty times the lyric genius

of Gray; we feel his fire in our cheeks. But Gray, but Akenside—both with a volition towards enthusiasm—have an under-constitution of most scholastic coldness: *Si vis me flere*, you must weep; but they only take out their pocket-handkerchiefs. We confess humbly, before gods and men, that we never read to the end of Akenside's *Pleasures*, albeit we have read Plato: some pleasures, say the moralists, are more trying than pains. Let us turn for refreshment to Goldsmith—that amiable genius, upon whose diadem we feel our hands laid ever and anon in familiar love,—to Goldsmith, half emerged from 'the system,' his forehead touched with the red ray of the morning; a cordial singer. Even Johnson, the ponderous critic of the system, who would hang a dog if he read *Lycidas* twice, who wrote the lives of the poets and left out the poets, even he loved Goldsmith! and Johnson was Dryden's critical bear—a rough bear, and with points of noble beardom. But while he growled the leaves of the greenwood fell; and oh, how sick to faintness grew the poetry of England! Anna Seward, 'by'r lady,' was the 'muse' of those days, and Mr. Hayley 'the bard,' and Hannah More wrote our dramas, and Helen Williams our odes, and Rosa Matilda our elegiacs,—and Blacklock, blind from his birth, our descriptive poems, and Mr. Whalley our 'domestic epics,' and Darwin our poetical philosophy, and Lady Millar encouraged literature at Bath, with red taffeta and 'the vase.' But the immortal are threatened vainly. It was the sickness of renewal rather than of death; St. Leon had his fainting hand on the elixir: the new era was alive in Cowper. We do not speak of him as the master of a transition, only as a hinge on which it slowly turned; only as an earnest, tender writer, and true poet enough to be true to himself. Cowper sang in England, and Thomas Warton also—of a weaker voice but in tune: and Beattie, for whom we have too much love to analyse it, seeing that we drew our childhood's first poetic pleasure from his

Minstrel. And Burns walked in glory on the Scotch mountain's side; and everywhere Dr. Percy's collected ballads were sowing the great hearts of some still living for praise with impulses of greatness. It was the revival of poetry —the opening of the fifth era—the putting down of the Dryden dynasty—the breaking of the serf bondage — the wrenching of the iron from the soul. And Nature and Poetry did embrace one another! and all men who were lovers of either and of our beloved England were enabled to resume the pride of their consciousness, and looking round the world say gently, yet gladly, 'OUR POETS.'

VI [1]

WHEN Mr. Wordsworth gave his first poems to the public it was not well with poetry in England. The 'system' riveted upon the motions of poetry by Dryden and his dynasty had gradually added to the restraint of slavery its weakness and emasculation. The change from poetry to rhetoric had issued in another change, to the commonplaces of rhetoric. We had no longer to complain of Pope's antithetic glories—there was 'a vile antithesis' for those also. The followers were not as the master; and the very facility with which the trick of acoustical mechanics was caught up by the former—admitting of 'singing for the million,' with ten fingers each for natural endowment, and the ability to count them for requirement—made wider and more apparent the difference of dignity between the Popes and the Pope Joans. Little by little, by slow and desolate degrees, Thought had perished out of the way of the appointed and most beaten rhythm; and we had the beaten rhythm, without the living footstep—we had the monotony of the military movement, without the heroic impulse—the cross of the Legion of Honour, hung, as

[1] Originally published in the *Athenaeum*, Aug. 27, 1842, as a review on Wordsworth's *Poems, chiefly of early and late years, including The Borderers, a Tragedy.*

it once was, in a paroxysm of converted Bourbonism, at a horse's tail; and the 'fork,' which expelled Nature, dropped feebly downward, blunted of its *point*. And oh! to see who sat then in England in the seats of the elders! The Elizabethan men would have gnashed their teeth at such a sight; the Queen Anne's men would have multiplied Dunciads. Of the third George's men ('Αχαιίδες οὐκ ἔτ' 'Αχαιοί), Hayley, too good a scholar to bear to be so bad a poet, was a chief hope; and Darwin, mistaker of the optic nerve for the poetical sense, an inventive genius.

But Cowper had a great name, and Burns a greater; and the *réveillé* of Dr. Percy's *Reliques of English Poetry* was echoed presently by the *Scottish Minstrelsy*. There was a change—a revival, an awakening—a turning, at least upon the pillow, of some who slept on in mediocrity, as if they felt the daylight on their shut eyelids: there was even a group of noble hearts (Coleridge, the idealist, poet among poets, in their midst), foreseeing the sun. Nature, the long banished, re-dawned like the morning—Nature, the true mother, cried afar off to her children, 'Children, I am here!—come to me.' It was a hard act to come, and involved the learning and the leaving of much. Conventionalities of phrase and rhythm, conventional dialects set apart for poets, conventional words, attitudes, and manners, consecrated by 'wits,'—all such Nessian trappings were to be wrenched off, even to the cuticle into which they had urged their poison. But it was an act not too hard for the doing. There was a visible movement towards Nature; the majority moving of course with reservation, but individuals with decision; some rending downward their garments of pestilent embroidery, and casting themselves at her feet. As the chief of the movement, the Xenophon of the return, we are bound to acknowledge this great Wordsworth, and to admire how, in a bravery bravest of all because born of love, in a passionate unreservedness sprung of genius, and to the actual scandal of the world which stared at the filial familiarity, he threw himself not at the feet of Nature, but straightway and right tenderly upon her bosom! And so, trustfully as child before mother, self-renouncingly as child after sin, absorbed away from the consideration of publics and critics as child at play-hours, with a simplicity startling to the *blasé* critical ear as inventiveness, with an innocent utterance felt by the competent thinker to be wisdom, and with a faithfulness to natural impressions acknowledged since by all to be the highest art—this William Wordsworth did sing his *Lyrical Ballads* where the 'Art of criticism' had been sung before, and 'the world would not let them die.'

The voice of Nature has a sweetness which few of us, when sufficiently tried, can gainsay; it penetrates our artificial 'tastes,' and overcomes us; and our ignorance seldom proves strong in proportion to our instincts. We recognize, like Ulysses' dog, with feeble joyous gesture the master's voice—and the sound is nearly always pleasant to us, however we may want strength to follow after it. But while, at the period we refer to, the recognition and gratulation were true and deep, the old conventionalities and prejudices hung heavily in bondage and repression. The great body of readers would recoil to the Drydenic rhythm, to the Queen Anne's poetical cant, to anti-Saxonisms, whether in Latin or French; or exacted, as a condition of a poet's faithfulness to Nature, such an effervescence of his emotions as had rendered Pope natural in the *Eloisa*. 'Let us all forsooth be Eloisa, and so natural,'—the want was an excuse for loving Nature; and the opinion went that the daily heart-beat was more obnoxious in poetry than the incidental palpitation. Poor Byron (true miserable genius, soul-blind great poet!) ministered to this singular need, identifying poetry and passion. Poetry ought to be the revelation of the complete man—and Byron's manhood having no completion nor entirety, consisting on the contrary of a one-sided

passionateness, his poems discovered not a heart, but the wound of a heart; not humanity, but disease; not life, but a crisis. It was not so—it was not in the projection of a passionate emotion—that William Wordsworth committed himself to Nature, but in full resolution and determinate purpose. He is scarcely, perhaps, of a passionate temperament, although still less is he cold; rather quiet in his love, as the stock-dove, and brooding over it as constantly, and with as soft an inward song lapsing outwardly—serene through deepness—saying himself of his thoughts, that they 'do often lie too deep for tears'; which does not mean that their painfulness will not suffer them to be wept for, but that their closeness to the supreme Truth hallows them, like the cheek of an archangel, from tears. Call him the very opposite of Byron, who, with narrower sympathies for the crowd, yet stood nearer to the crowd, because everybody understands passion. Byron was a poet through pain. Wordsworth is a feeling man because he is a thoughtful man; he knows grief itself by a reflex emotion; by sympathy, rather than by suffering. He is eminently and humanly expansive; and, spreading his infinite egotism over all the objects of his contemplation, reiterates the love, life, and poetry of his peculiar being in transcribing and chanting the material universe, and so sinks a broad gulf between his descriptive poetry and that of the Darwinian painter-poet school. Darwin was, as we have intimated, all optic nerve. Wordsworth's eye is his soul. He does not see that which he does not intellectually discern, and he beholds his own cloud-capped Helvellyn under the same conditions with which he would contemplate a grand spiritual abstraction. In his view of the exterior world—as in a human Spinozism—mountains and men's hearts share in a sublime unity of humanity; yet his Spinozism does in nowise affront God, for he is eminently a religious poet, if not, indeed, altogether as generous and capacious in his Christianity as in his poetry; and, being a true Christian poet, he is scarcely least so when he is not writing directly upon the subject of religion—just as we learn sometimes without looking up, and by the mere colour of the grass, that the sky is cloudless. But what is most remarkable in this great writer is his poetical consistency. There is a wonderful unity in these multiform poems of one man: they are 'bound each to each in natural piety,' even as his days are. And why? because they *are* his days—all his days, work days and Sabbath days—his *life*, in fact, and not the unconnected works of his life, as vulgar men do opine of poetry and do rightly opine of vulgar poems, but the sign, seal, and representation of his life—nay, the actual audible breathing of his inward spirit's life. When Milton said that a poet's life should be a poem he spoke a high moral truth; if he had added a reversion of the saying, that a poet's poetry should be his life, he would have spoken a critical truth, not low.

'Foole, saide my muse to mee, looke in thine hearte and write.' And not only, we must repeat, at feast times, fast times, or curfew times—not only at times of crisis and emotion, but at all hours of the clock; for that which God thought good enough to write, or permit the writing of, on His book, the heart, is not too common, let us be sure, to write again in the best of our poems. William Wordsworth wrote these common things of nature, and by no means in a phraseology nor in a style. He was daring in his commonness as any of your Tamerlanes may be daring when far fetching an alien image from an outermost world; and, notwithstanding the ribald cry of that *vox populi* which has, in the criticism of poems, so little the character of divinity, and which loudly and mockingly, at his first utterance, denied the sanctity of his simplicities—the Nature he was faithful to 'betrayed not the heart which loved her,' but, finally, justifying herself and him, 'DID'—without the *Edinburgh Review*.

'Hero-worshippers' as we are, and sitting for all the critical pretence—in right or wrong of which we speak at all —at the feet of Mr. Wordsworth,— recognizing him, as we do, as poet-hero of a movement essential to the better being of poetry, as poet-prophet of utterances greater than those who first listened could comprehend, and of influences most vital and expansive—we are yet honest to confess that certain things in the *Lyrical Ballads* which most provoked the ignorant innocent hootings of the mob do not seem to us all heroic. Love, like ambition, may overvault itself; and Betty Foys of the Lake school (so called) may be as subject to conventionalities as Pope's Lady Bettys. And, perhaps, our great poet might, through the very vehemence and nobleness of his hero and prophet-work for Nature, confound, for some blind moment, and by an association easily traced and excused, nature with rusticity, the simple with the bald; and even fall into a vulgar conventionality in the act of spurning a graceful one. If a trace of such confounding may occasionally be perceived in Mr. Wordsworth's earlier poetry, few critics are mad enough, to-day, to catch at the loose straws of the full golden sheaf and deck out withal their own arrogant fronts in the course of mouthing mocks at the poet. The veriest critic of straw knoweth well, at this hour of the day, that if Mr. Wordsworth was ever over-rustic, it was not through incapacity to be right royal; that of all poets, indeed, who have been kings in England, not one has swept the purple with more majesty than this poet, when it hath pleased him to be majestic. *Vivat rex*—and here is a new volume of his reign. Let us rejoice, for the sake of literature and the age, in the popularity which is ready for it, and in the singular happiness of a great poet living long enough to rebound from the 'fell swoop' of his poetical destiny, survive the ignorance of his public, and convict the prejudices of his reviewers. It is a literal 'poetical justice' and one rarest of all, that a great poet should stand in a permitted sovereignty, without doing so, like poor Inez de Castro, by right of death. It is almost wonderful that his country should clap her hands in praise of him before he has ceased to hear : the applause resembles an anachronism. Is Mr. Wordsworth startled at receiving from his contemporaries what he expected only from posterity?—is he asking himself 'Have I done anything wrong?' Probably not—it is at least with his usual air of calm and advised dignity that he addresses his new volume in its *Envoy*—

Go single,—yet aspiring to be joined
With thy forerunners, that through many a
    year
Have faithfully prepared each other's way—
Go forth upon a mission best fulfilled
When and wherever, in this changeful world,
*Power hath been given to please for higher
    ends
Than pleasure only ;* gladdening to prepare
For wholesome sadness, troubling to refine,
Calming to raise.

—words of the poet which form a nobler description of the character and uses of his poetry than could be given in any words of a critic.

We do not say that the finest of Mr. Wordsworth's productions are to be found, or should be looked for, in the present volume ; but the volume is worthy of its forerunners, consistent in noble earnestness and serene philosophy, true poet's work—the hand trembling not a jot for years or weariness—the full face of the soul turned hopefully and stilly as ever towards the True, and catching across its ridge the idealized sunlight of the Beautiful. And yet if we were recording angel, instead of only recording reviewer, we should drop a tear . . . another . . . and end by weeping out that series of sonnets in favour of capital punishments—moved that a hand which has traced *life*-warrants so long for the literature of England should thus sign a misplaced 'Benedicite' over the hangman and his victim. We turn away from them to other sonnets—to forget aught in Mr.

Wordsworth's poetry we must turn to his poetry !—and however the greatest poets of our country—the Shakespeares, Spensers, Miltons—worked upon high sonnet ground, not one opened over it such broad and pouring sluices of various thought, imagery, and emphatic eloquence as he has done. This is a worthy counsel from one worthy to counsel :—

A poet ! he hath put his heart to school,
Nor dares to move unpropped upon the staff
Which Art hath lodged within his hand—
    must laugh
By precept only, and shed tears by rule.
Thy Art be Nature ; the live current quaff,
And let the groveller sip his stagnant pool,
In fear that else, when Critics grave and cool
Have killed him, Scorn should write his
    epitaph.
How does the meadow-flower its bloom
    unfold ?
Because the lovely little flower is free
Down to its root, and, in that freedom, bold ;
And so the grandeur of the forest-tree
Comes not by casting in a formal mould,
But from its *own* divine vitality.

Here is a sonnet of softer sense, and not less true, referring, we have heard, to a portrait of that lovely ' Lady of her own ' which Nature made long ago for herself—and for the poet, we suppose—his sonnet being addressed to the painter :—

All praise the likeness by thy skill por-
    trayed,
But 'tis a fruitless task to paint for me,
Who, yielding not to changes Time has
    made,
By the habitual light of memory see
Eyes unbedimmed, see bloom that cannot
    fade,
And smiles that from their birthplace ne'er
    shall flee
Into the land where ghosts and phantoms
    be ;
And seeing this, own nothing in its stead.
Couldst thou go back into far-distant years,
Or share with me, fond thought ! that in-
    ward eye,
Then, and then only, Painter, could thy Art
The visual powers of Nature satisfy,
Which hold, whate'er to common sight
    appears,
Their sovereign empire in a faithful heart.

The tender Palinodia is beyond Petrarch:—

Though I beheld at first with blank surprise
This work, I now have gazed on it so long,
I see its truth with unreluctant eyes ;
Oh, my beloved ! I have done thee wrong,
Conscious of blessedness, but, whence it
    springs
Ever too heedless, as I now perceive :
Morn into noon did pass, noon into eve,
And the old day was welcome as the young,
As welcome and as beautiful—in sooth
More beautiful, as being a thing more holy ;
Thanks to thy virtues, to the eternal youth
Of all thy goodness, never melancholy ;
To thy large heart and humble mind, that
    cast
Into one vision, future, present, past !

That '*more beautiful*' is most beautiful !
all human love's cunning is in it ; besides
the full glorifying smile of Christian love !

Last in the volume is the tragedy of
The Borderers, which, having lain for
some fifty years 'unregarded' among
its author's papers—a singular destiny
for these printing days when our very
morning talk seems to fall naturally into
pica type—caused, in its announcement
from afar, the most faithful disciples to
tremble for the possible failure of their
master. Perhaps they trembled with
cause. The master, indeed, was a
prophet of humanity ; but he was wiser
in love than terror, in admiration than
pity, and rather intensely than actively
human ; capacious to embrace within
himself the whole nature of things and
beings, but not going out of himself to
embrace anything ; a poet of one large
sufficient soul, but not polypsychical
like a dramatist. Therefore his disciples
trembled : and we will not say that the
tragedy, taken as a whole, does not
justify the fear. There is something
grand and Greek in the intention which
hinges it, showing how crime makes
crime in cursed generation, and how
black hearts, like whiter ones (Topaze
or Ebéne), do cry out and struggle for
sympathy and brotherhood ; granting
that black heart (Oswald) may stand
something too much on the extreme
of evil to represent humanity broadly
enough for a drama to turn upon. The

action, too, although it does not, as
might have been apprehended, lose
itself in contemplation, has no unhesitating
firm dramatic march—perhaps it
' potters ' a little, to take a word from
Mrs. Butler ;—and when all is done we
look vainly within us for an impression,
the response to the unity of the whole.
But, again, when all is done, the work
is Mr. Wordsworth's, and the conceptions
and utterances living and voiceful
in it bear no rare witness to the master.
The old blind man, left to the ordeal
of the desert—the daughter in agony
hanging upon the murderer for consolation—knock
against the heart, and take
back answers ; and ever and anon there
are sweet gushings of such words as this
poet only knows, showing how, in a
' late remorse of love,' he relapses into
pastoral dreams, notwithstanding his
new vocation, and within the very sight
of the theatric *thymele* :—

A grove of darker and more lofty shade
I never saw. The music of the birds
Drops deadened from a roof so thick with
    leaves.

Who can overpass the image of the old
innocent man praying ?—

The name of daughter on his lips, he prays !
With nerves so steady, that the very flies
Sit unmolested on his staff.

And now to give a fragment from
a scene in which Oswald, the black
genius of the drama, brings his blackness
to bear on Marmaduke, who is no genius
at all. A passage, well known and
rightly honoured, will be recognized in
the extract :—

Osw.   It may be
That some there are, squeamish half-thinking
    cowards,
Who will turn pale upon you, call you
    murderer,
And you will walk in solitude among them.
A mighty evil for a strong-built mind !—
Join twenty tapers of unequal height
And light them joined, and you will see the
    less
How 'twill burn down the taller ; and they all
Shall prey upon the tallest. Solitude !—
The Eagle lives in Solitude !
Mar.   Even so,

The sparrow so on the house-top, and I,
The weakest of God's creatures, stand re-
    solved
To abide the issue of my act, alone.
    Osw. Now would you? and for ever?—
    My young friend,
As time advances either we become
The prey or masters of our own past deeds.
Fellowship we *must* have, willing or no ;
And if good Angels fail, slack in their duty,
Substitutes, turn our faces where we may,
Are still forthcoming ; some which, though
    they bear
Ill names, can render no ill services,
In recompense for what themselves re-
    quired.
So meet extremes in this mysterious world,
And opposites thus melt into each other.
    Mar. Time, since Man first drew breath,
    has never moved
With such a weight upon his wings as now ;
But they will soon be lightened.
    Osw. Aye, look up—
Cast round you your mind's eye, and you
    will learn
Fortitude is the child of Enterprise:
Great actions move our admiration, chiefly
Because they carry in themselves an earnest
That we can suffer greatly.
    Mar. Very true.
    Osw. Action is transitory—a step, a blow,
The motion of a muscle—this way or that—
'Tis done, and in the after-vacancy
We wonder at ourselves like men betrayed :
Suffering is permanent, obscure and dark,
And shares the nature of infinity.
    Mar. Truth—and I feel it.
    Osw. What ! if you had bid
Eternal farewell to unmingled joy
And the light dancing of the thoughtless
    heart ;
It is the toy of fools, and little fit
For such a world as this. The wise abjure
All thoughts whose idle composition lives
In the entire forgetfulness of pain.
    —I see I have disturbed you.
    Mar. By no means.
    Osw. Compassion !—pity !—pride can do
    without them ;
And what if you should never know them
    more !—
He is a puny soul who, feeling pain,
Finds ease because another feels it too.
If e'er I open out this heart of mine
It shall be for a nobler end—to teach
And not to purchase puling sympathy.
    —Nay, you are pale.
    Mar. It may be so.
    Osw. Remorse—

It cannot live with thought ; think on, think
    on,
And it will die. What ! in this universe,
Where the least things control the greatest,
    where
The faintest breath that breathes can move
    a world ;
What ! feel remorse, where, if a cat had
    sneezed,
A leaf had fallen, the thing had never been
Whose very shadow gnaws us to the vitals [1].

Anxious to conclude our extracts by
something truer to Mr. Wordsworth's
personal opinions than this strong black
writing we have hesitated, as we turned
the leaves, before many touching and
beautiful poems, wise in their beauty—
before the 'Grave of Burns,' for instance,
and the 'Widow of Windermere,' and
the 'Address to the Clouds,' and others
beyond meaning—a certain sonnet which
discovers our poet sitting on the chair
of Dante at Florence, tempting us for
many reasons. But the sun and air (by
courtesy) are heavy on us while we
write, and subdued besides by the charm
of the loveliest, freshest landscape-
making (oh, never say *painting*) in the
world, and by the prospect presently of
a ' little breeze,' we forget our difficulty
of breathing and selecting, and fall from
the elevation of Fahrenheit down in a
swoon in 'Airey-Force Valley' :—

        ——Not a breath of air
Ruffles the bosom of this leafy glen.
From the brook's margin, wide around, the
    trees
Are steadfast as the rocks ; the brook itself,
Old as the hills that feed it from afar,
Doth rather deepen than disturb the calm
Where all things else are still and motionless.
And yet, even now, a little breeze, perchance
Escaped from boisterous winds that rage
    without,
Has entered, by the sturdy oaks unfelt,
But to its gentle touch how sensitive
Is the light ash ! that, pendent from the
    brow
Of yon dim cave, in seeming silence makes
A soft eye-music of slow-waving boughs,
Powerful almost as vocal harmony
To stay the wanderer's steps and soothe his
    thoughts.

[1] *The Borderers*, Act III, ll. 1507-67.

But we start from the languor, and the dream floated upon our eyes by such charmed writing, and come hastily to the moral of our story,—seeing that Mr. Wordsworth's life does present a high moral to his generation, to forget which in his poetry would be an unworthy compliment to the latter. It is advantageous for us all, whether poets or poetasters, or talkers about either, to know what a true poet is, what his work is, and what his patience and successes must be, so as to raise the popular idea of these things, and either strengthen or put down the individual aspiration. 'Art,' it was said long ago, 'requires the whole man,' and 'Nobody,' it was said later, 'can be a poet who is anything else'; but the present idea of Art requires the segment of a man, and everybody who is anything at all is a poet in a parenthesis. And our shelves groan with little books over which their readers groan less metaphorically—there is a plague of poems in the land apart from poetry—and many poets who live and are true do not live by their truth, but hold back their full strength from Art because they do not *reverence* it fully; and all booksellers cry aloud and do not spare, that poetry will not sell; and certain critics utter melancholy frenzies, that poetry is worn out for ever—as if the morning-star was worn out from heaven, or 'the yellow primrose' from the grass! and Mr. Disraeli the younger, like Bildad comforting Job, suggests that we may content ourselves for the future with a rhythmetic prose, printed like prose for decency, and supplied, for comfort, with a parish allowance of two or three rimes to a paragraph. Should there be any whom such a 'New Poor Law' would content, we are far from wishing to disturb the virtue of their serenity—let them continue, like the hypochondriac, to be very sure that they have lost their souls, inclusive of their poetic instincts. In the meantime the hopeful and believing will hope—trust on; and, better still, the Tennysons and the Brownings, and other high-

gifted spirits, will work, wait on, until, as Mr. Horne has said—

> Strong deeds awake,
> And, clamouring, throng the portals of the hour.

It is well for them and all to count the cost of this life of a master in poetry, and learn from it what a true poet's crown is worth—to recall both the long life's work for its sake—the work of observation, of meditation, of reaching past models into Nature, of reaching past Nature unto God! and the early life's loss for its sake—the loss of the popular cheer, of the critical assent, and of the 'money in the purse.' It is well and full of exultation to remember *now* what a silent, blameless, heroic life of poetic duty this man has lived—how he never cried rudely against the world because he was excluded for a time from the parsley garlands of its popularity; nor sinned morally because he was sinned against intellectually; nor, being tempted and threatened by paymaster and reviewer, swerved from the righteousness and high aims of his inexorable genius. And it cannot be ill to conclude by enforcing a high example by some noble precepts which, taken from the *Musophilus* of old Daniel, do contain, to our mind, the very code of chivalry for poets :—

> Be it that my unseasonable song
>   Come out of Time, that fault is in the Time,
> And I must not do virtue so much wrong,
>   As love her aught the worse for other's crime.
> .   .   .   .   .   .
> And for my part, if only one allow
>   The care my labouring spirits take in this,
> He is to me a theatre large enow,
>   And his applause only sufficient is—
> All my respect is bent but to his brow;
>   That is my all, and all I am is his.
> And if some worthy spirits be pleased too,
>   It shall more comfort breed, but not more will.
> BUT WHAT IF NONE? *It cannot yet undo*
>   *The love I bear unto this holy skill.*
> *This is the thing that I was born to do:*
>   *This is my scene; this part must I fulfil.*

INDEX OF FIRST LINES

INDEX OF TITLES